MOUNT ROYAL COLLEGE

3 2047 00611 9864

D0843676

# HANDBOOK
## of
# PSYCHOLOGY

MOUNT ROYAL COLLEGE
LIBRARY

# HANDBOOK
## of
# PSYCHOLOGY

## VOLUME 8
## CLINICAL PSYCHOLOGY

George Stricker
Thomas A. Widiger

*Volume Editors*

Irving B. Weiner

*Editor-in-Chief*

**WILEY**

John Wiley & Sons, Inc.

This book is printed on acid-free paper. ∞

Copyright © 2003 by John Wiley & Sons, Inc. All rights reserved.

Published by John Wiley & Sons, Inc., Hoboken, New Jersey.
Published simultaneously in Canada.

No part of this publication may be reproduced, stored in a retrieval system or transmitted in any form or by any means, electronic, mechanical, photocopying, recording, scanning or otherwise, except as permitted under Sections 107 or 108 of the 1976 United States Copyright Act, without either the prior written permission of the Publisher, or authorization through payment of the appropriate per-copy fee to the Copyright Clearance Center, 222 Rosewood Drive, Danvers, MA 01923, (978) 750-8400, fax (978) 646-8600, or on the web at www.copyright.com. Requests to the Publisher for permission should be addressed to the Permissions Department, John Wiley & Sons, Inc., 111 River Street, Hoboken, NJ 07030, (201) 748-6011, fax (201) 748-6008.

Limit of Liability/Disclaimer of Warranty: While the publisher and author have used their best efforts in preparing this book, they make no representations or warranties with respect to the accuracy or completeness of the contents of this book and specifically disclaim any implied warranties of merchantability or fitness for a particular purpose. No warranty may be created or extended by sales representatives or written sales materials. The advice and strategies contained herein may not be suitable for your situation. The publisher is not engaged in rendering professional services, and you should consult a professional where appropriate. Neither the publisher nor author shall be liable for any loss of profit or any other commercial damages, including but not limited to special, incidental, consequential, or other damages.

This publication is designed to provide accurate and authoritative information in regard to the subject matter covered. It is sold with the understanding that the publisher is not engaged in rendering professional services. If legal, accounting, medical, psychological or any other expert assistance is required, the services of a competent professional person should be sought.

Designations used by companies to distinguish their products are often claimed as trademarks. In all instances where John Wiley & Sons, Inc. is aware of a claim, the product names appear in initial capital or all capital letters. Readers, however, should contact the appropriate companies for more complete information regarding trademarks and registration.

For general information on our other products and services please contact our Customer Care Department within the United States at (800) 762-2974, outside the United States at (317) 572-3993, or fax (317) 572-4002.

Wiley also publishes its books in a variety of electronic formats. Some content that appears in print may not be available in electronic books. For more information about Wiley products, visit our web site at www.wiley.com.

*Library of Congress Cataloging-in-Publication Data:*

Handbook of psychology / Irving B. Weiner, editor-in-chief.
    p.   cm.
    Includes bibliographical references and indexes.
    Contents: v. 1. History of psychology / edited by Donald K. Freedheim — v. 2. Research methods in psychology / edited by John A. Schinka, Wayne F. Velicer — v. 3. Biological psychology / edited by Michela Gallagher, Randy J. Nelson — v. 4. Experimental psychology / edited by Alice F. Healy, Robert W. Proctor — v. 5. Personality and social psychology / edited by Theodore Millon, Melvin J. Lerner — v. 6. Developmental psychology / edited by Richard M. Lerner, M. Ann Easterbrooks, Jayanthi Mistry — v. 7. Educational psychology / edited by William M. Reynolds, Gloria E. Miller — v. 8. Clinical psychology / edited by George Stricker, Thomas A. Widiger — v. 9. Health psychology / edited by Arthur M. Nezu, Christine Maguth Nezu, Pamela A. Geller — v. 10. Assessment psychology / edited by John R. Graham, Jack A. Naglieri — v. 11. Forensic psychology / edited by Alan M. Goldstein — v. 12. Industrial and organizational psychology / edited by Walter C. Borman, Daniel R. Ilgen, Richard J. Klimoski.
    ISBN 0-471-39263-4 (cloth : alk. paper : v. 8); ISBN 0-471-66671-8 (pbk.) — ISBN 0-471-66675-0 (set : pbk.)
    1. Psychology. I. Weiner, Irving B.

BF121.H1955 2003
150—dc21
                                                                    2002066380

Printed in the United States of America.

10  9  8  7  6  5  4  3  2  1

# Editorial Board

**Volume 1**
**History of Psychology**

Donald K. Freedheim, PhD
Case Western Reserve University
Cleveland, Ohio

**Volume 2**
**Research Methods in Psychology**

John A. Schinka, PhD
University of South Florida
Tampa, Florida

Wayne F. Velicer, PhD
University of Rhode Island
Kingston, Rhode Island

**Volume 3**
**Biological Psychology**

Michela Gallagher, PhD
Johns Hopkins University
Baltimore, Maryland

Randy J. Nelson, PhD
Ohio State University
Columbus, Ohio

**Volume 4**
**Experimental Psychology**

Alice F. Healy, PhD
University of Colorado
Boulder, Colorado

Robert W. Proctor, PhD
Purdue University
West Lafayette, Indiana

**Volume 5**
**Personality and Social Psychology**

Theodore Millon, PhD
Institute for Advanced Studies in
    Personology and Psychopathology
Coral Gables, Florida

Melvin J. Lerner, PhD
Florida Atlantic University
Boca Raton, Florida

**Volume 6**
**Developmental Psychology**

Richard M. Lerner, PhD
M. Ann Easterbrooks, PhD
Jayanthi Mistry, PhD

Tufts University
Medford, Massachusetts

**Volume 7**
**Educational Psychology**

William M. Reynolds, PhD
Humboldt State University
Arcata, California

Gloria E. Miller, PhD
University of Denver
Denver, Colorado

**Volume 8**
**Clinical Psychology**

George Stricker, PhD
Adelphi University
Garden City, New York

Thomas A. Widiger, PhD
University of Kentucky
Lexington, Kentucky

**Volume 9**
**Health Psychology**

Arthur M. Nezu, PhD
Christine Maguth Nezu, PhD
Pamela A. Geller, PhD

Drexel University
Philadelphia, Pennsylvania

**Volume 10**
**Assessment Psychology**

John R. Graham, PhD
Kent State University
Kent, Ohio

Jack A. Naglieri, PhD
George Mason University
Fairfax, Virginia

**Volume 11**
**Forensic Psychology**

Alan M. Goldstein, PhD
John Jay College of Criminal
    Justice–CUNY
New York, New York

**Volume 12**
**Industrial and Organizational Psychology**

Walter C. Borman, PhD
University of South Florida
Tampa, Florida

Daniel R. Ilgen, PhD
Michigan State University
East Lansing, Michigan

Richard J. Klimoski, PhD
George Mason University
Fairfax, Virginia

# *Handbook of Psychology* **Preface**

Psychology at the beginning of the twenty-first century has become a highly diverse field of scientific study and applied technology. Psychologists commonly regard their discipline as the science of behavior, and the American Psychological Association has formally designated 2000 to 2010 as the "Decade of Behavior." The pursuits of behavioral scientists range from the natural sciences to the social sciences and embrace a wide variety of objects of investigation. Some psychologists have more in common with biologists than with most other psychologists, and some have more in common with sociologists than with most of their psychological colleagues. Some psychologists are interested primarily in the behavior of animals, some in the behavior of people, and others in the behavior of organizations. These and other dimensions of difference among psychological scientists are matched by equal if not greater heterogeneity among psychological practitioners, who currently apply a vast array of methods in many different settings to achieve highly varied purposes.

Psychology has been rich in comprehensive encyclopedias and in handbooks devoted to specific topics in the field. However, there has not previously been any single handbook designed to cover the broad scope of psychological science and practice. The present 12-volume *Handbook of Psychology* was conceived to occupy this place in the literature. Leading national and international scholars and practitioners have collaborated to produce 297 authoritative and detailed chapters covering all fundamental facets of the discipline, and the *Handbook* has been organized to capture the breadth and diversity of psychology and to encompass interests and concerns shared by psychologists in all branches of the field.

Two unifying threads run through the science of behavior. The first is a common history rooted in conceptual and empirical approaches to understanding the nature of behavior. The specific histories of all specialty areas in psychology trace their origins to the formulations of the classical philosophers and the methodology of the early experimentalists, and appreciation for the historical evolution of psychology in all of its variations transcends individual identities as being one kind of psychologist or another. Accordingly, Volume 1 in the *Handbook* is devoted to the history of psychology as it emerged in many areas of scientific study and applied technology.

A second unifying thread in psychology is a commitment to the development and utilization of research methods suitable for collecting and analyzing behavioral data. With attention both to specific procedures and their application in particular settings, Volume 2 addresses research methods in psychology.

Volumes 3 through 7 of the *Handbook* present the substantive content of psychological knowledge in five broad areas of study: biological psychology (Volume 3), experimental psychology (Volume 4), personality and social psychology (Volume 5), developmental psychology (Volume 6), and educational psychology (Volume 7). Volumes 8 through 12 address the application of psychological knowledge in five broad areas of professional practice: clinical psychology (Volume 8), health psychology (Volume 9), assessment psychology (Volume 10), forensic psychology (Volume 11), and industrial and organizational psychology (Volume 12). Each of these volumes reviews what is currently known in these areas of study and application and identifies pertinent sources of information in the literature. Each discusses unresolved issues and unanswered questions and proposes future directions in conceptualization, research, and practice. Each of the volumes also reflects the investment of scientific psychologists in practical applications of their findings and the attention of applied psychologists to the scientific basis of their methods.

The *Handbook of Psychology* was prepared for the purpose of educating and informing readers about the present state of psychological knowledge and about anticipated advances in behavioral science research and practice. With this purpose in mind, the individual *Handbook* volumes address the needs and interests of three groups. First, for graduate students in behavioral science, the volumes provide advanced instruction in the basic concepts and methods that define the fields they cover, together with a review of current knowledge, core literature, and likely future developments. Second, in addition to serving as graduate textbooks, the volumes offer professional psychologists an opportunity to read and contemplate the views of distinguished colleagues concerning the central thrusts of research and leading edges of practice in their respective fields. Third, for psychologists seeking to become conversant with fields outside their own specialty and for persons outside of psychology seeking information about psychological matters, the *Handbook* volumes serve as a reference source for expanding their knowledge and directing them to additional sources in the literature.

The preparation of this *Handbook* was made possible by the diligence and scholarly sophistication of the 25 volume editors and co-editors who constituted the Editorial Board. As Editor-in-Chief, I want to thank each of them for the pleasure of their collaboration in this project. I compliment them for having recruited an outstanding cast of contributors to their volumes and then working closely with these authors to achieve chapters that will stand each in their own right as

valuable contributions to the literature. I would like finally to express my appreciation to the editorial staff of John Wiley and Sons for the opportunity to share in the development of this project and its pursuit to fruition, most particularly to Jennifer Simon, Senior Editor, and her two assistants, Mary Porterfield and Isabel Pratt. Without Jennifer's vision of the *Handbook* and her keen judgment and unflagging support in producing it, the occasion to write this preface would not have arrived.

IRVING B. WEINER
*Tampa, Florida*

# Volume Preface

Clinical psychology is currently the most popular and predominant specialization within psychology. It was not always this way. The beginning of psychology as a distinct profession is typically dated to the founding of Wilhelm Wundt's Psychological Institute in 1879. Wundt might today be classified more specifically as a cognitive or perceptual psychologist. In any case, clinical psychology was not a central or important interest of most of the early, original European or American psychologists who studied with Wundt.

By the time of the first meeting of the American Psychological Association (APA) in 1892, only a minority of American psychologists would be described as having interests consistent with today's clinical psychologists. The beginning of the explicit specialization of clinical psychology is often attributed to the child psychologist Lightner Witmer, who is credited with founding the first psychological clinic in Pennsylvania in 1896, analogous to the founding of the first laboratory by Wundt. Witmer called for the development of a profession of clinical psychology in the prescient inaugural issue of his journal, *The Psychological Clinic* (Witmer, 1907). However, as indicated by the psychology historian Benjamin (1996), "his words often fell on deaf ears" (p. 235).

Morton Prince, however, did share Witmer's vision. "Prince is said to have created the modern tradition of psychopathology and psychotherapy in the United States" (Hilgard, 1987, p. 306). Prince was a physician by education but a psychologist by preference. He founded the *Journal of Abnormal Psychology* in 1906. "It was the first journal of its kind with an emphasis on experimental psychopathology" (Hilgard, 1987, p. 307). Ernest Jones, the analyst and Sigmund Freud's biographer, was an early associate editor. Prince also founded the Harvard Psychological Clinic in 1927 and directed it within the university's psychology department. Upon his death two years later, his "young" assistant, Henry Murray, assumed its leadership. Murray (1956) stated that just prior to his death, Prince indicated that "I want no other monument than the Psychological Clinic" (p. 295).

Nevertheless, for many years, many clinical (and other applied) psychologists met and worked largely outside of the mainstream of the APA. It was not until World War II that the potential benefits and contributions of a profession of clinical psychology became readily apparent to the APA and to the federal government, resulting in the substantial reorganization of the APA to provide more explicit empowerment of the applied, clinical psychologist. Clinical psychologists who had previously been members of the American Association of Applied Psychology (AAAP) became members of the APA, and the *Journal of Consulting Psychology* (founded in 1937 by the AAAP) was added to the set of official APA journals, eventually becoming the *Journal of Consulting and Clinical Psychology*. The specialty of clinical psychology grew rapidly during the postwar years to the point that a strong majority of psychologists would now identify themselves as being clinical psychologists, and this growth has been evident with respect both to the study of psychopathology and to its treatment. "What began as a laboratory science to understand the nature of mind helped to evolve a companion profession to understand the problems of mind and to develop techniques to alleviate those problems" (Benjamin, 1996, p. 235).

This eighth volume of the *Handbook of Psychology* is devoted precisely to these primary concerns of the clinical psychologist: understanding the problems of the mind and the techniques for alleviating these problems, along with issues of particular importance to the profession of clinical psychology. We have attempted to provide within this volume a strong representation of what is currently known about the etiology, pathology, and treatment of psychopathology, as well as the likely future of its science and treatment. The first nine chapters are concerned with the diagnosis, course, etiology, and pathology of the problems of the mind; the next ten chapters are concerned with their treatment; and the concluding five chapters are concerned with professional issues. It should be noted that no chapter deals with assessment, a traditional area of strength for clinical psychology. This is because assessment is covered extensively in another volume of the Handbook. Similarly, attention to research is incorporated in each of the chapters, but there are no chapters solely concerned with research methods because those, too, are covered elsewhere.

The first chapter, by Peter E. Nathan and James Langenbucher, is devoted to the classification and diagnosis of psychopathology. A common language for describing the problems of the mind is necessary for clinical research and practice. The predominant taxonomy of psychopathology is provided by the American Psychiatric Association's (2000)

*Diagnostic and Statistical Manual of Mental Disorders–Fourth Edition, Text Revision*. There is much to applaud with respect to the value, utility, and validity of this diagnostic manual, but there is also much that is problematic and even controversial. Nathan and Langenbucher document well both the positive and negative aspects of this diagnostic nomenclature and point the way to the future of the classification of psychopathology.

Eric J. Mash and David A. Wolfe follow with an overview of major domains of child psychopathology. Beginning with disorders of childhood is an obvious starting point for understanding the development of psychopathology. However, as indicated by Mash and Wolfe, current knowledge of disorders of childhood and adolescence are hindered by a lack of sufficient development of child-specific theories. Some clinicians continue to believe that disorders of childhood and adolescence are the same as the disorders of adulthood, but psychopathology in fact develops and transforms over time. This developmental perspective not only is central to the chapter by Mash and Wolfe but is also emphasized in each of the following chapters within this text.

Eating disorders were classified as a disorder of childhood and adolescence in earlier diagnostic nomenclatures, but it is now recognized that eating disorders can have an onset into young adulthood. Eating disorders have been recognized since the beginning of medicine and are among the more frequently diagnosed and treated mental disorders. Howard Steiger, Kenneth R. Bruce, and Mimi Israël include within their chapter not only the well established disorders of anorexia nervosa and bulimia nervosa but also the burgeoning literature on binge eating disorder. They provide a compelling integrated conceptualization for these disorders that considers developmental, cognitive, social, dynamic, and neurophysiological contributions to their etiology and pathology.

Personality disorders were placed on a separate, distinct axis for diagnosis in the third edition of the *DSM-IV* (American Psychiatric Association, 2000) in recognition of their prevalence (very few persons fail to have maladaptive personality traits) and their contribution to the course and treatment of other mental disorders. Timothy J. Trull and Thomas A. Widiger cover in their chapter not only what is largely known and understood regarding the disorders of personality but also the controversies that bedevil this domain of psychopathology and how these issues might be addressed better from a broader perspective that is informed by the theory and research of "normal" personality psychologists.

Mood and anxiety disorders are the most frequent mental disorders and are probably the most frequently treated by clinical psychologists. As suggested by Constance Hammen, depressive disorders are so ubiquitous that they have been called the common cold of psychological disorders. However, Hammen documents well in her chapter on mood disorders that prevalence does not imply simplicity, and she again emphasizes the importance of considering etiology and pathology from divergent perspectives, including the cognitive, interpersonal, developmental, and neurobiological.

David Barlow, Donna Pincus, Nina Heinrichs, and Molly Choate provide a comparable overview of the etiology, development, and pathology of the many variations of anxiety disorder, including separation anxiety disorder of childhood, obsessive-compulsive disorder, specific phobia, social phobia, panic disorder, and generalized anxiety disorder. Anxiety is perhaps ubiquitous in clinical practice, and understanding the etiology and pathology of maladaptive anxiousness is of considerable importance to the practicing clinician. These authors provide a very thorough and sophisticated life span developmental understanding of these disorders, again well representing divergent perspectives within an integrated conceptualization.

The next two chapters separate themselves somewhat from the nomenclature of the American Psychiatric Association. Etzel Cardeña, Lisa D. Butler, and David Spiegel provide in their chapter on disorders of extreme stress the perspective that many of the disorders classified in different sections of *DSM-IV* might be better understood from a common perspective of stress-related psychopathology—specifically, for example, the dissociative, posttraumatic stress, acute stress, and conversion disorders. There is perhaps much to appreciate and understand through the integrated conceptualization of these disorders as different but related ways of responding to severe trauma.

In an analogous albeit different theoretical perspective, Kenneth J. Sher and Wendy Slutske provide an integration of disorders of impulse dyscontrol. They emphasize in particular dyscontrolled alcohol usage, drug usage, and gambling, but they note that deficits in self-control are important features of other disorders, including such childhood disorders as attention-deficit/hyperactivity disorder and adult paraphilia. They again provide a thorough and sophisticated presentation of what is currently known about these disorders and where future research is likely to go if a complete understanding of their etiologies and pathologies is ever to be found.

The final chapter devoted to a domain of psychopathology is Donald C. Fowles's chapter on schizophrenia and schizophrenia-related disorders. Fowles takes a developmental perspective that integrates neurobiology with stress-related research. He provides not only the predominant models for the etiology and pathology of schizophrenia but also provides a creative and sophisticated integration of these disorders with other domains of psychopathology that complement well many other chapters in this volume. Readers will find this chapter to be not only informative but also quite stimulating and invigorating for the future study of schizophrenic psychopathology.

Following the description of the range of psychopathology in Part I, the volume then moves into an account of the treatment of those disorders in Part II, which begins with three chapters that describe the major orientations toward psychotherapy—psychodynamic, cognitive-behavioral, and humanistic—and adds an account of an exciting new development that transcends single schools: psychotherapy integration.

The first chapter in Part II covers the oldest of the single schools of psychotherapy, psychodynamic psychotherapy, and it is described thoroughly and well by Nancy McWilliams and Joel Weinberger. Psychodynamic psychotherapy is not limited to the work of Freud; and although the contributions of the founder are described thoroughly, so are more recent developments in British object relations and American interpersonal theories, the self psychology movement, and contemporary intersubjective and relational theories. The research that supports much of this work also is described.

The primary single school alternative to psychodynamic psychotherapy is behavioral and cognitive-behavioral psychotherapy, and this is presented thoroughly and well by W. Edward Craighead and Linda Wilcoxon Craighead. This, too, is not a simple and unitary approach, but combines both behavior therapy and cognitive-behavioral psychotherapy, each of which has many variations. The clinical approach is integrated in the presentation with extensive research evidence, and the description of specific treatments for specific syndromes can be read in conjunction with many of the chapters in the Part I that describe these syndromes in more detail.

Along with psychodynamic psychotherapy and behavioral and cognitive-behavioral psychotherapy, there always has been a third force, the humanistic-experiential school. This is covered by Leslie Greenberg, Robert Elliott, and Germain Lietaer, and it also incorporates many individual approaches within the generic orientation, such as person-centered, Gestalt, existential, and experiential therapy. They all share a commitment to a phenomenological approach, a belief in the uniquely human capacity for reflective consciousness and growth, and a positive view of human functioning. Here, as in all the psychotherapy chapters, research evidence also is covered.

The fourth chapter that deals with individual psychotherapy does not recognize the boundaries established by

schools, which themselves, as we have seen, are more heterogenous than is commonly believed. Rather, psychotherapy integration seeks to take from each that which is most useful, and these attempts are described by Louis G. Castonguay, Marvin R. Goldfried, Gregory S. Halperin, and Jack J. Reid Jr. Just as the single schools are more complex than initially appears to be the case, psychotherapy integration is made up of many different attempts at rapprochement, drawing freely from all other theoretical and technical approaches and from research evidence. It is interesting to note that many of the leading practitioners of individual schools, including most of the authors of the chapters presenting those schools, are involved in attempts at a higher order integration of their work, which should work for the benefit of the patients that are served.

Aside from the individual approaches to psychotherapy, two other modalities are quite prominent. Patients are seen not only as individuals but also in groups or along with other members of their family. Group psychotherapy is described by Anne Alonso, Sarah Alonso, and William Piper. The goals of group therapy vary from overall personality reorganization to symptom-focused work and deal with patients in outpatient and inpatient settings. There also is a gamut of theoretical approaches that parallel the approaches that have been described in the chapters covering individual orientations to psychotherapy.

Family therapy is covered by Hamid Mirsalimi, Stephanie H. Perleberg, Erica L. Stovall, and Nadine J. Kaslow. Although an understanding of family systems theory is necessary for this work, the variations in application are every bit as great as in individual and group psychotherapy, if not greater. Alongside the typical approaches to psychotherapy, specific attention is given to culturally competent family therapy and gender-sensitive approaches to family therapy. In addition, specific applications of family therapy are described as they relate to medical problems, substance abuse, and family violence.

Two very popular approaches that represent applications of psychotherapy in specific situations or formats are crisis intervention therapy and brief psychotherapy. Crisis intervention is the focus of the chapter by Lisa M. Brown, Julia Shiang, and Bruce Bongar. Crisis intervention involves the provision of emergency mental health care to individuals and groups. Crises can refer to unusual and devastating events, such as the recent World Trade Center disaster, or to milestones in human life, such as divorce, that create upheavals in functioning. The immediate response to these crises can be of great help to the victim and also can provide the opportunity for much human growth. Cultural considerations, current research, and relevant legal issues are reviewed, along with the many theoretical approaches that are taken to resolving crises.

The brief psychotherapies are presented by Stanley B. Messer, William C. Sanderson, and Alan S. Gurman. Brief versions of each of the major orientations, including psychotherapy integration, are described, and a brief approach to marital and family psychotherapy is also covered. It may be a reflection of the current health care scene that there is more attention given to working in a more abbreviated fashion, but this is not necessarily second best, and the chapter makes clear how much good work can be done in a shorter time frame than is customarily considered.

Up to this point every chapter has focused on the adult population. However, in a life span framework, the other ends of the chronological spectrum also must be considered. Child psychotherapy is described by Richard J. Morris, Huijun Li, Patricia Sánchez Lizardi, and Yvonne P. Morris. Although the title is narrow, the conception includes adolescents as well as children, and the approaches cover the usual spectrum ranging from psychodynamic to cognitive-behavioral, including humanistic approaches. Given the formative importance of early experience, the treatment of younger people is an important contribution to the mental health of the population, and this chapter covers the various indications and approaches.

At the other end of the age spectrum, the approaches to treating the older patient are presented by Bob G. Knight, Inger Hilde Nordhus, and Derek D. Satre. They adopt an integrative model, drawing on the usual approaches to individual treatment and adopting methods, where necessary, to the needs of the older adult. A range of typical older adult disorders are considered, and evidence about treatment approaches is considered. A specific model, the Bergen model, is presented, along with a case example and much evidence for the necessity and efficacy of intervention.

In each of the chapters in Part II, concerned as they all are with psychotherapy, the picture arises of a field marked by great heterogeneity. The value of integration is presented, either in a specific chapter devoted to psychotherapy integration or as incorporated in many other chapters that deal with specific populations or modalities. Each chapter presents evidence for the approach being presented, and the picture of an evolving and developing field, marked by great promise and great accomplishment, is clear.

Clinical psychology is a science and a practice, and both elements have been presented consistently throughout the first two parts. It also is a profession, and issues that concern the profession are the topic of Part III. It is not sufficient for an individual to declare himself to be a clinical psychologist; rather, much training is required, and credentials are necessary so that members of the public who wish to use the service of professional psychologists. Concerns about the education, training, licensing, and credentialing of clinical psychologists are presented by Judy E. Hall and George Hurley. The authors are prominent in the United States and Canada, respectively, and they cover these issues as manifested in their countries, as well as, to a lesser degree, in Mexico, reflecting the recent emphasis on mobility and comparability of training and credentials that has characterized these discussions.

A profession must be self-regulating and serve the interests of the public if it is to be established and accepted. One necessary component of self-regulation is ethical practice, and issues about ethics that relate to clinical psychology are described by Stanley E. Jones. The APA ethics code is generic and applies to all psychologists, but this chapter focuses on those issues that are of most concern to the clinical psychologist. These include major ethical practice issues and frequent problems experienced by practitioners. Familiarity with these issues and their successful resolution are necessary for the sound practitioner, and this presentation should help to focus the potential problem areas and the models of understanding and resolving them.

Clinical psychology is practiced in a social context, and the changing context has had a marked effect on the nature of the practice. The health care marketplace in the United States is described by David J. Drum and Andrew Sekel. Their survey is both historical and conceptual, and it traces the evolution of health care in the United States from its early stage of self-regulation and independence to the current stage of input from multiple stakeholders in health care delivery. The implication this has for the future is not clear, of course, but some very educated guesses are offered, as well as the identification of key areas of concern.

The impact of technology on clinical psychology is described by Kjell Erik Rudestam, Ronald A. Giannetti, and B. Hudnall Stamm. Technology clearly is a cutting-edge area of development, and it has significant impact on clinical psychology. Telecommunication technology has been used to provide health information and intervention and for consultation and supervision across distances. There have been uses of the computer to provide testing and psychotherapy by computer, as well as to use it as a means of communication to facilitate more direct services from the provider. There is a great need for the validation of such services as well as a need for the development of ethical guidelines that are tied to this new method of service delivery.

Finally, we turn our attention to the future. Patrick H. DeLeon, Kristofer J. Hagglund, Stephen A. Ragusea, and Morgan T. Sammons explore areas of expanding roles for psychologists in future years. They also talk about technology but then go on to discuss other cutting-edge areas such as prescriptive authority and policy opportunities. As our society evolves, the field of clinical psychology also must evolve, and these authors lay out many possibilities for growth and development.

Clinical psychology is an expanding science and profession, and its capacity to continue to be relevant depends on its ability to adapt to changing social conditions, needs, and opportunities. We began with an account of historical factors, attempted to provide a context for the current state of the field, presented chapters that described these developments in detail, and concluded with a look toward the future. Clinical psychology has made major contributions to the discipline of psychology and to the welfare of society, and it shows every indication of continuing to grow and evolve with the world about it, and, by doing so, to retain its position at the forefront of scientific and professional developments. We hope that we have been successful in outlining these

possibilities and that we will be witness to continued growth and development.

## REFERENCES

American Psychiatric Association. (2000). *Diagnostic and statistical manual of mental disorders* (4th ed., Text Revision). Washington, DC: Author.

Benjamin, L. T. (1996). Lightner Witmer's legacy to American psychology. *American Psychologist, 51,* 235–236.

Hilgard, E. R. (1987). *Psychology in America: A historical survey.* New York: Harcourt Brace Jovanovich.

Murray, H. A. (1956). Morton Prince. *Journal of Abnormal Psychology, 52,* 291–295.

Witmer, L. (1907). Clinical psychology. *The Psychological Clinic, 1,* 1–9.

GEORGE STRICKER
THOMAS A. WIDIGER

# Contents

PART ONE
## PSYCHOPATHOLOGY

PART TWO
# PSYCHOTHERAPY

PART THREE
# PROFESSIONAL ISSUES

# Contributors

**Anne Alonso, PhD**
Harvard Medical School
Cambridge, Massachusetts

**Sarah Alonso, PhD**
Harvard Medical School/Cambridge Hospital
Cambridge, Massachusetts

**David H. Barlow, PhD**
Department of Psychology
Boston University
Boston, Massachusetts

**Bruce Bongar, PhD**
Clinical Psychology Program
Pacific Graduate School of Psychology
Palo Alto, California

**Lisa M. Brown, MS**
James Haley Veteran's Administration Hospital
Tampa, Florida

**Kenneth R. Bruce, PhD**
Eating Disorders Program
Douglas Hospital
McGill University
Montreal, Quebec, Canada

**Lisa D. Butler, PhD**
Department of Psychiatry and Behavioral Sciences
Stanford University
Stanford, California

**Etzel Cardeña, PhD**
Department of Psychology and Anthropology
University of Texas, Pan American
Edinburg, Texas

**Louis G. Castonguay, PhD**
The Pennsylvania State University
University Park, Pennsylvania

**Molly L. Choate, MA**
Center for Anxiety and Related Disorders
Boston University
Boston, Massachusetts

**Linda Wilcoxon Craighead, PhD**
Department of Psychology
University of Colorado
Boulder, Colorado

**W. Edward Craighead, PhD**
Department of Psychology
University of Colorado
Boulder, Colorado

**Patrick H. DeLeon, JD, PhD**
American Psychological Association
Washington, DC

**David J. Drum, PhD**
University of Texas
Austin, Texas

**Robert Elliott, PhD**
University of Toledo
Toledo, Ohio

**Donald C. Fowles, PhD**
Department of Psychology
University of Iowa
Iowa City, Iowa

**Ronald A. Giannetti, PhD**
Fielding Graduate Institute
Santa Barbara, California

**Marvin R. Goldfried, PhD**
SUNY at Stony Brook
Stony Brook, New York

**Leslie S. Greenberg, PhD**
Department of Psychology
York University
Toronto, Ontario, Canada

**Alan S. Gurman, PhD**
University of Wisconsin Medical School
Madison, Wisconsin

**Kristofer J. Hagglund, PhD**
School of Health Professions
University of Missouri–Columbia
Columbia, Missouri

**Judy E. Hall, PhD**
National Register of Health Service Providers
  in Psychology
Washington, DC

**Gregory S. Halperin, MS**
The Pennsylvania State University
University Park, Pennsylvania

**Constance Hammen, PhD**
Department of Psychology
University of California
Los Angeles, California

**Nina Heinrichs, Dipl-Psych**
Center for Anxiety and Related Disorders
Boston University
Boston, Massachusetts

**George Hurley, PhD**
Memorial University Counselling Centre
St. Johns, Newfoundland, Canada

**Mimi Israël, MD**
Eating Disorders Program
Douglas Hospital
McGill University
Montreal, Quebec, Canada

**Stanley E. Jones, PhD**
Fairview, North Carolina

**Nadine J. Kaslow, PhD**
Department of Psychiatry and
  Behavioral Sciences
Emory University
Atlanta, Georgia

**Bob G. Knight, PhD**
Andrus Gerontology Center
University of Southern California
Los Angeles, California

**James Langenbucher, PhD**
Department of Psychology
Rutgers, the State University of New Jersey
Piscataway, New Jersey

**Huijun Li**
Department of Special Education, Rehabilitation,
  and School Psychology
University of Arizona
Tucson, Arizona

**Germain Lietaer, PhD**
Katholieke Universiteit of Leuven
Leuven, Belgium

**Patricia Sánchez Lizardi**
Department of Special Education, Rehabilitation, and
  School Psychology
University of Arizona
Tucson, Arizona

**Eric J. Mash, PhD**
Department of Psychology
University of Calgary
Calgary, Alberta, Canada

**Nancy McWilliams, PhD**
Graduate School of Applied and Professional Psychology
Rutgers, the State University of New Jersey
Piscataway, New Jersey

**Stanley B. Messer, PhD**
Graduate School of Applied and Professional Psychology
Rutgers, the State University of New Jersey
Piscataway, New Jersey

**Hamid Mirsalimi, PhD**
Georgia School of Professional Psychology
Atlanta, Georgia

**Richard J. Morris, PhD**
Department of Special Education, Rehabilitation,
  and School Psychology
University of Arizona
Tucson, Arizona

**Yvonne P. Morris, PhD**
Tucson, Arizona

**Peter E. Nathan, PhD**
Department of Psychology
University of Iowa
Iowa City, Iowa

**Inger Hilde Nordhus, PhD**
University of Bergen
Bergen, Norway

**Stephanie H. Perleberg, PhD**
Marcus Institute
Atlanta, Georgia

**Donna B. Pincus, PhD**
Center for Anxiety and Related Disorders
Boston University
Boston, Massachusetts

**William Piper, PhD**
University of British Columbia
Vancouver, British Columbia, Canada

**Stephen A. Ragusea, PsyD**
Child, Adult, and Family Psychological Center
State College, Pennsylvania

**Jack J. Reid Jr., BA**
The Pennsylvania State University
University Park, Pennsylvania

**Kjell Erik Rudestam, PhD**
Fielding Graduate Institute
Santa Barbara, California

**Morgan T. Sammons, PhD**
Naval Medical Clinic
Annapolis, Maryland

**William C. Sanderson, PhD**
Graduate School of Applied and Professional Psychology
Rutgers, the State University of New Jersey
Piscataway, New Jersey

**Derek D. Satre, PhD**
University of California
San Francisco, California

**Andrew Sekel, PhD**
Summit Consulting Group, LLP
Austin, Texas

**Kenneth J. Sher, PhD**
Department of Psychology
University of Missouri
Columbia, Missouri

**Julia Shiang, EdD, PhD**
Clinical Psychology Program
Pacific Graduate School of Psychology
Palo Alto, California

**David Spiegel, MD**
Department of Psychiatry and Behavioral Sciences
Stanford University
Stanford, California

**Wendy S. Slutske**
Department of Psychology
University of Missouri
Columbia, Missouri

**B. Hudnall Stamm, PhD**
Idaho State University
Pocatello, Idaho

**Howard Steiger, PhD**
Eating Disorders Program
Douglas Hospital
McGill University
Montreal, Quebec, Canada

**Erica L. Stovall, PhD**
University of Tennessee
Knoxville, Tennessee

**Timothy J. Trull, PhD**
Department of Psychology
University of Missouri
Columbia, Missouri

**Joel Weinberger, PhD**
Derner Institute
Adelphi University
Garden City, New York

**Thomas A. Widiger, PhD**
Department of Psychology
University of Kentucky
Lexington, Kentucky

**David A. Wolfe, PhD**
Department of Psychology
University of Western Ontario
London, Ontario, Canada

# PART ONE
# PSYCHOPATHOLOGY

CHAPTER 1

# Diagnosis and Classification

PETER E. NATHAN AND JAMES LANGENBUCHER

Fundamental to the science and practice of clinical psychology is a valid diagnostic nomenclature. Clinicians and researchers need a common language with which to describe what they are treating and studying. However, the diagnosis and classification of psychopathology has been and continues to be difficult and controversial. This chapter begins with an overview of the nature of diagnosis and classification. The history of the diagnosis of psychopathology is then briefly described, including the recent editions of the American Psychiatric Association's (APA) diagnostic manual. Emphasis is given to issues of reliability, diagnostic stability, utility, cultural biases, and validity. Major controversies of the current diagnostic nomenclature are then discussed, including comorbidity, bias, the categorical-dimensional debate, and definitions of mental disorder. The chapter concludes with a presentation of new methods for diagnostic research.

## ON DIAGNOSIS AND CLASSIFICATION

### Folk Taxonomies

> Man is by nature a classifying animal. His continued existence depends on his ability to recognize similarities and differences between objects and events in the physical universe and to make known these similarities and differences linguistically. Indeed, the very development of the human mind seems to have been closely related to the perception of discontinuities in nature. (Raven, Berlin, & Breedlove, 1971, p. 1210)

Raven and his colleagues used the phrase *folk taxonomy* to emphasize their belief that peoples through the ages have developed taxonomies as ways of manipulating knowledge. Although this predisposition is particularly descriptive of specialist subgroups within cultures (e.g., mental health professionals), all cultures have developed taxonomies that—even across diverse cultures—nonetheless tend to take on strikingly similar characteristics.

Taxonomies recognize naturally occurring groups. They are readily identified as natural groups, at least by specialists; accordingly, they are treated as discontinuous from each other. This is certainly the case with psychopathology, in which such illnesses as schizophrenia, mood disorders, substance-related disorders, and others have been viewed as distinct from each other as well as from psychologically healthy states for many decades.

Taxonomies are developed for communication about items of interest to cultural groups that are acquainted with the properties of the items. They are, in effect, a kind of shorthand language that concentrates useful information in the hands of the specialists who require access to that information. The same is true of psychiatric diagnosis, which is the province of the mental health professionals, who daily trade information about their patients back and forth by means of a literature organized around diagnostic classes.

Taxonomies are also organized in a shallow hierarchy; this means that most folk taxonomies focus on generic taxa (categories at a low level of abstraction but not so specific as at the species level). These categories typically comprise a set that is memorizable (typically between 250 and 800) and consist of mutually separate and distinctively named categories with well-understood limits. The more specific or varietal the members of a genus, the more cultural importance that genus tends to have. Thus, the *DSM-IV* contains around 300 diagnostic categories, and those with the greatest degree of cultural significance—dementia praecox (schizophrenia) in the nineteenth century and (more recently) the mood, anxiety, and substance use disorders—are the most ramified and differentiated.

In other words, the traditions of modern syndromal diagnosis in psychiatry fit well within the limits of folk taxonomies as outlined by Raven and his coworkers. As clinical psychologists, we can take comfort in our adherence to an ancient natural scientific tradition, taxonomy. Said another way, we are not deviating from a putative scientific norm, as some critics of psychiatric diagnosis have alleged (e.g., Albee, 1970; Kanfer & Saslow, 1965; Zigler & Phillips, 1961), when we deploy diagnostic classification systems to categorize our patients. Humans indeed are classifying animals, and we mental health professionals are very human in this regard.

## Natural and Prototype Categorization

Rosch (1973) developed the useful concept of nonarbitrary *natural categories,* like names of colors, that form around perceptually salient *natural prototypes.* Natural categories have eight key attributes, which we illustrate here by using color as the example: (a) They are partitioned—not from discrete clusters but from continua (e.g., wavelength); (b) they cannot be further reduced to simpler attributes (e.g., attributes of color such as saturation and reflectance require a specialist's skills to describe and understand, and they must be specially learned); (c) some of the examples of these categories are better than others (e.g., true colors vs. off hues); (d) they are not arbitrary; (e) they are easily learned by novices; (f) they attract attention and are easily remembered because they are based on properties that are more salient perceptually than other stimuli in their domains (e.g., sky blue is more salient than aqua, forest green is more salient than lime, snow white is more salient than cream); (g) these salient properties of natural categories serve as natural prototypes for the organization of more knowledge; and (h) natural categories have fuzzy (indistinct) boundaries, so they will ultimately encompass both clear-cut and marginal examples. Lilienfeld and Marino (1995) subsequently extended this analysis specifically to psychiatric diagnosis by arguing that psychopathologic entities are Roschian or natural categories because they are partitioned from the continuum of human behavior, they are irreducible to simpler concepts, and some are better examples of firmly bounded categories than others are.

The view that mental disorders represent natural categories complements another influential conceptualization, *prototypic categorization,* first described by Cantor, Smith, French, and Mezzick (1980). Lamenting the tendency of numerous critics of psychiatric diagnosis to endorse the unhelpful classification standards of what they term the classical categorization model, Cantor and her colleagues proposed instead a prototype categorization model.

The classical categorization model makes the following assumptions about the items to be organized in a diagnostic process that the prototypic categorization model does not: (a) the presence of universally accepted criteria for class membership (e.g., all squares have four sides, and all schizophrenic individuals are autistic); (b) high agreement about class membership among classifiers (e.g., everyone agrees on what is a square, just as everyone agrees on who is schizophrenic); and (c) within-class homogeneity of members (e.g., all squares look alike, and all schizophrenic persons behave the same way). Obviously, this standard is inappropriate to judgments of mental disorder.

Cantor and colleagues' prototype categorization appears to characterize far better the process of syndromal classification epitomized by *DSM-III, DSM-III-R,* and *DSM-IV.* That approach assumes (a) correlated—not necessarily pathognomonic—criteria for class membership, (b) high agreement among classifiers only when classifying cases that demonstrate most of the correlated criteria for class membership, and (c) heterogeneity of class membership because criteria are only correlated, not pathognomonic.

> Psychiatric diagnosis and the diagnostic system look reasonably orderly when viewed within the context of [naturalistic classification] systems. Heterogeneity of class membership, borderline cases, and imperfect inter- and intrajudge reliability can all be accepted and studied as fundamental properties of the system, rather than branded as aberrations, errors in measurement or faulty utilization of an otherwise classical scientific system. Revisions in training procedures can be made to better mirror the system as it is actually conceptualized and utilized by practicing clinicians. (Cantor et al., 1980, p. 190)

### Utility of Classification and Diagnosis

Birley (1975) suggested that diagnosis should really be viewed as an art. He made this suggestion in the belief that the prime challenge to both the artist and the diagnostician is to grasp a complex and daunting slice of nature and transform it into a condensed, symbolic representation in such a way as to communicate a truth about that slice of nature. However, diagnosis is much more often viewed as a scientific tool. Viewing it this way, Blashfield and Draguns (1976) detailed its diverse scientific purposes as follows: (a) communication, because without a consensual language, practitioners could not communicate; (b) a means for organizing and retrieving information, because an item's name is a key to its literature and knowledge accrues to the type; (c) a template for describing similarities and differences between individuals; (d) a means of making predictions about course and outcome; and (e) a source of concepts to be used in theory and experimentation.

The view of diagnosis as a scientific tool is best exemplified in the work of members of the neo-Kraepelinian school of American psychiatry. This group of influential thinkers was drawn largely from psychiatry faculty at the Washington University School of Medicine in Saint Louis and the Columbia University College of Physicians and Surgeons in New York. Their diagnostic research during the decades of the 1960s and 1970s laid the groundwork for the revolutionary advances of the *DSM-III* (APA, 1980).

The neo-Kraepelinians, like their namesake, Emil Kraepelin, endorsed the existence of a boundary between pathological functioning and problems in living. Although this was seen as a permeable boundary (those who exist on one side of it sometimes cross over to the other), it was nonetheless an important distinction to make because the existence of pathology is an important mandate for professional attention. Second, viewing psychiatry as a branch of medicine, the neo-Kraepelinians viewed mental illness, like any other illness, as the purview of medicine. Mental illnesses are real, they are diverse, and—by applying a scientific method of discovery, the neo-Kraepelinians affirmed—they can be affected by studies of their etiology, course, prognosis, morbidity, associated features, family dynamics, and predisposing features.

## *DSM-I* AND *DSM-II*

### Historical Roots

Prior to the philosopher-physician Paracelsus, diagnoses were made on the basis of presumed etiology, as when Hippocrates rooted the illnesses he diagnosed in various imbalances of fluxes and humors (Zilboorg, 1941). This changed with Paracelsus' delineation of syndromal diagnosis, with the syndrome defined as a group of signs and symptoms that co-occur in a common pattern and characterize a particular abnormality or disease state. To our day, syndromal diagnosis has focused on the signs and symptoms of disease entities. Typically, it organizes them hierarchically, by the principles of descriptive similarity or shared symptom pictures. In Paracelsus' system, as well as in each succeeding step toward the modern approach epitomized by the *DSM-III* (APA, 1980) and *DSM-IV* (APA, 1994), the etiology of the illness was presumed to be unknown and hence unnecessary for the diagnostic task.

Notable and more complete nomenclatures were subsequently developed, first by Thomas Sydenham (1624–1663) and later by Francois de Sauvages (1706–1767); both developed what were for their time organized and comprehensive hierarchical classification systems. Shortly afterwards Phillippe Pinel, best known for his pioneering efforts to humanize the care of French patients in hospitals for the insane, developed an even more comprehensive classification system (Zilboorg, 1941). The appearance of this nomenclature coincided with the rise of asylums for the insane, for which Pinel was partly responsible. Both Pinel's system and the new availability of large numbers of patients in asylums paved the way for the marked increase in efforts to categorize psychopathology during the ensuing nineteenth century.

Predictably, superintendents of asylums for mentally ill patients in the nineteenth century were concerned almost entirely with cases of serious and protracted psychopathology—organic mental disorders, severe developmental disabilities, dementia, and what we today call schizophrenia and bipolar disorder (Nathan, 1998; Spitzer, Williams, & Skodol, 1980). Advances in the understanding of these serious disorders accelerated when the German psychiatrist Karl Kahlbaum (1828–1899) discovered the value of knowing premorbid course and risk factors as means of predicting outcome in dementia praecox (today we call the disorder schizophrenia). Additional advances followed Kraepelin's (1907) research on posthospital course, clinical outcome, and treatment response in cases of major mental illness (Zilboorg, 1941). Kraepelin synthesized these ideas and those of his intellectual forebears in his series called Lectures in Psychiatry, which developed the basic outlines of the first modern taxonomy of mental illnesses, from which many of our current concepts, procedures, and technical terms have developed.

In the twentieth century, psychiatrists and psychologists developed realms of clinical practice discrete from—and very different from—the mental asylums, including schools, the military services, private clinics, and other service outlets. Their experiences, especially during World War II, when psychological casualties took an unexpectedly high toll among combat personnel, required development of a nomenclature that provided substantially greater coverage of the nonpsychotic conditions. Nosologies grew increasingly complex in publications by the National Commission on Mental Hygiene/Committee on Statistics of the American Medico–Psychological Association (1917; Blashfield, 1984), the American Psychiatric Association/New York Academy of Medicine (APA, 1933), and especially the Veterans Administration in the aftermath of World War II. These developments formed the basis for the publication of the first formal nosologies sponsored by the American Psychiatric Association—*DSM-I* (APA, 1952) and *DSM-II* (APA, 1968).

## Deficiencies

The much-anticipated first edition of the *Diagnostic and Statistical Manual of Mental Disorders* (*DSM-I;* APA, 1952) was a pioneering comprehensive syndromal classification system. It enabled North American mental health professionals, at least in principle, to employ a common diagnostic language for the first time. At the same time, *DSM-I* and its like successor, *DSM-II* (1968), shared serious deficiencies.

The manuals contained relatively little material. The *DSM-I* contained 130 pages and fewer than 35,000 words; *DSM-II* was four pages longer but contained about as many words. As a result, they provided only brief, vague descriptions of each syndrome; typically, these descriptions consisted of one or two short paragraphs listing distinguishing signs and symptoms but not detailing them. This information proved insufficient for reliable diagnoses.

An additional problem was that the signs and symptoms linked to each syndrome were not empirically based; instead, they represented the accumulated clinical wisdom of the small number of senior academic psychiatrists who had drafted these two instruments. As a consequence, the diagnostic signs and symptoms were often inconsistent with the clinical experiences of mental health professionals working in public mental hospitals, mental health centers, and the like.

Consequently, clinicians often failed to agree with one another in assigning diagnoses based on *DSM-I* and *DSM-II*. They often failed to agree both when they were presented with the same diagnostic information (interclinician agreement; Beck, Ward, Mendelson, Mock, & Erbaugh, 1962; Nathan, Andberg, Behan, & Patch, 1969; Sandifer, Pettus, & Quade, 1964) and when they were asked to reevaluate the same patient after a short time had passed (diagnostic consistency; Zubin, 1967).

Predictably, the low reliability of *DSM-I* and *DSM-II* diagnoses affected both their validity and their clinical utility. If clinicians could not agree on a diagnosis, it was unlikely that they would be able to validate the diagnosis against other measures (Black, 1971). For the same reason, they would be unlikely to have confidence in predictions of the future course of diagnosed disorders (Nathan, 1967) or to create the diagnostically homogeneous groups of patients necessary to enable examination of etiological or treatment issues (Nathan & Harris, 1980).

The poor reliability and validity of diagnoses rendered according to *DSM-I* and *DSM-II* raised ethical concerns among some practitioners and scholars. Szasz (1960) wrote extensively of the dehumanizing, stigmatizing consequences of psychiatric labeling, ultimately concluding that the modern constructs of psychiatric illness categories were mere myths. Szasz's ideas were lent empirical substance in 1973 when Rosenhan published "On Being Sane in Insane Places." In this classic study, eight of Rosenhan's peers, friends, and graduate students self-referred to one of 12 psychiatric hospitals, complaining of hearing voices. Immediately upon admission, they ceased complaining of any abnormal perceptions and manifested no other symptoms. Nonetheless, all eight were diagnosed as psychotic, and their subsequent behavior was construed in conformance to that label. Summarizing his findings, Rosenhan concluded, "The normal are not detectably sane" (p. 252), a damning assertion indeed for advocates of then-current diagnostic systems in psychiatry.

## *DSM-III* AND *DSM-III-R*

The publication of *DSM-III* (APA, 1980) represented a substantial advance in the reliability, validity, and utility of syndromal diagnosis. *DSM-III-R,* published in 1987, was a selective revision of *DSM-III* that retained the advances of the 1980 instrument and incorporated generally modest changes in diagnostic criteria that new clinical research suggested should be a part of the diagnostic system.

## Development of *DSM-III*

In the late 1960s, psychiatrist Robert Spitzer and his colleagues at the New York State Psychiatric Institute undertook research on syndromal diagnosis that ultimately led to the development of several structured diagnostic interviews. These instruments were the first to have the capability of gathering the exhaustive data on clinical signs and symptoms required by an empirically based nomenclature. Chief among these structured interviews were the Mental Status Schedule (Spitzer, Fleiss, Endicott, & Cohen, 1967) and the Psychiatric Status Schedule (Spitzer, Endicott, Fleiss, & Cohen, 1970). Additionally, Spitzer and his colleagues developed two computer programs, called DIAGNO and DIAGNO-II, that were designed to use the clinical information gathered by the Mental Status Schedule to assign reliable clinical diagnoses (Spitzer & Endicott, 1968, 1969).

Diagnostic researchers at Washington University in Saint Louis shared a parallel interest in developing more systematic, empirically buttressed approaches to diagnosis. They published an article in 1972 (Feighner et al., 1972) that set forth explicit diagnostic criteria for the 16 major disorders about which the authors believed enough empirical data had accumulated to ensure reliability and validity. The intent of what came to be called the *Feighner criteria* was to replace the vague and unreliable material on these disorders in the *DSM-I* and *DSM-II* with formally organized, empirically supported diagnostic criteria. The hope was that these criteria could help researchers establish the diagnostically homogeneous experimental groups that diagnostic and treatment researchers were increasingly demanding. The format of the Feighner criteria anticipated—and influenced—the format of the diagnostic criteria subsequently adopted for *DSM-III*.

In 1975, the Research Diagnostic Criteria (RDC) were proposed. Developed jointly by the New York State Psychiatric Institute and Washington University groups (Spitzer, Endicott, & Robins, 1975), the RDC were designed to permit empirical testing of the presumed greater reliability and validity of the Feighner criteria. In fact, the reliability of the RDC did yield substantially greater diagnostic reliability for diagnoses of the same disorders based on *DSM-II* (Helzer, Clayton, et al., 1977; Helzer, Robins, et al., 1977). This finding foreshadowed the enhanced reliability of *DSM-III* diagnoses a few years later.

The *DSM-III* diagnostic criteria, based in large part on the RDC, constitute the nomenclature's most significant departure. They are designed to organize each syndrome's distinguishing signs and symptoms within a consistent format, so that each clinician who is called upon to use them can define each sign and symptom the same way and process the resulting diagnostic information in a similarly consistent manner. Many studies of the *DSM-III* diagnostic criteria have affirmed the criteria's success in inducing substantially higher diagnostic reliability, albeit not for every syndrome. However, as Skodol and Spitzer (1987) observed in describing five sources of variation among raters and ratings, not every factor contributing to less-than-perfect diagnostic reliability stems from inadequacies in the diagnostic system.

> Subject variance, as the patient's state changes over time; occasion variance, as the subject is in a different stage of the same condition, or at least reports different information about it; information variance, as different information is obtained from the patient as a result of different examinations; observer variance, as raters differ in their understanding or interpretation of phenomena, such as in rating blunted affect; and criterion variance, as subjects are allocated to different classes because different decision rules are followed. (Skodol & Spitzer, 1987, p. 15)

Around the time of publication of *DSM-III*, several structured and semistructured diagnostic interviews based on the *DSM-III* were published in recognition of the impact on diagnostic reliability of information, observer, and criterion variance, all associated with the process by which diagnostic information is gathered. The best known of these instruments is the National Institute of Mental Health (NIMH) Diagnostic Interview Schedule (DIS; Robins, Helzer, Croughan, & Ratcliff, 1981), a structured interview that was taught to nonclinician interviewers for use in the multisite Epidemiologic Catchment Area (ECA) study (Regier et al., 1984). The semistructured Structured Clinical Interview for *DSM-III* (SCID; Spitzer, 1983; Spitzer & Williams, 1986) was also published around the same time. Both have been widely used, and both appear to contribute to the enhanced diagnostic reliability of *DSM-III*. These important—and in most ways unprecedented—new instruments and ones like them provided the data-gathering structure both for major new epidemiological efforts (e.g., ECA study, Regier et al., 1984; National Comorbidity Survey, Kessler, Sonnega, Bromet, Hughes, & Nelson, 1995) and for a host of clinical and preclinical studies because such instruments ensured the internal validity of research by helping keep samples of human psychopathology well documented diagnostically.

## Reliability

The earliest direct tests of the interrater reliability of *DSM-III* were in the context of the field trials of the instruments that were conducted in the late 1970s. Data from two large field trials indicated that reliability was adequate but not outstanding, with overall kappa values of .68 and .72 for chance-correct agreement on Axis I disorders. Diagnoses for substance use disorder, schizophrenia, and organic mental disorder were significantly more reliable than were those for the adjustment and anxiety disorders (Spitzer, Forman, & Nee, 1979; Williams, Hyler, & Spitzer, 1982).

The reliability of the disorders of childhood was also examined in the *DSM-III* field trials; their reliability had been problematic through the years, in part because of the changeability of behavior during this era in a person's life. Field trial studies of the reliability of criteria for the new *DSM-III* childhood disorders, markedly expanded from *DSM-II* to *DSM-III*, were disappointing—in part because of clinicians' unfamiliarity with the radically new system (Cantwell, Russell, Mattison, & Will, 1979; Mattison, Cantwell, Russell, & Will, 1979). However, subsequent reliability studies of childhood disorder diagnoses attained from semistructured diagnostic interviews based on the *DSM-III* criteria and translated into Japanese (Hanada & Takahashi, 1983) and Norwegian (Larsen & Vaglum, 1986) were more promising.

A substantial number of reliability studies of the *DSM-III* and *DSM-III-R* diagnostic criteria have been published. In general, these studies point to greater diagnostic stability and greater interrater agreement for these instruments than for their predecessors, *DSM-I* and *DSM-II*. Enhanced reliability has been especially notable for the diagnostic categories of schizophrenia, bipolar disorder, major depressive disorder, and substance abuse and dependence. The reliability of the personality disorders, some of the disorders of childhood and adolescence, and some of the anxiety disorders, however, has been less encouraging (e.g., Chapman, Chapman, Kwapil, Eckblad, & Zinser, 1994; Fennig et al., 1994; Klein, Ouimette, Kelly, Ferro, & Riso, 1994; Mattanah, Becker, Lexy, Edell, & McGlashan, 1995), in part because of diagnostic stability problems.

## Diagnostic Stability

Even though the *DSM-III* and *DSM-III-R* diagnostic criteria markedly enhanced diagnostic reliability, diagnostic stability continued to affect the diagnostic process because of naturally occurring changes in clinical course over time. As the research summarized in this section suggests, diagnostic stability depends both on the reliability of the diagnostic instrument and on the variability of clinical course over time.

Fennig et al. (1994) investigated the 6-month stability of *DSM-III-R* diagnoses in a large group of first-admission patients with psychosis—a notably diagnostically unstable group. Affective psychosis and schizophrenic disorders showed substantial diagnostic stability, with 87–89% of patients remaining in the same broad category. Stability for subtypes of these conditions were less stable; only 62–86% of patients remained in the same subcategory. Forty-three percent of these diagnostic changes were attributed to clinical course, and the rest was assumed to reflect the imperfect reliability of the diagnostic process itself.

In a subsequent study of the stability of psychotic diagnoses, Chen, Swann, and Burt (1996) examined changes from schizophrenia diagnoses to those of other disorders and from those of other disorders to schizophrenia in inpatients hospitalized at an urban acute care hospital at least four times over a 7-year period. Only 22% of patients with a schizophrenia diagnosis at the beginning of the study received a different diagnosis during a subsequent hospitalization. Females and patients of Hispanic origin were more likely than others were to experience a diagnostic change from schizophrenia. However, 33% of patients with an initial diagnosis other than schizophrenia were later diagnosed with schizophrenia. Males and African Americans were more likely to change to a diagnosis of schizophrenia. These authors concluded that—contrary to widespread belief—the diagnosis of schizophrenia in current practice is not static.

Coryell et al. (1994) followed up a large group of patients initially diagnosed with major depressive disorder according to the Research Diagnostic Criteria (Spitzer et al., 1975) at 6-month intervals for 5 years and then annually for another 3 years. During this time, most patients had at least two recurrences of the disorder; some had three or four. The kappa statistic was used to quantify the likelihood that patients with psychotic, agitated-retarded, or endogenous subtypes of the disorder in a given episode would manifest the same subtype in subsequent episodes. The psychotic subtype showed the greatest diagnostic stability across multiple subsequent episodes; for all three subtypes, diagnostic stability was greater for contiguous episodes than for noncontiguous episodes.

Nelson and Rice (1997) tested the 1-year stability of *DSM-III* lifetime diagnoses of obsessive-compulsive disorder (OCD) in data from the ECA study. The temporal stability of OCD diagnoses over the course of a year turned out to be surprisingly poor: Of subjects in the ECA sample who met criteria for OCD, only 19% reported symptoms a year later that met the OCD criteria. These findings seemed to reflect an excess of false positives for OCD on initial diagnostic examination, raising concerns about the validity of diagnoses of other conditions reported in the ECA study.

Mattanah and his colleagues (1995) investigated the stability of a range of *DSM-III-R* disorders in a group of adolescent inpatients 2 years after hospitalization. Predictably, diagnostic stability for these subjects was lower than that for the same diagnoses in adults. Internalizing disorders (e.g., the affective disorders) turned out to be more stable but of uncertain reliability because of more new cases at follow-up, whereas externalizing disorders (e.g., attention-deficit/hyperactivity disorder; ADHD) were less stable but more reliable because of fewer new cases at follow-up. Surprisingly, personality disorder clusters and substance use disorders were both stable (53%) and reliable.

These studies of diagnostic stability emphasize the extent to which diagnostic reliability depends on both the clarity and the validity of diagnostic criteria, along with the inherent symptom variability of particular disorders over time, as influenced by alterations in environmental and individual circumstances. These findings also suggest that the stability component attributable to *DSM-III* and *DSM-III-R* diagnostic criteria caused problems for a number of diagnoses.

## Utility and Validity

The developers of *DSM-III* addressed its predecessors' disappointing clinical validity and utility in several ways (Spitzer et al., 1980). To begin with, the *DSM-III* and *DSM-III-R* volumes are much larger than their predecessors—in part to accommodate inclusion of more than three times as many diagnoses and in part to provide detailed information on each syndrome along with its defining diagnostic criteria. (Criticism of this proliferation of diagnoses in *DSM-III* is reviewed later in this chapter.) The substantial increase in numbers of syndromes made it easier for clinicians to locate and name more precisely the syndromes they observed in their patients. The information about the syndrome included in the volume provided concise summaries of empirical data permitting enhanced understanding of the likely context of the syndrome in the patient's milieu.

Another of *DSM-III*'s innovations was its introduction of the multiaxial diagnostic system, which provides for assessment of patients along five dimensions, or axes, rather than only one. The patient's psychopathology was to be recorded on Axes I and II; medical conditions impacting on the mental disorders were to appear on Axis III; the severity of psychosocial stressors that might affect the patient's behavior was to be located on Axis IV; and the patient's highest level of adaptive functioning was to be indicated on Axis V. The range of information available from multiaxial diagnosis was presumed to be more useful for treatment planning and disposition than was the single diagnostic label available from *DSM-I* and *DSM-II*.

Despite these substantial changes, it has not proven to be easy to document the enhanced validity and utility of *DSM-III*. The absence of the kind of definitive, documented etiological mechanisms, with associated laboratory findings, by which the diagnoses of many physical disorders are confirmed—a gold standard for comparative purposes—has made establishing the validity of many *DSM-III* diagnoses a good deal more difficult (Faraone & Tsuang, 1994). In recognition of the absence of a gold standard for the validation of clinical diagnoses, Robins and Guze (1970) proposed validating diagnoses against "internal criteria, such as consistency of the psychopathological symptoms and signs, and external criteria, like laboratory tests, genetic and family studies, course of illness, and delimitation from other illness" (Skodal & Spitzer, 1987, p. 18).

An editorial in *The American Journal of Psychiatry* by Andreasen (1995) recalled Robins and Guze's 1970 proposal for validation alluded to previously, a structure that would include existing validators like clinical description and family studies, but they add a new validator—neurophysiological and neurogenetic laboratory tests. Although she acknowledges that laboratory tests have not yet emerged as prime sources of validation information, Andreasen nonetheless believes that psychiatry's neuroscience base is key to the continuing evolution of validation. Specifically, she proposed "an additional group of validators . . . to link symptoms and diagnoses to their neural substrates (which) include molecular genetics and molecular biology, neurochemistry, neuroanatomy, neurophysiology, and cognitive neuroscience . . . (linking) psychiatric diagnosis to its underlying abnormalities in DNA" (p. 162). As what follows indicates, the search for neuronal, neurobiological, and genetic-familial validators, along with more traditional clinical and epidemiological ones, characterizes contemporary validation attempts.

### Schizophrenic Spectrum Disorders

Subsequent reports on efforts to validate the schizophrenic spectrum disorders have utilized Andreasen's (1995) "additional group of validators." Thus, Gur, Mozley, Shtasel, Cannon, and Gallacher (1994) sought to relate whole-brain volume to clinical subtypes of schizophrenia. Magnetic resonance imaging (MRI) measures of cranial, brain, and ventricular and sulcal cerebrospinal fluid volume were examined in schizophrenic men and women and healthy comparison subjects. The MRI measures differentiated males from females, including male patients from female patients, patients from comparison subjects, and subgroups of patients based on symptom profiles. The research revealed two patterns of neuroanatomic whole-brain abnormalities that differ in severity according to symptom differences and may reflect differential involvement of dysgenic and atrophic pathophysiological processes.

Two studies with related goals reported data from the epidemiologically based Roscommon Family Study. Kendler, Neale, and Walsh (1995) examined the familial aggregation and coaggregation of five hierarchically defined disorders—schizophrenia, schizoaffective disorder, schizotypal-paranoid personality disorder, other nonaffective psychoses, and psychotic affective illness—in siblings, parents, and relatives of index and comparison probands. The aim was to determine whether these patterns could be explained by a single underlying continuum of liability to the schizophrenic spectrum. Although schizophrenia and psychotic affective illness could be clearly assigned to the two extremes of the schizophrenia spectrum, the proper placement of schizoaffective disorder, schizotypal-paranoid personality disorder, and other nonaffective psychoses could not be clearly made. Nonetheless, Kendler and his colleagues considered these results to support the existence of a schizophrenic spectrum in which these five disorders manifest with varying severity an underlying vulnerability that is strongly transmitted within families. In a companion report, Kendler, McGuire, Gruenberg, and Walsh (1995) found that probands with schizoaffective disorder differed significantly from those with schizophrenia or affective illness in lifetime psychotic symptoms as well as in outcome and negative symptoms assessed at follow-up. Relatives of probands with schizoaffective disorder had significantly higher rates of schizophrenia than did relatives of probands with affective illness. These data are consistent with the hypotheses that schizoaffective disorder results from the co-occurrence of a high liability to both schizophrenia and affective illness and that *DSM-III-R* criteria for schizoaffective disorder define a syndrome that differs meaningfully from either schizophrenia or affective illness.

Strakowski (1994) examined antecedent, concurrent, and predictive validators of the *DSM-III/DSM-III-R* schizophreniform disorder diagnosis. Consistent data in support of the validity of the diagnosis as either a distinct diagnostic entity or a subtype of schizophrenia or affective illness could not be found. Instead, Strakowski concluded that these patients constitute a heterogeneous group with new-onset schizophrenia, schizoaffective disorder, and atypical affective disorder and a small subgroup with a remitting nonaffective psychosis.

In sum, this research on the schizophrenic spectrum disorders has succeeded in validating the disorders at the two ends of the continuum, but it has largely failed to identify distinct validators—either clinical or neurobiological—for those disorders between the extremes.

### Depressive Disorders

Kendler and Roy (1995) explored links between two common diagnostic sources of lifetime major depression—family history and personal history—and three independent validators. Although data from personal interview and family history agreed diagnostically at only a modest level, controlling for presence or absence of a personal interview diagnosis of major depression permitted family history diagnosis of the same disorder to predict future episodes of major depression, neuroticism, and familial aggregation of major depression significantly. Kendler et al. (1996) applied latent class analysis to 14 disaggregated *DSM-III-R* symptoms for major depression reported over the course of a year by members of more than a thousand female-female twin pairs. Three of the seven identified classes represented clinically significant depressive syndromes: mild typical depression, atypical depression, and severe typical depression. Depression was not etiologically homogeneous in this sample of twins; instead it was composed of several syndromes at least partially distinct from clinical, longitudinal, and familial-genetic perspectives. Both studies by this group, then, showed a convergence of old and new validators of major depression. In contrast to Kendler's research on the schizophrenic spectrum disorders, however, the validity of the major depression diagnostic syndrome was consistently supported.

Haslam and Beck (1994) tested the content and latent structure of five proposed subtypes of major depression. Analysis of self-reported symptom and personality profiles of more than 500 consecutively admitted outpatients with a primary major depressive diagnosis yielded clear evidence for discreteness only for the endogenous subtype; the other proposed forms lacked internal cohesion or were more consistent with a continuous or dimensional account of major depression.

### Interface of Depression and Anxiety

Clark, Watson, and Reynolds (1995) have sought to validate co-occurring depression and anxiety by means of a tripartite model that groups symptoms of these conditions into three subtypes: (a) largely nonspecific symptoms of general distress; (b) the manifestations of somatic tension and arousal that are relatively unique to anxiety; and (c) the symptoms of anhedonia specific to depression. The validity of this model was tested in five samples—three student samples, one adult sample, and one patient sample—in two studies reported in 1995. Watson, Weber, et al. (1995) used the Mood and Anxiety Symptom Questionnaire (MASQ) along with other symptom and cognition measures to validate these hypothesized symptom groups. Consistent with the tripartite model,

MASC Anxious Arousal and Anhedonic Depression scales differentiated anxiety and depression well and also showed excellent convergent validity. Watson, Clark, et al. (1995) conducted separate factor analyses of the 90 items of the MASQ. The same three factors (General Distress, Anhedonia vs. Positive Affect, Somatic Anxiety) emerged in each of the five data sets, suggesting that the symptom structure in this domain is highly convergent across diverse samples. Moreover, the factors broadly corresponded to the symptom groups proposed by the tripartite model.

Joiner and his colleagues provided additional support for the validity of the tripartite model's portrayal of anxiety and depression. In three separate studies, they reported that the model (a) distinguished among pure forms of depression and anxiety, comorbid depression and anxiety, and mixed anxiety-depression in a group of college students (Joiner & Blalock, 1995); (b) provided a good fit for data from self-report measures of depression, anxiety, self-esteem, and positive and negative affect completed by another group of undergraduates (Joiner, 1996); and (c) described validly the psychopathologic behavior of a group of child and adolescent psychiatric inpatients (Joiner, Catanzaro, & Laurent, 1996).

In an effort to validate Beck's cognitive model of depression and anxiety (Beck, 1976, 1987), which shares important assumptions with the tripartite model, Clark, Steer, and Beck (1994) explored both common and specific symptom dimensions of anxiety and depression proposed by both models in groups of psychiatric outpatients and undergraduates. Principal-factor analyses with oblique rotations on the items of the Beck Depression Inventory and the Beck Anxiety Inventory revealed two correlated factors: depression and anxiety. Second-order factor analyses yielded a large general distress or negative affect factor underlying the relationship between the two first-order factors. These results are consistent with both the tripartite and cognitive models, with cognitive and motivational symptoms found to be specific to depression and physiological symptoms found to be unique to anxiety.

Using five standard measures of anxiety and depression, Clark, Beck, and Beck (1994) compared symptom features of four *DSM-III* subtypes of depressive and anxiety disorders in a group of outpatients. Depression was distinguished by anhedonia, cognitions of personal loss and failure, and dysphoric mood, whereas anxiety was characterized by specific autonomic arousal symptoms, threat-related cognitions, and subjective anxiety and tension. Major depression and panic disorder were better differentiated by specific symptom markers than were dysthymia and generalized anxiety disorder.

Zinbarg and Barlow (1996) relied on a semistructured clinical interview and a self-report battery of questionnaires to identify central features of the anxiety disorders in a large group of patients seeking outpatient treatment. Their results were consistent with both the *DSM-III-R* and *DSM-IV* hierarchical models of anxiety and the anxiety disorders, as well as with Beck's and with Clark and Watson's trait models.

## Criticisms of *DSM-III* and *DSM-III-R*

*DSM-III* represented a major improvement in the diagnosis of psychopathology. Nevertheless, numerous criticisms have also been made. Discussed in the following sections are concerns regarding the propagation of diagnostic labels, definition of mental disorder, promotion of the medical model, and its atheoretical approach.

### *Propagation of Diagnostic Labels*

The number of diagnostic labels in *DSM-III* totaled more than three times the number contained within *DSM-I*. For this proliferation of diagnostic labels, the drafters of the instrument were severely criticized. Child clinical psychologist Norman Garmezy (1978), for example, expressed great concern about the marked increase in diagnoses for childhood and adolescent conditions. He feared that this many new diagnoses would tempt clinicians to label unusual but normal behaviors of childhood as pathological, thereby stigmatizing children who were simply behaving like children. Related concerns were expressed shortly after *DSM-IV* appeared. Social workers Kirk and Kutchins (1994), for example, accused the developers of the instrument of "diagnostic imperialism" by inappropriately labeling "insomnia, worrying, restlessness, getting drunk, seeking approval, reacting to criticism, feeling sad, and bearing grudges . . . (as) possible signs of a psychiatric illness" (p. A12).

### *Definition of Mental Disorder*

The definition of mental disorder developed for *DSM-III* and retained in *DSM-III-R* and *DSM-IV* has also been widely criticized. It has been viewed both as far too broad and encompassing of behaviors not necessarily pathological and criticized as insufficiently helpful to clinicians who must distinguish between uncommon or unusual behavior and psychopathological behavior. The definition states the following:

> Each of the mental disorders is conceptualized as a clinically significant behavioral or psychological syndrome or pattern that occurs in an individual and that is typically associated with either a painful symptom (distress) or impairment in one or more important areas of functioning (disability). In addition, there is an

inference that there is a behavioral, psychological, or biological dysfunction, and that the disturbance is not only in the relationship between the individual and society. (APA, 1980, p. 6)

Addressing these concerns, Spitzer and Williams (1982) defended the definition by noting their intention to construct a nomenclature that would cast as wide a clinical net as possible so that persons who were suffering from even moderately disabling or distressing conditions would receive the help they needed. The promise of alternative definitions of mental disorder proposed by Wakefield (1992, 1997) and Bergner (1997) is evaluated later in this chapter.

### Promotion of the Medical Model

Schacht and Nathan (1977), Schacht (1985), and others questioned the frequent emphasis in *DSM-III* on disordered brain mechanisms in its discussions of etiology as well as its apparent endorsement of pharmacological treatments in preference to psychosocial treatments for many disorders. In response, Spitzer (1983) justified these endorsements by noting that the *DSM-III* text was intended simply to reflect the state of knowledge of etiology and treatment. Similar concerns have been voiced about *DSM-IV* (Nathan & Langenbucher, 1999).

### Atheoretical Approach

*DSM-III* and its successors were also were criticized for their intentionally atheoretical, descriptive position on etiology. Critics (e.g., Klerman et al., 1984) charged that this stance ignored the contributions of psychodynamic theory toward fuller understanding of the pathogenesis of mental disorders and the relationships between emotional conflict and the ego's mechanisms of defense. Responding to these concerns in 1984 (Klerman, Vaillant, Spitzer, & Michels, 1984), Spitzer questioned the empirical basis for the claim that psychodynamic theory had established the pathogenesis of many of the mental disorders. In the foreword to *DSM-III-R* (APA, 1987), Spitzer (the primary author of the foreword) noted that the descriptive, atheoretical approach of *DSM-III* and *DSM-III-R* reflects "our current ignorance of the etiology and pathogenesis of most of the mental disorders" but added that "it is not intended to inhibit or denigrate the role of etiologic theories in psychiatry" (APA, 1987, p. xxiv).

### DSM-IV

The development of *DSM-III* and *DSM-III-R* was chaired by psychiatrist Robert Spitzer. The development of *DSM-IV* was given to another psychiatrist, Allen Frances, who was

given the mandates to provide a better documentation of the empirical support for the decisions that would be made, to improve the utility of the manual for the practicing clinician, and to improve congruency with International Classification of Diseases (ICD) 10.

### DSM-IV Process

The principal goal of the *DSM-IV* process (Frances, Widiger, & Pincus, 1989; Nathan, 1998; Nathan & Langenbucher, 1999; Widiger & Trull, 1993) was to create an empirically based nomenclature. To achieve this goal, a three-stage process was used. The process began with the appointment of 13 work groups, each consisting of four to six individuals. They covered the anxiety disorders; child and adolescent disorders; eating disorders; late luteal phase dysphoric disorder; mood disorders; the multiaxial system; delirium, dementia, amnesia, and other cognitive disorders; personality disorders; psychiatric system interface disorders; psychotic disorders; sexual disorders; sleep disorders; and substance-related disorders.

The work groups began their work by undertaking systematic literature reviews designed to address unresolved diagnostic questions. When the literature reviews failed to resolve outstanding questions, the work groups sought clinical data sets that might be capable of doing so; 36 reanalyses of existing patient data sets were ultimately completed. The work groups also designed and carried out 12 large-scale field trials involving more than 7,000 participants at more than 70 sites worldwide.

The *DSM-IV* process is thoroughly chronicled in four sourcebooks that archive literature reviews and summarize findings from data reanalyses and field trials. The first three (Widiger, Frances, et al., 1994; Widiger, Francis, et al., 1996; Widiger et al., 1997) include 155 detailed literature reviews commissioned by the *DSM-IV* work groups. Volume 4 (Widiger et al., 1998) includes summaries of the results of 36 data reanalyses completed by nine work groups, the key findings of 12 field trials, and each work group's final report.

### DSM-IV Field Trials

Although summaries of the field trials appear in Volume 4 of the sourcebooks, nine *DSM-IV* field trial reports have also been published in journals. Field trial reports on mixed anxiety-depression (Zinbarg et al., 1994) and oppositional defiant disorder and conduct disorder in children and adolescents (Lahey, Applegate, Barkley, Garfinkel, & McBurnett, 1994) appeared in August 1994, followed later the same year by field trial reports on sleep disorders (Buysse et al., 1994) and autistic disorder (Volkmar et al., 1994). The following year, field trial reports for obsessive-compulsive disorder (Foa & Kozak, 1995), somatization disorder (Yutzy et al., 1995), the mood disorders (Keller et al., 1995), and the substance-related disorders (Cottler et al., 1995) appeared. The field trial report for antisocial personality disorder was published in 1996 (Widiger, Hare, Rutherford, Corbitt, & Hart, 1996).

Most of the field trials contrasted the diagnostic sensitivity and specificity of alternative sets of existing diagnostic criteria—including those of ICD-10, *DSM-III-R*, and *DSM-III*—with one or more sets of new criteria. Many explored the impact on diagnostic reliability of changes in the wording of criteria. Some field trials also considered the diagnostic consequences of differing criterion thresholds and assessed the need for additional diagnostic categories.

Symptom data from the field trial for schizophrenia and related psychotic disorders were recently factor analyzed (Ratakonda, Gorman, Yale, & Amador, 1998) to determine whether the three common schizophrenic symptom domains—labeled positive, negative, and disorganized—also encompass the symptoms of psychotic disorders other than schizophrenia. These domains are apparently not exclusive to schizophrenia; they also describe the behavior of patients with schizoaffective disorder and primary mood disorder.

## Reliability and Validity

Most data reported to date on the reliability and validity of *DSM-IV* categories have come from the field trial reports. They suggest modest increments in the reliability of a few diagnostic categories (e.g., oppositional defiant disorder and conduct disorder in children and adolescents, substance abuse and dependence) and validity (e.g., autistic disorder, oppositional defiant disorder in childhood and adolescence). Unfortunately, they also report no real progress in addressing the substantial reliability problems of the personality disorders, the sleep disorders, the disorders of childhood and adolescence, and some of the disorders within the schizophrenic spectrum.

The Research Diagnostic Project (RDP) at Rutgers University has focused on diagnostic issues in substance abuse for several years. Initial RDP studies found the reliability of lifetime *DSM-IV* diagnoses of alcohol, cannabis, cocaine, and opiate abuse and dependence to be high (Langenbucher, Morgenstern, Labouvie, & Nathan, 1994b). The diagnostic concordance of *DSM-III, DSM-IV,* and ICD-10 for disorders involving alcohol, the amphetamines, cannabis, cocaine, the hallucinogens, the opiates, PCP, and the sedative-hypnotics was found to be high for severe disorders and less so for disorders barely reaching diagnostic threshold (Langenbucher, Morgenstern, Labouvie, & Nathan, 1994a). Langenbucher

and his colleagues (1997) also compared the predictive validity of four sets of dependence criteria and found the *DSM-IV* criteria for tolerance and dependence to be less discriminating than alternative criteria were. Finally, Langenbucher and Chung (1995) traced the onset and staging of symptoms of alcohol abuse and dependence. They identified three discrete stages—alcohol abuse, alcohol dependence, and accommodation to the illness—thereby supporting the construct validity of alcohol abuse as a discrete first illness phase and alcohol dependence as distinct from and succeeding abuse.

Three additional studies of *DSM-IV* reliability and validity have also appeared. The first (Eaton, Anthony, Gallo, Cai, & Tien, 1997) reported a 1-year incidence rate of 3.0 per 1,000 per year for major depression in Baltimore, diagnosed according to *DSM-IV* criteria; this rate was comparable to earlier estimates that used *DSM-III* criteria. Two other studies explored diagnostic issues raised by the personality disorders. Ball, Tennen, Poling, Kranzler, and Rounsaville (1997) examined relations between alcohol, cocaine, and opiate abusers' personality disorders and their responses to five- and seven-factor models of personality (respectively, the Neuroticism, Extraversion, Openness Personality Inventory, NEO-PI; Costa & McCrae, 1989 and the Temperament and Character Inventory, TCI; Cloninger, Svrakic, & Przybeck, 1993). NEO-PI scales were strongly linked with specific personality disorders and TCI scales somewhat less so, thereby adding to the growing literature attesting to the power of personality trait dimensions to portray personality disorder validly. On exploring differences in clinicians' uses of Axes I and II, Westen (1997) appeared to have identified an additional source of the diagnostic unreliability of the personality disorders. Whereas clinicians tended to use questions taken directly from the operational criteria to diagnose Axis I disorders, they made Axis II diagnoses more often by "listening to patients describe interpersonal interactions and observing their behavior with the interviewer" (p. 895). The latter practice may contribute to the unreliability of personality disorder assessment.

## Gender and Cultural Bias

Corbitt and Widiger (1995) lamented the paucity of empirical findings on gender prevalence rates in the personality disorders (PDs) that contributed to the controversy surrounding *DSM-III-R*'s estimates that more women than men merit the diagnoses of histrionic PD and dependent PD. The *DSM-IV* text now avoids specifying gender prevalence rates for these disorders. *DSM-IV* has also added three PDs (schizoid, schizotypal, and narcissistic) to the three (paranoid, antisocial, and obsessive-compulsive) disorders that *DSM-III-R* indicated were diagnosed more often in males than in females.

Corbitt and Widiger ask whether *DSM-IV* has unintentionally introduced diagnostic bias in the laudable effort to combat it, by going beyond the modest empirical data on gender prevalence rates for the histrionic and dependent PDs. Hartung and Widiger (1998) consider the question of gender prevalence rates in *DSM-IV* diagnoses more generally. Although conclusions about these rates were informed by data from several sources—the field trials, existing data sets, and systematic literature reviews—they could possibly have been compromised by sampling biases (e.g., disproportionate numbers of one or the other gender in sample populations) or biases within the diagnostic criteria themselves (e.g., lack of gender neutrality in criteria sets). Hartung and Widiger claim that as a result, *DSM-IV* may retain vestiges of the gender-based bias that characterized its predecessors.

### Criticisms of *DSM-IV*

There is general agreement on the strong empirical base that underlies *DSM-IV*. Yet even persons most involved in the development of the instrument acknowledge limitations on full utilization of the extensive empirical database because of unavoidable, biased, or misleading interpretations of the data (e.g., Kendler, 1990; Widiger & Trull, 1993).

Responding to criticisms that professional issues overshadowed scientific ones in the creation of *DSM-IV* (e.g., Caplan, 1991; Carson, 1991), Widiger and Trull (1993) defended attention to issues of utility that sometimes preempted issues of validity, such as when a valid diagnosis is de-emphasized because so few patients meet its criteria. Nonetheless, even though these authors admitted that the *DSM-IV* task force had to be sensitive to a variety of forensic, social, international, and public health issues, they saw the result as largely an empirically driven instrument. They also expected many of the decisions made during development of the instrument to continue to be debated, in part because the database for these decisions was often ambiguous or inadequate.

The lead review of *DSM-IV* in the *American Journal of Psychiatry* was written by Samuel Guze (1995), a key figure in the development of *DSM-III*. Although it was largely positive, Guze's review (1995) expressed concern that many *DSM-IV* diagnostic conditions failed to meet Robins and Guze's (1970) criteria for diagnostic validity. He criticized the apparent proliferation of less than fully validated diagnostic entities, a theme others (e.g., Grumet, 1995; Kirk & Kutchins, 1992, 1994) have also sounded. To this concern, Pincus, First, Frances, and McQueen (1996) note that although *DSM-IV* contains 13 diagnoses not in *DSM-III-R*, it has eliminated eight *DSM-III-R* diagnoses, for a net gain of only five.

## CONTINUING DIAGNOSTIC CONTROVERSIES

*DSM-IV* is a notable improvement over the prior editions of the APA diagnostic manual. Nevertheless, many diagnostic controversies remain. Discussed in the following sections are issues concerning excessive comorbidity, biases in diagnosis, the debate over categorical versus dimensional models, and new definitions of mental disorder.

### Comorbidity

In a conceptual consideration at diagnostic comorbidity, Klein and Riso (1993) revisited two fundamental issues: whether disorders are discrete and natural classes or artificial categories created by the establishment of arbitrary cutoffs on a continuum and whether categorical or dimensional models of psychopathology better capture the essence of psychopathology. (We review research on the first of these issues in this section and research on the second later.) A phenomenon that is pervasive in clinical research is that patients and community participants rarely meet diagnostic criteria for just one mental disorder, contrary to the intentions of the authors of the diagnostic manual to develop criteria sets that lead to the identification of one single pathology. Klein and Riso listed six conceptual and statistical methods that could be used to demonstrate the existence of discrete boundaries between disorders and 11 possible explanations for diagnostic co-occurrences; they ultimately concluded that even these sophisticated methods may not properly account for all instances of comorbidity.

Evaluating the impact of high rates of comorbidity on clinical practice and research design in a large sample of young adults, Newman, Moffit, Caspi, and Silva (1998) concluded that groups that underrepresent comorbidity (e.g., student samples) probably also underestimate effect sizes for relations between a disorder and its correlates (e.g., physical health problems, interference with daily living, use of treatments, etc.), whereas groups that overrepresent comorbidity (e.g., clinical samples) overestimate effect sizes.

Concerns about the nature and extent of comorbidity led to the development of the National Comorbidity Survey (NCS), a nationwide stratified multistage survey of the U.S. population from 15 through 54 years of age. In an initial NCS report, Blazer, Kessler, McGonagle, and Swartz (1994) reported higher 30-day and lifetime prevalence estimates of major depression than the estimates reported in the ECA study and confirmed the high rates of co-occurrence between major depression and a range of other mental disorders. Kessler et al. (1995) examined the prevalence and comorbidity of

*DSM-III-R* posttraumatic stress disorder (PTSD) in a second NCS article. PTSD was strongly comorbid with other lifetime *DSM-III-R* disorders in both men and women—especially the affective disorders, the anxiety disorders, and the substance use disorders. In another NCS report, Magee, Eaton, Wittchen, McGonagle, and Kessler (1996) reported that lifetime phobias are highly comorbid with each other, with other anxiety disorders, and with affective disorders; they were more weakly comorbid with alcohol and drug dependence. As with major depression, comorbid phobias are generally more severe than pure phobias.

Four additional comorbidity studies all investigated the frequent co-occurrence of substance-related and other psychiatric disorders. Two (Hudziak et al., 1996; Morgenstern, Langenbucher, Labouvie, & Miller, 1997) explored links between PDs and substance abuse; a third (Brown et al., 1995) traced the clinical course of depression in alcoholics; the fourth (Fletcher, Page, Francis, Copeland, & Naus, 1996) investigated cognitive deficits associated with long-term cannabis use. All confirmed that substance abuse and the PDs—especially borderline and antisocial PD—co-occur at high frequency, as does substance abuse and mood disorder as well as long-term substance abuse and cognitive dysfunction.

Reflecting recent clinical interest in comorbid mental and physical disorders, Sherbourne, Wells, Meredith, Jackson, and Camp (1996) reported that patients with anxiety disorder in treatment for chronic medical conditions like hypertension, diabetes, or heart disease functioned at levels lower than those of medical patients without comorbid anxiety. These differences were most pronounced in mental-health-related quality-of-life measures and when anxiety rather than depression was comorbid with the chronic medical conditions. A study with related aims (Johnson, Spitzer, Williams, Kroenke, & Linzer, 1995) reported that many of the primary care medical patients they studied also suffered from alcohol abuse or dependence; nearly half also had other co-occurring mental disorders. Although the substance abusers reported poorer health and greater functional impairment than did primary care patients without any mental disorders, they were less impaired than were patients who were diagnosed with mood, anxiety, eating, or somatoform disorders.

O'Connor, McGuire, Reiss, Hethering, and Plomin (1998) attempted to fit adolescent and parent reports and observational measures of depressive symptoms and antisocial behavior from a national sample of 720 same-sex adolescents to behavioral genetic models to determine the respective genetic and environmental influences on individual differences in and co-occurrence of the two psychopathological behaviors. Approximately half the variability in the depressive

symptoms and antisocial behaviors could be attributed to genetic factors, although shared and nonshared environmental influences were also significant.

Reflecting another major societal concern, a 1996 issue of *Archives of General Psychiatry* featured five reports on the co-occurrence of violence and mental illness (Eronen, Hakola, & Tiihonen, 1996; Hodgins, Mednick, Brennan, Schulsinger, & Engberg, 1996; Jordan, Schlenger, Fairbank, & Caddell, 1996; Teplin, Abram, & McClelland, 1996; Virkkunen, Eggert, Rawlings, & Linnoila, 1996). Summarizing the principal findings from these studies, Marzuk (1996) observed that this relationship "appears strongest for the severe mental illnesses, particularly those involving psychosis, and it is increased by the use of alcohol and other psychoactive substances" (pp. 484–485). Results from a 26-year prospective study of a 1966 Finnish birth cohort (Tiihonen, Isohanni, Rasanen, Koiranen, & Moring, 1997) supported the same conclusions: Risk for criminal behavior was significantly higher among persons with psychotic disorders, especially persons suffering from alcohol-induced psychoses or schizophrenia and coexisting substance abuse.

Overall, the extensive research on comorbidity to date has confirmed both the identity of the disorders most commonly comorbid (e.g., substance-related disorders, personality disorders, depression, anxiety) and comorbidity's substantial adverse social, physical, psychological, and psychiatric consequences.

## Diagnostic Bias

Diagnostic biases based on race and gender have recently been confirmed. Garb (1997) concluded that African American and Hispanic patients are less likely than Caucasians are to be diagnosed with psychotic mood disorder and more likely to be diagnosed with schizophrenia despite comparable symptoms. Becker and Lamb (1994) reported that females are more likely to be diagnosed with histrionic personality disorder than are males, whereas males are more likely than females are to be diagnosed with antisocial personality disorder despite equivalent symptoms. Depression is also diagnosed more often in women than it is in men, even when symptoms of mood disorder are comparable across the genders (Potts, Burnam, & Wells, 1991). Gender also influences the differential diagnosis of major depression and organic mental disorder (Wrobel, 1993). Both male and female clinicians show these gender-based diagnostic biases (Adler, Drake, & Teague, 1990).

An important question for future research is the source and nature of these apparent biases. Biases can be inherent to a diagnostic nomenclature (e.g., the presence of a particular diagnosis could reflect cultural biases within the organization that constructed the nomenclature), or they could be confined to the diagnostic criteria (i.e., the disorder does in fact exist but the criteria set is biased against a particular ethnic or gender group), clinicians' applications of the criteria set, or instruments of assessment. Biases in assessment are discussed in more detail within volume 10 (devoted entirely to the topic of assessment) of this series.

### The Categorical-Dimensional Debate

Categorical versus dimensional classification first became a matter of concern when *DSM-III* more than doubled the number of diagnoses included in its predecessors. As diagnoses proliferated with *DSM-III* and *DSM-IV*, the frequency of comorbidity substantially increased, causing clinicians to ask whether the comorbidity that resulted represented the co-occurrence of two or more separate mental disorders or a single disorder that had simply been labeled in different ways. As a consequence, the advantages and disadvantages of dimensional and categorical approaches to personality and diagnosis has begun to be debated and explored extensively (e.g., Clark, Livesley, & Morey, 1997; Clark, Watson, & Reynolds, 1995; Klein & Riso, 1993; Widiger, 1997b). The focus of these efforts has been primarily on the personality disorders, in which symptom overlap is greatest, but the issues and proposals apply to other sections of the manual as well. For example, Watson and Clark (1995), Watson, Clark, et al. (1995), and Watson, Weber, et al. (1995) have explored dimensions that underlie depression and anxiety. Some of that research has already been considered previously, in our review of efforts to validate *DSM-III* and *DSM-III-R* diagnoses. The research has also been reviewed extensively by Mineka, Watson, and Clark (1998), as well as by Clark (2000).

According to Clark (1999), dimensional approaches to personality disorder (a) are theoretically consistent with the complexity of symptom patterns that is observed clinically, (b) increase reliability, (c) are theoretically consistent with the observed lack of discrete boundaries between different types of psychopathology and between normality and psychopathology, and (d) provide a basis for understanding symptom heterogeneity within diagnoses by retaining information about component trait levels.

Clark (1999) distinguished between two different dimensional approaches to the personality disorders. The first, rooted in the traditional categorical system, conceptualizes each separate disorder as a continuum, so that in principle any patient could exhibit different levels of traits of several personality disorders. The alternative is the trait dimensional approach, in which assessment aims to create a profile of the personality traits that underlie the disorder. Although several instru-

ments that reflect the higher order factors describing normal personality have proven useful for studying relations between personality and personality disorders (e.g., Widiger, 1993), only recently have instruments been developed specifically for the purpose of tapping into the lower order traits relevant to personality disorders. These include the 15-dimension Schedule for Nonadaptive and Adaptive Personality (SNAP; Clark, 1993) and the 18-dimension Dimensional Assessment of Personality Pathology–Basic Questionnaire (DAPP-BQ; Livesley, 1990).

In unpublished research by Clark and her colleagues relating diagnostic and trait dimensional approaches to personality disorder (Clark, 1999), two patient samples were interviewed with the Structured Interview for *DSM-III-R* Personality Disorders–Revised (SIDP-R; Pfohl, Blum, Zimmerman, & Stangl, 1989) and completed the SNAP. Multiple correlations between SNAP scales and diagnostic interview scores revealed a great deal of common variance: The information in a SNAP profile enabled prediction of between one quarter and three quarters of the variance in the interview-based diagnostic ratings, suggesting that the trait dimensions assessed by the SNAP underlie clinical ratings of personality pathology. These findings are especially impressive in view of data reviewed by Clark et al. (1997) to the effect that obtaining convergent validity for measures of PD assessment has been extremely difficult.

> It is widely believed that categorical and dimensional models are inherently incompatible, and that one must choose between them. In actuality, however, it is more accurate to describe these models as existing in a hierarchical relation to one another, with dimensions being the blocks from which categories may be built. (Clark et al., 1997, p. 206)

O'Connor and Dyce (1998) recently reviewed the clinical data supporting the several models of PD configuration. They found moderate support for the *DSM-IV* dimensions and Cloninger's (1987) tridimensional theory, and they found stronger support for the five-factor model (Widiger, Trull, Clarkin, Sanderson, & Costa, 1994) and Cloninger and Svrakic's (1994) empirically derived seven-factor model. On balance, they concluded that four of the five factors within the five-factor model explain the bulk of the variance associated with PD. Unfortunately, these authors failed to include in their comparisons either the tripartite model or the trait dimensional approaches characterized by the SNAP and the DAPP-BQ. The integration of the SNAP and DAPP-BQ models with the five-factor model has been demonstrated in studies by Clark and Reynolds (2001) and Clark and Livesley (1994). However, although impressive progress has been made in recent years in amassing conceptual and historical support for dimensional versus categorical approaches to the personality disorders and other overlapping psychopathological entities, the ultimate utility of the trait dimensional approach will not be known until substantially more research data have been gathered that demonstrate empirically the advantages of this approach to these disorders.

## New Definitions of Mental Disorder

As previously indicated, a continuing criticism of *DSM-III* and *DSM-IV* has been their definition of mental disorders, which critics have seen as so broad and all-encompassing as to include many nonpathological behaviors within its purview. As a result, alternative definitions have been proposed. Two of the most widely discussed of these are briefly reviewed here.

### Wakefield's Harmful Dysfunction

Wakefield first defined mental disorder as *harmful dysfunction* in 1992 and in subsequent publications (e.g., 1997, 1999a, 1999b) defended and clarified the definition. To Wakefield, whether a condition is harmful requires a value judgment as to its desirability or undesirability, and *dysfunction* refers to a system's failure to function as shaped by processes of natural selection.

> A condition is a mental disorder if and only if (a) the condition causes some harm or deprivation of benefit to the person as judged by the standards of the person's culture (the value criterion), and (b) the condition results from the inability of some mental mechanism to perform its natural function, wherein a natural function is an effect that is part of the evolutionary explanation of the existence and structure of the mental mechanism (the explanatory criterion). (Wakefield, 1992, p. 385)

Bergner (1997), however, has argued that Wakefield's harmful dysfunction conceptualization requires clinicians to make judgments about patients' mental mechanisms and that many such judgments cannot reliably be made. Lilienfeld and Marino (1995, 1999) also take issue with Wakefield's definition. They argue that many mental functions are not direct evolutionary adaptations but are instead neutral by-products of adaptations. They also note that the concept of the evolutionarily designed response neglects the fact that natural selection often produces extreme behavioral variability across individuals and that many disorders that have achieved consensus are best portrayed as evolutionarily adaptive responses to danger, threat, or loss.

Disagreeing, Spitzer (1997) calls Wakefield's construct a "brilliant breakthrough" (p. 259) because it emphasizes

that what is not working in the organism is the function that we expect to be present and in operation by virtue of evolution and selection. Richters and Hinshaw (1997) also laud Wakefield's construct, even though they acknowledge that it requires a thorough knowledge of internal, neurobiological operations as well as value judgments about external, social data—both requirements that are difficult to satisfy.

### Bergner and Ossorio's Significant Restriction

Claiming that consensus on a definition of psychopathology has not been achieved despite years of trying, Bergner (1997) concluded that this situation has seriously affected efforts to study psychopathology, to treat it, and to deal with its social consequences. He endorsed a definition of psychopathology previously proposed by Ossorio (1985): Psychopathology is best defined as "significant restriction in the ability of an individual to engage in deliberate action and, equivalently, to participate in available social practices" (Bergner, 1997, p. 246). This definition "meets the intellectual criteria that an adequate definition represent a non-empirical articulation of the necessary and sufficient conditions for correct application of a concept, and that it successfully discriminate instances of a concept from non-instances."

Comparing Bergner's definition to his own (Wakefield, 1992), Wakefield (1997) concluded that it is neither necessary nor sufficient to define a disorder. Its most serious problem is its overinclusiveness: Many restrictions on deliberate action are imposed in normal mental functioning. By contrast, Wakefield understandably affirmed that his own harmful dysfunction analysis, criticized by Bergner (1997), adequately discriminates between disorder and nondisorder. Spitzer (1997), whose own attempt to define mental disorder is represented by *DSM-III* (APA, 1980) and its successors, admitted to fatigue at efforts to define psychopathology and expressed uncertainty over the value of a consensus definition. He wrote that the Bergner-Ossorio definition simply "muddles the issues," whereas he lauded Wakefield's harmful dysfunction conceptualization as a "brilliant breakthrough" because it clarifies important underlying issues (p. 259). Although Widiger (1997a) was pleased that Bergner addressed the fundamental issues and principal difficulties in defining mental illness, he agreed with others that the Bergner-Ossorio definition of mental disorder ultimately will not be more successful than earlier efforts were. A major reason is the absence of distinct boundaries between either physical disorders or normality for the construct proposed—an attraction for a scientist like Widiger who has espoused dimensional approaches to some forms of psychopathology. Finally, Nathan (1997) took issue with Bergner's statement that a consensus on a definition of mental disorder does not exist, in view of the widespread acceptance of the value of *DSM-IV* and its predecessors by mental health professionals. Moreover, Nathan (1997) noted, however attractive Bergner's construct may be, in the final analysis, data on utility—absent to this time—will be the ultimate arbiter of the construct's worth.

In a subsequent expansive articulation of his position, Bergner (in press) restated and defended his conception of pathology as behavioral disability or functional impairment, concluded that it unifies theoretically divergent explanations of psychopathology, offered a consequent model of integrative psychotherapy, and weighed the considerable scientific and clinical implications of this integrative framework.

## NEW QUANTITATIVE METHODS FOR DIAGNOSTIC AND CLASSIFICATION RESEARCH

The advanced quantitative techniques described in this section of the chapter increasingly have been brought to bear on problems of diagnosis and classification. The success to date of these efforts suggests even greater use of these approaches in the future.

### Event-History Analysis

Event-history techniques such as survival-hazard analysis (Cox & Oakes, 1984; Singer & Willett, 1991) appear to hold great promise for all levels of nosologic analysis—subcriterion, criterion, and composite algorithm—for which longitudinal data are available. To date, survival-hazard analysis has been applied to both the onset of depression, alcoholism, marijuana use, and other mental disorders at the syndrome level (e.g., Burke, Burke, Rae, & Regier, 1991) and the individual symptom level (Langenbucher & Chung, 1995; Martin, Langenbucher, Kaczynski, & Chung, 1996; Rosenberg & Anthony, 2001).

Survival methods generate two kinds of functions. The survival function estimates the proportion of individuals (cases) at each point in time to have escaped (survived) the onset of an index event such as the emergence of a psychological symptom or syndrome. Survival curves with steep slopes represent events that tend to occur relatively early; gradual slopes indicate that the events have occurred later. The hazard function estimates the likelihood that a case that has not yet experienced an event will do so during that period. An advantage of survival-hazard analysis for nosologic research on illness onset and symptom staging is its capacity to accommodate cases that have not yet developed the problem (so-called right-censored data); other methods

only use data from frankly ill or fully symptomatic subjects with (presumably) more severe illnesses. Another advantage is that survival-hazard analysis shows changes in risk and onset patterns across time rather than revealing only a cross-sectional view. The method produces a graphic plot of case survival and hazard, an intuitive and appealing mode of presenting data that often highlights relationships—such as symptom clusters or stages (e.g., Langenbucher & Chung, 1995)—that are otherwise obscure.

### Item Response Theory

Item response theory (IRT) focuses on the distribution of individuals' response patterns for a given set of items and offers the researcher a choice of models for understanding item or criterion behavior (Hambleton, Swaminathan, & Rogers, 1991).

The two-parameter logistic IRT model appears most relevant to the situation in which diagnostic symptoms are assessed by structured interview. Two-parameter IRT obtains estimates of each symptom's discrimination and threshold parameters. An item's discrimination is its ability to distinguish subjects with levels of the latent trait (the underlying dimension of illness severity) above or below the item's threshold. An item's threshold is the point on the underlying dimension or trait at which 50% of respondents endorse the item (i.e., report that they have the symptom). Threshold is therefore closely related to the construct of item difficulty in classical psychometrics. Discrimination and threshold, called the *a* and *b* parameters, respectively (Hambleton et al., 1991), can be presented graphically as an item response function or IRF. Plotted for each item or symptom, the IRF is an S-shaped normal ogive function that shows the probability that the symptom will be endorsed at each level of the latent trait. IRFs express discrimination as slope (gradually sloping IRFs indicate items with low discrimination and steeply sloping IRFs indicate items with high discrimination) and express threshold as horizontal displacement on the latent trait axis (IRFs displaced far to the right indicate items with high threshold and IRFs displaced to the left indicate items with low threshold). IRFs can be used to construct a scale that provides a parsimonious assessment of individual respondents' positions on the underlying or latent dimension. An optimally constructed scale consists of items with discrimination greater than 1.0 and thresholds relatively evenly dispersed from low to high, in order to cover the full range of the underlying dimension.

Two-parameter IRT appears especially useful for understanding patterns of responses to structured or semistructured diagnostic interviews. In this situation IRT assumes unidimensionality of the underlying dimension of psychopathology, requiring a preliminary stage of factor analysis to ensure that the diagnostic questions can be adequately modeled by a single underlying dimension—for example, depression, cognitive disorganization, and so forth. This is a limitation of the method because unidimensionality is a firm requirement for IRT. Although they are not yet widely used at this time, IRT-based analyses are powerfully heuristic and are beginning to surface in analyses of both discrete diagnostic instruments—for example, Cooke and Michie's (1997) analysis of the Hare Psychopathy Checklist–Revised (Hare, 1991) and Kirisci, Moss, and Tarter's (1996) analysis of the Situational Confidence Questionnaire (Annis & Graham, 1987)—and *DSM-IV* diagnostic criteria themselves (Langenbucher et al., 2000).

## Latent Class Analysis

Latent class analysis (LCA; McCutcheon, 1987) has been used to explore naturally occurring subtypes within a previously homogeneous collection of cases. LCA has much in common with and can be viewed as a categorical form of conventional factor analysis.

Different symptom profiles exist even for members of the same diagnostic category—for example, some alcoholics complain principally of physiological symptoms, whereas others experience loss of control, just as some schizophrenics complain of dramatic positive symptoms, whereas others are withdrawn, with predominantly negative symptom profiles. LCA assumes that these different profiles are the result of the presence within the diagnostic group of a limited number of mutually exclusive subtypes or latent classes, each with its own characteristic symptom profile. LCA identifies the structure and number of these latent classes by maximizing goodness of fit across models with different numbers and composition of latent classes. Results of LCA include membership probabilities—a statement of the expected prevalence of each latent class within the data set—and symptom endorsement probabilities (SEPs), which reflect the likelihood that a member of a particular class will endorse an item or symptom as present.

Although it is quite new, LCA has generated a great deal of excitement in subtyping research because it creates strong, falsifiable models. It has been applied successfully to studies of the latent classes of alcoholism (Bucholz et al., 1996), eating disorders (Bulik, Sullivan, & Kendler, 2000), depression (Chen, Eaton, Gallow, & Nestadt, 2000), and social phobia (Kessler, Stein, & Berglund, 1998), among other types of mental disorder. Bucholz et al.'s (1996) study underlined the centrality of substance-specific withdrawal in alcoholism and of nosologic instability—issues that have been a matter of debate for several decades. Kessler et al.'s (1998) study showed that social phobia is actually a conglomerate of two separate fear types—pure speaking fear versus more diffuse social fear—based on performance and interactional anxiety.

## Taxometric Analyses

Meehl and his colleagues have developed a variety of statistical techniques, coined *taxometrics,* for exploring the latent structure of psychological constructs. These techniques are statistical procedures that analyze relationships within and between variables that would be uniquely indicative of latent classes, referred to as *taxons* (Meehl, 1995; Widiger, 2001).

One of the first taxometric techniques was maximum covariance analysis or MAXCOV (Waller & Meehl, 1998). MAXCOV permits investigation of relationships among several fallible but valid indicators of a disorder. Two indicators are correlated with one another across groups identified by the scores obtained on the indicators. For example, two of the diagnostic criteria for a major depressive disorder could be correlated with one another in persons with only one, two, three, four, or more of the remaining diagnostic criteria for depression. The analyses are repeated using two other diagnostic criteria and are repeated again and again until all possible pairs of indicators have been correlated with one another. The average distribution of correlations is then obtained. If the distribution of averaged correlations lies flat along the levels of the other indicators, then the distribution is said to be consistent with a continuous, dimensional variable; if there is a clear peak in the distribution of correlations, then the distribution is said to be consistent with a categorical variable.

Additional taxometric techniques include mean above minus mean below a cut (MAMBAC; Waller & Meehl, 1998), maximum eigenvalue (MAXEIG; Waller & Meehl, 1998), and latent mode factor analysis (L-MODE; Waller & Meehl, 1998). MAXEIG is a multivariate generalization of MAXCOV. Like MAXCOV, MAXEIG examines the degree of covariation between indicators along successive points along another indicator. However, whereas MAXCOV considers the covariance between a pair of indicators, MAXEIG considers the eigenvalue (the multivariate analogue of covariance) of the first principal factor of the matrix of all remaining indicators.

MAMBAC creates a series of cuts along one indicator and examines differences in scores on a second indicator for cases falling above and below each cut. If the latent structure is taxonic, a plot of these differences should be peaked (suggesting the presence of an optimal cutting score). If there are no underlying latent class taxons, then the plot should take on a dish-shaped curve that would be characteristic of a dimensional latent structure. L-MODE works by factor analyzing all available indicators and examining the distribution of scores on the first principal factor. If the construct is taxonic, factor scores should be bimodally distributed; if the construct is dimensional, factor scores should be unimodally distributed.

Most researchers use more than one taxometric analysis in any given study because the consistency of findings across different taxometric techniques is considered to be most informative. These techniques have been used in many diagnostic studies, including studies of the latent class structure of depression (Haslem & Beck, 1994; Ruscio & Ruscio, 2000), schizotypia (Lenzenweger & Korfine, 1992), and dissociation (Waller, Putnam, & Carlson, 1996; Waller & Ross, 1994).

### Receiver-Operator Characteristic Analysis

Typically, *DSM-III, DSM-III-R,* or *DSM-IV* diagnoses are entered if a patient meets some minimum number of symptoms—three of a possible nine for a diagnosis of substance dependence, five of a possible nine for a major depressive episode. A shortcoming of the *DSM* tradition, however, has been the promulgation of these clinical thresholds or cut points in an essentially arbitrary way, as the result of expert consensus rather than empirical research. Receiver-operator characteristic (ROC) analysis represents an attractive alternative to this arbitrary approach because it is capable of suggesting symptom thresholds with optimum points of balance between diagnostic sensitivity and specificity (Hsiao, Bartko, & Potter, 1989)

At each possible cut point—one of seven possible symptoms, two of seven, three of seven, and so on—ROC plots diagnostic sensitivity (the proportion of ill cases diagnosed as ill) against specificity (the proportion of well cases diagnosed as well) in a simple bivariate space, so that the effect on diagnostic positivity and base rates of setting the cut point at different levels can be studied. A refinement, quality ROC (QROC; Clarke & McKenzie, 1994) compares different ROC curves for different symptom combinations, identifying threshold levels of particular symptom combinations that are more efficient than others. Although they are not yet widely used, ROC-based methods have begun to show substantial promise for selecting symptom thresholds and profiles that are most sensitive to cases of true illness. For example, Cassidy, Chapman, Kwapil, Eckblad, and Zinser (2000) have validated a proposed algorithm for mixed bipolar episode that requires two of a possible six dysphoric symptoms and Mota and Schachar (2000) developed, with ROC-based methods, specific combinations of ADHD symptoms; these combinations were two to three times more efficient than were stock *DSM-IV* algorithms in discriminating hyperactive from normal children.

## A FINAL WORD

Although we have worked hard to ensure that this chapter accurately reflects the problems—substantial, controversial, and perplexing—that continue to burden syndromal diagnosis, we have worked just as hard to represent the extensive empirical support for the validity of *DSM-IV* (APA, 1994). Nevertheless, few would disagree that substantial improvement will have to be made to the processes as well as the conceptual underpinnings of syndromal diagnosis more generally. We have suggested both some of the problems that must be faced and some of the research methods that will be deployed to address these problems if such substantial improvement in the performance of our diagnostic systems is, in fact, to be gained.

We are confident that very significant improvements in the reliability, external validity, coverage, and cultural coherence of our diagnostic systems will be made in *DSM-V* and its successors because nosology is a maturing field widely and rightly viewed as crucial to the development of the mental health sciences generally. It is possible that *DSM-IV*'s successors will take a very different form and perhaps even be based on a completely different set of underlying assumptions, such as a dimensional rather than categorical view of mental illness. Nonetheless, it is also true that *DSM-IV*'s current categorical structure conveys in easily accessible form valuable information on etiology, epidemiology, psychopathology, associated features, and treatment of most forms of human psychological suffering. The organization of the chapters that follow in this text attests to the utility and validity of this nomenclature, even though virtually every chapter author, if asked, could readily volunteer his or her own concerns with the present system.

## REFERENCES

Adler, D. A., Drake, R. E., & Teague, G. B. (1990). Clinicians' practices in personality assessment: Does gender influence the use of *DSM-III* Axis II? *Comprehensive Psychiatry, 31,* 125–133.

Albee, G. W. (1970). Notes toward a position paper opposing psychodiagnosis. In A. R. Mahrer (Ed.), *New approaches to personality classification* (pp. 385–398). New York: Columbia University Press.

American Psychiatric Association. (1933). Notes and comment: Revised classified nomenclature of mental disorders. *American Journal of Psychiatry, 90,* 1369–1376.

American Psychiatric Association. (1952). *Diagnostic and statistical manual of mental disorders.* Washington, DC: Author.

American Psychiatric Association. (1968). *Diagnostic and statistical manual of mental disorders* (2nd ed.). Washington, DC: Author.

American Psychiatric Association. (1980). *Diagnostic and statistical manual of mental disorders* (3rd ed.). Washington, DC: Author.

American Psychiatric Association. (1987). *Diagnostic and statistical manual of mental disorders* (3rd ed., rev.). Washington, DC: Author.

American Psychiatric Association. (1994). *Diagnostic and statistical manual of mental disorders* (4th ed.). Washington, DC: Author.

Andreasen, N. C. (1995). The validation of psychiatric diagnosis: New models and approaches. *American Journal of Psychiatry, 152,* 161–162.

Annis, H. M., & Graham, J. M. (1987). *Situational confidence questionnaire.* Toronto, Ontario, Canada: Addiction Research Foundation.

Ball, S. A., Tennen, H., Poling, J. C., Kranzler, H. R., & Rounsaville, B. J. (1997). Personality, temperament, and character dimensions and the DSM-IV personality disorders in substance abusers. *Journal of Abnormal Psychology, 106,* 545–553.

Beck, A. T. (1976). *Cognitive therapy of the emotional disorders.* New York: New American Library.

Beck, A. T. (1987). Cognitive models of depression. *Journal of Cognitive Psychotherapy, 1,* 2–27.

Beck, A. T., Ward, C. H., Mendelson, M., Mock, J. E., & Erbaugh, J. K. (1962). Reliability of psychiatric diagnoses: II. A study of consistency of clinical judgments and ratings. *American Journal of Psychiatry, 119,* 351–357.

Becker, D., & Lamb, S. (1994). Sex bias in the diagnosis of borderline personality disorder and post traumatic stress disorder. *Professional Psychology: Research & Practice, 25,* 55–61.

Bergner, R. M. (1997). What is psychopathology? And so what? *Clinical Psychology: Science and Practice, 4,* 235–248.

Bergner, R. M. (in press). Putting it all together: An integrative framework for psychopathology and psychotherapy. *Journal of Abnormal Psychology.*

Birley, J. L. T. (1975). The history of psychiatry as the history of an art. *British Journal of Psychiatry, 127,* 393–400.

Black, S. (1971). Labeling and psychiatry: A comment. *Social Science and Medicine, 5,* 391–392.

Blashfield, R. K. (1984). *The classification of psychopathology.* New York: Plenum.

Blashfield, R. K., & Draguns, J. G. (1976). Toward a taxonomy of psychopathology. *British Journal of Psychiatry, 42,* 574–583.

Blazer, D. G., Kessler, R. C., McGonagle, K. A., & Swartz, M. S. (1994). The prevalence and distribution of major depression in a national community sample: The National Comorbidity Survey. *American Journal of Psychiatry, 151,* 979–986.

Brown, S. A., Inaba, R. K., Gillin, M. D., Schuckit, M. A., Stewart, M. A., & Irwin, M. R. (1995). Alcoholism and affective disorder: Clinical course of depressive symptoms. *American Journal of Psychiatry, 152,* 435–452.

Bucholz, K. K., Heath, A. C., Reich, T., Hesselbrock, V. M., Kramer, J. R., Nurnberger, J. I., & Schuckit, M. A. (1996). Can we subtype alcoholism? A latent class analysis of data from relatives of alcoholics in a multicenter family study of alcoholism. *Alcoholism: Clinical and Experimental Research, 20,* 1462–1471.

Bulik, C. M., Sullivan, P. F., & Kendler, K. S. (2000). An empirical study of the classification of eating disorders. *American Journal of Psychiatry, 157,* 886–895.

Burke, K. C., Burke, J. D., Rae, D. S., & Regier, D. A. (1991). Comparing age of onset of major depression and other psychiatric disorders by birth cohorts in five US community populations. *Archives of General Psychiatry, 48,* 789–795.

Buysse, D. J., Reynolds, C. F., Hauri, P. J., Roth, T., Stepanski, E. J., Thorpy, M. J., Bixler, E. O., Kales, A., Manfredi, R. L., Vgontzas, A. N., Mesiano, D., Houck, P. R., & Kupfer, D. J. (1994). Diagnostic concordance for *DSM-IV* sleep disorders: A report from the APA/NIMH *DSM-IV* field trial. *American Journal of Psychiatry, 151,* 1351–1360.

Cantor, N., Smith, E. E., French, R. deS., & Mezzich, J. (1980). Psychiatric diagnosis as prototype categorization. *Journal of Abnormal Psychology, 89,* 181–193.

Cantwell, D. P., Russell, A. T., Mattison, R., & Will, L. (1979). A comparison of DSM-II and DSM-III in the diagnosis of childhood psychiatric disorders: I. Agreement with expected diagnosis. *Archives of General Psychiatry, 36,* 1208–1213.

Caplan, P. J. (1991). How do they decide who is normal? The bizarre, but true, tale of the *DSM* process. *Canadian Psychology, 32,* 162–170.

Carson, R. C. (1991). Dilemmas in the pathway of the *DSM-IV. Journal of Abnormal Psychology, 100,* 302–307.

Cassidy, F., Ahearn, E., Murry, E., Forest, K., & Carroll, B. J. (2000). Diagnostic depressive symptoms of the mixed bipolar episode. *Psychological Medicine, 30,* 403–411.

Chapman, L. J., Chapman, J. P., Kwapil, T. R., Eckblad, M., & Zinser, M. C. (1994). Putatively psychosis-prone subjects 10 years later. *Journal of Abnormal Psychology, 103,* 171–183.

Chen, L.-S., Eaton, W. W., Gallow, J. J., & Nestadt, G. (2000). Understanding the heterogeneity of depression through the triad of symptoms, course and risk factors: A longitudinal, population-based study. *Journal of Affective Disorders, 59,* 1–11.

Chen, Y. R., Swann, A. C., & Burt, D. B. (1996). Stability of diagnosis in schizophrenia. *American Journal of Psychiatry, 153,* 682–686.

Clark, L. A. (1993). *Manual for the Schedule for Nonadaptive and Adaptive Personality.* Minneapolis: University of Minnesota Press.

Clark, L. A. (1999). Dimensional approaches to personality disorder assessment and diagnosis. In C. R. Cloninger (Ed.), *Personality and psychopathology.* Washington, DC: American Psychiatric Press.

Clark, L. A. (2000). Mood, personality, and personality disorder. In R. Davidson (Ed.), *Anxiety, depression, and emotion* (pp. 171–200). New York: Oxford University Press.

Clark, L. A., Beck, A. T., & Beck, J. S. (1994). Symptom differences in major depression, dysthymia, panic disorder, and generalized anxiety disorder. *American Journal of Psychiatry, 151,* 205–209.

Clark, L. A., & Livesley, W. J. (1994). Two approaches to identifying the dimensions of personality disorder: Convergence on the five-factor model. In P. T. Costa & T. A. Widiger (Eds.), *Personality disorders and the five-factor model of personality* (pp. 261– 278). Washington, DC: American Psychological Association.

Clark, L. A., Livesley, W. J., & Morey, L. (1997). Special feature: Personality disorder assessment: The challenge of construct validity. *Journal of Personality Assessment, 11,* 205–231.

Clark, L. A., & Reynolds, S. K. (2001). Predicting dimensions of personality disorder from domains and facets of the Five-Factor model. *Journal of Personality, 69,* 199–222.

Clark, L. A., Steer, R. A., & Beck, A. T. (1994). Common and specific dimensions of self-reported anxiety and depression: Implications for the cognitive and tripartite models. *Journal of Abnormal Psychology, 103,* 645–654.

Clark, L. A., Watson, D., & Reynolds, S. (1995). Diagnosis and classification of psychopathology: Challenges to the current system and future directions. In J. T. Spence, J. M. Darley, & D. J. Foss (Eds.), *Annual review of psychology* (pp. 121–153). Palo Alto, CA: Annual Reviews.

Clarke, D. M., & McKenzie, D. P. (1994). A caution on the use of cut-points applied to screening instruments or diagnostic criteria. *Journal of Psychiatric Research, 28,* 185–188.

Cloninger, C. R. (1987). A systematic method for clinical description and classification of personality variants. *Archives of General Psychiatry, 44,* 573–588.

Cloninger, C. R., & Svrakic, D. M. (1994). Differentiating normal and deviant personality by the seven-factor personality model. In S. Strack & M. Lorr (Eds.), *Differentiating normal and abnormal personality* (pp. 40–64). New York: Springer.

Cloninger, C. R., Svrakic, D. M., & Przybeck, T. R. (1993). A psychobiological model of temperament and character. *Archives of General Psychiatry, 50,* 975–990.

Cooke, D. J., & Michie, C. (1997). An item response theory analysis of the Hare Psychopathy Checklist–Revised. *Psychological Assessment, 9,* 3–14.

Corbitt, E. M., & Widiger, T. A. (1995). Sex differences among the personality disorders: An exploration of the data. *Clinical Psychology: Science and Practice, 2,* 225–238.

Coryell, W., Winokur, G., Shea, T., Maser, J. D., Endicott, J., & Akiskal, H. S. (1994). The long-term stability of depressive subtypes. *American Journal of Psychiatry, 151,* 199–204.

Costa, P. T., & McCrae, R. R. (1989). *The NEO-PI/NEO-FFI manual supplement.* Odessa, FL: Psychological Assessment Resources.

Cottler, L. B., Schuckit, M. A., Helzer, J. E., Crowley, T., Woody, G. E., Nathan, P. E., & Hughes, J. (1995). The *DSM-IV* field trial for substance use disorders: Major results. *Drug and Alcohol Dependence, 38,* 59–69.

Cox, D. R., & Oakes, D. (1984). *Analysis of survival data.* London: Chapman and Hall.

Eaton, W. W., Anthony, J. C., Gallo, J., Cai, G., & Tien, A. (1997). Natural history of *Diagnostic Interview Schedule/DSM-IV* major depression. *Archives of General Psychiatry, 54,* 993–999.

Eronen, M., Hakola, P., & Tiihonen, J. (1996). Mental disorders and homicidal behavior in Finland. *Archives of General Psychiatry, 53,* 497–501.

Faraone, S. V., & Tsuang, M. T. (1994). Measuring diagnostic accuracy in the absence of a "gold standard." *American Journal of Psychiatry, 151,* 650–657.

Feighner, J. P., Robins, E., Guze, S. B., Woodruff, R. A., Winokur, G., & Munoz, R. (1972). Diagnostic criteria for use in psychiatric research. *Archives of General Psychiatry, 26,* 57–63.

Fennig, S., Kovasznay, B., Rich, C., Ram, R., Pato, C., Miller, A., Rubenstein, J., Carlson, G., Schwartz, J. E., Phelan, J., Lavelle, J., Craig, T., & Bromet, E. (1994). Six-month stability of psychiatric diagnoses in first-admission patients with psychosis. *American Journal of Psychiatry, 151,* 1200–1208.

Fletcher, J. M., Page, J. B., Francis, D. J., Copeland, K., & Naus, M. J. (1996). Cognitive correlates of long-term cannabis use in Costa Rican men. *Archives of General Psychiatry, 53,* 1051–1057.

Foa, E. B., & Kozak, M. J. (1995). *DSM-IV* field trial: Obsessive-compulsive disorder. *American Journal of Psychiatry, 152,* 90–96.

Frances, A. J., Widiger, T. A., & Pincus, H. A. (1989). The development of *DSM-IV. Archives of General Psychiatry, 46,* 373–375.

Garmezy, N. (1978). Never mind the psychologists: Is it good for the children? *The Clinical Psychologist, 31,* 1–6.

Grumet, G. W. (1995). What hath APA wrought? *American Journal of Psychiatry, 152,* 651–652.

Gur, R. E., Mozley, P. D., Shtasel, D. L., Cannon, T. D., & Gallacher, F. (1994). Clinical subtypes of schizophrenia: Differences in brain and CSF volume. *American Journal of Psychiatry, 151,* 343–350.

Guze, S. B. (1995). Review of *American Psychiatric Association Diagnostic and Statistical Manual of Mental Disorders–Fourth Edition. American Journal of Psychiatry, 152,* 1228.

Hambleton, R. K., Swaminathan, H., & Rogers, H. J. (1991). *Fundamentals of Item Response Theory.* Newbury Park, CA: Sage.

Hanada, K., & Takahashi, S. (1983). Multi-institutional collaborative studies of diagnostic reliability of DSM-III and ICD-9 in Japan. In R. L. Spitzer, J. B. W. Williams, & A. E. Skodal (Eds.), *International perspectives on DSM-III* (pp. 273–290). Washington, DC: American Psychiatric Association.

Hare, R. D. (1991). *The Hare Psychopathy Checklist–Revised.* Toronto, Ontario, Canada: Multi-Health Systems.

Hartung, C. M., & Widiger, T. A. (1998). Gender differences in the diagnosis of mental disorders: Conclusions and controversies of *DSM-IV. Psychological Bulletin, 123,* 260–278.

Haslam, N., & Beck, A. T. (1994). Subtyping major depression: A taxometric analysis. *Journal of Abnormal Psychology, 103,* 686–692.

Helzer, J. E., Clayton, P. J., Pambakian, R., Reich, T., Woodruff, R. A ., & Reveley, M. A. (1977). Reliability of psychiatric diagnosis: II. The test/retest reliability of diagnostic classification. *Archives of General Psychiatry, 34,* 136–141.

Helzer, J. E., Robins, L. N., Taibleson, M., Woodruff, R. A., Reich, T., & Wish, E. D. (1977). Reliability of psychiatric diagnosis: I. Methodological review. *Archives of General Psychiatry, 34,* 12(Suppl. 328), 18–21.

Hodgins, S., Mednick, S. A., Brennan, P. A., Schulsinger, F., & Engberg, M. (1996). Mental disorder and crime: Evidence from a Danish birth cohort. *Archives of General Psychiatry, 53,* 489–496.

Hsiao, J. K., Bartko, J. J., & Potter, W. Z. (1989). Diagnosing diagnoses: Receiver operating characteristic methods and psychiatry. *Archives of General Psychiatry, 46,* 664–667.

Hudziak, J. J., Boffeli, T. J., Kriesman, J. J., Battaglia, M. M., Stanger, C., & Guze, S. B. (1996). Clinical study of the relation of borderline personality disorder to Briquet's syndrome (hysteria), somatization disorder, antisocial personality disorder, and substance abuse disorders. *American Journal of Psychiatry, 153,* 1598–1606.

Johnson, J. G., Spitzer, R. L., Williams, J. B. W., Kroenke, K., & Linzer, M. (1995). Psychiatric comorbidity, health status, and functional impairment associated with alcohol abuse and dependence in primary care patients: Findings of the PRIME MD-1000 study. *Journal of Consulting & Clinical Psychology, 63,* 133–140.

Joiner, T. E. (1996). A confirmatory factor-analytic investigation of the tripartite model of depression and anxiety in college students. *Cognitive Therapy and Research, 20,* 521–539.

Joiner, T. E., & Blalock, J. A. (1995). Gender differences in depression: The role of anxiety and generalized negative affect. *Sex Roles, 33,* 91–108.

Joiner, T. E., Catanzaro, S. J., & Laurent, J. (1996). Tripartite structure of positive and negative affect, depression, and anxiety in child and adolescent psychiatric inpatients. *Journal of Abnormal Psychology, 105,* 401–409.

Jordan, B. K., Schlenger, W. E., Fairbank, J. A., & Caddell, J. M. (1996). Prevalence of psychiatric disorders among incarcerated women: II. Convicted felons entering prison. *Archives of General Psychiatry, 53,* 513–519.

Kanfer, F. H., & Saslow, G. (1965). Behavioral analysis: An alternative to diagnostic classification. *Archives of General Psychiatry, 12,* 529–538.

Keller, M. B., Klein, D. N., Hirschfeld, R. M. A., Kocsis, J. H., McCullough, J. P., Miller, I., First, M. B., Holzer, C. P., Keitner, G. I., Marin, D. B., & Shea, M. T. (1995). Results of the *DSM-IV* mood disorders field trial. *American Journal of Psychiatry, 152,* 843–849.

Kendler, K. S. (1990). Toward a scientific psychiatric nosology: Strengths and limitations. *Archives of General Psychiatry, 47,* 969–973.

Kendler, K. S., Eaves, L. J., Walters, E. E., Neale, M. C., Heath, A. C., & Kessler, R. C. (1996). The identification and validation of distinct depressive syndromes in a population-based sample of female twins. *Archives of General Psychiatry, 53,* 391–399.

Kendler, K. S., McGuire, M., Gruenberg, A. M., & Walsh, D. (1995). Examining the validity of *DSM-III-R* schizoaffective disorder and its putative subtypes in the Roscommon Family Study. *American Journal of Psychiatry, 152,* 755–764.

Kendler, K. S., Neale, M. C., & Walsh, D. (1995). Evaluating the spectrum concept of schizophrenia in the Roscommon Family Study. *American Journal of Psychiatry, 152,* 749–754.

Kendler, K. S., & Roy, M.-A. (1995). Validity of a diagnosis of lifetime major depression obtained by personal interview versus family history. *American Journal of Psychiatry, 152,* 1608–1614.

Kessler, R. C., Sonnega, A., Bromet, E., Hughes, M., & Nelson, C. B. (1995). Posttraumatic stress disorder in the National Comorbidity Survey. *Archives of General Psychiatry, 52,* 1048–1060.

Kessler, R. C., Stein, M. B., & Berglund, P. (1998). Social phobia subtypes in the National Comorbidity Survey. *American Journal of Psychiatry, 155,* 613–619.

Kirisci, L., Moss, H. B., & Tarter, R. E. (1996). Psychometric evaluation of the Situational Confidence Questionnaire in adolescents: Fitting a graded item response model. *Addictive Behaviors, 21,* 303–317.

Kirk, S. A., & Kutchins, H. (1992). *The selling of DSM: The rhetoric of science in psychiatry.* Hawthorne, NY: Walter de Gruyter.

Kirk, S. A., & Kutchins, H. (1994, May 28). Is bad writing a mental disorder? *New York Times,* p. A12.

Klein, D. N., Ouimette, P. C., Kelly, H. S., Ferro, T., & Riso, L. P. (1994). Test-retest reliability of team consensus best-estimate diagnoses of Axis I and Axis II disorders in a family study. *American Journal of Psychiatry, 151,* 1043–1047.

Klein, D. N., & Riso, L. P. (1993). Psychiatric disorders: Problems of boundaries and comorbidity. In C. G. Costello (Ed.), *Basic issues in psychopathology* (pp. 19–66). New York: Guilford Press.

Klerman, G. L., Vaillant, G. E., Spitzer, R. L., & Michels, R. (1984). A debate on *DSM-III. American Journal of Psychiatry, 141,* 539–553.

Kraepelin, E. (1907). *Clinical psychiatry: A textbook for students and physicians* (A. R. Diefendorf, Trans.). London: Macmillan.

Lahey, B. B., Applegate, B., Barkley, R. A., Garfinkel, B., & McBurnett, K. (1994). *DSM-IV* field trials for oppositional defiant disorder and conduct disorder in children and adolescents. *American Journal of Psychiatry, 151,* 1163–1171.

Langenbucher, J. W., & Chung, T. (1995). Onset and staging of *DSM-IV* alcohol dependence using mean age and survival/hazard methods. *Journal of Abnormal Psychology, 104,* 346–354.

Langenbucher, J. W., Chung, T., Morgenstern, J., Labouvie, E., Nathan, P. E., & Bavly, L. (1997). Physiological alcohol dependence as a "specifier" of risk for medical problems and relapse liability in *DSM-IV. Journal of Studies on Alcohol, 58,* 341–350.

Langenbucher, J. W., Labouvie, E., Sanjuan, P., Kirisci, L., Bavly, L., Martin, C., & Chung, T. (2000). Item Response Theory analysis of alcohol, cannabis and cocaine criteria in *DSM-IV.* Unpublished manuscript, Rutgers University.

Langenbucher, J. W., Morgenstern, J., Labouvie, E., & Nathan, P. E. (1994a). Diagnostic concordance of substance use disorders in DSM-III, DSM-IV and ICD-10. *Drug and Alcohol Dependence, 36,* 193–203.

Langenbucher, J. W., Morgenstern, J., Labouvie, E., & Nathan, P. E. (1994b). Lifetime *DSM-IV* diagnosis of alcohol, cannabis, cocaine and opiate dependence: Six-month reliability in a multisite clinical sample. *Addiction, 89,* 1115–1127.

Larsen, F., & Vaglum, S. (1986). Clinical experiences with the DSM-III system of classification: Interrater reliability of the DSM-III diagnoses in two Norwegian studies on psychiatric and super-obese patients. *Acta Psychiatrica Scandinavia, 73,* 18–21.

Lenzenweger, M. F., & Korfine, L. (1992). Confirming the latent structure and base rate of schizotypy: A taxometric analysis. *Journal of Abnormal Psychology, 101,* 567–571.

Lilienfeld, S. O., & Marino, L. (1995). Mental disorder as a Roschian concept: A critique of Wakefield's "harmful dysfunction" analysis. *Journal of Abnormal Psychology, 104,* 411–420.

Lilienfeld, S. O., & Marino, L. (1999). Essentialism revisited: Evolutionary theory and the concept of mental disorder. *Journal of Abnormal Psychology, 198,* 400–411.

Livesley, W. J. (1990). *Dimensional Assessment of Personality Pathology: Basic Questionnaire.* Unpublished manuscript, University of British Columbia.

Magee, W. J., Eaton, W. W., Wittchen, H.-U., McGonagle, K. A., & Kessler, R. C. (1996). Agoraphobia, simply phobia, and social phobia in the National Comorbidity Survey. *Archives of General Psychiatry, 53,* 159–168.

Martin, C. S., Langenbucher, J. W., Kaczynski, N. A., & Chung, T. (1996). Staging in the onset of *DSM-IV* alcohol symptoms in adolescents: Survival/hazard analyses. *Journal of Studies on Alcohol, 57,* 549–558.

Marzuk, P. M. (1996). Violence, crime, and mental illness: How strong a link? *Archives of General Psychiatry, 53,* 481–486.

Mattanah, J. J. F., Becker, D. F., Levy, K. N., Edell, W. S., & McGlashan, T. H. (1995). Diagnostic stability in adolescents followed up 2 years after hospitalization. *American Journal of Psychiatry, 152,* 889–894.

Mattison, R., Cantwell, D. P., Russell, A. T., & Will, L. (1979). A comparison of DSM-II and DSM-III in the diagnosis of childhood psychiatric disorders: II. Interrater agreement. *Archives of General Psychiatry, 36,* 1217–1222.

McCutcheon, A. L. (1987). *Latent class analysis.* Newbury Park, CA: Sage.

Meehl, P. E. (1995). Bootstrap taxometrics: Solving the classification problem in psychopathology. *American Psychologist, 50,* 266–274.

Mineka, S., Watson, D., & Clark, L. A. (1998). Comorbidity of anxiety and unipolar mood disorders. In J. T. Spence, J. M. Darley, & D. J. Foss (Eds.), *Annual review of psychology* (pp. 377–412). Palo Alto, CA: Annual Reviews.

Morgenstern, J., Langenbucher, J., Labouvie, E., & Miller, K. J. (1997). The comorbidity of alcoholism and personality disorders in a clinical population: Prevalence rates and relation to alcohol typology variables. *Journal of Abnormal Psychology, 106,* 74–84.

Mota, V. L., & Schachar, R. J. (2000). Reformulating attention-deficit/hyperactivity disorder according to signal detection theory. *Journal of the American Academy of Child and Adolescent Psychiatry, 39,* 1144–1151.

Nathan, P. E. (1967). *Cues, decisions, and diagnoses.* New York: Academic Press.

Nathan, P. E. (1997). In the final analysis, it's the data that count. *Clinical Psychology: Science and Practice, 4,* 281–284.

Nathan, P. E. (1998). *DSM-IV* and its antecedents: Enhancing syndromal diagnosis. In J. W. Barron (Ed.), *Making diagnosis meaningful: New psychological perspectives* (pp. 3–27). Washington, DC: APA Books.

Nathan, P. E., Andberg, M. M., Behan, P. O., & Patch, V. D. (1969). Thirty-two observers and one patient: A study of diagnostic reliability. *Journal of Clinical Psychology, 25,* 9–15.

Nathan, P. E., & Harris, S. L. (1980). *Psychopathology and society* (2nd ed.). New York: McGraw-Hill.

Nathan, P. E., & Langenbucher, J. W. (1999). Psychopathology: Description and classification. In J. T. Spence (Ed.), *Annual review of psychology* (Vol. 50, pp. 79–107). Palo Alto, CA: Annual Reviews.

Nelson, E., & Rice, J. (1997). Stability of diagnosis of obsessive-compulsive disorder in the Epidemiologic Catchment Area study. *American Journal of Psychiatry, 154,* 826–831.

Newman, D. L., Moffit, T. E., Caspi, A., & Silva, P. A. (1998). Comorbid mental disorders: Implications for clinical practice and psychopathology research. *Journal of Abnormal Psychology, 107,* 305–311.

O'Connor, B. P., & Dyce, J. A. (1998). A test of models of personality disorder configuration. *Journal of Abnormal Psychology, 107,* 3–16.

O'Connor, T. G., McGuire, S., Reiss, D., Hethering, E. M., & Plomin, R. (1998). Co-occurrence of depressive symptoms and antisocial behavior in adolescence: A common genetic liability. *Journal of Abnormal Psychology, 107,* 27–37.

Ossorio, P. (1985). Pathology. In K. Davis & T. Mitchell (Eds.), *Advances in descriptive psychology* (pp. 151–202). Greenwich, CT: JAI Press.

Pfohl, B., Blum, N., Zimmerman, M., & Stangl, D. (1989). *Structured Interview for DSM-III-R Personality.* Iowa City: University of Iowa.

Pincus, H. A., First, M., Frances, A. J., & McQueen, L. (1996). Reviewing *DSM-IV*. *American Journal of Psychiatry, 153,* 850.

Potts, M. K., Burnam, M. A., & Wells, K. B. (1991). Gender differences in depression detection: A comparison of clinician diagnosis and standardized assessment. *Psychological Assessment, 3,* 609–615.

Ratakonda, S., Gorman, J. M., Yale, S. A., & Amador, X. F. (1998). Characterization of psychotic conditions. *Archives of General Psychiatry, 55,* 75–81.

Raven, P. H., Berlin, B., & Breedlove, D. E. (1971). The origins of taxonomy. *Science, 174,* 1210–1213.

Regier, D. A., Myers, J. K., Kramer, M., Robins, L. N., Blazer, D. G., Hough, R. L., Eaton, W. W., & Locke, B. Z. (1984). The NIMH Epidemiologic Catchment Area program: Historical context, major objectives and study population characteristics. *Archives of General Psychiatry, 41,* 934–941.

Richters, J. E., & Hinshaw, S. (1997). Psychiatry's turbid solution. *Clinical Psychology: Science and Practice, 4,* 276–280.

Robins, E., & Guze, S. (1970). Establishment of diagnostic validity in psychiatric illnesses: Its application to schizophrenia. *American Journal of Psychiatry, 126,* 983–987.

Robins, L. N., Helzer, J. E., Croughan, J., & Ratcliff, K. S. (1981). National Institute of Mental Health Diagnostic Interview Schedule: Its history, characteristics, and validity. *Archives of General Psychiatry, 38,* 381–389.

Rosch, E. R. (1973). Natural categories. *Cognitive Psychology, 4,* 328–350.

Rosenberg, M. F., & Anthony, J. C. (2001). Early clinical manifestations of cannabis dependence in a community sample. *Drug and Alcohol Dependence, 64,* 123–131.

Rosenhan, D. L. (1973). On being sane in insane places. *Science, 179,* 250–258.

Ruscio, J., & Ruscio, A. M. (2000). Informing the continuity controversy: A taxometric analysis of depression. *Journal of Abnormal Psychology, 109,* 473–487.

Sandifer, M. G., Pettus, C., & Quade, D. (1964). A study of psychiatric diagnosis. *Journal of Nervous and Mental Disease, 139,* 350–356.

Schacht, T. E. (1985). DSM-III and the politics of truth. *American Psychologist, 40,* 513–526.

Schacht, T. E., & Nathan, P. E. (1977). But is it good for the psychologists? Appraisal and status of DSM-III. *American Psychologist, 32,* 1017–1025.

Sherbourne, C. D., Wells, K. B., Meredith, L. S., Jackson, C. A., & Camp, P. (1996). Comorbid anxiety disorder and the functioning and well-being of chronically ill patients of general medical providers. *Archives of General Psychiatry, 53,* 889–895.

Singer, J., & Willett, J. (1991). Modeling the days of our lives: Using survival analysis when designing and analyzing longitudinal studies of duration and timing of events. *Psychological Bulletin, 110,* 268–290.

Skodol, A. E., & Spitzer, R. L. (1987). *An annotated bibliography of DSM-III.* Washington, DC: American Psychiatric Press.

Spitzer, R. L. (1983). Psychiatric diagnosis: Are clinicians still necessary? *Comprehensive Psychiatry, 24,* 399–411.

Spitzer, R. L. (1997). Brief comments from a psychiatric nosologist weary from his own attempts to define mental disorder: Why Ossorio's definition muddles and Wakefield's "harmful dysfunction" illuminates the issues. *Clinical Psychology: Science and Practice, 4,* 259–266.

Spitzer, R. L., & Endicott, J. (1968). DIAGNO: A computer program for psychiatric diagnosis utilizing the differential diagnostic procedure. *Archives of General Psychiatry, 18,* 746–756.

Spitzer, R. L., & Endicott, J. (1969). DIAGNO II: Further developments in a computer program for psychiatric diagnosis. *American Journal of Psychiatry, 125,* 12–21.

Spitzer, R. L., Endicott, J., Fleiss, J. L., & Cohen, J. (1970). The Psychiatric Status Schedule: A technique for evaluating psychopathology and impairment of role functioning. *Archives of General Psychiatry, 23,* 41–55.

Spitzer, R. L., Endicott, J., & Robins, E. (1975). *Research Diagnostic Criteria (RDC) for a selected group of functional disorders.* New York: New York State Psychiatric Institute.

Spitzer, R. L., Fleiss, J. L., Endicott, J., & Cohen, J. (1967). Mental Status Schedule: Properties of a factor-analytically derived scale. *Archives of General Psychiatry, 16,* 479–493.

Spitzer, R. L., Forman, J. B., & Nee, J. (1979). *DSM-III* field trials: I. Initial interrater diagnostic reliability. *American Journal of Psychiatry, 136,* 815–817.

Spitzer, R. L., & Williams, J. B. W. (1982). The definition and diagnosis of mental disorders. *Sage Annual Reviews of Studies in Deviance, 6,* 15–31.

Spitzer, R. L., & Williams, J. B. W. (1986). *Structured Clinical Interview for DSM-III.* New York: New York State Psychiatric Institute, Biometrics Research Department.

Spitzer, R. L., Williams, J. B., & Skodol, A. E. (1980). *DSM-III:* The major achievements and an overview. *American Journal of Psychiatry, 137,* 151–164.

Strakowski, S. M. (1994). Diagnostic validity of schizophreniform disorder. *American Journal of Psychiatry, 151,* 815–824.

Szasz, T. S. (1960). The myth of mental illness. *American Psychologist, 15,* 113–118.

Teplin, L. A., Abram, K. M., & McClelland, G. M. (1996). Prevalence of psychiatric disorders among incarcerated women: I. Pretrial jail detainees. *Archives of General Psychiatry, 53,* 505–512.

Tiihonen, J., Isohanni, M., Rasanen, P., Koiranen, M., & Moring, J. (1997). Specific major mental disorders and criminality: A 26-year prospective study of the 1966 Northern Finland birth cohort. *American Journal of Psychiatry, 154,* 840–845.

Virkkunen, M., Eggert, M., Rawlings, R., & Linnoila, M. (1996). A prospective follow-up study of alcoholic violent offenders and fire setters. *Archives of General Psychiatry, 53,* 523–529.

Volkmar, F. R., Klin, A., Siegel, B., Szatmari, P., Lord, C., Campbell, M., Freeman, B. J., Cicchetti, D. V., Rutter, M., Kline, W., Buitelaar, J., Hattab, Y., Fombonne, E., Fuentes, J., Werry, J., Stone, W., Kerbeshian, J., Hoshino, Y., Bregman, J., Loveland, K., Szymanski, L., & Towbin, K. (1994). Field trial for autistic disorder in DSM-IV. *American Journal of Psychiatry, 151,* 1361–1367.

Wakefield, J. C. (1992). The concept of mental disorder: On the boundary between biological facts and social values. *American Psychologist, 47,* 373–388.

Wakefield, J. C. (1997). Normal inability versus pathological disability: Why Ossorio's definition of mental disorder is not sufficient. *Clinical Psychology: Science and Practice, 4,* 249–258.

Wakefield, J. C. (1999a). Evolutionary versus prototype analysis of the concept of disorder. *Journal of Abnormal Psychology, 108,* 374–399.

Wakefield, J. C. (1999b). Mental disorder as a black box essentialist concept. *Journal of Abnormal Psychology, 108,* 465–472.

Waller, N. G., & Meehl, P. E. (1998). *Multivariate taxonomic procedures: Distinguishing types from continua.* Newbury Park, CA: Sage.

Waller, N. G., Putnam, F. W., & Carlson, E. B. (1996). Types of dissociation and dissociative types: A taxometric analysis of dissociative experiences. *Psychological Methods, 1,* 300–321.

Waller, N. G., & Ross, C. A. (1997). The prevalence and biometric structure of pathological dissociation in the general population: Taxometric and behavior genetic findings. *Journal of Abnormal Psychology, 106,* 499–510.

Watson, D., & Clark, L. A. (1995). Depression and the melancholic temperament. *European Journal of Personality, 9,* 351–366.

Watson, D., Clark, L. A., Weber, K., Assenheimer, J. S., Strauss, M. E., & McCormick R. A. (1995). Testing a tripartite model: II. Exploring the symptom structure of anxiety and depression in student, adult, and patient samples. *Journal of Abnormal Psychology, 104,* 15–25.

Watson, D., Weber, K., Assenheimer, J. S., Clark, L. A., Strauss, M. E., & McCormick, R. A. (1995). Testing a tripartite model: I. Evaluating the convergent and discriminant validity of anxiety and depression symptom scales. *Journal of Abnormal Psychology, 104,* 3–14.

Westen, D. (1997). Divergences between clinical and research methods for assessing personality disorders: Implications for research and the evolution of Axis II. *American Journal of Psychiatry, 154,* 895–903.

Widiger, T. A. (1993). The *DSM-III-R* categorical personality disorder diagnoses: A critique and an alternative. *Psychological Inquiry, 4,* 75–90.

Widiger, T. A. (1997a). The construct of mental disorder. *Clinical Psychology: Science and Practice, 4,* 262–266.

Widiger, T. A. (1997b). Mental disorders as discrete clinical conditions: Dimensional versus categorical classification. In S. M. Turner & M. Hersen (Eds.), *Adult psychopathology and diagnosis* (pp. 3–23). New York: Wiley.

Widiger, T. A. (2001). What can we learn from taxometric analyses? *Clinical Psychology: Science and Practice.*

Widiger, T. A., Frances, A. J., Pincus, H. A., First, M. B., Ross, R., & Davis, W. (Eds.). (1994). *DSM-IV sourcebook* (Vol. 1). Washington, DC: American Psychiatric Association.

Widiger, T. A., Frances, A. J., Pincus, H. A., Ross, R., First, M. B., & Davis, W. (Eds.). (1996). *DSM-IV sourcebook* (Vol. 2). Washington, DC: American Psychiatric Association.

Widiger, T. A., Frances, A. J., Pincus, H. A., Ross, R., First, M. B., & Davis, W. (Eds.). (1997). *DSM-IV sourcebook* (Vol. 3). Washington, DC: American Psychiatric Association.

Widiger, T. A., Frances, A. J., Pincus, H. A., Ross, R., First, M. B., Davis, W., & Kline, M. (Eds.). (1998). *DSM-IV sourcebook* (Vol. 4). Washington, DC: American Psychiatric Association.

Widiger, T. A., Hare, R., Rutherford, M., Corbitt, E., & Hart, S. (1996). *DSM-IV* antisocial personality disorder field trial. *Journal of Abnormal Psychology, 105,* 3–16.

Widiger, T. A., & Trull, T. J. (1993). The scholarly development of *DSM-IV.* In J. A. C. de Silva & C. C. Nadelson (Eds.), *International review of psychiatry* (pp. 59–78). Washington, DC: American Psychiatric Press.

Widiger, T. A., Trull, T. J., Clarkin, J. F., Sanderson, C., & Costa, P. T. (1994). A description of the *DSM-III* and *DSM-IV* personality disorders with the five-factor model of personality. In P. T. Costa & T. A. Widiger (Eds.), *Personality disorders and the Five-Factor model of personality* (pp. 41–57). Washington, DC: American Psychological Association.

Williams, J. B. W., Hyler, S. E., & Spitzer, R. L. (1982). Reliability in the *DSM-III* field trials: Interview versus case summary. *Archives of General Psychiatry, 39,* 1275–1278.

Wrobel, N. H. (1993). Effect of patient age and gender on clinical decisions. *Professional Psychology: Research & Practice, 24,* 206–212.

Yutzy, S. H., Cloninger, C. R., Guze, S. B., Pribor, E. F., Martin, R. L., Kathol, R. G., Smith, G. R., & Strain, J. J. (1995). *DSM-IV* field trial: Testing a new proposal for somatization disorder. *American Journal of Psychiatry, 152,* 97–101.

Zigler, E., & Phillips, L. (1961). Psychiatric diagnosis: A critique. *Journal of Abnormal Psychology, 63,* 607–618.

Zilboorg, G. (1941). *A history of medical psychology.* New York: W. W. Norton.

Zinbarg, R. E., & Barlow, D. H. (1996). Structure of anxiety and the anxiety disorders. *Journal of Abnormal Psychology, 105,* 181–193.

Zinbarg, R. E., Barlow, D. H., Liebowitz, M., Street, L., Broadhead, E., Katon, W., Roy-Byrne, P., Lepine, J.-P., Teherani, M., Richards, J., Brantley, P. J., & Kraemenr, H. (1994). The *DSM-IV* field trial for mixed anxiety-depression. *American Journal of Psychiatry, 151,* 1153–1162.

Zubin, J. (1967). Classification of behavior disorders. *Annual Review of Psychology, 18,* 373–406.

CHAPTER 2

# Disorders of Childhood and Adolescence

ERIC J. MASH AND DAVID A. WOLFE

From the time that modern views of mental illness emerged in the late eighteenth and early nineteenth centuries, significantly less attention has been given to mental health problems in children than it has to problems in adults (Rie, 1971). Even today there are far fewer categories for diagnosing mental disorders in children, and these categories vary in their sensitivity to developmental parameters and context. Current knowledge of child and adolescent disorders is compromised by a lack of child-specific theories, by an unsystematic approach to research (Kazdin, 2001), and by the inherent conceptual and research complexities (Kazdin & Kagan, 1994), which may explain why there are far fewer empirically supported treatments for children than for adults (Chambless & Ollendick, 2001). Despite these caveats, tremendous advances have been made over the last decade (Mash & Barkley, 1996; Mash & Wolfe, 2002; Rutter & Sroufe, 2000).

New conceptual frameworks, new knowledge, and new research methods have greatly enhanced our understanding of childhood disorders (Cicchetti & Cohen, 1995; Sameroff, Lewis, & Miller, 2000) as well as our ability to assess and treat children with these problems (Mash & Barkley, 1998; Mash & Terdal, 1997b).

We begin with a discussion of the significance of children's mental health problems and the role of multiple interacting influences in shaping adaptive and maladaptive patterns of behavior. Next we provide a brief overview of disorders of childhood and adolescence and related conditions as defined by current diagnostic systems (American Psychiatric Association; APA, 2000). We then consider two common categories of problems in children and adolescents: externalizing disorders (disruptive behavior disorders; attention-deficit/hyperactivity disorder, ADHD), and internalizing disorders (mood disorders, anxiety disorders). We illustrate current issues and approaches to child and adolescent disorders by focusing on ADHD and anxiety disorders as examples. In doing so we consider the main characteristics, epidemiology,

During the writing of this chapter, Eric Mash was supported in part by a University of Calgary Killam Resident Fellowship.

developmental course, associated features, proposed causes, and an integrative developmental pathway model for each of these disorders. We conclude with a discussion of current issues and future directions for the field.

## THE SIGNIFICANCE OF CHILDREN'S MENTAL HEALTH PROBLEMS

Long-overdue concern for the mental health of children and adolescents is gradually coming to the forefront of the political agenda. For example, in the United States the new millennium witnessed White House meetings on mental health in young people and on the use of psychotropic medications with children. A Surgeon General's Conference on Children's Mental Health resulted in an extensive report and recommendations (U.S. Public Health Service, 2001a), closely followed by a similar report on youth violence (U.S. Public Health Service, 2001b). Increasingly, researchers in the fields of clinical child psychology, child psychiatry, and developmental psychopathology are becoming attentive to the social policy implications of their work and in effecting improvements in the identification of and services for youth with mental health needs (Cicchetti & Toth, 2000; Weisz, 2000c). Greater recognition is also being given to factors that contribute to children's successful mental functioning, personal well-being, productive activities, fulfilling relationships, and ability to adapt to change and cope with adversity (U.S. Department of Health and Human Services, 2000; U.S. Public Health Service, 2001a).

The increase in attention to children's mental health problems derives from a number of sources. First, many young people experience significant mental health problems that interfere with normal development and functioning. As many as one in five children in the United States experience some type of difficulty (Costello & Angold, 2000; Roberts, Attkisson, & Rosenblatt, 1998), and 1 in 10 have a diagnosable disorder that causes some level of impairment (B. J. Burns et al., 1995; Shaffer et al., 1996). These numbers likely underestimate the magnitude of the problem because they do not include a substantial number of children who manifest subclinical or undiagnosed disturbances that may place them at high risk for the later development of more severe clinical problems (McDermott & Weiss, 1995).

Moreover, the frequency of certain childhood disorders—such as antisocial behavior and some types of depression—may be increasing as the result of societal changes and conditions that create growing risks for children (Kovacs, 1997). Among these conditions are chronic poverty, family breakup, single parenting, child abuse, homelessness, problems of the rural

poor, adjustment problems of immigrant and minority children, and the impact of HIV, cocaine, and alcohol on children's growth and development (Duncan, Brooks-Gunn, & Klebanov, 1994; McCall & Groark, 2000). Evidence gathered by the World Health Organization suggests that by the year 2020, childhood neuropsychiatric disorders will rise proportionally by over 50% internationally—to become one of the five most common causes of morbidity, mortality, and disability among children (U.S. Public Health Service, 2001a).

For a majority of children who experience mental health problems, these problems go unidentified—only about 20% receive help, a statistic that has not changed for some time (B. J. Burns et al., 1995). Even when children are identified and receive help for their problems, this help may be less than optimal. For example, only about half of children with identified ADHD seen in real-world practice settings receive care that conforms to recommended treatment guidelines (Hoagwood, Kelleher, Feil, & Comer, 2000). The fact that so few children receive appropriate help is probably related to such factors as inaccessibility, cost, parental dissatisfaction with services, and the stigmatization and exclusion often experienced by children with mental disorders and their families (Hinshaw & Cicchetti, 2000).

Unfortunately, children with mental health problems who go unidentified and unassisted often end up in the criminal justice or mental health systems as young adults (Loeber & Farrington, 2000). They are at a much greater risk for dropping out of school and for not being fully functional members of society in adulthood, which adds further to the costs of childhood disorders in terms of human suffering and financial burdens. For example, average costs of medical care for youngsters with ADHD are estimated to be double those for youngsters without ADHD (Leibson, Katusic, Barberesi, Ransom, & O'Brien, 2001). Moreover, allowing just *one* youth to leave high school for a life of crime and drug abuse is estimated to cost society from $1.7 to $2.3 million (Cohen, 1998).

## UNDERSTANDING DISORDERS OF CHILDHOOD AND ADOLESCENCE

Much of what we know about disorders of childhood and adolescence is based on findings obtained at a single point in the child's development and in a single context. Although it is useful, such information is incomplete because it fails to capture dynamic changes in the expression and causal factors that characterize most forms of child psychopathology. Only in the last two decades have efforts to describe and explain psychopathology in children included longitudinal methods and conceptual models that are sensitive to developmental change and the sociocultural context (Cicchetti & Aber, 1998; Boyce et al., 1998; García Coll, Akerman, & Cicchetti, 2000).

The study of child psychopathology is further complicated by the fact that most childhood disorders do not present in neat packages, but rather overlap, co-exist, or both with other disorders. For example, symptoms of anxiety and depression in childhood are highly correlated (Brady & Kendall, 1992; Compas & Oppedisano, 2000), and there is also much overlap among emotional and behavioral disorders, child maltreatment, substance abuse, delinquency, and learning difficulties (e.g., Greenbaum, Prange, Friedman, & Silver, 1991). Many behavioral and emotional disturbances in children are also associated with specific physical symptoms, medical conditions, or both.

Furthermore, few childhood disorders can be attributed to a single cause. Although some rare disorders such as phenylketonuria (PKU) or Fragile X mental retardation may be caused by a single gene, current models in behavioral genetics recognize that more common and complex disorders are the result of multigene systems containing varying effect sizes (Plomin, 1995). Most childhood disorders are the result of multiple and interacting risk and protective factors, causal events, and processes (e.g., Ge, Conger, Lorenz, Shanahan, & Elder, 1995). Contextual factors such as the child's family, school, community, and culture exert considerable influence, one that is almost always equivalent to or greater than those factors usually thought of as residing within the child (Rutter, 2000b).

Like adult disorders, causes of child psychopathology are multifaceted and interactive. Prominent contributing causes include genetic influences, neurobiological dysfunction, difficult infant temperament, insecure child-parent attachments, problems in emotion regulation or impulse control, maladaptive patterns of parenting, social-cognitive deficits, parental psychopathology, marital discord, and limited family resources, among others. The causes and outcomes of child psychopathology operate in dynamic and interactive ways across time and are not easy to disentangle. The designation of a specific factor as a cause or an outcome of child psychopathology usually reflects the point in an ongoing developmental process that the child is observed and the perspective of the observer. For example, a language deficit may be viewed as a disorder (e.g., mixed receptive-expressive language disorder), the cause of other problems (e.g., impulsivity), or the result of some other condition or disorder (e.g., autism). In addition, biological and environmental determinants interact at all periods of development. For example, the characteristic styles used by parents in

responding to their infants' emotional expressions may influence the manner in which patterns of cortical mappings and connections within the limbic system are established during infancy (Dawson, Hessl, & Frey, 1994). Thus, early experiences may shape neural structure and function, which may then create dispositions that direct and shape the child's later experiences (Dawson, Ashman, & Carver, 2000).

The experience and the expression of psychopathology in children are known to have cognitive, affective, physiological, and behavioral components; consequently, many different descriptions and definitions of abnormality in children have been proposed (Achenbach, 2000). However, a central theme in defining disorders of childhood and adolescence is *adaptational failure* in one or more of these components or in the ways in which these components are integrated and organized (Garber, 1984; Mash & Dozois, 1996). Adaptational failure may involve a deviation from age-appropriate norms, an exaggeration or diminishment of normal developmental expressions, interference in normal developmental progress, a failure to master age-salient developmental tasks, a failure to develop a specific function or regulatory mechanism, or any combination of these (Loeber, 1991).

Numerous etiological models have been proposed to explain psychopathology in children. These models have differed in their relative emphasis on certain causal mechanisms and constructs, and they often use very different terminology and concepts to describe seemingly similar child characteristics and behaviors. Biological paradigms, for example, have emphasized genetic mutations, neuroanatomy, and neurobiological mechanisms as factors contributing to psychopathology, whereas psychological paradigms have focused on the interpersonal and family relationships that shape a child's cognitive, behavioral, and affective development. Although each of the various models places relative importance to certain causal processes versus others, most models recognize the role of multiple interacting influences. There is a growing recognition to look beyond the emphasis of single-cause theories and to integrate currently available models through intra- and interdisciplinary research efforts (cf. Arkowitz, 1992).

Interdisciplinary perspectives on disorders of childhood and adolescence mirror the considerable investment in children on the part of many different disciplines and professions, each of which has its own unique perspective of child psychopathology. Psychiatry-medicine, for example, has viewed and defined such problems categorically in terms of the presence or absence of a particular disorder or syndrome that is believed to exist within the child. In contrast, psychology has conceptualized psychopathology as an extreme occurrence on a continuum or dimension of characteristic(s) and has also focused on the role of environmental influences that operate outside the child. However, the boundaries are arbitrarily drawn between categories and dimensions, or between inner and outer conditions and causes, and there is growing recognition to find workable ways of integrating the two different worldviews of psychiatry-medicine and psychology (Richters & Cicchetti, 1993).

## CHILD AND ADOLESCENT DISORDERS: AN OVERVIEW

Many of the disorders that are present in adults are also present in children in one form or another, although admittedly the pathways are complex. Even though children can have similar mental health problems as adults, their problems often have a different focus. Children may experience difficulty with normal developmental tasks, such as beginning school, or they may lag behind other children their age or behave like a younger child during stressful periods. Even when children have problems that appear in adults, their problems may be expressed differently. For example, anxious children may be very concerned about their parents and other family members and may want to be near them at all times to be sure that everyone is all right.

The APA's *Diagnostic and Statistical Manual of Mental Disorders–Fourth Edition–Text Revision (DSM-IV-TR;* APA, 2000) recognizes the uniqueness of childhood disorders in a separate section for disorders usually first diagnosed in infancy, childhood, or adolescence. However, this designation is viewed primarily as a matter of convenience, recognizing that the distinction between disorders in children and those in adults is not always clear. For example, although most individuals with disorders display symptoms during childhood and adolescence, they sometimes are not diagnosed until adulthood. In addition, many disorders not included in the childhood disorders section of *DSM-IV-TR* often have their onset during childhood and adolescence, such as depression, schizophrenia, and bipolar disorder.

A brief overview of *DSM-IV-TR* disorders of childhood is presented in Table 2.1 for problems in development and learning and in Table 2.2 for behavior and other disorders. The disorders listed in these tables have traditionally been thought of as first occurring in childhood or as exclusive to childhood and as requiring child-specific operational criteria.

In addition to the separate listing of disorders of childhood and adolescence, many other *DSM-IV-TR* disorders apply to children and adolescents. As highlighted in Table 2.3, the most common of these are mood and anxiety disorders. For these disorders, the same diagnostic criteria are used for chil-

**TABLE 2.1**   *DSM-IV-TR* **Categories for Developmental and Learning Disorders Usually First Diagnosed in Infancy, Childhood, or Adolescence**

*Mental retardation*

Significantly below average intellectual functioning (an IQ of approximately 70 or less) with onset before age 18 years and associated deficits or impairments in adaptive functioning.

Level of Severity: Mild, moderate, severe, profound

*Pervasive developmental disorders*

Severe deficits and pervasive impairments in many areas of development, including reciprocal social interaction, communication, and the presence of stereotyped behavior, interests, and activities.

Categories: Autistic disorder, Rett's disorder, childhood disintegrative disorder, Asperger's disorder

*Learning disorders*

Academic functioning substantially below that expected given the youngster's chronological age, measured intelligence, and age-appropriate education.

Categories: Reading disorder, mathematics disorder, disorder of written expression

*Communication disorders*

Characterized by difficulties in speech and language.

Categories: Expressive language disorder, mixed receptive-expressive language disorder, phonological disorder, stuttering

*Motor skills disorder*

Motor coordination that is substantially less than expected given the youngster's chronological age and measured intelligence.

Category: Developmental coordination disorder

dren and adults with various adjustments made based on the age-appropriateness, duration, and—in some instances—the types of symptoms.

The *DSM-IV-TR* distinction between child and adult categories is recognized as being arbitrary—more a reflection of our current lack of knowledge concerning the continuities-discontinuities between child and adult disorders than of the existence of qualitatively distinct conditions (Silk, Nath, Siegel, & Kendall, 2000). Recent efforts to diagnose ADHD in adults illustrate this problem (Faraone, Biederman, Feighner, & Monuteaux, 2000). Whereas the criteria for ADHD were derived from work with children and the disorder is included in the child section of *DSM-IV-TR,* the same criteria are used to diagnose adults even though they may not fit the expression of the disorder in adults very well. Similarly, it is not clear that the degree of differentiation represented by the many *DSM-IV-TR* categories for anxiety disorders in adults fits with how symptoms of anxiety are expressed during childhood, which may reflect differences related to when symptoms appear in development rather than to the type of disorder (Zahn-Waxler, Klimes-Dougan, & Slattery, 2000). The more general issue here is whether there is a need for separate diagnostic criteria for children versus

**TABLE 2.2   Categories for Behavior and Other Disorders Usually First Diagnosed in Infancy, Childhood, or Adolescence**

*Attention-deficit/hyperactivity disorder (ADHD)*

Characterized by a persistent age-inappropriate pattern of inattention, hyperactivity-impulsivity, or both.

Subtypes: Predominantly inattentive type, predominantly hyperactive-impulsive type, combined type

*Oppositional defiant disorder (ODD)*

A recurrent pattern of negativistic, hostile, disobedient, and defiant behavior.

*Conduct disorder (CD)*

Characterized by a repetitive and persistent pattern of behavior that violates the basic rights of others or major age-appropriate societal norms or rules.

Subtypes: Childhood-onset type, adolescent-onset type

*Feeding and eating disorders of infancy or early childhood*

Persistent disturbances in eating or feeding such as the ingestion of non-nutritive substances, regurgitation and rechewing of food, and failure to eat adequately, resulting in a failure to gain weight or weight loss.

Categories: Pica, rumination disorder, feeding disorder of infancy or early childhood

*Tic disorders*

Prominent features are vocal and or motor tics. Tics may be simple (e.g., eye blinking, throat clearing) or complex (hand gestures, spontaneous expression of words or phrases).

Categories: Tourette's disorder, chronic motor or vocal tic disorder, transient tic disorder

*Elimination disorders*

Repeated and developmentally inappropriate passage of feces (encopresis) or voiding of urine (enuresis) into inappropriate places.

Categories: Encopresis, enuresis

*Other disorders of infancy, childhood, or adolescence*
*Separation anxiety disorder:* Anxiety concerning separation from primary attachment figures.

*Selective mutism:* Consistent failure to speak in specific social situations, despite speaking in other situations.

*Reactive attachment disorder:* Marked and developmentally inappropriate disturbances in social relatedness in the context of pathological care.

*Stereotypic movement disorder:* Repetitive, driven, and nonfunctional motor behavior (e.g., rocking, playing with hands, head banging).

**TABLE 2.3   Common Categories for Disorders of Childhood or Adolescence Not Listed Separately in *DSM-IV-TR* as Those Usually First Diagnosed in Infancy, Childhood, or Adolescence**

*Mood disorders*

Characterized by extreme, persistent, or poorly regulated emotional states such as excessive unhappiness or wide swings in mood from sadness to elation. A disturbance in mood is the predominant feature.

Categories: Major depressive disorder (MDD), dysthymic disorder (DD), bipolar disorders (BP)

*Anxiety disorders*[a]

Characterized by strong negative affect, bodily feelings of tension, and apprehensive anticipation of future danger or misfortune.

Categories: Specific phobia, social phobia, obsessive-compulsive disorder, posttraumatic stress disorder, acute stress disorder, generalized anxiety disorder, panic disorder, panic disorder with agoraphobia.

*Other disorders*

*Eating disorders*

*Sleep disorders*

*Somatoform disorders*

*Factitious disorders*

*Dissociative disorders*

*Sexual and gender identity disorders*

*Schizophrenia and other psychotic disorders*

*Substance-related disorders*

*Impulse-control disorders not elsewhere classified*

*Adjustment disorders*

*Personality disorders*

[a]see also Table 2.5.

**TABLE 2.4   Selected *DSM-IV-TR* Categories for Other Conditions That May Be a Focus of Clinical Attention During Childhood That Are Not Defined as Mental Disorders**

*Relational problems*

Characterized by patterns of parent-child or sibling interaction associated with clinically significant impairment in functioning, symptoms among one or more members of the relational unit, or impairment in the functioning of the unit itself.

Categories: Relational problem related to a general mental disorder or general medical condition, parent-child relational problem, partner relational problem, sibling relational problem

*Problems related to abuse or neglect*

Characterized by severe physical, sexual, or neglectful mistreatment of the child.

Categories: Physical abuse of child, sexual abuse of child, neglect of child.

*Other problems*

*Bereavement*

*Borderline intellectual functioning*

*Academic problem*

*Identity problem*

*Child or adolescent antisocial behavior*

*Acculturation problem*

adults or whether the same criteria can be used by adjusting them to take into account differences in developmental level and context.

There are a number of additional *DSM-IV-TR* categories for other conditions that are not defined as mental disorders but are frequently a focus of clinical attention during childhood. As highlighted in Table 2.4, these categories include relational problems, maltreatment, and academic and adjustment difficulties. The relational nature of most childhood disorders underscores the significance of these categories for diagnosing children and adolescents (Mash & Johnston, 1996). Although *DSM-IV-TR* does not provide the specifics needed to adequately diagnose these complex concerns, it does call attention to their importance.

In the sections that follow, we consider the two most common types of child and adolescent disorders: externalizing and internalizing problems. Youngsters with externalizing problems generally display behaviors that are disruptive and harmful to others (Campbell, Shaw, & Gilliom, 2000). In contrast, those with internalizing problems experience inner-directed negative emotions and moods such as sadness, guilt, fear, and worry (Zahn-Waxler et al., 2000). In reality, both types of disorders have behavioral, emotional, and cognitive components, and there is substantial overlap between the two.

## EXTERNALIZING DISORDERS: ATTENTION-DEFICIT/HYPERACTIVITY DISORDER (ADHD)

Externalizing disorders are characterized by a mix of impulsive, overactive, aggressive, and delinquent acts (G. L. Burns et al., 1997). They include a wide range of acting-out behaviors—from annoying but mild behaviors such as noncompliance and tantrums to more severe behaviors such as physical aggression and stealing (McMahon & Estes, 1997). The two major types of externalizing disorders are (a) disruptive behavior disorders and (b) ADHD. We limit our discussion to ADHD and discuss its symptoms and subtypes, epidemiology, developmental course, accompanying disorders, associated features, causes, and possible developmental pathways. Many of the issues that we address in discussing ADHD (e.g., prevalence estimates, comorbidity, gender and cultural factors, multiple and interacting causes, developmental pathways) have relevance for most other disorders of childhood.

ADHD is characterized by persistent and age-inappropriate symptoms of inattention, hyperactivity-impulsivity, or both (Campbell, 2000). Children with ADHD have great difficulty focusing on demands, are in constant motion, act without thinking, or any combination of these. Views of ADHD have changed dramatically over the past century as a result of new findings and discoveries (Barkley, 1998).

### Symptoms and Subtypes

The main attention deficit in ADHD appears to be one of sustained attention (Douglas, 1999). When presented with an uninteresting or repetitive task, the performance of a child with ADHD deteriorates over time compared to that of other children. However, findings are not always consistent and may depend on the definitions and tasks used to assess this construct (Hinshaw, 1994). Symptoms of hyperactivity and behavioral impulsivity are best viewed as a single dimension of behavior called hyperactivity-impulsivity (Lahey et al., 1988). The strong link between hyperactivity and behavioral impulsivity has led to suggestions that both are part of a more fundamental deficit in behavioral inhibition (Barkley, 1997; Quay, 1997).

The three core features of ADHD—inattention, hyperactivity, and impulsivity—are complex processes. The current view is that hyperactivity-impulsivity is an essential feature of ADHD. In contrast to inattention, it distinguishes children with ADHD from those with other disorders and from normal children (Halperin, Matier, Bedi, Sharma, & Newcorn, 1992). As such, impulsivity-hyperactivity appears to be a *specific marker* for ADHD, whereas inattention is not (Taylor, 1995). Children with ADHD display a unique constellation and severity of symptoms but do not necessarily differ from comparison children on all types and measures of inattention, hyperactivity, and impulsivity (Barkley, 1998).

*DSM-IV-TR* specifies three ADHD subtypes based on the child's primary symptoms, which have received growing empirical support (Eiraldi, Power, & Nezu, 1997; Faraone, Biederman, & Friedman, 2000; Gaub & Carlson, 1997a). Children with the *combined type* display symptoms of both inattention and hyperactivity; those with the *predominantly hyperactive-impulsive type* display primarily symptoms of hyperactivity-impulsivity; and those with the *predominantly inattentive type* display primarily symptoms of inattention. Children with the combined and predominantly hyperactive-impulsive types are more likely to display problems in inhibiting behavior and in behavioral persistence than are those who are predominantly inattentive. They are also more likely to be aggressive, defiant, and oppositional; to be rejected by their peers; and to be suspended from school or placed in special education classes (Lahey & Carlson, 1992). Because children who are predominantly hyperactive-impulsive are usually younger than those with the combined type, it is not yet known whether these are actually two distinct subtypes or the same type at different ages (Barkley, 1996).

Children who are predominantly inattentive are described as inattentive and drowsy, daydreamy, spacey, in a fog or easily confused, and they commonly experience a learning disability. They process information slowly and find it hard to remember things. Their main deficits seem to be speed of information processing and selective attention. Growing—but not yet conclusive—evidence suggests that children who are predominantly inattentive constitute a distinct subgroup from other two types (Maedgen & Carlson, 2000). They appear to display different symptoms, associated conditions, family histories, outcomes, and responses to treatment (Barkley, 1998).

The *DSM-IV-TR* criteria for ADHD have a number of limitations (Barkley, 1996), several of which apply to other childhood disorders as well. First, they are developmentally insensitive, using the same symptom criteria for individuals of all ages—even though some symptoms, such as running and climbing, apply more to young children. In addition, the number of symptoms needed to make a diagnosis is not adjusted for age or level of maturity even though many of these symptoms show a general decline with age. Second, according to *DSM-IV-TR*, ADHD is a disorder that the child either has or does not have. However, because the number and severity of symptoms are also a matter of degree, children who fall just below the cutoff for ADHD are not necessarily qualitatively different from those who are just above it. In fact, over time, some children move in and out of the *DSM-IV-TR* category as a result of fluctuations in their behavior. Third, there is some uncertainty about the *DSM-IV-TR* requirement that symptoms must have an onset prior to age 7. There seems to be little difference between children with an onset of ADHD before or after age 7 (Barkley & Biederman, 1997), and about half of children with ADHD who are predominantly inattentive do not manifest the disorder until *after* age 7 (Applegate et al., 1997). Finally, the requirement of persistence for 6 months may be too brief for young children. Many preschoolers display symptoms for 6 months, and the symptoms then go away. These limitations highlight the fact that *DSM-IV-TR* criteria are designed for specific purposes—classification and diagnosis. They help shape our understanding of ADHD and other childhood disorders but are also shaped by—and in some instances lag behind—new research findings.

## Epidemiology

As many as one half of all clinic-referred children display ADHD symptoms either alone or in combination with other disorders, making it one of the most common referral problems in North America (Barkley, 1998). The best estimate is that about 3–7% of all school-age children in North America have ADHD (APA, 2000; Jensen et al., 1999). However, as with other disorders, estimates can and do vary widely because informants in different settings do not always agree on symptoms or may emphasize different symptoms. Teachers, for example, are especially likely to rate a child as inattentive when oppositional symptoms are also present (Abikoff, Courtney, Pelham, & Koplewicz, 1993). Because adults may disagree, prevalence estimates are much higher when based on just one person's opinion than they are when based on a consensus (Lambert, Sandoval, & Sassone, 1978).

ADHD occurs much more frequently in boys than in girls, with estimates ranging from 6–9% for boys and from 2–3% for girls in the 6- to 12-year age range. In adolescence, overall rates of ADHD drop for both boys and girls, but boys still outnumber girls by the same ratio of 2:1 to 3:1. This ratio is even higher in clinic samples, in which boys outnumber girls by 6:1 or more—most likely because boys are referred more

frequently due to their defiance and aggression (Szatmari, 1992). ADHD in girls may go unrecognized and unreported because teachers may fail to recognize and report inattentive behavior unless it is accompanied by the disruptive symptoms normally associated with boys (McGee & Feehan, 1991). In fact, many of the *DSM-IV-TR* symptoms, such as excessive running around, climbing, and blurting out answers in class are generally more common in boys than in girls. Thus, sampling, referral, and definition biases may be a factor in the greater reported prevalence of ADHD in boys than in girls.

In the past, girls with ADHD were a highly under-studied group (Arnold, 1996). However, recent findings show that girls with ADHD are more likely to have conduct, mood, and anxiety disorders; lower IQ and school achievement scores; and greater impairment on measures of social, school, and family functioning than are girls without ADHD (Biederman et al., 1999; Greene et al., 2001; Rucklidge & Tannock, 2001). In addition, the expression, severity of symptoms, family correlates, and response to treatment are similar for boys and girls with ADHD (Faraone et al., 2000; Silverthorn, Frick, Kuper, & Ott, 1996). When gender differences are found, boys show more hyperactivity, more accompanying aggression and antisocial behavior, and greater impairment in executive functions, whereas girls show greater intellectual impairment (Gaub & Carlson, 1997b; Seidman, Biederman, Faraone, & Weber, 1997).

## Developmental Course

The symptoms of ADHD are probably present at birth, although reliable identification is difficult until the age of 3–4 years when hyperactive-impulsive symptoms become increasingly more salient (Hart, Lahey, Loeber, Applegate, & Frick, 1996). Preschoolers with ADHD act suddenly without thinking, dashing from activity to activity, grabbing at immediate rewards; they are easily bored and react strongly and negatively to routine events (Campbell, 1990; DuPaul, McGoey, Eckert, & VanBrakle, 2001). Symptoms of inattention emerge at 5–7 years of age, as classroom demands for sustained attention and goal-directed persistence increase (Hart et al., 1996). Symptoms of inattention continue through grade school, resulting in low academic productivity, distractibility, poor organization, trouble meeting deadlines, and an inability to follow through on social promises or commitments to peers (Barkley, 1996).

The child's hyperactive-impulsive behaviors that were present in preschool continue, with some decline, during the years from 6 to 12. During elementary school, oppositional defiant behaviors may also develop (Barkley, 1998). By 8–12 years, defiance and hostility may take the form of serious problems, such as lying or aggression. Through the school years, ADHD increasingly takes its toll as children experience problems with self-care, personal responsibility, chores, trustworthiness, independence, social relationships, and academic performance (Koplowicz & Barkley, 1995; Stein, Szumoski, Blondis, & Roizen, 1995). Although hyperactive-impulsive behaviors decline significantly by adolescence, they still occur at a level higher than in 95% of same-age peers (Barkley, 1996). The disorder continues into adolescence for at least 50% or more of clinic-referred elementary school children (Barkley, Fisher, Edelbrock, & Smallish, 1990; Weiss & Hechtman, 1993). Childhood symptoms of hyperactivity-impulsivity (more so than those of inattention) are generally related to poor adolescent outcomes (Barkley, 1998). Some youngsters with ADHD either outgrow their disorder or learn to cope with it. However, many continue to experience problems, leading to a lifelong pattern of suffering and disappointment (Mannuzza & Klein, 1992).

## Accompanying Disorders and Symptoms

As many as 80% of children with ADHD have a co-occurring disorder (Jensen, Martin, & Cantwell, 1997). About 25% or more have a specific learning disorder (Cantwell & Baker, 1992; Semrud-Clikeman et al., 1992) and 30–60% have impairments in speech and language (Baker & Cantwell, 1992; Cohen et al., 2000). About half of all children with ADHD—mostly boys—also meet criteria for oppositional defiant disorder (ODD) by age 7 or later, and 30–50% eventually develop conduct disorder (CD; Barkley, 1998; Biederman, Faraone, & Lapey, 1992). ADHD, ODD, and CD tend to run in families, which suggests a common causal mechanism (Biederman et al., 1992). However, ADHD is usually associated with cognitive impairments and neurodevelopmental difficulties, whereas conduct problems are more often related to family adversity, parental psychopathology, and social disadvantage (Schachar & Tannock, 1995).

About 25% of children with ADHD—usually younger boys—experience excessive anxiety (Tannock, 2000). It is interesting to note that the overall relationship between ADHD and anxiety disorders is reduced or eliminated in adolescence. The co-occurrence of an anxiety disorder may inhibit the adolescent with ADHD from engaging in the impulsive behaviors that characterize other youngsters with ADHD (Pliszka, 1992). As many as 20% of children with ADHD experience depression, and even more eventually develop depression or another mood disorder by early adulthood (Mick, Santangelo, Wypij, & Biederman, 2000; Willcutt, Pennington, Chhabildas, Friedman, & Alexander, 1999). The association between ADHD and depression may be a function of family risk for one disorder's increasing risk for the other (Biederman et al., 1995).

## Associated Features

Children with ADHD display many associated cognitive, academic, and psychosocial deficits. They consistently show deficits in executive functions—particularly those related to motor inhibition (Pennington & Ozonoff, 1996). Most children with ADHD are of at least normal overall intelligence, but they experience severe difficulties in school nevertheless (Fischer, Barkley, Edelbrock, & Smallish, 1990). In fact, the academic skills of children with ADHD have been found to be impaired even before they enter the first grade (Mariani & Barkley, 1997).

The association between ADHD and general health is uncertain at this time (Barkley, 1998; Daly et al., 1996), although a variety of health problems have been suggested (e.g., upper respiratory infections, asthma, allergies, bedwetting, and other elimination problems). Instability of the sleep-wake system is characteristic of children with ADHD, and sleep disturbances are common (Gruber, Sadeh, & Raviv, 2000). Resistance to going to bed and fewer total hours may be the most significant sleep problems (Wilens, Biederman, & Spencer, 1994), although the precise nature of the sleep disturbance in ADHD is not known (Corkum, Tannock, & Moldofsky, 1998). Up to 50% of children with ADHD are described as accident-prone, and they are more than twice as likely as other children to experience serious accidental injuries, such as broken bones, lacerations, severe bruises, poisonings, or head injuries (Barkley, 1998). As young adults, they are at higher risk for traffic accidents and offenses (Nada-Raja et al., 1997) as well as for substance abuse (Wilens, Biederman, Mick, Faraone, & Spencer, 1997) and risky sexual behaviors such as multiple partners and unprotected sex (Barkley, Fisher, & Fletcher, 1997).

Families of children with ADHD experience many difficulties, including interactions characterized by negativity, child noncompliance, high parental control, and sibling conflict (Whalen & Henker, 1999). Parents may experience high levels of distress and related problems; the most common ones are depression in mothers and antisocial behavior (i.e., substance abuse) in fathers. Further stress on family life stems from the fact that parents of children with ADHD may themselves have ADHD and other associated conditions (Johnston & Mash, 2001). It is critical to note that high levels of family conflict and the links between ADHD and parental psychopathology and marital discord seem to be related to the child's co-occurring conduct problems rather than to ADHD alone.

Children and adolescents with ADHD display little of the give and take, cooperation, and sharing that characterize other children (Dumas, 1998; Henker & Whalen, 1999). They are disliked and uniformly rejected by peers, have few friends, and are often unhappy (Gresham, MacMillan, Bocian,

Ward, & Forness, 1998; Landau, Milich, & Diener, 1998). Their difficulties in regulating their emotions (Melnick & Hinshaw, 2000) and the aggressiveness that frequently accompanies ADHD often lead to conflict and negative peer reputation (Erhardt & Hinshaw, 1994).

## Causes

Current research into causal factors provides strong evidence for ADHD as a disorder with neurobiological determinants (Biederman & Spencer, 1999; Tannock, 1998). However, biological and environmental risk factors together shape the expression of ADHD symptoms over time following several different pathways (Johnston & Mash, 2001; Taylor, 1999). ADHD is a complex and chronic disorder of brain, behavior, and development; its cognitive and behavioral outcomes affect many areas of functioning (Rapport & Chung, 2000). Therefore, any explanation of ADHD that focuses on a single cause and single outcome is likely to be inadequate (Taylor, 1999).

### Genetics

Several sources of evidence point to genetic influences as important causal factors in ADHD (Kuntsi & Stevenson, 2000). First, about one third of immediate and extended family members of children with ADHD are also likely to have the disorder (Faraone, Biederman, & Milberger, 1996; Hechtman, 1994). Of fathers who had ADHD as children, one third of their offspring have ADHD (Biederman et al., 1992; Pauls, 1991). Second, studies of biologically related and unrelated pairs of adopted children have found a strong genetic influence that accounts for nearly half of the variance in attention-problem scores on child behavior rating scales (van den Oord, Boomsma, & Verhulst, 1994). Third, twin studies report heritability estimates of ADHD averaging .80 or higher (Tannock, 1998). Both the symptoms and diagnosis of ADHD show average concordance rates for identical twins of 65%—about twice that of fraternal twins (Gilger, Pennington, & DeFries, 1992). Twin studies also find that the greater the severity of ADHD symptoms, the greater the genetic contributions (Stevenson, 1992).

Finally, genetic analysis suggests that specific genes may account for the expression of ADHD in some children (Faraone et al., 1992). Preliminary studies have found a relation between the dopamine transporter (DAT) gene and ADHD (Cook et al., 1995; Gill, Daly, Heron, Hawi, & Fitzgerald, 1997). Studies have also focused on the gene that codes for the dopamine receptor gene (DRD4), which has been linked to the personality trait of sensation seeking (high levels of thrill-seeking, impulsive, exploratory, and excitable

behavior; Benjamin et al., 1996; Ebstein et al., 1996). Findings that implicate specific genes within the dopamine system in ADHD are intriguing, and they are consistent with a model suggesting that reduced dopaminergic activity may be related to the behavioral symptoms of ADHD (Faraone et al., 1999; Winsberg & Comings, 1999). However, other genetic findings indicate that the serotonin system also plays a crucial role in mediating the hyperactive-impulsive components of ADHD (Quist & Kennedy, 2001). As with other disorders of childhood, it is important to keep in mind that in the vast majority of cases, the heritable components of ADHD are likely to be the result of multiple interacting genes on several different chromosomes. Taken together, the findings from family, adoption, twin, and specific gene studies suggest that ADHD is inherited, although the precise mechanisms are not yet known (Edelbrock, Rende, Plomin, & Thompson, 1995; Tannock, 1998).

### Pre- and Perinatal Factors

Many factors that compromise the development of the nervous system before and after birth—such as pregnancy and birth complications, low birth weight, malnutrition, early neurological insult or trauma, and diseases of infancy—may be related to ADHD symptoms (Milberger, Biederman, Faraone, Chen, & Jones, 1996; Milberger, Biederman, Faraone, Guite, & Tsuang, 1997). Although these early factors predict later symptoms of ADHD, there is little evidence that they are *specific* to ADHD because they also predict later symptoms of other disorders as well. A mother's use of cigarettes, alcohol, or other drugs during pregnancy can have damaging effects on her unborn child. Mild or moderate exposure to alcohol before birth may lead to inattention, hyperactivity, impulsivity, and associated impairments in learning and behavior (Streissguth, Bookstein, Sampson, & Barr, 1995). Other substances used during pregnancy—such as nicotine or cocaine—can adversely affect the normal development of the brain and lead to higher than normal rates of ADHD (Weissman et al., 1999).

### Neurobiological Factors

There is both indirect and direct support for neurobiological causal factors in ADHD (Barkley, 1998; Faraone & Biederman, 1998). There are known associations between events or conditions known to be related to neurological status and symptoms of ADHD. Among these are peri- and postnatal events and diseases; environmental toxins such as lead; language and learning disorders; and signs of neurological immaturity, such as clumsiness, poor balance and coordination, and abnormal reflexes. Other sources of indirect support include the improvement in ADHD symptoms produced by stimulant medications known to affect the central nervous system, the similarity between symptoms of ADHD and symptoms associated with lesions to the prefrontal cortex (Grattan & Eslinger, 1991), and the deficient performances of children with ADHD on neuropsychological tests associated with prefrontal lobe functions (Barkley, Grodzinsky, & DuPaul, 1992).

Neuroimaging studies have found that children with ADHD have a smaller right prefrontal cortex than do those without ADHD (Filipek et al., 1997) and show structural abnormalities in several parts of the basal ganglia (Semrud-Clikeman et al., 2000). Although simple and direct relations cannot be assumed between brain size and abnormal function, anatomic measures of frontostriatal circuitry are related to children's performance on response inhibition tasks (Casey et al., 1997). In adults with ADHD and in adolescent girls with ADHD, positron-emission tomography (PET) scan studies have found reduced glucose metabolism in the areas of the brain that inhibit impulses and control attention (Ernst et al., 1994). Significant correlations have also been found between diminished metabolic activity in the left anterior frontal region and severity of ADHD symptoms in adolescents (Zametkin et al., 1993). Taken together, the findings from neuroimaging studies suggest the importance of the frontostriatal region of the brain in ADHD. These studies tell us that in children with ADHD, there is a structural difference or less activity in certain regions of the brain, but they don't tell us why.

### Family Factors

Genetic studies find that psychosocial factors in the family account for only a small amount of the variance (less than 15%) in ADHD symptoms (Barkley, 1998), and explanations of ADHD based exclusively on negative family influences have received little support (Silverman & Ragusa, 1992; Willis & Lovaas, 1977). Nevertheless, family influences are important in understanding ADHD for several reasons (Johnston & Mash, 2001; Whalen & Henker, 1999). First, family influences may lead to ADHD symptoms or to a greater severity of symptoms. In some circumstances, ADHD symptoms may be the result of interfering and insensitive early caregiving practices (Jacobvitz & Sroufe, 1987). In addition, for children at risk for ADHD, family conflict may raise the severity of their hyperactive-impulsive symptoms to a clinical level (Barkley, 1996). Second, family problems may result from interacting with a child who is impulsive and difficult to manage (Mash & Johnston, 1990). The clearest support for this child-to-parent direction of effect comes from double-blind placebo control drug studies in which children's ADHD symptoms were decreased using stimulant

medications. Decreases in children's ADHD symptoms produced a corresponding reduction in the negative and controlling behaviors that parents had previously displayed when their children were unmedicated (Barkley, 1988; Humphries, Kinsbourne, & Swanson, 1978). Third, family conflict is probably related to the presence, maintenance, and later emergence of associated ODD and CD symptoms. Many interventions for ADHD try to change patterns of family interaction to head off an escalating cycle of oppositional behavior and conflict (Sonuga-Barke, Daley, Thompson, Laver-Bradbury, & Weeks, 2001). Family influences may play a major role in determining the outcome of ADHD and associated problems even if such influences are not the primary cause of ADHD (Johnston & Mash, 2001).

### Summary and Integration

ADHD has a strong biological basis, and for many children, it is an inherited condition. However, the specific cause of the disorder is not known. ADHD is probably the result of a complex pattern of interacting influences. We are just beginning to understand the complex causal pathways through which biological risk factors, family relationships, and broader system influences interact to shape the development and outcome of ADHD over time (Hinshaw, 1994; Taylor, 1999). Although data do not yet permit a comprehensive causal model, a possible developmental pathway for ADHD that highlights several known causal influences and outcomes is shown in Figure 2.1. Findings generally suggest that inherited variants of genes related to the transmission of dopamine and serotonin lead to structural and functional abnormalities in the frontal lobes and basal ganglia regions of the brain. Altered neurological function causes changes in psychological function involving a failure of children to adequately suppress inappropriate responses; this in turn leads to many failures in cognitive performance. The outcome involves a pattern of restless and disorganized behavior that is identified as ADHD, that also impairs social development and functioning, and that may lead to symptoms of ODD and CD (Barkley, 1997; Taylor, 1999).

### INTERNALIZING DISORDERS: ANXIETY DISORDERS

Internalizing disorders involve a core disturbance in emotions and moods such as worry, fear, sorrow, and guilt (Zahn-Waxler et al., 2000). The two major types of internalizing disorders are (a) mood disorders and (b) anxiety disorders. Children with mood disorders experience extreme, persistent, or poorly regulated emotional states such as excessive

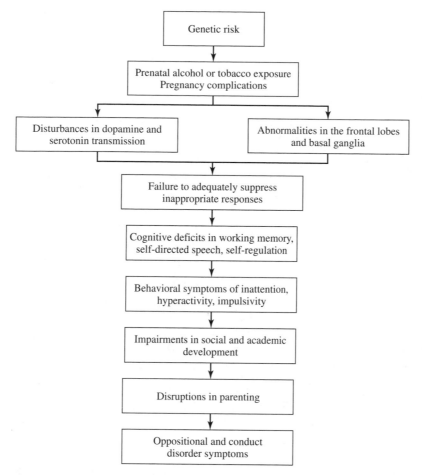

**Figure 2.1**   A possible developmental pathway for attention-deficit/hyperactivity disorder.

unhappiness or wide swings in mood from sadness to elation. The two most common mood disorders in childhood are major depressive disorder (MDD) and dysthymic disorder (DD; APA, 2000). MDD and DD are related; many children with DD eventually develop MDD, and some children may experience both disorders (Lewinsohn, Rohde, Seeley, & Hops, 1991). A third mood disorder, bipolar disorder, is rare in children, although there is growing interest in this problem in young people (Carlson, Bromet, & Sievers, 2000; Geller & Luby, 1997). In the sections to follow, we limit our discussion to anxiety disorders, highlighting many of the same features that we covered for ADHD. Once again, issues that we raise in discussing anxiety disorders have relevance for other childhood disorders as well.

Anxiety disorders are among most common mental health problems in young people (Majcher & Pollack, 1996; Vasey & Ollendick, 2000). However, because milder forms of anxiety are a common occurrence in normal development and because anxiety disorders are not nearly as damaging to other people or property as are ADHD and disruptive behavior disorders, anxiety disorders frequently go unnoticed, undiagnosed, and untreated (Albano, Chorpita, & Barlow, 1996). Anxiety was once thought of as a transient problem, but we now know that many children who experience anxiety continue to have problems well into adolescence and adulthood (Ollendick & King, 1994). Although isolated symptoms of fear and anxiety are usually short-lived, anxiety disorders in children have a more chronic course (March, 1995). In fact, nearly half of those affected have an illness duration of 8 years or more (Keller et al., 1992).

**Symptoms and Types**

Anxiety is a mood state characterized by strong negative emotion and bodily symptoms of tension in which an individual apprehensively anticipates future danger or misfortune (Barlow, 1988). The term *anxiety disorder* describes children who experience excessive and debilitating anxiety. However, as described in Table 2.5, these disorders take a number of different forms that vary in focus and severity as a function

**TABLE 2.5   Anxiety Disorders in Children: Main Features**

*Separation anxiety disorder (SAD):* Excessive and age-inappropriate anxiety about separation from the home or attachment figures that lasts for at least 4 weeks and begins before age 18 years.

*Specific phobia:* Age-inappropriate and marked fear in response to the presence or anticipation of a specific object or situation (e.g., animals, injections, seeing blood); the fear persists for at least 6 months and is excessive or unreasonable. Exposure provokes immediate anxiety and is avoided or endured with intense anxiety and distress; children may not recognize that their fear is excessive or unreasonable. Main subtypes involve phobias of animals and insects, blood-injection-injury, specific situations (e.g., elevators, flying, enclosed places), and other types (e.g., loud sounds, costumed characters).

*Social phobia (social anxiety disorder):* A marked and persistent fear of social or performance situations that expose the child to unfamiliar adults and peers, scrutiny, and possible humiliation or embarrassment; fear persists for at least 6 months.

*Generalized anxiety disorder (GAD):* Excessive and uncontrollable anxiety and worry (apprehensive expectation) about a number of events or activities (e.g., school performance, sporting events) on more days than not for at least 6 months. Child must display at least one of six characteristic symptoms: restlessness, fatigue, difficulty concentrating, irritability, muscle tension, and sleep disturbance.

*Obsessive-compulsive disorder (OCD):* Recurrent, time consuming (more than 1 hour a day), and disturbing obsessions (persistent and intrusive thoughts, ideas, impulses, or images) and compulsions (repetitive, purposeful, and intentional behaviors or mental acts) that are performed in response to an obsession. Children may not recognize their obsessions and compulsions as excessive or unreasonable. In children, common obsessions focus on contamination, fears of harm to self or others, and concerns with symmetry; common compulsions include excessive washing and bathing, checking, and ordering.

*Posttraumatic stress disorder (PTSD):* Persistent anxiety (a duration of at least 1 month) after an overwhelming traumatic event that is outside the range of usual human experience. The response to the event involved intense fear, helplessness, horror, or disorganized or agitated behavior. Symptoms include reexperiencing the traumatic event (e.g., intrusive recollections, repetitive play, frightening dreams), avoidance of associated stimuli and numbing of general responsiveness (e.g., avoidance of thoughts and feelings associated with the trauma, restricted range of emotion), and extreme arousal (e.g., sleep difficulties, hypervigilance).

*Panic disorder and agoraphobia:* Recurrent unexpected panic attacks followed by at least 1 month of persistent concern about having another, constant worry about the consequences of the attacks, or a significant change in behavior related to the attacks. The main feature of agoraphobia is anxiety about and avoidance of places or situations from which escape might be difficult or embarrassing or where help might be unavailable in the event of a panic attack or symptoms.

of development. It is important to keep in mind that there is substantial overlap among these disorders in childhood (Pine, Cohen, Cohen, & Brook, 2000). Many children suffer from more than one type—either at the same time or at different times during their development (Zahn-Waxler et al., 2000).

## Epidemiology and Accompanying Disorders

The overall prevalence rates for anxiety disorders in children range from about 6–18% (Costello & Angold, 2000). Rates vary as a function of whether functional impairment is part of the diagnostic criteria, with the informant, and with the type of anxiety disorder.

### Separation Anxiety Disorder (SAD)

SAD is the most common anxiety disorder in youths, occurring in about 10% of all children. It seems to be equally common in boys and girls, although when gender differences are found they tend to favor girls (Last, Perrin, Hersen, & Kazdin, 1992). Most children with SAD have another anxiety disorder—most commonly generalized anxiety disorder (Last, Perrin, Hersen, & Kazdin, 1996). About one third develop a depressive disorder within several months of the onset of SAD. They may also display specific fears of getting lost or of the dark. School reluctance or refusal is also quite common in older children with SAD (King & Bernstein, 2001).

### Specific Phobia

About 2–4% or more of all children experience specific phobias at some time in their lives (Essau, Conradt, & Petermann, 2000; Muris & Merckelbach, 2000). However, only a very small number of these children are referred for treatment, suggesting that most parents do not view specific phobias as a significant problem. Specific phobias—particularly blood phobia—are generally more common in girls than boys (Essau et al., 2000). The most common co-occurring disorder for children with a specific phobia is another anxiety disorder. Although comorbidity is frequent for children with specific phobias, it tends to be lower than it is for other anxiety disorders (Strauss & Last, 1993). Phobias involving animals, darkness, insects, blood, and injury typically have their onset at 7–9 years, which is similar to normal development. However, clinical phobias are much more likely to persist over time than are normal fears, even though both decline with age. Specific phobias can occur at any age but seem to peak between ages 10 and 13 years (Strauss & Last, 1993).

### Social Phobia (Social Anxiety Disorder)

Social phobia occurs in 1–3% of children, affecting slightly more girls than boys (Essau, Conradt, & Petermann, 1999). Girls may experience more social anxiety because they are more concerned with social competence than are boys and attach greater importance to interpersonal relationships (Inderbitzen-Nolan & Walters, 2000). Among children referred for treatment for anxiety disorders, as many as 20% have social phobia as their primary diagnosis, and it is also the most common secondary diagnosis for children referred for other anxiety disorders (Albano et al., 1996). Even so, many cases of social phobia are overlooked because shyness is common in our society and because these children are not likely to call attention to their problem even when they are severely distressed (Essau et al., 1999). Two thirds of children and adolescents with a social phobia have another anxiety disorder—most commonly a specific phobia or panic disorder (Beidel, Turner, & Morris, 1999). About 20% of adolescents with a social phobia also suffer from major depression. They may also use alcohol and other drugs as a form of self-medication and as a way of reducing their anxiety in social situations (Albano et al., 1996).

Social phobias generally develop after puberty, with the most common age of onset in early to midadolescence (Strauss & Last, 1993). The disorder is extremely rare in children under the age of 10. The prevalence of social phobia appears to increase with age, although little information is available to describe the natural course of the disorder or its long-term outcome.

### Generalized Anxiety Disorder (GAD)

Along with SAD, GAD is one of the most common anxiety disorders of childhood, occurring in 3–6% of all children (Albano et al., 1996). It is equally common in boys and girls, with perhaps a slightly higher prevalence in older adolescent females (Strauss, Lease, Last, & Francis, 1988). Children with GAD present with a high rate of other anxiety disorders and depression. For younger children, co-occurring SAD and ADHD are most frequent; older children with GAD tend to have specific phobias and major depression, impaired social adjustment, low self-esteem, and an increased risk for suicide (Keller et al., 1992; Strauss, Last, Hersen, & Kazdin, 1988). About half of children referred for treatment for anxiety disorders have GAD. This proportion is higher than it is for adults, in whom the disorder is more common, but fewer adults seek treatment (Albano et al., 1996).

The average age of onset for GAD is 10–14 years (Albano et al., 1996). In a community sample of adolescents with GAD, the likelihood of their having GAD at follow-up was higher if symptoms at the time of initial assessment were severe (Cohen, Cohen, & Brook, 1993). Nearly half of severe cases were rediagnosed after 2 years, suggesting that *severe* generalized anxiety symptoms persist over time, even in youngsters who have not been referred for treatment.

### Obsessive-Compulsive Disorder (OCD)

The prevalence of OCD in children and adolescents is 2–3%, which suggests that it occurs about as often in young people as in adults (Piacentini & Graae, 1997). Clinic-based studies of younger children indicate that OCD is twice as common in boys as it is in girls. However, this gender difference has not been found in community samples of adolescents, which may be a function of age, referral bias, or both (Albano et al., 1996). The most common comorbidities for OCD are other anxiety disorders, depressive disorders (especially in older children with OCD), and disruptive behavior disorders (Piacentini & Graae, 1997). Substance use disorders, learning disorders, and eating disorders are also overrepresented in children with OCD, as are vocal and motor tics (Peterson, Pine, Cohen, & Brook, 2001; Piacentini & Graae, 1997).

The mean age of onset of OCD is 9–12 years with two peaks—one in early childhood and another in early adolescence (Hanna, 1995). Children with an early onset of OCD (age 6–10) are more likely to have a family history of OCD than are those with a later onset, which indicates a greater role of genetic influences in such cases (Swedo, Rapoport, Leonard, Lenane, & Cheslow, 1989). These children have prominent motor patterns, engaging in compulsions without obsessions and displaying odd behaviors, such as finger licking or compulsively walking in geometric designs. One half to two thirds of children with OCD continue to meet the criteria for the disorder 2–14 years later. Although most children, including those treated with medication, show some improvement in symptoms, fewer than 10% show complete remission (Albano, Knox, & Barlow, 1995).

### Posttraumatic Stress Disorder (PTSD)

PTSD is common in children exposed to traumatic events (Perrin, Smith, & Yule, 2000). The prevalence of PTSD symptoms is greater in children who are exposed to life-threatening events than it is in those who are not. For example, nearly 40% of children exposed to the Buffalo Creek dam collapse in 1972 showed probable PTSD symptoms 2 years after the disaster (Fletcher, 1996). PTSD in children is also strongly correlated with degree of exposure. In children exposed to a school yard sniper attack, proximity to the attack was linearly related to the risk of developing PTSD symptoms (Pynoos et al., 1987). Traumatized children frequently exhibit symptoms of other disorders besides PTSD, and children with other disorders may have PTSD as a comorbid diagnosis (Famularo, Fenton, Kinscherff, & Augustyn, 1996). The PTSD that occurs in children traumatized by fires, hurricanes, or chronic maltreatment may worsen or lead to disruptive behavior disorders (Amaya-Jackson & March, 1995).

Because PTSD can strike at any time during childhood, its course depends on the age of the child when the trauma occurred and on the nature of the trauma. Because the traumatic experience is filtered cognitively and emotionally before it can be appraised as an extreme threat, how trauma is experienced depends on the child's developmental level. Some children appear to have different trauma thresholds, although exposure to horrific events is traumatic to nearly all children. Several trauma-related, child, and family factors appear to be important in predicting children's course of recovery from PTSD following exposure to a natural disaster (La Greca, Silverman, & Wasserstein, 1998). Among these are loss and disruption following the trauma, preexisting child characteristics (e.g., psychopathology), coping styles, and social support (Perrin et al., 2000).

Longitudinal findings suggest that PTSD can become a chronic psychiatric disorder, persisting for decades or a lifetime (Fletcher, 1996). Children with chronic PTSD may display a developmental course marked by remissions and relapses. Moreover, individuals exposed to a traumatic event may not exhibit symptoms until months or years afterwards, when a situation that resembles the original trauma triggers the onset of PTSD. For example, sexual abuse during childhood may lead to PTSD in adult survivors.

### Panic Disorder (PD)

Whereas panic attacks are common among adolescents (about 35–65%), panic disorder is much less common, affecting less than 1% to almost 5% of teens (Ollendick, Mattis, & King, 1994). Adolescent females are more likely to experience panic attacks than are adolescent males, and a fairly consistent association has been found between panic attacks and stressful life events (King, Ollendick, & Mattis, 1994; Last & Strauss, 1989). About half of adolescents with PD have no other disorder, and for the remainder an additional anxiety disorder and depression are the most common secondary diagnoses (Kearney, Albano, Eisen, Allan, & Barlow, 1997; Last & Strauss, 1989). After months or years of unrelenting panic attacks and the restricted lifestyle that results from avoidance behavior, adolescents and young adults with PD may develop severe depression and may be at risk for suicidal behavior. Others may begin to use alcohol or drugs as a way of alleviating their anxiety.

The average age of onset for a first panic attack in adolescents with PD is 15–19 years, and 95% of adolescents with the disorder are postpubertal (Bernstein, Borchardt, & Perwien, 1996; Kearney & Allan, 1995). PD occurs in otherwise emotionally healthy youngsters about half the time. The most frequent prior disturbance when there is one is a depressive disorder (Last & Strauss, 1989). Unfortunately, children and adolescents with PD have the lowest rate of remission for any of the anxiety disorders (Last et al., 1996).

### Gender, Ethnicity, and Culture

Studies have found a preponderance of anxiety disorders in girls during childhood and adolescence (Lewinsohn, Gotlib, Lewinsohn, Seeley, & Allen, 1998). By age 6, twice as many girls as boys have experienced symptoms of anxiety, and this discrepancy persists through childhood and adolescence. Such findings should be interpreted cautiously, however, because the possibility that girls are more likely than are boys to *report* anxiety cannot be ruled out as an alternative explanation.

Research into the relationship between ethnic and cultural factors and childhood anxiety disorders is limited and inconclusive. Studies comparing the number and nature of fears in African American and White youngsters have found the two groups to be quite similar (Ginsburg & Silverman, 1996; Treadwell, Flannery-Schroeder, & Kendall, 1994). However, African American children report more symptoms of anxiety than do White children (Cole, Martin, Peeke, Henderson, & Harwell, 1998). White children endorse more symptoms of social phobia and fewer symptoms of separation anxiety than do African American children (Compton, Nelson, & March, 2000). The underrepresentation of minorities and children of lower socioeconomic status (SES) for certain anxiety disorders such as OCD could also reflect a bias in which minority children are less likely to be referred for treatment (Neal & Turner, 1991).

Among children *referred* for anxiety disorders, Whites are more likely to present with school refusal and higher severity ratings, whereas African Americans are more likely to have a history of PTSD and a somewhat greater number of fears (Last & Perrin, 1993). Although anxiety may be similar in the two groups, patterns of referral, help-seeking behaviors, diagnoses, and treatment processes are likely to differ. For example, African Americans may be more likely to turn for help with their child's OCD symptoms to members of their informal social network, such as clergy or medical personnel, than to mental health professionals (Hatch, Friedman, & Paradis, 1996). Their family members are also less likely to be drawn into the child's OCD symptoms.

Research comparing phobic and anxiety disorders in Hispanic and White children finds marked similarities on most measures, including age at intake, gender, primary diagnoses, proportion of school refusal, and proportion with more than one diagnosis. Hispanic children are more likely to have a primary diagnosis of SAD. Hispanic parents also rate their children as more fearful than do White parents (Ginsburg & Silverman, 1996). Few studies have examined anxiety disorders in Native American children. Prevalence estimates from one study of Native American youth in Appalachia (mostly

Cherokee) indicate rates of anxiety disorders similar to those for White youth, with the most common disorder for both groups being SAD. Rates of SAD were slightly higher for Native American youth, especially for girls (Costello, Farmer, Angold, Burns, & Erkanli, 1997).

Although cross-cultural research into anxiety disorders in children is limited, specific fears in children have been studied and documented in virtually every culture. Developmental fears (e.g., a fear of loud noises or separation anxiety) occur in children of all cultures at about the same age. The number of fears in children tends to be highly similar across cultures, as does the presence of gender differences in pattern and content. Nevertheless, the expression and developmental course of fear and anxiety may be affected by culture. Cultures that favor inhibition, compliance, and obedience have increased levels of fear in children (Ollendick, Yang, King, Dong, & Akande, 1996).

## Accompanying Disorders and Symptoms

A child's risk for accompanying disorders varies with the type of anxiety disorder. Social phobia, GAD, and SAD are more commonly associated with depression than is specific phobia. Depression is also diagnosed more often in children with multiple anxiety disorders and in those who show severe impairments in their everyday functioning (Bernstein, 1991).

The strong and undeniable relationship between anxiety and depression in young people merits further discussion (Kendall & Brady, 1995; Mesman & Koot, 2000). Does anxiety lead to depression, are anxiety and depression the same disorder with different clinical features, are they on a continuum of severity, or are they distinct disorders with different causes but some overlapping features (Seligman & Ollendick, 1998; Zahn-Waxler et al., 2000)? Children with anxiety and depression are older at age of presentation than are children with anxiety alone, and in most cases symptoms of anxiety both precede and predict those of depression (Brady & Kendall, 1992; Cole, Peeke, Martin, Truglio, & Seroczynski, 1998). Symptoms of anxiety and depression may form a single indistinguishable dimension in younger children but are increasingly distinct in older children and in children with at least one diagnosable disorder (Cole, Truglio, & Peeke, 1997; Gurley, Cohen, Pine, & Brook, 1996). Recent studies of children's negative emotional symptoms generally support the three distinct constructs of anxiety, depression, and fear, with anxiety corresponding to negative affect, depression to low positive affect, and fear to physiological overarousal (Chorpita, Daleiden, Moffitt, Yim, & Umemoto, 2000; Joiner & Lonigan, 2000; Lonigan, Hooe, David, & Kistner, 1999).

## Associated Features

Children with anxiety disorders are typically of normal intelligence, and there is little evidence of a strong relationship between anxiety and IQ. However, excessive anxiety may be related to deficits in specific areas of cognitive functioning, such as memory, attention, and speech or language. High levels of anxiety can interfere with academic performance. One study found that anxiety in the first grade predicted anxiety in the fifth grade and significantly influenced fifth-grade achievement (Ialongo, Edelsohn, Werthamer-Larsson, Crockett, & Kellam, 1995). The specific mechanisms involved could include anything from frequent absences to direct interference on cognitive tasks, such as writing a test or solving a math problem.

Children with anxiety disorders selectively attend to information that may be potentially threatening, a tendency referred to as *anxious vigilance* or *hypervigilance* (Vasey, El-Hag, & Daleiden, 1996). Anxious vigilance is maintained because it permits the child to avoid potentially threatening events by means of early detection and with minimal anxiety and effort. Although this strategy may benefit the child in the short term, it has the negative long-term effect of maintaining and heightening anxiety by interfering with the information-processing and coping responses needed to learn that many potentially threatening events are not so dangerous after all (Vasey et al., 1996).

When faced with a clear threat, both normal and anxious children use rules to confirm information about danger and play down information about safety. However, high-anxious children often do this in the face of less obvious threats, suggesting that their perceptions of threat activate a danger-confirming reasoning strategy (Muris, Merckelbach, & Damsma, 2000). Anxious children generally engage in more negative self-talk than do nonanxious children. However, positive self-talk does not distinguish anxious children from controls, suggesting that their internal dialogue is more negative but not necessarily less positive than that of other children (Treadwell & Kendall, 1996). Although cognitive errors and distortions are associated with anxiety in children, their possible role in *causing* anxiety has not been established (Seligman & Ollendick, 1998).

Children with anxiety disorders often experience somatic symptoms such as stomachaches or headaches. These complaints are more common in youngsters with PD and SAD than in those with a specific phobia. Somatic complaints are also more frequent in adolescents than in younger children and in children who display school refusal. Children with anxiety disorders may also have sleep disturbances. Some may experience nocturnal panic—an abrupt waking in a state of extreme anxiety—that is similar to a daytime panic attack. Nocturnal panic attacks usually occur in adolescents with PD (Craske & Rowe, 1997).

Many children with anxiety disorders have low social competence and high social anxiety, and their parents and teachers are likely to view such children as anxious and socially maladjusted (Chansky & Kendall, 1997; Krain & Kendall, 2000; Strauss, Lease, Kazdin, Dulcan, & Last, 1989). Compared to their peers, these children are more likely to see themselves as shy and socially withdrawn and more likely to report low self-esteem, loneliness, and difficulties in starting and maintaining friendships. Some of their difficulties with peers may be related to specific deficits in emotion understanding—particularly in hiding and changing emotions (Southam-Gerow & Kendall, 2000). Findings are mixed regarding how children with anxiety disorders are viewed by other children (Kendall, Panichelli-Mindel, Sugarman, & Callahan, 1997). It appears that childhood anxiety disorders are most likely to be associated with diminished peer popularity when they coexist with depression (Strauss, Lahey, Frick, Frame, & Hynd, 1988).

## Causes

It is important to recognize that different anxiety disorders may require different causal models. For example, the affective, physiological, and interpersonal processes in GAD may differ from those in other anxiety disorders (T. M. Borkovec & Inz, 1990). Current models of anxiety emphasize the importance of interacting biological and environmental influences (Chorpita & Barlow, 1998; Zahn-Waxler et al., 2000).

### Early Temperament

Early temperament has been implicated as a precursor for anxiety disorders. Children differ markedly in their reactions to novel or unexpected events—perhaps because of genetics, gender, cultural background, prior experience, or a combination of factors. Orienting, attending, vigilance, wariness, and motor readiness in response to the unfamiliar are important mechanisms for survival. From an evolutionary perspective, abnormal fears and anxieties partly reflect variation among infants in their initial behavioral reactions to novelty (Kagan, 1997).

This variation is a reflection of inherited differences in the neurochemistry of structures that are thought to play an important role in detecting discrepant events (Kagan, Snidman, Arcus, & Reznick, 1994). These structures include the amygdala and its projections to the motor system, the cingulate and frontal cortex, the hypothalamus, and the sympathetic nervous system. Children who have a high threshold to novelty are presumed to be at low risk for developing anxiety disorders.

Other children are born with a tendency to become overexcited and to withdraw in response to novel stimulation—an enduring trait for some and a possible risk factor for the development of later anxiety disorders (Kagan & Snidman, 1999; Schwartz, Snidman, & Kagan, 1999).

The pathway from a shy-inhibited temperament in infancy and childhood to a later anxiety disorder is neither direct nor straightforward. Although a shy-inhibited temperament may contribute to later anxiety disorders, it is not an inevitable outcome (Prior, Smart, Sanson, & Oberklaid, 2000). Such an outcome probably depends on whether the inhibited child grows up in an environment that fosters this tendency (Kagan, Snidman, & Arcus, 1992). For example, a parent's use of firm limits that teach inhibited children how to cope with stress may reduce their risk for later anxiety. In contrast, it is possible that well-meaning but overprotective parents who shield their sensitive child from stressful events may inadvertently encourage a continuation of timidity by preventing the child from confronting fears and—by doing so—eliminating them. Such tendencies in the parents of inhibited children may be common (Hirshfeld et al., 1992; Rosenbaum et al., 1991). Thus, inhibited children may be at high risk not only because of their inborn temperament but also because of their elevated risk of exposure to anxious, overprotective parenting (Turner, Beidel, & Wolff, 1996).

### Genetics

Family and twin studies suggest a biological vulnerability to anxiety disorders, indicating that children's general tendencies to be inhibited, tense, or fearful are inherited (DiLalla, Kagan, & Reznick, 1994). However, little research exists at present to support a direct link between specific genetic markers and specific types of anxiety disorders. Contributions from multiple genes seem related to anxiety only when certain psychological and social factors are also present.

The overall concordance rates for anxiety disorders are significantly higher for monozygotic (MZ) twins than for dizygotic (DZ) twins (Andrews, Stewart, Allen, & Henderson, 1990). However, MZ twin pairs do not typically have the same types of anxiety disorders. This finding suggests that what is inherited is a disposition to become anxious, and the form that the disorder takes is a function of environmental influences. Twin and adoption studies of anxiety in children and adolescents may be summarized as follows: There is a genetic influence on anxiety in childhood that accounts for about one third of the variance in most cases; heritability for anxiety may be greater for girls than for boys; shared environmental influences or experiences that make children in the same family resemble one another (e.g., maternal psychopathology, ineffective parenting, or poverty) have a significant influence on anxiety disorders in children and adolescents (Eley, 1999).

Two lines of evidence suggest that anxiety disorders run in families. First, parents of children with anxiety disorders have increased rates of current and past anxiety disorders. Second, children of parents with anxiety disorders have an increased risk for anxiety disorders (McClure, Brennan, Hammen, & Le Brocque, 2001). Children of parents with anxiety disorders are about five times more likely to have anxiety disorders than are children of parents without anxiety disorders (Beidel & Turner, 1997). However, they are not necessarily the *same* anxiety disorders (Mancini, van Ameringen, Szatmari, Fugere, & Boyle, 1996). Nearly 70% of children of parents with agoraphobia meet diagnostic criteria for disorders such as anxiety and depression, and they report more fear and anxiety and less control over various risks than do children of comparison parents. However, the fears of parents with agoraphobia and the fears of their children are no more closely aligned than are those of nonanxious parents and their children, once again supporting the view that it is a general predisposition for anxiety that is perpetuated in families (Capps, Sigman, Sena, & Henker, 1996).

### Neurobiological Factors

The part of the brain most often connected with anxiety is the limbic system, which acts as a mediator between the brain stem and the cortex (Sallee & Greenawald, 1995). Signs of potential danger are monitored and sensed by the more primitive brain stem, which then relays them to the higher cortical centers via the limbic system. This brain system is referred to as the behavioral inhibition system and is believed to be overactive in children with anxiety disorders. Neuroimaging studies point to abnormalities in limbic-based amygdala, septohippocampal, and brain stem hypothalamic circuits as being associated with anxiety disorders (Pine & Grun, 1999).

A group of neurons known as the locus ceruleus is a major brain source for norepinephrine, an inhibitory neurotransmitter. Overactivation of this region is presumed to lead to a fear response, and underactivity is presumed to lead to inattention, impulsivity, and risk taking. Abnormalities of these systems appear to be related to anxiety states in children (Sallee & Greenawald, 1995). The neurotransmitter system that has been implicated most often in anxiety disorders is the gamma-aminobutyric acid (GABAergic) system.

### Family Factors

Surprisingly little is known about the relation between parenting styles or family factors and anxiety disorders. Parents of anxious children are often described as overinvolved, intrusive, or limiting of their child's independence. Observations of interactions between 9- to 12-year-old children with anxiety disorders and their parents found that parents of children with anxiety disorders were rated as granting less autonomy to their children than were other parents; the children rated their mothers and fathers as being less accepting (Siqueland, Kendall, Steinberg, 1996). Other studies have found that mothers of children previously identified as behaviorally inhibited are more likely to use criticism when interacting with their children and that emotional overinvolvement by parents is associated with an increased occurrence of SAD in their children (Hirshfeld, Biederman, Brody, & Faraone, 1997; Hirshfeld, Biederman, & Rosenbaum, 1997). These findings generally support the notion of excessive parental control as a parenting style associated with anxiety disorders in children, although the causal role of such a style is not yet known (Chorpita & Barlow, 1998; Rapee, 1997).

Not only do parents of children with anxiety disorders seem to be more controlling than do other parents, but they also have different expectations of their children. For example, when they thought the child was being asked to give a videotaped speech, mothers of children with anxiety disorders expected their children to become upset and had low expectations for their children's coping (Kortlander, Kendall, & Panichelli-Mindel, 1997). It is likely that parental attitudes shape—and are shaped by—interactions with the child, during which parent and child revise their expectations and behavior as a result of feedback from the other (Barrett, Rapee, Dadds, & Ryan, 1996).

Insecure early attachments may be a risk factor for the development of later anxiety disorders (Bernstein et al., 1996; Manassis & Bradley, 1994). Mothers with anxiety disorders have been found to have insecure attachments themselves, and 80% of their children are also insecurely attached (Manassis, Bradley, Goldberg, Hood, & Swinson, 1994). Infants who are ambivalently attached have more anxiety diagnoses in childhood and adolescence (Bernstein et al., 1996). Although it is a risk factor, insecure attachment may be a nonspecific one in that many infants with insecure attachments develop disorders other than anxiety (e.g., disruptive behavior disorder), and many do not develop any disorders.

### Summary and Integration

There is much debate regarding the distinctness of the *DSM-IV-TR* childhood anxiety disorders, with some individuals emphasizing the similarities among these disorders and others emphasizing the differences (Pine, 1997). An emphasis on similarities is consistent with the strong associations among the different disorders, the presence of shared risk factors such as female gender, and evidence of a broad genetic predisposition for anxiety. An emphasis on differences is consistent with different developmental progressions and outcomes as well as differences in the biological correlates of anxiety disorders in children versus adults (Pine et al., 2000). Children with anxiety disorders will most likely display features that are shared across the various disorders as well as other features that are unique to their particular disorder.

A possible developmental pathway for anxiety disorders in children is shown in Figure 2.2. In children with an inborn predisposition to be anxious or fearful, the child's sense that the world is not a safe place may create a psychological vulnerability to anxiety. After anxiety occurs, it feeds on itself. The anxiety and avoidance continue long after the stresses that provoked them are gone. In closing, it is important to keep in mind that many children with anxiety disorders do not continue to experience problems as adults. Therefore, it will be important to identify risk and protective factors that would explain these differences in outcomes (Pine & Grun, 1999).

## CURRENT ISSUES AND FUTURE DIRECTIONS

ADHD and anxiety—like most disorders of childhood and adolescence—involve broad patterns of behavior and dysfunction that unfold over time as the result of multiple interacting risk and protective factors in the child and the environment (Rutter & Sroufe, 2000). Building on our discussion of these disorders, we next highlight a number of current issues and future directions related to the study of child psychopathology more generally.

### Defining Disorders of Childhood and Adolescence

Defining child psychopathology and identifying the boundaries between abnormal and normal functioning are arbitrary processes at best—subject to meaning-based cultural interpretations (Hoagwood & Jensen, 1997). Traditional psychiatric approaches to defining mental disorders in children have emphasized concepts such as symptoms, diagnosis, and illness as residing within the child, and by doing so, they have strongly influenced the ways in which we think about child psychopathology and related questions (Richters &

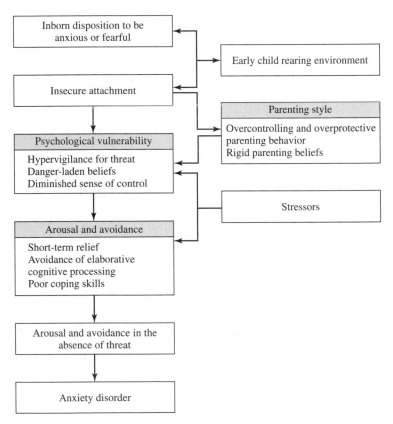

**Figure 2.2**    A possible developmental pathway for anxiety disorders.

Cicchetti, 1993). Implicit in these approaches was the view that a single primary cause would be found for each disorder and that this cause would be diagnosis specific (Rutter & Sroufe, 2000). They also gave little attention to causes as dynamic processes that operate over time, the role of context, direct and indirect influences, and developmental pathways.

The *DSM-IV-TR* diagnostic categories for childhood disorders clearly reflect this tradition. As a result, there has been ongoing concern about the subjective formulation and static nature of these categories, their insensitivity to developmental, age, gender, and contextual parameters, and their heterogeneity and overlap (Mash & Terdal, 1997a). In addition, many of the *DSM-IV-TR* categories for describing child psychopathology are downward extensions of concepts and categories developed for adults. There remains a need for a developmental system of classification.

Many childhood disorders such as anxiety, depression, and disruptive behavior appear to reflect dimensions of personality rather than categorical problems (Werry, 2001). Even disorders such as autism that have traditionally been viewed as categorical in nature can be conceptualized as an extreme on a continuum of social behavior (Baron-Cohen, 2000). For dimensional disorders, children who score just below the cutoff for a diagnosis may one day meet criteria and often show impairment that is comparable to that of children who score above the cutoff. Similarly, those above the cutoff may someday move below.

Current definitions of child psychopathology are cognizant of the need for standardized approaches to diagnosis and classification, and the *DSM-IV-TR* criteria represent a considerable improvement over the idiosyncratic definitions that characterized previous practices. However, the limitations of traditional diagnostic approaches indicate a need to broaden these perspectives to incorporate dimensional concepts and dynamic causal processes. This melding of ideas and approaches within the interdisciplinary framework known as developmental psychopathology (Cicchetti & Sroufe, 2000) will likely continue to advance our definition and understanding of childhood disorders and our ability to help children who suffer from them.

## Healthy Functioning

The study of child psychopathology requires attention to normal developmental processes for several reasons (Cicchetti & Richters, 1993). First, judgments of abnormality require knowledge about developmental functioning relative to same-age peers and to the child's own baseline of development. Second, normal and abnormal functioning represent two sides of the same coin in that dysfunction in a particular domain of development (e.g., cognitive) is usually accompanied by a failure to meet developmental tasks and expectations in the same domain (e.g., academic performance). Third, in addition to the specific problems that lead to referral and diagnosis, disturbed children are also likely to show impairments in other areas of adaptive functioning. Fourth, most children with specific disorders are known to cope effectively in some areas of their lives. Understanding the child's competencies informs our knowledge of the disorder and provides a basis for the development of effective treatment strategies. Finally, many child behaviors that are not classifiable as deviant at a particular point in time may nevertheless represent less extreme expressions or compensations of an already existing disorder or early expressions of a later progression to deviant extremes as development continues (Adelman, 1995). Therefore, any understanding of abnormality requires that we also attend to these less extreme problems. Future research on child psychopathology is likely to expand its focus on normal developmental processes, normative and representative community samples of children, and resilient children who show normal development despite adversity.

## Context

Any consideration of disorders of childhood and adolescence needs to consider the social context in which these disorders develop (Boyce et al., 1998; Cicchetti & Aber, 1998). Children's development and behavior changes rapidly such that descriptions taken at one point in time or in one context may yield information very different from that taken at other times or in other contexts. Understanding context requires a consideration of both proximal and distal events. Among these are events that impinge directly on the child in a particular situation at a particular point in time, extrasituational events that affect the child indirectly (e.g., a parent's work-related stress), and temporally remote events that continue to affect the child through their representation in memory. Defining context has been—and continues to be—a matter of some complexity (Mischel, 1968). For example, contextual events such as stress (Compas, Connor-Smith, Saltzman, Thomsen, & Wadsworth, 2001) and maltreatment (Wolfe, 1999) have been defined in numerous ways. Contexts for the development of psychopathology encompass heterogeneous sets of circumstances whose effects are likely to vary as a function of the configuration of these circumstances over time, when and where outcomes are assessed, and the specific domains of development that are affected.

## Comorbidity

Comorbidity refers to the manifestation of two or more disorders whose co-occurrence is greater than what would be expected by chance alone. As we saw for ADHD and anxiety disorders, supposedly distinct forms of psychopathology often co-occur in the same child (Angold, Costello, & Erkanli, 1999). In fact, rates of comorbidity as high as 50% have been reported in community samples, with even higher rates in clinical samples (Caron & Rutter, 1991).

Although research has become increasingly sensitive to the occurrence and pattern of co-occurring disorders, less attention has been given to the mechanisms underlying these associations (Rutter & Sroufe, 2000). At least some of the overlap may be due to sampling biases or false assumptions about diagnostic categories and boundaries (e.g., viewing anxiety disorders as distinct conditions rather than as overlapping conditions or as different points in the progression of the same disorder). Alternatively, both disorders may result from the same set of risk factors—for example, genetic risk or maternal psychopathology; or the presence of one disorder may predispose the child to developing another—for example, when the presence of early ADHD disrupts family relations and leads to later CD (Johnston & Mash, 2001). Comorbidity in childhood disorders may also be partly a function of developmental level—that is, of underlying processes that have not yet achieved full differentiation (Lilienfeld, Waldman, & Israel, 1994). Finally, differing rates of comorbidity with age may reflect the fact that the appearance of one disorder or problem may precede the appearance of another—for example, inattention preceding impulsivity or anxiety preceding depression (Brady & Kendall, 1992).

Because the presence and patterning of comorbidity can easily distort or confuse how findings are interpreted, a better understanding of the mechanisms underlying these associations may serve to increase our understanding of both the disorders of interest as well as related risk and protective factors. Whatever ambiguities surround the construct of comorbidity, the fact that many disorders cluster together has important implications for how child psychopathology is conceptualized and treated (Kazdin & Kagan, 1994). For example, the presence of certain comorbid conditions has been found to influence the effectiveness of both behavioral and pharmacological interventions in children with ADHD (Jensen et al., 2001).

## Prevalence

Prevalence estimates for most childhood disorders are directly related to changing diagnostic practices and trends. Earlier versions of *DSM* (APA, 1952, 1968) contained few separate child categories, and many forms of child psychopathology were constructed, so to speak, with the introduction of *DSM-III* in 1980 (APA, 1980) and reconstructed in subsequent revisions. For example, empirical findings in the 1980s did not support the category of attention deficit disorder *without* hyperactivity as a unique symptom cluster (Routh, 1990). As a result, this category was not included in *DSM-III-R;* however, as a result of new findings, it appeared in *DSM-IV* as the *predominantly inattentive* subtype. Similarly, several of the *DSM-III-R* categories for anxiety disorders for children changed in *DSM-IV,* lost their status as an independent category for children, or were dropped entirely (e.g., overanxious disorder; Albano et al., 1996).

Changes in diagnostic criteria based on new findings and other considerations (e.g., eligibility for services) are likely to continue to influence prevalence estimates. For example, current estimates of autism are about three times higher than previous ones (Fombonne, 1999; Tanguay, 2000), and this increase is primarily due to a broadening of the criteria used to diagnose autism and an increased recognition of milder forms of the disorder (Bryson & Smith, 1998; Gillberg & Wing, 1999). There is also ongoing debate about whether Asperger's disorder is a variant of autism or simply describes higher-functioning individuals with autism (Schopler, Mesibov, & Kunce, 1998; Volkmar & Klin, 2000). The resolution of this debate and prevalence estimates for both autism and Asperger's disorder will depend on how the diagnosis of Asperger's disorder is used, because no official definition for this disorder existed until it was introduced in *DSM-IV-TR* (Volkmar & Klin, 1998).

The most consistent conclusions to be drawn from epidemiological findings are that prevalence rates for childhood problems are generally high but that rates vary as a result of several factors. These include the criteria used to define the problem; the nature of the disorder; the age, gender, social class, and ethnicity of the child; the method and source of information; and sampling considerations such as the settings in which children are identified.

## Gender Differences

There are important differences in the prevalence, expression, accompanying disorders, underlying processes, outcomes, and developmental course of psychopathology in boys versus girls (Eme, 1979, 1992; Hops, 1995; Zahn-Waxler, 1993). ADHD, autism, childhood disruptive behavior disorders, and learning and communication disorders are all more common in boys than in girls, whereas the opposite is true for most anxiety disorders, adolescent depression, and eating disorders (Hartung & Widiger, 1998). Although gender differences are well established, the meaning of these differences is not well understood. For example, it is difficult to determine whether observed gender differences are a function of referral or reporting biases, the way in which disorders are currently defined, differences in the expression of the disorder (e.g., direct vs. indirect aggressive behavior), or sex differences in biological characteristics and environmental susceptibilities. All are possible, and there is a need for research into the processes underlying these gender differences. Clearly the mechanisms and causes of gender differences may vary for different disorders (e.g., ADHD vs. depression) or for the same disorder at different ages—for example, child versus adolescent OCD or early- versus late-onset CD.

Boys show greater difficulties than girls do during early or middle childhood—particularly with respect to disruptive behavior disorders. Girls' problems may increase during adolescence, with higher prevalence rates from midadolescence through adulthood. For example, conduct disorders and hyperactivity have been found to be more frequent in 12- to 16-year-old boys than they are in girls, whereas emotional problems have been found to be more frequent for girls than they are for boys in this age group (Boyle et al., 1987; Offord et al., 1987). Additionally, early signs of aggression have been found to predict later antisocial behavior for boys but not for girls (Tremblay et al., 1992).

Girls are less likely than boys are to be identified as having problems, largely due to sampling biases in which boys, who are more severely disruptive, are also more likely to be referred and studied (Spitzer, Davies, & Barkley, 1990). As a result, there is a predominance of externalizing problems in boys and of internalizing problems in adolescent girls in samples of children who are referred for treatment, but these differences are less in nonreferred samples of children (Achenbach, Howell, Quay, & Conners, 1991). Different factors may also be associated with psychopathology in boys versus girls. For example, in a population-based sample of 9- to 15-year-olds, headaches were associated with depression and anxiety in girls, but with conduct disorder in boys (Egger, Angold, & Costello, 1998). In addition, the types of child-rearing environments predicting resilience to adversity may differ for boys and girls. Resilience in boys is associated with households in which there is a male model (e.g., father, grandfather, older sibling), structure, rules, and some encouragement of emotional expressiveness. In contrast, resilient girls come from households that combine risk taking and independence with support from a female caregiver (e.g., mother, grandmother, older sister; Werner, 1995).

Although the prevalence of disruptive behavior is lower in girls than in boys, the risk of comorbid conditions such as anxiety is higher in girls. It may be that girls' heightened level of interpersonal sensitivity, caring, and empathy serves as a protective factor in insulating them from developing antisocial behavior. At the same time, however, girls' overreceptivity to the plight of others and their reluctance to assert their own needs in situations involving conflict and distress may elevate their risk for the development of internalizing problems (Zahn-Waxler, Cole, Welsh, & Fox, 1995).

## Socioeconomic Status

Although most children with mental health problems are from the middle class, mental health problems are disproportionately represented among the very poor. About 20% or more of children in the United States and Canada are living in poverty, and a significant number of them display impairments in their social, behavioral, and academic functioning. The impact of socioeconomic disadvantage on children derives from the fact that SES is a composite variable that includes many potential sources of negative influence. In addition to low income, low SES is often accompanied by low maternal education, a low level of employment, single-parent status, limited resources, and negative life events (e.g., poor nutrition, exposure to violence). Because overall indexes of SES may include one or more of these variables in any given study, the relationship that is reported between SES and child psychopathology may vary as a function of the particular index used as well as of racial and ethnic factors (McLeod & Nonnemaker, 2000).

Lower-SES children have been reported to display more psychopathology and other problems than do upper-SES children (e.g., Hollingshead & Redlich, 1958). However, although the reported relationships between SES and child psychopathology are statistically significant, the effects are small and should be interpreted cautiously (Achenbach et al., 1991). More important is that global estimates of SES often tell us little about the associated processes through which SES exerts its influence on the child. Knowledge of such processes is needed to inform our understanding of the disorder. For example, the effects of SES on aggression can be explained mostly by stressful life events and by beliefs that are accepting of aggression (Guerra, Huesmann, Tolan, Van-Acker, & Eron, 1995).

## Ethnicity and Culture

Despite the growing ethnic diversity of the North American population, ethnic representation in research studies and the study of ethnicity-related issues more generally have received relatively little attention in studies of child psychopathology, with most data drawn largely from European-American culture

(Foster & Martinez, 1995). Research into child psychopathology has generally been insensitive to possible differences in prevalence, age of onset, developmental course, and risk factors related to ethnicity (Kazdin & Kagan, 1994). In addition, few studies have compared ethnic groups while controlling for other important variables such as SES, sex, age, and geographic region (Achenbach et al., 1991). In recent comparisons that have controlled for these variables African American and Hispanic American children are identified and referred at the same rates as other children, but they are much less likely to actually receive specialty mental health services or psychotropic medications (García Coll, & Garrido, 2000). White and Native American children have been found to display similar mental health problems with the exception of substance abuse, which has higher rates for Native American youngsters (Costello, Farmer, & Angold, 1999).

Some studies that have included a small number of African American children in their samples have reported somewhat higher rates of externalizing problems for this group (Costello, 1989; Velez, Johnson, & Cohen, 1989). However, other studies with much larger national samples that included non-Hispanic White, African-American, and Hispanic children have reported either no or very small differences related to race or ethnicity when SES, sex, age, and referral status were controlled for (Achenbach & Edelbrock, 1981; Achenbach et al., 1991; Lahey et al., 1995). Thus, although externalizing problems have been reported to be more common among African American children, this finding is probably an artifact related to SES. Externalizing disorder is associated with both ethnicity and with SES; furthermore, because there is an overrepresentation of minority-status children in low-SES groups in North America, caution must be exercised in interpreting the relationships among SES, ethnicity, and aggression (Guerra et al., 1995; Lahey et al., 1995).

In contrast to the mixed findings for conduct disorder, race has not been found to be strongly associated with risk for eating disorders (Leon, Fulkerson, Perry, & Early-Zald, 1995). However, Catalano et al. (1993) have reported different patterns of substance abuse related to ethnicity. More research is needed, but these and other findings suggest that the effects of ethnicity probably vary with the problem under consideration. As was the case for SES, global comparisons of the prevalence of different types of problems for different ethnic groups are not likely to be very revealing. On the other hand, studies into the processes that influence the form, associated factors, and outcomes of different disorders for various ethnic groups hold promise for increasing our understanding of the relationship between ethnicity and child psychopathology.

Recent conceptualizations have looked at ethnicity-related sources of stress such as stereotype threat and stereotype confirmation concern and own group conformity pressure. Research suggests that members of ethnic minority groups are not passive recipients of prejudice and discrimination (this is true of mental health labels too); rather, they actively attempt to make sense of and cope with multiple and distinct ethnicity-related threats (Contrada et al., 2000).

The values, beliefs, and practices that characterize a particular ethnocultural group contribute to the development and expression of childhood distress and dysfunction, which in turn are organized into categories through cultural processes that further influence their development and expression (Harkness & Super, 2000). Through shared views about causality and intervention, culture also structures the way in which people and institutions react to the child's problems. Because the meaning of children's social behavior is influenced by cultural beliefs and values, it is not surprising that the form, frequency, and predictive significance of different forms of child psychopathology vary across cultures or that cultural attitudes influence diagnostic and referral practices (Lambert & Weisz, 1992).

Cross-cultural research on child psychopathology would suggest that the expression and experience of mental disorders in children is not universal (Fisman & Fisman, 1999). Patterns of onset and duration of illness and the nature and relationship among specific symptoms vary from culture to culture and across ethnic groups within cultures (Hoagwood & Jensen, 1997). However, few studies have compared the attitudes, behaviors, and biological and psychological processes of children with mental disorders across different cultures. Such information is needed to understand how varying social experiences and contexts influence the expression, course, and outcome of different disorders across cultures. For example, greater social connectedness and support in more traditional cultures and greater access to resources and opportunities in industrialized societies are examples of mechanisms that may alter outcomes across cultures. Sensitivity to the role of cultural influences in child psychopathology has increased (Evans & Lee, 1998; Lopez & Guarnaccia, 2000) and is likely to continue to do so as globalization and rapid cultural change become increasingly more common (García Coll et al., 2000).

## Causal Processes

As illustrated by the models we presented for ADHD and anxiety disorders, all forms of child psychopathology are influenced by multiple and complex interactional and transactional processes—between characteristics of the child and the changing environmental context for development and behavior—that unfold over time. This view has led to an increasingly integrative approach to the etiology of child psychopathology that recognizes the role of multiple causal processes, including neurobiological, psychological, social, and cultural influences (Rutter & Sroufe, 2000). Models based on this approach are complex—at times even overwhelming—but necessary if disorders of childhood and adolescence are to be understood (Cicchetti & Canon, 1999). Constraints on the amount of diversity that is possible and the fact that not all outcomes are equally likely makes the task of understanding individual patterns of adaptation and maladaptation during childhood and adolescence somewhat more manageable (Cicchetti & Sroufe, 2000).

Genetic, neurobiological, neurophysiological, and neuroanatomical evidence suggests a neurobiological basis for many childhood disorders, including ADHD, autistic disorder, adolescent depression, and OCD, to name a few. With respect to genetics, recent research using molecular genetics has identified specific genes for autism (International Molecular Genetic Study of Autism Consortium, 1998), ADHD (Kuntsi & Stevenson, 2000), and Rett's disorder (Amir et al., 1999). The identification of specific genes has the potential to greatly enhance our understanding of a disorder as well as its specific components (Stodgell, Ingram, & Hyman, 2000). However, the initial steps in identifying a specific gene for any disorder address only a small part of the genetic risk. Similar searches will be needed to identify other genes, and multiple interacting genes are a far more likely cause than is a single gene (Rutter, 2000a). Genetic influences are probabilistic, not deterministic, and environmental and genetic factors are generally of about equal importance (Plomin & Rutter, 1998). Most forms of child psychopathology are polygenic, involving a number of susceptibility genes that interact with one another and with environmental influences to result in observed levels of impairment (State, Lombroso, Pauls, & Leckman, 2000).

As our discussion of ADHD illustrated, research on brain structure and function using neuroimaging procedures has identified specific brain regions for ADHD and many other disorders. Neuroimaging studies tell us that one region or another may be involved but they do not tell us why, and the findings for particular disorders are not always consistent from study to study, for children of different ages, or for boys versus girls. Research into specific neurotransmitters has also provided promising leads, although findings have also been inconsistent. One of the difficulties in research in this area is that most forms of child psychopathology often involve the same brain structures and neurotransmitters, making it difficult to assess the specificity of their contributions to particular disorders. Such findings may reflect the limitations of existing categorical diagnostic systems that we discussed earlier.

Child psychopathology research has increasingly focused on the role of the family system, the complex relationships within families, and the reciprocal influences among various family subsystems (Fiese, Wilder, & Bickham, 2000). There is a need to consider the processes occurring within disturbed families and the common and unique ways in which these processes affect both individual family members and subsystems. Within the family, the role of the mother-child and marital subsystems have received the most research attention to date, with less attention given to the role of siblings or fathers (Hetherington, Reiss, & Plomin, 1994; Phares & Compas, 1992).

Research into family processes and child psychopathology has not kept pace with family theory and practice. Family members are frequently viewed as either the causes of childhood disorders or as passive responders. An integrative perspective in which family members are viewed as partners in a complex process of reciprocal interaction is needed (Hinshaw & Cicchetti, 2000). To accomplish this end, there is a need for the development of sophisticated methodologies and valid measures that will capture the complex relationships that are operative in disturbed and normal family systems (Bray, 1995; Bray, Maxwell, & Cole, 1995). This task is complicated by a lack of consensus concerning how dysfunctional or healthy family functioning should be defined or what specific family processes are important to assess (Bray, 1994; Mash & Johnston, 1996).

## Continuities and Discontinuities

A central issue for theory and research in child psychopathology concerns the continuity of disorders identified from one time to another and the relationship between child and adult disorders (Kazdin & Johnson, 1994; Rutter & Sroufe, 2000). Prior to the emergence of a disorder, certain pathways may suggest a failure to adapt to age-salient developmental tasks; this failure in turn increases the likelihood of later problems, given particular environmental events. Childhood disorders are not static entities, and many children experience periods of relapse, remission, or degrees of severity over the course of their development. The concept of developmental pathways is crucial for understanding continuities and discontinuities in psychopathology. A pathway defines the sequence and timing of behavioral continuities and transformations and relationships between successive behaviors (Loeber, 1991). Different pathways may lead to similar disorders (equifinality), and similar initial pathways may result in different disorders (multifinality), depending on the organization of the larger system in which they occur. The systematic delineation of developmental pathways, such as the ones that we presented for ADHD and anxiety disorders, attempts to capture the changing expressions of a given disorder and to assess causal process, the patterning of comorbid conditions over time, and diverse outcomes.

Evidence in support of the continuity between child and adult disorders is equivocal and depends on a number of methodological factors related to research design, assessment instruments, the nature of the study sample, and the type and severity of the disorder. In general, the literature suggests that child psychopathology is continuous with adult disorders for some but not all problems. Some evidence appears to favor the stability of externalizing problems over internalizing problems. However, previous findings may reflect the severity and pervasiveness of the disorders assessed, referral biases, and the fact that findings from longitudinal investigations of children with internalizing disorders are just beginning to accumulate.

Research has focused not only on continuities and discontinuities in childhood disorders but also on the identification of factors that predict them. One factor that has been studied in the context of CD is age of onset. It has been found that early onset of symptoms relates to higher rates and more serious antisocial acts over a longer period of time for both boys and girls. However, psychosocial variables that are present prior to and following onset may influence the seriousness and chronicity more than age of onset per se (Tolan & Thomas, 1995). An issue that needs to be addressed concerns whether early age of onset operates in a causal fashion for later problems—and if so, how?

Although research supports the notion of continuity of disorders, it does not support the continuity of identical symptoms over time (e.g., homotypic correspondence). Continuity over time for patterns of behavior rather than for specific symptoms is the norm. For example, although externalizing disorders in boys are stable over time, the ways in which these behavioral patterns are expressed change dramatically over the course of development (Olweus, 1979). Even with wide fluctuations in the expression of behavior over time, children may show consistency in the adaptive and maladaptive ways in which they organize their experiences and interact with the environment. For example, behavioral inhibition in infancy may affect later adjustment by influencing the way in which the child adapts to new and unfamiliar situations and the ensuing person-environment interactions over time. Certain genes and neural systems may also play a significant predisposing role in influencing the continuity of psychopathology (Pennington & Ozonoff, 1991). Discontinuities in observable behavior may obscure continuities in the mechanisms underlying observable behavior.

Given that developmental continuity is reflected in general patterns of organization over time rather than in isolated behaviors or symptoms, the relationships between early adaptation and later psychopathology are unlikely to be simple, direct, or uncomplicated. The links between early and later psychopathology are marked by continuities and by discontinuities. The degree of continuity or discontinuity will vary as a function of changing environmental circumstances and transactions between the child and environment that affect the child's developmental trajectory.

## Risk and Resilience

Resilience, which refers to successful adaptations in children who experience significant adversity has received a good deal of attention (Luthar, Cicchetti, & Becker, 2000). Early patterns of adaptation influence later adjustment in complex and reciprocal ways. Adverse conditions, early struggles to adapt, and failure to meet developmental tasks do not inevitably lead to a fixed and unchanging abnormal path. Rather, many different factors—including chance events and encounters—can provide turning points whereby success in a particular developmental task (e.g., educational advances, peer relationships) alters a child's course onto a more adaptive trajectory. Conversely, there are numerous events and circumstances that may deflect the child's developmental trajectory toward that of maladaptation (e.g., dysfunctional home environment, peer rejection, difficulties in school, parental psychopathology, intergenerational conflict).

Further attention needs to be directed to the conceptual and methodological problems that have plagued research on resilience (Luthar et al., 2000), not the least of which is the lack of a consistent vocabulary, conceptual framework, and methodological approach. It is particularly important to ensure that resilience is not defined as a universal, categorical, or fixed attribute of the child; individual children may be resilient in relation to some forms of environmental stress but not to others, and resilience may vary over time and across contexts. Rather than a direct causal pathway leading to a particular outcome, resilience involves ongoing interactions between risk and protective factors within the child and his or her environment. These factors need to be conceptualized as processes rather than as absolutes, because the same event or condition can operate as a protective or risk factor as a function of the overall context in which it occurs. More than a decade of research suggests that resilience is not indicative of any rare or special qualities of the child per se (i.e., the invulnerable child); rather, it is the result of the interplay of normal developmental processes such as brain development, cognition, caregiver-child relationships, regulation of emotion and behavior, and the motivation for learning (Masten, 2001).

## IMPLICATIONS FOR TREATMENT AND PREVENTION

As a result of the emergent concepts and findings discussed in this chapter, treatment approaches for children's mental health problems have grown tremendously in sophistication and breadth over the past two decades (Mash & Barkley, 1998). Many interventions today combine the most effective approaches to particular problems in an ongoing, developmentally sensitive manner (Kazdin, 2000). Moreover, because children's symptoms are often an expression of their unsuccessful attempts to adapt to their circumstances, more emphasis today is placed on the child's family, school, and peers—not just on the child (Howard & Kendall, 1996). Accordingly, treatment goals often focus on building children's skills for adapting to their social environment—skills that will facilitate long-term adjustment—not just on eliminating problem behaviors or reducing subjective distress in the short term.

Although many of the disorders discussed in this chapter begin early in life, accurate early identification is difficult. The reliability of many early symptoms such as social withdrawal, labile mood, and perceptual and cognitive disturbances in predicting later problems is in many cases unknown. Nevertheless, growing evidence for the early presence of subclinical symptoms for some childhood disorders (e.g., schizophrenia), the fact that certain symptoms (e.g., aggressive behavior) are known to predict later problems, and the early age of onset of many forms of child psychopathology have led to an increasing interest in prevention (Cicchetti, Rappaport, Sandler, & Weissberg, 2000). Prevention efforts for most forms of child psychopathology are now available, although their long-term effectiveness is still being evaluated; however, early findings are promising, suggesting that the early detection and treatment of childhood disorders may lead to a better prognosis and outcome in adolescence and adulthood (U.S. Public Health Service, 2001a).

Efforts to evaluate treatments for childhood disorders have intensified (Weisz, Donenberg, Han, & Weiss, 1995), resulting in several noteworthy conclusions based on carefully controlled research trials: (a) Changes achieved by children receiving psychotherapy are consistently greater than are those for children not receiving therapy; (b) the average child who is treated is better off at the end of therapy than at least 75% of those children who did not receive treatment; (c) treatments

have been shown to be equally effective for children with internalizing and externalizing disorders; (d) treatments are producing focused changes in targeted areas such as anxiety, rather than producing nonspecific or global effects such as changes in how the child feels (Kazdin, 1996; Weisz, 1998; Weisz & Weiss, 1993); and (e) the more outpatient therapy sessions children receive, the more improvement is seen in their symptoms (Angold, Costello, Burns, Erkanli, & Farmer, 2000).

In contrast to these findings for research therapy, however, studies of clinic therapy (i.e., in real-world settings) have resulted in less favorable outcomes (Andrade, Lambert, & Bickman, 2000; Weiss, Catron, Harris, & Phung, 1999; Weisz et al., 1995; for exceptions, see study by Angold et al., 2000; and meta-analytic review by Shadish, Matt, Navarro, & Phillips, 2000). These findings suggest that conventional services for children may be of limited effectiveness and that integrating these commonly used interventions into more coordinated systems of care also shows minimal support for the beneficial effects of treatment (Weisz, 1998). However, few studies exist of child therapy outcomes in settings where treatment is typically conducted; thus, it is premature to draw any conclusions from the findings from clinic and community studies until more empirical data about therapy in practice are available (Shadish et al., 1997). In order to address the differences in findings from research versus clinic studies, there is a growing interest in the development and evaluation of treatment strategies that reflect decision-making and service delivery as it occurs in clinical practice settings (T. D. Borkovec, 2001; Weisz, 2000a, 2000b). Further discussion of treatment and prevention is presented within subsequent chapters of this volume.

## REFERENCES

Abikoff, H., Courtney, M., Pelham, W., & Koplewicz, H. (1993). Teachers' ratings of disruptive behaviors: The influence of halo effects. *Journal of Abnormal Child Psychology, 21,* 519–533.

Achenbach, T. M. (2000). Assessment of psychopathology. In A. J. Sameroff & M. Lewis (Eds.), *Handbook of developmental psychopathology* (2nd ed., pp. 41–56). New York: Kluwer Academic/Plenum Publishers.

Achenbach, T. M., & Edelbrock, C. (1981). Behavioral problems and competencies reported by parents of normal and disturbed children aged four through sixteen. *Monographs of the Society for Research in Child Development, 46*(Serial No. 188, Whole No. 1).

Achenbach, T. M., Howell, C. T., Quay, H. C., & Conners, C. K. (1991). National survey of problems and competencies among four- to sixteen-year-olds: Parents' reports for normative and clinical samples. *Monographs of the Society for Research in Child Development, 56*(Serial No. 225, Whole No. 3).

Adelman, H. S. (1995). Clinical psychology: Beyond psychopathology and clinical interventions. *Clinical Psychology: Science and Practice, 2,* 28–44.

Albano, A. M., Chorpita, B. F., & Barlow, D. H. (1996). Childhood anxiety disorders. In E. J. Mash & R. A. Barkley (Eds.), *Child psychopathology* (pp. 196–241). New York: Guilford Press.

Albano, A. M., Knox, L. S., & Barlow, D. H. (1995). Obsessive-compulsive disorder. In A. R. Eisen, C. A. Kearney, & C. A. Schaefer (Eds.), *Clinical handbook of anxiety disorders in children and adolescents* (pp. 282–316). Northvale, NJ: Jason Aronson.

Amaya-Jackson, L., & March, J. S. (1995). Posttraumatic stress disorder. In J. S. March (Ed.), *Anxiety disorders in children and adolescents* (pp. 276–300). New York: Guilford Press.

American Psychiatric Association. (1952). *Diagnostic and statistical manual of mental disorders*. Washington, DC: Author.

American Psychiatric Association. (1968). *Diagnostic and statistical manual of mental disorders* (2nd ed.). Washington, DC: Author.

American Psychiatric Association. (1980). *Diagnostic and statistical manual of mental disorders* (3rd ed.). Washington, DC: Author.

American Psychiatric Association. (2000). *Diagnostic and statistical manual of mental disorders* (4th ed., Text Revision). Washington, DC: Author.

Amir, R. E., Van den Veyver, I. B., Wan, M., Tran, C. Q., Francke, U., & Zoghbi, H. Y. (1999). Rett Syndrome is caused by mutations in X-linked MECP2, encoding methyl-CpG-binding protein 2. *Nature Genetics, 23,* 185–188.

Andrade, A. R., Lambert, E. W., & Bickman, L. (2000). Dose effect in child psychotherapy: Outcomes associated with negligible treatment. *Journal of the American Academy of Child and Adolescent Psychiatry, 39,* 161–168.

Andrews, G., Stewart, G., Allen, B., & Henderson, A. S. (1990). The genetics of six neurotic disorders: A twin study. *Journal of Affective Disorders, 19,* 23–29.

Angold, A., Costello, J., Burns, B. J., Erkanli, A., & Farmer, E. M. Z. (2000). Effectiveness of nonresidential specialty mental health services for children and adolescents in the "real world." *Journal of the American Academy of Child and Adolescent Psychiatry, 39,* 154–160.

Angold, A., Costello, E., & Erkanli, A. (1999). Comorbidity. *Journal of Child Psychology and Psychiatry, 40,* 55–87.

Applegate, B., Lahey, B. B., Hart, E. L., Biederman, J., Hynd, G. W., Barkley, R. A., Ollendick, T., Frick, P. J., Greenhill, L., McBurnett, K., Newcorn, J. H., Kerdyk, L., Garfinkel, B., Waldman, I., & Shaffer, D. (1997). Validity of the age-of-onset criterion for ADHD: A report from the DSM-IV field trials. *Journal of the American Academy of Child and Adolescent Psychiatry, 36,* 1211–1221.

Arkowitz, H. (1992). Integrative theories of therapy. In D. K. Freedheim (Ed.), *History of psychotherapy: A century of change* (pp. 261–303). Washington, DC: American Psychological Association.

Arnold, L. E. (1996). Sex differences in ADHD: Conference summary. *Journal of Abnormal Child Psychology, 24,* 555–569.

Baker, L., & Cantwell, D. P. (1992). Attention deficit disorder and speech/language disorders. *Comprehensive Mental Health Care, 2,* 3–16.

Barkley, R. A. (1988). The effects of methylphenidate on the interactions of preschool ADHD children with their mothers. *Journal of the American Academy of Child and Adolescent Psychiatry, 27,* 336–341.

Barkley, R. A. (1996). Attention-deficit/hyperactivity disorder. In E. J. Mash & R. A. Barkley (Eds.), *Child psychopathology* (pp. 63–112). New York: Guilford Press.

Barkley, R. A. (1997). *ADHD and the nature of self-control*. New York: Guilford Press.

Barkley, R. A. (1998). *Attention-deficit hyperactivity disorder: A handbook for diagnosis and treatment* (2nd ed.). New York: Guilford Press.

Barkley, R. A., & Biederman, J. (1997). Toward a broader definition of the age-of-onset criterion for attention-deficit-hyperactivity disorder. *Journal of the American Academy of Child and Adolescent Psychiatry, 36,* 1204–1210.

Barkley, R. A., Fischer, M., Edelbrock, C. S., & Smallish, L. (1990). The adolescent outcome of hyperactive children diagnosed by research criteria: I. An 8-year prospective follow-up study. *Journal of the American Academy of Child and Adolescent Psychiatry, 29,* 546–557.

Barkley, R. A., Fischer, M., & Fletcher, K. (1997). *Young adult outcome of hyperactive children diagnosed by research criteria*. NIMH Grant, University of Massachusetts Medical Center.

Barkley, R. A., Grodzinsky, G., & DuPaul, G. J. (1992). Frontal lobe functions in attention deficit disorder with and without hyperactivity: A review and research report. *Journal of Abnormal Child Psychology, 20,* 163–188.

Barlow, D. H. (1988). *Anxiety and its disorders: The nature and treatment of anxiety and panic*. New York: Guilford Press.

Baron-Cohen, S. (2000). Is Asperger syndrome/high functioning autism necessarily a disability? *Development and Psychopathology, 12,* 489–500.

Barrett, P. M., Rapee, R. M., Dadds, M. M., & Ryan, S. M. (1996). Family enhancement of cognitive style in anxious and aggressive children. *Journal of Abnormal Child Psychology, 24,* 187–203.

Beidel, D. C., & Turner, S. M. (1997). At risk for anxiety: I. Psychopathology in the offspring of anxious parents. *Journal of the American Academy of Child and Adolescent Psychiatry, 36,* 918–924.

Beidel, D. C., Turner, S. M., & Morris, T. L. (1999). Psychopathology of childhood social phobia. *Journal of the American Academy of Child and Adolescent Psychiatry, 38,* 643–650.

Benjamin, J., Li, L., Patterson, C., Greenberg, B. D., Murphy, D. L., & Hamer, D. H. (1996). Population and familial association between the D4 dopamine receptor gene and measures of novelty seeking. *Nature Genetics, 12,* 81–84.

Bernstein, G. A. (1991). Comorbidity and severity of anxiety and depressive disorders in a clinic sample. *Journal of the American Academy of Child and Adolescent Psychiatry, 30,* 43–50.

Bernstein, G. A., Borchardt, C. M., & Perwien, A. R. (1996). Anxiety disorders in children and adolescents: A review of the past 10 years. *Journal of the American Academy of Child and Adolescent Psychiatry, 35,* 1110–1119.

Biederman, J., Faraone, S. V., & Lapey, K. (1992). Comorbidity of diagnosis in attention-deficit hyperactivity disorders. In G. Weiss (Ed.), *Child and adolescent psychiatric clinics of North America: Attention-deficit hyperactivity disorder* (pp. 335–360). Philadelphia: Saunders.

Biederman, J., Faraone, S. V., Mick, E., Williamson, S., Wilens, T. E., Spencer, T. J., Weber, W., Jetton, J., Kraus, I., Pert, J., & Zallen, B. (1999). Clinical correlates of ADHD in females: Findings from a large group of girls ascertained from pediatric and psychiatric referral sources. *Journal of the American Academy of Child and Adolescent Psychiatry, 38,* 966–975.

Biederman, J., & Spencer, T. (1999). Attention-deficit/hyperactivity disorder (ADHD) as a noradrenergic disorder. *Biological Psychiatry, 46,* 1234–1242.

Biederman, J., Wozniak, J., Kiely, K., Ablon, S., Faraone, S., Mick, E., Mundy, E., & Kraus, I. (1995). CBCL clinical scales discriminate prepubertal children with structured-interview-derived diagnosis of mania from those with ADHD. *Journal of the American Academy of Child and Adolescent Psychiatry, 34,* 464–471.

Borkovec, T. D. (2001, winter). Scientifically rigorous research in the practice setting: Practice research networks. *Clinical Science Newsletter* (winter), 2–3.

Borkovec, T. M., & Inz, J. (1990). The nature of worry in generalized anxiety disorder: A predominance of thought activity. *Behaviour Research and Therapy, 28,* 153–158.

Boyce, W. T., Frank, E., Jensen, P. S., Kessler, R. C., Nelson, C. A., & Stenberg, L. (1998). Social context in developmental psychopathology: Recommendations for future research from the MacArthur Network on Psychopathology and Development. *Development and Psychopathology, 10,* 143–164.

Boyle, M. H., Offord, D. R., Hoffman, H. G., Catlin, G. P., Byles, J. A., Cadman, D. T., Crawford, J. W., Links, P. S., Rae-Grant, N. I., & Szatmari, P. (1987). Ontario Child Health Study: I. Methodology. *Archives of General Psychiatry, 44,* 826–831.

Brady, E., & Kendall, P. C. (1992). Comorbidity of anxiety and depression in children and adolescents. *Psychological Bulletin, 3,* 244–255.

Bray, J. H. (1994). *Family assessment: Current issues in evaluating families.* Unpublished manuscript, Department of Family Medicine, Baylor College of Medicine, Houston, TX.

Bray, J. H. (1995). Methodological advances in family psychology research: Introduction to the special section. *Journal of Family Psychology, 9,* 107–109.

Bray, J. H., Maxwell, S. E., & Cole, D. (1995). Multivariate statistics for family psychology research. *Journal of Family Psychology, 9,* 144–160.

Bryson, S. E., & Smith, I. M. (1998). Epidemiology of autism: Prevalence, associated characteristics, and implications for research and service delivery. *Mental Retardation and Developmental Disabilities Research Reviews, 4,* 97–103.

Burns, B. J., Costello, E. J., Angold, A., Tweed, D., Stangl, D., Farmer, E. M. Z., & Erkanli, A. (1995). Data watch: Children's mental health service use across service sectors. *Health Affair, 14,* 147–159.

Burns, G. L., Walsh, J. A., Patterson, D. R., Holte, C. S., Somers-Flanagan, R., & Parker, C. M. (1997). Internal validity of the disruptive behavior disorder symptoms: Implications from parent ratings for a dimensional approach to symptom validity. *Journal of Abnormal Child Psychology, 25,* 307–319.

Campbell, S. B. (1990). *Behavior problems in preschool children: Clinical and developmental issues.* New York: Guilford Press.

Campbell, S. B. (2000). Attention-deficit/hyperactivity disorder: A developmental view. In A. J. Sameroff, M. Lewis, & S. M. Miller (Eds.), *Handbook of developmental psychopathology* (2nd ed., pp. 383–401). New York: Kluwer Academic.

Campbell, S. B., Shaw, D. S., & Gilliom, M. (2000). Early externalizing behavior problems: Toddlers and preschoolers at risk for later maladjustment. *Development and Psychopathology, 12,* 467–488.

Cantwell, D. P., & Baker, L. (1992). Association between attention deficit-hyperactivity disorder and learning disorders. In S. E. Shaywitz & B. A. Shaywitz (Eds.), *Attention deficit disorder comes of age: Toward the twenty-first century* (pp. 145–164). Austin, TX: Pro-ed.

Capps, L., Sigman, M., Sena, R., & Henker, B. (1996). Fear, anxiety and perceived control in children of agoraphobic parents. *Journal of Child Psychology and Psychiatry, 37,* 445–452.

Carlson, G. A., Bromet, E. J., & Sievers, S. (2000). Phenomenology and outcome of subjects with early and adult-onset psychotic mania. *American Journal of Psychiatry, 157,* 213–220.

Caron, C., & Rutter, M. (1991). Comorbidity in child psychopathology: Concepts, issues, and research strategies. *Journal of Child Psychology and Psychiatry, 32,* 1063–1080.

Casey, B. J., Castellanos, F. X., Giedd, J. N., Marsh, W. L., Hamburger, S. D., Schubert, A. B., Vauss, Y. C., Vaituzis, A. C., Dickstein, D. P., Sarfetti, S. E., & Rapoport, J. L. (1997). Implication of right frontostriatal circuitry in response inhibition and attention-deficit/hyperactivity disorder. *Journal of the American Academy of Child and Adolescent Psychiatry, 36,* 374–383.

Catalano, R. F., Hawkins, J. D., Krenz, C., Gilmore, M., Morrison, D., Wells, E., & Abbott, R. (1993). Using research to guide culturally appropriate drug abuse prevention. *Journal of Consulting and Clinical Psychology, 61,* 804–811.

Chambless, D. L., & Ollendick, T. H. (2001). Empirically supported psychological interventions: Controversies and evidence. *Annual Review of Psychology, 52,* 685–716.

Chansky, T. E., & Kendall, P. C. (1997). Social expectancies and self-perceptions in anxiety-disordered children. *Journal of Anxiety Disorders, 11,* 347–363.

Chorpita, B. F., & Barlow, D. H. (1998). The development of anxiety: The role of control in the early environment. *Psychological Bulletin, 124,* 3–21.

Chorpita, B. F., Daleiden, E. L., Moffitt, C., Yim, L., & Umemoto, L. A. (2000). Assessment of tripartite factors of emotion in children and adolescents: I. Structural validity and normative data of an affect and arousal scale. *Journal of Psychopathology and Behavioral Assessment, 23,* 141–160.

Cicchetti, D., & Aber, J. L. (Eds.). (1998). Contextualism and developmental psychopathology [Special issue]. *Development and Psychopathology, 10,* 137–426.

Cicchetti, D., & Cannon, T. D. (1999). Neurodevelopmental processes in the ontogenesis and epigenesis of psychopathology. *Development and Psychopathology, 11,* 375–393.

Cicchetti, D., & Cohen, D. J. (Eds.). (1995). *Developmental psychopathology: Vol. 1. Theory and methods.* New York: Wiley.

Cicchetti, D., Rappaport, J., Sandler, I., & Weissberg, R. P. (Eds.). (2000). *The promotion of wellness in children and adolescents.* Washington, DC: Child Welfare League of America, Inc.

Cicchetti, D., & Richters, J. E. (1993). Developmental considerations in the investigation of conduct disorder. *Development and Psychopathology, 5,* 331–344.

Cicchetti, D., & Sroufe, L. A. (2000). Editorial: The past as prologue to the future: The times, they've been a-changin'. *Development and Psychopathology, 12,* 255–264.

Cicchetti, D., & Toth, S. L. (2000). Social policy implications of research in developmental psychopathology, *Developmental Psychopathology, 12,* 551–554.

Cohen, M. (1998). The monetary value of saving a high risk youth. *Journal of Quantitative Criminology, 14,* 5–34.

Cohen, P., Cohen, J., & Brook, J. S. (1993). An epidemiological study of disorders in late childhood and adolescence: II. Persistence of disorders. *Journal of Child Psychology and Psychiatry, 34,* 869–877.

Cohen, N. J., Vallance, D. D., Barwick, M., Im, N., Menna, R., Horodezky, N. B., & Isaacson, L. (2000). The interface between ADHD and language impairment: An examination of language, achievement, and cognitive processing. *Journal of Child Psychology and Psychiatry, 41,* 353–362.

Cole, D. A., Martin, J. M., Peeke, L., Henderson, A., & Harwell, J. (1998). Validation of depression and anxiety measures in White and Black youths: Multitrait-multimethod analyses. *Psychological Assessment, 10,* 261–276.

Cole, D. A., Peeke, L., Martin, Truglio, & Seroczynski, A. D. (1998). A longitudinal look at the relation between depression and anxiety in children and adolescents. *Journal of Consulting and Clinical Psychology, 66,* 451–460.

Cole, D. A., Truglio, R., & Peeke, L. (1997). Relation between symptoms of anxiety and depression in children: A multitrait-multimethod-multigroup assessment. *Journal of Consulting and Clinical Psychology, 65,* 110–119.

Compas, B. E., Connor-Smith, J. K., Saltzman, H., Thomsen, A. H., & Wadsworth, M. E. (2001). Coping with stress during childhood and adolescence: Problems, progress, and potential in theory and research. *Psychological Bulletin, 127,* 87–127.

Compas, B. E., & Oppedisano, G. (2000). Mixed anxiety/depression in children and adolescents. In A. J. Sameroff, M. Lewis, & S. M. Miller (Eds.), *Handbook of developmental psychopathology* (2nd ed., pp. 531–548). New York: Kluwer Academic.

Compton, S. N., Nelson, A. H., & March, J. S. (2000). Social phobia and separation anxiety symptoms in community and clinical samples of children and adolescents. *Journal of the American Academy of Child and Adolescent Psychiatry, 39,* 1040–1046.

Contrada, R. J., Ashmore, R. D., Gary, M. L., Coups, E., Egeth, J. D., Sewell, A., Ewell, K., Goyal, T. M., & Chasse, V. (2000). Ethnicity-related sources of stress and their effects on well-being. *Current Directions in Psychological Science, 9,* 136–139.

Cook, E. H., Stein, M. A., Krasowski, M. D., Cox, N. J., Olkon, D. M., Kieffer, J. E., & Leventhal, B. L. (1995). Association of attention-deficit disorder and the dopamine transporter gene. *American Journal of Human Genetics, 56,* 993–998.

Corkum, P., Tannock, R., & Moldofsky, H. (1988). Sleep disturbances in children with attention-deficit/hyperactivity disorder. *Journal of the American Academy of Child and Adolescent Psychiatry, 37,* 637–646.

Costello, E. J. (1989). Developments in child psychiatric epidemiology. *Journal of the American Academy of Child and Adolescent Psychiatry, 28,* 836–841.

Costello, E. J., & Angold, A. C. (2000). Developmental epidemiology: A framework for developmental psychopathology. In A. Sameroff, M. Lewis, & S. Miller (Eds.), *Handbook of developmental psychopathology* (2nd ed., pp. 57–73). New York: Plenum.

Costello, E. J., Farmer, E. M. Z., & Angold, A. (1999). Same place, different children: White and American Indian children in the Appalachian mountains. In P. Cohen & C. Slomkowski (Eds.), *Historical and geographical influences on psychopathology* (pp. 279–298). Mahwah, NJ: Erlbaum.

Costello, E. J., Farmer, E. M. Z., Angold, A., Burns, B. J., & Erkanli, A. (1997). Psychiatric disorders among American Indian and white youth in Appalachia: The Great Smoky Mountains Study. *American Journal of Public Health, 87,* 827–832.

Craske, M. G., & Rowe, M. K. (1997). Nocturnal panic. *Clinical Psychology: Science and Practice, 4,* 153–174.

Daly, J. M., Biederman, J., Bostic, J. Q., Maraganore, A. M., Lelon, E., Jellinek, M., & Lapey, A. (1996). The relationship between childhood asthma and attention deficit hyperactivity disorder: A review of the literature. *Journal of Attention Disorders, 1,* 31–40.

Dawson, G., Ashman, S. B., & Carver, L. J. (2000). The role of early experience in shaping behavioral and brain development and its implications for social policy. *Development and Psychopathology, 12,* 695–712.

Dawson, G., Hessl, D., & Frey, K. (1994). Social influences on early developing biological and behavioral systems related to risk for affective disorder. *Development and Psychopathology, 6,* 759–779.

DiLalla, L. F., Kagan, J., & Reznick, J. S. (1994). Genetic etiology of behavioral inhibition among 2-year-old children. *Infant Behavior and Development, 17,* 405–412.

Douglas, V. I. (1999). Cognitive control processes in attention deficit/hyperactivity disorder. In H. C. Quay & A. E. Hogan (Eds.), *Handbook of disruptive behavior disorders* (pp. 105–138). New York: Kluwer Academic.

Dumas, M. C. (1998). The risk of social interaction problems among adolescents with ADHD. *Education & Treatment of Children, 21,* 447–460.

Duncan, G. J., Brooks-Gunn, J., & Klebanov, P. K. (1994). Economic deprivation and early-childhood development. *Child Development, 65,* 296–318.

DuPaul, G. J., McGoey, K. E., Eckert, T. L., & VanBrakle, J. (2001). Preschool children with attention-deficit/hyperactivity disorder: Impairments in behavioral, social, and school functioning. *Journal of the American Academy of Child and Adolescent Psychiatry, 40,* 508–515.

Ebstein, R. P., Novick, O., Umansky, R., Priel, B., Osher, Y., Blaine, D., Bennett, E. R., Nemanov, L., Katz, M., & Belmaker, R. H. (1996). Dopamine D4 receptor (D4DR) exon III polymorphism associated with the human personality trait of novelty seeking. *Nature Genetics, 12,* 78–80.

Edelbrock, C. S., Rende, R., Plomin, R., & Thompson, L. A. (1995). A twin study of competence and problem behavior in childhood and early adolescence. *Journal of Child Psychology and Psychiatry, 36,* 775–786.

Egger, H. L., Angold, A., & Costello, E. J. (1998). Headaches and psychopathology in children and adolescents. *Journal of the American Academy of Child and Adolescent Psychiatry, 37,* 951–958.

Eiraldi, R. B., Power, T. J., & Nezu, C. M. (1997). Patterns of comorbidity associated with subtypes of attention-deficit/hyperactivity disorder among 6- to 12-year-old children. *Journal of the American Academy of Child and Adolescent Psychiatry, 36,* 503–514.

Eley, T. C. (1999). Behavioral genetics as a tool for developmental psychology: Anxiety and depression in children and adolescents. *Clinical Child and Family Psychology Review, 2,* 21–36.

Eme, R. F. (1979). Sex differences in child psychopathology: A review. *Psychological Bulletin, 86,* 574–595.

Eme, R. F. (1992). Selective female affliction in development of disorders of childhood: A literature review. *Journal of Clinical Child Psychology, 21,* 354–364.

Erhardt, D., & Hinshaw, S. P. (1994). Initial sociometric impressions of attention-deficit hyperactivity disorder and comparison boys: Predictions from social behaviors and from nonbehavioral variables. *Journal of Consulting and Clinical Psychology, 62,* 833–842.

Ernst, M., Liebenauer, M. A., King, C., Fitzgerald, G. A., Cohen, R. M., & Zametkin, A. J. (1994). Reduced brain metabolism in hyperactive girls. *Journal of the Academy of Child and Adolescent Psychiatry, 33,* 858–868.

Essau, C. A., Conradt, J., & Petermann, F. (1999). Frequency and comorbidity of social phobia and social fears in adolescents. *Behaviour Research and Therapy, 37,* 831–843.

Essau, C. A., Conradt, J., & Petermann, F. (2000). Frequency, comorbidity, and psychosocial impairment of specific phobia in adolescents. *Journal of Clinical Child Psychology, 29,* 221–231.

Evans, B., & Lee, B. K. (1998). Culture and child psychopathology. In S. S. Kazarian & D. R. Evans (Eds.), *Cultural clinical psychology: Theory, research, and practice* (pp. 289–315). New York: Oxford University Press.

Famularo, R., Fenton, T., Kinscherff, R., & Augustyn, M. (1996). Psychiatric comorbidity in childhood posttraumatic stress disorder. *Child Abuse and Neglect, 20,* 953–961.

Faraone, S. V., & Beiderman, J. (1998). Neurobiology of attention deficit hyperactivity disorder. *Biological Psychiatry, 44,* 951–958.

Faraone, S. V., Biederman, J., Chen, W. J., Krifcher, B., Keenan, K., Moore, C., Sprich, S., & Tsuang, M. T. (1992). Segregation analysis of attention deficit hyperactivity disorder. *Psychiatric Genetics, 2,* 257–275.

Faraone, S. V., Biederman, J., Feighner, J. A., & Monuteaux, M. C. (2000). Assessing symptoms of attention deficit hyperactivity disorder in children and adults: Which is more valid? *Journal of Consulting and Clinical Psychology, 68,* 830–842.

Faraone, S. V., Biederman, J., & Friedman, D. (2000). Validity of DSM-IV subtypes of attention-deficit/hyperactivity disorder: A family study perspective. *Journal of the American Academy of Child and Adolescent Psychiatry, 39,* 300–307.

Faraone, S. V., Biederman, J., & Milberger, S. (1996). An exploratory study of ADHD among second degree relatives of ADHD children. *Society of Biological Psychiatry, 35,* 398–402.

Faraone, S. V., Biederman, J., Weiffenbach, B., Keith, T., Chu, M. P., Weaver, A., Spencer, T. J., Wilens, T. E., Frazier, J., Cleves, M., & Sakai, J. (1999). Dopamine D-sub-4 gene 7-repeat allele and attention deficit hyperactivity disorder. *American Journal of Psychiatry, 156,* 768–770.

Fiese, B. H., Wilder, J., & Bickham, N. L. (2000). Family context in developmental psychopathology. In A. J. Sameroff, M. Lewis, & S. M. Miller (Eds.), *Handbook of developmental psychopathology* (2nd ed., pp. 115–134). New York: Kluwer Academic.

Filipek, P. A., Semrud-Clikeman, M., Steingard, R. J., Renshaw, P. F., Kennedy, D. N., & Beiderman, J. (1997). Volumetric MRI analysis comparing subjects having attention-deficit hyperactivity disorder with controls. *Neurology, 48,* 589–601.

Fischer, M., Barkley, R. A., Edelbrock, C. S., & Smallish, L. (1990). The adolescent outcome of hyperactive children diagnosed by research criteria: II. Academic, attentional, and neuropsychological status. *Journal of Consulting and Clinical Psychology, 58,* 580–588.

Fisman, S., & Fisman, R. (1999). Cultural influences on symptom presentation in childhood. *Journal of the American Academy of Child and Adolescent Psychiatry, 38,* 782–783.

Fletcher, K. E. (1996). Childhood posttraumatic stress disorder. In E. J. Mash & R. A. Barkley (Eds.), *Child psychopathology* (pp. 242–276). New York: Guilford Press.

Fombonne, E. (1999). The epidemiology of autism: A review. *Psychological Medicine, 29,* 769–786.

Foster, S. L., & Martinez, C. R., Jr. (1995). Ethnicity: Conceptual and methodological issues in child clinical research. *Journal of Clinical Child Psychology, 24,* 214–226.

Garber, J. (1984). Classification of childhood psychopathology: A developmental perspective. *Child Development, 55,* 30–48.

García Coll, C., Akerman, A., & Cicchetti, D. (2000). Cultural influence on developmental processes and outcomes: Implications for the study of development and psychopathology. *Development and Psychopathology, 12,* 333–356.

García Coll, C., & Garrido, M. (2000). Minorities in the United States: Sociocultural context for mental health and developmental psychopathology. In A. J. Sameroff, M. Lewis, & S. M. Miller (Eds.), *Handbook of developmental psychopathology* (2nd ed., 177–195). New York: Kluwer Academic.

Gaub, M., & Carlson, C. L. (1997a). Behavioral characteristics of DSM-IV subtypes in a school-based population. *Journal of Abnormal Child Psychology, 25,* 103–111.

Gaub, M., & Carlson, C. L. (1997b). Gender differences in ADHD: A meta-analysis and critical review. *Journal of the American Academy of Child and Adolescent Psychiatry, 36,* 1036–1045.

Ge, X., Conger, R. D., Lorenz, F. O., Shanahan, M., & Elder, G. H., Jr. (1995). Mutual influences in parent and adolescent distress. *Developmental Psychology, 31,* 406–419.

Geller, B., & Luby, J. (1997). Child and adolescent bipolar disorder: A review of the past 10 years. *Journal of the American Academy of Child and Adolescent Psychiatry, 36,* 1168–1176.

Gilger, J. W., Pennington, B. F., & DeFries, J. C. (1992). A twin study of the etiology of comorbidity: Attention-deficit hyperactivity disorder and dyslexia. *Journal of the American Academy of Child and Adolescent Psychiatry, 321,* 343–348.

Gill, M., Daly, G., Heron, S., Hawi, Z., & Fitzgerald, M. (1997). Confirmation of a dissociation between attention deficit hyperactivity disorder and a dopamine transporter polymorphism. *Biological Psychiatry, 2,* 311–313.

Gillberg, C., & Wing, L. (1999). Autism: Not an extremely rare disorder. *Acta Psychiatrica Scandinavica, 99,* 399–406.

Ginsburg, G., & Silverman, W. (1996). Phobic and anxiety disorders in Hispanic and Caucasian youth. *Journal of Anxiety Disorders, 10,* 517–528.

Grattan, L. M., & Eslinger, P. J. (1991). Frontal lobe damage in children and adults: A comparative review. *Developmental Neuropsychology, 7,* 283–326.

Greenbaum, P. E., Prange, M. E., Friedman, R. M., & Silver, S. E. (1991). Substance abuse prevalence and comorbidity with other psychiatric disorders among adolescents with severe emotional disturbances. *Journal of the American Academy of Child and Adolescent Psychiatry, 30,* 575–583.

Greene, R. W., Biederman, J., Faraone, S. V., Monuteaux, M. C., Mick, E., DuPre, E. P., Fine, C. S., & Goring, J. C. (2001). Social impairment in girls with ADHD: Patterns, gender comparisons, and correlates. *Journal of the American Academy of Child and Adolescent Psychiatry, 40,* 704–710.

Gresham, F. M., MacMillan, D. L., Bocian, K. M., Ward, S. L., & Forness, S. R. (1998). Comorbidity of hyperactivity-impulsivity-inattention and conduct problems: Risk factors in social, affective, and academic domains. *Journal of Abnormal Child Psychology, 26,* 393–406.

Gruber, R., Sadeh, A., & Raviv, A. (2000). Instability of sleep patterns in children with attention-deficit/hyperactivity disorder. *Journal of the American Academy of Child and Adolescent Psychiatry, 39,* 495–501.

Guerra, N. G., Huesmann, L. R., Tolan, P. H., Van-Acker, R., & Eron, L. D. (1995). Stressful events and individual beliefs as correlates of economic disadvantage and aggression among urban children. *Journal of Consulting and Clinical Psychology, 63,* 518–528.

Gurley, D., Cohen, P., Pine, D. S., & Brook, J. (1996). Discriminating depression and anxiety in youth: A role for diagnostic criteria. *Journal of Affective Disorders, 39,* 191–200.

Halperin, J. M., Matier, K., Bedi, G., Sharma, V., & Newcorn, J. H. (1992). Specificity of inattention, impulsivity, and hyperactivity to the diagnosis of attention-deficit hyperactivity disorder. *Journal of the American Academy of Child and Adolescent Psychiatry, 31,* 190–196.

Hanna, G. (1995). Demographic and clinical features of obsessive-compulsive disorder in children and adolescents. *Journal of the American Academy of Child and Adolescent Psychiatry, 34,* 19–27.

Harkness, S., & Super, C. M. (2000). Culture and psychopathology. In A. J. Sameroff, M. Lewis, & S. M. Miller (Eds.), *Handbook of developmental psychopathology* (2nd ed., pp. 197–214). New York: Kluwer Academic.

Hart, E. L., Lahey, B. B., Loeber, R., Applegate, B., & Frick, P. J. (1996). Developmental change in attention-deficit hyperactivity disorder in boys: A four-year longitudinal study. *Journal of Abnormal Child Psychology, 23,* 729–749.

Hartung, C. M., & Widiger, T. A. (1998). Gender differences in the diagnosis of mental disorders: Conclusions and controversies of DSM-IV. *Psychological Bulletin, 123,* 260–278.

Hatch, M. L., Friedman, S., & Paradis, C. M. (1996). Behavioral treatment of obsessive-compulsive disorder in African Americans. *Cognitive and Behavioral Practice, 3,* 303–315.

Hechtman, L. (1994). Genetic and neurobiological aspects of attention deficit hyperactivity disorder: A review. *Journal of Psychiatric Neurosciences, 19,* 193–201.

Henker, B., & Whalen, C. K. (1999). The child with attention-deficit/hyperactivity disorder in school and peer settings. In H. C. Quay & A. E. Hogan (Eds.), *Handbook of disruptive behavior disorders* (pp. 157–178). New York: Kluwer Academic.

Hetherington, E. M., Reiss, D., & Plomin, R. (Eds.). (1994). *Separate social worlds of siblings: The impact of nonshared environment on development.* Hillsdale, NJ: Erlbaum.

Hinshaw, S. P. (1994). *Attention deficits and hyperactivity in children.* Thousand Oaks, CA: Sage.

Hinshaw, S. P., & Cicchetti, D. (2000). Stigma and mental disorder: Conceptions of illness, public attitudes, personal disclosure, and social policy. *Development and Psychopathology, 12,* 555–598.

Hirshfeld, D. R., Biederman, J., Brody, L., & Faraone, S. V. (1997). Associations between expressed emotion and child behavioral inhibition and psychopathology: A pilot study. *Journal of the American Academy of Child and Adolescent Psychiatry, 36,* 205–213.

Hirshfeld, D. R., Biederman, J., & Rosenbaum, J. F. (1997). Expressed emotion toward children with behavioral inhibition: Associations with maternal anxiety disorder. *Journal of the American Academy of Child and Adolescent Psychiatry, 36,* 910–919.

Hirshfeld, D. R., Rosenbaum, J. F., Biederman, J., Bolduc, E. A., Faraone, S. V., Snidman, N., Reznick, J. S., & Kagan, J. (1992). Stable behavioral inhibition and its association with anxiety disorder. *Journal of the American Academy of Child and Adolescent Psychiatry, 31,* 103–111.

Hoagwood, K., & Jensen, P. (1997). Developmental psychopathology and the notion of culture. *Applied Developmental Science, 1,* 108–112.

Hoagwood, K., Kelleher, K. J., Feil, M., & Comer, D. M. (2000). Treatment services for children with ADHD: A national perspective. *Journal of the American Academy of Child and Adolescent Psychiatry, 39,* 198–206.

Hollingshead, A. B., & Redlich, F. C. (1958). *Social class and mental illness.* New York: Wiley.

Hops, H. (1995). Age- and gender-specific effects of parental depression: A commentary. *Developmental Psychology, 31,* 428–431.

Howard, B. L., & Kendall, P. C. (1996). Cognitive-behavioral family therapy for anxiety-disordered children: A multiple-baseline evaluation. *Cognitive Therapy and Research, 20,* 423–443.

Humphries, T., Kinsbourne, M., & Swanson, J. (1978). Stimulant effects on cooperation and social interaction between hyperactive children and their mothers. *Journal of Child Psychology and Psychiatry, 19,* 12–22.

Ialongo, N., Edelsohn, G., Werthamer-Larsson, L., Crockett, L., & Kellam, S. (1995). The significance of self-reported anxious symptoms in first grade children: Prediction to anxious symptoms and adaptive functioning in fifth grade. *Journal of Child Psychology and Psychiatry, 36,* 427–437.

Inderbitzen-Nolan, H. M., & Walters, K. S. (2000). Social anxiety scale for adolescents: Normative data and further evidence of construct validity. *Journal of Clinical Child Psychology, 29,* 360–371.

International Molecular Genetic Study of Autism Consortium. (1998). A full genome screen for autism with evidence for linkage to a region on chromosome 7q. *Human Molecular Genetics, 7,* 571–578.

Jacobvitz, D., & Sroufe, L. A. (1987). The early caregiver-child relationship and attention-deficit disorder with hyperactivity in kindergarten: A prospective study. *Child Development, 58,* 1496–1504.

Jensen, P. S., Hinshaw, S. P., Kraemer, H. C., Lenora, N., Newcorn, J. H., Abikoff, H. B., March, J. S., Arnold, L. E., Cantwell, D. P., Connors, C. K., Elliott, G. R., Greenhill, L. L., Hechtman, L., Hoza, B., Pelham, W. E., Severe, J. B., Swanson, J. M., Wells, K. C., Wigal, T., & Vitiello, B. (2001). ADHD comorbidity findings from the MTA study: Comparing comorbid subgroups. *Journal of the American Academy of Child and Adolescent Psychiatry, 40,* 147–158.

Jensen, P. S., Kettle, L., Roper, R. S., Sloan, M. T., Dulcan, M. K., Hoven, C., Bird, H. R., Bauermeister, J. J., & Payne, J. D. (1999). Are stimulants overprescribed? Treatment of ADHD in four U.S. communities. *Journal of the American Academy of Child and Adolescent Psychiatry, 38,* 797–804.

Jensen, P. S., Martin, B. A., & Cantwell, D. P. (1997). Comorbidity in ADHD: Implications for research, practice, and DSM-IV. *Journal of the American Academy of Child and Adolescent Psychiatry, 36,* 1065–1079.

Johnston, C., & Mash, E. J. (2001). Families of children with Attention Deficit Hyperactivity Disorder: Review and recommendations for future research. *Clinical Child and Family Psychology Review, 4,* 183–207.

Joiner, T. E., Jr., & Lonigan, C. J. (2000). Tripartite model of depression and anxiety in youth psychiatric inpatients: Relations with diagnostic status and future symptoms. *Journal of Clinical Child Psychology, 29,* 372–382.

Kagan, J. (1997). Temperament and the reactions to unfamiliarity. *Child Development, 68,* 139–143.

Kagan, J., & Snidman, N. (1999). Early child predictors of adult anxiety disorders. *Biological Psychiatry, 46,* 1536–1541.

Kagan, J., Snidman, N., & Arcus, D. M. (1992). Initial reactions to unfamiliarity. *Current Directions in Psychological Science, 1,* 171–174.

Kagan, J., Snidman, N., Arcus, D. M., & Reznick, J. S. (1994). *Galen's prophecy: Temperament in human nature.* New York: Basic Books.

Kazdin, A. E. (1996). Developing effective treatments for children and adolescents. In E. D. Hibbs & P. S. Jensen (Eds.), *Psychosocial treatments for child and adolescent disorders: Empirically based strategies for clinical practice* (pp. 9–18). Washington, DC: American Psychological Association.

Kazdin, A. E. (2000). *Psychotherapy for children and adolescents: Directions for research and practice.* New York: Oxford University Press.

Kazdin, A. E. (2001). Bridging the enormous gaps of theory with therapy research and practice. *Journal of Clinical Child Psychology, 30,* 59–66.

Kazdin, A. E., & Johnson, B. (1994). Advances in psychotherapy for children and adolescents: Interrelations of adjustment, development, and intervention. *Journal of School Psychology, 32,* 217–246.

Kazdin, A. E., & Kagan, J. (1994). Models of dysfunction in developmental psychopathology. *Clinical Psychology: Science and Practice, 1,* 35–52.

Kearney, C. A., Albano, A. M., Eisen, A. R., Allan, W. D., & Barlow, D. A. (1997). The phenomenology of panic disorder in youngsters: An empirical study of a clinical sample. *Journal of Anxiety Disorders, 11,* 49–62.

Kearney, C. A., & Allan, W. D. (1995). Panic disorder with or without agoraphobia. In A. R. Eisen, C. A. Kearney, & C. A. Schaefer (Eds.), *Clinical handbook of anxiety disorders in children and adolescents* (pp. 251–281). Northvale, NJ: Jason Aronson.

Keller, M., Lavori, P., Wunder, J., Beardslee, W., Schwartz, C., & Roth, J. (1992). Chronic course of anxiety disorders in children and adolescents. *Journal of the American Academy of Child and Adolescent Psychiatry, 31,* 595–599.

Kendall, P. C., & Brady, E. (1995). Comorbidity in the anxiety disorders of childhood. In K. Craig & K. Dobson (Eds.), *Anxiety and depression in adults and children* (pp. 3–36). Newbury Park, CA: Sage.

Kendall, P. C., Panichelli-Mindel, S. M., Sugarman, A., & Callahan, S. A. (1997). Exposure to child anxiety: Theory, research, and practice. *Clinical Psychology: Science and Practice, 4,* 29–39.

King, N. J., & Bernstein, G. A. (2001). School refusal in children and adolescents: A review of the past 10 years. *Journal of the American Academy of Child and Adolescent Psychiatry, 40,* 197–205.

King, N. J., Ollendick, T. H., & Mattis, S. G. (1994). Panic in children and adolescents: Normative and clinical studies. *Australian Psychologist, 29,* 89–93.

Koplowicz, S., & Barkley, R. A. (1995). *Sense of time in children with attention deficit hyperactivity disorder and normal children.* Unpublished manuscript, University of Massachusetts Medical Center, Worcester.

Kortlander, E., Kendall, P. C., & Panichelli-Mindel, S. M. (1997). Maternal expectations and attributions about coping in anxious children. *Journal of Anxiety Disorders, 11,* 297–315.

Kovacs, M. (1997). Depressive disorders in childhood: An impressionistic landscape. *Journal of Child Psychology and Psychiatry, 38,* 287–298.

Krain, A. L., & Kendall, P. C. (2000). The role of parental emotional distress in parent report of child anxiety. *Journal of Clinical Child Psychology, 29,* 328–335.

Kuntsi, J., & Stevenson, J. (2000). Hyperactivity in children: A focus on genetic research and psychological theories. *Clinical Child Family Psychology Review, 3,* 1–23.

La Greca, A. M., Silverman, W. K., & Wasserstein, S. B. (1998). Children's predisaster functioning as a predictor of posttraumatic stress following Hurricane Andrew. *Journal of Consulting and Clinical Psychology, 66,* 883–892.

Lahey, B. B., & Carlson, C. L. (1992). Validity of the diagnostic category of attention deficit disorder without hyperactivity: A review of the literature. In S. E. Shaywitz & B. A. Shaywitz (Eds.), *Attention deficit disorder comes of age: Toward the twenty-first century* (pp. 119–144). Austin, TX: Pro-ed.

Lahey, B. B., Hartdagen, S. E., Frick, P. J., McBurnett, K., Connor, R., & Hynd, G. W. (1988). Conduct disorder: Parsing the confounded relationship between parental divorce and antisocial personality. *Journal of Abnormal Psychology, 97,* 334–337.

Lahey, B. B., Loeber, R., Hart, E. L., Frick, P. J., Applegate, B., Zhang, Q., Green, S. M., & Russo, M. F. (1995). Four-year longitudinal study of conduct disorder in boys: Patterns and predictors of persistence. *Journal of Abnormal Psychology, 104,* 83–93.

Lambert, N. M., Sandoval, J., & Sassone, D. (1978). Prevalence of hyperactivity in elementary school children as a function of social system definers. *American Journal of Orthopsychiatry, 48,* 446–463.

Lambert, M. C., & Weisz, J. R. (1992). Jamaican and American adult perspectives on child psychopathology: Further exploration of the threshold model. *Journal of Consulting and Clinical Psychology, 60,* 146–149.

Landau, S., Milich, R., & Diener, M. B. (1998). Peer relations of children with attention-deficit hyperactivity disorder. *Reading & Writing Quarterly: Overcoming Learning Difficulties, 14,* 83–105.

Last, C. G., & Perrin, S. (1993). Anxiety disorders in African-American and white children. *Journal of Abnormal Child Psychology, 21,* 153–164.

Last, C. G., Perrin, S., Hersen, M., & Kazdin, A. E. (1992). DSM-III-R anxiety disorders in children: Sociodemographic and clinical characteristics. *Journal of the American Academy of Child and Adolescent Psychiatry, 31,* 1070–1076.

Last, C. G., Perrin, S., Hersen, M., & Kazdin, A. E. (1996). A prospective study of childhood anxiety disorders. *Journal of the American Academy of Child and Adolescent Psychiatry, 35,* 1502–1510.

Last, C. G., & Strauss, C. C. (1989). Panic disorder in children and adolescents. *Journal of Anxiety Disorders, 3,* 87–95.

Leibson, C. L., Katusic, S. K., Barberesi, W. J., Ransom, J., & O'Brien, P. (2001). Use and costs of medical care for children and adolescents with and without attention-deficit/hyperactivity disorder (ADHD). *Journal of the American Medical Association, 285,* 60–66.

Leon, G. R., Fulkerson, J. A., Perry, C. L., & Early-Zald, M. B. (1995). Prospective analysis of personality and behavioral vulnerabilities and gender influences in later development of disordered eating. *Journal of Abnormal Psychology, 104,* 140–149.

Lewinsohn, P. M., Gotlib, I. H., Lewinsohn, M., Seeley, J. R., & Allen, N. B. (1998). Gender differences in anxiety disorders and anxiety symptoms in adolescents. *Journal of Abnormal Psychology, 107,* 109–117.

Lewinsohn, P. M., Rohde, P., Seeley, J. R., & Hops, H. (1991). The comorbidity of unipolar depression: Part 1. Major depression with dysthymia. *Journal of Abnormal Psychology, 100,* 205–213.

Lilienfeld, S. O., Waldman, I. D., & Israel, A. C. (1994). A critical examination of the use of the term and concept of comorbidity in psychopathology research. *Clinical Psychology: Science and Practice, 1,* 71–83.

Loeber, R. (1991). Questions and advances in the study of developmental pathways. In D. Cicchetti & S. L. Toth (Eds.), *Rochester symposium on developmental psychopathology: Vol. 3. Models and integrations* (pp. 97–116). Rochester, NY: University of Rochester Press.

Loeber, R., & Farrington, D. P. (2000). Young children who commit crime: Epidemiology, developmental origins, risk factors, early interventions, and policy implications. *Development and Psychopathology, 12,* 737–762.

Lonigan, C. J., Hooe, E. S., David, C. F., & Kistner, J. A. (1999). Positive and negative affectivity in children: Confirmatory factor analysis of a two-factor model and its relation to symptoms of anxiety and depression. *Journal of Consulting and Clinical Psychology, 67,* 374–386.

Lopez, S. R., & Guarnaccia, P. J. (2000). Cultural psychopathology: Uncovering the social world of mental illness. *Annual Review of Psychology, 51,* 571–598.

Luthar, S. S., Cicchetti, D., & Becker, B. (2000). The construct of resilience: A critical evaluation and guidelines for future work. *Child Development, 71,* 543–562.

Maedgen, J. W., & Carlson, C. L. (2000). Social functioning and emotional regulation in the attention deficit hyperactivity disorder subtypes. *Journal of Clinical Child Psychology, 29,* 30–42.

Majcher, D., & Pollack, M. H. (1996). Childhood anxiety disorders. In L. Hechtman (Ed.), *Do they grow out of it? Long-term outcomes of childhood disorders* (pp. 139–170). Washington, DC: American Psychiatric Press.

Manassis, K., & Bradley, S. (1994). The development of childhood anxiety disorders: Toward an integrated model. *Journal of Applied Developmental Psychology, 15,* 345–366.

Manassis, K., Bradley, S., Goldberg, S., Hood, J., & Swinson, R. P. (1994). Attachment in mothers with anxiety disorders and their children. *Journal of the American and Adolescent Psychiatry, 33,* 1106–1113.

Mancini, C., van Ameringen, M., Szatmari, P., Fugere, C., & Boyle, M. (1996). A high-risk pilot study of the children of adults with social phobia. *Journal of the American Academy of Child and Adolescent Psychiatry, 35,* 1511–1517.

Mannuzza, S., & Klein, R. (1992). Predictors of outcome of children with attention-deficit hyperactivity disorder. In G. Weiss (Ed.), *Child and adolescent psychiatric clinics of North America: Attention-deficit hyperactivity disorder* (pp. 567–578). Philadelphia: Saunders.

March, J. S. (Ed.). (1995). *Anxiety disorders in children and adolescents.* New York: Guilford Press.

Mariani, M. A., & Barkley, R. A. (1997). Neuropsychological and academic functioning in preschool boys with attention deficit hyperactivity disorder. *Developmental Neuropsychology, 13,* 111–129.

Mash, E. J., & Barkley, R. A. (Eds.). (1996). *Child psychopathology.* New York: Guilford.

Mash, E. J., & Barkley, R. A. (Eds.). (1998). *Treatment of childhood disorders.* New York: Guilford.

Mash, E. J., & Dozois, D. J. A. (1996). Child psychopathology: A developmental systems perspective. In E. J. Mash & R. A. Barkley (Eds.), *Child psychopathology* (pp. 3–60). New York: Guilford.

Mash, E. J., & Johnston, C. (1990). Determinants of parenting stress: Illustrations from families of hyperactive children and families of physically abused children. *Journal of Clinical Child Psychology, 19,* 313–328.

Mash, E. J., & Johnston, C. (1996). Family relational problems: Their place in the study of psychopathology. *Journal of Emotional and Behavioral Disorders, 4,* 240–254.

Mash, E. J., & Terdal, L. G. (1997a). Assessment of child and family disturbance: A behavioral-systems approach. In E. J. Mash & L. G. Terdal (Eds.), *Assessment of childhood disorders* (3rd ed., pp. 3–68). New York: Guilford Press.

Mash, E. J., & Terdal, L. G. (Eds.). (1997b). *Assessment of childhood disorders.* New York: Guilford.

Mash, E. J., & Wolfe, D. A. (2002). *Abnormal child psychology* (2nd ed.). Belmont, CA: Wadsworth.

Masten, A. (2001). Ordinary magic: Resilience processes in development. *American Psychologist, 56,* 227–238.

McCall, R. B., & Groark, C. J. (2000). The future of applied child development research and public policy. *Child Development, 71,* 197–204.

McClure, E. B., Brennan, P. A., Hammen, C., & Le Brocque, R. M. (2001). Parental anxiety disorders, child anxiety disorders, and the perceived parent-child relationship in an Australian high-risk sample. *Journal of Abnormal Child Psychology, 29,* 1–10.

McDermott, P. A., & Weiss, R. V. (1995). A normative typology of healthy, subclinical, and clinical behavior styles among American children and adolescents. *Psychological Assessment, 7,* 162–170.

McGee, R., & Feehan, M. (1991). Are girls with problems of inattention underrecognized? *Journal of Psychopathology and Behavioral Assessment, 13,* 187–198.

McLeod, J. D., & Nonnemaker, J. M. (2000). Poverty and child emotional and behavioral problems: Racial/ethnic differences in processes and effects. *Journal of Health and Social Behavior, 41,* 137–161.

McMahon, R. J., & Estes, A. M. (1997). Conduct problems. In E. J. Mash & L. G. Terdal (Eds.), *Assessment of childhood disorders* (3rd ed., pp. 130–193). New York: Guilford Press.

Melnick, S. M., & Hinshaw, S. P. (2000). Emotion regulation and parenting in AD/HD and comparison boys: Linkages with social behaviors and peer preference. *Journal of Abnormal Child Psychology, 28,* 73–86.

Mesman, J., & Koot, H. M. (2000). Child-reported depression and anxiety in preadolescence: I. Associations with parent- and teacher-reported problems. *Journal of the American Academy of Child and Adolescent Psychiatry, 39,* 1371–1378.

Mick, E., Santangelo, S. L., Wypij, D., & Biederman, J. (2000). Impact of maternal depression on ratings of comorbid depression in adolescents with attention-deficit/hyperactivity disorder. *Journal of the American Academy of Child and Adolescent Psychiatry, 39,* 314–319.

Milberger, S., Biederman, J., Faraone, S. V., Chen, L., & Jones, J. (1996). Is maternal smoking during pregnancy a risk factor for attention deficit hyperactivity disorder in children? *American Journal of Psychiatry, 153,* 1138–1142.

Milberger, S., Biederman, J., Faraone, S. V., Guite, J., & Tsuang, M. T. (1997). Pregnancy, delivery and infancy complications and attention deficit hyperactivity disorder: Issues of gene environment interaction. *Biological Psychiatry, 41,* 65–75.

Mischel, W. (1968). *Personality and assessment.* New York: Wiley.

Muris, P., & Merckelbach, H. (2000). How serious are common childhood fears? II. The parent's point of view. *Behaviour Research and Therapy, 38,* 813–818.

Muris, P., Merckelbach, H., & Damsma, E. (2000). Threat perception in nonreferred socially anxious children. *Journal of Clinical Child Psychology, 29,* 348–359.

Nada-Raja, S., Langley, J. D., McGee, R., Williams, S. M., Begg, D. J., & Reeder, A. I. (1997). Inattentive and hyperactive behaviors and driving offences in adolescence. *Journal of the American Academy of Child and Adolescent Psychiatry, 36,* 515–522.

Neal, A. M., & Turner, S. M. (1991). Anxiety disorders research with African Americans: Current status. *Psychological Bulletin, 109,* 400–410.

Offord, D. R., Boyle, M. H., Szatmari, P., Rae-Grant, N. I., Links, P. S., Cadman, D. T., Byles, J. A., Crawford, J. W., Blum, H. M., Byrne, C., Thomas, H., & Woodward, C. A. (1987). Ontario Child Health Study: II. Six-month prevalence of disorder and rates of service utilization. *Archives of General Psychiatry, 44,* 832–836.

Ollendick, T. H., & King, N. J. (1994). Diagnosis, assessment, and treatment of internalizing problems in children: The role of longitudinal data. *Journal of Consulting and Clinical Psychology, 62,* 918–927.

Ollendick, T. H., Mattis, S. G., & King, N. J. (1994). Panic in children and adolescents: A review. *Journal of Child Psychology and Psychiatry, 35,* 113–134.

Ollendick, T. H., Yang, B., King, N. J., Dong, Q., & Akande, A. (1996). Fears in American, Australian, Chinese, and Nigerian children and adolescents: A cross-cultural study. *Journal of Child Psychology and Psychiatry, 37,* 213–220.

Olweus, D. (1979). Stability of aggressive reaction patterns in males: A review. *Psychological Bulletin, 86,* 852–875.

Pauls, D. L. (1991). Genetic factors in the expression of attention-deficit hyperactivity disorder. *Journal of Child and Adolescent Psychopharmacology, 1,* 353–360.

Pennington, B. F., & Ozonoff, S. (1991). A neuroscientific perspective on continuity and discontinuity in developmental psychopathology. In D. Cicchetti & S. L. Toth (Eds.), *Rochester symposium on developmental psychopathology: Vol. 3. Models and integrations* (pp. 117–159). New York: University of Rochester Press.

Pennington, B. F., & Ozonoff, S. (1996). Executive functions and developmental psychopathology. *Journal of Child Psychology and Psychiatry, 37,* 51–87.

Perrin, S., Smith, P., & Yule, W. (2000). Practitioner review: The assessment and treatment of post-traumatic stress disorder in children and adolescents. *Journal of Child Psychology and Psychiatry, 41,* 277–289.

Peterson, B. S., Pine, D. S., Cohen, P., & Brook, J. S. (2001). Prospective, longitudinal study of tic, obsessive-compulsive, and attention-deficit/hyperactivity disorders in an epidemiological sample. *Journal of the American Academy of Child and Adolescent Psychiatry, 40,* 685–695.

Phares, V., & Compas, B. (1992). The role of fathers in child and adolescent psychopathology: Make room for daddy. *Psychological Bulletin, 111,* 387–412.

Piacentini, J., & Graae, F. (1997). Childhood OCD. In E. Hollander & D. Stein (Eds.), *Obsessive-compulsive disorders: Diagnosis, etiology, treatment* (pp. 23–46). New York: Marcel Dekker.

Pine, D. S. (1997). Childhood anxiety disorders. *Current Opinions in Pediatrics, 9,* 329–338.

Pine, D. S., Cohen, E., Cohen, P., & Brook, J. S. (2000). Social phobia and the persistence of conduct problems. *Journal of Child Psychology and Psychiatry, 41,* 657–665.

Pine, D. S., & Grun, J. (1999). Childhood anxiety: Integrating developmental psychopathology and affective neuroscience. *Journal of Child and Adolescent Psychopharmacology, 9,* 1–12.

Pliszka, S. R. (1992). Comorbidity of attention-deficit hyperactivity disorder and overanxious disorder. *Journal of the American Academy of Child and Adolescent Psychiatry, 31,* 197–203.

Plomin, R. (1995). Genetics and children's experiences in the family. *Journal of Child Psychology and Psychiatry, 36,* 33–38.

Plomin, R., & Rutter, M. (1998). Child development, molecular genetics, and what to do with genes once they are found. *Child Development, 69,* 1223–1242.

Prior, M., Smart, D., Sanson, A., & Oberklaid, F. (2000). Does shy-inhibited temperament in childhood lead to anxiety problems in adolescence. *Journal of the American Academy of Child and Adolescent Psychiatry, 39,* 461–468.

Pynoos, R. S., Frederick, C., Nader, K., Arroyo, W., Steinberg, A., Eth, S., Nunez, F., & Fairbanks, L. (1987). Life threat and posttraumatic stress in school-age children. *Archives of General Psychiatry, 44,* 1057–1063.

Quay, H. C. (1997). Inhibition and attention deficit hyperactivity disorder. *Journal of Abnormal Child Psychology, 25,* 7–13.

Quist, J. F., & Kennedy, J. L. (2001). Genetics of childhood disorders: XXIII. ADHD, part 7: The serotonin system. *Journal of the American Academy of Child and Adolescent Psychiatry, 40,* 253–256.

Rapee, R. M. (1997). Potential role of childrearing practices in the development of anxiety and depression. *Clinical Psychology Review, 17,* 47–67.

Rapport, M., & Chung, K. (2000). Attention deficit hyperactivity disorder. In M. Hersen & R. T. Ammerman (Eds.), *Advanced abnormal child psychology* (2nd ed., pp. 413–440). Mahwah, NJ: Erlbaum.

Richters, J. E., & Cicchetti, D. (1993). Mark Twain meets DSM-III-R: Conduct disorder, development, and the concept of harmful dysfunction. *Development and Psychopathology, 5,* 5–29.

Rie, H. E. (1971). Historical perspective of concepts of child psychopathology. In H. E. Rie (Ed.), *Perspectives in child psychopathology* (pp. 3–50). Chicago: Aldine-Atherton.

Roberts, R. E., Attkisson, C. C., & Rosenblatt, A. (1998). Prevalence of psychopathology among children and adolescents. *American Journal of Psychiatry, 155,* 715–725.

Rosenbaum, J. F., Biederman, J., Hirshfeld, D. R., Bolduc, E. A., Faraone, S. V., Kagan, J., Snidman, N., & Reznick, J. S. (1991). Further evidence of an association between behavioral inhibition and anxiety disorders: Results from a family study of children from a non-clinical sample. *Journal of Psychiatric Research, 25,* 49–65.

Routh, D. K. (1990). Taxonomy in developmental psychopathology: Consider the source. In M. Lewis & S. M. Miller (Eds.), *Handbook of developmental psychopathology* (pp. 53–62). New York: Plenum.

Rucklidge, J. J., & Tannock, R. (2001). Psychiatric, psychosocial, and cognitive functioning of female adolescents with ADHD. *Journal of the American Academy of Child and Adolescent Psychiatry, 40,* 530–540.

Rutter, M. (2000a). Genetic studies of autism: From the 1970s into the millennium. *Journal of Abnormal Child Psychology, 28,* 3–14.

Rutter, M. (2000b). Psychosocial influences: Critiques, findings, and research needs. *Development and Psychopathology, 12,* 375–405.

Rutter, M., & Sroufe, L. A. (2000). Developmental psychopathology: Concepts and challenges. *Developmental and Psychopathology, 12,* 265–296.

Sallee, R., & Greenawald, J. (1995). Neurobiology. In J. S. March (Ed.), *Anxiety disorders in children and adolescents* (pp. 3–34). New York: Guilford Press.

Sameroff, A. J., Lewis, M., & Miller, S. M. (Eds.). (2000). *Handbook of developmental psychopathology* (2nd ed.). New York: Kluwer Academic.

Schachar, R., & Tannock, R. (1995). Test of four hypotheses for the comorbidity of attention-deficit hyperactivity disorder and conduct disorder. *Journal of the American Academy of Child and Adolescent Psychiatry, 34,* 639–648.

Schopler, E., Mesibov, G. B., & Kunce, L. J. (Eds.). (1998). *Asperger syndrome or high-functioning autism?* New York: Plenum.

Schwartz, C. E., Snidman, N., & Kagan, J. (1999). Adolescent social anxiety as an outcome of inhibited temperament in childhood. *Journal of the American Academy of Child and Adolescent Psychiatry, 38,* 1008–1015.

Seidman, L. J., Biederman, J., Faraone, S. V., & Weber, W. (1997). A pilot study of neuropsychological function in girls with ADHD. *Journal of the American Academy of Child and Adolescent Psychiatry, 36,* 366–373.

Seligman, L. D., & Ollendick, T. H. (1998). Comorbidity of anxiety and depression in children and adolescents: An integrative review. *Clinical Child and Family Psychology Review, 1,* 125.

Semrud-Clikeman, M., Biederman, J., Sprich-Buckminster, S., Lehman, B. K., Faraone, S. V., & Norman, D. (1992). Comorbidity between ADHD and learning disability: A review and report in a clinically referred sample. *Journal of the American Academy of Child and Adolescent Psychiatry, 31,* 439–448.

Semrud-Clikeman, M., Steingard, R. J., Filipek, P., Biederman, J., Bekken, K., & Renshaw, P. F. (2000). Using MRI to examine brain-behavior relationships in males with attention deficit disorder with hyperactivity. *Journal of the American Academy of Child and Adolescent Psychiatry, 39,* 477–484.

Shadish, W. R., Matt, G. E., Navarro, A. M., & Phillips, G. (2000). The effects of psychological therapies under clinically representative conditions: A meta-analysis. *Psychological Bulletin, 126,* 512–529.

Shadish, W. R., Matt, G. E., Navarro, A. M., Siegle, G., Crits-Christoph, P., Hazelrigg, M. D., Jorm, A. F., Lyons, L. C., Nietzel, M. T., Prout, H. T., Robinson, L., Smith, M. L., Svartberg, M., & Weiss, B. (1997). Evidence that therapy works in clinically representative conditions. *Journal of Consulting and Clinical Psychology, 65,* 355–365.

Shaffer, D., Fisher, P., Dulcan, M. K., Davies, M., Piacentini, J., Schwab-Stone, M. E., Lahey, B. B., Bourdon, K., Jensen, P. S., Bird, H. R., Canino, G., & Regier, D. A. (1996). The NIMH Diagnostic Inverview Schedule for Children Version 2.3 (DISC-2.3): Description, acceptability, prevalence rates, and performance in the MECA study. *Journal of the American Academy of Child and Adolescent Psychiatry, 35,* 865–877.

Silk, J. S., Nath, S. R., Siegel, L. R., & Kendall, P. C. (2000). Conceptualizing mental disorders in children: Where have we been and where are we going? *Development and Psychopathology, 12,* 713–735.

Silverman, I. W., & Ragusa, D. M. (1992). Child and maternal correlates of impulse control in 24-month-old children. *Genetic, Social, and General Psychology Monographs, 116,* 435–473.

Silverthorn, P., Frick, P. J., Kuper, K., & Ott, J. (1996). Attention deficit hyperactivity disorder and sex: A test of two etiological models to explain the male predominance. *Journal of Clinical Child Psychology, 25,* 52–59.

Siqueland, L., Kendall, P. C., & Steinberg, L. (1996). Perceived family environment and observed family interaction styles. *Journal of Clinical Child Psychology, 25,* 225–237.

Sonuga-Barke, E. J. S., Daley, D., Thompson, M., Laver-Bradbury, C., & Weeks, A. (2001). Parent-based therapies for preschool attention-deficit/hyperactivity disorder: A randomized, controlled trial with a community sample. *Journal of the American Academy of Child and Adolescent Psychiatry, 40,* 402–408.

Southam-Gerow, M. A., & Kendall, P. C. (2000). A preliminary study of the emotion understanding of youths referred for treatment of anxiety disorders. *Journal of Clinical Child Psychology, 29,* 319–327.

Spitzer, R. L., Davies, M., & Barkley, R. A. (1990). The DSM-III-R field trial of disruptive behavior disorders. *Journal of the American Academy of Child and Adolescent Psychiatry, 29,* 690–697.

State, M. W., Lombroso, P. J., Pauls, D. L., & Leckman, J. F. (2000). The genetics of childhood psychiatric disorders: A decade of progress. *Journal of the American Academy of Child and Adolescent Psychiatry, 39,* 946–962.

Stein, M. A., Szumoski, E., Blondis, T. A., & Roizen, N. J. (1995). Adaptive skills dysfunction in ADD and ADHD children. *Journal of Child Psychology and Psychiatry, 36,* 663–670.

Stevenson, J. (1992). Evidence for a genetic etiology in hyperactivity in children. *Behavior Genetics, 22,* 337–343.

Stodgell, C. J., Ingram, J. L., & Hyman, S. L. (2000). The role of candidate genes in unraveling the genetics of autism. *International Review of Research in Mental Retardation, 23,* 57–82.

Strauss, C. C., Lahey, B. B., Frick, P., Frame, C. L, & Hynd, G. W. (1988). Peer social status of children with anxiety disorders. *Journal of Consulting and Clinical Psychology, 56,* 137–141.

Strauss, C. C., & Last, C. G. (1993). Social and simple phobias in children. *Journal of Anxiety Disorders, 7,* 141–152.

Strauss, C. C., Last, C. G., Hersen, M., & Kazdin, A. E. (1988). Association between anxiety and depression in children and adolescents with anxiety disorders. *Journal of Abnormal Child Psychology, 16,* 57–68.

Strauss, C. C., Lease, C. A., Kazdin, A. E., Dulcan, M. J., & Last, C. G. (1989). Multimethod assessment of the social competence of children with anxiety disorders. *Journal of Clinical Child Psychology, 18,* 184–189.

Strauss, C. C., Lease, C. A., Last, C. G., & Francis, G. (1988). Over-anxious disorder: An examination of developmental differences. *Journal of Abnormal Child Psychology, 16,* 433–443.

Streissguth, A. P., Bookstein, F. L., Sampson, P. D., & Barr, H. M. (1995). Attention: Prenatal alcohol and continuities of vigilance and attentional problems from 4 through 14 years. *Development and Psychopathology, 7,* 419–446.

Swedo, S. E., Rapoport, J. L., Leonard, H., Lenane, M., & Cheslow, D. (1989). Obsessive-compulsive disorder in children and adolescents: Clinical phenomenology of 70 consecutive cases. *Archives of General Psychiatry, 46,* 335–341.

Szatmari, P. (1992). The epidemiology of attention-deficit hyperactivity disorders. In G. Weiss (Ed.), *Child and adolescent psychiatric clinics of North America: Attention-deficit hyperactivity disorder* (pp. 361–372). Philadelphia: Saunders.

Tanguay, P. E. (2000). Pervasive developmental disorders: A 10-year review. *Journal of the American Academy of Child and Adolescent Psychiatry, 39,* 1079–1095.

Tannock, R. (1998). Attention deficit hyperactivity disorder: Advances in cognitive, neurobiological, and genetic research. *Journal of Child Psychology and Psychiatry, 39,* 65–99.

Tannock, R. (2000). Attention-deficit/hyperactivity disorder with anxiety disorders. In T. E. Brown (Ed.), *Attention deficit disorders and comorbidities in children, adolescents and adults* (pp. 125–170). Washington, DC: American Psychiatric Press.

Taylor, E. (1995). Dysfunctions of attention. In D. Cicchetti & D. J. Cohen (Eds.), *Developmental psychopathology: Risk disorder, and adaptation* (Vol. 2, pp. 243–273). New York: Wiley-Interscience.

Taylor, E. (1999). Developmental neuropsychology of attention deficit and impulsiveness. *Development and Psychopathology, 11,* 607–628.

Tolan, P. H., & Thomas, P. (1995). The implications of age of onset for delinquency risk: II. Longitudinal evidence. *Journal of Abnormal Child Psychology, 23,* 157–181.

Treadwell, K. H., Flannery-Schroeder, E. C., & Kendall, P. C. (1994). Ethnicity and gender in a sample of clinic-referred anxious children: Adaptive functioning, diagnostic status, and treatment outcome. *Journal of Anxiety Disorders, 9,* 373–384.

Treadwell, K. H., & Kendall, P. C. (1996). Self-talk in youth with anxiety disorders: States of mind, content specificity, and treatment outcome. *Journal of Consulting and Clinical Psychology, 64,* 941–950.

Tremblay, R. E., Masse, B., Perron, D., LeBlanc, M., Schwartzman, A., & Ledingham, J. E. (1992). Early disruptive behavior, poor school achievement, delinquent behavior, and delinquent personality: Longitudinal analyses. *Journal of Consulting and Clinical Psychology, 60,* 64–72.

Turner, S. M., Beidel, D. C., & Wolff, P. L. (1996). Is behavioral inhibition related to the anxiety disorders? *Clinical Psychology Review, 16,* 157–172.

U.S. Department of Health and Human Services. (2000, November). *Healthy people 2010: Understanding and improving health* (2nd ed.). Washington, DC: U.S. Government Printing Office.

U.S. Public Health Service. (2001a). *Report of the surgeon general's conference on children's mental health: A national action agenda*. Washington, DC: Department of Health and Human Services.

U.S. Public Health Service. (2001b). *Youth violence: Report from the surgeon general*. Washington, DC: Department of Health and Human Services.

van den Oord, E. J. C. G., Boomsma, D. I., & Verhulst, F. C. (1994). A study of problem behaviors in 10- to 15-year-old biologically related and unrelated international adoptees. *Behavior Genetics, 24,* 193–205.

Vasey, M. W., El-Hag, N., & Daleiden, E. L. (1996). Anxiety and the processing of emotionally threatening stimuli: Distinctive patterns of selective attention among high- and low-test anxious children. *Child Development, 67,* 1173–1185.

Vasey, M. W., & Ollendick, T. H. (2000). Anxiety. In A. J. Sameroff & M. L. Lewis (Eds.), *Handbook of developmental psychopathology* (2nd ed., pp. 511–529). New York: Kluwer Academic.

Velez, C. N., Johnson, J., & Cohen, P. (1989). A longitudinal analysis of selected risk factors for childhood psychopathology. *Journal of the American Academy of Child and Adolescent Psychiatry, 28,* 861–864.

Volkmar, F. R., & Klin, A. (1998). Asperger syndrome and nonverbal learning disabilities. In E. Schopler, G. B. Mesibov, & L. J. Kunce (Eds.), *Asperger syndrome or high-functioning autism?* (pp. 107–121). New York: Plenum.

Volkmar, F. R., & Klin, A. (2000). Asperger's Disorder and higher functioning autism: Same or different? *International Review of Research in Mental Retardation, 23,* 83–111.

Weiss, B., Catron, T., Harris, V., & Phung, T. M. (1999). The effectiveness of traditional child psychotherapy. *Journal of Consulting and Clinical Psychology, 67,* 82–94.

Weiss, G., & Hechtman, L. T. (1993). *Hyperactive children grown up: ADHD in children, adolescents, and adults* (2nd ed.). New York: Guilford Press.

Weissman, M. M., McAvay, G., Goldstein, R. B., Nunes, E. V., Verdeli, H., & Wickramaratne, P. J. (1999). Risk/protective factors among addicted mothers' offspring: A replication study. *American Journal of Drug and Alcohol Abuse, 25,* 661–679.

Weisz, J. R. (1998). Empirically supported treatments for children and adolescents: Efficacy, problems, and prospects. In K. S. Dobson & K. D. Craig (Eds.), *Empirically supported therapies: Best practice in professional psychology* (pp. 66–92). Newbury Park, CA: Sage.

Weisz, J. R. (2000a). Lab-clinic differences and what we can do about them: I. The clinic-based treatment development model. *Clinical Child Psychology Newsletter, 15*(1), 1–3, 10–11.

Weisz, J. R. (2000b). Lab-clinic differences and what we can do about them: II. Linking research and practice to enhance our public interest. *Clinical Child Psychology Newsletter, 15*(3), 1–4, 9.

Weisz, J. R. (2000c). Lab-clinic differences and what we can do about them: III. National policy matters. *Clinical Child Psychology Newsletter, 15*(3), 1–3, 6, 10.

Weisz, J. R., Donenberg, G. R., Han, S. S., & Weiss, B. (1995). Bridging the gap between laboratory and clinic in child and adolescent psychotherapy. *Journal of Consulting and Clinical Psychology, 63,* 688–701.

Weisz, J. R., & Weiss, B. (1993). *Effects of psychotherapy with children and adolescents*. Newbury Park, CA: Sage.

Werner, E. E. (1995). Resilience in development. *Current Directions in Psychological Science, 4,* 81–85.

Werry, J. S. (2001). Pharmacological treatments of autism, attention deficit hyperactivity disorder, oppositional defiant disorder, and depression in children and youth—commentary. *Journal of Clinical Child Psychology, 30,* 110–113.

Whalen, C. K., & Henker, B. (1999). The child with attention-deficit/hyperactivity disorder in family contexts. In H. C. Quay & A. E. Hogan (Eds.), *Handbook of disruptive behavior disorders* (pp. 139–155). New York: Kluwer Academic.

Wilens, T. E., Biederman, J., Mick, E., Faraone, S. V., & Spencer, T. (1997). Attention deficit hyperactivity disorder (ADHD) is associated with early onset substance use disorders. *Journal of Nervous and Mental Disease, 185,* 475–482.

Wilens, T. E., Biederman, J., & Spencer, T. (1994). Clonidine for sleep disturbances associated with attention-deficit hyperactivity disorder. *Journal of the American Academy of Child and Adolescent Psychiatry, 33,* 424–426.

Willcutt, E. G., Pennington, B. F., Chhabildas, N. A., Friedman, M. C., & Alexander, J. (1999). Psychiatric comorbidity associated with DSM-IV ADHD in a nonreferred sample of twins. *Journal of the American Academy of Child and Adolescent Psychiatry, 38,* 1355–1362.

Willis, T. J., & Lovaas, I. (1977). A behavioral approach to treating hyperactive children: The parent's role. In J. B. Milichap (Ed.), *Learning disabilities and related disorders* (pp. 119–140). Chicago: Yearbook Medical.

Winsberg, B. G., & Comings, D. E. (1999). Association of the dopamine transporter gene (DAT1) with poor methylphenidate response. *Journal of the American Academy of Child and Adolescent Psychiatry, 38,* 1474–1477.

Wolfe, D. A. (1999). *Child abuse: Implications for child development and psychopathology*. Thousand Oaks, CA: Sage.

Zahn-Waxler, C. (1993). Warriors and worriers: Gender and psychopathology. *Development and Psychopathology, 5,* 79–89.

Zahn-Waxler, C., Cole, P. M., Welsh, J. D., & Fox, N. A. (1995). Psychophysiological correlates of empathy and prosocial behaviors in preschool children with behavior problems. *Development and Psychopathology, 7,* 27–48.

Zahn-Waxler, C., Klimes-Dougan, B., & Slattery, M. J. (2000). Internalizing problems of childhood and adolescence. *Development and Psychopathology, 12,* 443–466.

Zametkin, A. J., Liebenauer, L. L., Fitzgerald, G. A., King, A. C., Minkunas, D. V., Herscovitz, P., Yamada, E. M., & Cohen, R. M. (1993). Brain metabolism in teenagers with attention-deficit hyperactivity disorder. *Archives of General Psychiatry, 50,* 333–340.

# CHAPTER 3

# Schizophrenia Spectrum Disorders

DONALD C. FOWLES

Schizophrenia, like all conceptualizations of psychopathology, is a hypothetical construct that clinicians and scientists have developed in an attempt to capture a complex reality (Morey, 1991). Generally speaking, *schizophrenia* is a label applied to individuals who manifest some combination of hallucinations, delusions, thought disorder (inferred from incoherent speech), and bizarre or disorganized behavior, which define an active (also called acute or florid) phase of the psychosis. Although the preceding features are seen in schizophrenia, the heterogeneity of schizophrenia (e.g., Kendler & Diehl, 1995; Tsuang & Faraone, 1995) has hindered attempts at simple conceptualizations, leaving current investigators talking about schizophrenia and other disorders as "complex illnesses" (Andreasen, 2001, p. 113). Although there are many issues in developing diagnostic criteria for schizophrenia, three have been particularly important: (a) a chronic versus an episodic course, (b) positive versus negative symptoms, and (c) the presence of affective symptoms.

## ISSUES IN DIAGNOSIS

### Chronicity, Negative Symptoms, and Affective Symptoms

Considerable debate has centered on the importance of a chronic course for a diagnosis of schizophrenia. Almost everyone agrees that individuals who follow a classic chronic course and manifest other symptoms of schizophrenia are true schizophrenia patients. Disagreement centers on those with an episodic course—especially with a small number of episodes. Since 1980 in the United States, the *Diagnostic and Statistical Manual of Mental Disorders Third Edition, Third*

*Edition–Revised, and Fourth Edition (DSM-III, DSM-III-R, and DSM-IV,* respectively) by the American Psychiatric Association (APA; 1980, 1987, 1994) have emphasized chronicity by requiring a 6-month duration for the diagnosis of schizophrenia. In *DSM-IV, schizophreniform disorder* applies to patients with episodes lasting between 1 and 6 months, whereas *brief psychotic disorder* applies to episodes of less than 1 month, and it is considered unclear whether either diagnosis is related to schizophrenia (Siris & Lavin, 1995).

In recent decades, extensive research has focused on negative symptoms (the absence or insufficiency of normal behavior), such as poverty of thought or speech, flat or blunted affect, apathy or anhedonia, and avolition or social withdrawal (Andreasen, 2001; Sommers, 1985). These negative symptoms are contrasted with positive symptoms (the presence of abnormal functioning), which may include hallucinations, delusions, thought disorder, disorganized behavior, and inappropriate emotions (Andreasen, 2001). Some theorists view negative symptoms as the fundamental deficiency of schizophrenia; others see them as a defect or residual state resulting from and following an active psychotic state (i.e., positive symptoms). A third perspective conceptualizes positive and negative symptoms as more or less equally important semi-independent processes (Lewine, 1985). The 6-month duration requirement for a diagnosis of schizophrenia that began with *DSM-III* made negative symptoms much more salient because the active phase symptoms often do not last for 6 months—placing the burden on negative symptoms to demonstrate chronicity. Negative symptoms are conceptualized as prodromal (preceding the onset of the active phase of psychotic symptoms) or residual (continuing after the active phase of psychotic symptoms) and either can be used to satisfy the duration requirement.

The separation of schizophrenia from the affective disorders (depression and mania) constitutes a third major diagnostic issue. The presence of many patients with both schizophrenic and affective symptoms (a schizoaffective clinical picture) challenges any attempt to dichotomize the distinction between schizophrenia and affective disorders (e.g., Kendell, 1982; Meltzer, 1984; Siris & Lavin, 1995). Decisions on this issue can profoundly affect the diagnosis of schizophrenia, and the presence of large numbers of patients with schizoaffective symptoms constitutes a major problem in conceptualizing schizophrenia.

## A Brief History of the Conceptualization of Schizophrenia

Many discussions of the concept of schizophrenia begin with Kraepelin's fundamental contributions toward the end of the nineteenth century and continuing into the early twentieth century (Johnstone, 1999c). Kraepelin grouped together syndromes with disparate clinical pictures on the basis of similarities in course, outcome, and age of onset, applying the name *dementia praecox* to this new diagnostic category. He viewed the disorder as having a youthful onset, intellectual and volitional disturbances, and a chronic course with intellectual deterioration as the outcome. For Kraepelin, these characteristics were a direct manifestation of an underlying organic disturbance (i.e., psychological or psychosocial factors were not emphasized). As valuable as Kraepelin's contribution was, three issues created tension regarding his position. First, the chronic, deteriorating course was a defining feature of dementia praecox (Andreasen & Carpenter, 1993), implying that treatment was impossible. Impossibility of treatment should not be a matter of definition of a disorder, but rather an empirical correlate (Chapman & Chapman, 1973). Second, a nonnegligible minority (about 13%) of his dementia praecox patients failed to run a chronic, deteriorating course (Johnstone, 1999a). Third, onset of the disorder was not limited to the youthful onset indicated by the term praecox (Andreasen, 2001).

In response to these problems, Bleuler (1911/1950) offered a very different conceptualization of the disorder, which he renamed schizophrenia. In place of course and outcome emphasized by Kraepelin, Bleuler emphasized signs and symptoms (Andreasen & Carpenter, 1993) and distinguished between fundamental symptoms (somewhat similar to negative symptoms), which he viewed as specific to schizophrenia and as permanent or chronic features of the disorder, and accessory symptoms (somewhat similar to positive symptoms), which may be completely absent during part or all of the course of the disorder or may be very prominent (Bleuler, 1911/1950). Like Kraepelin, Bleuler hypothesized a chronic underlying physical disease process that can progress on its own to produce the full schizophrenia syndrome, but this process was associated with fundamental symptoms. Influenced strongly by Freud, Bleuler proposed that stressful events and other psychological processes could substantially influence the course of the accessory symptoms—an early statement of the popular diathesis-stress model in which a genetic diathesis or vulnerability responds to psychosocial stress by producing symptoms of psychopathology (Rosenthal, 1970; Walker & Diforio, 1997).

Bleuler's conceptualization was much broader than Kraepelin's. First, the prototypical clinical picture included more than patients with a chronic, deteriorating course. Second, Bleuler described a continuum of severity, with milder cases blending into the normal range of personality variation. Third, clinical judgment as to the presence of a splitting in the basic functions of the mind replaced a more easily observed chronic deterioration as the basis for diagnosis, making it possible to perceive schizophrenic processes in a very large number of patients.

The emphasis on signs and symptoms introduced by Bleuler combined with the difficulty of making clinical judgments as to what signs and symptoms suffice for a diagnosis of schizophrenia inevitably led to attempts to more precisely identify symptoms specific to schizophrenia. In one particularly influential attempt to achieve this goal, Schneider developed a list of *first rank* symptoms he believed to be specific to schizophrenia (Andreasen & Carpenter, 1993). The resultant list was restricted to unusual and bizarre hallucinations (e.g., hearing voices speak one's thoughts aloud, discuss one in the third person, or describe one's actions) or delusions (e.g., believing that thoughts are inserted by an external force, that one's thoughts are broadcast to the outside world and heard by others, or that one's own actions are imposed by an outside force; Johnstone, 1999a). Schneider's approach, however, has not proven to predict outcome (i.e., chronicity) in schizophrenia or to be specific to schizophrenia (Andreasen & Carpenter, 1993). Similarly, genetic studies have yielded little support for the validity of first rank symptoms when such symptoms are employed as the sole basis for the diagnosis of schizophrenia (Gottesman, McGuffin, & Farmer, 1987; McGuffin, Farmer, Gottesman, Murray, & Reveley, 1984). Nevertheless, first rank symptoms have been a prominent part of the literature on schizophrenia and sometimes are incorporated into the list of active phase symptoms in other diagnostic approaches.

## Diagnostic Approaches

A number of well-known approaches to the diagnosis of schizophrenia have been developed. In the United States, the approach since *DSM-III* is especially noteworthy for requiring a 6-month duration before schizophrenia can be diagnosed, thereby opting for the view that true schizophrenia runs a relatively chronic course. *DSM-III* was strongly influenced by what are known as the Feighner criteria (Feighner et al., 1972) from the Washington University group and by the research diagnostic criteria (RDC; Spitzer, Endicott, & Robins, 1978) from the New York State Psychiatric Institute group. The Feighner criteria strongly emphasize a chronic course by requiring a 6-month duration, an absence of affective disorder diagnosis, and such predictors of chronicity as being single, showing poor premorbid adjustment, and having a family history of schizophrenia, while requiring only one positive or active symptom. In contrast, the RDC require two active-phase symptoms and only 2 weeks duration, aiming for a concept broader than that captured by chronic

schizophrenia. At the same time, the RDC also exclude patients who meet criteria for an affective disorder. As is discussed later in this chapter, in first-admission samples this exclusion can be quite restrictive.

Whereas the aforementioned diagnostic systems were created by consensus of committees attempting to interpret the clinical and research literature, other approaches have selected signs and symptoms that predict existing clinical diagnosis as the criterion. Further, one also hopes that by identifying features common to many diagnosticians, the essence or core features of the diagnosis will be preserved while eliminating more idiosyncratic aspects (Carpenter, Strauss, & Bartko, 1973)—although, of course, this approach depends on the wisdom of current clinical diagnosis. One such system was the New Haven Index (Astrachan et al., 1972), developed during an era of a very broad concept of schizophrenia. The New Haven Index was able to predict clinicians' diagnoses in New Haven hospitals by using only signs and symptoms without mention of affective symptoms or a minimal duration. Delusions, hallucinations, and thought disorder were emphasized by requiring at least one of them and making any two of them sufficient for a diagnosis.

A second system, sponsored by the World Health Organization, came from the International Pilot Study of Schizophrenia (IPSS; Carpenter et al., 1973) involving 1,202 patients from nine countries. Stepwise discriminant function analysis was used to identify 12 items that best discriminated between patients with hospital diagnoses of *schizophrenia* or *not schizophrenia* in half the sample and cross-validated on the other half. These items included delusions (four items reflecting different types), thought disorder, restricted or flat affect, poor insight, poor rapport during the interview, unreliable information during the interview, and the absence of three indications of affective disorders (elation, depressed facial expressions, waking early). One point was awarded for the presence of each of the nine positive indicators and for the *absence* of each of the three affective symptoms. A table indicating the agreement with hospital diagnoses of *schizophrenia* and *not schizophrenia* (in the two samples) as a function of the number of points required to make a diagnosis showed that requiring five or more points resulted in a relatively broad concept of schizophrenia—detecting 80–81% of hospital diagnoses of schizophrenia, while diagnosing as schizophrenic 13–22% of patients not diagnosed as having schizophrenia by the hospital. With the more restrictive criterion of six or more points, these numbers changed to 63–66% and 4–6%, respectively. The authors suggested choosing the criterion (e.g., five or six points) for a diagnosis of schizophrenia depending on the application—hence the term *Flexible System,* which has been applied to this approach.

If the different diagnostic systems all assessed the same clinical phenomenon but differed only in the threshold for making a diagnosis, they would show a hierarchical relationship: Broader systems, which diagnose more patients as having schizophrenia, would include all patients diagnosed as having schizophrenia by the narrower systems. Unfortunately, that is not the case, and even the narrow systems did not show high agreement (Gottesman et al., 1987). For example, Strauss and Gift (1977) applied seven diagnostic systems to 272 patients in their *first hospitalization* and found that 122 were diagnosed as schizophrenic by at least one system. The two broadest systems were the New Haven Index and the (IPSS) Flexible System-5 with 68 and 57 diagnoses, respectively. Even though they are very broad, these systems missed about half the 122 patients diagnosed as having schizophrenia by another system. The three narrowest systems were the RDC, Feighner criteria, and Flexible System-6 with 4, 9, and 34 diagnoses, respectively. To illustrate poor agreement even among narrower systems, the Feighner criteria and the RDC agreed on a schizophrenia diagnosis for only two patients, and the Flexible System-6 diagnosed as schizophrenic only 44% of those called schizophrenic by the Feighner criteria. For the broader systems, the Flexible System-5 diagnosed as schizophrenic only 65% of the New Haven Index cases. The authors noted that the exclusion criteria for affective symptoms were responsible for the extreme narrowness of the Feighner criteria and the RDC because affective symptoms are prominent in first-admission samples of hospitalized patients.

Although these diagnostic systems show greater agreement and a more hierarchical structure with more chronic hospitalized patients (Endicott et al., 1982), these data serve to illustrate significant diagnostic disagreement and the importance of chronicity and affective symptoms in making a diagnosis. Strauss and Gift (1977) make another important point about the implications of attempts to narrow the diagnosis of schizophrenia to a chronic, Kraepelinian view: Such attempts shift the problem rather than solving it, creating large numbers of undiagnosed (Feighner criteria) or schizoaffective patients (RDC). Logically, if such large groups of patients are not to be considered as having schizophrenia, then presumably alternative etiologic hypotheses need to be developed and evidence marshaled of discriminant validity vis-à-vis schizophrenia, which has not been done.

This underscoring of some uncertainties in diagnosis should not be taken to imply a chaotic situation. Quite to the contrary, even with our imperfect conceptualizations of schizophrenia, many reliable findings have been reported, especially in research on genetic influences. Indeed, the genetic data constitute some of the most compelling findings in all of psychopathology, and those findings in turn can inform diagnostic choices.

## THE CONTRIBUTION OF GENETICS

### Genetic Studies of Schizophrenia

The genetics of schizophrenia is one of the great stories in research on psychopathology. This research demonstrated unequivocally that genetic factors are important to the etiology of schizophrenia (e.g., Bassett, Chow, O'Neill, & Brzustowicz, 2001; Gottesman, 1991; Gottesman & Moldin, 1998; Kendler, 1999; Kendler & Diehl, 1995; Tsuang & Faraone, 1995). Having established that point, this research additionally provides a foundation for examining the validity of concepts of schizophrenia—that is, which ways of diagnosing schizophrenia produce the strongest findings from a genetic perspective?

The story begins with family risk for schizophrenia: It has long been known that schizophrenia runs in families (Kendler & Diehl, 1995). In these studies, one starts with a series of index cases or *probands* with a diagnosis of schizophrenia and then ascertains the risk of schizophrenia among their relatives. Risk for schizophrenia increases with genetic similarity. For example, using pooled European studies from 1920 to 1978, Gottesman et al. (1987) calculated the following risks of (definite) schizophrenia: first-degree relatives 7.3–9.35%, second-degree relatives 2.65–2.94%, and third-degree relatives 1.56%. Similarly, for seven more modern studies with improved methodology, Kendler and Diehl (1993) calculated an estimated morbid risk of schizophrenia among first-degree relatives to be 4.8% for schizophrenia probands compared with 0.5% for control probands, confirming a roughly tenfold increased risk reported by earlier family studies. Of course, in family studies environmental similarity is confounded with genetic similarity, creating a need for twin and adoption studies to clarify interpretation of family risk data.

Twin studies exploit an experiment of nature that creates monozygotic (MZ) and same-sex dizygotic (DZ) twins with 100% (exactly) and 50% (on average) of their genes in common, respectively. Because many aspects of the environment are equally similar for MZ and DZ twins (see Kendler & Diehl, 1995, for a discussion of this assumption), comparison of risk for schizophrenia in the cotwins of schizophrenia probands offers a strong test of the genetic hypothesis. As with family studies, twin studies from the first half of the twentieth century had reported results supportive of the genetic hypothesis: MZ cotwins of a schizophrenia proband have a higher probability of schizophrenia than do DZ cotwins.

These results seemed strongly supportive of the genetic hypothesis, but critics questioned them on methodological grounds. They argued that knowledge of zygosity contaminated the (nonblindfolded) diagnoses of schizophrenia, allowing the investigator's beliefs about heredity to bias the outcome (Gottesman, 1991). However, in a sophisticated twin study that laid to rest methodological criticisms, Gottesman and Shields (1966) reported 50% concordance in MZ twins compared with only 12% for DZ twins. Other modern twin studies yielded similar results. Gottesman (1991) further reported that a weighted average of the four recent (since 1963) European twin studies showed 48% MZ and 17% DZ twin concordance, a more recent British study showed 40.8% and 5.3% concordance (Cardno et al., 1999), and a summary of four European studies (including Cardno et al., 1999) and one Japanese twin study conducted in the 1990s reported heritabilities of the order of 80% (Cardno & Gottesman, 2000). Thus, twin studies strongly support the genetic hypothesis (Kendler & Diehl, 1995).

Adoption studies completed the final step, in which genetic and environmental similarity are unconfounded. Heston and Denney (1968) followed up the adopted-away but now-adult offspring of mothers hospitalized for schizophrenia in Oregon. At an average age of approximately 36 years, 5 of 47 experimental group (mother schizophrenic) adoptees had developed schizophrenia compared with none out of 50 matched control adoptees (mother not schizophrenic), strongly supporting the genetic explanation for the initial observation that schizophrenia runs in families.

A second, larger adoption study conducted in Denmark exploited excellent government records listing births (including adoption information), psychiatric diagnoses, and current addresses for everyone in the country. In the initial report on the Copenhagen sample, Kety and his colleagues (Kety, Rosenthal, Wender, & Schulsinger, 1968; Kety, Rosenthal, Wender, Schulsinger, & Jacobsen, 1978) selected adopted children who later developed schizophrenia, along with a control group with no psychiatric history; using hospital records, they ascertained the rate of *schizophrenic spectrum disorders* (a broad concept, intended to miss no one with possible schizophrenia) among the roughly 150 biological and 80 adoptive relatives of these index cases. Consistent with the genetic hypothesis, there was an elevated rate of schizophrenia among the biological relatives (8.7%) of the experimental index cases compared with biological relatives of control index cases (1.9%) and with the adoptive relatives of both the experimental group (2.7%) and the control group (3.6%). These results were confirmed in a later report based on interview-based diagnoses and data from all of Denmark (Kety et al., 1994), as well as a reanalysis of the Danish interview-based

data employing *DSM-III* diagnoses (Kendler, Gruenberg, & Kinney, 1994) and an independent adoption study in Finland (Tienari, 1991).

To summarize, the finding that schizophrenia runs in families could possibly be due to either genetic or environmental influences, but replicated findings from twin and adoption studies support the genetic interpretation. This conclusion raises two important questions: (a) What genetic model applies to schizophrenia and (b) what concepts of schizophrenia are supported by these data?

## Genetic Models

### Single-Gene Model

A single-gene model is attractive because it would be possible to locate the gene, study its properties, and ultimately understand its effects on brain structure or function that lead to schizophrenia. It would also be possible to identify non-schizophrenic carriers of the gene and to study those individuals to determine what environmental variables trigger the development of schizophrenia. Unfortunately, single-gene models have such a poor match to existing data that they can be rejected—at least for a large majority of cases of schizophrenia (Andreasen, 2001; Bassett et al., 2001; Faraone, Green, Seidman, & Tsuang, 2001; Gottesman & Moldin, 1998; Kendler, 1999; Kendler & Diehl, 1993, 1995; McGue & Gottesman, 1989; Tsuang & Faraone, 1997). Furthermore, attempts to identify a single gene through linkage with genetic markers in family pedigrees has been disappointing (Gottesman & Moldin, 1998; Kendler, 1999; Tsuang & Faraone, 1997).

### Multifactorial Polygenic Model

Gottesman and Shields (1967) were the first to apply the multifactorial polygenic (MFP) model to schizophrenia, in which a large number of genes—each often assumed to be of small effect—along with environmental influences contribute in an additive fashion to the overall liability for schizophrenia. The model assumes a threshold such that schizophrenia develops when total liability exceeds the threshold. In general, the genetic data are consistent with MFP models with a threshold (e.g., Andreasen, 2001; Faraone & Tsuang, 1985; Gottesman et al., 1987; Gottesman & Moldin, 1998; Kendler & Diehl, 1993; Tsuang & Faraone, 1997).

Parenthetically, there always has been some theoretical tension between the assumption of *additivity* in the MFP and the implication of an *interaction* effect in the diathesis-stress model—that is, stressors produce pathology only in those with a diathesis (Gottesman, 1991). The additivity assumption in the MFP is appropriate because most of the extant data fit this more parsimonious model, but interaction effects are to be expected, in which genetic vulnerability increases one's sensitivity to environmental influences that tend to induce schizophrenia (Gottesman & Moldin, 1998; Gottesman & Shields, 1972; Meehl, 1962). In recent years, evidence has accumulated of such greater effects of stressors among genetically vulnerable individuals (e.g., children or siblings of schizophrenia probands) for obstetric complications (Tsuang & Faraone, 1995), disturbed communication in adoptive parents (Gottesman & Moldin, 1998), and for inferred but unspecified stressors among second-generation African-Caribbean immigrants to the United Kingdom (Moldin & Gottesman, 1997). Additionally, there may well be interaction effects among genes, called epistasis (Bassett et al., 2001; Gottesman & Moldin, 1998).

### Mixed Models

Although the MFP model might be considered the default hypothesis because of the good fit with genetic data, intermediate and mixed models cannot be excluded and, in fact, are likely. In the limited-loci-polygenic model (Faraone & Tsuang, 1985) a small number of loci (e.g., two loci with two alleles each) contribute to schizophrenia. In order to fit the empirical findings, these models must assume a modest genetic contribution to schizophrenia, leaving a large environmental contribution. A similar situation obtains with mixed genetic models (a single gene combined with polygenes), which can be made consistent with either (a) a rare (e.g., 10% of schizophrenic cases) single gene with high penetrance (e.g., .60) or (b) a much more common single gene that has low penetrance (Gottesman & McGue, 1991; Kendler & Diehl, 1993). These latter two models probably are more interesting than the limited-loci-polygenic models because they are consistent with relatively high heritability overall (single gene plus polygenes) and potentially offer an explanation for some of the heterogeneity in the schizophrenia phenotype. The common single gene (or major gene) in particular is of interest because it might be associated with a more chronic course (Iacono, 1998). Nevertheless, the MFP model is a major component of any model consistent with genetic data on schizophrenia—even if there are one or more major genes with larger effects. Additionally, a broad review of the behavior genetics literature suggests that the kind of behavior represented by the construct of schizophrenia is likely to involve polygenic influences (Plomin, 1990; Plomin, DeFries, McLearn, & Rutter, 1997).

The preceding reasoning with respect to the MFP model applies to the majority of schizophrenia cases and does not exclude rare cases of schizophrenia or schizophrenia-like psychoses attributable to another etiology. For example, Tsuang and Faraone (1995) concluded that in some rare cases gross chromosomal abnormalities cause schizophrenia, and Gottesman (1991) listed numerous drugs, somatic disorders, and genetic and chromosomal factors that produce phenocopies of schizophrenia (i.e., schizophrenia-like psychoses that do not share the etiology of typical schizophrenia).

A small deletion of genetic material on the long arm of Chromosome 22 (22q) has been associated with a form of schizophrenia that develops in roughly 25% of individuals with the deletion and accounts for up to 2% of individuals with schizophrenia (Bassett et al., 2001). Although the 22q deletion is inherited in an autosomal dominant pattern, due to reproductive disadvantage such transmission is greatly reduced. Consequently, over 90% of the cases are due to de novo mutations, which in turn are more likely with increasing paternal age. More broadly, Gottesman (1991), when comparing schizophrenia to some extent with mental retardation, speculated that a mixed model will prove most appropriate for schizophrenia. In this model, some rare cases are attributed to single genes and others to primarily environmental factors, but the vast majority are attributed to one of two variations of the MFP. Of this MFP group, up to 10% might reflect the effect of a specific major gene combined with polygenic and environmental influences (the mixed genetic model with a more common single gene described previously), whereas the remaining 90% reflect the standard MFP model of polygenic and environmental influences. Although a specific major gene operating in a polygenic context has not yet been identified, identification of such a gene would constitute a major breakthrough.

### Specific and Nonspecific Liability

As noted previously, the MFP model assumes that polygenic and environmental influences combine to produce total liability with a threshold for the appearance of schizophrenia. The liability is further assumed to be distributed normally in the population as a whole and to consist of *specific* genetic, nonspecific genetic, and nonspecific environmental liability, as well as genetic and environmental assets that reduce liability (Gottesman, 1991). The modifier *specific* means that this aspect of the genetic contribution is specific to schizophrenia and not to any other disorders, whereas nonspecific factors affect liability but are not themselves specific to schizophrenia.

Relatively little has been said about the nature of nonspecific liability. As conceptualized within a diathesis-stress framework, environmental stress (physical or psychosocial) has nonspecific effects that influence but are not limited to the risk for schizophrenia. Similarly, it is reasonable to suggest that among the nonspecific genetic liability will be characteristics that influence the amount of stress the person experiences (Fowles, 1992b; also see Meehl's classic 1962 paper for discussion of nonspecific factors involving vulnerability to stress). Two examples can serve to illustrate this point. First, all other things being equal, individuals with an anxiety-prone or stress-reactive temperament will *experience* more stress than would less anxious individuals, thereby contributing to nonspecific liability. Second, individuals whose genetic endowment pushes toward lower intelligence are more likely to experience academic, occupational, economic, and even interpersonal aversive experiences that make the world objectively more stressful. These suggestions are consistent with Heston and Denney's (1968) report that among the adopted-away offspring of mothers with schizophrenia, there was a trend toward an increased rate of mental retardation and anxiety disorders. In selecting for mothers who clearly had schizophrenia, the authors may have selected for nonspecific genetic liability as well as specific genetic liability. On the other hand, inasmuch as presumably there are a large number of nonspecific effects, selection for any specific characteristic (e.g., low intelligence) would be weak and difficult to demonstrate. Furthermore, this nonspecific liability would segregate independently of specific liability, contributing to a varied collection of vulnerabilities and deficits among the relatives of schizophrenia probands—consistent with the impression of substantial rates of psychiatric abnormalities among relatives (Gottesman, 1991; Gottesman & Shields, 1976)—that add to the difficulty of identifying the true schizophrenic spectrum.

### Environmental Liability and Episodic Course

An important feature of the MFP model needs to be underscored. With a fixed threshold and additive genetic and environmental liability, a trade-off exists between the genetic and environmental liability. As genetic liability increases, less environmental liability is needed to reach threshold (Fowles, 1992b, 1994; Gottesman, 1991; Gottesman & Shields, 1982; Siris & Lavin, 1995; Zubin & Spring, 1977). We do not know how many genes are involved or how high the maximum liability can be, but it is generally assumed that there *can* be enough genetic liability so that relatively little environmental stress is needed to reach threshold. Such individuals are likely to run a chronic course because their total liability will be above threshold most or all of the time. As the genetic contribution to liability diminishes, it must be offset with greater contributions from the environment. In those cases, the course is likely to be episodic because most of the time the

individual will not encounter that much stress. Of course, stress can be more or less chronic, in which case even substantial contributions to liability from stress can be associated with chronicity (Wing, 1978). Finally, as the genetic liability diminishes even further, a point can be reached at which normal amounts of environmental stress will not be sufficient to bring total liability to threshold, making such fortunate individuals not schizophrenic for genetic reasons. In this conceptualization of the underlying etiology, episodic schizophrenia differs from chronic schizophrenia quantitatively but not qualitatively. It may be practical to distinguish between cases that—on average at least—are more genetic versus less genetic, but the etiologic model remains the same for both.

### Summary

It can be seen from this brief review that the MFP model accounts well for genetic data, but one cannot exclude contributions from single rare genes with relatively high penetrance, purely environmental etiologies, and more common single genes with low penetrance. It is important to note that all attempts to fit genetic models to extant data conclude that environmental factors cannot be neglected. Ironically, in this sense the genetic data provide the strongest evidence for environmental contributions to schizophrenia. This evidence is neutral with respect to whether the environmental contribution involves psychosocial factors or physical environmental factors. Two major lines of research provide support for the hypothesis that psychosocial stress does contribute to the onset of schizophrenia—life events and aversive family interactions, both of which are reviewed later in this chapter—but evidence also strongly supports physical environmental contributions.

## ENVIRONMENTAL INFLUENCES

### Variability in Outcome

A contribution of life events to the onset of schizophrenia became more likely after Bleuler broadened the concept of schizophrenia to include those who would show improvement. Additionally, with this outcome heterogeneity, it was inevitable that investigators would try to find predictors of good versus poor outcome. One approach distinguished between process and reactive schizophrenia (Chapman & Chapman, 1973; Neale & Oltmanns, 1980). *Reactive schizophrenia* has a rapid onset associated with a life event, a normal premorbid adjustment, and a good prognosis. *Process schizophrenia* has an insidious onset, poor premorbid social adjustment, affective flattening (a classic symptom of chronic schizophrenia), and a poor prognosis. Premorbid adjustment is the most powerful correlate of prognosis. In another tradition, the term *schizophreniform disorder* originally referred to psychoses with good prognoses in order to distinguish them from so-called genuine schizophrenia (Siris & Lavin, 1995)—that is, Kraepelinian chronic, deteriorating schizophrenia. The predictors of good outcome are now found in the good prognosis subtype of schizophreniform disorder in *DSM-IV* (American Psychiatric Association, 1994, 2000; see also Siris & Lavin, 1995) with confusion or perplexity during the episode and absence of blunted or flat affect being added to good premorbid adjustment and rapid onset as predictors of good outcome. The presence of affective symptoms also indicate a better prognosis (Siris & Lavin, 1995).

## Life Events

### Interpretation of Outcome Heterogeneity

A plausible interpretation of the process-reactive or poor versus good prognosis distinction is that the process or poor prognosis cases have greater (possibly largely genetic) vulnerability that adversely affects the premorbid personality and develops into schizophrenia without the additional liability of a noteworthy life event. In contrast, the reactive or good prognosis cases are somewhat less vulnerable to schizophrenia and develop normally until a stressful life event adds to liability and raises them above threshold for schizophrenia. In many cases, the stress response to negative life events does not last forever, the stress-based liability diminishes, and the person recovers from schizophrenic symptoms. This interpretation of the nature of the process-reactive distinction implies that life events and the associated stress response can contribute to the onset of schizophrenia but are likely to do so most obviously for individuals with a sudden onset of schizophrenic symptoms.

### Life Event Studies

In a classic study consistent with the aforementioned reasoning, Birley and Brown (1970) assessed life events during the 12 weeks prior to the onset of symptoms among patients whose symptom onset could be dated within a week. This datable-onset requirement necessarily precludes patients with an insidious onset and samples strongly in favor of reactive or good prognosis schizophrenia (approximately 50% of the schizophrenic patients were excluded by this criterion). Nonpatient controls from the community were asked about life events in the 12 weeks before the interview. The schizophrenic patients showed an increased rate of life events (60% of patients) in the 3 weeks prior to onset relative to earlier 3-week periods and relative to all 3-week periods for the controls (averaging about 21%).

For life events, there is a concern about the direction of effect—whether incipient psychotic symptoms cause the life event rather than the reverse. The authors rated the life events for their independence of the individual's behavior (e.g., losing one's job because a factory closed clearly would be independent). The results were similar to those previously mentioned for the restricted group of events classified as independent: 46% for the most recent 3 weeks for schizophrenic patients compared with 12–14% for other 3-week periods for patients and all 3-week periods for controls. Thus, this study found that life events were associated with onset of symptoms among the roughly 50% of patients with a datable onset and that the time frame for life event to symptoms was relatively short—about 3 weeks.

It was 17 years before a replication of this important finding was published. The World Health Organization reported data from eight cities around the world (Day et al., 1987), each site essentially constituting an attempt at independent replication. Because control subjects were not available, this study focused on the percentage of patients with life events in the 3 weeks before a datable onset relative to the three earlier 3-week periods. The predicted elevations were statistically significant at six of the eight sites for total life events and five of the eight sites for independent life events with identical trends at the remaining sites (not significant because of smaller numbers of patients).

Ventura, Nuechterlein, Lukoff, and Hardesty (1989) noted that the previous two studies involved retrospective memories of life events after the onset of schizophrenic symptoms (possibly permitting memory bias for patients who want to attribute the onset of schizophrenia to stress) and argued that it was important to replicate the results in a prospective study. They tracked 30 patients with schizophrenia following discharge from the hospital with assessment of schizophrenic symptoms biweekly (to detect relapse) and of life events monthly. Using data from the last life event interview before relapse-exacerbation, they found an increased number of life events (both total and independent) relative to other time periods for the 11-patient relapse group and relative to comparable months for the nonrelapse group. Although these patients were not selected for a datable onset, they had shown sufficient recovery that they could be monitored for relapse. At least in that sense they were selected not to include the most chronic, process cases of schizophrenia that tend to be less responsive to treatment. Thus, similar results were obtained in a prospective study, thereby eliminating the possibility of memory bias present in the Birley and Brown and the Day et al. studies.

### Extreme Life Events

The aforementioned studies were conducted with patients suffering from typical schizophrenia. Dohrenwend and Egri (1981) took the argument a step further and applied it to battlefield psychoses that—at a symptom level—are indistinguishable from schizophrenia, although they are likely to remit quickly. Finding that the individuals involved had shown no other evidence of schizophrenia, they proposed that very severe stress can contribute to a schizophrenic reaction in those without any obvious vulnerability. Although most would argue that these battlefield psychoses are not cases of true schizophrenia, a parsimonious model would suggest that these individuals may have some genetic liability to schizophrenia but only at a level that requires extreme stress to bring them to threshold. As soon as that extreme stress passes, they should recover and (hopefully) never again experience psychotic symptoms. Inasmuch as the vast majority of battlefield casualties do not involve symptoms of schizophrenia (Gottesman, 1991), the assumption that some degree of genetic liability combines with the extreme stress to produce a schizophrenic syndrome offers a possible explanation for why only certain individuals are afflicted. This perspective perhaps parallels that for amphetamine psychosis—in which massive increases in dopamine produced by stimulant drugs produce a schizophrenia-like condition in normal individuals—that routinely is cited as evidence of the involvement of dopaminergic activity in schizophrenia.

### Life Events Act on a Small Percent of the Population

The implications of this literature on life events—in the context of the MFP model—are that noteworthy stressful life events are not necessary for the small number of individuals with a heavy genetic loading for schizophrenia and are not sufficient for the large number (perhaps over 95% of the population) with a modest or no genetic loading (Gottesman, 1991). Between these extremes, a range of genetic liability for schizophrenia can be combined with stressful life events to bring the individual to the threshold for manifestation of schizophrenic symptoms. In a quantitative sense, the contribution of stress need not be large for the population as a whole because it centers on a small percentage of the population with enough genetic liability to be vulnerable to environmental stress (Fowles, 1992b, 1994; Gottesman & Shields, 1976; Siris & Lavin, 1995).

### Aversive Family Interactions

Not all stressful environments involve obvious life events. Some can be more subtle, as in the case of aversive family interactions. In a study that initiated an important line of research on family interactions and schizophrenia, Brown, Birley, and Wing (1972) monitored 9-month relapse among 101 patients with schizophrenia discharged from the hospital to live with family. At the patient's admission to the hospital, the authors rated an extensive interview with key relatives for number of critical comments and unusual emotional overinvolvement, these ratings being combined into a single index of family expressed emotion (EE). High EE was associated with more frequent relapse and interacted with both hours of contact with high-EE families and compliance with medication. This study was replicated by Vaughn and Leff (1976) and the pooled results summarized by Leff (1976) and Leff and Vaughn (1985). Based on these pooled data, 51% of patients returning to high-EE families relapsed versus 13% for those returning to low-EE families. Of those in high-EE families, 69% with more than 35 hours/week contact (in the same room) with their relatives relapsed compared with only 28% with less than 35 hours/week contact. Additionally, medication reduced relapse in high-EE families, with relapse ranging from 15% for those on medication and having fewer than 35 hours/week contact to 92% for the combination of high contact and no medication. Hours of contact and medication had no effect on relapse among patients with low-EE families.

The basic finding that aversive family interactions in the form of high EE predicts a higher rate of relapse has been replicated many times (Hooley & Hiller, 1998). Debate has centered on the direction of the effect: Does high EE cause relapse, or could both relapse and family reactions to the patient reflect the effects of a third variable, such as severity of the symptoms of schizophrenia? Although this question has not been fully resolved and possibly there are bidirectional effects, evidence suggests strongly that high EE among relatives does contribute in important ways to relapse of schizophrenic symptoms (Hooley & Hiller, 1998; Linszen et al., 1997; Nuechterlein, Snyder, & Mintz, 1992).

### Institutional Environments

In the famous three-hospital study, Wing and Brown (1970) found that negative symptoms in schizophrenia (slowness, underactivity, blunting of affect, and poverty of speech), called the *clinical poverty syndrome,* varied across time and hospitals as a function of the institutional environment—a phenomenon termed *institutionalism.* Clinical poverty was high on wards that placed many restrictions on patients and provided few opportunities for activities; in contrast, it was minimized on wards that placed fewer restrictions and required more socially positive activities. Wing (1978) attributed clinical poverty to "a protective reaction against the painful effects of social interaction when one has inadequate equipment for communication" (p. 606)—that is, some negative symptoms can be seen as a form of passive or active avoidance. In agreement, Carpenter, Heinrichs, and Wagman (1985) noted that in some cases, social withdrawal may reflect a combination of diminished social drive and a reaction to the development of positive symptoms and to aversive environments. In a similar observation, Manfred Bleuler (1974) described the elimination of what he called catastrophic schizophrenia by improved hospital care prior to the advent of antipsychotic medications. Catastrophic schizophrenia, which was the prototype for Kraepelin's dementia praecox, was characterized by an acute onset of a severe psychosis, followed with little improvement by a severe chronic psychosis lasting until death.

These phenomena reflect an interaction between a vulnerability among schizophrenia patients and the hospital environment. The fundamental point is that negative symptoms are not hard-wired manifestations of a genetic disease; rather, they are secondary to the schizophrenic process interacting with the environment. Thus, the environment contributes to some degree even to a classic Kraepelinian clinical picture.

## Cortisol as an Index of Stress During Episodes

If stress contributes to liability in schizophrenia, at least a portion of patients should be experiencing stress during episodes. Cortisol in blood or saliva in humans serves as an index of activation of the hypothalamic-pituitary-adrenal (HPA) axis, in turn a primary manifestation of the stress response in humans. Additionally, failure to suppress cortisol secretion in response to administration of the synthetic glucocorticoid dexamethasone reflects poor feedback HPA regulation. In studies reviewed by Walker and Diforio (1997), increased baseline cortisol levels were associated with positive psychotic symptoms among patients with schizophrenia in cross-sectional and longitudinal studies and were high immediately prior to psychotic episodes, consistent with precipitation of symptom exacerbation by increased cortisol levels. Failure to suppress cortisol in the dexamethasone suppression test (DST) was associated more strongly with negative than with positive symptoms, although the difference might have been due to greater reduction of positive symptoms by medication. Similarly, DST failure was associated with several indicators of poor prognosis—poor premorbid

adjustment, enlarged ventricals, worsening when medication is suspended, and poorer outcome over time. These findings strengthen the inference that psychosocial stress contributes to nonspecific liability in schizophrenia.

## Physical Environmental Influences

### Physical Environment as a Primary Cause of Schizophrenia

The possibility that schizophrenia is attributable to nongenetic biological factors has been attractive to many investigators. One favorite has been the hypothesis that an unspecified virus causes brain damage that presents—perhaps years later—as schizophrenia. However, one famous British advocate of that position later came to the conclusion that there was no evidence to support it (Crow in Liddle, Carpenter, & Crow, 1993). Invoking another important candidate, early trauma such as birth injury was proposed by Murray, Lewis, and Reveley (1985) to produce nongenetic forms of schizophrenia. They suggested that such trauma might account for the afflicted twin in discordant MZ twin pairs.

Gottesman and Bertelsen (1989) rebutted this argument by examining the risk of schizophrenia spectrum disorders among the offspring of both twins in discordant MZ twin pairs. They found an elevated risk of spectrum disorders that was equally high for the offspring of the healthy and afflicted cotwins and comparable to that for offspring of schizophrenia probands in general, exactly what would be predicted by a genetic hypothesis because of the identical genotype for the healthy cotwin. According to the Murray et al. hypothesis, there is no reason for increased risk for the offspring of the healthy twin (or the afflicted twin, for that matter; see Gottesman et al., 1987). The Gottesman and Bertelsen results demonstrate that the genetic hypothesis applies to a large majority of discordant MZ twins (and, by implication, to a large majority of all other cases of schizophrenia). Such evidence does not preclude the possibility that there are some cases of schizophrenia attributable to viral infection, obstetrical complications, or head injuries, but the number of such cases must be so few that they did not affect the results in the Gottesman and Bertelsen study, and there is little empirical support for environmental factors as a primary etiology of schizophrenia (Bassett et al., 2001).

### Physical Environment as Nonspecific Liability

In the context of the expectation of environmental contributions to schizophrenia in the MFP model, physical insults to the brain may constitute part of the nonspecific contribution of the environment, acting as a stressor to increase risk of schizophrenia in individuals with a genetic vulnerability (Walker & Diforio, 1997). As discussed previously in connection with the process-reactive distinction, patients whose onset of schizophrenia is associated with a life event should—on average—have less genetic liability than do patients without a life event. On that assumption, the relatives of persons with reactive schizophrenia should be at lower risk for schizophrenia than are the relatives of persons with a process schizophrenia. Gottesman (1991) cited an older study in Germany that included head injuries as somatic life events associated with the onset of schizophrenia. As expected from this reasoning, the siblings of patients with somatic stressors had a lower risk of schizophrenia (4.8%) than did siblings of patients with no stressors of any kind (10%). Along with other, more anecdotal (but nevertheless informative) evidence, these findings led Gottesman (1991) to include head injuries among the list of stressors that increase the risk of episodes among genetically vulnerable individuals.

Although the evidence is mixed, pregnancy and birth complications appear to be associated with an increased risk of schizophrenia (Johnstone, 1999b)—especially in the second trimester (Bunney & Bunney, 1999). Consistent with this finding, Gottesman (1991) cited a review of twin studies by McNeil and Kaij suggesting that obstetrical complications (pregnancy or birth complications and problems within 4 weeks of birth) may be stressors that combine with genetic vulnerability to produce schizophrenia. Similarly, Andreasen (2001) summarized findings that viral infections during pregnancy and other birth complications contribute to the development of schizophrenia, but they apparently do so in combination with genetic factors. Tsuang and Faraone (1995) found support for both obstetric complications and viral infections and proposed that their effects could best be conceptualized in the context of the MFP model.

### The Genain Quadruplets

The contribution of other than genetic factors to heterogeneity is underscored by a famous study of the Genain (identical) quadruplets (Mirsky et al., 2000; Rosenthal, 1963), all of whom developed schizophrenia. Although they were genetically identical, these four sisters showed very different clinical pictures, age at onset, course, and outcome. This varied manifestation of schizophrenia in spite of genetic identity underscores the importance of environmental factors—both physical (e.g., brain injury at birth) and psychosocial (e.g., differential treatment by parents)—as contributors to the heterogeneity of schizophrenia (Mirsky et al., 2000).

### Summary

To summarize, all attempts to fit genetic models to the data on family, twin, and adoption studies conclude that the environment makes some contribution to the etiology of schizophrenia; this conclusion is consistent with the diathesis-stress hypothesis. More direct evidence supports the inclusion of psychological stressors such as life events, aversive interpersonal interactions, and battlefield conditions as contributors to the onset of episodes of schizophrenia. Similarly, institutional environments influence negative symptoms in schizophrenia. Additionally, physical insults such as head injuries, obstetrical complications, and possibly viral infections contribute to the development of schizophrenia in genetically vulnerable individuals, although it may be that in relatively rare cases, physical insults alone produce a schizophrenia-like clinical condition. On average, the greater the contribution of psychological or physical stress to overall liability, the less the genetic contribution needs to be—with subsequent reduced risk of schizophrenia among the relatives.

## THE CONCEPT OF SCHIZOPHRENIA FROM A GENETIC PERSPECTIVE

In addition to pointing toward environmental contributions, the genetics literature provides an important perspective in a number of ways on the conceptualization of phenotypic heterogeneity. First, variation in genetic liability in the MFP model has implications for conceptualizing phenotypic heterogeneity. Second, it is possible to compare the validity of the diagnosis of schizophrenia for different diagnostic approaches from a genetic perspective. Assuming that invalid diagnoses will add error variance and undermine the magnitude of findings, diagnostic approaches that yield weaker results are less valid. Third, the genetic perspective can be used to evaluate different subtypes for inclusion in the schizophrenia spectrum.

### Severity of Genetic Loading

As already implied, one form of genetic heterogeneity with phenotypic consequences is to be expected from the MFP model: a dimension of severity of genetic liability (Gottesman, 1991; Gottesman et al., 1987) with consequences for family risk and course. This assumption has been documented most clearly with family risk data, in which family members of more severe phenotypes (e.g., nuclear, Kraepelin's hebephrenic and catatonic, process, chronic, negative symptom, Crow's

Type II) have a greater risk of schizophrenia than do relatives of those with other, less severe phenotypes (e.g., nonnuclear, Kraepelin's paranoid and simple, reactive, nonchronic, positive symptom, Crow's Type I). For example, children of those with hebephrenic and catatonic subtypes—sometimes called nuclear schizophrenia because of their chronic, severe course—have about a 20% risk of schizophrenia compared with only 10% for the children of the milder paranoid and simple schizophrenic subtypes (Gottesman, 1991). Additionally, differences in the severity of genetic liability will on average be related to differences in course—high genetic liability is associated with a more chronic course and less high genetic liability with a more episodic course combined with life events as precipitants of episodes (Gottesman, 1991; Siris & Lavin, 1995). In examining this question, Gottesman et al. (1987) found no results that could not be attributed to a continuum of severity within the concept of schizophrenia.

If these variations in family risk, course, and outcome are reflections of severity of liability in the MFP model and are not attributable to qualitatively different genetic etiologies, then subtypes should not breed true, so to speak, in family studies—that is, all subtypes or forms of schizophrenia should be found among relatives, regardless of the subtype of the index case. The results have been clear: Although there is some tendency for subtypes to breed true, all types of schizophrenia are found in family pedigrees, contradicting the hypothesis that schizophrenia can be subdivided on the basis of qualitatively different genetic effects (Gottesman, 1991; Gottesman et al., 1987; Gottesman & Shields, 1982). The polygenic model, then, can account for some of the heterogeneity in schizophrenia without recourse to hypothesizing qualitatively different underlying genetic etiologies. Of course, etiologic heterogeneity remains a possibility—as indicated previously—in the form of major genes in a polygenic context, rare single genes with high penetrance, and purely environmental effects (see also Kendler & Diehl, 1993).

## Breadth of the Concept of Schizophrenia

### Twin Studies

Twin studies have been used to advantage to examine the optimal breadth of the concept of schizophrenia. Gottesman (1991) had eight experts diagnose 120 case histories compiled in the course of the Gottesman and Shields (1966) Maudsley twin study. The breadth of the concept of schizophrenia varied across diagnosticians, ranging from a narrow approach that identified only 17 cases out of the 120 to a broad concept that diagnosed 79 cases. Each expert's diagnoses

were evaluated on the basis of the largest difference in MZ versus DZ concordance. A middle-of-the-road breadth of concept was found to be superior both to very broad and very narrow approaches.

Gottesman et al. (1987; Gottesman, 1991) used the Gottesman and Shields twin sample to evaluate *DSM-III,* RDC, and Feighner criteria. *DSM-III* yielded good results: 47.5% MZ, 9.5% DZ concordance. RDC and Feighner criteria yielded comparable results, but only if these stringent diagnostic systems were broadened to include probable schizophrenia. Use of Schneider first rank symptoms alone (presence of any one symptom justifies a diagnosis of schizophrenia) yielded very poor results: Only a small number of diagnoses of schizophrenia and the anomalous finding that DZ concordance was higher than MZ concordance. Use of Crow's Type II criteria (discussed later in this chapter) yielded only three cases, necessitating substitution of a mixed type (Type I plus Type II) for comparison with a positive-symptom-only type (cf. Fenton & McGlashan, 1992, for similar findings). It is important to underscore that this test of the diagnostic approaches was based on longitudinal research in which a great deal of information about the course of the disorder over a period of time had been collected. Diagnostic approaches requiring a chronic course do much better with such comprehensive data than they do when applied to cross-sectional studies involving a single assessment at one point in time. Gottesman et al. (1987), for example, cite a study in which the Feighner criteria failed to diagnose 32% of cases based on cross-sectional data when compared with later diagnoses based on longitudinal data.

In the original report using the Maudsley twin study sample with *DSM-III* diagnoses, Farmer, McGuffin, and Gottesman (1987) used the ratio of MZ concordance to DZ concordance to evaluate whether broadening the spectrum to include one additional diagnosis along with schizophrenia improved results. The ratio for schizophrenia alone was 5.01 (using data from the preceding paragraph). Improvements were found with adding schizotypal personality disorder (6.01), adding affective disorder with mood-incongruent delusions (6.31), and atypical psychosis (5.23), whereas there was no effect for adding schizophreniform disorder (5.00).

### Adoption and Family Studies

Adoption and family studies similarly can be used to provide clues as to which variations on the schizophrenia theme should be included in the schizophrenia spectrum. In the Danish adoption study, Kety et al. (1968) reported results based on hospital record diagnoses from the Copenhagen sample. Over time, these investigators enlarged the sample to include the rest of Denmark and conducted diagnostic interviews with all participants. Kendler et al. (1994) reported results based on *DSM-III* diagnoses for this national sample, which serves as an excellent illustration because of the relatively large sample size (for an adoption study) and high quality of the data. As in the original study, a broader concept of schizophrenia spectrum disorders was used, which included schizophrenia; schizoaffective disorder, mainly schizophrenia (SAD-MS); schizotypal personality disorder (SPD); and paranoid personality disorder (PPD). The risk of these spectrum disorders was elevated among the relatives of schizophrenic (13.0%), SAD-MS (12.8%), and SPD (19.1%) index case groups compared with a risk of only 3.0% among relatives of the control adoptees. The specific diagnoses were tallied among the relatives of the index cases and controls, and comparisons were made to see whether the particular diagnosis was elevated. When specific diagnoses were tallied, the diagnosis of SPD was elevated among the relatives of all three index case groups—schizophrenia (7.3%), SAD-MS (7.7%), and SPD (14.9%)—compared with relatives of controls (2.3%). The diagnosis of schizophrenia was elevated among the relatives of schizophrenic (3.3%) and SAD-MS (5.1%) but not SPD (0%) index groups compared with controls (0.3%). SAD-MS and PPD were not significantly elevated among the relatives of any index groups. Note that SPD was elevated among relatives of schizophrenia probands, but schizophrenia was not found among the relatives of SPD probands. In an opposite pattern, schizophrenia was found among relatives of SAD-MS probands, but SAD-MS was not found among the relatives of schizophrenia probands.

These analyses strongly support the inclusion of SPD in the spectrum, based on the elevated risk of SPD among relatives of schizophrenia probands. This conclusion consistently has been supported in reviews of the family, twin, and adoption literature (e.g., Asarnow et al., 2001; Battaglia & Torgersen, 1996; Kendler & Diehl, 1995). In a polygenic model in which SPD is a milder form, the risk of schizophrenia among relatives of SPD probands would be expected to be relatively low and difficult to detect with small samples (Battaglia & Torgersen, 1996), such as was the case in the Kendler et al. (1994) study when the data were reported separately for each spectrum diagnosis. Nevertheless, enough studies have found elevated risk of schizophrenia among relatives of SPD probands that Battaglia and Torgersen (1996) conclude the evidence is convincing.

Schizoaffective disorder clearly falls within the schizophrenic spectrum, as long as it is restricted to *mainly schizophrenic* subtypes. The unidirectional pattern of results for SAD-MS in the Kendler et al. (1994) study is consistent with the notion (discussed later in this chapter) that SAD-MS

involves a genetic contribution from schizophrenia with perhaps a synergistic but independent contribution of affective symptoms—such that the combination will emerge from the population as a whole when both happen to be present in moderate degree. However, when starting with schizophrenia in the proband, because of the independence of the two components, affective symptoms would not necessarily combine with schizophrenia symptoms among the relatives in high numbers. Consistent with this model, Kendler and Diehl (1995) report that in two large-scale studies, although there was no increase in risk of mood disorders among the relatives of schizophrenia probands (as expected), the risk of psychotic features was more than twice as likely among the affectively ill relatives of schizophrenia probands compared with relatives of controls. This finding supports the notion that genetic liability to schizophrenia combines with liability to affective disorder to produce psychotic reactions.

The results for PPD were equivocal in the Danish study. Similarly, some reviewers include it (e.g., Kendler & Diehl, 1995), whereas others find the evidence equivocal (Asarnow et al., 2001). PPD appears to be less strongly related to schizophrenia than is SPD but may well be included in the spectrum.

### Schizophreniform Disorder

Overall, the evidence for inclusion of schizophreniform disorder has been somewhat inconsistent, possibly as a function of varying conceptualizations of this disorder. As noted earlier, the diagnosis originally referred to psychotic patients with good prognosis in order to distinguish them from Kraepelinian chronic schizophrenia (Siris & Lavin, 1995). Since *DSM-III* (in the United States), the term has been narrowed to refer to a condition identical to schizophrenia except that it lasts less than 6 months and does not require deterioration in social and occupational functioning. In *DSM-IV*, a minimum of 1-month duration is required to distinguish schizophreniform disorder from brief psychotic disorder (APA, 1994, 2000). The latter diagnosis to some extent reflects a similar traditional Scandinavian concept of brief reactive psychosis that emphasized a severe stressor shortly before the onset of the psychosis, the understandability of the presenting symptoms as a result of the stressor, and full recovery to normal function, although it should be noted that the precise definition has varied over time and among authors (Siris & Lavin, 1995). Also, *DSM-IV* does not require a stressful event. Thus, the most salient aspect of these distinctions has to do with the duration of one or more episodes, combined with at least enough recovery to terminate an episode and an absence of chronic negative symptoms that would meet the 6-month duration requirement for schizophrenia in *DSM-IV.*

An episodic course per se is not an issue for inclusion in the concept of schizophrenia: Even with narrow diagnostic approaches, an episodic course is not precluded as long as the 6-month criterion is met at some point. Similarly, an initial presentation formally meeting the criteria for schizophreniform disorder is not incompatible with a later diagnosis of schizophrenia. In many studies, the diagnosis is changed to schizophrenia at follow-up, leaving a smaller (albeit still significant) number who show a remitting nonaffective psychosis (Siris & Lavin, 1995). Thus, it is only schizophreniform disorder based on a longitudinal perspective for which there is a question of relatedness to schizophrenia.

In the Danish adoption study (Kendler et al., 1994), schizophreniform disorder was included in a psychotic nonspectrum group (i.e., was not seen as part of the schizophrenia spectrum), but other evidence has been more supportive. In a *DSM-III* (lifetime diagnosis) reanalysis of the Iowa Family Study, Kendler, Gruenberg, and Tsuang (1986) reported as many schizophrenia cases among the relatives of schizophreniform probands (3.6%) as among the relatives of schizophrenia probands (3.7%), finding that the two diagnoses were indistinguishable from a familial perspective. Kendler and Diehl (1995) cited two large family studies that reported an increased risk of remitting or atypical psychoses (nonaffective psychoses that do not meet criteria for schizophrenia and thus would include schizophreniform disorder) among the relatives of probands with schizophrenia and suggested that family liability to schizophrenia increases the risk for several nonschizophrenic psychotic disorders.

From the perspective of a polygenic model, the shorter the episodes and the more complete the recovery, the lower is the presumed genetic liability—therefore, the more difficult it is to demonstrate genetic relatedness in family and adoption studies. Also, lower genetic liability (schizophreniform disorder) should be more easily seen among the relatives of probands with higher genetic liability (schizophrenia) than it is in the reverse direction. The evidence seems reasonably supportive of this expectation. As just noted, evidence from family studies for inclusion of schizophreniform disorder in the schizophrenia spectrum is reasonably strong. Furthermore, based on his reading of the genetics literature, Gottesman (1991) included many cases of schizophreniform disorder as part of schizophrenia: Although he accepted that there may be some psychogenic psychoses, he argued that schizophrenia can involve only one or two episodes, the duration criterion is arbitrary and can lead to underdiagnosis, and low-risk genotypes could develop mild and remitting schizophrenia, reflecting the unity of schizophrenia with manifestations along a broad continuum.

## *Brief Psychotic Disorder*

Little or no evidence supports the inclusion of brief psychotic disorder or brief reactive psychosis as part of the schizophrenia spectrum (Siris & Lavin, 1995). Several family studies (unfortunately often methodologically flawed) found that brief reactive psychosis tends to run in families and also may be related to mood disorder but is not associated with schizophrenia. Of even greater interest is that a Danish study of matings between persons with schizophrenia and reactive psychoses did not increase the risk of schizophrenia in offspring over that expected for children with one parent with schizophrenia and one with no psychopathology (Gottesman, 1991; Gottesman et al., 1987). Although the small sample size precludes firm conclusions, the result suggests no genetic or environmental contribution to liability for schizophrenia from brief reactive psychosis. Although it would be parsimonious to speculate that a very modest specific genetic liability for schizophrenia is required for a brief psychotic reaction and that this small genetic effect is undetectable without very large samples, it is also possible that processes having little or nothing to do with schizophrenia cause a portion of brief reactive psychoses.

## *Blurred Boundaries in the Polygenic Model*

It should be appreciated that—as emphasized previously—in a polygenic model the phenotypic manifestation of schizophrenia may be influenced by contributions from different types of nonspecific liability in different subgroups of patients. Due to the varying importance of these contributions, it will be difficult to demonstrate them with the sample sizes normally available. Stating this point another way, in such a model the boundaries of the spectrum are not distinct but rather fall off gradually with quantitative variations in specific and nonspecific genetic liability. Consequently, the boundaries of the schizophrenic spectrum may be inherently blurred; only the strongest and most common manifestations of schizophrenia may be reliably demonstrable.

## Summary

From the preceding examples, it can be seen that the genetics literature provides a valuable tool for evaluating the breadth of the concept of schizophrenia and the validity of specific diagnoses for inclusion in the schizophrenic spectrum (diagnoses with similarities to schizophrenia that are genetically related to schizophrenia). Based on the data reviewed so far, there has been no support for a subdivision of schizophrenia into two or more distinct genetic disorders, in spite of the heterogeneity of clinical features. A middle-of-the-road diagnosis is supported, comparable to *DSM-III* and to RDC and Feighner criteria diagnoses that were broadened to include *probably schizophrenia*—at least when these diagnoses are applied to longitudinal data. Additionally, the concept of schizophrenia needs to be broadened to include schizotypal personality disorder and—in some sense—schizoaffective disorder, mainly schizophrenic. Some phenotypic heterogeneity can be attributed to differences in the degree of genetic vulnerability with a higher genetic loading implicated for chronic, severe schizophrenia and the hebephrenic and catatonic subtypes. On the other hand, the life event, expressed emotion, and physical environmental studies and the example of the Genain quadruplets indicate that environmental factors affect the clinical picture.

## HETEROGENEITY: A CHALLENGE TO THE CONCEPTUALIZATION OF SCHIZOPHRENIA

Although differences in chronicity can be explained in terms of a dimension of severity of genetic loading, other aspects of the heterogeneity of schizophrenia continue to challenge the conceptualization of schizophrenia. In particular, the positive versus negative symptom distinction and the high frequency of a schizoaffective clinical picture represent major phenomena in need of explanation—that is, how can any unitary concept of schizophrenia account for these varied clinical pictures, or (alternatively) what other sources of variance might account for them? One neglected possibility is that nonspecific liability may account for some heterogeneity.

### Positive Versus Negative Symptoms

#### The Two-Dimensional Model

As noted previously, debate has centered on whether positive or negative symptoms constitute the core symptoms of schizophrenia. Rather than trying to subordinate one to the other, Strauss, Carpenter, and Bartko (1974) viewed positive and negative symptoms as representing semi-independent processes. In a well-known proposal consistent with semi-independence, Crow (1980, 1985) distinguished between Type I and Type II schizophrenia, which he held are two independent dimensions or pathological processes that underlie schizophrenic symptomatology. In his formulation, Type I schizophrenia is characterized by positive symptoms (e.g., delusions, hallucinations), acute onset, an episodic course, good premorbid adjustment, and good response to antipsychotic medication, whereas Type II schizophrenia is characterized by negative symptoms, insidious onset, intellectual deterioration, poor premorbid functioning, a chronic course, and a poorer response to antipsychotic medication. Crow further attributed Type I schizophrenia to a neurochemical disturbance involving the neurotransmitter dopamine and Type II schizophrenia to structural brain changes (e.g., enlarged cerebral ventricles as assessed by computed tomographic studies—discussed later in this chapter). Given the independence of these processes, patients may present with only Type I or only Type II symptoms or a combination of the two. However, patients with exclusively negative symptoms are rare (Andreasen, Flaum, Swayze, Tyrell, & Arndt, 1990; Gottesman et al., 1987).

Although Crow's hypothesis of an association between ventricular enlargement and negative symptoms has not been supported (Andreasen et al., 1990; Gottesman & Bertelsen, 1989; Liddle et al., 1993), involvement of dopaminergic activity in schizophrenia is indicated by three lines of evidence. First, the potency of typical antipsychotic medications correlates strongly with their ability to block dopamine receptors, especially D2 receptors (e.g., Byne, Kemether, Jones, Haroutunian, & Davis, 1999; Johnstone, 1999a). Second, dopamine agonists (e.g., amphetamine) in large doses can produce a clinical syndrome indistinguishable from paranoid schizophrenia in nonschizophrenic individuals (Krystal, Abi-Dargham, Laruelle, & Moghaddam, 1999). Third, the same drugs in small doses exacerbate symptoms in schizophrenic patients (Andreasen, 1985; Krystal et al., 1999) or cause transient symptoms in schizophrenic patients in remission (Losonczy, Davidson, & Davis, 1987). Additionally, as proposed by Crow, a good response to typical antipsychotic medication is associated with positive symptoms and a reactive schizophrenic pattern (e.g., Andreasen, 1985; Andreasen et al., 1990; Losonczy et al., 1987; Reynolds, 1989). On the other hand, after many years of research on this point it appears that although the dopamine hypothesis of the mechanism of traditional antipsychotic drugs is strongly supported, there is no positive support for a *primary* excess of dopamine (or dopamine receptors) in schizophrenia (Byne et al., 1999; Crow in Liddle et al., 1993; Weinberger & Lipska, 1995). Consistent with seeing dopamine as not a primary cause of schizophrenia, the newer, atypical antipsychotics (clozapine and risperidone) have pointed to the importance of inhibiting serotonergic activity, especially for treating negative symptoms (Kapur & Remington, 1996). Undoubtedly, dopamine plays an important role in schizophrenia, but it probably combines with other factors (Andreasen, 2001), possibly interacting with some other primary deficit in schizophrenia, to facilitate development of positive symptoms.

Like Crow, Carpenter (1992) addressed the theoretical implications of the divergence of positive and negative symptoms. He considered and rejected two traditional explanations for heterogeneity. One would reduce heterogeneity by dividing schizophrenia into several disease entities. The second would consider schizophrenia as a single disease entity and attribute the heterogeneity to the interaction between a primary pathology and other characteristics of the individual and the environment (cf. the MFP model discussed previously). Carpenter proposed instead that several distinct pathophysiological processes (with different neural circuits, pathophysiology, and etiology) combine differently in different individuals to produce the syndrome of schizophrenia. Rather than studying schizophrenia (comparing schizophrenic individuals with nonschizophrenic individuals) one should study the distinct pathophysiological processes (compare negative-symptom schizophrenic individuals with nonnegative-symptom schizophrenic individuals).

### The Three-Dimensional Model

With time, the positive and negative symptom two-dimensional model has been replaced by a three-dimensional model of schizophrenic symptoms in which the positive psychotic symptoms have split into two dimensions (Kirkpatrick, Buchanan, Ross, & Carpenter, 2001). Using factor analysis, Liddle (1987) found dimensions of psychomotor poverty (negative symptoms of poverty of speech, blunted affect, and decreased movement), reality distortion (positive symptoms of various delusions and hallucinations), and disorganization (formal thought disorder, inappropriate affect, and poverty of content of speech). Replication of these dimensions in later research and widespread acceptance of the findings (Andreasen, Arndt, Alliger, Miller, & Flaum, 1995; Cuesta, Peralta, & Caro, 1999; Johnstone, 1999a; Kirkpatrick et al., 2001; Liddle et al., 1993) make it clear that multiple dimensions of symptomatology must be incorporated into any fully adequate theory of schizophrenia; however, the implications of the addition of a third major symptom dimension have not been fully developed, and this chapter focuses on the two-dimensional model.

### Genetic Versus Pharmacological Approaches

The conceptual challenge of the independence of important symptom dimensions can be seen from another perspective. As noted earlier, more chronic cases—including negative-symptom cases (Gottesman et al., 1987)—seem to carry a greater genetic liability. This association of a strong genetic contribution to etiology with negative symptoms in contrast to the association of the pharmacological dopamine hypothesis with positive symptoms underscores the importance of understanding both negative and positive symptoms. Given that response to biological treatment and genetic contributions to etiology are the two cornerstones of biological theories of schizophrenia and yet are associated with semi-independent dimensions of schizophrenia, it is obvious that something more is needed for an adequate conceptualization of schizophrenia.

### Activity-Withdrawal

Although it is less frequently recognized as defining heterogeneity in schizophrenia, the activity-withdrawal dimension nevertheless is of some importance. Assessed by ward ratings on 10 items (Venables, 1957), patients with schizophrenia at the active end are described as restless, loud, overtalkative, overactive, and having many friends and interests (actually reminiscent of mania), whereas withdrawn cases are described by an absence of these features. In spite of being behaviorally inactive, withdrawn patients with schizophrenia were found to be more highly aroused on the basis of two perceptual measures of cortical reactivity and one autonomic measure (Venables, 1963a, 1963b, 1967; Venables & Wing, 1962), whereas active patients were low on arousal. Thus, the active schizophrenic patients showed a combination of behavioral activation, reward seeking, and low cortical arousal, whereas the withdrawn schizophrenic patients showed a pattern of anhedonia, behavioral inactivity, and high arousal (presumably aversive arousal or anxiety, discussed later in this chapter). Depue (1976) demonstrated a close congruence between activity-withdrawal and the good-poor premorbid adjustment distinction (withdrawn individuals showing poor premorbid adjustment). Wing's work on withdrawal in schizophrenia provided the background for the negative symptom component of Crowe's Type II symptom pattern (Crow, 1985), indicating the relevance of these findings to negative symptoms. The active cases have received little attention in the recent literature.

### Schizoaffective Symptoms

The traditional disease model implies a discrete, categorical distinction for different psychiatric disorders. Gradations of severity have long challenged that view, making it difficult to draw a sharp distinction between health and illness. Schizoaffective symptoms challenge the categorical approach in a different way: Even the boundaries between hypothesized disorders are blurred. Although it is not the concern of the present review, the past two decades or so have brought increasing awareness of the generality of comorbidity across many forms of psychopathology and the subsequent blurring of boundaries (Mineka, Watson, & Clark, 1998). Schizoaffective symptoms illustrate this phenomenon well.

As already noted, when patients are arranged along a continuum from pure schizophrenia at one end to pure affective disorder at the other end, the distribution is unimodal; patients with schizoaffective symptoms outnumber those with purely schizophrenic or purely affective symptoms (Kendell, 1982). The prevalence of schizoaffective disorder is far too common to be attributed to the chance occurrence of two relatively rare disorders (Procci, 1989; Siris & Lavin, 1995). Among hospital admissions for functional psychosis, depending on diagnostic criteria, 10–30% manifest schizoaffective disorder (Siris & Lavin, 1995). Even with narrow diagnostic systems that preclude a diagnosis of schizophrenia when prominent depression is present, significant depression is seen during the longitudinal course of 25–50% of schizophrenia patients (Sands & Harrow, 1999). The theoretical challenge of the large number of schizoaffective disorders is well recognized (Baron & Gruen, 1991; Crow, 1986, 1991; Grossman, Harrow, Goldberg, & Fichtner, 1991; Kendell, 1982; Maier et al., 1993; Meltzer, 1984; Sands & Harrow, 1999; Siris & Lavin, 1995; Taylor, 1992; Taylor, Berenbaum, Jampala, & Cloninger, 1993). Attempts to dichotomize the schizoaffective continuum on the basis of underlying etiology has failed, leading Crow (1998) to conclude that no objective genetic boundaries can be drawn between predominantly schizophrenic and predominantly affective patients.

Although for a while it was popular to argue that schizoaffective disorders are a variant of affective disorders (Meltzer, 1984), the evidence has not been consistent (Procci, 1989), and in any case, supportive studies tend to select patients for more prominent affective than schizophrenic symptomatology (Siris & Lavin, 1995; Williams & McGlashan, 1987). As noted earlier, when patients are selected to have schizoaffective symptoms with more prominent schizophrenic symptoms, they have more familial schizophrenia and less familial affective disorder (Kendler et al., 1994; Levinson & Levitt, 1987). Furthermore, when both the full schizophrenic syndrome and the full affective disorder syndrome are present, follow-up data point to a closer relationship to schizophrenia (Williams & McGlashan, 1987).

Such results are consistent with a continuum in which the vulnerability processes underlying affective disorders combine additively with vulnerability to schizophrenia to reach threshold for development of a psychotic episode (Braden,

1984; Fowles, 1992b; Siris & Lavin, 1995). In this model, the prominence of schizophrenic versus affective symptoms varies with the magnitude of the underlying contribution from schizophrenia or affective disorder. If vulnerability to schizophrenia is the major contributor and is combined with a small contribution from affective processes, then the clinical picture will be largely schizophrenic or schizoaffective, mainly schizophrenic. As the vulnerability to schizophrenia decreases, more liability from the processes underlying affective disorders is required to reach threshold for schizophrenia, and the associated affective symptoms become more prominent. This model can account for the continuum from schizophrenia to affective disorders, the temporal coupling between schizophrenic and affective symptomatology seen in many patients, the more favorable prognosis when affective symptoms are prominent, the higher number of schizoaffective diagnoses that is predicted on the basis of the chance occurrence of two relatively infrequent disorders, and the family and genetic findings (Siris & Lavin, 1995).

The model just presented can be strengthened by evidence that the processes underlying affective disorders *should* contribute to liability for schizophrenia—that is, some linkage between the two liabilities that makes affective liability relevant to the MFP model of schizophrenia. In order to make this argument effectively and to address contributors to positive and negative symptoms, it is necessary to consider the implications of the MFP model for the importance of affective processes and the associated underlying systems.

## AFFECTIVE NEUROBEHAVIORAL SYSTEMS AS A NONSPECIFIC LIABILITY

In considering the problem of heterogeneity in schizophrenia, the diathesis-stress and MFP models point to the processes associated with stress as the origin of an important component of nonspecific liability for schizophrenia—consistent with recent conclusions that genetic factors act via various dimensional risk factors involved in the multifactorial origins of psychopathology rather than producing discrete categorical diseases (Rutter, 1997). Neurobehavioral systems associated with affective-emotional responses are obviously relevant—both as affective responses to stressful environments and as dimensions of temperament-based individual differences in stress reactivity. Activity in these systems might be expected to constitute nonspecific liability and to influence the clinical presentation of schizophrenia. In this context, Fowles (1992b, 1994) cited Gray's and Depue's neurobehavioral theories as particularly useful. For Gray (1982, 1987; Gray & McNaughton, 1996, 2000) the motivational-affective systems in question are the behavioral approach or behavioral activation system (BAS), the behavioral inhibition system (BIS; Gray & McNaughton, 2000), and the fight-flight system (Gray & McNaughton, 2000), all derived from the literature on animal learning and motivation but integrated with findings in behavioral neuroscience. Depue (Depue & Collins, 1999; Depue, Collins, & Luciana, 1996; Depue & Iacono, 1989; Depue & Lenzenweger, 2001) uses the term behavioral facilitation system (BFS) to describe a system almost identical to the BAS, and he has written extensively on the relevance to personality and affective disorders. Depue's and Gray's primary contributions have been to the BFS and BIS, respectively; thus, those terms are used here.

## The BFS: Reward Seeking, Coping With Stress, Positive Affect, and Dopamine

The BFS facilitates goal-directed or reward-seeking behavior and increases nonspecific arousal in response to conditioned stimuli (CS) for reward. It is important to note that the BFS also facilitates punishment-avoiding behavior in response to cues for relieving nonpunishment in active avoidance situations (in which some instrumental response can avoid a threatened punishment). The positive affective states accompanying the behavioral activation are hope and relief, respectively. The substrate for the BAS-BFS centers on the ventral tegmental area (VTA) dopamine projection system—the VTA dopamine projection to the nucleus accumbens (the mesolimbic dopaminergic pathway) and other structures (see Depue & Collins, 1999, for additional dopamine projections in this system).

Several aspects of the BFS are especially important in the present context. First, its role in active avoidance means that it will be activated during any stressful situation in which the animal (or person) expects that some coping response may be effective in dealing with the potentially negative outcome. Second, the neurotransmitter dopamine is centrally involved in the substrate for the BAS (Gray, 1987) or the BFS (Depue & Collins, 1999; Depue & Iacono, 1989). The same dopaminergic pathways mediate the rewarding effects of many addictive drugs such as amphetamines, cocaine, and heroin (Leshner, 1997; Wise & Bozarth, 1987; Wise & Rompre, 1989). There is agreement, therefore, that dopamine pathways are involved in activating behavior in response to cues for reward, and both Gray and Depue describe a behavioral system that would be involved in coping with stress. Consistent with that view, it is well established that exposure to stress increases dopamine release (Walker & Diforio, 1997; Weinberger, 1987). Third,

the BFS has been implicated in mania and depression, making it relevant to schizoaffective disorders. Fourth, the BFS is likely to influence the degree of behavioral activation seen clinically in different subtypes of schizophrenia.

## The BIS: Passive Avoidance, Extinction, Anxiety, and Anxiolytic Drugs

The BIS inhibits behavior, increases nonspecific arousal, and facilitates attention to the environment in two important situations involving goal conflict: (a) approach-avoidance conflict (also called passive avoidance), in which an animal may receive punishment for making a rewarded response, such as crossing an electrified grid in order to reach food, or—in a more naturalistic setting—exploring for food when a predator might be present; and (b) extinction, in which the absence of an expected reward produces frustration. Both situations create a conflict between the desire to approach the reward and the desire to avoid the punishment or frustration by not approaching. All anxiolytic drugs—alcohol, barbiturates, benzodiazepines, the novel anxiolytics (e.g., buspirone), and the anxiolytic antidepressant imipramine—produce behavioral and neurobiological effects that can be conceptualized as weakening the BIS (Gray & McNaughton, 2000). These findings contribute to Gray's conclusion that the BIS is the anxiety system, and the BIS is seen as a substrate for Barlow's concept of anxiety that is common to all of the anxiety disorders (Barlow, Chorpita, & Turovsky, 1996; Fowles, 1992a). The BIS, therefore, processes stressful (i.e., anxiety-producing) stimuli, increases nonspecific arousal, and produces a clinical picture of reduced approach behavior. The substrate for the BIS centers on the septo-hippocampal system, which includes the hippocampus, the dentate gyrus, the subicular area, the entorhinal cortex, and the posterior cingulate cortex (Gray & McNaughton, 2000).

## The Fight-Flight System: Dealing With Imminent Threats

Gray has described a third system, the well-known fight-flight system, that prepares the organism for vigorous activity in the form of flight or flight. In his earlier work Gray (1987) said the fight-flight system is activated by unconditioned punishment stimuli, but recently Gray and McNaughton (2000) described the fight-flight system as activated when there is an actual threat (as opposed to a potential threat), such as when a predator is present. The term *fear* is commonly used (by Gray and others) to refer to activation of the fight-flight system. The fight-flight system, then, is a third stress-relevant system, but it is one that responds to imminent danger. The neurobiological substrate of the fight-flight system centers on the dorsal peri-aqueductal gray, but Gray and McNaughton (2000) suggested viewing it as part of a distributed system that also includes the hypothalamus, amygdala, anterior and posterior cingulate, and hippocampus.

## The BIS-BFS and Heterogeneity in Schizophrenia

Fowles (1992b, 1994) suggested that the concepts of a BFS and a BIS offer potential explanations for some aspects of heterogeneity in schizophrenia. The major considerations are that the BFS is associated with behavioral activation (active coping with stress, reward-seeking behaviors), positive affect, and dopaminergic activity, whereas BIS activation is associated with behavioral inhibition in conflict situations and with increased aversive arousal and negative affect in the form of anxiety. Although both systems are implicated in responding to threatening stimuli, both the behavioral effects and the underlying systems are quite different and can be expected to affect those vulnerable to schizophrenia differently.

The BFS is directly relevant to the manic form of schizoaffective disorder. Depue (Depue & Iacono, 1989; Depue, Krauss, & Spoont, 1987; Depue & Zald, 1993) argues that the features of manic episodes can be understood as resulting from uncontrolled activation of the BFS (with resultant high levels of dopaminergic activity) as a consequence of a breakdown of regulation. For example, the manic features of increased activity, positive affect, and uncritical optimism while engaging in risky activities are to be expected from uncontrolled activation of a moderately strong BFS. The resultant high levels of dopaminergic activity would combine with specific vulnerability to schizophrenia, as suggested previously, to produce a continuum of schizoaffective symptomatology involving positive symptoms (see Braden, 1984, for a similar proposal, albeit without notions of the BFS, in which he suggests that the dopamine-based behavioral activation seen in mania combines with vulnerability to schizophrenia to produce schizoaffective-manic disorder).

The activity-withdrawal dimension should reflect the balance between the BFS and the BIS. A temperamentally strong BFS would be expected to produce positive schizophrenic symptoms in connection with a behaviorally active, reward-seeking individual, as described previously for cases of active schizophrenia. Additionally, stressful situations that involve active coping by the individual would be expected to produce an increase in dopaminergic activity, triggering positive symptom episodes of schizophrenia in vulnerable individuals. In contrast, a temperamentally weak BFS would result in weak reward-seeking and active avoidance with little positive affect. Additionally, the finding of high arousal

in cases of withdrawn schizophrenia suggests that these negative-symptom patients suffer from high aversive arousal combined with behavioral inhibition (passive avoidance and extinction) due to activation of the BIS. The consequences of such temperament factors would be increased by an environment in which few responses were rewarded and aversive control was prominent and would also be increased by depression.

The first consideration in the application to schizoaffective disorder with depression is that depression involves low positive affect (e.g., Mineka et al., 1998; Tellegen, 1985), which can be seen as a result of greatly diminished activation of the BFS (e.g., Fowles, 1994). All behavioral theories of depression emphasize a blocking of reward-seeking behavior, punishment-avoiding behavior, or both as core etiologic factors (Eastman, 1976). Cognitive theories emphasize hopelessness, by which they mean a lack of hope that behavior will be effective in achieving desired goals (obtaining rewards or avoiding punishments). Furthermore, Depue (Depue & Iacono, 1989; Depue et al., 1987; Depue & Zald, 1993) concluded that depression in the context of bipolar disorder can be understood as a loss of BFS functioning—that is, the BFS no longer responds to the usual reward incentive cues. Thus, whether from a behavioral, cognitive, or biological perspective, depression is seen as involving a lack of the activities attributed to the BFS.

At the same time, depression, which shares a genetic diathesis with generalized anxiety disorder in the form of a predisposition to general distress (Kendler, Neale, Kessler, Heath, & Eaves, 1992), is associated with stress-related HPA activation (Walker & Diforio, 1997). This high level of negative affect-anxiety-distress should contribute nonspecifically to liability for schizophrenia, combining with specific liability to produce a continuum of schizoaffective-depressed symptomatology—a proposal also articulated by others. For example, Kendler and Diehl (1993) commented that "affective illness represents a stress that might precipitate a psychosis" (p. 269). More formally, Siris and Lavin (1995) articulated a shared diathesis in which "an episode of a major mood disorder may constitute a sufficient stressor" to elicit schizoaffective symptoms in individuals with a moderate schizophrenia diathesis (p. 1021). Presumably, it must be the high negative affect component of depression that functions as a stressor.

According to this analysis, the combination of minimal BFS functioning and high negative affect is one etiologic pathway to the withdrawn clinical picture, characterized by aversive arousal and lack of behavioral activation (prominent negative symptoms). The well-established evidence that depression can produce negative symptoms (e.g., Sommers, 1985) is consistent with this suggestion. Furthermore, the well-known negative symptom phenomenon of institutionalism, seen in schizophrenia patients exposed to nonstimulating and unrewarding psychiatric hospital environments (e.g., Sommers, 1985; Wing, 1978), can be understood as an extinction phenomenon that disrupts BFS activation and produces depression.

Thus, the BFS and the BIS are likely contributors to nonspecific liability in schizophrenia. Because of their different features, they offer explanations for some of the heterogeneity in schizophrenia. Although the precise conceptualization of these stress-relevant affective-motivational systems will evolve with additional research, the genetics literature in the form of the MFP model and its nonspecific contributors to liability suggests that they are relevant to understanding the etiology and heterogeneity in schizophrenia. The contribution of the fight-flight system and panic attacks is less clear, although it seems likely that panic attacks constitute biological stressors and that they promote withdrawal and avoidance of situations in which they occur.

## THE DEFICIT SYNDROME

Carpenter and his colleagues have focused on a deficit syndrome, reflecting Kraepelin's avolitional psychopathology (Carpenter, 1994; Carpenter, Heinrichs, & Wagman, 1988). A key to defining the deficit syndrome is the long-standing recognition that negative symptoms arise from a number of sources other than from schizophrenia per se (Sommers, 1985). To the institutionalism and postpsychotic depression mentioned previously can be added akinesia secondary to pharmacological treatment with dopamine antagonists. Narrowly defined, akinesia refers to extrapyramidal motor symptoms (diminished arm swing, shortened stride, and rigid posture); broadly defined, however, it includes a broad range of negative features (e.g., lack of emotional reactivity, lack of goal-directedness, lack of or retarded spontaneous speech, and masklike facial expressions very similar to flat affect), quite possibly due to impairment of a dopamine-based neurobehavioral system (Harrow, Yonan, Sands, & Marengo, 1994) conceptualized here as the BFS. Carpenter, Buchanan, Kirkpatrick, Thaker, and Tamminga (1991) developed diagnostic criteria that attempted to exclude secondary negative symptoms and to define a primary deficit syndrome. These criteria required the enduring presence of any two of the following: restricted affect, diminished emotional range, poverty of speech, curbing of interests, diminished sense of purpose, and diminished social drive. This definition is narrower than those of other commonly used scales for rating negative symptoms, which do not exclude secondary negative symptoms (Kirkpatrick et al., 2001).

Recently, Carpenter and his colleagues (Kirkpatrick et al., 2001) proposed that *deficit psychopathology* or a deficit schizophrenia subtype is a disease distinct from schizophrenia without deficit features, at least based on preliminary evidence to date. They estimated that the deficit schizophrenia is seen in about 15% of first-episode schizophrenia cases. In support of the view that deficit schizophrenia is a distinct disease, Kirkpatrick et al. (2001) cite a range of evidence comparing deficit and nondeficit schizophrenia, among which were (a) a worse premorbid adjustment with insidious onset; (b) poorer occupational and social functioning; (c) for relatives of deficit schizophrenia probands, an increased risk of schizophrenia, more severe social withdrawal, and a three-fold increase in the risk of deficit rather than nondeficit schizophrenia; (d) a small increase in the prevalence of antibodies for the Borna disease virus (and these antibodies are associated with greater severity of negative but not positive symptoms); (e) an increase in summer rather than winter births (suggesting that winter births are associated with a more benign course of nondeficit schizophrenia); (f) impairments on neurocognitive measures sensitive to frontal and parietal lobe dysfunction; (g) greater oculomotor (eye-tracking) dysfunction; and (h) decreased activity in the dorsolateral prefrontal cortex and the inferior parietal cortex that they suggest is consistent with dysfunction of the dorsolateral prefrontal basal ganglia-thalamocortical circuit (DLPFC).

If the deficit syndrome simply were a more severe version than the nondeficit syndrome of schizophrenia, then (the authors argued) the deficit syndrome should appear to be more extreme on a variety of problems characterizing schizophrenia in general. Contrary to this expectation, deficit schizophrenia patients have been found not to be more severe in terms of overall psychotic symptoms and have been found to be *less severe* in terms of (a) reduced frontal lobe white matter, (b) winter births, (c) and some measures of positive symptoms. The authors also cite less severe depression and other dysphoric affect even on follow-up, but it is not clear to what extent this correlate might be contaminated by excluding patients with depression in the initial diagnosis of deficit schizophrenia. Additionally, among the nonpsychotic relatives of deficit schizophrenia probands, dysphoria and psychotic-like symptoms are less severe than they are among the nonpsychotic relatives of nondeficit schizophrenia probands. Finally, among deficit schizophrenia patients, the disorganization symptom dimension is uncorrelated with impairment in the sequencing of complex motor acts, whereas among schizophrenia patients in general, there is a positive correlation.

These findings underscore the importance of the positive versus negative symptom distinction, and the authors have argued against a single dimension in which the negative symptom or deficit schizophrenia group is more severe on all dimensions. On the other hand, it does not appear to be the case that deficit schizophrenia breeds true, even with the more restrictive diagnostic approach developed by Carpenter and his colleagues (i.e., the risk of deficit schizophrenia among relatives of deficit probands is increased quantitatively, but nondeficit cases still appear).

An alternative interpretation would attribute their findings to greater severity of genetic loading combined with contributions from nonspecific liability. As noted previously, when examining negative symptom patients, Gottesman et al. (1987) found no results that could not be attributed to a continuum of severity. With an underlying continuum of severity, threshold effects are possible that create apparent discontinuous phenotypic variation (Gottesman & Shields, 1972). The difference in winter births and reduced frontal lobe white matter could reflect a need for additional stressors (in this case, physical environmental) for nondeficit schizophrenia that involves a lesser genetic loading, as suggested previously.

The implications of the association between negative symptoms and the presence of antibodies for the Borna disease virus are not clear. Borna disease is an immune-mediated meningoencephalitis known to infect a number of animal species and recently believed to infect humans as well. It is believed to cause damage to the hippocampus that (at least in theory), in turn, results in diminished activity in the frontal cortex (hypofrontality as discussed later) and a hypodopaminergic state (Waltrip et al., 1997). Thus, Borna disease might constitute a contributor to liability that is nonspecific with respect to schizophrenia but specific with respect to negative symptoms due to the hypodopaminergic state. Needless to say, more research is needed on the contribution of Borna disease.

However, the position adopted here is that some heterogeneity cannot be accounted for simply in terms of severity; rather, it reflects multidimensional components of nonspecific liability. The negative syndrome may reflect a weak BFS and a strong BIS in combination with an unrewarding and/or aversive environment, producing a failure to initiate approach and active avoidance behavior and a lack of positive affect—components of the avolitional syndrome. The increased BIS-related aversive arousal may constitute an important source of nonspecific liability in these patients. The reduced dopaminergic activity associated with reduced BFS activity would reduce positive symptomatology, making deficit syndrome patients appear less severe on positive symptoms. In addition to temperament variables, it is possible that more severe schizophrenia is associated with a central nervous system (CNS) dysfunction that directly or indirectly disrupts functioning of the BFS, adding to the effects of temperament variables. Such a CNS dysfunction could possibly reflect the effects of a single major gene, acting in a polygenic context in a minority of schizophrenic patients and producing a more severe form of schizophrenia. To date, no such gene has been identified, but as noted previously, it is not incompatible with existing data.

## BRAIN DYSFUNCTION HYPOTHESES

The features of schizophrenia are so extreme that it is difficult to imagine that they could be produced by psychosocial experiences alone as a normal part of learning. Consequently, a great many researchers believe that some type of brain dysfunction plays an important role in schizophrenia. Research on this hypothesis has been greatly facilitated by the development of modern technology that allows imaging of both brain structure and function. Improvements in resolution of these techniques have facilitated this effort. Two major findings have been enlarged ventricles and hypofrontality (diminished activation of the frontal cortex) in cases of schizophrenia.

### Enlarged Ventricles and Hypofrontality

Ventricles (pools of cerebrospinal fluid in the brain) can be measured with structural techniques such as magnetic resonance imagery. Enlarged ventricles (not attributable to medication) repeatedly have been found in a portion of cases, and it is also interesting to note that increased ventricular size is associated with the schizophrenic twin in discordant MZ twins (Berman & Weinberger, 1999; Bunney & Bunney, 1999). The enlarged ventricles imply smaller brain size but do not indicate the cause or locus. Although some evidence has supported reduced neural tissue in a number of areas, no clear picture has emerged at present (Andreasen, 2001; Berman & Weinberger, 1999; Bunney & Bunney, 1999), and it is quite likely that no single area accounts for the enlarged ventricles. Nevertheless, these findings strongly encourage theories of brain dysfunction. As discussed later in this chapter, those theories have suggested a problem in neural development rather than a degeneration.

Another well-replicated finding—relying on functional assessments of brain activity (changes in regional blood flow secondary to neural activity)—is that schizophrenia involves less activation of the prefrontal cortex during cognitive activation tasks, especially those involving working memory (Berman & Weinberger, 1999). This presumed deficit in prefrontal activity, which is not attributable to medication, is strongly supported by performance deficits on a wide range of neuropsychological tests tapping prefrontal cortical function, and both hypofrontality and neuropsychological deficits appear to be more characteristic of individuals with negative-symptom schizophrenia. Hypoactivation or hyperactivation have been reported in other regions of the brain, but the results have not been as consistent as those for the prefrontal cortex.

The findings of hypofrontality and its association with negative symptoms have served as the basis of speculations concerning a complex role of dopamine. In a classic paper, Weinberger (1987) suggested that a pathological process of unknown origin early in life interferes with the functioning of parts of the prefrontal cortex (especially the DLPFC) and limbic system, functionally compromising activity in the mesocortical dopamine pathways (i.e., producing *underactivity* of this dopamine pathway). The hypoactivity in the prefrontal cortex releases the mesolimbic dopamine pathways from feedback control, producing hyperactivity in this dopamine pathway. In this theory, negative symptoms are related to underactivity of the mesocortical dopamine pathways, whereas positive psychotic symptoms are related to overactivity of the mesolimbic pathways.

More recently, Byne et al. (1999) found support for an association between hypofrontality and decreased activity of mesocortical dopamine pathways, for a causal connection between hypofrontality and negative symptoms, and for an inverse relationship between prefrontal cortex dopamine activity and subcortical dopamine activity. However, evidence of increased subcortical $D_2$ dopamine receptors in schizophrenia is suggestive of underactivity of subcortical dopamine. An attempt to resolve this contradiction proposed that prefrontal cortical afferents fail to produce enough tonic mesolimbic dopamine release that results in up-regulation (i.e., an increase) of $D_2$ receptors. The increased $D_2$ receptors then respond more strongly to dopamine release caused by neural firing, producing a functional hyperactivity of this pathway in response to stimulation. This revised model permits the same predictions as the Weinberger (1987) model by virtue of modifications that take into account findings of up-regulation of $D_2$ receptors in mesolimbic pathways. The authors emphasize, however, that the model is speculation that has yet to be tested. Nevertheless, it serves to illustrate the complexity of current versions of the dopamine hypothesis.

## Neurodevelopmental Hypotheses: Distributed Networks and Poor Connectivity

Recent theorizing has shifted from searching for a deficit in a single area of the brain to an emphasis on interactions among many different regions, leading to hypotheses of abnormal

interconnectedness of different areas as a result of neurodevelopmental failures (Andreasen, 2001; Berman & Weinberger, 1999; Bunney & Bunney, 1999; Weinberger, 1987; Weinberger & Lipska, 1995). Weinberger and Lipska (1995) noted that during the second trimester of pregnancy, young neurons migrate and settle into their appropriate target sites; they suggested that schizophrenia involves a failure of this process in which neurons may not only fail to make some connections, but may also even make incorrect connections, resulting in inefficient, noisy processing (rather than no processing) between areas of the brain—specifically between the prefrontal and temporal and limbic areas, although other areas may be involved (see Berman & Weinberger, 1999). These neural systems are implicated not only in complex cognitive and psychological behaviors, but also in the regulation of subcortical dopamine systems during periods of stress. The authors suggested that this deficit is almost universally present in schizophrenia but falls on a continuum of severity. Animal data indicate that problems in dopaminergic regulation due to malfunction of the prefrontal-temporolimbic cortical neural systems do not appear until postpuberty, consistent with the age of onset of schizophrenia.

Bunney and Bunney (1999) suggested a similar neurodevelopmental model, also emphasizing abnormal functional connectivity between brain regions that arises especially during the second trimester of pregnancy. They focused on the cortical subplate, a transitory structure critical to formation of neural connections in the cortex during early brain development, a disturbance of which is suggested to lead to abnormal connections, particularly in the frontal and limbic regions and in thalamocortical connections. Disruption of this process during the second trimester by obstetrical complications and viral infections is seen as a second hit that adds to genetic vulnerability in a minority of schizophrenic patients. Although the authors did not explicitly suggest the idea, it is easy to imagine (as suggested previously) that these *second hits* play a critical role in individuals with a moderate degree of genetic liability for schizophrenia but are not required for individuals with greater genetic liability.

Andreasen (2001) also mentioned pregnancy and birth complications, but she proposed that negative influences on brain development probably occur at multiple times, acting in an additive manner and potentially extending from the intrauterine period to late adolescence or young adulthood (during which important neural connections are being made). The range of environmental influences that affect brain development include "head or birth injuries, viral infections, exposure to toxins and drugs of abuse, hormonal changes, and other factors" (p. 206). Although she cites evidence of decreased size of the prefrontal cortex and the hippocampus (a part of the limbic system), she reported that schizophrenic patients show abnormal patterns of neural activity (inferred from blood flow) in the thalamus and the cerebellum in addition to the prefrontal cortex to a wide variety of tasks. However, Andreasen concluded that no specific regional abnormalities have been identified in schizophrenia. She suggested that the fundamental problem is a dysfunction of functional connectivity between distributed neural circuits (different areas of the brain)—a misconnection syndrome. It is interesting to note that she encouraged further work on cognitive relearning treatment programs as an adjunct to medication for schizophrenia patients, in the hope that such extensive retraining may gradually form new neural connections.

Thus, there appears to be a convergence among different investigators that the brain dysfunction in schizophrenia is more subtle and complex than a lesion in a specific area and that it is more than likely that the problem arises as a failure of development. Additionally, the notions of faulty neural wiring or misconnections suggest a more diffuse deficit rather than the loss of a specific single psychological process. These theoretical models, then, are consistent with the complexity of deficits seen in schizophrenia and perhaps explain why it has been so difficult to identify a specific psychological deficit in schizophrenia (Chapman & Chapman, 1973; Strauss, 2001). These models also suggest that pharmacological manipulations can only partially ameliorate the problem, inasmuch as drugs cannot restore appropriate neural connections. Although this neurodevelopmental perspective has many positive features, it is an approach to looking for the neurobiological substrate of schizophrenia rather than providing support for any specific theory. Indeed, there is no consensus on the specific developmental insult that contributes to the etiology of schizophrenia (Meinecke, 2001).

## SUMMARY

The emotional, cognitive, and behavioral problems subsumed under the terms *schizophrenia* and *schizophrenia spectrum* constitute a complex and heterogeneous phenomenon that is only approximated by our current conceptualizations and diagnostic approaches. Opinions differ with respect to the importance of—and ways to conceptualize—chronicity, negative versus positive symptoms, and affective symptoms, and decisions on these issues exert a large effect on attempts to diagnose schizophrenia. In spite of these uncertainties, a large literature on family, twin, and adoption studies have documented a very large genetic contribution to schizophrenia. These same studies indicate that schizotypal personality disorder and schizoaffective disorder, mainly schizophrenic belong

in the schizophrenia spectrum and suggest that schizophreniform disorder and paranoid personality disorder may well be included. There is little or no positive support for inclusion of brief reactive psychosis.

The extant genetic data are most consistent with the MFP model, in which a large number of genes, each often assumed to be of small effect, and environmental influences contribute in an additive fashion to the overall liability for schizophrenia. Sources of liability include specific genetic, nonspecific genetic, and nonspecific environment. Schizophrenia develops when total liability exceeds a threshold. Although a large majority of cases of schizophrenia are attributed to the MFP model, it is quite possible that some rare cases eventually will be attributed primarily to single genes and others primarily to environmental factors. Furthermore, within the MFP majority, it is possible that a minority eventually will be attributable in part to a major gene (combined with polygenes and the environment) with low penetrance.

The phenotypic heterogeneity of schizophrenia challenges all theoretical approaches. This chapter attempted to conceptualize heterogeneity in terms of the MFP model, including a consideration of affective systems relevant to nonspecific liability. From the perspective of the MFP model, a greater genetic loading will on average be associated with a more chronic course, accounting for one aspect of heterogeneity. The frequent pairing of affective and schizophrenic symptoms suggests that the affective and schizophrenia vulnerabilities combine additively to produce a continuum from relatively pure schizophrenia to relatively pure affective disorder with many cases of schizoaffective symptomatology. Depue's work indicates that mania involves uncontrolled activation of the BFS, and it was suggested here that the dopaminergic activity central to this system contributes nonspecifically to schizophrenia liability. Depression involves suppression of this same system, combined with high negative affect–anxiety. It was proposed that the negative affect contributes nonspecifically to liability and that the failure to activate the BFS results in negative symptoms in the form of social withdrawal. Negative symptoms also were attributed to a temperamentally weak BFS combined with a temperamentally strong BIS, along with a social environment that is unrewarding and aversive. The extreme negative symptoms seen in the deficit schizophrenia subtype described by Carpenter and his colleagues are likely to reflect poor functioning of the BFS, possibly due to a CNS dysfunction that directly or indirectly disrupts the BFS or due to extremes of temperament combined with unrewarding-aversive environments.

Given the difficulty of accounting for schizophrenia symptoms in terms of psychosocial environmental events alone, intense interest naturally has focused on theories of brain dysfunction. These efforts, however, have been hindered by the crudeness of techniques for assessing CNS functioning and by the complexity of schizophrenia. Two major findings have been enlarged ventricles (a structural measure indirectly indicating smaller brain size) and hypofrontality (a functional measure showing diminished activation of the frontal cortex). Neither finding has resulted in clear conclusions concerning the neurobiological substrate for schizophrenia. More recently, the earlier search for a deficit in a single area of the brain has been replaced by an emphasis on interactions among many different regions, with hypotheses centering on abnormal interconnectedness of different areas as a result of neurodevelopmental failures. As interesting as these hypotheses are, again no firm conclusions have been reached.

The conceptualization of schizophrenia in the present chapter attempted to account for heterogeneity while retaining the parsimonious assumption of an underlying schizophrenic process varying in severity, to a substantial degree as a function of genetic liability. In that sense, it embraced Carpenter's (1992) second model, seeing schizophrenia as a single disease entity with heterogeneity attributed to the interaction between this primary pathology and other characteristics of the individual and the environment. By hypothesizing two affective neurobehavioral systems that contribute different types of nonspecific liability and have different effects on behavior, it was possible to account for important aspects of heterogeneity without giving up the concept of schizophrenia as a distinct phenomenon. While this approach, like all biological theories of schizophrenia, must be considered a work in progress, it is argued here that such important functional neurobehavioral systems cannot be ignored in any adequate approach to developing psychobiological theories of psychopathology.

## REFERENCES

American Psychiatric Association. (1980). *Diagnostic and statistical manual of mental disorders* (3rd ed.). Washington, DC: Author.

American Psychiatric Association. (1987). *Diagnostic and statistical manual of mental disorders* (3rd ed. Rev.). Washington, DC: Author.

American Psychiatric Association. (1994). *Diagnostic and statistical manual of mental disorders* (4th ed.). Washington, DC: Author.

American Psychiatric Association. (2000). *Diagnostic and statistical manual of mental disorders* (4th ed., Text Revision). Washington, DC: Author.

Andreasen, N. C. (1985). Positive vs. negative schizophrenia: A critical evaluation. *Schizophrenia Bulletin, 11,* 380–389.

Andreasen, N. C. (2001). *Brave new brain.* New York: Oxford University Press.

Andreasen, N. C., Arndt, S., Alliger, R., Miller, D., & Flaum, M. (1995). Symptoms of schizophrenia: Methods, meanings, and mechanisms. *Archives of General Psychiatry, 52,* 341–351.

Andreasen, N. C., & Carpenter, W. T., Jr. (1993). Diagnosis and classification of schizophrenia. *Schizophrenia Bulletin, 19,* 199–214.

Andreasen, N. C., Flaum, M., Swayze, V. W., II, Tyrell, G., & Arndt, S. (1990). Positive and negative symptoms in schizophrenia: A critical reappraisal. *Archives of General Psychiatry, 47,* 615–621.

Asarnow, R. F., Nuechterlein, K. H., Fogelson, D., Subotnik, K. L., Payne, D. A., Russell, A. T., Asamen, J., Kuppinger, H., & Kendler, K. S. (2001). Schizophrenia and schizophrenia-spectrum personality disorders in the first-degree relatives of children with schizophrenia. *Archives of General Psychiatry, 58,* 581–588.

Astrachan, B. M., Harrow, M., Adler, D., Brauer, L., Schwartz, A., Schwartz, C., & Tucker, G. (1972). A checklist for the diagnosis of schizophrenia. *British Journal of Psychiatry, 121,* 529–539.

Barlow, D. H., Chorpita, B. F., & Turovsky, J. (1996). Fear, panic, anxiety, and disorders of emotion. In D. A. Hope (Ed.), *Nebraska Symposium on Motivation* (Vol. 43, pp. 251–328). Lincoln: University of Nebraska Press.

Baron, M., & Gruen, R. S. (1991). Schizophrenia and affective disorder: Are they genetically linked? *British Journal of Psychiatry, 159,* 267–270.

Bassett, A. S., Chow, E. W. C., O'Neill, S., & Brzustowicz, L. M. (2001). Genetic insights into the neurodevelopmental hypothesis of schizophrenia. *Schizophrenia Bulletin, 27,* 417–430.

Battaglia, M., & Torgersen, S. (1996). Schizotypal disorder: At the crossroads of genetics and nosology. *Acta Psychiatrica Scandinavica, 94,* 303–310.

Berman, K. F., & Weinberger, D. R. (1999). Neuroimaging studies of schizophrenia. In D. S. Charney, E. J. Nestler, & B. S. Bunney (Eds.), *Neurobiology of mental illness* (pp. 246–257). Oxford, England: Oxford University Press.

Birley, J. L. T., & Brown, G. W. (1970). Crises and life changes preceding the onset or relapse of acute schizophrenia: Clinical aspects. *British Journal of Psychiatry, 116,* 327–333.

Bleuler, E. (1950). *Dementia praecox or the group of schizophrenias.* New York: International Universities Press. (Original work published 1911)

Bleuler, M. (1974). The long-term course of schizophrenic psychoses. *Psychological Medicine, 4,* 244–254.

Braden, W. (1984). Vulnerability and schizoaffective psychosis: A two-factor model. *Schizophrenia Bulletin, 10,* 71–86.

Brown, G., Birley, J. L. T., & Wing, J. K. (1972). Influence of family life on the course of schizophrenic disorder: A replication. *British Journal of Psychiatry, 121,* 241–258.

Bunney, W. E., Jr., & Bunney, B. G. (1999). Neurodevelopmental hypothesis of schizophrenia. In D. S. Charney, E. J. Nestler, & B. S.

Bunney (Eds.), *Neurobiology of mental illness* (pp. 225–235). Oxford, England: Oxford University Press.

Byne, W., Kemether, E., Jones, L., Haroutunian, V., & Davis, K. (1999). The neurochemistry of schizophrenia. In D. S. Charney, E. J. Nestler, & B. S. Bunney (Eds.), *Neurobiology of mental illness* (pp. 236–245). Oxford, England: Oxford University Press.

Cardno, A. G., & Gottesman, I. I. (2000). Twin studies of schizophrenia: From bow-and-arrow concordances to Star Wars Mx and functional genomics. *American Journal of Medical Genetics, 97,* 12–17.

Cardno, A. G., Marshall, E. J., Coid, B., Macdonald, A. M., Ribchester, T. R., Davies, N. J., Venturi, P., Jones, L. A., Lewis, S. W., Sham, P. C., Gottesman, I. I., Farmer, A. E., McGuffin, P., Reveley, A. M., & Murray, R. M. (1999). Heritability estimates for psychotic disorders: The Maudsley twin psychosis series. *Archives of General Psychiatry, 56,* 162–168.

Carpenter, W. T., Jr. (1992). The negative symptom challenge. *Archives of General Psychiatry, 49,* 236–237.

Carpenter, W. T., Jr. (1994). The deficit syndrome. *American Journal of Psychiatry, 151,* 327–329.

Carpenter, W. T., Jr., Buchanan, R. W., Kirkpatrick, B., Thaker, G., & Tamminga, C. (1991). Negative symptoms: A critique of current approaches. In A. Marneros, N. C. Andreasen, & M. T. Tsuang (Eds.), *Negative versus positive schizophrenia* (pp. 126–133). New York: Springer-Verlag.

Carpenter, W. T., Jr., Heinrichs, D. W., & Wagman, A. M. I. (1985). On the heterogeneity of schizophrenia. In M. Alpert (Ed.), *Controversies in schizophrenia: Changes and constancies* (pp. 38–47). New York: Guilford Press.

Carpenter, W. T., Jr., Heinrichs, D. W., & Wagman, A. M. I. (1988). Deficit and nondeficit forms of schizophrenia: The concept. *American Journal of Psychiatry, 145,* 578–583.

Carpenter, W. T., Jr., Strauss, J. S., & Bartko, J. J. (1973). Flexible system for the diagnosis of schizophrenia: Report from the WHO International Pilot Study of Schizophrenia. *Science, 182,* 1275–1278.

Chapman, L. J., & Chapman, J. P. (1973). *Disordered thought in schizophrenia.* Englewood Cliffs, NJ: Prentice-Hall.

Crow, T. J. (1980). Molecular pathology of schizophrenia: More than one disease process? *British Medical Journal, 180,* 66–68.

Crow, T. J. (1985). The two-syndrome concept: Origins and current status. *Schizophrenia Bulletin, 11,* 471–486.

Crow, T. J. (1986). The continuum of psychosis and its implications for the structure of the gene. *British Journal of Psychiatry, 149,* 419–429.

Crow, T. J. (1991). The search for the psychosis gene. *British Journal of Psychiatry, 158,* 611–614.

Crow, T. J. (1998). From Kraepelin to Kretschmer leavened by Schneider. *Archives of General Psychiatry, 55,* 502–504.

Cuesta, M. J., Peralta, V., & Caro, F. (1999). Premorbid personality in psychoses. *Schizophrenia Bulletin, 25,* 801–811.

Day, R., Nielsen, J. A., Korten, A., Ernberg, G., Dube, K. C., Gebhart, J., Jablensky, A., Leon, C., Marsella, A., Olatawura, M., Sartorius, N., Stromgren, E., Takahashi, R., Wig, N., & Wynne, L. C. (1987). Stressful life events preceding the acute onset of schizophrenia: A cross-national study from the World Health Organization. *Culture, Medicine, and Psychiatry, 11,* 123–205.

Depue, R. A. (1976). An activity-withdrawal distinction in schizophrenia: Behavioral, clinical brain damage, and neurophysiological correlates. *Journal of Abnormal Psychology, 85,* 174–185.

Depue, R. A., & Collins, P. F. (1999). Neurobiology of the structure of personality: Dopamine, facilitation of incentive motivation, and extraversion. *Behavioral and Brain Sciences, 22,* 491–569.

Depue, R. A., Collins, P. F., & Luciana, M. (1996). A model of neurobiology-environment interaction in developmental psychopathology. In M. F. Lenzenweger & J. J. Haugaard (Eds.), *Frontiers of developmental psychopathology* (pp. 44–77). New York: Oxford University Press.

Depue, R. A., & Iacono, W. G. (1989). Neurobehavioral aspects of affective disorders. *Annual Review of Psychology, 40,* 457–492.

Depue, R. A., Krauss, S. P., & Spoont, M. R. (1987). A two-dimensional threshold model of seasonal bipolar affective disorder. In D. Magnusson & A. Ohman (Eds.), *Psychopathology: An interactionist perspective* (pp. 95–123). New York: Academic Press.

Depue, R. A., & Lenzenweger, M. F. (2001). A neurobehavioral dimensional model. In W. J. Livesley (Ed.), *Handbook of personality disorders: Theory, research, and treatment* (pp. 136–176). New York: Guilford Press.

Depue, R. A., & Zald, D. (1993). Biological and environmental processes in nonpsychotic psychopathology: A neurobehavioral perspective. In C. G. Costello (Ed.), *Basic issues in psychopathology* (pp. 127–237). New York: Guilford Press.

Dohrenwend, B. P., & Egri, G. (1981). Recent stressful life events and episodes of schizophrenia. *Schizophrenia Bulletin, 7,* 12–23.

Eastman, C. (1976). Behavioral formulations of depression. *Psychological Review, 83,* 277–291.

Endicott, J., Nee, J., Fleiss, J., Cohen, J., Williams, J. B. W., & Simon, R. (1982). Diagnostic criteria for schizophrenia. *Archives of General Psychiatry, 39,* 884–889.

Faraone, S. V., Green, A. I., Seidman, L. J., & Tsuang, M. T. (2001). "Schizotaxia": Clinical implications and new directions for research. *Schizophrenia Bulletin, 27,* 1–18.

Faraone, S. V., & Tsuang, M. T. (1985). Quantitative models of the genetic transmission of schizophrenia. *Psychological Bulletin, 98,* 41–66.

Farmer, A. E., McGuffin, P., & Gottesman, I. I. (1987). Twin concordance for DSM-III schizophrenia. *Archives of General Psychiatry, 44,* 634–641.

Feighner, J. P., Robins, E., Guze, S. B., Woodruff, R. A., Winokur, G., & Munoz, R. (1972). Diagnostic criteria for use in psychiatric research. *Archives of General Psychiatry, 26,* 57–63.

Fenton, W. S., & McGlashan, T. H. (1992). Testing systems for assessment of negative symptoms in schizophrenia. *Archives of General Psychiatry, 49,* 179–184.

Fowles, D. (1992a). Motivational approach to anxiety disorders. In D. G. Forgays, T. Sosnowski, & K. Wrzesniewski (Eds.), *Anxiety: Recent developments in cognitive, psychophysiological, and health research* (pp. 181–192). Washington: Hemisphere.

Fowles, D. (1992b). Schizophrenia: Diathesis-stress revisited. *Annual Review of Psychology, 43,* 303–336.

Fowles, D. (1994). A motivational theory of psychopathology. In W. Spaulding (Ed.), *Nebraska Symposium on Motivation: Integrated views of motivation and emotion* (Vol. 41, pp. 181–238). Lincoln: University of Nebraska Press.

Gottesman, I. I. (1991). *Schizophrenia genesis.* New York: W. H. Freeman.

Gottesman, I. I., & Bertelsen, A. (1989). Confirming unexpressed genotypes for schizophrenia. *Archives of General Psychiatry, 46,* 867–872.

Gottesman, I. I., & McGue, M. (1991). Mixed and mixed-up models for the transmission of schizophrenia. In D. Cicchetti & W. M. Grove (Eds.), *Thinking clearly about psychology: Vol. 2. Personality and psychopathology (Essays in honor of Paul E. Meehl)* (pp. 295–312). Minneapolis: University of Minnesota Press.

Gottesman, I. I., McGuffin, P., & Farmer, A. E. (1987). Clinical genetics as clues to the "real" genetics of schizophrenia (A decade of modest gains while playing for time). *Schizophrenia Bulletin, 13,* 23–47.

Gottesman, I. I., & Moldin, S. O. (1998). Genotypes, genes, genesis, and pathogenesis in schizophrenia. In M. F. Lenzenweger & R. H. Dworkin (Eds.), *Origins and development of schizophrenia* (pp. 5–26). Washington, DC: American Psychological Association.

Gottesman, I. I., & Shields, J. A. (1966). Schizophrenia in twins: Sixteen years' consecutive admissions to a psychiatric clinic. *British Journal of Psychiatry, 112,* 809–818.

Gottesman, I. I., & Shields, J. A. (1967). A polygenic theory of schizophrenia. *Proceedings of the National Academy of Sciences, 58,* 199–205.

Gottesman, I. I., & Shields, J. A. (1972). *Schizophrenia and genetics: A twin study vantage point.* New York: Academic Press.

Gottesman, I. I., & Shields, J. A. (1976). A critical review of recent adoption, twin, and family studies of schizophrenia: Behavioral genetics perspective. *Schizophrenia Bulletin, 2,* 360–401.

Gottesman, I. I., & Shields, J. A. (1982). *Schizophrenia: The epigenetic puzzle.* New York: Cambridge University Press.

Gray, J. A. (1982). *The neuropsychology of anxiety: An enquiry into the functions of the septo-hippocampal system.* Oxford, England: Oxford University Press.

Gray, J. A. (1987). *The psychology of fear and stress* (2nd ed.). Cambridge, England: Cambridge University Press.

Gray, J. A., & McNaughton, N. (1996). The neuropsychology of anxiety: Reprise. In D. A. Hope (Ed.), *Nebraska Symposium on Motivation* (Vol. 43, pp. 61–134). Lincoln: University of Nebraska Press.

Gray, J. A., & McNaughton, N. (2000). *The neuropsychology of anxiety: An enquiry into the functions of the septo-hippocampal system* (2nd ed.). Oxford, England: Oxford University Press.

Grossman, L. S., Harrow, M., Goldberg, J. F., & Fichtner, C. G. (1991). Outcome of schizoaffective disorder at two long-term follow-ups: Comparisons with outcome of schizophrenia and affective disorders. *American Journal of Psychiatry, 148,* 1359–1365.

Harrow, M., Yonan, C. A., Sands, J. R., & Marengo, J. (1994). Depression in schizophrenia: Are neuroleptics, akinesia, or anhedonia involved? *Schizophrenia Bulletin, 20,* 327–338.

Heston, L. L., & Denney, D. (1968). Interactions between early life experience and biological factors in schizophrenia. In D. Rosenthal & S. S. Kety (Eds.), *The transmission of schizophrenia.* New York: Pergamon Press.

Hooley, J. M., & Hiller, J. B. (1998). Expressed emotion and the pathogenesis of relapse in schizophrenia. In M. F. Lenzenweger & R. H. Dworkin (Eds.), *Origins and development of schizophrenia: Advances in experimental psychopathology* (pp. 447–468). Washington, DC: American Psychological Association.

Iacono, W. G. (1998). Identifying psychophysiological risk for psychopathology: Examples from substance abuse and schizophrenia research. *Psychophysiology, 35,* 621–637.

Johnstone, E. C. (1999a). Diagnostic issues: Concepts of the disorder. In E. Johnstone, M. Humphreys, F. Lang, S. Lawrie, & R. Sandler (Eds.), *Schizophrenia: Concepts and clinical management* (pp. 20–43). Cambridge, England: Cambridge University Press.

Johnstone, E. C. (1999b). Epidemiology and genetics. In E. Johnstone, M. Humphreys, F. Lang, S. Lawrie, & R. Sandler (Eds.), *Schizophrenia: Concepts and clinical management* (pp. 145–160). Cambridge, England: Cambridge University Press.

Johnstone, E. C. (1999c). Introduction. In E. Johnstone, M. Humphreys, F. Lang, S. Lawrie, & R. Sandler (Eds.), *Schizophrenia: Concepts and clinical management* (pp. 1–19). Cambridge, England: Cambridge University Press.

Kapur, S., & Remington, G. (1996). Serotonin-dopamine interaction and its relevance to schizophrenia. *American Journal of Psychiatry, 153,* 466–476.

Kendell, R. E. (1982). The choice of diagnostic criteria for biological research. *Archives of General Psychiatry, 39,* 1334–1339.

Kendler, K. S. (1999). Molecular genetics of schizophrenia. In D. S. Charney, E. J. Nestler, & B. S. Bunney (Eds.), *Neurobiology of mental illness* (pp. 203–213). Oxford, England: Oxford University Press.

Kendler, K. S., & Diehl, S. R. (1993). The genetics of schizophrenia. *Schizophrenia Bulletin, 19,* 261–285.

Kendler, K. S., & Diehl, S. R. (1995). Schizophrenia: Genetics. In H. I. Kaplan & B. Sadock (Eds.), *Comprehensive textbook of psychiatry* (6th ed., pp. 942–957). Baltimore: Williams & Wilkins.

Kendler, K. S., Gruenberg, A. M., & Kinney, D., K. (1994). Independent diagnoses of adoptees and relatives as defined by DSM-III in the Provincial and National samples of the Danish Adoption Study of Schizophrenia. *Archives of General Psychiatry, 51,* 456–468.

Kendler, K. S., Gruenberg, A. M., & Tsuang, M. T. (1986). A DSM-III family study of the non-schizophrenic psychotic disorders. *American Journal of Psychiatry, 143,* 1098–1105.

Kendler, K. S., Neale, M. C., Kessler, R. C., Heath, A. C., & Eaves, L. J. (1992). Major depression and generalized anxiety disorder: Same genes, (partly) different environments? *Archives of General Psychiatry, 49,* 716–722.

Kety, S. S., Rosenthal, D., Wender, P. H., & Schulsinger, F. (1968). The types and prevalence of mental illness in the biological and adoptive families of adopted schizophrenics. In D. Rosenthal & S. S. Kety (Eds.), *The transmission of schizophrenia* (pp. 345–362). Oxford, England: Pergamon.

Kety, S. S., Rosenthal, D., Wender, P. H., Schulsinger, F., & Jacobsen, B. (1978). The biological and adoptive families of adopted individual who became schizophrenic: Prevalence of mental illness and other characteristics. In L. C. Wynne, R. L. Cromwell, & S. Matthysse (Eds.), *The nature of schizophrenia* (pp. 25–37). New York: Wiley.

Kety, S. S., Wender, P. H., Jacobsen, B., Ingraham, L. J., Jansson, L., Faber, B., & Kinney, D. K. (1994). Mental illness in the biological and adoptive relatives of schizophrenic adoptees: Replication of the Copenhagen study in the rest of Denmark. *Archives of General Psychiatry, 51,* 442–455.

Kirkpatrick, B., Buchanan, R. W., Ross, D. E., & Carpenter, W. T., Jr. (2001). A separate disease within the syndrome of schizophrenia. *Archives of General Psychiatry, 58,* 165–171.

Krystal, J. H., Abi-Dargham, A., Laruelle, M., & Moghaddam, B. (1999). Pharmacologic models of psychoses. In D. S. Charney, E. J. Nestler, & B. S. Bunney (Eds.), *Neurobiology of mental illness* (pp. 214–224). Oxford, England: Oxford University Press.

Leff, J. P. (1976). Schizophrenia and sensitivity to the family environment. *Schizophrenia Bulletin, 2,* 566–574.

Leff, J. P., & Vaughn, C. E. (1985). *Expressed emotion in families: Its significance for mental illness.* New York: Guilford Press.

Leshner, A. I. (1997). Addiction is a brain disease, and it matters. *Science, 278,* 45–47.

Levinson, D. F., & Levitt, M. E. M. (1987). Schizoaffective mania reconsidered. *The American Journal of Psychiatry, 144,* 415–425.

Lewine, R. J. (1985). Negative symptoms in schizophrenia: Editor's introduction. *Schizophrenia Bulletin, 11,* 361–363.

Liddle, P. F. (1987). The symptoms of chronic schizophrenia: A reexamination of the positive-negative dichotomy. *British Journal of Psychiatry, 151,* 145–151.

Liddle, P., Carpenter, W. T., & Crow, T. (1993). Syndromes of schizophrenia: Classic literature [Editorial]. *British Journal of Psychiatry, 165,* 721–727.

Linszen, D. H., Dingemans, P. M., Nugter, M. A., Van der Does, A. J. W., Scholte, W. F., & Lenior, M. A. (1997). Patient attributes and expressed emotion as risk factors for psychotic relapse. *Schizophrenia Bulletin, 23,* 119–130.

Losonczy, M. F., Davidson, M., & Davis, K. L. (1987). The dopamine hypothesis of schizophrenia. In H. Y. Meltzer (Ed.), *Psychopharmacology: The third generation of progress* (pp. 715–726). New York: Raven Press.

Maier, W., Lichtermann, D., Minges, J., Hallmayer, J., Heun, R., Benkert, O., & Levinson, D. F. (1993). Continuity and discontinuity of affective disorders and schizophrenia: Results of a controlled family study. *Archives of General Psychiatry, 50,* 871–883.

McGue, M., & Gottesman, I. I. (1989). Genetic linkage in schizophrenia: Perspectives from genetic epidemiology. *Schizophrenia Bulletin, 15,* 453–464.

McGuffin, P., Farmer, A. E., Gottesman, I. I., Murray, R. M., & Reveley, A. M. (1984). The concordance of operationally defined schizophrenia: Confirmation of familiality and heritability. *Archives of General Psychiatry, 41,* 541–545.

McNaughton, N., & Gray, J. A. (2000). Anxiolytic action on the behavioural inhibition system implies multiple types of arousal contribute to anxiety. *Journal of Affective Disorders, 61,* 161–176.

Meehl, P. E. (1962). Schizotaxia, schizotypy, schizophrenia. *American Psychologist, 17,* 827–838.

Meinecke, D. L. (2001). The developmental etiology of schizophrenia hypothesis: What is the evidence? Editor's introduction. *Schizophrenia Bulletin, 27,* 335–336.

Meltzer, H. Y. (1984). Schizoaffective disorder; Editor's introduction. *Schizophrenia Bulletin, 10,* 11–13.

Mineka, S., Watson, D., & Clark, L. A. (1998). Comorbidity of anxiety and unipolar mood disorders. *Annual Review of Psychology, 49,* 377–412.

Mirsky, A. F., Bieliauskas, L. A., French, L. M., Van Kammen, D. P., Jönsson, E., & Sedvall, G. (2000). A 39-year follow-up of the Genain quadruplets. *Schizophrenia Bulletin, 26,* 699–708.

Moldin, S. O., & Gottesman, I. I. (1997). At issue: Genes, experience, and chance in schizophrenia—positioning for the 21st century. *Schizophrenia Bulletin, 23,* 547–561.

Morey, L. C. (1991). Classification of mental disorder as a collection of hypothetical constructs. *Journal of Abnormal Psychology, 100,* 289–293.

Murray, R. M., Lewis, S., & Reveley, A. M. (1985). Towards an aetiological classification of schizophrenia. *Lancet, 1,* 1023–1026.

Neale, J. M., & Oltmanns, T. F. (1980). *Schizophrenia.* New York: Wiley.

Nuechterlein, K. H., Snyder, K. S., & Mintz, J. (1992). Paths to relapse: Possible transactional processes connecting patient illness onset, expressed emotion, and psychotic relapse. *British Journal of Psychiatry, 161,* 88–96.

Plomin, R. (1990). The role of inheritance in behavior. *Science, 248,* 183–188.

Plomin, R., DeFries, J. C., McLearn, G. E., & Rutter, M. (1997). *Behavioral genetics* (3rd ed). New York: W. H. Freeman.

Procci, W. R. (1989). Psychotic disorders not elsewhere classified. In H. Kaplan & B. Sadock (Eds.), *Comprehensive textbook of psychiatry*, (Vol. 5, pp. 830–842). Baltimore: Williams & Williams.

Reynolds, G. P. (1989). Beyond the dopamine hypothesis: The neurochemical pathology of schizophrenia. *British Journal of Psychiatry, 155,* 305–316.

Rosenthal, D. (Ed.). (1963). *The Genain quadruplets: A case study and theoretical analysis of heredity and environment in schizophrenia.* New York: Basic Books.

Rosenthal, D. (1970). *Genetic theory and abnormal behavior.* New York: McGraw-Hill.

Rutter, M. L. (1997). Nature-nurture integration. The example of antisocial behavior. *American Psychologist, 52,* 390–398.

Sands, J. R., & Harrow, M. (1999). Depression during the longitudinal course of schizophrenia. *Schizophrenia Bulletin, 25,* 157–171.

Siris, S. G., & Lavin, M. R. (1995). Schizoaffective disorder, schizophreniform disorder, and brief reactive psychotic disorder. In H. I. Kaplan & B. Sadock (Eds.), *Comprehensive textbook of psychiatry* (6th ed., pp. 1019–1031). Baltimore: Williams & Wilkins.

Snyder, S. H. (1978). Dopamine and schizophrenia. In L. C. Wynne, R. L. Cromwell, & S. Matthysse (Eds.), *The nature of schizophrenia* (pp. 87–94). New York: Wiley.

Sommers, A. A. (1985). "Negative symptoms": Conceptual and methodological problems. *Schizophrenia Bulletin, 11,* 364–379.

Spitzer, R. L., Endicott, J., & Robins, E. (1978). Research diagnostic criteria: Rationale and reliability. *Archives of General Psychiatry, 35,* 773–789.

Strauss, J., Carpenter, W. T., Jr., & Bartko, J. (1974). The diagnosis and understanding of schizophrenia: Part III. Speculations on the processes that underlie schizophrenic symptoms and signs [Experimental issue]. *Schizophrenia Bulletin, 1,* 61–69.

Strauss, J., & Gift, T. E. (1977). Choosing an approach for diagnosing schizophrenia. *Archives of General Psychology, 34,* 1248–1253.

Strauss, M. (2001). Demonstrating specific cognitive deficits: A psychometric perspective. *Journal of Abnormal Psychology, 110,* 6–14.

Taylor, M. A. (1992). Are schizophrenia and affective disorder related? A selective review of the literature. *American Journal of Psychiatry, 149,* 22–32.

Taylor, M. A., Berenbaum, S. A., Jampala, V. C., & Cloninger, C. R. (1993). Are schizophrenia and affective disorder related? Preliminary data from a family study. *American Journal of Psychiatry, 150,* 278–285.

Tellegen, A. (1985). Structures of mood and personality and their relevance to assessing anxiety, with an emphasis on self-report. In A. H. Tuma & J. D. Maser (Eds.), *Anxiety and the anxiety disorders* (pp. 681–706). Hillsdale, NJ: Erlbaum.

Tienari, P. (1991). Interaction between genetic vulnerability and family environment: The Finnish adoptive family study of schizophrenia. *Acta Psychiatrica Scandinavica, 84,* 460–465.

Tsuang, M. T., & Faraone, S. V. (1995). The case for heterogeneity in the etiology of schizophrenia. *Schizophrenia Research, 17,* 161–175.

Tsuang, M. T., & Faraone, S. V. (1997). *Schizophrenia: The facts* (2nd ed.). New York: Oxford University Press.

Vaughn, C., & Leff, J. (1976). The influence of family and social factors on the course of psychiatric illness. *British Journal of Psychiatry, 129,* 125–137.

Venables, P. H. (1957). A short scale for rating "Activity-Withdrawal" in schizophrenics. *Journal of Mental Science, 103,* 197–199.

Venables, P. H. (1963a). The relationship between level of skin potential and fusion of paired light flashes in schizophrenic and normal subjects. *Journal of Psychiatric Research, 1,* 279–287.

Venables, P. H. (1963b). Selectivity of attention, withdrawal, and cortical activation. *Archives of General Psychiatry, 9,* 74–78.

Venables, P. H. (1967). The relation of two flash and two click thresholds to withdrawal in paranoid and non-paranoid schizophrenics. *British Journal of Social and Clinical Psychology, 6,* 60–62.

Venables, P. H., & Wing, J. K. (1962). Level of arousal and the subclassification of schizophrenia. *Archives of General Psychiatry, 7,* 114–119.

Ventura, J., Nuechterlein, K. H., Lukoff, D., & Hardesty, J. P. (1989). A prospective study of stressful life events and schizophrenic relapse. *Journal of Abnormal Psychology, 98,* 407–411.

Walker, E., & Diforio, D. (1997). Schizophrenia: A neural diathesis-stress model. *Psychological Review, 104,* 667–685.

Waltrip, R. W., Buchanan, R. W., Carpenter, W. T., Kirkpatrick, B., Summerfelt, A., Breier, A., Rubin, S. A., & Carbone, K. M. (1997). Borna disease virus antibodies and the deficit syndrome of schizophrenia. *Schizophrenia Research, 23,* 253–257.

Weinberger, D. R. (1987). Implications of normal brain development for the pathogenesis of schizophrenia. *Archives of General Psychiatry, 44,* 660–669.

Weinberger, D. R., & Lipska, B. K. (1995). Cortical maldevelopment, anti-psychotic drugs, and schizophrenia: A search for common ground. *Schizophrenia Research, 16,* 87–110.

Williams, P. V., & McGlashan, T. H. (1987). Schizoaffective psychosis. *Archives of General Psychiatry, 44,* 130–137.

Wing, J. K. (1978). Social influences on the course of schizophrenia. In L. C. Wynne, R. L. Cromwell, & S. Matthysse (Eds.), *The nature of schizophrenia* (pp. 599–616). New York: Wiley.

Wing, J. K., & Brown, G. W. (1970). *Institutionalism and schizophrenia.* London: Cambridge University Press.

Wise, R. A., & Bozarth, M. A. (1987). A psychomotor stimulant theory of addiction. *Psychological Review, 94,* 469–492.

Wise, R. A., & Rompre, P.-P. (1989). Brain dopamine and reward. *Annual Review of Psychology, 40,* 191–225.

Zubin, J., & Spring, B. (1977). Vulnerability—A new view of schizophrenia. *Journal of Abnormal Psychology, 86,* 103–126.

CHAPTER 4

# Mood Disorders

CONSTANCE HAMMEN

*Mood disorders* are psychological disturbances defined by intense emotional experiences of depression or mania (or both). They are remarkably diverse in their features but share a focus on an excessive mood that colors and distorts the way the person thinks and views the world, accompanied by changed levels of movement, activity, and energy; disturbed patterns of sleep and appetite; and altered motivation and engagement in the world. Mood disorders encompass both commonplace and relatively rare disorders; their features may vary greatly from one individual to another, ranging from mild, transient changes to severe or enduring conditions. Some disorders of mood are apparently understandable reactions to life's adversities, while others may seem baffling in their origin and accompanied by psychotic departures from reality. No segment of the population is immune; mood disorders afflict the young and the old, men and women, and people of any culture. Depressive disorders are so frequent that they have been called the common cold of psychological disorders. Unlike the common cold, however, their consequences might be profoundly distressing and disruptive to the sufferer and his or her family. No matter how frequent and how impairing they may be, mood disorders are often misunderstood, both by society and by the sufferer and those in his or her life, and may be erroneously

viewed by others as weaknesses of will or character and failures of emotional self-control.

In the following chapter the topics discussed are unipolar depression and bipolar disorder, the two major forms of mood disorders, and their variants. Despite some similarities, the two disorders are viewed as distinct in their manifestations, underlying causes, and recommended treatments. Consequently, the chapter presents information on these disorders in separate sections.

## DEFINING AND DIAGNOSING UNIPOLAR DEPRESSION

### The Experience of Depression

*Depressed* is a word in such common usage that it is often used interchangeably with upset, disappointed, or some similar term to refer to a negative emotion following a bad experience. Depression may be a mood *state,* lasting only a few moments or hours—occasionally a few days—but in which other elements of the person's functioning are unchanged. It is, in fact, normal to have mild and brief depressed mood following an important loss or disappointment. Depression as a psychological *disorder* is more than a temporary, mild mood state. It is a constellation of experiences of mood, physical functioning, quality of thinking and outlook, and behaviors.

The depressed person may feel down or sad, but sadness may often be less apparent than a general lack of interest in activities that were once enjoyed. Irritability may be the dominant mood, rather than sadness. Changes in mood are accompanied by a gloomy outlook in which the future seems bleak and uninviting, and the person views himself or herself as flawed and inadequate, while circumstances may seem overwhelmingly difficult or unrelenting in their deprivation and capacity for disappointment. Because of the negative outlook, the sufferer's motivation and persistence may be impaired. The negative interpretations of the self and world that are typical of depression may seem illogical or distorted to others, and there appears to be a focus on negative possibilities to the neglect of positive or even neutral alternatives: "Even though I got this promotion at work, I will fail"; "my family is supportive of me, but I don't deserve it, and they will give up on me." Bodily changes may become pronounced with increasing severity of depression; sleep is interrupted by awakening in the night or early morning—although sometimes people sleep even more than usual. Some individuals may focus extensively on aches and pains and physical debility and medical symptoms. Energy flags, and for some depression sufferers, it is an immense chore to get out of bed, shower, and get dressed. Appetite may be lost, and loss of weight may result, although some individuals do not experience such changes and may even eat more than usual. Behaviors mirror the inner suffering; depressed individuals may withdraw from others or discontinue typical activities, having little pleasure or energy to sustain them—and even finding that being around others makes them feel worse. Of course, others do indeed find it difficult to enjoy the company of a silent or suffering person who cannot be cheered, and may be frustrated with the depressed person's seemingly willful exaggerations of negativity that they perceive inside and all around themselves. Some people experience depression as relentless suffering from which the only escape is death. For such sufferers, thoughts of death may be persistent, and unfortunately, for a significant minority of depressed people, suicidal acts may seem to be the only escape. What may seem to others as an irrational reaction or an excessive and selfish display of self-pity may even contribute to the depressed person's feeling of abandonment at the time of greatest need. A vicious cycle of negative thoughts and more depressed mood and behaviors may contribute to a prolonged period of depressive suffering.

## Diagnoses of Depression

The phenomenology of depression is relatively well recognized, and diagnostic systems have been developed to attempt to define key symptoms among the many possible manifestations, and to operationally define the point at which normal depressed mood becomes a clinical state. The current *Diagnostic and Statistical Manual of Mental Disorders–Fourth Edition* (*DSM IV;* American Psychiatric Association [APA], 1994a) and *International Classification of Diseases–10th Revision* (*ICD-10;* World Health Organization, 1992) have evolved from various efforts to provide systematic, reliable definitions. There are four key features of diagnoses of depressive disorders: presence of more than depressed or negative mood—requiring a variety of additional syndrome manifestations; duration over a period of weeks or months to distinguish depression from temporary mood shifts; and impairment, indicating that the depression interferes with normal functioning. The fourth feature is critical to distinguishing between unipolar and bipolar mood disorders: There must be information about prior symptomatology sufficient to determine whether the individual has ever experienced a manic or hypomanic episode (described later). Only if there has never been such an experience could a person receive a diagnosis of unipolar depression. Those with histories of mania are diagnosed with bipolar disorder.

### Major Depressive Episode and Dysthymic Disorder

The two most common unipolar diagnoses are *major depressive episode (MDE)* and *dysthymic disorder.* To meet diagnostic criteria for MDE, one must be depressed for at least two weeks, experience depressed mood nearly every day all day or have a loss of interest or pleasure, and at least four of the remaining nine symptoms (covering a range of cognitive, physical, and behavioral changes, such as diminished ability to think positively about the self or future or to concentrate; thoughts of death; changes in speed and spontaneity of movement). Dysthymic disorder is a milder, chronic form of depression that includes depressive experiences lasting for at least two years, accompanied by two or more of six milder depressive symptoms. Both MDE and dysthymic disorder diagnoses require the presence of impaired functioning in the person's important roles. Some individuals experience *double depression,* a pattern observed in about 25% of clinical patients in which major depressive episodes are superimposed on dysthymic disorder, an especially adverse disorder in terms of course and impairment in adults (e.g., Keller, Lavori, Endicott, Coryell, & Klerman, 1983; Klein, Taylor, Harding, & Dickstein, 1988). Children who meet criteria for both MDE and dysthymia also appear to function significantly worse than children with either of the disorders alone (Goodman, Schwab-Stone, Lahey, Shaffer, & Jensen, 2000).

Depression in children may be diagnosed with the same criteria as for adults, with minor modifications. For instance, irritability may be substituted for depressed mood, and dysthymic disorder may be diagnosed with only one year's duration. Although there may be developmental differences in expression of depressive symptoms (e.g., young children are unlikely to report subjective states), currently research suggests few reliable differences in symptom patterns in adults and children (reviewed in Garber & Flynn, 2001), and therefore the same criteria are to be used in the absence of validation of alternative procedures. At the same time, however, some have questioned the validity of distinguishing between MDE and dysthymic disorder in children and adolescents, noting that their correlates and impairments are similar (e.g., Goodman et al., 2000).

### Subclinical Depression

Diagnostic criteria for defining MDEs and dysthymia are somewhat arbitrary in their establishment of a cutoff of number and duration of symptoms. Depressive experiences may include subsyndromal symptoms that are milder or briefer than these two diagnoses, or that are intermittent but frequent, or that are mild but enduring. Although mild and short-lived symptoms may have little significance for a person's life and indeed might be considered normal reactions to losses and disappointments, even mild but persistent symptoms may be detrimental to a person's adjustment. Research has shown, for example, that subclinical depressions may predict future diagnosed depressions or other emotional problems, and may result in significant impairment in functioning affecting employment and social roles (e.g., Gotlib, Lewinsohn, & Seeley, 1995; Horwath, Johnson, Klerman, & Weissman, 1992; Wells et al., 1989; Zonderman, Herbst, Schmidt, Costa, & McCrae, 1993). Moreover, persisting mild symptoms following major depression (indicating lack of total recovery) may portend a more severe future course of disorder, including more frequent episodes and chronic symptomatology (Judd et al., 2000).

### Heterogeneity and Comorbidity of Depression

A particular challenge to the diagnosis of depression—and indeed, to the validity of diagnoses—is the fact that depressive experiences may be quite varied and they commonly overlap with or co-occur with other psychological disorders. The variability in presentation may range from premenstrual dysphoria to depressive delusions and psychotic states. Over the years, attempts to define meaningful subtypes have been based on the assumption that different forms of depression may result from different causes, and might have different effective treatments. A particular effort to define biologically based forms (endogenous rather than reactive or psychological forms) has permeated the field. The *DSM-IV* system defines a subtype of *melancholic* features of major depression based on phenomenology with emphasis on somatic symptoms. Although it is sometimes presumed to define a distinct form and perhaps biological origin, some have argued that it may simply represent a more severe version of depression. Another subtype distinction is a *seasonal pattern* of mood disorder, which may occur in both unipolar and bipolar patients. Further efforts to characterize potential etiological subtypes seem warranted, and an important corollary is that models of etiology or treatment methods that are successful with some depressions are unlikely to cover all depressions.

The diagnostic picture may be further complicated by comorbidity. The U.S. National Comorbidity Survey found that of all adult community residents who met criteria for current major depression, only 44% displayed pure depression, and the others had one or more additional diagnoses (Blazer, Kessler, McGonagle, & Swartz, 1994). Commonly co-occurring disorders are anxiety disorders (such as panic disorder, generalized anxiety, and posttraumatic stress disorder), substance abuse, and eating disorders. Moreover, Axis II pathology is extremely common among depressed individuals, with rates across different studies ranging from 23% to 87% (Shea, Widiger, & Klein, 1992). Such mixtures of depression and other disorders frequently portend more complicated courses of depression, and more difficulty in achieving success in treatment (Shea et al.).

In children, comorbidity is said to be the norm rather than the exception, with few children having pure depression rather than mixed with disruptive behavioral, anxiety, eating, and substance use disorders (e.g., reviewed in Angold & Costello, 1993; Hammen & Compas, 1994). High rates of comorbidity may reflect inadequacies in the diagnostic system in which some of the same symptoms may occur in different diagnoses, or over-narrowness in how disorders are conceived. Additionally, in children the indistinct boundaries of diagnoses may reflect a developmental reality in which nonspecific expressions of distress and behavioral disruption cannot readily be classified until further maturation and development occur. Continuing efforts to explore developmentally appropriate criteria for depression in children remain an important research priority (Garber & Flynn, 2001).

### Assessment of Depression

There are presently several widely used instruments available to diagnose unipolar depressive disorders, and to characterize the severity of symptomatology.

#### Diagnosing Depressive Disorders

To meet the goal of reliable, systematic application of diagnostic criteria to determine a person's past or current mood disorder, two methods have been widely used. The *Structured Clinical Interview for DSM-IV Axis I Disorders* (*SCID;* First, Spitzer, Gibbon, & Williams, 1995) has evolved from previous versions of research-oriented diagnostic criteria, including the *Schedule for Affective Disorders and Schizophrenia* (*SADS;* Endicott & Spitzer, 1978). It covers current and past symptomatology sufficient to diagnose most Axis I disorders, using semistructured questions and probes, administered by clinically trained interviewers whose task is to elicit examples and determine whether described experiences fulfill criteria to be included as definite symptoms. Interrater reliabilities for major depressive disorder and dysthymic disorder are high (First et al., 1995). The SCID is used in most research studies to select and define patient samples, and to evaluate the course of disorder.

The other major diagnostic instrument is the *Diagnostic Interview Scale* (*DIS;* Robins, Helzer, Croughan, & Ratcliff, 1981), developed for use in large epidemiological surveys. The major characteristic of the DIS is the highly structured administration of questions, eliciting yes-no answers from respondents, with no follow-up questions to determine the severity or significance of experiences with each symptom. Hence, the DIS requires relatively little training for administration, and does not require clinical experience. A computer algorithm is used to score the DIS, yielding diagnoses independent of clinician judgment. Thus, the DIS is used principally for epidemiological samples that are very large and for which costs of clinically trained interviewers would be prohibitive. The DIS has been reported to yield adequate reliabilities for depressive disorders. Some have feared that the DIS tends to overdiagnose depression because respondents may say *yes* to certain questions based on trivial negative emotional experiences. However, perhaps somewhat surprisingly, comparisons of rates of depressive diagnoses obtained from the DIS compared with a clinician-based interview indicated a tendency of the DIS to result in fewer diagnoses

(Eaton, Neufeld, Chen, & Cai, 2000). The authors suggest that the procedures vary by the threshold at which diagnoses are made, although agreement at the level of reporting syndrome features was fairly good.

It should be noted further that different diagnostic instruments, owing to differences in wording and procedures, may yield different estimates of rates of depression in the population. A recent modified version of the DIS, called the *Composite International Diagnostic Interview* (*CIDI;* e.g., Kessler et al., 1994) was used in the National Comorbidity Survey. Resulting data on incidence and prevalence of depression were notably higher than for the prior DIS-based Epidemiological Catchment Area studies. As Blazer et al. (1994) noted, the instruments differed slightly on the stem questions, with the CIDI asking more stem questions so that there were more opportunities for people to acknowledge a depressive mood. As Regier et al. (1998) observed, actual information about the occurrence of depressive (and other) disorders may be substantially affected by *how* the information is obtained.

#### Assessing Severity of Depressive Symptoms

There are a number of instruments available for research and clinical use to evaluate severity of current depressive symptoms. One type is a self-report questionnaire, exemplified by the *Beck Depression Inventory* (BDI), the most widely used such scale. Developed by Beck, Ward, Mendelsohn, Mock, and Erbaugh (1961), and recently revised as the BDI-II to be consistent with the *DSM-IV* (Beck, Steer, & Brown, 1996), the scale consists of 21 items, each containing four response options differing in severity. Individuals select the one response per item that corresponds most to their current clinical state "over the past two weeks." Total scores indicate level of depression, but like all self-report scales for which a cutoff is used to indicate significant symptoms, the scale is not a diagnostic instrument, and scores may be elevated temporarily due to environmental, medical, or other emotional difficulties. The BDI and BDI-II have been well studied and have excellent reliability and validity for measuring severity of depression (Beck, Steer, & Garbin, 1988; Beck et al., 1996). Further detailed information on additional self-report methods is reviewed in Nezu, Ronan, Meadows, and McClure (2000), *Practitioner's Guide to Empirically Based Measures of Depression*. Also, many instruments have been developed for use with specific populations, such as children and adolescents, geriatric samples, and with specialized content areas related to depression, such as hopelessness, suicidality, self-esteem, and others. There are also measures of depressed mood state, exclusive of additional symptomatology. These are beyond the scope of the current discussion.

Another type of assessment procedure for depression severity involves clinician-based interviews, representing the view that some of the symptoms of depression are more objectively characterized by a trained observer than by subjective self-report. The most widely used such instrument is the *Hamilton Rating Scale for Depression* (*HRSD;* Hamilton, 1960). It has been amended and altered several times over the years. It is focused much more on somatic and behavioral symptoms than on mood and cognitive symptoms as is typical in self-report questionnaires. In its most commonly administered form, the Hamilton is a 17-item scale measuring mood, guilt, suicidal ideation, sleep disorders, changes in work and interests, psychomotor agitation and retardation, anxiety, somatic symptoms, hypochondriasis, loss of insight, and loss of weight. It has been shown to have solid psychometric properties, and is nearly always included in clinical studies and treatment-outcomes research. Nevertheless, it does not cover all symptoms of the *DSM-IV* syndrome of depression, and has been criticized therefore as less adequate for assessing severity of bipolar depression. Revisions include the *Inventory of Depressive Symptomatology–Clinician rated* (*IDS-C;* Rush, Gullion, Basco, Jarrett, & Trivedi, 1996) and the *Revised Hamilton Rating Scale for Depression* (*RHRSD;* Warren, 1994).

## COURSE AND CONSEQUENCES OF UNIPOLAR DEPRESSION

Much of what clinicians once believed about depression—that it occurs mostly in middle and older adulthood and rarely in youngsters and that it is commonly expressed as a single episode with full recovery—has been found to be untrue. The following sections discuss key features of depression, and its consequences in the lives of sufferers and their families.

### Features of Unipolar Depression

#### Age of Onset

Researchers have documented that the most typical age of onset of major depression is adolescence and young adulthood (Burke, Burke, Regier, & Rae, 1990). Young women in particular have enormous liability for depression onset between ages 15 and 19 (Burke et al., 1990); 50% of respondents with depression histories reported onset by age 25 (Sorenson, Rutter, & Aneshensel, 1991). Generally speaking, the risk of first episode is significantly higher before age 40 than earlier (Coryell, Endicott, & Keller, 1992a). There are two important implications. One is that depression is especially likely to affect young people during critical periods

of their development, including marriage, childbearing, and establishment of careers. Impairment during these important functions might have persisting maladaptive consequences. A second implication is that relatively early onset of depression—or perhaps of any psychological disorder—may portend a relatively worse course of illness, both because of developmental disruptions and because earlier onset may reflect a more severe form of the disorder.

The issue of whether childhood or early adolescent onset of depression predicts higher rates of depression in adulthood has been examined in a small number of longitudinal studies. In the largest follow-up study of the continuity of childhood depression into adulthood, Weissman, Wolk, Wickramaratne, et al. (1999) determined that although the youngsters had relatively high rates of psychological disorders and maladjustment, there was poor specificity for depressive disorders—except in a small sample that had recurrent episodes in childhood and high rates of depressed relatives. Similar results were reported by Harrington, Fudge, Rutter, Pickles, and Hill (1990) in a follow-back study. Thus, childhood onset of depression may predict significant disorder, but not specifically recurring depression—suggesting that many cases labeled as *childhood depression* may reflect marked emotional and behavioral dysregulation. In contrast, several follow-up studies of adolescent-onset depression have shown relatively high risk for recurring episodes in adulthood (e.g., Bardone, Moffitt, Caspi, Dickson, & Silva, 1996; Harrington et al., 1990; Lewinsohn, Rohde, Klein, & Seeley, 1999; Rao, Hammen, & Daley, 1999; Weissman, Wolk, Goldstein, et al., 1999).

### Episode Length

Two trends are noteworthy concerning duration of major depressive episodes. One is that the majority of episodes appear to resolve within 6 months (including untreated depressions), as shown by longitudinal studies of the natural course of unipolar disorder. For instance, Coryell et al. (1994), in the National Institute of Mental Health (NIMH) Collaborative Depression Study (CDS), found that 55% of patients and 57% of nonclinical relatives who developed depression recovered by 6 months. The second trend, however, is that a substantial minority of depressions persist for long periods, and may even be chronic. For instance, the CDS follow-up reported that after 5 years, 12% of patients had still not recovered (Keller et al., 1992). Even among those who no longer meet diagnostic criteria for an episode, there may continue to be considerable residual symptomatology. Data from the CDS indicate that unipolar patients manifested symptoms during 59% of the weeks of the follow-up, with many never being free of some level of depressive symptoms (e.g., Judd et al., 1998).

### Risk for Recurrence of Depression

Whereas depression, except in its most severe forms, was once considered a relatively benign disorder with recovery as the norm, it is now recognized that depression is especially pernicious not only because of protracted symptomatology, but also because it is highly recurrent. More than 80% of depressed adults experience at least one recurrence—a figure increasing to 100% if minor or subsyndromal episodes are included; and the median number of MDEs is four (reviewed in Judd, 1997). Recurrent episodes of MDE last about 20 weeks (Solomon et al., 2000). An international study conducted under the auspices of the World Health Organization found that over 10 years, affected individuals experienced a mean of 2.7 episodes of major depression, and spent an average of 27.5% of their lives in depressive episodes (Thornicroft & Sartorius, 1993). Similar frequencies and probabilities of recurrent MDE have been observed in adolescent depressed populations including both community and clinical samples (e.g., McCauley et al., 1993; Rao et al., 1999).

Another feature of the recurrent nature of depressive episodes is the observation that each recurrence increases the probability of further episodes. Solomon et al. (2000) followed patients over a 10-year period, and found that the probability of recurrence after recovery from the index episode was 25% in the first year, 42% by two years, and 60% by 5 years. Moreover, as predicted, median time to recurrence decreased with subsequent episodes, and the converse also occurred: The longer the person remained well, the less likely he or she was to experience recurrence. The results suggest that episodes themselves increase likelihood of disorder, and the hypothesized mechanisms of the process are discussed in later sections.

### Impairment Associated With Depressive Disorders

It is hardly surprising that the low mood, loss of interest, decreased energy, sense of futility, and low self-esteem associated with depressive disorders would result in dysfunction in important roles such as work, marital, and parental adjustment. What is more surprising is the extent of debility, resulting in as much or even more self-reported impairment than many serious medical disorders (e.g., Wells et al., 1989). In the language of illness burden to society due to economic and social disability as well as mortality, the World Health Organization has termed major depression the number-one cause of disability in the world, and the fourth greatest cause of disease burden (expected to move to second most important by

the year 2020; Murray & Lopez, 1996). Depression is one of the few psychological disorders that can be said to be fatal. Mortality due to suicide has been estimated to affect about 15% of those with a diagnosis of major depressive episode (Clark & Fawcett, 1992), and some studies suggest that depression is also predictive of increased mortality associated with medical disorders such as heart attacks (e.g., Musselman, Evans, & Nemeroff, 1998).

In more specific terms of social disability, patients with major depression in the CDS sample compared with controls achieve lower educational and income levels, and have lower rates of employment and decreased occupational status (Coryell et al., 1993). Moreover, fewer of those with unipolar depression were married, and those who were married reported worse quality of relationships. Even relatively minor or subsyndromal depressions are also associated with impairment as noted previously (e.g., Gotlib et al., 1995; Wells et al., 1989). Detailed analyses of level of work and social adjustment as a function of level of symptomatology over several years of follow-up in the CDS sample indicated a fairly linear relationship between impairment and severity of depression (Judd et al., 2000). Individuals who suffer from double depression appear to be especially likely to have occupational and social impairment, and those with dysthymic disorder (including double depression) are more likely never married (Evans et al., 1996). Of additional interest is the finding in the Judd et al. study, as well as other reports, that impairment in role functioning persists, even when the person is no longer in an episode (e.g., Billings & Moos, 1985; Judd et al., 2000).

Not surprisingly, studies of the consequences of depression in children and adolescents also indicate significant impairment of functioning. Those with childhood or adolescent depression show relative difficulties in school performance and conduct, and problematic relationships with peers and family members (e.g., Lewinsohn et al., 1994; Puig-Antich et al., 1993; see reviews in Birmaher et al., 1996; Hammen & Rudolph, 1996). In addition to impaired current functioning, a unique concern for depressed youngsters is the possibility that depression interferes with acquisition of developmentally appropriate skills and attainments. As a consequence, depressed youngsters may be left behind in ways that may contribute to further stress and depressive experiences.

### Effects of Depression on Others

There has been considerable research on a further aspect of depression's toll: the effects of depression on others. A great deal of the social disability of depression is due to two particular aspects of impairment: maladaptive marital relationships and high risk for offspring of depressed parents to develop depression and other disorders. As noted previously, there is evidence of less frequency of marriage, or of greater marital dissatisfaction or divorce among depressed patients than nondepressed controls (Coryell et al., 1993; reviewed in Gotlib & Hammen, 1992). The romantic relationships of young women assessed over a 5-year period indicated that lower quality of the relationship at the end of the follow-up and the boyfriends' dissatisfaction were significantly correlated with the amount of time the woman had spent in major depressive episodes (Rao et al., 1999). Other research has indicated that depressed women are more likely to be romantically involved with men who themselves have psychological disorders (assortative mating), potentially creating a stressful home environment (e.g., Hammen, 1991a; Merikangas, Weissman, Prusoff, & John, 1988). The important question of whether intimate relationship difficulties are unique and specific to depressive disorders has been addressed by Zlotnick, Kohn, Keitner, and Grotta (2000) with community data from the National Comorbidity Survey. These investigators found that participants with current diagnoses of major depressive episode or dysthymic disorder were significantly more likely to report more negative and less positive quality of their marital or intimate relationships than participants with nonaffective disorders. Moreover, the relative negativity was especially pronounced in their romantic relationships, and not seen in their attitudes about friendships.

Overall, it appears that depressed persons themselves—as well as their spouses—experience difficulties in the marital relationship. The processes by which such problems occur are not fully understood. Certainly, depression symptoms themselves may create friction and mutual dissatisfaction. Depressed people may also have impaired interpersonal skills and dysfunctional cognitions that reflect poor interpersonal problem-solving, often leading to conflict (e.g., Hammen, 1991b). They are often dependent on others, and seek reassurance in ways that distance others (Barnett & Gotlib, 1988; Joiner & Metalsky, 1995). Spouses and significant others may view the depressed person as a burden, causing worry, reducing the sharing of pleasurable activities, and rejecting suggestions for help or support. A survey of the attitudes of spouses toward their depressed partners found that they acknowledged numerous such problems, and 40% of them were sufficiently distressed by the depressed person to warrant treatment themselves (Coyne et al., 1987).

The other major area of difficulty for depressed people is high likelihood that their children will have depressive or other disorders. Numerous studies have now shown that the risk to offspring for developing depression and other disorders is very high, likely greater than 50% (reviews in Beardslee, Versage, & Gladstone, 1998; Downey & Coyne,

1990). Indeed, the risk is so pronounced that being a child of a depressed parent is often said to be the strongest predictive factor for youth depression. Numerous studies have attempted to shed light on the mechanisms by which risk is imparted. Certainly, genetic transmission may be one pathway. Additionally, however, it seems apparent from many observational studies of depressed women with their infants, toddlers, and school-age children that the quality of the parent-child interaction is relatively more negative than for nondepressed mothers and their youngsters (e.g., reviewed in Goodman & Gotlib, 1999; Kaslow, Deering, & Racusin, 1994). Similarly, depressed children and adolescents have more negative relationships with their parents (Kaslow et al., 1994). Being a child in a family with a depressed parent also typically subjects the child to elevated levels of chronic stress (including parent marital disorder) and episodic life events, which may also contribute to children's risk for disorder (e.g., Hammen, 2002).

An important consequence of impaired marital and family relationships is that the impact of the depressed person on family members may create a context that endures even when the person is no longer depressed. Difficult marital issues and problematic relationships with ill children may present enduring challenges to depressed adults, contributing not only to the persistence of impairment but also to the risk for further depression.

## WHO IS AFFECTED BY UNIPOLAR DEPRESSION?

### Rates of Depression

In the United States, the most recent epidemiological survey of adults between the ages of 15 and 54, using the CIDI as described earlier, reported a rate of 4.9% current major depression, and 17% lifetime major depression (Kessler et al., 1994). Earlier surveys had reported substantially lower rates but used different methods as noted previously. An international collaborative study, using various methods to arrive at *DSM-III* diagnoses, indicated an annual rate of major depression ranging from 0.8% in Taiwan to 5.8% in New Zealand (with the United States at 3% annually; Weissman et al., 1996). This study also reported lifetime rates of MDE between 1.5% and 19% across the various sites. Additionally, dysthymic disorder is estimated to affect 2–4% of the population internationally (Smith & Weissman, 1992).

Depressive disorders in young children are relative rare, possibly affecting 2–3% of preadolescents and 1% of preschoolers (Angold & Costello, 1993; Kashani & Carlson, 1987). However, epidemiological surveys of diagnoses among children have been much more limited in scope than those for adults. Data on rates of adolescent depression generally indicate much higher rates than in childhood. For instance, the Oregon Adolescent Depression Study found that 3% met criteria for current major depression or dysthymia, and a total of 20% had a lifetime diagnosis of depressive disorder (Lewinsohn, Hops, Roberts, Seeley, & Andrews, 1993).

### Gender, Age, and Depression

#### Sex Differences in Depression

For many years a striking gender difference has been noted, with many more women reporting—or being treated—for depressive disorders than men. The Cross-National Collaborative Group (Weissman et al., 1996) found a gender difference in every culture studied, and overall, the rate of approximately 2:1 is cited indicating women's prevalence among those with unipolar depressive disorders.

The gender gap appears to emerge in early adolescence (e.g., Angold & Rutter, 1992; Cohen et al., 1993). The magnitude of the gender difference—and its emergence in early adolescence—have stimulated many theories and research efforts to explain the patterns (e.g., reviewed in Cyranowski, Frank, Young, & Shear, 2000; Nolen-Hoeksema, 1990; Nolen-Hoeksema & Girgus, 1994). A variety of biological and psychosocial perspectives have been pursued with no final resolution, including hormonal effects and timing of puberty; differential exposure to stressors; gender differences in self-esteem, cognition, and coping; societal expectations and access to achievement; and many others. A review of this literature is beyond the scope of the chapter, but the implications are significant for theoretical models of depression, treatments, and prevention programs.

#### Age Trends in Depression

A further challenge to models of understanding depression concerns evidence that young people are experiencing increasing rates of depression. Not only is the age of onset of depression now known to be in the teens or early 20s for most sufferers, but the rates of depression appear to be higher in more recently born people. For instance, the Cross-National Collaborative Group (1992) found that rates of depression increased in birth cohorts such that they were highest by age 25 in those who had been born since 1955. The rate appears to be continuing to increase in more recently born youngsters, with rates in adolescent and young women higher than 30% (e.g., Lewinsohn, Rohde, Seeley, & Fischer, 1993; Rao et al., 2000). Although methodological artifacts such as memory bias have been argued to be a partial cause, recent evidence

based on use of the same instrument over a 40-year period in the same community confirms that rates of depression have indeed increased in young women (Murphy, Laird, Monson, Sobol, & Leighton, 2000). Conversely, many studies have suggested that the rates of depression in older adults have been declining—although information on the very old is typically absent from most surveys (e.g., Murphy et al., 2000; see Wallace & O'Hara, 1992).

Theories of the origins of increased rates of depression in young people, especially females, abound. It has been suggested that changing cultural trends including family breakups and increasing social mobility diminishing supportive resources plus increased stress in the form of heightened expectations and increased competition for careers may have contributed. Such age trends appear to be a particular challenge to theories emphasizing biological diatheses. Nevertheless, the issue remains unresolved, while its consequences continue to be of considerable concern and interest.

## UNIPOLAR DEPRESSION: THEORIES OF ETIOLOGY AND VULNERABILITY

There are numerous biological and psychosocial perspectives on the origins of depression, and new findings emerge frequently following advances in the technologies for evaluating genetic and neurobiological processes. Consequently, the etiology sections can attempt only a brief statement of these approaches, and the current directions in which research is proceeding. It is safe to say that nearly all models adopt a diathesis-stress perspective, and many assume a biological predisposition that may require activation by environmental stressors. It is noted, however, that few studies have tested such interactions.

### Biological Approaches

#### Genetic Vulnerability to Unipolar Depression

Depression undeniably runs in families. Many studies of the first-degree relatives of depressed patients have reported rates of depression ranging between 7% and 30% across studies—considerably in excess of rates in the general population (Gershon, 1990; Winokur, Coryell, Keller, Endicott, & Leon, 1995). Studies of the children of depressed parents, as noted previously, have indicated that having a parent with a depressive disorder is one of the strongest predictors of youth depression (reviewed in Beardslee et al., 1998).

Of course, family studies do not prove a genetic mechanism of transmission, given potential effects of the family environment. Moreover, there is no evidence of a single depressive gene or defect—and likely never will be, given the apparent heterogeneity of depression and multiple causal pathways. However, genetic strategies that are less confounded with environmental factors are also suggestive. Twin studies using modern biometric model-testing analyses have proven to be highly suggestive. Kendler and colleagues (e.g., Kendler, Neale, Kessler, Heath, & Eaves, 1992) have published a series of studies based on a population-based twin registry in Virginia. Initially focused on female twins (Kendler et al., 1992), the authors found significantly higher monozygotic (MZ) concordance than dizygotic (DZ) concordance, recently replicated with male twin pairs (Kendler & Prescott, 1999). Biometric twin-modeling statistical analyses concluded that the genetic liability accounted for 39% of the risk for MDE in both male and female twin pairs, with the remaining 61% of the variance attributable to individual-specific factors (such as stressful events). McGuffin, Katz, Watkins, and Rutherford (1996) also conclude that there is a moderate role of genetic factors in depression, based on their inpatient sample. To date, however, there is no consensus on whether more severe forms of depression are especially likely to be genetically related (e.g., Kendler, Gardner, & Prescott, 1999; Lyons et al., 1998; McGuffin et al., 1996).

### Psychoneuroendocrinology of Depression

Even though suggestive, genetic studies to date do not tell what it is that might be transmitted. Brain functioning and neuroendocrine processes may provide possible mechanisms. Considerable evidence implicates dysregulation of the human stress response of the hypothalamic-pituitary-adrenal (HPA) axis in depressive disorders. Numerous studies have found elevated levels of cortisol, a hormone resulting in various forms of physical arousal and activation, in acutely depressed people compared to nondepressed people (as well as increased levels of corticotropin releasing factor, or CRF). When individuals are no longer depressed, cortisol levels return to normal. In addition to hypersecretion of cortisol, investigators have observed abnormalities in the regulation of cortisol. A review of 100 studies of abnormal cortisol regulation and clinical course concluded that the abnormalities themselves did not predict treatment outcome, but when the abnormalities continued even after treatment, they portended poorer prognosis and high likelihood of relapse (Ribeiro, Tandon, Grunhaus, & Greden, 1993). Thus, the subset of depressed people with abnormal HPA functioning may have a worse type of depression, or at least a form that perhaps stems from an underlying disorder of the stress response system.

Stress-related neuroendocrine processes may also affect brain development, predisposing to depression. Plotsky, Owens, and Nemeroff (1998) recently reviewed research on stress and HPA-related hormones and their effects on the brain. They speculated that early stress experiences may sensitize specific neural circuits, resulting in depressive reactions in later life in response to stressful life events (see also Gold, Goodwin, & Chrousos, 1988; Sapolsky, 2000). Most of the relevant research has been conducted on animals, but a growing body of human research has shown abnormal HPA axis functioning associated with adverse childhood experiences such as insecure attachment and abuse experiences (e.g., Gunnar, 1998; Heim, Ehlert, Hanker, & Hellhammer, 1998). However, information about continuity of effects into childhood or their direct and specific link with depressive reactions has yet to be established.

### Neurotransmitters and Depression Vulnerability

There has been considerable historical interest in the potential role of monoamine neurotransmitters such as serotonin, norepinephrine, and dopamine in mood disorders. These neurotransmitters are especially important in the limbic system of the brain, areas affecting drives and emotions, and pathways to other parts of the brain. The original catecholamine hypothesis of depression (Schildkraut, 1965) emphasizing relative deficits of these substances has proven to be far too simplistic, yielding to greater focus on amine receptor systems (McNeal & Cimbolic, 1986) and models of dysregulation of neurotransmitters (e.g., Siever & Davis, 1985). Recently, attention has turned particularly to serotonin (5-HT) models of depression (reviewed in Maes & Meltzer, 1995), suggesting that vulnerability to depression may arise from alterations in presynaptic 5-hydroxytryptamine (5HT) activity and postsynaptic serotonin receptor functioning. Moreover, since the hippocampus is a site of serotonergic innervation of the regulation of the HPA axis, it has been speculated that lowered central 5HT activity in depression may attenuate hippocampal feedback control over the HPA axis, inducing excessive corticosteroid secretion (Maes & Meltzer, 1995). Experimental analogue studies involving challenges with depletion of serotonin precursors that induce temporary depression in remitted patients (e.g., Smith, Fairburn, & Cowen, 1997) provide further suggestive evidence that serotonin processes may be involved in some forms of depression. Recent data also implicate a role of other neurotransmitters, such as norepinephrine and dopamine. It should be kept in mind that neurotransmitters are intimately interrelated with other neuroendocrine processes in the brain, and the interactions among them are extremely difficult to tease apart. Moreover, most of the cross-sectional designs of such studies make it difficult to draw definitive conclusions about whether depression results from—or causes—abnormalities of brain functioning.

## *Functional and Structural Brain Changes in Depression*

It has long been known that certain medical conditions with brain lesions cause depression (e.g., certain strokes, neurodegenerative diseases), prompting a search for particular areas of the brain associated with depressive symptoms. Neuroimaging studies have reported some evidence of structural abnormalities in the brains of depressed people, such as reduced frontal volume (Coffey et al., 1993). A review by Kennedy, Javanmard, and Vaccarino (1997) concludes that the evidence shows reduced metabolic rate and reduced blood flow during depressive states, and consistent evidence of abnormalities in the functions of the prefrontal and cingulate cortices—areas closely linked with limbic and paralimbic structures. However, as noted earlier, research designs have been unable to demonstrate when such observed abnormalities are stable, and whether they are the cause or the result of depressive disorders.

Electrophysiological research on frontal brain activity by Davidson and colleagues has resulted in a model of emotional reactivity that may have considerable promise as a vulnerability factor in negative emotional states such as depression (e.g., Davidson, 1993). He observed that depressed patients and even previously depressed but remitted patients showed relative left frontal hypoactivation. Davidson proposed that decreased left prefrontal activation represents an underactivation of an approach system, thus reducing the person's tendency to experience pleasure and positively engagement with the environment while enhancing the likelihood of developing depressive symptoms. Interestingly, several studies have found that infants and toddlers with depressed mothers display relative left frontal hypoactivation (e.g., Jones, Field, Fox, Lundy, & Davalos, 1997). Investigators have speculated that the patterns may be genetically transmitted—or acquired prenatally or in early stressful interactions with a depressed mother—and may represent a mechanism of risk for development of depression.

## *Additional Topics in the Biology of Depression*

Abnormalities of the circadian rhythms affecting the sleep-wake cycle as well as cortisol and other bodily processes have been hypothesized to contribute to mood disorders. Numerous studies have demonstrated not only clinical complaints of sleep disturbances but also abnormalities of sleep waves—in stages such as rapid eye movement (REM) and slow-wave sleep. Research on circadian rhythm abnormalities is discussed further in the section on bipolar disorder.

The relatively higher rates of depression among women has stimulated much speculation on a hormonal component to vulnerability to depression. To date, however, there is little evidence of a major role of hormones in clinical mood disorders. It has been noted that even massive changes in hormonal levels such as those accompanying childbirth are associated with only minor depressive symptoms, called *postpartum blues*. A recent review of changes involving such hormones as progesterone, estrogen, prolactin, and others associated with *postpartum major depression* notes the negative or inconsistent findings (Hendrick, Altshuler, & Suri, 1998). The authors conclude that while there is no evidence of an etiologic role for the hormones, some women may experience mood changes because they are extremely sensitive to hormone levels. It is noteworthy that this field of study has focused mainly on levels of hormones, while degrees of change and the interactions among ovarian and stress-related hormones are promising topics that merit further study pending methodological improvements.

## Psychological Models of Depression

Historically, psychodynamic theories of depression (melancholia) variously emphasized the experience of loss and intrapersonal dynamics including self-esteem and close relationships. Many of these same themes have been studied in more modern models of depression, and several themes are recognized as important contributors to depression vulnerability: stressful life events including loss; negative cognitive representations of the self and the world; quality of close relationships including childhood experiences.

### *Cognitive Vulnerability to Depression*

Aaron Beck's original (1967) cognitive model of depression was the first to illuminate the characteristically negative thinking of depressed people, and to assign causal significance in the phenomenology of depressive disorders to self-critical, pessimistic, helpless, and hopeless interpretations of the self and the world. Beck's approach gave rise to a veritable paradigm shift in clinical science in its focus on the significance and measurement of conscious thoughts and cognitive processes in psychopathology. Beck's approach was highly successful in describing depressive thinking, and stimulated the development of related but somewhat different approaches to understanding vulnerability to depression in adults (e.g., Abramson, Alloy, & Metalsky, 1989; see reviews in Ingram, Miranda, & Segal, 1998; Segal & Ingram, 1994) and in children (e.g., reviews in Garber & Flynn, 2001; Hammen & Rudolph, 1996). Both questionnaire-based and experimental information-processing methods are presently being employed by researchers to test the power of the cognitive vulnerability models to predict who is at risk for depression and under what conditions it might develop (e.g., Alloy et al., 2000).

The cognitive perspective has been the dominant psychological model of depression for more than two decades, and is bolstered both by research and common sense (i.e., that the way people think about the misfortunes that may befall them is what determines reactions to stressors, and that some people are prone to magnify the sense of being incompetent or diminished by negative events). However, these approaches have not been well supported as playing a causal role in the origin of depression, nor is it established that their contributions are necessary, substantial, and specific to depression (e.g., Hammen, 2000). Hammen emphasized the need for greater integration of the cognitive perspectives with developmental, contextual, and biological approaches.

### Stressful Life Events

There is strong empirical support for an association between significant stressful life events and depressive syndromes, in both community and clinical samples (e.g., Dohrenwend, Shrout, Link, Martin, & Skodol, 1986; Shrout et al., 1989). For instance, in Brown and Harris's (1989) review of seven community studies, approximately 70–95% of individuals who developed cases of depression experienced a prior severe life event, compared with 25–40% among those who did not develop depression.

Although these studies indicate that most depressions are triggered by a significant negative life event, the obverse raises the critical question of vulnerability: Most people who do experience even major negative events do not become depressed. Why do some people become depressed and others do not? One approach, a *multiple risk-factor model,* suggests that depression occurs in the context not only of stressors, but also of chronic strains and diminished resources for coping, such as social support (e.g., Lewinsohn, Hoberman, & Rosenbaum, 1988; Moos, Cronkite, & Moos, 1998). Brown and colleagues (e.g., Brown & Harris, 1978, 1989; Brown, Andrews, Harris, Adler, & Bridge, 1986) have shown empirical support for their model that includes life-event occurrence in the context of chronic stressors, reduced support, and psychological conditions such that the negative event is especially meaningful in terms of the person's values, commitments, and self-esteem.

Many studies have indicated that severe childhood adversities, such as physical or sexual abuse, may predict adult histories of depression among women (e.g., Kessler & Magee, 1993; McCauley et al., 1997). Such work has not revealed the mechanisms by which such experiences result in risk for

depression, and depression is by no means the specific consequence of childhood adversities.

A refinement of the life-stress approaches suggests that individuals may be particularly vulnerable to some stressors more than to others. Specifically, individuals differ in the sources of their self-esteem and sense of mastery, with some individuals experiencing personal worth as deriving from the achievement of highly valued goals and control (*autonomy*), whereas others are more likely to invest themselves and their self-definitions in personal relationships with others (*sociotropy*). Negative events occurring in the vulnerable domain may be especially interpreted as depletions of the sense of worth and competence, leading to depression. Several studies have found support for the life event–vulnerability matching approach in adults (e.g., Hammen, Marks, Mayol, & DeMayo, 1985; Segal, Shaw, Vella, & Katz, 1992) and children (Hammen & Goodman-Brown, 1990).

Another focus on stressful life events has emphasized the role that depressed people may play in the occurrence of stressful events. While research has clearly demonstrated the effects of stressors in precipitating depression among those who are vulnerable, other studies have shown that the behaviors of depressed women—even when not currently in a depressive episode—may contribute to the occurrence of stressors, especially stressors with interpersonal conflict themes (Daley et al., 1997; Hammen, 1991a). Depressed women may have difficult relationships with their children—and with their own spouses (e.g., Gotlib, Lewinsohn, & Seeley, 1998)—and may lack the skills to deal with problematic personal relationships. Moreover, depressed women are especially likely to marry men with psychopathology (e.g., Hammen, 1991b), thereby contributing to a stressful personal environment that may cause further depressive reactions. In a family or interpersonal context marked by conflict, repeated depressive experiences may occur.

An additional form of vulnerability to stressful life events may result from a sensitization process in which early exposure to significant stressors may increase the likelihood that subsequent stressors may trigger depression. Both psychological mechanisms of cognitive sensitization, as well as neurobiological changes in the developing brain, have been posited to account for such processes (e.g., Post, 1992; Sapolsky, 2000; Segal, Williams, Teasdale, & Gemar, 1996). Hammen, Henry, and Daley (2000) showed that young women's reports of early childhood adversity were associated with lowered levels of stress prior to depression onset compared with women who developed depression but who did not have early adversity. Clinical lore, and a few empirical studies, have suggested that repeated episodes of depression are progressively less associated with stress, such that triggering stressors may eventually become unnecessary for episodes to occur (e.g., Post, 1992). One recent longitudinal study appeared to support this model (Kendler, Thornton, & Gardner, 2000). Direct evidence of the neurobiological consequences of children's exposure to severe stressors, as well as for animal models (e.g., reviewed in Plotsky et al., 1998; Sapolsky, 2000) suggest that this integrative stress-biology perspective may hold considerable promise for understanding depression vulnerability.

### Interpersonal Approaches to Depression Vulnerability

There has been increasing research and theoretical interest in interpersonal aspects of depression. Initially, work in this area emphasized the debilitating social *consequences,* such as the effects of depression on marital relations and children's development, as noted previously. More recently, investigators have explored the role of interpersonal factors in the *origin* of depression, not only as social stressors precipitating episodes, but also in terms of the role that early parent-child relationships and interpersonal styles, needs, and cognitions may play in creating vulnerability to depression. No single model or theory defines this area, and readers may be referred to Gotlib and Hammen (1992), *Psychological Aspects of Depression: Toward a Cognitive-Interpersonal Integration,* and Joiner and Coyne (1999), *The Interactional Nature of Depression,* for more extended reviews. In the following sections, two interpersonal topics are discussed briefly.

### Dysfunctional Parent-Child Relations

From various theoretical perspectives, including *psychodynamic* (e.g., Bowlby's *attachment theory;* Bowlby, 1978, 1981) and *social learning* perspectives emphasizing the acquisition of interpersonal skills and self-views in the context of interactions with parents, many investigators have emphasized the important role of the quality of parent-child relations in vulnerability to depression. Studies have shown that depressed adults, as well as children and adolescents, report more negative relationships with their parents and show more evidence of insecure attachment (e.g., Kobak, Sudler, & Gamble, 1991; Rosenfarb, Becker, & Khan, 1994; reviewed in Gerlsma, Emmelkamp, & Arrindell, 1990; Kaslow et al., 1994). Insecure attachments are presumed to determine later beliefs, expectations, and behaviors in intimate relationships; maladaptive patterns may create vulnerability to depression. For example, a study of young women found that those with more negative cognitions about their ability to trust and depend on others were more likely to experience depression following a negative interpersonal life event than women who did not

have such beliefs (Hammen et al., 1995). Although more longitudinal and prospective studies are needed to further validate the role of such experiences in risk for depression, the sheer volume of supportive findings indicates that parent-child relationships, especially those characterized by negative affect and harsher parental control, may contribute to a sense of personal inadequacy that promotes susceptibility to depression.

### Dependency and Reassurance-Seeking

Dependency has long been recognized as a concomitant and risk factor for depression—as a trait, or as the diathesis in a diathesis-stress interaction (e.g., reviews by Barnett & Gotlib, 1988; Nietzel & Harris, 1990). As noted earlier, measures of sociotropy or dependency represent beliefs and schemas about the importance of contact and value by others, and when individuals high in such cognitions encounter negative interpersonal relationships, depressive reactions may result. Recently, Joiner and colleagues have speculated that *reassurance-seeking* may be an individual difference variable that serves as a vulnerability to develop depression. Reassurance-seeking is related to the construct of dependency—emotional reliance on others and the belief that affection, acceptance, and support of others are essential to well-being. Joiner and Metalsky (1995; see also Potthoff, Holahan, & Joiner, 1995) showed that a measure of reassurance-seeking predicted future depressive symptoms in students experiencing stressful situations.

## TREATMENT OF DEPRESSION

Since the chapter's focus is psychopathology rather than treatment, only a brief overview of treatment issues is noted. Only 25 years or so ago, there were few effective treatment options for depression. However, there is now solid empirical evidence for success in treating the acute phase of depression with short-term structured psychotherapy or with a variety of antidepressant medications. Cognitive-behavioral therapy (CBT; see review in Hollon, Haman, & Brown, 2002) and interpersonal psychotherapy (IPT; see review in Weissman & Markowitz, 2002), as well as various tricyclic and selective serotonin reuptake inhibitors (SSRIs) and atypical medications (reviewed in Gitlin, 2002) are all approximately equally effective. Recently, evidence has suggested that CBT and IPT, as well as SSRI medications, may also be effective in reducing depression in children and adolescents (e.g., Brent et al., 1997; Emslie et al., 1997; reviewed in Kaslow, McClure, & Connell, 2002). Overall, medication studies indicate about 60–70% effectiveness in reducing depressive symptoms.

Since depressive episodes tend to recur, a critical question is whether treatments prevent relapse and recurrence. It has become standard pharmacotherapy practice to continue medications for 6 to 9 months beyond symptom remission to prevent relapse, and *maintenance* medication at full dosage may be recommended for those whose histories indicate a significant risk for recurrence. Among the psychotherapies, CBT is especially oriented toward teaching patients skills they can use to prevent future episodes, and some evidence of the success in reducing rates of relapse has been reported especially for CBT (e.g., Hollon et al., 2002). Maintenance (periodic) IPT sessions have also been shown to lower recurrence rates (e.g., Frank, Kupfer, Wagner, McEachran, & Cornes, 1991). Remaining questions about whether there are some kinds of depression (e.g., more severe, more vegetative) that respond better to medications than to therapy are largely unresolved. Also, the question of whether combined medication-psychotherapy treatments are better than either alone has resulted in mixed results (Hollon et al., 2002).

Accordingly, future research is needed to refine the issue of the best match between treatment type and patient characteristics. Moreover, additional challenges remain. For one thing, most people do not seek treatment for depression, and those who do often are the ones most likely to be impaired and to have comorbid conditions. Adolescents, for example, may require more than medication alone to resolve their complex symptoms and maladjustment in social and academic roles. Also, many individuals are not adherent to the medication regimens, or may require unique combinations of treatments. Thus, finding ways to disseminate treatments to those in need, helping them to improve their lives as well as reduce depressive symptoms, improving treatments for more complex cases, and improving methods of preventing relapse are all important priorities in the treatment field.

# BIPOLAR DISORDER

Compared with unipolar depression, bipolar disorder is much more rare and is presumed to have a fundamentally biological origin with a genetic diathesis. Its severe, recurrent course necessitates lifelong pharmacological treatment for most sufferers. Also in comparison to unipolar depression, bipolar disorder has been less studied, in part because its diagnostic boundaries and differences from unipolar disorders were defined only relatively recently (in the late 1970s). Nevertheless, efforts to treat this potentially severe disorder with empirically tested medications helped to usher in an era of clearer diagnostic criteria and the study of neural mechanisms of pharmacotherapy effects, which in turn played an important role in the

development of modern neuroscience (Goodwin & Ghaemi, 1999). The following sections are relatively brief and descriptive, attempting to highlight the current understanding of this disorder and ongoing research activity on unresolved issues. A detailed account of bipolar disorder is presented in Goodwin and Jamison (1990), *Manic-Depressive Illness.*

## Defining and Diagnosing Bipolar Disorder

### Bipolar Diagnoses

The defining feature of bipolar disorder is the occurrence of a manic or hypomanic episode, or mixed states of mania and depression. The classical term *manic-depressive illness* has been replaced in recent years by the term *bipolar disorder,* because the former sometimes referred to recurrent depressive episodes in the absence of mania—a condition that nowadays would be called *unipolar depression.* Because both bipolar and unipolar disorder employ the same diagnostic criteria for presence of depressive episodes, diagnostic errors may occur. Individuals with current depression must be evaluated carefully for past history of mania or hypomania. *Mania* is defined as a period of persistently expansive, elevated, or irritable mood that is accompanied by at least three additional symptoms reflecting inflated self-esteem or grandiose thinking, marked cognitive changes such as distractibility or flight of ideas, pressured speech, decreased need for sleep, agitation or increased activity, and excessive involvement in pleasurable activities that have potentially harmful consequences. When similar symptoms are present but not severe enough to cause significant impairment of functioning or require hospitalization, the condition is termed *hypomania.* Mania must persist for at least a week, and hypomania for at least 4 days. Mania can be so severe as to include psychotic experiences and extremely destructive behaviors clearly signifying need for hospitalization, whereas hypomania may be brief and relatively mild—and therefore sometimes difficult to diagnose or recall. Mixed episodes refer to seemingly simultaneous or rapidly alternating manic and depressive symptoms. Bipolar I disorder is defined by presence of one or more manic episodes, whereas bipolar II disorder signifies history of hypomanic episodes and major depressive disorders.

Less severe mood swings that include numerous periods of highs and lows that do not meet criteria for mania or major depression may be diagnosed as *cyclothymic disorder.* Others have suggested that there may be additional variants of bipolar disorder in the subclinical bipolar spectrum, possibly portending risk for future bipolar I or II disorder or indicating stable bipolar temperaments or personalities (Akiskal, 1996; Depue, Krauss, Spoont, & Arbisi, 1989; Eckblad & Chapman,

1986; Lewinsohn, Klein, & Seeley, 1995). Research interest in further validation of bipolar diagnostic criteria or possible subtypes continues (e.g., Cassidy, Forest, Murry, & Carroll, 1998).

Diagnostic accuracy may be compromised by misperception of acute depressive episodes as unipolar when they are actually bipolar. Further problems may occur when severe psychotic symptoms of grandiosity or paranoia are misconstrued as schizophrenia. Also, the features of substance abuse and intoxication-related behaviors may make it difficult to recognize bipolar disorder. Such comorbid conditions or psychotic features may all contribute to the failure to recognize, accurately diagnose, and appropriate treat bipolar disorder. Indeed, as Goodwin and Ghaemi (1999) noted, about 40% of hospitalized patients they and colleagues had diagnosed as bipolar had not been diagnosed as bipolar by previous psychiatrists.

Substance abuse is an especially problematic comorbid condition (e.g., Kessler, Rubinow, Holmes, Abelson, & Zhao, 1997). For instance, Helzer and Pryzbeck (1988) found that individuals with bipolar I disorder had 6.2 times the likelihood of alcohol abuse as those in the general U.S. population. Not only may substance abuse problems prevent accurate diagnosis, but they are commonly associated with worse outcomes (e.g., Strakowski et al., 1998)—perhaps because they interfere with treatment adherence, but also because substances may affect biological brain processes that underlie the disorder. Personality disorders are also a common co-occurring problem among samples of bipolar patients, although potentially overlapping mood and behavioral symptoms require caution in interpretation. Studies that have attempted to examine personality disorder symptoms during remission of bipolar episodes have found particularly high rates of Cluster B disorders (e.g., Dunayevich et al., 1996; Peselow, Sanfilipo, & Fieve, 1995). Generally, as with other disorders, Axis II pathology generally predicts greater psychosocial maladjustment and more severe clinical course (e.g., Barbato & Hafner, 1998).

### Diagnosis of Bipolar Disorder in Children and Adolescents

Diagnosis of bipolar disorder in adolescents is now relatively well accepted, although it is potentially challenging if the first episode is depression. The disorder is frequently either misdiagnosed because of confusing comorbid conditions, or mislabeled as schizophrenia, substance abuse, or disruptive behavioral disorders. Some investigators have reported relatively higher rates of mixed episodes and more rapid cycling in adolescent bipolar patients than in adults (e.g., Kutcher, Robertson, & Bird, 1998; McElroy, Strakowski, West, Keck,

& McConville, 1997). Such cases may portend a relatively more difficult course of disorder than those who have relatively classic bipolar disorder (e.g., Stober et al., 1995).

Considerable controversy surrounds the question of childhood bipolar disorder (e.g., mania). Most investigators agree that such cases, although rare, definitely occur. Disagreement, however, concerns the frequency of occurrence and the accurate diagnosis of potentially ambiguous presentations, especially when longitudinal data are not available. A key problem is that childhood mania typically does not have features that help define adult mania: an acute onset, periods of relatively good functioning between episodes, and distinct periods of elevated mood or irritability. Geller et al. (1998) followed a well-defined sample of manic children with a mean onset age of 8.1 years, and reported that 75% had ultradian cycles (variation within 24 hr) and were chronically ill. Many presumed manic children show what appear to be mixed states, with intensely irritable moods and rages (e.g., Carlson & Kelly, 1998; Faraone, Biederman, Wozniak, et al., 1997). They are often aggressive and viewed as out of control, with severe impairment, and less evidence of euphoria and grandiosity than adults show (Faedda et al., 1995).

The apparent overlap of symptoms of mania and attention-deficit/hyperactivity disorder (ADHD) is especially confusing. Symptoms of hyperactivity, heightened energy and restlessness, distractibility, racing thoughts and pressure to talk, and impulsivity may make it difficult to distinguish between ADHD and mania. However, systematic comparisons indicate significantly higher scores for mania symptoms in bipolar children with ADHD than in children with ADHD alone (Geller et al., 1998). In contrast to typical ADHD, children with bipolar disorder may be purposefully destructive; may have prolonged rages, temper tantrums, and rapidly shifting moods; and may even show gross distortions in the perception of reality (Papolos & Papolos, 1999; Weller, Weller, & Dogin, 1998).

Biederman and colleagues (Biederman, 1998; Faraone, Biederman, Mennin, et al., 1997; Faraone, Biederman, Wozniak, et al., 1997) argue that ADHD and bipolarity are comorbid disorders, possibly reflecting an etiological genetically transmitted subtype of bipolar disorder. These investigators argue that comorbidity with ADHD may be a marker of childhood-onset bipolar disorder. Biederman (1998) further suggests that many cases of juvenile bipolar disorder may be missed or misdiagnosed because they are mistaken for severe cases of ADHD, when in fact they are a subtype of bipolar disorder. Geller et al. (1998), however, have suggested that ADHD in young bipolar samples may be a *phenocopy* ADHD, driven by developmentally prevalent high energy in children. Geller predicts that, with age, the ADHD will decrease to population levels by adulthood. Thus, ADHD may be either a prodrome or developmentally expressed version of bipolarity in children, rather than a separate disorder. On the other hand, some have argued that what is called *mania* in children may often be a mislabeled, nonspecific severe psychopathology found in children, possibly a "multiple complex developmental disorder"—which suggests that there are conditions of severe emotional and behavioral dysregulation that we simply have yet to characterize adequately (e.g., Carlson & Kelly, 1998; Carlson, Loney, Salisbury, & Volpe, 1998). Clearly, longitudinal studies of purported bipolar disorder in children are needed to help resolve the diagnostic issues. Meanwhile, some suggest that at the very least, diagnosis of prepubertal bipolar disorder be made only by very experienced clinicians (e.g., Nottelman & Jensen, 1998).

## Course of Bipolar Disorder

By definition, bipolar disorder is recurrent, with multiple lifetime episodes. One 5-year follow-up of patients with mood disorders indicated more total episodes for those with bipolar than for those with unipolar disorders (Winokur, Coryell, Keller, Endicott, & Akiskal, 1993). A subgroup of bipolar I patients (possibly 20–30%) seemingly do not experience depression, and therefore have only manic episodes (Kessler et al., 1997). Individuals vary additionally in whether they have depression following or preceding mania, whether they have polyphasic course patterns, and whether their patterns are consistent or inconsistent. Several studies have suggested that there may be prognostic significance to the patterning of episodes. The most extensive longitudinal study, the NIMH CDS, examined the association with patterning and outcome in patients with bipolar I over a period of up to 15 years (Turvey et al., 1999). They found that most bipolar patients had consistent polarity patterns, especially those whose episodes started with mania. Those with cycles that commenced with depressive episodes tended to have longer episodes and spent an average of 30% of the follow-up in an affective episode, compared to 18% in those with manic-onset patterns. Also, those whose episodes began with depression were more likely to have chronic illness courses over time. Based on close analysis of symptom patterns in bipolar patients in the same sample over a 15-year period, Coryell et al. (1998) concluded that there may be a depressive subtype of bipolar I disorder, marked by persistent depressive symptoms observable during the first 2 years of follow-up and continuing over the entire period, accompanied by poor prognosis in psychosocial adjustment.

Two additional bipolar I patterns have been especially associated with poor prognosis, as defined by multiple and frequent episodes, incomplete recovery, and psychosocial impairment. One concerns *rapid cycling,* defined as four or more episodes in a year's time. Rapid cycling is found to occur in approximately 5–15% of patients in treatment, and is more common among women (e.g., Coryell et al., 1992b). It is sometimes a side effect of antidepressant treatment, especially if treatment is administered in the absence of concurrent mood stabilizers. Also, *mixed state* episodes of concurrent manic and depressive symptoms also appear to portend worse outcomes (e.g., Keller, Lavori, Coryell, Endicott, & Mueller, 1993).

It has often been noted, since Kraepelin (1921), that episodes become more frequent after the first few, up to a point at which frequency may stabilize (see also Goodwin & Jamison, 1990). This pattern has implications that are discussed later, concerning kindling and the pathophysiology of bipolar disorder.

Age of onset of bipolar disorder has classically been viewed as occurring commonly in late teens and young adulthood. Kraepelin (1921) concluded that the greatest frequency of first episodes of manic depression occurs between the ages of 15 and 20. Supporting this observation, Faedda et al. (1995) summarized 28 studies that reported onset by age; overall, 25% of bipolar patients had onset before the age of 20. The authors suggest that this figure is probably inaccurate, noting that many of the original samples may have excluded child and early-onset cases owing to diagnostic biases and practices of the time. These findings are consistent with a retrospective self-report survey of 500 members of the National Depressive and Manic-Depressive Association (Lish, Dime-Meenan, Whybrow, Price, & Hirschfeld, 1994). When individuals with bipolar disorder were asked to indicate their best estimate of age of symptom onset, 60% reported onset in childhood and adolescence. Research on age of onset is, of course, also hampered by definitions of *onset.* As Carlson, Bromet, and Sievers (2000) asked, does one date onset of bipolar disorder from first symptoms, first episode, first treatment, or first hospitalization—or first diagnosis? Establishing age of onset of bipolar disorder may have the further complication that first episodes may be depression, followed by an indeterminate interval before manic episodes occur and thus establish the diagnosis. Exemplifying the potential difficulty of accurate diagnosis if the first episode is major depression, several longitudinal studies have shown a switch rate of about 15% from apparent unipolar depression to bipolar disorder (e.g., Akiskal et al., 1995; Coryell et al., 1995). For childhood- or adolescent-onset depression the rates may be even higher. A review of seven studies of more than 250 depressed children and adolescents followed for 2–4 years reported a mean switch rate from depression to mania of about 25% (Faedda et al., 1995; see also Kovacs, 1996; Weissman, Wolk, Wickramaratne, et al., 1999).

The implications of accurate diagnosis may be especially important for those with childhood or adolescent onset. Several studies have indicated that earlier onset of bipolar disorder portends a more pernicious clinical course with more social impairment (Carlson et al., 2000; Lish et al., 1994; Schurhoff et al., 2000). Moreover, it is commonly hypothesized that early detection and appropriate treatment may lessen the course of illness, based on the presumed neurobiological processes in which episodes actually alter the brain and accentuate a possible kindling mechanism (as will be discussed further).

Whereas bipolar I patients may experience both mania and hypomania along with major depressive episodes, bipolar II patients experience only hypomania and major depressive episodes. Over time, the pattern appears to be stable—this is, such individuals do not switch to manic episodes (Coryell et al., 1989). Episodes of depression are especially characteristic, and associated with impaired functioning.

## Impairment and Consequences of Bipolar Disorder

It was once believed that most bipolar patients were relatively symptom free between episodes, and that the disorder could be relatively successfully treated with lithium monotherapy. However, in recent years several longitudinal studies have demonstrated considerable variability in bipolar I patients' courses and social functioning, with a far less rosy picture of treatment success. Harrow, Goldberg, Grossman, and Meltzer (1990) and Tohen, Waternaux, and Tsuang (1990) found that only a minority of bipolar I patients had good clinical and functional outcomes, despite apparently adequate lithium treatment. Gitlin, Swendsen, Heller, and Hammen (1995) followed patients for a mean of more than 4 years, and found that despite adequate treatment with mood stabilizers, 73% had at least one major episode of depression or mania, and most had multiple episodes. Moreover, there was considerable subclinical symptomatology, paralleled by impaired work and social adjustment.

## Epidemiology of Bipolar Disorder

The rate of bipolar I disorder is generally about 1% of the population, although rates vary somewhat by country, and presumably, by diagnostic practices (Weissman et al., 1996). In the United States, somewhat different instruments in epidemiological surveys—the DIS versus the CIDI (as previously noted)—resulted in different rates. The former yielded a rate of bipolar I disorder of 0.8%, while the National Comorbidity Survey reported a rate of 1.6% (Kessler et al., 1994). These variations reflect not only diagnostic method

differences and unreliability, but also, as observed previously, the fact that diagnostic distinctions regarding bipolar disorder may be difficult, compounded by the relatively poor recognition or insight of affected individuals about their own manic and hypomanic experiences. Bipolar II disorder is estimated to affect somewhere between 0.3 and 3.0% of the population, and bipolar spectrum disorders, depending on how defined, may affect between 3.0 and 6.5% (Angst, 1998).

Unlike the rates of unipolar depression, the rates of bipolar I disorder are approximately the same for men and women (Weissman et al., 1996), although bipolar II disorder is diagnosed more frequently in women than men. Absence of striking gender differences is often seen as consistent with the view of a biological basis of bipolar disorder.

## Etiological Approaches to Bipolar Disorder

### Genetic Studies

There is solid evidence of heritability of bipolar disorder. Family studies have consistently revealed an interesting pattern: Both unipolar and bipolar disorders (mania) occur in relatives of bipolar patients, whereas only unipolar disorder is found among relatives of unipolar patients (e.g., Winokur et al., 1995). This distinctive pattern has helped to confirm that bipolar disorder is a separate disorder from unipolar depression. In addition to family studies, twin studies indicate heritability. A review by NIMH (1998) indicated that concordance rates for bipolar I disorder in monozygotic twins range between 33 and 80%.

For several years the focus of genetic research was on discovery of a single genetic locus, often based on isolated extended families with high rates of bipolar illness (e.g., Baron et al., 1987; Egeland et al., 1987). Most findings, however, were not replicated, and modern genetic techniques have identified multiple possible chromosome locations, including chromosomes 18, 21q, 11, and others (e.g., Bellivier et al., 1998; see review in Kelsoe, 1997). Despite interest in single-locus approaches, most research now suggests a polygenic disorder (Goodwin & Ghaemi, 1999). Current major bipolar genetic studies are underway to help resolve the genetic issues.

In addition to genetic research, there is considerable interest in discovery of potential markers of risk for bipolar disorder in children of bipolar parents. A meta-analysis of high-risk studies indicated that children of bipolar parents had a 52% likelihood of some diagnosis, with a risk of 26.5% of mood disorders (Lapalme, Hodgins, & LaRoche, 1997). Bipolar disorder occurred in 5.4% of the offspring of bipolar parents, whereas none of the children of non-ill parents were bipolar. Obviously this figure cannot be taken as the final estimate of risk for bipolarity, because most of the children had not passed—or even entered—the age of risk. The figure of 15–20% is often cited as the risk for developing bipolar disorders in offspring of a bipolar parent (e.g., Goodwin & Ghaemi, 1999). To date, high-risk research has yet to identify symptom, psychological, genetic, or biological markers of potential bipolar diathesis. Discovery of bipolar-related genes, for example, could help to identify children who might benefit from early treatment (see treatment section, later).

### Neuroregulatory Processes in Bipolar Disorder

Presuming genetic predisposition to bipolar disorder, the mechanism of the illness is unknown. However, any model must be able to explain clinical features of the disorder, such as recurrent episodes and the switches from one state to another, as well as apparent progression in severity and frequency of episodes. On the basis of animal research, Post (e.g., Post, 1992; Post, Rubinow, & Ballenger, 1984) has speculated that processes resembling *kindling* or *behavioral sensitization* may operate in which the brain is altered by repeated episodes of mood disorder, resulting in increased sensitivity to neurotransmitter and neurohormonal regulation of mood in response to stressors or other triggering experiences. This hypothesis is consistent with the clinical observation that the severity of untreated episodes worsens over time, and that early episodes are more likely triggered by stressors whereas later episodes are not. Several studies have shown nonspecific brain abnormalities but present conflicting evidence of correlation of extent of abnormality with length of illness (e.g., Altshuler et al., 1995; Dupont et al., 1995; Strakoswki et al., 1999). Recently, a study found neurocognitive impairments, especially those of memory and learning, that were strongly correlated with total duration of lifetime episodes (Van Gorp, Altshuler, Theberge, Wilkins, & Dixon, 1998). Consistent with Post's model, these authors speculated that repeated bipolar episodes may induce hippocampal dysfunction (with memory and learning impairment) through the toxic effects of episode- or stress-induced hypercortisolemia. Although the kindling model is intriguing, its empirical basis remains to be further developed.

Other models of brain and neurotransmitter functioning have been articulated over the years (e.g., Schildkraut, 1965; dopamine and the behavioral facilitation system, according to Depue & Iocono, 1989; and others). Simple neurotransmitter approaches have not captured much recent attention in isolation. However, relatively recent research on the mechanisms responsible for the effectiveness of lithium and antidepressants has led to important advances in understanding complex neurobiological processes. As Goodwin and Ghaemi (1999) phrase it, current thinking favors "the evolution from synaptic neurotransmitter-based hypotheses to . . . postsynaptic second messenger-based hypotheses" (p. 47). Research in this area promises to shed new light not only on possible bipolar illness–related abnormalities but on other disorders as well.

### Circadian-Rhythm Abnormalities

Neurotransmitter systems also may be a mechanism through which hypothesized abnormalities in circadian rhythms cause episodes. Wehr (e.g., Wehr & Goodwin, 1983) suggested that brain abnormalities affecting regulation of daily biological rhythms may cause desynchronization of the cycles, leading to clinical symptoms—as well as to seasonal patterns of mood episodes. Patterns of seasonal variation of mood and associated biological states—in both unipolar and bipolar patients—have contributed to considerable research interest in chronobiological processes in mood disorders (Goodwin & Jamison, 1990). Interestingly, disrupted sleep cycles are well known to trigger manic episodes in some bipolar patients, leading clinicians to urge individuals with bipolar I disorders to be cautious about sleep loss, international travel, and other sleep-altering patterns.

### Psychosocial Processes in Bipolar Disorder

Although modern theories of bipolar disorder do not view it as fundamentally caused by psychological processes, a small but growing body of research emphasizes the importance of such factors in potentially influencing the course of illness. It is also possible that psychological and environmental factors play a role in triggering the disorder among those who may be biologically predisposed. It is clear that psychological factors play a role in treatment outcome and adherence to medication.

A number of studies have shown that stressful life events may affect the course of disorder by triggering episodes of depression and mania (e.g., reviewed in Johnson & Roberts, 1995). Quality of family and spouse support also appear to affect outcome, in that more negative family attitudes toward the patient significantly predict increased likelihood of relapse (Miklowitz, Goldstein, Nuechterlein, Snyder, & Mintz, 1988), and better social support in general appears to predict a more favorable course of disorder (Johnson, Winett, Meyer, Greenhouse, & Miller, 1999). To date, however, research has not been designed to test potentially important predictors of manic versus depressive experiences, and such questions are important. Also, considerably more work is needed to help understand the psychosocial predictors of the vastly different outcomes—both clinical and functional—that are observed among bipolar patients.

## Treatment of Bipolar Disorder

Medications are the primary treatment for bipolar disorders, and are indicated for reduction of manic (antimanic drugs) or depressive (antidepressant drugs) symptoms in the short run, and prevention of episodes over time (mood stabilizers). Lithium is the most frequently used and effective antimanic and mood stabilizer medication. Up to 2 weeks of lithium treatment may be needed to achieve significant reduction of manic symptoms (APA, 1994b), and treatment of acute mania may also include use of neuroleptics. Regarding lithium's prophylactic effect, a review of 10 double-blind, placebo-controlled studies indicated a significantly lower probability or intensity of an episode in those taking lithium, compared with placebo (Goodwin & Jamison, 1990). Despite the enormous treatment advances that lithium brought about in the early 1960s, however, recent studies, as indicated previously, have shown that many patients have relatively high rates of relapse and symptoms despite adequate lithium treatment. It has been argued that recent investigations may include many patients who have more treatment-resistant forms of disorder, or who have problems with medication compliance. It is also suspected that lithium is especially effective for those who have classic bipolar I disorder, with manic and depressive episodes, but less so for those with mixed or cycling episodes. Moreover, due to lithium's potential toxicity and various side effects—as well as to patients' reduced insight about the need for continuous medication—compliance with lithium may be problematic, requiring continuing medical monitoring and support. It has also been suggested, although not empirically resolved, that periodic discontinuation of lithium may reduce its effectiveness in episode prevention.

In recent years, several additional mood stabilizer medications that are pharmacological antiseizure drugs have been used with apparently good results in treatment of acute mania—and apparently (although less well established empirically) with prophylactic effects as well. Sodium valproate, for example, is suspected to be more effective than lithium for patients who have mixed states and rapid cycling (APA, 1994b). Although it, too, is associated with bothersome side effects (such as weight gain), it is not toxic. Carbamazepine is also apparently effective as an antimanic and mood stabilizer medication, but may have serious adverse side effects including fatal toxicity.

Use of antidepressants to treat depression in bipolar patients is problematic, because they may trigger manic episodes and have been implicated in the emergence of rapid-cycling bipolar episodes. Indeed, it has been speculated that recent studies of the relatively poor showing for lithium prophylaxis may reflect illness courses that are more difficult to treat in part because of the widespread use of antidepressants without concurrent mood stabilizers (e.g., Goodwin & Ghaemi, 1999). Psychiatrists are urged to use antidepressants with caution in bipolar patients. New drugs with safer antidepressant properties are currently being evaluated.

An intriguing issue in treatment concerns the implications of the previously mentioned *kindling hypothesis*: the idea that early intervention in the course of disorder may prevent the development of future episodes by eliminating the cumulative pathological effects of episodes themselves. There is considerable interest in detection of bipolar disorder in children and those at risk due to genetic factors to enable early intervention. Lithium treatment of children and adolescents is relatively well established, but the long-term effects have not been evaluated in terms of the kindling hypothesis.

There is also increasing interest in psychotherapy and psychosocial interventions for bipolar patients as an adjunct to pharmacological treatment (e.g., APA, 1994b). A number of issues have been targeted: education about the illness, identification of prodromal signs of impending episodes, management of lifestyles to promote stable sleep and social patterns conducive to more stable moods, dealing with issues of personal identity and self-esteem in the face of destructive mood swings, encouragement of adherence to medication, and improved personal and family communications and problem solving. Family process, cognitive-behavioral, and interpersonal psychotherapy models are currently being applied and studied (e.g., Frank, Swartz, & Kupfer, 2000; reviewed in Johnson, Greenhouse, & Bauer, 2000).

## CONCLUSIONS AND FUTURE DIRECTIONS

The past two decades have seen enormous amounts of research on mood disorders, contributing substantially to the understanding of unipolar and bipolar disorders in children, adolescents, and adults. Future work on the further identification of the disorder, the clarification of risk markers, and the longitudinal course of disorders in children will be a high priority, especially to test the hypotheses that early intervention may quell the severity of the course of recurrent mood disorders. High-risk studies of the offspring of unipolar parents have been highly informative, but new ground will be broken by more integrative approaches that include multiple and interacting factors, including both biological and psychosocial variables. High-risk research in bipolar families is of great interest but in need of further attention.

Additional clarification of possible subtypes of unipolar and bipolar disorders, including subclinical variants, will be necessary to fully understand the ranges and courses of the disorders and their distributions in the population. However, it would be unfortunate to focus only on syndromal conditions, since specific symptoms and constellations of characteristics—such as negative affectivity or behavioral activation—may also be productive for further study.

Research on etiological factors will continue to mine the advances in genetic and neuroscience models and techniques. However, a hugely important issue is the integration of biological and psychosocial models. Although there are increasing signs of such integration, important advances in mood disorders will require developments in conceptualization and methods that employ strategies from multiple fields.

Both pharmacological and psychological treatments have proven to be successful in reducing depressive symptomatology. The challenge in this topic is to extend the effectiveness of such interventions to reduce recurrence and prevent future episodes. Among bipolar patients, treatment options are somewhat more limited, but advances are being made on both the medication and psychotherapy fronts. However, an important consideration in both unipolar and bipolar populations is dissemination of treatments, and encouragement of those in need to get treatment. Surprisingly large numbers of both depressed and bipolar patients are not being treated at all, or are not being treated aggressively enough. The obstacles appear to include recognition of the illnesses as well as lack of widespread use of treatment guidelines and limited availability of empirically supported therapies outside the university communities. Treatments of children are particularly challenging and important, and preventive interventions require continued exploration.

Finally, the demographics of mood disorders command ongoing interest: Depression has increased in young people and continues to affect women disproportionately. All our assessment, etiological models, and treatments need to contend with and shed further light on this reality.

## REFERENCES

Abramson, L. Y., Alloy, L. B., & Metalsky, G. I. (1989). Hopelessness depression: A theory-based subtype of depression. *Psychological Review, 96,* 358–372.

Akiskal, H. S. (1996). The prevalent clinical spectrum of bipolar disorders: Beyond DSM-IV. *Journal of Clinical Psychopharmacology, 16,* 4S–14S.

Akiskal, H. S., Maser, J. D., Zeller, P. J., Endicott, J., Coryell, W., Keller, M., Warshaw, M., Clayton, P., & Goodwin, F. (1995). Switching from "unipolar" to bipolar II: An 11-year prospective study of clinical and temperamental predictors in 559 patients. *Archives of General Psychiatry, 52,* 114–123.

Alloy, L. B., Abramson, L. Y., Hogan, M. E., Whitehouse, W. G., Rose, D. T., Robinson, M. S., Kim, R. S., & Lapkin, J. B. (2000). The Temple-Wisconsin Cognitive Vulnerability to Depression Project: Lifetime history of Axis I psychopathology in individuals at high and low cognitive risk for depression. *Journal of Abnormal Psychology, 109,* 403–418.

Altshuler, L. L., Curran, J. G., Hauser, P., Mintz, J., Denicoff, K., & Post, R. (1995). T$_2$ hyperintensities in polar disorder: Magnetic resonance imaging comparison and literature meta-analysis. *American Journal of Psychiatry, 152,* 1139–1144.

American Psychiatric Association. (1994a). *Diagnostic and statistical manual of mental disorders* (4th ed.). Washington, DC: Author.

American Psychiatric Association. (1994b). Practice guideline for the treatment of patients with bipolar disorder. *Supplement to the American Journal of Psychiatry, 151,* 1–36.

Angold, A., & Costello, E. J. (1993). Depressive comorbidity in children and adolescent: Empirical, theoretical, and methodological issues. *American Journal of Psychiatry, 150,* 1779–1791.

Angold, A., & Rutter, M. (1992). Effects of age and pubertal status on depression in a large clinical sample. *Development & Psychopathology, 4,* 5–28.

Angst, J. (1998). The emerging epidemiology of hypomania and bipolar II disorder. *Journal of Affective Disorders, 50,* 143–151.

Barbato, N., & Hafner, R. J. (1998). Comorbidity of bipolar and personality disorder. *Australian and New Zealand Journal of Psychiatry, 32,* 276–280.

Bardone, A., Moffitt, T., Caspi, A., Dickson, N., & Silva, P. (1996). Adult mental health and social outcomes of adolescent girls with depression and conduct disorder. *Development and Psychopathology, 8,* 811–829.

Barnett, P. A., & Gotlib, I. H. (1988). Psychosocial functioning and depression: Distinguishing among antecedents, concomitants, and consequences. *Psychological Bulletin, 104,* 97–126.

Baron, M., Risch, N., Hamburger, R., Mandel, B., Kushner, S., Newman, M., Drumer, D., & Belmaker, R. H. (1987). Genetic linkage between X-chromosome markers and bipolar affective illness. *Nature, 326,* 289–292.

Beardslee, W. R., Versage, E. M., & Gladstone, T. R. (1998). Children of affectively ill parents: A review of the past 10 years. *Journal of the American Academy of Child and Adolescent Psychiatry, 37,* 1134–1141.

Beck, A. T. (1967). *Depression: Clinical, experimental, and theoretical aspects.* New York: Harper & Row.

Beck, A. T., Steer, R. A., & Brown, G. K. (1996). *Manual for the BDI-II.* San Antonio, TX: Psychological Corporation.

Beck, A. T., Steer, R. A., & Garbin, M. G. (1988). Psychometric properties of the Beck Depression Inventory: Twenty-five years of evaluation. *Clinical Psychological Review, 8,* 77–100.

Beck, A. T., Ward, C. H., Mendelsohn, M., Mock, J., & Erbaugh, J. (1961). An inventory for measuring depression. *Archives of General Psychiatry, 4,* 561–571.

Bellivier, F., Leboyer, M., Courtet, P., Buresi, C., Beaufils, B., Samolyk, D., Allilaire, J., Feingold, J., Mallet, J., & Malafosse, A. (1998). Association between the tryptophan hydroxylase gene and manic-depressive illness. *Archives of General Psychiatry, 55,* 33–37.

Biederman, J. (1998). Resolved: Mania is mistaken for ADHD in prepubertal children. *Journal of the American Academy of Child and Adolescent Psychiatry, 37*(10), 1091–1093.

Billings, A. G., & Moos, R. H. (1985). Psychosocial processes of remission in unipolar depression: Comparing depressed patients with matched community controls. *Journal of Consulting and Clinical Psychology, 53,* 314–325.

Birmaher, B., Ryan, N. D., Williamson, D. E., Brent, D. A., Kaufman, J., Dahl, R. E., Perel, J., & Nelson, B. (1996). Childhood and adolescent depression: Pt. 1. A review of the past 10 years. *Journal of the American Academy of Child and Adolescent Psychiatry, 35,* 1427–1439.

Blazer, D. G., Kessler, R. C., McGonagle, K. A., & Swartz, M. S. (1994). The prevalence and distribution of major depression in a national community sample: The national comorbidity survey. *American Journal of Psychiatry, 151,* 979–986.

Bowlby, J. (1978). *Attachment and loss: Vol. 2. Separation: Anxiety and anger.* Harmondsworth, England: Penguin.

Bowlby, J. (1981). *Attachment and loss: Vol. 3. Loss: Sadness and depression.* Harmondsworth, England: Penguin.

Brent, D. A., Holder, D., Kolko, D., Birmaher, B., Baugher, M., Roth, C., Iyengar, S., & Johnson, B. A. (1997). A clinical psychotherapy trial for adolescent depression comparing cognitive, family, and supportive therapy. *Journal of the American Academy of Child and Adolescent Psychiatry, 54,* 877–885.

Brown, G. W., Andrews, B., Harris, T. O., Adler, Z., & Bridge, L. (1986). Social support, self-esteem, and depression. *Psychological Medicine, 16,* 813–831.

Brown, G. W., & Harris, T. O. (1978). *Social origins of depression.* London: Free Press.

Brown, G. W., & Harris, T. O. (1989). Depression. In G. W. Harris & T. O. Harris (Eds.), *Life events and illness* (pp. 49–93). New York: Guilford Press.

Burke, K. C., Burke, J. D., Regier, D. A., & Rae, D. S. (1990). Age at onset of selected mental disorders in five community populations. *Archives of General Psychiatry, 47,* 511–518.

Carlson, G. A., Bromet, E. J., & Sievers, S. (2000). Phenomenology and outcome of subjects with early- and adult-onset psychotic mania. *American Journal of Psychiatry, 157*(2), 213–219.

Carlson, G. A., & Kelley, K. L. (1998). Manic symptoms in psychiatrically hospitalized children—what do they mean? *Journal of Affective Disorders, 51,* 123–135.

Carlson, G. A., Loney, J., Salisbury, H., & Volpe, R. J. (1998). Young referred boys with DICA-P manic symptoms vs. two comparison groups. *Journal of Affective Disorders, 121,* 113–121.

Clark, D. C., & Fawcett, J. (1992). Review of empirical risk factors for evaluation of the suicidal patient. In B. M. Bongar (Ed.), *Suicide: Guidelines for assessment, management, and treatment* (pp. 16–48). New York: Oxford University Press.

Coffey, C. E., Wildinson, W. E., Weiner, R. D., Parashos, I. A., Djang, W. T., Webb, M. C., Figiel, G. S., & Spritzer, C. E. (1993). Quantitative cerebral anatomy in depression: A controlled magnetic resonance imaging study. *Archives of General Psychiatry, 50,* 7–16.

Cohen, P., Cohen, J., Kasen, S., Velez, C. N., Hartmark, C., Johnson, J., Rojas, M., Brook, J., & Streuning, E. L. (1993). An epidemiological study of disorders in late childhood and adolescence: I. Age and gender-specific prevalence. *Journal of Child Psychology and Psychiatry, 34,* 851–867.

Coryell, W., Akiskal, H., Leon, A., Winokur, G., Maser, J., Mueller, T., & Keller, M. (1994). The time course of nonchronic major depressive disorder: Uniformity across episodes and samples. *Archives of General Psychiatry, 51,* 405–410.

Coryell, W., Endicott, J., & Keller, M. (1992a). Major depression in a nonclinical sample: Demographic and clinical risk factors for first onset. *Archives of General Psychiatry, 49,* 117–125.

Coryell, W., Endicott, J., & Keller, M. (1992b). Rapid cycling affective disorder: Demographics, diagnosis, family history, and course. *Archives of General Psychiatry, 49,* 126–131.

Coryell, W., Endicott, J., Maser, J. D., Keller, M. B., Leon, A. C., & Akiskal, H. S. (1995). Long-term stability of polarity distinctions in the affective disorders. *American Journal of Psychiatry, 152,* 385–390.

Coryell, W., Keller, M., Endicott, J., Andreasen, N., Clayton, P., & Hirschfeld, R. (1989). Bipolar II illness: Course and outcome over a five-year period. *Psychological Medicine, 19,* 129–141.

Coryell, W., Scheftner, W., Keller, M., Endicott, J., Maser, J., & Klerman, G. L. (1993). The enduring psychological consequences of mania and depression. *American Journal of Psychiatry, 150,* 720–727.

Coryell, W., Turvey, C., Endicott, J., Leon, A. C., Mueller, T., Solomon, D., & Keller, M. (1998). Bipolar I affective disorder: Predictors of outcome after 15 years. *Journal of Affective Disorders, 50,* 109–116.

Coyne, J. C., Kessler, R. C., Tal, M., Turnbull, J., Wortman, C. B., & Greden, J. F. (1987). Living with a depressed person. *Journal of Consulting and Clinical Psychology, 55,* 347–352.

Cross-National Collaborative Group. (1992). The changing rate of major depression: Cross-national comparisons. *Journal of the American Medical Association, 268,* 3098–3105.

Cyranowski, J. M., Frank, E., Young, E., & Shear, M. (2000). Adolescent onset of the gender difference in lifetime rates of major depression: A theoretical model. *Archives of General Psychiatry, 57,* 21–27.

Daley, S., Hammen, C., Burge, D., Davila, J., Paley, B., Lindberg, N., & Herzberg, D. (1997). Predictors of the generation of episodic stress: A longitudinal study of late adolescent women. *Journal of Abnormal Psychology, 106,* 251–259.

Davidson, R. J. (1993). Cerebral asymmetry and emotion: Conceptual and methodological conundrums. *Cognition and Emotion, 7,* 115–138.

Depue, R. A., & Iacono, W. G. (1989). Neurobehavioral aspects of affective disorders. *Annual Review of Psychology, 40,* 457–492.

Depue, R. A., Krauss, S., Spoont, M. R., & Arbisi, P. (1989). General Behavior Inventory identification of unipolar and bipolar affective conditions in a nonclinical university population. *Journal of Abnormal Psychology, 98,* 117–126.

Dohrenwend, B. P., Shrout, P. E., Link, B., Martin, J., & Skodol, A. (1986). Overview and initial results from a risk-factor study of depression and schizophrenia. In J. E. Barrett (Ed.), *Mental disorder in the community: Progress and challenges* (pp. 184–215). New York: Guilford Press.

Downey, G., & Coyne, J. C. (1990). Children of depressed parents: An integrative review. *Psychological Bulletin, 108,* 50–76.

Dunayevich, E., Strakowski, S. M., Sax, K. W., Sorter, M. T., Keck, P. E., Jr., McElroy, S. L., & McConville, B. J. (1996). Personality disorders in first- and multiple-episode mania. *Psychiatry Research, 64,* 69–75.

Dupont, R. M., Jernigan, T. L., Heindel, W., Butters, N., Shafer, K., Wilson, T., Hesselink, J., & Gillin, C. (1995). Magnetic resonance imagining and mood disorders: Localization of white matter and other subcortical abnormalities. *Archives of General Psychiatry, 52,* 747–755.

Eaton, W. W., Neufeld, K., Chen, L., & Cai, G. (2000). A comparison of self-report and clinical diagnostic interviews for depression. *Archives of General Psychiatry, 57,* 217–222.

Eckblad, M., & Chapman, L. J. (1986). Development and validation of a scale for hypomanic personality. *Journal of Abnormal Psychology, 95,* 214–222.

Egeland, J. A., Gerhard, D. S., Pauls, D. L., Sussex, J. N., Kidd, K. K., Allen, C. R., Hostetter, A. M., & Housman, D. E. (1987). Bipolar affective disorders linked to DNA markers on chromosome 11. *Nature, 325,* 783–787.

Emslie, G. J., Rush, A. J., Weinberg, W. A., Kowatch, R. A., Hughes, C. W., Carmody, T., & Rintelmann, J. (1997). A double-blind, randomized, placebo-controlled trial of fluoxetine in children and adolescents with depression. *Archives of General Psychiatry, 54,* 1031–1037.

Endicott, J., & Spitzer, R. L. (1978). A diagnostic interview: The schedule for affective disorders and schizophrenia. *Archives of General Psychiatry, 35,* 837–844.

Evans, S., Cloitre, M., Kocsis, J. H., Keitner, G. I., Holzer, C. P., & Gniwesch, L. (1996). Social-vocational adjustment in unipolar mood disorders: Results of the DSM-IV field trial. *Journal of Affective Disorders, 38,* 73–80.

Faedda, G., Baldessarini, R., Suppes, T., Tondo, L., Becker, I., & Lipschitz, D. (1995). Pediatric-onset bipolar disorder: A neglected clinical and public health problem. *Harvard Review of Psychiatry, 3,* 171–195.

Faraone, S. V., Biederman, J., Mennin, D., Wozniak, J., & Spencer, T. (1997). Attention-deficit hyperactivity disorder with bipolar disorder: A familial subtype? *Journal of the American Academy of Child and Adolescent Psychiatry, 36,* 1378–1387.

Faraone, S. V., Biederman, J., Wozniak, J., Mundy, E., Mennin, D., & O'Donnell, D. (1997). Is comorbidity with ADHD a marker for juvenile-onset mania? *Journal of the American Academy of Child and Adolescent Psychiatry, 36*(8), 1046–1055.

First, M. B., Spitzer, R. L., Gibbon, M., & Williams, J. B. W. (1995). *Structured clinical interview for DSM-IV Axis I disorders.* Washington, DC: American Psychiatric Press.

Frank, E., Kupfer, D. J., Wagner, E. F., McEachran, A. B., & Cornes, C. (1991). Efficacy of interpersonal psychotherapy as a maintenance treatment of recurrent depression. *Archives of General Psychiatry, 48,* 1053–1059.

Frank, E., Swartz, H., & Kupfer, D. (2000). Interpersonal and social rhythm therapy: Managing the chaos of bipolar disorder. *Biological Psychiatry, 48,* 593–604.

Garber, J., & Flynn, C. (2001). Vulnerability to depression in childhood and adolescence. In R. Ingram & J. Price (Eds.), *Vulnerability to psychopathology: Risk across the lifespan* (pp. 175–225). New York: Guilford Press.

Geller, B., Williams, M., Zimerman, B., Frazier, J., Beringer, L., & Warner, K. L. (1998). Prepubertal and early adolescent bipolarity differentiate from ADHD by manic symptoms, grandiose delusions, ultra-rapid or ultradian cycling. *Journal of Affective Disorders, 51,* 81–91.

Gerlsma, C., Emmelkamp, P. M. G., & Arrindell, W. A. (1990). Anxiety, depression, and perception of early parenting: A meta-analysis. *Clinical Psychology Review, 10,* 251–277.

Gershon, E. S. (1990). Genetics. In F. K. Goodwin & K. R. Jamison (Eds.), *Manic depressive illness* (pp. 373–401). New York: Oxford University Press.

Gitlin, M. J. (2002). Pharmacologic treatment for depression. In I. H. Gotlib & C. Hammen (Eds.), *Handbook of depression* (pp. 360–382). New York: Guilford Press.

Gitlin, M., Swendsen, J., Heller, T., & Hammen, C. (1995). Relapse and impairment in bipolar disorder: A longitudinal study. *American Journal of Psychiatry, 152,* 1635–1640.

Gold, P. W., Goodwin, F. K., & Chrousos, G. P. (1988). Clinical and biochemical manifestations of depression: Relation to the neurobiology of stress. *The New England Journal of Medicine, 319,* 348–419.

Goodman, S., & Gotlib, I. (1999). Risk for psychopathology in the children of depressed mothers: A developmental model for understanding mechanisms of transmission. *Psychological Review, 106,* 458–490.

Goodman, S. H., Schwab-Stone, M., Lahey, B. B., Shaffer, D., & Jensen P. S. (2000). Major depression and dysthymia in children and adolescents: Discriminant validity and differential consequences in a community sample. *Journal of the American Academy of Child and Adolescent Psychiatry, 39,* 761–770.

Goodwin, F., & Ghaemi, S. N. (1999). Bipolar disorders: State of the art. *Dialogues in Clinical Neuroscience, 1,* 41–51.

Goodwin, F. K., & Jamison, K. R. (1990). *Manic-depressive illness.* New York: Oxford University Press.

Gotlib, I. H., & Hammen, C. L. (1992). *Psychological aspects of depression: Toward a cognitive-interpersonal integration*. London: Wiley.

Gotlib, I. H., Lewinsohn, P. M., & Seeley, J. R. (1995). Symptoms versus a diagnosis of depression: Differences in psychosocial functioning. *Journal of Consulting and Clinical Psychology, 65,* 90–100.

Gotlib, I., Lewinsohn, P., & Seeley, J. (1998). Consequences of depression during adolescence: Marital status and marital functioning in early adulthood. *Journal of Abnormal Psychology, 107,* 686–690.

Gunnar, M. R. (1998). Quality of early care and buffering of neuroendocrine stress reactions: Potential effects on the developing human brain. *Preventive Medicine, 27,* 208–211.

Hamilton, M. (1960). A rating scale for depression. *Journal of Neurology, Neurosurgery and Psychiatry, 12,* 56–62.

Hammen, C. L. (1991a). *Depression runs in families: The social context of risk and resilience in children of depressed mothers.* New York: Springer-Verlag.

Hammen, C. L. (1991b). The generation of stress in the course of unipolar depression. *Journal of Abnormal Psychology, 100,* 555–561.

Hammen, C. L. (2000). Vulnerability to depression in adulthood. In R. Ingram & J. Price (Eds.), *Handbook of vulnerability to psychopathology: Risk across the lifespan* (pp. 226–257). New York: Guilford Press.

Hammen, C. L. (2002). The context of stress in families of children with depressed parents. In S. Goodman & I. Gotlib (Eds.), *Children of depressed parents: Alternative pathways to risk for psychopathology* (pp. 175–179). Washington, DC: American Psychological Association.

Hammen, C. L., Burge, D., Daley, S., Davila, J., Paley, B., & Rudolph, K. (1995). Interpersonal attachment cognitions and prediction of symptomatic responses to interpersonal stress. *Journal of Abnormal Psychology, 104,* 436–443.

Hammen, C. L., & Compas, B. (1994). Unmasking unmasked depression: The problem of comorbidity in childhood depression. *Clinical Psychology Review, 14,* 585–603.

Hammen, C. L., & Goodman-Brown, T. (1990). Self-schemas and vulnerability to specific life stress in children at risk for depression. *Cognitive Therapy and Research, 14,* 215–227.

Hammen, C. L., Henry, R., & Daley, S. (2000). Depression and sensitization to stressors among young women as a function of childhood adversity. *Journal of Consulting and Clinical Psychology, 68,* 782–787.

Hammen, C. L., Marks, T., Mayol, A., & deMayo, R. (1985). Depressive self-schemas, life stress, and vulnerability to depression. *Journal of Abnormal Psychology, 94,* 308–319.

Hammen, C., & Rudolph, K. (1996). Childhood depression. In E. J. Mash & R. A. Barkley (Eds.), *Child psychopathology* (pp. 153–195). New York: Guilford Press.

Harrington, R., Fudge, H., Rutter, M., Pickles, A., & Hill, J. (1990). Adult outcomes of childhood and adolescent depression: Psychiatric status. *Archives of General Psychiatry, 47,* 465–473.

Harrow, M., Goldberg, J. F., Grossman, L. S., & Meltzer, H. Y. (1990). Outcome in manic disorders: A naturalistic follow-up study. *Archives of General Psychiatry, 47,* 665–671.

Heim, C., Ehlert, U., Hanker, J. P., & Hellhammer, D. H. (1998). Abuse-related post-traumatic stress disorder and alterations of the hypothalamic-pituitary-adrenal axis in women with chronic pelvic pain. *Psychosomatic Medicine, 60,* 309–318.

Helzer, J. E., & Pryzbeck, T. R. (1988). The co-occurence of alcoholism with other psychiatric disorders in the general population and its impact on treatment. *Journal of Studies on Alcohol, 49,* 219–224.

Hendrick, V., Altshuler, L. L., & Suri, R. (1998). Hormonal changes in the postpartum and implications for postpartum depression. *Psychosomatics, 39,* 93–101.

Hollon, S. D., Haman, K. L., & Brown, L. L. (2002). Cognitive behavioral treatment of depression. In I. H. Gotlib & C. Hammen (Eds.), *Handbook of depression* (pp. 383–403). New York: Guilford Press.

Horwath, E., Johnson, J., Klerman, G. L., & Weissman, M. M. (1992). Depressive symptoms as relative and attributable risk factors for first-onset major depression. *Archives of General Psychiatry, 49,* 817–823.

Ingram, R. E., Miranda, J., & Segal, Z. V. (1998). *Cognitive vulnerability to depression.* New York: Guilford Press.

Johnson, S., Greenhouse, W., & Bauer, M. (2000). Psychosocial approaches to the treatment of bipolar disorder. *Current Opinions in Psychiatry, 13,* 69–72.

Johnson, S. L., & Roberts, J. R. (1995). Life events and bipolar disorder: Implications from biological theories. *Psychological Bulletin, 117,* 434–449.

Johnson, S. L., Winett, C., Meyer, B., Greenhouse, W., & Miller, I. (1999). Social support and the course of bipolar disorder. *Journal of Abnormal Psychology, 108,* 558–566.

Joiner, T., & Coyne, J. C. (Eds.). (1999). *The interactional nature of depression: Advances in interpersonal approaches.* Washington, DC: American Psychological Association.

Joiner, T. E., Jr., & Metalsky, G. I. (1995). A prospective test of an integrative interpersonal theory of depression: A naturalistic study of college roommates. *Journal of Personality and Social Psychology, 69,* 778–788.

Jones, N. A., Field, T., Fox, N. A., Lundy, B., & Davalos, M. (1997). EEG activation in 1-month-old infants of depressed mothers. *Development and Psychopathology, 9,* 491–505.

Judd, L. L. (1997). The clinical course of unipolar major depressive disorders. *Archives of General Psychiatry, 54,* 989–991.

Judd, L., Akiskal, A., Maser, J. D., Zeller, P. J., Endicott, J., Coryell, W., Paulus, M. P., Kunovac, J. L., Leon, A. C., Mueller, T. I., Rice, J. A., & Keller, M. B. (1998). A prospective 12-year study of subsyndromal and syndromal depressive symptoms in unipolar major depressive disorders. *Archives of General Psychiatry, 55,* 694–700.

Judd, L. L., Akiskal, H. S., Zeller, P. J., Paulus, M., Leon, A. C., Maser, J. D., Endicott, J., Coryell, W., Kunovac, J. L., Mueller, T. I., Rice, J. P., & Keller, M. B. (2000). Psychosocial disability during the long-term course of unipolar major depressive disorder. *Archives of General Psychiatry, 57,* 375–380.

Kashani, J. H., & Carlson, G. A. (1987). Seriously depressed preschoolers. *American Journal of Psychiatry, 144,* 348–350.

Kaslow, N. J., Deering, C. G., & Racusin, G. R. (1994). Depressed children and their families. *Clinical Psychology Review, 14,* 39–59.

Kaslow, N., McClure, E., & Connell, A. (2002). Treatment of depression in children and adolescents. In I. H. Gotlib & C. Hammen (Eds.), *Handbook of depression* (pp. 441–464). New York: Guilford Press.

Keller, M. B., Lavori, P. W., Coryell, M. D., Endicott, J., & Mueller, T. I. (1993). Bipolar I: A five-year prospective follow-up. *The Journal of Nervous and Mental Disease, 181,* 238–245.

Keller, M. B., Lavori, P. W., Endicott, J., Coryell, W., & Klerman, G. L. (1983). "Double depression": Two year follow-up. *American Journal of Psychiatry, 140,* 689–694.

Keller, M., Lavori, P. W., Mueller, T. I., Endicott, J., Coryell, W., Hirschfeld, R. M. A., & Shea, T. (1992). Time to recovery, chronicity, and levels of psychopathology in major depression. *Archives of General Psychiatry, 49,* 809–816.

Kelsoe, J. R. (1997). The genetics of bipolar disorder. *Psychiatric Annals, 27,* 285–292.

Kendler, K. S., Gardner, C. O., & Prescott, C. A. (1999). Clinical characteristics of major depression that predict risk of depression in relatives. *Archives of General Psychiatry, 56,* 322–327.

Kendler, K. S., Neale, M. C., Kessler, R. C., Heath, A. C., & Eaves, L. J. (1992). A population-based twin study of major depression in women. *Archives of General Psychiatry, 49,* 257–266.

Kendler, K. S., & Prescott, C. A. (1999). A population-based twin study of lifetime major depression in men and women. *Archives of General Psychiatry, 56,* 39–44.

Kendler, K. S., Thornton, L. M., & Gardner, C. O. (2000). Stressful life events and previous episodes in the etiology of major depression in women: An evaluation of the "Kindling" hypothesis. *American Journal of Psychiatry, 157,* 1243–1251.

Kennedy, S. H., Javanmard, M., & Vaccarino, F. J. (1997). A review of functional neuroimaging in mood disorders: Positron emission tomography and depression. *The Canadian Journal of Psychiatry, 42,* 467–475.

Kessler, R., & Magee, W. (1993). Childhood adversities and adult depression: Basic patterns of association in a U.S. national survey. *Psychological Medicine, 23,* 679–690.

Kessler, R., McGonagle, K., Zhao, S., Nelson, C., Hughes, M., Eshelman, S., Wittchen, H., & Kendler, K. (1994). Lifetime and 12-month prevalence of DSM-III-R psychiatric disorders in the United States: Results from the National Comorbidity Survey. *Archives of General Psychiatry, 51,* 8–19.

Kessler, R. C., Rubinow, D. R., Holmes, C., Abelson, J. M., & Zhao, S. (1997). The epidemiology of DSM-III-R bipolar I disorder in a general population survey. *Psychological Medicine, 27,* 1079–1089.

Klein, D. N., Taylor, E. B., Harding, K., & Dickstein, S. (1988). Double depression and episodic major depression: Demographic, clinical, familial, personality, and socioenvironmental characteristics and short-term outcomes. *American Journal of Psychiatry, 145,* 1226–1231.

Kobak, R. R., Sudler, N., & Gamble, W. (1991). Attachment and depressive symptoms during adolescence: A developmental pathways analysis. *Development and Psychopathology, 3,* 461–474.

Kovacs, M. (1996). Presentation and course of major depressive disorder during childhood and later years of the life span. *Journal of the American Academy of Child and Adolescent Psychiatry, 35*(6), 705–715.

Kraepelin, E. (1921). *Manic-depressive insanity and paranoia* (R. M. Barclay, Trans.). Edinburgh, Scotland: Livingstone.

Kutcher, S. P., Robertson, H. A., & Bird, D. (1998). Premorbid functioning in adolescent onset bipolar I disorder: A preliminary report from an ongoing study. *Journal of Affective Disorders, 51,* 137–144.

Lapalme, M., Hodgins, S., & LaRoche, C. (1997). Children of parents with bipolar disorder: A meta-analysis of risk for mental disorders. *Canadian Journal of Psychiatry, 42*(6), 623–631.

Lewinsohn, P. M., Hoberman, H., & Rosenbaum, M. (1988). A prospective study of risk factors for unipolar depression. *Journal of Abnormal Psychology, 97,* 251–264.

Lewinsohn, P. M., Hops, H., Roberts, R. E., Seeley, J. R., & Andrews, J. A. (1993). Adolescent psychopathology: I. Prevalence and incidence of depression and other DSM-III-R disorders in high school students. *Journal of Abnormal Psychology, 102,* 133–144.

Lewinsohn, P. M., Klein, D. N., & Seeley, J. R. (1995). Bipolar disorders in a community sample of older adolescents: Prevalence, phenomenology, comorbidity, and course. *Journal of the American Academy of Child and Adolescent Psychiatry, 34*(4), 454–463.

Lewinsohn, P. M., Roberts, R. E., Seeley, J. R., Rohde, P., Gotlib, I. H., & Hops, H. (1994). Adolescent psychopathology: II. Psychosocial risk factors for depression. *Journal of Abnormal Psychology, 103,* 302–315.

Lewinsohn, P. M., Rohde, P., Klein, D. M., & Seeley, J. R. (1999). Natural course of adolescent major depressive disorder: I. Continuity into young adulthood. *Journal of the American Academy of Child and Adolescent Psychiatry, 38,* 56–63.

Lewinsohn, P. M., Rohde, P., Seeley, J. R., & Fischer, S. A. (1993). Age-cohort changes in the lifetime occurrence of depression and other mental disorders. *Journal of Abnormal Psychology, 102,* 110–120.

Lish, J. D., Dime-Meenan, S., Whybrow, P. C., Price, R. A., & Hirschfeld, R. M. A. (1994). The National Depressive and Manic-Depressive Association (DMDA) survey of bipolar members. *Journal of Affective Disorders, 31,* 281–294.

Lyons, M. J., Eisen, S. A., Goldberg, J., True, W., Lin, N., Meyer, J. M., Toomey, R., Faraone, S. V., Merla-Ramos, M., & Tsuang, M. T. (1998). A registry-based twin study of depression in men. *Archives of General Psychiatry, 55,* 468–472.

Maes, M., & Meltzer, H. Y. (1995). The serotonin hypothesis of major depression. In F. E. Bloom & D. J. Kupfer (Ed.), *Psychopharmacology: The fourth generation of progress* (pp. 933–944). New York: Raven Press.

McCauley, E., Myers, K., Mitchell, J., Calderon, R., Schloredt, K., & Treder, R. (1993). Depression in young people: Initial presentation and clinical course. *Journal of the American Academy of Child and Adolescent Psychiatry, 32,* 714–722.

McCauley, J., Kern, D., Kolodner, K., Dill, L., Schroeder, A., DeChant, H., Ryden, J., Derogatis, L., & Bass, E. (1997). Clinical characteristics of women with a history of childhood abuse: Unhealed wounds. *Journal of the American Medical Association, 277,* 1362–1368.

McElroy, S. L., Strakowski, S. M., West, S. A., Keck, P. E., Jr., & McConville, B. J. (1997). Phenomenology of adolescent and adult mania in hospitalized patients with bipolar disorder. *American Journal of Psychiatry, 154*(1), 44–49.

McGuffin, P., Katz, R., Watkins, S., & Rutherford, J. (1996). A hospital-based twin register of the heritability of DSM-IV unipolar depression. *Archives of General Psychiatry, 53,* 129–136.

McNeal, E. T., & Cimbolic, P. (1986). Antidepressants and biochemical theories of depression. *Psychological Bulletin, 99,* 361–374.

Merikangas, K., Weissman, M., Prusoff, B., & John, K. (1988). Assortative mating and affective disorders: Psychopathology in offspring. *Psychiatry, 51,* 48–57.

Miklowitz, D. J., Goldstein, M. J., Nuechterlein, K. H., Snyder, K. S., & Mintz, J. (1988). Family factors and the course of bipolar affective disorder. *Archives of General Psychiatry, 45,* 225–231.

Moos, R. H., Cronkite, R. C., & Moos, B. S. (1998). Family and extra family resources and the 10-year course of treated depression. *Journal of Abnormal Psychology, 107,* 450–460.

Murphy, J. M., Laird, N. M., Monson, R. R., Sobol, A. M., & Leighton, A. H. (2000). A 40-year perspective on the prevalence of depression: The Stirling County Study. *Journal of the American Medical Association, 57,* 209–215.

Murray, C. J., & Lopez, A. D. (1996). *The global burden of disease.* Cambridge, MA: Harvard University Press.

Musselman, D., Evans, D., & Nemeroff, C.B. (1998). The relationship of depression to cardiovascular disease: Epidemiology, biology, and treatment. *Archives of General Psychiatry, 55,* 580–592.

National Institute of Mental Health. (1998). *Genetics and mental disorders: Report of the NIMH genetics workgroup* (NIMH Publication No. NIH-98-4268). Bethesda, MD: Author.

Nezu, A. M., Ronan, G. F., Meadows, E. A., & McClure, K. S. (Eds.). (2000). *Practitioner's guide to empirically based measures of depression.* New York: Kluwer Academic/Plenum.

Nietzel, M. T., & Harris, M. J. (1990). Relationship of dependency and achievement/autonomy to depression. *Clinical Psychology Review, 10,* 279–297.

Nolen-Hoeksema, S. N. (1990). *Sex differences in depression.* Stanford, CA: Stanford University Press.

Nolen-Hoeksema, S. N., & Girgus, J. S. (1994). The emergence of gender differences in depression during adolescence. *Psychological Bulletin, 115,* 424–443.

Nottelmann, E. D., & Jensen, P. S. (1998). Current issues in childhood bipolarity. *Journal of Affective Disorders, 51,* 77–80.

Papolos, D., & Papolos, J. (1999). *The bipolar child: The definitive and reassuring guide to childhood's most misunderstood disorder.* New York: Broadway Books.

Peselow, E. D., Sanfilipo, M. P., & Fieve, R. R. (1995). Relationship between hypomania and personality disorders before and after successful treatment. *The American Journal of Psychiatry, 152*(2), 232–238.

Plotsky, P. M., Owens, M. J., & Nemeroff, C. B. (1998). Psychoneuroendocrinology of depression. *Psychoneuroendocrinology, 21,* 293–307.

Post, R. M. (1992). Transduction of psychosocial stress into the neurobiology of recurrent affective disorder. *American Journal of Psychiatry, 149,* 999–1010.

Post, R. M., Rubinow, D. R., & Ballenger, J. C. (1984). Conditioning, sensitization, and kindling: Implications for the course of affective illness. In R. Post & J. Ballenger (Eds.), *Neurobiology of mood disorders* (pp. 432–466). Baltimore: Williams & Wilkins.

Potthoff, J. G., Holahan, C. J., & Joiner, T. E., Jr. (1995). Reassurance-seeking, stress generation, and depressive symptoms: An integrative model. *Journal of Personality and Social Psychology, 68,* 664–670.

Puig-Antich, J., Kaufman, J., Ryan, N. D., Williamson, D., Dahl, R. E., Lukens, E., Todak, G., Ambrosini, P., Rabinovich, H., & Nelson, B. (1993). The psychosocial functioning and family environment of depressed adolescents. *Journal of the American Academy of Child and Adolescent Psychiatry, 32,* 244–253.

Rao, U., Hammen, C., & Daley, S. (1999). Continuity of depression during the transition to adulthood: A 5-year longitudinal study of young women. *Journal of the American Academy of Child and Adolescent Psychiatry, 38,* 908–915.

Regier, D. A., Kaelber, C. T., Rae, D. S., Farmer, M. E., Knauper, B., Kessler, R. C., & Norquist, G. S. (1998). Limitations of diagnostic criteria and assessment instruments for mental disorders. *Archives of General Psychiatry, 55,* 109–115.

Ribeiro, S. C. M., Tandon, R., Grunhaus, L., & Greden, J. F. (1993). The DST as a predictor of outcome in depression: A meta-analysis. *American Journal of Psychiatry, 150,* 1618–1629.

Robins, L. N., Helzer, J. E., Croughan, J., & Ratcliff, K. S. (1981). National Institute of Mental Health Diagnostic Interview Schedule: Its history, characteristics, and validity. *Archives of General Psychiatry, 38,* 381–389.

Rosenfarb, I. S., Becker, J., & Khan, A. (1994). Perceptions of parental and peer attachments with mood disorders. *Journal of Abnormal Psychology, 103,* 637–644.

Rush, A. J., Gullion, C. M., Basco, M. R., Jarrett, R. B., & Trivedi, M. H. (1996). The Inventory of Depression Symptomatology (IDS): Psychometric properties. *Psychological Medicine, 26,* 477–486.

Sapolsky, R. M. (2000). Glucocorticoids and hippocampal atrophy in neuropsychiatric disorders. *Archives of General Psychiatry, 57,* 925–935.

Schildkraut, J. J. (1965). The catecholamine hypothesis of affective disorders: A review of supporting evidence. *American Journal of Psychiatry, 122,* 509–522.

Schurhoff, F., Bellivier, F., Jouvent, R., Mouren-Simeoni, M. C., Bouvard, M., Allilaire, J. F., & Leboyer, M. (2000). Early and late onset bipolar disorders: Two different forms of manic-depressive illness? *Journal of Affective Disorders, 58,* 215–221.

Segal, Z. V., & Ingram, R. E. (1994). Mood priming and construct activation in tests of cognitive vulnerability to unipolar depression. *Clinical Psychology Review, 14,* 663–695.

Segal, Z. V., Shaw, B. F., Vella, D. D., & Katz, R. (1992). Cognitive and life stress predictors of relapse in remitted unipolar depressed patients: A test of the congruency hypothesis. *Journal of Abnormal Psychology, 101,* 26–36.

Segal, Z. V., Williams, J. M., Teasdale, J. D., & Gemar, M. (1996). A cognitive science perspective on kindling and episode sensitization in recurrent affective disorder. *Psychological Medicine, 26,* 371–380.

Shea, M. T., Widiger, T. A., & Klein, M. H. (1992). Comorbidity of personality disorders and depression: Implications for treatment. *Journal of Consulting and Clinical Psychology, 60,* 857–868.

Shrout, P. E., Link, B. G., Dohrenwend, B. P., Skodol, A. E., Stueve, A., & Mirttznik, J. (1989). Characterizing life events as risk factors for depression: The role of fateful loss events. *Journal of Abnormal Psychology, 98,* 460–467.

Siever, L. J., & Davis, K. L. (1985). Overview: Toward a dysregulation hypothesis of depression. *American Journal of Psychiatry, 142,* 1017–1031.

Smith, A. L., & Weissman, M. M. (1992). Epidemiology. In E. S. Paykel (Ed.), *Handbook of affective disorders* (pp. 111–129). New York: Guilford Press.

Smith, K. A., Fairburn, C. G., & Cowen, P. J. (1997). Relapse of depression after rapid depletion of tryptophan. *The Lancet, 349,* 915–919.

Solomon, D. A., Keller, M. B., Leon, A. C., Mueller, T. I., Lavori, P. W., Shea, T., Coryell, W., Warshaw, M., Turvey, C., Maser, J. D., & Endicott, J. (2000). Multiple recurrences of major depressive disorder. *The American Journal of Psychiatry, 157,* 229–233.

Sorenson, S. B., Rutter, C. M., & Aneshensel, C. S. (1991). Depression in the community: An investigation into age of onset. *Journal of Consulting Clinical Psychology, 59,* 541–546.

Strakowski, S. M., DelBello, M. P., Sax, K. W., Zimmerman, M. E., Shear, P, K., Hawkins, J. M., & Larson, E. R. (1999). Brain magnetic resonance imaging of structural abnormalities in bipolar disorder. *Archives of General Psychiatry, 56,* 254–260.

Strakowski, S. M., Keck, P. E., McElroy, S. L., West, S. A., Sax, K. W., Hawkins, J. M., Kmetz, G. F., Upadhyaya, V. H., Tugrul, K. C., & Bourne, M. L. (1998). Twelve-month outcome after a first hospitalization for affective psychosis. *Archives of General Psychiatry, 55,* 49–55.

Strober, M., Schmidt-Lackner, S., Freeman, R., Bower, S., Lampert, C., & DeAntonio, M. (1995). Recovery and relapse in adolescents with bipolar affective illness: A five-year naturalistic, prospective follow-up. *Journal of the American Academy of Child and Adolescent Psychiatry, 34*(6), 724–731.

Thornicroft, G., & Sartorius, N. (1993). The course and outcome of depression in different cultures: 10-year follow-up of the WHO collaborative study on the assessment of depressive disorders. *Psychological Medicine, 23,* 1023–1032.

Tohen, M., Waternaux, C. M., & Tsuang, M. T. (1990). Outcome in mania: A 4-year prospective follow-up of 75 patients utilizing survival analysis. *Archives of General Psychiatry, 47,* 1106–1111.

Turvey, C. L., Coryell, W. H., Arndt, S., Solomon, D. A., Leon, A. C., Endicott, J., Mueller, T., Keller, M., & Akiskal, H. (1999). Polarity sequence, depression, and chronicity in bipolar I disorder. *Journal of Nervous and Mental Disease, 187,* 181–187.

Van Gorp, W. G., Altshuler, L., Theberge, D. C., Wilkins, J., & Dixon, W. (1998). Cognitive impairment in euthymic bipolar patients with and without prior alcohol dependence. *Archives of General Psychiatry, 55,* 41–46.

Wallace, J., & O'Hara, M. W. (1992). Increases in depressive symptomatology in the rural elderly: Results from a cross-sectional and longitudinal study. *Journal of Abnormal Psychology, 101,* 398–404.

Warren, W. L. (1994). *Revised Hamilton Rating Scale for Depression (RHRSD): Manual.* Los Angeles: Western Psychological Services.

Wehr, T. A., & Goodwin, F. K. (1983). Biological rhythms in manic-depressive illness. In T. A. Wehr & F. K. Goodwin (Eds.), *Circadian rhythms in psychiatry* (pp. 129–184). Pacific Grove, CA: Boxwood.

Weissman, M. M., Bland, R. C., Canino, G. J., Faravelli, C., Greenwald, S., Hwu, H. G., Joyce, P. R., Karam, E. G., Lee,

C. K., Lellouch, J., Lepine, J. P., Newman, S. C., RubioStipec, M., Wells, J. E., Wickramaratne, P. J., Wittchen, H. U., & Yeh, E. K. (1996). Cross-national epidemiology of major depression and bipolar disorder. *Journal of the American Medical Association, 276,* 293–299.

Weissman, M. M., & Markowitz, J. C. (2002). Interpersonal psychotherapy for depression. In I. H. Gotlib & C. Hammen (Eds.), *Handbook of depression* (pp. 404–421). New York: Guilford Press.

Weissman, M. M., Wolk, S., Goldstein, R. B., Moreau, D., Adams, P., Greenwald, S., Klier, C. M., Ryan, N. D., Dahl, R. E., & Wickramaratne, P. (1999). Depressed adolescents grown up. *Journal of the American Medical Association, 281*(18), 1707–1713.

Weissman, M. M., Wolk, S., Wickramaratne, P., Goldstein, R., Adams, P., Greenwald, S., Ryan, N., Dahl, R., & Steinberg, D. (1999). Children with prepubertal-onset major depressive disorder and anxiety grown up. *Archives of General Psychiatry, 56,* 794–801.

Weller, E., Weller, R. A., & Dogin, J. W. (1998). A rose is a rose is a rose. *Journal of Affective Disorders, 51,* 189–193.

Wells, K. B., Stewart, A., Hays, R. D., Burnam, A., Rogers, W., Daniels, M., Berry, S., Greenfield, S., & Ware, J. (1989). The functioning and well-being of depressed patients. *Journal of the American Medical Association, 262,* 914–919.

Winokur, G., Coryell, W., Keller, M., Endicott, J., & Akiskal, H. (1993). A prospective follow-up of patients with bipolar and primary unipolar affective disorder. *Archives of General Psychiatry, 50,* 457–465.

Winokur, G., Coryell, W., Keller, M., Endicott, J., & Leon, A. (1995). A family study of manic-depressive (bipolar I) disease: Is it a distinct illness separable from primary unipolar depression? *Archives of General Psychiatry, 52,* 367–373.

World Health Organization. (1992). *International statistical classification of diseases and related health problems* (10th ed.). Geneva, Switzerland: Author.

Zlotnick, C., Kohn, R., Keitner, G., & Grotta, S. A. D. (2000). The relationship betweeen quality of interpersonal relationships and major depressive disorder: Findings from the National Comorbidity Survey. *Journal of Affective Disorders, 59,* 205–215.

Zonderman, A. B., Herbst, J. H., Schmidt, C., Costa, P. T., & McCrae, R. R. (1993). Depressive symptoms as a nonspecific, graded risk for psychiatric diagnoses. *Journal of Abnormal Psychology, 102,* 544–552.

CHAPTER 5

# Anxiety Disorders

DAVID H. BARLOW, DONNA B. PINCUS, NINA HEINRICHS, AND MOLLY L. CHOATE

Anxiety disorders are complex and mysterious, but we have learned much about them in the past decade. Knowledge of these disorders is complicated by the fact that each one may take a very different form with different symptom manifestations, from the presence of intrusive, uncontrollable, negative thoughts to fainting at the sight of blood. Yet anxiety disorders have two fundamental emotions in common: anxiety and fear. We have learned in the last decade that anxiety and fear are clearly distinct emotions, although they are related in fundamental ways. We have also learned that anxiety is implicated heavily across the full range of psychopathology. *Anxiety* is a future-oriented emotion characterized by marked negative affect, bodily symptoms of tension, and chronic apprehension. The focus of anxiety is on potentially threatening or dangerous events that may occur at some time in the future, from the next minute to the next year and beyond. Fear, on the other hand, is an immediate alarm reaction to present danger characterized by strong escape-action tendencies. We have also learned that one can experience the emotion of fear when there is really nothing to be afraid of. This experience has been labeled *panic*. These emotions are the building blocks of anxiety disorders, and they arrange themselves in different ways in that they focus on varying internal and external stimuli that had become imbued with threat or danger to form the variety of anxiety disorders. In this chapter we will briefly review the nature and treatment of each anxiety disorder with an emphasis on the symptomatic expression of each one across the lifespan. Posttraumatic stress disorder will not be covered in this chapter due in part to space limitations and its coverage within the chapter concerned with disorders of extreme stress.

## SEPARATION ANXIETY DISORDER

Separation anxiety disorder (SAD) is the most common anxiety disorder experienced by children, accounting for approximately one-half of children seen for mental health treatment of anxiety disorders (Bell-Dolan, 1995). SAD has also been associated with later risk of anxiety disorders such as panic disorder in adolescence and adulthood (Lease & Strauss, 1993). The key feature of SAD is excessive anxiety and fear concerning separation from home or from those to whom the child is attached. Such anxiety must be inappropriate given the age and expected developmental level of the child. Although separation anxiety has been recognized and studied as a characteristic of normal development for many years (Bowlby, 1970; Freud, 1958) it was not treated as a distinct clinical diagnostic category until the 1980 publication of the *Diagnostic and Statistical Manual of Mental Disorders–Third Edition (DSM-III),* which described SAD as one of three distinct anxiety disorders of childhood.

### Clinical Presentation

Separation anxiety is well recognized as one of the normal, developmentally related fears that arise and dissipate at reasonably predictable times during childhood (Pianta, 1999). Separation fears are said to peak between the ages of 9 and 13 months, and occur among children all over the world (Barlow, 2002; Marks, 1987b). For most children, separation anxiety begins to decrease after about 2 years 6 months of age. This typically occurs through a process of experiencing progressively longer and gradual separation experiences that are not accompanied by aversive consequences (Bernstein & Borchardt, 1991). Given that separation anxiety is a normal developmental phenomenon in infancy and toddlerhood, the SAD diagnosis is given only if the child's level of anxiety during separation is inappropriate considering the child's age and developmental level, and significantly interferes with the child's healthy functioning.

The defining feature of SAD is an excessive and unrealistic fear of separation from an attachment figure, usually a parent. This anxiety reaction must persist for a period of 2 weeks and must be well beyond that normally seen in other children of the child's developmental level (American Psychiatric Association [APA], 1994, p. 113). This fear is expressed through excessive and persistent worry about separation, behavioral and somatic distress when faced with separation situations, and persistent avoidance of or attempts to escape from such situations (Albano, Chorpita, & Barlow, 1996; Bell-Dolan, 1995). Children's separation worries include worries that a parent will leave and never return, or worries that they themselves will be lost, kidnapped, or killed. In younger children, repeated nightmares containing themes of separation are common (Francis, Last, & Strauss, 1987).

Young children with SAD often display disruptive, oppositional behaviors as well as avoidance behaviors that cause significant interference in child and family functioning and in normal social development (Tonge, 1994). It is not uncommon for young children with SAD to begin to avoid social situations that involve separation from a caregiver, such as playing with friends or going to birthday parties. Young children may be very clingy with parents, often refusing to play in a different room of the house or outside unless a parent is present. Young children may become desperate in their attempts to contact parents. Academic performance may be compromised by repeated requests to leave class or a refusal to attend school, or by the child's preoccupation with separation concerns. In addition, young children with SAD often display disruptive behaviors at bedtime, including refusing to sleep in their own rooms, begging to sleep with a parent, and crying and pleading to have siblings sleep with them. For older children, the avoidance of separation may cause them to refuse to engage in appropriate peer activities (e.g., sports, clubs, sleepovers) without a parent present (Albano et al., 1996).

Children diagnosed with SAD are more likely to report somatic complaints than children diagnosed with phobic disorders (Last, 1991). Children often complain of physical symptoms, such as headaches or gastrointestinal upset, and display disruptive behaviors such as temper tantrums, crying, or pleading. These physical symptoms and somatic complaints can lead to secondary consequences that further complicate matters for the child and family. Frequent visits to the family doctor occur and often lead to costly medical investigations. In a review of 95 children admitted to a psychiatry inpatient unit, children with SAD reported a significantly greater number of medically unexplained physical symptoms than those with other diagnoses (Livingstone, Taylor, & Crawford, 1988). Reports of abdominal pain and heart palpitations were significantly more likely in children with separation anxiety than in children with other psychopathological disorders. Pediatric headache, which is often associated with a high state of general arousal and muscle tension in the head and neck (Tonge, 1994), is another symptom often seen in children with SAD. These physical symptoms often lead to immediate care and attention from the parent, which results in positive reinforcement and secondary gain that may further perpetuate the problem.

### Prevalence and Demographics

In the past 10 years there have been a number of epidemiological studies reporting the prevalence rates of various anxiety disorders in nonreferred young children. These studies indicate that anxiety disorders are probably one of the most common (if not *the* most common) categories of childhood disorder (Bernstein & Borchardt, 1991; Eisen, Engler, & Geyer, 1998). SAD has been said to be the most common anxiety disorder seen in children and adolescents, with epidemiological studies reporting that as many as 41% of children experience separation concerns, while between 5% and 10% show a clinical level of separation anxiety (Costello & Angold, 1995). Most clinical researchers agree that it is quite common for even very young children (aged 3 years and older) to experience excessive separation distress that causes significant interference in social, academic, and family functioning.

## Comorbidity

Children with SAD often report a variety of specific fears in addition to their separation fears. These include fears of monsters, animals, and insects, fear of the dark, and fear of getting lost, although such fears may or may not be of phobic proportion (Last, Francis, & Strauss, 1989). In addition, there is considerable evidence of a high level of comorbidity between SAD and depression (Werry, 1991). For example, Werry (1991) indicated that one-third of children with SAD presented with a comorbid depressive disorder that developed several months following the onset of SAD. In more severe cases, children with SAD may threaten to harm themselves in attempts to escape or avoid separation situations (Last, 1991).

## Cultural Influences

There has been relatively little research conducted about the possible influences of ethnic and cultural factors on the development and phenomenology of SAD in children, and some of these studies have had conflicting results. For example, one study found that children with SAD were primarily Caucasian (Last, Hersen, Kazdin, Finkelstein, & Strauss, 1987), yet other studies have reported that anxiety symptoms are more common in black than white childern. Such findings may have been biased, however, by the demography of the area served by the clinic, and the extent to which various ethnic groups used clinical services.

Other research has shown that children all over the world have reported feelings of anxiety upon separation (e.g., Chiland & Young, 1990). However, for some children who are raised in cultures that have extended families living together, it is possible that these children would have less opportunity to be left alone, or to have to separate from a primary caregiver. It is possible children from certain cultures may have the opportunity to develop secure attachments with several

caregivers. For children whose schooling is conducted in or close to the home, there may be fewer opportunities for children to develop such separation fears. Overall, very little research has been conducted to date on the influence of culture on the epidemiology, symptom presentation, or progression of anxiety disorders in children, leaving the area relatively uncharted and open to future research.

## Developmental Changes and Course

Although SAD first presents in the preschool child, the mean age of presentation of the disorder to a clinical setting has been reported to be around 9 years (Last, Francis, Hersen, & Kazdin, 1987). SAD has also been found to be more prevalent in prepubertal children than in adolescents (Geller, Chestnut, Miller, Price, & Yates, 1985). There are a number of developmental differences in the presentation and phenomenology of SAD. Francis et al. (1987) evaluated 45 children and adolescents (aged 5–16) with SAD and found no gender differences on each of the symptom criteria for the disorder. However, there were age differences with regard to which criteria were most frequently endorsed. Young children (aged 5–8) endorsed the greatest number of symptoms, and were most likely to report fears of unrealistic harm, nightmares about separation, or school refusal; older children (aged 9–12) endorsed excessive and severe distress at the time of separation; adolescents (aged 13–16) most often endorsed somatic complaints and school refusal.

## Etiology

### Role of Temperament

There are no empirically validated theories on the development of SAD. Because separation anxiety is normal and adaptive for infants and small children, SAD has been conceptualized as a failure to transition from this developmental stage. However, recent research about the development of SAD indicates that its onset is most likely due to the interaction of environmental events and stresses, temperamental characteristics, developmental experiences of care and attachment, and various biological vulnerabilities. Studies by Kagan and colleagues (Kagan, 1989; Kagan, Reznick, & Snidman, 1987) have carefully demonstrated the persistence of the temperamental characteristic of behavioral inhibition from early childhood to the age of 7 years. It has been suggested that this behavioral inhibition might indicate *anxiety proneness*. Specific temperamental characteristics such as behavioral inhibition have not yet been associated with the specific development of SAD, and this hypothesis remains to be explored.

## Attachment

Developmental theorists have identified the period of early childhood as a critical period for the development of attachment, and the organization of the child-caregiver system during this period will set the stage for later development (Hofer, 1994; Thompson, 1991). Thus, developmentally oriented theories of psychopathology highlight the importance of targeting the child-caregiver dyadic system in assessment and intervention of early childhood disorders (Lieberman, 1992; Sroufe, 1985). Child-parent relationships are frequently identified as predictors and correlates of childhood adjustment or psychopathology (Pianta, 1999). According to *attachment theory,* an early attachment pattern characterized by consistency, responsiveness, and warmth is considered an antecedent to healthy development (Campbell, 1989; Greenberg, Speltz, & DeKlyen, 1993). Thus, common and successful treatment regimens for the period of early childhood frequently involve rearranging dyadic caregiving interactions or family interactions to promote secure, healthy attachment between parents and children (e.g., Kazdin, 1992; Schuhmann, Foote, Eyberg, Boggs, & Algina, 1998).

Main, Kaplan, and Cassidy (1985) have reported a strong relation between security of infant attachment and separation anxiety at 6 years of age. Children in this study who were securely attached as infants responded to the question of what they would do during a 2-week separation from their parents, with answers indicating effective behavior directed toward others (e.g., express disappointment to the parents, persuade them not to leave), thus showing a working model of accessibility pertaining to the attachment figures. Main et al. (1985) suggested that such an internal sense would help the child deal with real separations. Children in the study who were insecurely attached infants, however, indicated that they did not know what they would do during a 2-week separation from their parents, although some children gave responses characterized by fears of harm on themselves or their parents.

## Parenting Style and Family Factors

Evidence is accumulating that problems also exist in the family relationships of children with anxiety disorders. Research indicates that parenting styles characterized by high control and low warmth are more prevalent in families with anxious children than in families in which the child does not have a psychiatric diagnosis (Hudson & Rapee, 2000; Siqueland, Kendall, & Steinberg, 1996). Compared to the parents of children without psychiatric disorders, parents of anxious children tend to grant less psychological autonomy and evidence less warmth and acceptance. This parental overcontrol

and lack of warmth may contribute to the child's experience of diminished control, leading to greater anxiety in the child (Barlow, 2000; Chorpita & Barlow, 1998). It has been suggested that child anxiety researchers begin to integrate parent-child interaction strategies and incorporate interventions that attempt to directly alter this parenting style and promote warmth, acceptance, and positive interactions between parents and children.

A considerable number of studies have produced evidence that familial factors are involved in the etiology of childhood anxiety disorders. One of the research approaches that have been pursued in this area has been to assess the children of adults with an anxiety disorder; the other has been to assess the mental state and psychiatric history of parents of children with anxiety disorders. Turner, Beidel, and Costello (1987) studied the children of parents with an anxiety disorder, using a semistructured interview to derive a *DSM-III* diagnosis, and compared their children with the offspring of parents with dysthymia and parents without a psychiatric disorder. They found that in the group of parents with an anxiety disorder, 25–30% of their children had SAD. This study demonstrated a significantly increased risk of anxiety disorder in children with either anxious or dysthymic parents compared to normal controls, but there was no difference between the two patient groups.

Another, larger study (Tonge, 1994) examined the lifetime psychiatric histories of mothers of a group of 58 children with SAD and compared them with a group of nonanxious psychiatric controls. The study revealed that the mothers of anxiety-disordered children had a much higher lifetime rate of anxiety disorders (83%) than the control-group mothers (40%). They also found that 57% of the mothers of the anxious children were currently suffering from an anxiety disorder compared to 20% of the mothers from the control group. These findings show a surprisingly high level of mother-child linkage. In sum, it seems quite likely that familial factors are involved in the development of childhood anxiety disorders, including SAD, although there is not yet any convincing evidence that specific childhood anxiety disorders such as SAD are associated with specific types of psychiatric disorders in the parents. The field awaits twin and adoption studies to determine whether a hereditary component is present.

## Learned Behavior

Another theory on the development of SAD incorporates a learned behavior model in which the child's behaviors are reinforced through the parent's reaction to the separation anxiety. For example, certain types of parental child-management patterns have also been discussed in the literature as being associated with fearful and anxious behaviors (e.g., Bush, Melamed, Sheras, & Greenbaum, 1986; Melamed, 1992). Melamed, for example, described how parental use of positive reinforcement, modeling, and persuasion have been associated with low levels of child fear. However, parental reinforcement of dependency has been associated with higher levels of child fear. It is possible that parents who have inadequate parenting or child-management skills may use inappropriate methods to manage their children's fearful displays or avoidant behaviors, using physical punishment, force, or shame. Other parents, through repeatedly overprotecting their children and providing extra attention during their children's episodes of separation distress inadvertently reinforce their children's behavior, and thus, the fearful behavior increases.

## OBSESSIVE-COMPULSIVE DISORDER

Obsessive-compulsive disorder (OCD) is an anxiety disorder characterized by intrusive and distressing thoughts, urges, and images as well as repetitive behaviors aimed at decreasing the discomfort caused by these obsessive thoughts. Although most people experience occasional intrusive thoughts or engage in repetitive compulsive rituals from time to time, these occasional thoughts and behaviors do not pose a significant problem. In contrast, persons suffering from OCD experience obsessions and compulsions that cause significant distress and interference across many life domains (Antony, Roth, Swinson, Huta, & Devins, 1998). OCD is substantially more common in children, adolescents, and adults than was previously believed. Although clinicians and researchers have long been interested in the features of OCD, knowledge about this disorder has increased exponentially over the past few decades (Antony, Downie, & Swinson, 1998), and as a result, there have been great advances in the area of OCD and its treatment.

### Clinical Presentation

In the *DSM-IV* (APA, 1994), the hallmark of OCD is the presence of obsessions or compulsions. *Obsessions* are defined as persistent thoughts, images, or impulses that occur repeatedly and are experienced as intrusive, inappropriate, and distressing. Some examples include fears of contamination, doubts about one's actions, and aggressive impulses. Since obsessions provoke anxiety, a person with OCD attempts to ignore or suppress these obsessions or try to neutralize them with another thought or action (i.e., a compulsion). Obsessions are not simply worries about real-life problems, and according to the *DSM-IV*, individuals with OCD recognize that their obsessions are products of their own minds.

*Compulsions* are defined as repetitive behaviors, such as washing, cleaning, or repeating, or mental acts, such as counting or checking, that an individual feels compelled to perform in response to an obsession or according to certain rigid rules. Typically, compulsions are carried out to reduce discomfort or to prevent a dreaded event. However, they are clearly excessive and unconnected in a realistic way to the event they are aimed to prevent. Adults with OCD must recognize at some point during the course of the disorder that the obsessions or compulsions are unreasonable or excessive. In addition to these primary symptoms, other affective symptoms of fear, anxiety, chronic worry, and depression most usually accompany OCD. Individuals with OCD may be irritable, angry, and demanding. Not surprisingly, OCD symptoms often cause significant distress and functional impairment in patients' lives and family functioning.

Manifestation of the symptoms of OCD in childhood is similar to that in adults. Common childhood obsessions include fears of contamination, fears of harm to self or others, and urges related to a need for symmetry or exactness. These obsessions are typically followed by compulsions of cleaning, checking, counting, repeating, touching, and straightening (Swedo et al., 1989). Children may also demonstrate hoarding, self-doubt, mental rituals such as counting or praying, and concerns of things being out of order. Some children have displayed excessive religious concerns (scrupulosity), such as worries that they have sinned. These symptoms often change over time, with no clear pattern or progression, and many children report having more than one OCD symptom at a time. By the end of adolescence, many children will have experienced many of the classic OCD symptoms (Rettew, Swedo, Leonard, Lenane, & Rappaport, 1992). It is rare for children to report only obsessions or only compulsions (Geffken, Pincus, & Zelikovsky, 1999). In addition, as many as 50–60% of children receiving diagnoses of OCD experience severe impairment in their social, personal, and academic functioning (Last & Strauss, 1989; Whitaker et al., 1990). Unlike adults, children may not recognize their obsessions and compulsions to be problematic.

### Prevalence and Demographics

The prevalence of OCD is now estimated to be about 2.5% (Karno, Golding, Sorensen, & Burnam, 1988). The average age of onset of the disorder ranges from early adolescence to the mid-20s, and it typically occurs earlier in males (peak onset at 13–15 years of age) than in females (peak onset at 20–24 years of age). The onset of OCD is usually gradual, but acute onset has been reported in some cases. The disorder tends to be chronic, with symptoms waxing and waning in severity. However, episodic and deteriorating courses have been observed in about 10% of patients (Rasmussen & Eisen, 1989). Many individuals with OCD suffer for years before seeking treatment. The disorder may cause severe impairment in functioning, resulting in job loss and disruption of marital and other interpersonal relationships. A number of studies have examined gender differences in the prevalence rates for particular types of obsessions and compulsions (Castle, Deale, & Marks, 1995; Hanna, 1995). Lensi, Cassano, Correddu, Ravagli, and Kunovac (1996) found that men reported more sexual obsessions than women (27.0% vs. 12.7%), more obsessions concerning symmetry and exactness (28.6% vs. 8.0%), and more odd rituals (34.8% vs. 22.1%). Women reported more aggressive obsessions (26.2% vs. 15.3%) and cleaning rituals (59.6% vs. 43.7%) than did men.

March and Mulle (1998) report that approximately 1 in 200 children and adolescents, or approximately 3–4 children in elementary school and up to 20 teenagers in most average-sized high schools, have OCD. Leonard, Lenane, Swedo, and Rettew (1993) have suggested that these numbers are probably low due to the secrecy manifested by patients with this disorder. OCD has been referred to as the *hidden epidemic* because it is largely underdiagnosed and undertreated due to factors such as patient secrecy, lack of patient access to treatment resources, and health care providers' lack of familiarity with proven treatments.

Although research on OCD has increased, very little is known about this disorder in the elderly (Calamari, Faber, Hitsman, & Poppe, 1994). In general, much more attention has been given to depression in the elderly than to anxiety disorders. A number of studies have noted that the rate of OCD tends to decline somewhat as individuals age (Nestadt, Bienvenu, Cai, Samuels, & Eaton, 1998). In general, additional research is needed to determine the symptom presentation of OCD in elderly populations.

## Comorbidity

There is a high comorbidity of OCD with other anxiety disorders. In one sample of OCD patients, 15–30% of patients had a comorbid anxiety or depressive disorder (Karno et al., 1988; Rasmussen & Tsuang, 1986). Approximately 40% of patients report sleep disturbance in conjunction with their symptoms of OCD. In addition to these disorders, there is some evidence supporting a relationship between OCD and eating disorders. Approximately 10% of women with OCD had a history of anorexia nervosa (Kasvikis, Tsakiris, Marks, Basoglu, & Noshirvani, 1986), and more than 33% of individuals with bulimia report a history of OCD (Hudson, Pope, Yurgelun-Todd, Jonas, & Frankenburg, 1987). Lastly, tic

disorders such as Tourette's syndrome also appear related to OCD. Estimates of the comorbidity of Tourette's and OCD range from 36% to 52% (Leckman & Chittenden, 1990).

Comorbid psychiatric disorders occur in 62–74% of children and adolescents with OCD, with anxiety disorders the most prevalent and mood disorders less prevalent than reported in adults (Last & Strauss, 1989). Similar to the rates among adults, high rates of tics and Tourette's syndrome have been associated with this population.

## Cultural Influences

Recent epidemiological studies show some consistent differences in the prevalence of OCD in different ethnic groups. In one community sample of 819 individuals, Nestadt, Samuels, Romanowki, and Folstein (1994) found the prevalence of obsessions and compulsions to be 2.1% among Caucasians and 0.5% among non-Caucasians. These findings were consistent with those in other studies (e.g., Karno et al., 1988), which showed that OCD tends to be relatively rare in Hispanic and African American individuals relative to Caucasian individuals.

Relatively little is known about the impact of ethnicity on the expression of OCD. Researchers have just recently begun to study the nature and prevalence of anxiety disorders across ethnic groups. Studies are needed to elucidate the ways in which ethnic diversity relates to the types of obsessions and compulsions experienced, as well as the usefulness of the established assessment and treatment methods in ethnically diverse groups.

## Developmental Changes

Most (if not all) children display normal, age-dependent obsessive-compulsive behaviors and rituals that appear to dissipate with time (March & Mulle, 1998). For example, young children frequently like things done just so or insist on elaborate bedtime rituals. Such behaviors can often be understood in terms of developmental issues involving mastery and control and are usually replaced by collecting, hobbies, and focused interests in middle childhood. Clinically, normal childhood obsessive-compulsive behaviors can be discriminated from OCD on the basis of timing, content, and severity. Developmentally sanctioned obsessive behaviors occur early in childhood, are rare during adolescence, are common to large numbers of children, and are associated with mastery of important developmental transitions. In contrast, clinically significant OCD behaviors occur somewhat later, appear bizarre to adults and to other children, and produce disruption of the child or adolescent's life.

Common obsessions and compulsions seen in pediatric OCD patients are fear of contamination, fear of harm to oneself and to others, and urges for symmetry or exactness. Most children develop washing and checking rituals at some time during the course of the illness. OCD symptoms change over time, often with no clear pattern of progression, and many children will have experienced almost all the classic OCD symptoms by the end of adolescence. Children who have only obsessions or compulsions are extremely rare.

## Etiology

### Behavioral Influences

There are several theoretical accounts of the etiology and maintenance of OCD. Mowrer's (1939) two-stage theory for the acquisition and maintenance of fear and avoidance behavior has been commonly adopted to explain phobias and OCD. This theory's first stage proposes that a neutral event comes to elicit fear after being experienced along with an event that causes distress. Distress can be conditioned to mental events as well as to physical events. Once fears are acquired, escape or avoidance patterns (i.e., compulsions) develop to reduce fear and are maintained by the negative reinforcement of fear reduction. Thus, in the second stage of this model, the escape or avoidance responses are developed to reduce the anxiety or discomfort evoked by the various conditioned stimuli and are maintained by the success of those responses. Dollard and Miller (1950) adopted Mower's two-stage theory to account for phobias and obsessive-compulsive neurosis. For persons with OCD, active avoidance patterns in the form of ritualistic behaviors are developed and are maintained by their success in alleviating the person's distress and anxiety. Thus, obsessions give rise to anxiety and discomfort, and compulsions reduce this discomfort.

### Cognitive Influences

Cognitive theorists argue that OCD is founded in ideas of exaggerated negative consequences (Carr, 1974; McFall & Wollersheim, 1979). Specifically, Carr proposed that obsessive-compulsives have unusually high expectations of negative outcome, and that they overevaluate the negative consequences for a variety of actions. Carr's explanation of OCD suggests that the cognitive processes and distortions are similar to individuals with generalized anxiety disorder, agoraphobia, and social phobia.

McFall and Wollersheim (1979) suggest that persons with OCD hold erroneous beliefs such as the belief that failure to live up to ideals should be punished and that certain magical

rituals can prevent catastrophes. These mistaken beliefs lead to erroneous perceptions of threat, which in turn provoke anxiety. Persons with OCD tend to devalue their ability to deal adequately with such threats, which results in feelings of uncertainty, discomfort, and helplessness. Foa and Kozak (1985) proposed that in addition to the pathological content of the cognitions of persons with OCD, such persons have impairments in their information-processing abilities. Specifically, OCD patients have difficulty making inferences about harm, and erroneously conclude that a situation is dangerous based on the absence of evidence of safety. As a result, these patients make inductive leaps and must perform rituals to reduce the likelihood of harm.

### Biological Influences

The prevailing biological account of OCD hypothesizes that abnormal serotonin metabolism is expressed as OCD symptoms. The efficacy of selective serotonin reuptake inhibitors (SSRIs) for OCD as compared with nonserotonergic compounds and to a pill placebo (PBO) has provided a compelling argument for this hypothesis (Zohar & Insel, 1987). Significant correlations between clomipramine plasma levels and improvement in OCD have led researchers to suggest that serotonin function mediates obsessive-compulsive symptoms, lending further support to the serotonin hypothesis. However, inconsistent with the serotonin hypothesis is the finding that clomipramine, a nonselective serotonergic medication, appears to produce greater OCD symptom reduction than do such SSRIs as fluoxetine, fluvoxamine, and sertraline (Franklin & Foa, 1998). Numerous studies also suggest that there may be a neuroanatomical basis to OCD. For example, some studies have indicated that individuals with OCD have some deficits in frontal lobe functioning (e.g., Head, Bolton, & Hymas, 1989), but other studies have failed to support these findings. Results of several studies using positron emission tomography (PET) to assess metabolic activity in the brain suggest that persons with OCD show increased metabolic rates in the prefrontal cortex. Currently, OCD is understood as a disorder of the neural circuitry involving the corticostriatothalamo-cortical (CSTC) pathways.

## SPECIFIC PHOBIA

*Specific phobias* are irrational and persistent fears of certain objects or animals (Merckelbach, de-Jong, Muris, & van den Hout, 1996). Although descriptions of phobic behavior have remained remarkably consistent throughout history, theories explaining this behavior have changed dramatically, and during the past decades our understanding of the origins of specific phobias has steadily increased. It is now well recognized that learning mechanisms, developmental processes, and cognitive processes all contribute to the etiology and maintenance of phobic symptoms.

## Clinical Presentation

The central features of specific phobias listed in the *DSM-IV* (APA, 1994) can be summarized as follows: (a) Fear and anxiety are directed at a limited set of stimuli; (b) contact with these stimuli elicits intense fear, anxiety, and avoidance behavior; and (c) fear and anxiety are unreasonable and excessive to the degree that they interfere in a person's daily functioning. Fears are nonrandomly distributed, and in the general population, some fears are far more prevalent than others. The *DSM-IV* differentiates among four highly prevalent types of specific phobia: animal type (e.g., spider phobia), natural environment type (e.g., phobia of dark or heights), blood-injection-injury type (e.g., dental phobia), and situational type (e.g., elevators). Although most adult patients with intense phobias are able to admit that their fears are excessive and irrational, this is not always the case with children.

Because fears are a normal response to a threat of harm, fears can serve an adaptive function by facilitating avoidance of dangerous situations. Since genuine threats are plentiful during childhood, it is not surprising that specific fears are common in infancy and throughout childhood. When asked, most children will readily identify multiple fears (Ollendick, 1983). Typically, such fears are mild and transient, and follow a predictable developmental sequence (Marks, 1987b). However, some children experience fears that persist, interfere with daily functioning, and are not age appropriate. When these fears are excessive, and not associated with an actual threat, they suggest a clinical level of fear, or a phobic disorder. Similar to adults, the characteristic feature of phobic disorders in children is the presence of excessive fear or anxiety that leads to avoidance of a feared object, event, or situation, and the experience of extreme levels of fear and anxiety when confronted with the perceived threat. With only minor exceptions, the same criteria are used to classify phobic disorders in adults and in children.

## Prevalence and Demographics

Epidemiological evidence indicates that phobias may affect more than 12.5% of the general U.S. population (e.g., Regier et al., 1988). This indicates that phobias are the most common of the mental disorders. Kessler et al. (1994) found lifetime and 12-month prevalence rates of 11.3% and 8.8%, respectively.

All recent epidemiological studies show very high rates of prevalence for specific phobia; Epidemiologic Catchment Area (ECA) data, for example, indicate a lifetime prevalence rate ranging from 7.8% to 23.3% across three different sites (Robins et al., 1984) and 11.25% overall (Eaton et al., 1989). Thus, the prevalence of specific phobias is quite high. The 30-day prevalence rate for specific phobia is 5.5%, making it more common than social phobia (4.5%) or agoraphobia (2.3%). Among the various specific phobias, Fredrikson, Annas, Fischer, and Gustav (1996) found that situational and environmental phobias had the highest point-prevalence rate (13.2%), followed by animal phobias and blood-injection-injury phobias (7.9% and 3.0%, respectively). Additionally, studies indicate that most specific phobias are diagnosed more often in women than in men (Chapman, Fyer, Mannuzza, & Klein, 1993; Fredrikson et al., 1996). Despite the prevalence of specific phobia in the population, relatively few persons seek treatment.

Recent epidemiological surveys suggest that between 2 and 4% of children in the general population have clinical levels of fear that would qualify as a specific phobia (Bird et al., 1988). Phobias are not a frequent reason for seeking psychological services, accounting for fewer than 7% of the referrals for mental health services for children (Graziano & De Giovanni, 1979; Silverman & Kearney, 1992). The prognosis for children with specific phobias (without comorbidity) is excellent. Most phobias dissipate over time, even without treatment. It appears that those children who are brought to clinics for treatment often have additional anxiety-related disorders (Last et al., 1989). These more severe problems may prompt parents to seek treatment.

## Cultural Influences

Assessments of the excessiveness of fears, worries, or concerns about the dangerousness of situations or objects must be made within the cultural context of the individual's reference group. The content of phobias as well as their prevalence varies with culture and ethnicity. Many important phobic responses in other cultural groups may not be contained in the *DSM-IV* or may present themselves differently across cultures. For example, in certain cultures, apprehension or vigilance toward magic or spirits or a concern with being possessed or bewitched could be seen, in most cases, as a symptom of anxiety or a specific phobia rather than a sign of a thought disorder. Although ethnic comparisons within the United States have not identified major symptom differences for specific phobias between persons of different ethnicities, cross-cultural studies have indicated that there may be significant differences in the ways phobias and fears are described and, potentially, experienced (Guarnaccia, 1997). Both psychiatric researchers and clinicians need to develop a more complex understanding of culture and its relationship to the expression of emotion and experience of fear of specific stimuli. Although physiological reactions underlying anxiety and fear appear to be universal, culture may define the situations that arouse anxiety and fear and determine how it is expressed and reacted to by the individual and his or her group (Al-Issa & Oudji, 1998).

## Developmental Changes

Childhood fears are common and usually transient, adaptive, age-appropriate behaviors with no long-lasting sequelae. Numerous studies have shown that most children experience multiple fears of mild to moderate severity that appear to be age related, following a progression associated with cognitive development (King, Hamilton, & Ollendick, 1988). These specific fears appear to follow a predictable course. For example, Wenar (1990) described the period of infancy as characterized by fear reactions in response to loud noise, pain, falling, and sudden, unexpected movement, while middle childhood is characterized by an increase in realistic fears (e.g., fears of bodily injury from traffic accidents or fires) accompanied by a decrease in fantasy-based fears (e.g., fears of ghosts and imaginary creatures). These findings are consistent with previous research (Bauer, 1976). Interestingly, both the number and the intensity of fears experienced by children and adolescents have been shown to decrease steadily with age, and thus, childhood fears are usually considered normal, short lived, adaptive reactions to either real or perceived threatening stimuli. Yet in some cases, fears persist and become debilitating and disruptive to the child and family. In general, specific phobias seem to have an early onset, with a substantial proportion of phobias beginning in childhood. For example, Ost (1987) reported mean onset ages of 7 and 9 years for animal and blood-injury-injection phobias, respectively, and a similar early onset for natural environmental phobias. Studies evaluating specific fears in children have generally found that girls report more fears than boys, yet there are also indications that gender differences are modulated by age (Ollendick & King, 1991a).

## Etiology

The etiology of normal, age-appropriate fears has been conceptualized from several different theoretical perspectives. The past 40 years have produced a substantial shift away from psychoanalytic and phenomenological theorizing toward more behavioral conceptualizations (Morris & Kratochwill, 1983).

### Behavioral Influences

For years, it was widely assumed that all phobias were learned through simple traumatic conditioning. As weaknesses in this model became apparent a number of modifications were proposed, inducing *two-factor theory* (Mowrer, 1947), *observational learning* (Bandura, 1969), and *preparedness* (Seligman, 1971). At present, we are aware of a number of psychosocial pathways to fear acquisition, with traumatic fear conditioning representing only one path.

According to the work of Pavlov (1927), Skinner (1953), and Mowrer (1939), fear is considered to be learned, as a function of conditioning history. Multiple fears are thought to be learned separately, each having its own environmental contingencies and conditions. Fears are considered to be situation specific, caused by the environment, with unconscious factors playing no essential role. Thus, behavioral perspectives on the etiologies of fears can be thought of as being based primarily on respondent-conditioning, operant-conditioning, and vicarious-conditioning principles.

Other behavioral theorists have expanded on this perspective. Rather than being rooted in one particular conditioning history, several theorists have attributed the emergence, persistence, and dissipation of fears to multiple sources. Rachman's (1977) theory of fear acquisition identified three main pathways by which fears develop and are transmitted. The first pathway is *traumatic conditioning,* the second is through *vicarious* or *observational learning,* and the third is through *informational transmission.* While Rachman's theory proposes that there are three separate possible pathways of fear, recent research (Ollendick & King, 1991a) indicates that these three pathways are unlikely to be independent but rather are integrative and interactive, thus pointing to a theory of fear acquisition in which a particular fear is multiply determined. Some studies support a role for direct or indirect conditioning (King, Clowes-Hollins, & Ollendick, 1997), but other studies find less empirical support for conditioning theories (McNally & Steketee, 1985). For example, in a classic study, di Nardo, Guzy, and Bak (1988) found that 50% of dog phobics could report having had a frightening encounter with a dog. However, 50% of a matched control group without phobia reported similar experiences with dogs.

### Nonassociative Theories of Fear Acquisition

In contrast to the conditioning theories of fear acquisition, the nonassociative account suggests that evolutionarily relevant fears emerge in the absence of associative learning (Menzies & Clark, 1995). Indeed, retrospective reports of associative-learning events have been found to be extremely rare in studies examining the acquisition of evolutionarily relevant fears, including fear of heights (Menzies & Clark, 1993b, 1995), water (Menzies & Clark, 1993a), and spiders (Jones & Menzies, 1995). Pury and Mineka (1997) also reported that, regardless of their blood-injection-injury fear levels, humans show an associative bias to associate blood-injection-injury stimuli selectively with adverse outcomes, suggesting a predisposition to more readily acquire fears of stimuli that may have once posed a threat to our early ancestors. This *covariation bias* has been widely replicated (e.g., Tomarken, Sutton, & Mineka, 1995). These data support the preparedness theories of etiology in some phobias (e.g., Seligman, 1971). In general, many studies examining the etiology of specific phobias have found that at least a sizeable minority of people with specific phobias report a history of direct conditioning experiences, although many additional subjects fail to report any clear-cut psychosocial antecedents of their fear. In addition, most investigators reporting direct experiences have found that a relatively large number of phobic subjects also report either a history of vicarious experiences with the phobic stimulus, or having received negative information regarding the stimulus. Ollendick and King (1991b) have concluded that the three pathways of fear acquisition may be interactive rather than independent, with fear more likely to occur when two or more sources of fear acquisition are combined.

### Biological Influences

Research examining anxiety disorders suggests that there is a proneness to experience both anxiety and fear that may be at least partially heritable (Barlow, 1988; Biederman et al., 1990). Genetic predisposition also appears to play an important role in the acquisition of many irrational fears and specific phobias. Specifically, researchers have reported greater concordance among monozygotic than dizygotic twins for a variety of fears, including specific fears of animals or mutilation, and social fears (Rose & Ditto, 1983). Similarly, in a genetic analysis of twin data derived from the Fear Survey Schedule for Children–Revised (FSSC-R), Stevenson, Batten, and Cherner (1992) reported significant heritabilities for the Fear of the Unknown, Fear of Injury and Small Animals, Fear of Danger, and Total Fear Score. Interestingly, they found no evidence of enhanced heritability at more extreme levels of fearfulness. Kendler and colleagues (Kendler et al., 1995) conducted an epidemiologically based study of psychiatric disorders in female twins. Both genetic factors and phobia-specific environmental events were implicated in the development of specific phobias. There are also some other data indicating that specific phobia is familial (Fyer et al., 1990). For instance, in a retrospective study of parental

history and experiential factors in the development of snake and spider phobias, Fredrikson, Annas, and Wik (1997) found that a history of indirect fear exposures was more common among phobic women who also reported having a phobic parent compared with those who did not. Such family studies do not isolate the role of genetic factors in the etiology of specific phobias, and the specific pathways of familial transmission are still unclear.

### A Diathesis-Stress Framework

The development of specific phobias may be conceptualized in terms of a diathesis-stress model (e.g., Barlow, 1988), which predicts that both high levels of the diathesis and exposure to psychosocial factors are necessary for the development of specific phobia. Thus, the major factors placing an individual at risk for specific phobia include psychosocial experiences (i.e., direct conditioning, indirect conditioning, and instruction-information) as well as a biologically influenced propensity to experience fear and anxiety.

## SOCIAL PHOBIA (SOCIAL ANXIETY DISORDER)

Social fears are a universal experience. Social phobia, however, goes beyond appropriate and helpful fear reactions to social situations. Social phobia was discussed as early as 1966 (Marks & Gelder, 1966); however, it did not find its way into the diagnostic nomenclature until 1980, when the third edition of the *DSM* (APA, 1980) was published. In the previous version (*DSM-II;* APA, 1968), social fears were thought to be similar to a specific phobia of social situations, or an excessive fear reaction to being observed or scrutinized by others. This perspective was challenged when it became clear that social phobia often includes fear of multiple social situations, is more debilitating and more prevalent than initially assumed, and is often under-recognized, probably because either individuals with social phobia do not bring their fears directly to the physician's attention or the physician does not recognize them adequately (Den-Boer & Dunner, 1999; Liebowitz, Gorman, Fyer, & Klein, 1985; Liebowitz, Heimberg, Fresco, Travers, & Stein, 2000). In 1985, social phobia was still viewed as the neglected anxiety disorder (Liebowitz et al., 1985). In 1994 an alternative term for social phobia—*social anxiety disorder*—was introduced into the *DSM-IV* to indicate how generalized and pervasive these fears can be and to indicate that the term *phobia* might be inappropriate to describe the disorder (Liebowitz et al., 2000).

## Clinical Presentation

Individuals suffering from social phobia often fear being humiliated, embarrassed, or judged negatively in social situations. They may fear that they will behave inappropriately or possibly be scrutinized by others. Patients are often concerned about making a mistake or acting somewhat awkwardly, or that others will notice their anxiety and their physical symptoms in particular. Typical situations that are avoided or endured with distress are initiating or maintaining a conversation; speaking, performing, eating, drinking, or writing in front of people; meeting new people; attending social gatherings; and talking on the phone. When exposed to social situations, individuals with social phobia experience a range of physical symptoms that may culminate in a panic attack. Muscle twitches, blushing, heart racing, sweating, and trembling often occur as part of a fear reaction to social situations (Amies, Gelder, & Shaw, 1983). However, physical reactions need to be limited to social situations in order to qualify for a social phobia diagnosis.

## Prevalence and Demographics

Social phobia is the third most common mental disorder with a lifetime U.S. prevalence of 13% (Kessler et al., 1994). In European studies the lifetime prevalence seems to be lower, from 2% (Norway; Den-Boer et al., 1999) to 7% (Italy; Faravelli et al., 2000). The prevalence of social phobia in general appears to have increased over time, although the prevalence of the fear of public speaking in particular seems to have remained consistent. (Heimberg, Stein, Hiripi, & Kessler, 2000). The disorder usually begins during late adolescence (between ages 13 and 20) and follows a chronic, unremitting course (Hazen & Stein, 1995; Ost, 1987; Wittchen, Stein, & Kessler, 1999). New cases of social phobia have been found in all age groups with an incidence rate of 4–5 per 1,000 per year (Neufeld, Swartz, Bienvenu, Eaton, & Cai, 1999). In a recent study in Norway, social phobia was found to be the most chronic anxiety disorder (Alnaes & Torgersen, 1999). In epidemiological studies, woman are more likely to receive a diagnosis of social phobia; however, in treatment samples, social phobia is equally distributed across gender (Heimberg & Juster, 1995; Turk et al., 1998).

## Comorbidity

Individuals with social phobia are often very self-critical (Cox et al., 2000; Heckelman & Schneier, 1995), self-conscious (Boegels, Alberts, & de Jong, 1996; Jostes, Pook, & Florin, 1999), and self-focused in their attention (Hofmann, 1999;

Mellings & Alden, 2000). They tend to evaluate their own performance as being worse than that of others (Rapee & Lim, 1992) and they generate a negative impression of how they appear to others by imagining how they look from an observer's vantage point (Wells, Clark, & Ahmad, 1998; Wells & Papageorgiu, 1998, 1999). People with social phobia often live in social isolation and occupational maladjustment. Their quality of life is significantly reduced in a variety of areas, including education, career, friendships, and romantic relationships (Wittchen, Fuetsch, Sonntag, Mueller, & Liebowitz, 2000). Depression, increased suicidal ideation, general anxiety, and alcohol abuse have repeatedly been found to be associated with social phobia (Den-Boer et al., 1999; Kessler, Stang, Wittchen, Stein, & Walters, 1999). In adolescence, social anxiety and social phobia have also been found to be associated with higher rates of nicotine dependence (Sonntag, Wittchen, Hoefler, Kessler, & Stein, 2000)

Avoiding a variety of social situations often leads to a significant phenomenological overlap with avoidant personality disorder (APD). Most studies support the assumption that there is no dividing line between social phobia and APD, either conceptually or diagnostically (Noyes, Woodman, Holt, & Reich, 1995; Reich, 2000). Individuals with an additional diagnosis of APD are typically characterized by greater social anxiety and greater overall psychopathology than individuals with generalized social phobia alone, who in turn show greater psychopathology than individuals with nongeneralized social phobia (Boone et al., 1999; Stemberger, Turner, Beidel, & Calhoun, 1995; Turner, Beidel, Borden, Stanley, & Jacob, 1991). Another Axis II disorder that often co-occurs with social phobia is obsessive-compulsive personality disorder (Turner et al., 1991).

It might be difficult to differentiate social phobia from other Axis I disorders at times. The focus and extensiveness of reported worries are helpful characteristics in discriminating social anxiety disorder from generalized anxiety disorder. Panic disorder and social phobia share the concern that others might notice physical symptoms. In addition, panic attacks can also occur in either disorder. However, many differences exist, including age of onset, gender distribution, help-seeking and avoidance behavior, and neurobiological and physical reactions (Reich, Noyes, & Yates, 1988; Uhde, Tancer, Black, & Brown, 1991).

## Cultural Influences

Social phobia is expressed differently across cultures (e.g., Kleinknecht, Dinnel, Kleinknecht, Hiruma, & Harada, 1997; Lee & Oh, 1999). In East Asia, *offensive social phobia* is a common type of social anxiety disorder (Kleinknecht et al.,

1997; Lee & Oh, 1999). Individuals with offensive social phobia are obsessed with embarrassing or offending others by blushing, emitting offensive odors, or staring inappropriately (*taijin kyofusho;* Kleinknecht et al., 1997), or they are fearful of offending other persons with certain parts of their body (*taein kong po*). This type seems to occur most often among Japanese and Korean individuals. It has been suggested that a submissive, collectivist social structure and the nonverbal social communication in East Asian culture favors the development of this social phobia type (Kleinknecht et al., 1997; Lee & Oh, 1999). Recently, the influence of Arab-Muslim culture on social phobia has also been reviewed (Takriti & Ahmad, 2000), but more empirical evidence is needed to come to a conclusion about the cultural influence on social anxiety disorder in this population.

## Developmental Changes

Developmental variables that have been considered in relation to social phobia are shyness, neuroticism, introversion, and behavioral inhibition (Kagan, Snidman, & Arcus, 1992; Stemberger et al., 1995). In a retrospective study, 72% of individuals with social phobia reported a childhood history of shyness and indicated significantly higher neuroticism scores and lower extraversion scores than individuals without social phobia (Stemberger et al.). Similar results were obtained in previous studies (Amies et al., 1983; Watson, Clark, & Carey, 1988). Similarly, shy children with no mental disorder were more often found to have mothers with social phobia (Cooper & Eke, 1999). The onset of shyness is usually very early, is often transitory, and, in contrast to social phobia, is considered a temperament trait of social reticence and not an emotional disorder. Furthermore, although a number of individuals in epidemiological studies endorsed shyness, only a small portion met criteria for social phobia (e.g., Robins et al., 1984). This indicates that the two concepts are not interchangeable. Similarly, behavioral inhibition (BI), which is a behavioral pattern characterized by discomfort with novelty and heightened physiological arousal that can be observed at 4 months and persists until age 7 or 8 years, has been viewed as a vulnerability factor for social phobia (Kagan et al., 1987, 1992). Although some studies indicate that subsequent fear development predominantly relates to social situations (Biederman et al., 1990), children who show this behavior pattern are more likely to be anxious in general, as well. However, data on the relationship among shyness, behavioral inhibition, and social phobia are rare, and despite the remarkably similar expression of these concepts, it remains unclear whether shyness or behavioral inhibition are vulnerability factors for social phobia or if they are milder versions of social phobia (Turner, Beidel, & Townsley, 1990).

Social phobia itself expresses similarly in both childhood and adulthood (Spence, Donovan, & Brechman-Toussaint, 1999). However, different diagnostic criteria apply to childhood social phobia, specifying that the child needs to be developmentally capable of engaging in social interactions and that social-evaluative fears need to occur in interactions with peers, not only in interactions with adults. Furthermore, social anxiety in children can be expressed in tantrums, freezing, or crying in social situations. Social anxiety in childhood also seems to be associated with a reduced general facial activity, a restricted facial repertoire, and less accurate facial expression of emotions (Melfsen, Osterlow, & Florin, 2000).

## Etiology

### Biological Influences

Family studies of social phobia show higher prevalence of this disorder in relatives of patients with social phobia than in relatives of patients with other anxiety disorders or of participants with no mental disorder (Knowles, Mannuzza, & Fyer, 1995; M. B. Stein et al., 1998). Several twin studies suggest moderate heritability for social fears; however, no data exist for heritability of social anxiety disorder as defined by *DSM-IV* (APA, 1994). Differences in physiological reactions to social situations between the generalized and nongeneralized subtype (Hofmann, Newman, Ehlers, & Roth, 1995) lead to the speculation that individuals with generalized social phobia are biologically more vulnerable to developing social phobia than are individuals with nongeneralized social phobia (Zuckerman, 1999). A recent family study supports this suggestion, finding an increased risk for generalized social phobia in first-degree relatives of individuals with generalized social phobia only, not in relatives of individuals with nongeneralized social phobia (M. B. Stein et al., 1998). A high comorbidity between Parkinson's disease and social phobia has been observed, suggesting that dopamine depletion is possibly related to the development of social phobia (Lauterbach & Duvoisin, 1991; M. B. Stein, 1998; M. B. Stein, Heuser, Juncos, & Uhde, 1990). Recent single photon emission computed tomography studies in patients with social phobia found that striatal dopamine reuptake site densities were lower in patients with social phobia than in individuals without a mental disorder (Schneier et al., 2000; Tiihonen et al., 1997), and that chronic amphetamine abuse seems to be capable of causing social phobia through dopamine depletion (Williams, Argyropoulos, & Nutt, 2000). Results from numerous pharmacotherapy studies also point to the contribution of the dopaminergic system in social phobia (e.g., Blanco, Schneier, & Liebowitz, in press);

however, it remains unclear whether dopamine depletion is a cause or consequence of social phobia.

### Behavioral Influences

Several researchers have discussed the role of conditioning in the development of social phobia (Hofmann, Ehlers, & Roth, 1995; D. J. Stein & Bouwer, 1997). Often, ethological considerations are integrated in this debate, providing reasons for the evolution of vulnerability to social threat (Ohman, 1986; D. J. Stein & Bouwer, 1997). Zuckerman (1999) suggested that the greater physiological reactivity of nongeneralized social phobics to specific social situations such as public speaking likely indicates conditioning processes in the development of this disorder (see also Hofmann, Ehlers, & Roth, 1995). Although traumatic experiences have been reported from speech-phobic individuals, these events often occurred after the phobia began (Hofmann et al., 1995). Similarly to public-speaking anxiety, fear of blushing has been discussed in terms of conditioning (Mulkens & Boegels, 1999). Highly fearful individuals reported more negative learning experiences with regard to blushing. Individuals with social phobia differ from healthy individuals in the classical conditioning processes of aversive emotional reactions, indicating that learning processes contribute to some extent to the development and persistence of social anxiety disorder.

### Cognitive Influences

Individuals with social phobia share typical negative beliefs about themselves in social situations (e.g., "What I say sounds stupid," "I'm boring," "I will make a fool out of myself," "I won't have anything to say"). Clark and Wells (1995) assume that individuals with social phobia activate a series of negative beliefs about themselves as social subjects when they are faced with social situation. These assumptions likely cause social phobics to perceive threat in such circumstances. In particular, they overestimate the likelihood that they will behave inadequately in social situations, and they tend to believe that this behavior will result in a personal catastrophe, such as rejection or loss of worth (Clark & Wells, 1995). These thoughts elicit anticipatory anxiety and avoidance, leading to short-term anxiety reduction. This way, cognitive responses and applied strategies to control increasing anxiety result in a vicious circle that maintains social anxiety. A more detailed outline of this cognitive model can be found in Clark and Wells. The model has stimulated extensive research on the cognitive basis of social anxiety disorder (discussed later in this chapter), particularly with regard to information processes. Individuals with social phobia seem

to attend selectively to socially threatening information (Amir, Foa, & Coles, 1998b; Gilboa-Schechtman, Foa, & Amir, 1999; Horenstein & Segui, 1997; Maidenberg, Chen, Craske, Bohn, & Bystritsky, 1996), and they also seem more prone to interpret and judge information in a socially threatening way (Amir, Foa, & Coles, 1998a; Foa, Franklin, Perry, & Herbert, 1996; Stopa & Clark, 2000)—for example, by overestimating the likelihood and the cost of negative social outcomes (Foa et al.) or by drawing more negative inferences from available social stimuli (Amir et al., 1998a, 1998b; Stopa & Clark; Wallace & Alden, 1997). Furthermore, individuals with social phobia show a rather unique cognitive process after facing a social situation in which they review the previous interaction in detail (*post-event processing;* Clark & Wells). This review seems to be dominated by negative self-perception that enhances future avoidance tendencies. For a review of information-processing biases in social phobia and their relation to Clark and Wells' cognitive model, see Heinrichs and Hofmann (2001).

Other cognitive models of social phobia focus more on expectancies (Trower & Gilbert, 1989) or on interpersonal goals that persons aim to achieve and their low confidence in their ability to achieve these goals (*self-presentation model;* Leary & Kowalski, 1995a, 1995b). According to this approach, individuals with social phobia are extraordinarily motivated to make desired impressions on others because of certain dispositional traits that predispose them to develop social anxiety. Most research conducted to test this model involved individuals with subclinical social anxiety (for a review see Leary & Kowalski, 1995a, 1995b).

## PANIC DISORDER WITH AND WITHOUT AGORAPHOBIA

*Panic disorder* is a syndrome that has stimulated a significant amount of research, particularly since 1987 (McNally, 1994). Today, it is probably the most researched anxiety disorder. In *DSM-III,* panic disorder (PD) was classified as an anxiety neurosis that is best characterized and differentiated from other anxiety disorders by the presence of spontaneous panic attacks. *Agoraphobia* was conceptualized as a consequence of spontaneous panic attacks (APA, 1980; Barlow, 1988, 2002; Klein & Klein, 1989a). Three types of panic attacks are distinguished (*DSM-IV;* APA, 1994): unexpected or spontaneous attacks, situationally bound attacks, and situationally predisposed attacks. If panic attacks are exclusively triggered by a phobic stimulus, the attacks are *situationally bound* (e.g., a person experiences panic attacks if and always if faced with heights). *Situationally predisposed* attacks tend to occur more in some situations than in others; however, they are not inevitably experienced in those situations (e.g., in a large mall). *Spontaneous* panic attacks seem to occur "out of the blue," with no evident situational trigger. This conceptualization of panic attacks reflects a dimension of predictability on which situationally bound attacks are predictable but spontaneous attacks are not.

Panic attacks occur across all anxiety disorders, and can also be found in the general population (Barlow, 2002; Katerndahl & Realini, 1993); they are not specific to PD. This knowledge was clarified in *DSM-IV,* which defines panic attacks separately from PD. Situationally predisposed and spontaneous attacks are most relevant to PD and agoraphobia.

## Clinical Presentation

*Panic attacks* are defined as sudden episodes of fear accompanied by distressing physical sensations such as dizziness, heart racing, palpitations, chest pain, shortness of breath, choking sensations, sweating, or nausea. The particular symptoms of panic vary across different individuals. If a patient has 4 or more symptoms, the experience is defined as a full-blown (vs. limited-symptom) attack. During a panic attack, the individual often fears dying, losing control, or going crazy. Patients with PD worry persistently about potential adverse implications or consequences of panic attacks. As a result, they usually engage in behavioral strategies to prevent the feared consequences. Active avoidance behaviors range from subtle (e.g., unzipping one's jacket to be able to breathe) to obvious (e.g., not going into movie theaters), and may include different forms of distraction and safety behaviors (e.g., turning up the volume on the radio, or carrying around a bottle of water). To qualify for a PD diagnosis, these worries or behavioral changes due to a panic attack need to persist for at least 1 month (APA, 1994).

As a result of their worries, individuals with recurrent panic attacks often feel vulnerable in places or situations that would be difficult to leave, or where help might not be readily available in the event of sudden need. Examples include open spaces, unfamiliar or unpopulated areas, crowds, modes of public transportation, elevators, bridges, limited-access highways, restaurants, malls, and movie theaters. If such situations are physically avoided or cause significant distress, the person is said to have *agoraphobia.* Severe agoraphobia can prevent individuals from leaving their homes, resulting in a variety of occupational, social, and personal disadvantages. Panic disorder and agoraphobia typically coexist, although either one can also occur separately. About 95% of individuals presenting in clinical settings with agoraphobia also have PD (APA, 2000). The development of agoraphobia in PD

seems to be more closely associated with an earlier onset of PD, with a fear of losing control and with experiencing chills or hot flushes, whereas chest pain was found more often in PD alone (Langs et al., 2000). If agoraphobia occurs alone, the fear often relates to experiencing panic-like sensations. A predominant fear of embarrassment due to others' noticing these effects (e.g., diarrhea, loss of bladder control, vomiting, excessive sweating) can sometimes make it difficult to distinguish agoraphobia from social phobia. Guidelines for a differential diagnosis of panic disorder with agoraphobia (PDA) versus other anxiety disorders can be found in Baker, Patterson, and Barlow (2002).

The core of PD is a strong fear of physical sensations, even in the absence of any noticeable sensations (fear of the fear). As a consequence, patients with PD usually avoid situations (e.g., exercising, sexual activity) that are naturally capable of eliciting physical sensations similar to those of a panic attack. Environmental factors such as humidity and hot weather may also contribute to panic attacks (Asnis, Faisal, & Sanderson, 1999).

Panic attacks can occur at any time, including at night. Awakening from sleep in a state of sudden, uncued panic is referred to as a *nocturnal panic attack.* Similar to daytime panic attacks, these attacks are not limited to PD but rather occur across all anxiety disorders. They are often misconceptualized as some form of a sleeping disorder (Craske & Rowe, 1997). Differential diagnoses can best be established by a focus on the time at which panic occurs (e.g., nocturnal panic attacks usually occur in Stage 2 and 3 sleep [Craske & Rowe, 1997], whereas symptoms of sleep apnea typically occur in Stage 1 or 2 sleep or during rapid eye movement [George, Millar, & Kryger, 1988]).

Patients with PD often seek medical advice for their physical sensations, and if the unexpected sensations are severe, they may seek intensive medical services such as emergency rooms (Barsky, Delamater, & Orav, 1999; Klerman, Weissman, Oullette, Johnson, & Greenwald, 1991). Quality of life is significantly reduced in patients with PD (Birehall, Brandon, & Taub, 2000; Kessler et al., 1994; Rubin et al., 2000), and patients with PD are more likely to initiate disability payments (Kouzis & Eaton, 2000). Panic disorder is therefore associated with high social and economic costs (Hofmann & Barlow, 1999).

## Prevalence and Demographics

PDA is a prevalent and chronic condition: The lifetime prevalence is estimated to be 1–4% (APA, 2000). A recent survey of panic in a general practice population found a lifetime prevalence of 8.6% (Birehall et al. 2000). Women are twice as likely to have PDA than men (Katerndahl & Realini, 1993). The median age of onset is 24 years (Burke, Burke, Regier, & Rae, 1990). PDA has also been observed in children; however, there is an ongoing controversy regarding at which age PDA can occur (e.g., Klein, Mannuzza, Chapman, & Fyer, 1992; Moreau & Follet, 1993). In older adults, increasing prevalence of medical conditions and physical complaints (e.g., shortness of breath, rapid heart rate; Zarit & Zarit, 1998) make it reasonable to also assume a higher prevalence of PDA. Furthermore, in the ECA study, a second peak age of onset was found (45–54 years; Eaton, Kessler, Wittchen, & Magee, 1994), indicating the existence of late-onset PDA. It has been stated repeatedly, however, that PD is rather uncommon in elderly, among whom agoraphobia without PD occurs more often, frequently subsequent to a traumatic event (Flint, 1998). Epidemiological studies with the elderly, however, are rare, preventing any firm conclusions on the prevalence of PDA in older adults. Two studies that analyzed sociodemographic and clinical characteristics of late-onset PD found that this PD type may be associated with less severe panic symptoms and general mental health complaints, a less likely family history of PD, more distress from sensations of choking and numbness, less utilization of mental health services, and more likely use of physical health services (e.g., family physicians; Katerndahl & Realini, 1995; Katerndahl & Talamantes, 2000; Segui et al., 2000). PDA typically takes an unremitting course. As do most other anxiety disorders, it seems to be a chronic condition with spontaneous remissions occurring rather rarely (for a recent review see Pollack & Marzol, 2000).

## Comorbidity

Panic disorder also was found to be associated with and predictive of suicide risks (Clayton, 1993; Cox, Direnfeld, Swinson, & Norton, 1994). However, the suicidal risk seems to be associated with comorbid Axis I (e.g., major depression) and II (e.g., borderline personality disorder; Friedman, Jones, Chernen, & Barlow, 1992; Johnson, Weissman, & Klerman, 1990). More recent studies of PD and suicidal ideation did not find an increased suicidal risk in PD patients alone (Hornig & McNally, 1995; Starcevic, Bogojevic, Marinkovic, & Kelin, 1999). Whether patients with PD are at risk of committing suicide seems, therefore, to depend strongly on the presence of comorbid conditions. Depression often co-occurs with PDA (Roy-Byrne et al., 2000), and PDA was found less likely to precede the first depressive episode than to emerge subsequently (Fava et al., 2000).

M. B. Stein, Shea, and Uhde (1989) stated that 46% of patients with PDA have also been diagnosed with social phobia. In our clinical setting, these disorders co-occur less often

(15%; Brown, Campbell, Lehman, Grisham, & Mancill, 2001). It is unclear whether these two disorders are, in fact, so strongly associated or the association is due to differential diagnosis difficulties.

PDA often co-occurs with personality disorders (Brooks, Baltazar, & Munjack, 1989; Dammen, Ekeberg, Arnesen, & Friis, 2000). Closely associated with PD are dependent, avoidant, and histrionic personality disorders (Chambless, Renneberg, Goldstein, & Gracely, 1992; Diaferia et al., 1993).

Several medical conditions are also associated with PD (e.g., Jeejeebhoy, Dorian, & Newman, 2000). The prevalence of PD in patients with coronary artery disease (CAD) ranges from 10 to 50% (Fleet, Lavoie, & Beitman, 2000). Asthma and panic attacks also frequently co-occur (Feldman, Giardino, & Lehrer, 2000), and asthma has been noted as a risk factor for the development of PDA (Carr, 1998, 1999) because of the shared sensations between an asthma and a panic attack (e.g., feeling of suffocation). In most instances it is unclear whether these medical conditions are conceptually associated with PDA. A specific pathophysiological mechanism for PD has not been found (Jeejeebhoy et al., 2000). Fleet and colleagues (2000) conclude their review of the PD-CAD association by stating that PD is prevalent in CAD patients, but that there is no evidence that PD puts a patient at risk for developing CAD. This seems also true for cardiovascular problems such as mitral valve prolapse (MVP; Bowen, D'Arcy, & Orchard, 1991; Yang, Tsai, Hou, Chen, & Sim, 1997). Similarly, the presence of a direct association between pulmonary impairment and PD has been subject to debate (Ley, 1998; Spinhoven, Sterk, van der Kamp, & Onstein, 1999) with no concluding evidence that PD is associated with pulmonary impairment. Medical conditions in general are more likely to heighten body awareness and thus contribute to PDA by exacerbating symptoms.

## Cultural Influences

Panic disorder seems to occur less frequently in Hispanic Americans and Asian Americans than in Whites in the United States (Zhang & Snowden, 1999). Hispanics show a culturally bound reaction—*ataques de nervios*—that seems related to PD (Guarnaccia, Canino, Rubio-Stipec, & Bravo, 1993; Guarnaccia, Rubio-Stipec, & Canino, 1989). During such an attack, PD-like symptoms are experienced (e.g., palpitations, shaking, numbness, etc.). The attacks, however, are triggered by stressful life events such as funerals or accidents, and afterward there is no recollection of the attacks. Although these attacks may be related to PD, they also show some important differences (e.g., the missing recollection). Other transcultural research focusing on how cultural beliefs may influence the expression of PDA demonstrated that, in Khmer culture,

PDA-related complaints have been found: Khmer refugees in a clinical setting in the United States reported *sore neck attacks* (Hinton, Ba, Peou, & Um, in press a, in press b). A sore neck attack is a state of autonomic arousal (e.g., heart racing, shortness of breath, sudden headaches, blurry vision, dizziness, and buzzing in the ears) that emerges as a consequence of *Kyol Goeu* (*wind overload,* which is assumed to occur if blood and wind cannot be carried through the body because important vessels in the neck are blocked).

Despite a similar clinical presentation of PD, African Americans were found to have a later age of onset for PDA than do European Americans, and the groups differ in the coping strategies they use to face their PDA (Smith, Friedman, & Nevid, 1999). African Americans experienced more needless psychiatric hospitalizations, more frequent emergency room visits, higher incidence of childhood trauma (Friedman, Paradis, & Hatch, 1994), and higher comorbidity with posttraumatic stress disorder (PTSD; Smith et al., 1999).

## Developmental Changes

Panic disorder has also been found in adolescence; however, it is assumed that the clinical presentation does not differ from that of adults. Panic disorder in childhood is extremely rare and thus not much research has been conducted (Moore & Carr, 2000). In a study investigating the prevalence of mitral valve prolapse in children with anxiety disorders, no association with PD was found; of 52 anxious children, 9.6% were diagnosed with PD (Toren et al., 1999). It has been suggested that PD and SAD may be different clinical manifestations of the same underlying disorder (e.g., Black, 1995; Black & Robins, 1990) in different developmental stages. A recent study attempted to explore childhood risk factors such as SAD for onset of panic attacks in adolescents (Hayward, Killen, Kraemer, & Taylor, 2000). Negative affectivity and anxiety sensitivity in childhood, but not SAD, were found to predict onset of panic attacks. Other studies also failed to provide reasonable evidence that SAD in childhood continues as PD in adulthood (Manicavasagar, Silove, Curtis, & Wagner, 2000).

## Etiology

Different theoretical models for PD have been presented (for a balanced review of research from different perspectives see McNally, 1994, and White & Barlow, 2002). Recently, the most common models have been integrated into a biopsychosocial approach (Barlow, 2002) in which the initial panic attack is conceptualized as a misfiring of the fear system under stressful life circumstances in physiologically vulnerable individuals. The panic reaction is similar to the emergence of

the biologically based mechanism of fear in response to immediate survival threat, whereas anxiety is a response to future threats. An overly reactive autonomic nervous system (biological basis) puts an individual at risk of experiencing a panic attack in response to stress. The (false) alarm reaction becomes associated with internal sensations, leading to further false alarms in response to internal sensations (behavioral basis).

### *Biological Influences*

Biological research on panic focuses on estimating heritability, biological challenges, neuroendocrine functioning, and neuroanatomy. With respect to heritability, the tendency to panic runs in families and has a genetic component (Barlow, 2002; Scherrer et al., 2000). Zuckerman (1999) estimates a modest heritability for PD. The disorder shares a genetic factor with agoraphobia, but not with generalized anxiety disorder or depression (Kendler et al., 1995). Chromosome studies using the quantitative trait loci method showed that chromosomes 1, 12, 15 and other nearby chromosomes are associated with a tendency to be uptight and anxious (Flint et al., 1995).

Patients with PDA are more likely to experience a panic attack in response to carbon dioxide inhalation ($CO_2$ *hypersensitivity*) than patients with other anxiety disorders (Beck & Shipherd, 1997; Biber & Alkin, 1999; Schmidt, 1999; Schmidt, Trakowski, & Staab, 1997; Sinha et al., 1999). This hypersensitivity was also found to run in families (van Beek & Griez, 2000). Recent studies found evidence, however, that it is not the $CO_2$ sensitivity that causes exaggerated anxiety, but rather a change in breathing involving either increased $CO_2$ or decreased oxygen (Beck, Ohtake, & Shipherd, 1999) and that patients with predominantly respiratory symptoms may be more affected by breathing challenges than others (Biber & Alkin, 1999; Schmidt, 1999). Results from other studies suggest a biological sensitivity to sympathetic stimulation (van Zijderveld, Veltman, van Dyck, & van Doornen, 1999).

**Neuroendocrine Functioning.** The brain circuit involved in panic is the *fight-or-flight system* (*FFS;* Gray, 1982; Gray & McNaughton, 1996). When stimulated in animals, this circuit triggers a response that resembles panic in humans (Gray & McNaughton, 1996).

The FFS originates in the brain stem and is also connected to the limbic system. Recently, developments in the neurobiology of fear have been integrated into a comprehensive neuroanatomical hypothesis of PD (Gorman, Kent, Sullivan, & Coplan, 2000). The authors suggest that fear responses are mediated by a fear network that is centered in the amygdala, which interacts with the hippocampus and medial prefrontal cortex. These projections may account for conditioned fear responses.

### Behavioral Influences

Behavioral approaches to panic (e.g., Mineka, 1985; Wolpe & Rowan, 1988) are based on classical conditioning processes assuming that an initial fear reaction (*unconditioned response, or UCR*) occurs in response to a dangerous or stressful situation (*unconditioned stimulus, or UCS*). During this response a variety of stimuli (*conditioned stimuli, or CSs*), both external (e.g., open spaces) and internal (e.g., cardiorespiratory symptoms such as hyperventilation, rapid heartbeat); are present and may become associated with this fear reaction. Subsequently, these cues will be able to provoke a similar fear reaction (*conditioned response, or CR*) despite the absence of a dangerous or stressful situations (UCS), resulting in panic attacks. The behavioral approach is based on Razran's (1961) model of *interoceptive conditioning*. Furthermore, internal cues such as breathing alterations can also cause a panic attack when they are provoked by normal circumstances, including exercising, due to the associative power they acquired during the conditioning process. Near-drowning or other suffocation experiences have been emphasized as initial traumatic situations that can elicit the first panic attack and were found to precede the onset of PD in a subsample of patients with the disorder (Alkin, 1999; Bouwer & Stein, 1997). Furthermore, one year after traumatic brain injury, the rates of PD were much higher in this population than in the general population (Deb, Lyons, Koutzoukis, Ali, & McCarthy, 1999). The frequency of panic attacks in patients who had already developed PD, however, was unaffected by a traumatic event (Sasson, Zohar, Gross, Taub, & Fux, 1999).

The behavioral approach to PD was criticized because of the conceptual ambiguity of the CS, CR, and UCS in regard to internal sensations (McNally, 1990, 1994), and because the behavioral approach could explain neither why these sensations become conditioned only for PD patients nor why they do not always result in full-blown panic attacks. Answers to these puzzles have been suggested in the context of an up-to-date learning-theory conceptualization of the development of PD (Barlow, 2002).

### Cognitive Influences

As an alternative to the interoceptive conditioning model, Clark (1986, 1989) emphasized catastrophic misinterpretations of bodily sensations as the primary cause of PD. Typical panic-related thoughts are "I will have a heart attack," "I will collapse," "I will go crazy," or "I will lose control." Impending insanity is often associated with feelings of derealization,

whereas thoughts about heart failure are often triggered by heart-related sensations such as palpitations. In his cognitive model, Clark assumes that sensations, regardless of their origins, will not lead to panic unless they are interpreted as a threat to one's physical or mental integrity. Furthermore, stimuli related to panic concerns were found to be processed differently than stimuli that were not related to panic concerns (McNally, 1994; Pauli et al., 1997). Improvements in panic symptoms have been associated with changes in information-processing characteristics (e.g., Dengler, Wiedemann, & Pauli, 1999). Further evidence for this model comes from biological challenge studies. As discussed previously, patients with PDA are more sensitive to artificially provoked breathing alterations. Clark believes that these challenge procedures provoke sensations in all participants, but that only patients with PD experience fear in response to these sensations because they tend to misinterpret them. In fact, it has been found that challenges produce similar bodily sensations both in patients with PD and in participants without a mental disorder (Gaffney, Fenton, Lane, & Lake, 1988). Furthermore, providing safety information makes it less likely that patients with PD will panic in challenge situations (Salkovskis & Clark, 1990). In addition, physical sensations alone are not sufficient to predict panic development (Moore & Zebb, 1999). Clark's (1989) cognitive theory was criticized several times (e.g., Klein & Klein, 1989b; Seligman, 1988) because, for example, it does not explain why catastrophic beliefs persist despite contrary information (e.g., information that one has repeatedly survived panic attacks).

Recent developments focus on the concept of sensitivity to anxiety. Catastrophic cognitions can occur at the time of the attack (i.e., they are acute) or can be more persistent. A persistent tendency to misinterpret certain bodily sensations as catastrophic or imminently dangerous can be considered a trait called *anxiety sensitivity (AS)*. Persons with high AS dislike intense arousal and perceive it as frightening. The concept of AS has stimulated a significant amount of research, which is summarized in Taylor (1999). Anxiety sensitivity was found to significantly predict panic symptoms after a biological challenge task in nonclinical participants (Eifert, Zvolensky, Sorrell, Hopko, & Lejuez, 1999). Other cognitive factors that contribute to panic attacks are predictability, controllability, and expectancies (see Barlow, 2002; McNally, 1990, 1994).

## GENERALIZED ANXIETY DISORDER

*Generalized anxiety disorder (GAD)* is characterized by excessive anxiety and worry about a number of events or activities. Individuals with GAD tend to find this worry difficult to control. The worry is also associated with several physical symptoms such as muscle tension, fatigue, and restlessness (APA, 1994). In comparison with other anxiety disorders, GAD has less well established theoretical understanding; and, compared with other anxiety disorders, GAD is the diagnostic category that has changed the most over the past 20 years (Campbell & Brown, 2002).

For example, in *DSM-III,* the diagnostic criteria for GAD required the presence of persistent anxiety as evidenced by symptoms from at least three of four categories, including motor tension, autonomic hyperactivity, apprehensive expectation, and vigilance and scanning of the environment (APA, 1980). However, this diagnostic description of GAD made it difficult for both researchers and clinicians to distinguish between generalized and anticipatory anxiety (Brown, O'Leary, & Barlow, 1993). Accordingly, in *DSM-III-R* (APA, 1987), the symptom criteria were changed to specify that the worry was not due to another Axis I diagnosis. The time required to make a diagnosis of GAD was also extended from 1 to 6 months, to differentiate the disorder from transient worry due to stressful events (APA, 1987). After *DSM-III-R* and by the time of publication of *DSM-IV,* GAD was conceptualized by defining features of chronic worry and persistent somatic symptoms (Brown et al., 1993). *DSM-IV* stipulated that a worried individual must have at least three of six physical symptoms of anxiety for 6 months or more in order to receive a diagnosis of GAD.

In part because of the changing view of GAD, treatments developed or adapted for the disorder are less well established. In recent years, the nature of GAD has been more fully explored and effective psychological treatments have been critically evaluated. The following section will describe the clinical presentation, models of etiology, and understanding of the current treatments for GAD.

## Clinical Presentation

In general, GAD tends to be a chronic condition that fluctuates with the current level of stress in the patient's life (Brown, 1997). The majority of patients report an onset of GAD before the age of 20, although a subset of patients report that their worries began in adulthood (Brown et al., 1993). Although the results vary, several studies suggest that the age of onset for GAD may be earlier than for other anxiety disorders (Massion, Warshaw, & Keller, 1993; Woodman, Noyes, Black, Schlosser, & Yagla, 1999).

## Prevalence and Demographics

Prevalence data for GAD are determined from epidemiological studies. In the United States, the National Comorbidity Survey (NCS) estimated the current prevalence rate of GAD to be 1.6% of the population (Wittchen, Zhao, Kessler, & Eaton, 1994). The NCS also found that GAD affects approximately 5.1% of the population over the course of a lifetime (Kessler et al., 1994). In the general population, GAD appears to be less common than specific or social phobia but is currently slightly more common than PD (Roemer, Orsillo, & Barlow, 2002).

Outside the United States, prevalence rates for GAD have also been estimated. In Italy, current and lifetime GAD prevalence estimates based on *DSM-III-R* criteria were found to be 2.8 and 5.4%, respectively (Faravelli, Degl'Innocenti, & Giardinelli, 1989). Alternately, a two-stage epidemiological study of a rural area in South Africa found a prevalence rate of 3.7% based on *DSM-IV* criteria (Bhagwanjee, Parekh, Paruk, Petersen, & Subedar, 1998, as cited in Roemer et al., 2002).

In general, the research suggests that GAD occurs more frequently in women. For example, GAD appears to be about twice as common for women as for men in both community and clinical samples (Wittchen et al., 1994). However, cultural factors may also play a role in determining the prevalence of GAD among different groups of individuals. For example, the epidemiological study conducted in South Africa found that men showed a higher prevalence of GAD than women (Bhagwanjee et al., 1998).

GAD is frequently comorbid with other disorders. Some symptoms of GAD, such as irritability and fatigue, overlap with other disorders, such as depression. However, research suggests that GAD is a separate diagnostic factor (Brown, Chorpita, & Barlow, 1998). At the same time, GAD commonly co-occurs with other disorders. For example, clinical data suggest 68% current and 92% lifetime comorbidity with another Axis I disorder (Brown et al., 2001). Mood disorders and social phobia seem to be the disorders most frequently diagnosed in addition to GAD (Brown et al., 2001).

It may be difficult at times for clinicians to distinguish GAD from normal worry or anxious cognitions associated with other anxiety disorders (Campbell & Brown, 2002). Borkovec, Shadick, and Hopkins (1991) describe worry as a predominantly verbal, conceptual activity aimed at problem solving. Borkovec (1994) suggests that worry is an attempt to control uncertainty and avoid the negative affect associated with a lack of control. However, the long-term consequences of avoidance may lead to the maintenance of worry. Thus, pathological worry is hypothesized to be maintained by the negative reinforcement associated with the avoidance of negative affect. Avoidance of negative affect also may inhibit the processing of emotionally threatening material, which is considered necessary in the reduction of anxiety (Brown, 1997).

Pathological worry is associated with the perception that the world is threatening and that one is unable to cope with or control uncertain future events (Brown, 1997). Pathological worry in GAD patients is distinguished from normal worry by the percentage of the day that is taken up with worry, as well as the impairment and distress caused by the worry. Additionally, some researchers suggest that the distinguishing factor between GAD and normal worry is the amount of meta-worry—that is, the concern that the worry causes the individual (Wells & Carter, 1999). This model suggests that pathological worry results from the interaction between positive beliefs concerning the advantages of worry as a coping strategy and negative appraisals of worry. For example, Wells and Carter suggest that the GAD patients' worry is maintained by avoidance of the thoughts associated with negative beliefs regarding worry, along with the continued use of worry as a coping strategy. Both models stress the importance of avoidance and cognitions in the maintenance of GAD. A theoretical framework for understanding GAD is an important element of developing and evaluating treatment to address this disorder.

Children as well as adults with GAD manifest excessive anxiety concerning a number of different spheres, including the future, world events, school or work, and the health of themselves and their families. The clinician must distinguish between developmentally appropriate levels of anxiety and clinically significant levels of worry. Anxiety and fear naturally develop in children but become clinically significant when they begin to interfere in the child's life. GAD should be distinguished from other anxiety disorders by the nature and specificity of the worry. For example, if the worry in different areas, such as relationships and work, is focused on one principal concern, such as the negative evaluation of others, a diagnosis of social phobia instead of GAD would better describe the individual's anxiety (Campbell & Brown, 2002). Conversely, if the individual has diffuse and varied concerns in a number of different areas, a diagnosis of GAD may best capture the client's anxiety.

## Developmental Changes

As with other anxiety disorders, the expression of GAD changes throughout the lifetime. Because GAD emphasizes worry or uncontrollable cognitions, it is seldom diagnosed in very young children. However, children as young as 7 years of age can express their worries about a number of areas. Often parents provide information concerning the nature of their child's worries. Interestingly, the parents of some chil-

dren may provide the model and initial negative evaluation of worry for their children (Chorpita & Barlow, 1998).

Children who are overanxious may innately have the higher baselines of arousal associated with excessive worry and elevated tension. However, expression of worry does seem to change over time. For example, older and younger children report differences in their worry. Data derived from self-report inventories demonstrates significantly more state and trait anxiety, worry, and oversensitivity, and higher levels of depression in older than younger children with GAD. Children of different ages also report differences in the number of worry symptoms, displayed patterns of comorbidity, and severity of anxiety. However, GAD is equally likely to occur in younger and older age groups.

In some cases, GAD may be considered to be a chronic, lifelong illness. When GAD is diagnosed in adulthood, many patients report that GAD began during childhood (Brown, 1997). However, other individuals report that GAD began during adulthood, usually in response to a stressful life event. Brown (1997) suggests that there may be two separate pathways to the development of GAD. Interestingly, both models of GAD correctly reflect one of the separate mechanisms that may result in the expression of GAD.

Although GAD does not disappear with age, little is known about its expression in the elderly population. The NCS found that GAD was most common in the group over age 45, and least common in the youngest group (aged 15–24; Wittchen et al., 1994). Flint (1994) reported prevalence rates of GAD among older adults to be as high as 7%. More recent research revealed that 25% of older adults with depression also met criteria for GAD, and that the additional presence of symptoms of GAD was associated with a higher level of suicidality (Lenze et al., 2000, as cited in Roemer et al., 2002). However, the elder adult population seems to have been neglected by researchers for the most part (Blazer, 1997). The lack of information on GAD in the elderly may be attributed in part to difficulties associated with conducting research in this population (e.g., many of the physical symptoms associated with GAD could also be due to other medical conditions or factors associated with aging; Blazer, 1997). Thus, good assessment instruments and treatment studies are lacking for elder adults, largely due to a lack of sufficient research interest (Beck & Stanley, 1997).

Additionally, a diagnosis of GAD also requires a rule-out of medical conditions, which may be more difficult to determine in an older individual. Although some treatment techniques may be beneficial for those elderly individuals who are not cognitively impaired, no research has been conducted in this area (Blazer, 1997). As yet there is little known or understood about the expression of GAD in the elderly.

## Etiology

In general, GAD is considered to develop as neurobiological and psychological vulnerabilities are activated by negative or stressful life events (Roemer et al., 2002). These neurobiological and psychological vulnerabilities are considered to develop as the result of early experience and patterns of interaction. In GAD, when an individual's vulnerabilities are activated by life events, the attentional focus remains on these generally negative life events. This attention to the negative events distinguishes GAD from other anxiety disorders, which focus attention on discrete external events such as phobic objects, or on internal events as with panic attacks (Roemer et al., 2002). Thus, a sensitivity to relatively minor inconveniences develops. Additionally, the individual's reaction to these events is accompanied by arousal associated with negative affect. The individual develops a sense that these events are proceeding in an unpredictable, uncontrollable fashion, reflecting a psychological diathesis arising out of early experience (Roemer et al., 2002).

Thus begins a maladaptive process of shifting the focus of attention from the task at hand to self-evaluative modes, which further increases arousal (Roemer et al., 2002). As noted previously, psychological and neurobiological vulnerabilities lead to a fundamental perception of a lack of control over potential threats. The perceived lack of control leads to distortions in information processing, as occurs with the narrowing of attention to the focus of the concern and the increasing of vigilance (Roemer et al., 2002). The process of worry becomes negatively reinforcing in an attempt to control this spiraling process.

It is hypothesized that the isolated presence of either a psychological or a neurobiological vulnerability would be insufficient to lead to the development of GAD. Rather, one would expect to see a personality style characterized by some combination of pessimism, arousability, low self-confidence, or, perhaps, no clinical manifestations (Roemer et al., 2002). However, the synergistic effect of the combination of genetic vulnerabilities and early experiences would be most likely to lead to the clinical manifestation of GAD (Roemer et al., 2002).

## CONCLUSIONS

We have learned much about anxiety disorders in the last decade—but we still have much to learn. Currently, we categorize anxiety disorders based on presenting symptoms that often comprise the focus of anxiety and fear. The implication of this classification is that we need to develop individual treatments for each specific anxiety disorder as well as specific assessment strategies. It may be, however, that we categorize anxiety (and mood) disorders more parsimoniously by focusing on the commonalities rather than on the differences among them. Work is currently proceeding along these lines in anticipation of the next edition of the *DSM* (namely, the *DSM-V*). These developments may, in turn, open up a new perspective on the nature and treatment of anxiety, mood, and related disorders.

## REFERENCES

Albano, A. M., Chorpita, B. F., & Barlow, D. H. (1996). Childhood anxiety disorders. In E. J. Mash & R. A. Barkley (Eds.), *Child psychopathology* (pp. 196–241). New York: Guilford Press.

Al-Issa, I., & Oudji, S. (1998). Culture and anxiety disorders. In S. S. Kazarian & D. R. Evans (Eds.), *Cultural clinical psychology: Theory, research, and practice* (pp. 127–151). New York: Oxford University Press.

Alkin, T. (1999). Near-drowning experiences and panic disorder. *American Journal of Psychiatry, 156,* 667.

Alnaes, R., & Torgersen, S. (1999). A 6-year follow-up study of anxiety disorders in psychiatric outpatients: Development and continuity with personality disorders and personality traits as predictors. *Nordic Journal of Psychiatry, 53,* 409–416.

American Psychiatric Association. (1968). *Diagnostic and statistical manual of mental disorders* (2nd ed.). Washington, DC: Author.

American Psychiatric Association. (1980). *Diagnostic and statistical manual of mental disorders* (3rd ed.). Washington, DC: Author.

American Psychiatric Association. (1987). *Diagnostic and statistical manual of mental disorders* (3rd ed., rev.). Washington, DC: Author.

American Psychiatric Association. (1994). *Diagnostic and statistical manual of mental disorders* (4th ed.). Washington, DC: Author.

American Psychiatric Association. (2000). *Diagnostic and statistical manual of mental disorders* (4th ed., Text Revision). Washington, DC: Author.

Amies, P. L., Gelder, M. G., & Shaw, P. M. (1983). Social phobia: A comparative clinical study. *British Journal of Psychiatry, 142,* 174–179.

Amir, N., Foa, E. B., & Coles, M. E. (1998a). Automatic activation and strategic avoidance of threat-relevant information. *Journal of Abnormal Psychology, 107,* 285–290.

Amir, N., Foa, E. B., & Coles, M. E. (1998b). Negative interpretation bias in social phobia. *Behavior Research and Therapy, 36,* 945–957.

Antony, M. M., Downie, F., & Swinson, R. P. (1998). Diagnostic issues and epidemiology in obsessive-compulsive disorder. In R. P. Swinson, M. M. Antony, S. Rachman, & M. A. Richter (Eds.), *Obsessive-compulsive disorder: Theory, research and treatment* (pp. 3–32). New York: Guilford Press.

Antony, M. M., Roth, D., Swinson, R. P., Huta, V., & Devins, G. M. (1998). Illness intrusiveness in individuals with panic disorder, obsessive-compulsive disorder, or social phobia. *Journal of Nervous and Mental Disease, 186*(5), 311–315.

Asnis, J., Faisal, A., & Sanderson, W. (1999). Environmental factors in panic disorder. *Journal of Clinical Psychiatry, 60,* 264.

Baker, S. L., Patterson, M. D., & Barlow, D. H. (2002). Panic disorder and agoraphobia. In M. M. Anthony & D. H. Barlow (Eds.), *Handbook of assessment and treatment planning for psychological disorders* (pp. 67–112). New York: Guilford Press.

Bandura, A. (1969). *Principles of behavior modification.* New York: Holt, Rinehart, & Winston.

Barlow, D. H. (1988). Anxiety and its disorders. New York: Guilford Press.

Barlow, D. H. (2000). Unraveling the mysteries of anxiety and its disorders from the perpective of emotion theory. *American Psychologist, 55,* 1245–1263.

Barlow, D. H. (2002). *Anxiety and its disorders: The nature and treatment of anxiety and panic* (2nd ed.). New York: Guilford Press.

Barsky, A. J., Delamater, B. A., & Orav, J. E. (1999). Panic disorder patients and their medical care. *Psychosomatics, 40,* 50–56.

Bauer, D. H. (1976). An exploratory study of developmental changes in children's fears. *Journal of Child Psychology and Psychiatry and Allied Disciplines, 17*(1), 69–74.

Beck, G. J., Ohtake, P. J., & Shipherd, J. C. (1999). Exaggerated anxiety is not unique to $CO_2$ in panic disorder: A comparison of hypercapnic and hypoxic challenges. *Journal of Abnormal Psychology, 108,* 473–482.

Beck, G. J., & Shipherd, J. C. (1997). Repeated exposure to interoceptive cues: Does habituation of fear occur in panic disorder patients? A preliminary report. *Behaviour Research and Therapy, 35,* 551–557.

Beck, J. G., & Stanley, M. A. (1997). Anxiety disorders in the elderly: The emerging role of behavior therapy. *Behavior Therapy, 28*(1), 83–100.

Bell-Dolan, D. (1995). Separation anxiety disorder. In R. T. Ammerman & M. Hersen (Eds.), *Handbook of child behavior therapy in the psychiatric setting* (pp. 217–298). New York: Wiley.

Bernstein, G. A., & Borchardt, C. M. (1991). Anxiety disorders of childhood and adolescence: A critical review. *Journal of the American Academy of Child and Adolescent Psychiatry, 30*(4), 519–532.

Biber, B., & Alkin, T. (1999). Panic disorder subtypes: Differential responses to $CO_2$ challenge. *American Journal of Psychiatry, 156,* 739–744.

Biederman, J., Rosenbaum, J. F., Hirshfeld, D. R., Faraone, S. V., Bolduc, E. A., Gersten, M., Meminger, S. R., Kagan, J., Snidman, N., & Reznick, S. (1990). Psychiatric correlates of behavioral inhibition in young children of parents with and without psychiatric disorders. *Archives of General Psychiatry, 47,* 21–26.

Bird, H. R., Canino, G., Rubio-Stipec, M., Gould, M. S., Ribera, J., Sesman, M., Woodbury, M., Huertas-Goldman, S., Pagan, A.,

Sanchez-Lacay, A., & Moscoso, M. (1988). Estimates of the prevalence of childhood maladjustment in a community survey in Puerto Rico: The use of combined measures. *Archives of General Psychology, 45*(12), 1120–1126.

Birehall, H., Brandon, S., & Taub, N. (2000). Panic in a general practice population: Prevalence, psychiatric comorbidity, and associated disability. *Social Psychiatry and Psychiatric Epidemiology, 35,* 235–241.

Black, B. (1995). Separation anxiety disorder and panic disorder. In J. S. March (Ed.), *Anxiety disorders in children and adolescents* (pp. 212–234). New York: Guilford Press.

Black, B., & Robins, D. R. (1990). Panic disorder in children and adolescents. *Journal of the American Academy of Child and Adolescent Psychiatry, 29,* 36–44.

Blanco, C., Schneier, F. R., & Liebowitz, M. R. (in press). Psychopharmacology. In S. G. Hofmann & P. M. DiBartolo (Eds.), *Social phobia and social anxiety: An integration.* Needham Heights, MA: Allyn & Bacon.

Blazer, D. G. (1997). Generalized anxiety disorder and panic disorder in the elderly: A review. *Harvard Review of Psychiatry, 5,* 18–27.

Boegels, S. M., Alberts, M., & de Jong, P. J. (1996). Self-consciousness, self-focused attention, blushing propensity and fear of blushing. *Personality and Individual Differences, 21,* 573–581.

Boone, M. L., McNeil, D. W., Masia, C. L., Turk, C. L., Carter, L. E., Reis, B. J., & Lewin, M. R. (1999). Multimodal comparison of social phobia subtypes and avoidant personality disorder. *Journal of Anxiety Disorders, 13,* 271–292.

Borkovec, T. D. (1994). The nature, functions, and origins of worry. In G. C. Davey & F. Tallis (Eds.), *Worrying: Perspectives on theory, assessment, and treatment* (pp. 5–33). New York: Wiley.

Borkovec, T. D., Shadick, R., & Hopkins, M. (1991). The nature of normal and pathological worry. In R. M. Rapee & D. H. Barlow (Eds.), *Chronic anxiety: Generalized anxiety disorder, and mixed anxiety depression* (pp. 29–51). New York: Guilford Press.

Bouwer, C., & Stein, D. J. (1997). Association of panic disorder with a history of traumatic suffocation. *American Journal of Psychiatry, 154,* 1566–1570.

Bowen, R. C., D'Arcy, C., & Orchard, R. C. (1991). The prevalence of anxiety disorders among patients with mitral valve prolapse syndrome and chest pain. *Psychosomatics, 32,* 400–406.

Bowlby, J. (1970). Disruption of affectional bonds and its effects on behavior. *Journal of Contemporary Psychotherapy, 2,* 75–86.

Brooks, R. B., Baltazar, P. L., & Munjack, D. J. (1989). Co-occurrence of personality disorders with panic disorder, social phobia, and generalized anxiety disorder: A review of the literature. *Journal of Anxiety Disorders, 3,* 259–285.

Brown, T. A. (1997). The nature of generalized anxiety disorder and pathological worry: Current evidence and conceptual models. *Canadian Journal of Psychiatry, 42,* 817–825.

Brown, T. A., Campbell, L. A., Lehman, C. L., Grisham, J. R., & Mancill, R. B. (2001). Current and lifetime comorbidity of the

DSM-IV anxiety and mood disorders in a large clinical sample. *Journal of Abnormal Psychology, 110*, 585–599.

Brown, T. A., Chorpita, B. F., & Barlow, D. H. (1998). Structural relationships among dimensions of the DSM-IV anxiety and mood disorders and dimensions of negative affect, positive affect, and autonomic arousal. *Journal of Abnormal Psychology, 107*, 179–192.

Brown, T. A., O'Leary, T. A., & Barlow, D. H. (1993). Generalized anxiety disorder. In D. H. Barlow (Ed.), *Clinical handbook of psychological disorders: A step-by-step treatment manual* (2nd ed., pp. 137–188). New York: Guilford Press.

Burke, K. C., Burke, J. D., Jr., Regier, D. A., & Rae, D. S. (1990). Age at onset of selected mental disorders in five community populations. *Archives of General Psychiatry, 47*, 511–518.

Bush, J. P., Melamed, B. G., Sheras, P. L., & Greenbaum, P. E. (1986). Mother-child patterns of coping with anticipatory medical stress. *Health Psychology, 5*(2), 137–157.

Calamari, J. E., Faber, S. D., Hitsman, B. L., & Poppe, C. J. (1994). Treatment of obsessive-compulsive disorder in the elderly: A review and case example. *Journal of Behavior Therapy and Experimental Psychiatry, 25*(2), 95–104.

Campbell, L. A., & Brown, T. A. (2002). Assessment of generalized anxiety disorder. In M. M. Antony & D. H. Barlow (Eds.), *Handbook of assessment, treatment planning, and outcome evaluation: Empirically supported strategies for psychological disorders* (pp. 147–181). New York: Guilford Press.

Campbell, S. B. (1989). Developmental perspectives. In T. H. Ollendick & M. Hersen (Eds.), *Handbook of child psychopathology* (pp. 5–28). New York: Plenum.

Carr, A. T. (1974). Compulsive neurosis: A review of the literature. *Psychological Bulletin, 81*, 311–318.

Carr, R. E. (1998). Panic disorder and asthma: Causes, effects and research implications. *Journal of Psychosomatic Research, 44*, 43–52.

Carr, R. E. (1999). Panic disorder and asthma. *Journal of Asthma, 36*, 143–152.

Castle, D. J., Deale, A., & Marks, I. M. (1995). Gender differences in obsessive-compulsive disorder. *Australian and New Zealand Journal of Psychiatry, 29*(1), 114–117.

Chambless, D. L., Renneberg, B., Goldstein, A., & Gracely, E. J. (1992). MCMI-diagnosed personality disorders among agoraphobic outpatients: Prevalence and relationship to severity and treatment outcome. *Journal of Anxiety Disorders, 6*, 193–211.

Chapman, T. F., Fyer, A. J., Mannuzza, S., & Klein, D. F. (1993). A comparison of treated and untreated simple phobia. *American Journal of Psychiatry, 150*(5), 816–818.

Chiland, C., & Young, B. F. (1990). Why children reject school: Views from seven countries. New Haven, CT: Yale University Press.

Chorpita, B. F., & Barlow, D. H. (1998). The development of anxiety: The role of control in the early environment. *Psychological Bulletin, 124*(1), 3–21.

Clark, D. M. (1986). A cognitive approach to panic. *Behaviour Research and Therapy, 24*, 461–470.

Clark, D. M. (1989). A cognitive model of panic attacks. In S. Rachman & J. D. Maser (Eds.), *Panic: Psychological perspectives* (pp. 71–89). Hillsdale, NJ: Erlbaum.

Clark, D. M., & Wells, A. (1995). A cognitive model of social phobia. In R. G. Heimberg, M. R. Liebowitz, D. A. Hope, & F. R. Schneier (Eds.), *Social phobia: Diagnosis, assessment, and treatment* (pp. 69–93). New York: Guilford Press.

Clayton, P. I. (1993). Suicide in panic disorder and depression. *Current Therapeutic Research, 54*, 825–831.

Cooper, P. J., & Eke, M. (1999). Childhood shyness and maternal social phobia: A community study. *British Journal of Psychiatry, 174*, 439–443.

Costello, E. J., & Angold, A. (1995). Epidemiology. In J. March (Ed.), *Anxiety disorders in children and adolescents* (pp. 109–124). New York: Guilford Press.

Cox, B. J., Direnfeld, D. M., Swinson, R. P., & Norton, R. G. (1994). Suicidal ideation and suicide attempts in panic disorder and social phobia. *American Journal of Psychiatry, 151*, 882–887.

Cox, B. J., Rector, N. A., Bagby, R. M., Swinson, R. P., Levitt, A. J., & Joffe, R. T. (2000). Is self-criticism unique for depression? A comparison with social phobia. *Journal of Affective Disorder, 57*, 223–228.

Craske, M. G., & Rowe, M. K. (1997). Nocturnal panic. *Clinical Psychology: Science and Practice, 4*, 153–174.

Dammen, T., Ekeberg, O., Arnesen, H., & Friis, S. (2000). Personality profiles in patients referred for chest pain: Investigation with emphasis on panic disorder patients. *Psychosomatics, 41*, 269–276.

Deb, S., Lyons, I., Koutzoukis, C., Ali, I., & McCarthy, G. (1999). Rate of psychiatric illness 1 year after traumatic brain injury. *American Journal of Psychiatry, 156*, 374–378.

Den-Boer, J.-A., Baldwin, D. S., Bobes, J., Katschnig, H., Westenberg, H., & Wittchen, H.-U. (1999). Social anxiety disorder: Our current understanding. *International Journal of Psychiatry in Clinical Practice, 3*(Suppl. 3), 3–12.

Den-Boer, J.-A., & Dunner, D. L. (1999). Physician attitudes concerning diagnosis and treatment of social anxiety disorder in Europe and North America. *International Journal of Psychiatry in Clinical Practice, 3*(Suppl. 3), 13–19.

Dengler, W., Wiedemann, G., & Pauli, P. (1999). Association between cortical slow potentials and clinical rating scales in panic disorder: A 1.5-year follow-up study. *European Psychiatry, 14*, 399–404.

Diaferia, G., Sciuto, G., Perna, G., Barnardeschi, L., Battaglia, M., Rusmini, S., & Bellodi, L. (1993). DSM-III-R personality disorders in panic disorders. *Journal of Anxiety Disorders, 7*, 153–161.

diNardo, P. A., Guzy, L. T., & Bak, R. M. (1988). Anxiety response patterns and etiological factors in dog-fearful and non-fearful subjects. *Behavior Research and Therapy, 26*(3), 245–251.

Dollard, J., & Miller, N. E. (1950). *Personality and psychotherapy: An analysis in terms of learning, thinking, and culture.* New York: McGraw-Hill.

Eaton, W. W., Kessler, R. C., Wittchen, H. U., & Magee, W. J. (1994). Panic and panic disorder in the United States. *American Journal of Psychiatry, 151,* 413–420.

Eaton, W. W., Kramer, M., Anthony, J. C., Dryman, A., Shapiro, S., & Locke, B. Z. (1989). The incidence of specific DIS/DSM-III mental disorders: Data from the NIMH Epidemiologic Catchment area program. *Acta Psychiatrica Scandinavica, 79*(2), 163–178.

Eifert, G. H., Zvolensky, M. J., Sorrell, J. T., Hopko, D. R., & Lejuez, C. W. (1999). Predictors of self-reported anxiety and panic symptoms: An evaluation of anxiety sensitivity, suffocation fear, heart-focused anxiety, and breath-holding duration. *Journal of Psychopathology and Behavioral Assessment, 21,* 293–305.

Eisen, A. R., Engler, L. B., & Geyer, B. (1998). Parent training for separation anxiety disorder. In J. M. Briesmeister & C. E. Schaefer (Eds.), *Handbook of parent training: Parents as co-therapists for childrens' behavior problems* (2nd ed., pp. 205–224). New York: Wiley.

Faravelli, C., Degl'Innocenti, B. G., & Giardinelli, L. (1989). Epidemiology of anxiety disorders in Florence. *Acta Psychiatrica Scandinavica, 79*(4), 308–312.

Faravelli, C., Zucchi, T., Viviani, B., Salmoria, R., Perone, A., Paionni, A., Scarpato, A., Vigliaturo, D., Rosi, S., D'Adamo, D., Bartolozzi, D., Cecchi, C., & Abrardi, L. (2000). Epidemiology of social phobia: A clinical approach. *European Psychiatry, 15,* 17–24.

Fava, M., Rankin, M. A., Wright, E. C., Alpert, J. E., Nierenberg, A. A., Pava, J., & Rosenbaum, J. F. (2000). Anxiety disorders in major depression. *Comprehensive Psychiatry, 41,* 97–102.

Feldman, J. M., Giardino, N. D., & Lehrer, P. M. (2000). Asthma and panic disorder. In D. L. Mostofsky & D. H. Barlow (Eds.), *The management of stress and anxiety in medical disorders* (pp. 220–239). Boston: Allyn & Bacon.

Fleet, R., Lavoie, K., & Beitman, B. D. (2000). Is panic disorder associated with coronary artery disease? A critical review of the literature. *Journal of Psychosomatic Research, 48,* 347–356.

Flint, A. J. (1994). Epidemiology and comorbidity of anxiety disorders in the elderly. *American Journal of Psychiatry, 151,* 640–649.

Flint, A. J. (1998). Management of anxiety in late life. *Journal of Geriatric Psychiatry and Neurology, 11,* 194–200.

Flint, J., Corley, R., DeFries, J. C., Fulker, D. W., Gray, J. A., Miller, S., & Collins, A. C. (1995). Chromosomal mapping of three loci determining quantitative variation of susceptibility to anxiety in the mouse. *Science, 268,* 1432–1435.

Foa, E. B., Franklin, M. E., Perry, K. J., & Herbert, J. D. (1996). Cognitive biases in generalized social phobia. *Journal of Abnormal Psychology, 105,* 433–439.

Foa, E. B., & Kozak, M. J. (1985). Treatment of anxiety disorders: Implications for psychopathology. In A. H. Tuma & J. D. Maser (Eds.), *Anxiety and the anxiety disorders* (pp. 421–452). Hillsdale, NJ: Erlbaum.

Francis, G., Last, C. G., & Strauss, C. C. (1987). Expression of separation anxiety disorder: The roles of age and gender. *Child Psychiatry and Human Development, 18*(2), 82–89.

Franklin, M. E., & Foa, E. B. (1998). Cognitive-behavioral treatments for obsessive-compulsive disorder. In P. E. Nathan & J. M. Gorman (Eds.), *A guide to treatments that work* (pp. 339–357). New York: Oxford University Press.

Fredrikson, M., Annas, P., Fischer, H., & Gustav, W. (1996). Gender and age differences in the prevalence of specific fears and phobias. *Behaviour Research and Therapy, 34*(1), 33–39.

Fredrikson, M., Annas, P., & Wik, G. (1997). Parental history, aversive exposure and the development of snake and spider phobia in women. *Behavior Research and Therapy, 35*(1), 23–28.

Freud, A. (1958). *Psychoanalytic study of the child.* New Haven, CT: Yale University Press.

Friedman, S., Jones, J. C., Chernen, L., & Barlow, D. H. (1992). Suicidal ideation and suicide attempts among patients with panic disorder: A survey of two outpatient clinics. *American Journal of Psychiatry, 149,* 680–685.

Friedman, S., Paradis, C. M., & Hatch, M. (1994). Characteristics of African-American and White patients with panic disorder and agoraphobia. *Hospital and Community Psychiatry, 45,* 798–803.

Fyer, A. J., Manuzza, S., Gallups, M. S., Martin, L. Y., Aaronson, C., Gorman, J. M., Liebowitz, M. R., & Klein, D. F. (1990). Familial transmission of simple phobias and fears: A preliminary report. *Archives of General Psychiatry, 47*(3), 252–256.

Gaffney, F. A., Fenton, B. J., Lane, L. D., & Lake, C. R. (1988). Hemodynamic, ventilatory, and biochemical responses of panic patients and normal controls with sodium lactate infusion and spontaneous panic attacks. *Archives of General Psychiatry, 45,* 53–60.

Geffken, G. R., Pincus, D. B., & Zelikovsky, N. (1999). Obsessive-compulsive disorder in children and adolescents: Review of background, assessment, and treatment. *Journal of Psychological Practice, 5*(1), 15–31.

Geller, B., Chestnut, E. C., Miller, M. D., Price, O. T., & Yates, E. (1985). Preliminary data on DSM-III associated features of major depressive disorders in children and adolescents. *American Journal of Psychiatry, 142*(5), 643–644.

George, C. F., Millar, T. W., & Kryger, M. H. (1988). Sleep apnea and body position during sleep. *Sleep, 11*(1), 90–99.

Gilboa-Schechtman, E., Foa, E. B., & Amir, N. (1999). Attentional biases for facial expressions in social phobia: The face-in-the-crowd paradigm. *Cognition and Emotion, 13,* 305–318.

Gorman, J. M., Kent, J. M., Sullivan, G. M., & Coplan, J. D. (2000). Neuroanatomical hypothesis of panic disorder, revised. *American Journal of Psychiatry, 157,* 493–505.

Gray, J. A. (1982). *The neuropsychology of anxiety.* New York: Oxford University Press.

Gray, J. A., & McNaughton, N. (1996). The neuropsychology of anxiety: Reprise. In D. A. Hope (Ed.), *Perspectives on anxiety, panic and fear (The 43rd Annual Nebraska Symposium on Motivation)* (pp. 61–134). Lincoln: Nebraska University Press.

Graziano, A. M., & De Giovanni, I. S. (1979). The clinical significance of childhood phobias: A note on the proportion of child-clinical referrals for the treatment of children's fears. *Behaviour Research and Therapy, 17*(2), 161–162.

Greenberg, M. T., Speltz, M. L., & DeKlyen, M. (1993). The role of attachment in early development of disruptive problems. *Development and Psychopathology, 5*(1-2), 191–213.

Guarnaccia, P. J. (1997). A cross-cultural perspective on anxiety disorders. In S. Friedman (Ed.), *Cultural issues in the treatment of anxiety* (pp. 3–20). New York: Guilford Press.

Guarnaccia, P. J., Canino., G., Rubio-Stipec, M., & Bravo, M. (1993). The prevalence of ataques de nervios in the Puerto Rico Disaster Study. *Journal of Nervous and Mental Disease, 181,* 157–165.

Guarnaccia, P. J., Rubio-Stipec, M., & Canino, G. J. (1989). Ataques de nervios in the Puerto Rican Diagnostic Interview Schedule: The impact of cultural categories on psychiatric epidemiology. *Culture, Medicine, and Psychiatry, 13,* 275–295.

Hanna, G. L. (1995). Demographic and clinical features of obsessive-compulsive disorder in children and adolescents. *Journal of the American Academy of Child and Adolescent Psychiatry, 34*(1), 19–27.

Hayward, C., Killen, J. D., Kraemer, H. C., & Taylor, C. B. (2000). Predictors of panic attacks in adolescents. *Journal of the American Academy of Child and Adolescent Psychiatry, 39,* 207–214.

Hazen, A. L., & Stein, M. B. (1995). Clinical phenomenology and comorbidity. In M. B. Stein (Ed.), *Social phobia: Clinical and research perspectives* (pp. 3–41). Washington, DC: American Psychiatric Press.

Head, D., Bolton, D., & Hymas, N. (1989). Deficit in cognitive shifting ability in patients with obsessive-compulsive disorder. *Biological Psychiatry, 25*(7), 929–937.

Heckelman, L. R., & Schneier, F. R. (1995). Diagnostic issues. In R. G. Heimberg, M. R. Liebowitz, D. A. Hope, & F. R. Schneier (Eds.), *Social phobia: Diagnosis, assessment, and treatment* (pp. 3–20). New York: Guilford Press.

Heimberg, R. G., & Juster, H. R. (1995). Cognitive-behavioral treatments: Literature review. In R. G. Heimberg, M. R. Liebowitz, D. A. Hope, & F. R. Schneier (Eds.), *Social phobia: Diagnosis, assessment, and treatment* (pp. 261–309). New York: Guilford Press.

Heimberg, R. G., Stein, M. B., Hiripi, E., & Kessler, R. C. (2000). Trends in the prevalence of social phobia in the United States: A synthetic cohort analysis of changes over four decades. *European Psychiatry, 15,* 29–37.

Heinrichs, N., & Hofmann, S. G. (2001). Information processing biases in social phobia: A critical review. *Clinical Psychology Review, 21*(5), 751–770.

Hinton, D., Ba, P., Peou, S., & Um, K. (in press a). Kyol Goeu ("wind overload"): Part I. Cultural syndromes, catastrophic cognitions, and the generation of panic; or, Kyol Goeu and orthostatic panic among Khmer refugees attending a psychiatric clinic. *Transcultural Psychiatry.*

Hinton, D., Ba, P., Peou, S., & Um, K. (in press b). Kyol Goeu ("wind overload"): Part II. The prevalence of Kyol Goeu ("wind overload") and near-Kyol Goeu episodes in a Khmer psychiatric population. *Transcultural Psychiatry.*

Hofer, M. A. (1994). Hidden regulators in attachment, separation, and loss. In A. C. Huston (Ed.), *Children in poverty: Child development and public policy* (pp. 1–22). New York: Cambridge University Press.

Hofmann, S. G. (1999). Self-focused attention before and after treatment of social phobia. *Behaviour Research and Therapy, 38,* 717–725.

Hofmann, S. G., & Barlow, D. H. (1999). The costs of anxiety disorders: Implications for psychosocial interventions. In N. E. Miller & K. M. Magruder (Eds.), *Cost-effectiveness of psychotherapy: A guide for practitioners, researchers, and policymakers* (pp. 224–234). New York: Oxford University Press.

Hofmann, S. G., Ehlers, A., & Roth, W. T. (1995). Conditioning theory: A model for the etiology of public speaking anxiety? *Behaviour Research and Therapy, 33,* 567–571.

Hofmann, S. G., Newman, M. G., Ehlers, A., & Roth, W. T. (1995). Psychophysiological differences between subgroups of social phobia. *Journal of Abnormal Psychology, 104,* 224–231.

Horenstein, M., & Segui, J. (1997). Chronometrics of attentional processes in anxiety disorders. *Psychopathology, 30,* 25–35.

Hornig, C. D., & McNally, R. J. (1995). Panic disorder and suicide attempt: A reanalysis of data from the Epidemiologic Catchment Area study. *British Journal of Psychiatry, 167,* 76–79.

Hudson, J. I., Pope, H. G., Yurgelun-Todd, D., Jonas, J. M., & Frankenburg, F. R. (1987). A controlled family history study of bulimia. *Psychological Medicine, 17*(4), 883–890.

Hudson, J. L., & Rapee, R. M. (2000). The origins of social phobia. *Behavior Modification, 24,* 102–129.

Jeejeebhoy, F. M., Dorian, P., & Newman, D. M. (2000). Panic disorder and the heart: A cardiology perspective. *Journal of Psychosomatic Research, 48,* 393–403.

Jones, M. K., & Menzies, R. G. (1995). The etiology of fear of spiders. *Anxiety, Stress, and Coping: An International Journal, 8*(3), 227–234.

Jostes, A., Pook, M., & Florin, I. (1999). Public and private self-consciousness as specific psychopathological features. *Personality and Individual Differences, 27,* 1285–1295.

Kagan, J. (1989). Temperamental contributions to social behavior. *American Psychologist, 44,* 668–674.

Kagan, J., Reznick, J. S., & Snidman, N. (1987). The physiology and psychology of behavioral inhibition in children. *Child Development, 58,* 1459–1473.

Kagan, J., Snidman, N., & Arcus, D. M. (1992). Initial reactions to unfamiliarity. *Current Directions in Psychological Science, 1,* 171–174.

Karno, M., Golding, J. M., Sorenson, S. B., & Burnam, M. A. (1988). The epidemiology of obsessive-compulsive disorder in five U.S. communities. *Archives of General Psychiatry, 45*(12), 1094–1099.

Kasvikis, Y. G., Tsakiris, F., Marks, I. M., Basoglu, M., & Nashirvani (1986). Past history of anorexia nervosa in women with obsessive-compulsive disorder. *International Journal of Eating Disorders, 5*(6), 1069–1075.

Katerndahl, D. A., & Realini, J. P. (1993). Lifetime prevalence of panic states. *American Journal of Psychiatry, 150,* 246–249.

Katerndahl, D. A., & Realini, J. P. (1995). Where do panic sufferers seek care? *Journal of Family Practice, 40,* 237–243.

Katerndahl, D. A., & Talamantes, M. (2000). A comparison of persons with early- versus late-onset panic attacks. *Journal of Clinical Psychiatry, 61*(6), 422–427.

Kazdin, A. E. (1992). Overt and covert antisocial behaviour: Child and family characteristics among psychiatric inpatient children. *Journal of Child and Family Studies, 1*(1), 3–20.

Kendler, K. S., Walters, E. E., Neale, M. C., Kessler, R. C., Heath, A. C., & Eaves, L. J. (1995). The structure of the genetic and environmental risk factors for six major psychiatric disorders in women. *Archives of General Psychiatry, 52,* 374–383.

Kessler, R. C., McGonagle, K. A., Zhao, S., Nelson, C. B., Hughes, M., Eshleman, S., Wittchen, H.-U., & Kendler, K. S. (1994). Lifetime and 12-month prevalence of DSM-III-R psychiatric disorders in the United States: Results from the National Comorbidity Study. *Archives of General Psychiatry, 51*(1), 8–19.

Kessler, R. C., Stang, P., Wittchen, H. U., Stcin, M., & Walters, E. E. (1999). Lifetime comorbidities between social phobia and mood disorders in the US National Comorbidity Survey. *Psychological Medicine, 29*(3), 555–567.

King, N. J., Clowes-Hollins, V., & Ollendick, T. H. (1997). The etiology of childhood dog phobia. *Behaviour Research and Therapy, 35*(1), 77.

King, N. J., Hamilton, D. I., & Ollendick, T. H. (1988). *Children's phobias: A behavioral perspective.* London: Academic Press.

Klein, D. F., & Klein, H. M. (1989a). The definition and psychopharmacology of spontaneous panic and phobia. In P. Tyrer (Ed.), *Psychopharmacology of anxiety* (pp. 135–162). New York: Oxford University Press.

Klein, D. F., & Klein, H. M. (1989b). The nosology, genetics, and theory of spontaneous panic and phobia. In P. Tyrer (Ed.), *Psychopharmacology of anxiety* (pp. 163–195). New York: Oxford University Press.

Klein, D. F., Mannuzza, S., Chapman, T., & Fyer, A. J. (1992). Child panic revisited. *Journal of the American Academy of Child and Adolescent Psychiatry, 31,* 112–114.

Kleinknecht, R. A., Dinnel, P. L., Kleinknecht, E. E., Hiruma, N., & Harada, N. (1997). Cultural factors in social anxiety: Comparison of social phobia symptoms and taijin kyofusho. *Journal of Anxiety Disorders, 11,* 157–177.

Klerman, G. L., Weissman, M. M., Ouellette, R., Johnson, J., & Greenwald, S. (1991). Panic attacks in the community: Social morbidity and health care utilization. *Journal of the American Medical Association, 265,* 742–746.

Knowles, J. A., Mannuzza, S., & Fyer, A. J. (1995). Heritability of social anxiety. In M. B. Stein (Ed.), *Social phobia: Clinical and research perspectives* (pp. 147–161). Washington, DC: American Psychiatric Press.

Kouzis, A. C., & Eaton, W. W. (2000). Psychopathology and the initiation of disability payments. *Psychiatric Services, 51,* 908–913.

Langs, G., Quehenberger, F., Fabisch, K., Klug, G., Fabisch, H., & Zapotoczky, H.-G. (2000). The development of agoraphobia in panic disorder: A predictable process? *Journal of Affective Disorders, 58,* 43–50.

Last, C. G. (1991). Somatic complaints in anxiety disordered children. *Journal of Anxiety Disorders, 5*(2), 125–138.

Last, C. G., Francis, G., Hersen, M., & Kazdin, A. E. (1987). Separation anxiety and school phobia: A comparison using DSM-III criteria. *American Journal of Psychiatry, 144*(5), 653–657.

Last, C. G., Francis, G., & Strauss, C. C. (1989). Assessing fears in anxiety-disordered children with the Revised Fear Survey Schedule for Children (FSSC-R). *Journal of Clinical Child Psychology, 18*(2), 137–141.

Last, C. G., Hersen, M., Kazdin, A. E., Finkelstein, R., & Strauss, C. C. (1987). Comparison of DSM-III separation anxiety and overanxious disorders: Demographic characteristics and patterns of comorbidity. *Journal of the American Academy of Child and Adolescent Psychiatry, 26*(4), 527–531.

Last, C. G., & Strauss, C. C. (1989). Panic disorder in children and adolescents. *Journal of Anxiety Disorders, 3,* 221–241.

Lauterbach, E. C., & Duvoisin, R. C. (1991). Anxiety disorders in familial parkinsonism. *American Journal of Psychiatry, 148,* 274.

Leary, M. R., & Kowalski, R. M. (1995a). The self-presentation model. In R. G. Heimberg, M. R. Liebowitz, D. A. Hope, & F. R. Schneier (Eds.), *Social phobia: Diagnosis, assessment, and treatment* (pp. 94–112). New York: Guilford Press.

Leary, M. R., & Kowalski, R. M. (1995b). *Social anxiety.* New York: Guilford Press.

Lease, C. A., & Strauss, C. C. (1993). Separation anxiety disorder. In R. T. Ammerman & M. Hersen (Eds.), *Handbook of behavior therapy with children and adults: A developmental and longitudinal perspective* (Vol. 171, pp. 93–107). Needham Heights, MA: Allyn and Bacon.

Leckman, J. F., & Chittenden, E. H. (1990). Gilles de La Tourette's syndrome and some forms of obsessive-compulsive disorder may share a common genetic diathesis. *Encephale, 16*(1), 321–323.

Lee, S.-H., & Oh, K. S. (1999). Offensive type of social phobia: Cross-cultural perspectives. *International Medical Journal, 6,* 271–279.

Lensi, P., Cassano, G. B., Correddu, G., Ravagli, S., & Kunovac, J. J. (1996). Obsessive-compulsive disorder. Familial-developmental history, symptomatology, comorbidity and course with special reference to gender-related differences. *British Journal of Psychiatry, 169*(1), 101–107.

Leonard, H. L., Lenane, M. C., Swedo, S. E., & Rettew, D. C. (1993). Tics and Tourette's disorder: A 2- to 7-year follow-up of 54 obsessive-compulsive children. *Annual Progress in Child Psychiatry and Child Development,* 402–417.

Ley, R. (1998). Pulmonary function and dyspnea/suffocation theory of panic. *Journal of Behavior Therapy and Experimental Psychiatry, 29,* 1–11.

Lieberman, A. F. (1992). Infant parent psychotherapy with toddlers. *Development and Psychopathology, 4*(4), 559–574.

Liebowitz, M. R., Gorman, J. M., Fyer, A. J., & Klein, D. F. (1985). Social phobia: Review of a neglected anxiety disorder. *Archives of General Psychiatry, 42*(7), 729–736.

Liebowitz, M. R., Heimberg, R. G., Fresco, D. M., Travers, J., & Stein, M. B. (2000). Social phobia or social anxiety disorder: What's in a name? *Archives of General Psychiatry, 57*(2), 191–192.

Livingstone, R., Taylor, J. L., & Crawford, S. L. (1988). A study of somatic complaints and psychiatric diagnosis in children. *Journal of the American Academy of Child and Adolescent Psychiatry, 27*(2), 185–187.

Maidenberg, E., Chen, E., Craske, M., Bohn, P., & Bystritsky, A. (1996). Specificity of attentional bias in panic disorder and social phobia. *Journal of Anxiety Disorders, 10,* 529–541.

Main, M., Kaplan, N., & Cassidy, J. (1985). Security in infancy, childhood, and adulthood: A move to the level of representation. *Monographs of the Society for Research in Child Development, 50*(1-2), 66–104.

Manicavasagar, V., Silove, D., Curtis, J., & Wagner, R. (2000). Continuities of separation anxiety from early life into adulthood. *Journal of Anxiety Disorders, 14,* 1–18.

March, J. S., & Mulle, K. (1998). OCD in children and adolescents: *A cognitive-behavioral treatment manual.* New York: Guilford Press.

Marks, I. M. (1987a). Behavioral aspects of panic disorder. *American Journal of Psychiatry, 144,* 1160–1165.

Marks, I. M. (1987b). The development of normal fear: A review. *Journal of Child Psychiatry and Allied Disciplines, 28*(5), 667–697.

Marks, I. M., & Gelder, M. G. (1966). Different ages of onset in varieties of phobia. *American Journal of Psychiatry, 123,* 218–221.

Massion, A. O., Warsaw, M. G., & Keller, M. B. (1993). Quality of life and psychiatric morbidity in panic disorder and generalized anxiety disorder. *American Journal of Psychiatry, 150*(4), 600–607.

McFall, M. E., & Wollersheim, J. P. (1979). Obsessive-compulsive neurosis: A cognitive-behavioural formulation and approach to treatment. *Cognitive Therapy and Research, 3*(4), 333–348.

McNally, R. J. (1990). Psychological approaches to panic disorder: A review. *Psychological Bulletin, 108,* 403–419.

McNally, R. J. (1994). *Panic disorder: A critical analysis.* New York: Guilford Press.

McNally, R. J., & Steketee, G. S. (1985). The etiology and maintenance of severe animal phobias. *Behavior Research and Therapy, 23*(4), 430–435.

Melamed, B. G. (1992). Family factors predicting children's reaction to anesthesia induction. In A. M. La Greca & L. J. Siegel (Eds.), *Stress and coping in child health: Advances in pediatric psychology* (pp. 140–156). New York: Guilford Press.

Melfsen, S., Osterlow, J., & Florin, I. (2000). Deliberate emotional expressions of socially anxious children and their mothers. *Journal of Anxiety Disorders, 14,* 249–261.

Mellings, T. M. B., & Alden, L. E. (2000). Cognitive processes in social anxiety: The effects of self-focus, rumination and anticipatory processing. *Behaviour Research and Therapy, 38,* 243–257.

Menzies, R. G., & Clarke, J. C. (1993a). The etiology of childhood water phobia. *Behaviour Research and Therapy, 31*(5), 499–501.

Menzies, R. G., & Clarke, J. C. (1993b). The etiology of fear of heights and its relationship to severity and individual response patterns. *Behaviour Research and Therapy, 31*(4), 355–365.

Menzies, R. G., & Clarke, J. C. (1995). The etiology of phobias: A nonassociative account. *Clinical Psychology Review, 15*(1), 23–48.

Merckelbach, H., de-Jong, P. J., Muris, P., & van den Hout, M. A. (1996). The etiology of specific phobias: A review. *Clinical Psychology Review, 16*(4), 337–361.

Mineka, S. (1985). Animal models of anxiety based disorders: Their usefulness and limitations. In A. H. Tuma & J. D. Maser (Eds.), *Anxiety and the anxiety disorders* (pp. 199–244). Hillsdale, NJ: Erlbaum.

Moore, M. C., & Carr, A. (2000). Anxiety disorders. In A. Carr (Ed.), *What works with children and adolescents? A critical review of psychological interventions with children, adolescents, and their families* (pp. 178–202). New York: Routledge.

Moore, M. C., & Zebb, B. J. (1999). The catastrophic misinterpretation of physiological distress. *Behaviour Research and Therapy, 37,* 1105–1118.

Moreau, D., & Follet, C. (1993). Panic disorder in children and adolescents. *Child and Adolescent Psychiatric Clinics of North America, 2,* 581–602.

Morris, R. J., & Kratochwill, T. R. (1983). *Treating children's fears and phobias: A behavioral approach.* New York: Pergamon Press.

Mowrer, O. H. (1939). A stimulus-response analysis of anxiety and its role as a reinforcing agent. *Psychological Review, 46*(1), 553–566.

Mowrer, O. H. (1947). On the dual nature of learning—a reinterpretation of "conditioning" and "problem-solving." *Harvard Educational Review, 17,* 102–148.

Mulkens, S., & Boegels, S. M. (1999). Learning history in fear of blushing. *Behaviour Research and Therapy, 37,* 1159–1167.

Nestadt, G., Bienvenu, O. J., Cai, G., Samuels, J. F., & Eaton, W. W. (1998). Incidence of obsessive-compulsive disorder in adults. *Journal of Nervous and Mental Disease, 186*(7), 401–406.

Nestadt, G., Samuels, J. F., Romanowski, A. J., & Folstein, M. F. (1994). Obsessions and compulsions in the community. *Acta Psychiatrica Scandinavica, 89*(4), 219–224.

Neufeld, K. J., Swartz, K. L., Bienvenu, O. J., Eaton, W. W., & Cai, G. (1999). Incidence of DIS/DSM-IV social phobia in adults. *Acta Psychiatrica Scandinavica, 100*(3), 186–192.

Noyes, R., Woodman, C. L., Holt, C. S., & Reich, J. H. (1995). Avoidant personality traits distinguishing social phobic and panic disorder subjects. *Journal of Nervous and Mental Disease, 183,* 145–153.

Ohman, A. (1986). Face the beast and fear the face: Animal and social fears as prototypes for evolutionary analysis of emotion. *Psychophysiology, 23,* 123–145.

Ollendick, T. H. (1983). Reliability and validity of the Revised Fear Schedule for Children (FSSC-R). *Behavior Research and Therapy, 21,* 685–692.

Ollendick, T. H., & King, N. J. (1991a). Developmental factors in child behavioral assessment. In P. R. Martin (Ed.), *Handbook of behavior therapy and psychological science: Vol. 164. An integrative approach* (pp. 57–72). Elmsford: Pergamon.

Ollendick, T. H., & King, N. J. (1991b). Origins of childhood fears: An evaluation of Rachman's theory of fear acquisition. *Behaviour Research and Therapy, 29*(2), 117–123.

Ost, L. G. (1987). Age of onset in different phobias. *Journal of Abnormal Psychology, 96,* 223–229.

Pauli, P., Dengler, W., Wiedemann, G., Montoya, P., Flor, H., Birbaumer, N., & Buchkremer, G. (1997). Behavioral and neurophysiological evidence for altered processing of anxiety-related words in panic disorder. *Journal of Abnormal Psychology, 106,* 213–220.

Pavlov, I. P. (1927). *Conditioned reflexes* (G. V. Anrep, Trans.). London: Oxford University Press.

Pianta, R. C. (1999). Early childhood. In W. K. Silverman & T. H. Ollendick (Eds.), *Developmental issues in the clinical treatment of children* (pp. 88–107). Needham Heights, MA: Allyn and Bacon.

Pollack, M. H., & Marzol, P. C. (2000). Panic: Course, complications and treatment of panic disorder. *Journal of Psychopharmacology, 14*(Suppl. 1), 25–30.

Pury, C. L. S., & Mineka, S. (1997). Covariation bias for blood-injury stimuli and aversive outcomes. *Behaviour Research and Therapy, 35*(1), 35–47.

Rachman, S. (1977). The conditioning theory of fear acquisition: A critical examination. *Behavior Research and Therapy, 15,* 375–387.

Rapee, R. M., & Lim, L. (1992). Discrepancy between self- and observer ratings of performance in social phobics. *Journal of Abnormal Psychology, 101*(4), 728–731.

Rasmussen, S. A., & Eisen, J. L. (1989). Clinical features and phenomenology of obsessive-compulsive disorder. *Psychiatric Annals, 19*(2), 67–73.

Rasmussen, S. A., & Tsuang, M. T. (1986). Clinical characteristics and family history in DSM-III obsessive-compulsive disorder. *American Journal of Psychiatry, 143*(3), 317–322.

Razran, G. (1961). The observable unconscious and the inferable conscious in current Soviet psychophysiology. Interoceptive conditioning, semantic conditioning, and the orienting reflex. *Psychological Review, 68,* 81–147.

Regier, D. A., Boyd, J. H., Burke, J. D., Rae, D. S., Myers, J. K., Kramer, M., Robins, L. N., George, L. K., Karno, M., & Locke, B. Z. (1988). One-month prevalence of mental disorders in the United States: Based on five epidemiologic catchment area sites. *Archives of General Psychiatry, 45*(11), 977–986.

Reich, J. H. (2000). The relationship of social phobia to avoidant personality disorder: A proposal to reclassify avoidant personality disorder based on clinical empirical findings. *European Psychiatry, 15,* 151–159.

Reich, J. H., Noyes, R., & Yates, W. (1988). Anxiety symptoms distinguishing social phobia from panic and generalized anxiety disorders. *Journal of Nervous and Mental Diseases, 176*(8), 510–513.

Rettew, D. C., Swedo, S. E., Leonard, H. L., Lenane, M. C., & Rappaport, M. (1992). Obsessions and compulsions across time in 79 children and adolescents with obsessive-compulsive disorder. *Journal of the American Academy of Child and Adolescent Psychiatry, 31*(6), 1050–1056.

Robins, L. N., Helzer, J. E., Weissman, M. M., Orvaschel, H., Gruenberg, B., Burke, J. D., Jr., & Regier, D. A. (1984). Lifetime prevalence of specific psychiatric disorders in three sites. *Archives of General Psychiatry, 41*(10), 949–958.

Roemer, L., Orsillo, S., & Barlow, D. H. (2002). Generalized anxiety disorder. In D. H. Barlow (Ed.), *Anxiety and its disorders: The nature and treatment of anxiety and panic* (2nd ed., pp. 477–518). New York: Guilford Press.

Rose, R. J., & Ditto, W. B. (1983). A developmental-genetic analysis of common fears from early adolescence to early adulthood. *Child Development, 54*(2), 361–368.

Roy-Byrne, P. P., Stang, P., Wittchen, H.-U., Ustun, B., Walters, E. E., & Kessler, R. C. (2000). Lifetime panic-depression comorbidity in the National Comorbidity Survey: Association with symptoms, impairment, course, and help-seeking. *British Journal of Psychiatry, 176,* 229–235.

Rubin, H. C., Rapaport, M. H., Levine, B., Gladsjo, J. K., Rabin, A., Aurbach, M., Judd, L. L., & Kaplan, R. (2000). Quality of well being in panic disorder: The assesment of psychiatric and general disability. *Journal of Affective Disorders, 57*(1-3), 217–221.

Salkovskis, P. M., & Clark, D. M. (1990). Affective responses to hyperventilation: A test of the cognitive model of panic. *Behaviour Research and Therapy, 28,* 51–61.

Sasson, Y., Zohar, J., Gross, R., Taub, M., & Fux, M. (1999). Response to missile attacks on civilian targets in patients with panic disorder. *Journal of Clinical Psychiatry, 60,* 385–388.

Scherrer, J. F., True, W. P., Xian, H., Lyons, M. J., Eisen, S. A., Goldberg, J., Lin, N., & Tsuang-Ming, T. (2000). Evidence for genetic influences common and specific to symptoms of generalized anxiety and panic. *Journal of Affective Disorders, 57,* 25–35.

Schmidt, N. B. (1999). Examination of differential anxiety sensitivities in panic disorder: A test of anxiety sensitivity subdomains predicting fearful responding in a 35% $CO_2$ challenge. *Cognitive Therapy and Research, 23,* 3–20.

Schmidt, N. B., Trakowski, J. H., & Staab, J. P. (1997). Extinction of panicogenic effects of a 35% $CO_2$ challenge in patients with panic disorder. *Journal of Abnormal Psychology, 106,* 630–638.

Schneier, F. R., Liebowitz, M. R., Abi-Dargham, A., Zea-Ponce, Y., Lin, S.-H., & Laruelle, M. (2000). Low dopamine $D_2$ receptor binding potential in social phobia. *American Journal of Psychiatry, 157,* 457–459.

Schuhmann, E. M., Foote, R. C., Eyberg, S. M., Boggs, S. R., & Algina, J. (1998). Efficacy of parent-child interaction therapy: Interim report of a randomized trial with short-term maintenance. *Journal of Clinical Child Psychology, 27*(1), 34–45.

Segui, J., Salvador-Carulla, L., Marquez, M., Garcia, L., Canet, J., & Ortiz, M. (2000). Differential clinical features of late-onset panic disorder. *Journal of Affective Disorders, 57,* 115–124.

Seligman, M. E. (1971). Phobias and preparedness. *Behavior Therapy, 2*(3), 307–320.

Seligman, M. E. P. (1988). Competing theories of panic. In S. Rachman & J. D. Maser (Eds.), *Panic: Psychological perspectives* (pp. 321–329). Hillsdale, NJ: Erlbaum.

Silverman, W. K., & Kearney, C. A. (1992). Listening to our clinical partners: Informing researchers about children's fears and phobias. *Journal of Behavior Therapy and Experimental Psychiatry, 23*(2), 71–76.

Sinha, S. S., Coplan, J. D., Pine, D. S., Martinez, J. A., Klein, D. F., & Gorman, J. M. (1999). Panic induced by carbon dioxide inhalation and lack of hypothalamic-pituitary-adrenal axis activation. *Psychiatry Research, 86,* 93–98.

Siqueland, L., Kendall, P. C., & Steinberg, L. (1996). Anxiety in children: Perceived family environments and observed family interaction. *Journal of Clinical Child Psychology, 25*(2), 225–237.

Skinner, B. F. (1953). *Science and human behavior.* New York: Macmillan.

Smith, L. C., Friedman, S., & Nevid, J. (1999). Clinical and sociocultural differences in African American and European American patients with panic disorder and agoraphobia. *Journal of Nervous and Mental Disease, 187,* 549–560.

Sonntag, H., Wittchen, H.-U., Hoefler, M., Kessler, R. C., & Stein, M. B. (2000). Are social fears and DSM-IV social anxiety disorder associated with smoking and nicotine dependence in adolescents and young adults? *European Psychiatry, 15,* 67–74.

Spence, S. H., Donovan, C., & Brechman-Toussaint, M. (1999). Social skills, social outcomes, and cognitive features of childhood social phobia. *Journal of Abnormal Psychology, 108,* 211–221.

Spinhoven, P., Sterk, P. J., van der Kamp, L., & Onstein, E. J. (1999). The complex association of pulmonary function with panic disorder: A rejoinder to Ley (1998). *Journal of Behavior Therapy and Experimental Psychiatry, 30,* 341–346.

Sroufe, L. A. (1985). Attachment classification from the perspective of infant-caregiver relationships and infant temperament. *Child Development, 56,* 1–14.

Starcevic, V., Bogojevic, G., Marinkovic, J., & Kelin, K. (1999). Axis I and II comorbidity in panic/agoraphobic patients with and without suicidal ideation. *Psychiatric Research, 88,* 153–161.

Stein, D. J., & Bouwer, C. (1997). Blushing and social phobia: A neuroethological speculation. *Medical Hypotheses, 49,* 101–108.

Stein, M. B. (1998). Neurobiological perspectives on social phobia: From affiliation to zoology. *Biological Psychiatry, 44,* 1277–1285.

Stein, M. B., Chartier, M. J. D., Hazen, A. L., Kozak, M. V., Tancer, M. E., Landers, S., Furer, P., Chubory, D., & Walker, J. R. (1998). A direct-interview family study of generalized social phobia. *American Journal of Psychiatry, 151,* 90–97.

Stein, M. B., Heuser, I. J., Juncos, J. L., & Uhde, T. W. (1990). Anxiety disorders in patients with Parkinson's disease. *American Journal of Psychiatry, 147,* 217–221.

Stein, M. B., Shea, C. A., & Uhde, T. W. (1989). Social phobic symptoms in patients with panic disorder: Practical and theoretical implications. *American Journal of Psychiatry, 146,* 235–238.

Stemberger, R. T., Turner, S. M., Beidel, D. C., & Calhorn, K. S. (1995). Social phobia: An analysis of possible developmental factors. *Journal of Abnormal Psychology, 104,* 526–531.

Stevenson, J., Batten, N., & Cherner, M. (1992). Fears and fearfulness in children and adolescents: A genetic analysis of twin data. *Journal of Child Psychology and Psychiatry and Allied Disciplines, 33*(6), 977–985.

Stopa, L., & Clark, D. M. (2000). Social phobia and interpretation of social events. *Behaviour Research and Therapy, 38,* 273–283.

Swedo, S. E., Rapoport, J. L., Leonard, H. L., & Lenane, M. (1989). Obsessive compulsive disorder in children and adolescents: Clinical phenomenology of 70 consecutive cases. *Archives of General Psychology, 46*(4), 335–341.

Takriti, A., & Ahmad, T. (2000). Anxiety disorders and treatment in Arab-Muslim culture. In I. Al-Issa et al. (Eds.), *Al-Junnun: Mental illness in the Islamic world* (pp. 235–250). Madison, CT: International Universities Press.

Taylor, S. (1999). *Anxiety sensitivity: Theory, research, and treatment of the fear of anxiety.* Mahwah, NJ: Erlbaum.

Thompson, R. A. (1991). Emotion regulation and emotional development. *Educational Psychology Review, 3,* 269–307.

Tiihonen, J., Kuikka, J., Bergstroem, K., Lepola, U., Koponen, H., & Leinonen, E. (1997). Dopamine reuptake site densities in patients with social phobia. *American Journal of Psychiatry, 154,* 239–242.

Tomarken, A. J., Sutton, S. K., & Mineka, S. (1995). Fear-relevant illusory correlations: What type of associations promote judgmental bias? *Journal of Abnormal Psychology, 104*(2), 312–326.

Tonge, B. (1994). Separation anxiety disorder. In T. H. Ollendick, N. J. King, & W. Yule (Eds.), *International handbook of phobic and anxiety disorders in children and adolescents* (pp. 145–167). New York: Plenum.

Toren, P., Eldar, S., Cendorf, D., Wolmer, L., Weizman, R., Zubadi, R., Koren, S., & Laor, N. (1999). The prevalence of mitral valve prolapse in children with anxiety disorders. *Journal of Psychiatric Research, 33,* 357–361.

Trower, P., & Gilbert, P. (1989). New theoretical conceptions of social anxiety and social phobia. *Clinical Psychology Review, 9,* 19–35.

Turk, C. L., Heimberg, R. G., Orsillo, R. M., Holt, C. S., Gitow, A., Street, L. L., Schneier, F. R., & Liebowitz, M. R. (1998). An investigation of gender differences in social phobia. *Journal of Anxiety Disorders, 12*(3), 209–223.

Turner, S. M., Beidel, D. C., Borden, J. W., Stanley, M. A., & Jacob, R. G. (1991). Social phobia: Axis I and II correlates. *Journal of Abnormal Psychology, 100,* 102–106.

Turner, S. M., Beidel, D. C., & Costello, A. (1987). Psychopathology in the offspring of anxiety disorder patients. *Journal of Consulting and Clinical Psychology, 55*(2), 229–235.

Turner, S. M., Beidel, D. C., & Townsley, (1990). Social phobia: Relationship to shyness. *Behaviour Research and Therapy, 28*(6), 497–505.

Uhde, T. W., Tancer, M. E., Black, B., & Brown, T. M. (1991). Phenomenology and neurobiology of social phobia: Comparison with panic disorder. *Journal of Clinical Psychiatry, 52*(Suppl. 11), 31–40.

van Beek, N., & Griez, E. (2000). Reactivity to a 35% $CO_2$ challenge in health first-degree relative of patients with panic disorder. *Biological Psychiatry, 47,* 830–835.

van Zijderveld, G. A., Veltman, D. J., van Dyck, R., & van Doornen, I. J. P. (1999). Epinephrine-induced panic attacks and hyperventilation. *Journal of Psychiatric Research, 33,* 73–78.

Watson, D., Clark, L. A., & Carey, G. (1988). Positive and negative affectivity and their relation to axiety and depressive disorders. *Journal of Abnormal Psychology, 97*(3), 346–353.

Wells, A., & Carter, T. (1999). Preliminary tests of a cognitive model of generalized anxiety disorder. *Behaviour Research and Therapy, 37,* 585–594.

Wells, A., Clark, D., & Ahmad, S. (1998). How do I look with my minds eye: Perspective taking in social phobic imagery. *Behaviour Research and Therapy, 36,* 631–634.

Wells, A., & Papageorgiu, C. (1998). Social phobia: Effects of external attention on anxiety, negative beliefs and perspective taking. *Behavior Therapy, 29,* 357–370.

Wells, A., & Papageorgiu, C. (1999). The observer perspective: Biascd imagery in social phobia, agoraphobia, and blood/injury phobia. *Behaviour Research and Therapy, 37,* 653–658.

Wenar, C. (1990). Childhood fears and phobias. In M. Lewis & S. M. Miller (Eds.), *Handbook of developmental psychopathology: Perspectives in developmental psychology* (pp. 281–290). New York: Plenum.

Werry, J. S. (1991). Overanxious disorder: A review of its taxonomic properties. *Journal of the American Academy of Child and Adolescent Psychiatry, 30*(4), 533–544.

Whitaker, A., Johnson, J., Shaffer, D., Rapoport, J., Kalikow, K., Walsh, B. T., Davies, M., Braiman, S., & Dolinsky, A. (1990). Uncommon troubles in young people: Prevalence estimates of selected psychiatric disorders in a nonreferred adolescent population. *Archives of General Psychiatry, 47,* 487–496.

White, K. S., & Barlow, D. H. (2002). Panic disorder and agoraphobia. In D. H. Barlow (Ed.), *Anxiety and its disorders: The nature and treatment of anxiety and panic* (2nd ed., pp. 328–379). New York: Guilford Press.

Williams, K., Argyropoulos, S., & Nutt, D. J. (2000). Amphetamine misuse and social phobia. *American Journal of Psychiatry, 157,* 834–835.

Wittchen, H.-U., Fuetsch, M., Sonntag, H., Muellen, N., & Liebowitz, M. R. (2000). Disability and quality of life in pure and comorbid social phobia: Findings from a controlled study. *European Psychiatry, 15,* 46–58.

Wittchen, H.-U., Stein, M. B., & Kessler, R. C. (1999). Social fears and social phobia in a community sample of adolescents and young adults: Prevalence, risk factors and comorbidity. *Psychological Medicine, 29,* 309–323.

Wittchen, H., Zhao, S., Kessler, R. C., & Eaton, W. W. (1994). DSM-III-R generalized anxiety disorder in the National Comorbidity Study. *Archives of General Psychiatry, 51,* 355–364.

Wolpe, J., & Rowan, V. C. (1988). Panic disorder: A product of classical conditioning. *Behaviour Research and Therapy, 26,* 441–450.

Woodman, C. L., Noyes, R., Black, D. W., Schlosser, S., & Yagla, S. J. (1999). A 5-year follow-up study of generalized anxiety disorder and panic disorder. *Journal of Nervous and Mental Disease, 187*(1), 3–9.

Yang, S., Tsai, T. H., Hou, Z. Y., Chen, C. Y., & Sim, C. B. (1997). The effect of panic attack on mitral valve prolapse. *Acta Psychiatrica Scandinavica, 96,* 408–411.

Zarit, S. T., & Zarit, J. M. (1998). *Mental disorders in older adults: Fundamentals of assessment and treatment.* New York: Guilford Press.

Zhang, A. Y., & Snowden, L. R. (1999). Ethnic characteristics of mental disorders in five U.S. communities. *Cultural Diversity and Ethnic Minority Psychology, 5,* 134–146.

Zohar, J., & Insel, T. R. (1987). Obsessive-compulsive disorder: Psychobiological approaches to diagnosis, treatment and pathophysiology. *Biological Psychiatry, 22*(6), 667–687.

Zuckerman, M. (1999). *Vulnerability to psychopathology: A biosocial model.* Washington, DC: American Psychological Association.

# CHAPTER 6

# Personality Disorders

TIMOTHY J. TRULL AND THOMAS A. WIDIGER

The American Psychiatric Association (APA) includes 10 personality disorders in their *Diagnostic and Statistical Manual of Mental Disorders–Fourth Edition* (*DSM-IV;* APA, 1994, 2000): paranoid, schizoid, schizotypal, antisocial, borderline, histrionic, narcissistic, avoidant, dependent, and obsessive-compulsive. We discuss each of these personality disorders individually later in this chapter. The 10 officially recognized personality disorders are further organized into three clusters based on descriptive similarities: Cluster A (odd-eccentric) includes paranoid, schizoid, and schizotypal; Cluster B (dramatic-erratic-emotional) includes antisocial, borderline, histrionic, and narcissistic; and Cluster C (anxious-fearful) includes avoidant, dependent, and obsessive-compulsive. Two additional personality disorders (passive-aggressive and depressive) are provided within an appendix to *DSM-IV* for diagnoses that are not yet officially recognized. *DSM-IV* also includes the diagnosis of personality disorder not otherwise specified (PDNOS), a diagnosis clinicians can provide when they believe that a personality disorder is present but the symptomatology of the patient is not adequately represented by one of the 10 officially recognized diagnoses.

## Definition of Personality Disorder

"Personality traits are enduring patterns of perceiving, relating to, and thinking about the environment and oneself that are exhibited in a wide range of social and personal contexts" (APA, 2000, p. 686). It is when "personality traits are inflexible and maladaptive and cause significant functional impairment or subjective distress [that] they constitute personality disorders" (APA, 2000, p. 686). *DSM-IV* (1994, 2000) provides a formal and general definition of personality disorder that is particularly important to consider when using the PDNOS diagnosis. Table 6.1 presents these general diagnostic criteria.

The general diagnostic criteria are concerned primarily with documenting that the symptomatology concerns personality functioning (i.e., an enduring pattern of inner experience that is pervasive across a broad range of personal and social functioning) rather than another domain of psychopathology (e.g., mood or anxiety disorder). Further details regarding the concept and assessment of personality are provided within the fifth volume of this Handbook. However, we want to highlight here three of the general diagnostic criteria.

**TABLE 6.1  General Diagnostic Criteria for a Personality Disorder**

A.  An enduring pattern of inner experience and behavior that deviates markedly from the expectations of the individual's culture. This pattern is manifested in two (or more) of the following areas:

- Cognition (i.e., ways of perceiving and interpreting self, other people, and events).
- Affectivity (i.e., the range, intensity, lability, and appropriateness of emotional response).
- Interpersonal functioning.
- Impulse control.

B.  The enduring pattern is inflexible and pervasive across a broad range of personal and social situations.

C.  The enduring pattern leads to clinically significant distress or impairment in social, occupational, or other important areas of functioning.

D.  The pattern is stable and of long duration, and its onset can be traced back at least to adolescence or early adulthood.

E.  The enduring pattern is not better accounted for as a manifestation or consequence of another mental disorder.

F.  The enduring pattern is not due to the direct physiological effects of a substance (e.g., a drug of abuse, a medication) or a general medical condition (e.g., head trauma).

*Note.* Adapted from American Psychological Association (2000, p. 689).

First, it is stated in *DSM-IV* that a personality disorder "leads to clinically significant distress or impairment in social, occupational, or other important areas of functioning" (APA, 2000, p. 689). A difficulty many clinicians have with personality disorder (and other mental disorder) diagnosis is the absence of any definition or guidelines for what is meant by a *clinically significant* impairment (Spitzer & Wakefield, 1999; Widiger & Corbitt, 1994). *DSM-IV* states only that it is "an inherently difficult clinical judgment" (APA, 2000, p. 8).

*DSM-III* through *DSM-IV* have provided specific rules for when enough features of a specific personality disorder, such as schizoid or borderline, are present in order for it to be diagnosed, but the rationale for these diagnostic thresholds are unexplained and do not appear to bear a relationship to the presence of a clinically significant level of impairment (Widiger & Corbitt, 1994). In the absence of any guidelines or rationale for the diagnostic thresholds, it is not surprising to find substantial variation in the diagnostic thresholds across each edition. For example, Morey (1988) reported an 800% increase in the number of persons beyond the threshold for a schizoid diagnosis in *DSM-III-R* as compared to *DSM-III* and a 350% increase for the narcissistic diagnosis. Some of this shift in prevalence might have been intentional (Widiger, Frances, Spitzer, & Williams, 1988), but much of it was unanticipated (Blashfield, Blum, & Pfohl, 1992). An important focus of future research and *DSM-V* will be the development of a clearer distinction between the presence and absence of a mental disorder (Spitzer & Wakefield, 1999; Widiger, 2001).

A second point of emphasis with respect to the general definition of personality disorder is that personality disorder symptomatology is stable over time and of long duration. The onset of a personality disorder must be traceable back to adolescence or early adulthood. Temporal stability is fundamental to the concept of personality and to the diagnosis of personality disorders (Tickle, Heatherton, & Wittenberg, 2001). However, the extent to which this fundamental component of personality is in fact assessed by researchers and clinicians is unclear. Clinicians and researchers tend to emphasize current symptomatology, and they may do so at the neglect of determining whether the symptomatology has in fact been present throughout much of a person's life; this at times contributes to overdiagnosis and to a failure to adequately distinguish personality disorders and other mental disorders.

Finally, the symptoms of a personality disorder are said in the general definition to deviate from the expectations of one's culture. The purpose of this *DSM-IV* cultural deviation requirement is to decrease the likelihood that clinicians will impose the expectations of their own culture onto a patient (Rogler, 1996). The *DSM-IV* cultural deviation requirement emphasizes that a behavior pattern that appears to be deviant from the perspective of one's own culture might be quite normative and adaptive within another culture. Therefore, the expectations or norms within the clinician's culture might not necessarily be relevant or applicable to a patient from a different cultural background. For example, "what is considered to be excessively inhibited in one culture may be courteously dignified within another" (Widiger, Mangine, Corbitt, Ellis, & Thomas, 1995, p. 212).

However, one should not infer from the cultural deviation requirement that a personality disorder is simply a deviation from a cultural norm. Optimal, healthy functioning does not necessarily involve adaptation to cultural expectations, nor does adaptation to cultural expectations necessarily ensure the absence of maladaptive personality traits (Wakefield, 1992). In fact, some of the personality disorders may represent—at least in part—excessive or exaggerated expressions of traits that a culture values or encourages, at least within some members of that culture (Alarcon, 1996; Rogler, 1996; Widiger & Spitzer, 1991). For example, it is usually adaptive to be confident but not to be arrogant, to be agreeable but not to be submissive, or to be conscientious but not to be perfectionistic.

## Clinical Importance of Personality Disorders

The diagnosis of personality disorders can be quite difficult and even controversial. Nevertheless, the importance in assessing for the presence of personality disorders in clinical practice equals the difficulties of their diagnosis. A formal recognition by the American Psychiatric Association of the importance of personality classification to clinical diagnosis and treatment planning was demonstrated by the provision of a separate diagnostic axis (Axis II) devoted to personality disorders in *DSM-III* (APA, 1980; Frances, 1980). Personality disorders (along with mental retardation) continue to be placed on a separate axis for diagnosis in *DSM-IV;* all other mental disorders are diagnosed on Axis I (APA, 2000).

The valid, accurate assessment of personality disorders is important for several reasons. First, the existing large-scale studies that have assessed individuals for the full range of Axis I and Axis II disorders indicate that personality disorders are prevalent in both clinical and nonclinical populations (Mattia & Zimmerman, 2001). For example, Koenigsberg, Kaplan, Gilmore, and Cooper (1985) reported that 36% of over 2,000 psychiatric patients in their sample received a personality disorder diagnosis, whereas Zimmerman and Coryell (1989) reported that approximately 18% of a nonclinical, community sample received a personality disorder diagnosis. Prevalence rates of personality disorders are also substantial outside of the United States. For example, the World Health Organization (WHO) and Alcohol, Drug Abuse, Mental Health Administration (ADAMHA) Joint Program on the Diagnosis and Classification of Mental Disorders, Alcoholism, and Drug Abuse initiated the International Pilot Study of Personality Disorders (Loranger et al., 1994). The first report from a field trial evaluating 716 patients from 11 countries indicated that 51.1% of the patients met criteria for at least one *DSM-III-R* personality disorder.

Although a number of large-scale, community epidemiological studies on Axis I disorders have been conducted, we know much less about the prevalence of personality disorders in the general population. Antisocial personality disorder was the only personality disorder included in the Epidemiological Catchment Area (ECA) study (Robins & Regier, 1991) and the National Comorbidity Study (NCS; Kessler, 1999), from which most of our estimates on the prevalence of mental disorders in the community are drawn. Table 6.2 presents our best estimates of the prevalence of the full range of *DSM* personality disorders, drawn from the *DSM-IV* text (APA, 2000), several empirical studies (Maier, Lichtermann, Klinger, & Heun, 1992; Samuels, Nestadt, Romanoski, Folstein, & McHugh, 1994; Zimmerman & Coryell, 1989), and prior reviews (Lyons, 1995; Mattia & Zimmerman, 2001; Weissman, 1993). Across studies that used the *DSM* criteria to estimate the prevalence of current personality disorder (i.e., one or more diagnoses) the average estimate was 11.25% (range = 7.3–17.9%). For comparison, the past year prevalence estimates for major depressive episode were 3.7% (ECA) and 10.3% (NCS), for generalized anxiety disorder were 3.8% (ECA) and 3.1% (NCS), for alcohol use disorder were 6.3% (ECA) and 9.7% (NCS), and for drug use disorder were 1.2% (ECA) and 3.6% (NCS). Therefore, personality disorder does appear to be relatively prevalent in the community. The Cluster B disorders (especially antisocial, borderline, and histrionic) appear to be the most prevalent personality disorders.

Many studies have also documented that personality disorders are associated with significant social and

**TABLE 6.2   Estimates of the Prevalence of DSM Personality Disorders in the Community**

| Personality Disorder | DSM-IV General Population | Zimmerman & Coryell (1989) DSM-III; Nonclinical (n = 797) | Samuels et al. (1994) [def or prov] DSM-III; Nonclinical (n = 762) | Maier et al. (1992) DSM-III-R; Nonclinical (n = 452) | Moldin et al. (1994) DSM-III-R; Nonclinical (n = 302) | Weissman (1993) Review of Literature through 1990; US only |
|---|---|---|---|---|---|---|
| Cluster A | ? | ? | 0.1% | ? | ? | ? |
| Paranoid | 0.5–2.5% | 0.9% | 0.0% | 1.8% | 0.0% | 0.4–1.8% |
| Schizoid | ? | 0.9% | 0.0% | 0.4% | 0.0% | 0.48–0.7% |
| Schizotypal | 3% | 2.9% | 0.1% | 0.7% | 0.7% | 0.6–3.0% |
| Cluster B | ? | ? | 5.4% | ? | ? | ? |
| Antisocial | 1–3% | 3.3% | 1.8% | 0.2% | 2.6% | 2.3–3.2% |
| Borderline | 2% | 1.6% | 0.5% | 1.1% | 2.0% | 0.2–1.8% |
| Histrionic | 2–3% | 3.0% | 3.6% | 1.3% | 0.3% | 1.3–3.0% |
| Narcissistic | <1% | 0.0% | 0.0% | 0.0% | 0.0% | 0.0% |
| Cluster C | ? | ? | 4.0% | ? | ? | ? |
| Avoidant | 0.5–1.0% | 1.3% | 0.0% | 1.1% | 0.7% | 1.1–1.3% |
| Dependent | ? | 1.8% | 0.2% | 1.5% | 1.0% | 1.6–1.7% |
| Obsessive Compulsive | 1% | 2.0% | 3.4% | 2.2% | 0.7% | 1.7–2.2% |
| Passive Aggressive | N/A | 3.3% | 0.3% | 1.8% | 1.7% | 1.8–3.0% |
| Any PD | ? | 17.9% | 9.3% | 10.0% | 7.3% | 10–13.5% |

occupational dysfunction, comorbid Axis I psychopathology, and even suicidal state (e.g., Bernstein et al., 1993; Daley, Burge, & Hammen, 2000; Johnson, Cohen, Brown, Smailes, & Bernstein, 1999; Trull, Useda, Conforti, & Doan, 1997), and these relations remain significant after controlling for Axis I disorder and demographic variables (e.g., age, gender). For example, one of the more well-validated personality disorders is the antisocial or psychopathic (Stoff, Breiling, & Maser, 1997). Persons who have met the diagnostic criteria for this personality disorder have been shown to be at significant risk for unemployment, impoverishment, injury, violent death, substance and alcohol abuse, incarceration, recidivism (parole violation), and significant relationship instability (Hart & Hare, 1997; L. N. Robins, Tipp, & Przybeck, 1991).

Maladaptive personality traits will be evident among many patients seeking treatment for an Axis I mental disorder. For example, Trull, Sher, Minks-Brown, Durbin, and Burr (2000) estimated that approximately 57% of patients with borderline personality disorder will meet criteria for one or more substance use disorders (primarily alcohol use disorder), whereas approximately 27% of those with one or more substance use disorders should also receive a borderline diagnosis. Thus, the comorbidity rates for the substance use and borderline personality disorder are quite substantial, and the presence of a personality disorder will often result in an increased utilization of mental health services (Bender et al., 2001).

Investigators have reported that a comorbid diagnosis of personality disorder in depressed, substance-abusing, and anxiety-disordered patients suggests poorer prognosis (Dolan-Sewell, Krueger, & Shea, 2001; Trull et al., 2000). Antisocial patients can be irresponsible, unreliable, or untrustworthy; paranoid patients can be mistrustful, accusatory, and suspicious; dependent patients can be excessively needy; passive-aggressive patients can be argumentative and oppositional; and borderline patients can be intensely manipulative and unstable (Sanderson & Clarkin, 1994; Stone, 1993). The manner and extent to which a patient's personality facilitates and hinders clinical treatment—and the extent to and manner in which they result in clinically significant maladaptive functioning—should be a routine consideration of every clinician (Harkness & Lilienfeld, 1997). "In the *DSM-III*, then, personality not only attained a nosological status of prominence in its own right but was assigned a contextual role that made it fundamental to the understanding and interpretation of other psychopathologies" (Millon & Frances, 1987, p. ii).

In sum, the placement of personality disorders on a separate axis does have a meaningful rationale and justification, but the separate placement has also become controversial and perhaps misunderstood. Some have interpreted the placement on a separate axis to imply that personality disorders (along with mental retardation) are largely untreatable. Personality disorders are indeed among the most difficult of mental disorders to treat, in part because they involve pervasive and entrenched behavior patterns that have been present throughout much of a person's life. In addition, people consider many of their personality traits to be integral to their sense of self, and they may even value particular aspects of their personality that a clinician considers to be important targets of treatment (Stone, 1993). Nevertheless, contrary to popular perception, personality disorders are not untreatable. Maladaptive personality traits are often the focus of clinical treatment (Beck, Freeman, & Associates, 1990; Linehan, 1993; Millon et al., 1996; Soloff, Siever, Cowdry, & Kocsis, 1994; Stone, 1993), and there is compelling empirical support to indicate that meaningful responsivity to treatment does occur (Perry, Banon, & Ianni, 1999; Sanislow & McGlashan, 1998). Treatment of a personality disorder is unlikely to result in the development of a fully healthy or ideal personality structure (whatever that may entail), but clinically and socially meaningful change to personality structure and functioning can occur.

## Assessment of *DSM-IV* Personality Disorders

There are five methods commonly used for the assessment of personality disorders in research and general clinical practice: self-report inventories, unstructured clinical interviews, semistructured clinical interviews, projective techniques, and informant reports. Each of these methods is discussed briefly in turn.

First, several self-report inventories have been developed that include items that purportedly assess individual *DSM-IV* personality disorder criteria (e.g., the Personality Diagnostic Questionnaire–4; Hyler, 1994). However, because these instruments do not include appropriate time frames in their instructions (e.g., do not assess whether the diagnostic criteria were evident since young adulthood) and do not assess whether a clinically significant level of impairment or distress is associated with the endorsed personality disorder symptoms, self-report personality disorder inventories may be best suited for screening measures—not as diagnostic instruments. The prevalence rates obtained by these inventories tend to be dramatically higher than those estimated by interview measures of personality disorders and well beyond theoretical expectations for most of the personality disorders (Clark & Harrison, 2001; Kaye & Shea, 2000; Westen, 1997; Zimmerman, 1994). On the other hand, the tendency of self-report inventories to err in the direction of overdiagnosis does make them suitable as screening measures. The administration of a self-report inventory prior to a clinical interview can save a considerable amount of interviewing time and alert the clinician to areas of personality dysfunction that might have otherwise not have been anticipated or noticed (Widiger, 2002). The generally preferred method of assessment in clinical practice is an unstructured clinical interview (Westen, 1997), whereas the preferred method within clinical research is the semistructured interview (Rogers, 1995; Zimmerman, 1994). Unstructured clinical interviews can be highly problematic because they are often idiosyncratic, less reliable, and more susceptible than are semistructured interviews to attributional errors, halo effects, and false assumptions, including gender biases (Garb, 1997; Widiger, 1998). Convergent validity data have been consistently weakest when one of the measures was an unstructured clinical interview (Widiger, 2002). A variety of studies have indicated that clinicians relying upon unstructured clinical interviews routinely fail to assess for the presence of the specified diagnostic criteria. One of the more compelling demonstrations of this failure was provided by Morey and Ochoa (1989). Morey and Ochoa provided 291 clinicians with the 166 *DSM-III* (APA, 1980) personality disorder diagnostic criteria and asked them to indicate, for one of their patients, which *DSM-III* personality disorder(s) were present and which of the 166 *DSM-III* personality disorder diagnostic criteria were present. Kappa for the agreement between their diagnoses and the diagnoses that would be given based upon their own assessment of the diagnostic criteria was poor, ranging from .11 (schizoid) to .58 (borderline), with a median kappa of only .25. These findings were subsequently replicated by Blashfield and Herkov (1996). "It appears that the actual diagnoses of clinicians do not adhere closely to the diagnoses suggested by the [diagnostic] criteria" (Blashfield & Herkov, 1996, p. 226).

Patients often meet the *DSM-IV* diagnostic criteria for more than one personality disorder, yet clinicians typically provide only one diagnosis to each patient (Gunderson, 1992). Clinicians tend to diagnose personality disorders hierarchically. After a patient is identified as having a particular personality disorder (e.g., borderline), clinicians often fail to assess whether additional personality traits are present (Herkov & Blashfield, 1995). Adler, Drake, and Teague (1990) provided 46 clinicians with case histories of a patient that met the *DSM-III* criteria for four personality disorders (i.e., histrionic, narcissistic, borderline, and dependent). "Despite the directive to consider each category separately . . . most clinicians assigned just one [personality disorder] diagnosis" (Adler et al., 1990, p. 127). Sixty-five percent of the clinicians provided only one diagnosis, 28% provided two, and none

provided all four. Comorbidity among mental disorders is a pervasive phenomenon that can have substantial significance and importance to clinical treatment and outcome research (Clark, Watson, & Reynolds, 1995; Sher & Trull, 1996; Widiger & Clark, 2000), yet comorbidity may be grossly underrecognized in general clinical practice. Zimmerman and Mattia (1999b) compared the Axis I clinical diagnoses provided for 500 patients who were assessed with unstructured clinical interviews with the diagnoses provided by a semistructured interview. More than 90% of the patients receiving the unstructured clinical interview were provided with only one Axis I diagnosis, whereas more than a third of the patients assessed with the semistructured interview were discovered to have met the diagnostic criteria for at least two additional Axis I disorders. Zimmerman and Mattia (1999a) also reported that clinicians diagnosed less than 1% of the patients with borderline personality disorder, whereas 14% were diagnosed with this disorder when a semistructured interview was used. Zimmerman and Mattia (1999a) then provided the clinicians with the additional information obtained by the more systematic semistructured interview. "Providing the results of [the] semistructured interview to clinicians prompts them to diagnose borderline personality disorder much more frequently" (Zimmerman & Mattia, 1999a, p. 1570). The rate of diagnosis increased from .4% to 9.2%.

The reluctance to use semistructured interviews in general clinical practice is understandable because they are constraining, may at times be impractical, and can appear to be superficial (Westen, 1997). However, they are particularly advisable when questions regarding the reliability or validity of an assessment are likely to be raised (Widiger, 2002). Semistructured interviews are helpful in ensuring that the interview will be systematic, comprehensive, replicable, and objective (Widiger & Coker, 2002). Diagnoses derived from the administration of a semistructured interview have often been used as the standard by which the validity of other measures are evaluated. Minimally, semistructured interviews are useful in providing to the clinician a set of useful suggestions for a variety of possible inquiries to use for the assessment of each diagnostic criterion.

Several semistructured interviews for the assessment of *DSM-IV* personality disorders are available (Clark & Harrison, 2001; Kaye & Shea, 2000; Widiger, 2002; Widiger & Coker, 2002; Zimmerman, 1994). Regrettably, there have been only a few studies concerned with their convergent validity. This limited research has suggested questionable validity with respect to agreement for the presence of categorical diagnoses but acceptable to good convergent validity with respect to the assessment of the extent to which respective personality disorder symptomatology are present (e.g., Skodol, Oldham, Rosnick, Kellman, & Hyler, 1991).

A potential disadvantage of self-report inventories and semistructured interviews is their emphasis on self-report (Bornstein, 1995; Westen, 1997). Personality disorders are characterized in part by distortions in self-image and self-presentation, which may not be assessed adequately simply by asking respondents if they have each diagnostic criterion. However, it is important to emphasize that neither self-report inventories nor semistructured interviews rely upon accurate self-report. Semistructured interviews include many open-ended questions, indirect inquiries, and observations of the respondents' manner of relating to the interviewer. Interviewers administering a semistructured interview do not simply record respondents' answers to queries, but are instead using their clinical expertise to rate each diagnostic criterion based in part on direct, indirect, and open-ended questions that have been found by experienced investigators to be effective for assessing whether a particular diagnostic criterion is present.

Projective tests are less dependent on the ability or willingness of a person to provide an accurate self-description (Bornstein, 1995), but there is currently only limited empirical support for the use of projective techniques for the assessment of the *DSM-IV* personality disorders. Supportive research has been reported for the assessment of histrionic, narcissistic, antisocial, and borderline personality traits (e.g., Blais, Hilsenroth, & Fowler, 1998; Hilsenroth, Handler, & Blais, 1996), but no projective test currently provides a systematic or comprehensive assessment of the *DSM-IV* personality disorders. There is also disagreement concerning the extent of the empirical support for projective tests (Acklin, 1999; Archer, 1999; Garb, 1999; Weiner, 1999; Wood & Lilienfeld, 1999).

An underutilized method of personality disorder assessment is informant report (Clark, Livesley, & Morey, 1997). Informants (e.g., family members, close friends) can provide an historical perspective on an individual's personality functioning and thus may lack the significant personality or Axis I pathology that can complicate a patient's self-description. Self- and informant assessments of personality disorder symptomatology often fail to agree, and it is not yet certain which perspective should be considered to be more valid (Bernstein et al., 1997; Riso, Klein, Anderson, Ouimette, & Lizardi, 1994; Widiger, 2002; Zimmerman, 1994). Relatives and close friends will not know everything about a person that would be necessary to provide a valid description, they may have their own axes to grind, and they may have false assumptions or expectations concerning the identified target. Nevertheless, informant reports of personality disorder features remains a promising method that deserves more research attention. Oltmanns and

his colleagues have been conducting a particularly creative and intriguing investigation of the agreement and disagreement between self-descriptions and peer nominations of air force recruits (Oltmanns, Turkheimer, & Strauss, 1998).

## THE *DSM-IV* PERSONALITY DISORDERS

Up to this point, we have reviewed the definition of personality disorder, its clinical importance, and its assessment. In the following sections we describe briefly each of the 10 personality disorders included in *DSM-IV*.

### Paranoid Personality Disorder

#### Description

Paranoid personality disorder (PPD) is characterized by an all-pervasive distrust and suspiciousness of others (Miller, Useda, Trull, Burr, & Minks-Brown, 2001). To receive a *DSM-IV* PPD diagnosis, one must exhibit at least four of seven diagnostic criteria that are—for the most part—indicators of a suspicious interpersonal style and a tendency to read malevolent intentions into what are truly innocuous or neutral interactions or events (APA, 1994, 2000). As one might guess, individuals with PPD are rather difficult to get along with, and they are likely to be argumentative, hostile, and overly sarcastic. They may blame others for their own difficulties and misfortunes and are unlikely to be able to work collaboratively or closely with others. They might maintain a steady employment but will often be difficult coworkers because they tend to be rigid, controlling, critical, blaming, and prejudicial. They might become involved in lengthy, acrimonious, and litigious disputes that are difficult if not impossible to resolve.

#### Epidemiology

*DSM-IV* estimates that only 0.5–2.5% of the general population qualify for a PPD diagnosis, and epidemiological studies of community samples (see Table 6.2) support this estimate. Although PPD may be more prevalent in clinical samples, it is unlikely that PPD will be the patient's presenting problem. The available studies indicate that more men than women are diagnosed with PPD (Corbitt & Widiger, 1995; Miller et al., 2001). There are no strong empirical data to suggest that members of certain racial or ethnic groups are more likely to receive a PPD diagnosis. In fact, *DSM-IV* cautions against overinterpreting anger and frustration in response to perceived neglect or guardedness sometimes exhibited by individuals from other cultures or backgrounds.

## Etiology

There is little research to indicate a direct inheritance of PPD (McGuffin & Thapar, 1992; Nigg & Goldsmith, 1994). There has been research to indicate a genetic contribution to the development of paranoid personality traits, if these traits are conceptualized as being on a continuum with general personality functioning (Jang, McCrae, Angleitner, Reimann, & Livesley, 1998; Livesley, Jang, & Vernon, 1998; Nigg & Goldsmith, 1994). There is some support for a genetic relationship of PPD with schizophrenia and delusional disorder (persecutory type), but these findings have not always been replicated and the positive results may have been due in part to the overlap of PPD with the schizotypal personality disorder (Miller et al., 2001; Siever, 1992).

There has been speculation on the neurophysiology that might underlie the personality disorders within the odd-eccentric cluster (Cloninger, 1998; Siever & Davis, 1991) but research has been confined largely to the schizotypal personality disorder. There has been little consideration given to the neurophysiological concomitants of nonpsychotic paranoid personality traits.

Attention has been given to cognitive and interpersonal models for the development of paranoid personality traits. Paranoid beliefs may have a self-perpetuating tendency due to the focus on signs of and evidence for malicious intentions (Beck et al., 1990). From this perspective, the pathology of PPD would be inherent to the irrationality of the belief systems and would be sustained by biased information processing. There might also be an underlying motivation or need to perceive threats in others and to externalize blame that help to sustain the accusations and distortions (Stone, 1993).

There are few systematic studies on psychosocial contributions to the development of PPD. There are retrospective data indicating that persons with this personality disorder considered their parents to be excessively critical, rejecting, withholding, and at times even abusive (e.g., Modestin, Oberson, & Erni, 1998; Norden, Klein, Donaldson, Pepper, & Klein, 1995); however, the retrospective nature of these studies is problematic (paranoid persons might not be providing accurate descriptions of prior relationships) and the childhood experiences that have been identified are not specific to this personality disorder (Miller et al., 2001). There are presently no prospective longitudinal studies that have explored the development of paranoid personality traits.

Premorbid traits of PPD that might be evident prior to adolescence include isolation, hypersensitivity, hypervigilance, social anxiety, peculiar thoughts, and idiosyncratic fantasies (APA, 1994, 2000). As children, they may appear odd and peculiar to their peers and may not have achieved to

their capacity in school. Mistrust and suspicion is often evident in members of minority groups, immigrants, refugees, and other groups for whom such distrust is often a realistic and appropriate response to their social environment. It is conceivable that a comparably sustained experience through childhood and adolescence could contribute to the development of excessive paranoid beliefs that are eventually applied inflexibly and inappropriately to a wide variety of persons, but it can be very difficult to determine what is excessive or unrealistic suspicion and mistrust within a member of an oppressed minority (Alarcon & Foulks, 1996; Whaley, 1997). Paranoid suspiciousness could in fact be more closely associated with prejudicial attitudes, wherein a particular group in society becomes the inappropriate target of one's anger, blame, and resentment.

## Schizoid Personality Disorder

### Description

Schizoid personality disorder (SZPD) is characterized by social detachment and isolation as well as by restricted emotional experience and expression (APA, 2000; Miller et al., 2001). Individuals with this personality disorder not only choose to be by themselves, but they also have little interest in establishing or maintaining interpersonal relationships. In addition, SZPD individuals show little emotional expression and may not even appear to experience much pleasure, joy, or sadness. They have few friendships. Those that do occur are likely to have been initiated by the other person. They will have had few sexual relationships and may never marry. Relationships will fail to the extent to which the other person desires or needs emotional support, warmth, and intimacy. Persons with SZPD may do well within an occupation as long as substantial social interaction is not required. They would prefer to work in isolation. They may eventually find employment and a relationship that is relatively comfortable or tolerable to them, but they could also drift from one job to another and remain isolated throughout much of their lives. If they do eventually become parents, they have considerable difficulty providing warmth and emotional support and may appear neglectful, detached, and disinterested.

### Epidemiology

SZPD, as diagnosed by *DSM-IV,* does appear to be relatively uncommon in both clinical and nonclinical settings. Estimates of this disorder in the general population have been less than 1% (see Table 6.2). Over the years, the definition of SZPD has become more restricted, and many of the features once associated with this disorder prior to *DSM-III* (APA, 1980) are now part of the criterion sets of other disorders (e.g., avoidant and schizotypal; Miller et al., 2001). *DSM-IV* states that SZPD is diagnosed more frequently in men than in women; however, the empirical findings are mixed (Corbitt & Widiger, 1995). It is also important to caution against over-diagnosing SZPD in individuals from other cultures or minority ethnic backgrounds. Such individuals may appear somewhat introverted or isolated, as well as emotionally aloof, simply because they are being interviewed or observed by someone from another culture or because their culture is not, on average, as affiliative or emotionally expressive as the majority cultures in the United States.

*Etiology*

There is little research to indicate a direct inheritance of SZPD (McGuffin & Thapar, 1992; Nigg & Goldsmith, 1994). A substantial amount of research has supported the heritability for the general personality dimension of introversion (Jang & Vernon, 2001; Plomin & Caspi, 1999), and SZPD does appear to be essentially equivalent to the social withdrawal and anhedonia evident within extreme introversion (Trull, 1992; Trull et al., 1998). A genetic association with schizophrenia has at times been reported, but this association might be explained by the overlap of SZPD with schizotypal personality traits (Fulton & Winokur, 1993; Miller et al., 2001; Siever, 1992).

Psychosocial models for the etiology of SZPD are lacking. It is possible that a sustained history of isolation during infancy and childhood, with an encouragement or modeling by parental figures of interpersonal withdrawal, social indifference, and emotional detachment could contribute to the development of schizoid personality traits, but there is no systematic research to support this hypothesis. Persons with SZPD are likely to have been socially isolated and withdrawn as children. They may not have been accepted well by their peers and may have even been the brunt of some ostracism (APA, 1994, 2000). However, systematic research on the childhood development of SZPD is lacking (Bernstein & Travaglini, 1999; Miller et al., 2001). The central pathology of SZPD might be anhedonic deficits, or an excessively low ability to experience positive affectivity (Rothbart & Ahadi, 1994; Siever, 1992). A fundamental distinction of schizophrenic symptomatology is between positive and negative symptoms. Positive symptoms include hallucinations, delusions, inappropriate affect, and loose associations; negative symptoms include flattened affect, alogia, and avolition. SZPD may represent subthreshold negative symptoms, comparable to the subthreshold positive symptoms (cognitive-perceptual aberrations) that predominate schizotypal PD.

## Schizotypal Personality Disorder

### Description

Schizotypal personality disorder (STPD) is characterized by a pervasive pattern of interpersonal deficits, cognitive and perceptual aberrations, and behavioral eccentricities (APA, 2000; Miller et al., 2001). Persons with STPD exhibit excessive social anxiety that is related to paranoid fears. They also appear odd, eccentric, or peculiar in their behavior or appearance, display inappropriate or constricted affect, and have few (if any) friends or confidants outside of their immediate family. Also striking are the STPD individual's unusual ideas, beliefs, and communication. Those with this personality disorder tend to misinterpret or overpersonalize events, to hold unusual ideas that influence behavior (e.g., telepathy, clairvoyance), and to have difficulty being understood by others. They may drift toward esoteric, fringe groups that support their magical thinking and aberrant beliefs. These activities can provide structure for some persons with STPD, but they can also contribute to a further loosening and deterioration if there is an encouragement of psychotic-like or dissociative experiences.

Persons with STPD are most likely to seek treatment for anxiety or mood disorders rather than seek treatment for the symptoms specific to STPD. Individuals with STPD may experience transient psychotic episodes especially in response to stress. However, these episodes are relatively brief (i.e., lasting a few minutes to a few hours) and are typically of insufficient duration to warrant an Axis I psychotic diagnosis. Only a small proportion of persons with STPD develop schizophrenia, but many may eventually develop a major depression. The symptomatology of STPD does not appear to remit with age (Siever, 1992). The course appears to be relatively stable, with some proportion of schizotypal persons remaining marginally employed, withdrawn, and transient though much of their lives.

### Epidemiology

Although *DSM-IV* reports that STPD may occur in up to 3% of the population, most estimates using structured diagnostic interviews to assess STPD are lower and closer to 1% (see Table 6.2). STPD appears to be slightly more common in men. Little is known about the prevalence of this disorder in nonwestern cultures.

### Etiology

There is empirical support for a genetic association of STPD with schizophrenia (McGuffin & Thapar, 1992; Nigg & Goldsmith, 1994), which is consistent with the fact that the diagnostic criteria for STPD were obtained from studies of the biological relatives of persons with schizophrenia (Miller et al., 2001). A predominant model for the psychopathology of STPD is deficits or defects in the attention and selection processes that organize a person's cognitive-perceptual evaluation of and relatedness to his or her environment (Siever & Davis, 1991). These deficits may lead to discomfort within social situations, misperceptions and suspicions, and to a coping strategy of social isolation. Correlates of central nervous system dysfunction seen in persons with schizoprenia have been observed in laboratory tests of persons with STPD, including performance on tests of visual and auditory attention (e.g., backward masking and sensory gating tests) and smooth pursuit eye movement that might be associated with dysregulation along dopaminergic pathways (Siever, 1992). As children, persons with STPD are likely to have been notably isolated. They may have appeared peculiar and odd to their peers, and may have been teased or ostracized. Achievement in school was likely to have been impaired, and they may have been heavily involved in esoteric fantasies and peculiar games—particularly those that do not involve peers (APA, 1994, 2000). Empirical support for the childhood development of STPD, however, is limited.

## Antisocial Personality Disorder

### Description

Antisocial personality disorder (ASPD) is characterized by a pattern of behavior that reflects an extreme disregard for and violation of the rights of others. The *DSM-IV* diagnostic criteria for ASPD include deceitfulness, impulsivity, irritability-aggressiveness, acts of criminality, and irresponsibility (APA, 2000). Persons with ASPD often commit reckless acts that neglect to consider the safety of others, and they lack remorse for the harm they have inflicted. Additional features of ASPD not included within the *DSM-IV* diagnostic criteria include arrogance, superficial charm, exploitativeness, and a lack of empathy (Hare, 1991; Sutker & Allain, 2001). Persons with ASPD are unlikely to maintain steady employment. Some persons with ASPD can obtain professional and criminal success for periods of time, as long as their exploitations, violations, deceptions, and manipulations are not discovered. Their success, however, may at some point unravel, due in part to their impulsivity, negligence, and lack of foresight. A similar pattern may occur within their social and sexual relationships. They may at first appear to be quite successful socially, as they can be charming, fun, and engaging, but many of their relationships will eventually fail as a result of their lack of empathy, fidelity, and responsibility, as well as episodes of abuse, exploitation, and angry hostility.

ASPD is evident in childhood in the form of a conduct disorder (e.g., aggression toward persons and animals, destruction of property, deceitfulness or theft, and serious violations of laws and rules). Evidence of conduct disorder before the age of 15 is in fact required for the *DSM-IV* diagnosis of ASPD (APA, 2000). However, it is important to emphasize that not all children with conduct disorder will meet the criteria for ASPD as an adult. A continuation into adulthood is more likely to occur if multiple delinquent behaviors are evident before the age of 10 (Hinshaw, 1994).

### Epidemiology

It is estimated that the prevalence rate for ASPD is about 3% in men and about 1% in women (L. N. Robins et al., 1991). High rates of this personality disorder are seen in substance abuse treatment settings and in forensic settings. Up to 50% of males within prison settings meet the *DSM-IV* criteria for ASPD, but this could be due in part to a lack of adequate specificity of the diagnostic criteria within prison settings (Hare, 1991). Although ASPD is more common among those from lower socioeconomic classes and those in urban settings, the direction of the causality for this relationship is unclear. This correlation may reflect that persons with ASPD migrate to urban settings and become more socially or economically impoverished or that economic impoverishment contributes to the development of antisocial traits.

### Etiology

There is considerable support from twin, family, and adoption studies for a genetic contribution to the etiology of the criminal, delinquent tendencies of persons with ASPD (McGuffin & Thapar, 1992; Nigg & Goldsmith, 1994; Stoff et al., 1997; Sutker & Allain, 2001). The genetic disposition can be more evident in females with ASPD due in part to a greater social pressure on females against the development of aggressive, exploitative, and criminal behavior.

Abnormally low levels of anxiousness, constraint, and arousal have been implicated in the development of ASPD. Research has suggested that individuals with ASPD demonstrate a hyperreactive electrodermal response to stress that is associated with a commonly studied domain of normal personality functioning—neuroticism or negative affectivity (Patrick, 1994). These findings are consistent with developmental research concerned with the interaction of parenting and temperament (e.g., low anxiousness and low inhibition) on the development of a moral conscience (Kochanska, 1991). From this perspective, the pathology of psychopathy might not be a deficit that is qualitatively distinct from general personality functioning (Widiger & Lynam, 1998). "The observed absence of startle potentiation in psychopaths . . . may reflect a temperamental deficit in the capacity for negative affect" (Patrick, 1994, p. 425).

Activities that the average person would find stimulating might be found by psychopathic persons to be dull, impelling them perhaps to engage in risky, reckless, prohibited, and impulsive activities. Abnormally low levels of arousal would also minimize feelings of anxiety, guilt, or remorse and help resist aversive conditioning. The development of normal levels of guilt, conscience, and shame may require a degree of distress-proneness (neuroticism or negative affectivity) and attentional self-regulation (constraint). Normal levels of anxiousness promote the internalization of conscience (the introjection of the family's moral values) by associating distress and anxiety with wrongdoing, and the temperament of self-regulation helps modulate impulses into a socially acceptable manner (Kochanska, 1991).

There are also substantial data to support the contribution of family, peer, and other environmental factors, although no single environmental factor appears to be specific to its development (Stoff et al., 1997; Sutker & Allain, 2001). Modeling of exploitative, abusive, and aggressive behavior by parental figures and peers; excessively harsh, lenient, or erratic discipline; and a tough, harsh environment in which feelings of empathy and warmth are discouraged (if not punished) and tough-mindedness, aggressiveness, and exploitation are encouraged (if not rewarded) have all been associated with the development of ASPD. For example, ASPD in some cases could be the result of an interaction of early experiences of physical or sexual abuse, exposure to aggressive parental models, and erratic discipline that develop a view of the world as a hostile environment, which is further affirmed over time through selective attention on cues for antagonism, encouragement and modeling of aggression by peers, and the immediate benefits that result from aggressive behavior (Dodge & Schwartz, 1997; Farrington, 1997).

## Borderline Personality Disorder

### Description

Borderline personality disorder (BPD) is characterized by a pattern of impulsivity and instability in affect, interpersonal relationships, and self-image. According to *DSM-IV,* at least five of nine criteria must be present for a BPD diagnosis (APA, 2000). Table 6.3 provides these diagnostic criteria for BPD. As can be seen from Table 6.3, those diagnosed with BPD frequently experience strong, intense negative emotions and are prone to suicidal threats, gestures, or attempts. They are unsure of their self-image as well as their own views of

**TABLE 6.3   Diagnostic Criteria for Borderline Personality Disorder**

A pervasive pattern of instability of interpersonal relationships, self-image, and affects, and marked impulsivity beginning by early adulthood and present in a variety of contexts, as indicated by five (or more) of the following:

1. Frantic efforts to avoid real or imagined abandonment. *Note:* Do not include suicidal or self-mutilating behavior covered in Criterion 5.

2. A pattern of unstable and intense interpersonal relationships characterized by alternating between extremes of idealization and devaluation.

3. Identity disturbance: markedly and persistently unstable self-image or sense of self.

4. Impulsivity in at least two areas that are potentially self-damaging (e.g., spending, sex, substance abuse, reckless driving, binge eating). *Note:* Do not include suicidal or self-mutilating behavior covered in Criterion 5.

5. Recurrent suicidal behavior, gestures, threats, or self-mutilating behavior.

6. Affective instability due to a marked reactivity of mood (e.g., intense episodic dysphoria, irritability, or anxiety usually lasting a few hours and only rarely more than a few days).

7. Chronic feelings of emptiness.

8. Inappropriate, intense anger or difficulty controlling anger (e.g., frequent displays of temper, constant anger, recurrent physical fights).

9. Transient, stress-related paranoid ideation or severe dissociative symptoms.

*Note.* Adapted from American Psychiatric Association (2000, p. 710).

other people. They harbor intense abandonment fears and feelings of emptiness. Stressful situations may invoke transient paranoid ideation or dissociation. Associated features include a propensity for engaging in self-defeating behavior (e.g., making a bad decision that destroys a good relationship), high rates of mood or substance use disorders, and premature death from suicide. Approximately 3–10% will have committed suicide by the age of 30 (Gunderson, 2001).

### Epidemiology

It is estimated that approximately 2% of the general population meets diagnostic criteria for BPD. BPD is the most frequently diagnosed personality disorder in both inpatient and outpatient settings (Adams, Bernat, & Luscher, 2001; Gunderson, 2001). It is believed that more women than men meet the criteria for BPD, but this belief is based primarily on clinical studies. It is important to distinguish BPD symptoms, which are chronic and pervasive, from borderline behaviors that may be exhibited for short periods of time in adolescence. Studies that have followed over time children and adolescents who initially received a BPD diagnosis find that only a small percentage still have a BPD diagnosis years later. This finding raises the possibility that BPD may be overdiagnosed in children and adolescents.

*Etiology*

There are studies to suggest a genetic disposition specific to BPD, but research has also suggested an association with mood and impulse disorders (McGuffin & Thapar, 1992; Nigg & Goldsmith, 1994). There is also empirical support for a childhood history of physical abuse, sexual abuse, or both, as well as parental conflict, loss, and neglect (Gunderson, 2001; Johnson et al., 1999; Silk, Lee, Hill, & Lohr, 1995; Zanarini, 2000). It appears that past traumatic events are important in many if not most cases of BPD, contributing to the development of malevolent perceptions of others (Ornduff, 2000) and a comorbidity with posttraumatic stress, mood, and dissociative disorders. BPD may involve the interaction of a genetic disposition for lack of mood and impulse control with an evolving series of intense and unstable relationships (Bartholomew, Kwong, & Hart, 2001; Paris, 2001). Linehan (1993) hypothesizes that persons with a borderline personality disorder failed to learn important and useful skills for regulating emotional arousal and tolerating emotional distress; they learned instead that drug abuse, promiscuity, and self-injurious behavior produce temporary relief from stress.

There are numerous theories regarding the pathogenic mechanisms of BPD; most concern expectations of abandonment, separation, exploitative abuse, or any combination of these (Gunderson, 2001). Persons with BPD have usually had quite intense, disturbed, or abusive relationships with the significant persons of their lives, including their parents. They continue to expect and may even recreate unstable and intense relationships throughout their adult lives. Persons with BPD may require numerous hospitalizations due to their lack of affect and impulse control, psychotic-like and dissociative symptomatology, and risk of suicide (Stone, 2001). Minor problems quickly become crises as the intensity of affect and impulsivity contribute to disastrous life decisions. They are at a high risk for developing depressive, substance-related, bulimic, and posttraumatic stress disorders (Adams et al., 2001). The potential for suicide is increased with a comorbid mood and substance-related disorder.

**Histrionic Personality Disorder**

*Description*

Histrionic personality disorder (HPD) is characterized by pervasive and excessive emotionality and attention seeking (Widiger & Bornstein, 2001). The *DSM-IV* criteria for HPD include actions and behaviors that serve to place one in the center of attention, behavior that is provocative or inappropriately intimate, fleeting and superficial emotional expression, and suggestibility (APA, 2000). Persons with HPD tend to experience difficulty both in romantic relationships and in friendships. They have trouble balancing their strong needs for attention and intimacy with the reality of the situation. It is often difficult for those with HPD to delay gratification, and they are prone to act impulsively. Persons with this disorder are said to have a pathologic need to be loved, desired, and involved with others on an intimate basis, and they use a variety of means to get this involvement (Horowitz, 1991). They use their physical appearance to draw attention to themselves, they are melodramatically emotional, and they are inappropriately seductive. They may even perceive a relationship as being more intimate than is really the case, in part because of their need for romantic fantasy.

*Epidemiology*

As indicated in Table 6.2, about 2–3% of the general population is believed to meet criteria for an HPD diagnosis. HPD is more prevalent among women, but it is important to keep cultural, gender, and age norms in mind when judging whether a given behavioral feature is indicative of HPD. The diagnostic criteria for HPD resemble closely stereotypic femininity, and clinicians at times overdiagnose HPD in women (Widiger, 1998). Cultural groups also differ in their degrees of emotional expression. It is only when the degree of emotional expression is excessive (within a cultural group) and causes distress or impairment that it should be considered symptomatic of HPD. HPD is likely to be diagnosed in some cultural groups more than in others. For example, the disorder might be seen less frequently in Asian cultures, in which overt sexual seductiveness is less frequent (Johnson, 1993) and more frequently within Hispanic and Latin American cultures, in which more overt and uninhibited sexuality is evident (Padilla, 1995). It can be difficult to determine when or how adjustments to the diagnostic criteria should be made within these different cultural contexts because the *DSM-IV* criteria may also reflect biases or assumptions regarding seductiveness that are not shared within other societies (Alarcon, 1996; Rogler, 1996).

*Etiology*

There has been little research on the etiology of HPD. There is some limited support for the heritability of histrionic personality traits, but there has not yet been a familial aggregation, twin, or adoption study of this disorder (Jang & Vernon, 2001; McGuffin & Thapar, 1992; Nigg & Goldsmith, 1994). There are data to suggest that HPD is a constellation of maladaptive variants of common personality traits within the broad domains of neuroticism and extraversion (Trull, 1992;

Trull et al., 1998). For example, normal extraversion includes the dispositions to be outgoing, talkative, and affectionate; to be convivial, to have many friends, and to seek social contact; to be energetic, fast-paced, and vigorous; to be flashy, seek stimulation, and take risks; and to be high-spirited (Costa & McCrae, 1992). Traits of extraversion are for the most part desirable and adaptive, but persons who are at the most extreme variants of these traits are likely to be histrionic and experience a number of maladaptive consequences (Trull, 1992). To the extent that HPD does indeed include maladaptively extreme variants of the personality traits of extraversion, there would be support for its heritability (Jang et al., 1998; Nigg & Goldsmith, 1994).

A variety of parent-child relationships may contribute to the development of HPD (Bornstein, 1999). Histrionic needs may develop in part through an overly eroticized parent-child relationship. For example, a father might repeatedly indicate through a variety of verbal and nonverbal communications that his love and attention for a daughter are largely contingent upon her being attractive, desirable, and provocative to him. Her sense of self-worth and meaning might be dependent in large part on how he relates to her, and she might then value herself primarily in terms of how she is valued by men (Millon et al., 1996; Stone, 1993). Empirical support for this developmental model of HPD, however, is lacking.

Neurochemical models of the disorder have emphasized a hyperresponsiveness of the noradrenergic system. This dysregulation in catecholamine functioning may contribute to a pronounced emotional reactivity to signs of rejection (Klein, 1999). There may be a naturally occurring neurochemical mechanism for the regulation of mood in response to signs of social applause and rejection. This regulatory mechanism would be helpful sociobiologically in making a person appropriately responsive to cues of social interest, but excessive responsivity of the noradrenergic system might also result in oversensitivity to attention and rejection.

## Narcissistic Personality Disorder

### Description

Narcissistic personality disorder (NPD) is characterized by grandiosity, a need for admiration, and a lack of empathy for others (APA, 2000; Widiger & Bornstein, 2001). Persons with NPD tend to have an exaggerated sense of self-importance and to believe that they are so unique that they can only be understood by similarly special people. These self-views lead to interpersonal behaviors that prove to be problematic—arrogance, exploitativeness, and a sense of

entitlement. Despite the veneer of high self-confidence and self-esteem, those with NPD are quite vulnerable to real or perceived threats to their status. Therefore, it is not uncommon to see rage or counterattacks. As might be expected, NPD individuals tend to have serial friendships, which end when others discontinue their willingness to express admiration or envy. NPD individuals' intolerance of criticism or perceived defeat may keep them from high levels of achievement.

### Epidemiology

According to estimates (see Table 6.2), NPD seems relatively rare in the general population (i.e., less than 1%). NPD is also among the least frequently diagnosed personality disorders within clinical settings (Widiger & Bornstein, 2001). This personality disorder does appear to be more prevalent among men, but systematic epidemiological studies have not been conducted. It is important not to mistake an idealism that is characteristic of adolescents and young adults (e.g., stating a strong belief that one will become a surgeon) with the traits and behaviors of NPD. It is only when such beliefs are excessive (i.e., extremely unrealistic) and cause significant distress or impairment that we see them as indicative of NPD.

Cross-cultural studies of narcissism and narcissistic personality disorder would be of interest. NPD is the only *DSM-IV* personality disorder that is not given official recognition within the WHO's (1992) international nomenclature. Some theorists have in fact suggested that NPD is distinctly cultural, arguing that pathological narcissism is the manifestation of a modern, Western society that has become overly self-centered and materialistic, coupled with a decreasing importance of familial (interpersonal) bonds (Cooper & Ronningstam, 1992).

### Etiology

There has not yet been a familial aggregation, twin, or adoption study of NPD (McGuffin & Thapar, 1992). The predominant models for the etiology of narcissism have been largely social learning or psychodynamic. One model proposes that narcissism develops through an excessive idealization by parental figures, which is then incorporated by the child into his or her self-image (Millon et al., 1996). Narcissism may also develop through unempathic, neglectful, inconsistent, or even devaluing parental figures who have failed to adequately mirror a child's natural need for idealization (Cooper & Ronningstam, 1992). The child may find that the attention, interest, and perceived love of a parent are contingent largely on achievements or successes. They may fail to perceive the parents as valuing or loving them for their own sake but may instead recognize that the love and attention are largely conditional on successful accomplishments (Widiger & Bornstein, 2001). They might then develop the belief that their own feelings of self-worth are dependent upon a continued recognition of their achievements and successes by others. Conflicts and deficits with respect to self-esteem do appear to be central to the pathology of the disorder (Stone, 1993). Narcissistic persons continually seek and obtain signs and symbols of recognition to compensate for conscious or perhaps even unconscious feelings of inadequacy. Empirical support for the validity of hypotheses concerning narcissistic pathology are being provided by social-psychological (as well as clinical) research. Rhodewalt, Madrian, and Cheney (1998), for example, indicated how narcissism is more highly correlated with instability in self-esteem than with simply a consistently high self-confidence. Narcissism is perhaps a maladaptive process of regulating or protecting a fragile self-esteem in part through gaining the approval and admiration of others (Raskin, Novacek, & Hogan, 1991). Baumeister and his colleagues have been exploring the contribution of narcissistic conflicts to the occurrence of aggressive, violent behavior (Baumeister, Smart, & Boden, 1996; Bushman & Baumeister, 1998). They demonstrated empirically, for example, that neither low nor high self-esteem was predictive of reacting aggressively to threat. It was instead a combination of vulnerable self-esteem and injurious insult.

## Avoidant Personality Disorder

### Description

Avoidant personality disorder (AVPD) is characterized by a pervasive pattern of timidity, inhibition, feelings of inadequacy, and social hypersensitivity (APA, 2000; Bernstein & Travaglini, 1999). Those with AVPD for the most part avoid situations (occupational or otherwise) that require significant interpersonal contact. Therefore, they are seen as shy or loners. This interpersonal stance seems driven by the belief that they are inept, unappealing, or inferior. AVPD individuals are afraid of being embarrassed or rejected by others. They only become involved with others in situations in which they feel certain they will be accepted or liked. AVPD individuals want close relationships, but their fears keep them from initiating and maintaining contacts. Associated features of AVPD include hypervigilance (especially in social situations), low self-esteem, and a proneness both to anxiety disorders and to mood disorders.

Occupational success may not be significantly impaired as long as there is little demand for public performance.

Through a job or career, persons with AVPD may in fact find considerable gratification and esteem that they are unable to find within their relationships. The job can serve as a distraction from intense feelings of loneliness. Their avoidance of social situations impairs their ability to develop adequate social skills, and their impaired social skills then further handicap their efforts to develop relationships. However, they may eventually develop an intimate relationship to which they often cling dependently. Persons with AVPD are prone to mood and anxiety disorders—particularly depression and social phobia.

### Epidemiology

Timidity, shyness, social insecurity, and other features of AVPD are not uncommon problems, and AVPD is one of the more prevalent personality disorders within clinical settings (Mattia & Zimmerman, 2001). However, AVPD may be diagnosed in only 1% of the general population (see Table 6.2). It appears to occur equally among males and females, with some studies reporting more males and others reporting more females.

### Etiology

AVPD appears to be an extreme variant of the general personality traits of introversion and neuroticism (Trull, 1992; Trull et al., 1998), both of which have substantial heritability (Jang & Vernon, 2001; Plomin & Caspi, 1999). Most children and adolescents have many experiences of interpersonal embarrassment, rejection, or humiliation, but these experiences are particularly devastating to the person who is already lacking in self-confidence and is temperamentally anxious and introverted (Rothbart & Ahadi, 1994). Persons with AVPD will have been shy, timid, and anxious as children. Many will have been diagnosed with a social phobia. Adolescence will have been a particularly difficult developmental period, due to the importance at this time of attractiveness, dating, and popularity.

AVPD may involve elevated peripheral sympathetic activity and adrenocortical responsiveness, resulting in excessive autonomic arousal, fearfulness, and inhibition. Just as ASPD may involve deficits in the functioning of a behavioral inhibition system, AVPD may involve excessive functioning of this same system. The pathology of AVPD, however, may also be more psychological than neurochemical; the timidity, shyness, and insecurity may be a natural result of a cumulative history of denigrating, embarrassing, and devaluing experiences. Underlying AVPD may be excessive self-consciousness, feelings of inadequacy or inferiority, and irrational cognitive schemas that perpetuate introverted, avoidant behavior (Beck et al., 1990).

## Dependent Personality Disorder

### Description

Dependent personality disorder (DPD) is characterized by a pervasive, excessive need to be cared for, leading to submissiveness, clinging behavior, and fears of separation (APA, 2000; Widiger & Bornstein, 2001). DPD individuals tend to give their lives over to others—they ask for advice and guidance about even the smallest of decisions, exude helplessness, and readily abdicate responsibility for most areas of their lives. They are so fearful that others may reject or leave them that they do not express disagreements and may even volunteer to do unpleasant, demeaning tasks in order to gain nurturance and approval. As might be expected, DPD individuals are prone to low self-esteem, self-doubt, and self-derogation, leading to mood and anxiety disorders. Their neediness and desperation often prevents them from carefully selecting a person who will in fact be protective and supportive. They often choose their partners indiscriminately and become quickly attached to persons who are unreliable, unempathic, and even exploitative or abusive. They might feel that either they deserve an inadequate partner or may even select an inadequate partner to try to work through or resolve their long-standing interpersonal conflicts and feelings of inadequacy (Stone, 1993).

### Epidemiology

DPD appears to be among the more prevalent of the personality disorders in clinical settings. However, the rate of DPD in the general population does not appear to be very high (see Table 6.2). Most studies that have been conducted report higher prevalence rates of DPD in women than in men (Corbitt & Widiger, 1995). The prevalence and diagnosis of dependent personality disorder may also vary across cultures (Foulks, 1996) because there are profound differences in the extent to which societies encourage and value dependency-related behaviors. Many Western societies do appear to place more emphasis and value upon expressions of autonomy and self-reliance and might then be prone to overdiagnose the disorder (Bornstein, 1992). In some cultures, such as the Japanese or Indian cultures, interpersonal connectedness and interdependency are more highly valued, and what is considered dependency within the American culture might not be considered pathological within another culture.

### Etiology

O'Neill and Kendler (1998) reported the results of a longitudinal study of 2,230 twins who had been administered a measure of interpersonal dependency. The results suggested a modest genetic influence and a large specific environmental contribution. DPD may represent an interaction of an anxious, fearful temperament with an insecure attachment to an inconsistent or unreliable parental figure (McGuffin & Thapar, 1992). Dependent persons may turn to a parental figure to provide a reassurance and sense of security that they are unable to generate for themselves. This empirically supported etiological model (Rothbart & Ahadi, 1994) is consistent with current object relations theory in which dependent personality traits are considered to be an internalization of the mental representation of the self as weak and ineffectual, contributing to a disposition to look to others to provide protection and support, to become preoccupied with fears of abandonment, and to develop feelings of helplessness and insecurity (Blatt, Cornell, & Eshkol, 1993; Bornstein, 1992). In an intriguing cross-generational laboratory study, Thompson and Zuroff (1998) demonstrated how dependent mothers tended to reward mediocre over excellent performances by their daughters.

A number of studies have documented a relationship between the dependent person's weak and ineffectual self-image, excessive need to please others, and a variety of interpersonal problems (Bornstein, 1999). For example, Santor and Zuroff (1997) demonstrated how dependent persons were excessively concerned with maintaining interpersonal relatedness, adopting the responses of friends, and minimizing disagreement. Studies have also indicated that dependent personality traits provide a vulnerability to the development of clinically significant episodes of depression—particularly in response to interpersonal rejection or loss (Blatt & Zuroff, 1992). Methodological concerns have been raised with respect to this research (Coyne & Whiffen, 1995; Widiger, Verheul, & van den Brink, 1999), but there does appear to be a sufficient number of replicated, well-designed prospective studies to support the hypothesis that dependency does provide a vulnerability to episodes of depression (C. J. Robins, Hayes, Block, Kramer, & Villena, 1995). For example, Hammen et al. (1995) obtained 6-month and 12-month follow-up assessments of 129 high school senior women. They conducted multiple regression analyses to predict depression on the basis of dependency cognitions, prior interpersonal stress, and the interaction between them, controlling for initial levels of depression. All of the young women experienced stressful life events during this period of their lives, including moving away from home, separation from an important relationship, and loss of a romantic partner, but most of them did not become depressed. "It was the women with cognitions about relationships representing concerns about rejection or untrustworthiness of others who were especially challenged by normative changes" (Hammen et al., 1995, p. 441).

## Obsessive-Compulsive Personality Disorder

### Description

Obsessive-compulsive personality disorder (OCPD) is characterized by a preoccupation with orderliness, perfectionism, and control (APA, 2000; McCann, 1999). OCPD individuals tend to be rigid, stubborn, and perfectionistic to the point of impairment (e.g., tasks never get completed). Their preoccupation with rules, details, and morality cause them trouble both at work and outside of work. They are seen as inflexible and miserly and may be described by others as control freaks and workaholics. Other features of this personality disorder include hoarding, indecisiveness, reluctance to delegate tasks, being devoid of affection, ruminative, and prone to outbursts of anger. OCPD individuals often have comorbid anxiety disorders or mood disorders.

Many persons with OCPD obtain good to excellent success within a job or career. They can be excellent workers to the point of excess, sacrificing their social and leisure activities, marriage, and family for their job. Relationships with a spouse and children are likely to be strained due to their tendency to be detached and uninvolved but also authoritarian and domineering. A spouse may complain of a lack of affection, tenderness, and warmth. Relationships with colleagues at work may be equally strained by the excessive perfectionism, domination, indecision, worrying, and anger. Jobs that require flexibility, openness, creativity, or diplomacy may be particularly difficult (McCann, 1999). Persons with OCPD may be prone to various anxiety and physical disorders that are secondary to their worrying, indecision, and stress. Those with concomitant traits of angry hostility may be prone to cardiovascular disorders. Mood disorders may not develop until the person recognizes the sacrifices that have been made by their devotion to work and productivity, which may at times not occur until middle age. However, most experience early employment or career difficulties and even failures that may result in depression.

### Epidemiology

OCPD is characteristic of about 2% of the general population (see Table 6.2). It is believed that rates of OCPD in men are about twice those found in women. Clinicians must be careful not to overdiagnose OCPD. A number of individuals are conscientious, devoted to their work, very organized, and have perfectionistic tendencies. However, it is only when these features are associated with significant distress or impairment that they can be considered indicators of OCPD.

### Etiology

A variety of studies have indicated heritability for the trait of obsessiveness (Nigg & Goldsmith, 1994). OCPD may also relate to the general personality trait of constraint or conscientiousness (Trull, 1992; Trull et al., 1998) and the childhood temperament of attentional self-regulation, both of which have demonstrated substantial heritability (Plomin & Caspi, 1990). As children, some persons with OCPD may have appeared to be relatively well-behaved, responsible, and conscientious. However, they may have also been overly serious, rigid, and constrained (Rothbart & Ahadi, 1994).

Early psychoanalytic theories regarding OCPD concerned issues of unconscious guilt or shame. A variety of underlying conflicts have subsequently been proposed, including a need to maintain an illusion of infallibility to defend against feelings of insecurity, an identification with authoritarian parents, or an excessive, rigid control of feelings and impulses (McCann, 1999; Oldham & Frosch, 1991). Any or all of the aforementioned conflicts may in fact be important for a particular person with OCPD. OCPD involves an extreme variant of traits that are highly valued within most cultures (i.e., conscientiousness). Some persons may exaggerate cultural expectations as a result of excessive demands or pressures by parental figures. However, there have been few systematic studies on the developmental history or etiology of OCPD.

## FUTURE DIRECTIONS IN PERSONALITY DISORDER RESEARCH

Personality disorders were placed on a separate axis in *DSM-III* in recognition of their unique importance to clinical practice (Frances, 1980; Spitzer, Williams, & Skodol, 1980). The placement on a separate axis may have also in turn contributed to an increased interest in the study of personality disorders by clinicians and researchers. Prior to *DSM-III*, only ASPD received much systematic empirical research. Since *DSM-III* was published, BPD (Gunderson, 2001) and STPD (Siever, 1992) have received a considerable amount of attention by researchers. Researchers have also been turning their attention to the dependent and narcissistic personality disorders (Bornstein, 1992, 1999; Bushman & Baumeister, 1998). Regrettably, very little attention has been given to the others, outside of their inclusion within broad, nonspecific studies in which all of the personality disorders are considered without much attention to hypotheses that are specific to individual personality disorders (e.g., Johnson et al., 1999; Modestin et al., 1998; Norden et al., 1995).

In this last section, we would like to highlight what we view to be important future directions in personality disorder research. We emphasize in particular research concerning the childhood, developmental precursors to adult personality disorder and their biological mechanisms. We also suggest that a better understanding of the *DSM-IV* personality disorders will be achieved when their conceptualization is integrated within more general models of personality functioning. A considerable amount of research has been devoted to the study of general personality functioning (see volume 5 within this Handbook), and the science of personality disorders may progress to the extent that it incorporates this knowledge.

## Childhood Development of Maladaptive Personality Traits

One of the more remarkable gaps in knowledge is the childhood antecedents for personality disorders (Widiger & Clark, 2000). Included in *DSM-III* (APA, 1980) were four childhood antecedents of the personality disorders: identity disorder as an antecedent of BPD, avoidant disorder as an antecedent of AVPD, oppositional defiant disorder for passive-aggressive personality disorder, and conduct disorder for ASPD. Only the childhood antecedents for ASPD are still included within the diagnostic manual. Empirical support for the childhood antecedents of ASPD are so compelling that evidence of their presence is required for its diagnosis (APA, 2000), yet there are almost no data on the childhood antecedents for most of the other personality disorders.

Prospective longitudinal studies from childhood into adulthood are needed to document empirically how maladaptive personality traits develop, sustain, alter, or remit in their presentation across the life span (Caspi, 1998; Sher & Trull, 1996; Widiger & Sankis, 2000). For example, Trull, Useda, Conforti, and Doan (1997) and Lenzenweger, Loranger, Korfine, and Neff (1997) are conducting prospective longitudinal studies of *DSM-IV* personality disorder symptomatology in young adults who have not yet developed a clinically significant psychopathology but are presumably at risk for doing so. Trull et al. identified from a sample of 1,700 college students persons who presented with a sufficient number of borderline personality traits to consider them to represent premorbid cases. "These initial studies . . . mark an important step in identifying young adults with significant levels of borderline features who may go on to experience significant dysfunction in

later years" (Trull et al., 1997, p. 308). Lenzenweger et al. likewise identified 708 college students from a sample 1,646 who provided sufficiently elevated scores on a measure of personality disorder symptomatology to consider them to be at risk for future mental disorders. "Clearly, the prospective study of these particular subjects, currently under way through the Longitudinal Study of Personality Disorders, will shed light on their long-term social and occupational functioning and their mental health" (Lenzenweger et al., 1997, p. 350).

Ideally, the personality dispositions studied in adulthood would have conceptually meaningful and empirically valid relationships to the behavior patterns and temperaments that are of interest in current developmental research. We referred to some of this research in our discussion of individual personality disorders (e.g., ASPD, AVPD, and DPD). For example, there has been substantial research on the contributions of sexual and psychological abuse to the etiology of BPD (Zanarini, 2000). Linehan (1993) has hypothesized that BPD is the result of a heritable temperament of emotional instability interacting with a severely invalidating (e.g., abusive) environment. However, the broad BPD diagnostic category may not capture well the specific traits that are especially vulnerable or responsive to abusive experiences. Progress in the understanding of the development of BPD might be obtained by an integration of BPD research with existing developmental studies on the interaction between parenting, temperament, and attachment (Bartholomew et al., 2001).

Research has indicated that much of the phenomenology of BPD can be understood as extreme variants of a general domain of personality functioning described as neuroticism or negative affectivity (Trull, 1992; Trull et al., 1998). Neuroticism is a domain of personality functioning along which all persons vary, including persons diagnosed with a personality disorder (Widiger & Costa, 1994), and much of the BPD symptomatology can be understood as facets of neuroticism—specifically, angry hostility, vulnerability, impulsivity, anxiousness, depression, and impulsivity (Clarkin, Hull, Cantor, & Sanderson, 1993). Persons who are the very highest levels of angry hostility, vulnerability, impulsivity, anxiousness, and depression would be diagnosed with BPD. Although they are generally critical of this conceptualization of BPD, Morey and Zanarini (2000) did report obtaining better temporal stability over a 4-year period for neuroticism in comparison to the symptomatology of BPD. They suggested that BPD is perhaps "a disorder that waxes and wanes in severity over time, whereas neuroticism reflects a putatively stable trait configuration" (Morey & Zanarini, 2000, p. 737). "From this perspective, [neuroticism] could indicate a temperamental vulnerability to a disorder that is then triggered by developmental events (such as childhood neglect or abuse), resulting in functional levels that may be quite variable in response to situational elements even while the underlying traits remain relatively stable" (Morey & Zanarini, 2000, p. 737).

## Biological Mechanisms of Maladaptive Personality Traits

We have left the decade of the brain to perhaps enter a decade of the brain disease (Hyman, 1998). The emphasis being given to neurophysiological models of psychopathology can be to the detriment of adequate attention to cognitive, interpersonal, and other psychosocial models of etiology and pathology (Gunderson, 2001; Miller, 1996; Widiger & Sankis, 2000). Nevertheless, there is also much that is neurophysiological in psychopathology and the progress that has been made in understanding biogenetic and neurophysiological etiologies and pathologies has been remarkable (Kandel, 1998). Regrettably, there has been comparably little progress in understanding the neurophysiology of most of the personality disorders.

Biogenetic and heritability research has been confined largely to ASPD, BPD, and STPD, with very little research specific to the narcissistic, obsessive-compulsive and other personality disorders (McGuffin & Thapar, 1992; Nigg & Goldsmith, 1992). On the other hand, there has been a considerable amount of biogenetic and heritability research on general personality functioning (Plomin & Caspi, 1999). Progress in understanding the biogenetics of the *DSM-IV* personality disorders might be obtained through a consideration of the biogenetic research of general personality functioning—as we suggested previously in our discussion of some of the individual personality disorders (e.g., AVPD, DPD, and HPD).

An important area of future research is the clarification of the physiological substrates of maladaptive personality traits (Cloninger, 1998; Depue & Lenzenweger, 2001). For example, clinical studies have suggested that low serotonergic (5-hydroxytryptamine or 5HT) activity might be related to angry, hostile, and aggressive behavior. This research has included personality disordered populations (e.g., antisocial and borderline) but "one of the most remarkable aspects of this literature is the general consistency of these findings across different study samples and using various assessments of 5HT function" (Coccaro, 1998, p. 2). In other words, the 5HT findings have not been specific to any particular mental disorder; rather, they are associated instead with more fundamental dimensions of impulsivity and aggression that cut across diagnostic categories.

The anatomy and physiology of humans is quite similar to that of nonhuman animals, and research on the neurobiology of animal behavior can contribute to an understanding of the neurophysiology of human personality functioning. For example, the personality domain of extraversion (positive emotionality) is quite analogous to the search, foraging, and approach system studied in various animal species, at times more globally referred to as a behavioral facilitation system (BFS). Depue (1996) and his colleagues are exploring the neurobiology of the personality domains of positive affectivity (extraversion), negative affectivity (neuroticism), and constraint (conscientiousness) through pharmacological challenge studies.

"One of the more exciting directions for genetic research on personality involves the use of molecular genetic techniques to identify some of the specific genes responsible for genetic influence on personality" (Plomin & Caspi, 1999, p. 261). This research may ultimately lead to an understanding of the causal pathways from cells to social systems that will elucidate how genes affect the development of personality disorders (Hyman, 1998). Support for hypotheses concerning domains of personality functioning that are hypothesized to underlie the *DSM-IV* personality disorders have been obtained (e.g., Osher, Hamer, & Benjamin, 2000). For example, individuals with the long-repeat DRD4 allele are thought to be dopamine deficient and to seek novelty to increase dopamine release (Cloninger, 1998). However, failures to replicate these findings have also occurred (e.g., Hamer, Greenberg, Sabol, & Murphy, 1999; Herbst, Zonderman, McCrae, & Costa, 2000). One possible reason for replication failures is that the effect sizes for broad personality dispositions provided by single genes is quite small, but other methodological concerns need to be addressed as well (Ordway, 2000; Hamer et al., 1999; Plomin & Caspi, 1999).

## Integration With General Models of Personality Functioning

It is apparent from our discussion of developmental and biogenetic research that we feel that progress in the understanding of the *DSM-IV* personality disorders will be obtained by an integration of the APA (2000) personality disorders with our current understanding of general personality functioning (Trull, 2000; Widiger & Costa, 1994). Much of what we know about normal personality functioning should provide a strong empirical, scientific basis for what could be known about abnormal personality functioning.

A variety of studies and methodologies have raised compelling concerns regarding the validity of the *DSM-IV* categorical model of personality disorder, and the existing research suggests that the maladaptive personality traits that constitute the *DSM-IV* personality disorders might be better understood as maladaptive variants of common personality traits (Clark et al., 1997; Livesley, 1998; Trull, 2000; Widiger, 1993). Alternative dimensional models for the personality disorders have been proposed, including the 15-factor model of Clark (1993), the interpersonal circumplex (Wiggins & Pincus, 1989), the seven-factor model of Cloninger (1998), the 18-factor model of Livesley (1998), and the five-factor model (Widiger & Costa, 1994).

The five-factor model (FFM) of personality was derived originally from studies of the English language to identify the domains of personality functioning most important in describing the personality traits of oneself and other persons. This lexical research has emphasized five broad domains of personality, identified as extraversion (surgency or positive affectivity), agreeableness, conscientiousness (or constraint), neuroticism (negative affectivity), and openness (intellect or unconventionality; John & Srivastava, 1999). Each of these five domains can be further differentiated into underlying facets or components. Costa and McCrae (1992) have proposed six facets within each domain. For example, they suggest that the domain of agreeableness (vs. antagonism) can be usefully differentiated into more specific facets of trust (vs. mistrust, skepticism), straightforwardness (vs. deception, manipulation), altruism (vs. egocentrism, exploitation), compliance (vs. oppositionalism, aggression), modesty (vs. arrogance), and tendermindedness (vs. toughmindedness, callousness). Table 6.4 provides an abbreviated description of the 30 facets of the FFM.

Empirical support for the construct validity of the FFM is extensive both at the domain and at the facet levels, including convergent and discriminant validation across self, peer, and spouse ratings, temporal stability, cross-cultural replication, and heritability (John & Srivastava, 1999; McCrae & Costa, 1999). The FFM has been used successfully as a model for integrating a broad and diverse array of personality research in such fields as industrial and organizational psychology and behavioral medicine. There does appear to be sufficient empirical support for the FFM to consider it for use as a possible dimensional model of personality disorder (Widiger & Costa, 1994).

Widiger, Trull, Clarkin, Sanderson, and Costa (1994) indicated how each of the *DSM-III-R* personality disorders could be understood in terms of the 30 facets of the FFM identified by Costa and McCrae (1992). These descriptions were updated for *DSM-IV* by Trull and Widiger (1997), and they informed some of our earlier discussions of individual personality disorders. For example, the normal domain of conscientiousness concerns a person's degree of organization, persistence, order, and achievement orientation (Costa & McCrae, 1992). Conscientious persons tend to be organized, reliable, hard-working, self-

**TABLE 6.4   Brief Summary of Five-Factor Model of Personality**

1. Neuroticism vs. Emotional Stability:
   Anxiousness: fearful, apprehensive vs. relaxed, unconcerned, cool.
   Angry hostility: bitter, angry vs. even-tempered.
   Depressiveness: pessimistic, glum, despondent vs. optimistic.
   Self-consciousness: timid, embarrassed vs. self-assured, glib, shameless.
   Impulsivity: tempted, urgency vs. controlled, restrained.
   Vulnerability: fragile, helpless vs. stalwart, brave, fearless, unflappable.

2. Extraversion vs. Introversion:
   Warmth: affectionate, attached vs. cold, aloof, indifferent.
   Gregariousness: sociable, outgoing, involved vs. withdrawn, isolated.
   Assertiveness: forceful, dominant vs. unassuming, quiet, resigned.
   Activity: active, energetic, vigorous vs. passive, lethargic.
   Excitement Seeking: daring, reckless vs. cautious, monotonous, dull.
   Positive Emotions: high-spirited vs. placid, anhedonic.

3. Openness vs. Closedness to Experience:
   Fantasy: imaginative, dreamer, unrealistic vs. practical, concrete.
   Aesthetic: aesthetic vs. unaesthetic.
   Feelings: responsive, sensitive vs. unresponsive, constricted, alexythymic.
   Actions: unpredictable, unconventional vs. routine, habitual, stubborn.
   Ideas: odd, peculiar, strange, indiscriminate vs. pragmatic, rigid.
   Values: broad-minded, permissive vs. traditional, dogmatic, inflexible.

4. Agreeableness vs. Antagonism:
   Trust: trusting, gullible vs. skeptical, cynical, suspicious, paranoid.
   Straightforwardness: honest, naive vs. cunning, manipulative, deceptive.
   Altruism: giving, sacrificial vs. selfish, stingy, greedy, exploitative.
   Compliance: cooperative, docile vs. oppositional, combative, aggressive.
   Modesty: self-effacing, meek vs. confident, boastful, arrogant.
   Tender-Mindedness: empathic, soft-hearted vs. callous, ruthless.

5. Conscientiousness vs. Undependability:
   Competence: efficient, perfectionistic vs. lax, negligent.
   Order: organized, methodical, ordered vs. haphazard, disorganized, sloppy.
   Dutifulness: reliable, dependable, rigid vs. casual, undependable, unethical.
   Achievement-Striving: ambitious, workaholic vs. aimless, desultory.
   Self-Discipline: devoted, dogged, perseverative vs. negligent, hedonistic.
   Deliberation: reflective, thorough, ruminative vs. careless, hasty, rash.

disciplined, businesslike, and punctual. Persons who are overly conscientious will be excessively devoted to work, perfectionistic, and preoccupied with organization, rules, and details, resembling quite closely OCPD. AVPD is likewise readily understood as being simply maladaptively extreme variants of self-consciousness, anxiousness, and vulnerability facets of neuroticism, coupled with facets of introversion (Trull, 1992).

Wiggins and Pincus (1989) were the first to provide published data concerned with the relationship of the FFM to the APA (1980, 1987) personality disorder symptomatology. Since that original effort, more than 50 additional published studies have indicated a close relationship between the FFM and personality disorder symptomatology (Widiger & Costa,

2002). These studies, using a variety of measures and populations, have supported the hypothesis that each of the *DSM-IV* personality disorders could be readily understood as maladaptive variants of the personality traits included within the FFM (e.g., Ball, Tennen, Poling, Kranlem, & Rousanville, 1997; O'Connor & Dyce, 1998; Trull, 1992; Trull, Widiger, & Burr, 2001). The future of FFM personality disorder research will include a reproduction of the theoretical, nomological network surrounding the *DSM-IV* personality disorders, indicating how the etiology, pathology, and treatment of personality disorders can be best understood when the personality disorders are conceptualized as maladaptive variants of common personality traits.

# REFERENCES

Acklin, M. V. (1999). Behavioral science foundations of the Rorschach test: Research and clinical applications. *Assessment, 6,* 319–324.

Adams, H. E., Bernat, J. A., & Luscher, K. A. (2001). Borderline personality disorder: An overview. In P. B. Sutker & H. E. Adams (Eds.), *Comprehensive handbook of psychopathology* (3rd ed., pp. 491–508). New York: Plenum.

Adler, D. A., Drake, R. E., & Teague, G. B. (1990). Clinicians' practices in personality assessment: Does gender influence the use of *DSM-III* Axis II? *Comprehensive Psychiatry, 31,* 125–133.

Alarcon, R. D. (1996). Personality disorders and culture in *DSM-IV:* A critique. *Journal of Personality Disorders, 10,* 260–270.

Alarcon, R. D., & Foulks, E. F. (1996). Cultural factors and personality disorders. In T. A. Widiger, A. J. Frances, H. A. Pincus, R. Ross, M. B. First, & W. Davis (Eds.), DSM-IV *Sourcebook* (Vol. 3, pp. 975–982). Washington, DC: American Psychiatric Association.

American Psychiatric Association. (1980). *Diagnostic and statistical manual of mental disorders* (3rd ed.). Washington, DC: Author.

American Psychiatric Association. (1987). *Diagnostic and statistical manual of mental disorders* (3rd ed., Rev. ed.). Washington, DC: Author.

American Psychiatric Association. (1994). *Diagnostic and statistical manual of mental disorders* (4th ed.). Washington, DC: Author.

American Psychiatric Association. (2000). *Diagnostic and statistical manual of mental disorders* (4th ed., text revision). Washington, DC: Author.

Archer, R. (1999). Some observations on the debate currently surrounding the Rorschach. *Assessment, 6,* 309–311.

Ball, S. A., Tennen, H., Poling, J. C., Kranler, H. R., & Rousanville, B. J. (1997). Personality, temperament, and character dimensions in substance abusers. *Journal of Abnormal Psychology, 106,* 545–553.

Bartholomew, K., Kwong, M. J., & Hart, S. D. (2001). Attachment. In W. J. Livesley (Ed.), *Handbook of personality* (pp. 196–230). New York: Guilford.

Baumeister, R. F., Smart, L., & Boden, J. M. (1996). Relation of threatened egoism to violence and aggression: The dark side of high self-esteem. *Psychological Review, 103,* 5–33.

Beck, A. T., Freeman, A., & Associates. (1990). *Cognitive therapy of personality disorders.* New York: Guilford.

Bender, D. S., Dolan, R. T., Skodol, A. E., Sanislow, C. A., Dyck, I. R., McGlashan, T. H., Shea, M. T., Zanarini, M. C., Oldham, J. M., & Gunderson, J. G. (2001). Treatment utilization by patients with personality disorders. *American Journal of Psychiatry, 158,* 295–302.

Bernstein, D. P., Cohen, P., Velez, C. N., Schwab-Stone, M., Siever, L., & Shinsato, L. (1993). Prevalence and stability of the *DSM-III-R* personality disorders in a community-based survey of adolescents. *American Journal of Psychiatry, 150,* 1237–1243.

Bernstein, D. P., Kasapis, C., Bergman, A., Weld, E., Mitropoulou, V., Horvath, T., Klar, H., Silverman, J., & Siever, L. J. (1997). Assessing Axis II disorders by informant interview. *Journal of Personality Disorders, 11,* 158–167.

Bernstein, D. P., & Travaglini, L. (1999). Schizoid and avoidant personality disorders. In T. Millon, P. H. Blaney, & R. D. Davis (Eds.), *Oxford textbook of psychopathology* (pp. 523–534). New York: Oxford University Press.

Black, D. W., Noyes, R., Pfohl, B., Goldstein, R. B., & Blum, N. (1993). Personality disorder in obsessive-compulsive volunteers, well comparison subjects, and their first degree relatives. *American Journal of Psychiatry, 150,* 1226–1232.

Blais, M. A., Hilsenroth, M. J., & Fowler, J. C. (1998). Rorschach correlates of the *DSM-IV* histrionic personality. *Journal of Personality Assessment, 70,* 355–364.

Blashfield, R. K., Blum, N., & Pfohl, B. (1992). The effects of changing Axis II diagnostic criteria. *Comprehensive Psychiatry, 33,* 245–252.

Blashfield, R. K., & Herkov, M. J. (1996). Investigating clinician adherence to diagnosis by criteria: A replication of Morey and Ochoa (1989). *Journal of Personality Disorders, 10,* 219–228.

Blatt, S. J., Cornell, C. E., & Eshkol, E. (1993). Personality style, differential vulnerability, and clinical course in immunological and cardiovascular disease. *Clinical Psychology Review, 13,* 421–450.

Blatt, S. J., & Zuroff, D. (1992). Interpersonal relatedness and self-definition: Two prototypes for depression. *Clinical Psychology Review, 12,* 527–562.

Bornstein, R. F. (1992). The dependent personality: Developmental, social, and clinical perspectives. *Psychological Bulletin, 112,* 3–23.

Bornstein, R. F. (1995). Sex differences in objective and projective dependency tests: A meta-analytic review. *Assessment, 2,* 319–331.

Bornstein, R. F. (1999). Dependent and histrionic personality disorders. In T. Millon, P. Blaney, & R. Davis (Eds.), *Oxford textbook of psychopathology* (pp. 535–554). Oxford, England: Oxford University Press.

Bushman, B. J., & Baumeister, R. F. (1998). Threatened egotism, narcissism, self-esteem, and direct and displaced aggression: Does self-love or self-hate lead to violence? *Journal of Personality and Social Psychology, 75,* 219–229.

Caspi, A. (1998). Personality development across the life course. In W. Damon & N. Eisenberg (Eds.), *Handbook of child psychology: Vol. 3. Social, emotional, and personality development* (pp. 311–388). New York: Wiley.

Clark, L. A. (1993). *Manual for the Schedule for Nonadaptive and Adaptive Personality.* Minneapolis: University of Minnesota Press.

Clark, L. A., & Harrison, J. A. (2001). Assessment instruments. In W. J. Livesley (Ed.), *Handbook of personality disorders* (pp. 277–306). New York: Guilford.

Clark, L. A., Livesley, W. J., & Morey, L. (1997). Personality disorder assessment: The challenge of construct validity. *Journal of Personality Disorders, 11,* 205–231.

Clark, L. A., Watson, D., & Reynolds, S. (1995). Diagnosis and classification of psychopathology: Challenges to the current system and future directions. *Annual Review of Psychology, 46,* 121–153.

Clarkin, J. F., Hull, J. W., Cantor, J., & Sanderson, C. (1993). Borderline personality disorder and personality traits: A comparison of SCID-II BPD and NEO-PI. *Psychological Assessment, 5,* 472–476.

Cloninger, C. R. (1998). The genetics and psychobiology of the seven-factor model of personality. In K. R. Silk (Ed.), *Biology of personality disorders* (pp. 63–92). Washington, DC: American Psychiatric Press.

Coccaro, E. F. (1998). Neurotransmitter function in personality disorders. In K. Silk (Ed.), *Biology of personality disorders* (pp. 1–25). Washington, DC: American Psychiatric Press.

Cooper, A. M., & Ronningstam, E. (1992). Narcissistic personality disorder. In A. Tasman & M. B. Riba (Eds.), *Review of psychiatry* (Vol. 11, pp. 80–97). Washington, DC: American Psychiatric Press.

Corbitt, E. M., & Widiger, T. A. (1995). Sex differences among the personality disorders: An exploration of the data. *Clinical Psychology: Science and Practice, 2,* 225–238.

Costa, P. T., Jr., & McCrae, R. R. (1992). *Revised NEO-Personality Inventory (NEO-PI-R) and NEO Five Factor Inventory (FFI) manual.* Odessa, FL: Psychological Assessment Resources.

Coyne, J. C., & Whiffen, V. E. (1995). Issues in personality as diathesis for depression: The case of sociotropy-dependency and autonomy-self-criticism. *Psychological Bulletin, 118,* 358–378.

Daley, S. E., Burge, D., & Hammen, C. (2000). Borderline personality disorder symptoms as predictors of 4-year romantic relationship dysfunction in young women: Addressing issues of specificity. *Journal of Abnormal Psychology, 109,* 451–460.

Depue, R. A. (1996). A neurobiological framework for the structure of personality and emotion: Implications for personality disorders. In J. F. Clarkin & M. F. Lenzenweger (Eds.), *Major theories of personality disorder* (pp. 347–390). New York: Guilford.

Depue, R. A., & Lenzenweger, M. F. (2001). A neurobehavioral dimensional model. In W. J. Livesley (Ed.), *Handbook of personality disorders* (pp. 136–176). New York: Guilford.

Dodge, K. A., & Schwartz, D. (1997). Social information processing mechanisms in aggressive behavior. In D. M. Stoff, J. Breiling, & J. D. Maser (Eds.), *Handbook of antisocial behavior* (pp. 171–180). New York: Wiley.

Dolan-Sewell, R. G., Krueger, R. F., & Shea, M. T. (2001). Co-occurrence with syndrome disorders. In W. J. Livesley (Ed.), *Handbook of personality disorders* (pp. 84–104). New York: Guilford.

Farrington, D. P. (1997). A critical analysis of research on the development of antisocial behavior from birth to adulthood. In D. M. Stoff, J. Breiling, & J. D. Maser (Eds.), *Handbook of antisocial behavior* (pp. 234–241). New York: Wiley.

Foulks, E. F. (1996). Culture and personality disorders. In J. E. Mezzich, A. Kleinman, H. Fabrega, & D. L. Parron (Eds.), *Culture and psychiatric diagnosis. A DSM-IV perspective* (pp. 243–252). Washington, DC: American Psychiatric Press.

Frances, A. J. (1980). The *DSM-III* personality disorders section: A commentary. *American Journal of Psychiatry, 137,* 1050–1054.

Fulton, M., & Winokur, G. (1993). A comparative study of paranoid and schizoid personality disorders. *American Journal of Psychiatry, 150,* 1363–1367.

Garb, H. N. (1997). Race bias, social class bias, and gender bias in clinical judgment. *Clinical Psychology: Science and Practice, 4,* 99–120.

Garb, H. N. (1999). Call for a moratorium on the use of the Rorschach inkblot test in clinical and forensic settings. *Assessment, 6,* 313–315.

Gunderson, J. G. (1992). Diagnostic controversies. In A. Tasman & M. B. Riba (Eds.), *Review of psychiatry* (Vol. 11, pp. 9–24). Washington, DC: American Psychiatric Press.

Gunderson, J. G. (2001). *Borderline personality disorder. A clinical guide.* Washington, DC: American Psychiatric Press.

Hamer, D. H., Greenberg, B. D., Sabol, S. Z., & Murphy, D. L. (1999). Role of the serotonin transporter gene in temperament and character. *Journal of Personality Disorders, 13,* 312–328.

Hammen, C. L., Burge, D., Daley, S. E., Davila, J., Paley, B., & Rudolph, K. D. (1995). Interpersonal attachment cognitions and predictions of symptomatic responses to interpersonal stress. *Journal of Abnormal Psychology, 104,* 436–443.

Hare, R. D. (1991). *The Revised Psychopathy Checklist.* Toronto, Ontario, Canada: Multi-Health Systems.

Harkness, A. R., & Lilienfeld, S. O. (1997). Individual differences science for treatment planning: Personality traits. *Psychological Assessment, 9,* 349–360.

Hart, S. D., & Hare, R. D. (1997). Psychopathy: Assessment and association with criminal conduct. In D. M. Stoff, J. Breiling, & J. D. Maser (Eds.), *Handbook of antisocial behavior* (pp. 22–35). New York: Wiley.

Herbst, J. H., Zonderman, A. B., McCrae, R. R., & Costa, P. T. (2000). Do the dimensions of the Temperament and Character Inventory map a simple genetic architecture? Evidence from molecular genetics and factor analysis. *American Journal of Psychiatry, 157,* 1285–1290.

Herkov, M. J., & Blashfield, R. K. (1995). Clinicians' diagnoses of personality disorder: Evidence of a hierarchical structure. *Journal of Personality Assessment, 65,* 313–321.

Hilsenroth, M. J., Handler, L., & Blais, M. A. (1996). Assessment of narcissistic personality disorder: A multi-method review. *Clinical Psychology Review, 16,* 655–683.

Hinshaw, S. P. (1994). Conduct disorder in childhood: Conceptualization, diagnosis, comorbidity, and risk status for antisocial functioning in adulthood. In D. C. Fowles, P. B. Sutker, & S. H. Goodman (Eds.), *Progress in experimental personality and psychopathology research* (Vol. 15, pp. 3–44). New York: Springer.

Horowitz, M. J. (1991). *Hysterical personality style and the histrionic personality disorder.* Northvale, NJ: Jason Aronson.

Hyler, S. E. (1994). *Personality Diagnostic Questionnaire-4 (PDQ-4)* [Unpublished test]. New York: New York State Psychiatric Institute.

Hyman, S. E. (1998). NIMH during the tenure of Director Steven E. Hyman, M.D. (1996-present): The now and future of NIMH. *American Journal of Psychiatry, 155*(Suppl.), 36–40.

Jang, K. L., McCrae, R. R., Angleitner, A., Riemann, R., & Livesley, W. J. (1998). Heritability of facet-level traits in a cross-cultural twin sample: Support for a hierarchical model of personality. *Journal of Personality and Social Psychology, 74,* 1556–1565.

Jang, K. L., & Vernon, P. A. (2001). Genetics. In W. J. Livesley (Ed.), *Handbook of personality disorders* (pp. 177–195). New York: Guilford.

John, O. P., & Srivastava, S. (1999). The Big Five trait taxonomy: History, measurement, and theoretical perspectives. In L. A. Pervin & O. P. John (Eds.), *Handbook of personality. Theory and research* (2nd ed., pp. 102–138). New York: Guilford.

Johnson, F. F. (1993). *Dependency and Japanese socialization.* New York: New York University Press.

Johnson, J. G., Cohen, P., Brown, J., Smailes, E. M., & Bernstein, D. P. (1999). Childhood maltreatment increases risk for personality disorders during early adulthood. *American Journal of Psychiatry, 56,* 600–606.

Kandel, E. R. (1998). A new intellectual framework for psychiatry. *American Journal of Psychiatry, 155,* 457–469.

Kaye, A. L., & Shea, M. T. (2000). Personality disorders, personality traits, and defense mechanisms measures. In H. A. Pincus, A. J. Rush, M. B. First, & L. E. McQueen (Eds.), *Handbook of psychiatric measures* (pp. 713–750). Washington, DC: American Psychiatric Association.

Kessler, R. C. (1999). The World Health Organization International Consortium in psychiatric epidemiology. Initial work and future directions: The NAPE lecture. *Acta Psychiatrica Scandinavica, 99,* 2–9.

Klein, D. F. (1999). Harmful dysfunction, disorder, disease, illness, and evolution. *Journal of Abnormal Psychology, 108,* 421–429.

Kochanska, G. (1991). Socialization and temperament in the development of guilt and conscience. *Child Development, 62,* 1379–1392.

Koenigsberg, H. W., Kaplan, R. D., Gilmore, M. M., & Cooper, A. M. (1985). The relationship between syndrome and personality disorder in *DSM-III:* Experience with 2,462 patients. *American Journal of Psychiatry, 142,* 207–212.

Lenzenweger, M. F., Loranger, A. W., Korfine, L., & Neff, C. (1997). Detecting personality disorders in a nonclinical population. *Archives of General Psychiatry, 54,* 345–351.

Linehan, M. M. (1993). *Cognitive-behavioral treatment of borderline personality disorder.* New York: Guilford Press.

Livesley, W. J. (1998). Suggestions for a framework for an empirically based classification of personality disorder. *Canadian Journal of Psychiatry, 43,* 137–147.

Livesley, W. J., Jang, K. L., & Vernon, P. A. (1998). Phenotypic and genetic structure of traits delineating personality disorder. *Archives of General Psychiatry, 55,* 941–948.

Loranger, A. W., Sartorius, N., Andreoli, A., Berger, P., Buchheim, P., Channabasavanna, S. M., et al. (1994). The International Personality Disorder Examination. The World Health Organization/ Alcohol, Drug Abuse, and Mental Health Administration international pilot study of personality disorders. *Archives of General Psychiatry, 51,* 215–224.

Lyons, M. J. (1995). Epidemiology of personality disorders. In M. T. Tsuang, M. Tohen, & G. E. P. Zahner (Eds.), *Textbook in psychiatric epidemiology.* New York: Wiley-Liss.

Maier, W., Lichtermann, D., Klinger, T., & Heun, R. (1992). Prevalences of personality disorders (DSM-III-R) in the community. *Journal of Personality Disorders, 6,* 187–196.

Mattia, J. I., & Zimmerman, M. (2001). Epidemiology. In W. J. Livesley (Ed.), *Handbook of personality disorders* (pp. 107–123). New York: Guilford.

McCann, J. T. (1999). Obsessive-compulsive and negativistic personality disorders. In T. Millon, P. Blaney, & R. Davis (Eds.), *Oxford textbook of psychopathology* (pp. 585–604). Oxford, England: Oxford University Press.

McCrae, R. R., & Costa, P. T. (1999). A five-factor theory of personality. In L. A. Pervin & O. P. John (Eds.), *Handbook of personality* (2nd ed., pp. 139–153). New York: Guilford.

McGuffin, P., & Thapar, A. (1992). The genetics of personality disorder. *British Journal of Psychiatry, 160,* 12–23.

Miller, G. A. (1996). How we think about cognition, emotion, and biology in psychopathology. *Psychophysiology, 33,* 615–628.

Miller, M. B., Useda, J. D., Trull, T. J., Burr, R. M., & Minks-Brown, C. (2001). Paranoid, schizoid, and schizotypal personality disorders. In P. B. Sutker & H. E. Adams (Eds.), *Comprehensive handbook of psychopathology* (3rd ed., pp. 535–558). New York: Plenum.

Millon, T., Davis, R. D., Millon, C. M., Wenger, A. W., Van Zuilen, M. H., Fuchs, M., & Millon, R. B. (1996). *Disorders of personality: DSM-IV and beyond.* New York: Wiley.

Millon, T., & Frances, A. J. (1987). Editorial. *Journal of Personality Disorders, 1,* i-iii.

Modestin, J., Oberson, B., & Erni, T. (1998). Possible antecedents of *DSM-III-R* personality disorders. *Acta Psychiatrica Scandinavica, 97,* 260–266.

Morey, L. C. (1988). Personality disorders in DSM-III and DSM-III-R: Convergence, coverage, and internal consistency. *American Journal of Psychiatry, 145,* 573–577.

Morey, L. C., & Ochoa, E. (1989). An investigation of adherence to diagnostic criteria: Clinical diagnosis of the *DSM-III* personality disorders. *Journal of Personality Disorders, 3,* 180–192.

Morey, L. C, & Zanarini, M. C. (2000). Borderline personality: Traits and disorder. *Journal of Abnormal Psychology, 109,* 733–737.

Nigg, J. T., & Goldsmith, H. H. (1994). Genetics of personality disorders: Perspectives from personality and psychopathology research. *Psychological Bulletin, 115,* 346–380.

Norden, K. A., Klein, D. N., Donaldson, S. K., Pepper, C. M., & Klein, L. M. (1995). Reports of the early home environment in *DSM-III-R* personality disorders. *Journal of Personality Disorders, 9,* 213–223.

O'Connor, B. P., & Dyce, J. A. (1998). A test of models of personality disorder configuration. *Journal of Abnormal Psychology, 107,* 3–16.

Oldham, J. M., & Frosch, W. A. (1991). Compulsive personality disorder. In R. Michels (Ed.), *Psychiatry* (Vol. 1, pp. 1–8). Philadelphia: Lippincott.

Oltmanns, T. F., Turkheimer, E., & Strauss, M. E. (1998). Peer assessment of personality traits and pathology. *Assessment, 5,* 53–65.

O'Neill, F. A., & Kendler, K. S. (1998). Longitudinal study of interpersonal dependency in female twins. *British Journal of Psychiatry, 172,* 154–158.

Ordway, G. A. (2000). Searching for the chicken's egg in transporter gene polymorphism. *Archives of General Psychiatry, 57,* 739–740.

Ornduff, S. R. (2000). Childhood maltreatment and malevolence: Quantitative research findings. *Clinical Psychology Review, 20,* 991–1018.

Osher, Y., Hamer, D., & Benjamin, J. (2000). Association and linkage of anxiety-related traits with a functional polymorphism of the serotonin transporter gene regulatory region in Israeli sibling pairs. *Molecular Psychiatry, 5,* 216–219.

Padilla, A. M. (1995). *Hispanic psychology: Critical issues in theory and research.* Newbury Park, CA: Sage.

Paris, J. (2001). Psychosocial adversity. In W. J. Livesley (Ed.), *Handbook of personality disorders* (pp. 231–241). New York: Guilford.

Patrick, C. J. (1994). Emotion and psychopathy: Startling new insights. *Psychophysiology, 31,* 415–428.

Perry, J. C., Banon, E., & Ianni, F. (1999). Effectiveness of psychotherapy for personality disorders. *American Journal of Psychiatry, 156,* 1312–1321.

Plomin, R., & Caspi, A. (1999). Behavioral genetics and personality. In L. Pervin & O. John (Eds.), *Handbook of personality* (2nd ed., pp. 251–276). New York: Guilford.

Raskin, R., Novacek, J., & Hogan, R. (1991). Narcissistic self-esteem management. *Journal of Personality and Social Psychology, 60,* 911–918.

Rhodewalt, F., Madrian, J. C., & Cheney, S. (1998). Narcissism, self-knowledge, organization, and emotional reactivity: The effect of daily experience on self-esteem and affect. *Personality and Social Psychology Bulletin, 24,* 75–87.

Riso, L. P., Klein, D. N., Anderson, R. L., Ouimette, P. C., & Lizardi, H. (1994). Concordance between patients and informants on the Personality Disorder Examination. *American Journal of Psychiatry, 151,* 568–573.

Robins, C. J., Hayes, A. H., Block, P., Kramer, R. J., & Villena, M. (1995). Interpersonal and achievement concerns and the depressive vulnerability and symptom specificity hypothesis: A prospective study. *Cognitive Therapy and Research, 19,* 1–20.

Robins, L. N., & Regier, D. A. (Eds.). (1991). *Psychiatric disorders in America.* New York : Free Press.

Robins, L. N., Tipp, J., & Przybeck, T. (1991). Antisocial personality. In L. N. Robins & D. A. Regier (Eds.), *Psychiatric disorders in America. The epidemiologic catchment area study* (pp. 258–290). New York: Free Press.

Rogers, R. (1995). *Diagnostic and structured interviewing. A handbook for psychologists.* Odessa, FL: Psychological Assessment Resources.

Rogler, L. H. (1996). Framing research on culture in psychiatric diagnosis: The case of the *DSM-IV. Psychiatry, 59,* 145–155.

Rothbart, M. K., & Ahadi, S. A. (1994). Temperament and the development of personality. *Journal of Abnormal Psychology, 103,* 55–66.

Samuels, J. F., Nestadt, G., Romanoski, A. J., Folstein, M. F., & McHugh, P. R. (1994). *DSM-III* personality disorders in the community. *American Journal of Psychiatry, 151,* 1055–1062.

Sanderson, C., & Clarkin, J. F. (1994). Use of the NEO-PI personality dimensions in differential treatment planning. In P. T. Costa & T. A. Widiger (Eds.), *Personality disorders and the five-factor model of personality* (pp. 219–235). Washington, DC: American Psychological Association.

Sanislow, C. A., & McGlashan, T. H. (1998). Treatment outcome of personality disorders. *Canadian Journal of Psychiatry, 43,* 237–250.

Santor, D. A., & Zuroff, D. C. (1997). Interpersonal responses to threats of status and interpersonal relatedness: Effects of dependency and self-criticism. *British Journal of Clinical Psychology, 36,* 521–541.

Sher, K. J., & Trull, T. J. (1996). Methodological issues in psychopathology research. *Annual Review of Psychology, 47,* 371–400.

Siever, L. J. (1992). Schizophrenia spectrum disorders. In A. Tasman & M. B. Riba (Eds.), *Review of psychiatry* (Vol. 11, pp. 25–42). Washington, DC: American Psychiatric Press.

Siever, L. J., & Davis, K. L. (1991). A psychobiological perspective on the personality disorders. *American Journal of Psychiatry, 148,* 1647–1658.

Silk, K. S., Lee, S., Hill, E. M., & Lohr, N. E. (1995). Borderline personality disorder symptoms and severity of sexual abuse. *American Journal of Psychiatry, 152,* 1059–1064.

Skodol, A. E., Oldham, J. M., Rosnick, L., Kellman, H. D., & Hyler, S. E. (1991). Diagnosis of *DSM-III-R* personality disorders: A comparison of two structured interviews. *International Journal of Methods in Psychiatric Research, 1,* 13–26.

Soloff, P. H., Siever, L., Cowdry, R., & Kocsis, J. H. (1994). Evaluation of pharmacologic treatment in personality disorders. In R. F. Prien & D. S. Robinson (Eds.), *Clinical evaluation of psychotropic drugs: Principles and guidelines* (pp. 651–673). New York: Raven.

Spitzer, R. L., & Wakefield, J. C. (1999). The *DSM-IV* diagnostic criterion for clinical significance: Does it help solve the false positives problem? *American Journal of Psychiatry, 156,* 1856–1864.

Spitzer, R. L., Williams, J. B. W., & Skodol, A. E. (1980). *DSM-III:* The major achievements and an overview. *American Journal of Psychiatry, 137,* 151–164.

Stoff, D. M., Breiling, J., & Maser, J. D. (Eds.). (1997). *Handbook of antisocial behavior.* New York: Wiley.

Stone, M. H. (1993). *Abnormalities of personality: Within and beyond the realm of treatment.* New York: Norton.

Stone, M. H. (2001). Natural history and long-term outcome. In W. J. Livesley (Ed.), *Handbook of personality disorders* (pp. 259–273). New York: Guilford.

Sutker, P. B., & Allain, A. N. (2001). Antisocial personality disorder. In P. B. Sutker & H. E. Adams (Eds.), *Comprehensive handbook of psychopathology* (3rd ed., pp. 445–490). New York: Plenum.

Thompson, S., & Zuroff, D. C. (1998). Dependent and self-critical mothers' responses to adolescent autonomy and competence. *Personality and Individual Differences, 24,* 311–324.

Tickle, J. F., Heatherton, T. F., & Wittenberg, L. G. (2001). Can personality change? In W. J. Livesley (Ed.), *Handbook of personality disorders* (pp. 242–258). New York: Guilford.

Trull, T. J. (1992). *DSM-III-R* personality disorders and the five-factor model of personality: An empirical comparison. *Journal of Abnormal Psychology, 101,* 553–560.

Trull, T. J. (2000). Dimensional models of personality disorder. *Current Opinion in Psychiatry, 13,* 179–184.

Trull, T. J., Sher, K. J., Minks-Brown, C., Durbin, J., & Burr, R. (2000). Borderline personality disorder and substance use disorders: A review and integration. *Clinical Psychology Review, 20,* 235–254.

Trull, T. J., Useda, D., Conforti, K., & Doan, B.-T. (1997). Borderline personality disorder features in nonclinical young adults: 2. Two-year outcome. *Journal of Abnormal Psychology, 106,* 307–314.

Trull, T. J., & Widiger, T. A. (1997). *Structured Interview for the five-factor model of personality.* Odessa, FL: Psychological Assessment Resources.

Trull, T. J., Widiger, T. A., & Burr, R. (2001). A structured interview for the assessment of the five-factor model of personality: 2. Facet-level relations to the Axis II personality disorders. *Journal of Personality, 69,* 175–198.

Trull, T. J., Widiger, T. A., Useda, J. D., Holcomb, J., Doan, B.-T., Axelrod, S. R., Stern, B. L., & Gershuny, B. S. (1998). A structured interview for the assessment of the five-factor model of personality. *Psychological Assessment, 10,* 229–240.

Wakefield, J. C. (1992). Disorder as harmful dysfunction: A conceptual critique of *DSM-III-R*'s definition of mental disorder. *Psychological Review, 99,* 232–247.

Weiner, I. B. (1999). What the Rorschach can do for you: Incremental validity in clinical applications. *Assessment, 6,* 327–338.

Weissman, M. M. (1993). The epidemiology of personality disorders: A 1990 update. *Journal of Personality Disorders, 7,* 44–62.

Westen, D. (1997). Divergences between clinical and research methods for assessing personality disorders: Implications for research and the evolution of Axis II. *American Journal of Psychiatry, 154,* 895–903.

Whaley, A. (1997). Ethnicity/race, paranoia, and psychiatric diagnosis: Clinician bias versus sociocultural differences. *Journal of Psychopathology and Behavorial Assessment, 19,* 1–20.

Widiger, T. A. (1993). The *DSM-III-R* categorical personality disorder diagnoses: A critique and an alternative. *Psychological Inquiry, 4,* 75–90.

Widiger, T. A. (1998). Sex biases in the diagnosis of personality disorders. *Journal of Personality Disorders, 12,* 95–118.

Widiger, T. A. (2001). Official classification systems. In W. J. Livesley (Ed.), *Handbook of personality disorders* (pp. 60–83). New York: Guilford.

Widiger, T. A. (2002). Personality disorders. In M. M. Antony & D. H. Barlow (Eds.), *Handbook of assessment, treatment planning, and outcome* (pp. 453–480). New York: Guilford.

Widiger, T. A., & Bornstein, R. F. (2001). Histrionic, dependent, and narcissistic personality disorders. In P. B. Sutker & H. E. Adams (Eds.), *Comprehensive handbook of psychopathology* (3rd ed., pp. 509–531). New York: Plenum.

Widiger, T. A., & Clark, L. A. (2000). Toward *DSM-V* and the classification of psychopathology. *Psychological Bulletin, 126,* 946–963.

Widiger, T. A., & Coker, L. A. (2002). Assessing personality disorders. In J. N. Butcher (Ed.), *Clinical personality assessment. Practical approaches* (2nd ed., pp. 407–434). New York: Oxford University Press.

Widiger, T. A., & Corbitt, E. (1994). Normal versus abnormal personality from the perspective of the *DSM*. In S. Strack & M. Lorr (Eds.), *Differentiating normal and abnormal personality* (pp. 158–175). New York: Springer.

Widiger, T. A., & Costa, P. T. (1994). Personality and personality disorders. *Journal of Abnormal Psychology, 103,* 78–91.

Widiger, T. A., & Costa, P. T. (in press). Five factor model personality disorder research. In P. T. Costa & T. A. Widiger (Eds.), *Personality disorders and the five factor model of personality* (2nd ed.). Washington, DC: American Psychological Association.

Widiger, T., Frances, A., Spitzer, R., & Williams, J. (1988). The *DSM-III-R* personality disorders: An overview. *American Journal of Psychiatry, 145,* 786–795.

Widiger, T. A., & Lynam, D. R. (1998). Psychopathy from the perspective of the five-factor model of personality. In T. Millon, E. Simonsen, & M. Birket-Smith (Eds.), *Psychopathy: antisocial, criminal, and violent behaviors* (pp. 171–187). New York: Guilford.

Widiger, T. A., Mangine, S., Corbitt, E. M., Ellis, C. G., & Thomas, G. V. (1995). *Personality Disorder Interview-IV: A semistructured interview for the assessment of personality disorders.* Odessa, FL: Psychological Assessment Resources.

Widiger, T. A., & Sankis, L. (2000). Adult psychopathology: Issues and controversies. *Annual Review of Psychology, 51,* 377–404.

Widiger, T. A., & Spitzer, R. L. (1991). Sex bias in the diagnosis of personality disorders: Conceptual and methodological issues. *Clinical Psychology Review, 11,* 1–22.

Widiger, T. A., Trull, T. J., Clarkin, J. F., Sanderson, C., & Costa, P. T., Jr. (1994). A description of the *DSM-III-R* and *DSM-IV* personality disorders with the five-factor model of personality. In P. T. Costa & T. A. Widiger (Eds.), *Personality disorders and the five-factor model of personality* (pp. 41–56). Washington, DC: American Psychological Association.

Widiger, T. A., Verheul, R., & van den Brink, W. (1999). Personality and psychopathology. In L. Pervin & O. John (Eds.), *Handbook of personality* (2nd ed., pp. 347–366). New York: Guilford.

Wiggins, J. S., & Pincus, A. (1989). Conceptions of personality disorder and dimensions of personality. *Psychological Assessment, 1,* 305–316.

Wood, J. M., & Lilienfeld, S. O. (1999). The Rorschach inkblot test: A case of overstatement? *Assessment, 6,* 341–349.

World Health Organization. (1992). *The ICD-10 classification of mental and behavioural disorders. Clinical descriptions and diagnostic guidelines.* Geneva, Switzerland: Author.

Zanarini, M. C. (2000). Childhood experiences associated with the development of borderline personality disorder. *Psychiatric Clinics of North America, 23,* 89–101.

Zimmerman, M. (1994). Diagnosing personality disorders: A review of issues and research methods. *Archives of General Psychiatry, 51,* 225–245.

Zimmerman, M., & Coryell, W. H. (1989). *DSM-III* personality disorder diagnoses in a nonpatient sample. *Archives of General Psychiatry, 46,* 682–689.

Zimmerman, M., & Mattia, J. I. (1999a). Differences between clinical and research practices in diagnosing borderline personality disorder. *American Journal of Psychiatry, 156,* 1570–1574.

Zimmerman, M., & Mattia, J. I. (1999b). Psychiatric diagnosis in clinical practice: Is comorbidity being missed? *Comprehensive Psychiatry, 40,* 182–191.

# CHAPTER 7

# Eating Disorders

HOWARD STEIGER, KENNETH R. BRUCE, AND MIMI ISRAËL

The current system of psychiatric classification, the *Diagnostic and Statistical Manual of Mental Disorders–Fourth Edition* (*DSM-IV;* American Psychiatric Association [APA], 1994), includes two official eating disorder (ED) syndromes: anorexia nervosa and bulimia nervosa, and a third (still provisional) diagnosis, binge-eating disorder. Binge-eating disorder, however, is likely to become officially recognized in future editions of the diagnostic manual and we therefore include it in this chapter. Anorexia, bulimia, and binge eating are polysymptomatic syndromes, defined by maladaptive attitudes and behaviors around eating, weight, and body image, including as well nonspecific disturbances of self-image, mood, impulse regulation, and interpersonal functioning. In this chapter, we review pathognomonic features of the EDs and findings on concurrent traits and comorbid psychopathology. We also discuss the putative set of factors, biological, psychological, and social (as well as eating-specific and more generalized) that may explain ED development.

## DEFINING CHARACTERISTICS

### Anorexia Nervosa

Anorexia nervosa (AN) is defined by a relentless pursuit of thinness and a morbid fear of the consequences of eating (usually expressed as a dread of weight gain or obesity). The result is a willful (and often dramatic) restriction of food intake. The person with AN imposes upon herself a state of gradual weight loss and (sometimes) dangerous emaciation.

(Recognizing different proportions of EDs among females and males, we use feminine personal pronouns. This convention is not intended to disregard eating syndromes in males.) At the core of such behavior appears to be a literal phobia of weight gain, so intense that the individual avoids behaviors (e.g., eating unfamiliar foods, eating without exercising) that could lead to weight gain and thus incrementally loses further weight.

Individuals with AN typically eat a restricted range of safe (usually low-calorie) foods or avoid social eating situations so that they will have full control over what, how much, and in what way they can eat. In some cases, anorexics purge after eating through vomiting, misuse of laxatives, or other means, due to fears that they may have overeaten. About half of sufferers eventually develop binge-eating episodes—that is, periodic dyscontrol over eating, or incapacity to satiate (DaCosta & Halmi, 1992). Consequently, a distinction is usually made between AN, restricting subtype, in which the sufferer limits food intake but does not engage in binge eating or purging (i.e., self-induced vomiting; misuse of laxatives, diuretics, or enemas), and AN, binge-eating/purging subtype, in which (as the label implies) binge or purge episodes are prominent.

### Bulimia Nervosa

In apparent contrast to AN, the main feature of bulimia nervosa (BN) is *binge eating* (i.e., appetitive *dyscontrol*, vs. AN's overcontrol). Bulimia nervosa is diagnosed in relatively normal or overweight individuals (not anorexics) who display recurrent eating binges, and who then compensate for overeating through self-induced vomiting, laxative misuse, intensive exercise, fasting, or other means. It is the combination of binge eating and compensation that define BN and that differentiates it from an apparently related syndrome, binge-eating disorder (which we will introduce shortly). In BN, binges are characterized by consumption, with a terrifying sense of dyscontrol, of sometimes massive quantities of calories. Binges can provoke profound feelings of shame, anxiety, or depression, and the bulimic's sense of self-worth and well-being often shifts quite dramatically in concert with her sense of control around eating and body image. This lends to BN a characteristic unpredictability or lability, as people with this syndrome will shift rapidly (depending upon felt control over eating) from a sense of well-being, expansiveness, or excitability, to profound despair, irritability, and depression. Although the validity of BN as a unique diagnostic category seems well supported (Gleaves, Lowe, Snow, Green, & Murphy-Eberenz, 2000), the distinction (in *DSM-IV* criteria) between purging and nonpurging bulimic subtypes may be of dubious merit in identifying truly different populations of sufferers (Tobin, Griffing, & Griffing, 1997).

### Binge-Eating Disorder and Eating Disorders Not Otherwise Specified

Other variations on EDs occur, classified in the *DSM-IV* system as eating disorder not otherwise specified (EDNOS). For example, anorexic-like weight preoccupations and pursuit of thinness in individuals who retain menses, are given the diagnosis of EDNOS. Most important of the EDNOS variants is, however, an apparently quite prevalent pattern characterized by recurrent eating binges in the absence of compensatory behaviors such as vomiting or fasting. This pattern, which (eventually) renders the sufferer overweight, is currently labeled *binge-eating disorder (BED)*. According to provisional criteria, defining characteristics include eating more rapidly than normal, eating until uncomfortably full, eating when not hungry, eating alone due to embarrassment around the quantity one eats, or feeling intense guilt, disgust, or depression after eating. In BED, binge episodes must be markedly distressing.

Compared to individuals with BN, BED patients are noted to binge over considerably longer periods of time (Fairburn, 1995), with individuals in some cases showing day-long binges. Eating in individuals with BED is noted to have a less desperate or driven character than in BN, and BED patients apparently consume more proteins than do bulimics, who preferentially binge on sweets or carbohydrates (Fitzgibbon & Blackman, 2000). In addition, BED subjects are reportedly more likely than bulimics to find the food on which they binge soothing or relaxing (Mitchell et al., 1999).

There has been controversy surrounding the BED diagnosis—a concern being that BED may not isolate a truly psychological or behavioral disturbance. However, data show obese people with BED to have more fear of weight gain, more body dissatisfaction, more problems of self-esteem and dysphoric mood, and poorer maintenance of weight loss (once achieved) than do non-BED obese people (Marcus, Wing, & Hopkins, 1988; Streigel-Moore, Wilson, Wilfley, Elder, & Brownell, 1998). Also lending credence to the validity of BED as a unique entity, data indicate taxonomic and genetic distinctiveness of the syndrome. A latent-class analysis applied in a large cohort of female twins ($N = 2,163$) identified a distinct BED syndrome and showed greater resemblance for the syndrome among monozygotic versus dizygotic twins (Bulik, Sullivan, & Kendler, 1998).

### The Restrictor-Binger Distinction

A distinction between restrictors (those anorexic patients who restrict food intake without binging and purging) and bingers (those ED patients, sometimes anorexic, sometimes bulimic, sometimes obese, who binge and purge) has been introduced by various theorists as an alternative to the formal anorexic-bulimic distinction (see DaCosta & Halmi, 1992). The restrictor-binger distinction has been thought to correspond to important phenomenological and etiological differences, including differences as to key personality features, family interaction styles, and associations with biological processes (all will be reviewed presently).

Where relevant, throughout this chapter, we will address and clarify the rationale for the restrictor-binger distinction concept.

### EPIDEMIOLOGY

Anorexia nervosa and bulimia nervosa occur disproportionately, often in industrialized (vs. economically less developed) nations, but are otherwise reported to occur with surprisingly uniform prevalences in developed parts of Europe, Asia, and the Americas. Reported prevalences in school-aged females of strictly defined AN generally fall in the 0.5% to 1% range (Wakeling, 1996), and of BN generally in the 1% to 2% range (e.g., Garfinkel et al., 1995). However, it is probably fair to assume that in subthreshold forms, identified using less stringent diagnostic criteria, EDs occur in larger numbers (Garfinkel et al.). At least 10% of school-aged females in the industrialized world display partial anorexic or bulimic syndromes, associated with significant dietary, psychological, and medical distress.

Although a popular stereotype is the young adolescent AN sufferer, actual peak prevalences of EDs are observed in young adult women, reflecting the (unfortunate) tendency of EDs to run a chronic course and of BN to develop later in the life cycle (during the transition to adulthood). Although they occur about one-tenth as often in men as in women, classical anorexic and bulimic syndromes are also noted in males (e.g., Wakeling, 1996) and there are some indications to suggest that if ED prevalences are rising in any group, it is doing so especially among males. Eating disorders appear to occur less frequently in certain racial and ethnic groups, for example, among Black and Asian-American versus White females (Crago, Shisslak, & Estes, 1996). A comparison of White, Hispanic, and Black adolescent females, both athletic ($N = 571$) and nonathletic ($N = 463$), for example, showed reliably lower rates of disordered eating in both of the Black female groups, compared to those obtained in White and Hispanic groups (Rhea, 1999). However, some findings suggest that Black women may yet be especially susceptible to certain aspects of eating disturbance: For example, a telephone-interview survey involving 1,628 Black and 5,741 White urban women found Blacks to report more fasting, abuse of laxatives or diuretics, and high-frequency binge eating than did the White women (Striegel-Moore, Wilfley, Pike, Dohm, & Fairburn, 2000).

Although changes in diagnostic and record-keeping practices make it difficult to pin the issue down, evidence suggests an increasing ED incidence (Wakeling, 1996). Reviewing annual incidence rates for AN in the United States published between the early 1960s and the mid-1980s, Mitchell and Eckert (1987) concluded that there had been a progressive increase, from 0.35 to 4.06 per 100,000. Similarly, an incidence study in the Rochester, Minnesota, area concluded, after screening 2,806 medical records for new cases of AN, that there had been a long-term increase in AN, especially among 15- to 24-year-old females (Lucas, Crowson, O'Fallon, & Melton, 1999). In a similar vein, it is commonly believed that EDs are disorders of affluent, urban society. However, current data show surprisingly limited linkage to upper socioeconomic status, and unexpectedly high numbers of EDs found in rural communities suggest that EDs may not be as much an urban phenomenon as may once have been believed (Gard & Freeman, 1996).

Only limited epidemiological data are available for BED, given its more recent addition to the diagnostic nomenclature. Nonetheless, studies suggest a disturbingly common syndrome that may affect from 1% to 5% of the general population and about 8% of the population of obese people. In selected subgroups, such as obese people undergoing weight-loss treatment, BED prevalences apparently run as high as 30–50% (Spitzer et al., 1992). Intriguingly, data show BED to have a more even gender-based distribution than do other EDs, probably affecting 2 males for every 3 females (Streigel-Moore et al., 1998), and to affect a broader age group, with peak age being about 40 years, compared to 28 years for BN (Fitzgibbon & Blackman, 2000). Binge-eating disorder, therefore, seems to be less gender and age dependent than either AN or BN.

## Comorbidity With Other Psychopathology

Paradoxically, it seems that if one assertion can be made about EDs, it is that they are not only about eating. Rather, EDs frequently co-occur with other forms of psychopathology, for example, mood, anxiety, substance-abuse, posttraumatic stress, and personality disorders.

### Mood Disorders

Among comorbid tendencies noted in ED sufferers, comorbid mood disorders figure very prominently. Råstam (1992) reported a 40% rate for currently comorbid major depression in her anorexic sample, a 70% rate for overall mood disorders, and a rate of lifetime mood disorder in excess of 90%. A comparable, or perhaps even more pronounced, tendency toward comorbid mood disorder is noted in binge-purge syndromes. One study, comparing point prevalences of major depression across restricting and binging-purging anorexics, noted the disorder in about 30% of restrictors and in 53% of binger-purgers (Herzog, Keller, Sacks, Yeh, & Lavori, 1992). Other investigations have suggested that from 20% to more than 40% of bulimics are clinically depressed (Brewerton et al., 1995; Garfinkel et al., 1995).

Co-aggregation with other mood-disorder variants is also apparently considerable. A community study by Zaider, Johnson, and Cockell (2000) points to an important affinity between EDs and dysthymia, a milder chronic mood disturbance. In addition, evidence has shown a strong association of BN with seasonal affective disorder (SAD), implying cyclical season-dependent recurrences in depressed mood. In one study, 69% of BN patients were noted to show comorbid SAD (Levitan, Kaplan, Levitt, & Joffe, 1994). Furthermore, a study by our group demonstrated stronger SAD comorbidity in bulimic rather than anorexic ED variants. In a sample of 259 patients presenting at our specialized ED clinic, 27.0% were rated as showing SAD—71.4% diagnosed with BN, 18.6% with AN, and 10.0% with EDNOS (Ghadirian, Marini, Jabalpurlawa, & Steiger, 1999).

Various areas of etiological overlap can be postulated to explain eating disorder–mood disorder convergence. Both syndromes are believed to depend upon similar familial or developmental substrates (e.g., developmental neglect or familial overprotection), and both have been thought to have similar neurobiological substrates. Pertinent to questions of shared causality, a genetic-epidemiological study by Wade, Bulik, Neale, and Kendler (2000), involving 850 female twin pairs indicates that both genetic and environmental factors contribute significantly to shared risk for AN and major depression. Given the implication of serotonergic factors in mood disorders in general and in seasonality in particular, there is ample potential for serotonin-mediated crossover of risk for BN, mood disorders, and SAD—a notion that has been partially corroborated by findings showing serotonin abnormalities to be more pronounced in BN patients with a seasonal profile (Levitan et al., 1997).

### Anxiety Disorders

Anxiety disorders in AN reportedly vary from 20% (Herzog et al., 1992) to more than 80% (Godart, Flament, Lecrubier, & Jeammet, 2000), and reported rates in BN vary from 13% (Herzog et al.) to about 60% (Garfinkel et al., 1995). Godart and colleagues reported 83% of persons with AN and 71% of those with BN to have at least one lifetime anxiety-disorder diagnosis. Most common among the conditions they studied was social phobia (present in 55% of anorexics and 59% of bulimics).

Although studies report generalized anxiety disorder, social and simple phobias, agoraphobia, panic disorder, and obsessive compulsive disorder (OCD) in the EDs, we pay particular attention to data on the convergence between OCD and the EDs. This is because the structure of the EDs so closely resembles that of OCD—intrusive obsessions with weight and body image that are appeased by apparently compulsive gestures, such as fasting or purging. Lifetime prevalences of OCD are reported to range from 15% to 70% in anorexics, and from 3% to 30% in bulimics. Thornton and Russell (1997) reported that OCD was more prevalent in 35 women with AN (27%) than in 33 women with BN (3%), suggesting stronger co-aggregation of OCD with anorexic ED variants. Arguing for a specific affinity, one study indicated that obsessive-compulsive symptoms in adolescent anorexics are more common than are depressive symptoms (Cassidy, Allsopp, & Williams, 1999). Arguing that OCD characteristics may constitute an equally common (and apparently stable) trait in those susceptible to BN, von Ranson, Kaye, Weltzin, Rao, and Matsunaga (1999) found scores measuring OCD to be higher in 31 active bulimics and 29 recovered bulimics (abstinent for more than 1 year) than

in 19 healthy comparison women, with scores on measures of symmetry and exactness being as abnormal in recovered bulimics as they were in active cases.

Various additional studies have examined the temporal sequence of onset for anxiety and eating syndromes, testing the idea that in vulnerable individuals, EDs actually may evolve from anxiety disorders. Thornton and Russell (1997) and Godart et al. (2000) both concluded that anxiety disorders often precede ED onset, implying that an anxious (and often obsessive-compulsive) disposition predisposes to ED development—or may be a manifestation of an incipient ED.

### Substance-Abuse Disorders

Studies consistently indicate bulimic ED variants to be more strongly associated with alcohol and chemical dependencies than is the AN-restrictive type (see Holderness, Brooks-Gunn, & Warren, 1994). Relevant findings show from 10% to 55% of women with BN to abuse substances, whereas from 25% to 40% of *females* with alcohol dependence show some form of (often bulimia-spectrum) ED. Schuckit and colleagues (1996) found BN, but not AN, to occur at a greater-than-expected rate among alcoholic women. Corroborating the impression of syndrome-specific aggregation, a study implicating 1,031 adolescent girls and 888 adolescent boys showed binge eating, especially when associated with compensatory weight-control behaviors, to coincide with elevated substance abuse (Ross & Ivis, 1999). Not surprisingly, studies examining psychopathological implications of substance abuse in the EDs report that concurrent substance abuse predicts greater comorbidity. Lilenfeld and colleagues (1997), for example, found substance abusers in an eating-disordered population to show significantly more social phobia, panic disorder, and personality disorders.

Holderness and colleagues (1994) discuss sources for etiological overlap between bulimic ED variants and substance-abuse disorders. A so-called *addictive personality* (one prone to misuse of substances) has been postulated to underlie both types of syndromes, but evidence of such a personality style is unconvincing. It remains viable to consider shared biological substrates underlying substance-abuse and binge-eating behaviors, mediated by shared genetic diathesis, or shared factors related to serotonin, endorphin, or other neurotransmitters or neurohormones.

### Posttraumatic and Dissociative Disorders

Eating disorders are, in an alarming proportion of cases, associated with adverse (potentially traumatic) life experiences (Everill & Waller, 1995; Wonderlich, Brewerton, Jocic, Dansky, & Abbott, 1997)—a link that we discuss more fully in a later section on developmental factors. Consistent with such observations, findings have suggested a remarkable coincidence between EDs and posttraumatic stress disorder (PTSD). One study reported PTSD in about half of 294 women with AN, BN, or EDNOS (Gleaves, Eberenz, & May, 1998). Severity of PTSD, however, was not found to predict subtype or severity of ED symptoms, suggesting that trauma (and associated posttraumatic stress) may not specifically control eating symptoms. On a related theme, there is a sizable body of data addressing the connection between EDs and dissociative disorders. Characterized by disturbances in memory (e.g., amnesias), consciousness (e.g., problems of identity, or apparent fragmentation of the personality), and sensorimotor function (e.g., conversion-type symptoms), dissociative disorders are sometimes regarded as failed adaptive responses to traumatic stress. Applying the dissociative-disorder concept to EDs, several groups have noted that individuals with BN and BED both produce elevations, relative to normal subjects, psychiatric comparison subjects, and restrictor anorexics, on validated self-report instruments measuring dissociation (e.g., Vanderlinden, Vandereycken, van Dyk, & Vertommen, 1993). Likewise, one study reported that 29 obese women with BED showed significantly more dissociative symptoms on a self-report questionnaire, and more traumatic experiences, than did 35 obese women with no binge-eating symptoms (Grave, Oliosi, Todisco, & Vanderlinden, 1997).

Although evidence suggests a link between dissociative phenomena and bulimic symptoms, the extent to which dissociative symptoms correspond to binge eating, per se, or to general psychopathological indicators that (only incidentally) co-occur with bulimic eating problems, remains to be established. Various relevant studies suggest that dissociation coincides more closely with nonspecific than eating-specific components of psychopathology in ED patients. For example, a study by Gleaves and Eberenz (1995) linked dissociative symptoms more closely to severity of anxiety and depressive symptoms than to bulimic or anorexic symptoms in 53 ED patients. Similarly, Demitrack, Putnam, Brewerton, Brandt, and Gold (1990) concluded that the propensity toward self-mutilation in BN patients is linked more strongly to dissociative pathology than to severity of eating symptoms. In contrast, indicating some degree of specificity in the dissociative disorder–eating disorder connection, Everill, Waller, and Macdonald (1995) found self-reported dissociation, and especially the style of absorption (e.g., daydreaming), to predict frequency of binging in 26 clinical BN sufferers; whereas Katz and Gleaves (1996), studying 52 females diagnosed as having either an ED with dissociation, ED alone, dissociation alone, or neither condition, found that even those ED patients who showed no comorbid dissociative disorder tended to display dissociative-spectrum psychopathology.

Various pathways might account for an etiological link, direct or indirect, between the EDs and traumatic events. Where traumata impact directly upon the body, intuition leads to consideration of relatively direct effects acting upon bodily experience, and in turn upon eating and weight-control behaviors. Alternatively, abusive experiences might impact upon regulation of self, mood, and impulse, and in these ways indirectly heighten the risk of maladaptive eating behavior or moderate the intensity of eating symptoms such as binging or purging. Full discussions of direct and indirect pathways thought to link trauma and EDs are available elsewhere (see Everill & Waller, 1995; Wonderlich et al., 1997). Our group has documented a tendency for more severely abused bulimics to show greater abnormalities on indices reflecting serotonin and cortisol function (Steiger, Gauvin, et al., 2001). Such results could imply neurobiological factors, associated with childhood abuse, that could heighten the risk of over-reactivity to stress and of self- and appetitive dysregulation.

## Personality Disorders

Among various comorbid propensities in the EDs, that with personality disorders is arguably the strongest (see Vitousek & Manke, 1994). A recent meta-analysis (Rosenvinge, Martinussen, & Ostensen, 2000) of 28 studies on this area of comorbidity represents well the general tendencies in findings. In particular, Rosenvinge and colleagues found a higher proportion (58%) of eating-disordered than of comparison women (28%) to have a personality disorder. Furthermore, whereas AN and BN patients were found to show comparable likelihood of *DSM* Cluster-C (anxious-fearful) personality disorders (45% and 44%, respectively), BN patients showed higher proportions of Cluster-B (dramatic-erratic) personality disorders (44% overall) and of borderline personality disorder (31%) than did AN patients or controls. Such findings are representative of themes noted in earlier reviews: Personality disorders are frequently present in anorexic and bulimic syndromes, and results imply differential co-aggregation of personality-disorder subtypes with restrictive and bulimic ED variants. Restrictive AN seems to be associated with a high concentration of anxious-fearful personality-disorder diagnoses (characterized by anxiousness, orderliness, introversion, and preference for sameness and control). Eating-disorder variants characterized by binge-purge symptoms coincide with more heterogeneous personality-disorder subtypes than do restrictive forms, and more importantly, with more pronounced affinity for the dramatic-erratic personality disorders (characterized by prominent attention and sensation seeking, extraversion, mood lability, and proneness to excitability or impulsivity). In other words, the dietary overcontrol that characterizes restrictive AN seems to be paralleled by generalized overcontrol, as a personality or adaptive style, whereas the dietary dyscontrol that characterizes binge-purge syndromes seems, in many cases, to be paralleled by generalized dyscontrol.

Malnutrition can have adverse effects upon personality functioning (Keys, Brozek, Henschel, Mickelson, & Taylor, 1950). This raises the concern that apparent personality disturbances seen in ED sufferers (and, in turn, personality-disorder diagnoses) may reflect state disturbances associated with an active ED rather than trait tendencies. In other words, caution around the use of personality-disorder diagnoses in active ED patients is warranted. Nonetheless, various findings associate the EDs with stable underlying personality disturbances. One investigation reports 26% of women recovered from AN or BN to show some form of ongoing personality disorder, with Cluster-B personality disorders' being more closely associated with bulimic subtypes (Matsaunaga, Kaye, et al., 2000). Another study, comparing 51 weight-restored adolescent-onset anorexics to 51 matched comparison cases, concluded that anorexics often show persistent obsessions, compulsions, and social-interaction problems (Nilsson, Gillberg, Gillberg, & Råstam, 1999).

## ETIOLOGY

Contemporary etiological theory on the EDs invokes a multidimensional, biopsychosocial causality (Garfinkel & Garner, 1982; Striegel-Moore, Silberstein, & Rodin, 1986). In general form, such theory postulates that EDs implicate a collision among biological factors (e.g., heritable influences on mood, temperament, and impulse controls), social pressures (promoting body-consciousness or generalized self-definition problems), psychological tendencies (autonomy disturbances, perfectionism, preference for order and control, hypersensitivity to social approval), and developmental processes (conducive to self-image or adjustment problems). In the following sections, we review evidence pertaining to biological, psychological, and social factors that may act in ED development.

### Psychological Factors

#### Developmental Theories

Psychological theories on ED development are very diverse. However, there is some consensus concerning convergence of psychological characteristics, developmental dynamics, and ED variants. Restrictive AN has been widely associated with traits of compliance and anxiousness in individuals who gravitate to orderliness or control, whereas bulimic subtypes of EDs (including AN, binge-purge subtype) have been linked to

self-regulatory deficits, dramatic fluctuations in self-concept, and erratic efforts to regulate inner tensions. Early *psychodynamic models* interpreted anorexic symptoms as a defense against conflicting drives (e.g., sexual drives); eating was thought to invoke forbidden sexual fantasies, and food refusal to reduce associated anxiety (e.g., Waller, Kaufman, & Deutsch, 1940). Crisp (1980), in a related vein, formulated AN as a *phobic-avoidance response,* reinforced by a literal escape from maturational changes at puberty. In her conceptualization, Bruch (1973) emphasized *maternal overinvolvement* and failure to respond appropriately to the child's self-affirming behaviors, believing such parenting problems to underlie autonomy deficits and pervasive feelings of ineffectiveness on the child's part. Strober's (1991) *organismic-developmental paradigm* again addressed pathological adaptations to adolescence, but emphasized an incompatibility between developmental imperatives surrounding puberty and a heritable temperament characterized by *harm-avoidance, hyperreactivity to social approval,* and *preference for sameness.* Related theories regard food refusal as a gesture of self-assertion, mounted by some children in the face of excessive familial controls or emotional overinvestment; in other words, as an adaptation to familial intrusions and overprotectiveness (e.g., Humphrey, 1991; Johnson, 1991).

From a developmental perspective, bulimic ED variants have been thought to be linked to family-wide interaction patterns tinged with greater hostility, neglect, criticism, rejection, and blaming (Humphrey, 1991; Johnson, 1991). For example, Johnson linked bulimic symptoms to parental neglect, in his view spanning a continuum from nonmalevolent forms (in families in which parents' perfectionistic needs place excessive demands upon children) to malevolent forms (occurring in frankly chaotic or abusive families). Humphrey referred to family-wide deficits in nurturance and tension regulation and systems that ensnare members in mutually destructive, hostile, blaming projections. In both views, bulimic behaviors are conceived to play self- and mood-regulatory functions and to be metaphors for chaotic family interactions, tinged with desperate attempts to achieve closeness and hostile rejections.

### Empirical Findings: Individual Psychological Characteristics

Empirical findings on personality and on cognitive and emotional functioning in individuals with EDs provide qualified support for tendencies outlined previously in the theoretical accounts.

**Personality Characteristics.** Early psychometric studies showed anorexic patients to be neurotic, socially anxious, and often depressed (Sohlberg & Strober, 1994). In addition, various findings pointed to a systematic co-aggregation between restrictor and binger-purger subtypes (on the one hand) and personality traits with an overcontrolled or dyscontrolled style (on the other)—the binger-purgers' being noted to show greater emotional lability, impulsivity, or oppositionality than the restrictors, and lesser extraversion and novelty seeking (risk taking). The same concept is reiterated, although imperfectly, in various contemporary studies. Findings with the Millon Clinical Multiaxial Inventory have, for example, suggested more schizoid or avoidant tendencies among restrictors and more histrionic tendencies among normal- or anorexic-weight bingers (Norman, Blais, & Herzog, 1993). With the Multidimensional Personality Questionnaire, Casper, Hedeker, and McClough (1992) found normal-weight bulimics to be less conforming and more impulsive than were either restrictor or binger-purger anorexics, but found the restrictors to show the greatest self-control, conscientiousness, and emotional inhibition. With the Tridimensional Personality Questionnaire, Bulik, Sullivan, Weltzin, and Kaye (1995) found normal-weight bulimics to be more novelty seeking than restrictor or binger anorexics, and restrictor anorexics to be more reward dependent than bulimic anorexics, but bulimic anorexics to be more harm avoidant than restrictors.

Taken together, available findings seem to support two theoretically important generalizations (seen also in data reviewed earlier on comorbid personality disorders): (a) Restrictive AN is associated with relatively circumscribed personality characteristics, with particular emphasis on traits of rigidity, emotional constriction, and compulsivity. (b) Binge-purge syndromes, on the other hand, are associated with relatively heterogeneous psychopathological characteristics that sometimes implicate greater behavioral disinhibition and affectivity. We illustrate this combination of tendencies in Figure 7.1, making the assumption that overcontrol and dyscontrol can be regarded as spanning a continuum along various theoretically related dimensions (e.g., compulsivity vs. impulsivity; preference for sameness vs. novelty seeking; introversion vs. extroversion; etc.). The figure depicts a tendency for there to be a circumscribed convergence, in restrictive ED variants, of overcontrolled tendencies, but greater heterogeneity as to characteristics in bulimic (binge-purge) variants. Some bulimic cases show overcontrol, as has been associated with restrictive AN, but many others show marked erraticism and dyscontrol. Given trait heterogeneity among bulimics, theorists have proposed the existence of multiple pathways to bulimic eating disturbances, with some individuals being vulnerable due to underlying dysregulatory processes that manifest themselves in the form of mood and impulse dysregulation. What is believed is that, in some individuals, processes that correspond to generalized behavioral disinhibition may also underlie appetitive dysregulation (see Vitousek & Manke, 1994).

**Specific Traits of Importance.** Clinical observations consistently associate AN with specific personality traits, including perfectionism and impulsivity. For example, one study reported 322 anorexic women (restrictors and binger-purgers alike) to have higher Multidimensional Perfectionism Scale scores than do 44 healthy control women, and notes a coincidence between degree of perfectionism and severity of eating symptomatology (Halmi et al., 2000). Perfectionism is also noted to be elevated in BN probands and their relatives (Lilenfeld et al., 2000), but not in individuals with BED (Fairburn et al., 1998). In addition, data show perfectionism to be evident in AN after long-term weight recovery (Srinivasagam et al., 1995), suggesting that the dimension may be an exophenotypic characteristic of AN. Following from this view, studies have attempted to link perfectionism causally to ED development. Perfectionism has been noted to be elevated premorbidly in those with AN and BN, compared to those with other mental disorders (Fairburn, Cooper, Doll, & Welch, 1999). However, assessed prospectively, perfectionism has not emerged as a predictor of individuals who, among healthy adolescents, would develop later ED symptoms (Calam & Waller, 1998).

We have already noted that bulimic patients can show remarkable propensities toward nonreflectiveness, behavioral disinhibition, self-harming behaviors, or other impulsive characteristics. Almost half of a cohort of normal-weight bulimics studied by Newton, Freeman, and Munro (1993), for example, met criteria for a *multi-impulsive* syndrome characterized by substance abuse, multiple overdoses, recurrent self-harm, sexual disinhibition, or shoplifting. Such findings corroborate the impression (described earlier) that impulse-control problems are prominent in many BN sufferers. Pronounced impulsivity in BN has been linked, in different reports, to more severe eating disturbances

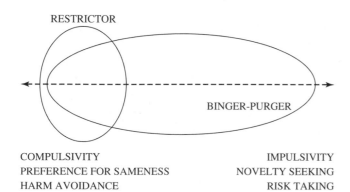

RESTRICTOR

BINGER-PURGER

| COMPULSIVITY | IMPULSIVITY |
| PREFERENCE FOR SAMENESS | NOVELTY SEEKING |
| HARM AVOIDANCE | RISK TAKING |
| INTROVERSION | EXTRAVERSION |
| OVERREGULATION | DYSREGULATION |

**Figure 7.1** Hypothetical relationship between eating-disorder subtypes and personality-trait dimensions.

(binge eating, vomiting, laxative abuse, and drive for thinness), greater body-image problems, and greater generalized psychopathology—including substance abuse, self-injurious behaviors, and borderline traits (e.g., Wiederman & Pryor, 1996). However, impulsivity has not been shown to correspond to severity of bulimic symptoms in other studies (e.g., Wolfe, Jimerson, & Levine, 1994). In consequence, controversy remains around the question of whether impulsivity drives bulimic symptoms (and hence corresponds to their severity), or whether it should be regarded as an independent comorbid dimension that may heighten susceptibility but that is otherwise independent of symptom severity.

**Gender Identifications.**    Given its gender distribution, there has been interest among ED theorists in variables reflecting gender-role adherence and gender identifications. Early findings suggested that eating-disordered women tended (in the most traditional sense of the term) to be hyperfeminine, or overidentified with traditional female roles (Sitnick & Katz, 1984). A recent meta-analysis of 22 studies on the relationship between gender-role adherence and EDs provides modest corroboration of this proposal, finding clinical eating problems to be related positively with femininity and negatively with masculinity (Murnen & Smolak 1997).

**Body-Image Perception.**    Given that the defining characteristics of AN and BN include disturbed body perception and experience, there has been a surprising degree of controversy around the body-image disturbance concept in the EDs. Although many empirical findings suggest overestimation of bodily proportions or unusually harsh attitudes toward body image in ED patients, many others suggest that eating-disordered individuals have body-image perceptions and attitudes that are quite normal (see Hsu & Sobkiewicz, 1991). Where abnormalities in bodily experience are identified, current findings tend to emphasize emotional and attentional factors and not perceptual ones (e.g., Carter, Bulik, Lawson, Sullivan, & Wilson, 1996). The actual origins of bodily disturbances in the EDs remain uncertain and have been postulated to reflect various factors; from social-learning influences, to effects of biological abnormalities that alter thought and perception, to the impact of body-relevant trauma.

**Body Dysmorphic Disorder.**    Although its relationship to the EDs is uncertain, body-image disturbance is as much a central characteristic of body dysmorphic disorder (APA, 1994) as it is of EDs, and we therefore provide a special comment on this syndrome. *Body dysmorphic disorder* is defined by distress or functional impairment due to a preoccupation with a real (but minor) or an imagined physical defect. Because it involves an intense, distressing preoccupation (in this case with bodily characteristics) and the drive to correct perceived imperfections, it is often thought to represent a variant of OCD. Hence, one possible common pathway linking body dysmorphic disorder and eating disorders might be an underlying obsessive-compulsive structure. Regardless of whether this is true, body dysmorphic disorder appears to be prevalent in people with EDs, and it has been proposed that this convergence reflects common pathogenesis—especially at a neurobiological level (Olivardia, Pope, & Hudson, 2000)—and possible etiological convergence with OCD (see Widiger & Sankis, 2000). Consistent with the possibility of an ontological relationship, symptoms of body dysmorphic disorder have been reported to precede onset of anorexic symptoms in some anorexic patients. Indeed, some theorists have proposed that the thinness preoccupations seen in anorexic and bulimic women may represent gender-specific variants of the more generalized bodily preoccupations that manifest as body dysmorphic disorder—and which may be more focused upon fitness than on thinness among men (Widiger & Sankis, 2000). However, despite a common object of concern (i.e., the body), various differences are noted. Eating-disordered patients are noted to be mainly concerned about weight and body shape, whereas sufferers of body dysmorphic disorder have more diverse physical complaints and more pronounced negative self-evaluation and social avoidance due to appearance (Gupta & Johnson, 2000). Furthermore, EDs are, in at least some studies, noted to have broader implications for psychopathology. Hence, although speculations on commonalities remain appealing, it is premature to assume that EDs and body dysmorphic disorder are truly comparable syndromes at either phenomenological or etiological levels.

### State versus Trait Issues on Personality Dimensions

Given the known effects of malnutrition (and other ED sequelae) upon the mental status, it is necessary, when studying affinities between psychological characteristics and eating disturbances, to differentiate stable, underlying *traits* from effects of being in an eating-disordered *state*. One approach to this question has been to assess characteristics in formerly eating-disordered individuals after recovery. Certain tendencies have seemed to represent likely ED sequelae. For example, data have indicated recovered anorexics to display less harm avoidance and oppositionality and a more external locus of control than do actively ill anorexics (Bulik, Sullivan, Fear, & Pickering, 2000). Similarly, a study by our group showed rather marked illness-related sequelae (in the form of increased depression, anxiety, suicidality, interpersonal problems, and compulsivity in actively ill bulimics) that were not evident in recovered ones (Lehoux, Steiger, & Jabalpurlawa, 2000). In contrast, enduring traits of rigidity, overcautiousness, and obsessionality have been reported to persist (over several years) in recovered anorexics (Windauer, Lennerts, Talbot, Touyz, & Beumont, 1993), whereas enduring narcissistic disturbances are reported in recovered bulimics (Lehoux et al., 2000).

### Binge Antecedents and Consequences

Cognitive components of dietary restraint—so-called *restrictive eating attitudes* (e.g., the belief that one should always eat low-calorie foods, or compensate when one eats more than usual)—are thought to make an important contribution to the development of disinhibited (binge-like) eating behaviors. Polivy and Herman's (1985) *restraint theory* specifically postulates that chronic attitudinal restraint of eating potentiates the breakdown of cognitive controls upon appetitive behaviors, and eventual counterregulation (or overeating). It also proposes that counterregulation has specific cognitive and emotional triggers. An impressive catalogue of findings, derived mainly from laboratory studies in nonclinical populations, shows counterregulation of eating behavior to be induced (in attitudinally restrained eaters) by manipulations that generate (a) beliefs that one has exceeded an allowable calorie limit; (b) negative affects; (c) feelings of self-inadequacy; or (d) global disinhibition, as is induced following alcohol consumption. Clinical experience dictates that all of these factors are relevant as binge precipitants in clinical BN patients.

The connection between binge eating and emotional factors deserves specific comment. Functional analyses of binge-eating antecedents (usually performed using on-line experience-sampling procedures) suggest that the proximal antecedents to binge episodes often include negative emotions (depression, anger, emptiness, worry), aversive social experiences, or negative self-perceptions (e.g., Polivy & Herman, 1993; Steiger, Gauvin, Jabalpurlawa, Séguin, & Stotland, 1999; Stickney, Miltenberger, & Wolff, 1999). Furthermore, data show that, compared with nonclinical dieters and nondieter controls, bulimic patients respond to laboratory stressors with increases in both hunger and the desire to binge (e.g., Tuschen-Caffier & Vogele, 1999). As for sequelae, binge episodes are reported to provide transient relief from negative feelings and thoughts and to decrease hunger and food cravings (e.g., Stickney et al.), but to heighten negative affect, poor self-esteem, and probability of further binge eating (Steiger, Gauvin, et al.) over the long term. Such consequences of binge-eating behaviors may be ingredients in the tendency for binge eating to become entrenched and self-perpetuating.

The preceding suggests that binge antecedents may include states characterized by caloric deprivation, negative affects, high social stress, and negative self-concepts. Intriguingly, available literature has also suggested that different antecedents may influence binge-eating behaviors in different individuals. In support, studies have documented a subgroup of binge eaters who deny dieting prior to the onset of eating binges (e.g., Borman Spurrel, Wilfley, Tanofsky, & Brownell, 1997). Moreover, Borman Spurrell et al. noted that people in whom binge eating preceded onset of dieting showed more evidence of personality pathology. These findings resonate with data from our research group, suggesting that restraint may be a weaker hour-to-hour antecedent to binge episodes in highly impulsive versus in less-impulsive bulimics (Steiger, Gauvin, et al., 1999). We interpret these findings as implying that processes associated with impulsivity may contribute directly to the propensity to binge. In this regard, it is noteworthy that some of our findings (described in the section titled "Neurobiology"), have linked impulsivity in bulimics to greater disturbance of central serotonin mechanisms that are also thought to underlie problems with satiety mechanisms.

### Cognitive Functioning

Anorexic and bulimic ED variants have both been linked to (generally mild) neuropsychological impairments associated with higher-level cognitive functions such as active memory, attention, and problem solving (e.g., Szmukler et al., 1992). In addition, some neuropsychological data corroborate the theme of general restrictor-binger differences. Blanz, Detzner, Lay, Rose, and Schmidt (1997) found that BN but not AN patients to show better nonverbal than verbal performance, and Toner, Garfinkel, and Garner (1987) indicated bulimic anorexics to be more likely than restrictor anorexics to commit errors of commission, suggesting problems with response inhibition. Studies that examine the prospective course of neuropsychological impairments in ED patients report improvements that coincide with ED-symptom remission for both AN (Szmukler et al.) and BN (Lauer, Gorzewski, Gerlinghoff, Backmund, & Zihl, 1999). However, some findings indicate alarmingly permanent structural and neuropsychological alterations (Lambe, Katzman, Mikulis, Kennedy, & Zipursky, 1997).

### Family and Developmental Characteristics

Suggestive themes emerge in family findings pertaining to the EDs. However, there are several important limitations of the literature in this area: (1) Very few of the available studies apply appropriate psychiatric control groups to establish specificity of observed patterns to eating syndromes. (2) Studies rarely provide for corroboration, by family members, of observations from actively eating-disordered participants. (3) Even when systematic tendencies are identified (ED-specific or otherwise), there remains a need to clarify whether they express dynamic family patterns (transmitted via psychosocial pathways), or effects of temperamental traits (representing inherited tendencies). These concerns aside, available data have provided partial corroboration of developmental theories on EDs (reviewed earlier).

Studies on anorexic individuals and their relatives have provided general corroboration of the concepts of enmeshment, overprotection, separation problems, and conflict avoidance. Studies report anorexics' families to limit members' autonomy, or to show unusually low levels of conflict. Crisp, Hsu, Harding, and Hartshorn (1980) reported disturbed parent-child interactions in about half of 102 cases of AN, with enmeshment being the most commonly reported theme. Goldstein (1981), using coded records of parent-child interactions, discriminated families of hospitalized anorexics from those of hospitalized nonanorexics, on dimensions reflecting requests for protection and conflict avoidance. Similarly, families of anorexics have been noted to show unusually low expressed emotion, indicating low levels of conflictual or disapproving interactions (Hodes & leGrange, 1993). Such observations are compatible with the concept of an enmeshed or underseparated familial organization. However, Kog, Vertommen, and Vandereycken's (1987) study of families with an eating-disordered daughter indeed identified a subset that displayed low conflict, although they found this pattern to coincide with bulimic ED variants as frequently as it did with restrictive ones. Their finding raises some doubts about the specificity of the conflict-avoiding, enmeshed family concept for AN.

Observational studies of families in which binge-purge syndromes develop have tended to corroborate the perspective that such syndromes coincide relatively more often with overt familial discord and hostility. For example, Sights and Richards (1984) noted bulimics' families to display marked parent-daughter stress and rated bulimics' mothers as being domineering and demanding. Similar themes are conveyed by Humphrey's rather extensive observational work with eating-disordered families (see Humphrey, 1991). In studies comparing bulimic-anorexic mother-father-daughter triads to those of normal triads, her findings showed the bulimic-anorexic families to be more blameful, rejecting, and neglectful, and less nurturant and comforting. Likewise, in a series of studies contrasting family processes in females with normal-weight bulimia, bulimic AN, restrictive AN, or no

ED, Humphrey found the families of both bulimic subgroups to be prone to deficits in parental nurturance and (to some extent) empathy. In keeping with this notion, studies have indicated *expressed emotion* (i.e., open conflict and critical comments) to be greater in bingers' than in restrictors' families (Hodes & leGrange, 1993).

Data on family interaction patterns in BED are very rare, making it premature to draw conclusions. However, Hodges, Cochrane, and Brewerton (1998) obtained self-reports on family functioning in 23 anorexic-restrictor, 45 bulimic, 20 anorexic-binger, and 43 BED women. The BED patients reported less family cohesion than did anorexic ones and less familial expressiveness than did bulimic ones. The BED women also indicated their families to show less cohesion, expressiveness, independence, and intellectual-cultural and active-recreational pursuits than did women in a normal control group. Relative to the normal control women, BED patients reported their families to be higher on dimensions measuring conflict and control. In other words, BED patients seemed to be reporting a constellation of family interaction patterns that was at least partially reminiscent of those of BN patients.

Although there are systematic convergences between family interaction patterns (on the one hand) and ED subtypes (on the other), recent thinking on family factors in the EDs is close to abandoning the probably unrealistic notion that there may be ED-specific family interaction variants. Instead, theorists address more interesting questions about the possible modulating role of family functioning in the development and maintenance of eating symptoms. Schmidt, Humfress, and Treasure (1997) noted that severity of family dysfunction corresponds closely to severity of personality pathology in affected individuals, suggesting a modulating influence of family functioning enacted through concurrent psychopathological traits.

### Psychosocial Induction

It is appealing to presume that the EDs depend upon psychosocial induction effects in which parents convey maladaptive concerns with body image, weight, and eating to their children. Indeed, in clinical populations, many studies report parents of ED sufferers to show abnormal eating and body-image attitudes (e.g., Hall & Brown, 1983). However, many others report an absence of differences between parents with and without eating-disordered daughters (e.g., Hall, Leibrich, Walkley, & Welch, 1986). At the same time, various findings are consistent with parental influences upon children's eating behavior. Miller, McCluskey-Fawcett, and Irving (1993) compared perceptions of early mealtime experiences across normal eaters, repeat dieters, and bulimics, and found the bulimics to display more eating-related issues in the early family context. In a related vein, a recent study of 369 adolescent girls and their parents found that parents' encouragements to daughters to lose weight were more significant as predictors of daughters' dietary restraint than were parents' own dietary restraint levels, and mothers' encouragements were more influential than were fathers' (Wertheim, 1999). Such findings may be sensitive to retrospective reporting biases but they are consistent with the idea that the family's eating and body-image-relevant attitudes can convey risk for an ED.

Yet another source of parental influence over children's eating patterns is suggested by data showing a disturbing degree of association between mothers' EDs and feeding problems in children. Whelan and Cooper (2000) rated a filmed family meal in three groups of 4-year-olds: Children with feeding problems ($N = 42$), children with a nonfeeding form of disturbance (e.g., shyness or behavioral disturbance; $N = 79$), and children with no disturbance ($N = 29$). They found mothers of children with feeding problems, when compared to mothers in the other two groups, to have higher rates of current and past EDs but not mood disorders.

## Attachment

On the basis of a review of studies concerning parent-child and familial attachment patterns in the EDs, Ward, Ramsay, Turnbull, Benedettini, and Treasure (2000) concluded that ED patients display pathological attachment tendencies. Various studies have indicated that individuals with anorexia, relative to healthy controls, report one or both parents to be less affectionate, empathic, caring, or protective (Rhodes & Kroger, 1992; Steiger, Van der Feen, Goldstein, & Leichner, 1989). Rhodes and Kroger found anorexic individuals to be anxious about parental separation and engulfment, whereas Armstrong and Roth (1989) found AN subjects to have more anxious attachments and separation depression than controls. While such findings are suggestive, we note that they do not necessarily imply ED-specific anomalies.

Data indicate parallel attachment problems in BN. Individuals with bulimia report themselves to form dependent or insecure attachments (Jacobsin & Robins, 1989), to be mistrustful of others, anxious about revealing imperfections, and fearful of intimacy (Pruitt, Kappins, & Gorman, 1992). An experience-sampling study by our group highlights the potential importance of relationship factors in BN, in that stressful social experiences emerged as relatively direct antecedents to binge episodes in actively bulimic women (Steiger, Gauvin, et al., 1999).

## Childhood Sexual Abuse

Modal figures indicate roughly 30% of ED sufferers to report some form of unwanted sexual experience during childhood (e.g., Everill & Waller, 1995; Wonderlich et al., 1997). Given that they implicate such markedly disturbed bodily experience, it is enticing to think that EDs may be specifically (and causally) linked to body-relevant trauma occurring during childhood. However, it should be noted that observed rates of trauma in ED sufferers do not consistently exceed those obtained in females with other psychopathology, an implication that there is a strong but nonspecific association of the EDs with childhood trauma.

Data comparing prevalence of childhood sexual trauma in restricting and binging subgroups have suggested that bulimic ED variants might be associated with the more unfavorable developmental experiences. Schmidt et al. (1997), for example, conclude that findings have consistently associated childhood abuse more strongly with binge-purge than with restrictive ED variations. In keeping with the suggested tendency, Webster and Palmer (2000) found that women with bulimic symptomatology (but not restrictive AN) reported more troubled childhood experiences than did normal-eater comparison women, but reported experiences comparable to those of women with depression. Although such observations could reflect greater repression in restrictors, or protectiveness of the family, the trend in question would also be consistent with an overall portrait of the bulimic family as being the more destructive, abusive, or neglectful, rendering the child subject to a heightened risk of abuse. These data also reiterate the point made earlier about relative nonspecificity of the link between EDs and childhood abuse.

Community-survey data have corroborated the notion that BN coincides with relative elevations of victimization experiences. A telephone survey of 3,006 women linked history of forcible assault or rape to BN more than to BED or non–eating disordered status. Furthermore, in this study, reliance upon compensatory behaviors was associated with higher rates of victimization (Dansky, Brewerton, Kilpatrick, & O'Neil, 1997). Even if childhood traumata are more strongly linked to bulimic than to restrictive ED variants, however, this need not imply bulimia-specific pathogenic effects. Several studies in BN have noted that severity of childhood abuse predicts severity of personality pathology, impulsivity, dissociative potentials, and other forms of comorbid psychopathology more directly than it does severity of bulimic symptoms. For example, a study comparing 50 sexually abused versus 83 nonsexually abused eating-disordered women showed elevations in the sexually abused women, not on ED symptoms, but on various self-reported personality dimensions: schizotypal, avoidant, schizoid, passive-aggressive, and borderline (Moreno, Selby, & Neal, 1998). One study of 44 former bulimics found that those with a history of sexual or physical abuse ($N = 20$) had more posttraumatic symptoms and more substance dependence (Matsunaga, Kaye, et al., 1999).

## Sociocultural Context

Eating disorders occur disproportionately often in Western industrialized nations, implying that cultural ideals prevailing in the West may be conducive to ED development. It is obvious that Western social values to some extent equate slimness with cultural ideals of success, beauty, power, and self-control, and there is little doubt that such factors play some role in the development of clinical EDs (see Garfinkel & Garner, 1982). Changing ideals for female body shape are thought to be associated with the apparent increase in incidence of EDs that occurred in the West during the decades since 1960 (see the section titled "Epidemiology"). This period coincided with a dramatic shift in a cultural ideal—from a voluptuous form represented by such icons as Marilyn Monroe, Elizabeth Taylor, or Sophia Loren to a thin (and often relatively androgynous) ideal for female appearance that became popular in the early 1960s, and that remains prominent in celebrity and media images in the 2000s. Attesting to the importance of peer and pop culture influences in the development of maladaptive eating, a 1-year prospective study of 6,982 girls showed that measures of the felt importance of looking like the females that are seen on television, in movies, or in magazines predict the onset of regular vomiting or laxative abuse as a means of weight control (Field, Camargo, Taylor, Berkey, & Colditz, 1999). Further supporting the concept that social values pertinent to thinness have a causal role in EDs, the work of Garner and Garfinkel (see Garfinkel & Garner, 1982) shows AN to occur exceptionally often in individuals whose social milieu emphasizes weight control (e.g., ballet dancers, models, or athletes). In a related vein, various findings suggest that Western cultural values have a special role in generating risk for ED development. Davis and Katzman (1999) noted that level of eating and body-image concerns corresponded quite directly to the level of acculturation to American values of Chinese university students studying in the United States. Likewise, Lake, Staiger, and Glowinski (2000) compared Australian-born and Hong Kong–born Australian university students on eating attitudes and body-shape perceptions, and found that Australian-born and Western-acculturated Hong Kong–born women showed greater body-image problems.

Although risk for EDs is certainly linked to Western social contexts, such social effects may yet have only a limited influence in ED etiology. For example, systematic cross-cultural research indicates anorexia-like syndromes, characterized by food refusal, to be prevalent in diverse (non-Western) contexts (Pate, Pumariega, Hester, & Garner, 1992), suggesting that anorexia-like syndromes may not be as culture-bound as once thought. A self-report assessment of attitudes toward eating among undergraduate women studying in Pennsylvania ($N = 111$) and South Korea ($N = 115$) showed similar percentages (21% and 18%, respectively) of respondents reporting elevations on an ED-screening instrument (Lippincott & Hwang, 1999). Indeed, some cross-cultural data reduce emphasis upon the role of cultural pressures favoring slimness in ED pathogenesis altogether. Lee, Ho, and Hsu (1993), for example, provided a well-constructed study of individuals with anorexia in Hong Kong—all of whom were clearly anorexic according to criteria reflecting self-imposed weight loss, resistance to others' encouragements to eat, and amenorrhea (or loss of libido, in one male case). However, unlike individuals with anorexia encountered in American contexts, roughly 60% were noted to display no conscious fear of becoming fat. They justified their food refusal instead by stating a desire to avoid gastric bloating. Given similar findings from other Asian studies, Lee and colleagues proposed that *fat phobia* may be characteristic of weight-conscious Western societies but not definitive of AN at large. These findings imply that culture may exert pathoplastic effects that shape ultimate ED expression.

Other cross-cultural studies have reported an absence of cultural influences or culture-free universals that apply to the EDs. For example, bulimic tendencies and proneness to generalized impulse-control problems have been noted to coincide as much in Japanese samples as in Western cases (Matsunaga, Kiriike, et al., 2000). Similarly, cross-cultural data make a case that, regardless of cultural context, EDs and OCD converge (Matsunaga, Kiriike, et al., 1999). Emphasizing a universal importance of maladaptive family interactions as an ED correlate, one study has shown that the degree of maladaptive eating attitudes and behaviors in British Asian schoolgirls correlates with measures of familial overprotection and conflicts around socializing (Furnham & Husain, 1999).

## Biological Factors

### Family Studies

Findings from available family studies provide unequivocal support for the conclusion that there is familial aggregation for the EDs, a prerequisite if one assumes biological transmission. The largest case-controlled study available examined the prevalence of EDs among first-degree relatives of 300 probands with AN or BN (Strober, Freeman, Lampert, Diamond, & Kaye, 2000). This investigation found substantially higher risks for AN in female relatives of anorexic and bulimic probands (relative risks of 11.3 and 12.3, respectively) compared to those obtained in relatives of normal-eater comparison subjects. A familial propensity was also indicated for BN, with relative risks of 4.2 for relatives of anorexic probands and 4.4 for bulimic probands, respectively. These findings suggest a strong family tendency for both anorexic and bulimic ED variants, but stronger aggregation for AN than for BN. Results of another recent family study have suggested that relatives of AN and BN probands both show similarly elevated risk for ED, without AN or BN specificity (Lilenfeld et al., 1998). These findings are consistent with familial transmission for a general factor that heightens susceptibility to EDs, but not specifically to AN or BN.

## Cotransmission in Families With Other Syndromes

Family data need not imply disorder-specific transmission effects. Rather, they could reflect a liability that is conveyed by linkage within the family to another heritable disturbance or syndrome. Relationships of this type have been explored for the EDs with respect to various forms of psychopathology. Family studies suggest substantially higher rates of mood disorders, especially unipolar depression, among relatives of anorexic (e.g., Strober, Lampert, Morrell, Burroughs, & Jacobs, 1990) and bulimic (e.g., Logue, Crowe, & Bean, 1989) probands. However, when distinctions between ED probands with and without an ascertained history of mood disorder have been made, findings reveal increased risk of affective disorders in only the relatives of those ED probands who themselves suffer from mood disturbance (Lilenfeld et al., 1998; Strober et al.). In other words, while shared vulnerability factors may be implicated, there does not seem to be any simple or direct cotransmission for eating and affective disturbances.

Similarly, various studies have documented an increased rate of alcohol and drug abuse in ED patients and their relatives, especially in the relatives of bulimic probands (Lilenfeld et al., 1998). However, as noted for mood disorders, evidence on the co-aggregation of eating and substance-use disorders favors belief in independent transmission because only the relatives of ED probands who themselves abuse substances show consistently higher risk of substance-abuse problems (e.g., Lilenfeld et al.). Likewise, Lilenfeld and colleagues report that only eating-disordered probands who themselves show heightened OCD have family histories characterized by higher OCD prevalence. In other words, familial transmission of OCD appears also to occur independently of EDs.

In an intriguing contrast to the preceding, Lilenfeld and colleagues (1998) have also suggested shared familial transmission of obsessive-compulsive *personality* disorder (OCPD) with AN (but not BN). In their study, relatives of anorexic probands showed elevated OCPD, regardless of the presence of OCPD in the anorexic proband. Such findings are in keeping with the notion that there may be a relatively AN-specific transmission, within families, of personality traits of perfectionism, rigidity, and harm avoidance (i.e., OCPD) and risk for AN.

## Twin Studies

Through comparison of concordance rates in genetically identical (i.e., monozygotic) versus nonidentical (i.e., dizygotic) twins, it becomes possible to isolate genetic factors that contribute to a disorder. Twin data can, furthermore (using behavioral-genetic models), be analyzed to tease apart the relative contributions of additive-genetic effects (i.e., inherited liabilities) , shared-environmental effects (i.e., liabilities resulting from such influences as general family-interaction patterns, or the family's socioeconomic status), and effects of the nonshared or individual-specific environment (i.e., liabilities related to having experienced childhood trauma, or having had a particular type of relationship with one parent). Various twin studies of EDs have now been completed, providing intriguing yet equivocal findings.

In a clinically ascertained sample of 31 monozygotic and 28 dizygotic anorexic twins, Treasure and Holland (1989) found substantially higher concordance in monozygotic than in dizygotic pairs (45% vs. 2%, respectively). Furthermore, when diagnostic criteria were narrowed to accept only restricting AN (i.e., excluding patients with binge or purge symptoms), differences between mono- and dizygotic twins became even more striking—with concordance increasing to 65% for monozygotic and falling to 0% for dizygotic. Such findings imply rather striking heritability for a restrictive AN factor, and based on their results, Treasure and Holland estimated a 70% liability for restrictive AN attributable to additive genetic effects. Raising controversy around such conclusions, however, Walters and Kendler (1995), in a population-based (vs. clinically ascertained) sample, obtained no evidence of heightened risk for AN in monozygotic compared to dizygotic twins.

A reanalysis of combined data from the early-available twin studies on BN revealed 46% concordance for monozygotic twins versus 26% concordance for dizygotic twins, with an estimated 47% of the variance attributable to additive genetic effects, 30% to shared environment, and 23% to nonshared environment (Bulik, Sullivan, Wade, et al., 2000). Similarly, a population-based study of 2,163 female twins found concordance rates for BN to be 22.9% for monozygotic and 8.7% for dizygotic twins (Kendler et al., 1991), with an estimated 55% of variance from additive genetic effects, 0% from shared environment, and 45% from individual-specific environmental effects. Other studies have examined genetic effects acting upon more broadly defined (subthreshold) variants of BN. For example, Bulik, Sullivan, and Kendler (1998) estimated heritability of broadly defined BN to be 83% in a sample of 854 twin pairs, suggesting that BN is quite a heritable syndrome.

### Genetic Linkage Studies

Genetic linkage studies seek to identify genes, in affected individuals and their relatives, that may underlie risk for a specific disorder. Studies aimed at candidate genes underlying ED vulnerability have focused on genes coding for dopamine, serotonin, and noradrenaline systems, under the assumption (which will be explained further) that these monoamines may regulate eating behavior. To date, relevant studies in anorexic samples have failed to find systematic linkage of particular variants of dopamine (Bruins-Slot et al., 1998) or $\beta_3$-adrenergic receptor (Hinney et al., 1997) genes in AN. The search for candidate genes within the serotonin (5-hydroxytryptamine, or 5HT) system has, however, yielded somewhat more promising results. Association has been reported between AN and a polymorphism ($-1438$G/A) in the promoter region of the $5HT_{2A}$ receptor (Enoch et al., 1998). Furthermore, this $5HT_{2A}$ finding has been found to be associated with both AN restrictor subtype and OCD, but not with bulimic ED variants. Together, such findings argue that the 5HT gene variation in question may correspond to both "anorexic" and "generalized" obsessions and compulsions.

Possible genetic substrates for BN are also identified. Levitan et al. (2000) reported an association between the C218 allele of the gene encoding for tryptophan hydroxylase (or TPH, the rate-limiting enzyme for 5HT synthesis) and BN. It is pertinent to note that Nielsen and colleagues (1998) reported a similar association, in male offenders, between a TPH gene variant (on the one hand) and suicidality and alcoholism (on the other hand), suggesting that this gene variant may correspond to an impulsive–behaviorally dysregulated phenotype. Such findings, viewed together, are consistent with the tendency of bulimic ED variants to be characterized by impulsivity and behavioral dyscontrol.

### Neurobiology

The search for neurobiological agents that are implicated in the pathophysiology of EDs has led to the exploration of neurotransmitter, neuropeptide, and hormone systems involved in appetite, feeding behaviors, affect regulation, and temperament.

**Neurotransmitters.** Various monoamine neurotransmitters play a role in appetite regulation. Actions upon appetitive behaviors of noradrenaline and dopamine appear to include both excitatory and inhibitory effects upon feeding behavior, depending upon receptor sites stimulated. In contrast, serotonin (5HT), via its action on hypothalamic receptors, is believed to act mainly in the mediation of satiety. Animal and human studies indicate experimental manipulations that increase 5HT neurotransmission to lead to suppression of food intake, whereas antagonism of 5HT leads to hyperphagia (see Brewerton, 1995). We shall review the findings obtained for AN and BN in studies of each of these systems.

Several investigations have studied the noradrenergic system in AN. Anorexia nervosa has been associated with reduced concentrations of noradrenaline and its major metabolite, 3-methoxy-4-hydroxyphenylglycol (MHPG) in cerebrospinal fluid (CSF), as well as with increased density and sensitivity of platelet $\alpha_2$-adrenergic receptors (see Fava, Copeland, Schweiger, & Herzog, 1989). However, after nutritional rehabilitation, CSF MHPG levels in women with AN are found to compare to those of control women (Kaye, Frank, & McConaha, 1999), suggesting that changes in the noradrenergic system may mainly constitute adaptations to starvation. Studies of dopamine activity in AN have yielded contradictory results. Kaye, Ebert, Raleigh, and Lake (1984) reported anorexic women to show lower CSF homovanillic acid (HVA, a dopamine metabolite) than did control women, and then, in a 1999 study, reported lower CSF HVA in a group of recovered anorexic restrictors and a tendency toward lower HVA in recovered anorexic bingers. Although such findings imply lowered dopamine activity in active or recovered AN, Johnston, Leiter, Burrow, Garfinkel, and Anderson (1984) found no differences when comparing HVA levels in women with anorexia to those in controls.

Studies of the serotonin system have revealed various 5HT abnormalities, consistent with reduced 5HT tone, in active anorexics, including (a) decreased platelet binding of serotonin uptake inhibitors (Weizman, Carmi, Tyano, Apter, & Rehavi, 1986); (b) blunted prolactin and cortisol responses to 5HT agonists and partial agonists (Monteleone, Brambilla, Bortolotti, La Rocca, & Maj, 1998); and (c) reduced CSF levels of 5HT metabolites (Kaye et al., 1984). Some investigators have reported normalization of prolactin response to a 5HT releasing agent, d-fenfluramine, in recovered anorexics (Ward, Brown, Lightman, Campbell, & Treasure, 1998), as might indicate a state-related 5HT abnormality. In contrast,

Kaye, Gwirtsman, George, and Ebert (1991) found *elevated* CSF 5-hydroxyindoleacetic acid (or 5HIAA, a 5HT metabolite) in a sample of weight-restored anorexics. They interpreted this apparently anomalous finding as an indication that AN and associated traits (e.g., harm avoidance, perfectionism) may actually be linked to a primary state of increased 5HT tone that is then masked by malnutrition-induced *reductions* in 5HT activity during active stages of the disorder. Further work is needed to clarify this possibility.

As with AN, findings in BN have been consistent with decreased noradrenaline activity. For example, women with BN have been reported to show low resting levels of plasma noradrenaline (Kaye et al., 1990). Given a study reporting normal CSF MHPG levels in recovered bulimics, however, it appears that noradrenaline abnormalities in BN may need to be regarded as state-dependent effects (Kaye et al., 1998). Studies focused on dopaminergic activity in BN have documented low CSF HVA (a dopamine metabolite) in active BN (Jimerson, Lesem, Kaye, & Brewerton, 1992). However, again, one study reports normal CSF HVA levels in recovered bulimics (Kaye et al., 1998).

More extensive than that in AN, study of the 5HT system in BN has consistently suggested reduced 5HT activity. Bulimia nervosa patients are noted to display (a) decreased CSF 5HIAA (Jimerson et al., 1992), (b) reduced platelet binding of 5HT uptake inhibitors (Steiger et al., 2000), and (c) blunted neuroendocrine responses to 5HT precursors and 5HT agonists or partial agonists (e.g., Levitan et al., 1997; Steiger, Koerner, et al., 2001). Such findings have been taken to suggest decreased brain 5HT turnover and down-regulation of postsynaptic 5HT receptors mediating neuroendocrine responses. Other studies have used dietary manipulations to explore links between 5HT levels and bulimic symptoms. For instance, tryptophan depletion, which lowers brain tryptophan and subsequent 5HT synthesis, has been shown to exacerbate bulimic symptoms in actively bulimic women (Kaye et al., 2000) and to lead to transient reappearance of bulimic symptoms in recovered bulimics (Smith, Fairburn, & Cowen, 1999). These results appear to reflect a particular vulnerability within the 5HT system of women at risk for BN and establishes a potential neurobiological substrate for antecedent effects of dieting in BN.

Given their marked co-aggregation, there has been an interest in the possibility that bulimic symptoms and impulsivity have a common serotonergic basis. In non–eating disordered populations, data document a clear association between impulsivity and low 5HT (Coccaro et al., 1989). Paralleling such findings, Steiger, Koerner, et al. (2001b) found correspondence between the extent of apparent reduction in 5HT activity and the severity of impulsive symptoms. Such findings imply that 5HT abnormalities may mediate both binge eating and impulsive symptoms, and may (in part) account for the frequent convergence of BN with problems of impulse regulation.

**Appetite-Regulating Peptides and Hormones.**    Cholecystokinin (CCK), a peptide secreted by the gut, acts on the hypothalamus to produce satiety. Available data suggest low basal and postprandial (after-eating) plasma CCK in BN, but not in AN (Pirke, Kellner, Frieβ, Krieg, & Fichter, 1994). It is not known to what extent low CCK in BN may preexist disorder onset or may result from abnormal eating behaviors. Regardless, once established, low CCK could help perpetuate binge-eating behavior via its impact on satiety.

Leptin is a newly identified hormone secreted by fat cells. Leptin acts on the hypothalamus to regulate appetite and energy expenditure in accordance with fat stores. In active AN, findings have shown reductions in serum and CSF leptin levels corresponding to decreased body mass (Grinspoon et al., 1996). Findings have also shown restoration of normal levels upon weight recovery (Hebebrand et al., 1997). However, although low leptin levels in AN may, therefore, be partly attributable to low fat stores, one study found decreased leptin in restricting but not purging anorexics, despite equally low body weight in both groups (Mehler, Eckel, & Donahoo, 1999). A study of bulimic women has also reported low leptin levels, despite normal body weight (Monteleone, Di Lieto, Tortorella, Longobardi, & Maj, 2000). Leptin levels may, therefore, not be modulated by body weight alone, and further work is needed to investigate the full interplay that may exist between leptins and the EDs.

**Neuroimaging Studies.**    Neuroimaging studies aim to establish structural or functional brain abnormalities and use techniques like computerized tomography (CT) and magnetic resonance imaging (MRI) to allow visualization of gross brain structure. Functional neuroimaging techniques, including positron emission tomography (PET) and proton magnetic resonance spectroscopy (H-MRS), are used to analyze specific chemical and electrical activity within the brain. With the use of CT and MRI, structural brain changes have been detected in both anorexic and bulimic patients. Findings include enlarged ventricles and sulcal widening, gray- and white-matter abnormalities, and lateralization of deficits (e.g., Hoffman et al., 1989). Reversible and irreversible components have been identified, including persistent gray-matter (but not white-matter) volume deficits in weight-recovered anorexics (Lambe et al., 1997). Taken together, imaging studies suggest that many abnormalities constitute transient effects of nutritional deprivation, but that some may be disturbingly permanent sequelae.

## AN INTEGRATED (MULTIDIMENSIONAL) ETIOLOGICAL CONCEPT

In a social context that equates thinness with many social values, it is not surprising to find that most people display body-image and diet consciousness, and that an alarming number of these persons (especially young women) progress to the development of full-blown EDs. However, as much as the EDs are defined by pathognomonic preoccupations with eating, weight-control, and body image, they are also polysymptomatic syndromes, invariably including characterological, affective, interpersonal, and self-regulatory disturbances. Syndromes with this degree of phenomenological complexity are likely to implicate diverse causal processes. An adequate etiological model for the EDs will need to account for roles of converging biological, psychological, familial, and sociocultural processes.

In attempting to understand ED etiology, we have often found it heuristic to contemplate two classes of causal agents, each having its own character and each (presumably) its own multiple (biopsychosocial) etiological agents. One factor relates to eating-specific aspects of disturbance (surrounding eating, weight, and body image); the other relates to more generalized vulnerabilities, psychopathology, or maladaptation. This proposal, that EDs implicate eating-specific and generalized components of pathology, was first addressed in the *two-component model* of eating disorders proposed by Garner, Olmstead, Polivy, and Garfinkel (1984). A basic aspect of this view is that eating-specific concerns are not sufficient to explain the development of clinical ED, and that the concurrent presence of a more generalized psychopathology, expressed through broad mood and behavioral dysregulation, is required. How might generalized and eating-specific factors interact in ED pathology? To reflect a diversity of possible pathways, we provide some illustrative examples.

1. Constitutional vulnerabilities (e.g., inherited problems of serotonin neurotransmission) may, along with their predictable effects on mood and impulse regulation, confer vulnerability to disorders of satiation (and hence bulimic eating patterns) in individuals disposed by social or family pressures emphasizing thinness to restrict their food intake. This might, in part, explain an affinity of bulimic eating syndromes for manifestations including mood or impulse dyscontrol and, in part, findings showing BN to be associated with reduced serotonin functioning. In other words, BN may (at least sometimes) implicate a generalized (serotonin-linked) risk factor, related to susceptibility to impulsiveness and appetitive dysregulation, but what might be needed to trigger the expression of this vulnerability is a specific pressure or encouragement toward dietary restraint.

2. Given a social context that overvalues thinness and that links body-esteem to overall self-esteem (especially in women), generalized self-image problems in females (along with a propensity to be perfectionistic or overly sensitive to social approval) might indirectly heighten susceptibility to dieting and, eventually, to pathological eating practices. In this eventuality, one would expect (as tends to be the case) to find perfectionism, self-criticism, reward dependence, and related characteristics in AN-prone individuals. We presume that such (generalized) tendencies heighten the likelihood that normal (eating-specific) social concerns about slimness may be carried, in clinical ED sufferers, to the pathological extreme.

3. Parental overprotection or overcontrol, while alone insufficient to explain ED development, might support the progression from compulsive dieting to frank eating obsession in the weight-conscious adolescent. Furthermore, the adolescent's rejection of parental controls might, if the parents themselves showed propensities toward compulsiveness or anxious overcontrol, mobilize destructively intrusive overreactions on the part of the parents. The child's further opposition would gradually feed into an escalating spiral of parental intrusiveness followed by angry oppositionality on the part of the affected child. Self-starvation seems, at least sometimes, to be mobilized as a weapon in such an escalation of conflict.

In each of the preceding examples, we assume that development of a clinical ED requires that thresholds be surpassed in key areas of vulnerability, some eating-specific, some more generalized. A main implication of this view is that diffuse psychopathology, while not representing an ED-specific ingredient, might be a manifestation of a process that serves to enhance risk of ED development. At the same time, it is also necessary to contemplate the full range of interactions (among biological, psychological, and social factors) that may occur once an ED has developed, such that increasingly more severe and more entrenched eating and generalized disturbances may ensue. Consider the following hypothetical examples.

In the first example, an insecure adolescent girl with an anxious, perfectionistic bent (prone to difficulties with establishing limits around her own performance) begins dieting to bolster her self-esteem. Weight loss produces various social rewards as peers and parents pay her more positive attention. However, dieting also leads to alteration of normal neurobiological systems (known sequelae of intensive dieting). One consequence can be an exacerbation of anxiety and obsessionality and, gradually, increasing preoccupation with thinness. Her natural tendency to demand too much of herself evolves, under new biological influences, into full-blown obsession—and intensive dieting gradually evolves into a full-blown ED.

Alternatively, consider the effects, in a second adolescent, in whom a very-destructive developmental environment characterized by parental hostility and physical abuse has (aside from having damaging effects upon her sense of self-worth) been a manifestation of a family wide tendency towards impulse dysregulation. Assume that the family tendency of impulse dysregulation may have been borne, in part, by genes that code for lowered serotonin synthesis and neurotransmission. For this girl, dieting to achieve a better self-image (which would reduce brain serotonin activity even further) may not only lower the threshold for the expression of impulsive tendencies, but may lower the threshold for binge eating by creating impairment in satiety mechanisms. She might gradually develop binge eating, while at the same time becoming progressively more disinhibited, irritable, labile, and self-damaging. An implicit concept, especially important in designing eventual treatments, is that ED symptoms can become quite self-perpetuating, and in time, quite divorced from the psychobiological and sociocultural factors that may have originally contributed to the development of the disorder.

If ED etiology is as genuinely biopsychosocial as findings lead us to believe, then the study of eating disorders may inform theory on psychopathology in many ways, including the manner in which psychopathology can represent the activation of latent genetic vulnerabilities through specific environmental pressures; the manner in which latent traits and tendencies can be shaped by developmental experiences; and how maladaptive traits within the at-risk individual can mobilize destructive responses from the social environment. In addition, the EDs teach us to appreciate the ways in which socially prescribed responses (even those as apparently innocuous as a young girl's dieting) can, in specifically vulnerable individuals, generate multiple and highly maladaptive repercussions that can come to broadly affect an individual's global psychological development and functioning.

# REFERENCES

American Psychiatric Association. (1994). *Diagnostic and statistical manual of mental disorders* (4th ed.). Washington, DC: Author.

Armstrong, J., & Roth, D. M. (1989). Attachment and separation difficulties in eating disorders: A preliminary investigation. *International Journal of Eating Disorders, 8,* 141–155.

Blanz, B. J., Detzner, U., Lay, B., Rose, F., & Schmidt, M. H. (1997). The intellectual functioning of adolescents with anorexia nervosa and bulimia nervosa. *European Child and Adolescent Psychiatry, 6,* 129–135.

Borman Spurrel, E. B., Wilfley, D. E., Tanofsky, M. B., & Brownell, K. D. (1997). Age of onset for binge eating: Are there different pathways to binge eating? *International Journal of Eating Disorders, 21,* 55–65.

Brewerton, T. D. (1995). Toward a unified theory of serotonin dysregulation in eating and related disorders. *Psychoneuroendocrinology, 20,* 561–590.

Brewerton, T. D., Lydiard, R. B., Herzog, D. B., Brotman, A. W., O'Neil, P. M., & Ballenger, J. C. (1995). Comorbidity of Axis I psychiatric disorders in bulimia nervosa. *Journal of Clinical Psychiatry, 56,* 77–80.

Bruch, H. (1973). *Eating disorders: Obesity, anorexia nervosa and the person within.* New York: Basic Books.

Bruins-Slot, L., Gorwood, P., Bouvard, M., Blot, P., Ades, J., Feingold, J., Schwartz, J., & Mouren-Simeoni, M. (1998). Lack of association between anorexia nervosa and D3 dopamine receptor gene. *Biological Psychiatry, 43,* 76–78.

Bulik, C. M., Sullivan, P. F., Fear, J. L., & Pickering, A. (2000). Outcome of anorexia nervosa: Eating attitudes, personality, and parental bonding. *International Journal of Eating Disorders, 28,* 139–147.

Bulik, C. M., Sullivan, P. F., & Kendler, K. S. (1998). Heritability of binge-eating and broadly defined bulimia nervosa. *Biological Psychiatry, 44,* 1210–1218.

Bulik, C. M., Sullivan, P. F., Wade, T. D., & Kendler, K. S. (2000). Twin studies of eating disorders: A review. *International Journal of Eating Disorders, 27,* 1–20.

Bulik, C. M., Sullivan, P. F., Weltzin, T. F., & Kaye, W. H. (1995). Temperament in eating disorders. *International Journal of Eating Disorders, 17,* 251–261.

Calam, R., & Waller, G. (1998). Are eating disorders and psychosocial characteristics in early teenage years useful predictors of eating characteristics in adult years? A 7-year longitudinal study. *International Journal of Eating Disorders, 24,* 351–362.

Carter, F. A., Bulik, C. M., Lawson, R. H., Sullivan, P. F., & Wilson, J. S. (1996). Effect of mood and food cues on body image in women with bulimia and controls. *International Journal of Eating Disorders, 20,* 65–76.

Casper, R. C., Hedeker, D., & McClough, J. F. (1992). Personality dimensions in eating disorders and their relevance for subtyping. *Journal of the American Academy of Child and Adolescent Psychiatry, 31,* 830–840.

Cassidy, E., Allsopp, M., & Williams, T. (1999). Obsessive-compulsive symptoms at initial presentation of adolescent eating disorders. *European Child & Adolescent Psychiatry, 8,* 193–199.

Coccaro, E. F., Siever, L. J., Klar, H. M., Maurer, G., Cochrane, K., Cooper, T. B., Mohs, R. C., & Davis, K. L. (1989). Serotonergic studies in patients with affective and personality disorders:

Correlates with suicidal and aggressive behavior. *Archives of General Psychiatry, 46,* 587–599.

Crago, M., Shisslak, C. M., & Estes, L. S. (1996). Eating disturbances among American minority groups: A review. *International Journal of Eating Disorders, 19,* 239–248.

Crisp, A. H. (1980). *Anorexia nervosa: Let me be.* London: Academic Press.

Crisp, A. H., Hsu, L., Harding, B., & Hartshorn, J. (1980). Clinical features of anorexia nervosa: A study of a consecutive series of 102 female patients. *Journal of Psychosomatic Research, 24,* 179–191.

DaCosta, M., & Halmi, K. A. (1992). Classifications of anorexia nervosa: Question of subtypes. *International Journal of Eating Disorders, 11,* 305–313.

Dansky, B. S., Brewerton, T. D., Kilpatrick, D. G., & O'Neil, P. M. (1997). The National Women's Study: Relationship of victimization and posttraumatic stress disorder to bulimia nervosa. *International Journal of Eating Disorders, 21,* 213–228.

Davis, C., & Katzman, M. A. (1999). Perfection as acculturation: Psychological correlates of eating problems in Chinese male and female students living in the United States. *International Journal of Eating Disorders, 25,* 65–70.

Demitrack, M. A., Putnam, F. W., Brewerton, T. D., Brandt, H. A., & Gold, P. W. (1990). Relation of clinical variables to dissociative phenomena in eating disorders. *American Journal of Psychiatry, 147,* 1184–1188.

Enoch, M. A., Kaye, W. H., Rotondo, A., Greenberg, B. D., Murphy, D. L., & Goldman, D. (1998). 5-HT$_{2A}$ promoter polymorphism-1438G/A, anorexia nervosa, and obsessive-compulsive disorder. *Lancet, 351,* 1785–1786.

Everill, J., & Waller, G. (1995). Reported sexual abuse and eating psychopathology: A review of evidence for a causal link. *International Journal of Eating Disorders, 18,* 1–11.

Everill, J., Waller, G., & Macdonald, W. (1995). Dissociation in bulimic and non-eating-disordered women. *International Journal of Eating Disorders, 17,* 127–134.

Fairburn, C. G. (1995). *Overcoming binge eating.* New York: Guilford Press.

Fairburn, C. G., Cooper, Z., Doll, H. A., & Welch, S. L. (1999). Risk factors for anorexia nervosa: Three integrated case-controlled comparisons. *Archives of General Psychiatry, 56,* 468–476.

Fairburn, C. G., Doll, H. A., Welch, S. L., Hay, P. J., Davies, B. A., & O'Connor, M. E. (1998). Risk factors for binge eating disorders: A community-based study. *Archives of General Psychiatry, 55,* 425–432.

Fava, M., Copeland, P. M., Schweiger, U., & Herzog, D. (1989). Neurochemical abnormalities of anorexia nervosa and bulimia nervosa. *American Journal of Psychiatry, 146,* 963–971.

Field, A. E., Camargo, C. A., Taylor, C. B., Berkey, C. S., & Colditz, G. A. (1999). Relation of peer and media influences to the development of purging behaviors among preadolescent and adolescent girls. *Archives of Pediatrics & Adolescent Medicine, 153,* 1184–1189.

Fitzgibbon, M. L., & Blackman, L. R. (2000). Binge eating disorder and bulimia nervosa: Differences in the quality and quantity of binge eating episodes. *International Journal of Eating Disorders, 27,* 238–243.

Furnham, A., & Husain, K. (1999). The role of conflict with parents in disordered eating among British Asian females. *Social Psychiatry & Psychiatric Epidemiology, 34,* 498–505.

Gard, M. C. E., & Freeman, C. P. (1996). The dismantling of a myth: A review of eating disorders and socioeconomic status. *International Journal of Eating Disorders, 20,* 1–12.

Garfinkel, P., & Garner, D. (1982). *Anorexia nervosa: A multidimensional perspective.* New York: Brunner/Mazel.

Garfinkel, P. E., Lin, E., Goering, P., Spegg, C., Goldbloom, D. S., Kennedy, S., Kaplan, A. S., & Woodside, D. B. (1995). Bulimia nervosa in a Canadian community sample: Prevalence and comparison of subgroups. *American Journal of Psychiatry, 152,* 1052–1058.

Garner, D., Olmsted, M., Polivy, J., & Garfinkel, P. (1984). Comparison between weight preoccupied women and anorexia nervosa. *Psychosomatic Medicine, 46,* 255–266.

Ghadirian, A. M., Marini, N., Jabalpurlawa, S., & Steiger, H. (1999). Seasonal mood patterns in eating disorders. *General Hospital Psychiatry, 21,* 354–359.

Gleaves, D. H., & Eberenz, K. P. (1995). Correlates of dissociative symptoms among women with eating disorders. *Journal of Psychiatric Research, 29,* 417–426.

Gleaves, D. H., Eberenz, K. P., & May, M. C. (1998). Scope and significance of posttraumatic symptomatology among women hospitalized for an eating disorder. *International Journal of Eating Disorders, 24,* 147–156.

Gleaves, D. H., Lowe, M. R., Snow, A. C., Green, B. A., & Murphy-Eberenz, K. P. (2000). Continuity and discontinuity models of bulimia nervosa: A taxometric investigation. *Journal of Abnormal Psychology, 109,* 56–68.

Godart, N. T., Flament, M. F., Lecrubier, Y., & Jeammet, P. (2000). Anxiety disorders in anorexia nervosa and bulimia nervosa: Comorbidity and chronology of appearance. *European Psychiatry, 15,* 38–45.

Goldstein, H. J. (1981). Family factors associated with schizophrenia and anorexia nervosa. *Journal of Youth and Adolescence, 10,* 385–405.

Grave, R. D., Oliosi, M., Todisco, P., & Vanderlinden, J. (1997). Self-reported traumatic experiences and dissociative symptoms in obese women with and without binge-eating disorder. *Eating Disorders: The Journal of Treatment and Prevention, 5,* 105–109.

Grinspoon, S., Gulick, T., Askari, H., Landt, M., Vignati, L., Bowsher, R., Herzog, D., & Klibanski, A. (1996). Serum leptin levels in women with anorexia nervosa. *Journal of Clinical Endocrinology and Metabolism, 81,* 3861–3863.

Gupta, M. A., & Johnson, A. M. (2000). Nonweight-related body image concerns among female eating-disordered patients and nonclinical controls: Some preliminary observations. *International Journal of Eating Disorders, 27,* 304–309.

Hall, A., & Brown, L. B. (1983). A comparison of the attitudes of young anorexia nervosa patients and non-patients with those of their mothers. *British Journal of Medical Psychology, 56,* 39–48.

Hall, A., Leibrich, J., Walkley, F., & Welch, G. (1986). Investigation of "weight pathology" of 58 mothers of anorexia nervosa patients and 204 mothers of schoolgirls. *Psychological Medicine, 16,* 71–76.

Halmi, K. A., Sunday, S. R., Strober, M., Kaplan, A., Woodside, D. B., Fichter, M., Treasure, J., Berrettini, W. H., & Kaye, W. H. (2000). Perfectionism in anorexia nervosa: Variation by clinical subtype, obsessionality, and pathological behavior. *American Journal of Psychiatry, 157,* 1799–1805.

Hebebrand, J., Blum, W. F., Barth, N., Coners, H., Englaro, P., Juul, A., Ziegler, A., Rascher, W., & Remschmidt, H. (1997). Leptin levels in patients with anorexia nervosa are reduced in the acute stage and elevated upon short-term weight restoration. *Molecular Psychiatry, 2,* 330–334.

Herzog, D. B., Keller, M. B., Sacks, N. R., Yeh, C. J., & Lavori, P. W. (1992). Psychiatric comorbidity in treatment-seeking anorexics and bulimics. *Journal of the American Academy of Child and Adolescent Psychiatry, 31,* 810–818.

Hinney, A., Lentes, K. U., Rosenkrantz, K., Barth, N., Roth, H., Ziegler, A., Henninghausen, K., Coners, H., Wurmser, H., Romer, J. K., Winnikes, G., Mayer, H., Herzog, W., Lehmkuhl, G., Poustka, F., Schmidt, M. H., Blum, W. F., Pirke, K. M., Schafer, H., Greschik, K. H., Remschmidt, H., & Hebebrand, J. (1997). Beta 3-adrenergic receptor allele distributions in children, adolescents and young adults with obesity, underweight or anorexia nervosa. *International Journal of Obesity Related Metabolic Disorders, 21,* 224–230.

Hodes, M., & leGrange, D. (1993). Expressed emotion in the investigation of eating disorders: A review. *International Journal of Eating Disorders, 13,* 279–288.

Hodges, E. L., Cochrane, C. E., & Brewerton, T. D. (1998). Family characteristics of binge-eating disorder patients. *International Journal of Eating Disorders, 23,* 145–151.

Hoffman, G. W., Ellinwood, E. H., Rockwell, W. J., Herfkens, R. J., Nishita, J. K., & Guthrie, L. F. (1989). Cerebral atrophy in bulimia. *Biological Psychiatry, 25,* 894–902.

Holderness, C., Brooks-Gunn, J., & Warren, M. (1994). Comorbidity of eating disorders and substance abuse: Review of the litertaure. *International Journal of Eating Disorders, 16,* 1–34.

Hsu, L. K. G., & Sobkiewicz, T. A. (1991). Body image disturbance: Time to abandon the concept for eating disorders. *International Journal of Eating Disorders, 10,* 15–30.

Humphrey, L. L. (1991). Object relations and the family system: An integrative approach to understanding and treating eating disorders. In C. Johnson (Ed.), *Psychodynamic treatment of anorexia nervosa and bulimia* (pp. 321–353). New York: Guilford Press.

Jacobsin, R., & Robins, C. J. (1989). Social dependency and social support in bulimic and nonbulimic women. *International Journal of Eating Disorders, 8,* 665–670.

Jimerson, D. C., Lesem, M. D., Kaye, W. H., & Brewerton, T. D. (1992). Low serotonin and dopamine metabolite concentrations in cerebrospinal fluid from bulimic patients with frequent binge episodes. *Archives of General Psychiatry, 49,* 132–138.

Johnson, C. (1991). Treatment of eating-disordered patients with borderline and false-self/narcissistic disorders. In C. Johnson (Ed.), *Psychodynamic treatment of anorexia nervosa and bulimia* (pp. 165–193). New York: Guilford Press.

Johnston, J. L., Leiter, L. A., Burrow, G. N., Garfinkel, P. E., & Anderson, G. H. (1984). Excretion of urinary catecholamine metabolites in anorexia nervosa: Effect on body composition and energy intake. *American Journal of Clinical Nutrition, 40,* 1001–1006.

Katz, B. E., & Gleaves, D. H. (1996). Dissociative symptoms with eating disorders: Associated feature or artifact of a comorbid dissociative disorder. *Dissociation, 9,* 28–36.

Kaye, W. H., Ebert, M. H., Raleigh, M. H., & Lake, R. (1984). Abnormalities in CNS monoamine metabolism in anorexia nervosa. *Archives of General Psychiatry, 41,* 350–355.

Kaye, W. H., Frank, G. K. W., & McConaha, C. (1999). Altered dopamine activity after recovery from restricting-type anorexia nervosa. *Neuropsychopharmacology, 21,* 503–506.

Kaye, W. H., Gendall, K. A., Fernstrom, M. H., Fernstrom, J. D., McConaha, C. W., & Weltzin, T. E. (2000). Effects of acute tryptophan depletion on mood in bulimia nervosa. *Biological Psychiatry, 47,* 151–157.

Kaye, W. H., Greeno, C. G., Moss, H., Fernstrom, J. D., Fernstrom, M. H., Lilenfeld, L. R, Weltzin, T. E., & Mann, J. (1998). Alterations in serotonin activity and psychiatric symptoms after recovery from bulimia nervosa. *Archives of General Psychiatry, 55,* 927–935.

Kaye, W. H., Gwirtsman, H. E., George, D. T., & Ebert, M. H. (1991). Altered serotonin activity in anorexia nervosa after long-term weight restoration. Does elevated cerebrospinal fluid 5-hydroxyindoleacetic acid level correlate with rigid and obsessive behavior? *Archives of General Psychiatry, 48,* 556–562.

Kaye, W. H., Gwirtsman, H. E., George, D. T., Jimenson, D. C., Ebert, M. H., & Lake, R. (1990). Disturbances of noradrenergic systems in normal weight bulimia: Relationship to diet and menses. *Biological Psychiatry, 27,* 4–21.

Kendler, K. S., Maclean, C., Neale, M. C., Kessler, R. C., Heath, A. C., & Eaves, L. J. (1991). The genetic epidemiology of bulimia nervosa. *American Journal of Psychiatry, 148,* 1627–1637.

Keys, A., Brozek, J., Henschel, A., Mickelson, O., & Taylor, H. (1950). *The biology of human starvation.* Minneapolis: University of Minnesota Press.

Kog, E., Vertommen, H., & Vandereycken, W. (1987). Minuchin's psychosomatic family model revised: A concept validation study using a multitrait-multimethod apporach. *Family Process, 26,* 235–253.

Lake, A. J., Staiger, P. K., & Glowinski, H. (2000). Effect of western culture on women's attitudes to eating and perceptions of body shape. *International Journal of Eating Disorders, 27,* 83–89.

Lambe, E. K., Katzman, D. K., Mikulis, D. J., Kennedy, S. H., & Zipursky, R. B. (1997). Cerebral gray matter volume deficits after weight recovery from anorexia nervosa. *Archives of General Psychiatry, 54,* 537–542.

Lauer, C. J., Gorzewski, B., Gerlinghoff, M., Backmund, H., & Zihl, J. (1999). Neuropsychological assessments before and after treatment in patients with anorexia nervosa and bulimia nervosa. *Journal of Psychiatry Research, 33,* 129–138.

Lee, S., Ho, P., & Hsu, L. K. G. (1993). Fat phobic and non-fat phobic anorexia nervosa: A comparative study of 70 Chinese patients in Hong Kong. *Psychological Medicine, 23,* 999–1017.

Lehoux, P., Steiger, H., & Jabalpurlawa, S. (2000). State/trait distinctions in bulimic syndromes. *International Journal of Eating Disorders, 27,* 36–42.

Levitan, R. D., Kaplan, A. S., Brown, G. M., Joffe, R. T., Levitt, A. J., Vaccarino, F. J., & Kennedy, S. (1997). Low plasma cortisol in bulimia nervosa patients with reversed neurovegetative symptoms of depression. *Biological Psychiatry, 41,* 366–368.

Levitan, R. D., Kaplan, A. S., Levitt, A. J., & Joffe, R. T. (1994). Seasonal fluctuations in mood and eating behavior in bulimia nervosa. *International Journal of Eating Disorders, 16,* 295–299.

Levitan, R., Maselis, M., Kaplan, A., Basile, V., Kennedy, S., Lam, R., Vaccarino, F., Macciardi, F., & Kennedy, J. (2000, May). *Serotonin genetic polymorphism in bulimia nervosa and seasonal affective disorder.* Paper presented at the Ninth International Conference on Eating Disorders, New York.

Lilenfeld, L. R., Kaye, W. H., Greeno, C. G., Merikangas, K. R., Plotnicov, K., Pollice, C., Rao, R., Strober, M., Bulik, C. M., & Nagy, L. (1997). Psychiatric disorders in women with bulimia nervosa and their first-degree relatives: Effects of comorbid substance dependence. *International Journal of Eating Disorders, 22,* 253–264.

Lilenfeld, L. R., Kaye, W. H., Greeno, C. G., Merikangas, K. R., Plotnicov, K., Pollice, C., Rao, R., Strober, M., Bulik, C. M., & Nagy, L. (1998). A controlled family study of anorexia nervosa and bulimia nervosa: Psychiatric disorders in first-degree relatives and effects of proband comorbidity. *Archives of General Psychiatry, 55,* 603–610.

Lilenfeld, L. R., Stein, D., Bulik, C. M., Strober, M., Plotnicov, K., Pollice, C., Rao, R., Merikangas, K. R., Nagy, L., & Kaye, W. H. (2000). Personality traits among currently eating disordered, recovered and never ill first-degree female relatives of bulimic and control women. *Psychology Medicine, 30,* 1399–1410.

Lippincott, J. A., & Hwang, H. S. (1999). On cultural similarities in attitudes toward eating of women students in Pennsylvania and South Korea. *Psychological Reports, 85,* 701–702.

Logue, C. M., Crowe, R. R., & Bean, J. A. (1989). A family study of anorexia nervosa. *British Journal of Psychiatry, 30,* 179–188.

Lucas, A. R., Crowson, C. S., O'Fallon, W. M., & Melton, L. J. (1999). The ups and downs of anorexia nervosa. *International Journal of Eating Disorders, 26,* 397–405.

Marcus, M. D., Wing, R. R., & Hopkins, J. (1988). Obese binge eaters: Affect, cognitions and response to behavioral weight control. *Journal of Consulting and Clinical Psychology, 13,* 433–439.

Matsunaga, H., Kaye, W. H., McConaha, C., Plotnicov, K., Pollice, C., & Rao, R. (2000). Personality disorders among subjects recovered from eating disorders. *International Journal of Eating Disorders, 27,* 353–357.

Matsunaga, H., Kaye, W. H., McConaha, C., Plotnicov, K., Pollice, C., Rao, R., & Stein, D. (1999). Psychopathological characteristics of recovered bulimics who have a history of physical or sexual abuse. *Journal of Nervous and Mental Disease, 187,* 472–477.

Matsunaga, H., Kiriike, N., Iwasaki, Y., Miyata, A., Matsui, T., Nagata, T., Yamagami, S., & Kaye, W. H. (2000). Multi-impulsivity among bulimic patients in Japan. *International Journal of Eating Disorders, 27,* 348–352.

Matsunaga, H., Kiriike, N., Miyata, A., Iwasaki, Y., Matsui, T., Fulimtot, K., Kasai, S., & Kaye, W. H. (1999). Prevalence and symptomatology of comorbid obsessive-compulsive disorder among bulimic patients. *Psychiatry and Clinical Neurosciences, 54,* 661–666.

Mehler, P. S., Eckel, R. H., & Donahoo, W. T. (1999). Leptin levels in restricting and purging anorectics. *International Journal of Eating Disorders, 26,* 189–194.

Miller, D. A., McCluskey-Fawcett, K., & Irving, L. M. (1993). Correlates of bulimia nervosa: Early mealtime experiences. *Adolescence, 28,* 621–635.

Mitchell, J. E., & Eckert, E. D. (1987). Scope and significance of eating disorders. *Journal of Consulting and Clinical Psychology, 55,* 628–634.

Mitchell, J. E., Mussell, M. P., Peterson, C. B., Crow, S., Wonderlich, S. A., Crosby, R. D., Davis, T., & Weller, C. (1999). Hedonics of binge eating in women with bulimia nervosa and binge eating disorder. *International Journal of Eating Disorders, 26,* 165–170.

Monteleone, P., Brambilla, F., Bortolototti, F., LaRocca, A., & Maj, M. (1998). Prolactin response to d-fenfluramine is blunted in people with anorexia nervosa. *British Journal of Psychiatry, 172,* 438–442.

Monteleone, P., Di Lieto, A., Tortorella, A., Longobardi, N., & Maj, M. (2000). Circulating leptin in patients with anorexia nervosa, bulimia nervosa or binge-eating disorder: Relationship to body weight, eating patterns, psychopathology and endocrine changes. *Psychiatry Research, 94,* 121–129.

Moreno, J. K., Selby, M. J., & Neal, S. (1998). Psychopathology in sexually abused and non-sexually abused eating-disordered women. *Psychotherapy in Private Practice, 17,* 1–9.

Murnen, S. K., & Smolak, L. (1997). Femininity, masculinity, and disordered eating: A meta-analytic review. *International Journal of Eating Disorders, 22,* 231–242.

Newton, J. R., Freeman, C. P., & Munro, J. (1993). Impulsivity and dyscontrol in bulimia nervosa: Is impulsivity an independent phenomenon or a marker of severity? *Acta Psychiatrica Scandinavia, 87,* 389–394.

Nielsen, D., Virkkunen, M., Lappalainen, J., Eggert, M., Brown, G., Long, J., Goldman, D., & Linnoila, M. (1998). A tryptophan hydroxylase gene marker for suicidality and alcoholism. *Archives of General Psychiatry, 55,* 593–602.

Nilsson, E. W., Gillberg, C., Gillberg, I. C., & Rastam, M. (1999). Ten-year follow-up of adolescent onset anorexia nervosa: Personality disorders. *Journal of the American Academy of Child and Adolescent Psychiatry, 38,* 1389–1395.

Norman, D. K., Blais, D., & Herzog, D. (1993). Personality characteristics of eating-disordered patients as identified by the Millon Clinical Multiaxial inventory. *Journal of Personality Disorders, 7,* 1–9.

Olivardia, R., Pope, H. G., Jr., & Hudson, J. I. (2000). Muscle dysmorphia in male weightlifters: A case-control study. *American Journal of Psychiatry, 157,* 1291–1296.

Pate, J. E., Pumariega, A. J., Hester, C., & Garner, D. M. (1992). Cross-cultural patterns in eating disorders: A review. *Journal of the American Academy of Child and Adolescent Psychiatry, 31,* 802–809.

Pirke, K. M., Kellner, M. B., Frieβ, E., Krieg, J.-C., & Fichter, M. M. (1994). Satiety and cholecystokinin. *International Journal of Eating Disorders, 15,* 63–69.

Polivy, J., & Herman, C. P. (1985). Dieting and binging: A causal analysis. *American Psychologist, 40,* 193–201.

Polivy, J., & Herman, C. P. (1993). Etiology of binge eating: Psychological mechanisms. In C. G. Fairbairn & G. T. Wilson (Eds.), *Binge eating: Nature, assessment, and treatment* (pp. 173–205). New York: Guilford Press.

Pruitt, J. A., Kappins, R. E., & Gorman, P. W. (1992). Bulimia and fear of intimacy. *Journal of Clinical Psychology, 48,* 472–476.

Råstam, M. (1992). Anorexia nervosa in 51 Swedish adolescents: Premorbid problems and comorbidity. *Journal of the American Academy of Child and Adolescent Psychiatry, 31,* 819–829.

Rhea, D. J. (1999). Eating disorder behaviors of ethnically diverse urban female adolescent athletes and non-athletes. *Journal of Adolescence, 22,* 379–388.

Rhodes, B., & Kroger, J. (1992). Parental bonding and separation-individuation difficulties among late adolescent eating disordered women. *Child Psychiatry & Human Development, 22,* 249–263.

Rosenvinge, J. H., Martinussen, M., & Ostensen, E. (2000). The comorbidity of eating disorders and personality disorders: A meta-analytic review of studies published between 1983 and 1998. *Eating and Weight Disorders, 5,* 52–61.

Ross, H. E., & Ivis, F. (1999). Binge eating and substance use among male and female adolescents. *International Journal of Eating Disorders, 26,* 245–260.

Schmidt, U., Humfress, H., & Treasure, J. (1997). The role of general family environment and sexual and physical abuse in the origins of eating disorders. *European Eating Disorders Review, 5,* 184–207.

Schukit, M. A., Tipp, J. E., Anthenelli, R. M., Bucholz, K. K., Hesselbrock, V. M., & Nurnberger, J. I., Jr. (1996). Anorexia nervosa and bulimia nervosa in alcohol-dependent men and women and their relatives. *American Journal of Psychiatry, 153,* 74–82.

Sights, J. R., & Richards, H. C. (1984). Parents of bulimic women. *International Journal of Eating Disorders, 3,* 3–13.

Sitnick, T., & Katz, J. (1984). A study of sex role identity and anorexia nervosa. *International Journal of Eating Disorders, 3,* 81–87.

Smith, K. A., Fairburn, C. G., & Cowen, P. J. (1999). Symptomatic relapse in bulimia nervosa following acute tryptophan depletion. *Archives of General Psychiatry, 56,* 171–176.

Sohlberg, S., & Strober, M. (1994). Personality in anorexia nervosa: An update and a theoretical integration. *Acta Psychiatrica Scandinavica, 89*(Suppl. 378), 1–15.

Spitzer, R. L., Devlin, M., Walsh, B. T., Hasin, D., Wing, R., Marcus, M., Stunkard, A., Wadden, T., Yanovski, S., Agras, S., Mitchell, J., & Nonas, C. (1992). Binge eating disorder: A multi-site field trial of diagnostic criteria. *International Journal of Eating Disorders, 11,* 191–203.

Srinivasagam, N. M., Kaye, W. H., Plotnicov, K. H., Greeno, C., Weltzin, T. E., & Rao, R. (1995). Persistent perfectionism, symmetry, and exactness after long-term recovery from anorexia nervosa. *American Journal of Psychiatry, 152,* 1630–1634.

Steiger, H., Gauvin, L., Israel, M., Koerner, Ng Ying Kin, N. M. K., Paris, J., & Young, S. N. (2001). Association of serotonin and cortisol indices with childhood abuse in bulimia nervosa. *Archives of General Psychiatry, 58,* 837–843.

Steiger, H., Gauvin, L., Jabalpurlawa, S., Séguin, J. R., & Stotland, S. (1999). Hypersensitivity to social interactions in bulimic eating syndromes: Relationship to binge-eating. *Journal of Consulting and Clinical Psychology, 67,* 765–775.

Steiger, H., Koerner, N. M., Engleberg, M., Israel, M., Ng Ying Kin, N. M. K., & Young, S. N. (2001). Self-destructiveness and serotonin function in bulimia nervosa. *Psychiatry Research, 103,* 15–26.

Steiger, H., Leonard, S., Ng Ying Kin, N. M. K., Ladouceur, C., Ramdoyal, D., & Young, S. N. (2000). Childhood abuse and tritiated paroxetine binding in bulimia nervosa. *Journal of Clinical Psychiatry, 61,* 428–435.

Steiger, H., Van der Feen, J., Goldstein, C., & Leichner, P. (1989). Defense styles and parental bonding in eating-disordered women. *International Journal of Eating Disorders, 8,* 131–140.

Stickney, M. I., Miltenberger, R. G., & Wolff, G. (1999). A descriptive analysis of factors contributing to binge eating. *Journal of Behavior Therapy and Experimental Psychiatry, 30,* 177–189.

Striegel-Moore, R. H., Silberstein, L. R., & Rodin, J. (1986). Toward an understanding of risk factors for bulimia. *Amercan Psychologist, 41,* 246–248.

Striegel-Moore, R. H., Wilfley, D. E., Pike, K. M., Dohm, F. A., & Fairburn, C. G. (2000). Recurrent binge eating in black American women. *Archives of Family Medicine, 9,* 83–87.

Striegel-Moore, R. H., Wilson, G. T., Wilfley, D. E., Elder, K. A., & Brownell, K. D. (1998). Binge eating in an obese community sample. *International Journal of Eating Disorders, 23,* 27–37.

Strober, M. (1991). Disorders of the self in anorexia nervosa: An organismic-developmental paradigm. In C. Johnson (Ed.), *Psychodynamic treatment of anorexia nervosa and bulimia* (pp. 354–372). New York: Guilford Press.

Strober, M., Freeman, R., Lampert, C., Diamond, J., & Kaye, W. (2000). Controlled family study of anorexia nervosa and bulimia nervosa: Evidence of shared liability and transmission of partial syndromes. *American Journal of Psychiatry, 157,* 393–401.

Strober, M., Lampert, C., Morrell, W., Burroughs, J., & Jacobs, C. (1990). A controlled family study of anorexia nervosa: Evidence of familial aggregation and lack of shared transmission with affective disorders. *International Journal of Eating Disorders, 9,* 239–253.

Szmukler, G. I., Andrewes, D., Kingston, K., Chen, L., Stargatt, R., & Stanley, R. (1992). Neuropsychological impairment in anorexia nervosa: Before and after refeeding. *Journal of Clinical and Experimental Neuropsychology, 14,* 347–352.

Thornton, C., & Russell, J. (1997). Obsessive-compulsive comorbidity in the dieting disorders. *International Journal of Eating Disorders, 21,* 83–87.

Tobin, D. L., Griffing, A., & Griffing, S. (1997). An examination of subtype criteria for bulimia nervosa. *International Journal of Eating Disorders, 22,* 179–186.

Toner, B. B., Garfinkel, P. E., & Garner, D. M. (1987). Cognitive style of patients with bulimic and diet-restricting anorexia nervosa. *American Journal of Psychiatry, 144,* 510–512.

Treasure, J. L., & Holland, A. J. (1989). Genetic vulnerability to eating disorders: Evidence from twin and family studies. In H. Remschmidt & M. H. Schmidt (Eds.), *Anorexia nervosa* (pp. 59–68). Toronto, Ontario, Canada: Hogrefe & Huber.

Tuschen-Caffier, B., & Vogele, C. (1999). Psychological and physiological reactivity to stress: An experimental study on bulimic patients, restrained eaters and controls. *Psychotherapy and Psychosomatics, 68,* 333–340.

Vanderlinden, J., Vandereycken, W., van Dyk, R., & Vertommen, H. (1993). Dissociative experiences and trauma in eating disorders. *International Journal of Eating Disorders, 13,* 187–194.

Vitousek, K., & Manke, F. (1994). Personality variables and disorders in anorexia nervosa and bulimia nervosa. *Journal of Abnormal Psychology, 103,* 137–147.

von Ranson, K. M., Kaye, W. H., Weltzin, T. E., Rao, R., & Matsunaga, H. (1999). Obsessive-compulsive disorder symptoms before and after recovery form bulimia nervosa. *American Journal of Psychiatry, 156,* 1703–1708.

Wade, T. D., Bulik, C. M., Neale, M., & Kendler, K. S. (2000). Anorexia nervosa and major depression: Shared genetic and environmental risk factors. *American Journal of Psychiatry, 157,* 469–471.

Wakeling, A. (1996). Epidemiology of anorexia nervosa. *Psychiatry Research, 62,* 3–9.

Waller, J. V., Kaufman, M. R., & Deutsch, F. (1940). Anorexia nervosa: A psychosomatic entity. *Psychosomatic Medicine, 2,* 3–16.

Walters, E. E., & Kendler, K. S. (1995). Anorexia nervosa and anorexic-like syndromes in a population-based female twin sample. *American Journal of Psychiatry, 152,* 64–71.

Ward, A., Brown, N., Lightman, S., Campbell, I. C., & Treasure, J. (1998). Neuroendocrine, appetitive and behavioral responses to d-fenfluramine in women recovered from anorexia nervosa. *British Journal of Psychiatry, 172,* 351–358.

Ward, A., Ramsay, R., & Treasure, J. (2000). Attachment research in eating disorders. *British Journal of Medical Psychology, 73,* 35–51.

Ward, A., Ramsay, R., Turnbull, S., Benedettini, M., & Treasure, J. (2000). Attachment patterns in eating disorders past in the present. *International Journal of Eating Disorders, 28,* 370–376.

Webster, J. J., & Palmer, R. L. (2000). The childhood and family background of women with clinical eating disorders: A comparison with women with major depression and women without psychiatric disorder. *Psychological Medicine, 30,* 53–60.

Weizman, R., Carmi, M., Tyano, S., Apter, A., & Rehavi, M. (1986). High affinity [3H]imipramine binding and serotonin uptake to platelets of adolescent females suffering from anorexia nervosa. *Life Sciences, 38,* 1235–1242.

Wertheim, E. H. (1999). Relationships among adolescent girls' eating behviors and their parents' weight-related attitudes and behaviors. *Sex Roles, 41,* 169–187.

Whelan, E., & Cooper, P. J. (2000). The association between childhood feeding problems and maternal eating disorder: A community study. *Psychological Medicine, 30,* 69–77.

Widiger, T. A., & Sankis, L. M. (2000). Adult psychopathology: Issues and controversies. *Annual Review of Psychology, 51,* 377–404.

Wiederman, M. W., & Pryor, T. (1996). Multi-impulsivity among women with bulimia nervosa. *International Journal of Eating Disorders, 20*(4), 359–365.

Windauer, U., Lennerts, W., Talbot, P., Touyz, S., & Beumont, P. (1993). How well are "cured" anorexia nervosa patients? An investigation of 16 weight-recovered anorexic patients. *British Journal of Psychiatry, 163,* 195–200.

Wolfe, B. E., Jimerson, D. C., & Levine, J. M. (1994). Impulsivity ratings in bulimia nervosa: Relationship to binge eating behaviors. *International Journal of Eating Disorders, 15,* 289–292.

Wonderlich, S. A., Brewerton, T. D., Jocic, Z., Dansky, B., & Abbott, D. W. (1997). Relationship of childhood sexual abuse and eating disorders. *Journal of the American Academy of Child and Adolescent Psychiatry, 36,* 1107–1115.

Zaider, T. I., Johnson, J. G., & Cockell, S. J. (2000). Psychiatric comorbidity associated with eating disorder symptomatology among adolescents in the community. *International Journal of Eating Disorders, 28,* 58–67.

# CHAPTER 8

# Disorders of Impulse Control

KENNETH J. SHER AND WENDY S. SLUTSKE

In this chapter we review research and theory across several different conditions that appear to have deficits in impulse control in common. The construct of disorders of impulse control is similar to *disinhibitory psychopathology,* a term used by Gorenstein and Newman (1980) to refer to a range of conditions across the life span marked by a failure of self-control. The unifying themes across these related yet distinct conditions include deficits in inhibition and excesses in rule-breaking or norm-violating behavior. The chapter focuses on a select subset of clinical disorders, specifically substance use disorders and pathological gambling. However, deficits in self-control clearly are important features of some personality disorders (such as antisocial and borderline personality disorders), of childhood disorders such as attention-deficit/hyperactivity disorder and conduct disorder, and of other clinical conditions such as mania, some paraphilias, and what the *Diagnostic and Statistical Manual (DSM)* of the American Psychiatric Association (APA, 1994) terms *impulse-control disorders not elsewhere classified* (including intermittent explosive disorder, characterized by discrete episodes of failure to resist aggressive impulses; kleptomania; pyromania; and trichotillomania, characterized by recurrent pulling out of

one's hair for pleasure, gratification, or relief of tension that results in noticeable hair loss).

In addition to reflecting a failure of impulse control (i.e., a tendency to engage in the behavior despite attempts or desires to resist), we could also characterize these disorders as indicating excessive appetite (i.e., a strong underlying drive toward engaging in the behavior; Orford, 2001). Orford proposes that the core central processes underlying conditions such as alcohol dependence, drug dependence, nicotine dependence, pathological gambling, excessive eating, and sexual addiction are related to both "deterrence and restraint" and "primary, positive incentive learning mechanisms" (pp. 19–20). That is, these disorders might be viewed as conditions resulting from a conflict between inclination and inhibition, and an adequate conceptualization of the problem places emphases on both the compelling and the restraining (i.e., inhibitory) aspects of the phenomenon.

## DISINHIBITION

Although it is not unusual for psychologists to discuss impulsivity and inhibition as unitary constructs, it is clear that they are not. For example, impulsivity has been operationalized in myriad ways and some alternative measures of impulsivity are not highly correlated (e.g., White et al., 1994). In a probing review, Nigg (2000) distinguishes eight specific forms of inhibition described by psychologists, each with different functional relations to behavior and neurological substrates. Probably of greatest relevance for understanding disorders of impulse control are those inhibition systems related to so-called *behavioral inhibition* (e.g., suppression of prepotent responses), response to punishment cues, and response to novelty.

Prior to discussing individual disorders we first consider evidence supporting the hypothesis that there is a broad class of disorder sharing a common factor of disinhibition. This evidence stems from studies showing both high co-occurrence (i.e., comorbidity) of ostensibly different disorders and common etiologically relevant correlates.

## Comorbidity Among Impulse Control Disorders

The categorical approach to diagnosis exemplified by the *DSM* (versions III, III-R, and IV) of the APA (1980, 1987, 1994) is predicated upon the idea of distinct diagnostic entities. Although similarities among disorders can be represented by membership in the same class or subclass of a hierarchical diagnostic system, disorders are still represented as distinct entities. Within the tradition of the *DSM,* high co-occurrence between two disorders (i.e., comorbidity) suggests the possibility that the two disorders are members of the same general class of disorders. An alternative approach to classification is the factor-analytic approach whereby varying forms and degree of psychopathology are represented as dimensional constructs and an individual's symptomatology can be represented as a score on multiple dimensions. Although there is considerable debate regarding whether psychopathology is best represented as distinct classes or multiple dimensions (Klein & Riso, 1993; Widiger, 1997), both categorical and dimensional approaches indicate high comorbidity.

For example, in one large epidemiological study (Kessler, Crum, Warner, & Nelson, 1997), the diagnosis of alcohol dependence was strongly associated with other disorders characterized by disinhibition (e.g., conduct disorder, antisocial personality disorder, drug use disorders, and mania) as well as disorders for which affective disturbance is the cardinal feature (e.g., anxiety and depressive disorders). This high comorbidity could suggest either shared etiological processes or that the presence of one of these disorders increases the likelihood of developing a second disorder. (It is also possible that overlap in the diagnostic criteria could be responsible as well.) Regardless of the underlying mechanism, comorbidity

among disorders of impulse control is common and implies some form of causal mechanism related to inhibitory processes.

However, some ostensible comorbidity might merely represent short-term, transient psychiatric disturbances induced by acute substance intoxication or by a withdrawal syndrome that mimics independent disorders. In the *DSM-IV,* criteria are set out for a number of *substance-induced disorders* (e.g., substance-induced mood disorder, substance-induced psychotic disorder). The issue is more than academic; the course and treatment implications of substance-induced and independent disorders are quite different because substance-induced disorders are, by definition, likely to remit or improve after a prolonged period of abstinence (Kadden, Kranzler, & Rounsaville, 1995; Schuckit, 1994). Attribution of substance induction might be straightforward in some cases, as with, for example, an alcohol dependent individual whose depression remits within a couple of weeks of detoxification (and whose depression never occurs during prolonged period of sobriety). However, in many cases, determining whether conditions such as anxiety disorders, mood disorders, and psychotic disorders are independent or substance induced can be difficult in practice, especially when a substance use disorder and another condition have coexisted for many years, have insidious onsets, or have fluctuating courses. Moreover, by early adolescence there is often co-occurrence of symptoms (e.g., negative affect and drinking) prior to any morbidity in a formal diagnostic sense (Costello, Erkanli, Federman, & Angold, 1999). Thus, although useful conceptually and clinically, the distinction between independent and substance-induced disorders can sometimes be problematic.

In childhood and adolescence, there is considerable evidence for the existence of a broad class of symptomatology usually labeled as *externalizing disorders.* Almost 25 years ago, Achenbach and Edelbrock (1978) reviewed the empirical literature on the structure of childhood behavior problems and concluded there was consistent evidence for two broadband factors of psychopathology, which they termed *overcontrolled* and *undercontrolled.* The broadband undercontrolled factor subsumed behaviors labeled as "aggressive, externalizing, acting out, [and] conduct disorder" (p. 1284), which suggests that these problems may share some common features. Subsequent research has strongly supported the validity of the broadband factor of undercontrolled behavior, now usually referred to as *externalizing behavior,* which represents a higher order factor subsuming delinquent and aggressive behavior (see Achenbach, 1995). Additional factor-analytic studies of samples of adolescents and young adults by Jessor and his colleagues (Donovan & Jessor, 1985; Donovan,

Jessor, & Costa, 1988; Jessor, Donovan, & Costa, 1991) offer strong support for a broad class of problem behaviors indicated by problem drinking, marijuana use, other illicit drug use, cigarette smoking, and what they termed *general deviant behavior* (e.g., vandalism, fighting, theft). They labeled this factor the *syndrome of problem behavior* while acknowledging that there is considerable unique variability in each of the problem behaviors that is not accounted for by the general problem-behavior factor.

The construct of a broadband externalizing factor appears to generalize to adults. Krueger (1999; Krueger, Caspi, Moffitt, & Silva, 1998) provided evidence of this from two different studies employing structured diagnostic interviews (a nationally representative survey of mental disorders in the United States, and a New Zealand birth cohort studied prospectively from age 18 to age 21). Factor analyses of diagnoses from both studies offered strong support for a broadband externalizing psychopathology factor indicated by alcohol dependence, drug dependence, and antisocial personality disorder, and this externalizing factor showed high temporal stability over a 3-year interval.

Overall, there appears to be strong evidence for the view that covariation among symptoms of substance use disorders and general antisociality can be modeled as reflecting a higher order factor indicative of externalizing psychopathology or behavioral undercontrol (see also Zuckerman, 1999) suggesting that these correlated disorders may share common, core etiological processes. In principle, identification of these core processes would provide support for the validity of the construct of externalizing psychopathology and would also provide a foundation for identifying factors that are unique to individual disorders.

## Common Childhood Correlates

Conditions such as substance use disorders, pathological gambling, and antisocial behavior have their roots in childhood and adolescence. To the extent that there is some degree of developmental continuity, common childhood precursors are strongly implied. For example, childhood antisocial behavior and poor parental monitoring are common precursors of adult antisocial behavior, early alcohol involvement, and drug involvement (for reviews see Caspi & Moffitt, 1995; Dishion, French, & Patterson, 1995; Zucker, Fitzgerald, & Moses, 1995). This is not to say that these different outcomes are functionally the same, only that there appears to be an overlap of etiological factors. Longitudinal, behavior genetic-findings can help shed further light on the nature of common etiological antecedents. For example, in a study of adults, Slutske et al. (1998) showed a strong genetic correlation

between childhood conduct disorder and alcohol dependence, indicating that much of the overlap between these disorders is due to common genetic influences and that genetic variation in the personality dimension of behavioral undercontrol (impulsivity, interpersonal exploitativeness, and social nonconformity) can explain nearly all of this common underlying genetic predisposition (Slutske et al., 2002). Such studies of the genetic causes of comorbidity would help to further identify underlying, heritable dimensions or traits contributing to the range of impulse-control disorders.

## Personality Correlates

The assumption that disorders of impulse control are related at the level of personality is implicit in much clinical thinking and is explicit in some older diagnostic schemes (*DSM-I;* APA, 1952). Influential theorists (e.g., Cloninger, 1987a, 1987b; Gorenstein & Newman, 1980) have postulated a common underlying vulnerability to multiple disorders associated with disinhibition. Indeed, Cloninger (1987a, 1987b) proposes an identical configuration of personality traits underlying both a subtype of alcohol dependence and antisocial personality disorder (APD).

In recent reviews of the personality literature on alcoholism and APD (Sher & Trull, 1994) and on alcoholism and other substance use disorders (Sher, Trull, Bartholow, & Vieth, 1999) we have arrived at similar conclusions: There are consistent patterns of association between certain broadband personality characteristics (specifically, impulsivity and neuroticism) and a wide range of externalizing psychopathology. Research on the personality correlates of pathological gambling (PG) is not as well developed as it is for substance use disorders, with most studies of PG based upon small samples of patients in treatment. For example, there are no studies of the personality correlates of those at high versus low risk for the development of PG, and very limited relevant prospective data. Despite the lack of strong empirical foundations, theories of the etiology of PG implicate the personality dimensions of neuroticism–negative emotionality (e.g., Dickerson & Baron, 2000; Hand, 1998) and impulsivity-disinhibition (e.g., Dickerson & Baron, 2000) as important risk factors for the subsequent development of PG. Moreover, existing studies are generally consistent in demonstrating a pattern of personality correlates for PG similar to what has been obtained for the substance use disorders. Individuals in treatment for PG have elevated levels of neuroticism–negative emotionality (Blaszczynski, Buhrish, & McConaghy, 1985; Blaszczynski, Steel, & McConaghy, 1997; Blaszczynski, Wilson, & McConaghy, 1986; Ciarrocchi, Kirschner, & Fallik, 1991; Graham & Lowenfeld, 1986) and impulsivity-disinhibition (Blaszczynski et al., 1985, 1986,

1997; Ciarrocchi et al., 1991; Graham & Lowenfeld, 1986; McCormick, Taber, Kruedelbach, & Russo, 1987; Steel & Blaszczynski, 1998) compared to unaffected controls. The results for extraversion-sociability are mixed, with some studies failing to find an association with PG (Blaszczynski et al., 1985, 1986; Ciarrocchi et al., 1991; Graham & Lowenfeld, 1986), and with others finding either a positive association (McCormick et al., 1987) or a negative association (Blaszczynski et al., 1997).

### Neuroticism–Negative Emotionality

Findings from several major longitudinal studies of substance use disorders do not suggest a strong causal role for neuroticism–negative emotionality (e.g., Jackson, Sher, & Wood, 2000; Jones, 1968; Robins, Bates, & O'Neal, 1962; Sher, Bartholow, & Wood, 2000; Vaillant & Milofsky, 1982). In contrast, other prospective studies do implicate negative emotionality as predictive of later alcohol involvement (Caspi et al., 1997; Chassin, Curran, Hussong, & Colder, 1996; Cloninger, Sigvardsson, Reich, & Bohman, 1988; Labouvie, Pandina, White, & Johnson, 1990; Sieber, 1981). However, it should be noted that Cloninger et al. specify that *low* negative affectivity (characterized by low scores on the Harm Avoidance scale of the Tridimensional Personality Questionnaire [TPQ], Cloninger, 1987c) is most relevant to the development of early-onset alcoholism, whereas people high in negative affect are susceptible to the occurance of alcohol dependence later in life.

This divergent pattern of findings indicates that our understanding of the role played by neuroticism–negative emotionality in substance use disorder is far from complete, particularly given that the existing database of informative prospective studies remains relatively sparse. Furthermore, the issue may be best resolved by considering moderating variables influencing the relationship between negative emotionality and substance use (e.g., Greeley & Oei, 1999; Sher, 1987).

### Impulsivity-Disinhibition

The broad personality dimension that appears to be most relevant to impulse-control disorders is that of impulsivity-disinhibition. This dimension incorporates traits such as sensation seeking, aggressiveness, impulsivity, and psychoticism, and has been termed *impulsive, undersocialized sensation-seeking* by Zuckerman (1994). The high rates of comorbidity between alcohol use disorders and both antisocial and borderline personality disorders (discussed later) provide support for the idea that clinical alcoholics tend to be impulsive (e.g., Regier et al., 1990), and alcoholics tend to score high on psychometric measures assessing this

dimension (e.g., Bergman & Brismar, 1994; Plutchik & Plutchik, 1988). Moreover, alcoholics with comorbid APD experienced a more severe and chronic course of alcoholism, and engaged in more drug use, compared to those without this comorbid diagnosis (e.g., Holdcraft, Iacono, & McGue, 1998).

Additionally, cross-sectional high-risk studies (e.g., Alterman et al., 1998; Sher, 1991) demonstrate that traits reflecting impulsivity-disinhibition are elevated in the offspring of alcoholics. Most importantly, prospective studies consistently indicate that impulsive-disinhibited individuals are at elevated risk for the development of substance-related problems (e.g., Bates & Labouvie, 1995; Caspi et al., 1997; Cloninger et al., 1988; Hawkins, Catalano, & Miller, 1992; Pederson, 1991; Schuckit, 1998; Sher et al., 2000; Zucker & Gomberg, 1986; Zucker et al., 1995). Although there are no prospective studies of personality and PG, Vitaro, Arsenault, and Tremblay (1997) found that a five-item self-report measure of impulsiveness completed at age 13 predicted gambling *problems* at age 17 among 754 boys. Additionally, in a subsample of 154 boys it predicted gambling problems even after controlling for socioeconomic status, frequency of gambling involvement at age 13, and measures of anxiety and aggressiveness (Vitaro, Arsenault, & Tremblay, 1999). The importance of impulsivity-disinhibition as an early predictor of later alcohol problems has been outlined in detail by Zucker et al. (1995). These authors hypothesize that the prospective relation between childhood impulsivity-disinhibition (or childhood conduct disorder) and later drinking problems marks an etiologic process whereby these traits lead to poor school performance and relational problems. These troubles in turn may lead such individuals to associate with similar peers, who are likely to begin using alcohol and other drugs early in adolescence. Moreover, conduct disorder and alcohol dependence have been linked to the influence of genes that increase the risk for both disorders (Slutske et al., 1998).

Because it has been argued that antisociality reflects merely behavior and not personality as defined by classic personality theorists (see Nathan, 1988), studies demonstrating that personality variables can statistically explain the relation between antisocial behavior and alcoholism can be of theoretical relevance. In one such study, Earleywine and Finn (1991) demonstrated that the cross-sectional relation between alcohol use and a scale that heavily samples antisocial behavior can be statistically explained by the effect of sensation seeking on both variables. Stronger support for a common underlying vulnerability related to personality traits is provided by Jang, Vernon, and Livesley (2000), who found some common genetic influence upon alcohol misuse and personality traits related to antisociality (specifically sensation-seeking, recklessness, and impulsivity) as well as to narcissism (grandiosity and attention seeking), and by Slutske et al. (2002), who found that about 40% of the genetic susceptibility for alcohol dependence was shared with genetic variation in the personality dimension of behavioral undercontrol (impulsivity, interpersonal exploitativeness, and social nonconformity). It would be useful to extend these types of analyses to a broader range of impulse-control disorders.

### Extraversion-Sociability

The evidence concerning the relationship between extraversion-sociability and impulse-control disorders can best be described as mixed. Most reviews of the clinical literature (e.g., Barnes, 1983; Cox, 1987) do not suggest that, as a group, individuals with substance use disorders differ from controls on the dimension of extraversion-sociability, although as dependence becomes severe, levels of extraversion-sociability may decrease (Rankin, Stockwell, & Hodgson, 1982). Moreover, high-risk, cross-sectional studies do not typically indicate that children of alcoholics differ from controls on this trait (Sher, 1991), although sociability predicted substance use for adolescent children of alcoholics but not for controls in one study (Molina, Chassin, & Curran, 1994). On the other hand, at least one other recent cross-sectional study did not find a significant relationship between extraversion and either alcohol use frequency or alcohol problems using a nonclinical sample (Stacy & Newcomb, 1998). However, prospective studies have noted the possibility that extraversion-sociability may be etiologically relevant to the development of substance use problems. For example, Jones (1968) reported that prealcoholics were rated as being high in expressiveness and gregariousness. Also, sociability has been found to prospectively predict frequency of intoxication (Sieber, 1981). Another, more recent prospective study found that higher extraversion scores predicted alcohol dependence among young adults over a 3.5-year interval (Kilbey, Downey, & Breslau, 1998).

There may be more consistency in the mixed patterns of findings than appears on the surface. For example, it seems possible that extraversion-sociability is a risk factor for the *development* of substance involvement (especially because substance initiation usually occurs in a social context), and that this trait becomes increasingly masked in those whose levels of dependence increase over time. Another possibility is that other third variables may play a role in determining the influence of extraversion on substance use disorders. For example, some recent evidence suggests a gender difference wherein high extraversion scores may be more relevant for predicting alcohol problems in women than in men (e.g., Heath et al., 1997; Prescott, Neale, Corey, & Kendler, 1997). Furthermore, it is currently unclear whether these outgoing

characteristics most accurately reflect true sociability or (misattributed) disinhibition (Tarter, 1988). Additional systematic investigations of this association with prospective data, including consideration of other potential moderating and mediating processes, would prove helpful in better identifying the importance of traits related to extraversion.

### Common Biological Substrates

There is a scattered but large literature linking biological variables to individual differences in the trait of impulsivity in general and to disorders of impulse control in particular (Zuckerman, 1991). Note that because of acute and chronic effects of psychoactive substances on the individual, it can be very difficult to attribute differences in brain function to a predisposing vulnerability versus a consequence of substance use (e.g., Hare, 1984).

One of the most actively researched questions currently is whether deficits in so-called *executive functioning* (e.g., planning, organizing, selective attention, some forms of inhibitory control) are related to disorders of impulse control. Because these functions are associated with activity located in the frontal cortex (Luria, 1980; Stuss & Benson, 1985), they are sometimes described as *frontal functions*. However, because of extensive connections between the frontal lobes and other brain regions, localization of any complex executive function is probably an oversimplification. *Hypofrontality* (i.e., decreased frontal lobe activity) and related impaired executive functions have been hypothesized to be related to certain forms of impulsivity in general (e.g., Nigg, 2000), conduct disorder, and adult antisocial behavior and substance use disorders (e.g., Gorenstein, 1987). In a recent meta-analysis, Morgan and Lilienfeld (2000) reported an overall negative association between executive functions and antisociality across a variety of ages and populations. Children of alcoholics, who are at high risk for a range of disorders of impulse control (esp. substance use disorders), have been shown to have a range of cognitive deficits, some of these related to executive functions (Pihl & Bruce, 1995; Polich, Pollock, & Bloom, 1994; Sher, 1991). Although, to date, the neuropsychology of pathological gamblers has not been well studied, there have been recorded cases of the development of PG subsequent to frontal lobe injury (Blaszczynski, Hyde, & Sandanam, 1991). Thus there are a number of converging findings suggesting that deficits in cognitive functions subsumed under the rubric of executive control relate to a range of disorders of impulse control. However, much of the primary literature is characterized by serious design limitations: There is great variability among researchers in how various cognitive functions are classified; the specificity to executive functions (as opposed to nonexecutive functions) is not always clear; and some disorders not typically thought of as disorders of impulse control (e.g., schizophrenia, obsessive-compulsive disorder) may also be associated with similar deficits. Thus, there is a need for studies bringing a higher degree of resolution in relating specific forms of neurocognitive deficits to specific symptoms and syndromes.

Impulsivity and associated disorders have also been associated with several distinct neuropharmacological systems, in particular the serotonin, dopamine, and norepinephrine systems (Zuckerman, 1991). Many of these studies have sought to establish correlations between the presence of a disorder (e.g., alcohol dependence; Major & Murphy, 1978; PG; Blanco, Orensanz-Munoz, Blanco-Jerez, & Saiz-Ruiz, 1996) or variations in a personality trait (e.g., sensation seeking; Schooler, Zahn, Murphy, & Buchsbaum, 1978) and differing levels of neurotransmitter metabolites or enzymes responsible for neurotransmitter metabolism. Other studies have employed acute pharmacological challenges in order to alter the functioning of a neurotransmitter system (e.g., LeMarquand, Benkelfat, Pihl, Palmour, & Young, 1999) and examine the effect on impulsive behavior. Additionally, treatment outcome studies of impulse-control disorders investigating medications known to have effects on specific neurotransmitter systems (e.g., selective serotonin reuptake inhibitors, or SSRIs) have relevance to understanding the biological bases of these conditions.

Research on biological markers of impulsivity and associated disorders has been going on for more than 20 years, and numerous intriguing findings implicate functionally high levels of dopaminergic activity and low levels of noradrenergic and serotonergic activity (Zuckerman, 1991, 1999) in impulsivity and in disorders of impulse control. However, it is difficult to point to many results that implicate a robust, specific deficit. For example, although low serotonergic activity is posited to play a role in substance use disorders, clinical outcome trials of SSRIs have had inconsistent results (Litten & Allen, 1998). Additionally, a low level of monoamine oxidase (an enzyme important in the breakdown of dopamine, norepinephrine, and serotonin) activity is claimed to be "one of the most reliable biological markers for sensation seeking and impulsivity traits and disinhibitory disorders such as [APD], alcohol and substance abuse, and other disorders characterized by poor impulse control . . . [including PG]" (Zuckerman, 1999, p. 309). However, the association often is small and it is possible, if not likely, that even this relationship is an artifact of comorbid tobacco use (Anthenelli et al., 1998; Sher, Bylund, Walitzer, Hartmann, & Ray-Prenger, 1994).

Given heterogeneity within primary diagnostic groups, it is possible that strong relations between disorders and biological markers are obscured by mixtures of disorder subtypes. For example, Linnoila, Virkkunen, George, and Higley (1993) review evidence suggesting that although early-onset alcoholism is characterized by low levels of serotonin metabolites in cerebrospinal fluid, later onset alcoholism is not; and this early versus late onset maps onto a distinction between more and less impulsivity (e.g., see discussion of alcoholism typologies later in this chapter). Pettinati et al. (2001) reported that sertraline (a specific serotonin reuptake inhibitor) was effective at reducing drinking in alcoholics *without* a history of depression. It seems fair to say that we are still at an early stage of understanding the neuropharmacological foundation of impulsivity and related disorders. Presumably, progress in *behavioral genomics* (which will identify specific genes associated with specific biological processes) will help guide the next leg of this important research direction.

## SUBSTANCE USE DISORDERS AND PATHOLOGICAL GAMBLING

In the following sections, we focus on three disorders of impulse control: (a) alcohol use disorders, (b) drug use disorders, and (c) pathological gambling. As operationalized by the *DSM-IV*, these conditions share in common a number of features, including preoccupation with engaging in the behavior (i.e., either substance use or gambling); inability to abstain from the behavior; tolerance (e.g., either using more of a substance or increasing the stakes in gambling to get the desired effect); and withdrawal (e.g., discomfort or irritability when abstaining from the behavior). Although each of these disorders have unique features (e.g., PG's chasing losses) their underlying commonalities permit a more in-depth analysis of basic mechanisms likely common to a number of conceptually distinct conditions.

Before separately discussing alcohol use disorders and drug use disorders, we first consider the concepts of substance abuse and substance dependence. The abuse-dependence distinction is applicable to both alcohol use and drug use disorders, and dependence-related concepts are increasingly being applied to other conditions such as PG and other types of addictive behaviors (e.g., so-called sexual addiction, Internet addiction).

## THE ABUSE AND DEPENDENCE SYNDROMES

Most theory and research on the distinction between abuse and dependence has been targeted on the use of alcohol, and so our discussion will focus on this substance. More than 150 years ago, the term *alcoholism* was introduced by Magnus

Huss to indicate a condition resulting from excessive consumption of alcohol (Keller & Doria, 1991). Subsequently, alcoholism has been alternately construed as any use of alcohol that negatively affects the drinker or society (Jellinek, 1960), as a syndrome of problem drinking (*ICD-8;* World Health Organization [WHO], 1967), as a personality disorder (*DSM-I;* APA, 1952), or as a disease marked by signs of physiological adaptation (e.g., tolerance or withdrawal) or loss of control over drinking (Feighner et al., 1972; National Council on Alcoholism [NCA] Criteria Committee, 1972). Eventually, classification systems formally contrasted *dependence* on alcohol with alcohol *abuse*—a pattern of maladaptive alcohol use characterized by negative social, legal, or occupational consequences (*DSM-III;* APA, 1980). In this way, the hazardous use of alcohol was contrasted with a more severe form of dependency on alcohol characterized by physiological symptoms.

Early operationalizations of alcohol dependence, such as the *DSM-III* (APA, 1980), NCA Criteria Committee (1972), and the World Health Organization (1967) criteria for alcohol dependence, required evidence of *physiological* dependence, indicated by tolerance or withdrawal. At about the same time the NCA and *DSM-III* criteria were being drafted, Edwards and Gross (1976) proposed an alternate dependence concept, the *Alcohol Dependence Syndrome (ADS),* in which physiological signs and symptoms of dependence were indicators of but not necessary criteria for the diagnosis of dependence. Edwards and Gross's conception of alcohol dependence referred to a syndrome composed of a variety of signs and symptoms that signified the importance that alcohol consumption plays in the life of the drinker. These signs and symptoms include what Edwards (1982, 1986; Edwards & Gross) described as "a narrowing of the drinking repertoire"; centrality of drinking in the person's life relative to other life tasks and responsibilities; tolerance and withdrawal; "awareness of the compulsion to drink"; and rapid reinstatement of dependence symptoms after a period of abstinence. The broadened construct of dependence introduced by Edwards and Gross was clearly influential in later revisions of the *DSM,* and symptoms of tolerance or withdrawal were no longer required for the diagnosis of substance dependence in *DSM-III-R* (APA, 1987) and *DSM-IV* (APA, 1994; note, however, that "with physiological dependence" remains a specifier of a subtype of dependence in the present *DSM*).

Edwards (1986) was careful to distinguish *alcohol dependence* from *alcohol-related consequences* (or disabilities). *Alcohol-related consequences* refer to a variety of negative life events that are directly the result of alcohol consumption. These consequences include social problems (e.g., physical or verbal aggression, marital difficulties, loss of important social relationships), legal problems (e.g., arrests for driving while intoxicated, public inebriation), vocational problems (e.g., termination from employment, failure to achieve career goals), and medical problems (e.g., physical injury, liver disease, central nervous system disease). Both substance-related consequences and the dependence syndrome can be viewed as dimensional constructs that can be graded in intensity from absent to severe and do not explicitly reference the *amount* of substance consumed as a criterion.

The *DSM-IV* describes two major categories of substance use disorder, specifically substance abuse and substance dependence, that roughly correspond to Edwards and Gross's (1976) distinction between alcohol-related disabilities and the alcohol dependence syndrome. Within *DSM-IV,* substance dependence is the more severe disorder and its presence (or its history) excludes the diagnosis of substance abuse.

Factor analysis of alcohol symptom scales in clinical samples of alcoholics tend to suggest a multidimensional structure with at least one factor representing dependence (e.g., Skinner, 1981; Svanum, 1986), but factor analyses employing population-based samples paint a less clear-cut picture. More specifically, mixed abuse and dependence indicators can be well represented by a single factor (e.g., Hasin, Muthen, Wisnicki, & Grant, 1994). When evidence for more than one factor is found, the item content of the factors are not consistent with the *DSM* criteria sets (e.g., Muthen, Grant, & Hasin, 1993) for separate abuse and dependence symptoms. Moreover, when multiple dimensions are empirically identified, correlations among the factors appear to be exceptionally high, calling into question the value of a multidimensional approach (e.g., Allen, Fertig, Towle, & Altschuler, 1994; Hasin et al., 1994).

Recently, some investigators have begun to question the broadening of the dependence construct that took place in the transition from *DSM-III* to *DSM-III-R,* and argue for a narrower definition based on physiological dependence. For example, Langenbucher et al. (2000) propose a *withdrawal gate model* in which the symptom of withdrawal is both necessary and sufficient for the diagnosis of dependence. Withdrawal-based dependence diagnoses were found to be more reliable and proved to show a stronger pattern of validity along diverse criteria than *DSM-IV*-based dependence diagnoses. Schuckit et al. (1998) also endorsed the importance of physiological dependence (especially withdrawal) as being an important severity indicator, as evidenced by its association with a range of clinical variables (both psychiatric and substance related). Thus, recent work indicates that substance withdrawal is particularly important clinically and suggests that it should be considered for special attention in future diagnostic revisions. Because this symptom is fairly rare in both adolescent samples (Langenbucher et al., 2000) and nonclinical samples (Helzer, Burnam, & McEvoy, 1991), prevalence estimates of withdrawal-based dependence diagnoses would likely be much lower in both clinical adolescent samples and in nonclinical samples than is currently reported using *DSM-III-R* and *DSM-IV* criteria. In typological research using *latent-class analysis* (a multivariate technique designed to uncover latent classes underlying a set of observations), withdrawal symptoms typically are found only in the most severe subtype of alcohol dependence identified. This appears to be true in both clinical (Bucholz, Heath, Reich, & Hesselbrock, 1996) and nonclinical samples (Heath, Bucholz, Slutske, & Madden, 1994; Nelson, Heath, & Kessler, 1998).

It is unclear why the other putative indicator of physiological dependence, *tolerance,* has not been found to be as important an indicator of dependence; both tolerance and withdrawal are thought to reflect neurological adaptations related to chronic use. One possibility is that current questionnaire- and interview-based assessments of tolerance that rely upon subjective inferences concerning changes in drug sensitivity over time are of limited validity. O'Neill and Sher (2000) found that the course of subjective reports of tolerance over time, in young adulthood, did not conform to prediction (e.g., self-reported tolerance appeared to decrease during young adulthood, even among consistent heavy drinkers). Thus, it may be that current assessment strategies for tolerance are limited and conclusions regarding the importance of tolerance as a dependence criterion await improved assessments of tolerance.

Moving beyond the issue of assessment, research on behavioral aspects of tolerance over the past 35 years has highlighted the role of nonpharmacological factors in tolerance development and expression and, in doing so, has downplayed the concept of tolerance as one of simple neuroadaptation to a psychoactive substance (Siegel, Baptista, Kim, McDonald, & Weise-Kelly, 2000). Siegel and his colleagues have repeatedly demonstrated that *conditioned* compensatory responses (i.e., opposite in direction to the unconditioned response) to drug effects develop over repeated administrations of a drug along with its associated stimuli (e.g., beverage taste, hypodermic needle, social setting). Over time, these associated stimuli become capable of eliciting conditioned compensatory responses that counteract the direct effects of the drug. Thus, tolerance can be highly situational or context dependent. Consequently, use of a drug in novel circumstances (that lack the situational cues that elicit conditioned compensatory responses) can result in an escape from tolerance (and perhaps even overdose). These situational tolerance effects have been noted for a range of psychoactive substances including opiates, alcohol, and caffeine (Siegel et al.). Such

associative processes might be used to explain tolerance for nonpharmacological stimuli such as gambling (e.g., the need to gamble with increasing amounts of money in order to achieve the desired excitement). Siegel and Allen (1998) have shown how nonpharmacological processes, such as the visual-aftereffect phenomenon known as the *McCollough effect,* appear to involve conditioned compensatory responses; this suggests that conditioning plays a role in a range of homeostatic adjustments, not just those involving drugs.

Similar to Siegel and colleagues' (2000) associative theory of tolerance is a nonassociative theory proposed by Solomon and Corbit's (1974) *opponent-process theory.* According to this theory, a positive (or negative) hedonic state (or A-state) elicits a countervailing negative (or positive) hedonic state (or B-state) that serves to counteract the initial state as part of a natural homeostatic mechanism. Over time, the B-state is thought to strengthen, thereby reducing the reaction to the drug (i.e., the opponent B-state reduces the initial A-state). In this way, tolerance is thought to develop. Koob and colleagues (e.g., Koob & Le Moal, 2001) have extended opponent-process theory to account for changes in homeostatic set-point, or *allostasis.* That is, over time, there is a change in the natural homeostatic set-point so that the B-state no longer balances the evoking A-state and actually serves to overshoot the initial homeostatic set-point. This type of allostatic derangement is thought to characterize chronic dependence, and this deviation from the (original) natural set-point to the allostatic set-point is believed to represent significant cost to the individual. That is, according to this model, chronic adaptive changes to drug taking dynamically resets homeostatic mechanisms altering the basic hedonic set-point. From this perspective, but also from conditioning models such as Siegel's, withdrawal phenomena can be viewed as opponent processes acting in the absence of reward and involving the same underlying brain systems (albeit in the opposite direction). It is for this reason that resumption of drug intake (initiating a new A-state) counteracts withdrawal.

In general, the concepts of tolerance and neuroadaptation suggest that many problem behaviors may escalate over time, leading to greater problem involvement. Although the focus on impulse-control disorders is on notions of inclination and inhibition, it may be fruitful to determine the extent that both acute and chronic homeostatic adjustments to the effects of reward tend to maintain these disorders.

## ALCOHOL USE DISORDERS

Pathological alcohol use is both prevalent and costly in North America and represents a serious health threat in many other developed and developing nations (Helzer & Canino, 1992).

It bears noting that much of the societal cost of alcohol consumption (e.g., unintended injury, motor vehicle crashes) is attributable to the large proportion of individuals who do not necessarily suffer from an alcohol use disorder (AUD), abuse, or dependence, but who do misuse alcohol on occasion. Consequently, effective prevention of alcohol-related harm needs to be broadly based and not targeted only at those with AUDs (Institute of Medicine, 1990; Kreitman, 1986).

## History and Evolution of the Concept of Alcoholism

"Alcoholic beverages have been known to almost all people from before the dawn of history" (Poznanski, 1959, p. 42). Seneca (4 B.C.–65 A.D.; 1942) distinguished between two distinct definitions of the word *drunken,* one definition referring to someone who is acutely intoxicated and poorly self-controlled, and the other to someone who is a habitual drinker and "a slave to the habit." As was true for many psychological disorders, it was during the nineteenth century that leading European physicians attempted to define and describe the condition we now call *alcohol dependence.*

Perhaps the best known early scholar in the area of alcohol dependence was Magnus Huss, who is credited with creating the term *chronic alcoholism* and who noted that there was little in the way of a clear boundary between this condition and other mental disorders. However, most modern conceptions of alcohol dependence are more closely associated with the writings of E. M. Jellinek (1960; Bowman & Jellinek, 1941) who described five varieties of alcoholism based on the configuration of etiological elements, alcohol process elements (including both symptom profile and the nature of symptom progression), and the nature of damage. Over the past century, clinicians and researchers have proposed a number of additional typologies (see Babor, 1996) based on a variety of criteria including personality characteristics, drinking patterns, developmental course, heritability, age of onset, and psychiatric comorbidity. Although these various typologies differ in number and kind of types proposed, there appears to be consistent evidence for at least two types.

One type frequently described involves comorbid antisocial tendencies and early onset—for example, Babor et al.'s Type B (1992); Cloninger's Type 2 (1987a); Knight's essential (1938); and Zucker's antisocial (1987). The other type involves later onset and more negative affectivity—for example, Babor et al.'s Type A (1992); Cloninger's Type 1 (1987a); Knight's reactive (1938); and Zucker's negative affect (1987). Still, the value of subtyping alcohol dependence into two or more discrete types remains to be definitively established. Such typologies invariably represent prototypic cases and many affected individuals fail to fit clearly into a single subtype. Moreover, the association between alcohol dependence and subtyping variables such as antisociality (and presumably others, such as age of onset) appears to be graded across the range of levels of antisociality (Sher, 1994), and it is not only high levels of antisociality that are associated with alcohol-related difficulties. Regardless of whether one subscribes to a categorical or dimensional approach with respect to conceptualizing AUDs, there is little question that there is significant heterogeneity with respect to etiological factors, symptoms, and course.

## Epidemiology

Over the past 20 years, three large-scale, population-based epidemiological surveys using structured diagnostic interviews have provided estimates of AUDs in the United States. These include the Epidemiologic Catchment Area (ECA) Survey (Helzer et al., 1991; Robins, Bates, & O'Neal, 1991); the National Comorbidity Survey (NCS; Kessler et al., 1994, 1997); and the National Longitudinal Alcohol Epidemiologic Survey (NLAES; Grant, 1997; Grant & Pickering, 1996; Grant et al., 1994). Both the NCS and NLAES employed nationally representative samples that provide a scientific basis for generating prevalence estimates for the United States.

Each of these major studies indicates very high past-year and lifetime prevalences of AUDs in the U.S. population (13.8% lifetime and 6.8% past-year *DSM-III* in ECA; 23.5% lifetime and 7.7% past-year *DSM-III-R* in NCS; and 18.2% lifetime and 7.41% past-year *DSM-IV* in NLAES). Additionally, each of these studies documented that AUDs are most prevalent in men and in young adulthood; dependence is more prevalent than abuse in the NCS and NLAES.

Focusing on the NLAES data (because of that survey's size and its use of the *DSM-IV*), we note several important findings that help characterize the relation between AUDs and important demographic variables. First, AUDs are more than twice as prevalent in men than in women, with larger sex differences in older cohorts than in younger cohorts (e.g., AUDs are 4.4 times as prevalent in men vs. women in the 65+ age group, but only 2.2 times as prevalent in men vs. women in the 18–20 age group; Grant et al., 1994). Also, alcohol dependence is lower in Blacks than in Whites and Hispanics, and is lower among those who are married and who have higher family incomes (Grant, 1997).

Examination of Figure 8.1 shows how strongly age-graded AUDs (especially alcohol dependence) are in the NLAES study. With the exception of Black women (who tend to have comparatively low rates of alcohol dependence in early adulthood), there is a steep, negative prevalence gradient with age across the other demographic strata. This suggests either a marked developmentally limited condition that tends to remit in the 3rd decade of life, or secular changes

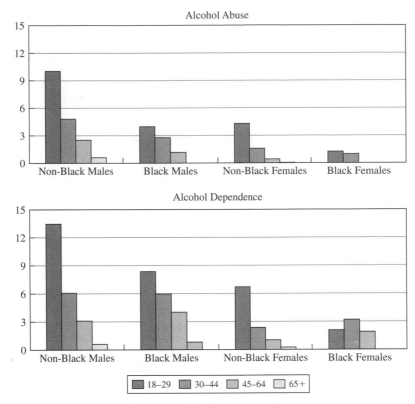

**Figure 8.1**    Prevalence of (past-year) *DSM-IV* alcohol use disorders.

occurring in the prevalence of AUDs such that more recently born cohorts have higher prevalences. (It is also possible that high early mortality is partially responsible for the decline, but the size of the decline from the 18–29 group to the 30–44 group is far too large to make this a viable explanation for the most dramatic part of the curve.) Although there is some evidence to suggest that there are secular changes in the age of onset of AUDs, with recent cohorts showing an earlier onset than older cohorts (Reich, Cloninger, Van Eerdewegh, Rice, & Mullaney, 1988), existing data suggest that the age-related decline in prevalence is primarily a developmental phenomenon and is not attributable to secular trends in consumption patterns (Grant, 1997). Perhaps the most compelling data suggesting that AUDs are strongly developmentally graded come from prospective studies of heavy, episodic alcohol use and AUDs in young adulthood (e.g., Chen & Kandel, 1995; Schulenberg, O'Malley, Bachman, Wadsworth, & Johnston, 1996; Sher & Gotham, 1999).

Beyond revealing a mean decreasing trend in heavy drinking during the 20s, these same studies also indicate considerable variability in course. Schulenberg et al. (1996) identified several distinct trajectories of (so-called) *binge drinking* (defined here as five or more drinks in a row during the previous 2 weeks) over the age span of 18 to 24. None of these trajectories closely resembled the mean trajectory of relatively low

levels of bingeing at age 18, slight increases from age 18 to age 19–20, stability, and then decreases beginning at age 21–22. These trajectories as were described as *chronic* (high levels of bingeing at all time points), *decreased* (high levels at age 18 that monotonically decreased to very low levels by age 23–24), *increased* (low levels at 18 monotonically increasing over time to very high levels by age 23–24), and *fling* (low levels at 18 and at 23–24 but moderately high levels during the middle years), with a *rare* trajectory that was characterized by infrequent bingeing at all time points.

These different trajectories were found to be distinguishable from each other on the basis of a range of etiologically relevant predictors such as gender, personality, drinking motivations, and the social context of drinking. Similarly, other data suggest that young adults show a decreasing likelihood of diagnosing with an AUD over time but with significant variation in course; some individuals tend to diagnose chronically, others show apparent remission after diagnosing early, and still others tending to increase in their likelihood of diagnosing over time (Sher & Gotham, 1999). Thus, although the mean trend of pathological alcohol involvement in young adulthood is toward maturing-out, so to speak, we also see the beginning stages of what might become a persistent life-course pattern in early adulthood. In addition, there is a small group of late starters who begin to show problematic alcohol involvement when their peers are recovering from such patterns. Thus, variability in course can be conceptualized as mixture of distinct trajectories.

An alternative perspective on variability in course is the *state-trait model* of psychopathology (Jackson et al., 2000). This model proposes that the tendency to diagnose over time is attributable to a stable trait that is indicated by the presence or absence of symptoms at multiple assessment occasions. From this perspective, the occurrence of an AUD at a particular point in time is a joint function of trait AUD and situational variables that tend to inhibit or facilitate the expression of the trait. Both trajectory and state-trait perspectives suggest that cross-sectional current diagnoses (based on recent symptom clustering) and retrospectively assessed, lifetime diagnoses (based on meeting of diagnostic criteria at some point in the individual's life) fail to capture developmental aspects of AUDs and the related dimension of chronicity. Diagnostic approaches that attend more fully to course may prove to be important etiologically and clinically.

## Comorbidity

As noted earlier, there is high comorbidity between AUDs and other Axis I and Axis II disorders. In the NCS (Kessler et al., 1997), lifetime *alcohol dependence* was robustly associated with higher rates of lifetime diagnoses of all anxiety, affective, drug, and antisocial behavior disorders surveyed; and this was true for both men and women. Consistent with data from the ECA (Helzer & Pryzbeck, 1988; Helzer et al., 1991), the disorders most strongly associated with alcohol dependence were mania, drug use disorder, and antisocial personality disorder. However, comorbidity with *alcohol abuse* was less consistent and those relations that were significant were less generalizable across gender.

Most NCS participants with an AUD had at least one of the disorders surveyed. Establishing whether the comorbidity with AUD was potentially causal, consequential, or attributable to some common etiological process is a major area of current interest. In order to characterize the nature of comorbidity better, many investigators have attempted to classify AUDs as either primary or secondary (Schuckit, 1985). This primary-secondary distinction is based upon the sequencing of onset of AUDs and of comorbid conditions. That is, when an AUD occurs prior to a comorbid condition it is considered *primary;* when it occurs subsequent to a comorbid condition it is considered *secondary.*

In the NCS, alcohol dependence was typically found to be secondary to other comorbid disorders (Kessler et al., 1997). In particular, alcohol dependence was found to be secondary to anxiety disorders (especially social phobia) and antisocial

disorders (especially conduct disorder); and primary to drug use disorders and affective disorders. This is not surprising because, *by definition,* some disorders (e.g., conduct disorder) onset before midadolescence, and some disorders (e.g., depression) tend to have relatively late onset. Moreover, prior lifetime disorders tended to positively predict the onset of lifetime alcohol dependence across all disorders assessed. However, other prior lifetime disorders did not predict the onset of alcohol abuse consistently, and when they did predict, the patterns were difficult to interpret. For example, depression, mania, and drug dependence were found to be negatively associated with subsequent alcohol abuse in men and positively associated in women (Kendler et al., 1997). It seems likely that these seemingly anomalous results represent a statistical artifact of segregating out a mild form of AUD (abuse) from more severe forms (dependence). Alternatively, it might be useful to consider broadband diagnosis (abuse and dependence combined) and narrow-band dependence separately.

The retrospective analyses in both the NCS and ECA, although of interest, assume the accuracy of retrospective symptom reporting when trying to sequence disorders that may have been experienced decades earlier . . . a big assumption. Moreover, there can be co-occurrence between alcohol consumption and minor symptomatology prior to any formal symptom onset, and many symptoms (e.g., tolerance to alcohol, worry) can have insidious onsets and be difficult to date.

Unfortunately, there are few prospective studies of AUD comorbidity that would help unravel direction of causality. Those studies that do exist either cover early periods of development (e.g., Costello et al., 1999) during which participants have yet to pass through much of the period of risk for disorders, or begin later in development (e.g., Kushner, Sher, & Erickson, 1999) when extensive symptomatology is already in place. Costello et al.'s findings indicate that comorbidity processes can begin in childhood, further highlighting the difficulty of disentangling cause and effect using retrospective reports in adults.

To date, population-based epidemiology of comorbidity between AUDs and psychopathology has focused on the *DSM* Axis I disorders with the important exception of APD (and its childhood precursors), which was assessed in the ECA and NCS. Although the database for examining AUD/Axis II comorbidity is not well developed, existing studies suggest a strong relation between AUDs and both antisocial and borderline personality disorders (Sher et al., 1999), two disorders characterized by disinhibition. Other personality disorders associated with AUDs in multiple studies include borderline, histrionic, narcissistic, and avoidant. It is possible that much of the comorbidity among AUDs and

Axis I comorbidity might be mediated via personality disorder or closely related traits.

Even well-conducted prospective studies beginning early in development are not capable of disentangling direction of effect between alcohol involvement and psychiatric symptomatology because it is possible that common third variables influence both alcohol involvement and comorbid conditions. For example, behavior-genetic investigations suggest that common genetic vulnerabilities are partially responsible for comorbidity between alcohol dependence and nicotine dependence (True et al., 1999), conduct disorder (Jang et al., 2000; Slutske et al., 1998), and to a lesser degree, anxiety disorders (Kendler et al., 1995; Merikangas et al., 1998) and depression (Prescott, Aggen, & Kendler, 2000). Identifying common vulnerability factors represents just a first step toward identifying the functional mechanisms transducing genetic influences. Differences in neurocognitive abilities and personality discussed earlier may represent heritable vulnerabilities mediating genetic influences on AUD and comorbid conditions.

## Genetics

It has long been known that AUDs are strongly familial, that is, they tend to aggregate in the same families (e.g., Cotton, 1979). However, only in the past 20 years has a strong consensus developed that the cause of this familiality is genetic inheritance. This is because modern adoption and twin studies have clearly shown that much of the variation in risk for AUDs is attributable to genes rather than to the effect of living in a family environment that promotes AUD development. For example, adoption studies indicate that it is alcoholism in biological relatives and not alcoholism in the family of rearing that increases risk for offspring. Similarly, twin studies indicate higher concordance rates for AUDs in identical (monozygotic) twins than in fraternal (dizygotic) twins (see McGue, 1999b, for review; and note that there is also strong evidence for genetic effects on measures of alcohol intake [Heath, 1995a]). Nevertheless, there is some controversy in the genetic epidemiology literature concerning a number of issues, including whether there are distinct heritable subtypes or whether genetics play as important a role in women as in men (Hesselbrock, 1995; McGue, 1999b; Searles, 1988). Much of this inconsistency probably arises from the fact that many primary studies are underpowered and have variation in the operationalization of the phenotype studied, and that ascertainment biases surrounding use of clinical samples can lead to inaccurate estimates (Heath, 1995b; Searles). At present there appears to an emerging consensus that genetic factors are important in men and women,

that multiple genes are responsible for the genetic effect, and that the nature of the genetic vulnerability remains to be discovered (McGue; National Institute on Alcohol Abuse and Alcoholism [NIAAA], 2000).

The search for identifying specific genes contributing to alcoholism risk is still at an early stage, but recent advances in molecular genetics now allow us to scan many genetic loci for possible association with alcoholism. Several chromosomal regions that appear to contain genes associated with alcoholism have been tentatively identified (Reich et al., 1998) and it seems likely that in the next several years, specific genes associated with alcoholism risk will be definitively identified and the mode of influence characterized.

One source of genetic influence on alcoholism risk appears to be mediated by individual differences in ethanol metabolism, at least in some populations. First, variation in two of the genes (alcohol dehydrogenase 2 and 3 [ADH2 and ADH3]) responsible for the enzymes that break down alcohol into its metabolite, acetaldehyde, appear to be related to alcoholism risk in Asian populations (Reich et al., 1998). One recent review concludes, "It can now be regarded as firmly established that . . . [genetic variants] encoding faster metabolizing forms of ADH2 and ADH3 reduce the risk that carriers of these [genetic variants] will develop alcoholism" (NIAAA, 2000, p. 176). Additionally, variation in one of the genes for aldehyde dehydrogenase (the enzyme that breaks down acetaldehyde, the toxic metabolite of alcohol, into acetic acid) is associated with alcoholism risk in Asians (e.g., Harada, Agarwal, Goedde, Tagaki, & Ishikawa, 1982). Those with a specific variant of the gene are at very low risk for alcoholism (i.e., they are protected). The relevance of this effect to those of European ancestry, however, is unclear because the prevalence of this genetic variation is very rare in Caucasians. Still, this finding indicates how specific genes could have an effect on alcoholism risk.

Much of the current research on the search for specific genes for alcoholism has focused on genes related to central nervous system functioning. As reviewed by Diamond and Gordon (1995), there are a number of plausible candidate genes related to different neurotransmitter mechanisms. These include genetic variation associated with the gamma-aminobutyric acid (GABA)/benzodiazepine (BZ) receptor complex (important in anxiolysis), the N-methyl-D-aspartate (NMDA) receptor (an excitatory glutamate receptor known to be extremely sensitive to alcohol in physiological doses), calcium channels, cyclic adenosine monophosphate (cAMP), and G proteins. Additionally, there has been recent interest in genes regulating dopamine and serotonin transport (Lichtermann et al., 2000; Repo et al., 1999). However, to date, no genes related to brain function have been firmly linked to alcoholism risk. Previous reports that one genetic variant of the dopamine D2 receptor is associated with alcoholism have proven controversial and are not widely accepted (McGue, 1999; NIAAA, 2000). However, there is currently much interest in the possible association between the D4 receptor gene and a range of impulse-control disorders, including alcohol misuse (Zuckerman & Kuhlman, 2000). At this juncture, it seems likely that research currently underway will begin providing more definitive links between specific genes and alcohol dependence and point to specific etiological mechanisms.

### Etiological Models

There are a number of theories of alcoholism etiology that have empirical support and that continue to be under active investigation. These various models are not mutually incompatible and there are likely to be multiple pathways into pathological alcohol involvement both between and within individuals. Four etiological models are highlighted here: (1) *positive affect regulation,* (2) *negative affect regulation,* (3) *pharmacological vulnerability,* and (4) *deviance proneness.* To varying degrees, each of these models is probably applicable not only to other forms of substance use disorder (e.g., cocaine dependence, opiate dependence) but, with the exception of the pharmacological vulnerability model, they are also likely applicable to PG and other impulse-control disorders.

### *Positive Affect Regulation*

Most drinkers expect alcohol to be a positively transforming experience that directly produces pleasurable experiences

(Goldman, Del Boca, & Darkes, 1999). Although expectations concerning the effects of alcohol begin early in childhood and prior to direct pharmacological experience (e.g., Noll, Zucker, & Greenberg, 1990), these expectations strengthen during adolescence with increasing alcohol experience (Smith, Goldman, Greenbaum, & Christiansen, 1995). Moreover, drinking for positive reinforcement or enhancement (e.g., drinking "to get high" and "because it makes you feel good"; Cooper, Russell, Skinner, & Windle, 1992) appears to be a primary dimension of drinking motives and is strongly associated both with positive expectancies for enhancement and with personality traits related to reward seeking (i.e., sensation seeking; Cooper, Frone, Russell, & Mudar, 1995) and appears to mediate these expectancy and personality effects on alcohol use.

Presumably, these motivations for positive reinforcement from alcohol are based on alcohol's neuropharmacological effects on the brain centers involved in basic reward mechanisms. For example, alcohol, like other drugs of abuse, has been shown to stimulate mesolimbic dopamine activity that is believed to be involved in basic reward mechanisms (Koob, 2000). In addition, alcohol has been shown to increase activity in brain opioid systems (Gianoulakis, 1996). As illustrated in Table 8.1, alcohol has effects on a range of neurotransmitter systems; several of these are related to positive reinforcement and others to negative reinforcement. Note that the chronic effect of ethanol is often in the opposite direction of the acute effect. For example, the profile of neuropharmacological activity and associated affects during withdrawal are in opposition to the corresponding profile of acute effects. This suggests that in early stages of alcohol

**TABLE 8.1  Acute and Chronic Effects of Alcohol Use**

| Neurochemical | Acute Effects | Behavioral Correlates | Withdrawal & Chronic Effects | Behavioral Correlates |
|---|---|---|---|---|
| GABA | Increase | Sedation, anxiety reduction | Decrease | Heightened anxiety |
| Glutamate | Decrease | Impaired memory formation | Increase | Seizures |
| Dopamine | Increase | Reward; exploratory behavior, attention | Decrease | Craving; dysphoria |
| Norepinephrine | Increase[a] | Arousal | Decrease[b] | Cognitive deficits; craving |
| Serotonin | Increase | Behavioral activation; attention to salient cues | Decrease[c] | Deficits in cognitive processing |
|  |  |  | Increase[c] | Tolerance |
| Opioid peptides | Increase | Reward; self-administration of alcohol | Decrease | Anhedonia |

*Source:* From "Neurobiological Bases of Alcohol's Psychological Effects," by K. Fromme and E. J. D'Amico, 1999, in *Psychological Theories of Drinking and Alcoholism* (2nd ed.), edited by K. E. Leonard and H. T. Blane (pp. 422–455). New York: Guilford Publications. Copyright 1999 by Guilford Publications. Reprinted with permission.
[a]At low doses, alcohol increases norepinephrine, whereas at higher doses alcohol decreases norepinephrine.
[b]Chronic alcohol use is associated with decreased norepinephrine levels, whereas acute withdrawal from chronic alcohol use is associated with increased norepinephrine levels.
[c]Alcohol increases or decreases serotonin activity depending on the receptor subtype and brain region involved.

involvement, reinforcement from use may predominate—but with chronic exposure, negative affect starts to develop, setting up a "spiraling addiction cycle" (Koob & Le Moal, 2001). That is, chronic use leads to dependence phenomena that provide further motivation for use.

### Negative Affect Regulation

One of the most enduring etiological perspectives on alcoholism is that AUDs become established because of the relief of negative affect. There is certainly considerable evidence in support of this general model, which has sometimes been referred to as *self-medication* or the *tension-reduction hypothesis* (Cappell & Herman, 1972; Greeley & Oei, 1999; Sayette, 1999; Sher, 1987). As is true for expectancies for positive reinforcement, individuals hold strong expectations that alcohol reduces anxiety or stress (Fromme, Stroot, & Kaplan, 1993). They also report drinking to cope with negative affect (e.g., "to relax," "to forget your worries," "because it helps when you feel depressed or worried") as a primary reason-for-drinking dimension (Cooper et al., 1992). These coping motivations are strongly related to both alcohol consumption and problems (see Sher, 1987) and mediate the effects of negative affect and tension-reduction expectancies on drinking outcomes (Cooper et al., 1995).

The animal literature indicates that alcohol can have powerful anxiolytic effects in certain paradigms. For example, alcohol has been shown to reliably decrease passive avoidance (i.e., it increases approach to reward in the presence of cues for punishment) in a way much like that of well-known anxiety-reducing compounds such as benzodiazepines and barbiturates (Cappell & Herman, 1972). Additionally, alcohol is known to affect the GABA/BZ receptor in many of the same ways that benzodiazepines do (see Table 8.1), although some paradigms for assessing emotions in humans suggest that the effect of alcohol is quite different than that of benzodiazepines (Stritzke, Patrick, & Lang, 1995).

The picture is further clouded because negative affective states, by themselves, have not been found to be strongly related to alcohol consumption or problems, and laboratory-based investigations of the effect of alcohol on negative affect have yielded confusing and contradictory evidence (Greeley & Oei, 1999; Sayette, 1999; Sher, 1987; Stritzke, Lang, & Patrick, 1996). Greeley and Oei (p. 41) concluded a recent review with the statement that "some individuals, for example, those who may be genetically predisposed to experience greater stress-buffering effects from alcohol, who hold certain beliefs about alcohol, will under certain circumstances consume alcohol for its stress-response-dampening effects." Thus, contemporary research has demonstrated that

alcohol can have negatively reinforcing properties and is consumed for these effects, but that the alcohol–negative affect relation is highly conditional upon a range of individual-difference, contextual, and response parameters.

Perhaps one of the most important formulations regarding the relation between alcohol effects and negative affect is that proposed by Steele and Josephs' (1990) *alcohol myopia* model. According to this model, many of alcohol's "prized and dangerous" effects are mediated by alcohol's effects on attentional processes. Quite simply, alcohol narrows attentional capacity so that one can attend to only the most salient cues in the environment. Whether alcohol is found to be stress reducing can be moderated by the nature of the environmental context. If pleasant distractors are present and salient, these can take attentional precedence over less salient cues for punishment (or internal aversive thoughts) and serve to mitigate stress or anxiety. However, in the absence of cues to divert attention, alcohol can actually amplify negative affect by narrowing the attentional focus to only salient negative stimuli. That is, the affective consequences of intoxication are heavily moderated by contextual factors and, as discussed next, individual difference variables.

### Pharmacological Vulnerability

The *pharmacological vulnerability model* (Sher, 1991) proposes that individuals differ in their responses to the acute or chronic effects of alcohol and that these individual differences are etiologically relevant. More than 100 years ago, Fere (1899) posited that "all subjects do not offer the same susceptibility to the actions of medicaments and poisons," and noted that "Lasegue has specially insisted upon the differences of aptitude for intoxication." The model itself incorporates several submodels that would appear to offer opposing predictions. For example, it can be hypothesized that some individuals are at risk for alcohol-related difficulties because they are especially sensitive to reinforcement (either positive or negative) and are therefore more likely to use alcohol because they get comparatively great effect from it. Alternatively, it can be hypothesized that some individuals are relatively insensitive to reinforcement and thus must consume relatively high amounts of alcohol to achieve a desired effect and thus expose themselves to high blood-alcohol levels, putting themselves at higher risk for alcohol-related organ damage and possibly physiological dependence.

Because of acquired tolerance, it is problematic to compare the alcohol sensitivities of alcohol-dependent individuals and controls. To get around this important methodological difficulty, a number of studies have compared nonalcoholics at high risk for later alcohol dependence with those at low risk. In these studies, risk status is predicated on family history of alcoholism. Reviews of the literature (Newlin & Thomson, 1990; Pollock, 1992) reveal a confusing pattern of findings, with some studies indicating that those at high risk show more pronounced alcohol effects (e.g., increased stress reduction or heart rate), whereas other studies show less pronounced alcohol effects (e.g., decreased body sway, decreased reports of intoxication). Newlin and Thomson (1990) reconciled these seeming discrepancies in noting that high-risk individuals show greater sensitivity when blood alcohol is rising and less sensitivity when blood alcohol is dropping. Because reward is more associated with rising blood alcohol and punishment with descending blood alcohol, they suggest that high-risk individuals are likely to experience both more reinforcement and less punishment than their low-risk counterparts, and that this pattern represents a very powerful form of pharmacological vulnerability.

Most data relevant to the pharmacological vulnerability model are based upon cross-sectional, high-risk versus low-risk comparisons. Stronger evidence for the etiological relevance of individual differences in the pharmacological effect of alcohol involves the prospective prediction of later alcohol use disorders from baseline differences in alcohol sensitivity. Schuckit and Smith (1996) found, in an 8-year follow-up study of 450 men, that decreased alcohol sensitivity (especially with respect to subjective intoxication) was associated with the later development of AUDs. These findings are the strongest to date in implicating individual differences in alcohol sensitivity as a risk factor for alcoholism. However, because it is unethical to give alcohol-naive subjects alcohol in the laboratory, it is unclear to what extent these individual differences reflect constitutional differences in alcohol sensitivity or acquired tolerance. The mechanisms underlying variability in sensitivity remain unclear, but it does not appear to be due to differences in ethanol metabolism.

### Deviance Proneness

A final model to consider concerns what has been termed *deviance proneness* (Sher, 1991). The key notion here is that excessive alcohol involvement comes about not so much because of attempts at regulating affective states or because of any particular vulnerability to alcohol as a drug but because alcohol use is part of a more general, deviant pattern that has its roots in childhood and is attributable to deficient socialization. In a probing review of the early development of alcohol problems, Zucker et al. (1995; see also Zucker & Gomberg, 1986) note consistency across extant longitudinal studies of alcoholism that begin in childhood. These studies highlight a number of commonalities, including a history of childhood antisocial behavior problems, childhood achievement problems, poorer childhood interpersonal relations, heightened activity in childhood, less parent-child contact, and inadequate parenting. Several explanatory models have been put forth to explain the relation between these correlates and early alcohol use and other problem behaviors. Perhaps the best known of these is *problem-behavior theory* (Donovan & Jessor, 1985; Jessor & Jessor, 1977), which posits that a range of personality, family, peer, and other environmental variables causally relate to involvement in a range of deviant behaviors including early alcohol use, illicit drug use, precocious sexual activity, and school failure. From this perspective alcohol involvement is only one indicator of a broader factor of general deviance, although the hypothesized causal structure among problem behaviors and their mediators differs (Kaplan, 1975; Oetting & Beauvais, 1986; Windle & Davies, 1999).

Although this model emphasizes deficient socialization as evidenced by decreased attachments to family, school, and religious institutions and increased involvement with deviant peers, personality and temperamental variables are often viewed as distal influences on these social, developmental processes (Petraitis, Flay, & Miller, 1995). Consequently, genetic influences on personality are probably very relevant to these ostensibly social processes. Moreover, the same personality traits that put into place these problematic behavior trajectories (e.g., impulsivity) can also have proximal effects on alcohol use in the form of risky decisions about alcohol use and other behaviors (Sher et al., 1999).

## DRUG USE DISORDERS

A recent report commissioned by the Robert Wood Johnson Foundation chronicles the consequences of drug use in the United States (Horgan et al., 2001). The number of deaths directly attributable to drug use has more than doubled over the last two decades, and is approaching the number of deaths directly attributable to alcohol. Most of these deaths directly attributable to drugs were associated with overdoses of heroin or cocaine, especially a lethal combination of heroin or cocaine with alcohol or other drugs. There are also many deaths that are indirectly associated with drug use, such as deaths from suicide, hepatitis, and tuberculosis, and from AIDS among injecting drug users. Drug use is also associated with motor vehicle crashes, other types of accidents, and crime (Horgan, Skwara, & Strickler, 2001).

Despite all of the negative publicity, heroin, especially if it is not adulterated, does not cause as much physical harm as many of the more common drugs of abuse. Much of the medical harm associated with heroin use is due to poor nutrition, the use of adulterated heroin, the sharing of needles, and other lifestyle factors. Inhalant use disorders, compared to the other drug use disorders, are the most likely to cause medical harm to those affected. Inhalants are especially toxic to the nervous system, but can also cause damage to the heart, lungs, kidney, liver, blood, and other systems (Kuhn, Swartzwalder, & Wilson, 1998).

## History of Drug Use Disorders in the United States

In this section, we cover drugs that are illegal or, legal when prescribed by a health professional, are used for nonmedical purposes. The problem of drug abuse in the United States is inextricably linked with the history of the legislation that has led to the regulation and eventual criminalization of these drugs. Perhaps the single piece of legislation that most reduced drug use disorders in the United States was also the first law dealing with the regulation of drugs: the Food and Drug Act of 1906 (Bonnie & Whitebread, 1974), which required manufacturers to provide lists of the ingredients in their products. Prior to this, many Americans were unwittingly becoming addicted to opiates and cocaine simply by using products readily available at their local stores or from traveling salesmen.

In response to the mounting problem of opiate and cocaine addiction in the early twentieth century, the Harrison Tax Act was passed in 1914 and represented the first attempt of the U.S. government to control drug addiction through criminal sanctions. Individuals who were found in possession of heroin or cocaine were arrested for tax evasion, rather than for criminal possession of a drug (Bonnie & Whitebread, 1974). Soon after, several Supreme Court rulings made it illegal for doctors to prescribe drugs to those who were addicted, which meant that the only means for acquiring drugs were illegal (King, 1972) and many addicts were imprisoned. In response to the growing problem of overcrowding in federal prisons, Congress authorized the U.S. Public Health Service to establish hospitals (one opening in Lexington, Kentucky, in 1935, and the other in Ft. Worth, Texas, in 1938) where addicted individuals convicted in federal courts could serve their terms (King, 1972).

In 1915, Utah became the first state to pass a criminal law against the use of marijuana, and many other states soon followed. In 1937, the United States passed the Marijuana Tax Act, which heralded the beginning of the U.S. national prohibition of marijuana. Over the ensuing years, the U.S. government and individual states dealt with the problem of drug addiction by imposing increasingly strict penalties for drug possession that were often harsher than penalties for violent crimes like rape (Bonnie & Whitebread, 1974). In 1970, in order to bring some order to a complex array of antidrug laws, the U.S. Comprehensive Drug Abuse Prevention and Control Act repealed, replaced, or updated all previous antidrug laws (King, 1972). This act classified the drugs of abuse into *schedules*, according to their medical utility and abuse potential (Goode, 1999), and linked penalties for distribution and possession to these schedules. The Schedule I drugs (the most severe category) included heroin, LSD, hallucinogens, and marijuana; these drugs were considered to have no acceptable medical use and high potential for abuse. (Since passage of this act, many states have decriminalized the possession and use of small amounts of marijuana.) As new drugs of abuse enter the marketplace (e.g., 3, 4-Methylenedioxymethamphetamine [MDMA, or Ecstasy]), they are placed into this schedule. Despite decades of criminalization of drug use and prevention, the drug problem is probably as severe now as it was prior to regulation and prohibition.

Another perspective on the history of drug abuse in the United States comes from changes in drug-use disorder classifications over successive revisions of the *DSM*. The drug use disorders have been recognized as a mental illness since the *DSM-I* (APA, 1952), but as with alcohol use disorder, they were considered a subtype of sociopathy until the *DSM-III* (APA, 1980), when a new substance use disorder section was added. The *DSM-III* described drug use disorders associated with seven different substances (in addition to alcohol and tobacco): sedative-hypnotic-anxiolytics, opiates, amphetamines, cannabis, cocaine, phencyclidine (PCP), and hallucinogens. The *DSM-III* recognized drug abuse for all seven substances, but drug dependence was possible for only four of the seven because there was no evidence at the time that tolerance or withdrawal were associated with cocaine, PCP, or the hallucinogens (APA, 1980). It was not until the *DSM-III-R* in 1987 that cocaine withdrawal and cocaine dependence were officially recognized (APA, 1987). Although tolerance is probably associated with all of the drugs considered in the *DSM*, problems in assessment (discussed with respect to alcohol earlier in this chapter), variability in the potency of street drugs due to their unregulated nature and potency differences among drugs within a class can make it difficult to establish.

In the *DSM-III-R,* inhalants were added and the diagnostic criteria for the substance use disorders were standardized to be the same across substances, and both abuse and dependence were recognized for all eight drug classes listed. In the *DSM-IV,* a drug dependence was further specified as being with or without physiological dependence for all substances except hallucinogens and PCP, for which the existence of a withdrawal syndrome is still somewhat uncertain (APA, 2000).

## Epidemiology

In the NLAES study, the combined lifetime prevalence of drug use disorders according to *DSM-IV* criteria was 6.1%. (It is worth noting that the ECA study provided an estimate of [*DSM-III*] lifetime drug use disorder prevalence of 6.2%; Anthony & Helzer, 1991.) In NLAES, the highest prevalences were for cannabis use disorder (4.6%); a composite category of prescription drug use disorder incorporating sedatives, tranquilizers, opiates, and amphetamines (2.0%); cocaine use disorder (1.7%); and amphetamine use disorder (1.5%). The lifetime prevalences of disorder for the remaining drug classes (sedatives, tranquilizers, and hallucinogens) were each less than 1.0% each (Grant & Pickering, 1996). Because of the relatively low prevalences of specific drug use disorders and the substantial comorbidity among them (discussed shortly), most of the epidemiologic research (other than the behavioral genetic studies, again, discussed shortly) focuses on composite diagnoses of drug use disorder.

Although the NCS provided higher lifetime (n.b., *DSM-III-R*) prevalence estimates than did NLAES for drug dependence (7.5%) and abuse (4.4%; Kessler et al., 1994), there was consistency with NLAES in the relative prevalence of specific drug dependence, with cannabis being the most prevalent at more than 4.0%, following by cocaine (2.7%) and amphetamines (1.7%). The remaining lifetime prevalences of dependence for the remaining drug classes were each less than 1.2% (Anthony, Warner, & Kessler, 1994). Because drug use disorders tend to be developmentally limited, past-year prevalence estimates are much lower than lifetime estimates. For example, the past-year prevalence of any drug use disorder in the NCS study was 1.8% (Warner, Kessler, Hughes, Anthony, & Nelson, 1995) as compared to a lifetime prevalence of 11.9%. In general, lifetime drug use disorders are higher among young white men with fewer years of education and lower incomes, and residing in urban areas (Anthony & Helzer, 1991; Anthony et al.).

## Comorbidity

In the ECA study (Anthony & Helzer, 1991) individuals with a *DSM-III* lifetime drug use disorder were 2 to 11 times more likely to have a comorbid psychiatric disorder than those without a history of drug use disorder, with the largest increases in relative risk for drug use disorder among those with mania and APD, followed by schizophrenia, depression, alcohol use disorder, and the anxiety disorders. The patterns of comorbidity were similar for men and women, except that the increased rates of drug use disorders among women with APD and alcohol use disorders were relatively much higher than among men.

Large national samples have conclusively demonstrated high comorbidity among specific drug use disorders and between alcohol use disorders and drug use disorders. For example, in NLAES (Grant & Pickering, 1996), each of the specific drug use disorders was strongly associated with alcohol use disorder, with odds ratios ranging from 13 to 27. Lyons et al. (1998) present the associations of the specific lifetime *DSM-III-R* drug use disorders with each other, using a large national community-based sample of middle-aged men. Again, the various drug use disorders were all strongly associated with each other, with odds ratios ranging from 12 (between opiate and cannabis use disorders) to 68 (between amphetamine and a combined category including hallucinogen and PCP use disorders). In sum, there is substantial comorbidity within the drug use disorder category, between drug use disorders and alcohol use disorders, and between drug use disorders and other psychiatric disorders. Polysubstance abuse–dependence and comorbidity appear to be the rule, rather than the exception.

## Genetics

There has been much less published research on the genetics of drug use and drug use disorders compared to alcoholism, although it is presumed that the genetic risk for drug use disorders will overlap with the genetic risk factors for alcohol use disorders. Because there have been increases in the lifetime prevalence of drug use and drug use disorders in more recently born cohorts, the interpretation of studies that examine intergenerational patterns (e.g., family studies and adoption studies) is problematic because of secular changes in drug exposure and availability. Consequently, within-generation behavioral genetic studies of drug use disorders are the most straightforward to interpret.

Two recent large community-based twin studies of drug use disorders provide valuable within-generation information on the familial transmission of a composite diagnosis of drug use disorder and the specific drug use disorders. Tsuang et al. (1996) conducted a study of *DSM-III-R* drug use disorders in a large sample of twins from the Vietnam Era Twin Registry, a national sample of male twin pairs (born between 1939 and 1957) in which both men served in the U.S. military during the Vietnam era. Kendler and colleagues (Kendler & Prescott, 1998a, 1998b; Kendler, Karkowski, & Prescott, 1999; Kendler, Karkowski, Neale, & Prescott, 2000) conducted a population-based study of *DSM-IV* drug use disorders among male (born between about 1936 and 1978) and female (born between about 1933 and 1975) adult twin pairs born in the state of Virginia. With only a few exceptions, the results of these two studies support the existence of substantial genetic influences and very modest family environmental influences on the risk for drug use disorders. Heritability estimates for different classes of drugs ranged from .25 to .76 among men and from .72 to .79 among women for more broadly-defined drug use disorder (drug abuse or dependence), and from .58 to .97 for more narrowly-defined drug use disorder (drug dependence) amongs men (results for drug dependence among women are not available; Kendler & Prescott, 1998a, 1998b; Kendler, Karkowski, & Prescott, 1999; Kendler et al., 2000; Tsuang et al., 1996). In contrast, estimates of the proportion of variation in risk due to family environmental influences ranged from 0 to .32 among men and stood consistently at 0 among women (Kendler & Prescott, 1998a, 1998b; Kendler, Karkowski, & Prescott, 1999; Kendler et al., 2000; Tsuang et al., 1996).

In a follow-up multivariate analysis, Tsuang et al. (1998) examined the extent to which the familial risk for each specific drug use disorder was shared versus the extent to which it was specific to the drug. They found that most of the familial risk for the different drug use disorders could be explained by common genetic and environmental factors, with significant specific genetic influences on the risk for opiate use disorder and specific family environmental influences on the risk for cannabis use disorder. Kendler, Karkowski, Corey, et al. (1999) examined the extent to which genetic variation in risk for drug use disorder could be explained by genetic factors associated with the *initiation of substance use,* and found that, on average, about half of the genetic variation in drug use disorder was associated with genetic effects on substance use initiation. These findings are extremely important in that they indicate that different etiological processes are involved in substance use experimentation (a necessary precondition for drug use disorders) and the development of drug abuse or dependence once drug use is initiated. Future behavioral genetic studies of drug use disorders focusing on the influence of genetic and environmental factors across the various stages in the disorders' development, starting with initiation and culminating with the final outcome of disorder, will be extremely valuable (Tsuang et al., 1999) but also difficult given the large sample sizes and the complexity of models that will be required.

### Neurobiological Substrates of Drug Effects

Different drugs of abuse vary in their spectrum of effects on neurotransmitter systems, specific brain regions, and associated motivational systems. However, there are some important, shared commonalities among these pharmacologically distinct agents. As noted in Table 8.2, all commonly abused psychoactive drugs involve dopamine systems and, to a

**TABLE 8.2    Neurobiological Substrates for the Acute Reinforcing Effects of Drugs of Abuse**

| Drug of Abuse | Neurotransmitter | Sites |
|---|---|---|
| Cocaine and amphetamines | Dopamine<br>Serotonin | Nucleus accumbens<br>Amygdala |
| Opiates | Dopamine<br>Opioid peptides | Ventral tegmental area<br>Nucleus accumbens |
| THC | Dopamine<br>Opioid peptides | Ventral tegmental area |
| Alcohol | Dopamine<br>Opioid peptides<br>Serotonin<br>GABA<br>Glutamate | Ventral tegmental area<br>Nucleus accumbens<br>Amygdala |

*Source:* Reprinted by permission of Elsevier Science from "Drug Addiction, Dysregulation of Reward, and Allostatis," by G. F. Koob and M. Le Moal, Neuropsychopharmacology, Vol. 24, pp. 97–129, 2001, by American College of Neuropsychopharmacology.

slightly lesser extent, the opioid peptide system (which is intimately linked to the dopamine system; e.g., Koob & Le Moal, 2001). One influential theory of addiction (Wise & Bozarth, 1987) posits that "all addictive drugs have psychomotor stimulant properties and that the biological mechanism of the psychomotor stimulant properties is the same as, or has common elements with, the biological mechanism of the reinforcing effects of these drugs" (p. 482). That is, there is a common reward mechanism underlying the effects of different addictive drugs. This is not to say, however, that different drugs of abuse exert their addictive properties through only one site of action. Indeed, different drugs of abuse show affinities to distinct classes of receptors, and their effects on dopamine and opioid systems may be indirect. As noted by Koob and Le Moal (2001, p. 103), "drugs may enter into this neurocircuitry at different points and via different molecular/cellular mechanisms."

From a neurobiological perspective, vulnerability to drug abuse can come about either because of individual differences in the initial reinforcing properties of a drug or because of individual differences in compensatory mechanisms (e.g., initial opponent processes or allostatic progression) discussed earlier. Unfortunately, longitudinal research in humans that attempts to chart neurobiological changes associated with differing patterns or trajectories of drug involvement have yet to be conducted.

### Etiological Models

Etiological theories of drug use disorders tend to parallel those described under alcohol use disorders (i.e., positive and negative affect regulation, pharmacological vulnerability, and deviant socialization). However, a major distinction between alcohol use and illicit drug use is the fact that alcohol use is legal for adults, whereas use of illicit drugs, by definition, is not. Consequently, use of alcohol is more readily integrated into mainstream culture, and initial exposure, even for minors, is inherently less of a deviant social behavior. Thus, models of deviant socialization are particularly relevant to drug use disorders, especially as they relate to experimental substance use.

Petraitis et al. (1995) recently reviewed 14 models of experimental substance use that have received empirical evaluation in the research literature. Based on their synthesis of these theories, which varied widely with respect to focus and constructs employed, they developed a matrix of influences on experimental use. This matrix is defined by types of influence (i.e., social-interpersonal, cultural-attitudinal, and intrapersonal) and level of influence (i.e., ultimate, distal, and proximal), yielding nine cells of this matrix. For example, ultimate influences include parental divorce or separation (social-interpersonal), local crime and unemployment (cultural-attitudinal), and temperament or personality (intrapersonal). Distal influences include attachment to parents and peers (social-interpersonal); weak commitment to conventional values, school, and religion (cultural-attitudinal); and psychological distress (intrapersonal). Proximal influences include perceived norms for use (social-interpersonal), expected utilities of substance use (cultural-attitudinal), and refusal skills and intentions to use substances (intrapersonal). Petraitis et al. argue that a comprehensive theory of experimental substance use needs to address both the level and the type of influence in order to be complete. This approach appears to be a useful first step toward organizing constructs involved in the literature and illustrates why some types of models (e.g., models that focuses more on proximal as opposed to distal or ultimate processes) should predict initiation of use better than others. However, it is more of a framework than a theory in that it is relatively agnostic toward identifying key causal mechanisms.

## PATHOLOGICAL GAMBLING

It is a matter of continuing controversy whether the overall costs to society of PG, including costs associated with indebtedness, unemployment, and loss in productivity; thefts and criminal justice system costs; welfare costs; and treatment costs for individuals with PG and their spouses are outweighed by the economic benefits to society of gambling (National Research Council, 1999). What is not controversial is that PG has considerable negative economic and psychological effects on individuals and families. Although there is little direct evidence supporting a causal link, there seems to

be little disagreement that PG can precipitate the types of stressful life events that are associated with an increased risk of depression and suicide (Blaszczynski & Farrell, 1998). Perhaps it is no coincidence that Las Vegas has the highest suicide rate of any city in the United States (Phillips, Welty, & Smith, 1997).

### History of Pathological Gambling in the United States

The legality and availability of gambling have changed dramatically over the past two decades, and currently most adults have engaged in some form of gambling (86%; Gerstein et al., 1999). Prior to the late 1980s, the only legal gambling options in the United States were gambling in Nevada and Atlantic City, and state-run lotteries. In the late 1980s, gambling on Native American land or on riverboat casinos was legalized, and in the mid-1990s Internet-gambling Web sites were introduced. By 1999, gambling in some form was legal in 48 states; 21 states had casinos, 37 states had a lottery, and there were more than 650 Internet gambling sites worldwide. The number of Internet gambling sites has since doubled. The prevalences of gambling participation (Gerstein et al.), and of PG and problem gambling (Shaffer, Hall, & Bilt, 1999), have increased along with the growth of gambling venues.

Pathological gambling was introduced into the official diagnostic nomenclature with the publication of the ninth edition of the *International Classification of Diseases* in 1977, followed by its inclusion into the *DSM-III* in 1980 (APA, 1980). However, the concept of compulsive gambling was widely accepted prior to its inclusion in the *DSM-III:* Gambling problems were recognized by Freud (1928/1961) and other psychoanalysts (e.g., Bergler, 1936, 1943, 1957) in the first half of the twentieth century, the self-help community of Gamblers Anonymous was founded in 1957, and the first specialty treatment program for gambling problems was created in 1968 (Petry & Armentano, 1999).

Pathological gambling is classified as an impulse-control disorder along with kleptomania, trichotillomania, pyromania, and intermittent explosive disorder. Although the diagnostic criteria for PG have changed over the subsequent revisions of the *DSM,* the essential feature remains the same: persistent and recurrent maladaptive gambling behavior that disrupts personal, family, or vocational pursuits (APA, 1994). With the revision of the *DSM-III* (*DSM-III-R;* APA, 1987) the diagnostic criteria for PG were modified to be parallel to the criteria for the substance use disorders, and included concepts of preoccupation, loss of control, tolerance, and withdrawal. In support of this conceptualization, surveys of individuals in treatment for PG have found that 45% to 89% felt that they needed to gamble progressively more to achieve the desired excitement (Bradford, Geller, Lesieur, Rosenthal, & Wise, 1996; Griffiths, 1995), and 33% to 87% felt irritable or restless after stopping or cutting back on their gambling (Bergh & Kuehlhorn, 1994; Bradford et al.; Wray & Dickerson, 1981). A distinctive feature of PG not shared with the substance use disorders is *chasing*—that is, returning to a gambling activity in an attempt to win back losses. Chasing losses is considered by some experts to be a pathognomonic symptom of PG, and represents the mechanism by which individuals who gamble can become ensnared in the downward spiral of problems (Lesieur, 1984).

## The Nature of Gambling Activities

The variety of gambling activities available differ along several dimensions that may make them more or less likely to lead to PG or problem gambling (i.e., problematic gambling that does not reach threshold for a diagnosis of PG). By definition, gambling involves a certain amount of chance, but different activities vary in the amount of chance versus skill involved. The outcome of a bet can be decided in a matter of seconds to as long as several weeks, and either the winnings can either be immediately reinvested or there may be a time interval before the next bet can be made. For some gambling activities the bet-to-win ratio is extremely large, and for others the odds are nearly even. Finally, some activities are readily available and convenient whereas others are relatively less convenient; some gambling activities are solitary, whereas others require interacting with other people. The two dimensions that have been most consistently linked with PG and problem gambling are the chance-skill continuum and the continuous-discontinuous continuum. It has been suggested that games that require some skill (or perceived skill) and are more continuous, or high action, are more likely to be related to the development of problems (Walker, 1992). However, the strongest and most consistent predictor of PG or problem gambling is not necessarily the type of activity, but rather the number of gambling activities (Sproston, Erens, & Orford, 2000; Volberg & Banks, 1994).

It is possible that different gambling activities represent indicators of an underlying continuum of gambling involvement, with some activities being very common and indicative of lower levels on this continuum and other activities being less common and indicative of higher levels. Evidence consistent with this comes from a nationally representative survey of adolescents and adults in Great Britain (Sproston et al., 2000). Respondents were divided into groups according to whether they had participated in one, two, three, four, five, or six or more different gambling activities in the past year. With each additional activity, all of the activities of the less involved groups were endorsed by the majority of the individuals in the more involved groups. That is, gambling activities appeared to conform to a Guttman scale progressing from participation in the national lottery, to scratchcards, to fruit (slot) machines, to private betting with friends, to horse races, and to dog races. Thus, in Great Britain, lottery playing is much less strongly associated with pathological and problem gambling than is betting on dog races.

## Epidemiology

A recent meta-analysis of 119 North American PG prevalence studies conducted between 1977 and 1997 estimated the lifetime prevalence of diagnosable PG among adults at 1.6%, and the lifetime prevalence of subclinical PG, or *problem gambling* (i.e., endorsing at least one symptom of PG but not meeting the full criteria for a diagnosis; Shaffer et al., 1999) at 3.9%. The estimated lifetime prevalences of PG and problem gambling in a recent, nationally representative survey of 2,417 adults in the United States were 0.8% and 9.2%, respectively (Gerstein et al., 1999). Thus, between 5 and 10% of the U.S. population will experience problems with gambling at some point in their lives.

These gambling problems are unevenly distributed throughout the population. The prevalence of PG is higher (a) among men than women, (b) among younger than older individuals, (c) among individuals with fewer years of formal education than those with more education, (d) among individuals with lower income levels than the more advantaged, and (e) among indigenous peoples than other racial and ethnic groups (Volberg & Abbott, 1997; Welte, Barnes, Wieczorek, Tidwell, & Parker, 2000). The prevalence of PG is also higher among Blacks (Gerstein et al., 1999; Welte et al.) and Asian Americans (Welte et al.). It is unclear the extent to which these demographic correlates reflect differences in access to gambling venues, differences in the propensity to gamble, or differences in the propensity to fall prey to gambling problems given participation in gambling activities.

Comparisons of the prevalences of PG and problem gambling across geographic regions that differ in the availability of gambling suggest that greater access to regulated forms of gambling may be responsible for higher rates of PG and problem gambling. For example, comparisons across the eight states and territories within Australia yielded a correlation of about 0.65 between the per capita number of electronic gaming machines in a state or territory and the past-year prevalence of PG or problem gambling (Productivity Commission, 1999). Because of the historical and geographic variation in the accessibility of legal forms of gambling, it is important to know when and where a particular study took place because the prevalence, correlates, and causes of PG may vary with these different environmental contexts.

## Genetics

Numerous studies have demonstrated that gambling involvement and problems run in families (e.g., Gambino, Fitzgerald, Shaffer, & Renner, 1993), although all of the extant studies relied on the family history method rather than on directly interviewing family members of index cases. Many experts attribute the familial transmission of gambling and PG to social-modeling influences (e.g., Gupta & Derevensky, 1997), but this conclusion is based upon the observation of parent-offspring transmission in nuclear families, which could be due to genetic as well as environmental factors. The role of a possible underlying biological diathesis in the development of PG has not been ignored by researchers; in fact, the search for putative indicators of biological vulnerability for PG (Blanco et al., 1996; Carrasco, Saiz-Ruiz, Hollander, Cesar, & Lopez-Ibor, 1994; Roy et al., 1988) and specific susceptibility genes associated with PG (Comings et al., 1996) actually preceded the behavioral genetic research documenting the importance of genetic influences on the risk for PG. Thus far, molecular genetic research on PG has focused on genes that have been claimed to show promise for explaining genetic variation associated with alcohol dependence (the dopamine D2 receptor [Comings et al.] and serotonin transporter [de Castro, Ibanez, Saiz-Ruiz, & Fernandez, 1999] genes) and the personality trait of novelty seeking (the dopamine D4 receptor gene [Comings et al.]).

Compared to research on substance use disorders, the behavioral genetic literature on PG is scant, consisting of a single study. In the Vietnam Era Twin Registry, the lifetime rates of *DSM-III-R* PG were significantly elevated among the monozygotic (23%) and dizygotic (10%) co-twins of men with PG, compared to the lifetime prevalence in the full sample (1.4%; Eisen et al., 1998). It was not possible to discern whether this familial similarity for PG was due to genetic or environmental factors because of the low base rate of PG, but it was possible to estimate that the total percentage of variation in the risk for PG that was accounted for by all familial factors (genetic and environmental) was 62%. In a follow-up combined (and more powerful) analysis of PG and alcohol dependence, Slutske et al. (2000) found that 64% of the variation in the risk for PG could be accounted for by genetic factors, with the remaining variation accounted for by individual-specific environmental factors or errors of measurement. Familial environmental factors did not significantly contribute to variation in PG, although these factors may still be important either in mediating genetic effects or in their

interaction with an existing genetic predisposition. The results of this study suggest that PG is as heritable as alcohol dependence, and that genetic factors, rather than social modeling, predominantly explain the familial transmission of PG. However, it is unclear the extent to which this single study of PG among middle-aged men conducted in the early 1990s can be generalized to women, adolescents, or certain minority groups, or to the current gambling milieu.

## Comorbidity

Reviews of the (primarily) clinical literature suggest that the rates of substance use disorders (Crockford & el-Guebaly, 1998; Spunt, Dupont, Lesieur, Liberty, & Hunt, 1998), mood and anxiety disorders (Crockford & el-Guebaly), and antisocial behavior disorders (Slutske et al., 2001) are significantly elevated in treatment-seeking individuals with PG compared to those without PG. However, comparisons of individuals with PG in treatment and in the community suggest that treatment samples are not representative of individuals with PG in the community (Volberg & Steadman, 1988) because less than 2% of individuals with PG report having ever received PG treatment (Wallisch, 1996). Six studies have reported the rates of comorbid psychopathology among individuals with PG recruited from the community, and only three of these studies were based upon randomly selected representative samples that included appropriate controls (Bland, Newman, Orn, & Stebelsky, 1993; Cunningham-Williams, Cottler, Compton, & Spitznagel, 1998; Smart & Ferris, 1996).

Although PG was not included in the ECA or NCS studies, it was included in one of the particular ECA sites. Symptoms of PG were assessed in the St. Louis ECA study in 1981, prior to the introduction of legal gambling to the St. Louis area (Cunningham-Williams et al., 1998). In the St. Louis ECA sample, problem gambling was significantly associated with alcohol abuse or dependence and nicotine dependence, but not with other substance use disorders. Problem gambling was also significantly associated with major depression and phobias, but not with panic disorder, generalized anxiety disorder, or obsessive-compulsive disorder. The strongest association obtained was between problem gambling and APD. Problem gambling was also significantly associated with schizophrenia and somatization disorder (Cunningham-Williams et al.). These findings are consistent with other community-based studies in finding elevated rates of alcohol use disorders (Black & Moyer, 1998; Bland et al., 1993; Slutske et al., 2000; Smart & Ferris, 1996) and APD (Black & Moyer; Bland et al.; Cunningham-Williams, Cottler, Compton, Spitznagel, & Ben-Abdallah, 2000; Slutske et al., 2001) among individuals with PG or problem gambling. These are the most robust findings in the PG comorbidity literature. Results on the associations of PG with the mood and anxiety disorders are more mixed, and most studies since the St. Louis ECA study have found increased prevalences of other substance use disorders among individuals with PG or problem gambling (Black & Moyer; Bland et al.). There are also studies suggesting that the prevalences of *DSM* personality disorders from all three clusters (i.e., odd-eccentric, dramatic-erratic, and anxious-inhibited) are elevated among individuals with PG (Black & Moyer; Blaszczynski & Steel, 1998).

The causes of comorbidity of PG with other substance use and psychiatric disorders have not been extensively studied and there is little in the way of prospective longitudinal research tracking the temporal course of PG and comorbid conditions. Retrospective studies suggest that substance use disorders tend to precede PG in the majority of cases (Cunningham-Williams et al., 1998, 2000; Ramirez, McCormick, Russo, & Taylor, 1983). These findings are difficult to interpret because the apparent temporal sequencing may merely reflect age-related differences in the availability of gambling activities, disposable income, and psychoactive substances.

It is clear that alcohol and drug use often accompany gambling (e.g., Giacopassi, Stitt, & Vandiver, 1998), and concurrent gambling and substance use may be especially common among individuals with gambling problems (Spunt et al., 1998; Wallisch, 1996). Thus, the situational covariation of gambling and substance use may increase the likelihood of developing, maintaining, or exacerbating both gambling-related and substance use–related problems.

Alcohol intoxication may alter the perception of the likelihood of negative consequences of risky activities (Fromme, Katz, & D'Amico, 1997), or may lead to more general impairments in cognition and judgment that may result in poor decisions during gambling that may increase the likelihood of an adverse outcome. Several experimental studies have demonstrated that subjects are more willing to gamble or gamble more when under the influence of a moderate dose of alcohol than when given a placebo (Kyngdon & Dickerson, 1999; Sjoberg, 1969; Steele, 1986), although there are also studies that fail to find a causal link between alcohol use and willingness to gamble in a laboratory task (see Breslin, Sobell, Cappell, Vakili, & Poulos, 1999, for a review). To our knowledge, there are no experimental investigations testing the reverse-causal hypothesis that gambling may lead to an increased use of alcohol or other drugs, although the possibility is quite plausible.

Behavior genetic studies suggest that some proportion of comorbid substance use disorder and PG is due to a shared diathesis. Rates of alcohol-related problems among parents and other family members of individuals with PG appear to be higher than in the general population (Dell, Ruzicka, & Palisi, 1981; Lesieur, Blume, & Zappa, 1986; Lesieur et al., 1991; Linden, Pope, & Jonas, 1986; Ramirez et al., 1983; Roy et al., 1988). In the Vietnam Era Twin Study, there was significant familial cross-transmission of PG and alcohol dependence, suggesting a common vulnerability. Most of the genetic and environmental variation in the risk for PG was unique and not shared with alcohol dependence, but a significant fraction of genetic (12–20%) and individual-specific environmental (3–8%) vulnerability for PG was shared with alcohol dependence. It is important to recognize that these estimates subsume all possible reasons for the association between the genetic risk for PG and alcohol dependence, including *pleiotropy* (i.e., the presence of a genetic locus that jointly increases the risk for both PG and alcohol dependence) and indirect causal chains such as gene(s) Æ PG Æ AD and gene(s) Æ AD Æ PG.

There are two main lines of research linking PG and the antisocial disorders—the literature on delinquent youth suggesting a strong association of delinquency with PG and problem gambling, and the literature on adults with PG suggesting that PG can be a cause of criminal activities. Among youth, antisocial behavior appears to be the best concurrent predictor of gambling frequency in both boys and girls (Stinchfield, 2000). Although adults with PG are more likely to retrospectively report a history of childhood conduct disorder than adults without PG (Slutske et al., 2001), and the retrospectively reported age of onset of comorbid APD typically predates the onset of PG (Cunningham-Williams et al., 2000), the few attempts to predict gambling or problem gambling among adolescents or young adults from earlier involvement in delinquent activities have yielded mostly negative findings (Vitaro, Ladouceur, & Bujold, 1996; Winters, Stinchfield, Botzet, & Anderson, 2001). Thus, a causal influence of antisocial behavior on later PG has not been established.

Conclusions about the causal influence of PG on crime are based upon (a) retrospectively reported ages of onset of PG and crime, (b) the types of criminal activities that are involved, and (c) judgments of individuals with PG concerning the extent to which their crimes were gambling related (see Blaszczynski & Silove, 1996). Although there are no prospective studies or any experimental evidence supporting a causal link, the evidence is still quite convincing that crime is in some cases a consequence of PG. In fact, gambling-related crime constituted two of the seven diagnostic criteria for PG in the *DSM-III:* "arrest for forgery, fraud, embezzlement, or income tax evasion due to attempts to obtain money," and "borrowing of money from illegal sources (loan sharks)" (APA, 1980, p. 293). One of these criteria has been modified and reinstated in the criteria for PG in *DSM-IV:* "has committed illegal acts such as forgery, fraud, theft, or embezzlement to finance gambling" (APA, 1994, p. 618). In the *DSM-IV* field trials, this item was less sensitive than the other symptoms of PG (endorsed by 65% of individuals with a PG diagnosis compared to 78–94% for other symptoms) but was more specific (endorsed by none of the participants without a PG diagnosis; Bradford et al., 1996). Involvement in illegal activities to finance gambling appears to be a more psychometrically difficult indicator of PG, suggesting that only individuals with more severe problems and who have hit bottom, so to speak, will resort to such behaviors.

A genetic basis for comorbidity between antisociality and PG is supported by the finding of significant familial cross-transmission of PG with childhood conduct disorder, adult antisocial behavior (the adult criterion for APD), and APD in the Vietnam Era Twin Study (Slutske et al., 2001). As with alcohol dependence, there was a significant fraction of genetic (26%) and individual-specific environmental (7%) vulnerability for PG that was shared with the antisocial behavior disorders, and all of the shared genetic vulnerability could be explained by the genetic risk for conduct disorder. Further analyses suggested that risk factors common to the antisocial behavior disorders and alcohol dependence accounted for 28% of the genetic variation and 8% of the individual-specific variation in PG risk; thus, most of the genetic and environmental variation in PG risk is left unexplained after accounting for the most likely sources of shared vulnerability. However, these results from the Vietnam Era Twin Study suggest that the comorbidity between PG and alcohol dependence and the antisocial behavior disorders is mainly due to genetic factors (Slutske et al., 2000, 2001).

## Etiological Models

To date, a number of variables and processes have been proposed as etiological factors in PG, and several of these are described later. Because the diagnosis of PG involves a high diagnostic threshold, by the time someone's behavior warrants the diagnosis, the individual has typically suffered considerable psychological, economic, interpersonal, and social harm. Consequently, potentially mutable variables associated with the diagnosis of PG (e.g., personality traits, affective state, biological markers) might not characterize prepathological gamblers. Because there is a dearth of detailed prospective data, we are not yet in a position to make strong claims about those variables that predispose someone to gamble problematically or pathologically.

### Positive Affect Regulation (hypoarousal)

Surveys of gamblers indicate that the most commonly endorsed reason for gambling is "because it's fun" (e.g., Wallisch, 1996). It has been suggested that individuals with PG experience and become dependent upon achieving an aroused, euphoric state similar to a drug-induced high (Griffiths, 1995; Leary & Dickerson, 1985; Lesieur & Blume, 1993; Sharpe, Tarrier, Schotte, & Spence, 1995). Experiences of wins or near-wins are hypothesized to be the stimuli that initially elicit this state of subjective and physiological arousal (Griffiths, 1991). Using the allostatic model of Koob and Le Moal (2001) described earlier, one could predict opponent processes to develop into gambling-related reinforcements that set up tolerance of gambling and, ultimately, into an allostatic process in which gambling is needed to achieve homeostatic levels of arousal.

From this general perspective, individual differences in baseline levels of arousal would be expected to be a vulnerability factor. However, individual differences in gambling behavior are not consistently related to sensation seeking, a trait that would be expected to predict reward-seeking behavior. In particular, pathological gamblers in treatment and following treatment tend to be average or even low in sensation seeking (Zuckerman, 1999). However, in active gamblers, there is a positive relation between sensation seeking and the number of gambling activities a gambler engages in, bet size, the tendency to chase losses, and loss of control (Coventry & Brown, 1993).

Zuckerman (1999) notes that measures of impulsivity tend to fare better than measures of sensation seeking in distinguishing pathological gamblers from controls. This suggests that it is not simply reward seeking but perhaps reward seeking in the context of punishment that represents a critical vulnerability to PG. For example, Newman and colleagues (e.g., Newman, Patterson, & Kosson, 1987) found that individuals with psychopathology did particularly poorly on a card-playing task when payouts are initially likely but then are manipulated to become unlikely; in such a situation, the subjects tend to play more cards and lose more money than controls because they fail to extinguish their reward-seeking behavior when the contingencies change. Using a similar task, Breen and Zuckerman (1999) found that a paper-and-pencil measure of impulsivity but not sensation seeking was related to poorer task performance (i.e., losing more money).

### Negative Affect Regulation

The negative-affect-regulation model of PG is embodied in the *DSM-IV* PG criterion "gambles as a way of escaping from problems or relieving a dysphoric mood (e.g., feelings of helplessness, guilt, anxiety, depression)" (APA, 1994, p. 618). Individuals with PG have higher rates of anxiety disorders and depression than individuals without PG, and tend to score higher on questionnaire measures of negative affectivity. In addition, depressed mood at the start of a session of gambling predicts persistence in that activity (Dickerson, Cunningham, England, & Hinchy, 1991).

There are several explanations for why gambling may help some people cope with negative emotions. Many individuals with PG describe experiencing altered states of consciousness during gambling, such as being in a trance state or feeling removed from reality (Bergh & Kuehlhorn, 1994; Bradford et al., 1996). Alternatively, gambling may help alleviate stress in some individuals by giving an illusion of control (Friedland, Keinan, & Reger, 1992). For those who are experiencing distress because of financial difficulties, gambling can serve as an active (but maladaptive) coping device that provides short-term hope for resolving these problems (Walker, 1992), and this might be particularly true of pathological gamblers with low socioeconomic status.

### Deviance Proneness

The deviance proneness model emphasizes the roles of parents and peers in the development of PG. Parents are assumed to exert their influence by not providing an adequate rearing environment or by serving as gambling role models. For example, in the *DSM-III* (APA, 1980), the predisposing factors described for PG disorder are "loss of a parent by death, separation, divorce, or desertion before the child is 15 years of age, inappropriate parental discipline (absence, inconsistency, harshness), exposure to gambling activities as an adolescent . . . lack of family emphasis on saving, planning, and budgeting" (p. 292). Pathological gambling may be part of a constellation of associated behaviors characterized by deviance proneness or behavioral undercontrol (Stinchfield & Winters, 1998) similar to Jessor and colleagues' syndrome of problem behavior discussed earlier. For example, studies (as reviewed in Slutske et al., 2001) have shown that problem-gambling adolescents and young adults, compared to non-problem-gambling adolescents and young adults, are more likely to skip school (Wallisch, 1996), drop out of high school (Wallisch), use alcohol and other drugs (Lesieur et al., 1991; Proimos, DuRant, Pierce, & Goodman, 1998; Stinchfield, Cassuto, Winters, & Latimer, 1997; Vitaro et al., 1996; Wallisch; Winters, Stinchfield, & Fulkerson, et al., 1993), be sexually active (Proimos et al.), engage in physical fights (Proimos et al.; Vitaro et al.), have committed an illegal act or been arrested (Lesieur et al.; Stinchfield et al.; Vitaro et al.;

Wallisch; West & Farrington, 1970; Winters et al.), and have friends who carry weapons or belong to gangs (Wallisch).

### Cognitive Vulnerability

One set of models specific to PG, as opposed to substance use disorders, concerns specific cognitive biases that are thought to predispose an individual to gambling. Much of the research on gambling cognitions has used been based on naturalistic observations of the verbalizations of gamblers (Walker, 1992) and studies in which gamblers are asked to think out loud while they are gambling (e.g., Ladouceur & Gaboury, 1988). Based on the results of this research, several typologies of gambling-related cognitive biases have been developed (Rogers, 1998; Toneatto, 1999; Walker, 1992).

Perhaps the most familiar cognitive bias is the *gambler's fallacy* or *law of averages*. This is the belief that the outcome of a particular bet is not independent, but rather is dependent on the outcome of previous bets. Thus, gamblers might believe that a win is more likely after a series of losses. This belief may be one mechanism that leads to chasing losses. Other biases of gamblers include a magnification of gambling skill; superstitious beliefs about how certain objects, rituals, or thoughts can increase one's chances of winning; and more generally, the belief that the random and uncontrollable is lawful and predictable. The common theme underlying the cognitive biases engaged in by gamblers is that they help gamblers maintain optimism about the outcome of future gambling even in the face of substantial losses.

## CONCLUDING COMMENTS

Disorders of impulse control are prevalent in our society and place high costs on the affected individuals, their friends and families, the larger community, and the criminal justice and health care systems. Because they often co-occur with each other as well as with other psychological disorders, it is important to consider them through an understanding of psychopathology in general.

These disorders often manifest themselves in youth and show developmental continuities with childhood psychopathology, and are probably related to basic temperamental proclivities. Perhaps more than other psychological disorders, their manifestation requires availability of certain types of stimuli (e.g., psychoactive substances, gambling activities), and it is thus understandable that attempts at control of these problems have often led to attempts at social control via policies that seek to restrict access to the stimulus and to impose legal sanctions on those who engage in the behavior. Although clearly certain types of environments are necessary for the development of the disorder (e.g., one can not be alcohol dependent in a culture that has effectively eliminated the making and sale of alcoholic beverages), these disorders appear to have strong genetic determinants that are likely manifested in temperamental traits such as reward seeking and self-control. The exact nature of constitutional vulnerability will probably continue to be refined in the near future.

For each of the disorders considered, there appear to be multiple etiological mechanisms that convey risk for the development of disorder. We have termed these mechanisms *positive affect regulation, negative affect regulation, pharmacological vulnerability* (in the case of substance use disorders), and *deviance proneness*. These risk mechanisms can be viewed as a starting point for developing new and refining existing approaches to prevention and treatment. Although we have emphasized similarities in the etiology and clinical manifestations of these distinct disorders, it also appears that each disorder has unique characteristics. Indeed, as implied by the multiple etiological mechanisms just mentioned, there is considerable heterogeneity within each disorder category. It seems likely that attention to underlying mechanisms will permit us to refine our diagnostic notions and derive more clearly resolved sets of diagnostic criteria.

## REFERENCES

Achenbach, T. M. (1995). Developmental issues in assessment, taxonomy, and diagnosis of child and adolescent psychopathology. In D. Cicchetti, Dante, & D. J. Cohen (Eds.), *Developmental psychopathology: Vol. 1. Theory and methods* (pp. 57–80). New York: Wiley.

Achenbach, T. M., & Edelbrock, C. S. (1978). The classification of child psychopathology: A review and analysis of empirical efforts. *Psychological Bulletin, 85,* 1275–1301.

Allen, J. P., Fertig, J. B., Towle, L. H., & Altshuler, V. B. (1994). Psychometric analyses of the Alcohol Dependence Scale among United States and Russian clinical samples. *International Journal of the Addictions, 29,* 71–87.

Alterman, A. I., Bedrick, J., Cacciola, J. S., Rutherford, M. J., Searles, J. S., McKay, J. R., & Cook, T. G. (1998). Personality pathology and drinking in young men at high and low familial risk for alcoholism. *Journal of Studies on Alcohol, 59,* 495–502.

American Psychiatric Association. (1952). *Diagnostic and statistical manual of mental disorders* (1st ed.). Washington, DC: Author.

American Psychiatric Association. (1980). *Diagnostic and statistical manual of mental disorders* (3rd ed.). Washington, DC: Author.

American Psychiatric Association. (1987). *Diagnostic and statistical manual of mental disorders* (3rd ed., rev.). Washington, DC: Author.

American Psychiatric Association. (1994). *Diagnostic and statistical manual of mental disorders* (4th ed.). Washington, DC: Author.

American Psychiatric Association. (2000). *Diagnostic and statistical manual of mental disorders* (4th ed., Text Revision). Washington, DC: Author.

Anthenelli, R. M., Tipp, J., Li, T. K., Magnes, L., Schuckit, M. A., Rice, J., Daw, W., & Nurnberger, J. I., Jr. (1998). Platelet monoamine oxidase activity in subgroups of alcoholics and controls: Results from the Collaborative Study on the Genetics of Alcoholism. *Alcoholism: Clinical & Experimental Research, 22,* 598–604.

Anthony, J. C., & Helzer, J. (1991). Syndromes of drug abuse and dependence. In L. N. Robins & D. A. Regier (Eds.), *Psychiatric disorders in America: The Epidemiologic Catchment Area Study.* New York: Macmillan.

Anthony, J. C., Warner, L. A., & Kessler, R. C. (1994). Comparative epidemiology of dependence on tobacco, alcohol, controlled substances, and inhalants: Basic findings from the National Comorbidity Survey. *Experimental & Clinical Psychopharmacology, 2,* 244–268.

Babor, T. F. (1996). The classification of alcoholics: Typology theories from the nineteenth century to the present. *Alcohol Health and Research World, 20*(1), 6–14.

Babor, T. F., Hofmann, M., DelBoca, F. K., Hesselbrock, V., Meyer, R. E., Dolinsky, Z. S., & Rounsaville, B. (1992). Types of alcoholics: I. Evidence for an empirically derived typology based on indicators of vulnerability and severity. *Archives of General Psychiatry, 49,* 599–608.

Barnes, G. E. (1983). Clinical and prealcoholic personality characteristics. In B. Kissin & H. Begleiter (Eds.), *The pathogenesis of alcoholism: Psychosocial factors* (pp. 113–195). New York: Plenum Press.

Bates, M. E., & Labouvie, E. W. (1995). Personality environment constellations and alcohol use: A process-oriented study of intraindividual change during adolescence. *Psychology of Addictive Behaviors, 9,* 23–35.

Bergh, C., & Kuehlhorn, E. (1994). The development of pathological gambling in Sweden. *Journal of Gambling Studies, 10,* 261–274.

Bergler, E. (1936). Psychology of the gambler. *Imago (Leipzig), 22,* 409–441.

Bergler, E. (1943). The gambler: A misunderstood neurotic. *Journal of Criminal Psychopathology, 4,* 379–393.

Bergler, E. (1957). *The psychology of gambling.* Madison, CT: International Universities Press.

Bergman, B., & Brismar, B. (1994). Hormone levels and personality traits in abusive and suicidal male alcoholics. *Alcoholism: Clinical and Experimental Research, 18,* 311–316.

Black, D. W., & Moyer, T. (1998). Clinical features and psychiatric comorbidity of subjects with pathological gambling behavior. *Psychiatric Services, 49,* 1434–1439.

Blanco, C., Orensanz-Munoz, L., Blanco-Jerez, C., & Saiz-Ruiz, J. (1996). Pathological gambling and platelet MAO activity: A psychobiological study. *American Journal of Psychiatry, 153,* 119–121.

Bland, R. C., Newman, S. C., Orn, H., & Stebelsky, G. (1993). Epidemiology of pathological gambling in Edmonton. *Canadian Journal of Psychiatry, 38,* 108–112.

Blaszczynski, A. P., Buhrish, N., & McConaghy, N. (1985). Pathological gamblers, heroin addicts, and controls compared on the E.P.Q. "Addiction Scale." *British Journal of Addiction, 80,* 315–319.

Blaszczynski, A., & Farrell, E. (1998). A case series of 44 completed gambling-related suicides. *Journal of Gambling Studies, 14,* 93–109.

Blaszczynski, A., Hyde, J., & Sandanam, J. (1991). Pathological gambling secondary to brain trauma: A case study. *Journal of Gambling Studies, 7,* 65–71.

Blaszczynski, A., & Silove, D. (1996). Pathological gambling: Forensic issues. *Australian and New Zealand Journal of Psychiatry, 30,* 358–369.

Blaszczynski, A., & Steel, Z. (1998). Personality disorders among pathological gamblers. *Journal of Gambling Studies, 14,* 51–71.

Blaszczynski, A., Steel, Z., & McConaghy, N. (1997). Impulsivity in pathological gambling: The antisocial impulsivist. *Addiction, 92,* 75–87.

Blaszczysnski, A. P., Wilson, A. C., & McConaghy, N. (1986). Sensation seeking and pathological gambling. *British Journal of Addiction, 81,* 113–117.

Bonnie, R., & Whitebread, C. (1974). *The marijuana conviction: A history of marijuana prohibition in the United States.* New York: Lindesmith Center.

Bowman, K. M., & Jellinek, E. M. (1941). Alcoholic mental disorders. *Quarterly Journal of Studies on Alcohol, 2,* 312–390.

Bradford, J., Geller, J., Lesieur, H. R., Rosenthal, R., & Wise, M. (1996). Impulse control disorders. In T. A. Widiger, A. J. Frances, H. A. Pincus, R. Ross, M. B. First, & D. W. Wakefield (Eds.), *DSM-IV sourcebook: Vol. 2.* Washington, DC: American Psychiatric Association.

Breen, R. B., & Zuckerman, M. (1999). "Chasing" in gambling behavior: Personality and cognitive determinants. *Personality & Individual Differences, 27,* 1097–1111.

Breslin, F. C., Sobell, M. B., Cappell, H., Vakili, S., & Poulos, C. X. (1999). The effects of alcohol, gender, and sensation seeking on the gambling choices of social drinkers. *Psychology of Addictive Behaviors, 13,* 243–252.

Bucholz, K. K., Heath, A. C., Reich, T., & Hesselbrock, V. M. (1996). Can we subtype alcoholism? A latent class analysis of data from relatives of alcoholics in a multicenter family study of alcoholism. *Alcoholism: Clinical & Experimental Research, 20,* 1462–1471.

Cappell, H., & Herman, C. P. (1972). Alcohol and tension reduction. A review. *Quarterly Journal of Studies on Alcohol, 33,* 33–64.

Carrasco, J. L., Saiz-Ruiz, J., Hollander, E., Cesar, J., & Lopez-Ibor, J. J., Jr. (1994). Low platelet monoamine oxidase activity in pathological gambling. *Acta Psychiatrica Scandinavica, 90,* 427–431.

Caspi, A., Begg, D., Dickson, N., Harrington, H., Langley, J., Moffitt, T. E., & Silva, P. A. (1997). Personality differences predict health-risk behaviors in young adulthood: Evidence from a longitudinal study. *Journal of Personality & Social Psychology, 73,* 1052–1063.

Caspi, A., & Moffitt, T. E. (1995). The continuity of maladaptive behavior: From description to understanding in the study of antisocial behavior. In D. Cicchetti & D. J. Cohen (Eds.), *Developmental psychopathology: Vol. 2. Risk, disorder, and adaptation* (pp. 472–511). New York: Wiley.

de Castro, I. P., Ibanez, A., Saiz-Ruiz, J., & Fernandez, P. J. (1999). Genetic contribution to pathological gambling: Possible association between a functional DNA polymorphism at the serotonin transporter gene (5-HTT) and affected men. *Pharmacogenetics, 9,* 397–400.

Chassin, L., Curran, P. J., Hussong, A. M., & Colder, C. R. (1996). The relation of parent alcoholism to adolescent substance use: A longitudinal follow-up study. *Journal of Abnormal Psychology, 105,* 70–80.

Chen, K., & Kandel, D. B. (1995). The natural history of drug use from adolescence to the mid-thirties in a general population sample. *American Journal of Public Health, 85,* 41–47.

Ciarrocchi, J. W., Kirschner, N. M., & Fallik, F. (1991). Personality dimensions of male pathological gamblers, alcoholics, and dually addicted gamblers. *Journal of Gambling Studies, 7,* 133–141.

Cloninger, C. R. (1987a). Neurogenetic adapative mechanisms in alcoholism. *Science, 236,* 410–416.

Cloninger, C. R. (1987b). A systematic method for clinical description and classification of personality variants. *Archives of General Psychiatry, 44,* 573–588.

Cloninger, C. R. (1987c). *Tridimensional Personality Questionnaire, version 4.* Unpublished manuscript.

Cloninger, C. R., Sigvardsson, S., Reich, T., & Bohman, M. (1988). Childhood personality predicts alcohol abuse in young adults. *Alcoholism: Clinical and Experimental Research, 12,* 494–505.

Comings, D. E., Gonzalez, N., Wu, S., Gade, R., Muhleman, D., Saucier, G., Johnson, P., Verde, R., Rosenthal, R. J., Lesieur, H. R., Rugle, L. J., Miller, W. B., & MacMurray, J. P. (1999). Studies of the 48 bp repeat polymorphism of the DRD4 gene in impulsive, compulsive, addictive behaviors: Tourette Syndrome, ADHD, pathological gambling, and substance abuse. *American Journal of Medical Genetics (Neuropsychiatric Genetics), 88,* 358–368.

Comings, D. E., Rosenthal, R. J., Lesieur, H. R., Rugle, L. J., Muhleman, D., Chiu, C., Dietz, G., & Gade, R. (1996). A study of the dopamine D2 receptor gene in pathological gambling. *Pharmacogenetics, 6,* 223–234.

Cooper, M. L., Frone, M. R., Russell, M., & Mudar, P. (1995). Drinking to regulate positive and negative emotions: A motivational model of alcohol use. *Journal of Personality & Social Psychology, 69,* 990–1005.

Cooper, M. L., Russell, M., Skinner, J. B., & Windle, M. (1992). Development and validation of a three-dimensional measure of drinking motives. *Psychological Assessment, 4,* 123–132.

Costello, E. J., Erkanli, A., Federman, E., & Angold, A. (1999). Development of psychiatric comorbidity with substance abuse in adolescents: Effects of timing and sex. *Journal of Clinical Child Psychology, 28,* 298–311.

Cotton, N. (1979). The familial incidence of alcoholism: A review. *Journal of Studies on Alcohol, 40,* 89–116.

Coventry, K. R., & Brown, R. I. (1993). Sensation seeking, gambling and gambling addictions. *Addiction, 88,* 541–554.

Cox, W. M. (1987). Personality theory and research. In H. T. Blane & K. E. Leonard (Eds.), *Psychological theories of drinking and alcoholism* (pp. 55–84). New York: Guilford Press.

Crockford, D. N., & el-Guebaly, N. (1998). Psychiatric comorbidity in pathological gambling: A critical review. *Canadian Journal of Psychiatry, 43,* 43–50.

Cunningham-Williams, R. M., Cottler, L. B., Compton, W. M., III, & Spitznagel, E. L. (1998). Taking chances: Problem gamblers and mental health disorders: Results from the St. Louis Epidemiologic Catchment Area study. *American Journal of Public Health, 88,* 1093–1096.

Cunningham-Williams, R. M., Cottler, L. B., Compton, W. M., Spitznagel, E. L., & Ben-Abdallah, A. (2000). Problem gambling and comorbid psychiatric and substance use disorders among drug users recruited from drug treatment and community settings. *Journal of Gambling Studies, 16,* 347–376.

Dell, L., Ruzicka, M., & Palisi, A. (1981). Personality and other factors associated with the gambling addiction. *International Journal of the Addictions, 16,* 149–156.

Diamond, I., & Gordon, A. (1995). Biochemical phenotypic markers in genetic alcoholism. In H. Begleiter & B. Kissin (Eds.), *Alcohol and alcoholism: Vol. 1. The genetics of alcoholism* (pp. 259–268). New York: Oxford University Press.

Dickerson, M., & Baron, E. (2000). Contemporary issues and future directions for research into pathological gambling. *Addiction, 95,* 1145–1159.

Dickerson, M., Cunningham, R., England, S. L., & Hinchy, J. (1991). On the determinants of persistent gambling: III. Personality, prior mood, and poker machine play. *International Journal of the Addictions, 26,* 531–548.

Dishion, T. J., French, D. C., & Patterson, G. R. (1995). The development and ecology of antisocial behavior. In D. Cicchetti & D. J. Cohen (Eds.), *Developmental psychopathology: Vol. 2. Risk, disorder, and adaptation* (pp. 421–471). New York: Wiley.

Donovan, J. E., & Jessor, R. (1985). Structure of problem behavior in adolescence and young adulthood. *Journal of Consulting and Clinical Psychology, 53,* 890–904.

Donovan, J. E., Jessor, R., & Costa, F. M. (1988). Syndrome of problem behavior in adolescence: A replication. *Journal of Consulting and Clinical Psychology, 56,* 762–765.

Earleywine, M., & Finn, P. R. (1991). Sensation seeking explains the relation between behavioral disinhibition and alcohol consumption. *Addictive Behaviors, 16,* 123–128.

Edwards, G. (1982). *The treatment of drinking problems: A guide for the helping professions.* New York: McGraw-Hill.

Edwards, G. (1986). The alcohol dependence syndrome: A concept as stimulus to enquiry. *British Journal of Addiction, 81,* 171–183.

Edwards, G., & Gross, M. (1976). Alcohol dependence: Provisional decription of a clinical syndrome. *British Medical Journal, 1,* 1058–1061.

Eisen, S. A., Lin, N., Lyons, M. J., Scherrer, J. F., Griffith, K., True, W. R., Goldberg, J., & Tsuang, M. T. (1998). Familial influences on gambling behavior: An analysis of 3359 twin pairs. *Addiction, 93,* 1375–1384.

Feighner, J. P., Robins, E., Guze, S. B., Woodruff, R. A., Winokur, G., & Munoz, R. (1972). Diagnostic criteria for use in psychiatric research. *Archives of General Psychiatry, 26,* 57–63.

Fere, C. (1899). *The pathology of emotions* (R. Park, Trans.). London: University Press.

Freud, S. (1961). *Dostoevsky and parricide.* In J. Strachey (Ed. & Trans.), *Standard edition of the complete psychological works of Sigmund Freud* (Vol. 21, pp. 175–196). London: Hogarth. (Original work published 1928)

Friedland, N., Keinan, G., & Regev, Y. (1992). Controlling the uncontrollable: Effects of stress on illusory perceptions of controllability. *Journal of Personality and Social Psychology, 63,* 923–931.

Fromme, K., Katz, E., & D'Amico, E. (1997). Effects of alcohol intoxication on the perceived consequences of risk taking. *Experimental and Clinical Psychopharmacology, 5,* 14–23.

Fromme, K., Stroot, E. A., & Kaplan, D. (1993). Comprehensive effects of alcohol: Development and psychometric assessment of a new expectancy questionnaire. *Psychological Assessment, 5,* 19–26.

Gambino, B., Fitzgerald, R., Shaffer, H. J., & Renner, J. (1993). Perceived family history of problem gambling and scores on SOGS. *Journal of Gambling Studies, 9,* 169–184.

Gerstein, D., Volberg, R., Hoffmann, J., Larison, C., Engelman, L., Murphy, S., Palmer, A., Chuchro, L., Toce, M., Johnson, R., Buie, T., & Hill, M. A. (1999). *Gambling impact and behavior study.* New York: Christiansen/Cummings Associates.

Giacopassi, D., Stitt, B. G., & Vandiver, M. (1998). An analysis of the relationship of alcohol to casino gambling among college students. *Journal of Gambling Studies, 14,* 135–149.

Gianoulakis, C. (1996). Implications of endogenous opioids and dopamine in alcoholism: Human and basic science studies. *Alcohol & Alcoholism, 31,* 33–42.

Goldman, M. S., Del Boca, F. K., & Darkes, J. (1999). Alcohol expectancy theory: The application of cognitive neuroscience. In K. E. Leonard & H. T. Blane (Eds.), *Psychological theories of drinking and alcoholism* (2nd ed., pp. 203–246). New York: Guilford Press.

Goode, E. (1999). *Drugs in American society* (5th ed.). New York: McGraw-Hill.

Gorenstein, E. E. (1987). Cognitive-perceptual deficit in an alcoholism spectrum disorder. *Journal of Studies on Alcohol, 48,* 310–318.

Gorenstein, E. E., & Newman, J. P. (1980). Disinhibitory psychopathology: A new perspective and a model for research. *Psychological Review, 87,* 301–315.

Graham, J. R., & Lowenfeld, B. H. (1986). Personality dimensions of the pathological gambler. *Journal of Gambling Behavior, 2,* 58–66.

Grant, B. F. (1997). Prevalence and correlates of alcohol use and DSM-IV alcohol dependence in the United States: Results of the National Longitudinal Alcohol Epidemiologic Survey. *Journal of Studies on Alcohol, 58,* 464–473.

Grant, B. F., Harford, T., Dawson, D., Chou, P., Dufour, M., & Pickering, R. (1994). Prevalence of DSM-IV alcohol abuse and dependence. *Alcohol Health and Research World, 18,* 243–248.

Grant, B. F., & Pickering, R. P. (1996). Comorbidity between DSM-IV alcohol and drug use disorders: Results from the National Longitudinal Alcohol Epidemiologic Survey. *Alcohol Health & Research World, 20*(1), 67–72.

Greeley, J., & Oei, T. (1999). Alcohol and tension reduction. In K. Leonard & H. T. Blane (Eds.), *Psychological theories of drinking and alcoholism* (2nd ed., pp. 14–53). New York: Guilford Press.

Griffiths, M. D. (1991). Psychobiology of the near-miss in fruit machine gambling. *Journal of Psychology, 125,* 347–357.

Griffiths, M. D. (1995). The role of subjective mood states in the maintenance of fruit machine gambling behaviour. *Journal of Gambling Studies, 11,* 123–135.

Gupta, R., & Derevensky, J. (1997). Familial and social influences on juvenile gambling behavior. *Journal of Gambling Studies, 13,* 179–192.

Hand, I. (1998). Pathological gambling: A negative state model and its implications for behavioral treatments. *CNS Spectrums, 3,* 58–71.

Harada, S., Agarwal, D. P., Goedde, H. W., Tagaki, S., & Ishikawa, B. (1982). Possible protective role against alcoholism for aldehyde dehydrogenase isozyme deficiency in Japan. *Lancet, 2*(8302), 827.

Hare, R. D. (1984). Performance of psychopaths on cognitive tasks related to frontal lobe function. *Journal of Abnormal Psychology, 93,* 133–140.

Hasin, D. S., Muthen, B., Wisnicki, K. S., & Grant, B. (1994). Validity of the bi-axial dependence concept: A test in the U.S. general population. *Addiction, 89,* 573–579.

Hawkins, J. D., Catalano, R. F., & Miller, J. Y. (1992). Risk and protective factors for alcohol and other drug problems in adolescence and early adulthood: Implications for substance abuse prevention. *Psychological Bulletin, 112,* 64–105.

Heath, A. C. (1995a). Genetic influences on alcoholism risk: A review of adoption and twin studies. *Alcohol Health and Research World, 19*(3), 166–171.

Heath, A. C. (1995b). Genetic influences on drinking behavior in humans. In H. Begleiter & B. Kissin (Eds.), *Alcohol and alcoholism: Vol. 1. The genetics of alcoholism* (pp. 82–121). New York: Oxford University Press, Inc.

Heath, A. C., Bucholz, K. K., Madden, P. A. F., Dinwiddie, S. H., Slutske, W. S., Bierut, L. J., Statham, D. J., Dunne, M. P., Whitfield, J., & Martin, N. G. (1997). Genetic and environmental contributions to alcohol dependence risk in a national twin sample: Consistency of findings in women and men. *Psychological Medicine, 27,* 1381–1396.

Heath, A. C., Bucholz, K. K., Slutske, W. S., & Madden, P. A. F. (1994). The assessment of alcoholism in surveys of the general community: What are we measuring? Some insights from the Australian twin panel interview survey. *International Review of Psychiatry, 6,* 295–307.

Helzer, J. E., Burnam, A., & McEvoy, L. T. (1991). Alcohol abuse and dependence. In L. N. Robins & D. A. Regier (Eds.), *Psychiatric disorders in America: The Epidemiologic Catchment Area Study* (pp. 81–115). New York: Macmillan.

Helzer, J. E., & Canino, G. J. (Eds.). (1992). *Alcoholism in North America, Europe, and Asia.* New York: Oxford University Press.

Helzer, J. E., & Pryzbeck, T. R. (1988). The co-occurrence of alcoholism with other psychiatric disorders in the general population and its impact on treatment. *Journal of Studies on Alcohol, 49,* 219–224.

Hesselbrock, V. M. (1995). The genetic epidemiology of alcoholism. In H. Begleiter & B. Kissin (Eds.), *Alcohol and alcoholism: Vol. 1. The genetics of alcoholism* (pp. 17–39). New York: Oxford University Press.

Holdcraft, L. C., Iacono, W. G., & McGue, M. K. (1998). Antisocial Personality Disorder and depression in relation to alcoholism: A community-based sample. *Journal of Studies on Alcohol, 59,* 222–226.

Horgan, C., Skwara, K., & Strickler, G. (2001). *Substance abuse: The nation's number one health problem.* Princeton, NJ: Schneider Institute for Health Policy, Brandeis University.

Institute of Medicine. (1990). *Broadening the base of treatment for alcohol problems.* Washington, DC: National Academy Press.

Jackson, K. M., Sher, K. J., & Wood, P. K. (2000). Prospective analysis of comorbidity: Tobacco and alcohol use disorders. *Journal of Abnormal Psychology, 109,* 679–694.

Jang, K. L., Vernon, P. A., & Livesley, W. J. (2000). Personality disorder traits, family environment, and alcohol misuse: A multivariate behavioural genetic analysis. *Addiction, 95,* 873–888.

Jellinek, E. M. (1960). *The disease concept of alcoholism.* New Haven, CT: Hillhouse.

Jessor, R., Donovan, J. E., & Costa, F. M. (1991). *Beyond adolescence: Problem behavior and young adult development.* New York: Cambridge University Press.

Jessor, R., & Jessor, S. (1977). *Problem behavior and psychosocial development: A longitudinal study of youth.* New York: Academic Press.

Jones, M. C. (1968). Personality correlates and antecedents of drinking patterns in adult males. *Journal of Consulting & Clinical Psychology, 32,* 2–12.

Kadden, R. M., Kranzler, H. R., & Rounsaville, B. J. (1995). Validity of the distinction between "substance-induced" and "independent" depression and anxiety disorders. *American Journal on Addictions, 4,* 107–117.

Kaplan, H. B. (1975). Increase in self-rejection as an antecedent of deviant responses. *Journal of Youth and Adolescence, 4,* 281–292.

Keller, M., & Doria, J. (1991). On defining alcoholism. *Alcohol Health & Research World, 15,* 253–259.

Kendler, K., Karkowski, L., Corey, L., Prescott, C., & Neale, M. (1999). Genetic and environmental risk factors in the atiology of illicit drug initiation and subsequent misuse in women. *The British Journal of Psychiatry, 175,* 351–356.

Kendler, K. S., Karkowski, L., Neale, M., & Prescott, C. (2000). Illicit psychoative substance use, heavy use, abuse, and dependence in a US population-based sample of male twins. *Archives of General Psychiatry, 57,* 261–269.

Kendler, K. S., Karkowski, L., & Prescott, C. A. (1999). Hallucinogen, opiate, sedative and stimulant use and abuse in a population-based sample of female twins. *Acta Psychiatrica Scandinavica, 99,* 368–376.

Kendler, K. S., & Prescott, C. A. (1998a). Cannabis use, abuse, and dependence in a population-based sample of female twins. *American Journal of Psychiatry, 155,* 1016–1022.

Kendler, K. S., & Prescott, C. A. (1998b). Cocaine use, abuse and dependence in a population-based sample of female twins. *British Journal of Psychiatry, 173,* 345–350.

Kendler, K. S., Walters, E. E., Neale, M. C., Kessler, R. C., Heath, A. C., & Eaves, L. J. (1995). The structure of the genetic and environmental risk factors for six major psychiatric disorders in women: Phobia, generalized anxiety disorder, panic disorder, bulimia, major depression and alcoholism. *Archives of General Psychiatry, 52,* 374–383.

Kessler, R. C., Crum, R. M., Warner, L. A., & Nelson, C. B. (1997). Lifetime co-occurrence of DSM-III-R alcohol abuse and dependence with other psychiatric disorders in the National Comorbidity Survey. *Archives of General Psychiatry, 54,* 313–321.

Kessler, K., McGonagle, K., Zhao, S., Nelson, C., Hughes, M., Eshleman, S., Wittchen, H., & Kendler, K. (1994). Lifetime and 12 month prevalence of DSM-III-R psychiatric disorders in the United States. *Archives of General Psychiatry, 51,* 8–19.

Kilbey, M. M., Downey, K., & Breslau, N. (1998). Predicting the emergence and persistence of alcohol dependence in young adults: The role of expectancy and other risk factors. *Experimental & Clinical Psychopharmacology, 6,* 149–156.

King, R. (1972). *The drug hang-up: America's fifty year folly.* New York: W. W. Norton.

Klein, D. N., & Riso, L. P. (1993). Psychiatric disorders: Problems of boundaries and comorbidity. In C. G. Costello (Ed.), *Basic issues in psychopathology* (pp. 19–66). New York: Guilford Press.

Knight, R. P. (1938). The psychoanalytic treatment in a sanatorium of chronic addiction to alcohol. *Journal of the American Medical Association, 111,* 1443–1448.

Koob, G. (2000). Drug addiction. *Neurobiology of Disease, 7,* 543–545.

Koob, G. F., & Le Moal, M. (2001). Drug addiction, dysregulation of reward, and allostasis. *Neuropsychopharmacology, 24,* 97–129.

Kreitman, N. (1986). Alcohol consumption and the preventive paradox. *British Journal of Addiction, 81,* 353–363.

Krueger, R. F. (1999). The structure of common mental disorders. *Archives of General Psychiatry, 56,* 921–926.

Krueger, R. F., Caspi, A., Moffitt, T. E., & Silva, P. A. (1998). The structure and stability of common mental disorders (DSM-III-R): A longitudinal-epidemiological study. *Journal of Abnormal Psychology, 107,* 216–227.

Kuhn, C., Swartzwalder, S., & Wilson, W. (1998). *Buzzed: The straight facts about the most used and abused drugs from alcohol to ecstasy.* New York: W. W. Norton.

Kushner, M. G., Sher, K. J., & Erickson, D. J. (1999). Prospective analysis of the relation between DSM-III anxiety disorders and alcohol use disorders. *American Journal of Psychiatry, 156,* 723–732.

Kyngdon, A., & Dickerson, M. (1999). An experimental study of the effect of prior alcohol consumption on a simulated gambling activity. *Addiction, 94,* 697–707.

Labouvie, E. W., Pandina, R. J., White, H. R., & Johnson, V. (1990). Risk factors of adolescent drug use: An affect-based interpretation. *Journal of Substance Abuse, 2,* 265–285.

Ladouceur, R., & Gaboury, A. (1988). Effects of limited and unlimited stakes on gambling behavior. *Journal of Gambling Behavior, 4,* 119.

Langenbucher, J., Martin, C. S., Labouvie, E., Sanjuan, P. M., Bavly, L., & Pollock, N. K. (2000). Toward the DSM-V: The withdrawal-gate model versus the DSM-IV in the diagnosis of alcohol abuse and dependence. *Journal of Consulting & Clinical Psychology, 68,* 799–809.

Leary, K., & Dickerson, M. G. (1985). Levels of arousal in high and low frequency gamblers. *Behavior Research and Therapy, 23,* 635–640.

LeMarquand, D. G., Benkelfat, C., Pihl, R. O., Palmour, R. M., & Young, S. N. (1999). Behavioral disinhibition induced by tryptophan depletion in nonalcoholic young men with multigenerational family histories of paternal alcoholism. *American Journal of Psychiatry, 156,* 1771–1779.

Lesieur, H. R. (1984). *The chase: Career of the compulsive gambler.* Rochester, VT: Schenkman Books.

Lesieur, H. R., & Blume, S. B. (1993). Pathological gambling, eating disorders, and the psychoactive substance use disorders. *Journal of Addictive Diseases, 12,* 89–102.

Lesieur, H. R., Blume, S. B., & Zoppa, R. M. (1986). Alcoholism, drug abuse, and gambling. *Alcoholism: Clinical & Experimental Research, 10,* 33–38.

Lesieur, H. R., Cross, J., Frank, M., Welch, M., White, C. M., Rubenstein, G., Moseley, K., & Mark, M. (1991). Gambling and pathological gambling among university students. *Addictive Behaviors, 16,* 517–527.

Lichtermann, D., Hranilovic, D., Trixler, M., Franke, P., Jernej, B., Delmo, C. D., Knapp, M., Schwab, S. G., Maier, W., & Wildenauer, D. B. (2000). Support for allelic association of a polymorphic site in the promoter region of the serotonin transporter gene with risk for alcohol dependence. *American Journal of Psychiatry, 157,* 2045–2047.

Linden, R. D., Pope, H. G., & Jonas, J. M. (1986). Pathological gambling and major affective disorder: Preliminary findings. *Journal of Clinical Psychiatry, 47,* 201–203.

Linnoila, M., Virkkunen, M., George, T., & Higley, D. (1993). Impulse control disorders. *International Clinical Psychopharmacology, 8,* 53–56.

Litten, R. Z., & Allen, J. P. (1998). Advances in development of medications for alcoholism treatment. *Psychopharmacologia, 139,* 20–33.

Luria, A. R. (1980). Neuropsychology in the local diagnosis of brain damage. *International Journal of Clinical Neuropsychology, 2,* 1–7.

Lyons, M. J., Eisen, S. A., Goldberg, J., True, W., Lin, N., Meyer, J. M., Toomey, R., Faraone, S. V., Merla-Ramos, M., & Tsuang, M. T. (1998). A registry-based twin study of depression in men. *Archives of General Psychiatry, 55,* 468–472.

Major, L. F., & Murphy, D. L. (1978). Platelet and plasma amine oxidase activity in alcoholic individuals. *British Journal of Psychiatry, 132,* 548–554.

McCormick, R. S., Taber, J., Kruedelbach, N., & Russo, A. (1987). Personality profiles of hospitalized pathological gamblers: The California Personality Inventory. *Journal of Clinical Psychology, 43,* 521–572.

McGue, M. (1999). Behavioral genetic models of alcoholism and drinking. In K. E. Leonard & H. T. Blane (Eds.), *Psychological theories of drinking and alcoholism* (2nd ed., pp. 372–421). New York: Guilford Press.

Merikangas, K. R., Stevens, D. E., Fenton, B., Stolar, M., O'Malley, S., Woods, S. W., & Risch, N. (1998). Co-morbidity and familial aggregation of alcoholism and anxiety disorders. *Psychological Medicine, 28,* 773–788.

Molina, B. S. G., Chassin, L., & Curran, P. J. (1994). A comparison of mechanisms underlying substance use for early adolescent children of alcoholics and controls. *Journal of Studies on Alcohol, 55,* 269–275.

Morgan, A. B., & Lilienfeld, S. O. (2000). A meta-analytic review of the relation between antisocial behavior and neuropsychological measures of executive function. *Clinical Psychology Review, 20,* 113–136.

Muthen, B. O., Grant, B., & Hasin, D. (1993). The dimensionality of alcohol abuse and dependence: Factor analysis of DSM-III-R and proposed DSM-IV criteria in the 1988 National Health Interview Survey. *Addiction, 88,* 1079–1090.

Nathan, P. (1988). The addictive personality is the behavior of the addict. *Journal of Consulting and Clinical Psychology, 56,* 183–188.

National Council on Alcoholism. (1972). Criteria for the diagnosis of alcoholism. *American Journal of Psychiatry, 129,* 127–135.

National Council on Alcoholism, Criteria Committee. (1972). Criteria for the diagnosis of alcoholism. *Annals of Internal Medicine, 77,* 249–258.

National Institute on Alcohol Abuse and Alcoholism. (2000). *10th special report to the U.S. Congress on alcohol and health.* Washington, DC: U.S. Department of Health and Human Services.

National Research Council. (1999). *Pathological gambling: A critical review.* Washington, DC: National Academy Press.

Nelson, C. B., Heath, A. C., & Kessler, R. C. (1998). Temporal progression of alcohol dependence symptoms in the U.S. household population: Results from the National Comorbidity Survey. *Journal of Consulting & Clinical Psychology, 66,* 474–483.

Newlin, D. B., & Thomson, J. B. (1990). Alcohol challenge with sons of alcoholics: A critical review and analysis. *Psychological Bulletin, 108,* 383–402.

Newman, J. P., Patterson, C. M., & Kosson, D. S. (1987). Response preservation in psychopaths. *Journal of Abnormal Psychology, 96,* 145–148.

Nigg, J. T. (2000). On inhibiton/disinhibition in development psychopathology: Views from cognitive and personality psychology and a working inhibition taxonomy. *Psychological Bulletin, 126,* 220–246.

Noll, R. B., Zucker, R. A., & Greenberg, G. S. (1990). Identification of alcohol by smell among preschoolers: Evidence for early socialization about drugs occurring in the home. *Child Development, 61,* 1520–1527.

Oetting, E. R., & Beauvais, F. (1986). Peer cluster theory: Drugs and the adolescent. *Journal of Counseling & Development, 65,* 17–22.

O'Neill, S., & Sher, K. J. (2000). Physiological alcohol dependence symptoms in early adulthood: A longitudinal perspective. *Experimental and Clinical Psychopharmacology, 8,* 493–508.

Orford, J. (2001). Addiction as excessive appetite. *Addiction, 96,* 15–31.

Pederson, W. (1991). Mental health, sensation seeking and drug use patterns: A longitudinal study. *British Journal of Addiction, 86,* 195–204.

Petraitis, J., Flay, B. R., & Miller, T. Q. (1995). Reviewing theories of adolescent substance use: Organizing pieces in the puzzle. *Psychological Bulletin, 117,* 67–86.

Petry, N. M., & Armentano, C. (1999). Prevalence, assessment, and treatment of pathological gambling: A review. *Psychiatric Services, 50,* 1021–1027.

Pettinati, H. M., Volpicelli, J. R., Luck, G., Kranzler, H. R., Rukstalis, M. R., & Cnaan, A. (2001). Double-blind clinical trial of sertraline treatment for alcohol dependence. *Journal of Clinical Psychopharmacology, 21,* 143–153.

Phillips, D. P., Welty, W. R., & Smith, M. M. (1997). Evaluated suicide levels associated with legalized gambling. *Suicide & Life-Threatening Behavior, 27,* 373–378.

Pihl, R. O., & Bruce, K. R. (1995). Cognitive impairment in children of alcoholics. *Alcohol Health and Research World, 19*(2), 142–147.

Plutchik, A., & Plutchik, R. (1988). Psychosocial correlates of alcoholism. *Integrative Psychiatry, 6,* 205–210.

Polich, J., Pollock, V. E., & Bloom, F. E. (1994). Meta-analysis of P300 amplitude from males at risk for alcoholism. *Psychological Bulletin, 115,* 55–73.

Pollock, V. E. (1992). Meta-analysis of subjective sensitivity to alcohol in sons of alcoholics. *American Journal of Psychiatry, 149,* 1534–1538.

Poznanski, A. (1959). Our drinking heritage. In R. G. McCarthy (Ed.), *Drinking and intoxication: Selected reading in social attitudes and controls* (pp. 42–43). New Haven, CT: College and University Press.

Prescott, C. A., Aggen, S. H., & Kendler, K. S. (2000). Sex-specific genetic influences on the comorbidity of alcoholism and major depression in a population-based sample of US twins. *Archives of General Psychiatry, 57,* 803–811.

Prescott, C. A., Neale, M. C., Corey, L. A., & Kendler, K. S. (1997). Predictors of problem drinking and alcohol dependence in a population-based sample of female twins. *Journal of Studies on Alcohol, 58,* 167–181.

Productivity Commission. (1999). *Australia's gambling industries* (Inquiry Report, Vol. 1, No. 10).

Proimos, J., DuRant, R. H., Pierce, J. D., & Goodman, E. (1998). Gambling and other risk behaviors among 8th- to 12th-grade students. *Pediatrics, 102,* 23.

Ramirez, L., McCormick, R., Russo, A., & Taber, J. (1983). Patterns of substance abuse in pathological gamblers undergoing treatment. *Addictive Behaviors, 8,* 425–428.

Rankin, H., Stockwell, T., & Hodgson, R. (1982). Personality and alcohol dependence. *Personality & Individual Differences, 3,* 145–151.

Reich, T., Cloninger, C. R., Van Eerdewegh, P., Rice, J. P., & Mullaney, J. (1988). Secular trends in the familial transmission of alcoholism. *Alcoholism: Clinical & Experimental Research, 12,* 458–464.

Reich, T., Edenberg, H. J., Goate, A., Williams, J. T., Rice, J. P., Van Eerdewegh, P., Foroud, T., Hesselbrock, V., Schuckit, M. A., Bucholz, K. K., Porjesz, B., Li, T. K., Conneally, P. M., Nurnberger, J. I., Jr., Tischfield, J. A., Crowe, R. R., Cloninger, C. R., Wu, W., Shears, S., Carr, K., Crose, C., Willig, C., &

Begleiter, H. (1998). Genome-wide search for genes affecting the risk for alcohol dependence. *American Journal of Medical Genetics, 81,* 207–215.

Regier, D. A., Farmer, M. E., Rae, D. S., Locke, B. Z., Keith, S. J., Judd, L. L., & Goodwin, F. K. (1990). Comorbidity of mental disorders with alcohol and other drug abuse: Results from the Epidemiologic Catchment Area (ECA) Study. *Journal of American Medical Association, 264,* 2511–2518.

Repo, E., Kuikka, J. T., Bergstroem, K. A., Karhu, J., Hiltunen, J., & Tiihonen, J. (1999). Dopamine transporter and D-sub-2-receptor density in late-onset alcoholism. *Psychopharmacology, 147,* 314–318.

Robins, L., Bates, W., & O'Neal, P. (1962). Adult drinking patterns of former problem children. In D. Pittman & C. R. Synder (Eds.), *Society, culture, and drinking patterns* (pp. 395–412). New York: Wiley.

Robins, L. N., Bates, W. M., & O'Neal, P. (1991). Adult drinking patterns of former problem children. In D. Pittman & H. R. White (Eds.), *Society, culture, and drinking patterns reexamined. Alcohol, culture, and social control monograph series* (pp. 460–479). Piscataway, NJ: Rutgers Center of Alcohol Studies.

Rogers, P. (1998). The cognitive psychology of lottery gambling: A theoretical review. *Journal of Gambling Studies, 14,* 111–134.

Roy, A., Adinoff, B., Roehrich, L., Lamparski, D., Custer, R., Lorenz, V., Barbaccia, M., Guidotti, A., Costa, E., & Linnoila, M. (1988). Pathological gambling. *Archives of General Psychiatry, 45,* 369–373.

Sayette, M. A. (1999). Does drinking reduce stress? *Alcohol Health and Research World, 23*(4), 250–255.

Schooler, C., Zahn, T. P., Murphy, D. L., & Buchsbaum, M. S. (1978). Psychological correlates of monoamie oxidase in normals. *Journal of Nervous and Mental Disease, 166,* 177–186.

Schuckit, M. A. (1985). Genetics and the risk for alcoholism. *Journal of the American Medical Association, 253,* 2614–2617.

Schuckit, M. A. (1994). The relationship between alcohol problems, substance abuse and psychiatric problems. In T. A. Widiger, A. J. Frances, H. A. Pincus, M. B. First, R. Ross, & W. Davis (Eds.), *DSM-IV sourcebook* (Vol. 1, pp. 45–66). Washington, DC: American Psychiatric Association.

Schuckit, M. A. (1998). Biological, psychological and environmental predictors of the alcoholism risk: A longitudinal study. *Journal of Studies on Alcohol, 59,* 485–494.

Schuckit, M. A., & Smith, T. L. (1996). An 8-year follow-up of 450 sons of alcoholic and control subjects. *Archives of General Psychiatry, 53,* 202–210.

Schuckit, M. A., Smith, T. L., Daeppen, J. B., Eng, M., Li, T. K., Hesselbrock, V. M., Nurnberger, J. I., Jr., & Bucholz, K. K. (1998). Clinical relevance of the distinction between alcohol dependence with and without a physiological component. *American Journal of Psychiatry, 155,* 733–740.

Schulenberg, J., O'Malley, P. M., Bachman, J. G., Wadsworth, K. N., & Johnston, L. D. (1996). Getting drunk and growing up: Trajectories of frequent binge drinking during the transition to young adulthood. *Journal of Studies on Alcohol, 57,* 289–304.

Searles, J. S. (1988). The role of genetics in the pathogenesis of alcoholism. *Journal of Abnormal Psychology, 97,* 153–167.

Seneca. (1942). Epistle LXXXIII: On drunkenness—Classics of the alcohol literature. *Quarterly Journal of Studies on Alcohol, 3,* 302–307.

Shaffer, H., Hall, M., & Bilt, J. (1999). Estimating the prevalence of disordered gambling behavior in the United States and Canada: A research synthesis. *American Journal of Public Health, 89,* 1369–1376.

Sharpe, L., Tarrier, N., Schotte, D., & Spence, S. (1995). The role of autonomic arousal in problem gambling. *Addiction, 90,* 1529–1540.

Sher, K. J. (1987). Stress response dampening. In H. T. Blane & K. E. Leonard (Eds.), *Psychological theories of drinking and alcoholism* (pp. 227–271). New York: Guilford Press.

Sher, K. J. (Ed.). (1991). *Children of alcoholics: A critical appraisal of theory and research.* Chicago: University of Chicago Press.

Sher, K. J. (1994). There are two types of alcoholism researchers: Those who believe in two types of alcoholism and those who don't. *Addiction, 89,* 1061–1064.

Sher, K. J., Bartholow, B. D., & Wood, M. D. (2000). Personality and substance use disorders: A prospective study. *Journal of Consulting and Clinical Psychology, 68,* 818–829.

Sher, K. J., Bylund, D. B., Walitzer, K. S., Hartmann, J., & Ray-Prenger, C. (1994). Platelet MAO activity: Personality, substance use, and the stress-response-dampening effect of alcohol. *Experimental and Clinical Psychopharmacology, 2,* 53–81.

Sher, K. J., & Gotham, H. (1999). Pathological alcohol involvement: A developmental disorder of young adulthood. *Development and Psychopathology, 11,* 933–956.

Sher, K. J., & Trull, T. (1994). Personality and disinhibitory psychopathology: Alcoholism and antisocial personality disorder. *Journal of Abnormal Psychology, 103,* 92–102.

Sher, K. J., Trull, T. J., Bartholow, B., & Vieth, A. (1999). Personality and alcoholism: Issues, methods, and etiological processes. In H. Blane & K. Leonard (Eds.), *Psychological theories of drinking and alcoholism* (2nd ed., pp. 55–105). New York: Plenum Press.

Sieber, M. F. (1981). Personality scores and licit and illicit substance abuse. *Personality and Individual Differences, 2,* 235–241.

Siegel, S., & Allan, L. G. (1998). Learning and homeostasis: Drug addiction and the McCollough effect. *Psychological Bulletin, 124,* 230–239.

Siegel, S., Baptista, M. A., Kim, J. A., McDonald, R. V., & Weise-Kelly, L. (2000). Pavlovian psychopharmacology: The associative basis of tolerance. *Experimental & Clinical Psychopharmacology, 8,* 276–293.

Sjoberg, L. (1969). Alcohol and gambling. *Psychopharmacologia, 14,* 284–298.

Skinner, H. A. (1981). Primary syndromes of alcohol abuse: Their measurement and correlates. *British Journal of Addiction, 76,* 63–76.

Slutske, W. S., Eisen, S., True, W., Lyons, M., Goldberg, J., & Tsuang, M. (2000). Common genetic vulnerability for pathological gambling and alcohol dependence in men. *Archives of General Psychiatry, 57,* 666–673.

Slutske, W. S., Eisen, S., Xian, H., True, W., Lyons, M., Goldberg, J., & Tsuang, M. (2001). A twin study of the association between pathological gambling and antisocial personality disorder. *Journal of Abnormal Psychology, 110,* 297–308.

Slutske, W. S., Heath, A. C., Dinwiddie, S., Madden, P. A. F., Bucholz, K. K., Dunne, M., Statham, D., & Martin, N. (1998). Common genetic risk factors for conduct disorder and alcohol dependence. *Journal of Abnormal Psychology, 107,* 363–374.

Slutske, W. S., Heath, A. C., Madden, P. A. F., Bucholz, K. K., Statham, D. J., & Martin, N. G. (2002). Personality and the genetic risk for alcohol dependence. *Journal of Abnormal Psychology, 111,* 124–133.

Smart, R. G., & Ferris, J. (1996). Alcohol, drugs and gambling in the Ontario adult population, 1994. *Canadian Journal of Psychiatry, 41,* 36–45.

Smith, G. T., Goldman, M. S., Greenbaum, P. E., & Christiansen, B. A. (1995). Expectancy for social facilitation from drinking: The divergent paths of high-expectancy and low-expectancy adolescents. *Journal of Abnormal Psychology, 104,* 32–40.

Solomon, R. L., & Corbit, J. D. (1974). An opponent-process theory of motivation: I. Temporal dynamics of affect. *Psychological Review, 81,* 119–145.

Sproston, K., Erens, B., & Orford, J. (2000). *Gambling behaviour in Britain: Results from the British Gambling Prevalence Survey.* London: National Centre for Social Research.

Spunt, B., Dupont, I., Lesieur, H., Liberty, H. J., & Hunt, D. (1998). Pathological gambling and substance misuse: A review of the literature. *Substance Use & Misuse, 33,* 2535–2560.

Stacy, A. W., & Newcomb, M. D. (1998). Memory association and personality as predictors of alcohol use: Mediation and moderator effects. *Experimental & Clinical Psychopharmacology, 6,* 280–291.

Steel, Z., & Blaszczynski, A. (1998). Impulsivity, personality disorders and pathological gambling severity. *Addiction, 93,* 895–905.

Steele, C. M. (1986). What happens when you drink too much? *Psychology Today,* 48–52.

Steele, C. M., & Josephs, R. A. (1990). Alcohol myopia: Its prized and dangerous effects. *American Psychologist, 45,* 921–933.

Stinchfield, R. (2000). Gambling and correlates of gambling among Minnesota public school students. *Journal of Gambling Studies, 16,* 153–173.

Stinchfield, R., Cassuto, N., Winters, K., & Latimer, W. (1997). Prevalence of gambling among Minnesota public school students in 1992 and 1995. *Journal of Gambling Studies, 13,* 25–48.

Stinchfield, R., & Winters, K. C. (1998). Gambling and problem gambling among youths. *The Annals of the American Academy of Political and Social Science, 556,* 172–185.

Stritzke, W. G. K., Lang, A. R., & Patrick, C. J. (1996). Beyond stress and arousal: A reconceptualization of alcohol-emotion relations with respect to psychophysiological methods. *Psychological Bulletin, 120,* 376–395.

Stritzke, W. G., Patrick, C. J., & Lang, A. R. (1995). Alcohol and human emotion: A multidimensional analysis incorporating startle-probe methodology. *Journal of Abnormal Psychology, 104,* 114–122.

Stuss, D., & Benson, D. (1985). *The frontal lobes.* New York: Raven.

Svanum, S. (1986). Alcohol-related problems and dependence: An elaboration and integration. *International Journal of the Addictions, 21,* 539–558.

Tarter, R. E. (1988). Are there inherited behavioral traits that predispose to substance abuse? *Journal of Consulting & Clinical Psychology, 56,* 189–196.

Toneatto, T. (1999). Cognitive psychopathology of problem gambling. *Substance Use and Misuse, 34,* 1593–1604.

True, W. R., Xian, H., Scherrer, J. F., Madden, P. A. F., Bucholz, K. K., Heath, A. C., Eisen, S. A., Lyons, M. J., Goldberg, J., & Tsuang, M. (1999). Common genetic vulnerability for nicotine and alcohol dependence in men. *Archives of General Psychiatry, 56,* 655–661.

Tsuang, M., Lyons, M., Eisen, S., Goldberg, J., True, W., Lin, N., Meyer, J., Toomey, R., Faraone, S., & Eaves, L. (1996). Genetic influences on DSM-III-R drug abuse and dependence: A study of 3,372 twin pairs. *American Journal of Medical Genetics, 67,* 473–477.

Tsuang, M. T., Lyons, M. J., Harley, R. M., Xian, H., Eisen, S., Goldberg, J., True, W. R., & Faraone, S. V. (1999). Genetic and environmental influences on transitions in drug use. *Behavior Genetics, 29,* 473–479.

Tsuang, M. T., Lyons, M. J., Meyer, J. M., Doyle, T., Eisen, S. A., Goldberg, J., True, W., Lin, N., Toomey, R., & Eaves, L. (1998). Co-occurrence of abuse of different drugs in men: The role of drug-specific and shared vulnerabilities. *Archives of General Psychiatry, 55,* 967–972.

Vaillant, G. E., & Milofsky, E. S. (1982). The etiology of alcoholism: A prospective viewpoint. *American Psychologist, 37,* 494–503.

Vitaro, F., Arsenault, L., & Tremblay, R. E. (1997). Dispositional predictors of problem gambling in male adolescents. *American Journal of Psychiatry, 154,* 1769–1770.

Vitaro, F., Arsenault, L., & Tremblay, R. E. (1999). Impulsivity predicts problem gambling in low SES adolescent males. *Addiction, 94,* 565–575.

Vitaro, F., Ladouceur, R., & Bujold, A. (1996). Predictive and concurrent correlates of gambling in early adolescent boys. *Journal of Early Adolescence, 16,* 211–228.

Volberg, R. A., & Abbott, M. W. (1997). Gambling and problem gambling among indigenous peoples. *Substance Use & Misuse, 32,* 1525–1538.

Volberg, R. A., & Banks, S. M. (1994). *A new approach to understanding gambling and problem gambling in the general population.* Paper presented at the Ninth International Conference on Gambling and Risk Taking, Las Vegas, NV.

Volberg, R. A., & Steadman, H. J. (1988). Refining prevalence estimates of pathological gambling. *American Journal of Psychiatry, 145,* 502–505.

Walker, M. (1992). *Psychology of gambling.* Woburn, MA: Butterworth-Heinemann.

Wallisch, L. (1996). *Gambling in Texas: 1995 surveys of adult and adolescent gambling behavior.* Austin: Texas Commission on Alcohol and Drug Abuse.

Warner, L., Kessler, R., Hughes, M., Anthony, J., & Nelson, C. (1995). Prevalence and correlates of drug use and dependence in the United States. *Archives of General Psychiatry, 52,* 219–229.

Welte, J., Barnes, G., Wieczorek, W., Tidwell, M., & Parker, J. (2000). *Alcohol dependence and pathological gambling: Comorbidity and comparative epidemiology in the U.S.* New York: Research Institute on Addictions, and Center for Health and Social Research, Buffalo State College.

West, D. J., & Farrington, D. P. (1973). *Who becomes delinquent?* London: Heinemann.

White, J. L., Moffitt, T. E., Avshalom, C., Bartush, D. J., Needles, D. J., & Stouthamer-Loeber, M. (1994). Measuring impulsivity and examining its relationship to delinquency. *Journal of Abnormal Psychology, 103,* 192–205.

Widiger, T. A. (1997). Mental disorders as discrete clinical conditions: Dimensional versus categorical classification. In S. M. Turner & M. Hersen (Eds), *Adult psychopathology and diagnosis* (3rd ed.). New York: Wiley.

Windle, M., & Davies, P. T. (1999). Depression and heavy alcohol use among adolescents: Concurrent and prospective relations. *Development & Psychopathology, 11,* 823–844.

Winters, K. C., Stinchfield, R., Botzet, A., & Anderson, N. (2001). *Prospective studies of youth gambling behaviors.* Unpublished manuscript.

Winters, K. C., Stinchfield, R., & Fulkerson, J. (1993). Patterns and characteristics of adolescent gambling. *Journal of Gambling Studies, 9,* 371–386.

Wise, R. A., & Bozarth, M. A. (1987). A psychomotor stimulant theory of addiction. *Psychological Review, 94,* 469–492.

World Health Organization. (1967). *Manual of the International Statistical Classification of Diseases, Injuries, and Causes of Death* (8th ed.). Geneva, Switzerland: Author.

Wray, I., & Dickerson, M. (1981). Cessation of high frequency gambling and "withdrawal" symptoms. *British Journal of Addiction, 76,* 401–405.

Zucker, R. A. (1987). The four alcoholisms: A developmental account of the etiologic process. In P. C. Rivers (Ed.), *Alcohol and addictive behaviors: Nebraska Symposium on Motivation* (pp. 27–83). Lincoln: University of Nebraska Press.

Zucker, R. A. (1995). Pathways to alcohol problems and alcoholism: A developmental account of the evidence for multiple alcoholisms and for contextual contributions to risk. In R. A. Zucker, G. M. Boyd, & J. Howard (Eds.), *The development of alcohol problems: Exploring the biopsychosocial matrix of risk* (NIAAA Research Monograph No. 26, pp. 255–289). Rockville, MD: Department of Health and Human Services.

Zucker, R. A., Fitzgerald, H. E., & Moses, H. D. (1995). Emergence of alcohol problems and the several alcoholisms: A developmental perspective on etiologic theory and life course trajectory. In D. Cicchetti & D. J. Cohen (Eds.), *Developmental psychopathology: Vol. 2. Risk, disorder, and adaptation. Wiley*

*series on personality processes* (pp. 677–711). New York: Wiley.

Zucker, R. A., & Gomberg, E. S. L. (1986). Etiology of alcoholism reconsidered: The case for a biopsychosocial process. *American Psychologist, 41,* 783.

Zuckerman, M. (1991). *Psychobiology of personality.* New York: Cambridge University Press.

Zuckerman, M. (1994). *Behavioral expressions and biosocial bases of sensation seeking.* New York: Cambridge University Press.

Zuckerman, M. (1999). *Vulnerability to psychopathology: A biosocial model.* Washington, DC: American Psychological Association.

Zuckerman, M., & Kuhlman, D. M. (2000). Personality and risk-taking: Common biosocial factors. *Journal of Personality, 68,* 999–1029.

CHAPTER 9

# Stress Disorders

ETZEL CARDEÑA, LISA D. BUTLER, AND DAVID SPIEGEL

*We are healed of a suffering only by experiencing it to the full.*

MARCEL PROUST (1871–1922)

In this chapter we review the concepts of stress and trauma and describe conditions within the American Psychiatric Association's (APA) *Diagnostic and Statistical Manual of Mental Disorders–Fourth Edition* (*DSM-IV;* APA, 1994, 2000) that include trauma as an etiological criterion (i.e., acute stress disorder and posttraumatic stress disorder or PTSD), as well as disorders strongly associated with extreme stress and trauma—namely, the dissociative and conversion disorders. Although they are not covered in this chapter, depression, anxiety, substance abuse, and adjustment disorders can also occur as responses to traumatic stress.

## STRESS AND TRAUMA

Stress is usually defined as the product of circumstance that threatens the homeostasis of the organism and requires adjustment to reestablish homeostasis or develop a new cognitive and emotional organization to accommodate the challenging experience or irretrievable loss. Hans Selye (1976) developed a theory of stress, which he considered a syndrome of "nonspecifically-induced changes within a biological system" (p. 64). However, for the purpose of this chapter, the definition of stress by Mason (1971) as a reaction to threatening or unpleasant factors is more appropriate. Selye discussed both psychological and physiological factors

and described negative (distress) and positive (eustress) types of stress responses. His work implicated the autonomic nervous system in the stress response, but it had little in the way of cognitive components to it. The stress response was understood to be—in essence—a cortical reflex to stress. Subsequent theories have taken cognitive appraisal of the nature of a stressor into greater account. This later work was facilitated through the development of life event inventories—such as the Holmes-Rahe inventory (Rahe, Meyer, Smith, Kjaer, & Holmes, 1964), which attempted to quantify life stressors and which are being improved by newer approaches (Carson, Butcher, & Mineka, 2000).

Stimuli and circumstances that produce stress are called *stressors,* and there have been various categorizations of them, including that of frustrations, conflicts, and pressures (Carson et al., 2000). Although there is no absolute demarcation, extreme stressors would include severely intense or chronic frustrations, conflicts, or pressures of any kind, whereas traumatic events can be defined in a more circumscribed way. We consider trauma as an event caused by humans or nature that reduces the individual to an object and challenges deeply held assumptions of safety, fairness, ability to control events, and predictability. The discontinuity of circumstances in trauma contributes to a discontinuity of cognitive, emotional, and somatic experience among the persons who experience it. The 1987 edition of the *Diagnostic and Statistical Manual of Mental Disorders–Third Edition–Revised* (*DSM-III-R;* APA, 1987) defined traumas as events outside of the range of typical normal experience, but epidemiological studies have shown that the majority of individuals—even inhabitants of countries not at war—have witnessed or experienced some form of trauma during their lifetime. An example is the study by Norris (1992) in which 69% of respondents had reported at least one traumatic incident during their lifetime.

Partly to correct the false notion that trauma is an uncommon event, the *DSM-IV* (APA, 1994, 2000) redefined it as experiencing or witnessing events that involve actual or threatened death or injury or jeopardize the physical integrity of self or others. Furthermore, it is required that the individual's response include intense fear, helplessness, or horror—or agitated or disorganized behavior in children. There are problems with this conceptualization. The first criterion limits trauma to actual or threat of violence and death, but other factors such as property loss and serious medical or psychological disorder can bring about PTSD (McFarlane & de Girolamo, 1996). The second criterion, although it seeks to address the importance of the subjective response, was partly designed for forensic rather than scientific reasons (McFarlane & de Girolano, 1996) and disregards the possibility that an individual may respond initially with numbing and dissociation rather than with intense emotion (Lindemann, 1944; Spiegel & Cardeña, 1991).

Bearing in mind both the limitations of the current *DSM-IV* definition of trauma and the fact that the posttraumatic response always involves an interaction between the characteristics of the stressor and those of the experiencing individual, we examine now salient dimensions of trauma. Traumatic events vary with regard to their source (e.g., natural vs. human-made victimization), nature (e.g., sexual abuse vs. physical abuse), chronicity (e.g., being a prisoner of war or POW for a week vs. being a POW for months or years), severity (e.g., being exposed to combat without casualties vs. a combat with multiple casualties), extent of areas affected (e.g., an earthquake that affects only the self or personal property vs. one that produces disruptions in food supplies, transportation, and other resources), type of exposure (e.g., witnessing an accident vs. personal experience of the grotesque or handling of dead bodies), relationship to perpetrator (e.g., a stranger vs. a parental figure committing sexual abuse), and so on. Although the data are not unequivocal, it has been generally observed that traumatic events with a greater negative impact are instigated by humans, are chronic and severe, affect various living functions and the social network, and involve sexual rather than just physical abuse—especially abuse of an incestuous nature (Dancu, Riggs, Hearst-Ikeda, Shoyer, & Foa, 1996; Freyd, DePrince, & Zurbriggen, 2001; Labbate, Cardeña, Dimitreva, Roy, & Engel, 1998; van der Kolk, McFarlane, & Weisaeth, 1996). Green (1993) has categorized trauma of a violent nature according to eight dimensions: threat to life and limb, severity of

physical harm, receiving intentional injury or harm, exposure to the grotesque, violent or sudden loss of a loved one, witnessing or learning of violence to a loved one, learning of exposure to noxious agent, and causing death or severe harm to another.

Individual psychological differences are at least as important as the characteristics of the stressor. Whereas some severe and chronic traumas such as chronic maltreatment as a POW can produce lifetime or current PTSD prevalences as high as 85% and 59%, respectively (Engdahl, Dikel, Eberly, & Blank, 1997; Ursano & Rundell, 1995), there are marked differences in the effect of less severe stressors (Yehuda & McFarlane, 1995). In a recent and important meta-analysis on predictors of PTSD, Brewin, Andrews, and Valentine (2000) found that previous psychiatric history, childhood abuse, family psychiatric history, low socioeconomic status (SES), lack of education, low levels of intelligence, other previous trauma or adverse childhood factors, trauma severity, lack of social support, and life stress were consistent or homogeneous predictors, whereas being a woman, younger, and of minority status seemed to be significant predictors only in some populations.

After extreme stress or trauma has occurred, there is a wide range of possible and sometimes overlapping reactions. Some traumatic events only have a transient effect, whereas others have life-transforming consequences—both positive and negative. Besides the dysfunctional responses that are described in later sections of this chapter, many individuals report positive changes as a result of the struggle with a traumatic event (Calhoun & Tedeschi, 2000). These changes include greater investment in and appreciation of life, interpersonal relationships, spirituality, personal resources, and an immediate or delayed increase in the sense of mastery to deal with difficult situations (Fullerton & Ursano, 1997; Tedeschi & Calhoun, 1995). Such benefits have been found among various populations, including survivors of cancer (e.g., Taylor, 2000), bereavement (Bower, Kemeny, Taylor, & Fahey, 1998), disaster (McMillen, Smith, & Fisher, 1997), combat (Fontana & Rosenheck, 1998), war captivity (Sledge, Boydstun, & Rabe, 1980), and severe accidents (Brickman, Coates, & Janoff-Bulman, 1978). Women tend to report more benefits from traumatic experiences than do men (Cordova, Cunninghman, Carlson, & Andrykowski, 2001).

The majority of people react to most time-limited traumas such as a disaster with transient mild to moderate symptoms (e.g., Cardeña & Spiegel, 1993), but particularly violent events such as rape may have a greater impact (e.g., Dancu et al., 1996; Engdahl et al., 1997). An important area of investigation is the impact of early responses to trauma on current and chronic dysfunction. The scant and not fully consistent data suggest that severe dissociation may jeopardize survival at the time of the stressor (Koopman, Classen, & Spiegel, 1994, 1996), despite its overall possible species survival value (Nijenhuis, 2000). The *DSM-IV* diagnosis of acute stress disorder (ASD; APA, 1994, 2000) has triggered a growing number of studies of dysfunctional reactions around the time of trauma (i.e., peritraumatic) and their potential to develop into chronic severe psychopathology.

The vast majority of clinical and research attention has focused on severe chronic or delayed-onset symptoms (mostly under the rubric of PTSD). In the sections that follow, we give an overview of ASD, PTSD, and complex PTSD, a proposed variant of PTSD that encompasses broader posttraumatic responses than does simple PTSD, including dysfunctions in areas such as personality structure, identity, and relational abilities. After reviewing these posttraumatic disorders, (ASD and PTSD are included in the anxiety disorders section of the *DSM-IV*), we cover the literature on dissociative and conversion disorders (currently classified elsewhere in the *DSM-IV* nosology).

## ACUTE STRESS DISORDER

The main reasons to include acute stress disorder (ASD) in the *DSM-IV* were the lack of a diagnosis for acute and dysfunctional reactions within the first month after trauma, the partial disregard of dissociative symptomatology in the concept and criteria of PTSD, and a greater convergence with the International Classification of Diseases (ICD) classification of *acute stress reaction* (Cardeña, Lewis-Fernández, Beahr, Pakianathan, & Spiegel, 1996). The original proposal of *brief reactive dissociative disorder* (Spiegel & Cardeña, 1991) underwent a number of transformations and compromises until it emerged as the current *acute stress disorder* diagnosis. Its final criteria include exposure to direct or witnessed trauma involving intense negative emotions; at least three dissociative symptoms (e.g., numbing, depersonalization, derealization, being in a daze, and amnesia); reexperiencing or intrusion of the traumatic event (one symptom required); marked avoidance of stimuli related to trauma (one symptom required); marked anxiety or hyperarousal (one symptom required); clinically significant distress or impairment for a minimum of 2 days and a maximum of 4 weeks; and the absence of a direct cause by a psychoactive substance or a general medical condition (APA, 1994, 2000).

Critics of the ASD criteria point out some problems, including the mismatch of ASD and PTSD symptoms (even though the *DSM-IV* considers that the former, if continuing past 1 month, can be rediagnosed as PTSD), the question of the extent to which dissociative symptoms are as central to

the diagnosis as the other criteria are, and the need for greater refinement in diagnostic criteria (e.g., Bryant & Harvey, 1997). A more severe critique of the validity of ASD and of the importance of peritraumatic dissociation as a predictor of PTSD (Marshall, Spitzer, & Leibowitz, 1999) has called for greater accuracy in the diagnosis of acute stress responses, but this critique also seems to have misinterpreted data on the predictive value of peritraumatic dissociative responses (Butler, 2000; Simeon & Guralnik, 2000; Spiegel, Classen, & Cardeña, 2000). The conceptualization of both PTSD and ASD and the nature of their relationship clearly need further elucidation.

The relationship between traumatic stressors and dissociative reactions is quite robust. The current conception of this relationship is based on observations by clinical pioneers such as Breuer and Freud, Charcot, James, Janet, and others (van der Kolk, Weisaeth, & van der Hart, 1996), on extensive literature reviews (Butler, Duran, Jasiukaitis, Koopman, & Spiegel, 1996; Spiegel & Cardeña, 1991), and on international data reanalyses (Cardeña et al., 1998) of reactions to traumatic events that support a strong association between traumatic events and disssociative reactions. Prospective studies assessing dissociation shortly after an earthquake (Cardeña & Spiegel, 1993) and before and after acute stress during military training (Morgan, Hazlett, Richardson, Schnurr, & Southwick, 2001) also challenge the skepticism about a robust trauma-dissociation relationship (Merckelbach & Muris, 2001).

In addition to the commonly reported alterations in memory, perception, and a sense of detachment associated with exposure to human-made or natural trauma (Spiegel & Cardeña, 1991), dissociation and PTSD subscales have a high correlation (Gold & Cardeña, 1998), and more patients with posttraumatic disorders manifest state and trait dissociative symptomatology (e.g., Cardeña, 1998; Hyer, Albrecht, Poudewyns, Woods, & Brandsma, 1993) and show higher hypnotizability than do most other clinical and nonclinical groups (Spiegel, Hunt, & Dondershine, 1988).

The most important finding seems to be that acute dissociative reactions are significant, strong, and independent predictors of long-term psychopathology. Retrospective studies reporting a substantially higher dissociation around the time of trauma for PTSD patients compared with other groups include Vietnam (Bremner et al., 1992) and Gulf War (Cardeña, 1998) veterans, individuals exposed to typhoons (Staab, Grieger, Fullerton, & Ursano, 1996) and emergency rescue workers (Grieger et al., 2000). Prospective studies show similar findings, including numbing as the single best predictor of later PTSD among Israeli soldiers (Cardeña et al., 1998) and dissociative symptoms as significant predictors of later PTSD symptomatology among victims of a firestorm (Koopman et al., 1994, 1996); bystanders of a mass shooting (Classen, Koopman, Hales, & Spiegel, 1998); individuals with mild traumatic brain injury (Bryant & Harvey, 1998); survivors of disastrous flooding (Waelde, Koopman, Rierdan, & Spiegel, 2001); and victims of motor vehicle accidents, other accidents, or terrorist attacks (Brewin, Andrews, Rose, & Kirk, 1999; Ehlers, Mayou, & Bryant, 1998; Harvey & Bryant, 1998; Shalev, Peri, Canetti, & Schreiber, 1996). Although there is a dearth of research with children, Saxe and collaborators (Saxe, 2002) have reported that among child burn patients, dissociation as evaluated by adults was a significant predictor of later PTSD symptomatology.

Some studies that have not replicated these findings have methodological problems, including a lack of specific measures to evaluate ASD (Barton, Blanchard, & Hickling, 1996) or low statistical power and a measurement time frame inconsistent with ASD criteria (McFarlane, Atchison, & Yehuda, 1997). Nevertheless, a number of issues about ASD require more investigation, including criteria that might optimize diagnostic sensitivity and specificity of dissociative and other ASD symptoms (Brewin et al., 1999), the biology of peritraumatic dissociation (Griffin, Resick, & Mechanic, 1997), and risk predictors for peritraumatic dissociation (Morgan et al., 2001). Valid and reliable instruments to help this inquiry have been developed (Bryant & Harvey, 1997; Cardeña, Koopman, Classen, Waelder, & Spiegel, 2000). It will be useful to evaluate peritraumatic biological indicators as well, because there is evidence that increased heart rate and lower cortisol levels at that time may predict later PTSD (Yehuda, McFarlane, & Shalev, 1998).

Some evidence indicates that compared with men, women experience—or at least report—greater peritraumatic dissociation. In a reanalysis of our earlier study on professional students exposed to an earthquake (Cardeña & Spiegel, 1993), we found that about 2 weeks after the incident, women reported significantly greater time distortion, derealization, and depersonalization reactions than did men ($df = 95$, $p < .001$), but this difference disappeared 4 months after the incident ($p > .1$). A gender difference was also found in a general sample exposed to a firestorm (Koopman et al., 1996). There is also some evidence that younger people experience or report more peritraumatic dissociation (Marmar, Weiss, Metzler, & Delucchi, 1996). Recently, Koopman and collaborators (2001) reported that minority Vietnam veterans with PTSD reported more peritraumatic dissociation than did nonminority veterans, but that study did not control for SES. Zatzick, Marmar, Weiss, and Metzler (1994) controlled for that factor and found no independent contribution of ethnicity. Marshall and Orlando (2002), in a study on victims of community violence, found

evidence that degree of acculturation in their minority Latino sample was negatively correlated to peritraumatic dissociation.

## POSTTRAUMATIC STRESS DISORDER

### History

Although posttraumatic pathology has been described for centuries, it was not until the twentieth century that systematic research and theory started in earnest. Some earlier antecedents of the PTSD construct include so-called traumatic neurosis, soldier's heart, and shell shock (van der Kolk, Weisaeth, et al., 1996). Some of the great clinical pioneers—Charcot, Janet, and Freud among them—wrote on posttraumatic conditions, and the psychiatrist Stierlin concluded in the early part of the twentieth century that posttraumatic reactions (fright neurosis) were not rare and did not require a psychopathological predisposition (van der Kolk, Weisaeth, et al., 1996). World War I brought forth important theoretical and clinical work by Charles Myers and W. H. Rivers in Great Britain; this work continued being developed during World War II by Kardiner, Grinker and Spiegel, and other eminent figures. At about the same time, Lindemann (1944), in his classic paper on the symptomatology and management of acute grief, documented the fundamental categories of PTSD symptoms—intrusion, avoidance, and hyperarousal—that form the basis of the diagnostic criteria today (APA, 1994). He noted that the severe disruption that followed trauma, with physical agitation, emotional distress, and disturbed patterns of sleep, seemed to be a necessary processing of loss—a kind of grief work that prepared the traumatized individual to reenter life and relationships. Later, Horowitz (1986) noted the importance of affective dysregulation in the posttraumatic period. Related symptoms were either undermodulated, as with intrusion and hyperarousal symptoms, or overmodulated, as with avoidance symptoms, and both could occur in sequence in the same person.

### Symptomatology

The *DSM-IV* (APA, 1994, 2000) diagnostic criteria for PTSD include—in addition to exposure to the criterion stressor criteria discussed previously—at least *one* intrusion, *three* numbing, and *two* hyperarousal symptoms. The intrusion symptoms include recurrent and intrusive distressing recollections of the traumatic event, dreams or nightmares about the event, reliving the experience, flashback episodes, illusions or hallucinations (related to the event), intense distress at exposure to cues that represent an aspect of the traumatic event, and physiological reactivity on exposure to cues concerning the event (APA, 1994, 2000). The numbing-avoidance symptoms include efforts to avoid thoughts, feelings, or conversations associated with the trauma, efforts to avoid activities, places, or people that arouse recollections of the trauma, inability to recall an important aspect of the trauma, markedly diminished interest or participation in significant activities, feelings of detachment or estrangement from others, restricted range of affect (e.g., inability to have loving feelings), and sense of a foreshortened future (APA, 1994, 2000). The hyperarousal symptoms include difficulty falling or staying asleep, irritability or outbursts of anger, difficulty concentrating, hypervigilance, and exaggerated startle response (APA, 1994, 2000). The disorder must also last at least 1 month. It is considered acute if it lasts less than 3 months and chronic if it lasts more than 3 months. It must cause significant distress or impairment in social, occupational, or other important areas of functioning.

Those with PTSD often have other comorbid psychiatric symptoms and disorders, such as social anxiety (e.g., Crowson, Frueh, Beidel, & Turner, 1998), other anxiety and mood disorders (e.g., Breslau & Davis, 1992), suicide attempts (e.g., Davidson, Hughes, Blazer, & George, 1991), dissociative symptoms (Yehuda et al., 1996), substance abuse (e.g., Cottler, Compton, Mager, Spitznagel, & Janca, 1992; Kessler, Sonnega, Bromet, Hughes, & Nelson, 1995), and personality disorders (e.g., Southwick, Yehuda, & Giller, 1993).

## Etiology

Ideas about the etiology of PTSD have fluctuated between an emphasis on the nature of the stressed person and the nature of the stressor. In the middle of the twentieth century, psychiatry in the United States came under the increasing domination of psychoanalytic theory. Freud had postulated that combat neurosis was a variation of other neuroses arising from unresolved dynamic conflicts based on problems in psychosexual development (Freud, Ferenczi, Abraham, Caligor, & Jones, 1921). His theory held that early life difficulties in development determined psychopathology more than did the combat trauma itself. This perspective led to attempts to link combat trauma to what are now called personality disorders (Henderson & Moore, 1944). Freud developed his metapsychology (Freud, 1916–1917/1963) after he abandoned the trauma theory of the etiology of the neuroses. He formulated symptoms as expressions of dynamic unconscious conflict between incestuous libidinal wishes and harsh superego strictures against such wishes. The linking of personality disorders to posttraumatic symptomatology had the disadvantage of scapegoating emotional casualties of combat—in essence, blaming the victims rather than the combat trauma for the disorder.

There is a fundamental conflict between the psychodynamic and the PTSD models. Preoccupation with early childhood development and the world of the unconscious tends to minimize the importance of the role of trauma and the intrusion of reality later in life—that is, unconscious language tends to be extreme and dramatic, blurring the distinction between fantasy and reality. Initially, one of the reasons that the diagnosis of PTSD was overlooked or minimized was a prevailing assumption that the diathesis was more important than the stress—that people who developed symptoms after trauma such as combat had serious psychiatric problems, especially personality disorders, prior to the trauma that accounted for the response to it. From this point of view, the trauma was merely a trigger for an exacerbation of symptoms of a preexisting disorder.

Reaction to this viewpoint spawned several decades of research with the opposite point of view—that is, that PTSD developed in a minority of normal individuals who were subjected to serious physical stress independent of their personality or early life experience. A study of World War II veterans found that only a quarter of acute psychiatric casualties of combat had a preexisting psychiatric diagnosis (Torrie, 1944), and some later studies posited no relationship between prior psychopathology and PTSD (e.g., Ursano, 1981).

More recently, however, the pendulum has begun to swing a bit back to the earlier position. Several studies indicate that a history of previous PTSD due to earlier life trauma does sensitize individuals to the reoccurrence of PTSD when they endure subsequent trauma (Brewin et al., 2000). These individuals may be asymptomatic prior to the trauma, but they seem to retain a vulnerability that may elicit memories and symptoms related to earlier life trauma. For example, Baider and colleagues (Baider, Peretz, & Kaplan De-Nour, 1992) observed that Holocaust survivors who develop cancer often experience a recrudescence of their long-dormant posttraumatic stress symptoms.

Even though early life trauma may predispose individuals to the development of PTSD in the wake of subsequent trauma, this phenomenon does not reduce the salience of the stress itself in the production of PTSD symptoms (Figley, 1978; Spiegel et al., 1988). There is growing evidence that exposure to traumatic stressors is almost the norm rather than the exception. In one study of 1,007 young adults from an HMO practice in Detroit, Breslau and collaborators (Breslau, Davis, Andreski, & Peterson, 1991) found a high lifetime prevalence of exposure to traumatic events of

39.1%. The rate of PTSD among those exposed was 23.6%, yielding a lifetime prevalence of PTSD in this sample of 9.2%. Those with PTSD also suffered increased risk for anxiety and mood disorders. A similar prevalence rate of combat-related PTSD (Keane & Fairbank, 1983) provides compelling evidence that trauma exposure frequently leads to PTSD. However, such data leave open the question of what differentiates those who were symptomatic from the three out of four who are exposed but did *not* develop PTSD symptoms. A comprehensive meta-analysis of risk factors (Brewin et al., 2000) concluded that pretrauma factors have a consistent but weak relationship to subsequent PTSD, whereas such posttrauma factors as lack of social support may have a higher impact.

Sensitization theory (Silver & Wortman, 1980) holds that prior exposure to trauma takes a toll on an individual's resources for coping with subsequent trauma. This can occur by a reactivation of memories of prior trauma during exposure to subsequent trauma, adding to its burden. Indeed, it has been commonly observed in Vietnam veterans that even comparatively mild subsequent stressors, such as a minor auto accident, can elicit major traumatic responses (Spiegel, 1981), especially in those with previous significant trauma exposure (Breslau, Chilcoat, Kessler, & Davis, 1999). Even the unexposed offspring of Holocaust survivors show physiological and psychological signs of PTSD sensitization (Yehuda, Halligan, & Bierer, 2001).

There is also fascinating recent evidence of permanent hypothalamic-pituitary-adrenal (HPA) dysregulation in adults who suffered sexual and physical abuse as children and have symptoms of depression and PTSD (Heim et al., 2000). A vast number of psychobiological abnormalities involving psychophysiology, neurohormonal systems, and neuroanatomical and immunological effects have been related to PTSD (van der Kolk, 1996). One of the areas that has received more attention is hippocampal atrophy among individuals with PTSD. Various studies have found decreased dendritic branching and smaller hippocampal volume among these individuals, although not every study has replicated these results (Bremner, 2002).

Another compelling theory is that certain personality characteristics such as neuroticism and extroversion predispose some to trauma exposure and therefore to a higher prevalence of PTSD (Breslau, Davis, & Andreski, 1995). Secondary losses and gains subsequent to trauma may either reinforce or diminish the odds that a transient symptom picture will become chronic. We now turn our attention to a proposed and severe variant of PTSD that is spawning a wealth of research, clinical observations, and treatment strategies.

# COMPLEX PTSD

## Concept

Historically, PTSD has been defined as a syndromic response to a specific delimited traumatic event (APA, 1994), with the symptom constellation and comorbidity mentioned previously. However, in 1992, Judith Herman proposed that the traditional diagnostic categories neither suited nor captured the features associated with conditions of extreme and protracted traumatic stress, such as some cases of childhood sexual and physical abuse, prolonged persecution or captivity as a hostage or POW, or chronic domestic battery. Herman (1992a) noted that there were three broad areas of disturbance among such patients: the complexity and tenacity of their symptom profiles, the event-related characterological changes they undergo that undermine their experience of relatedness and identity, and their vulnerability to repeated self- or other-inflicted harm. Conventional diagnostic groupings, including PTSD symptom criteria, either simply overlooked these aspects or fitted such clinical presentations into traditional categories. Thus, Herman (1992a, 1992b) proposed a new diagnostic category, complex PTSD, noting that "responses to trauma are best understood as a spectrum of conditions rather than a single disorder. They range from a brief stress reaction that gets better by itself and never qualifies for a diagnosis, to classic or simple post-traumatic stress disorder, to the complex syndrome of prolonged, repeated trauma" (Herman, 1992b, p. 119).

Herman's proposal addressed observations made and issues raised by earlier commentators, including clinical reflections that the simple PTSD concept was inadequate to describe or account for the severity and multiplicity of effects seen in Holocaust survivors or refugees (Kroll et al., 1989; Niederland, 1968). Additionally, Terr (1991) had observed that childhood traumatic stressor events came in two types: "single-blow" traumas (Type I; p. 14) and traumas that result from "long-standing or repeated ordeals" (Type II; p. 11) and that each was associated with a different constellation of emotional, cognitive, and behavioral symptoms. Similarly, in reviewing the long-term effects of childhood sexual abuse, Finkelhor (1988) argued that PTSD was not the appropriate diagnostic label for these outcomes because it did not capture the functional impairment and other abuse-specific symptomatology present in the condition.

## Diagnosis

The diagnosis of complex PTSD (also known within the literature as a *disorder of extreme stress not otherwise specified;* DESNOS) that Herman (1992b) proposed required that the individual must have suffered a *history of subjection to totalitarian control over a prolonged period.* Additionally, it included diagnostic symptomatic and characterological features not addressed in the classic PTSD diagnosis:

- *Alterations in affect regulation,* including persistent dysphoria, suicidal preoccupation, self-injury, under- or over-regulated anger, and compulsive or inhibited sexuality.

- *Alterations in consciousness,* including memory disturbances, transient dissociative experiences, depersonalization-derealization, and reliving experiences.

- *Alterations in self-perception,* including feelings of helplessness; paralysis of initiative; defilement; stigma; difference from others; and shame, guilt, and self-blame.

- *Alterations in perception of the perpetrator,* including preoccupation with the relationship, idealization or paradoxical gratitude, a sense of a special or supernatural relationship, unrealistic attribution of total power to perpetrator, and acceptance of the belief system or rationalizations of the perpetrator.

- *Alterations in relations with others,* including isolation and withdrawal, disruption of romantic relationships, distrust, repeated failures of self-protection, and repeated search for a rescuer.

- *Alterations in systems of meaning,* which may manifest as a loss of sustaining faith, a sense of hopelessness and despair, or both.

- *Disturbances in somatic functioning,* such as somatization symptoms, a central feature of this disorder often not included in measures of complex PTSD and DESNOS (Herman, 1992a; Pelcovitz et al., 1997; Roth, Newman, Pelcovitz, van der Kolk, & Mandel, 1997; van der Kolk, 1996).

Empirical support for this new diagnosis has come from a number of studies. Zlotnick and colleagues (1996) found that women with a history of childhood sexual abuse showed increased severity of symptoms of somatization, dissociation, hostility, anxiety, alexithymia, social dysfunction, maladaptive schemas, self-destruction, and adult victimization when compared to women without such histories. van der Kolk, Pelcovitz, and colleagues (1996) found that participants in the *DSM-IV* field trial for PTSD who had experienced physical or sexual assaults in childhood (before age 14) were significantly more likely than were participants who had experienced a disaster at some time in their lives to report difficulties with all three of the following DESNOS symptom areas: affect regulation, dissociation, and somatization; they

were also more likely to endorse various individual DESNOS-related items.

There is also evidence that a DESNOS diagnosis has different treatment implications. Ford (1999) found that the DESNOS (but not the PTSD) classification was associated with early childhood trauma, extreme levels of reexperiencing, impaired characterological functioning, and use of intensive psychiatric services in military veterans seeking inpatient PTSD treatment (see also Newman, Orsillo, Herman, Niles, & Litz, 1995). Ford and Kidd (1998) reported that a DESNOS diagnosis predicted poor PTSD treatment outcome independent of the effects of a PTSD diagnosis or early childhood trauma history, indicating that the presence of DESNOS should be assessed and considered in planning treatment for those with chronic PTSD. Ford (1999) concluded that although PTSD and DESNOS are often comorbid, they are distinct syndromes.

The *DSM-IV* PTSD field trial (Pelcovitz et al., 1997; Roth et al., 1997; van der Kolk, Pelcovitz, et al., 1996) also sought to evaluate the feasibility and utility of the complex PTSD and DESNOS categorization. Preliminary findings from a study of 234 participants with a history of sexual abuse, physical abuse, or both (Roth et al., 1997) found that for women, sexual abuse—particularly in combination with physical abuse—was a risk factor for complex PTSD (see also Hall, 1999). Patients with a history of both sexual and physical abuse were 14.5 times more likely to warrant a complex PTSD diagnosis than were patients who had not experienced both types of abuse. In addition, preliminary findings in the trials indicated that complex PTSD was rarely found among non-trauma-exposed survivors (those who did not meet the stressor criterion for PTSD) and rarely occurred without concurrent PTSD. In the same field trials, a useful, psychometrically sound, structured interview for disorders of extreme stress was developed (Pelcovitz et al., 1997).

Although Herman's (1992a, 1992b) classification was not included in *DSM-IV* (APA, 1994), 9 of 12 of the associated features listed for PTSD are derived from her formulation (Roth et al., 1996). Additionally, the *International Classification of Diseases–10th Revision* (*ICD-10;* World Health Organization), published in 1992, included a similar disorder named *enduring personality change after catastrophic experience.* Commenting on the inclusion of this disorder, Kinzie and Goetz (1996) observed, "the absence of a similar disorder in the *DSM-IV* is puzzling" (p. 173). Given the growing evidence supporting the plurality of traumatic stress responses and the demonstrated utility of assessing complex PTSD or DESNOS in some traumatized samples, it seems likely that complex PTSD will be incorporated into future American psychiatric nosologies; it is already informing clinicians who treat patients with histories of extreme, repeated trauma.

## DISSOCIATIVE AND CONVERSION DISORDERS

What are now called the dissociative and conversion disorders in *DSM-IV* would map quite directly onto the hysterical symptoms that were a central concern of the clinical pioneers in France, Austria, and the United States at the end of the nineteenth century (Spiegel & Cardeña, 1991). Nonetheless, the investigation of pathological (or normal) alterations of consciousness and their relationship to somatic functioning were neglected during later decades and have just recently gained preeminence among many clinicians and researchers (Cardeña, 1997a; Hilgard, 1994). This interest, however, has not gone unchallenged; some critics have questioned the validity of dissociative amnesia and dissociative identity disorder (DID). We discuss these controversies later in this chapter.

Our review emphasizes dissociative disorders among adults, although there is a small but growing literature on children and adolescents (e.g., Putnam, 1994) going back at least to the eighteenth century. Because the term *dissociation* is used to signify different areas of inquiry in psychology and other disciplines, it is worthwhile to establish some distinctions at the beginning. In cognitive psychology, general dissociation implies differential performance in apparently related cognitive tasks such as comprehension of nouns and adjectives. For our purposes in clinical and personality psychology, the term *dissociation* has three main senses (Cardeña, 1994):

1. It is a descriptive construct for a lack of association between psychological processes that should be integrated and cannot be explained merely by overlearning or inattention (e.g., *he cannot recall his name even though there is no neurological damage that can explain this amnesia*).

2. It is a descriptive construct for an alteration of consciousness characterized by experiential detachment from the self or the environment (e.g., *I felt that my body was moving on its own*).

3. It is an explanatory construct denoting an intentional defense mechanism (e.g., *she dissociated her body sensation to tolerate the rape while it was occurring;* see Nemiah, 1995).

Other distinctions can also be made. Dissociative *phenomena* are not necessarily pathological and can occur in benign contexts such as hypnosis, meditation, or religious rituals (Cardeña, 1997b). Distressing or dysfunctional dissociative *symptoms* can be secondary symptoms of neurological (e.g.,

seizure disorder) or psychiatric conditions (e.g., panic attacks), whereas dissociative *disorders,* which we cover in this chapter, involve dissociative symptoms as the main presenting problem and have a mainly psychological rather than neurological etiology.

Dissociation can occur in every major psychological process, including the sense of self, sense of the environment, or both (e.g., depersonalization, derealization); emotions (e.g., disconnection between emotional behaviors and awareness of them); physical sensations and agency (e.g., conversion disorders); memory (e.g., psychogenic or dissociative amnesia); and identity (e.g., DID; Butler et al., 1996; Cardeña, 1997b). One final distinction, first made by Pierre Janet, distinguishes positive symptoms (exaggerations or additions to normal processes such as the flashbacks in PTSD) and negative symptoms (diminution of normal processes, such as lack of memory for one's name; Janet, 1907/1965). The *DSM-IV* defines a *dissociative disorder* as a "disruption in the usually integrated functions of consciousness, memory, identity, or perception of the environment" (APA, 1994, p. 477) that is distressing, impairs basic areas of functioning, or both.

*Repression* and *dissociation* have often been used interchangeably to explain the same manifestations (e.g., the inability to remember a traumatic event), with some authors defining repression as a defense mechanism to ward off internal pressures and dissociation as an alteration in consciousness to deflect the overwhelming impact of ongoing trauma. The first term is readily identifiable with Sigmund Freud, whereas dissociation is closely linked to the work of Pierre Janet. In the view of Janet, as elaborated by Hilgard, dissociation refers to a different model of mental structure in which information is stored in units that are separate from but relatively accessible to consciousness, unlike the traditional psychodynamic repression model that views the contents of the unconscious as disguised and in need of translation (Hilgard, 1994). Notwithstanding these perspectives, *dissociation* can be used to describe the lack of integration among psychological processes such as memory or identity or to refer to an experienced disconnection with the self or the environment, without necessarily having to endorse either Janet's or Freud's position.

### Etiology

The *DSM-IV,* following decades of clinical observations and studies, asserts that the dissociative disorders are commonly linked to severe stress (e.g., serious emotional conflict) and traumatic events (e.g., early abuse, especially if the events are chronic and severe; e.g., Terr, 1991). Nonetheless, they do not constitute a sufficient cause; otherwise, every seriously traumatized individual would end up having a dissociative disorder, which is clearly not the case. It should also be noted that, for instance, a home where abuse occurs is also one where neglect and chaos can be expected (Widom, 1999), so it is difficult to disentangle traumatic events from related circumstances. Nonetheless, there is new and strong evidence, based on an extensive twin study, that reported childhood sexual abuse has various deleterious consequences, even after controlling for family background (Nelson et al., 2002). Proposed diatheses for development of dissociative disorders include an inborn disposition to dissociate (Jang, Paris, Zweig-Frank, & Livesley, 1998; but see Waller & Ross, 1997) or to be highly hypnotizable (Butler et al., 1996). More recently, a growing database has been providing compelling evidence that specific forms of early attachment (especially avoidant and disorganized) are strong predictors of pathological dissociation (e.g., Ogawa, Sroufe, Weinfield, Carlson, & Egeland, 1997).

The account of dissociative symptoms and disorders originating—at least in part—in actual experiences of trauma (or traumatogenic theory) has been challenged by skeptics of the validity of dissociative amnesia and DID. This latter account posits that these disorders are brought about by the shaping and reinforcement of symptoms by therapists (the iatrogenic theory) or the culture (the sociocognitive theory). We address these proposals in the sections for amnesia and dissociative identity disorders.

**Epidemiology and Demographics**

Regrettably, major nationwide epidemiological surveys have not systematically evaluated the prevalence of the dissociative disorders, probably following the conclusion by Mezzich, Fabrega, Coffman, and Haley (1989) that such disorders are rare even in a psychiatric population; however, more recent studies with community and clinical samples show that this is not the case. Gleaves (1996) reviewed studies on the prevalence of dissociative disorders among various clinical populations, which ranged between 10% (clients with obsessive-compulsive anxiety disorder) and 88% (women reporting sexual abuse). Studies in countries other than the United States have also found significant rates of dissociative disorders, including 10% in a Turkish university clinic (Tutkun, Sar, Yargic, Ozpulat, Yanik, & Kiziltan, 1998), and 8% in a Dutch clinical sample (Friedl & Draijer, 2000). Ross (1991) sampled a nonclinical Canadian population (*n* = 454) and found that 11% seemed to have a dissociative disorder of some type, although this latter figure may be an inflated estimate of the actual prevalence in a nonclinical population, at least using *DSM-IV* criteria.

With respect to age, various studies in the United States and Europe (Vanderlinden, van der Hart, & Varga, 1996) suggest that dissociation reaches its peak somewhere in early adolescence and then gradually declines in a manner similar to that of hypnotizability (Hilgard, 1968).

Moving to the impact of SES on the prevalence of dissociative phenomena, a study with a Canadian community sample found no significant relationship (Ross, 1991; see also Vanderlinden et al., 1996). With respect to peritraumatic dissociation, one study (Koopman et al., 2001) found a significant effect for ethnicity; however, in another study that controlled for SES, the difference disappeared (Zatzick et al., 1994). With respect to the culture-bound syndromes with a dissociative component, both pathological spirit possession and *ataque de nervios* are predominantly found among women of lower SES, whereas *amok, berserk* and similar assault conditions are mostly found among men (Lewis-Fernández, 1994; Simons & Hughes, 1985).

Other than those for DID, wherein the vast majority of identified clients are female, findings do not appear to be consistent as to the gender distribution of other dissociative disorders (e.g., Varnderlinden et al., 1996). Nonetheless, Kluft (1996) cautions that the reported ratio of about 9:1 female to male DID patients may be skewed because some males with DID end up in the legal system and are not assessed in epidemiological studies (see also Lewis, Yeager, Swica, Pincus, & Lewis, 1997). Although it has not been studied systematically, there are reports that DID patients seem to come from middle- to low-SES groups (Barach, personal communication, 1996; Coons, 1996).

**Disorders**

Many varieties of dissociative manifestations in technological and nontechnological cultures are unrelated to distress or dysfunction (Cardeña, 1997b). In the following sections, we confine our discussion to the dissociative pathological manifestations included in the *DSM-IV:* Dissociative amnesia and dissociative fugue, DID, depersonalization, DDNOS, and the related conversion disorder.

*Dissociative Amnesia*

According to the *DSM-IV,* dissociative amnesia (previously called psychogenic amnesia) is characterized by one or more instances of amnesia for important personal information that cannot be explained by ordinary forgetfulness, the common developmental amnesia for the first years of life, or an organic condition. Dissociative amnesia typically involves problems with explicit memory (awareness of personal information or previous experience), whereas implicit memory (i.e., general knowledge such as language, habits, conditioned responses, etc.) is generally but not always preserved (van der Hart & Nijenhuis, 2001). Another general distinction is that dissociative amnesia is typically partially or fully reversible, whereas amnesias with a neurological etiology generally show no (or very gradual and slight) recovery. Careful research does not support a malingering explanation for this condition.

Episodes of amnesia can differ with regard to frequency, extent, and temporal parameters. Patients can have one or few episodes of amnesia, or they can have a chronic condition. The episodic type may involve an individual's sudden forgetfulness of some or most aspects of his or her life, often after a severe traumatic event. In contrast to this presentation, Coons and Milstein (1992) described chronic forms of amnesia typically associated with reported history of early abuse and involving one or more of the following: episodes of missing time, unexplainable forgetfulness, chronic amnesia for periods that should be remembered (e.g., not remembering events before the person was 13 years of age), and so on.

Amnesic episodes can also be characterized as generalized, selective, localized, or systematized. *Generalized amnesia* involves amnesia for all or most personal information, including name and personal history, whereas *selective amnesia* involves forgetting some (but not all) aspects of an event (e.g., remembering just some aspects of a rape incident). *Localized amnesia* refers to amnesia for a certain period of time—hours, days, or longer. Finally, *systematized amnesia* refers to the inability to remember certain categories of information, such as all memories about one's family. Coons and Milstein (1992), in a study with 25 patients, found that the majority of cases were chronic and selective. The loss of memory following a traumatic event is typically concurrent or retrograde to the event, and the person is still able to learn new material. This pattern contrasts with a number of neurologically caused amnesias in which the inability to remember new information is continuous (e.g., various dementias, alcohol amnestic syndrome).

The onset of dissociative amnesia is closely related to severe stress or exposure to trauma, including war experiences, natural disaster, violence, childhood abuse, serious legal or marital problems, depression, and suicide attempts (Coons & Milstein, 1992; Loewenstein, 1991). The precipitating event(s) for dissociative amnesia can be complex and involve idiosyncratic elements; the traumatic events may interact with a preexisting tendency to dissociate and with personal psychodynamics.

As with the other dissociative disorders, comorbid symptomatology of dissociative amnesia frequently includes depression, anxiety, and episodes of depersonalization and unawareness of the surroundings. If there is a history of early and chronic abuse, a more complex syndrome that also includes self-injurious behavior, substance abuse, and sexual problems may be present (Cardeña & Spiegel, 1996; see also this chapter's section on complex PTSD).

The differential diagnosis of dissociative amnesia includes other dissociative disorders that are superordinate to amnesia (i.e., dissociative fugue, DID, ASD, PTSD, and somatization). Medical conditions that can produce amnesias should also be considered, including transient global amnesia (Rollinson, 1978), amnestic alcohol or Korsakoff's syndrome, head injury, epilepsy, dementia, amnesic stroke, postoperative amnesia, postinfectious amnesia, alcoholic blackout, and anoxic amnesia (Kopelman, 1987; Sivec & Lynn, 1995). The effect of psychoactive drugs and malingering, when likely, should also be ruled out (Good, 1993). The clinician should be mindful that amnesia may not be a presenting problem because clients may have amnesia for the amnesic episodes, or they may assume that these episodes of forgetfulness are shared by everybody else.

Earlier reports of dissociative amnesia and fugue concentrated on male soldiers in time of war, whereas more recent work (e.g., Coons & Milstein, 1992) has reported a preponderance of females. As with the other dissociative disorders, dissociative amnesia seems to be a condition affecting mostly young adults (Cardeña & Spiegel, 1996).

A thorough discussion of the current controversy about what have been called recovered memories is beyond the scope of this chapter, but notwithstanding some skepticism (e.g., Loftus, 1993), there is considerable evidence confirming the existence of this clinical phenomenon. First, the literature contains dozens of studies—retrospective, prospective, and using various samples, types of trauma, and measurements, including current videotaping (Corwin & Olafson, 1997)—that support the reality of dissociative amnesia and the recovery of corroborated previously forgotten memories (Brown, Scheflin, & Hammond, 1998; van der Hart & Nijenhuis, 2001). Second, the triggers to recover memories involve many mechanisms other than therapy (e.g., Herman & Harvey, 1997). Third, it is more useful to consider the amnesia process as fluctuating and involving different levels of awareness of the forgotten material (Kopelman, Christensen, Puffett, & Stanhope, 1994; Schooler, 1994) than it is to think of such memories as completely irretrievable. Fourth, there are both cognitive (Schooler, 1994) and neurophysiological (Bremner, Krystal, Southwick, & Charney, 1995) mechanisms that may explain both dissociative amnesia and the recovery of the forgotten material. Fifth, the external validity of some recovered memories does not in any way negate the reality of confabulation and suggestive influences on memory (Loftus, 1993). In fact, both processes are two sides of the same coin, showing the malleability of memory and the effect of suggestive influences (self- or other-generated) to forget matters that did occur or remember matters that did not occur (Butler & Spiegel, 1997).

## *Dissociative Fugue*

Some use the term *fugue* to describe temporary unawareness of surroundings, but the term has a different connotation in psychopathology. Dissociative fugue is defined by the *DSM-IV* (APA, 1994, 2000) as a sudden wandering away from home or place of employment; it is associated with global amnesia for one's past and confusion about personal identity or adoption of a new identity. The *DSM-IV* follows the tradition of presenting amnesia and fugue as distinct diagnoses, although it can be argued that dissociative fugue is simply a variant of generalized amnesia.

Before the *DSM-IV*, the diagnosis was restricted to individuals who actually adopted a new identity, as in William James' description of the Reverend Ansel Bourne, who left his hometown, adopted a new name and profession, and did not recall his previous identity until much later (Kenny, 1986). Although it is not too uncommon to read in newspapers of modern-day Bournes, recent studies show that the most common presentation is confusion about one's identity rather than adoption of a new one (Loewenstein, 1991; Riether & Stoudemire, 1988). Of course, an undetected and unresolved case of identity confusion may develop a new identity.

As for the nature of this confusion of identity, William James (1890/1923) saw it as a long-lasting trance, and Stengel (1941, in Loewenstein, 1991, p. 255) described it as "states of altered or narrowed consciousness with the impulse to wander," consistent with Janet's view of dissociation as involving a focusing and narrowing of consciousness (van der Kolk, Weisaeth, et al., 1996) and with some more recent studies (Cardeña & Spiegel, 1993; Christianson & Loftus, 1987). As in the case of amnesia, traumatic events and severe stress are the common precipitants of this condition. Older references on dissociative amnesia and fugue centered on soldiers at time of war (e.g., Grinker & Spiegel, 1945; Kardiner & Spiegel, 1947), but most current cases involve civilians fleeing the terrors of urban life. In a comprehensive review, Loewenstein (1991) noted that in our nomadic modern societies, some patients do not complain of fugue unless they are queried about it, and some abused individuals may have episodes of fugue without anybody noticing it.

Regarding differential diagnosis, a DID diagnosis is superordinate to that of fugue. Conditions that should be ruled out include postictal episodes of aimless wandering or so-called poriomania (Mayeux, Alexander, Benson, Brandt, & Rosen, 1979), which are typically of shorter duration; manic and psychotic episodes accompanied by traveling; neurological conditions such as brain tumors; and drug-related episodes of amnesia and wandering.

## *Dissociative Identity Disorder*

By far the most widely studied and controversial dissociative condition is DID, a new term for what used to be called multiple personality disorder. According to the *DSM-IV*, it involves the presence within the person of two or more identities or personality states (also known as *alters*)—with characteristic behaviors, moods, memories, and other characteristics—that recurrently manifest themselves to take control of the individual (APA, 1994, 2000). Psychogenic amnesia is another criterion, although in the case of DID the issue of amnesia is complex because an alter may claim to remember events that another alter cannot recall. The inter-alter amnesia is both complex and inconsistent with a simple malingering hypothesis (Eich, Macaulay, Loewenstein, & Patrice, 1997). As with the other diagnoses, the symptoms must produce distress or impairment.

There were two main reasons that the name of this condition was changed from multiple personality disorder to DID in the *DSM-IV*. The first was that the older term emphasized the concept of various personalities (as though different people inhabited the same body), whereas the current view is that DID patients experience a failure in the integration of aspects of their personality into a complex and multifaceted integrated identity. The International Society for the Study of Dissociation (1997) states it this way: "The DID patient is a single person who experiences himself/herself as having separate parts of the mind that function with some autonomy. The patient is not a collection of separate people sharing the same body."

Another reason for the name change is that the term *personality* refers to characteristic pattern of thoughts, feelings, moods, and behaviors of the whole individual. The fact that patients with DID consistently switch between different identities, behavior styles, and so on is a feature of the individual's overall personality. Other phrasing changes in diagnostic criteria clarified that although alters may be personalized by the individual, they are not to be considered as having an objective, independent existence.

It is generally considered that DID is the most severe of the dissociative disorders, and it is certainly the most studied. Originally only a few authors were responsible for most of the research in this area, but there has been a steady growth in the number of contributors to the field. Although it may be true that the majority of clinicians have not treated a DID patient, acceptance of the diagnosis among psychologists and psychiatrists is considerable (Dunn, Paolo, Ryan, & van Fleet, 1994).

DID is the most controversial of all of the dissociative disorders, partly because of the recent increase in its diagnosis (Boor, 1982). Positions range from those who believe that the condition is mostly or completely iatrogenic (e.g., Aldridge-Morris, 1989), produced by naive therapists and the media; to those who state that the condition is not necessarily iatrogenic but is molded by cultural expectations and social roles and strategies (e.g., Spanos, 1994); to those who believe that DID is a valid and specific diagnosis (e.g., Putnam, 1989).

Proponents of the iatrogenic explanation point out that DID patients show significantly higher hypnotizability than do other clinical groups and normal individuals (Frischholz, Lipman, Braun, & Sachs, 1992) and are thus prone to follow manifest or subtle suggestions provided by hypnotists probing for possible hidden personalities or alters. At least two studies (Putnam, Guroff, Silberman, Barban, & Post, 1986; Ross, Norton, & Fraser, 1989) have answered this objection by showing that neither the use of hypnosis nor other proposed therapist characteristics account for who gets a DID diagnosis. Also, if the majority of DID patients were just following clinicians' suggestions, they would have adopted other diagnoses or their symptoms would have been suggested away because the vast majority of such patients had received a number of other previous diagnoses, and many clinicians do not believe in or use the DID diagnosis (Coons, Bowman, & Milstein, 1988; Putnam et al., 1986). In a balanced overview of the DID controversy, Horevitz (1994, p. 447) stated that "critics who claim multiple personality disorder [DID] is nonexistent, rare, iatrogenic, or overdiagnosed may be right or they may be wrong. However, no data at present exists to directly support these contentions" (see also Gleaves, 1996). In fact, there is good evidence for the diagnostic validity of DID using standard clinical criteria (Gleaves, May, & Cardeña, 2001). Also, recent studies using brain imaging technology provide independent corroboration for the reality of switching from one alter to another (Tsai, Condie, Wu, & Chang, 1999) and for the diagnosis as a whole (Sar, Unal, Kiziltan, Kundakci, & Ozturk, 2001).

The fact remains, however, that DID is more frequently diagnosed in the United States than it is in other countries, although there is growing evidence for its validity, reliable diagnosis, and similar prevalence in other places (e.g., Boon & Draijer, 1991; Coons, Bowman, Kluft, & Milstein, 1991; Tutkun et al., 1998). In addition to the iatrogenetic account of this phenomenon, there are other possible explanations, including (a) clinicians in the United States may have greater knowledge of diagnosis and treatment of this disorder, whereas other countries are lagging behind; (b) the etiological circumstances that spawn the condition—namely childhood sexual and other abuse—may be more common in the United States than in other places; or (c) DID may be a more acceptable idiom of distress, so to speak, in the United States than in other countries.

It is also worth noting that a number of studies have found independent corroboration (e.g., medical or legal records; corroboration from family members) for DID patients' reports of abuse (Coons, 1994; Lewis et al., 1997). This does not mean, of course, that all reports, or all details of every report, are valid or accurate, but it shows that at least a significant proportion of DID patients have verifiable histories of abuse.

The course and prognosis of DID depend on the symptom severity and characterological fragility of the patient, and there is evidence of a wide variety of recovery trajectories (Kluft, 1994). It is widely accepted that therapy for these patients typically takes a number of years (Putnam & Loewenstein, 1993). There is substantial comorbidity between DID, depression, affective lability (including self-injury attempts), anxiety, conversion and other somatoform disorders (headaches are almost always found among DIDs), personality disorders (especially avoidant and borderline) and schizophrenic-like first rank symptoms; substance abuse and eating disorders are not infrequent in DID either (Cardeña & Spiegel, 1996). By definition, DID includes psychogenic amnesia, and this condition is also associated with other dissociative symptoms, including fugue, depersonalization, and "trancelike" states. Although individuals with DID report some first rank symptoms such as auditory hallucinations, they typically have adequate reality testing outside of specific events such as fugues or flashbacks, and they do not usually present the negative symptoms of schizophrenia.

### Depersonalization

The *DSM-IV* (APA, 1994) defines depersonalization as clinically significant persistent or recurrent experiences of feeling detached from one's mental processes or body, without loss of reality testing. The person may experience a sense of being unreal, dead, or unfeeling. Whereas psychotic episodes involve delusional beliefs, depersonalization episodes describe *experiences* of alienation from the self but without the impairment in reality testing encountered in psychosis. A depersonalized individual may feel like a robot or as if body movements are mechanical, whereas psychosis might entail holding delusional beliefs that one is turning into metal. Although it is sometimes used interchangeably with depersonalization—

and typically co-occurs with it—derealization refers to a sense of unreality about the environment rather than the self.

The range of phenomena that involve alteration in the sense of self is very broad (Cardeña, 1997b), and some authors have tried to distinguish between various self-experience alterations such as out-of-body experiences, autoscopy, and depersonalization proper (Gabbard, Twemlow, & Jones, 1982). Jacobs and Bovasso (1992) proposed five different types of depersonalization: inauthenticity, self-negation, self-objectification, derealization, and body detachment. In their sample of students, self-objectification was more closely related to psychological disorganization than the other types were. The four most common features of depersonalization may be (a) an altered sense of self (e.g., *my body doesn't belong to me*), (b) a precipitating event (e.g., an accident, marijuana use), (c) a sense of unreality or a dreamlike state (e.g., *nothing seems real; I'm not real*), and (d) sensory alterations (e.g., *colors are less vibrant; voices sound strange;* Cardeña, 1997b).

Depersonalization *disorder* should be distinguished from isolated or transient symptoms. The former involves psychologically caused depersonalization as the predominant disturbance, with recurrent and chronic episodes that cause distress or maladjustment. Depression and anxiety frequently co-occur with the condition. In contrast, depersonalization *symptoms* may be part of a larger clinical syndrome (e.g., DID, panic attacks) or may be unrelated to clinically significant distress or dysfunction. They may have psychological or neurological etiology (e.g., seizure disorders; Litwin & Cardeña, 2000). When depersonalization symptoms occur exclusively in the presence of another psychological disorder, the latter is the superordinate diagnosis. Depersonalization episodes are not uncommon among nonclinical populations and frequently occur during or shortly after a traumatic event (Koopman, Classen, Cardeña, & Spiegel, 1995; Noyes & Kletti, 1977) or as a byproduct of meditation (Lazarus, 1976), hypnosis (Cardeña & Spiegel, 1991), or the use of psychoactive substances (Good, 1993).

Because of the co-occurrence of depersonalization and anxiety symptoms, there has been discussion as to the validity of the depersonalization diagnosis, but recent systematic research (Simeon et al., 1997) has supported this construct.

Until recently, there was a dearth of systematic research on this condition (Coons, 1996), but in the last few years Simeon and collaborators have carried out a series of important studies. Their findings about depersonalization include related attentional and memory problems (Guralnik, Schmeidler, & Simeon, 2000), functional abnormalities in cortical areas associated with sensory integration and body schema (Simeon, Guralnik, Hazlett, et al., 2000), and hypothalamic-pituitary-adrenal dysregulation (Simeon, Guralnik, Knutelska,

Hollander, & Schmeidler, 2001). Consistent with the clinical literature, these authors have also concluded that reports of early abuse—especially emotional abuse—are strongly associated with later depersonalization (Simeon, Guralnik, Schmeidler, Sirof, & Knutelska, 2000).

### Dissociative Disorders Not Otherwise Specified

This category includes dissociative pathologies of consciousness, identity, memory, or perception that do not fulfill the criteria of the disorders described so far. Examples from the *DSM-IV* include cases similar to DID that do not fulfill all the criteria, derealization without depersonalization, dissociative states produced by coercion, dissociative trance disorder, loss of consciousness without a medical condition, and Ganser's syndrome. Many dissociative diagnoses in this and other cultures fall under this category. For instance, in a large general psychiatric sample ($N = 11,292$), Mezzich et al. (1989) found the majority (57%) of dissociative disorder diagnoses to be atypical (a pre-*DSM-IV* designation of DDNOS). This figure is very similar (60%) to the one obtained by Saxe and collaborators (1993) in a subgroup of general psychiatric patients reporting clinical levels of dissociation. However, the epidemiological research by Ross (1991) did not find a large percentage of DDNOS diagnoses in that sample.

The studies of Lynn and Rhue (1988), H. Spiegel (1974), and Hartmann (1984) have respectively described subgroups of high fantasizers, hypnotic virtuosos, and thin-boundaried individuals who are vulnerable to distressing fantasies, excessive suggestibility, and uncontrolled loss of boundaries—traits that increase their risk for psychopathology. Some of these individuals may fulfill criteria for DDNOS because uncontrolled and disorganized fluctuations of consciousness are associated with psychopathology in this and other cultures (Cardeña, 1992). Nonetheless, the mere presence of unusual experiences is not indicative of psychological dysfunction (Cardeña, Lynn, & Krippner, 2000).

A substantial proportion of dissociative patients in other cultures have presentations that differ from the ones described so far, including unwanted and uncontrolled spirit possession (Cardeña et al., 1996; Saxena & Prasad, 1989) and medically unexplained loss of consciousness (van Ommeren et al., 2001). There are also various culture-bound syndromes that have dissociation as a central component, including *ataque de nervios* (which includes paresthesias, unawareness of surroundings and amnesia), startle responses such as *latah,* and emotional dysregulation syndromes such as *amok* (Simons & Hughes, 1985). A thorough consideration of social, political, gender, and cultural variables is required to understand these syndromes (Littlewood, 1998).

## Conversion Disorder

Conversion disorder is included under the somatoform disorders section of the *DSM-IV*. This section groups syndromes suggestive of a general medical condition but whose etiology is judged to be primarily psychological. Although we only discuss conversion disorder, much of the research literature we review in the following also applies to other somatoform conditions, such as somatization disorder (similar to the earlier Briquet's syndrome) and at least some forms of somatoform pain disorder. The *DSM-IV* criteria for conversion include one or more symptoms or deficits affecting voluntary motor (e.g., seizure-like movement or paralysis) or sensory function (e.g., somesthesias) that suggest a medical condition and psychological factors associated with the symptoms. These symptoms should not be intentionally produced or feigned and cannot be fully explained by a medical condition, the effects of a substance, or culturally sanctioned behavior or experience.

As mentioned previously, many of the so-called hysterical cases described at the turn of the century involved the joint presentation of somatoform and dissociative phenomena (Kihlstrom, 1994). The *DSM* taxonomy kept these phenomena as a hysterical neurosis of either dissociative or conversion disorder until its third edition, when it subsumed conversion types of reactions under the somatoform disorders (APA, 1980). The avowed reason was to alert clinicians to "the need to exclude occult general medical conditions or substance-induced etiologies for the bodily symptoms" (APA, 2000, p. 485).

Critics of this decision have adduced historical, conceptual, and empirical reasons to challenge this view (Cardeña, 1994; Kihlstrom, 1994; Nemiah, 1991). In support of this position, some studies have reported a substantial overlap of the somatization disorders, trauma history, and dissociative symptomatology in Western (e.g., Pribor, Yutzi, Dean, & Wetzel, 1993; Saxe et al., 1994) and non-Western (van Ommeren et al., 2001) cultures. The most formidable challenge to the separation of conversion and dissociative phenomena has come from the programmatic research of Ellert Nijenhuis and his collaborators (reviewed in Nijenhuis, 2000; see also Cardeña & Nijenhuis, 2000). Advancing the work originally described by Pierre Janet, W. H. Rivers, Charles Myers, and others, Nijenhuis has developed the Somatoform Dissociation Questionnaire, proposed an evolutionary account (based on animal defensive reactions), and carried out various studies showing the relationship between what he calls psychoform (i.e., cognitive and experiential dissociative phenomena) and somatoform dissociation (e.g., somatic dissociative phenomena such as anesthesia, immobility, and pain) and trauma. As is the case with depersonalization, programmatic research on somatoform dissociation has produced a qualitative advance in our understanding of this and related areas.

## CONCLUSIONS

The previous sections provide an overview of the posttraumatic, dissociative, and conversion disorders. Considering the brief span in which systematic research on the disorders of extreme stress has been conducted, it is impressive how much information has accumulated on these disorders, so it is likely that the conception of their diagnosis and treatment may change in the future. Some of these changes will come out of programmatic research and new brain imaging techniques, whereas others may follow a reconceptualizaton of disorders of extreme stress in particular and psychopathology in general. For instance, it can be argued that the categorical-prototypal scheme for psychological disturbances that the *DSM* adopts may not be as valuable as a dimensional approach. In the latter, rather than having a set of criteria that need to be present for a diagnosis, the individual is evaluated quantitatively (i.e., dimensionally) with respect to symptoms related to a particular problem. Although the dimensional approach to diagnosis has been most developed in relation to various dimensions of depression, anxiety, and personality disorders (Mineka, Watson, & Clark, 1998; Widiger & Clark, 2001), it could be used for posttraumatic conditions.

More specific problems remain, including the relationship between ASD and PTSD criteria (e.g., the latter minimizes dissociative reactions) and their relationship to other symptoms such as depression. Furthermore, as we have mentioned, the value of separating somatoform dissociative phenomena from psychological forms can be challenged in various ways. The dissociative disorders have been mired in controversy for a number of years, but empirical investigation on such areas as the psychophysiology of DID and depersonalization has been gradually replacing uninformed speculation. Nonetheless, a number of areas remain open for systematic research, among them the longitudinal courses of posttraumatic reactions, the personal characteristics that predispose individuals to react to trauma with dissociation rather than with other symptoms, the encoding of traumatic memories, and so on.

In a world of never-ending disasters, violence, and increasingly sophisticated terrorism, the study of the disorders of extreme stress and trauma remains a vital human endeavor.

# REFERENCES

Aldridge-Morris, R. (1989). *Multiple personality: An exercise in deception*. Hillsdale, NJ: Erlbaum.

American Psychiatric Association. (1980). *Diagnostic and statistical manual of mental disorders* (3rd ed.). Washington, DC: Author.

American Psychiatric Association. (1987). *Diagnostic and statistical manual of mental disorders* (3rd ed., Rev.). Washington, DC: Author.

American Psychiatric Association. (1994). *Diagnostic and statistical manual of mental disorders* (4th ed.). Washington, DC: Author.

American Psychiatric Association. (2000). *Diagnostic and statistical manual of mental disorders* (4th ed., text revision). Washington, DC: Author.

Baider, L., Peretz, T., & Kaplan De-Nour, A. (1992). Effect of the Holocaust on coping with cancer. *Social Science and Medicine, 34*, 11–15.

Barton, K. A., Blanchard, E. B., & Hickling, E. J. (1996). Antecedents and consequences of acute stress disorder among motor vehicle accident victims. *Behavioral Research Therapy, 34*, 805–813.

Boon, S., & Draijer, N. (1991). Diagnosing dissociative disorders in the Netherlands: A pilot study with the Structured Clinical Interview for the *DSM-III-R* dissociative disorders. *American Journal of Psychiatry, 148*, 458–462.

Boor, M. (1982). The multiple personality epidemic. *Journal of Nervous and Mental Disease, 170*, 302–304.

Bower, J. E., Kemeny, M. E., Taylor, S. E., & Fahey, J. L. (1998). Cognitive processing, discovery of meaning, CD4 decline, and AIDS-related mortality among bereaved HIV-seropositive men. *Journal of Consulting and Clinical Psychology, 66*, 979–986.

Bremner, J. D. (2002, January). *Alterations in brain structure and function in PTSD*. Paper presented at the conference on Early trauma responses and psychopathology: Theoretical and empirical directions, National Institute of Mental Health, Bethesda, MD.

Bremner, J. D., Krystal, J. H., Southwick, S. M., & Charney, D. S. (1995). Functional neuroanatomical correlates of the effects of stress on memory. *Journal of Traumatic Stress, 8*, 527–553.

Bremner, J. D., Southwick, S., Brett, E., Fontana, A., Rosenheck, R., & Charney, D. S. (1992). Dissociation and posttraumatic stress disorder in Vietnam combat veterans. *American Journal of Psychiatry, 149*, 328–332.

Breslau, N., Chilcoat, H. D., Kessler, R. C., & Davis, G. C. (1999). Previous exposure to trauma and PTSD effects of subsequent trauma: Results from the Detroit area survey of trauma. *American Journal of Psychiatry, 156*, 902–907.

Breslau, N., & Davis, G. C. (1992). Posttraumatic stress disorder in an urban population of young adults: Risk factors for chronicity. *American Journal of Psychiatry, 149*, 671–675.

Breslau, N., Davis, G. C., & Andreski, P. (1995). Risk factors for PTSD-related traumatic events: A prospective analysis. *American Journal of Psychiatry, 152*, 529–535.

Breslau, N., Davis, G. C., Andreski, P., & Peterson, E. (1991). Traumatic events and posttraumatic stress disorder in an urban population of young adults. *Archives of General Psychiatry, 48*, 216–222.

Brewin, C. R., Andrews, B., Rose, S., & Kirk, M. (1999). Acute stress disorder and posttraumatic stress disorder in victims of violent crime. *Journal of Consulting and Clinical Psychology, 156*, 360–366.

Brewin, C., Andrews, B., & Valentine, J. D. (2000). Meta-analysis of risk factors for posttraumatic stress disorder in trauma-exposed adults. *Journal of Consulting and Clinical Psychology, 68*, 748–766.

Brickman, P., Coates, D., & Janoff-Bulman, R. (1978). Lottery winners and accident victims: Is happiness relative? *Journal of Personality and Social Psychology, 36*, 917–927.

Brown, D., Scheflin, A. W., & Hammond, D. C. (1998). *Memory, trauma, treatment, and the law*. New York: Norton.

Bryant, R. A., & Harvey, A. G. (1997). Acute stress disorder: A critical review of diagnostic issues. *Clinical Psychology Review, 17*, 757–773.

Bryant, R. A., & Harvey, A. G. (1998). Relationship between acute stress disorder and posttraumatic stress disorder following mild traumatic brain injury. *American Journal of Psychiatry, 155*, 625–629.

Butler, L. D. (2000). Validity and utility of the acute stress disorder (ASD) symptom criteria and diagnosis. *American Journal of Psychiatry, 157*, 189.

Butler, L. D., Duran, R. E., Jasiukaitis, P., Koopman, C., & Spiegel, D. (1996). Hypnotizability and traumatic experience: A diathesis-stress model of dissociative symptomatology. *American Journal of Psychiatry, 153*, (Festschrift Suppl. 7), 42–63.

Butler, L. D., & Spiegel, D. (1997). Trauma and memory. In L. J. Dickstein, M. B. Riba, & J. O. Oldham (Eds.), *Review of psychiatry* (Vol. 16, pp. II13-II53). Washington, DC: American Psychiatric Press.

Calhoun, L. G., & Tedeschi, R. G. (2000). Early posttraumatic interventions: Facilitating possibilities for growth. In J. M. Violant, D. Paton, & C. Dunning (Eds.) *Posttraumatic stress intervention: Challenges, issues, and perspectives* (pp. 135–152). Springfield, IL: Charles C. Thomas.

Cardeña, E. (1992). Trance and possession as dissociative disorders. *Transcultural Psychiatric Research Review, 29*, 283–297.

Cardeña, E. (1994). The domain of dissociation. In S. J. Lynn & J. Rhue (Eds.), *Dissociation* (pp. 15–31). New York: Guilford.

Cardeña, E. (1997a). Dissociative disorders: Phantoms of the self. In S. M. Turner & M. Hersen (Eds.), *Adult psychopathology and diagnosis* (pp. 384–408). New York: Wiley.

Cardeña, E. (1997b). The etiologies of dissociation. In S. Powers & S. Krippner (Eds.), *Broken images, broken selves* (pp. 61–87). New York: Brunner.

Cardeña, E. (1998). The relationship between cortical activity and dissociativity among PTSD and non-PTSD Gulf War veterans. *International Journal of Clinical and Experimental Hypnosis, 45,* 400–401.

Cardeña, E., Holen, A., McFarlane, A., Solomon, Z., Wilkinson, C., & Spiegel, D. (1998). A multi-site study of acute-stress reaction to a disaster. In T. A. Widiger, A. J. Frances, H. A. Pincus, R. Ross, M. B. First, W. Davis, & M. Kline (Eds.), *Sourcebook for the DSM-IV* (Vol. 4, pp. 377–391). Washington, DC: American Psychiatric Press.

Cardeña, E., Koopman, C., Classen, C., Waelde, L., & Spiegel, D. (2000). Psychometric properties of the Stanford Acute Stress Reaction Questionnaire (SASRQ): A valid and reliable measure of acute stress reactions. *Journal of Traumatic Stress, 13,* 719–734.

Cardeña, E., Lewis-Fernández, R., Beahr, D., Pakianathan, I., & Spiegel, D. (1996). Dissociative disorders. In T. A. Widiger, A. J. Frances, H. J. Pincus, R. Ross, M. B. First, & W. W. Davis (Eds.), *Sourcebook for the DSM-IV* (Vol. 2, pp. 973–1005). Washington, DC: American Psychiatric Press.

Cardeña, E., Lynn, S. J., & Krippner, S. (2000). *Varieties of anomalous experience.* Washington, DC: American Psychological Association.

Cardeña, E., & Nijenhuis, E. (Eds.). (2000). Somatoform dissociation [Special issue]. *Journal of Trauma and Dissociation, 1*(4).

Cardeña, E., & Spiegel, D. (1991). Suggestibility, absorption, and dissociation: An integrative model of hypnosis. In J. F. Schumaker (Ed.), *Human suggestibility: Advances in theory, research and application* (pp. 93–107). New York: Routledge.

Cardeña, E., & Spiegel, D. (1993). Dissociative reactions to the Bay Area Earthquake. *American Journal of Psychiatry, 150,* 474–478.

Cardeña, E., & Spiegel, D. (1996). Diagnostic issues, criteria and co-morbidity of dissociative disorders. In L. Michelson & W. Ray (Eds.), *Handbook of dissociation: Theoretical, empirical and clinical perspectives* (pp. 227–250). New York: Plenum Press.

Carson, R. C., Butcher, J. N., & Mineka, S. (2000). *Abnormal psychology and modern life.* Boston: Allyn and Bacon.

Christianson, S. A., & Loftus, E. F. (1987). Memory for traumatic events. *Applied Cognitive Psychology, 1,* 225–239.

Classen, C., Koopman, C., Hales, R., & Spiegel, D. (1998). Acute stress disorder as a predictor of posttraumatic stress symptoms. *American Journal of Psychiatry, 155,* 620–624.

Coons, P. M. (1994). Confirmation of childhood abuse in child and adolescent cases of multiple personality and dissociative disorder not otherwise specified. *Journal of Nervous and Mental Disease, 182,* 461–464.

Coons, P. M. (1996). Depersonalization and derealization. In L. Michelson & W. Ray (Eds.), *Handbook of dissociation: Theoretical, empirical, and clinical perspectives* (pp. 291–305). New York: Plenum.

Coons, P. M., Bowman, E. S., Kluft, R. P., & Milstein, V. (1991). The cross-cultural occurrence of MPD: Additional cases from a recent survey. *Dissociation, 4,* 124–128

Coons, P. M., Bowman, E. S., & Milstein, V. (1988). Multiple personality disorder: A clinical investigation of 50 cases. *Journal of Nervous and Mental Disorder, 176,* 519–527.

Coons, P. M., & Milstein, V. (1992). Psychogenic amnesia: A clinical investigation of 25 cases. *Dissociation, 5,* 73–79.

Cordova, M. J., Cunningham, L. L. C., Carlson, C. R., & Andrykowski, M. A. (2001). Posttraumatic growth following breast cancer: A controlled comparison study. *Health Psychology, 3,* 176–185.

Corwin, D. L., & Olafson, E. (1997). Videotaped discovery of a reportedly unrecallable memory of child sexual abuse: Compared with a childhood interview videotaped 11 years before. *Child Maltreatment, 2,* 91–112.

Cottler, L. B., Compton, W. M. D., Mager, D., Spitznagel, E. L., & Janca, A. (1992). Posttraumatic stress disorder among substance users from the general population. *American Journal of Psychiatry, 149,* 664–670.

Crowson, J. J., Jr., Frueh, B. C., Beidel, D. C., & Turner, S. M. (1998). Self-reported symptoms of social anxiety in a sample of combat veterans with posttraumatic stress disorder. *Journal of Anxiety Disorders, 6,* 605–612.

Dancu, C. V., Riggs, D. S., Hearst-Ikeda, D., Shoyer, B. G., & Foa, E. B. (1996). Dissociative experiences and posttraumatic stress disorder among female victims of criminal assault and rape. *Journal of Traumatic Stress, 9,* 253–266.

Davidson, J. R., Hughes, D., Blazer, D. G., & George, L. K. (1991). Post-traumatic stress disorder in the community: An epidemiological study. *Psychological Medicine, 3,* 713–721.

Dunn, G. E., Paolo, A. M., Ryan, J. J., & van Fleet, J. N. (1994). Belief in the existence of multiple personality disorder among psychologists and psychiatrists. *Journal of Clinical Psychology, 50,* 454–457.

Ehlers, A., Mayou, R. A., & Bryant, B. (1998). Psychological predictors of chronic posttraumatic stress disorder after motor vehicle accidents. *Journal of Abnormal Psychology, 107,* 508–519.

Eich, E., Macaulay, D., Loewenstein, R., & Patrice, H. (1997). Memory, amnesia, and dissociative identity disorder. *Psychological Science, 8,* 417–422.

Engdahl, B., Dikel, T. N., Eberly, R., & Blank, A., Jr. (1997). Posttraumatic stress disorder in a community group of former prisoners of war: A normative response to severe trauma. *American Journal of Psychiatry, 154,* 1567–1581.

Figley, C. R. (1978). Psychosocial adjustment among Vietnam veterans: An overview of the research. In C. R. Figley (Ed.), *Stress disorders among Vietnam veterans* (pp. 57–70). New York: Brunner/Mazel.

Finkelhor, D. (1988). The trauma of child sexual abuse: Two models. In G. E. Wyatt & G. J. Powell (Eds.), *Lasting effects of child sexual abuse* (pp. 61–82). Newbury Park, CA: Sage.

Fontana, A., & Rosenheck, R. (1998). Psychological benefits and liabilities of traumatic exposure in the war zone. *Journal of Traumatic Stress, 11,* 485–503.

Ford, J. D. (1999). Disorders of extreme stress following war-zone military trauma: Associated features of posttraumatic stress disorder or comorbid but distinct syndromes? *Journal of Consulting & Clinical Psychology, 67,* 3–12.

Ford, J. D., & Kidd, P. (1998). Early childhood trauma and disorders of extreme stress as predictors of treatment outcome with chronic posttraumatic stress disorder. *Journal of Traumatic Stress, 11,* 742–761.

Freud, S. (1963). Introductory lectures on psycho-analysis. In J. Strachey (Ed. and Trans.), *The standard edition of the complete psychological works of Sigmund Freud* (Vol. 15, pp. 1–240; Vol. 16, pp. 241–496). London: Hogarth Press. (Original work published 1916–1917)

Freud, S., Ferenczi, S., Abraham, K., Caligor, L., & Jones, E. (1921). *Psychoanalysis and the war neurosis.* New York: International Psycho-Analytic Press.

Freyd, J. J., DePrince, A. P., & Zurbriggen, E. L. (2001). Self-reported memory for abuse depends upon victim-perpetrator relationship. *Journal of Trauma and Dissociation, 2,* 5–16.

Friedl, M., & Draijer, N. (2000). Dissociative disorders in Dutch psychiatric inpatients. *American Journal of Psychiatry, 157,* 1012–1013.

Frischholz, E. J., Lipman, L. S., Braun, B. G., & Sachs, R. G. (1992). Psychopathology, hypnotizability, and dissociation. *American Journal of Psychiatry, 149,* 1521–1525.

Fullerton, C. S., & Ursano, R. (1997). *Posttraumatic stress disorders: Acute and long-term responses to trauma and disaster.* Washington, DC: American Psychiatric Press.

Gabbard, G. O., Twemlow, S. W., & Jones, F. C. (1982). Differential diagnosis of altered mind/body perception. *Psychiatry, 45,* 361–369.

Gleaves, D. H. (1996). The sociocognitive model of dissociative identity disorder: A reexamination of the evidence. *Psychological Bulletin, 120,* 42–59.

Gleaves, D. H., May, M. C., & Cardeña, E. (2001). An examination of the diagnostic validity of dissociative identity disorder. *Clinical Psychology Review, 21,* 577–608.

Gold, J., & Cardeña, E. (1998). Convergent validity of 3 PTSD inventories among adult sexual abuse survivors. *Journal of Traumatic Stress, 11,* 173–180.

Good, M. I. (1993). The concept of an organic dissociative disorder: What is the evidence? *Harvard Review of Psychiatry, 1,* 145–157.

Green, B. L. (1993). Identifying survivors at risk. Trauma and stressors across events. In J. P. Wilson & B. Raphael (Eds.), *International handbook of traumatic stress syndromes* (pp. 135–144). New York: Plenum.

Grieger, T. A., Staab, J. P., Cardeña, E., McCarroll, J. E., Brandt, G. T., Fullerton, C. S., & Ursano, R. J. (2000). Acute stress disorder and subsequent posttraumatic stress disorder in a group of disaster workers. *Anxiety and Depression, 11,* 183–184.

Griffin, M. G., Resick, P. A., & Mechanic, M. B. (1997). Objective assessment of peritraumatic dissociation: Psychophysiological indicators. *American Journal of Psychiatry, 154,* 1081–1088.

Grinker, R. R., & Spiegel, J. P. (1945). *Men under stress.* Philadelphia: Blakiston.

Guralnik, O., Schmeidler, J., & Simeon, D. (2000). Feeling unreal: Cognitive processes in depersonalization. *American Journal of Psychiatry, 157,* 103–109.

Hall, D. K. (1999). "Complex" posttraumatic stress disorder/disorders of extreme stress (CP/DES) in sexually abused children: An exploratory study. *Journal of Child Sexual Abuse, 8,* 51–71.

Hartmann, E. (1984). *The nightmare.* New York: Basic Books.

Harvey, A. G., & Bryant, R. A. (1998). The relationship between acute stress disorder and posttraumatic stress disorder: A prospective evaluation of motor vehicle accident survivors. *Journal of Consulting and Clinical Psychology, 66,* 507–512.

Heim, C., Newport, D. J., Graham, Y. P., Wilcox, M., Bonsall, R., Miller, A., & Nemeroff, C. (2000). Pituitary-adrenal and autonomic responses to stress in women after sexual and physical abuse in childhood. *Journal of the American Medical Association, 284,* 592–597.

Henderson, J., & Moore, M. (1944). The psychoneurosis of war. *New England Journal of Medicine, 230,* 274–278.

Herman, J. L. (1992a). Complex PTSD: A syndrome in survivors of prolonged and repeated trauma. *Journal of Traumatic Stress, 3,* 377–391.

Herman, J. (1992b). *Trauma and recovery.* New York: Basic Books.

Herman, J. L., & Harvey, M. R. (1997). Adult memories of childhood trauma: A naturalistic clinical study. *Journal of Traumatic Stress, 4,* 557–571.

Hilgard, E. R. (1968). *The experience of hypnosis.* New York: Harcourt, Brace & World.

Hilgard, E. R. (1994). Neodissociation theory. In S. J. Lynn & J. Rhue (Eds.), *Dissociation* (pp. 32–51). New York: Guilford.

Horevitz, R. (1994). Dissociation and multiple personality: Conflicts and controversies. In S. J. Lynn & J. Rhue (Eds.), *Dissociation* (pp. 434–461). New York: Guilford.

Horowitz, M. J. (1986). *Stress response syndromes.* New York: Aronson.

Hyer, L. A., Albrecht, W., Poudewyns, P. A., Woods, M. G., & Brandsma, J. (1993). Dissociative experiences of Vietnam veterans with chronic posttraumatic stress disorder. *Psychological Reports, 73,* 519–530.

International Society for the Study of Dissociation. (1997). *Guidelines for treating dissociative identity disorder (multiple personality disorder) in adults.* Retrieved June 27, 2002, from http://www.issd.org/indexpage/isdguide.htm

Jacobs, J. R., & Bovasso, G. B. (1992). Toward the clarification of the construct of depersonalization and its association with affective and cognitive dysfunctions. *Journal of Personality Assessment, 59,* 352–365.

James, W. (1923). *The principles of psychology.* New York: Holt. (Original work published 1890)

Janet, P. (1965). *The major symptoms of hysteria* (2nd ed.). New York: Hafner. (Original work published 1907)

Jang, K. L., Paris, J., Zweig-Frank, H., & Livesley, W. J. (1998). Twin study of dissociative experience. *Journal of Nervous and Mental Disease, 186,* 345–351.

Kardiner, A., & Spiegel, H. (1947). *War stress and neurotic illness.* New York: Hoeber.

Keane, T. M., & Fairbank, J. A. (1983). Survey analysis of combat-related stress disorders in Vietnam veterans. *American Journal of Psychiatry, 140,* 348–350.

Kenny, M. G. (1986). *The passion of Ansel Bourne.* Washington, DC: Smithsonian Institution Press.

Kessler, R. C., Sonnega, A., Bromet, E., Hughes, M., & Nelson, C. B. (1995). Posttraumatic stress disorder in the National Comorbidity Survey. *Archives of General Psychiatry, 52,* 1048–1060.

Kihlstrom, J. F. (1994). One hundred years of hysteria. In S. J. Lynn & J. W. Rhue (Eds.), *Dissociation: Clinical and theoretical perspectives* (pp. 365–394). New York: Guilford.

Kinzie, J. D., & Goetz, R. R. (1996). A century of controversy surrounding posttraumatic stress-spectrum syndromes: The impact on *DSM-III* and *DSM-IV. Journal of Traumatic Stress, 9,* 159–179.

Kluft, R. P. (1994). Treatment trajectories in multiple personality disorder. *Dissociation, 7,* 63–76.

Kluft, R. P. (1996). Dissociative identity disorder. In L. K. Michelson & W. J. Ray (Eds.), *Handbook of dissociation: Theoretical, empirical and clinical perspectives* (pp. 337–366). New York: Plenum.

Koopman, C., Classen, C., Cardeña, E., & Spiegel, D. (1995). When disaster strikes, acute stress disorder may follow. *Journal of Traumatic Stress, 8,* 29–46.

Koopman, C., Classen, C., & Spiegel, D. (1994). Predictors of posttraumatic stress symptoms among survivors of the Oakland/Berkeley, Calif., firestorm. *American Journal of Psychiatry, 151,* 888–894.

Koopman, C., Classen, C., & Spiegel, D. (1996). Dissociative responses in the immediate aftermath of the Oakland/Berkeley firestorm. *Journal of Traumatic Stress, 9,* 521–540.

Koopman, C., Drescher, K., Bowles, S., Gusman, F., Blake, D., Dondershine, H., Chang, V., Butler, L. D., & Spiegel, D. (2001). Acute dissociative reactions in veterans with PTSD. *Journal of Trauma and Dissociation, 2,* 91–111.

Kopelman, M. D. (1987). Amnesia: Organic and psychogenic. *British Journal of Psychiatry, 150,* 428–442.

Kopelman, M. D., Christensen, H., Puffett, A., & Stanhope, N. (1994). The great escape: A neuropsychological study of psychogenic amnesia. *Neuropsychologia, 32,* 675–691.

Kroll, J., Habenicht, M., Mackenzie, R., Yang, M., Chan, S., Vang, T., Nguyen, T., Ly, M., Phommasouvann, B., & Nguyen, H. (1989). Depression and posttraumatic stress disorder in Southeast Asian refugees. *American Journal of Psychiatry, 146,* 1592–1597.

Labbate, L. A., Cardeña, E., Dimitreva, J., Roy, M., & Engel, C. C. (1998). Psychiatric syndromes in Persian Gulf War veterans: An association of handling dead bodies with somatoform disorders. *Psychotherapy and Psychosomatics, 67,* 275–279.

Lazarus, A. (1976). Psychiatric problems precipitated by Transcendental Meditation. *Psychological Reports, 10,* 39–74.

Lewis, D. O., Yeager, C. A., Swica, Y., Pincus, J. H., & Lewis, M. (1997). Objective documentation of child abuse and dissociation in 12 murderers with dissociative identity disorder. *American Journal of Psychiatry, 154,* 1703–1710.

Lewis-Fernández, R. (1994). Culture and dissociation. A comparison of *ataque de nervios* among Puerto Ricans and possession syndrome in India. In D. Spiegel (Ed.), *Dissociation. Culture, mind, and body* (pp. 123–167). Washington, DC: American Psychiatric Press.

Lindemann, E. (1944). Symptomatology and management of acute grief. *American Journal of Psychiatry, 101,* 141–148.

Littlewood, R. (1998). Mental illness as ritual theatre. *Performance Research, 3,* 41–52.

Litwin, R., & Cardeña, E. (2000). Demographic and seizure variables, but not hypnotizability or dissociation, differentiated psychogenic from organic seizures. *Journal of Trauma and Dissociation, 1,* 99–122.

Loewenstein, R. J. (1991). Psychogenic amnesia and psychogenic fugue: A comprehensive review. In A. Tasman & S. M. Goldfinger (Eds.), *Review of psychiatry* (Vol. 10, pp. 189–222). Washington, DC: American Psychiatric Press.

Loftus, E. F. (1993). The reality of repressed memories. *American Psychologist, 48,* 518–537.

Lynn, S. J., & Rhue, J. W. (1988). Fantasy proneness: Hypnosis, developmental antecedents, and psychopathology. *American Psychologist, 43,* 35–44.

Marmar, C. R., Weiss, D. S., Metzler, T. J., & Delucchi, K. (1996). Characteristics of emergency services personnel related to peritraumatic dissociation during critical incident exposure. *American Journal of Psychiatry, 153,* 94–102.

Marshall, G. N., & Orlando, M. (2002). Acculturation and peritraumatic dissociation in young adult Latino survivors of community violence. *Journal of Abnormal Psychology, 111,* 166–174.

Marshall, R., Spitzer, R., & Leibowitz, M. (1999). Review and critique of the new *DSM-IV* diagnosis of acute stress disorder. *American Journal of Psychiatry, 156,* 1677–1685.

Mason, J. W. (1971). A re-evaluation of the concept of "nonspecificity" in stress theory. *Journal of Psychiatric Research, 8,* 323–333.

Mayeux, R., Alexander, M. P., Benson, F., Brandt, J., & Rosen, J. (1979). Poriomania. *Neurology, 29,* 1616–1619.

McFarlane, A. C., Atchison, M., & Yehuda, R. (1997). The acute stress response following motor vehicle accidents and its relation to PTSD. In R. Yehuda & A. C. McFarlane (Eds.), *Psychobiology of posttraumatic stress disorder* (Vol. 821, pp. 437–441). New York: Annals of the New York Academy of Sciences.

McFarlane, A. C., & de Girolamo, G. (1996). The nature of traumatic stressors and the epidemiology of posttraumatic reactions. In B. A. van der Kolk, A. C. McFarlane, & L. Weisaeth (Eds.), *Traumatic stress: The effects of overwhelming experience on mind, body, and society* (pp. 129–154). New York: Guilford.

McMillen, J. C., Smith, E. M., & Fisher, R. H. (1997). Perceived benefit and mental health after three types of disaster. *Journal of Consulting and Clinical Psychology, 65,* 733–739.

Merckelbach, H., & Muris, P. (2001). The causal link between self-reported trauma and dissociation: A critical review. *Behavior Research and Therapy, 39,* 245–254.

Mezzich, J. E., Fabrega, H., Coffman, G. A., & Haley, R. (1989). *DSM-III* disorders in a large sample of psychiatric patients: Frequency and specificity of diagnoses. *American Journal of Psychiatry, 146,* 212–219.

Mineka, S., Watson, D., & Clark L. A. (1998). Comorbidity of anxiety and unipolar mood disorders. *Annual Review of Psychology, 49,* 377–412.

Morgan, C. A., III, Hazlett, Maj. G., Richardson, E. G., Jr., Schnurr, P., & Southwick, S. M. (2001). Symptoms of dissociation in humans experiencing acute, uncontrollable stress: A prospective investigation. *American Journal of Psychiatry, 158,* 1239–1247.

Nelson, E. C., Heath, A. C., Madden, P. A., Cooper, M. L., Dinwiddle, S. H., Bucholz, K. K., Glowinski, A., McLaughlin, T., Dunne, M. P., Astatham, D. J., & Martin, N. G. (2002). Association between self-reported childhood sexual abuse and adverse psychosocial outcomes. *Archives of General Psychiatry, 59,* 139–145.

Nemiah, J. (1991). Dissociation, conversion and somatization. In A. Tasman & S. M. Goldfinger (Eds.), *American psychiatric press review of psychiatry* (Vol. 10, pp. 248–260). Washington, DC: American Psychiatric Press.

Nemiah, J. C. (1995). Dissociative disorders. In H. I. Kaplan & B. J. Sadock (Eds.), *Comprehensive textbook of psychiatry* (Vol. 6, pp. 1281–1293). Baltimore: Williams & Wilkins.

Newman, E., Orsillo, S. M., Herman, D. S., Niles, B. L., & Litz, B. T. (1995). Clinical presentation of disorders of extreme stress in combat veterans. *Journal of Nervous & Mental Disease, 183,* 628–632.

Niederland, W. G. (1968). Clinical observations on the "survivor syndrome." *International Journal of Psycho-Analysis, 2-3,* 313–315.

Nijenhuis, E. (2000). Somatoform dissociation: Major symptoms of dissociative disorders. *Journal of Trauma & Dissociation, 1,* 7–29.

Norris, F. H. (1992). Epidemiology of trauma: Frequency and impact of different potentially traumatic events on different demographic groups. *Journal of Consulting and Clinical Psychology, 60,* 409–418.

Noyes, R., & Kletti, R. (1977). Depersonalization in response to life-threatening danger. *Comprehensive Psychiatry, 18,* 375–384.

Ogawa, J. R., Sroufe, L. A., Weinfield, N. S., Carlson, E. A., & Egeland, B. (1997). Development and the fragmented self: Longitudinal study of dissociative symptomatology in a nonclinical sample. *Development and Psychopathology, 9,* 855–879.

Pelcovitz, D., van der Kolk, B., Roth, S., Mandel, F., Kaplan, S., & Resick, P. (1997). Development of a criteria set and a structured interview for disorders of extreme stress (SIDES). *Journal of Traumatic Stress, 10,* 3–16.

Pribor, E. E., Yutzi, S. H., Dean, T. J., & Wetzel, R. D. (1993). Briquet's syndrome, dissociation, and abuse. *American Journal of Psychiatry, 150,* 1507–1511.

Putnam, F. W. (1989). *Diagnosis and treatment of multiple personality disorder.* New York: Guilford.

Putnam, F. W. (1994). Dissociative disorders in children and adolescents. In S. J. Lynn & J. Rhue (Eds.), *Dissociation* (pp. 175–189). New York: Guilford.

Putnam, F. W., Guroff, J. J., Silberman, E. K., Barban, L., & Post, R. M. (1986). The clinical phenomenology of multiple personality disorder: Review of 100 recent cases. *Journal of Clinical Psychiatry, 47,* 285–293.

Putnam, F. W., & Loewenstein, R. J. (1993). Treatment of multiple personality disorder: A survey of current practices. *American Journal of Psychiatry, 150,* 1048–1052.

Rahe, R. H., Meyer, M., Smith, M., Kjaer, G., & Holmes, T. (1964). Social stress and illness onset. *Journal of Psychosomatic Research, 8,* 35–44.

Riether, A. M., & Stoudemire, A. (1988). Psychogenic fugue states: A review. *Southern Medical Journal, 81,* 568–571.

Rollinson, R. D. (1978). Transient global amnesia: A review of 213 cases from the literature. *Australian and New Zealand Journal of Medicine, 8,* 547–549.

Ross, C. A. (1991). Epidemiology of multiple personality and dissociation. *Psychiatric Clinics of North America, 14,* 503–517.

Ross, C. A., Norton, G. R., & Fraser, G. A. (1989). Evidence against the iatrogenesis of multiple personality disorder. *Dissociation, 2,* 61–65.

Roth, S., Newman, E., Pelcovitz, D., van der Kolk, B., & Mandel, F. S. (1997). Complex PTSD in victims exposed to sexual and physical abuse: Results from the *DSM-IV* field trial for posttraumatic stress disorder. *Journal of Traumatic Stress, 10,* 539–555.

Sar, V., Unal, S. N., Kiziltan, E., Kundakci, T., & Ozturk, E. (2001). HMPAO SPECT study of regional cerebral blood flow in dissociative identity disorder. *Journal of Trauma and Dissociation, 2,* 5–25.

Saxe, G. N. (2002, January). *ASD and PTSD in children with burns.* Paper presented at the conference on Early trauma responses and psychopathology: Theoretical and empirical directions, National Institute of Mental Health, Bethesda, MD.

Saxe, G. N., Chinman, G., Berkowitz, R., Hall, K., Lieberg, G., Schwartz, J., & van der Kolk, B. A. (1994). Somatization in patients with dissociative disorders. *American Journal of Psychiatry, 151,* 1329–1334.

Saxe, G. N., van der Kolk, B. A., Berkowitz, R., Chinman, G., Hall, K., Lieberg, G., & Schwartz, J. (1993). Dissociative disorders in psychiatric patients. *American Journal of Psychiatry, 150,* 1037–1042.

Saxena, S., & Prasad, K. V. (1989). *DSM-III* subclassification of dissociative disorders applied to psychiatric outpatients in India. *American Journal of Psychiatry, 146,* 261–262.

Schooler, J. W. (1994). Seeking the core: The issues and evidence surrounding recovered accounts of sexual trauma. *Consciousness and Cognition, 3,* 452–469.

Selye, H. (1976). *The stress of life* (2nd ed.). New York: McGraw Hill.

Shalev, A.Y., Peri, T., Canetti, L., & Schreiber, S. (1996). Predictors of PTSD in injured trauma survivors: A prospective study. *American Journal of Psychiatry, 153,* 219–225.

Silver, R. L., & Wortman, C. B. (1980). Coping with undesirable life events. In J. Garber & M. E. Seligman (Eds.), *Human helplessness*. New York: Academic Press.

Simeon, D., Gross, S., Guralnik, O., Stein, D., Schmeidler, J., & Hollander, E. (1997). Feeling unreal: 30 cases of *DSM-III-R* depersonalization disorder. *American Journal of Psychiatry, 154,* 1107–1113.

Simeon, D., & Guralnik, O. (2000). Letter to the editor. *American Journal of Psychiatry, 157,* 1888–1889.

Simeon, D., Guralnik, O., Hazlett, E. A., Spiegel-Cohen, J., Hollander, E., & Buchsbaum, M. S. (2000). Feeling unreal: A PET study of depersonalization disorder. *American Journal of Psychiatry, 11,* 1782–1788.

Simeon, D., Guralnik, O., Knutelska, M., Hollander, E., & Schmeidler, J. (2001). Hypothalamic-pituitary-adrenal axis dysregulation in depersonalization disorder. *Neuropsychopharmacology, 5,* 793–795.

Simeon, D., Guralnik, O., Schmeidler, J., Sirof, B., & Knutelska, M. (2000). The role of childhood interpersonal trauma in depersonalization disorder. *American Journal of Psychiatry, 157,* 1027–1033.

Simons, R. C., & Hughes, C. C. (Eds.). (1985). *The culture bound syndromes*. Dordrecht, the Netherlands: Reidel.

Sivec, H. J., & Lynn, S. J. (1995). Dissociative and neuropsychological symptoms: The question of differential diagnosis. *Clinical Psychology Review, 15,* 297–316.

Sledge, W. H., Boydstun, J. A., & Rabe, A. J. (1980). Self-concept changes related to war captivity. *Archives of General Psychiatry, 37,* 430–443.

Southwick, S. M., Yehuda, R., & Giller, E., Jr. (1993). Personality disorders in treatment-seeking combat veterans with post-

traumatic stress disorder. *American Journal of Psychiatry, 150,* 1020–1023.

Spanos, N. P. (1994). Multiple identity enactments and multiple personality disorder: A sociocognitive perspective. *Psychological Bulletin, 116,* 143–165.

Spiegel, D. (1981). Vietnam grief work using hypnosis. *American Journal of Clinical Hypnosis, 24,* 33–40.

Spiegel, D., & Cardeña, E. (1991). Disintegrated experience: The dissociative disorders revisited. *Journal of Abnormal Psychology, 100,* 366–378.

Spiegel, D., Classen, C., & Cardeña, E. (2000). Letter to the editor. *American Journal of Psychiatry, 157,* 1890.

Spiegel, D., Hunt, T., & Dondershine, H. E. (1988). Dissociation and hypnotizability in posttraumatic stress disorder. *American Journal of Psychiatry, 145,* 301–305.

Spiegel, H. (1974). The grade 5 syndrome: The highly hypnotizable person. *International Journal of Clinical & Experimental Hypnosis, 22,* 303–319.

Staab, J. P., Grieger, T. A., Fullerton, C. S., & Ursano, R. J. (1996). Acute stress disorder, subsequent posttraumatic stress disorder and depression after a series of typhoons. *Anxiety, 16,* 219–225.

Taylor, E. (2000). Transformation of tragedy among women surviving breast cancer. *Oncology Nursing Forum, 27,* 781–788.

Tedeschi, R. G., & Calhoun, L. G. (1995). *Trauma and transformation: Growing in the aftermath of suffering*. Thousand Oaks, CA: Sage.

Terr, L. C. (1991). Childhood traumas: An outline and overview. *American Journal of Psychiatry, 148,* 10–20.

Torrie, L. (1944). Psychosomatic casualties in the Middle East. *Lancet, 29,* 139–143.

Tsai, G. E., Condie, D., Wu, M. T., & Chang, I. W. (1999). Functional magnetic resonance imaging of personality switches in a woman with dissociative identity disorder. *Harvard Review of Psychiatry, 7,* 119–122.

Tutkun, H., Sar, V., Yargic, I., Ozpulat, T., Yanik, M., & Kiziltan, E. (1998). Frequency of dissociative disorders among psychiatric inpatients in a Turkish university clinic. *American Journal of Psychiatry, 155,* 800–805.

Ursano, R. J. (1981). The Vietnam era prisoner of war: Precaptivity personality and the development of psychiatric illness. *American Journal of Psychiatry, 138,* 315–318.

Ursano, R. J., & Rundell, J. R. (1995). The prisoner of war. In F. Jones, L. R. Sparacino, V. L. Wilcox, J. M. Rothberg, & J. W. Stokes (Eds.), *Textbook of military medicine: War psychiatry* (Vol. 2, pp. 431–455). Washington, DC: U. S. Government Printing Office.

van der Hart, O., & Nijenhuis, E. (2001). Generalized dissociative amnesia: Episodic, semantic and procedural memories lost and found. *Australian and New Zealand Journal of Psychiatry, 5,* 589–600.

van der Kolk, B. A. (1996). The body keeps the score. In B. A. van der Kolk, A. C. McFarlane, & L. Weisaeth (Eds.), *Traumatic stress: The effects of overwhelming experience on mind, body, and society* (pp. 214–241). New York: Guilford Press.

van der Kolk, B. A., McFarlane, A. C., & Weisaeth, L. (Eds.). (1996). *Traumatic stress: The effects of overwhelming experience on mind, body, and society.* New York: Guilford.

van der Kolk, B. A., Pelcovitz, D., Roth, S., Mandel, F., McFarlane, A., & Herman, J. L. (1996). Dissociation, affect dysregulation, and somatization: The complexity of adaptation to trauma. *American Journal of Psychiatry, 153,* (Festschrift Suppl.), 83–93.

van der Kolk, B., Weisaeth, L., & van der Hart, O. (1996). History of trauma in psychiatry. In B. A. van der Kolk, A. C. McFarlane, & L. Weisaeth (Eds.), *Traumatic stress* (pp. 47–74). New York: Guilford.

Vanderlinden, J., van der Hart, O., & Varga, K. (1996). European studies of dissociation. In L. K. Michelson & W. J. Ray (Eds.), *Handbook of dissociation: Theoretical, empirical and clinical perspectives* (pp. 25–49). New York: Plenum.

van Ommeren, M. V., Sharma, B., Komproe, I., Sharma, G. K., Cardeña, E., de Jong, J. T., Poudyal, B., & Makaju, R. (2001). Trauma and loss as determinants of medically unexplained epidemic illness in a Bhutanese refugee camp. *Psychological Medicine, 31,* 1259–1267.

Waelde, L. C., Koopman, C., Rierdan, J., & Spiegel, D. (2001). Symptoms of acute stress disorder and posttraumatic stress disorder following exposure to disastrous flooding. *Journal of Trauma and Dissociation, 2,* 37–52.

Waller, N. G., & Ross, C. (1997). The prevalence and biometric structure of pathological dissociation in the general population: Taxometric and behavior genetic findings. *Journal of Abnormal Psychology, 106,* 499–510.

Widiger, T. A., & Clark, L. E. A. (2001). Toward *DSM-V* and the classification of psychopathology. *Psychological Bulletin, 126,* 946–963.

Widom, C. (1999). Posttraumatic stress disorder in abused and neglected children grown up. *American Journal of Psychiatry, 8,* 1223–1229.

World Health Organization. (1992). *ICD-10: International Statistics Classification of Diseases and Related Health Problems, 10th Revision.* Geneva: Author.

Yehuda, R., Elkin, A., Binder-Brynes, K., Kahana, B., Southwick, S. M., Schmeidler, J., & Giller, E. L., Jr. (1996). Dissociation in aging Holocaust survivors. *American Journal of Psychiatry, 153,* 935–940.

Yehuda, R., Halligan, S. L., & Bierer, L. M. (2001). Relationship of parental trauma exposure and PTSD to PTSD, depressive and anxiety disorders in offspring. *Journal of Psychiatric Research, 5,* 261–270.

Yehuda, R., & McFarlane, A. C. (1995). Conflict between current knowledge about posttraumatic stress disorder and its original conceptual basis. *American Journal of Psychiatry, 152,* 1705–1713.

Yehuda, R., McFarlane, A. C., & Shalev, A. Y. (1998). Predicting the development of posttraumatic stress disorder from the acute response to a traumatic event. *Biological Psychiatry, 44,* 1305–1313.

Zatzick, D. F., Marmar, C. R., Weiss, D. S., & Metzler, T. (1994). Does trauma-linked dissociation vary across ethnic groups? *Journal of Nervous and Mental Disease, 182,* 576–582.

Zlotnick, C., Zakriski, A. L., Shea, M. T., Costello, E., Begin, A., Pearlstein, T., & Simpson, E. (1996). The long-term sequelae of sexual abuse: Support for a complex posttraumatic stress disorder. *Journal of Traumatic Stress, 9,* 195–205.

PART TWO

# PSYCHOTHERAPY

# CHAPTER 10

# Psychodynamic Psychotherapy

NANCY McWILLIAMS AND JOEL WEINBERGER

Psychodynamic psychotherapy originated in the efforts of Sigmund Freud to understand and treat the perplexing array of severe psychopathologies diagnosed as hysteria in the nineteenth century. The language and metaphors in which early analytic thinking was framed reflect a European sensibility that includes post-Darwinian excitement about tracing origins, Cartesian assumptions that the mind controls the body, and Enlightenment-era optimism about the promise of science to propel civilization upward from savagery or the so-called state of nature depicted by philosophers such as Locke and Hobbes. More than a century later, it is hard to grasp the passion Freud conveyed about the prospect of understanding and alleviating miseries that had tormented human beings throughout history.

There is still a passionate temperament or romantic-intuitive world view embedded in psychoanalytic theories that inclines some of us to embrace them and others to disparage them (Messer & Winokur, 1980; Schneider, 1998). Mitchell and Black (1995) summarized the convictions held in common by diverse analytic thinkers as involving respect for "the complexity of the mind, the importance of unconscious mental processes, and the value of a sustained inquiry into subjective experience" (p. 206). Most psychodynamic thinking has emerged from clinical practice rather than from the research tradition of academic psychology. In this chapter we first cover developments in psychoanalytic clinical theory and then review empirical findings relevant to psychodynamic treatment. After more than a century of complicated, contentious evolution in psychodynamic metapsychology, practice, and research, we can hit only the high spots.

## HISTORICAL BACKGROUND OF CONTEMPORARY PSYCHODYNAMIC PSYCHOTHERAPY

When Freud was formulating his early theories, diagnostic conventions reflected the work of Emil Kraepelin, whose nosology was descriptive. He divided psychological afflictions into neuroses and psychoses. In neuroses, the patient kept in touch with

The authors wish to thank Stanley Messer and Kerry Gordon for their helpful critiques of an earlier draft of this chapter.

reality. Psychoses included *dementia praecox* (schizophrenia, considered organic and incurable) and *manic-depressive psychosis* (bipolar illness with psychotic features), viewed as having a complex etiology and as potentially treatable. Under neurosis in Kraepelin's era were four syndromes: *phobias, obsessive-compulsive disorders, nonpsychotic depressions,* and the *hysterias.* The first three correspond roughly to the same categories in current taxonomies. The last included physical and mental disabilities with no physiological explanation—for example, inexplicable blindness, deafness, epileptiform seizures, anesthesia, paralysis, amnesia, and out-of-control acts at odds with a sufferer's usual self.

Freud became fascinated by neurosis: How do human beings become terrified by an object they know not to be dangerous, become immobilized by anxiety if they cannot perform a ritual, believe themselves unworthy despite all evidence to the contrary, or suffer a physical illness with no physical cause? Nineteenth-century doctors were exasperated by hysteria—improbable complaints voiced by people who often had self-dramatizing, provocative personalities. Freud's determination to take (mostly female) sufferers of hysteria seriously attests to both his relentless curiosity and his admiration for Jean Charcot, who was demonstrating that hysterical symptoms can be made to disappear via hypnotic suggestion.

## CLASSICAL DRIVE-CONFLICT THEORY

Inspired by Charcot, Freud began experimenting with hypnosis and with entreaties to patients with hysterical problems to think out loud about the origins of their symptoms. His discovery of the superiority of *free association* over hypnosis is attributable to a talented patient of his collaborator Josef Breuer. Anna O. (the pseudonym given to Bertha Pappenheim) insisted that simply reporting her stream of consciousness led to relief from her suffering; she called it chimney sweeping. When this activity led to an emotionally charged memory of something deeply upsetting, specific symptoms would disappear. On the basis of this kind of work, Freud and Breuer postulated that hysterical symptoms express traumatic memories that need to be *abreacted*—that is, remembered and experienced in their original intensity.

### Freud's Topographic, Economic, and Dynamic Models

Freud began developing a model of the mind envisioned as containing a vast unconscious reservoir of primitive urges, affects, thoughts, and memories that—despite the Victorian conceit that civilized adults outgrow their childish preoccupations—continue to affect human impulses, emotions,

thoughts, and reactions to stress. He argued that the psyche is like an iceberg: Most of it (the *unconscious* system) is submerged; a smaller part (the *preconscious* system) is potentially in awareness; the tiniest part (the *conscious* system) consists of what is at any time in mind. Freud's earliest conception of therapy involved trying to connect with material in a patient's unconscious life that was exerting a negative influence on her functioning. This formulation has been called the *topographical model,* as it involves progressively "deeper" layers of mentation.

From working with hysterical patients, Freud and Breuer concluded that people can keep disturbing, intolerable experiences out of consciousness—a process they termed *repression.* Much as contemporary psychologists feel defensive about the place of their field relative to the "hard sciences" and consequently convey ideas in terms of models from more prestigious disciplines, Freud tried to stress the scientific nature of his conclusions by expropriating concepts from seminal physicists such as Hermann Helmholtz and Gustav Fechner. Concepts like psychic energy, cathexis, dynamics, abreaction, and repression are all nineteenth-century physics terms.

Freud posited that although the mental effort required to achieve repression may have been necessary in childhood, its continued operation in adults is not warranted: Unlike children, adults can understand traumatic events, articulate reactions to them, and protect themselves from potential abusers. The energy required to keep their traumatic memories unconscious drains and depletes their general psychology. Hence, Freud inferred, treatment that undoes repression will free up the patient's energy for use in positive directions. This idea of shifting quantities of psychic energy from one area to another has been called his *economic model.*

Hysterical symptoms were seen as products of a repressive process that did not entirely succeed; hints of the original trauma abide in the symptom. For example, an adult who had been traumatically shamed for masturbating as a child might develop a paralysis of the hand (glove anesthesia, a condition perhaps as common in Freud's era and culture as anorexia is in ours). The symptom was believed to have the *primary gain* of ruling out masturbation, without the patient's feeling either painful temptation or humiliating prohibition. It had the *secondary gain* of getting the now-disabled patient some loving attention. The site of the paralysis suggested that the trauma was related to an activity of the hand. Similarly, hysterical blindness or deafness implied that the patient had seen or heard something that had been too overwhelming to take in: The disability thus was seen as containing "the return of the repressed" (Freud, 1896, p. 169).

The term *conversion* was coined to refer to the mind's capacity to transform traumatic experiences into bodily states that both resolve a painful conflict and symbolize its nature. Intolerably coexisting ideas are *converted* into a compromise-formation, the symptom. The construal of hysterical disorders as expressions of unconscious conflict was the origin of the general tendency in psychoanalysis to view psychological problems as expressing a subterranean tension and compromise between at least two contradictory aims: social respectability versus uninhibited expression, conscience versus impulse, and so on. Freud soon applied this model to other neuroses, including obsessive and compulsive syndromes, depressions, phobias, and some instances of paranoia. This emphasis on the dynamics of internal forces operating in opposition—and the consequent disposition to attribute psychological suffering to failed attempts to resolve unconscious conflicts—is the core of what is called the *dynamic model* in psychoanalytic theory.

Freud initially believed that neurotic symptoms result from sexual abuse or seduction of the young child. Like many discoverers of dissociation in the 1980s, he originally assumed that events recalled in therapy are veridical with early experiences. Readers who have seen clients relive a trauma with all its affect may appreciate how credulous a sympathetic observer can be about the historical accuracy of the memory; the emotional power of the description feels too authentic to be contrived. Later, however, Freud concluded that not all of what his patients "remembered" could have happened. Reluctantly (Masson, 1985, p. 264) he postulated that some of the recollections of hysterical patients stand for experiences even more disturbing than traumatic memories—experiences in which the patient felt not only like a victim but also like an actor in a perverse drama. To account for the prevalence of unsubstantiated convictions about childhood molestation, Freud had to devise a more complex theory. Therapy then evolved from the effort to remember and abreact into a more complex process; this process widened the explanatory power of psychoanalytic thinking about symptom formation and created possibilities for helping people with problems outside the hysterical realm, but it also contributed to minimizing the harm done by early sexual abuse. It disposed therapists toward skepticism about reports of incest and molestation, thereby doing a grave disservice to patients with trauma histories.

## The Genetic Model: Psychoanalytic Developmental Theory

Eventually, Freud concluded that although beliefs in childhood sexual molestations are sometimes based on valid recollections, often they are *screen memories*—partial expressions, partial disguises—for children's erotic longings. Screen memories were seen as condensations of wishes, fears, and

experiences of some kind of sexual overstimulation. Freud began emphasizing (as pathogenic) certain outcomes of what he considered a universal *Oedipus complex,* the desire of children between about 3 and 6 years of age to possess one parent sexually and be rid of the other, combined with fears (magnified by projections of the child's aggression) that the parent one wished to displace would retaliate by murder or mutilation. He postulated that it is the strength of these fears—along with the "civilized" person's horror of acknowledging primitive incestuous wishes—that provide the impetus for repression.

This emphasis on children's oedipal fantasies was grafted on to Freud's existing ideas about infant development. His assumptions about child rearing betray both Platonic and Victorian tendencies to idealize self-knowledge and self-discipline (controlling one's baser instincts, taming the beast within). He saw infants as insatiable, striving animals—and parenting as a balancing act between gratifying and thwarting the instinctual drives of offspring as they move through an invariant sequence of preoccupation with *oral, anal,* and *genital* satisfactions. According to Freud, a child can develop a *fixation* on the issues of a particular phase if he or she is either traumatically frustrated or seductively overgratified at that stage or if the constitutional intensity of that child's oral, anal, or oedipal drives is particularly strong.

Following Darwin, Freud assumed that the essence of the primitive continues to exist in the form of the evolved. Applying this concept to individuals, he began to view neuroses as representing a stress-related *regression* to the passions of an early stage at which one is fixated unconsciously. For example, he argued that frugality, stubbornness, and fastidiousness—a triad of traits noted in people with obsessive and compulsive symptoms—betray a fixation on the anal phase of development, with its issues of expelling versus withholding, complying versus rebelling, and cleanliness versus mess. This idea of an orderly progression of conflicts organized around erogenous zones has been called the *genetic model,* meaning that the *genesis* of neurosis lies in normal maturational sequences and the drives and fantasies that accompany them.

This shift of emphasis from assumed seduction to infantile sexual striving and associated terrors led to substantial revisions in early psychoanalytic technique. Although Freud still aimed to make the unconscious conscious, the problematic contents of the unconscious mind were seen not so much as traumatic memories as they were unacceptable wishes and terrifying, primordial fears. Rather than urging his patients to have the courage to remember traumatic events, Freud began to lecture them about the normality of children's erotic fantasies and about how they were behaving as if their natural sexual and competitive strivings were somehow dangerous. Instead of seeing them essentially as victims of incestuous perpetrators who needed to recount their ordeal, Freud began viewing his patients as agents coping with powerful sensual and aggressive urges—agents whose energies were being put into symptom formation rather than into achievements in love and work. Psychotherapy became an effort to put a person's impeded development back on track rather than a mission to heal the unconscious scars of trauma.

The language of drive and energy in which Freud couched his economic, dynamic, and genetic models is referred to as *drive theory*. The Freudian term for the drive toward closeness, physical satisfaction in touch, and eventually adult sexuality is *libido* or *libidinal energy*. His early theories treated this energy as the wellspring of all human motivation. Later, possibly in reaction to World War I, he developed a dualistic theory, emphasizing the equivalent importance of the drive toward separateness, difference, antagonism, and ultimately death, usually referred to simply as *aggression* or the *aggressive drive*. Freud's early notion of symptom formation is termed the *drive-conflict model*. This conceptualization originated when Freud was still thinking topographically, but it carried over into his structural model, explicated about 30 years later. Certain concepts from the early theory have been remarkably persistent: Practitioners still refer to secondary gain when they describe circumstances that reinforce a problematic condition, conversion disorder remains an official diagnosis in *DSM-IV*, and the term *psychodynamic* endures as the umbrella label under which psychoanalytically influenced ideas are categorized.

Although contemporary practitioners reject the nineteenth-century drive models in which Freud's first theories were grounded, clinical experience has so consistently noted the value of both free association and emotional expression that these early emphases persist. There are now substantial bodies of empirical literature attesting to the associative nature of unconscious cognition (see Westen, 1998) and to the value of expressing feelings (Frey, 1985; Pennebaker, 1997). Some widely repudiated drive-conflict concepts live on in psychoanalytic language, presumably because of a combination of familiarity and intuitive resonance. Even in nonprofessional conversation, one sometimes hears comments like *What did you do with your anger?*—as if anger contains a finite amount of energy that must be *put* somewhere to avoid some intrapsychic cost. Such is the legacy of Freud's debt to the physics of his time.

### Clinical Implications of Freud's Early Theories

Freud wrote surprisingly little about therapeutic technique. His own was highly variable. Even after he gave up hypnosis

and suggestion, he was hardly the stereotype of the silent, withholding analyst (Lipton, 1977). Over time, he made changes in how he worked, eventually adopting an approach that put more responsibility on the patient as a coinvestigator. In the second decade of the twentieth century (Freud, 1911, 1912a, 1912b, 1913, 1914, 1915), he laid out his ideas about how to conduct a psychoanalysis in quite nondogmatic language, comparing treatment to chess, in which opening and closing moves "admit of an exhaustive systematic presentation" (1912, p. 123), but everything else requires art and judgment. He explained practices such as using the couch and charging a fee for missed sessions as expressing his personal preferences rather than as rigid rules. His main emphases included urging free expression, avoiding formulaic interpretations, expecting and respecting resistances to change, and not exploiting feelings (especially erotic ones) transferred from old love objects to the therapist. The use of *free association* and the analysis of *transference* and *resistance* in a relationship marked by *abstinence* and *neutrality* gradually became definitional of psychoanalytic treatment.

Transference was originally an unwelcome discovery. Freud found that although he was trying to come across as a benignly concerned doctor, he was instead being experienced as if he were a significant figure from a patient's past. At first, he tried to talk people out of these attitudes with lectures about *displacement* (shifting the target of a drive from one object to a less disturbing one) and *projection* (attribution of one's disowned strivings to others), but eventually he concluded that it was only in the context of a relationship dominated by transference that healing takes place. "It is impossible to destroy anyone *in absentia* or *in effigie*" (Freud, 1912a, p. 108), he commented, referring to how in analysis a person can have the experience of having a different outcome to a problematic early relationship. Resistance, the unconscious effort to cling to the familiar even when it is self-damaging, was also first subjected to frontal attack (Freud was not above complaining *You're resisting!*) but later became understood as an inevitable process that must be respected and worked through. Abstinence referred to the avoidance of exploitation, especially when a patient's transference was romantic or idealizing; neutrality referred to the commitment that the therapeutic role not be used in the pursuit of the analyst's personal ambitions, goals, and values.

Freud saw people an hour a day, 5 or 6 days a week. When doctor and patient were together this often, with one party urged to say anything and the other saying rather little, patients had more than passing transference reactions; they tended to develop a *transference neurosis,* a set of attitudes, affects, and fantasies about the analyst expressing themes and conflicts from their individual childhoods. Eventually, psychoanalysis became defined as the process by which a transference neurosis is allowed to emerge and is then analyzed and re-solved (Etchegoyen, 1991; Greenson, 1967). Resolution meant *working through* an understanding of the diverse effects of one's core conflicts, ultimately substituting knowledge and agency for the unreflective, involuntary expressions of conflict that had required treatment. With some justification, intellectuals of the early Freudian era quipped that analysts create a disease in order to cure it.

## FREUD'S STRUCTURAL MODEL AND THE DEVELOPMENT OF EGO PSYCHOLOGY

In 1923, for complex reasons including a growing appreciation of the unconscious nature of defenses and the superego (Arlow & Brenner, 1964), Freud replaced his topographical model with a *structural theory,* the famous division of the mind into intrapsychic agencies. The *id,* roughly equivalent to the topographic unconscious, was envisioned as a seething cauldron of drives, impulses, primitive affects, and prelogical cognition (*primary process thought*); the *ego,* a term Freud often used synonymously with *self,* emerges as the child matures, to cope with reality and its limits on instant gratification. The id follows Fechner's *pleasure principle;* the ego operates according to the *reality principle.* Ego processes were seen as involving such activities as language, problem solving, and logical cognition (*secondary process thought*). Eventually, as the child identifies with caregivers' values, the *superego* arises from the ego as the voice of conscience and personal ideals. Freud described the id (it, in German) as entirely unconscious and the ego (I or me) and superego (above me) as partly conscious and partly unconscious. Prophetically, Freud believed that these metaphorical concepts would eventually be replaced by an understanding of neurophysiological processes.

Unconscious aspects of the ego include habitual ways of functioning, such as reliance on *defense mechanisms* like repression. Unconscious superego functions were inferred from self-punishing behaviors that imply a sense of guilt. An enduring literature—theoretical, clinical, and empirical—arose on ego processes and defense mechanisms (A. Freud, 1936; Hartmann, 1958; Laughlin, 1970/1979; Vaillant, 1992). Analysts began distinguishing between higher-order defenses and putatively more infantile processes such as *withdrawal, denial, splitting of the ego, omnipotent control, projective identification* (M. Klein, 1946), and primitive forms of *idealization* and *devaluation.* It was observed that patients with classically neurotic problems rely mainly on less global, less reality-distorting defenses such as *repression, regression, reaction-formation, isolation of affect,* and *reversal,* whereas more disturbed clients depend heavily on less mature ways to handle anxiety and other negative states.

The tripartite image of the psyche ushered in the era of *ego psychology.* This term refers to the change from attention to the nature of the id to the study and treatment of the functions of the ego (and to a lesser extent, those of the superego). The ego psychology period saw important revisions of Freudian epistemologies. Erikson (1950), for example, recast Freud's psychosexual stages in terms of the *psychosocial* tasks faced by the baby, restating Freud's oral, anal, and oedipal sequence to describe the young child's negotiation of trust, autonomy, and initiative, respectively. Later, Mahler (e.g., 1968) rethought the same phases in terms of symbiosis, separation-individuation, and object constancy. These contributions had wide-ranging consequences for the emerging discipline of psychotherapy (Blanck & Blanck, 1974, 1979).

### Clinical Implications of Ego Psychology

Ego psychology concepts eventually changed the nature of therapists' interventions. Instead of trying to expose the *contents* of the unconscious part of the mind (thoughts, feelings, fantasies, and impulses of the id), practitioners began to address the ego and superego *processes* that were keeping them out of consciousness. This clinical paradigm shift allowed patients to have more of a sense of discovery of their own dynamics. It translates into the difference between saying *You desired your mother* and *I notice that every time we talk about your mother's beauty, you get sleepy,* or the difference between *You're obviously angry at me,* and *You seem to be disagreeing with everything I say today. What comes to mind about that?*

The structural model ushered in a more collaborative version of therapy. Treatment was seen as requiring a *therapeutic alliance* (Zetzel, 1956) or *working alliance* (Greenson, 1967) between the clinician and the *observing ego* of the patient (the conscious parts of the person's ego and superego that can describe feelings, thoughts, impulses, actions, and ideals). Together, both parties would examine the client's *experiencing ego,* especially its defensive patterns. The goal of treatment became the modification of maladaptive, habitual defenses that manifest themselves as symptoms. Such defenses were understood as the residue of efforts to cope with a childhood situation for which they had been adaptive. Resistance was reconceptualized as an expression of the patient's core defenses, *as they manifest themselves in the therapy relationship.*

The shift to the structural model also allowed practitioners to frame the therapeutic task differently depending on whether a patient was neurotic or psychotic, hysterical or obsessional or phobic or depressed, troubled by a sudden response to stress or burdened by a rigid character structure (Fenichel, 1945). For example, it became conventional clinical wisdom that one should *undermine* the defenses of people with neurotic-level problems (so that they would become less frightened of derivatives from their id), whereas one should *support* defenses of people with psychotic-level pathology (thus helping them recover from having been overwhelmed with material from their id). Types of psychopathology were associated with particular defenses (e.g., hysterical problems with regression, repression, and conversion; obsessive-compulsive problems with isolation of affect and undoing; phobic reactions with symbolization and displacement) that required different styles of therapeutic response. This emphasis gave clinicians a set of interventions that were much more powerful than simply relating symptoms to levels of psychosexual fixation.

A distinction arose between *symptom neurosis* and *character neurosis,* one still echoed in Axis I versus Axis II disorders, respectively, in recent editions of the *DSM*. People with symptom neuroses were described as able to remember not having their current problems and as feeling anxious about them and consequently motivated to change. Their difficulties were hence dubbed *ego-alien* or *ego-dystonic*. Because they could readily ally with a therapist and adopt mutual goals, patients with symptom neuroses could do brief, problem-focused work (some early analyses lasted only a few weeks). Clients with character pathology (personality disorders) were depicted as *not* notably anxious about what others saw as their psychological problems; their histories suggested they had "always" had what a therapist would see as maladaptive defenses. Their psychopathology was thus termed *ego-syntonic*. For these people, long-term work was required in order to develop a working alliance in which the patient gradually accepts the therapist's idea of the problem and develops a vision of what it would be like not to have it.

Psychotherapy was conceived as a process that aims *to strengthen the ego* (including making defensive processes less automatic and more flexible), *to modify the superego* (making a person's moral precepts more consistent with what is achievable instead of infantile fantasies of purity or perfection), and *to put the energies of the id under the agency of the ego and superego* (directing the powerful, primitive contents of the id into positive directions instead of self-defeating or socially destructive ones). By 1933, Freud was describing the ideal outcome of treatment with the aphorism "Where id was, there shall ego be" (p. 80).

### Psychoanalysis and Psychodynamic Psychotherapy

The term *psychoanalysis* can refer, confusingly, to a theoretical position, a body of knowledge, or a type of psychotherapy. As to the therapy, some have followed Freud's more catholic definition of psychoanalysis as any procedure that deals with transference and resistance. Others have reserved *psychoanalytic* for references to classical, intensive treatment, preferring the term *psychodynamic* for any therapy or theoretical stance informed primarily by analytic theory (Westen, 1990). The ego psychology era inaugurated efforts to define psychoanalysis as a therapy and to stipulate its efficacy for various problems. The issue of who is analyzable became a hot topic theoretically and empirically (Erle, 1979; Erle & Goldberg, 1984). Distinctions were made between analysis proper (classical psychoanalysis) and more focused, analytically influenced therapies. For reasons of both expense (classical analysis is costly) and applicability (it is contraindicated for patients in whom it precipitates disorganization), analysts began developing definitions of the differences between—and the differential applications of—psychoanalysis and analytically oriented psychotherapy.

The critical difference between an analysis and a therapy is, of course, the content of what happens. Psychoanalysis is a comprehensive, open-ended effort to understand all of one's central fantasies, desires, fears, defenses, identifications, and expectations; psychotherapy has the more modest goal of relieving a particular symptom or problem. Analysis was assumed to be ideal for resolving difficulties inhering in a person's character, whereas therapy might adequately ameliorate a symptom neurosis. To accomplish the ambitious task of a full analysis, clinical experience suggested that patients must undergo a contained regression in the treatment, in which the analyst gradually attains the emotional power previously held by early caregivers—hence the centrality of a transference neurosis to both cure and prevention. Such a regression is more likely to happen under conditions of frequent contact between therapist and patient.

Freud had stressed that to help others explore their darkest places, the analyst must have been there. It quickly became an article of faith in the psychoanalytic community that the most important preparation for practice is to undergo a thoroughgoing personal analysis (see Fromm-Reichmann, 1950). Training institutes specified conditions, in the form of requirements, that would increase the probability that trainees would develop and analyze a transference neurosis. The question of how closely appointments must be spaced to ensure a full analytic process is still hotly debated. Most current analysts define analysis as requiring three to five sessions per week and psychodynamic therapy as requiring two or fewer.

An interesting controversy of the ego psychology period involved the mechanisms of therapeutic change. Alexander and French (1946) disquieted a community whose reigning gods were insight and interpretation with the proposition that what is therapeutic in analytic treatment is not so much acquired self-knowledge as a *corrective emotional experience*.

Accounting for therapeutic progress in learning theory terms, they recommended that clinicians deliberately aim to be experienced as different from pathogenic early influences. Most mainstream analysts found their departure from traditional norms of neutrality suspect, and yet much subsequent clinical and empirical work (reviewed later in this chapter) has supported their general position.

Psychoanalysis underwent a remarkable popularization during World War II, when Roy Grinker and John Spiegel treated posttraumatic conditions in combatants with a combination of sodium pentothal and cathartic psychoanalytic therapy. Public interest in getting soldiers back on the front lines—along with the dramatic nature of traumatic symptoms and recoveries—produced a spate of stories in the media about the new treatments for war trauma (Hale, 1995) along with ebullient claims for the efficacy of psychoanalysis. At the same time, films like *Spellbound* and Broadway shows like *Lady in the Dark* were fanning public fascination with unconscious processes. This idealistic period had both positive and negative effects—prompting an increase in resources to treat mental illness, yet spawning an uncritical overvaluation of analysis and an unseemly smugness among some analysts. Disillusionment predictably set in as grandiose claims were contrasted with the relatively modest effects of psychodynamic therapies. The certainty of many analysts that the psychoanalytic movement had brought revolutionary, irreversible progress in mental health permitted an attitude of indifference to efforts to evaluate their treatments scientifically—an indifference that has returned to haunt them in a more skeptical era.

## THE OBJECT RELATIONS AND INTERPERSONAL CONTRIBUTIONS

As the ego psychology paradigm took shape, a different sensibility was stirring in several places. While keeping the Freudian emphasis on unconscious processes, this emerging paradigm replaced drive and conflict with *relationship* as a core construct, looked to preoedipal rather than oedipal origins of pathology, gave more weight to social and cultural contributors to individual dynamics, and attended to archaic modes of experiencing believed to predate the development of repression, conversion, displacement, and other defenses of interest to ego psychologists. Many analysts embodying these attitudes were influenced directly or indirectly by Freud's Hungarian colleague Sandor Ferenczi, whose warmth and flexibility moved him to experiment with a more personally interrelated kind of therapy from very early on. In the United States, such analysts called their discipline *interpersonal psychoanalysis* (e.g., Fromm, 1941; Fromm-Reichmann, 1950; Horney, 1945;

Sullivan, 1953); in Europe, a roughly comparable movement was becoming known as *object relations theory* (Fairbairn, 1952; Guntrip, 1971; Winnicott, 1958).

There are serious differences between and within these schools of thought, but for this review, we are stressing their shared thrust and similar divergences from drive-conflict theory and ego psychology, along with their joint contributions to the evolution of psychodynamic treatment. Together, they created the architecture of the *relational movement* in psychoanalysis (Aron, 1996; S. Mitchell, 1993, 1997, 2000). As individuals, the early relational theorists were more attuned than Freud was to mental processes that predate oedipal concerns. More critical to the nature of their thought, they were trying to help clients—children, impulsive and addicted people, schizophrenic and manic-depressive patients, and a group that was eventually labeled borderline—for whom classical concepts seemed tangential to the central pathological issues.

By the second half of the twentieth century, some of the most vital clinical writing was coming from people with interpersonal and object-relational emphases. Many of these thinkers were deeply influenced by post-Freudian research on *attachment*. The work of Spitz (1965), Bowlby (1969, 1973, 1982), Mahler (1968; Mahler, Pine, & Bergmann, 1975), and others who conducted observational studies of babies and mothers was crucial to the maturation of psychodynamic theories and therapies. Winnicott's ideas about infant mentation—shaped by his years of practice as a pediatrician—captured critical aspects of development about which drive theory was frustratingly silent. Because advocates of relational ideas lacked Freud's need to root their theories in biological science and because they saw infants and mothers as fundamentally interrelated rather than as separate motivational units (Balint, 1968; Winnicott, 1965), they could consider ultimately psychological rather than biological explanations for psychopathology.

Meanwhile, the discipline of clinical psychology was maturing. When World War II created a pressing need for evaluations and treatment, academic psychology programs began contributing graduates to the effort—professionals who found the theories of the psychoanalytic movement highly relevant to their tasks. Some psychologists began to publish empirical research on analytic ideas. Medical analysts, too (Wallerstein, 1986), were conducting empirical investigations. The existence of a number of psychoanalytic journals with differing ideological and institutional orientations allowed clinicians to publish their experiences of applying analytic concepts and to share their knowledge across an international community of professionals.

All of these developments produced a creative ferment in psychoanalytic theory, practice, and scholarship. The appearance of new institutes with divergent theoretical biases reinforced the fissiparous tendency that Freud had inaugurated via his disposition to equate disagreement with heresy (Breger, 2000). At the same time, however, seminal thinkers like Otto Kernberg struggled to synthesize and integrate—combining object relations theory with ego psychology and relationship with drive. While analytic celebrities haggled over which approach was the most epistemologically defensible and therapeutically effective, ordinary clinicians tended to draw from different theorists depending on the specific psychologies of their clients and were grateful for any angle of vision that threw light on the suffering of someone they were trying to help.

## Clinical Implications of the Object Relations and Interpersonal Traditions

One outcome of efforts to extend analytic help to previously untreatable conditions was the rejection of Kraepelin's dichotomy between neurosis and psychosis—sanity and insanity. As Sullivan, Fromm-Reichmann, Bion, Milner, Searles, and others worked with psychotic patients, continuities between their experiences and those of putatively normal people emerged. The more therapists could feel their way into their deeply disturbing subjective worlds, the more Freud's belief that human beings are all in some fundamental way psychotic became increasingly persuasive—until by the latter part of the twentieth century, psychoanalysts were referring to the psychotic core in all of us (Eigen, 1986). This conviction opened up possibilities for much deeper therapeutic work and contributed to a lengthening of psychodynamic therapies.

At the same time, awareness of a range of pathology lying *between* the psychotic and neurotic levels began to be noted by three different groups of professionals: those in outpatient practice, those in inpatient settings, and those with expertise in testing. Therapists in office practice reported that some people they took into analysis were unable to contain the regression fostered by standard approaches. Instead of settling into a relationship in which they could safely *feel* regressed, they would *become* regressed—swamped by intense feelings, impulsive behaviors, and transferences so unmitigated by reflection as to be considered psychotic. They tended to react to well-meaning interventions as if attacked, and they got worse rather than better in therapy. Their mental organization was not easily describable in terms of id, ego, and superego; they seemed to career from one *ego state* to another, in which self and others were alternately seen as all good or all bad. In hospital and clinic settings, observers were describing patients admitted as schizophrenic who—once safely in the institution—no longer looked psychotic and began to pose dismaying management problems. Typically, some of the medical personnel had intense rescue fantasies toward such a person, whereas the rest found him or her manipulative and hateful (T. Main, 1957). Among psychological testers, it was observed that some individuals appear psychotic on relatively unstructured tests like the Rorschach or thematic apperception test (TAT), yet they appear neurotic on structured instruments like the Wechsler Adult Intelligence Scales (WAIS) and the Minnesota Multiphasic Personality Inventory (MMPI; see Edell, 1987).

From these converging observations came the notion that there is a type of person on the *border* between psychosis and neurosis, someone with a kind of stable instability (Grinker, Werble, & Drye, 1968). Thus arose the concept of borderline personality organization. Eventually, enough research was done with people with this kind of psychology (Gunderson, 1984; Stone, 1980) to justify including an operationalized version of borderline dynamics in the personality disorders section of *DSM-III*. Meanwhile, a sizable literature was appearing on how treatment of such clients should differ from therapy for either psychotic or neurotic individuals.

Practitioners had already followed Freud in noting that the uncovering, exploratory kind of work he had devised to help neurotic patients is unsuited to psychotic individuals, children, and people in crisis. Some clients respond better to educative interventions, judicious advice, explicit support of their self-esteem, concrete evidence of the therapist's humanity, reinforcement of their most adaptive defenses, the involvement of external support services, and medication. This kind of work was eventually called *supportive psychotherapy* (Pinsker, 1997; Rockland, 1992). Conceptually, supportive therapy was described in ego psychology terms as an effort to strengthen a weak ego (as opposed to dismantling the defenses of a basically strong one to foster reconfiguration along healthier lines) and to encourage more adaptive behavior without trying to change the dynamics that had given rise to maladaptive responses.

As noted, the discovery of borderline pathology derived from clinical experience with clients for whom supportive therapy is infantilizing and uncovering therapy too disorganizing. It led to a flurry of efforts to devise appropriate treatments for people in this large group. The most visible early formulators of approaches for treating borderline clients were Masterson (1972, 1976) and Kernberg (1975, 1984), who hold somewhat different views but agree on the value of staying in the here and now (as opposed to dwelling on the client's history), of establishing contingencies that support mature responses and discourage immature ones, and of addressing primitive defenses like splitting (the tendency to divide experience into all-good and all-bad categories) and projective identification (the tendency to ascribe disowned qualities to another person while behaving in ways that subtly induce that person to react with just those qualities).

One of Kernberg's pivotal contributions was his argument that people in borderline states rely not on *weak* defenses against disorganization, as potentially psychotic people do, but rather on *strong but primitive* defenses. He originally called his approach *expressive therapy* but recently renamed his method *transference focused psychotherapy* (Clarkin, Kernberg, & Yeomans, 1998) to avoid its confusion with exploratory therapy. Thus, by the 1980s, three kinds of therapy had emerged from psychoanalytic theory and practice. Depending on the inferred character structure of the client, clinicians worked (a) in an exploratory way, letting transference reactions develop and become understood; (b) in a focused, expressive way, confronting the patient with defenses in the here and now; or (c) in a supportive way, behaving as an active mentor. For therapists learning to work psychodynamically with different kinds of people, the warm-up is the same, but the delivery is highly specific to the patient in question.

Not surprisingly, work with psychotic and borderline clients led dynamic therapists to a sensitivity to psychological processes that were seen as antedating oedipal conflicts and mature forms of identification and adaptation. Even less surprisingly, concepts relevant to the ways in which human beings symbolize and represent their preverbal experiences proved anything but irrelevant to higher functioning people. Attention to *introjects*—stark internalizations of comforting and persecutory images of others—supplemented efforts to understand ego defenses. If a client stated, for example, *I'm terribly selfish,* a therapist might respond, *Who's saying that?* in an effort to identify the internal object and help the person stand apart from it—as opposed to simply noting that he or she tends to turn negative feelings against the self.

The object relations movement constituted a transformation in which therapists found themselves asking new questions. Instead of looking for fixation at a particular maturational stage, they looked for the *nature of relationship* across all phases of development. It was argued that a mother who is rigid about toilet training is apt to be equally rigid about feeding schedules, sleep arrangements, appropriate gender roles, and deference to authority. To understand the child of such a parent, the concept of maternal rigidity seemed to have more explanatory power than did that of anal fixation. Furthermore, clinicians reported more progress when they told clients that they may have had a certain kind of mother—one from whom they could now differentiate themselves—than when they told clients they were fixated at the anal stage and needed to pursue genitality.

An example of the clinical value of the shift toward relational thinking concerns how therapists respond to clients

with an incest history. Freud viewed molestation as the premature gratification of a drive, thus emphasizing biological excitability and utterly missing the child's experience of being used, scared by the incomprehensible phenomenon of adult sexual arousal, and made to feel confusing mixtures of intense pain and premature genital responsiveness. The language of drive gratification or frustration cannot capture the atmosphere of an incestuous enactment or appreciate why it can be so destructive. But when one talks in terms of what kind of *relationship* a child needs to feel safe, agentic, and understood, both the subjective world of the molested child and the damage to that child are much clearer (Davies & Frawley, 1993).

## THE SELF PSYCHOLOGY MOVEMENT

As the twentieth century advanced, psychoanalytic therapy flourished. Yet experienced practitioners noted that the types of problems prevalent at midcentury—especially in Americans—differed from those that had intrigued the early European analysts. Many clients complained of emptiness, meaninglessness, and envy. They could not maintain a realistic, positively valued sense of themselves and found it hard to love others. They were perfectionistic, were consumed with how they were perceived, and were either grandiose and contemptuous or self-loathing and ashamed, depending on their perceptions of others' reactions to them. In therapy, they did not develop familiar analyzable transferences, and they tended to perceive interpretation as criticism.

By the 1970s the effort to extend psychoanalytic help to people with these self-esteem problems had led to a vast literature on narcissism. A focus on how people come to understand and accept who they are had been foreshadowed by Erikson's (1959) writing on identity and by observations of many previous analysts interested in how people develop a stable sense of self (Balint, 1968; Fairbairn, 1952; Guntrip, 1971; Jacobson, 1964, 1971; Mahler, 1968; Sullivan, 1953, 1956; Winnicott, 1958, 1965, 1971). But it was Heinz Kohut (1971, 1977) who radically reformulated psychoanalytic theories and therapies of narcissism; in the process, he created a movement that saw the formation of a positively valued sense of self as far more central to mental health than was the struggle with drive and conflict.

### Clinical Implications of Self Psychology

Although Kohut originally wrote about the specific challenges of treating patients with narcissistic problems or disorders of the self, his ideas quickly grew into a general psychology that his successors consider universal (e.g., Basch, 1988; Goldberg, 1988; Shane, Shane, & Gales, 1997; Wolf, 1988). Contributions to the art of therapy from Kohut and his students are manifold, but the most important include his depiction of previously unidentified kinds of transferences, his elevation of empathy to a preeminent role, and his emphasis on and recommendations for dealing with the inadvertent injuries that therapists inevitably inflict on patients' self-esteem.

Psychodynamic clinicians trying to help clients with narcissistic problems had become frustrated with their inability to develop analyzable transferences. Efforts to show such patients that they were experiencing the therapist as an early object elicited not interest, but rather boredom and irritation. Queries like *How are you feeling about me?* would evoke only suspicions about the therapist's insecurity or vanity. Then Kohut argued that although narcissistically preoccupied people do not generate transferences like those Freud wrote about, they do develop *selfobject transferences:* They unconsciously regard the analyst not as a separate object resembling someone from the past (an *object transference*); rather, the analyst is seen as a means to consolidate self-esteem. In other words, they need the therapist in the emotional role that an affirming parent plays in the years before a child appreciates the parent's separate identity. Among the selfobject transferences, Kohut delineated idealizing, mirroring, and twinship or alter ego transferences.

*Idealizing transferences* handle self-esteem problems with the fantasy that the analyst is perfect and omnipotent; the client feels elevated by associating with this ideal figure. (Kernberg was more impressed with the tendency of narcissistic clients to develop *devaluing* transferences, in which the person gets self-esteem from feeling superior to the therapist.) *Mirroring transferences* refer to the experience of being seen and validated, allowing the client to feel deeply known and prized despite whatever shameful states of mind appear in therapy. *Twinship* or *alter ego transferences* occur when the patient sees the therapist as radically similar, aiding self-esteem because "there is someone basically like me out there." Identification of these processes helped clinicians to appreciate divergent ways in which people experience the therapeutic relationship, to devise means of working with them, and to stop trying to push clients to find reactions that are alien to their most basic ways of organizing interpersonal information.

The promotion of *empathic attunement* from facilitating attitude to the *sine qua non* of therapy was a significant corrective to the privileged status of interpretation of defense in ego psychology. Whereas drive-conflict models emphasize the importance of frustrating a client's wish for closeness or penchant to idealize so that such urges can be analyzed, self

psychologists saw what classical analysts termed *gratification* as a prerequisite for healing. The acceptance by therapists of patients' need to see them in self-esteem-restorative roles led to subtle but significant changes in intervention. Questions like *Why do you suppose you need to see me as perfectly attuned?* became comments like *You feel deeply understood by me.* The analysis of identification as a defense (*I wonder why you selectively perceive us as so similar*) became the appreciation of identification as a need (*You take pleasure in noticing how we are alike*).

Flexibility in practice was legitimated by self psychology. Whereas the classical analyst would avoid answering a question in order to explore the thoughts and feelings that had inspired it, a self psychologist would answer it when the patient might perceive failure to answer as a breach of empathy. Drive-oriented analysts had been trained to reject small gifts from clients because gratification of the impulse to give would allow that impulse to remain unanalyzed; following Kohut, it became permissible to accept a gift if it would wound the patient not to do so. Many clinicians heaved sighs of relief to have a respected psychoanalytic theory that justified departures from standard technique—departures that they were already making on an intuitive basis.

Comparable changes had long been urged by Carl Rogers (1951), with arguments from a different metapsychology but based on similar clinical observations (Stolorow, 1976). Kohut went significantly beyond the nondirective therapists, however, in his belief that no matter how exquisitely empathic, genuine, and congruent a therapist tries to be, he or she will eventually be experienced as injurious. Just as a child is inevitably disappointed by the devoted parent who cannot always get it right, the therapy client will sometimes feel misunderstood by the most sensitive clinician. This insight ushered in a new way of handling mistakes. Instead of simply exploring how the client had experienced an error and associated it with early disappointments, Kohut (1984) and his followers advised therapists to express regret for their empathic failures. Such behavior, they argued, not only is realistic and humane, but it also models how to be an imperfect person who nonetheless maintains self-esteem, thereby demonstrating an alternative to the client's doomed, self-defeating "narcissistic pursuit of perfection" (Rothstein, 1980).

## CONTEMPORARY RELATIONAL AND INTERSUBJECTIVE VIEWS

Recently, there has been a shift in perspective that has become framed as the question of whether clinical psychoanalysis represents a one-person or a two-person psychology (Aron,

1996). Freud had labeled as *countertransference* any feelings toward clients that exceed ordinary professional concern. Strong emotional reactions to patients, he believed, reflect unresolved aspects of the analyst's psychology and must be mastered in his or her own analysis, lest they unwittingly thwart the unfolding of the patient's transference. Inherent in this stance was the ideal of scientific objectivity—the capacity to stand apart and see clients' psychologies as created by their own temperament and personal history, uncontaminated by a therapist's dynamics. Stolorow and Atwood (1992) call this position "the myth of the isolated mind" (p. 115). Freud (1912b) even urged colleagues to emulate the surgeon, "who puts aside all his feelings, even his human sympathy, and concentrates his mental forces on the single aim of performing the operation as skillfully as possible" (p. 115). His strikingly sterile analogy was doubtless meant to shame some of his colleagues into better behavior; by 1912 he was alarmed at the number of analysts who were acting out sexually with patients. Unfortunately, his metaphor was taken literally by many second-generation analysts who took pains to appear formal to the point of coldness with their analysands, lest they contaminate the transference (Gay, 1988).

Despite the master's entreaty, when post-Freudian therapists spoke frankly, they admitted to intense countertransferences, regardless of how well analyzed they were (e.g., Searles, 1979; Winnicott, 1949). They noted that it is unrealistic to expect only mild, benign feelings toward unhappy, difficult people; more important, however, was that countertransferences contain valuable information (Ehrenberg, 1992; Gill & Hoffman, 1982; Maroda, 1991; Racker, 1968). It was not a big stretch to rethink the analytic relationship as involving two mutually influencing subjectivities. Appreciation of projective identification and similar types of emotional contagion (Bion, 1959; Ogden, 1982) led to efforts to describe the interpersonal *field* between therapist and patient (Langs, 1976; Ogden, 1994) rather than the dynamics of the patient as seen by a neutral onlooker. Joseph Sandler (1976) began writing about inevitable *role-responsiveness;* Irwin Hoffman (1983) spoke of the *co-construction* of the transference.

This sea change emerged from many sources: heirs of Ferenczi's work and of the American interpersonal and British object relations movements (Balint, 1953; Bollas, 1987; Greenberg & S. Mitchell, 1983; Joseph, 1989; Levenson, 1972, 1983); theorists in France (A. Green, 1999; Lacan, 1977; McDougall, 1980); Gill and his Chicago group (Gill, 1982, 1994; Gill & Hoffman, 1982); Heidigger's student, Hans Loewald (e.g., 1980); American feminists (e.g., Benjamin, 1988, 1995; Chodorow, 1978, 1989; Gilligan, 1982; J. Mitchell, 1974); developmental scholars (Beebe & Lachmann, 1988; Lichtenberg, 1983; Pine, 1985, 1990; D. Silverman,

1998; Stern, 1985, 1995); and writers drawing on George Klein (1976) and Kohut who stressed *intersubjectivity* and *contextualism* (Orange, Atwood, & Stolorow, 1997; Stolorow, Brandchaft, & Atwood, 1987). At the same time, research on therapy was generating relational explanations for its effectiveness, even when treatment was conducted classically (Weiss, Sampson, & The Mount Zion Psychotherapy Research Group, 1986). The intersubjective, two-person vision of therapy can be seen as a democratization of the more authoritarian Freudian model—an egalitarian, postmodern slant more suited to our era and culture.

## Clinical Implications of a Relational-Intersubjective Orientation

For therapists who resonate to more intersubjective versions of psychoanalytic therapy, certain articles of faith of classical technique are called into question (Buirski & Hagland, 2001). Because objectivity is seen as impossible, *authenticity* replaces neutrality as a cardinal stance. The ideal that a therapist dispassionately interprets a patient's *acting out* of transference feelings becomes the assumption that both parties will find themselves involved in *enactments* they must figure out together. Bion's (1970) notion that the analyst becomes the *container* for disavowed contents of the patient's psychology or Winnicott's (1965) argument that substantial movement comes from the patient's sense of therapy as a *holding environment* find expression in the therapist's suspension of interpretation for more tentative ways of working. Rather than being assumed to represent distortion, the patient's transferences may be seen as containing knowledge about the analyst's psychology that the analyst would sometimes prefer to disown (Aron, 1991).

Tolerating *not knowing* becomes easier. Self-disclosure is not taboo, although a special discipline is required of relational therapists in deciding what and when to disclose (Aron, 1996; Maroda, 1991, 1999; Renik, 1995). Insight is regarded as the *by-product* of the internalization of a new relationship—not as the cause of change. Relational theorists often equate the work of therapy with Winnicott's (1971) notion of *play,* carried out in the potential space (Ogden, 1986) generated by the analytic dyad. Sometimes the language of contemporary analysts becomes almost mystical in its effort to find metaphors that convey preverbal experience and the sense of intimate connection between therapist and client.

It is unclear how different actual behavior is between relationally oriented clinicians and therapists who think more traditionally. Some research suggests that effective treaters of different theoretical stripes—even markedly different stripes—do substantially similar things (Fiedler, 1950;

Wachtel, 1977). Contemporary psychoanalytic practitioners may identify with the ego psychologists, the self psychologists, or the relational analysts—or they may synthesize several points of view. Many also integrate into their work the ideas of early psychoanalytic dissidents (especially Jung, Adler, and Rank), of systems theorists (Gerson, 1996; Leupnitz, 1988), and of more recent philosophers and scholars in other fields. Moreover, now that the behavioral movement has embraced cognition, there are myriad possibilities for integration between therapists trained in psychoanalytic theory and those who come from a learning theory or cognitive science background (Arkowitz & Messer, 1984; Frank, 1999; Wachtel, 1977, 1993).

## EMPIRICAL RESEARCH ON PSYCHODYNAMIC PSYCHOTHERAPY

Empirical research on psychodynamic psychotherapy is not nearly as plentiful or rich as is the theoretical work in this area. There are no studies comparing various psychoanalytic schools with one another, nor are there investigations comparing long-term dynamic therapy with the nondynamic short-term treatments currently in vogue. Without including interpersonal psychotherapy (e.g., Klerman, Weissman, Rounsaville, & Chevron, 1984), which is arguably psychodynamic, we must note the paucity of studies comparing dynamic therapies to nondynamic treatments. Studies relevant to dynamic therapy do exist, however. We begin with empirically identified factors that distinguish dynamic therapies—that is, with what makes psychodynamic therapy unique. We then cover research pertaining to the relevance of each factor in human functioning generally and in therapeutic efficacy specifically. Finally, we review research on the effects of long-term psychotherapy and psychoanalysis.

### What Is Psychodynamic Psychotherapy Made Of?

Blagys and Hilsenroth (2000) reviewed the comparative psychotherapy process literature in order to identify those processes that distinguish psychodynamic and cognitive-behavioral therapies. To qualify as a distinguishing feature, a process had to differentiate a treatment in at least two studies, conducted in at least two different research venues. They identified seven such factors: (a) a focus on affect and expression of emotion; (b) exploration of the patient's efforts to avoid certain topics or engage in activities that retard therapeutic progress (i.e., defense and resistance); (c) identification of patterns in the patient's actions, thoughts, feelings, experiences, and relationships (object relations); (d) emphasis on

past experiences; (e) focus on interpersonal experiences; (f) emphasis on the therapeutic relationship (transference and the therapeutic alliance); (g) explorations of wishes, dreams, and fantasies (intrapsychic dynamics). Missing from the list but implicit in all factors is the assumption of ubiquitous unconscious processes, the defining feature of psychoanalysis as described by Freud (e.g., 1926). Ablon and E. E. Jones (1998, 1999) and E. E. Jones and Pulos (1993) have shown that these factors in combination lead to successful psychotherapeutic outcome. In fact, they do so in cognitive-behavioral as well as in psychodynamic therapies. We next examine the evidence for each factor individually.

### Focus on Affect

The best evidence that expression of affectively meaningful material is therapeutic has been supplied by Pennebaker (1995, 1997). In a typical experiment, his participants were asked to write or speak of upsetting incidents in their lives. Compared with members of a control group, they had fewer stressful physiological reactions (Pennebaker, 1997), healthier immune functioning (Petrie, Booth, & Pennebaker, 1998), and fewer health problems (Suedfeld & Pennebaker, 1997) months after this intervention. These results are all the more remarkable because the participants, who were not patients, were not seeking either emotional relief or health benefits. Unfortunately, there are as yet no studies relating such processes—as they specifically occur in dynamic psychotherapy—to outcome. Still, it is safe to say that emotional expression as it routinely occurs in the psychodynamic therapies is clearly good for people.

### Focus on Defense

According to a model propounded by Weiss and Sampson (Weiss, 1971; Weiss et al., 1986), patients are troubled by unconscious pathogenic beliefs that interfere with their abilities to cope adaptively and that create psychological symptoms with their attendant guilt and shame. In order for treatment to work, patients must access warded-off (defended-against) material related to their pathogenic beliefs. After these beliefs become conscious, they can be disconfirmed. After they are disconfirmed, they lose their power. Patients come equipped with unconscious plans for achieving these ends; therapists must identify these plans and help each patient carry them out. This model was derived from a case-by-case examination of analytic treatments of numerous patients, after which Weiss and Sampson derived testable hypotheses and then subjected them to rigorous investigation. First, they assumed the existence of identifiable unconscious pathogenic beliefs. Second, the model proposed that a patient will test his or her pathogenic beliefs in relation to the analyst. Third, warded-off material ought to emerge so long as the therapist's words and behavior do not confirm the pathogenic beliefs. Fourth, interventions that are compatible with a patient's unconscious plan should further therapeutic progress, as evidenced by the emergence of previously warded-off material.

To test these hypotheses, Weiss and Sampson used transcribed audiotapes and process notes of psychoanalytic treatment, rated by clinicians blind as to hypotheses and critical aspects of the treatment. Scales measured analyst interventions for plan compatibility and patient verbalizations for warded-off material, insight, and therapeutic improvement. The units of analysis were analyst verbalizations and segments of patient speech. The most comprehensive research concerned the treatment of a patient dubbed Mrs. C. All hypotheses were strongly supported: Raters were able to agree about the nature of Mrs. C's unconscious plan; without explicit interpretation, Mrs. C made use of her therapist to test her unconscious beliefs; she became conscious of previously warded-off material; and she showed favorable reactions and therapeutic improvement when the analyst's interventions accorded with her unconscious plan.

There are also empirical data on repression, the conceptual grandparent of psychoanalytic notions of defense. Although experimental efforts to produce discrete incidents of repression have been largely unsuccessful (Eagle, 2000; Holmes, 1990), when repression is considered as a personality trait or style, there is a great deal of supporting data for this phenomenon. The most influential research of this sort is that of Daniel Weinberger's group (D. Weinberger, 1990; D. Weinberger & Schwartz, 1990), who originally measured repressive style via two self-report scales assessing trait anxiety and social desirability (D. Weinberger, Schwartz, & Davidson, 1979). Individuals describing themselves as low in anxiety but high in social desirability were identified as repressors, on the assumption that they were being defensive about their anxiety.

Weinberger et al. (1979) found that repressors reported experiencing little reaction to a stressful task but were physiologically and behaviorally affected in a way that indicated considerable stress. Newton and Contrada (1992) reported that repressors claimed to experience little anxiety when asked to give a talk, yet they evidenced substantially increased heart rate. Derakshan and Eysenck (1997) had people rate videotapes of themselves giving a speech. Repressors claimed to have experienced and rated themselves as having exhibited little anxiety. Their high heart rate, however, told a different story. Moreover, independent judges viewing the videotapes

rated the repressors as high in anxiety. Their defensiveness was further suggested by their response when informed of their elevated heart rate: They ascribed it to the excitement and challenge of giving the talk, not to anxiety.

Further evidence for the existence of a repressive or defensive kind of personality—and its costs—can be found in the work of Shedler and colleagues (Karliner, Westrich, Shedler, & Mayman, 1996; Shedler, Mayman, & Manis, 1993), Myers and Brewin (1994, 1995), and Davis and colleagues (Bonanno, Davis, Singer, & Schwartz, 1991; Davis, 1987; Davis & Schwartz, 1987). In summary, a group of people can be identified who manifest the sorts of defensive behaviors identified and ostensibly treated by psychodynamic clinicians. Such individuals tend to deny anxiety while physically displaying it and fail to recall negative events or stimuli. This style has been shown to have negative health consequences.

### Identification of Patient Patterns

Surprisingly, there are no empirical data relating specifically to therapeutic interpretations in which patients are alerted to their recurrent patterns of thinking, feeling, perceiving, and acting. Insight has often been the stated goal of pointing out patterns to one's clients. If this leads to insight and insight is associated with positive outcome, this factor would be supported. But there are no data directly linking the therapist's identifying patterns to the patient's achievement of insight. Because this connection is a central premise of classical psychoanalytic theory and case studies, this area would be fruitful for future research.

There is a vast literature, however, on devising treatment to fit patients' patterns. Individual personality dynamics and defenses are contained implicitly in diagnostic labels—especially those for the personality disorders (McWilliams, 1994; Millon, 1996); in the clinical literature on treating personality disorders and softening rigid character structure, one finds scattered references to empirical research on psychodynamic therapy with individuals in the various categories. In the literature on depression, Blatt's (2000) writing on the robust finding of a difference between introjective and anaclitic personality styles, who have different kinds of depressive dynamics and respond differentially to psychodynamic treatments, is notable.

Luborsky's work, discussed later in this chapter, emphasizes a client-specific pattern of relationship, contributing to predictable feelings, thoughts, and behaviors. The working models concept of attachment theory, also discussed later in this chapter, has similar clinical implications. Weiss and Sampson, as noted previously, found support for the value of identifying patterns in order to determine a patient's plan. Other empirically derived ways of understanding patients' relational patterns for therapeutic purposes include concepts such as Henry, Schacht, and Strupp's (1986) cyclical maladaptive pattern, Horowitz's (1988) personal schemas, Dahl's (1988) fundamental repetitive and maladaptive emotional structures, and Lachmann and Lichtenberg's (1992) model scenes. Finally, there is research that addresses *indirectly* the question of identifying patient patterns with the purpose of conveying insight to the patient. Ablon and E. E. Jones (1998, 1999) and E. E. Jones and Pulos (1993) found that insight was related to positive outcome in both psychodynamic and cognitive-behavioral psychotherapy.

### Emphasis on Past Experiences

The characteristic psychoanalytic emphasis on a mutual effort by therapist and patient to understand the patient's personal history and its effects has also been largely unresearched. Although a focus on the past is usually carried out in the service of insight, there are no data currently linking exploration of an individual's prior history to that person's attainment of therapeutic insight. This area is another in which research is badly needed.

### Focus on Interpersonal Experiences

The most comprehensive research enterprise examining interpersonal experiences from a psychoanalytic (as well as ethological and systems) perspective is the development and testing of attachment theory, inspired by Bowlby's (1969, 1972, 1982) three-volume work on attachment and separation. Bowlby postulated an inborn need of the infant to maintain proximity to the mother or primary caregiver. How the caregiver responds and what environmental contingencies enhance or retard the fulfillment of this need are seen as having critical implications for the child's attachment to the main caregiver and for his or her later relationships. Experiences and images of relationship arising from transactions between the infant and the mothering figure are internalized in what Bowlby called working models, which then influence how the person relates to others and responds to the challenges of life.

Levy, Blatt, and Shaver (1998) found that attachment styles predicted parental representations. Thus, attachment style is closely akin to object representations. Ainsworth, who also related object representations to attachment, studied the effects of attachment on children (Ainsworth, 1969, 1978), whereas Mary Main and her associates expanded the domain of the theory to adults (M. Main, Kaplan, & Cassidy,

1985). Waters and his colleagues (Waters, Hamilton, & Weinfield, 2000; Waters, Weinfield, & Hamilton, 2000) have demonstrated the stability of attachment style—and therefore object representations—from early childhood through adolescence and young adulthood. Of 60 infants identified as having a particular attachment style, 72% showed the same style in early adulthood. Of those who had changed styles, most had suffered presumably traumatic events such as parental loss or abuse. This finding suggests that object representations tend to remain stable in the absence of outside forces that radically change relationships—exactly what psychoanalytic theory would predict.

Attachment and its associated object representations have also been shown to relate to diagnosed psychopathology in adults. Parkes, Stevenson-Hinde, and Marris (1991) have compiled a review of research relating childhood attachment patterns to adult psychopathology in general; Brennan and Shaver (1998) have related them to personality disorders. Slade and Aber (1992) and M. Main (1995, 1996) have reviewed much of this literature.

### Emphasis on the Therapeutic Relationship

Research on the therapeutic relationship and its connection to outcome has focused on two areas: the therapeutic alliance and transference.

**The Therapeutic Alliance.**    Data on the therapeutic alliance are clear and consistent. It has repeatedly been shown to be an important and positive factor in psychotherapy (Safran & Muran, 2000; J. Weinberger, 1995). Hovarth and Symonds (1991) conducted a meta-analysis of 24 studies examining the working alliance and found its effect to be reliably positive and not unique to psychodynamic psychotherapy. Gaston, Marmar, Gallagher, and Thompson (1991) reported a very large effect for the alliance even when controlling for initial symptomatology and symptom change. What we do not know from an empirical standpoint, however, is how best to foster the alliance or how it works. These questions await further empirical investigation.

**Transference.**    The experimental study of transference has been spearheaded by Andersen (Andersen & Baum, 1994; Andersen & Berk, 1998; Anderson & Glassman, 1996; Andersen, Reznik, & Chen, 1997; Glassman & Andersen, 1999). Her conception of transference goes beyond representations of childhood parental figures as they manifest themselves in the relationship with a therapist; it involves representations of all significant others and applies to all interpersonal relationships in all settings. Andersen's orientation is the empirical information-processing perspective of social cognition, which is closer to the kinds of internalizations described by object relations theory than it is to classical Freudian ideas of transference (see Westen, 1991, for a thorough comparison of social cognition and object relations theory, and Singer, 1985, for a translation of the concept of transference into information-processing terms).

Several studies (e.g., Andersen & Baum, 1994; Andersen, Reznik, & Manzella, 1996) have shown that people are more likely to remember information about a new or fictitious person that is consistent with significant-other representations. In fact, they will infer and claim to recall representation-consistent information that was never presented (Andersen & Baum, 1994; Andersen & Cole, 1990; Andersen, Glassman, Chen, & Cole, 1995; Andersen et al., 1996; Hinkley & Andersen, 1996). They will also respond affectively to new people in a manner consonant with their existing representation (Andersen & Baum, 1994)—that is, they find themselves feeling emotionally close to the new person (Andersen et al., 1996). Moreover, subjects' self-concepts shift so as to be more consistent with how they feel in the presence of the significant other whose representation has been activated (Hinkley & Andersen, 1996). Such effects can be obtained even when the significant-other representation is activated subliminally (Glassman & Andersen, 1998).

Andersen's team has provided impressive evidence for the existence and operation of representations of significant others, representations that affect memory, emotions, and self-concept and that operate even when we are unaware of their activation. Their findings give powerful support to Sullivan's (1953) assertion that we have as many personalities as we do relationships with the important people in our lives. These data say nothing directly, however, about the operation of such representations in psychotherapy.

The work of Luborsky and his colleagues (Luborsky & Crits-Cristoph, 1990; Luborsky, Crits-Cristoph, & Mellon, 1986) does speak to the operation of transference representations in clinical practice. Their research with the Core Conflictual Relationship Theme (CCRT), designed to identify patterns of relationships as they appear in therapeutic sessions, shows that the frequency of unrealistic transference wishes diminishes in successful analytic treatment—as classical psychoanalytic theory would predict. In addition, self- and other-evaluations become less negatively toned and more three-dimensional (e.g., Crits-Christoph, Cooper, & Luborsky, 1988, 1990). Although there are some unresolved reliability problems with this research (Galatzer, Bachrach, Skolnikoff, & Waldron, 2000), the concept of transference

has been shown to have validity and to relate to psychotherapeutic process and outcome.

### Exploration of Wishes, Dreams, and Fantasies

An emphasis on inner subjective life—the intrapsychic factor of the psychoanalytic approach to therapy—has been studied in terms of unconscious dynamic conflicts and wish-fulfilling fantasies. Shevrin and his associates (Shevrin, Bond, Brakel, Hertel, & Williams, 1996) have for decades collected data showing that unconscious conflicts have unique effects on individuals. Their method has involved a rigorous combination of psychoanalytic assessment and modern electrophysiological measurement. Each person seeking treatment at the clinic associated with Shevrin's laboratory underwent a thorough psychodynamic evaluation (three clinical interviews, the WAIS-R, the Rorschach, and the TAT). Clinical judges studied the material, inferred the person's conscious description of relevant symptomatology, and specified the unconscious conflict presumably underlying it. Based on these formulations, the judges selected words that reflected, respectively, the patients' conscious experience of their symptoms and the unconscious conflicts from which they were assumed to derive. These words were then presented both subliminally and supraliminally to the patients while event-related potentials (ERPs) were recorded from their brains. To control for affective valence of the words, pleasant and unpleasant words not chosen by the judges were also shown.

Results showed that unconscious-conflict words evidenced unique ERPs only when presented subliminally, whereas conscious-conflict words did so only when presented supraliminally. Participants did not respond differentially to control words, no matter how they were presented. These findings—that psychoanalytically oriented judges can identify relevant unconscious conflicts as confirmed by physiological (brain-wave) measures—demonstrate a clear connection between psychodynamic clinical judgment and brain functioning.

Research conducted by Silverman and his colleagues (L. Silverman, 1976, 1983; L. Silverman, Lachmann, & Milich, 1982; L. Silverman & J. Weinberger, 1985; J. Weinberger & L. Silverman, 1987) demonstrated a link between unconscious dynamic processes and behavior. Silverman termed his method *subliminal psychodynamic activation* (SPA). In an SPA experiment, one chooses a psychodynamic proposition and operationalizes it into a phrase. For example, Silverman operationalized the aggression that analytic theory posits as underlying depressive symptomatology in the phrase *destroy mother*. Then the chosen phrase or a control phrase is presented subliminally to individuals held to be susceptible to it.

Early SPA studies investigated the proposition that many behaviors are at least partly motivated by conflict over libidinal and aggressive wishes. They revealed that the relevant dynamic stimuli affected behaviors in the targeted populations in ways that control stimuli did not. Such effects were obtained *only* when the stimuli were presented subliminally. Populations tested by Silverman and his associates included schizophrenic, stuttering, and depressive individuals. Later SPA studies focused on the effects of stimuli designed to tap interpersonal fantasies. These were derived from Mahler's notion of symbiosis and on the claim of some analysts (e.g., Limentani, 1956; Searles, 1965; Sechehaye, 1951) that therapy is more successful when symbiotic-like wishes are gratified. The stimulus used to test this assertion was *mommy and I are one* (MIO). To see whether subliminal MIO stimulation could enhance outcome, patients were given MIO or a control stimulus before they began treatment. Over a dozen studies using this strategy were conducted, with interventions ranging from systematic desensitization to counseling like that of Alcoholics Anonymous. Most found better outcomes in the MIO group than in controls (both groups improved, presumably as a result of the treatment). Meta-analyses have confirmed the reliability and strength of the MIO effects (Hardaway, 1990; J. Weinberger & Hardaway, 1990). The SPA studies show that there is validity to psychoanalytically posited unconscious intrapsychic dynamics and that these dynamics can be related to positive outcomes in therapy.

Joel Weinberger (e.g., 1992) has created a TAT measure of the fantasy associated with MIO, terming it the *oneness motive* (OM). Scores on OM have been found to predict outcome in a behavioral medicine study (Siegel & J. Weinberger, 1998) and in inpatient psychiatric treatment (J. Weinberger, Bonner, & Barra, 1999). This research shows that the types of unconscious fantasies posited by psychoanalytic theory can be operationalized and—in at least one case—predict outcome consistent with the theory's assumptions.

## OUTCOME IN PSYCHOANALYSIS AND LONG-TERM PSYCHODYNAMIC PSYCHOTHERAPY

Most of the work reviewed thus far has concerned short-term treatment. Some of it was purely experimental and involved no treatment whatsoever. Most psychodynamic therapy, however, is open-ended (decisions to continue or stop are within the client's control) and thus typically of long duration, and all of psychoanalysis is long-term. We have taken psychodynamic

therapy apart and looked at its components. Now let us move from process to outcome, putting it back together to see what empirical research says about its effectiveness.

Studies of psychoanalytic outcome began almost as soon as psychoanalytic clinics were established (Alexander, 1937; Coriat, 1917; E. Jones, 1936; Kessel & Hyman, 1933). Although Knight's (1941) review of these early investigations paints a highly positive picture of outcome, all had employed a retrospective strategy using no control groups or independent observations; the sole arbiter of change was the treating analyst. Consequently, these findings are suspect. Later studies corrected for the flaws of retrospective report and independent observation but not for the lack of control groups. The first prospective and still the most impressive such study was the Menninger Foundation Psychotherapy Research Project (Appelbaum, 1977; Kernberg et al., 1972; Wallerstein, 1986). Initiated in 1954, this project tracked its participants for more than 30 years. Forty-two adult patients (22 in analysis and 20 in psychodynamic therapy) were studied. Psychotic, organically damaged, and mentally deficient patients were excluded. Nonetheless, many subjects were extremely troubled individuals with histories of unsuccessful treatment. Six had to be switched from psychoanalysis to psychodynamic psychotherapy because of unmanageable transferences. This research project generated a huge amount of data—hundreds of pages for each participant. Five books and 60 papers on this data set have appeared so far.

Overall, although the study reported substantial and equivalent general improvement for both psychoanalytic and dynamic psychotherapy patients, there was considerable variability. Treatment helped individuals to modify repetitive, long-standing, and characterological problems as well as to diminish their presenting symptoms. This finding was compelling because—as noted previously—many of the patients had not been helped by other treatments. Therapist support was the major curative factor identified by this study. Insight did not contribute to outcome—that is, improvement did not correlate with interpretive activity of the therapist or with the development of insight on the part of the patient. In contrast, the use of the positive dependent transference, corrective emotional experiences, assistance with reality testing, and other more supportive measures did correlate with outcome. Before one accepts these findings as representative of analytic treatment, a caveat applies: These patients were severely ill and may not have been suited for engaging in an exploratory, regression-promoting psychoanalytic process.

Another important study was conducted by the Columbia University Department of Psychiatry Center for Psychoanalytic Training and Research. Over 250 psychoanalytic patients (less disturbed than the Menninger clients), the largest sample ever examined in one research project, were studied from 1945 to 1961. A second wave of data collection involving about 90 patients ran from 1962 through 1971. Data included case records and reports of patients, analysts, and supervisors. Judges with adequate reliability evaluated these sources. Outcome was assessed through judge evaluation of circumstances of termination, clinical judgment of improvement by independent judges and treating therapists, and change scores based on judges' evaluations of records at the beginning and end of treatment. Overall, patients benefited from treatment. Length of therapy and development of an analytic process were strongly related to the benefits obtained. Reviews and analyses of these data may be found in Bachrach, Weber, and Solomon (1985) and Weber, Bachrach, and Solomon (1985a, 1985b).

In later research at Columbia, Vaughan and her colleagues (Vaughan et al., 2000) investigated whether psychoanalysis and long-term analytic therapy could be feasibly subjected to the degree of methodological rigor necessary to establish their effectiveness. Methodology that has been used to study brief therapies and pharmacological studies—including self-report data, therapist data, and blind ratings at baseline, 6 months, and 1 year—was applied to nine patients in analysis and 15 in dynamic psychotherapy. Significant therapeutic effects on a variety of measures were seen at 1 year, despite the small sample, in both psychoanalysis and dynamic therapy. The authors did note, however, some resistance by clinicians to having their work studied—a problem if psychologists are to attain reliable data on outcome.

The Boston Psychoanalytic Institute conducted a retrospective study covering the years 1959 to 1966 (Sashin, Eldred, & Van Amerowgen, 1975) that showed positive effects of both treatment in general and treatment length in particular. A prospective and therefore less potentially biased study was undertaken at the same institute in 1972 (Kantrowitz, Katz, Paolitto, Sashin, & Solomon, 1987a, 1987b). Measures taken at the beginning and end of treatment included the Rorschach, TAT, Draw-a-Person Test, Cole Animal Test, and WAIS verbal subtests. These were evaluated by two judges for reality testing, object relations, motivation for treatment, availability of affect, and affect tolerance. Both intake and termination interviewers also made these judgments, based on their respective experiences of each patient. A year after treatment, the therapist was interviewed, and his or her comments were rated for analytic process and for outcome. Therapeutic benefit was assessed in terms of changes in the tests (pre- to posttest) and in terms of therapist assessment. Again, patients showed improvement, and level of improvement was positively related to treatment length.

A follow-up on these patients, collected up to 10 years after termination (Kantrowitz, Katz, & Paolitto, 1990a, 1990b,

1990c; Kantrowitz et al., 1989), showed that most had developed self-analytic capabilities and were maintaining their gains. Individual improvement was variable: Some kept improving, some maintained their gains, some had ups and downs, and a few got worse. Despite the variability, this result is impressive because 10-year follow-ups are extremely rare in the literature. That most patients had stayed better and acquired a lifelong skill of engaging in a self-analytic process is a remarkable finding.

The New York Psychoanalytic Institute collected data from 1967 to 1969 (Erle, 1979; Erle & Goldberg, 1984), showing that treatment length was strongly related to outcome and that most patients improved. Similar results were obtained with a retrospective study. Because all variables were collected from the treating therapists and were not confirmed through independent report or even by the patients involved, these data are not very reliable. Erle and Goldberg (1984) acknowledge the limitations of their findings, calling them preliminary.

A methodologically stronger study has recently been carried out in Sweden. Sandell and his colleagues (2000) collected data on 450 patients (a 66% response rate from a pool of 756), using normed interview and questionnaire data from patients and therapists, as well as absenteeism and health care utilization data. Patients were in a range of analytic therapies, including 74 in analysis three or more times per week. Findings were complex, but overall, patients in both analysis and therapy improved in treatment in direct proportion to its duration and frequency. Oddly, improvement was high on self-rating measures of symptom relief and general morale but not in the area of social relations.

Taken together, these studies support the efficacy of psychoanalysis and psychoanalytic therapy. They also demonstrate that deeply entrenched problems are amenable to psychoanalysis and psychodynamic treatment. Bachrach, Galatzer-Levy, Skolnikoff, and Waldron (1991); Doidge (1997); and Galatzer-Levy et al. (2000) provide excellent reviews of these and other psychoanalytic outcome studies.

A method for studying long-term psychotherapy that is popular in psychology today falls under the heading of "effectiveness" research. It was not designed with psychoanalytic principles in mind; rather, it was created as a counterpoint to rigorous, internally valid but somewhat artificial psychotherapy outcome studies termed *efficacy research*. In a nutshell, effectiveness studies are concerned with how actual patients fare in the real world. The goal of these naturalistic studies is ecological validity. Therapy investigated by effectiveness research includes long-term treatment, and long-term treatment as currently practiced is still overwhelmingly psychodynamic. We therefore review this area of research here.

The first effectiveness study was conducted by *Consumer Reports* magazine (Seligman, 1995, 1996), whose editors sent readers a questionnaire on their experiences in psychotherapy. More than 4,000 respondents reported having been in some kind of treatment; almost 3,000 had seen mental health professionals. Treatments were not standardized, diagnostic information was not obtained, and before and after measures were not taken. Data were obtained only from clients and were analyzed as to length and frequency of treatment and type of professional providing it. Results indicated that therapy was helpful. Psychiatrists, psychologists, and social workers obtained better results than did other professionals such as physicians and marriage counselors. Of particular relevance to our concerns is that greater improvement was associated with long-term as opposed to short-term treatment and with higher session frequency. Results were not limited to symptom relief; people reported that the quality of their lives had improved as well. These findings are controversial because they consist of self-report data, which are notoriously subject to bias, in a study that lacked a control group (see Vanden Bos, 1996).

For our purposes, a significant limitation of the *Consumer Reports* study is that although the treatments can be assumed to have been largely psychodynamic, this was not shown. Freedman, Hoffenberg, Vorus, and Frosch (1999) solved this problem by applying effectiveness methodology to psychoanalysis. Patients in their study were treated at a clinic associated with the Institute for Psychoanalytic Therapy and Research (IPTAR); thus, this study concerned itself specifically with psychoanalytic treatments. The investigators sent out 240 questionnaires, of which 99 were returned (41%). Treatment duration ranged from 1 month to 2 years, and session frequency from once a month to three times a week. Measures were the same as those used in the *Consumer Reports* study. Results from the IPTAR study replicated those of the *Consumer Reports* survey. Length of treatment was positively related to outcome, especially when therapies of under 6 months were compared with treatment lasting over a year. Frequency was also related to outcome: Both two- and three-times-a-week appointments proved superior to once-weekly sessions, although they did not differ significantly from each other. Moreover, frequency and duration contributed separately to outcome—that is, each was related to outcome independently of the other (cf. Roth & Fonagy, 1996).

Taken together, these studies indicate that long-term psychoanalytic psychotherapy is effective. They also support the conclusion that duration and frequency of treatment are important variables. Prior to these findings, psychoanalytic clinicians had only personal and anecdotal experience to support their conviction that psychoanalysis and psychodynamic therapy are beneficial to their patients and that more is better. Currently, a collaborative analytic multisite program, spearheaded by the American Psychoanalytic Association, is gathering process and outcome data from numerous research groups in the United States and elsewhere, in which a common database of audiotaped and transcribed psychoanalytic sessions will be analyzed in methodologically sophisticated ways that correct for design flaws in the earlier studies. Regrettably, costs of implementing this project are high enough—and funding dicey enough—that Wallerstein (2001) has wryly referred to the fulfillment of the aim to integrate these process and outcome studies as "music for the future" (p. 263). We look forward to hearing this music.

## CURRENT DIRECTIONS IN PSYCHODYNAMIC PSYCHOTHERAPY

Changes in health care financing have required psychoanalytically oriented therapists to confront treatment exigencies radically at odds with their sensibilities. One positive effect of the managed care movement has been to stimulate research on psychoanalytic therapies. Meanwhile, more and more psychodynamic clinicians are practicing on a fee-for-service basis outside health maintenance plans because the values and goals of analytic work are hard to graft on a symptom-focused, limited-session model in which drug treatment is privileged (cf. McWilliams, 1999).

Peripheral to managed care and its political context, there are some areas of current psychoanalytic exploration that have significant implications for therapy. For example, there is an impressive clinical and empirical literature about infancy that permits preventive interventions of a precise nature (e.g., Greenspan, 1992; Stern, 1995). Psychoanalytic therapy with children has matured into a sophisticated discipline with empirical as well as theoretical underpinnings (Chethik, 2000; Heineman, 1998). There is a growing body of psychoanalytic work that illuminates the psychologies and the treatment needs of previously ill-served populations such as people in sexual minorities (e.g., Glassgold & Iasenza, 1995; Isay, 1989, 1994), in cultures of poverty (Altman, 1995), and in racial and ethnic subgroups (e.g., Foster, Moskowitz, & Javier, 1996; Jackson & Greene, 2000).

Psychoanalytically influenced feminists have been contributing to an increasingly sophisticated interdisciplinary conversation on gender (e.g., Young-Breuhl, 2000). Connections between psychoanalytic theory and diverse religious and spiritual traditions are being forged (e.g., Epstein, 1998; Suler, 1993). Philosophical explorations of psychoanalysis are enjoying a recrudescence, in the contemporary context of hermeneutic, postmodernism, and social constructivist ideas (e.g., Hoffman, 1991, 1992; Messer, Sass, & Woolfolk, 1994). Other scholars are integrating analytic theory and cognitive neuroscience (e.g., Schore, 1994).

We hope that we have conveyed the richness and diversity of the psychodynamic tradition. In the new millennium, when the talking cure has been subject to unforgiving scrutiny and penetrating criticism, the need for well-controlled research on psychoanalytic therapies—and on conventional long-term treatment in particular—is especially pressing.

# REFERENCES

Ablon, J. S., & Jones, E. E. (1998). How expert clinicians' prototypes of an ideal treatment correlate with outcome in psychodynamic and cognitive-behavioral therapy. *Psychotherapy Research, 8,* 71–83.

Ablon, J. S., & Jones, E. E. (1999). Psychotherapy process in the National Institute of Mental Health Treatment of Depression Collaborative Research Program. *Journal of Counseling and Clinical Psychology, 67,* 64–75.

Ainsworth, M. D. S. (1969). Object relations, dependency, and attachment: A theoretical review of the mother-infant relationship. *Child Development, 40,* 969–1025.

Ainsworth, M. D. S. (1978). *Patterns of attachment: A psychological study of the strange situation.* Hillsdale, NJ: Erlbaum.

Alexander, F. (1937). *Five year report of the Chicago Institute for Psychoanalysis.* Chicago: Chicago Psychoanalytic Institute.

Alexander, F., & French, T. M. (1946). *Psychoanalytic therapy: Principles and application.* New York: Ronald Press.

Altman, N. (1995). *The analyst in the inner city: Race, class, and culture through a psychoanalytic lens.* Mahwah, NJ: Analytic Press.

Andersen, S. M., & Baum, A. (1994). Transference in interpersonal relations: Inferences and affect based on significant-other representations. *Journal of Personality, 62,* 459–498.

Andersen, S. M., & Berk, M. S. (1998). Transference in everyday experience: Implications of experimental research for relevant clinical phenomena. *Review of General Psychology, 2,* 81–120.

Andersen, S. M., & Cole, S. W. (1990). "Do I know you?": The role of significant others in general social perception. *Journal of Personality and Social Psychology, 59,* 383–399.

Andersen, S. M., & Glassman, N. S. (1996). Responding to significant others when they are not there: Effects on interpersonal inference, motivation, and affect. In R. M. Sorrentino & E. T. Higgins (Eds.), *Handbook of motivation and cognition* (Vol. 3, pp. 262–321). New York: Guilford.

Andersen, S. M., Glassman, N. S., Chen, S., & Cole, S. W. (1995). Transference in social perception: The role of chronic accessibility in significant-other representations. *Journal of Personality and Social Psychology, 69,* 41–57.

Andersen, S. M., Reznik, I., & Chen, S. (1997). The self in relation to others: Cognitive and motivational underpinnings. In J. G. Snodgrass & R. L. Thompson (Eds.), *The self across psychology: Self-recognition, self awareness, and the self-concept* (pp. 233–275). New York: New York Academy of Science.

Andersen, S. M., Reznik, I., & Manzella, L. M. (1996). Eliciting facial affect, motivation, and expectancies in transference: Significant-other representations in social relations. *Journal of Personality and Social Psychology, 71,* 1108–1129.

Appelbaum, S. A. (1977). *The anatomy of change: A Menninger Foundation report on testing the effects of psychotherapy.* New York: Plenum.

Arkowitz, H., & Messer, S. B. (Eds.). (1984). *Psychoanalytic therapy and behavior therapy: Is integration possible?* New York: Plenum Press.

Arlow, J. A., & Brenner, C. (1964). *Psychoanalytic concepts and the structural theory.* New York: International Universities Press.

Aron, L. (1991). The patient's experience of the analyst's subjectivity. *Psychoanalytic Dialogues, 1,* 29–51.

Aron, L. (1996). *A meeting of minds: Mutuality in psychoanalysis.* Hillsdale, NJ: Analytic Press.

Bachrach, H., Galatzer-Levy, R., Skolnikoff, A., & Waldron, S. (1991). On the efficacy of psychoanalysis. *Journal of the American Psychoanalytic Association, 39,* 871–916.

Bachrach, H., Weber, J., & Solomon, M. (1985). Factors associated with the outcome of psychoanalysis (clinical and methodological considerations) of the Columbia Psychoanalytic Center research project (IV). *International Review of Psychoanalysis, 43,* 161–174.

Balint, M. (1953). *Primary love and psycho-analytic technique.* New York: Liveright.

Balint, M. (1968). *The basic fault: Therapeutic aspects of regression.* London: Tavistock.

Basch, M. (1988). *Understanding psychotherapy.* New York: Basic Books.

Beebe, B., & Lachmann, F. M. (1988). The contribution of mother-infant mutual influence to the origins of self and object representations. *Psychoanalytic Psychology, 5,* 305–337.

Benjamin, J. (1988). *The bonds of love: Psychoanalysis, feminism, and the problem of domination.* New York: Pantheon.

Benjamin, J. (1995). *Like subjects, love objects: Essays on recognition and sexual difference.* New Haven, CT: Yale University Press.

Bion, W. R. (1959). *Experiences in groups.* New York: Basic Books.

Bion, W. R. (1970). *Attention and interpretation.* London: Tavistock.

Blagys, M. D., & Hilsenroth, M. J. (2000). Distinctive of short-term psychodynamic-interpersonal psychotherapy: A review of the comparative psychotherapy process literature. *Clinical Psychology: Science and Practice, 7,* 167–189.

Blanck, G., & Blanck, R. (1974). *Ego psychology: Theory and practice.* New York: Columbia University Press.

Blanck, G., & Blanck, R. (1979). *Ego psychology II: Psychoanalytic developmental psychology.* New York: Columbia University Press.

Blatt, S. J. (2000, April). *Relatedness and self-definition: A fundamental psychological polarity and its implications for psychotherapy research.* Paper presented at the annual Spring meeting, Division of Psychoanalysis (39) of the American Psychological Association, San Francisco.

Bollas, C. (1987). *The shadow of the object: Psychoanalysis of the unthought known.* London: Free Association Books.

Bonanno, G. A., Davis, P. J., Singer, J. L., & Schwartz, G. E. (1991). The repressor personality and avoidant information processing: A dichotic listening study. *Journal of Research in Personality, 25,* 386–401.

Bowlby, J. (1969). *Attachment and loss: Vol. 1. Attachment.* New York: Basic Books.

Bowlby, J. (1973). *Attachment and loss: Vol. 2. Separation: Anxiety and anger.* New York: Basic Books.

Bowlby, J. (1982). *Attachment and loss: Vol. 3. Loss.* New York: Basic Books.

Breger, L. (2000). *Freud: Darkness in the midst of vision: An analytical biography.* New York: Wiley.

Brennan, K. A., & Shaver, P. R. (1998). Attachment styles and personality disorders: Their connections to each other and to parental divorce, parental death, and perceptions of parental caregiving. *Journal of Personality, 66,* 835–878.

Buirski, P., & Hagland, P. (2001). *Making sense together: The intersubjective approach to psychotherapy.* Northvale, NJ: Jason Aronson.

Chethik, M. (2000). *Techniques of child therapy: Psychodynamic strategies.* New York: Guilford Press.

Chodorow, N. J. (1978). *The reproduction of mothering: Psychoanalysis and the sociology of gender.* Berkeley: University of California Press.

Chodorow, N. J. (1989). *Feminism and psychoanalytic theory.* New Haven, CT: Yale University Press.

Clarkin, J. F., Kernberg, O. F., & Yeomans, F. E. (1998). *Psychotherapy for borderline personality.* New York: Wiley.

Coriat, T. (1917). Some statistical results of the psychoanalytic treatment of the psychoneuroses. *Psychoanalytic Review, 4,* 209–216.

Crits-Christoph, P., Cooper, A., & Luborsky, L. (1988). The accuracy of therapists' interpretations and the outcome of dynamic psychotherapy. *Journal of Counseling and Clinical Psychology, 56,* 490–495.

Crits-Christoph, P., Cooper, A., & Luborsky, L. (1990). The measurement of accuracy of interpretations. In L. Luborsky & P. Crits-Christoph (Eds.), *Understanding transference: The CCRT method* (pp. 173–188). New York: Basic Books.

Dahl, H. (1988). Frames of mind. In H. Dahl, H. Kachele, & H. Thomae (Eds.), *Psychoanalytic process research for clinical*

work with children, adolescents and adults (pp. 51–66). New York: Springer-Verlag.

Davies, J. M., & Frawley, M. G. (1993). *Treating the adult survivor of childhood sexual abuse.* New York: Basic Books.

Davis, P. J. (1987). Repression and the inaccessibility of affective memories. *Journal of Personality and Social Psychology, 53,* 585–593.

Davis, P. J., & Schwartz, G. E. (1987). Repression and the inaccessibility of affective memories. *Journal of Personality and Social Psychology, 53,* 155–162.

Derakshan, N., & Eysenck, M. W. (1997). Repression and repressors: Theoretical and experimental approaches. *European Psychologist, 2,* 235–246.

Doidge, N. (1997). Empirical evidence for the efficacy of psychoanalytic psychotherapies and psychoanalysis: An overview. *Psychoanalytic Inquiry, 15*(Suppl. 5), 102–150.

Eagle, M. (2000). Repression: Part II of II. *Psychoanalytic Review, 87,* 161–187.

Edell, W. S. (1987). Role of structure in disordered thinking in borderline and schizophrenic disorders. *Journal of Personality Assessment, 51,* 23–41.

Ehrenberg, D. (1992). *The intimate edge.* New York: Norton.

Eigen, M. (1986). *The psychotic core.* Northvale, NJ: Jason Aronson.

Epstein, M. (1998). *Going to pieces without falling apart: A Buddhist perspective on wholeness (Lessons from meditation and psychotherapy).* New York: Broadway Books.

Erikson, E. H. (1950). *Childhood and society.* New York: Norton.

Erikson E. H. (1959). *Identity and the life cycle.* New York: Norton.

Erle, J. (1979). An approach to the study of analyzability and analyses: The course of forty consecutive cases selected for supervised analysis. *Psychoanalytic Quarterly, 48,* 198–228.

Erle, J., & Goldberg, D. (1984). Observations on assessment of analyzability of experienced analysts. *Journal of the American Psychoanalytic Association, 32,* 715–737.

Etchegoyen, R. H. (1991). *The fundamentals of psychoanalytic technique.* New York: Karnac Books.

Fairbairn, W. R. D. (1952). *An object-relations theory of the personality.* New York: Basic Books.

Fenichel, O. (1945). *The psychoanalytic theory of neurosis.* New York: Norton.

Fiedler, F. E. (1950). The concept of an ideal therapeutic relationship. *Journal of Consulting Psychology, 14,* 239–245.

Foster, R. P., Moskowitz, M., & Javier, R. A. (1996). *Reaching across boundaries of culture and class: Widening the scope of psychotherapy.* Northvale, NJ: Jason Aronson.

Frank, K. A. (1999). *Psychoanalytic participation: Action, interaction, and integration.* Hillsdale, NJ: Analytic Press.

Freedman, N., Hoffenberg, J. D., Vorus, N., & Frosch, A. (1999). The effectiveness of psychoanalytic psychotherapy: The role of treatment duration, frequency of sessions, and the therapeutic relationship. *Journal of the American Psychoanalytic Association, 47*, 741–772.

Freud, A. (1966). *The ego and the mechanisms of defense.* New York: International Universities Press. (Original work published 1936)

Freud, S. (1896). The neuro-psychoses of defense. *Standard Edition, 3*, 169–170.

Freud, S. (1911). The handling of dream-interpretation in psycho-analysis. *Standard Edition, 12*, 91–96.

Freud, S. (1912a). The dynamics of transference. *Standard Edition, 12*, 99–108.

Freud, S. (1912b). Recommendations to physicians practising psycho-analysis. *Standard Edition, 12*, 111–120.

Freud, S. (1913). On beginning the treatment (Further recommendations on the technique of psycho-analysis I). *Standard Edition, 12*, 123–144.

Freud, S. (1914). Remembering, repeating and working-through (Further recommendations on the technique of psycho-analysis II). *Standard Edition, 12*, 147–156.

Freud, S. (1915). Observations on transference-love (Further recommendations on the technique of psycho-analysis III). *Standard Edition, 12*, 159–171.

Freud, S. (1923). The ego and the id. *Standard Edition, 19*, 13–59.

Freud, S. (1926). Psycho-analysis. *Standard Edition, 20*, 263–270.

Freud, S. (1933). New introductory lectures in psycho-analysis. *Standard Edition, 22*, 3–182.

Frey, W. H., II (1985). *Crying: The mystery of tears.* Minneapolis, MN: Winston Press.

Fromm, E. (1941). *Escape from freedom.* New York: Rinehart.

Fromm-Reichmann, F. (1950). *Principles of intensive psychotherapy.* Chicago: University of Chicago Press.

Galatzer-Levy, R. M., Bachrach, H. Skolnikoff, A., & Waldron, S., Jr. (2000). *Does psychotherapy work?* New Haven, CT: Yale University Press.

Gaston, L., Marmar, C. R., Gallagher, D., & Thompson, L. W. (1991). Alliance prediction of outcome beyond in-treatment symptomatic change in psychotherapy processes. *Psychotherapy Research, 1*, 104–113.

Gay, P. (1988). *Freud: A life for our time.* New York: Norton.

Gerson, J. (1996). *The embedded self: A psychoanalytic guide to family therapy.* Hillsdale, NJ: Analytic Press.

Gill, M. M. (1982). *The analysis of transference* (Vol. 1). New York: International Universities Press.

Gill, M. M. (1994). *Psychoanalysis in transition: A personal view.* Hillsdale, NJ: The Analytic Press.

Gill, M. M., & Hoffman, I. Z. (1982). *Analysis of transference* (Vol. 2). New York: International Universities Press.

Gilligan, C. (1982). *In a different voice: Psychological theory and women's development.* Cambridge, MA: Harvard University Press.

Glassgold, J. M., & Iasenza, S. (Eds.). (1995). *Lesbians and psychoanalysis: Revolutions in theory and practice.* New York: Free Press.

Glassman, N. S., & Andersen, S. M. (1998). *Activating transference without consciousness: Using significant-other representations to go beyond the subliminally given information.* Unpublished manuscript, New York University.

Glassman, N. S., & Andersen, S. M. (1999). Streams of thought about the self and significant other: Transference and construction of interpersonal meaning. In J. A. Singer & P. Salovey (Eds.), *At play in the fields of consciousness: Essays in honor of Jerome L. Singer* (pp. 103–142). Mahwah, NJ: Erlbaum.

Goldberg, A. (1988). *A fresh look at psychoanalysis: The view from self psychology.* Hillsdale, NJ: Analytic Press.

Green, A. (1999). *The fabric of affect and psychoanalytic discourse.* London: Routledge, Kegan & Paul.

Greenberg, J. R., & Mitchell, S. A. (1983). *Object relations in psychoanalytic theory.* Cambridge, MA: Harvard University Press.

Greenson, R. R. (1967). *The technique and practice of psychoanalysis.* New York: International Universities Press.

Greenspan, S. I. (1992). *Infancy and early childhood: The practice of clinical assessment and intervention with emotional and developmental challenges.* Madison, CT: International Universities Press.

Grinker, R. R., Werble, B., & Drye, R. C. (1968). *The borderline syndrome: A behavioral study of ego functions.* New York: Basic Books.

Gunderson, J. G. (1984). *Borderline personality disorder.* Washington, DC: American Psychiatric Press.

Guntrip, H. (1971). *Psychoanalytic theory, therapy and the self.* New York: Basic Books.

Hale, N. G. (1995). *The rise and crisis of psychoanalysis in the United States: Freud and the Americans, 1917–1985.* New York: Oxford University Press.

Hardaway, R. (1990). Subliminally activated symbiotic fantasies: Facts and artifacts. *Psychological Bulletin, 107*, 177–195.

Hartmann, H. (1958). *Ego psychology and the problem of adaptation.* New York: International Universities Press.

Heineman, T. V. (1998). *The abused child: Psychodynamic understanding and treatment.* New York: Guilford Press.

Henry, W. P., Schacht, T. E., & Strupp, H. H. (1986). Structural analysis of social behavior: Application to a study of interpersonal process in differential psychotherapeutic outcome. *Journal of Counseling and Clinical Psychology, 54*, 27–31.

Hinkley, K., & Anderson, S. M. (1996). The working self-concept in transference: Significant-other activation and self change. *Journal of Personality and Social Psychology, 71*, 1279–1295.

Hoffman, I. Z. (1983). The patient as interpreter of the analyst's experience. *Contemporary Psychoanalysis, 19*, 389–422.

Hoffman, I. Z. (1991). Discussion: Toward a social-constructivist view of the analytic situation. *Psychoanalytic Dialogues, 1*, 74–105.

Hoffman, I. Z. (1992). Some practical implications of a social-constructivist view of the analytic situation. *Psychoanalytic Dialogues, 2*, 287–304.

Holmes, D. S. (1990). The evidence for repression: An examination of sixty years of research. In J. Singer (Ed.), *Repression and dissociation: Implications of personality theory, psychopathology, and health.* Chicago: University of Chicago Press.

Horney, K. (1945). *Our inner conflicts: A constructive theory of neurosis.* New York: Norton.

Horowitz, M. (1988). *Introduction to psychodynamics: A new synthesis.* New York: Basic Books.

Hovarth, A. O., & Symonds, B. D. (1991). Relation between working alliance and outcome in psychotherapy: A meta-analysis. *Journal of Counseling Psychology, 38,* 139–149.

Isay, R. A. (1989). *Being homosexual: Gay men and their development.* Northvale, NJ: Jason Aronson.

Isay, R. A. (1994). *Becoming gay: The journey to self-acceptance.* New York: Holt.

Jackson, L. C., & Greene, B. (Eds.). (2000). *Psychotherapy with African American women: Innovations in psychodynamic perspectives and practice.* New York: Guilford Press.

Jacobson, E. (1964). *The self and the object world.* New York: International Universities Press.

Jacobson, E. (1971). *Depression.* New York: International Universities Press.

Jones, E. (1936). *Decannual report of the London clinic of psychoanalysis: 1926–1936.*

Jones, E. E., & Pulos, S. M. (1993). Comparing the process in psychodynamic and cognitive-behavioral therapies. *Journal of Consulting and Clinical Psychology, 61,* 306–316.

Joseph, B. (1989). *Psychic equilibrium and psychic change.* London: Tavistock/Routledge.

Kantrowitz, J., Katz, A., Greenman, D., Morris, H., Paolitto, F., Sashin, J., & Solomon, L. (1989). The patient-analyst match and the outcome of psychoanalysis: A study of 13 cases. *Journal of the American Psychoanalytic Association, 37,* 893–920.

Kantrowitz, J., Katz, A., & Paolitto, F. (1990a). Follow up of psychoanalysis five to ten years after termination: Part 1. Stability of change. *Journal of the American Psychoanalytic Association, 38,* 637–654.

Kantrowitz, J., Katz, A., & Paolitto, F. (1990b). Follow up of psychoanalysis five to ten years after termination: Part 2. The development of the self-analytic function. *Journal of the American Psychoanalytic Association, 38,* 637–654.

Kantrowitz, J., Katz, A., & Paolitto, F. (1990c). Follow up of psychoanalysis five to ten years after termination: Part 3. The relation between the resolution of the transference and the patient-analyst match. *Journal of the American Psychoanalytic Association, 38,* 655–678.

Kantrowitz, J., Katz, A., Paolitto, F., Sashin, J., & Solomon, L. (1987a). Changes in the level and quality of object relations in psychoanalysis: Follow-up of a longitudinal, prospective study. *Journal of the American Psychoanalytic Association, 35,* 23–46.

Kantrowitz, J., Katz, A., Paolitto, F., Sashin, J., & Solomon, L. (1987b). The role of reality testing in psychoanalysis: Follow-up of 22 cases. *Journal of the American Psychoanalytic Association, 35,* 367–385.

Karliner, R., Westrich, E. K., Shedler, J., & Mayman, M. (1996). Bridging the gap between psychodynamic and scientific psychology: The Adelphi Early Memory Index. In J. M. Masling & R. F. Bornstein (Eds.), *Empirical studies of psychoanalytic theories: Vol. 6. Psychoanalytic perspectives on developmental psychology* (pp. 43–67). Washington, DC: APA Press.

Kernberg, O. F. (1975). *Borderline conditions and pathological narcissism.* New York: Jason Aronson.

Kernberg, O. F. (1984). *Severe personality disorders: Psychotherapeutic strategies.* New Haven, CT: Yale University Press.

Kernberg, O. F., Burstein, E., Coyne, L., Appelbaum, S. A., Horowitz, L., & Voth, H. (1972). Psychotherapy and psychoanalysis: Final report of the Menninger Foundation's psychotherapy research project. *Bulletin of the Menninger Clinic, 36,* 1–275.

Kessel, L., & Hyman, H. (1933). The value of psychoanalysis as a therapeutic procedure. *Journal of the American Medical Association, 101,* 1612–1615.

Klein, G. (1976). *Psychoanalytic theory.* New York: International Universities Press.

Klein, M. (1946). Notes on some schizoid mechanisms. In R. Money-Kyrle (Ed.), *The writings of Melanie Klein* (Vol. 3, pp. 1–24). London: Hogarth Press.

Klerman, G. L., Weissman, M. M., Rounsaville, B. J., & Chevron, E. S. (1984). *Interpersonal psychotherapy of depression.* New York: Basic Books.

Knight, R. (1941). Evaluation of the results of psychoanalytic therapy. *American Journal of Psychiatry, 98,* 434–446.

Kohut, H. (1971). *The analysis of the self.* New York: International Universities Press.

Kohut, H. (1977). *The restoration of the self.* New York: International Universities Press.

Kohut, H. (1984). *How does analysis cure?* Chicago: University of Chicago Press.

Lacan, J. (1977). *Ecrits: A selection* (A. Sheridan, Trans.). New York: Norton.

Lachmann, F. M., & Lichtenberg, J. D. (1992). Model scenes: Implications for psychoanalytic treatment. *Journal of the American Psychoanalytic Association, 40,* 117–137.

Langs, R. (1976). *The bipersonal field.* New York: Jason Aronson.

Laughlin, H. P. (1979). *The ego and its defenses.* New York: Jason Aronson. (Original work published 1970)

Leupnitz, D. A. (1988). *The family interpreted: Psychoanalysis, feminism, and family therapy.* New York: Basic Books.

Levenson, E. A. (1972). *The fallacy of understanding: An inquiry into the changing structure of psychoanalysis.* New York: Basic Books.

Levenson, E. A. (1983). *The ambiguity of change*. New York: Basic Books.

Levy, K. N., Blatt, S. J., & Shaver, P. R. (1998). Attachment styles and parental representations. *Journal of Personality and Social Psychology, 74*, 407–419.

Lichtenberg, J. D. (1983). *Psychoanalysis and infant research*. Hillsdale, NJ: Analytic Press.

Limentani, D. (1956). Symbiotic identification in schizophrenia. *Psychiatry, 19*, 231–236.

Lipton, S. D. (1977). The advantages of Freud's technique as shown in his analysis of the Rat-In Man. *International Journal of Psycho-Analysis, 58*, 255–273.

Loewald, H. W. (1980). *Papers on psychoanalysis*. New Haven, CT: Yale University Press.

Luborsky, L., & Crits-Christoph, P. (Eds.). (1990). *Understanding transference: The core conflictual relationship theme method*. New York: Basic Books.

Luborsky, L., Crits-Christoph, P., & Mellon, J. (1986). Advent of objective measures of the transference concept. *Journal of Consulting and Clinical Psychology, 54*, 39–47.

Mahler, M. (1968). *On human symbiosis and the vicissitudes of individuation: Vol. 1. Infantile psychosis*. New York: International Universities Press.

Mahler, M., Pine, F., & Bergmann, A. (1975). *The psychological birth of the human infant*. New York: Basic Books.

Main, M. (1995). Recent studies in attachment: Overview, with selected implications for clinical work. In S. Goldberg, J. Kerr, & R. Muir (Eds.), *Attachment theory: Social, developmental, and clinical perspectives* (pp. 407–474). Hillsdale, NJ: Analytic Press.

Main, M. (1996). Introduction to the special section on attachment and psychopathology: 2. Overview of the field of attachment. *Journal of Consulting and Clinical Psychology, 64*, 237–243.

Main, M., Kaplan, N., & Cassidy, J. (1985). Security in infancy, childhood, and adulthood: A move to the level of representation. *Monographs of the Society for Research in Child Development, 50*(1-2, Serial No. 209).

Main, T. F. (1957). The ailment. *British Journal of Medical Psychology, 30*, 129–145.

Maroda, K. (1991). *The power of countertransference*. Chichester, England: Wiley.

Maroda, K. (1999). *Seduction, surrender, and transformation: Emotional engagement in the analytic process*. Hillsdale, NJ: Analytic Press.

Masson, J. M. (trans.). (1985). *The complete letters of Sigmund Freud to Wilhelm Fliess, 1887–1904*. Cambridge, MA: Belknap Press of Harvard University Press.

Masterson, J. F. (1972). *Treatment of the borderline adolescent: A developmental approach*. New York: Wiley-Interscience.

Masterson, J. F. (1976). *Psychotherapy of the borderline adult: A developmental approach*. New York: Brunner/Mazel.

McDougall, J. (1980). *Plea for a measure of abnormality*. New York: International Universities Press.

McWilliams, N. (1994). *Psychoanalytic diagnosis: Understanding personality structure in the clinical process*. New York: Guilford Press.

McWilliams, N. (1999). *Psychoanalytic case formulation*. New York: Guilford Press.

Messer, S. B., Sass, L. A., & Woolfolk, R. L. (1994). *Interpretive perspectives on personality, psychotherapy, and psychopathology*. New Brunswick, NJ: Rutgers University Press.

Messer, S. B., & Winokur, M. (1980). Some limits to the integration of psychoanalytic and behavior therapy. *American Psychologist, 35*, 818–827.

Millon, T. (1996). *Personality and psychopathology: Building a clinical science*. New York: Wiley-Interscience.

Mitchell, J. (1974). *Psychoanalysis and feminism: Freud, Reich, Laing, and women*. New York: Pantheon.

Mitchell, S. A. (1993). *Hope and dread in psychoanalysis*. New York: Basic Books.

Mitchell, S. A. (1997). *Influence and autonomy in psychoanalysis*. Hillsdale, NJ: Analytic Press.

Mitchell, S. A. (2000). *Relationality: From attachment to intersubjectivity*. Hillsdale, NJ: Analytic Press.

Mitchell, S. A., & Black, M. J. (1995). *Freud and beyond: A history of modern psychoanalytic thought*. New York: Basic Books.

Myers, L. B., & Brewin, C. R. (1994). Recall of early experience and the repressive coping style. *Journal of Abnormal Psychology, 103*, 288–292.

Myers, L. B., & Brewin, C. R. (1995). Repressive coping and the recall of emotional material. *Cognition & Emotion, 9*, 637–642.

Newton, T. L., & Contrada, R. J. (1992). Repressive coping and verbal-autonomic response dissociation: The influence of social context. *Journal of Personality and Social Psychology, 62*, 159–167.

Ogden, T. H. (1982). *Projective identification and psychotherapeutic technique*. New York: Jason Aronson.

Ogden, T. H. (1986). *The matrix of the mind: Object relations and the psychoanalytic dialogue*. Northvale, NJ: Jason Aronson.

Ogden, T. H. (1994). *Subjects of analysis*. New York: Jason Aronson.

Orange, D. M., Atwood, G. E., & Stolorow, R. D. (1997). *Working intersubjectively: Contextualism in psychoanalytic practice*. Hillsdale, NJ: Analytic Press.

Parkes, E. M., Stevenson-Hinde, J., & Marris, P. (Eds.). (1991). *Attachment across the life cycle*. London: Routledge.

Pennebaker, J. W. (Ed.). (1995). *Emotion, disclosure and health*. Washington, DC: APA Press.

Pennebaker, J. W. (1997). *Opening up: The healing power of expressing emotions* (Rev. ed.). New York: Guilford Press.

Petrie, K. J., Booth, R. J., & Pennebaker, J. W. (1998). The immunological effects of thought suppression. *Journal of Personality and Social Psychology, 75*, 1264–1272.

Pine, F. (1985). *Developmental theory and clinical process.* New Haven, CT: Yale University Press.

Pine, F. (1990). *Drive, ego, object, and self: A synthesis for clinical work.* New York: Basic Books.

Pinsker, H. (1997). *A primer of supportive psychotherapy.* Hillsdale, NJ: Analytic Press.

Racker, H. (1968). *Transference and countertransference.* New York: International Universities Press.

Renik, O. (1995). The ideal of the anonymous analyst and the problem of self-disclosure. *Psychoanalytic Quarterly, 62,* 553–571.

Rockland, L. H. (1992). *Supportive therapy: A psychodynamic approach.* New York: Basic Books.

Rogers, C. R. (1951). *Client-centered therapy: Its current practice, implications, and theory.* Boston: Houghton Mifflin.

Roth, A., & Fonagy, P. (1996). *What works for whom? A critical review of psychotherapy research.* New York: Guilford Press.

Rothstein, A. (1980). *The narcissistic pursuit of perfection.* New York: International Universities Press.

Safran, J. D., & Muran, J. C. (2000). *Negotiating the therapeutic alliance: A relational treatment guide.* New York: Guilford Press.

Sandell, R., Blomberg, J., Lazar, A., Carlsson, J., Broberg, J., & Schubert, J. (2000). Varieties of long-term outcome among patients in psychoanalysis and long-term psychotherapy: A review of findings in the Stockholm outcome of Psychoanalysis and Psychotherapy Project (STOPP). *International Journal of Psychoanalysis, 81,* 921–942.

Sandler, J. (1976). Countertransference and role-responsiveness. *International Review of Psycho-Analysis, 3,* 43–47.

Sashin, J., Eldred, S., & Van Amerowgen, A. (1975). A search for predictive factors in institute supervised cases: A retrospective study of 183 cases from 1959–1966 at the Boston Psychoanalytic Society and Institute. *International Journal of Psychoanalysis, 56,* 343–359.

Schneider, K. J. (1998). Toward a science of the heart: Romanticism and the revival of psychology. *American Psychologist, 53,* 277–289.

Schore, A. N. (1994). *Affect regulation and the origin of the self: The neurobiology of emotional development.* Hillsdale, NJ: Erlbaum.

Searles, H. F. (1965). Integration and differentiation in schizophrenia. In H. F. Searles (Ed.), *Collected papers on schizophrenia and related subjects* (pp. 304–348). New York: International Universities Press.

Searles, H. F. (1979). *Countertransference and related subjects: Selected papers.* New York: International Universities Press.

Sechehaye, M. (1951). *Symbolic realization: A new method of psychotherapy applied to a case of schizophrenia.* New York: International Universities Press.

Seligman, M. E. P. (1995). The effectiveness of psychotherapy: The *Consumer Reports* Study. *American Psychologist, 50,* 965–974.

Seligman, M. E. P. (1996). A creditable beginning. *American Psychologist, 51,* 1086–1087.

Shane, E., Shane, M., & Gales, M. (1997). *Intimate attachments: Toward a new self psychology.* New York: Guilford Press.

Shedler, J., Mayman, M., & Manis, M. (1993). The illusion of mental health. *American Psychologist, 48,* 1117–1131.

Shevrin, H., Bond, J. A., Brakel, L. A., Hertel, R. K., & Williams, W. J. (1996). *Conscious and unconscious process.* New York: Guilford Press.

Siegel, P., & Weinberger, J. (1998). Capturing the "Mommy and I are one" merger fantasy: The oneness motive. In R. F. Bornstein & J. M. Masling (Eds.), *Empirical perspectives on the psychoanalytic unconscious* (pp. 71–98). Washington, DC: APA Press.

Silverman, D. (1998). The tie that binds: Affect regulation, attachment, and psychoanalysis. *Psychoanalytic Psychology, 15,* 187–212.

Silverman, L. H. (1976). Psychoanalytic theory: The reports of my death are greatly exaggerated. *American Psychologist, 31,* 621–637.

Silverman, L. H. (1983). The subliminal psychodynamic method: Overview and comprehensive listing of studies. In J. Masling (Ed.), *Empirical studies of psychoanalytic theory* (Vol. 1, pp. 69–103). Hillsdale, NJ: Erlbaum.

Silverman, L. H., Lachmann, F. M., & Milich, R. H. (1982). *The search for oneness.* New York: International Universities Press.

Silverman, L. H., & Weinberger, J. (1985). Mommy and I are one: Implications for psychotherapy. *American Psychologist, 40,* 1296–1308.

Singer, J. L. (1985). Transference and the human condition: A cognitive-affective perspective. *Psychoanalytic Psychology, 2,* 189–219.

Slade, A., & Aber, L. A. (1992). Attachments, drives, and development: Conflicts and convergences in theory. In J. W. Barron, M. N. Eagle, & D. L. Wolitzky (Eds.), *Interface of psychoanalysis and psychology* (pp. 154–185). Washington, DC: APA Press.

Spitz, R. A. (1965). *The first year of life.* New York: International Universities Press.

Stern, D. N. (1985). *The interpersonal world of the infant: A view from psychoanalysis and developmental psychology.* New York: Basic Books.

Stern, D. N. (1995). *The motherhood constellation: A unified view of parent-infant psychotherapy.* New York: Basic Books.

Stolorow, R. D. (1976). Psychoanalytic reflections on client-centered therapy in the light of modern conceptions of narcissism. *Psychotherapy: Theory, Research and Practice, 13,* 26–29.

Stolorow, R. D., & Atwood, G. E. (1992). *Contexts of being: The intersubjective foundations of psychological life.* Hillsdale, NJ: Analytic Press.

Stolorow, R. D., Brandchaft, B., & Atwood, G. E. (1987). *Psychoanalytic treatment: An intersubjective approach.* Hillsdale, NJ: Analytic Press.

Stone, M. H. (1980). *The borderline syndromes: Constitution, personality, and adaptation.* New York: McGraw-Hill.

Suedfeld, P., & Pennebaker, J. W. (1997). Health outcomes and cognitive aspects of recalled negative life events. *Psychosomatic Medicine, 59,* 172–177.

Suler, J. R. (1993). *Contemporary psychoanalysis and Eastern thought.* Albany: State University of New York Press.

Sullivan, H. S. (1953). *The interpersonal theory of psychiatry.* New York: Norton.

Sullivan, H. S. (1956). *Clinical studies in psychiatry.* New York: Norton.

Vaillant, G. E. (1992). *Ego mechanisms of defense.* Washington, DC: American Psychiatric Press.

Vanden Bos, G. R. (Ed.). (1996). Outcome assessment of psychotherapy [Special issue]. *American Psychologist, 51*(10).

Vaughan, S., Marshall, R. D., Mackinnon, R. A., Vaughan, R., Mellman, L., & Roose, S. P. (2000). Can we do psychoanalytic outcome research? A feasibility study. *International Journal of Psychoanalysis, 81,* 513–527.

Wachtel, P. L. (1977). *Psychoanalysis and behavior therapy: Toward an integration.* New York: Basic Books.

Wachtel, P. L. (1993). *Therapeutic communication: Knowing what to way when.* New York: Guilford Press.

Wallerstein, R. S. (1986). *Forty-two lives in treatment: A study of psychoanalysis and psychotherapy.* New York: Guilford Press.

Wallerstein, R. S. (2001). The generations of psychotherapy research: An overview. *Psychoanalytic Psychology, 18,* 243–267.

Waters, E., Hamilton, C. E., & Weinfield, N. S. (2000). The stability of attachment security from infancy to adolescence and early adulthood: General introduction. *Child Development, 71,* 684–689.

Waters, E., Weinfield, N. S., & Hamilton, C. E. (2000). The stability of attachment security from infancy to adolescence and early adulthood: General introduction. *Child Development, 71,* 703–706.

Weber, J., Bachrach, H., & Solomon, M. (1985a). Factors associated with the outcome of psychoanalysis: Report of the Columbia Psychoanalytic Center Research Project, part 2. *International Review of Psychoanalysis, 12,* 127–141.

Weber, J., Bachrach, H., & Solomon, M. (1985b). Factors associated with the outcome of psychoanalysis: Report of the Columbia Psychoanalytic Center Research Project, part 3. *International Review of Psychoanalysis, 12,* 251–262.

Weinberger, D. A. (1990). The construct validity of the repressive coping style. In J. L. Singer (Ed.), *Repression and dissociation: Implications for personality theory, psychopathology, and health* (pp. 337–386). Chicago: University of Chicago Press.

Weinberger, D. A., & Schwartz, G. E. (1990). Distress and restraint as superordinate dimensions of self-reported adjustments: A typological perspective. *Journal of Personality, 58,* 381–417.

Weinberger, D. A., Schwartz, G. E., & Davidson, R. J. (1979). Low-anxious, high-anxious, and repressive coping styles: Psychometric patterns and behavioral and physiological responses to stress. *Journal of Abnormal Psychology, 88,* 369–380.

Weinberger, J. (1992). Demystifying subliminal psychodynamic activation. In R. Bornstein & T. Pittman (Eds.), *Perception without awareness.* New York: Guilford Press.

Weinberger, J. (1995). Common factors aren't so common: The common factors dilemma. *Clinical Psychology: Science and Practice, 2,* 45–69.

Weinberger, J., Bonner, E., & Barra, M. (1999). *Reliability and validity for the oneness motive.* Paper presented at American Psychological Association convention, Boston.

Weinberger, J., & Hardaway, R. (1990). Separating science from myth in subliminal psychodynamic activation. *Clinical Psychology Review, 10,* 727–756.

Weinberger, J., & Silverman, L. H. (1987). Subliminal psychodynamic activation: A method for studying psychoanalytic dynamic propositions. In R. Hogan & H. Jones (Eds.), *Perspectives in personality* (Vol. 2, pp. 251–287). Greenwich, CT: JAI Press.

Weiss, J. (1971). The emergence of new themes: A contribution to the psychoanalytic theory of therapy. *International Journal of Psychoanalysis, 52,* 459–467.

Weiss, J., Sampson, H., & the Mount Zion Psychotherapy Research Group. (1986). *The psychoanalytic process: Theory, clinical observations, and empirical research.* New York: Guilford Press.

Westen, D. (1990). Psychoanalytic approaches to personality. In L. Pervin (Ed.), *Handbook of personality theory and research* (pp. 21–39). New York: Guilford Press.

Westen, D. (1991). Social cognition and object relations. *Psychological Bulletin, 109,* 429–455.

Westen, D. (1998). The scientific legacy of Sigmund Freud: Toward a psychodynamically informed psychological science. *Psychological Bulletin, 124,* 333–371.

Winnicott, D. W. (1949). Hate in the countertransference. In D. W. Winnicott (Ed.), *Collected papers* (pp. 194–203). New York: Basic Books.

Winnicott, D. W. (1958). *Through pediatrics to psychoanalysis.* London: Tavistock.

Winnicott, D. W. (1965). *The maturational process and the facilitating environment.* New York: International Universities Press.

Winnicott, D. W. (1971). *Playing and reality.* New York: Basic Books.

Wolf, E. S. (1988). *Treating the self: Elements of clinical self psychology.* New York: Guilford Press.

Young-Breuhl, E. (2000). *Subject to biography: Psychoanalysis, feminism and writing women's lives.* Cambridge, MA: Harvard University Press.

Zetzel, E. R. (1956). Current concepts of transference. *International Journal of Psycho-Analysis, 37,* 369–376.

CHAPTER 11

# Behavioral and Cognitive-Behavioral Psychotherapy

W. EDWARD CRAIGHEAD AND LINDA WILCOXON CRAIGHEAD

Behavior therapy (BT), which began in earnest during the 1960s, and Cognitive Behavior Therapy (CBT), which began during the 1970s, are now among the mainstream models of psychosocial clinical interventions. Training in these conceptual models and in the related interventions is central to most doctoral and internship programs in Clinical, Counseling, and School Psychology. Because the therapies are so compatible with the prevailing biological models of modern Psychiatry, training and clinical use of these therapies (along with Interpersonal Psychotherapy) have even made their way into most departments of Psychiatry.

BT and CBT interventions have not always enjoyed such valued status. For example, in a debate conducted during the late 1960s at the University of Illinois between Leonard Ullmann (a behaviorist) and Charles Patterson (a distinguished Rogerian therapist and writer), the latter described BT as only a "passing fad." When we first began using BT procedures at Pennsylvania State University in the early 1970s, a Philosophy professor called for a faculty council meeting to prohibit these interventions in the Psychology Clinic, even labeling them "unethical." Although controversial in the beginning, BT and subsequently CBT overcame and survived such criticisms, as well as the widely held view that direct modifications of clinical problems would result in "symptom substitution." A description of the background and brief history of BT and CBT will elucidate how these psychotherapies achieved the positive stature they currently enjoy.

## ORIGINS, BACKGROUND, AND BRIEF HISTORY

### Development of Behavior Therapy

BT grew out of the conceptual framework of Behaviorism, which may be traced to a variety of influences from around the world. In the United States, John B. Watson (1878–1958) is usually credited with changing the focus of psychology from introspection of Structuralism and Functionalism to the study of observable behaviors. Watson defined Psychology as the "science of behavior," which limited the scope of psychological inquiry to directly observable, objectively verifiable events and behaviors. Because of Watson's influence in America as well as the research on conditioning in Russia and animal behavioral research in Europe (especially England), behaviorism became the primary conceptual framework underlying most basic psychological research from the 1920s through the 1970s.

Although there were sporadic studies evaluating the clinical application of behavioral interventions prior to World War II, it was the emergence of Clinical Psychology following that war that produced more extensive developments within BT (see W. E. Craighead, Craighead, & Ilardi, 1995). The primary defining characteristic of BT was the application of principles of behaviorism to clinical phenomena as psychology moved from the basic science laboratories to inform clinical interventions. Behaviorism focused on how learning occurs, and several theories of learning emerged over the 50-year period dominated by Behaviorism (see Kazdin, 1978, for details). However, principles of learning from two of these learning theories guided the development of BT during the 1950s: (a) the application of principles of operant conditioning (first labeled behavior modification, but now most commonly called applied behavior analysis) championed by Skinner (1953) and his colleagues; and (b) the application of principles of classical conditioning (at least metaphorically) by Wolpe (1958) in his description of behavioral treatments for anxiety. Similar developments, exemplified by Eysenck (1960) and his colleagues at the Institute of Psychiatry in London, occurred concurrently in Europe.

In addition to utilizing principles drawn from learning theory to guide the development of intervention procedures, another fundamental hallmark of BT has been its insistence on the empirical evaluation of the BT interventions. In the final analysis, it has been this empirical emphasis that has given BT its staying power and supported its efficacy with a wide range of clinical disorders (see L. W. Craighead, Craighead, Kazdin, & Mahoney, 1994; Kazdin, 1994). BT began with a focus on treatment of "anxiety" problems, largely because anxiety was viewed as the core of "neuroses" within the prevailing psychodynamic model of psychopathology and treatment. As we shall see later in this chapter, applications were soon developed for a variety of other clinical disorders. During the 1970s, however, a confluence of factors resulted in a large percentage of behavior therapists shifting their focus to internal cognitive processes; these factors produced the therapies now subsumed under the rubric of CBT.

## Emergence of Cognitive-Behavior Therapy

The fundamental factor effecting a shift to a more cognitive focus within BT was the shift in the focus of basic psychology. During the late 1960s and the early 1970s basic psychology underwent what Kuhn has labeled a "paradigm shift" (Kuhn, 1962). Because it focused on observable behaviors (stimulus-response relationships), basic psychology, guided by Behaviorism, had eschewed the human "black box," but with the "cognitive revolution" (see Dember, 1974) there was a shift to the study of internal cognitive processes (e.g., information processing, memory, problem solving, etc.).

Because behavior therapists were guided by basic psychology, the cognitive shift in basic psychology had a direct impact on the models and procedures of their clinical endeavors. This shift implied a central role for cognitive processes in the mediation of behavior and thereby legitimized cognition as a viable target for clinical intervention. Just as with BT, the specific definition of CBT has not been monolithic, and over 20 different approaches to CBT have been identified (Mahoney & Lyddon, 1988). We can now trace these CBT therapies to three major influences. First (as just noted) was the application of basic cognitive psychology constructs by empirically oriented clinicians to the development of models and procedures of clinical intervention (e.g., Bandura's 1969 use of information processing in the development of his social learning theory). The second major influence was the reformulation of behavioral self-control procedures as cognitive interventions (e.g., Thoresen & Mahoney, 1974). Finally, there was the emergence of Ellis's (1962) and A. T. Beck's (1964, 1970) cognitive therapies (CT), which were developed within a clinical setting and initially based on clinical experience rather than findings of basic psychology (see W. E. Craighead et al., 1995, for detailed discussion of these influences).

BT and CBT share the same basic assumptions; namely, basic psychological research can inform clinical models and procedures, and one should evaluate the efficacy and effectiveness of clinical interventions. The major difference between BT and CBT lies in the conceptualization of the psychopathology and the specific intervention programs for the various clinical disorders. Many behavior therapists who label themselves applied behavior analysts may still avoid the use of cognitive models and strategies. Similarly, there are those who see themselves as strict cognitive therapists, and they may view behaviors as important only because they can become the basis for discussion and modification of cognitive styles associated with those behaviors. In the main, however, BT and CBT models are conceptually quite similar, and the procedures from both are complementary in the clinical process. J. S. Beck (2001) recently suggested a need to distinguish between CT and CBT, but then she described an intervention program for a depressed patient that was as behavioral as it was cognitive. Her description also demonstrated an extremely important clinical factor, which we shall note in several places in this chapter: Both BT and CBT are usually compatible with appropriate medication interventions.

Within the remainder of this chapter we describe and discuss BT and CBT interventions for most of the major clinical disorders. We have organized the following section according to the disorders treated, rather than according to the various clinical procedures employed. In order to avoid redundancy, we describe each treatment program (e.g., A. T. Beck's form of CBT) only the first time it is noted. We conclude with some comments about future directions for relevant conceptual issues and clinical research.

# CLINICAL RESEARCH ON BEHAVIOR THERAPY AND COGNITIVE-BEHAVIOR THERAPY

## Anxiety Disorders

### Phobias

Because the treatment of anxiety disorders with BT began with an emphasis on fear, anxiety, and avoidance, we begin our discussion with phobias. Wolpe (1958) provided the first comprehensive discussion of BT treatments of anxiety in his classic book, *Psychotherapy by Reciprocal Inhibition.* Concurrently, Eysenck (1960) and his colleagues were challenging the psychodynamic concept of anxiety as the core of neuroses. Wolpe argued that anxiety, and specifically phobias, represented conditioned autonomic nervous system responses to certain environmental situations or stimuli. Based on laboratory research, primarily with cats, he posited several BT interventions to alleviate the conditioned anxiety responses. Two of those procedures that have been widely studied are systematic desensitization (including relaxation training) and assertion training.

The diagnostic system at that time did not include the level of differentiation currently in place for anxiety disorders. Nevertheless, systematic desensitization was evaluated for a number of problems that currently would be labeled phobia or social phobia (see Paul, 1969). Systematic desensitization comprises three procedures: training in progressive muscular relaxation; development of a hierarchy of stimulus situations ranging from those that trigger very low levels of anxiety to the one (e.g., flying in a plane) that elicits the phobic reaction; and sequential visualization of the hierarchy of situations while remaining relaxed in the therapist's office. Early BT research demonstrated that systematic desensitization was effective in reducing anxiety associated with social interactions, public speaking, and a variety of phobic situations (Paul, 1969). Progressive muscular relaxation continues to be widely used as a part of BT/CBT treatments for virtually all anxiety disorders. Systematic desensitization is primarily used for treatment of those disorders for which exposure-based treatments (described in the next paragraph) are not appropriate or as a first step in an exposure treatment program.

Utilizing principles of both operant and classical conditioning, other behavior therapists in the United States (e.g., Agras, Leitenberg, & Barlow, 1968) and in England (e.g., Marks, 1969) developed another procedure, "*in vivo* exposure," to treat phobias. With in vivo exposure, the phobic individual, frequently accompanied by the therapist, is gradually placed in the presence of the phobic object. The person is asked not to avoid or escape the situation until the anxiety is habituated or significantly decreased. Although some anxiety situations (e.g., anxiety regarding sexual interactions) necessitate the use of imaginal exposure as used in systematic desensitization, in vivo exposure has generally been found to be the more efficacious of the two procedures (see Barlow, 1988). Consistent with his social learning model of therapeutic change, Bandura added a cognitive component (e.g., self-instruction training) to both systematic desensitization and in vivo exposure and suggested that the therapist model both the behaviors and the cognitive component as part of the therapy (see Bandura, 1977).

In the *Diagnostic and Statistical Manual of Mental Disorders–Fourth Edition* (*DSM-IV;* American Psychological Association [APA], 1994), phobias were divided into five categories: blood-injection-injury, situational, natural environment, animal, and other (e.g., choking). With all types of phobias for which it is possible, an exposure-based intervention, structured and implemented by a clinician, is the most effective BT method. In addition, because of the risk of fainting during in vivo exposure for blood-injection-injury phobia, the patient needs to be taught how to tense various muscle groups in order to keep the blood pressure high enough to prevent fainting (Ost, 1992). Recently, Ost and his colleagues have utilized massed (e.g., all-day) exposure, which is effective for most individuals with phobias and may be completed in one session (Hellstrom, Fellenius, & Ost, 1996; Ost, Ferebee, & Furmark, 1997). Although these procedures may seem simple, they need to be implemented by a clinician according to principles of learning and extinction. Self administration or administration by an untrained therapist is typically not effective and can even make the problem worse because of inadequate or inappropriate exposure.

One of the clinical problems for which exposure therapies have been especially useful is now called *agoraphobia.* Research has gradually demonstrated that patients diagnosed with agoraphobia frequently suffered from panic attacks and that exposure therapy alone was not a particularly effective intervention for those comorbid panic attacks. This led to the development of BT and CBT interventions designed specifically for the treatment of panic disorder (PD) with and without agoraphobia (see Barlow & Lehman, 1996, for discussion of this issue as well as treatments of other anxiety disorders).

### Panic Disorder

Barlow and his colleagues (e.g., Barlow & Craske, 1994) have developed an effective CBT program called *Panic Control Therapy* (PCT), for treating PD. The treatment consists of: (a) progressive muscular relaxation and breathing retraining; (b) interoceptive exposure (exposure to clinically induced physiological arousal cues that mimic panic attack symptoms, e.g., by use of hyperventilation, exercise, etc.); and (c) cognitive restructuring aimed at correcting misconceptions about anxiety and pain as well as overestimates of the threat and danger of panic attacks. Clark and his colleagues (Clark, 1989; Salkovskis & Clark, 1991), working in England and utilizing a cognitive theoretical model of PD, developed a program that is quite similar to Barlow's PCT. It has the same major components, including the focus on correction of misperceived physiological cues, but it places greater emphasis on the intervention's cognitive restructuring phase, which is more similar to the cognitive approach of A. T. Beck's CBT.

Barlow's PCT program, which has been extensively evaluated by its originators, was recently compared to imipramine (Tofranil), CBT plus imipramine, CBT plus placebo, and placebo alone in a four-site randomized control trial (RCT; Barlow, Gorman, Shear, & Woods, 2000). All active treatments were more effective than placebo alone. Imipramine produced a slightly higher initial quality of response, but CBT was more durable and somewhat better tolerated. Only CBT alone and CBT plus placebo were superior to placebo alone at the 6-month follow-up. It is interesting to note that the combined CBT-imipramine condition, which produced slightly superior acute treatment results, had a large relapse rate and was not superior to placebo alone at the 6-month follow-up.

Research with Clark's CBT has provided results fairly similar to those obtained with Barlow's PCT. For example, Clark et al. (1994) found that approximately 75% of panic patients treated with CBT were panic free, and this compared to 70% for those who received imipramine and 40% who received applied relaxation training. At a 9-month follow-up, only 15% of the CBT patients had relapsed, whereas the relapse rate for the imipramine patients was 40% and for the applied relaxation patients was 53%; CBT was significantly more effective than either of the other two conditions at follow-up.

The combination of CBT with high-potency benzodiazepines appears to be one of the areas in which CBT and medications are incompatible. For example, both Brown and Barlow (1995) and Otto, Pollack, and Sabatino (1995) have found that the effects of CBT are weakened by the concurrent administration of benzodiazepines. Because of this and because of the high rate of relapse following typical termination of benzodiazepines, which are frequently prescribed by physicians for anxiety disorders, Otto et al. (1993) and Spiegel, Bruce, Gregg, and Nuzzarello (1994) have developed effective programs for the tapering of benzodiazepines while patients receive CBT/PCT.

The cumulative data for these CBT programs suggest that CBT may very well be the treatment of choice for PD. It appears to be as effective as medications, and it appears to be more enduring. Of course, these findings will have to be replicated in subsequent comparisons to newer medications (e.g., selective serotonin reuptake inhibitors, SSRIs) in order for this conclusion to stand.

### Obsessive-Compulsive Disorder

The most effective psychosocial treatment for obsessive-compulsive disorder (OCD) is a BT procedure called *exposure and ritual prevention* (EX/RP; Franklin & Foa, 2002). EX/RP derives from the following conceptualization of OCD: Obsessions evoke pathological and unrealistic anxiety, and compulsions are performed in order to reduce that obsessional anxiety. Treatment consists of repeated exposures to situations (stimuli) that evoke the obsessions and the associated urges to perform compulsions (i.e., ritualize). These procedures produce a gradual reduction (i.e., habituation) of the obsessional anxiety and, consequently, a decrease of urges to ritualize. In EX/RP individuals suffering from OCD are exposed to the stimuli that trigger obsessional thoughts, and the therapist assists in preventing ritualistic behaviors and obsessional thoughts by verbally guiding the patient in their abstinence. In addition to overt behaviors, the program can also be implemented with mental rituals such as fear of swearing in church or continuous counting.

Treatment programs vary with respect to the length, number, and spacing of exposure sessions (Foa & Franklin, 1999). In the "intensive program," developed by Foa and her colleagues (Franklin, Kozak, Levitt, & Foa, 2000), patients typically participate in 15 exposure sessions (imaginal and in vivo) of 90-min duration conducted over 3 to 4 weeks. The program utilizes homework assignments, which require the patient to practice EX/RP between sessions.

Foa and Liebowitz and their colleagues (Kozak, Liebowitz, & Foa, 2000) conducted an extensive two-site RCT comparing EX/RP to clomipramine, their combination, and pill placebo conditions. Preliminary results indicate that EX/RP was more effective than clomipramine alone (which was more effective than placebo), and the combination of clomipramine and EX/RP was no more effective than was EX/RP alone. Furthermore, meta-analytic studies of EX/RP and SSRIs revealed the treatment effect sizes to be somewhat greater for EX/RP (van Balkom et al., 1994).

The few treatment studies with adequate follow-up data have demonstrated a very high relapse for medication treatments but only modest relapse for EX/RP, particularly when a relapse-prevention component is included in the treatment program (Hiss, Foa, & Kozak, 1994). Nevertheless, some patients are reluctant to participate in EX/RP because they fear that their OCD symptoms will increase rather than diminish; such patients may benefit from treatment that begins with medication (an SSRI or clomipramine) followed by EX/RP (Foa & Wilson, 2000). Use of EX/RP requires expertise in BT, in general, and training in the specific intervention procedures; thus, it is not yet widely available even though it appears to be the treatment of choice for OCD when properly delivered.

### Social Phobia

Although there were several early studies regarding BT procedures for public speaking anxiety (e.g., Paul, 1966), it is only recently that the treatment of social phobia has been systematically studied. Social phobia is a very prevalent disorder that interferes substantially with work (including school), social interactions, and intimate relationships. Several studies have demonstrated that exposure therapy and cognitive restructuring are effective BT-CBT interventions (see Barlow, 1988).

Heimberg, Liebowitz, and their colleagues have conducted the most extensive and clinically relevant work. Heimberg and his colleagues developed a group behavioral and cognitive therapy (GBCT) that includes social exposure exercises and cognitive restructuring implemented within a group therapy setting. In their first systematic study, they compared GBCT to an educational supportive group therapy (ESGT; Heimberg et al., 1990). GBCT was superior to ESGT on most measures employed in the study, and these superior effects were sustained at various follow-ups concluding at 5 years.

The results of the preceding study led to a multisite study comparing GBCT with the monoamine oxidase inhibitor (MAOI) phenelzine, pill placebo, and ESGT (Heimberg et al., 1998). Because one site developed GBCT and the other is well known for the treatment of social phobia with medications and because of the inclusion of appropriate control groups, this study provided an excellent test of treatment efficacy and allegiance effects. Both phenelzine and GBCT were found to be superior to both control groups. However, phenelzine appeared to work faster and was superior on a few of the outcome measures, although these were minimal differences. There were no substantial effects for treatment sites, suggesting that therapeutic allegiance made little difference in this study. Liebowitz et al. (1999) followed the patients in the phenelzine and the GBCT conditions for 6 months of maintenance therapy and an additional 6 months during which they received no treatment. Slightly more phenelzine patients relapsed during the treatment-free period, so that by the end of follow-up there were very few differences between the two groups. The slight superiority of phenelzine during active treatment seems to be offset by the greater relapse during the follow-up, so the treatments appear to be equally effective for social phobia.

### Posttraumatic Stress Disorder

BT treatments of posttraumatic stress disorder (PTSD) have included a variety of exposure-based procedures. CBT approaches have been broader and typically include some type of exposure procedure plus training in progressive muscular relaxation, problem solving, emotional regulation, and cognitive restructuring. Most of the studies evaluating these interventions have included patients who have suffered from a specific traumatic event (e.g., rape) rather than patients who have suffered repeated traumas such as having been in an incestuous relationship (many of these patients suffer from primary problems in addition to PTSD). The major exception to this has been the treatment of war-related traumas (e.g., Keane, Fairbank, Caddell, & Zimering, 1989).

Exposure-based therapies for PTSD have been evaluated as treatments for sexual and nonsexual assault as well as war-related traumas (see Bryant, 2000; Rothbaum, Meadows, Resick, & Foy, 2000). In general, in vivo exposure has been more effective than imaginal exposure, and whenever possible in vivo exposure should be incorporated into the intervention program. About 50% of PTSD patients are responsive to the best exposure therapies (Foa & Meadows, 1997; Marks, Lovell, Noshirvani, Livanou, & Thrasher, 1998). Nevertheless, exposure therapy appears to be superior to wait-list and usual treatments for PTSD and indeed among the most effective treatments available for this serious and complicated clinical problem (Bryant, 2000).

As with OCD, some patients choose not to participate in exposure therapy because of fear that it will exacerbate their problems. Some of these individuals may be making an adaptive choice because preliminary data suggest that individuals with extreme levels of anxiety (Ehlers et al., 1998) and high levels of anger (Riggs, Rothbaum, & Foa, 1995) may not be appropriate candidates for this type of therapy. However, Lovell, Marks, Noshirvani, Thrasher, and Livanou (2001) demonstrated that exposure was equivalent to CBT in alleviating both behavioral and emotional symptoms of PTSD; both were superior to a placebo control group. Nevertheless, it needs to be noted that *incorrect* use of exposure procedures (e.g., not following standard time parameters) has the potential to be detrimental to various types of anxious patients, and especially patients suffering from PTSD (Bleich, Shalev, Shoham, Solomon, & Kotler, 1992; Pitman et al., 1991). As noted in the treatment of OCD, exposure therapy is among the most powerful interventions, and it should be used cautiously by well-trained mental health professionals.

Because of the hypothesized role of cognitive factors in the development and maintenance of PTSD, several authors have developed typical CBT programs for the treatment of this disorder, although there is a greater than usual emphasis on emotional regulation. Resick and Schicke (1992) developed a specific CBT program, *cognitive processing therapy,* which they have found to be effective for the treatment of rape trauma. Both Marks et al. (1998) and Tarrier et al. (1999) found CBT to be an effective treatment for trauma caused by a wide range of multiple events in patients' lives. As noted, however, exposure was just as effective as CBT in the Marks et al. study (Lovell et al., 2001).

The most controversial treatment for PTSD is probably Eye Movement Desensitization and Reprocessing (EMDR; Shapiro, 1995). In EMDR the client, while tracking the therapist's finger as it is moved within the client's field of vision, visualizes or remembers as vividly as possible the traumatic situation. Most of the research on this procedure has been seriously flawed, and the only firm conclusion that can currently be reached is that the eye movement component of the therapy is not critical to whatever gains may be attained by EMDR (Pitman et al., 1996). If EMDR does prove to be effective for some PTSD patients, it is likely that "exposure" is the effective ingredient inherent in the procedure; more efficacious exposure procedures clearly are available for the clinician (see Bryant, 2000).

## Eating Disorders and Obesity

### Anorexia Nervosa

Operant techniques (BT), primarily returning privileges or delivering reinforcers contingent on weight gain and contracting to maintain the weight gained, were first introduced into inpatient settings for the treatment of anorexia nervosa (AN) in the early 1960s. The approach was so effective it has been incorporated, either implicitly or explicitly, into most current hospital programs (see review by Touyz & Beumont, 1997). Touyz and colleagues demonstrated that more flexible BT programs were as effective as were the early, rigid programs. Both programs promoted weight gain at a rate of about .2/kg per day, but the flexible program required less nursing time and was more acceptable to patients, and the same percentage of patients were able to reach goal weight. CBT interventions, developed initially for bulimia (discussed later), have been adapted to the treatment of AN (see the description in Garner, Vitousek, & Pike, 1997). These procedures are widely used clinically, but they have not been rigorously evaluated. It has

not been possible to determine the specific contribution of the cognitive component, particularly within comprehensive inpatient programs. Only one outpatient trial has been reported; Channon, De Silva, Hemsley, and Perkins (1989) found no differences in outcome among BT, CBT, or traditional weight monitoring, but the study's small sample size precludes definite conclusions. The most recent innovation has been the incorporation of motivational interviewing into treatment for AN (see Treasure et al., 1999) as a way to address the client's ambivalence about weight gain. Behaviorally oriented family systems therapy has been applied to AN; the one study available supported its effectiveness compared to ego-oriented psychotherapy (Robin, Siegel, & Moye, 1995).

### Bulimia Nervosa

In contrast to AN, there are over 50 randomized clinical trials that clearly establish CBT as the treatment of choice for bulimia nervosa (BN; see review by Wilson & Fairburn, 2002). This intervention, first described by Fairburn (1981), has been evaluated in both group and individual formats. CBT typically consists of about 19 outpatient sessions occurring during a 20-week period. Two treatment manuals are available (Apple & Agras, 1997; Fairburn, Marcus, & Wilson, 1993). CBT utilizes behavioral strategies to interrupt the cycle of restraint, binge eating, and purging; establish a normalized eating pattern (3 meals and 2 snacks); and reintroduce forbidden foods. Cognitive restructuring is added to challenge the dysfunctional attitudes and beliefs that perpetuate disordered eating. Relapse prevention strategies are used to facilitate maintenance of changes.

Wilson and Fairburn's (2002) review supports the following conclusions. CBT leads to significant improvements on the focal symptoms, binge eating and purging (average 85% reduction in frequency; 55% remitted), attitudes toward weight and shape, and general psychological functioning. Maintenance at 1-year follow-up is favorable, and one 6-year follow-up has been reported (Fairburn et al., 1995). A subset of BN patients can be effectively treated with abbreviated, guided self-help versions of CBT (Treasure et al., 1994). A specific behavioral procedure, *exposure and response prevention* (for purging), does not appear to add significantly to the CBT package. Comorbid personality disorder is a negative predictor for all interventions for BN. Intensive day treatment and inpatient programs are available for outpatient nonresponders; however, only one study (Maddocks, Kaplan, Woodside, Langdon, & Piran, 1992) has reported on such a program.

CBT is more effective at the end of treatment than are any nondirective, supportive, or psychodynamically oriented psychotherapies (see Wilson & Fairburn, 2002). Recently, a large multisite, controlled trial (Agras, Walsh, Fairburn, Wilson, & Kraemer, 2000) replicated an earlier finding that patients receiving Interpersonal Psychotherapy (IPT) do not improve as much by the end of treatment. However, they continue to improve during follow-up, whereas CBT subjects maintain their improvement. Thus, the differences at 1-year follow-up (40% remitted with CBT vs. 27% with IPT) no longer reached significance. Unfortunately, no predictors of differential response to the two treatments have been found.

Comparisons between CBT and pharmacotherapy (antidepressant medication) generally favor CBT at follow-up assessments, even when end-of-treatment effects have been equivalent (see Wilson & Fairburn, 2002). Support for additive effects of combining the two treatments is relatively weak. Walsh et al. (1997) combined CBT with a two-stage antidepressant medication protocol (a second antidepressant was employed if the first was ineffective or poorly tolerated). This combined condition reduced depression (but not focal symptoms) more than did CBT alone. However, medication was most effective for patients with a family history of depression and patients with a positive dexamethasone suppression test. Thus, future research is likely to identify subgroups of patients who benefit from this combination of treatments.

## Obesity

Obesity was a very popular treatment target of early (1960s) behavioral weight loss (BWL) interventions; this was probably due to the clearly observable outcome measure of weight. These BWL programs were short-term interventions that had a relatively narrow focus on altering eating behavior and used functional analyses of behavior. Stimulus control procedures were used to alter antecedents to eating, and contingency management was used to alter consequences for eating. It quickly became clear that while superior to other available interventions, these BWL programs led to quite modest weight losses that were not well maintained (see review by Grilo, 1996). Thus, longer, more comprehensive programs were developed. Currently, BWL interventions include multiple components such as nutrition education, exercise programs, lifestyle change, and relapse prevention strategies.

Grilo (1996) summarized the major conclusions that can be reached about BWL programs. BWL is moderately effective in the short run, but the long-term outcome is not as positive. Weight loss seems to peak at about 6 months of treatment. Few patients achieve goal weight; most lose about 10% to 15% of their body weight. On average patients regain one third to one half of the weight lost during the year after treatment. Very low calorie diets do not improve the long-term results achieved

with the more moderate restriction advocated in BWL. Sustained exercise consistently emerges as a correlate of successful long-term maintenance, even though initiating exercise by itself does not generally lead to significant weight loss. It is not clear whether adding specific cognitive interventions is helpful, but participants like them. The addition of relapse prevention strategies or booster sessions has not been shown significantly to improve long-term outcome.

Recognition of the strong genetic and metabolic components of obesity has led to a growing consensus that obesity may be better conceptualized as a chronic disease. It may require intermittent or even continuous treatment to be effective, at least with more severe cases. Wilson (1994) argued that pharmacological interventions will likely need to be added to BWL programs for some patients. Unfortunately, at the current time no effective appetite suppressant medications have turned out to be safe for long-term use. Research continues to evaluate medications, including antidepressants such as buproprion (e.g., Wellbutrin) and fluoxetine (e.g., Prozac), which may be found to be safe and effective adjuncts to BWL.

## Binge Eating Disorder

The subset of obese patients who also have difficulty with binge eating (eating large amounts and feeling loss of control) have been given the (provisional) diagnosis of binge eating disorder (BED). Although it is not clear whether individuals with BED who participate in standard BWL programs do more poorly, some evidence suggests that they drop out at higher rates and show greater relapse (see Johnson, Tsoh, & Varnado, 1996). Because CBT interventions successfully reduced binge eating in BN, they were adapted (see Marcus, 1997) for use with BED. Several trials support the effectiveness of CBT for BED in reducing binge eating, but it did not lead to weight loss.

Only one study has directly compared CBT to BWL (Marcus, 1995). Both interventions were effective in stopping binge eating, but only BWL led to modest weight loss—about half of which was maintained at follow-up. Agras, Telch, Arnow, Eldredge, and Marnell (1997) found that abstinence from binge eating was critical to sustaining weight lost in a BWL phase (which followed the initial CBT phase). For clients who are resistant to the food monitoring central to CBT, appetite monitoring is an equally effective alternative (Craighead, Elder, Niemeier, & Pung, 2002). Findings from Agras et al. (1994) suggest that antidepressants may lead to modest improvements in weight loss. Other psychosocial interventions, specifically IPT, are as effective as CBT in the long run but are less effective at the end of treatment, just as with BN (see Wilfley et al., in press). Regardless of weight loss, reductions in binge eating are clearly associated with improvements in psychosocial functioning and with prevention of further weight gain—a substantial accomplishment for individuals with BED.

### Summary

For AN, BT procedures are clearly effective in promoting weight gain during inpatient hospitalization, but the utility of cognitive techniques in addressing the broader issues associated with AN has not yet been adequately documented. For BN, CBT is clearly the treatment of choice; no other intervention has been shown to work as quickly to reduce binge eating, purging, and dietary restraint. The cognitive component also effectively addresses weight and shape concerns and low self-esteem. For obesity, comprehensive BWL programs are clearly the treatment of choice, although long-term outcome is still far from satisfactory. For obese individuals with BED, CBT effectively reduces binge eating, but BWL is also needed to achieve even modest weight loss. Thus, it appears that BT/CBT procedures are quite effective in altering *current* problematic eating behaviors; normal eating patterns can be established. These more normal patterns are adequate to achieve some weight gain (in AN) as well as to prevent weight gain (in BED). However, achieving substantial, long-term weight loss is far more difficult. Long-term, and possibly medical, approaches are likely to be needed.

## Major Depressive Disorder

### Individual Behavior Therapy

Several variants of BT have been developed for the treatment of major depressive disorder (MDD); they all share the assumption that MDD is related to a decrease in behaviors that produce positive reinforcement. Behavior therapies for depression have, therefore, focused largely on monitoring and increasing positive daily activities, improving social and communication skills, increasing adaptive behaviors such as positive and negative assertion, increasing response-contingent positive reinforcement for adaptive behaviors, and decreasing negative life experiences.

In several studies during the 1970s and early 1980s, Lewinsohn and his group demonstrated that relative to various control groups, BT increased pleasant experiences and reduced aversive experiences, which produced concomitant decreases in depression symptomatology (see summary in Lewinsohn & Gotlib, 1995). Building on Lewinsohn's work, Bellack, Hersen, and Himmelhoch (1981, 1983) and Hersen, Bellack, Himmelhoch, and Thase (1984) studied the effects

of BT with clinical patients. They found that BT was as effective as was the antidepressant amitriptyline (Elavil) in reducing depression during a 12-week treatment period; these effects were maintained over a 6-month follow-up period during which patients were given 6 to 8 BT booster sessions.

McLean and Hakstian (1979) added problem solving and self-control (see Rehm, 1977) procedures to BT and conducted a 10-week clinical trial comparing this expanded BT intervention to relaxation therapy, insight-oriented psychotherapy, and amitriptyline. The BT program was equal or superior to each of the other treatment conditions. These results were maintained at a 27-month follow-up, at which time the BT group was more socially active and productive than were participants in the other treatment conditions (McLean & Hakstian, 1990). Rehm's (1977) self-control therapy, when administered alone, has also been found to be superior to nonspecific psychosocial treatments and no-treatment controls (Rehm, 1990), but it has not been compared to standard antidepressant treatment.

Keller and colleagues (2000) recently completed an extremely important and well-designed evaluation of a form of BT. They treated 681 adults with chronic major depression (MDD of at least 2 years' duration, current MDD superimposed on a preexisting dysthymic disorder, or recurrent MDD with incomplete remission between episodes and a total duration of continuous illness of at least 2 years). These individuals were randomly assigned to 12 weeks of treatment consisting of either the cognitive-behavioral analysis system of psychotherapy (CBASP), the antidepressant nefazodone (Serzone), or the combination of CBASP and nefazodone. CBASP (McCullough, 2000) focuses on the consequences of patient's behavior and the use of social problem solving to address interpersonal difficulties. Patients receiving nefazodone had a more rapid reduction in symptoms during the first four weeks of treatment, but the overall rate of response was equivalent for the CBASP and nefazodone groups. Furthermore, at posttreatment the combination of CBASP and nefazodone was superior to either treatment given alone. Follow-up data for this trial have not yet been published.

In summary, consistent findings support the efficacy of BT for depression; nevertheless, BT has been overshadowed by subsequent outcome studies that have focused on CBT and IPT as psychosocial interventions for MDD. However, given the relative efficacy, efficiency, and endurance of behavioral interventions, as well as the recent results for CBASP, it seems that this has been a premature turn of events. From a historical perspective, it was most likely due to the exclusion of BT from the well-publicized National Institute of Mental Health (NIMH) Treatment of Depression Collaborative Research Program (TDCRP; Elkin, Parloff, Hadley, & Autry,

1985), rather than to the relative scientific merit and empirical outcomes of the comparative treatment studies.

## Behavior Marital Therapy

Behavioral marital therapy (BMT) has been evaluated as a treatment for individuals suffering concurrently from MDD and marital distress. Both O'Leary and colleagues' and Jacobson and colleagues' standard BMT (Beach, Sandeen, & O'Leary, 1990; Jacobson, Dobson, Fruzetti, Schmaling, & Salusky, 1991; O'Leary & Beach, 1990) have been demonstrated to be equal to individual CBT for the alleviation of depression among individuals with *both* MDD and marital discord. BMT appears to have the added advantage of being superior to individual CBT in the reduction of marital discord. None of these studies employed appropriate follow-up procedures to permit a determination of whether BMT confers greater prophylactic effects than individual CBT for the prevention of relapse of an MDD following successful treatment. However, given that "marital disputes" is the most frequently discussed topic among depressed patients in maintenance therapy (Weissman & Klerman, 1973) and that marital friction is an enduring problem among formerly depressed patients even when they become asymptomatic (Bothwell & Weissman, 1977), it seems likely that successful BMT is likely to reduce the rate of relapse among successfully treated MDD patients in discordant marriages. Because these BMT studies have included small numbers of *severely* depressed patients, it is not known whether the presence of severe depression will necessitate treatment with antidepressants administered either alone or in combination with BMT.

## Cognitive-Behavior Therapy

The most extensively evaluated psychosocial treatment for MDD is A. T. Beck's CBT (A. T. Beck, Rush, Shaw, & Emery, 1979). This form of CBT is a short-term (16 to 20 sessions over a period of 12 to 16 weeks), directive therapy designed to change the depressed patient's negative view of the self, world, and future. The therapy begins with the presentation of the rationale, which is designed to inform the client of the cognitive formulation and conceptualization of the process of therapeutic change (A. T. Beck, 2001). Following this, early CBT sessions consist of the implementation of behavioral strategies. The purpose of increasing behaviors is to provide the future opportunity for monitoring the behaviors and their associated thoughts and feelings; behavioral changes are not posited to be responsible directly for decreases in depression. During the third week, expanded self-monitoring techniques are introduced in order to demonstrate the relationship

between thoughts and feelings; subsequently, patients are taught to evaluate their thought processes for logical errors, which include arbitrary inference, selective abstraction, overgeneralization, magnification and minimalization, personalization, and dichotomous thinking (A. T. Beck, 1976). At about the middle of therapy (around session 8 or 9), the concept of *schemata,* or beliefs underlying negative and positive thoughts, is introduced, and therapy begins to focus on changing those negative schemata that are posited to have been activated, thus precipitating the MDD. Near the end of therapy (around sessions 14 to 16), the focus shifts to termination and the use of cognitive strategies to prevent relapse or a future recurrence of depression.

A number of studies have compared the effectiveness of CBT to several tricyclic antidepressant medications (Elkin et al., 1989; Hollon et al., 1992; Rush, Beck, Kovacs, & Hollon, 1977; Simons, Murphy, Levine, & Wetzel, 1986). With the possible exception of the TDCRP (Elkin et al., 1989), the bottom-line finding in all these studies is that CBT is as effective as tricyclic antidepressant medication in alleviating MDD among outpatients. Similarly, CBT is as effective as the MAOI phenelzine (Nardil), and is more effective than pill placebo, in the treatment of atypical depression (Jarrett et al., 1999). CBT also was as effective as antidepressant medication when study physicians were free to prescribe the antidepressant of their choice (and free to switch medications during the treatment trial), provided that they prescribed at or above established therapeutic doses (Blackburn & Moore, 1997). Currently, trials comparing CBT and SSRIs are in progress, but because the efficacies of the tricyclics and the SSRIs are very similar, it seems unlikely that different conclusions will be reached in these studies.

Jacobson et al. (1996) tested A. T. Beck's hypothesized theory of mechanisms of change in cognitive therapy by comparing the full CBT package to its component parts: behavioral activation (BA) and behavioral activation plus modification of automatic dysfunctional thoughts (AT). The BA treatment was similar to the behavioral interventions previously reviewed and included such techniques as monitoring daily activities, assessing pleasure and mastery of activities, assigning increasingly difficult activities, imaging behaviors to be performed, discussing specific problems and identification of behavioral solutions to those problems, and intervening to ameliorate social skills deficits. The major finding of this study was that BA was as effective as both AT and the full CBT package, both immediately after the 20-session treatment trial and at 6-month follow-up. Furthermore, BA performed equally well over a 2-year follow-up period, with patients across the three treatments having equivalent rates of relapse, time to relapse, and number of well weeks (Gortner,

Gollan, Dobson, & Jacobson, 1998). This is currently the only direct comparison of BT and CBT. However, in a study initiated by the late N. S. Jacobson, investigators at the University of Washington are currently conducting a replication study in which they are comparing BA to CBT, antidepressant medication (paroxetine), and pill placebo among 400 depressed adults (Dobson et al., 2000).

In summary, typically, 50% to 70% of MDD patients who complete a course of CBT no longer meet criteria for MDD at posttreatment, and 30–40% are rated as "recovered." Furthermore, among the samples studied, CBT appeared to confer some enduring prophylactic effects; only 20% to 30% of those successfully treated relapsed during the first year following treatment. Indeed, 16 weeks of CBT produced a 1-year follow-up success rate that equaled or slightly exceeded that achieved by a full year of antidepressant treatment (Evans et al., 1992). Furthermore, CBT's maintenance effects are clearly superior to short-term (16-week) antidepressant treatment; of course, 16 weeks is not the recommended treatment period, but it is, unfortunately, fairly comparable if not worse in clinical practice (Hirschfeld et al., 1997; Keller et al., 1986).

Perhaps the major issue in psychotherapy research regarding MDD is whether BT, CBT, and IPT are effective for *severely* depressed patients (see W. E. Craighead, Hart, Craighead, & Ilardi, 2002). This issue arose primarily because the outcomes of the TDCRP suggested that CBT was not equally effective to the antidepressant with severely depressed patients. The TDCRP (Elkin et al., 1989) was the first large-sample RCT for MDD, and it compared the effects of a tricyclic (imipramine), a pill placebo plus clinical management, and CBT and IPT treatments; study sites included three major medical centers. Even though the overall sample sizes were fairly large (*N* about 60 per condition at beginning of treatment), unfortunately there were 15 or fewer severely depressed patients in each condition. Furthermore, as Jacobson and Hollon noted (1996), there was a treatment by severity by site interaction for the major outcome measures. Nevertheless, based largely on the TDCRP, the American Psychiatric Association published treatment guidelines (APA, 1993), which indicated that psychosocial treatments alone were not appropriate for severely depressed patients. This conclusion, based on one study with a small sample of severely depressed patients, was unwarranted (W. E. Craighead et al., 2002; Persons, Thase, & Crits-Christoph, 1996). This question of whether severely depressed patients should be treated with psychotherapy alone is currently being extensively investigated in a multisite study by Hollon and DeRubeis and also by Jacobson's successors. Thus, a clearer answer regarding this important issue should soon be available from these clinical research centers.

## Bipolar Disorder

There have been several studies evaluating the effects of combining BT and CBT with mood-stabilizing medications. The following sections describe and review the individual and family therapy studies; a summary and critique of the group therapy studies, which are based largely on other therapeutic models, are available in Huxley, Parikh, and Baldessarini (2000).

### Individual Cognitive-Behavior Therapy

A small number of very well conducted studies have evaluated the efficacy of individual CBT used in conjunction with mood stabilizing medications for the treatment of bipolar disorder (BD). CBT assumes that BD mood swings are partially a function of negative thinking patterns (self-statements, cognitive processes, and core dysfunctional schemata) that can be alleviated by a combination of BA and cognitive restructuring interventions. CBT for BD includes education regarding the disorder, a focus on medication compliance, behavioral management (e.g., assertion training, anger management), and cognitive restructuring.

In the first systematic study of individual CBT for BD, 14 out of 28 newly admitted lithium-treated outpatients were randomly assigned to receive only lithium, whereas the other 14 received both lithium and an additional preventive compliance CBT intervention (Cochran, 1984). The CBT program, comprising six weekly, individual, 1-hr therapy sessions, was designed to alter specific cognitive styles and behavioral patterns hypothesized to interfere with medication adherence. At both posttreatment and 6-month follow-up assessments, patients who received the combined CBT/lithium intervention exhibited significantly greater medication adherence. During the 6-month follow-up period, the combined intervention group also had significantly fewer hospitalizations (2 vs. 8). Although the groups did not differ significantly in total number of relapses (9 vs. 14), patients in the CBT/lithium group had significantly fewer mood disorder episodes (5 episodes experienced by 3 patients vs. 11 episodes experience by 8 standard-treatment patients) judged to be precipitated by medication nonadherence.

A randomized pilot study (Lam et al., 2000) further supports the short-term efficacy of CBT for BD. This 6-month CBT program was allowed to vary between 12 and 20 sessions; it focused on strategies for relapse prevention, sleep-wake stabilization (similar to the Frank's et al., 1999, Interpersonal and Social Rhythm Theory, or IPSRT, approach), and BA. The investigators randomized 25 patients to CBT plus medication management or medication management alone. The 12-month follow-up data indicated that CBT plus medication management was more effective than was medication management alone in reducing rates of relapse, improving medication adherence, and improving psychosocial functioning.

In the largest randomized CBT study ($N = 69$) of treatment of BD, Perry, Tarrier, Morriss, McCarthy, and Limb (1999) compared patients who received medication management alone with patients who received medication management and a 7- to 12-session CBT intervention. The focus of the CBT differed from that employed by Cochran (1984); rather than focusing on medication compliance as Cochran had done, Perry et al. taught patients to recognize emerging symptoms of bipolar disorder when they occurred and to seek appropriate preventive interventions. During an 18-month follow-up period, time to manic relapse was significantly longer among bipolar patients in the CBT versus the medication-only group; no differences were found in survival times for depressive relapses. CBT and medical management also had a stronger impact on social and occupational functioning than did medication management alone. There were no between-group differences for compliance with medication regimens. The effects of CBT and medication management were primarily on the manic phase of the disorder; thus, it may be wise to combine CBT with interpersonally oriented or family-marital psychoeducational interventions, which seem to have a larger impact on depressive phases of the disorder (Frank et al., 1999; Miklowitz et al., 2000).

Although the previous studies have employed small samples, they have consistently found positive effects for supplementing mood-stabilizing medications with individual CBT. The mechanisms of action of the adjunctive CBT treatments—whether they have a direct impact on patients' cognitive styles and core dysfunctional beliefs or whether they increase the patients' knowledge of BD and use of disorder management strategies (e. g., medication adherence, seeking emergency interventions prior to relapses, or BA)—have not been examined. Effectiveness studies, including more participants in clinical settings and with a longer follow-up, are currently needed.

### Behavioral Family Therapy

Research groups at the University of Colorado, the University of California–Los Angeles (UCLA), and Brown Medical Center have conducted systematic studies of family dysfunction associated with BD. Each group has also developed an intervention program that is loosely based on principles of BT and is designed for use in conjunction with mood-stabilizing medications. Clarkin and his colleagues have also conducted family and marital therapy studies for families

with an adult member who has BD, but these therapies appear to be less behaviorally focused (see W. E. Craighead & Miklowitz, 2000).

**The University of Colorado and UCLA Studies of Family-Focused Treatment.** Family-focused treatment (FFT; Miklowitz & Goldstein, 1997) is a 9-month psychoeducational treatment for bipolar patients in any type of family milieu. It is delivered in three modules over 21 sessions (weekly for 12 weeks, biweekly for 12 weeks, and monthly for 3 months). In the first module, called psychoeducation, patients and relatives learn about the nature of, etiology of, and treatments for BD. They are taught to recognize the signs and symptoms of new episodes and to develop a relapse prevention plan. The second module focuses on behavior rehearsal exercises designed to enhance communication between patients and relatives (e.g., active listening, delivering positive feedback). The third module trains patients and relatives to define and solve specific family problems.

One RCT of FFT has been conducted at the University of Colorado (Miklowitz et al., 2000; Simoneau, Miklowitz, Richards, Saleem, & George, 1999) and another at UCLA (Goldstein, Rea, & Miklowitz, 1996; Rea et al., in press). In both studies patients had suffered a recent and acute episode of BD and were being maintained on mood-stabilizing medications (typically lithium or one of the anticonvulsants, with adjunctive medications as needed). In the Colorado study, FFT was compared to a crisis management group, which was given two sessions of family education and individual crisis sessions as needed over 9 months. The UCLA study compared FFT to an individual intervention that focused on symptom management and problem solving, and it was delivered on the same schedule as FFT (21 sessions over 9 months).

In the Colorado study, FFT-medication patients reported lower rates of relapse than did patients in the comparison medication–crisis management intervention (29% vs. 53%). Survival analysis found FFT to produce longer delays prior to relapse over the 12 months than crisis management. Among treatment completers ($n = 79$), patients in FFT had less severe depressive symptoms over the 12 months than did those in the crisis management control, a difference that was not observed until 9 months into treatment. Medication regimes or compliance did not account for the results. In evaluating changes in communication patterns among patients who participated in FFT, Simoneau et al. (1999) found that both patients and relatives increased the number of positive interactions in FFT relative to crisis management, but there were no differences for negative interactions. Additional analyses demonstrated that the effects of FFT were largely on positive nonverbal (e.g., smiling, nodding, affectionate voice tone) rather than verbal (e.g., statements of acceptance or acknowledgement) behaviors.

In the UCLA study ($N = 53$) no effects of FFT were found for the first year of treatment. However, during the 2-year follow-up, FFT was consistently more effective in reducing time to relapse and time to rehospitalization. Again, results could not be accounted for by medication variables. The delay in observed effects of FFT in both studies suggests that patients and family members require some time to absorb the education and skill-training materials into their day-to-day lives before these new skills have ameliorative effects on BD.

**The Brown Study of Group Family Therapy.**    Miller, Keitner, and their colleagues at Brown Medical Center have completed two studies of behaviorally oriented family therapy for BD. The first was a small study that compared the effects of adding family therapy to standard medication treatment. Based on pilot studies of families that included an adult BD patient, they predicted that an intervention that focused on improving family functioning might lead to both improved family functioning and decreased rates of relapse or recurrence of the disorder as well as decreased rehospitalizations. In a pilot study of 14 patients they found that family therapy for bipolar patients in dysfunctional families improved the quality of family life and decreased the rate of relapse of bipolar disorder (Miller, Keitner, Bishop, & Ryan, 1991).

In a larger follow-up study (Miller, Keitner, Ryan, & Solomon, 2000) these investigators studied 92 very carefully diagnosed patients with BD. They compared the effects of three treatments: (a) standard treatment (medication plus clinical management), (b) standard treatment plus family therapy given separately to each participating family, and (c) standard treatment plus multifamily therapy, in which treatment was delivered to groups of families. Family therapy consisted of 6 to 8 sessions delivered during the first 4 months of treatment with booster sessions as clinically indicated. Multifamily therapy comprised 4 to 6 patients and their families, who met for 90 min for 6 consecutive weeks; there were "reunion" meetings every 6 months. In all patients, treatment continued for 28 months. Using strictly defined criteria, slightly over 30% of the patients in each of the family therapy conditions were recovered, but fewer than 20% of the standard treatment patients were recovered. Perhaps the most important finding of this study was that the effects of family interventions on the symptomatic outcome of patients were especially pronounced for families who exhibited poor family functioning prior to treatment. Among dysfunctional families, there was a significant difference favoring the two family therapy conditions over the standard treatment in terms of the proportion recovered;

however, the two family therapy conditions did not differ from each other. There were no significant treatment effects for families with good functioning prior to treatment; indeed, patients in these families showed very little symptomatic improvement regardless of the treatment condition in which they participated.

The results of these three studies suggest that behaviorally based family therapies are efficacious adjuncts to pharmacotherapy for bipolar patients who are recovering from an episode of mood disorder. Positive changes in the postepisode family interactions may reduce external life stressors and protect the patient from early relapse. The subtypes of bipolar patients who do and do not benefit from family intervention have not yet been clearly identified, although the Brown study suggests that family therapy is most appropriate for dysfunctional families that include a bipolar patient.

### Schizophrenia

Appropriate psychotropic medications, currently atypical antipsychotics, are the primary interventions for schizophrenia. The following BT/CBT interventions, however, are useful as adjunctive therapies to antipsychotic medications: behavior modification, social skills training, family therapy, cognitive coping strategies, and supported employment (see Penn & Mueser, 1996, and Kopelowicz, Liberman, & Zarate, 2002, for detailed reviews).

Specific maladaptive behaviors or deficits associated with chronic schizophrenia were the targets of early behavioral interventions. Starting in the 1970s, extensive research established the usefulness of behavior modification–token economy programs (see Paul & Lentz, 1977) for treating chronic, severely debilitated, and treatment-refractory schizophrenic patients. It is important to note that as a result of these BT interventions many patients were able to function at least semi-independently in community settings. During the past two decades, enormous progress has been made in broader applications of BT with a greater range of patients diagnosed with schizophrenia. These programs, focused largely on *social skills training,* have improved levels of social functioning and quality of life beyond those obtained with medications and case management, but reductions in relapse and improvements in community functioning have been less clear (see Liberman, DeRisi, & Mueser, 1989; Penn & Mueser, 1996).

*Family therapy,* in conjunction with medication, has also been used extensively in the treatment of schizophrenia. There are many forms of family therapy, but behavioral family therapy and psychoeducational family therapy have been the most extensively studied. The components of these family therapies typically include education, communication coping skills (focused on reducing "expressed emotion" in family members, i.e., criticism, intrusiveness, and negative verbal interactions), and problem-solving skills (see Goldstein & Miklowitz, 1995). In their review of several family therapy studies, Penn and Mueser (1996) wrote, "The studies reviewed all lead to the conclusion that long-term family intervention is effective for lowering relapse rate, reducing expressed emotion, and improving outcome (e.g., social functioning) among individuals with schizophrenia. The superiority of family intervention over customary outpatient care has been demonstrated. Furthermore, there is some evidence that family intervention reduces family burden" (p. 612).

Another important recent development has been the programs, based on principles of BT, that are best referred to as *supported employment* (see Wehman & Moon, 1988). Such programs lead to more successful vocational adjustment and less relapse than do more standard vocational follow-up procedures. Supported employment focuses both on rapid job identification and placement and on long-term support for the patient to engage in competent work behaviors.

A. T. Beck (1952) and Hole, Rush, and Beck (1979) first described case studies utilizing *cognitive techniques* to reduce delusional beliefs. This approach was more fully developed and evaluated by a number of English researchers over the next two decades. Tarrier et al. (1993) utilized the term *coping strategy enhancement* to refer to applications of CT/CBT techniques to reducing the frequency, or negative impact, of delusions and hallucinations.

Cognitive coping strategies are employed as an adjunct to pharmacotherapy and also have been used to enhance compliance with medications (Kemp, Hayward, Appleyard, Everitt, & David, 1996). Generally, psychotic activity is considered too severe and overwhelming for the patient to be responsive to a purely psychological intervention, so treatment is typically instituted after an appropriate medication regime has been established. Most of the empirical studies have focused on the reduction of residual psychotic symptoms that have not responded to medication. However, Drury, Birchwood, Cochrane, and MacMillan (1996) demonstrated that CT might be a useful treatment during the acute stage of schizophrenia; CBT resulted in decreased positive symptoms and reduced times to recovery compared with a minimal treatment control.

The cognitive model of schizophrenia clearly acknowledges the presence of neurodevelopmental abnormalities that render individuals more sensitive to normal life stressors. It is hypothesized that internal biological processes generate affective responses that are usually activated only by external events. The activated person searches for a cause or interpretation for this activation, but the explanations arrived at are likely to appear inexplicable ("delusional") to others. Once

such a "delusional" belief (explanation) is in place, the CT model contends that it is maintained by the same biased thinking processes that are involved in the maintenance of irrational beliefs in other disorders. These irrational beliefs in turn lead to maladaptive behaviors. Cognitive interventions (see Nelson's, 1997, treatment manual) are designed to activate patients' latent rationality to correct the cognitive errors maintaining their maladaptive beliefs or delusions; correct their maladaptive beliefs about their psychotic symptoms and about suffering from a chronic, severe disorder; and combat their apathy and social withdrawal (negative symptoms). Typical procedures include: providing a normalizing rationale for delusions and hallucinations; recognizing and labeling delusional ideas; developing challenges and reality tests relevant to those ideas; developing cards with coping statements and strategies; developing strategies to reduce the interference of voices; and challenging beliefs that voices "speak the truth" and must be obeyed.

Recent, larger RCTs (Kuipers et al., 1998; Pinto, La Pia, Menella, Giorgino, & De Simone, 1999; Tarrier et al., 2000) have clearly supported the effectiveness of CBT plus routine care in reducing positive symptoms. Effects on negative symptoms were weaker. Low dropout rates and high patient satisfaction with the intervention were also reported. The superiority of CBT was maintained at 2-year follow-ups. However, the specific effectiveness of the cognitive restructuring component is not yet clearly established (Sensky et al., 2000; Tarrier et al., 2000).

In summary, BT/CBT interventions (specifically social skills training, family therapy, supported employment, and cognitive coping skills training) are important, effective adjunctive psychosocial interventions for schizophrenia. Because most programs include several components, investigators have not yet identified which aspects of the programs account for their positive effects. It is clear that BT and CBT of various types enhance the effects of medication and appear to be more beneficial than the minimal supportive counseling that comprises "routine care" for this severe disorder. As noted by Kopelowicz et al. (2002), these interventions are "most efficacious when delivered in a continuous, comprehensive, and well-coordinated manner through a service delivery systems" (p. 201).

## Personality Disorders

Early behaviorists eschewed the concept of "personality," focusing instead on changing specific problem behaviors. Evolutionary changes in the diagnostic criteria for personality disorders (PDs), however, have rendered them more behaviorally based. This has led to improved diagnostic reliabilities, which has made these disorders more amenable to the empirical evaluation required by the behavioral approach. Cognitive therapists, in particular, have extended their conceptual model to address PDs and have provided extensive clinical descriptions of the application of CT for these disorders (A. T. Beck & Freeman, 1990). Nevertheless, RCTs evaluating these applications have been almost nonexistent; this is likely due to the unique methodological problems of dealing with more chronic, less clearly distinguishable problems. Unfortunately, no other types of psychosocial interventions have been evaluated either, so there is little scientific basis for recommending specific treatments for PDs. There are some data suggesting the efficacy of specific BT/CBT interventions for avoidant personality disorder (APD) and borderline personality disorder (BPD).

Behavioral treatments that were first developed for social phobia have been applied to APD. Three variations of group BT (graded exposure, social skills training, and intimacy-focused social skills training) were all superior to no treatment at 10 weeks (posttest) and follow-up (Alden, 1989). Unfortunately, these patients were still not functioning at the level of "normal" comparison samples; this suggested that longer treatment might be necessary for this more pervasive disorder. Post hoc analyses of these data suggested that patients with problems with distrust and anger benefited primarily from exposure; those who were less assertive benefited from all three treatments, although they did somewhat better as a result of the intimacy-focused social skills training therapy.

BPD is the only PD for which a specific CBT approach has been systematically developed and evaluated. Emerging from a behavioral tradition, Linehan's work first targeted a population with a specific problem behavior, *chronic parasuicidal behavior*. It was only later that she began to use the descriptor BPD because it became clear that the majority of the individuals with whom she worked met those criteria. Linehan (1993) provided a model of BPD that assumes that individuals with BPD have a basic dysfunction in emotion regulation, which presumably begins as a biologically based dysfunction. She posits that the emotion dysregulation is exacerbated by developmental experiences with significant others, who not only invalidate the individuals' inner experiences but also fail to teach them appropriate emotion regulation skills that they need even more than do less vulnerable people.

Linehan's CBT (also referred to as dialectical behavior therapy; DBT) for BPD is a complex, long-term (1 to 3 years), and intensive (weekly group and individual) intervention with multiple components including emotion regulation skills training, interpersonal skills training, distress tolerance–reality acceptance, problem solving, and extensive use of supportive-validating techniques. Although DBT might be claimed as an example of a broadly integrated model of psychotherapy, Linehan (1993) clearly presented her model as having derived

from and maintaining a behavioral focus. The first controlled trial, Linehan, Hubert, Suarez, Douglas, and Heard (1991), found that 1 year of DBT resulted in fewer and less severe episodes of parasuicidal behavior and fewer days of hospitalization than treatment as usual (TAU) in the community. However, there were no differences in depression, hopelessness, or suicidal ideation. The treatment did appear to be well tolerated by this difficult-to-treat population that may even be difficult to retain in treatment. Attrition was quite low (17%), especially when compared to the TAU (58%). Results at 1-year follow-up continued to be favorable (Linehan, Heard, & Armstrong, 1993). Similar positive findings were reported comparing 1 year of her CBT to TAU with substance-dependent women with BPD (Linehan et al., 1999). Additionally, uncontrolled studies have reported favorable adaptations of this intervention for adult inpatient units and for use with suicidal teens (Bohus et al., 2000; Miller, Rathus, Linehan, Wetzler, & Leigh, 1997). More extensive RCTs are in progress in Sweden; these studies are comparing different types of psychotherapy, including Linehan's CBT, with BPD patients.

## Other Disorders

BT and CBT have been used in the successful treatment of several other disorders, but space limitations preclude a detailed discussion of these interventions. These include sexual dysfunction, paraphilia, trichotillamania, drug and alcohol abuse and dependence (Hester & Miller, 1995), and a variety of physical health–related problems (e.g., pain, headache, etc.; see Baum, Singer, & Revenson, 2000). Recent descriptions of the procedures and systematic reviews of the relevant outcome studies are available (see Barlow, 1993; L. W. Craighead et al., 1994; Nathan & Gorman, 2002).

## CONCLUSIONS AND FUTURE DIRECTIONS

### Conclusions

BT, which began in earnest during the 1960s, can trace its origins to the basic psychology laboratory and learning theory. CBT has multiple origins, including applications of basic cognitive psychology, cognitive conceptualizations of self-control, and cognitive therapy. Specific BT and CBT procedures vary according to the nature of the disorder being treated. Some variant of BT and CBT has been demonstrated to be effective for most *DSM-IV* Axis I disorders and some Axis II disorders. Appropriate utilization of BT and CBT in the clinical setting requires a thorough understanding of the therapeutic model and treatment rationale as well as training in implementation of the specific procedures, even when they might appear simple to use. The endurance (maintenance) following these successful treatments are the best among psychotherapeutic interventions.

With many disorders, BT and CBT have been combined with pharmacological interventions to enhance acute treatment effects (e.g., schizophrenia and bipolar disorders), although with other disorders (e.g., depression) the value of combining BT and CBT with medications is less well established. In fact, with some disorders (e.g., bulimia nervosa) the addition of medications appears to weaken the acute effects of BT and CBT. Furthermore, with some disorders combining BT and CBT with medications to improve acute treatment effects appears to compromise the well-established maintenance or enduring effects of BT and CBT (e.g., panic disorder).

## Future Directions

There are several exciting future directions for BT-CBT clinical research. For example, the relationship of behavioral and cognitive symptoms to neurobiological dysregulation may provide new conceptualizations of psychopathology as well as the refinement of current forms of these therapies and the development of new interventions. Indeed, some clinical scientists have begun to evaluate the mechanisms of change in BT and CBT compared to the biological changes of pharmacological agents; for example, Baxter et al. (1992) found that the neurobiological changes associated with BT for OCD are quite similar to those obtained with clomipramine.

BT and CBT need to be further evaluated as treatments for additional Axis II disorders. The limited evidence for treatment of APD and BPD has been encouraging. Empirical data clearly demonstrate that individuals suffering from Axis II personality disorders are among the most difficult to treat successfully, and pharmacological interventions do not appear to be particularly promising for these individuals (Ilardi & Craighead, 1994/1995). Even stronger evidence indicates that individuals with comorbid Axis I and personality disorders are much more likely to have a relapse or recurrence of the Axis I disorder even when they have been successfully treated. Thus, development of effective treatments for personality disorders, either alone or when comorbid with Axis I problems, is an essential step for BT-CBT research.

The investigation of the relationship of *emotion* to behavioral, cognitive, and neurobiological components of various disorders (especially Axis II personality disorders) is another area for future investigation. Clinical data suggest that it will be important to develop and systematically evaluate programs that include attention to emotional dysfunction, volatility, and dysregulation. One avenue of increasing attention to emotion would be the integration of BT and CBT with IPT. It is also possible that new findings in basic neuroscience of emotion

may lead to the modification of current programs or the creative development of new interventions.

Even when treated with the most effective psychotherapy procedures available and pharmacotherapy, a goodly percentage of patients will suffer a relapse or recurrence of the disorder. Thus, it is important to expand current BT-CBT treatments to include a relapse prevention emphasis toward the end of therapy; some of the programs reviewed in this chapter have already done this. Alternatively, for those patients who have been successfully treated or have made it through an episode of a disorder and are essentially symptom free, BT-CBT programs might be developed specifically for the prevention of relapse or recurrence of the disorder.

Because the probability of recurrence of most disorders increases with each episode, it is important to develop BT-CBT primary prevention programs. Such programs are needed especially for individuals who can be identified as being clearly at risk for a disorder. Although such research is expensive and difficult to complete, even modest preventive effects could be of great personal and societal benefit.

## REFERENCES

Agras, W. S., Leitenberg, H., & Barlow, D. H. (1968). Social reinforcement in the modification of agoraphobia. *Archives of General Psychiatry, 19*(4), 423–427.

Agras, W. S., Telch, C. F., Arnow, B., Eldredge, K., & Marnell, M. (1997). One-year follow-up of cognitive-behavioral therapy for obese individuals with binge eating disorder. *Journal of Consulting and Clinical Psychology, 65*(2), 343–347.

Agras, W. S., Telch, C. F., Arnow, B., Eldredge, K., Wilfley, D. E., Raeburn, S. D., Henderson, J., & Marnell, M. (1994). Weight loss, cognitive-behavioral, and desipramine treatments in binge eating disorder: An additive design. *Behavior Therapy, 25*(2), 225–238.

Agras, W. S., Walsh, B. T., Fairburn, C. G., Wilson, G. T., & Kraemer, H. C. (2000). A multicenter comparison of cognitive-behavioral therapy and interpersonal psychotherapy for bulimia nervosa. *Archives of General Psychiatry, 57*(5), 459–466.

Alden, L. (1989). Short-term structured treatment for avoidant personality disorder. *Journal of Consulting and Clinical Psychology, 57*(6), 756–764.

American Psychiatric Association. (1993). Practice guidelines for major depressive disorder in adults. *American Journal of Psychiatry, 150*(Suppl. 4), 1–26.

American Psychological Association. (1994). *Diagnostic and statistical manual of mental disorders* (4th ed.). Washington, DC: Author.

Apple, R. F., & Agras, W. S. (1997). *Overcoming eating disorders: Client workbook.* San Antonio, TX: Psychological Corporation.

Bandura, A. (1969). *Principles of behavior modification.* New York: Holt, Rinehart & Winston.

Bandura, A. (1977). *Social learning theory.* Englewood Cliffs, NJ: Prentice-Hall.

Barlow, D. H. (1988). *Anxiety and its disorders: The nature and treatment of anxiety and panic.* New York: Guilford Press.

Barlow, D. H. (Ed.). (1993). *Clinical handbook of psychological disorders* (2nd ed.). New York: Guilford Press.

Barlow, D. H., & Craske, M. G. (1994). *Mastery of your anxiety and panic* (Vol. 2). Albany, NY: Graywind.

Barlow, D. H., Gorman, J. M., Shear, M. K., & Woods, S. W. (2000). Cognitive-behavioral therapy, imipramine, or their combination for panic disorder. *Journal of the American Medical Association (JAMA), 283*(19), 2529–2536.

Barlow, D. H., & Lehman, C. L. (1996). Advances in the psychosocial treatment of anxiety disorders: Implications for National Health Care. *Archives of General Psychiatry, 53*(8), 727–735.

Baum, A. W., Singer, J. E., & Revenson, T. A. (Eds.). (2000). *Handbook of health psychology* (Vol. 8). New York: Erlbaum.

Baxter, L. R., Schwartz, J. M., Bergman, K. S., Szuba, M. P., Guze, B. H., Mazziotta, J. C., Alazraki, A., Selin, C. E., Ferng, H. K., & Munford, P. (1992). Caudate glucose metabolic rate changes with both drug and behavior therapy for obsessive-compulsive disorder. *Archives of General Psychiatry, 49*(9), 681–689.

Beach, S. R. H., Sandeen, E. E., & O'Leary, K. D. (1990). *Depression in marriage: A model for etiology and treatment.* New York: Guilford.

Beck, A. T. (1952). Successful outpatient psychotherapy of a chronic schizophrenic with a delusion based on borrowed guilt. *Psychiatry, 15,* 305–312.

Beck, A. T. (1964). Thinking and depression: II. Theory and therapy. *Archives of General Psychiatry, 10,* 561–571.

Beck, A. T. (1970). Cognitive therapy: Nature and relation to behavior therapy. *Behavior Therapy, 1,* 184–200.

Beck, A. T. (1976). *Cognitive therapy and the emotional disorders.* New York: International Universities Press.

Beck, A. T., & Freeman, A. (1990). *A cognitive therapy of personality disorders.* New York: Guilford Press.

Beck, A. T., Rush, A. J., Shaw, B. F., & Emery, G. (1979). *Cognitive therapy of depression: A treatment manual.* New York: Guilford Press.

Beck, J. S. (2001). Why distinguish between cognitive therapy and cognitive behavior therapy. *Cognitive Therapy Today, 6,* 1–4.

Bellack, A. S., Hersen, M., & Himmelhoch, J. (1981). Social skills training compared with pharmacotherapy and psychotherapy in the treatment of unipolar depression. *American Journal of Psychiatry, 138,* 1562–1566.

Bellack, A. S., Hersen, M., & Himmelhoch, J. (1983). A comparison of social skills training, pharmacotherapy and psychotherapy for depression. *Behaviour Research and Therapy, 21,* 101–107.

Blackburn, I. M., & Moore, R. G. (1997). Controlled acute and follow-up trial of cognitive therapy and pharmacotherapy in out-patients with recurrent depression. *The British Journal of Psychiatry, 171,* 328–334.

Bleich, A., Shalev, A., Shoham, S., Solomon, Z., & Kotler, M. (1992). Theoretical and practical considerations as reflected through Koach: An innovative treatment project. *Journal of Traumatic Stress, 5,* 265–271.

Bohus, M., Haaf, B., Stiglmayr, C., Pohl, U., Boehme, R., & Linehan, M. (2000). Evaluation of inpatient dialectical-behavioral therapy for borderline personality disorder: A prospective study. *Behaviour Research and Therapy, 38,* 875–887.

Bothwell, S., & Weissman, M. M. (1977). Social impairments four years after an acute depressive episode. *American Journal of Orthopsychiatry, 47,* 231–237.

Brown, T. A., & Barlow, D. H. (1995). Long-term outcome in cognitive behavioral treatment of panic disorder. *Journal of Consulting and Clinical Psychology, 63,* 754–765.

Bryant, R. A. (2000). Cognitive behavioral therapy of violence-related posttraumatic stress disorder. *Aggression and Violent Behavior, 5,* 79–97.

Channon, S., De Silva, P., Hemsley, D., & Perkins, R. (1989). A controlled trial of cognitive-behavioural and behavioural treatment of anorexia nervosa. *Behaviour Research and Therapy, 27,* 529–535.

Clark, D. M. (1989). Anxiety states: Panic and generalized anxiety. In K. Hawton, P. M. Salkovskis, J. Kirk, & D. M. Clark (Eds.), *Cognitive behavior therapy for psychiatric problems: A practical guide* (pp. 52–96). Oxford, England: Oxford University Press.

Clark, D. M., Salkovskis, P. M., Hackmann, A., Middleton, H., Anastasiades, P., & Gelder, M. (1994). A comparison of cognitive therapy, applied relaxation, and imipramine in the treatment of panic disorder. *British Journal of Psychiatry, 164,* 759–769.

Cochran, S. D. (1984). Preventing medical noncompliance in the outpatient treatment of bipolar affective disorders. *Journal of Consulting and Clinical Psychology, 52,* 873–878.

Craighead, L. W., Craighead, W. E., Kazdin, A. E., & Mahoney, M. J. (Eds.). (1994). *Cognitive and behavioral interventions: An empirical approach to mental health problems.* Boston: Allyn & Bacon.

Craighead, L. W., Elder, K. A., Niemeier, H. N., & Pung, M. A. (2002, November). *Food versus appetite monitoring in CBWL for binge eating disorder.* Paper presented at the meetings of the Association for Advancement of Behavior Therapy, Reno, NV.

Craighead, W. E., Craighead, L. W., & Ilardi, S. S. (1995). Behavior therapies in historical perspective. In B. M. Bongar & L. E. Beutler (Eds.), *Comprehensive textbook of psychotherapy: Vol. 1. Theory and practice* (pp. 64–83). New York: Oxford University Press.

Craighead, W. E., Hart, A. B., Craighead, L. W., & Ilardi, S. S. (2002). Unipolar depression. In P. E. Nathan & J. M. Gorman (Eds.), *A guide to treatments that work* (2nd ed., pp. 245–261). New York: Oxford University Press.

Craighead, W. E., & Miklowitz, D. J. (2000). Psychosocial interventions for bipolar disorder. *Journal of Clinical Psychiatry, 61,* 58–64.

Dember, W. N. (1974). Motivation and the cognitive revolution. *American Psychologist, 29,* 161–168.

Dobson, K. S., Dimidgian, S., Hollon, S. D., Shilling, E., Steiman, M., & McGlinchey, J. (2000, November). *The University of Washington treatments for depression study: Design, subject, assessment, and treatment evaluation considerations.* Paper presented at the annual meeting of the Association for the Advancement of Behavior Therapy, New Orleans, LA.

Drury, V., Birchwood, M., Cochrane, R., & MacMillan, F. (1996). Cognitive therapy and recovery from acute psychosis: A controlled trial. I. Impact on psychotic symptoms. *British Journal of Psychiatry, 169,* 593–601.

Ehlers, A., Clark, D., Winston, E., Jaycox, L., Meadows, E., & Foa, E. B. (1998). Predicting response to exposure treatment in PTSD: The role of mental defeat and alienation. *Journal of Traumatic Stress, 11,* 457–471.

Elkin, I., Parloff, M. B., Hadley, S. W., & Autry, J. H. (1985). NIMH treatment of depression collaborative research program: Background and research plan. *Archives of General Psychiatry, 42,* 305–316.

Elkin, I., Shea, M. T., Watkins, J. T., Imber, S. D., Sotsky, S. M., Collins, J. F., Glass, D. R., Pilkonis, P. A., Leber, W. R., Docherty, J. P., Fiester, S. J., & Parloff, M. B. (1989). National Institute of Mental Health Treatment of Depression Collaborative Research Program: General effectiveness of treatments. *Archives of General Psychiatry, 46,* 971–982.

Ellis, A. (1962). *Reason and emotion in psychotherapy.* New York: Lyle Stuart.

Evans, M. D., Hollon, S. D., DeRubeis, R. J., Piasecki, J. M., Grove, W. M., Garvey, M. J., & Tuason, V. B. (1992). Differential relapse following cognitive therapy and pharmacotherapy for depression. *Archives of General Psychiatry, 49,* 802–808.

Eysenck, H. J. (1960). *Behavior therapy and the neuroses.* Oxford, England: Pergamon Press.

Fairburn, C. G. (1981). A cognitive-behavioral approach to the management of bulimia. *Psychological Medicine, 11,* 707–711.

Fairburn, C. G., Marcus, M. D., & Wilson, G. T. (1993). Cognitive behavioral therapy for binge eating and bulimia nervosa: A comprehensive treatment manual. In C. G. Fairburn & G. T. Wilson (Eds.), *Binge eating: Nature, assessment, and treatment* (pp. 361–404). New York: Guilford Press.

Fairburn, C. G., Norman, P. A., Welch, S. L., O'Connor, M. E., Doll, H. A., & Peveler, R. C. (1995). A prospective study of outcome in bulimia nervosa and the long-term effects of three psychological treatments. *Archives of General Psychiatry, 52,* 304–312.

Foa, E. B., & Franklin, M. E. (1999). Obsessive compulsive disorder: Behavior therapy. In M. Hersen & A. S. Bellack (Eds.), *Handbook of comparative interventions for adult disorders* (2nd ed., pp. 359–377). New York: Wiley.

Foa, E. B., & Meadows, E. A. (1997). Psychosocial treatments for posttraumatic stress disorder: A critical review. *Annual Review of Psychology, 48,* 449–480.

Foa, E. B., & Wilson, R. (2000). *Stop obsessing: How to overcome your obsessions and compulsions* (2nd ed.). New York: Bantam Books.

Frank, E., Swartz, H. A., Mallinger, A. G., Thase, M. E., Weaver, E. V., & Kupfer, D. J. (1999). Adjunctive psychotherapy for bipolar disorder: Effects of changing treatment modality. *Journal of Abnormal Psychology, 108,* 579–587.

Franklin, M. E., & Foa, E. B. (2002). Cognitive-behavioral treatments for obsessive compulsive disorder. In P. E. Nathan & J. M. Gorman (Eds.), *A guide to treatments that work* (2nd ed., pp. 367–386). New York: Oxford University Press.

Franklin, M. E., Kozak, M. J., Levitt, J. T., & Foa, E. B. (2000). Effectiveness of exposure and ritual prevention for obsessive compulsive disorder: Randomized versus nonrandomized samples. *Journal of Consulting and Clinical Psychology, 68,* 594–602.

Garner, D. M., Vitousek, K. M., & Pike, K. M. (1997). Cognitive-behavioral therapy for anorexia nervosa. In D. M. Garner & P. E. Garfinkel (Eds.), *Handbook for eating disorders* (2nd ed., pp. 94–144). New York: Guilford Press.

Goldstein, M. J., & Miklowitz, D. J. (1995). The effectiveness of psychoeducational family therapy in the treatment of schizophrenic disorders. *Journal of Marital and Family Therapy, 21,* 361–376.

Goldstein, M. J., Rea, M. M., & Miklowitz, D. J. (1996). Family factors related to the course and outcome of bipolar disorder. In C. Mundt, M. J. Goldstein, K. Hahlweg, & P. Fiedler (Eds.), *Interpersonal factors in the origin and course of affective disorders* (pp. 193–203). London: Gaskell Books.

Gortner, E. T., Gollan, J. K., Dobson, K. S., & Jacobson, N. S. (1998). Cognitive-behavioral treatment for depression: Relapse prevention. *Journal of Consulting and Clinical Psychology, 66,* 377–384.

Grilo, C. M. (1996). Treatment of obesity: An integrative model. In J. K. Thompson (Ed.), *Body image, eating disorders, and obesity* (pp. 425–441). Washington, DC: American Psychological Association.

Heimberg, R. G., Dodge, C. S., Hope, D. A., Kennedy, C. R., Zollo, L., & Becker, R. E. (1990). Cognitive-behavioral group treatment of social phobia: Comparison to a credible placebo control. *Cognitive Therapy and Research, 14,* 1–23.

Heimberg, R. G., Liebowitz, M. R., Hope, D. A., Schneier, F. R., Holt, C. S., Welkowitz, L. A., Juster, H. R., Campeas, R., Bruch, M. A., Cloitre, M., Fallon, B., & Klein, D. F. (1998). Cognitive behavioral group therapy vs. phenelzine therapy for social phobia. *Archives of General Psychiatry, 55,* 1133–1141.

Hellstrom, K., Fellenius, J., & Ost, L.-G. (1996). One versus five sessions of applied tension in the treatment of blood phobia. *Behaviour Research and Therapy, 34,* 101–112.

Hersen, M., Bellack, A. S., Himmelhoch, J. M., & Thase, M. E. (1984). Effects of social skill training, amitriptyline, and psychotherapy in unipolar depressed women. *Behavior Therapy, 15,* 21–40.

Hester, R. K., & Miller, W. R. (Eds.). (1995). *Handbook of alcoholism treatment approaches: Effective alternatives.* Boston: Allyn & Bacon.

Hirschfeld, R. M., Keller, M. B., Panico, S., Arons, B. S., Barlow, D. H., Davidoff, F., Endicott, J., Froom, J., Goldstein, M. J., Gorman, J. M., Guthrie, D., Marek, R. G., Maurer, T. A., Meyer, R., Phillips, K., Ross, J., Schwenk, T. L., Sharfstein, S. S., Thase, M. E., & Wyatt, R. J. (1997). The National Depressive and Manic-Depressive Association consensus statement on the undertreatment of depression. *Journal of the American Medical Association (JAMA), 277,* 333–340.

Hiss, H., Foa, E. B., & Kozak, M. J. (1994). Relapse prevention program for treatment of obsessive-compulsive disorder. *Journal of Consulting and Clinical Psychology, 62*(4), 801–808.

Hole, R. W., Rush, A. J., & Beck, A. T. (1979). A cognitive investigation of schizophrenic delusions. *Psychiatry, 42,* 312–319.

Hollon, S. D., DeRubeis, R. J., Evans, M. D., Wiemer, M. J., Garvey, M. J., Grove, W. M., & Tuason, V. B. (1992). Cognitive therapy and pharmacotherapy for depression: Singly and in combination. *Archives of General Psychiatry, 49,* 774–781.

Huxley, N. A., Parikh, S. V., & Baldessarini, R. J. (2000). Effectiveness of psychosocial treatments in bipolar disorder: State of the evidence. *Harvard Review of Psychiatry, 8,* 126–140.

Ilardi, S. S., & Craighead, W. E. (1994/1995). Personality pathology and response to somatic treatments for major depression: A critical review. *Depression, 2,* 200–217.

Jacobson, N. S., Dobson, K. S., Fruzetti, A. E., Schmaling, K. B., & Salusky, S. (1991). Marital therapy as a treatment for depression. *Journal of Consulting and Clinical Psychology, 59,* 547–557.

Jacobson, N. S., Dobson, K. S., Truax, P. A., Addis, M. E., Koerner, K., Gollan, J. K., Gortner, E., & Prince, S. E. (1996). A component analysis of cognitive-behavioral treatment for depression. *Journal of Consulting and Clinical Psychology, 64,* 295–304.

Jacobson, N. S., & Hollon, S. D. (1996). Cognitive-behavior therapy versus pharmacotherapy: Now that the jury's returned its verdict, it's time to present the rest of the evidence [see comments]. *Journal of Consulting and Clinical Psychology, 6*(1), 74–80.

Jarrett, R. B., Schaffer, M., McIntire, D., Witt-Browder, A., Kraft, D., & Risser, R. C. (1999). Treatment of atypical depression with cognitive therapy or phenelzine: A double-blind, placebo-controlled trial. *Archives of General Psychiatry, 56*(5), 431–437.

Johnson, G. F., Tsoh, W. G., & Varnado, P. J. (1996). Eating disorders: Efficacy of pharmacological and psychological interventions. *Clinical Psychology Review, 16*(6), 457–478.

Kazdin, A. E. (1978). *History of behavior modification: Experimental foundations of contemporary research.* Baltimore: University Park Press.

Kazdin, A. E. (1994). *Behavior modification in applied settings* (5th ed.). Pacific Grove, CA: Brooks/Cole.

Keane, T. M., Fairbank, J. A., Caddell, J. M., & Zimering, R. T. (1989). Implosive flooding therapy reduces symptoms of PTSD in Vietnam combat veterans. *Behavior Therapy, 20,* 245–260.

Keller, M. B., Lavori, P. W., Coryell, W., Andreasen, N. C., Endicott, J., Clayton, P. J., Klerman, G. L., & Hirschfeld, R. M. (1986). Differential outcome of pure manic, mixed/cycling, and pure depressive episodes in patients with bipolar illness. *Journal of the American Medical Association (JAMA), 255,* 3138–3142.

Keller, M. B., McCullough, J. P., Klein, D. N., Arnow, B., Dunner, D. L., Gelenberg, A. J., Markowitz, J. C., Nemeroff, C. B., Russell, J. M., Thase, M. E., Trivedi, M. H., & Zajecka, J. (2000). A comparison of nefazodone, the cognitive behavioral-analysis system of psychotherapy, and their combination for the treatment of chronic depression [see comments]. *New England Journal of Medicine, 342*(20), 1462–1470.

Kemp, R., Hayward, P., Appleyard, G., Everitt, B., & David, A. (1996). Compliance therapy in psychotic patients: Randomized controlled trial. *British Medical Journal, 312*(7027), 345–349.

Kopelowicz, A., Liberman, R. P., & Zarate, R. (2002). Psychosocial treatments for schizophrenia. In P. E. Nathan & J. M. Gorman (Eds.), *A guide to treatments that work* (2nd ed., pp. 201–228). New York: Oxford University Press.

Kozak, M. J., Liebowitz, M. R., & Foa, E. B. (2000). Cognitive behavior therapy and pharmacotherapy for OCD: The NIMH-sponsored collaborative study. In W. K. Goodman, M. Rudorfer, & J. Maser (Eds.), *Treatment challenges in obsessive compulsive disorder: Contemporary issues in treatment* (pp. 501–530). Mahwah, NJ: Erlbaum.

Kuhn, T. S. (1962). *The structure of scientific revolutions.* Chicago: University of Chicago Press.

Kuipers, E., Fowler, D., Garety, P., Chishom, D., Freeman, D., Dunn, G., Bebbington, P., & Hadley, C. (1998). London-East Anglia randomized controlled trial of cognitive behaviour therapy for psychosis: III. Follow-up and economic evaluation at 18 months. *British Journal of Psychiatry, 173,* 61–68.

Lam, D. H., Bright, J., Jones, S., Hayward, P., Schuck, N., Chisholm, D., & Sham, P. (2000). Cognitive therapy for bipolar illness: Pilot study of relapse prevention. *Cognitive Therapy Research, 24,* 503–520.

Lewinsohn, P. M., & Gotlib, I. H. (1995). Behavioral theory and treatment of depression. In E. E. Becker & W. R. Leber (Eds.), *Handbook of depression* (pp. 352–375). New York: Guilford Press.

Liberman, R. P., DeRisi, W. J., & Mueser, K. T. (1989). *Social skills training for psychiatric patients.* Elmsford, NY: Pergamon Press.

Liebowitz, M. R., Heimberg, R. G., Schneier, F. R., Hope, D. A., Davies, S., Holt, C. S., Goetz, D., Juster, H. R., Lin, S.-H., Bruch, M. A., Marshall, R. D., & Klein, D. F. (1999). Cognitive-behavioral group therapy versus phenelzine in social phobia: Long term outcome. *Depression and Anxiety, 10,* 89–98.

Linehan, M. M. (1993). *Cognitive-behavioral treatment of borderline personality disorder.* New York: Guilford Press.

Linehan, M. M., Heard, H. L., & Armstrong, H. E. (1993). Naturalistic follow up of a behavioral treatment for chronically parasuicidal borderline patients. *Archives of General Psychiatry, 50,* 971.

Linehan, M. M., Hubert, A. E., Suarez, A., Douglas, A., & Heard, H. L. (1991). Cognitive-behavioral treatment of chronically parasuicidal borderline patients. *Archives of General Psychiatry, 48,* 1060–1064.

Linehan, M. M., Schmidt, H., Dimeff, L. A., Craft, J. C., Kanter, J., & Comtois, K. A. (1999). Dialectical behavior therapy for patients with borderline personality disorder and drug-dependence. *American Journal on Addictions, 8,* 279–292.

Lovell, K., Marks, I. M., Noshirvani, H., Thrasher, S., & Livanou, M. (2001). Do cognitive and exposure treatments improve various PTSD symptoms differently? A randomized controlled trial. *Behavioural and Cognitive Psychotherapy, 29,* 107–112.

Maddocks, S. E., Kaplan, A. S., Woodside, D. B., Langdon, L., & Piran, N. (1992). Two year followup of bulimia nervosa: The importance of abstinence as the criterion of outcome. *International Journal of Eating Disorders, 12,* 133–141.

Mahoney, M. J., & Lyddon, W. J. (1988). Recent developments in cognitive approaches to counseling and psychotherapy. *The Counseling Psychologist, 16,* 190–234.

Marcus, M. D. (1995). Introduction—Binge eating: Clinical and research directions. *Addictive Behaviors, 20*(6), 691–693.

Marcus, M. D. (1997). Adapting treatment for patients with binge-eating disorder. In D. M. Garner & P. E. Garfinkel (Eds.), *Handbook of treatment for eating disorders* (pp. 484–493). New York: Guilford Press.

Marks, I. M. (1969). *Fears and phobias.* London: Heineman.

Marks, I. M., Lovell, K., Noshirvani, H., Livanou, M., & Thrasher, S. (1998). Treatment of posttraumatic stress disorder by exposure and/or cognitive restructuring. *Archives of General Psychiatry, 55,* 317–325.

McCullough, J. P. (2000). *Treatment of chronic depression: Cognitive behavioral analysis system of psychotherapy.* New York: Guilford Press.

McLean, P. D., & Hakstian, A. R. (1979). Clinical depression: Comparative efficacy of outpatient treatments. *Journal of Consulting and Clinical Psychology, 47,* 818–836.

McLean, P. D., & Hakstian, A. R. (1990). Relative endurance of unipolar depression treatment effects: Longitudinal follow-up. *Journal of Consulting and Clinical Psychology, 58*(4), 482–488.

Miklowitz, D. J., & Goldstein, M. J. (1997). *Bipolar disorder: A family-focused treatment approach.* New York: Guilford Press.

Miklowitz, D. J., Simoneau, T. L., George, E. A., Richards, J. A., Kalbag, A., Sachs-Ericsson, N., & Suddath, R. (2000). Family-focused treatment of bipolar disorder: 1-year effects of a psychoeducational program in conjunction with pharmacotherapy. *Biological Psychiatry, 48,* 582–592.

Miller, A. L., Rathus, J. H., Linehan, M. M., Wetzler, S., & Leigh, E. (1997). Dialectical behavioral therapy adapted for suicidal adolescents. *Journal of Practical Psychiatry and Behavioral Health, 3,* 78–86.

Miller, I. W., Keitner, G. I., Bishop, D. S., & Ryan, C. E. (1991, November). *Families of bipolar patients: Dysfunction, course of illness, and pilot treatment study.* Paper presented at the Association for the Advancement of Behavior Therapy, New York.

Miller, I. W., Keitner, G. I., Ryan, C. E., & Solomon, D. S. (2000, June). *Family treatment of bipolar disorder.* Paper presented at the Society for Psychotherapy Research, Braaga, Portugal.

Nathan, P. E., & Gorman, J. M. (Eds.). (2002). *A guide to treatments that work* (2nd ed.). New York: Oxford University Press.

Nelson, H. E. (1997). *Cognitive behavior therapy with schizophrenia: A practice manual.* Chichester, England: Thornes.

O'Leary, K. D., & Beach, S. R. H. (1990). Marital therapy: A viable treatment for depression and marital discord. *American Journal of Psychiatry, 147,* 183–186.

Ost, L.-G. (1992). Blood and injection phobia: Background and cognitive, physiological, and behavioral variables. *Journal of Abnormal Psychology, 101,* 68–74.

Ost, L.-G., Ferebee, I., & Furmark, T. (1997). One-session group therapy of spider phobia: Direct vs. indirect treatments. *Behaviour Research and Therapy, 35,* 731–732.

Otto, M. W., Pollack, M. H., & Sabatino, S. A. (1995). *Maintenance of remission following CBT for panic disorder: Possible deleterious effects for concurrent medication treatment.* Paper presented at the World Congress of Behavioural and Cognitive Therapies, Copenhagen, Denmark.

Otto, M. W., Pollack, M. H., Sachs, G. S., Teiter, S. R., Meltzer-Brody, S., & Rosenbaum, J. F. (1993). Discontinuation of benzodiazepine treatment: Efficacy of cognitive-behavioral therapy for patients with panic disorder. *American Journal of Psychiatry, 150,* 1485–1490.

Paul, G. L. (1966). *Insight versus desensitization in psychotherapy: An experiment in anxiety reduction.* Stanford, CA: Stanford University Press.

Paul, G. L. (1969). Outcome of systematic desensitization: II. Controlled investigations of individual treatment, technique variations and current status. In C. M. Frank (Ed.), *Behavior therapy: Appraisal and status* (pp. 105–159). New York: McGraw-Hill.

Paul, G. L., & Lentz, R. J. (1977). *Psychosocial treatment of chronic mental patients: Milieu versus social-learning programs.* Cambridge, MA: Harvard University Press.

Penn, D. L., & Mueser, K. T. (1996). Research update on the psychosocial treatment of schizophrenia. *American Journal of Psychiatry, 153*(5), 607–617.

Perry, A., Tarrier, N., Morriss, R., McCarthy, E., & Limb, K. (1999). Randomized controlled trial of efficacy of teaching patients with bipolar disorder to identify early symptoms of relapse and obtain treatment. *British Medical Journal, 16,* 149–153.

Persons, J. B., Thase, M. E., & Crits-Christoph, P. (1996). The role of psychotherapy in the treatment of depression: Review of two practice guidelines. *Archives of General Psychiatry, 53,* 283–290.

Pinto, A., La Pia, S., Menella, R., Giorgino, D., & De Simone, L. (1999). Cognitive behavioral therapy and clozapine for clients with treatment-refractory schizophrenia. *Psychiatric Services, 50,* 901–904.

Pitman, R. K., Altman, B., Greenwald, E., Longpre, R. E., Macklin, M. L., Poire, R. E., & Steketee, G. S. (1991). Psychiatric complications during flooding therapy for posttraumatic stress disorder. *Journal of Clinical Psychiatry, 52,* 17–20.

Pitman, R. K., Orr, S. P., Altman, B., Longpre, R. E., Poire, R. E., & Macklin, M. L. (1996). Emotional processing during eye movement desensitization and reprocessing therapy of Vietnam veterans with chronic posttraumtic stress disorder. *Comprehensive Psychiatry, 37,* 419–429.

Rea, M. M., Tompson, M., Miklowitz, D. J., Goldstein, M. J., Hwang, S., & Mintz, J. (in press). Family-focused treatment vs. individual treatment for bipolar disorder: Results of a randomized clinical trial. *Journal of Consulting and Clinical Psychology.*

Rehm, L. P. (1977). A self-control model of depression. *Behavior Therapy, 8,* 787–804.

Rehm, L. P. (1990). Cognitive and behavioral theories. In B. B. Wolman & G. Stricker (Eds.), *Depressive disorders: Facts, theories, and treatment methods* (pp. 64–91). New York: Wiley.

Resick, P. A., & Schicke, M. K. (1992). Cognitive processing therapy for sexual assault victims. *Journal of Consulting and Clinical Psychology, 60,* 748–756.

Riggs, D. S., Rothbaum, B. O., & Foa, E. B. (1995). A prospective examination of symptoms of posttraumatic stress disorder in victims of nonsexual assault. *Journal of Interpersonal Violence, 10,* 201–213.

Robin, A. L., Siegel, P. T., & Moye, A. (1995). Family versus individual therapy for anorexia: Impact on family conflict. *International Journal Eating Disorders, 17,* 313–322.

Rothbaum, B. O., Meadows, E. A., Resick, P. A., & Foy, D. W. (2000). Cognitive-behavioral therapy. In E. B. Foa, T. M. Keane, & M. J. Friedman (Eds.), *Effective treatments for PTSD: Practice guidelines from the International Society for Traumatic Stress Studies* (pp. 60–83). New York: Guilford Press.

Rush, A. J., Beck, A. T., Kovacs, M., & Hollon, S. (1977). Comparative efficacy of cognitive therapy in the treatment of depressed outpatients. *Cognitive Therapy and Research, 1,* 17–37.

Salkovskis, P. M., & Clark, D. M. (1991). Cognitive therapy for panic disorder. *Journal of Cognitive Psychotherapy, 5,* 215–226.

Sensky, T., Turkington, D., Kingdon, D., Scott, J. L., Scott, J., Siddle, R., O'Coarroll, M., & Barnes, T. R. E. (2000). A randomized controlled trial of cognitive-behavioral therapy for persistent symptoms in schizophrenia resistant to medication. *Archives of General Psychiatry, 57,* 165–172.

Shapiro, F. (1995). *Eye movement desensitization and reprocessing: Basic principles, protocols, and procedures.* New York: Guilford.

Simoneau, T. L., Miklowitz, D. J., Richards, J. A., Saleem, R., & George, E. L. (1999). Bipolar disorder and family communication: Effects of a psychoeducational treatment program. *Journal of Abnormal Psychology, 108,* 588–597.

Simons, A. D., Murphy, G. E., Levine, J. L., & Wetzel, R. D. (1986). Cognitive therapy and pharmacotherapy for depression. *Archives of General Psychiatry, 43,* 43–48.

Skinner, B. F. (1953). *Science and human behavior.* New York: Free Press.

Spiegel, D. A., Bruce, T. J., Gregg, S. F., & Nuzzarello, A. (1994). Does cognitive behavior therapy assist slow-taper alprazolam discontinuation in panic disorder? *American Journal of Psychiatry, 151,* 876–881.

Tarrier, N., Beckett, R., Harwood, S., Baker, A., Yusupoff, L., & Ugarteburu, I. (1993). A trial of two cognitive-behavioural methods of treating drug-resistant residual psychotic symptoms in schizophrenic patients. *British Journal of Psychiatry, 162,* 524–532.

Tarrier, N., Kinney, C., McCarthy, E., Humphreys, L., Wittkowski, A., & Morris, J. (2000). Two-year follow-up of cognitive-behavioral therapy and supportive counseling in the treatment of persistent symptoms in chronic schizophrenia. *Journal of Consulting and Clinical Psychology, 68,* 917–922.

Tarrier, N., Pilgrim, H., Sommerfield, C., Faragher, B., Reynolds, M., Graham, E., & Barrowclough, C. (1999). A randomized trial of cognitive therapy and imaginal exposure in the treatment of chronic posttraumatic stress disorder. *Journal of Consulting and Clinical Psychology, 67,* 13–18.

Thoresen, C. E., & Mahoney, M. J. (1974). *Behavioral self-control.* New York: Holt, Rinehart & Winston.

Touyz, S. W., & Beumont, P. J. V. (1997). Behavioral treatment to promote weight gain in anorexia nervosa. In D. M. Garner & P. E. Garfinkel (Eds.), *Handbook of treatments for eating disorders* (2nd ed., pp. 361–371). New York: Guilford Press.

Treasure, J. L., Schmidt, U., Troop, N., Tiller, J., Todd, T., Keilen, M., & Dodge, E. (1994). First step in managing bulimia nervosa: Controlled trial of therapeutic manual. *British Medical Journal, 308,* 686–689.

Treasure, J. L., Katzman, M., Schmidt, U., Troop, N., Todd, G., & de Silva, P. (1999). Engagement and outcome in the treatment of bulimia nervosa: First phase of sequential design comparing motivation enhancement therapy and cognitive behavioural therapy. *Behaviour Research and Therapy, 37,* 405–418.

van Balkom, A. J. L. M., van Oppen, P., Vermeulen, A. W. A., van Dyck, R., Nauta, M. C. E., & Vorst, H. C. M. (1994). A meta analysis on the treatment of obsessive compulsive disorder: A comparison of anti-depressants, behavior, and cognitive therapy. *Clinical Psychology Review, 5,* 359–381.

Walsh, B. T., Wilson, G. T., Loeb, K., Devlin, M., Pike, K. M., Roose, S. P., Fleiss, J., & Waternaux, C. (1997). Medication and psychotherapy in the treatment of bulimia nervosa. *American Journal of Psychiatry, 154,* 523–531.

Wehman, P., & Moon, M. S. (1988). *Vocational rehabilitation and supported employment.* Baltimore: Brookes.

Weissman, M. M., & Klerman, G. L. (1973). Psychotherapy with depressed women: An empirical study of content themes and reflection. *British Journal of Psychiatry, 123,* 55–61.

Wilfley, D. E., Welch, R. R., Stein, R. I., Spurrell, E. B., Cohen, L. R., Saelens, B. E., Dounchis, J. Z., Frank, M. A., Wiseman, C. V., & Matt, G. E. (in press). A randomized comparison of group cognitive-behavioral therapy and group Interpersonal Psychotherapy for the treatment of overweight individuals with Binge Eating Disorder. *Archives of General Psychiatry.*

Wilson, G. T. (1994). Evaluating behavioral interventions for obesity: Thirty years and counting. *Behavioural Research and Therapy, 16*(1), 31–75.

Wilson, G. T., & Fairburn, C. G. (2002). Treatments for eating disorders. In P. E. Nathan & J. M. Gorman (Eds.), *A guide to treatments that work* (2nd ed., pp. 559–592). New York: Oxford University Press.

Wolpe, J. (1958). *Psychotherapy by reciprocal inhibition.* Stanford, CA: Stanford University Press.

CHAPTER 12

# Humanistic-Experiential Psychotherapy

LESLIE S. GREENBERG, ROBERT ELLIOTT, AND GERMAIN LIETAER

In this chapter the humanistic-experiential orientation to psychotherapy is defined. The major approaches within this orientation are discussed as well as aspects of related approaches with an experiential-humanistic flavor. The emergence of contemporary experiential therapy, based on a neo-humanistic reformulation of classic humanistic values, is presented, followed by a presentation of an experiential therapy that derives from this reformulation.

The major subapproaches within the humanistic tradition are the client-centered (or person-centered), Gestalt, and existential approaches. Other influential approaches have been psychodrama (Verhofstadt-Denève, 1999; Wilkins, 1999) and the body therapies and, more recently, the interpersonal views of such authors as Kiesler (1996), Yalom (1995), and Schmid (1995). More recently, humanistic approaches have begun to be grouped together under the experiential umbrella (Greenberg, Elliott, & Lietaer, 1994; Greenberg, Watson, & Lietaer, 1998). The process-experiential approach is one current expression of the contemporary humanistic-experiential tradition in psychotherapy. It integrates client-centered and gestalt therapy traditions (Greenberg, Rice, & Elliott, 1993). Gendlin's (1996) focusing-oriented approach is another current expression. This approach emphasizes the creation of new meaning by focusing on bodily felt referents. Dialogical gestalt therapy (Hycner & Jacobs, 1995; Yontef, 1993) and some more integrative forms of person-centered or experiential psy-

chotherapy (Finke, 1994; Lietaer & Van Kalmthout, 1995; Mearns & Thorne, 2000) are further current expressions. In practice, these contemporary approaches strive to maintain a creative tension or dialectic between the client-centered emphasis on creating a genuinely empathic and prizing therapeutic relationship (Barrett-Lennard, 1998; Biermann-Ratjen, Eckert, & Schwartz, 1995; Rogers, 1961) and a more active, task-focused, process-directive style of engagement that promotes deeper experiencing (Gendlin, 1996; Perls, Hefferline, & Goodman, 1951).

## HUMANISTIC-EXPERIENTIAL THEORY

Humanistic theories (Greenberg & Rice, 1997) take a positive view of human nature and see subjectivity and awareness as essential for understanding human beings. They oppose views that cast the person as an object to be viewed from an external vantage point because these ignore the individual's existential reality. Drawing on existential writers such as Kierkegaard (1843/1954) and Sartre (1943/1956), humanists believe that peoples' uniquely human, subjective reality must be respected in order to grasp their reality. The European philosophers Husserl (1925/1977), Heidegger (1949/1962), Jaspers (1963), Marcel (1951), and Merleau-Ponty (1945/1962) were also influential in explicating and extending this position.

Heidegger's understanding of being-in-the-world and the importance of understanding phenomena as they appear to the subject are strong themes throughout humanistic-existential psychology.

## Classical Humanistic Assumptions and Values

Humanistic theorists, often spoken of as the third force in psychology, have written extensively on the nature of human existence, on methods by which these uniquely human modes of functioning can be studied and grasped, and on the implications of humanistic assumptions for the goals and processes of psychotherapy.

The first and most central characteristic of humanistic psychology and psychotherapy is its focus on promoting in-therapy *experiencing*. Methods that stimulate emotional experience are used within the context of an empathic facilitative relationship. The word "experiential" is defined in the Concise Oxford Dictionary (1990) as "involving or based on experience," whereas experience is defined in turn as the "actual observation of, or practical acquaintance with facts or events" or "to feel or be affected by (an emotion etc.)." The distinction between two ways of knowing—knowledge by acquaintance (experiential) and knowledge by description (conceptual)—was first made by St. Augustine and later emphasized in the epistemologies of William James and Bertrand Russell. In these terms the essence of experiential therapy is its focus on promoting knowledge by acquaintance. Thus, a person does not come to know something about him- or herself conceptually but rather through emotional experience of the self interacting with others and the world. In experiential therapy the client's ongoing experiencing process is kept as a continuous point of reference for all therapist responses; change is seen as occurring through the promotion of new in-session experiencing.

A commitment to a *phenomenological* approach flows directly from this central interest in experiencing. This approach is grounded in the belief in the uniquely human capacity for reflective consciousness, as well as in the belief that it is this capacity that can lead to self-determination and freedom. All humanistic psychotherapists agree on the inescapable uniqueness of human consciousness and on the importance of understanding peoples' perceptions of reality as a way of understanding their experiences and behaviors. They all build on the uniquely human capacity for self-reflective consciousness and on the human search for meanings, choices, and growth.

A *positive view* of human functioning and the operation of some form of growth tendency are also highly significant issues for humanistic therapists. All would agree with the importance of the view of human beings as goal directed, striving toward growth and development rather than merely toward the maintenance of stability. All would agree that peoples' choices are guided more by their awareness of the future and of the immediate present than by the past. Consciousness in this view transforms the growth tendency in the organism into a directional tendency that places the self as a center of intentionality in a more or less constant search for meaning. The self is seen as an agent in the process of change.

The belief in the human capacity for *self-determination* is an important and sometimes controversial focus of humanistic theorists. The ways in which this capacity is developed and the ways in which its development can be facilitated or blocked is a key issue for humanistic therapies. Individuals are determined solely neither by their pasts nor by their environments but are agents in the construction of their worlds. All humanistic views attempt to move beyond what they regard as the restricted deterministic views of human functioning represented in the other major orientations. Although all humanistic theories have explicated views of pathological functioning, their primary focus has always been on understanding ways in which people could be helped to move toward healthy or even ideal functioning.

Humanistic approaches also are consistently *person centered*. This involves concern and real respect for each person. The person is viewed holistically, neither as a symptom-driven case nor as best characterized by a diagnosis. Each person's subjective experience is of central importance to the humanist, and in an effort to grasp this experience, the therapist attempts empathically to enter into the other person's world in a special way that goes beyond the subject-object dichotomy. Being allowed to share another person's world is viewed as a special privilege requiring a special kind of relationship.

## Theory of Human Functioning

As just outlined, humanistic-experiential therapies assume that human beings are aware, experiencing organisms who function holistically to organize their experience into coherent forms (Gendlin, 1962; Mahrer, 1978; May, Angel, & Ellenberger, 1958; May & Schneider, 1995; Perls et al., 1951; Rogers, 1951). People therefore are viewed as meaning-creating, symbolizing agents whose subjective experience is an essential aspect of their humanness. In addition, the operation of an integrative, formative tendency oriented toward survival, growth, and the creation of meaning has governed a humanistic-experiential view of functioning. Finally, in this view behavior is seen as the goal-directed attempt of people to satisfy their perceived needs (Perls et al., 1951; Rogers, 1951).

A general principle that has united all experientially oriented theorists is that people are wiser than their intellects alone. In an experiencing organism, consciousness is seen as being at the peak of a pyramid of nonconscious organismic functioning. Of central importance is that tacit experiencing is an important guide to conscious experience, is fundamentally adaptive, and is potentially available to awareness. Internal tacit experiencing is most readily available to awareness when the person turns his or her attention internally within the context of a supportive interpersonal relationship. Interpersonal safety and support are thus viewed as key elements in enhancing the amount of attention available for self-awareness and exploration. Experiments in directed awareness, in addition, help focus and concentrate attention on unformed experience and intensifying its vividness.

The classical humanistic-experiential theories of functioning posited two main structural constructs, self-concept and organismic experience, as well as one major motivational construct, a growth tendency.

### Self/Self-Concept

The self is central in explaining human functioning. In devising his self theory, James (1890/1950) drew on a fundamental distinction between two aspects of self: self as subject-agent-process ("I") and self as object-structure-content ("me"). In developing a more systematic self theory, Rogers (1959) appears to have emphasized the self as self-concept, that is, object-content. On the other hand, Gestalt theory is less clear but appears to have characterized the self as more of an integrated whole and the agent of growth. Finally, existentialists have viewed self as a quality of existence ("being" or, more specifically, "being-for-itself"). In the end, however, all have endorsed the idea of an active integrating self.

For Rogers, the self-concept was an organized *conceptual* gestalt consisting of the individual's perceptions of self and self in relation to others, together with the *values* attached to these perceptions. The self-concept is not always in awareness but always is available to awareness. In this view, the self has a twofold nature: It is both a changing process and, at any moment, a fixed entity. My self-concept is the view I have of myself ("me"), plus my evaluation of that view. A person may, for example, perceive herself as a good student, of superior intelligence and as loving her parents, and may value these positively; at the same time, this person may see herself as unattractive to the opposite sex and as competitive, and may in fact view these characteristics negatively. Gestalt theory also held that there is a conflict between an image

(self-concept) that the person is trying to actualize and what in Gestalt is called the self-actualizing tendency. In these traditions, introjected conditions of worth are seen as crucial in forming self-concept "shoulds" by which people try to manipulate their selves to behave and experience in accord with certain dictates.

Some form of agency ("I") is seen as an agent that is variedly identified with, or alienated from, aspects of spontaneous, organismic, preverbal levels of experiencing to form a "me" (James, 1890/1950). In addition, a core set of interruptive mechanisms were posited. These were seen as preventing the owning of emerging experience as well as preventing contact between the person and the environment. In Gestalt theory the person was also viewed as being constituted by parts and as functioning by the integration of polarities. In essence, a modular theory of self was postulated in which there existed different parts of the person that needed to be integrated.

### Organismic Experience

According to Rogers (1959), experience includes everything going on within the organism that is potentially available to awareness; to experience means to receive the impact of concurrent sensory or physiological events. According to Gendlin (1962), experiencing is the process of concrete bodily feeling that constitutes the basic matter of psychological phenomena. Experience is thus a datum; it is what happens as we live. Awareness of this basic datum is seen as essential to healthy living.

### The Growth Tendency

Most humanistic theorists have drawn on Goldstein's (1939) description of a holistic actualizing tendency to describe the human tendency to organize resources and capacities so as to cope optimally. Rogers developed his notion of an actualizing tendency from his initial view of the operation of a growth and development tendency. This tendency came to be defined as the "inherent tendency of the organism to develop all its capacities in ways which serve to maintain or enhance the organism" (Rogers, 1959, p. 196). The latter view added the idea of the actualizing of all capacities to the notion of the adaptive function of a growth and development tendency. The actualizing tendency was highly important in that it offered a nonhomeostatic view of functioning. The person is not guided by deficiencies but is instead proactive.

Perls (1947) took from Gestalt psychology the view of people as active organizers of their world, including a tendency toward closure or completion of experience. This was offered as an alternative to views of people as determined, either by their history or by the unfolding of a genetic blueprint. Perls was committed to the idea of an inherent organizing tendency. This tendency leads infants to learn to walk and to develop, and people in general to learn to maintain themselves, to use tools, to develop verbal concepts, to strive for meaningful interpersonal contact, and to develop a sense of personal mastery. The holistic nature of this formative tendency was emphasized over any specific drives or needs. Maslow (1968) subsequently defined the actualizing tendency in terms of a hierarchy of needs, moving from lower level biological survival ("deficiency") needs to higher level, growth-oriented ("being") needs. Perls, however, rejected this level concept and adopted the more dynamic principle that the most dominant need in the situation emerges to organize the field.

All the theorists originally emphasized the growth tendency's thrust toward autonomy from external control, a view that fitted the male-gender-role-based, autonomy-oriented view of psychological health prevalent at the time. Perls, for example, stressed that maturation involves moving from environmental support to self-support. Perls and the existentialists also emphasized the importance of choice and the integration of polarities over any inherent tendency toward goodness. Rogers (1961), on the other hand, strongly emphasized the prosocial nature of the actualizing tendency. He believed that when people are guided by this tendency, they are trustworthy, reliable, and constructive.

Existential therapists, although seeing life as purposive and the organism as active in choosing its own destiny, have not explicitly posited a growth tendency. In existential terms, no innate "essence" precedes existence; rather, people determine themselves. People are born morally neutral, with a penchant both for health and sickness, and for good and bad. However, people are seen as having innate worth in the sense that they have the ability to know the difference between good and evil and the capacity to choose. Thus, a growth-like principle is implicit in existential thinking. Frankl (1963), for example, proposed a "will to meaning," and May and Yalom (1989) suggested that the therapist cannot create engagement or wishing that but the desire to engage in one's life is always there. In his first book, *The Doctor and the Soul,* Frankl (1955) proposed that people live in three dimensions: the somatic, the mental, and the spiritual. He equated the search for meaning with a spiritual struggle, and one that appears only in humans. For Frankl (1963), the will to meaning is the fundamental human drive.

## Theory of Dysfunction

In the humanistic-experiential tradition, dysfunction has generally been seen as resulting from the disowning of

experience. According to Rogers (1959), dysfunction is caused by *incongruence between self-concept and experience.* A state of incongruence exists when the self-concept differs from the actual experience of the organism. Thus, if I see myself as loving but feel angry and vengeful, then I am incongruent. When the organismic valuing process and externally imposed conditions of worth are in agreement, organismic experiencing is accurately perceived and symbolized. However, experiences that contradict conditions of worth compromise the need for positive self-regard, if accurately perceived and assimilated. Therefore, these experiences are selectively perceived, distorted, or simply denied in order to make them consistent with self-worth. This leads to progressively greater estrangement from oneself, so that the person can no longer live as an integrated whole, but is instead internally divided.

Threat or anxiety thus occurs if accurately symbolized experience violates the self-concept, leaving the person vulnerable. When a discrepancy between self-concept and experience threatens to enter awareness, the person responds by becoming anxious. However, in response to strong organismic needs, behavior inconsistent with the self-concept nevertheless occurs. Furthermore, the tacit perception (*subception*) of incongruence between self-concept and organismic experiencing leads to healthy acceptance, immediate distortion or disowning of experience, or (in severe instances) fragmentation of the self-concept.

Similarly, according to Gestalt theory, health involves the owning of emerging experience, whereas dysfunction involves the automatic *disowning* or *alienation* of this experience. A variety of interruptive mechanisms, including introjections, projections, and retroflections, prevents need satisfaction. Other phenomena such as conflict between polarities, habits, unfinished business, avoidance, and catastrophizing are also seen as important processes that produce dysfunction.

Different views of dysfunction and change coexist in this tradition. One, reflecting a psychoanalytic influence, held that awareness or discovery of previously unaware contents was curative, implying that hidden contents were pathogenic. Alternatively, pathology was seen as resulting from the inability to integrate one's representations and reactions to certain experiences into one's existing self-organization. In this view, the unacceptable is dealt with not by expelling it from consciousness (repression), but by failing to experience it as one's own (disowning). Rather than making the unconscious conscious, therapy needs to promote reowning or the fuller experiencing of what one was talking about and already knew in some way. The important thing about this view is that what is disowned is not in itself pathogenic; instead, it is the healthy or the traumatic that has been disowned. Dysfunction occurs because of the disowning of healthy growth-oriented resources and needs or because of the avoidance of pain. It is the owning and reprocessing of experience to assimilate it into existing meaning structures, as opposed to consciousness of repressed contents, that is the key change process in this view. This is an essential difference from classical psychoanalytic views, where dysfunction arises from denial of indirect efforts to gratify infantile or nonadaptive needs.

Among the existentialists, Boss (1963) viewed psychopathology as a narrowing of the attunement that a person has to his or her world. Instead of being able to attend to numerous events in the world, the client is able to attend only to a narrower range of phenomena, so that in neurosis the person's world of possibilities shrinks. This narrowing of attunement or attending leaves the person with only a partial view of his or her world (Boss, 1963). For May (1977), pathology develops because of the anxiety that arises from the defensive unawareness of the possibility of nonbeing. The anxiety of nonbeing (*ontological anxiety*) is resolved by using this angst to gain an appreciation for being. "To grasp what it means to exist, one needs to grasp the fact that he might not exist" (May, 1977, p. 51). Heidegger phrased it more strongly: To grasp what it means to exist, one needs to grasp the fact that one will, in some number of years, not exist (Heidegger, 1949/1962). In existential theory, dysfunction has been seen as resulting from lack of authenticity and alienation from experience, and the resultant lack of meaning. Therapy thus needs to promote fuller experiencing of what one is talking about and already knows tacitly. In existential theory, dysfunction therefore is seen as resulting from lack of authenticity, alienation from experience, and ontological anxiety, and the resultant lack of meaning.

## Experiential Theory: A Neo-Humanistic Synthesis

The classical views of humanistic therapy described in the previous section have been complemented recently by an additional set of ideas from current psychological theory in order to provide the basis for a more complete understanding of human function, dysfunction, and change (Greenberg & Van Balen, 1998; Greenberg, Watson, & Lietaer 1998). This reformulated perspective has added certain "neo-humanistic" (Elliott, 1999; Elliott, Watson, Goldman, & Greenberg, in press) principles, which provide the basis for experiential and emotion-focused therapies. The traditional humanistic assumptions have been expanded to incorporate modern views on emotion, dynamic systems, constructivism, and the importance of a process view of functioning to help clarify the humanistic views of growth and self-determination.

Contemporary *emotion theory* (Frijda, 1986; Greenberg & Paivio, 1997; Greenberg & Safran, 1987) holds that emotion is fundamentally adaptive in nature and provides the basis for

the growth tendency. In this view, emotion helps the organism to process complex situational information rapidly and automatically in order to produce action appropriate for meeting important organismic needs (e.g., self-protection, support). Emotions provide rapid appraisals of the significance of situations to peoples' well-being and therefore guide adaptive action.

In addition, humanistic perspectives on subjectivity and perception have been connected to *constructivist* epistemology and views of functioning. In this view people are seen as dynamic systems in which various elements continuously interact to produce experience and action (Greenberg & Pascual-Leone, 1995, 1997; Greenberg & Van Balen, 1998). These multiple, interacting self-organizations can be described metaphorically as "voices" or parts of self (Elliott & Greenberg, 1997; Mearns & Thorne, 2000). In this view, the "I" is an agentic self-aspect or self-narrating voice that constructs a coherent story of the self by integrating different aspects of experience in a given situation; however, this voice has no special status as an "executive self." Of particular importance are two sets of voices, which can be referred to broadly as "internal" and "external," or as "experiential" and "conceptual."

Furthermore, change is a dynamic, *dialectically constructive* process that requires that there be a clear separation between different modules, self-aspects, or voices within the person, especially between the internal-experiential and the external-conceptual aspects. These modules, aspects, or voices are then brought into direct contact with each other so that *discords* and *harmonies* can be heard. When this dialogue is successful, some form of newness is generated. As is true for all dialectically constructive processes, the precise nature of this new experience is impossible to predict in advance, although it should be understandable in retrospect (cf. Gendlin, 1996). Most important, it involves change in both aspects or voices; that is, both assimilation and accommodation occur.

## *Reformulation of the Self as Process and Self-Narration*

Over time, the original humanistic structural theories came to be supplemented and somewhat replaced by a process conception. In his initial attempts to develop a process conception, Rogers (1958) offered a conceptualization of health that saw change as a transition from stability to flux, from rigidity to flow, and from structure to process. In his theory of experiencing, Gendlin (1962, 1964) more fully articulated this process-oriented view of experiencing and moved away from denial-incongruence models. He started from the premise that people are experiencing beings and stressed the interactional character of all naturally occurring forms of life.

Excessive stability, tied to the absence of forms of interaction that carry processes forward, was seen as the major cause of disturbance in spontaneous organismic process, or what he referred to as a bodily way of being-in-the world. Gendlin (1962) argued that optimal self-process involves an ever-increasing use of experiencing as a process in which felt meanings *interact* with verbal symbols to produce an explicit meaning.

Gestalt theorists also proposed a self-as-process model (Perls et al., 1951). This theory made two proposals. One was that the self is the *synthesizing agent,* the artist of life, who creates contact at the organism-environment boundary. The second, and somewhat different, was that the *self is contact* with the environment and that it comes into being at the moment of contact. According to the first view of self, the self creates solutions to problems that arise at the contact boundary. According to the second view of self, when there is full contact, there is full self; and when there is little contact, there is little self. Thus, the self comes into existence in the experience of contact, and I "am" my experience. The self is removed from "inside" the person and becomes a field process. Self, in process terms, is thus the meeting point of internal and external, achieved by a process of dynamic synthesis of all elements of the field (Perls et al., 1951; Wheeler, 1991; Yontef, 1993). The self is on the surface, not somewhere deep inside, and it forms continually, *at the ever-changing boundary* between the organism and the environment, in order to fulfill needs, solve problems, and deal with obstacles. With this field view, culture is given an important role in understanding experience.

In the process-oriented Gestalt view, it is awareness of the *process* of identification and alienation of experience that are the road to health. Awareness of functioning provides people with the option to choose, if and when, to own experience (Perls et al., 1951). Therapy, then, offers clients experiments of deliberate awareness in order to promote the experience of being an active agent in experience; this allows the person to begin to experience what Perls et al. (1951) described as "It is me who is thinking, feeling or doing this" (p. 251).

Integrating and developing experiential process theory in line with modern views on emotion, constructive cognition, and the operation of dynamic systems, a dialectical constructivist model of experiential therapy has been proposed (Greenberg et al., 1993; Greenberg & Pascual-Leone, 1995, 1997; Watson & Greenberg, 1997). In this view, people are seen as active agents in the construction of their own realities, and the self is seen as a process in a continual state of self-organization. Humans are seen as symbolizing, meaning-creating beings who act as dynamic systems, constantly synthesizing conscious experience out of many levels of processing and from both internal and external sources.

Three major levels of processing—innate sensorimotor, emotional schematic memory, and conceptual level processing—have been identified (Greenberg & Safran, 1987; Greenberg et al., 1993). In addition, people are seen as organizing experience into emotion-based schemes that then play a central role in functioning.

This dynamic view supports a form of practice in which emotion plays an important role in the construction of reality and both therapeutic relationship and therapeutic work on specific problems are seen as aiding change. Emotional experience, although seen as a basically healthy resource, is viewed as capable of either providing healthy adaptive information based on its biologically adaptive origins or, in certain instances, becoming maladaptive through learning and experience. The most basic process for the individual in therapy is thus one of developing awareness of emotion and discriminating which emotional responses are healthy and can be used as a guide and which are maladaptive and need to be changed (Greenberg & Paivio, 1997). Change is seen as occurring by the coconstruction of new meaning in a dialogue between client and therapist, in which the therapist plays an active role in confirming clients' emotional experiencing and helping them synthesize an identity based on strengths and possibilities.

In this view, it is the dialectical interaction among emotion schemes and levels of processing to synthesize new meaning that becomes the central process. This suggests that a principle of *coherence* can be viewed as supplementing the traditional principle of congruence in explaining healthy functioning. Thus, it is not simply that "I" become aware of my "feelings," or that my self-concept and experience are consistent with one another. Rather, I form a coherent sense of myself, as, say, angry or sad; this form successfully organizes aspects of my experience together into a coherent whole that is viable in a given situation. In this view, adaptive functioning involves coordination among aspects of experience as well as levels of processing, with mutually affiliative relationships to one another, generating a coherent whole that makes sense and is identified as a part of one's self-organization. This view helps overcome the problem, in both language and thought, of presuming the operation of any preexisting hidden content or meaning that comes to awareness or is accepted into a self-concept. Rather, there is an ongoing process of synthesizing levels of processing and modules of experience in a complex internal field. In addition, reowning is seen as integrating aspects of experience into coherent forms, and this involves meaning creation as well as identification with the disowned.

In this dialectical view, the person is emphasized as an *active agent* (cf. Bohart & Tallman, 1999) constantly organizing or configuring experience and reality into meaningful wholes. Both discovery of experience and creation of meaning operate in tandem, neither process being privileged over the other (Greenberg et al., 1993). In addition, both emerging internal experience and interpersonal support are seen as active ingredients in the process of change. Meaning is created by human activity, in dialogue with others, and people are seen as creators of the self they find themselves to be.

In this process, the self is the agent that acts to become aware of needs and creatively resolve problems that arise from interactions with the environment. Need emergence is seen as a field event rather than as an inner drive; it occurs as the self synthesizes internal and external elements into coherent forms. Needs and goals, along with meaning, are thus both created and discovered. The inability to identify and form needs and a clear coherent sense of self leads to weak self-organization.

In this view, the term "self" refers not to an entity or object but to a tacit integrating organization that separates what is "me" from what is "not me." The self is a dynamic system organizing the elements of experience into a coherent whole by a process of dynamic-dialectical synthesis (Pascual-Leone, 1991; Smith & Thelen, 1993; Whelton & Greenberg, 2000). There is thus no central control; all elements add weight in an ongoing synthesis, producing a succession of momentary self-organizations, such as feeling shy or being assertive. Conscious control is but one aspect that can influence the synthesis process but is always itself influenced by tacit knowing.

The self-concept, in this view, is replaced by a *self-narration,* that is, by a story we tell others and ourselves in order to make sense of our lives. This self-narration is not a structure or a concept but instead is an ongoing process by which we organize our experiences and provide accounts of our actions. The self-narration is a conscious conceptual process influenced by learning, by values, and by a variety of different cognitive and evaluative processes. People do not possess a self-concept; they actively narrate their experience, constructing views of who they and others are, as well as how and why things happened (Greenberg & Pascual-Leone, 1995; Watson & Greenberg, 1997).

Once we develop a conscious representation of our experience, this acts as an identity or becomes our self-narration. We then reflect on this leading to further new experiencing. We have many views of our self and are constantly revising these. Thus, we do not *have* a self-concept but are constantly forming it. We are engaged in an ongoing process of creating coherence and unity. In each moment we are the expression of one of many possible selves.

## Experiencing

Experiencing has often been treated as the given datum. It just happens. In contrast, according to the neo-humanistic view, experiencing can be understood as the synthesized product of a variety of sensorimotor responses and emotion schemes, tinged with conceptual memories, all activated in a situation (Greenberg et al., 1993). In this view, multiple patterns of neural activation (schemes) are evoked by the same releasers and function together to produce a complex, coordinated internal field (Greenberg & Pascual-Leone, 1995, 1997; Pascual-Leone, 1991). This field provides the person with a sense of internal complexity to which to refer, and in which much more is contained at any one moment than any one explicit representation can capture.

Imagine, for example, telling the story to a friend of one of two versions of an experience the previous evening: While standing in line for a movie, you turned around and suddenly saw someone whom you either (a) wished desperately to avoid or (b) were amorously longing to meet. Depending on which experience occurred, you might be able to speak at length from two entirely different senses of internal complexity, generated in the moment by complex tacit synthesis. You could talk about how you felt in, and about, this moment, drawing on many different images and explicating complex felt meanings and their implications. All these tacit meanings occurred in the field of internal complexity but were not necessarily processed consciously in the moment that you greeted the other person.

It is important to note that this bodily felt sense of internal complexity is not only *multidetermined* by many modalities and modes of processing, such as auditory visual, kinesthetic, emotional, and semantic; it is also *overdetermined.* The sense of internal complexity is the result of many determinant causes stemming from the many compatible processes involved in the experience. Experiencing is overdetermined in the sense that many schemes or aspects are coordinated in its production (Greenberg & Pascual-Leone, 1995). A subset of these schemes might suffice to produce the same result. An experience thus means both "this" and "that," even though the two determinants may differ and either could have sufficed to produce the result. Explanation of why one feels or does something is thus not a simple rational or linearly causal process. Conscious meaning then occurs by the symbolization of aspects of internal complexity into symbols that create distinctions in experience. These symbols in turn can be further organized by reflection to generate new felt meanings (Greenberg & Pascual-Leone, 1997; Watson & Greenberg, 1997).

Tacit decentralized control in a synthesis system of this nature makes it always possible to perceive more than we currently experience and to experience more than we currently attend to. New sets of tacit experience are always available to be explicated in consciousness. Experiencing is thus a tacit level of meaning generated by a dynamic synthesis of sensory, schematic, and conceptual levels of processing that integrate by a type of summation of related or mutual elements into a gestalt with figural and background aspects. In symbolizing experiencing, making the implicit explicit is not simply a process of representation but rather a process of construction, always limited and incomplete. Not all tacit information is used in any construction. Thus we can always explore for what more there is and reconfigure it in a new way. Explicit knowledge needs to fit adequately, to make sense of, and to integrate elements into a coherent, meaningful whole.

Growth is seen as emerging not only through the self-organization of some type of biological tendency, but also from genuine dialogue with another person. In such an I-thou dialogue (Buber, 1957), each person is made present to and by the other. In therapy, the therapist both *contacts* and *confirms* the client by focusing on particular aspects of the client's experiencing. Contact involves a continual focus by the therapist on the client's subjective experience, confirming the person as an authentic source of experience. Confirmation derives from the therapist's selective focus on strengths and on what is adaptive and promotes growth. It is the therapist's focus on subjective experience and strengths that helps guide client growth and development. In our view, people are often struggling and confused. Both "good" and "bad" inclinations exist as possibilities. Therapy is a coconstructive dialogue in which both the therapist and the client struggle to discern and confirm the client's health-promoting tendencies and possibilities. Growth truly emerges from the "in-between," from two people working together in a collaborative alliance toward the client's survival, enhancement, and affirmation of life. The therapist's ability to help the client explicate his or her experiencing, and to see and focus on implicit growth-oriented possibilities, is an important element of promoting the client's directional tendency.

Experience, then, is rich with not-yet-articulated implications. New meanings always can be created from a person's field of internal complexity. Thus, developing oneself is really the unfolding of the implications of internal experiencing. This involves discovering some of the tacit constituents and organizing them into coherent wholes in interaction with another person. The growth tendency is thus seen as being dialectically guided both from within and from without. The internal aspect is guided by the emotion system, which evaluates situations in relation to well-being (Frijda, 1986; Greenberg et al., 1993; Greenberg & Safran, 1987; Lazarus, 1991). External guidance and support of the growth process comes from another person who sees the first person's coping efforts, confirms them, and focuses on strengths, potentials, and possibilities. In other words, growth occurs in an interpersonal field. It is

strengthened by being focused on, symbolized, and confirmed in dialogue.

### Dysfunction

In the neo-humanistic process view, dysfunction occurs not through a single process, such as incongruence (Rogers, 1959), interruptions of contact (Perls et al., 1951), or a blocking of the meaning-symbolization process (Gendlin, 1962). Instead, dysfunction arises via many possible routes. This provides a more useful, flexible view of dysfunction—one that includes discerning varied current determinants and maintainers of problems.

At the most global level, we see the *inability to integrate* aspects of functioning into coherent harmonious internal relations as a major source of dysfunction. Thus, one's wishes and fears, one's strengths and vulnerabilities, or one's autonomy and dependence may at any moment be in conflict or at any moment in danger of being disowned. Notice that conflict here is between different self organizations, not conscious versus unconscious or moral versus immoral. This view incorporates both Rogers's and Perls's views of incongruence and integration, as well as Mahrer's (1978) view of the importance of affiliation and disaffiliation between operating potentials. However, these problems are attributed to the synthesizing and self-organizing functions of the self.

In line with Gendlin, Perls, and Rogers, we also see the *inability to symbolize bodily felt experience* in awareness as another central source of dysfunction. Thus, one may not be aware or be able to make sense of the increasing tension in one's body, of the anxiety one feels, or of unexpressed resentment.

A third major source of dysfunction involves the activation of *core maladaptive emotion schemes,* often trauma-based (Greenberg & Paivio, 1997). This leads either to painful emotions or maladaptive emotional experience and expression. The operation of this process implies that not all basic internal experience is an adaptive guide and that in addition to the benefits of becoming aware of basic experience, basic experience itself sometimes requires therapeutic change. For example, in posttraumatic stress the emotion system often signals an alarm when no danger is present. Similarly, poor attachment histories can lead to maladaptive experience of desire for, or mistrust of, interpersonal closeness.

The previous three general processes of dysfunction are supplemented by the operation of a large variety of more specific cognitive-affective processing difficulties that help explain different types of dysfunction. Greenberg et al. (1993) described a variety of particular experiential difficulties, including difficulties such as problematic reactions, in which one's view of an experience and one's reaction don't fit; self evaluative splits, in which one part of the self negatively evaluates another; unfinished business, involving unresolved emotional memories; and statements of vulnerability involving a fragile sense of self. All involve different types of underlying schematic processing problems. Each state requires different interventions designed to deal with the specific cognitive-affective processing problems. This offers a differential view of dysfunction in which current determinants and maintainers of disorders are identified by a form of process diagnosis in which therapists identify markers of in-session opportunities for implementing specific types of interventions and change processes.

For example, specific problems in living such as depression might be seen as involving some of the above general processes of inability to integrate, symbolize, and separate past from present experience, but all also involve specific determinants and processing difficulties unique to different types of depressive problems or persons. For example, self-critical depressions manifest primarily in self-evaluative conflicts in the person, whereas dependence-based depressions are organized around unfinished business with significant others (Greenberg, Watson, & Goldman, 1998).

### Summary of Neo-Humanistic Theory

In the neo-humanistic view, people are seen as dynamic systems attempting to maintain the coherence of their organizing processes by continuous synthesis and restructuring. The person grows toward greater and greater complexity and coherence by constantly assimilating experience, integrating incongruities and polarities. Growth is inherently dialectical and dialogical. This view does not privilege an internal process of feeling and attending over meaning-creating processes of symbolization and reflection; nor does it privilege internal experience over contact with others. Rather, it sees a dialectical synthesis of all elements, emotion and cognition, internal and external, biological and social, as the crucial process in the creation of meaning. Culture, experience, and biology are given equally important roles.

Dysfunction occurs via different general and specific types of processing problems. In addition, any notion of a genetic or predetermined blueprint for whom the person "truly is" is rejected. In its place is an interpersonally facilitated growth tendency oriented toward increased complexity, coherence, and adaptive flexibility. Therapy involves attending to this adaptive capacity, confirming it, and promoting different types of processing to facilitate different types of problem resolution. In addition, therapy promotes awareness of blocks and interruptions of the person's strengths and problem-solving capacities so that awareness becomes fluid rather than fixated on

reworking unfinished situations. Therapy provides a relational environment that helps strengthen the adaptive self, creates process-enhancing interactions that will not interfere with or block healthy self-organizing processes, and will recognize the client as expert on his or her own experiencing. In addition, therapy emphasizes evoking maladaptive schemes in order to make them accessible to new experiencing. Different active methods are used to facilitate the resolution of different specific processing difficulties, always recognizing clients as having privileged access to their experience and as having the right to choose their direction, both in and outside therapy (Greenberg et al., 1993).

Realizing that emotion is a basic biologically adaptive system solves the problem of the scientific basis of the organismic valuing process (the "wisdom of the body"). This system operates by evaluating situations in relation to our well-being, thus serving as an organizing function for experience. This formative tendency works by means of a dynamic system process involving the dialectical coordination of many different elements to form inclusive, coherent syntheses of activated elements. This dialectical process works both through the medium of a basic biologically adaptive emotion system and via the human symbolic capacity and drive to make sense of things, in the service of goals to survive and to maintain and enhance the self. Thus, the organism is always producing a directional tendency informed by all its learning, experience, and interaction.

Further, human beings live and grow in the context of relationships and function by allocating attention to aspects of the organism-environment field. Attention operates under the control of emotion, interest, reason, conscious effort, and salient environmental stimuli. Attending leads to the creation of emotional meaning that organizes the person for action. At the point of symbolization, reasoning, aided by imagination, invents possible solutions and guides action. Goals, as well as plans for their attainment, are reflected on and evaluated, and the person decides on a course of action. Action on the chosen alternative then follows. This process involves emotion, reason, choice, and, above all, an ongoing process of dynamic synthesis of many elements including feelings, memories, beliefs, values, learnings, and anticipations, all constantly integrated as the self reorganizes itself to meet the environment.

## THE PRACTICE OF HUMANISTIC-EXPERIENTIAL PSYCHOTHERAPY

Having summarized humanistic-experiential theory, including a neo-humanistic, process-oriented reformulation, we now review the basic elements of humanistic-experiential therapy based on this reformulation.

## Goals

The general goals of treatment are to promote more fluid and integrative self-organizations. Therapy focuses on the whole person; that is, it is person-centered rather than problem or symptom focused, but within this holistic focus the underlying determinants of different types of self-dysfunction are also an important point of focus. Both a change in manner of functioning of the whole self and changes in particular problems in self-organization are viewed as important. For example, a client may be seen as changing a general manner of functioning by becoming both more empathic toward self and better able to symbolize bodily felt experience, while also resolving a specific problem such as unfinished business with a significant other. In addition to promoting self-acceptance and a strengthening of the self, treatment also aims at solving particular problems of self-organization that emerge in treatment. The problems that are focused on emerge in a collaborative fashion over the course of treatment. The goal of treatment is to increase awareness and promote self-reorganization by integrating disparate parts of the self. In addition, awareness of the processes that regulate what enters awareness and what does not is emphasized.

## The Therapeutic Relationship

In the most general terms, humanistic-experiential therapy is based on two basic principles: first, the importance of the relationship as a stubborn attempt by two human beings to meet each other in a genuine manner in order to provide help to one of them; and second, the consistent and gentle promotion of the deepening of the client's experience. The relationship is seen as both curative, in and of itself, and as facilitating of the main task of therapy, that is, the deepening of client experiencing. The relationship is built on a genuinely prizing empathic relation and on the therapist's guiding clients' experiential processing toward their internal experience. An active collaboration is created between client and therapist in which neither feels led, or simply followed, by the other. Instead, the ideal is an easy sense of coexploration. Although the relationship is collaborative, when disjunction or disagreement does occur, the therapist defers to the client as the expert on his or her own experience. Thus, therapist interventions are offered in a nonimposing, tentative manner, as conjectures, perspectives, "experiments," or offers, rather than as expert pronouncements or statements of truth. Interventions are construed as offering tasks on which clients who are active agents can work if they so choose. The relationship always takes precedence over the pursuit of a task. Although the therapist may be an expert on the possible therapeutic steps that might facilitate task resolution, it is made clear that the therapist is a

facilitator of client discovery, not a provider of "truth" or a psycho-educator. The role of a "life mentor" or an "internal exploration coach," however, is compatible with a humanistic perspective.

Experiential therapy thus recognizes both the power of the understanding relationship and the importance of different in-therapy tasks in promoting different types of therapeutic change. The quality of the bond between participants as well as collaboration on the tasks and goals of therapy are seen as essential in creating a good therapeutic alliance. The bond is warm, respectful, empathic, and validating, whereas the goals and tasks focus on increasing awareness, deepening experience, and resolving specific in-session emotional problems.

The relational bond is seen as involving three main healing ingredients. First is a more transcendent aspect, the human *presence* of the therapist, witnessing and validating the other's humanness; second is a set of more explicit facilitative *attitudes* that create a safe working environment; and the last is a set of specific interpersonal *behaviors* that facilitate growth and provide new interpersonal experience. Buber's (1957) I-thou relationship, involving such elements as presence, commitment to dialogue, and nonexploitiveness, and the Rogerian triad (Rogers, 1957) of empathy, positive regard, and congruence, describe the general nature of the relationship. Empathy is seen as a complex cognitive-affective process of imaginative entry into the world of the other and involves understanding the other, including the other's deeper experience. This process helps the client to feel connected, to regulate affect, and to construct new meaning.

A relational bond of this type is seen as both confirming the client as an authentic source of experience and as providing the optimal context for helping the client to attend to and become aware of prereflective experience and to communicate and explore it without fear of evaluation. The facilitative relationship, in addition to being curative in and of itself, also provides a safe environment for working on particular problems. Finally, not only does the relationship serve as a confirming environment and as a context for specific forms of intrapsychic work, but it is itself also a medium for specific corrective interpersonal experiences. Thus, certain forms of work on the relationship between client and therapist are also seen as mutative.

The experience of the therapist's genuine and unconditional empathic prizing is viewed as freeing the client from the "conditions of worth" that have been assimilated from early experiences with parents and others (Rogers, 1959) and as providing new interpersonal experience that disconfirms pathogenic beliefs about self and relationship. These relationship conditions of personal genuineness and empathic prizing enable clients to express and explore their moment-to-moment experience as they describe the issues, events, and frustrations in their daily lives. The therapist's empathic reflections of the most poignant feelings and other inner experiences enable the client to explore these inner experiences more deeply and to access aspects that have never before been fully expressed to others or even to themselves. The therapist's clear, nonjudgmental caring reduces clients' interpersonal anxiety and thus enables them to tolerate their own intrapersonal anxiety as they explore more and more deeply. Thus the relationship is not only a primary change agent in itself, but it also establishes a climate of inner awareness in which clients can engage in the exploratory process.

Buber's (1957) I-thou relationship has also been adopted as an important model of relating for humanists. In this view, the therapist relates with immediacy and is fully present to the other, letting the other in on his or her own inner experience. The genuine dialogue is mutual and nonexploitive, with both participants caring about each other's side of the dialogue. Buber sees the I-thou relationship as a genuine meeting between two people in which both openly respect the essential humanity of the other. Healing is viewed as occurring in the meeting (van Deurzen-Smith, 1996). In this sense the relationship is an active change agent. More recent interpretations of contact reflect the influence of Buber's philosophy on Gestalt therapy and include Yontef's (1998) concept of dialogue, a special form of contact in which people seek to be psychologically present to each other and to share what they experience as an end in itself. In experiential therapies this is considered to be the basis of effective therapy (Hycner & Jacobs, 1995).

Presence and contact are major principles of relating. Essentially, contact means that the therapist and client are fully present and engaged in a congruent fashion in whatever is occurring for the client in the moment. To the degree that the client's internal processes interrupt the his or her contact with the self or with the therapist, the therapist attempts to bring this to the client's awareness by inquiring about what happened at the point of interruption. Humanistic therapists believe that ultimately it is only in the context of an authentic relationship that the uniqueness of the individual can be truly recognized. Thus, the therapist strives for the genuine contact of a true encounter. This authenticity does not, however, mean overwhelming clients with self-disclosure or honesty without consideration for their needs or personal readiness.

## Deepening Awareness of Client Experiencing: The Key Therapeutic Task

In addition to the provision of a "healing" relationship, facilitating work on particular therapeutic tasks is also seen as a core ingredient of experiential therapy (Greenberg et al., 1993). The most central task of experiential therapy is that of deepening the client's experiencing. This involves focusing clients on their internal experiences, helping them to symbolize them in words and create new meaning. The therapist promotes different internal processes at different times to aid experiential processing. The processes facilitated range from symbolizing a bodily felt sense, to evoking memories, to allowing an intense feeling to form, to expressing feelings, to reflecting on experience to create new meaning. In addition, the client is encouraged to engage in such activities as psychodramatic enactments or exercises in imagination to help address particular emotional issues.

The humanistic-experiential approaches all attempt to promote client awareness and discovery, with the client viewed as the expert on his or her own experience. Drawing on existentialists such as Boss (1963) and Binswanger (1963), meaning is seen as resting in the phenomena (experiences) themselves. The view of the unconscious is not one of experience that is inaccessible to awareness other than through an external agent's understanding and interpretation of it. Even if an experience is not available to first view, it is potentially accessible to awareness. The humanist position does not claim that there is no unconscious processing of information but subscribes to a view of a cognitive rather than a dynamic unconscious. The key difference is that in a cognitive-affective schematic processing view, the unconscious does not motivate behavior but rather influences perception and construal. Much of that which is unconscious is simply not currently in awareness and can be made aware by attentional focusing.

Empathic reflection and exploration of the client's moment-by-moment inner awareness is viewed as an important way of both guiding attention and offering symbols that enable the client to discover for his or her experience. The therapist's reflections carry the message of empathic understanding, as well as the explicit or implicit expectation that the client will be able to correct this reflected understanding and will carry it further. The assumption is that the personal meaning of the client's experience is in the experience itself, and under optimal conditions clients can grasp these meanings for themselves. Thus, the therapist works consistently within the client's frame of reference, reflecting what it is like to be the person at that moment and making sure not to assume the position of being more expert than the client about the client's experience. The therapist conveys to clients that they are the best judges of their own realities. This is a very important active ingredient of therapy because the process provides an experience that is viewed as an antidote to one of the client's major psychological problems—not trusting their own experience because of learned conditions of worth.

Humanistic therapists integrate leading and following in their responses to clients. The therapist at times directs the process by influencing the client's depth of experiencing and manner of processing, always guiding the client toward his or her inner experience. Therapists create experiments in order to help clients to discover aspects of their experience, share hunches about what may be occurring, and teach clients about specific interruptive and avoidance processes. Therapists train clients to become aware both of their experience and of how they interfere with their experience, directing them to attend to sensations, nonverbal expressions, and interruptive and avoidant processes (Sachse, 1996; Lietaer, Rombauts, & Van Balen, 1990; Polster & Polster, 1973).

Humanists use a combination of discovery, interpretation, and confrontation. They might challenge and interpret obstacles to choice and action. Existential therapists, for example, view the anxiety aroused by awareness of the "ultimate concerns" such as death, freedom, isolation, and meaninglessness as leading to defense mechanisms such as repression, distortion, or avoidance. It is these kinds of avoidances that are often directly challenged by the therapist. Thus, therapists may at times confront blocks or avoidances; however, the primary emphasis is on supporting clients in discovering for themselves what it is that they are experiencing, especially what they feel and need. The ultimate belief is that clients must discover the truth for themselves from their own internal experiences and that therapists cannot provide that truth or insight.

Awareness is regarded as central to change. Therapists give feedback in the form of observations about clients' current process, particularly on nonverbal aspects of client expression, and thus, to some degree, therapists view the client as not having immediate access to all experience without help. Conflicts between aspects of experience are seen as interfering with functioning and awareness, and a confrontation between these different aspects of experience, if suitably facilitated, is seen as important in the therapeutic process.

With regard to the complex issue of the possibility of knowing oneself, although humanists would not deny the constructed nature of the creation of meaning, they believe that there is an experiential reality for each person and that awareness of this reality can be progressively approximated. Although there may be no one single truth that can be attained, there will be many perspectives that would not fit the experiential data, and only a few that will provide a good fit. People know their worlds through their bodily felt experiences (Gendlin, 1962; Johnson, 1987). Once they accurately symbolize their bodily experience (e.g., that they feel tense or afraid or angry), they can construct a variety of meanings from this. But symbolizing tension as calmness, the experience of fear as grief, or anger as joy would be inherently inaccurate and distorting. People are seen as being able to determine the right paths for themselves from an intensive process of discovery,

leading to an inner sense of certitude. Thus, although the person is always constructing the meaning of the experience by a synthesizing process, the elements of the synthesis have an experiential validity and can be symbolized more or less accurately.

Therapists thus work to enable clients to turn inward and get in touch with their own present organismic experience and to value it as a trustworthy guide. The emphasis is on process rather than on choosing goals, and therapy is not viewed primarily as a struggle against resistance, but as something that can be achieved under the right conditions. The therapeutic conditions of empathy, unconditional prizing, and genuineness are viewed by many as being sufficient to release and foster the actualizing tendency. The therapist is seen as needing to be very active in fostering inward experiential search, but not in judging what is best for this person.

Growth becomes possible when people fully identify with themselves as growing, changing organisms and clearly discriminate their feelings and needs. Effective self-regulation depends on discriminating feelings and needs by means of sensory awareness. This leads to awareness of intuitive appraisals of either what is good for the person and should be assimilated or of what is bad and should be rejected. The assumption is that the healthy organism "knows" what is good for it—this is organismic wisdom. This wisdom works by a spontaneous emergence of needs to guide action. Life is the process of a need arising and being satisfied and another need emerging and being satisfied.

The graded experiment was introduced in Gestalt therapy as an addition to the predominant interventions of the time, namely interpretation, reflection, or goal setting. This experimental method drew from psychodrama the use of enactment and set up in-session tasks for clients, not necessarily to be completed, but to be tried out to discover something. Experimenting in the session with tasks such as two-chair work and dream work was emphasized, but many other experiments were created in the moment to help clients intensify and embody their experiences. Creative experiments were produced to meet the client's situation. Experiments were created such as asking the client to express resentment to an imagined other, to assert or disclose something intimate to the therapist, to curl up into a ball, to express a desire in order to make it more vivid, or to move freely and fluidly like water. The client's experience and expression were then analyzed for what prevented or interrupted completion of these experiments. The experimental method focuses on bringing peoples' difficulties with task completion to the surface. Therapists ask clients to become aware of and experience the interruptive processes that prevent their feelings or needs from being expressed or acted upon. In this manner, clients are seen as gaining insight into their own experience by discovery rather than interpretation.

Creative use of imagery and experiment involve "try this," followed by "what do you experience now?" In addition to the experiment, Gestalt therapists used a set of key questions designed to get at particular aspects of clients' functioning and to promote creative adjustment to the environment. Key questions oriented at experience include the following: What are you aware of? What do you experience? What do you need? and What do you want or want to do? Finally, identity-related questions of the form "Who are you?" or "What do you want to be?" were also used at appropriate times.

With more fragile clients who have not developed a strong sense of self or boundary between self and other, the development of awareness was seen as more of a long-term objective. Promotion of experience and asking these clients feeling-oriented questions was seen as pointless, as these clients had yet to develop an awareness of their internal worlds. With these clients, the relationship was seen as the therapeutic point of departure. Thus, more fragile clients need a more relational form of work, with the focus on the process of contact with the therapist.

Much therapeutic work thus involved helping people become more aware of sensation or experience. Blocking of arousal or excitement results from dampening or disavowal of emotional experience. Therapeutic work at times may focus on increasing awareness of muscular constriction and becoming aware of one's other methods of suppressing emotional experience. At other times, the focus is on promoting awareness of and action to satisfy organismic needs that have been interrupted by introjected attitudes and values that create a split between wants and shoulds. Two-chair dialogues often are used at this point to resolve the split. Interruption can also occur at the completion stage when the person does not allow him- or herself to experience the satisfaction of the need. At this stage, awareness work is again implemented in order to help the person become aware of the experience of satisfaction and how he or she may be preventing it. Ultimately, awareness is seen as leading to choice; with enough awareness, the person can then make the most adaptive choices.

Gestalt therapists, such as Polster and Polster (1973), give work with dreams a central place in Gestalt therapy. A number of techniques are used to give dream work immediacy. The client is asked to start by telling the dream as if it is occurring in the present, which helps the dreamer relate more directly to the dream's content. The client may also be asked to act out the dream, to identify with a figure or a mood and narrate his or her dream experiences from a subjective perspective.

Frankl (1969) writes about the two main logotherapeutic techniques. These are dereflection and paradoxical intention. Dereflection attempts to remove the "demand quality" from future events so that the person can live more spontaneously.

The technique of dereflection basically involves telling a person to stop focusing on him- or herself and to look for meaning in the outside world (Yalom, 1980). Often helpful for phobias, paradoxical intention encourages the client to wish for the very thing that he or she fears. Paradoxical intention uses the logotherapeutic principle that goals that are focused on become difficult to achieve. For example, if individuals try to gain fame and wealth, they are likely to fail. However, if people pursue something that is meaningful to them, fame and wealth may follow. Similarly, if individuals fear public speaking because they know that they will sweat, they are encouraged paradoxically to attend to the sweating and to try to force as much sweat as possible. In this way, the client's *anticipatory anxiety* can be overcome. In anticipatory anxiety, a client avoids a fearful stimulus that creates the possibility that that event will occur. This is because the feared stimulus is never engaged, but always feared, thus creating a vicious cycle. By paradoxically attending to the experience of the feared stimulus, the myth of its danger dissipates.

## Experiential Therapy as Process Theory

An important distinguishing characteristic of experiential therapy is that it offers a process theory of how to facilitate knowledge by acquaintance, rather than a content theory of personality or psychopathology. A process theory of this type specifies both the moment-by-moment steps in the client's process of change and the therapist's interventions that will facilitate these steps. The emphasis in each step always is on how to promote the direct sensing of what is concretely felt in the moment to create new meaning.

Experiential theorists and researchers have also specified patterned sequences of change processes that occur in sessions, sequences such as attending to bodily felt sensation, and symbolizing this in words, or arousing emotion followed by accessing needs. These sequence models can be used to facilitate client work in therapy sessions. The therapist is seen as an expert in the use of methods that promote experiencing and facilitate new steps rather than as an expert on what people are experiencing.

There is an explicit assumption that within each individual there is a flow of experiencing to which the person can refer in order to be informed about the personal meaning of particular experiences. The main principle of the experiential method is to have people check whatever is said or done against their own concretely felt experiences. Change is seen as emerging from a growing awareness of previously unsymbolized experience and the bringing of this experience into dialectical interaction with words or symbols and other aspects of experience to create new meaning.

The key to experiential therapy is to have clients experience content in a new way so that this new experience will produce a change in the way that they view themselves, others, and the world. Experiential therapy thus adds the emphasis that symbols, schemes, and even behavior must interact with the body-based, experiential level of existence in order to produce change. It thus offers a process theory of how body and symbol interact, as well as a set of methods for promoting this process.

Experiential therapy theorists have specified patterned sequences of change processes and events, the explicit connections of which are spelled out by their process theories of particular types of change. Three such characteristic sequences are described here. One sequence offered by Gendlin (1996) describes a series of three fundamental client change processes: (a) The client focuses on a directly felt meaning. (b) The client allows feelings, words, and pictures to arise from this inward focusing and attends to the generated feeling. (c) The client receives a new felt meaning that emerges from the ensuing shift in body experience. Another experiential sequence (Mahrer, 1989) consists of four client basic change processes: (a) The client attains a level of strong feeling. (b) The client welcomes and appreciates the accessed inner experiencing. (c) The client becomes (identifies with) the inner experiencing in the context of earlier life scenes. (d) The client becomes and behaves according to the inner experiencing in the context of imminent future life scenes.

A third sequence, specified by Greenberg and Paivio (1997), involves a series of six basic change processes: (a) The client experiences the problematic bad feelings in the session. (b) The client accesses, allows, and receives deeper core emotions and needs in the session. (c) The client and therapist together explore whether the core emotion is adaptive or maladaptive. (d) If judged to be adaptive, the core feelings are used as a guide; if judged to be maladaptive, alternate adaptive emotions and needs are accessed. (e) Any core maladaptive emotions and associated beliefs are challenged from within the client by the newly accessed adaptive emotions and needs. (f) New meaning is created based on the new experience that emerges from the dialectical interaction of adaptive and maladaptive parts of self.

In these processes the therapist is seen as an expert on how to facilitate new steps in the client's experiencing, rather than as an expert on the content of the client's experience. Therapists thus avoid interpretations of the content of clients' experiences that tell the client why they do things and that are theory-driven rather than experience-near. Responses that are conceptual or explanatory, or are expressed as fact, or that convey the message that truth comes from the therapists' professional knowledge, are avoided in favor of phenomenologically refined exploration of the client's experiencing. Experiential therapy thus attempts to eliminate any interpretations that are based on the therapist's theory of how people are, or should be, or that attempt to reveal hidden "truths."

Instead, the experiential approach places great emphasis on, and holds great respect for, what the client experiences and pays special attention to what the client experiences in the session with the therapist. Experiential therapy involves consistent listening from within the client's frame of reference. Sustained empathic inquiry is a central part of practice. However, although this empathic emphasis is necessary for good psychotherapy, it is not necessarily sufficient for the best psychotherapy. The most effective psychotherapy also requires therapist practices of a technical nature, such as experiential focusing and within-session experimentation (Gendlin, 1996; Perls et al., 1951). Diagnostic understanding of the individual, as well as understanding of the social, cultural, and institutional forces affecting the individual, is also required.

Notwithstanding the fact that what the client experiences is the indispensable essence of psychotherapy, and that it is imperative that this be the subject of respectful ongoing inquiry by therapist and client, what the client does not experience is also an indispensable and critical component of what happens in therapy. Important factors that are current outside the client's conscious awareness may also need to be explored. In experiential therapy there is a special emphasis on bringing into awareness the processes that regulate this process of awareness-unawareness (Polster & Polster, 1973; Yontef, 1993). This work is codirected by therapist and client and is not based on any alleged higher truth of the therapist. It is based on a joint empathic exploration that may include in-session process observation, experimentation, and dialogue.

## Basic Principles of Practice

Greenberg et al. (1993) laid out six principles describing the balance between relationship and work in experiential therapies. These guiding principles are themselves divided evenly between relationship and task facilitation elements, with the relationship principles coming first and ultimately receiving priority over the task facilitation principles.

**Relationship Principles.** The relationship principles involve facilitation of shared engagement in a relationship that is both secure and focused enough to encourage the client to express and explore his or her key personal difficulties and emotional pain. These involve the following:

1. *Empathic attunement to the client's subjective experiencing.* Throughout, the therapist tries to enter the world of

the other imaginatively in order to make contact with and maintain an understanding of the client's internal experience as it evolves from moment to moment (Bohart & Greenberg, 1997).

2. *Creating a therapeutic bond.* The therapist seeks to develop a strong therapeutic bond with the client, by conveying understanding and empathy, acceptance and prizing, and presence and genuineness. The therapist's presence as an authentic and, where appropriate, transparent human being encourages client openness and risk taking and helps to break down the client's sense of isolation (May & Yalom, 1989). Authenticity and transparency also support the therapist's empathic attunement and prizing, making them believable for the client. Genuineness refers to facilitative, disciplined, nonexploitive transparency, based on the therapist's accurate self-awareness and an intention to help rather than to obtain personal gratification or simply to express self (Greenberg & Geller, 2001).

3. *Facilitating task collaboration.* An effective therapeutic relationship also entails involvement by both client and therapist in the overall treatment goals, immediate within-session tasks, and specific therapeutic activities to be carried out in therapy (Bordin, 1979).

**Task Principles.** The other three principles are based on the general assumption that human beings are active, purposeful organisms, with an innate need for exploration and mastery of their environments. These principles are expressed in the therapist's attempts to help the client resolve internal, emotion-related problems through work on personal goals and within-session tasks.

1. *Facilitate optimal client experiential processing.* Based on the recognition that optimal client in-session activities vary between and within therapeutic tasks, the therapist helps the client to work in different ways at different times (Leijssen, 1998).

2. *Facilitate client completion of key therapeutic tasks.* The therapist begins by helping the client to develop clear treatment foci and then tracks the client's current task within each session. Typically, the therapist gently persists in helping the client stay with key therapeutic tasks rather than wandering off into material that does not relate to the theme of the task.

3. *Foster client growth and self-determination.* The therapist supports the client's potential and motivation for self-determination, mature interdependence, mastery, and self-development by listening carefully for, helping the client explore, and validating the "growing edges" of new client experience.

## Therapist Experiential Response Modes

In carrying out the six treatment principles, therapists use a number of specific speech acts or response modes to help clients (cf. Greenberg et al., 1993). Most of what the therapist does in experiential therapy involves empathic understanding, empathic exploration, process directing, and experiential presence responses (Elliott, 1999; Greenberg et al., 1993). These basic building blocks comprise the vast majority of what the therapist does in this treatment (Davis, 1995).

### *Empathic Understanding Responses*

Empathic reflection seeks to communicate understanding of the client's message and includes simple reflections and related responses (uh-huh's). In addition to expressing the therapist's empathic attunement, such responses commonly serve to enhance the client-therapist relationship, to offer prizing and support to the client (through understanding), and to underline issues as they emerge within therapeutic tasks. For example, a client who is talking about her shattered security after a trauma says,

C: I mean that's the biggest grief, that's my biggest sadness, to lose my sense of confidence in everything.

In response, the therapist reflected with,

T: That's what you grieve for, the loss of safety, of a sense of being able to trust that things will be OK.

### *Empathic Exploration Responses*

The most characteristic therapist response in experiential therapy is empathic exploration. These simultaneously communicate understanding and help clients move toward the unclear or emerging edges of their experience. Empathic exploration responses take a number of different forms, including evocative and leading-edge reflections, exploratory questions, and empathic conjectures. Following is a brief excerpt with the same client illustrating first an evocative empathic exploratory response followed by a response that focuses on the leading edge of the client's experience.

C: I just want enough of who I used to be, so that I again could live like a human being.

T: "I don't feel like a human being right now. Maybe more like a stalked animal?"

C: Just like a paranoid little girl, ya know. I just need something of what I had.

T: It's like I need what I had—I need some of the courage and strength of what I was before it all happened.

**C:** Yeah. Just to feel able to face things again.

A little later, the therapist asks an *exploratory question:*

> **T:** What's it like inside? What do you feel now in this part?
> **C:** Happy. [laughs softly]

### Process Directives

These interventions are directive in process rather than in content. There are a variety of ways of being process directive, but telling the client what to do to solve problems outside the therapy session is inconsistent with the principle of client self-determination. However, the therapist can suggest in a nonimposing way that the client try engaging in particular *in-session* activities. This includes experiential teaching (giving orienting information, treatment rationales), attention suggestions (directives to attend to immediate experience), task structuring (to help the client enter into therapeutic tasks), action suggestions (directives to do or try something in the session), and task focusing (used to help the client "stay with" or "come back to" a therapeutic task after a sidetrack). These are illustrated by this sample of process directives used to help the same client grieve and reaccess her "lost strong self":

> **T:** Can you stay with that hurt and sadness for a minute, and just feel what that's about and what that's like? [Attention suggestion about her discouragement at not overcoming her fears.]
> **T:** One way to try to work with the grief is to put that part of you that you've lost in the chair and talk to her. [Suggesting a potentially useful therapeutic task.]

Once the task is in process the therapist directs the process:

> **T:** Can you go over and *be* in the strong part?
> **C:** I would but I wouldn't know how.
> **T:** Tell her, "I'd like you to have that strength."
> **C:** I'd like you to have my strength.
> **T:** What's that feel like?
> **C:** Like a—like a mom.

*Experiential homework* is an additional kind of process directive, as in the following example involving a client who suffers from sudden inexplicable episodes of suicidal feelings:

> **T:** During the next week, it might be useful for you to try to pay attention to what is going on when you have these "black funnel" experiences and see if you can remember exactly what is going through your mind right before them.

### Experiential Presence

Therapist empathic attunement, prizing, transparency, and collaboration—attitudes involved in fostering the therapeutic relationship—are communicated primarily through the therapist's "presence" or manner of being with the client. The exact configuration of therapist paralinguistic and nonverbal behaviors, including silence, vocal quality, and appropriate posture and expression, is difficult to describe. There is, however, an easily recognized, distinctive style. For example, the therapist typically uses a gentle, prizing voice (and sometimes humor) to deliver the process directives just described, while empathic exploration responses often have a tentative, pondering quality intended to support client experiential search. Presence is also indicated by direct eye contact at moments of connection between client and therapist. It is important to recognize that the therapist cannot fake these behaviors, which must come naturally from the therapist's genuine experience of being attuned, caring, and joining with the client in shared, emotionally involving therapeutic work.

Therapist *process* and *personal disclosure* responses are commonly used forms of experiential presence. Here the therapist uses a personal disclosure to help the client explore her feelings:

> **C:** I just wish I could stop that part of me from feeling so scared.
> **T:** I understand; it's hard to feel so scared. But I feel sad for how alone that frightened little girl in you must feel.

### Nonexperiential Responses

Although therapist responses such as interpretation, extratherapy advisement, and reassurance are typically avoided or minimized, they may at times be useful or even necessary. For example, they may be needed for clinical management of crises, suicidality, and impulsiveness or for dealing with other important practical issues. The important thing is for the therapist to say them briefly and from his or her perspective.

## Experiential Tasks

As noted earlier, experiential therapy uses a variety of different sequential process experiential tasks, drawn from client-centered, Gestalt, and existential therapy traditions. These tasks all include three elements: a *marker* of a problem state that signals the client's readiness to work on a particular issue or experiential task, a *task performance* sequence of therapist and client task-relevant actions, and a desired *resolution* or end state. It is useful to divide experiential tasks into three major groupings:

1. Experiential search tasks generally emphasize exploration of inner experiencing, usually ending with some form of new symbolic representation.
2. Active expression tasks are most distinctive for promoting client enactment of experiences or aspects of self in order to heighten and access underlying emotion schemes.
3. Interpersonal contact tasks center around genuine person-to-person contact between client and therapist.

*Experiential search tasks* are those in which clients present some form of problematic experience that requires them to examine closely and put into words painful or puzzling aspects of inner experience. Two experiential search tasks are described here.

First, *focusing* has been described by Gendlin (1984, 1996) as a general task for working with client experiencing, and, in particular, with unclear felt sense markers. Or the client may be *distancing* emotionally in the session, in the form of speaking in an intellectual or externalizing manner, talking around in circles without getting to what is important to him or her. When this occurs, the therapist can gently intervene:

T: I wonder, as you are talking, what are you experiencing?
C: I'm not sure. I feel like I'm just going on talking and not really saying anything.
T: I wonder if we could try something here? [Client nods.] Can you take a minute, maybe slow down . . . and close your eyes, and look inside, to the part of you where you feel your feelings. . . . And ask yourself, "What's going on with me right now?" . . . See what comes to you . . . Don't force it; just let it come . . . and tell me what comes to you. . . .

Resolution involves symbolizing a felt sense, accompanied by an experienced sense of easing or relief and a sense of direction for carrying this "felt shift" into life outside the therapy session.

Second, *systematic evocative unfolding* is used for *problematic reaction points,* or instances in which the client is puzzled by an overreaction to a specific situation (Greenberg et al., 1993).

When the client presents a problematic reaction point, the therapist suggests that the client take him or her through the puzzling episode, including what led up to it and exactly what it was to which the client reacted. The therapist helps the client alternately explore both the perceived situation and the inner emotional reaction in the situation. As the client imaginally reenters the situation, he or she commonly reexperiences the reaction while the therapist begins by encouraging

the client in an experiential search for the exact instant of the reaction and its trigger. As with the other tasks, resolution is a matter of degree; at a minimum, resolution involves reaching an understanding of the reason for the puzzling reaction; this is referred to as a *meaning bridge*. Nevertheless, the meaning bridge is usually just the beginning of a self-reflection process in which the client examines and symbolizes important self-related emotion schemes and explores alternative ways of viewing self. Full resolution involves a clear shift in view of self, together with a sense of empowerment to make life changes consistent with the new view of self.

The next set of tasks, *active expression tasks,* come out of Gestalt and psychodrama traditions and ask the client to enact aspects of self or others in order to evoke and access underlying emotion schemes. They are also used for helping clients access disowned or externally attributed aspects of self, especially anger; and they are particularly useful to help clients change how they act toward themselves (e.g., moving from self-attacking to self-supporting). The major empirically investigated active expression tasks have been extensively described elsewhere (Rice & Greenberg, 1984; Greenberg et al., 1993). Note that these active, evocative tasks generally require a stronger therapeutic alliance and thus are rarely attempted before session three.

*Two-chair dialogues* are used when the client presents some form of conflict split marker. While some conflicts are easily recognized, others are not:

- *Decisional conflict:* client feels torn between two alternative courses of action (e.g., whether to end a relationship).
- *Self-evaluation split:* client criticizes self; this is seen as a conflict between critic and self aspects of the person.
- *Attribution split:* client describes an overreaction to a perceived critical or controlling other person or situation; this is understood as a conflict between the self aspect and the client's own critical aspect, projected onto the other person.

For obvious reasons, traumatized, anxious, and depressed clients often present self-evaluation splits. Frequently, the internal critical or threatening process is attributed to the environment and experienced as coming back at the self. For example, anxiety splits often involve a fear-inducing situation being infused with attributed meaning to which the client overreacts with the weak self (Elliott, Davis, & Slatick, 1998). This type of split can present as "X (e.g., driving on the freeway) makes me afraid." A catastrophizing critic is often central in this experience, and as the person enacts the terrorizing road, threatening the self, the attributed catastrophizing-protective part of the self is reowned. The client then becomes an agent, enacting the warning-protective aspect of self that tries to prevent future harm by continually scaring the other aspect of the self, with the unintended consequence of making it feel weak and vulnerable.

The therapist initiates the two-chair dialogue by suggesting that the client move back and forth between two chairs, each representing one self-aspect, in order to enact the internal conversation between the two parts. (Examples of therapist process directive responses used to set up and maintain this task were given earlier in the presentation of process directing responses.) In the case of an attributional split, the client is asked to enact the other or external situation. For example, a traumatized client with a fear of driving on the freeway can be asked to "be" the freeway and "show how you scare her." This gives the client the opportunity to identify with and reown the powerful, frightening part of the self. This reowning would constitute a partial resolution, whereas a full resolution would require some kind of mutual understanding and accommodation between the fearful self and the fear-inducing aspect. The fearful self would express its primary fear and access the core emotion scheme and needs, and the fear-inducing critic self would soften its stance toward the self aspect.

*Two-chair enactments* for self-interruptions are relevant for addressing immediate within-session episodes of emotional avoidance or for distancing indicative self-interruption. Depressed, anxious, and traumatized clients often suffer from an underlying emotional processing split between emotional-experiencing and intellectual-distancing aspects of self. These processing splits result in emotional blocking or stuckness and often manifest in the form of secondary reactive emotions such as hopelessness or resignation. Self-interruptions are most readily recognized when the client begins to feel something (e.g., anger) in the session, then stops him- or herself, often with some kind of nonverbal action (e.g., squeezing back tears) or reported physical sensation (e.g., headache). However, self-interruptions are also indicated by statements of resignation, numbness, stuckness, or reports of feeling weighted down, all typical of clinical depression.

Asking the client to enact the process of self-interruption facilitates resolution of this task. In a two-chair enactment the therapist directs the client's attention to the interruption (the stuck or blocked state) and then suggests the experiment by asking him or her to "show how you stop (the client) from feeling (whatever was interrupted)." The intervention helps the client bring the automatic avoiding aspect of self into awareness and under deliberate control; this in turn helps the client become aware of the previously interrupted emotion so that it can be expressed in an appropriate, adaptive manner. Minimal resolution involves expression of the interrupted emotion, and more complete resolution requires expression of underlying needs and self-empowerment.

*Empty chair work* is based specifically on the assumption, discussed earlier, that primary adaptive emotions (e.g., sadness at loss, anger at violation) need to be fully expressed; to access their adaptive actions and to be processed more completely. Thus, this task is aimed at helping clients resolve lingering bad feelings (usually sadness and anger) toward developmentally significant others (most commonly parents). The marker, referred to as *unfinished business,* involves partial expression of the bad feelings, often in the form of complaining or blaming; this indicates that the client is blocked from fully expressing the feelings.

Empty chair work has been used extensively by therapists working with individuals who were abused or maltreated as children (e.g., Briere, 1989). Research by Paivio (1997; see also Paivio & Greenberg, 1995) supports its effectiveness for helping the client resolve unfinished emotional business. There is, however, some controversy about the therapeutic value of putting the perpetrator in the empty chair (Briere, 1989), and, in any case, the method appears to be less useful in single victimizations by strangers. Nevertheless, victimization experiences almost always involve significant others who are perceived by the person as having failed to provide adequate protection during and after the trauma (Elliott et al., 1998). Unfinished business markers also appear to be common in depressed clients as well, especially those whose depression is characterized by interpersonal loss issues.

Thus, in the presence of a strong therapeutic alliance and the unfinished business marker, the therapist suggests that the client imagine the other in the empty chair and express any previously unexpressed feelings toward him or her. The therapist may also suggest that the client take the role of the other and speak to the self. Resolution consists, at a minimum, of expression of unmet needs to the other; full resolution requires restructuring of unmet needs and a shift toward a more positive view of self and a more differentiated view of the other.

Empty chair work is highly evocative and emotionally arousing. If the client is already in a strong emotional state, he or she is likely to feel overwhelmed even by the suggestion to speak to the other in the empty chair. In any of these more expressive tasks, if emotional arousal is high to start with, it is preferable to work with the creation of meaning than to encourage further arousal because this helps the client to symbolize and contain painful emotion (Clarke, 1993). In general, in empty chair work the therapist needs to maintain constant empathic attunement to the client's level of emotional arousal and to whether the client feels safe enough with the therapist to undertake this task.

*Interpersonal contact tasks* constitute the final set of experiential tasks we discuss. These tasks return to the relational strand of the therapy tradition and include three kinds of genuine person-to-person contact between client and therapist, in which change is believed to emerge directly from a therapeutic relationship characterized by empathic attunement, prizing, genuineness and collaboration. These tasks take priority over all others.

*Empathic affirmation* is offered when clients present a *vulnerability marker,* indicating the emergence of general, self-related emotional pain or shame. The client reluctantly confesses to the therapist, sometimes for the first time, that he or she is struggling with powerful feelings of personal shame, unworthiness, vulnerability, despair, or hopelessness. The sense is that the client is experiencing a pervasive, painful, shameful feeling and has run out of resources. Vulnerability markers are relatively common in work with traumatized clients (Elliott et al., 1996) and are also found in depression. When vulnerability emerges in the course of working on some other task, it takes priority.

In emotional vulnerability, the client's need is to face and admit to another person an intense, feared aspect of self that had been previously kept hidden. The therapist's task is to offer a nonintrusive empathic presence, accepting and prizing whatever the client is experiencing, and allowing the client to descend into his or her pain, despair, or humiliation as far as he or she cares to go. The therapist does not push for inner exploration and indeed does not try to "do" anything with the client's experience, except to understand and accept it. When the therapist follows and affirms the client's experience in this way, it helps to heighten the vulnerability to the point where the client "hits bottom" before beginning spontaneously to turn back toward hope. It is very important for the therapist to maintain the faith that the client's innate growth tendencies will enable him or her to come back up after hitting bottom. Resolution consists of enhanced client self-acceptance and wholeness, together with decreased sense of isolation and increased self-direction.

*Alliance dialogue* takes place when the client expresses some form of complaint or difficulty with the treatment, as in the following examples (cf. Safran, Crocker, McMain, & Murray, 1990):

- I feel stuck, like I'm not progressing anymore, or maybe even going backward.
- There you go, exaggerating again.
- I know you're not supposed to give advice, but I really think I need someone to tell me what to do about these fear attacks I keep having.

Although such alliance difficulties are relatively rare in empathic experiential therapies because of the empathic attunement of the therapist, they nevertheless occur and warrant immediate attention and the suspension of any other

therapeutic tasks. Furthermore, therapeutic errors, empathic failures, and mismatches between client expectations and treatment are inevitable in any therapy. These result in disappointment and sometimes anger in the client. In addition, this task is particularly relevant to work with clients who have extensive or severe histories of abuse or other forms of victimization; such persons routinely perceive the therapist as just another potential victimizer. It is therefore very important that therapists listen carefully for and respond to *therapy complaint markers.*

The therapist begins alliance dialogue work by offering a solid empathic reflection of the potential difficulty, trying to capture it as accurately and thoroughly as possible. The therapist suggests to the client that it is important to discuss the difficulty in order to understand what is going on, including what the therapist may be doing to bring about the problem. The difficulty is presented as a shared responsibility for client and therapist to work on together. The therapist models and fosters this process by genuinely considering and disclosing his or her own possible role. In this way, the client is encouraged to examine his or her own part in the difficulty as well, and the client and therapist explore what is at stake for the client in the difficulty, as well as how it might be resolved between them. Resolution consists, at minimum, of client and therapist together arriving at an understanding of the sources of the problem; full resolution entails genuine client satisfaction with the outcome of the dialogue, along with renewed enthusiasm for the therapy.

*Experiential interactional work* involves focusing with high immediacy on what is occurring in the interaction between client and therapist, under the assumption that there is a link between a person's problems and the person's interactional style with the therapist (van Kessel & Lietaer, 1998).

The marker here is internal to the therapist in that he or she begins to feel some difficulty or distress in the interpersonal interaction with the client. The therapist then focuses on this internal experience in order to discern what interactional pull is being responded to. This occurs when the client's typical style of communication calls for a response from the therapist such as humor, caretaking, or humiliation. Through a process of disciplined genuineness, the therapist needs to become clear on what his or her internal response is. The intervention involves metacommunicating about the internal reaction, elucidating the interactional pattern and providing a new experience in the relationship to help change the pattern (Kiesler, 1996; Lietaer, 1993; Rennie, 1998).

Although this task is psychodynamically derived, the experiential approach to this situation of working through transference patterns emphasizes the importance of the here-and-now interactional process with the client. This task is only when the therapist notices that a recurrent problematic interaction is currently occurring and is able to avoid being caught up in the automatic complementary response. This allows the therapist to offer his or her current, genuine response in the relationship, giving the client the experience of being known and engaged in a vital, searching human relationship. Of great importance in an experiential approach to this task is that it is engaged in only when currently relevant. Thus, rather than this being the main avenue of treatment, or the relationship being structured to evoke the pattern, the problematic interactional pattern is responded to only when it keeps reappearing overtly as an issue in the relationship and is acting as a block to the experiencing process. In addition, in experiential interaction work, the emphasis is on a new, corrective emotional experience emerging within the relationship rather than on understanding the pattern or its psychogenetic origins.

Resolution of this task involves clients' experiencing themselves in new ways and being able to move forward in the session and experience and relate to the therapist in a new way. Therapist self-reflection, presence, and genuineness are vital here. The therapist must be able to share his or her experience of the interaction in a facilitative way so that the client truly experiences a moment of healing in the encounter with the therapist.

For example, rather than responding to repeated client ridicule with annoyance, the therapist uses his or her annoyance as a marker for a problematic client interactional style; he or she then turns attention inward, focuses, and identifies a sense of embarrassment and helplessness underneath the annoyance. Instead of self-disclosing the annoyance, the therapist shares the embarrassment and helplessness, communicating both the genuine response and the desire to help the client examine the problematic interaction process. Together, client and therapist each disclose their reactions to the other, including their hopes and fears, and also exploring what has happened between them as an instance of a general way in which the client relates to other people.

## Case Formulation

Historically, humanistic therapists have resisted the notion of case formulation, as traditional diagnosis and formulation were seen as potentially creating an imbalance of power and setting the therapist up to play the role of the expert. Case formulation, however, has been redefined in neo-humanistic terms as process diagnosis (Goldman & Greenberg, 1997). From this perspective, case formulation occurs within an egalitarian relationship and ultimately communicates that clients are expert on their own experience and that the therapeutic process is coconstructive. Process-oriented case formulation gives priority to the person's experience in the moment. Therapists do not

conduct a factual history taking conducted prior to or at the onset of therapy because such information is often incomplete and lacking the proper context to establish its true significance in the person's life. Material that emerges later within a safe relationship and in a vivid emotional context will reveal whether the material is important and what aspects of it are of emotional significance.

Case formulation in this approach thus involves an unfolding, coconstructive process of establishing a focus on the key components of the presenting problems. Formulation emphasizes making process diagnoses of current in-session states and exploring these until a clear focus on underlying determinants emerge through the exploratory process. Formulation emerges from the dialogue and is a shared construction involving deeper understandings of the problem and goals of treatment. In developing a case formulation, the therapist focuses first on salient poignant feelings and meanings and notices the client's initial manner of cognitive-affective processing and what will be needed to help the client focus internally. Then, working together, client and therapist develop a shared understanding of the main emotional problems and tasks and, finally, of the client's emerging foci and themes.

For example, a therapist listening to a depressed man who has recently failed to get a promotion will first hear how poignant is his sense of hopelessness and loss. The client's difficulty in focusing on his internal experience acts as an indicator that the therapist will need to direct attention toward the client's bodily felt experience in order to access this information. As they develop an alliance, the therapist may begin to hear how much the client's divorce three years prior is affecting him now. Over time, the therapist might notice that the client continues to return to that topic, describing the pain of the loss and the fear of continuing loss. Through their ongoing process, client and therapist may come to understand that unresolved anger and sadness about the divorce are affecting the way in which the client is navigating through current relationships and daily life. What begins to emerge out of the process is a need to focus on the loss around the divorce, the necessary grieving the client has not done, and the meaning that the divorce has for the client. After two or three sessions, the therapist would then suggest an unfinished business dialogue task with the ex-spouse in an empty chair. The therapist's decision to initiate that dialogue would emerge from the process. The meaning of the recent loss for the client would become apparent only when the client feels safe enough to disclose it, and only then could the therapist absorb the full gravity of it. The loss, for example, may connect to unresolved losses earlier in the person's life or to a pervasive theme of failure. It is only through material that emerges out of the safety of the relationship (bond) and the exploratory process that both come to understand the significance of the loss and the importance of resolving it (goal) and to know the appropriate tasks that will best facilitate working it through (task alliance).

## Differential Treatment

One of the major developments in practice in humanistic-experiential approaches has been the move toward specification of differential treatments for different disorders and problems. A number of books have appeared on client-centered therapy in Europe, mainly in Dutch and German, emphasizing its application to different problems and disorders (Eckert, Höger, & Linster, 1997; Finke, 1994; Lietaer & Van Kalmthout, 1995; Sachse, 1996; Swildens, 1997). For example, Eckert and Biermann-Ratjen (1998) studied client-centered treatment of clients with borderline processes, and Teusch studied client-centered treatment of clients with anxiety disorders (Teusch & Boehme, 1999). In North America, Warner (1998) focused on working with the fragile self, and Prouty (1994) worked on the experiential treatment of clients with schizophrenic and related psychotic processes. Similarly, Gestalt therapists have begun to look at disturbances of awareness and psychological contact that occur in the personality disorders (Delisle, 1991), as well as at the importance of the differential application of a variety of aspects of Gestalt therapy to different types of clients. Practice has thus shifted from a "one treatment fits all" approach to the differential application of aspects of the different experiential approaches to different disorders (Greenberg, Watson, & Lietaer, 1998). Most notable are the development of special methods for working with hallucinations (Prouty & Pietrzak, 1988), trauma and childhood maltreatment (Kepner, 1996; Paivio & Greenberg, 1995), depression (Greenberg, Watson, & Goldman, 1998), and psychosomatic disorders (Sachse, 1998).

## THE EFFECTIVENESS OF HUMANISTIC THERAPY

A series of meta-analyses of controlled and uncontrolled studies on the outcome of humanistic-experiential therapies have demonstrated their effectiveness (Elliott, 1996, 2002; Greenberg et al., 1994). In the latest version (Elliott, 2002), nearly 100 treatment groups were analyzed, incorporating studies with a very wide variety of characteristics. The main conclusions of this analysis follow:

1. The average effect size of change over time ($d = 1.06$; $N = 99$) for clients who participate in humanistic-experiential therapies is considered to be large.

2. Posttherapy gains in humanistic-experiential therapies are stable; that is, they are maintained over early ($<12$ months) and late (12 months) follow-ups.

3. In randomized clinical trials against wait-list and no-treatment controls, clients in humanistic-experiential therapies, in general, show substantially more change than comparable untreated clients ($d = 0.99$; $n = 36$).

4. In randomized clinical trials against comparative treatment, clients in humanistic therapies generally show amounts of change equivalent to clients in nonhumanistic therapies, including cognitive-behavioral treatments ($d = 0.0$; $n = 48$).

5. Client presenting problem, treatment setting, and therapist experience level did not affect outcome; however, other study characteristics did, including treatment modality (couples conjoint), researcher theoretical allegiance (in comparative treatment studies), and type of humanistic-experiential therapy (process-directive treatments had larger effects).

6. If researcher theoretical allegiance is ignored, cognitive-behavioral treatments show a modest superiority to client-centered and nondirective-supportive treatments ($d = -.33$; $n = 23$); however, this advantage disappeared ($d = -.05$) when allegiance was controlled for.

7. Process-directive therapies may be slightly superior to cognitive-behavior therapies ($d = .29$; $n = 9$), but this advantage also disappeared ($d = -.04$) after controlling for researcher allegiance.

Thus, while more research is needed, the available evidence clearly runs against the claims of critics of client-centered and other humanistic therapies (e.g., Grawe, Donati, & Bernauer, 1994).

The outcome of individual process-experiential therapy has been subjected to the largest number of recent empirical investigation ($n = 14$). This has covered various clinical populations, including major depression (Elliott et al., 1990; Greenberg & Watson, 1998) and a number of traumatic situations. The latter have included childhood abuse, unresolved relationships with significant others, and crime-related post-traumatic stress disorder (PTSD; Clarke, 1993; Paivio & Greenberg, 1995; Paivio & Nieuwenhuis, 2001). Populations with other personal and interpersonal difficulties have also been investigated (Clarke & Greenberg, 1986; Greenberg & Webster, 1982; Lowenstein, 1985; Toukmanian & Grech, 1991).

A series of meta-analyses of controlled and uncontrolled studies on the outcome of humanistic-experiential therapies have demonstrated the effectiveness of this approach in this tradition (Elliott, 1996; Greenberg et al., 1994). Results of meta-analyses for both client-centered and Gestalt therapies have provided evidence of their effectiveness. The outcome of the contemporary form of neo-humanistic therapy emphasized in this chapter (process-experiential therapy) has been subjected to empirical investigation in at least 14 separate studies with various clinical populations, including clients with major depression (Gibson, 1998; Greenberg & Watson, 1998; Jackson & Elliott, 1990); traumatic situations, including childhood sexual abuse, other unresolved relationships with significant others, and crime-related PTSD (Clarke, 1993; Elliott et al., 1998; Paivio, 1997; Paivio & Greenberg, 1995); and other personal and interpersonal difficulties (Clarke & Greenberg, 1986; Greenberg & Webster, 1982; Lowenstein, 1985; Toukmanian & Grech, 1991).

The most recent meta-analysis yielded very large prepost effect sizes (mean effect size: 1.06 *SD*). In addition, in 36 controlled evaluations (involving comparison to wait-list or no-treatment conditions), the overall effect size was .99 *SD*, almost as large as the uncontrolled prepost effect. Moreover, in 48 comparisons between humanistic-experiential and other (mostly cognitive-behavioral) therapies, the average difference was .00, supporting the claim that experiential therapies are statistically equivalent to nonexperiential therapies in effectiveness. Finally, although very few direct comparisons exist, the available data tentatively suggest that the newer process-directive experiential therapies may be somewhat more effective than the older nondirective or client-centered therapies, although this may reflect research artifacts.

## CONCLUSION

In the humanistic-experiential orientation described here, an empathic focus on the client's actual experience is seen as indispensable, but the therapist is also seen as making contributions in addition to sustained empathic inquiry. Therapists complement their empathic inquiry with a variety of therapeutic interventions. These can help the client learn how to focus awareness efficiently, differentiate actual subjective experience, and highlight the processes essential to the client's self-organization, building on a sophisticated theoretical understanding of human psychological function and dysfunction.

The strength of this orientation lies in its theory of personality change. Rather than focusing on theory of functioning or diagnosis, it has focused on understanding how people change. Macro theories (Gendlin, 1964; Perls et al.,

1951; Rogers, 1959) do exist, but progress is being made on the meso (intermediate) and micro levels (Greenberg et al., 1993), where more concrete and differentiated theories on specific subprocesses of change, on both specific intrapsychic and interpersonal tasks, are taking place. Progress also is occurring in dialogue with academic psychology particularly in relation to emotion theories, constructivism, and interpersonal processes. As a consequence, the orientation is becoming more specific, suggesting different types of processes for different types of problems. A therapy-oriented process diagnostics has been proposed and will hopefully be developed to allow the construction of "manuals" for ways of treating specific process blocks in specific ways, without losing the "humanistic" essence of focusing on the unique in the whole person. Process research and comprehensive qualitative research, which have contributed to this study of specific events and experiences, will continue to be the hallmark of a humanistic contribution to research on psychotherapy.

This process-diagnostic approach to treatment and research will promote the integration that is taking place within the experiential-humanistic family, one that will lead to a Gestalt that is larger than the sum of its parts (Greenberg et al., 1998). Pure-form approaches are still dominant within the humanistic orientation. In this a person is trained or practices only as a Rogerian, only as a focusing-oriented therapist, only Gestalt, only process-oriented, only existential, or only as a psychodramatist. Cross-fertilization within these approaches will lead to a richer and more well-balanced approach and will allow trainees to search for their own styles within a more integrated orientation. This kind of integration will force a broadening of the humanistic framework and will sharpen its views on the core aspects of a humanistic identity in spite of differences between subapproaches.

Finally, it is encouraging to see that international organizations have developed over the last decade, and this augurs well for future developments in this orientation. Both the World Association of Person-Centered and Experiential Psychotherapy (WAPCEP) and an International Gestalt Therapy Organization have held a number of meetings in the last decade, and two new journals reflecting the membership of theses organization have emerged. These are the newly planned *Person-Centered and Experiential Psychotherapy Journal* as well as the *Gestalt Review,* which was first published in 1997. In these there is recognition of the need for more scholarly writing and more research in this orientation, which until recently has focused predominantly on experiential learning and teaching. More scholarly publishing will help promote the development of this orientation.

# REFERENCES

Barrett-Lennard, G. T. (1998). *Carl Rogers' helping system: Journey and substance.* London: Sage.

Biermann-Ratjen, E.-M., Eckert, J., & Schwartz, H.-J. (1995). *Gesprächspsychotherapie. Verändern durch Verstehen* (7th rev. ed.). Stuttgart, Germany: Kohlhammer.

Binswanger, L. (1963). *Being in the world* (J. Needleman, Trans.). New York: Basic Books. (Original work published 1951)

Bohart, A. C., & Greenberg, L. S. (Eds.). (1997). *Empathy reconsidered. New directions in psychotherapy.* Washington, DC: American Psychological Association.

Bohart, A. C., & Tallman, K. (1999). *How client make therapy work: The process of active self-healing.* Washington, DC: American Psychological Association.

Bordin, E. S. (1979). The generalizability of the psychoanalytic concept of working alliance. *Psychotherapy: Theory, Research and Practice, 16,* 252–260.

Boss, M. (1963). *Psychoanalysis and daseinsanalysis* (L. B. Lefebre, Trans.). New York: Basic Books. (Original work published 1957)

Briere, J. (1989). *Therapy for adults molested as children: Beyond survival.* New York: Springer-Verlag.

Buber, M. (1957). *I and thou.* New York: Scribners.

Clarke, K. M. (1993). Creation of meaning in incest survivors. *Journal of Cognitive Psychotherapy, 7,* 195–203.

Clarke, K. M., & Greenberg, L. S. (1986). Differential effects of the gestalt two-chair intervention and problem solving in resolving decisional conflict. *Journal of Counseling Psychology, 33,* 11–15.

Delisle, G. (1991). A gestalt perspective of personality disorders. *British Gestalt Journal, 1,* 42–50.

Eckert, J., & Biermann-Ratjen, E.-M. (1998). The treatment of borderline personality disorder. In L. S. Greenberg, J. C. Watson, & G. Lietaer (Eds.), *Handbook of experiential psychotherapy* (pp. 349–367). New York: Guilford Press.

Eckert, J., Höger, D., & Linster, H. W. (Eds.). (1997). *Praxis der Gesprächspsychotherapie. Störungsbezogene Falldarstellungen.* Stuttgart, Germany: Kohlhammer.

Elliott, R. (1996). Are client-centered/experiential therapies effective? A meta-analysis of outcome research. In U. Esser, H. Pabst, & G.-W. Speierer (Eds.), *The power of the person-centered-approach: New challenges-perspectives-answers* (pp. 125–138). Köln, Germany: GwG Verlag.

Elliott, R. (1999). Prozeß-Erlebnisorientierte Psychotherapie–Ein Überblick [The process-experiential approach to psychotherapy: An overview]. *Psychotherapeut, 44,* 203–213, 340–349.

Elliott, R. (2002). Research on the effectiveness of humanistic therapies: A meta analysis. In D. Cain & J. Seeman (Eds.), *Handbook of research and practice in humanistic psychotherapies.* Washington, American Psychological Association.

Elliott, R., Clark, C., Wexler, M., Kemeny, V., Brinkerhoff, J., & Mack, C. (1990). The impact of experiential therapy of depression: Initial results. In G. Lietaer, J. Rombauts, & R. Van Balen (Eds.), *Client-centered and experiential psychotherapy in the nineties* (pp. 549–577). Leuven, Belgium: Leuven University Press.

Elliott, R., Davis, K., & Slatick, E. (1998). Process-experiential therapy for post-traumatic stress difficulties. In L. Greenberg, G. Lietaer, & J. Watson (Eds.), *Handbook of experiential psychotherapy* (pp. 249–271). New York: Guilford Press.

Elliott, R., & Greenberg, L. S. (1997). Multiple voices in process-experiential therapy: Dialogues between aspects of the self. *Journal of Psychotherapy Integration, 7*(3), 225–239.

Elliott, R., Suter, P., Manford, J., Radpour-Markert, L., Siegel-Hinson, R., Layman, C., & Davis, K. (1996). A process-experiential approach to post-traumatic stress disorder. In R. Hutterer, G. Pawlowsky, P. F. Schmid, & R. Stipsits (Eds.), *Client-centered and experiential psychotherapy: A paradigm in motion* (pp. 235–254). Frankfurt am Main, Germany: Peter Lang.

Elliott, R., Watson, J., Goldman, R., & Greenberg, L. S. (in press). Learning process experiential therapy: An introduction to emotionally-focused therapy. Washington, DC: American Psychological Association.

Finke, J. (1994). *Empathie und Interaktion. Methodik und Praxis der Gesprächspsychotherapie* [Empathy and interaction. Method and practice in client centered psychotherapy]. Stuttgart, Germany: Thieme.

Frankl, V. (1955). *The doctor and the soul: From psychotherapy to logotherapy.* New York: Vintage Books.

Frankl, V. (1963). *Man's search for meaning.* New York: Pocket Book.

Frankl, V. (1969). *The will to meaning: Foundations and applications of logotherapy.* Cleveland, Ohio: World Publishing.

Frijda, N. H. (1986). *The emotions.* Cambridge, England: Cambridge University Press.

Gendlin, E. T. (1962). *Experiencing and the creation of meaning.* New York: Free Press of Glencoe.

Gendlin, E. T. (1964). A theory of personality change. In P. Worchel & D. Byrne (Eds.), *Personality change.* New York: Wiley.

Gendlin, E. T. (1984). *Focusing* (Rev. ed.). New York: Bantam Books.

Gendlin, E. T. (1996). *Focusing-oriented psychotherapy: A manual of the experiential method.* New York: Guilford Press.

Goldman, R., & Greenberg, L. S. (1997). Case formulation in process-experiential therapy. In T. D. Eels (Ed.), *Handbook of psychotherapy case formulation.* New York: Guilford Press.

Goldstein, K. (1939). *The organism: A holistic approach derived from pathological data in man.* New York: American Book.

Grawe, K., Donati, R., & Bernauer, F. (1994). *Psychotherapie im Wandel: Von der Konfession zur Profession.* Göttingen, Germany: Hogrefe.

Greenberg, L. S. (1984). A task-analysis of intrapersonal conflict resolution. In L. N. Rice & L. S. Greenberg (Eds.), *Patterns of change* (pp. 67–123). New York: Guilford Press.

Greenberg, L. S., Elliott, R., & Lietaer, G. (1994). Research on experiential psychotherapy. In A. Bergin & S. Garfield (Eds.), *Handbook of psychotherapy and behavior change*. New York: Wiley.

Greenberg, L. S., & Paivio, S. (1997). *Working with emotion in psychotherapy*. New York: Guilford Press.

Greenberg, L. S., & Pascual-Leone, J. (1995). A dialectical constructivist approach to experiential change. In R. A. Neimeyer & M. J. Mahoney (Eds.), *Constructivism in psychotherapy* (pp. 169–191). Washington, DC: American Psychological Association.

Greenberg, L. S., & Pascual-Leone, J. (1997). Emotion in the creation of personal meaning. In M. Power & C. (Eds.), Brewin. *Transformation of meaning*. London: Wiley.

Greenberg, L. S., & Rice, L. N. (1997). Humanistic approaches to psychotherapy. In P. Wachtel & S. Messer (Eds.), *Theories of psychotherapy: Origins and evolution*. Washington, DC: American Psychological Association.

Greenberg, L. S., Rice, L. N., & Elliott, R. (1993). *Facilitating emotional change: The moment-by-moment process*. New York: Guilford Press.

Greenberg, L. S., & Safran, J. D. (1987). *Emotion in psychotherapy*. New York: Guilford Press.

Greenberg, L. S., & Van Balen, R. (1998). The theory of experience-centered therapies. In L. S. Greenberg, J. C. Watson, & G. Lietaer (Eds.), *Handbook of experiential psychotherapy* (pp. 28–57). New York: Guilford Press.

Greenberg, L. S., & Watson, J. (1998). Experiential therapy of depression: Differential effects of client-centered relationship conditions and active experiential interventions. *Psychotherapy Research, 8,* 210–224.

Greenberg, L. S., Watson, J., & Lietaer, G. (Eds.). (1998). *Handbook of experiential psychotherapy*. New York: Guilford Press.

Greenberg, L. S., Watson, J., & Goldman, R. (1998). Process-experiential therapy of depression. In L. S. Greenberg, J. C. Watson, & G. Lietaer (Eds.), *Handbook of experiential psychotherapy* (pp. 227–248). New York: Guilford Press.

Greenberg, L. S., & Webster, M. (1982). Resolving decisional conflict by means of two-chair dialogue and empathic reflection at a split in counseling. *Journal of Counseling Psychology, 29,* 468–477.

Heidegger, M. (1962). *Being and time* (J. Macquarrie & E. S. Robinson, Trans.). New York: Harper and Row. (Original work published 1949)

Husserl, E. (1977). *Phenomenological psychology* (J. Scanlon, Trans.). The Hague, The Netherlands: Nijhoff. (Original work published 1925)

Hycner, R., & Jacobs, L. M. (1995). *The healing relationship in Gestalt therapy: A dialogic/self psychology approach*. Highland, NY: Gestalt Journal Press.

Jackson, L., & Elliott, R. (1990, June). *Is experiential therapy effective in treating depression?: Initial outcome data*. Paper presented at Society for Psychotherapy Research, Wintergreen, VA.

James, W. (1950). *Principles of psychology*. New York: Dover. (Original work published 1890)

Jaspers, K. (1963). *General psychopathology*. Chicago: University of Chicago Press.

Kierkegaard, S. (1954). *Fear and trembling and the sickness unto death* (W. Lowrie, Trans.). Garden City, NY: Doubleday Anchor. (Original work published 1843)

Kiesler, D. J. (1996). *Contemporary interpersonal theory and research: Personality, psychopathology and psychotherapy*. New York: Wiley.

Lazarus, R. S. (1991). Progress on a cognitive-emotional-relational theory of emotion. *American Psychologist, 46,* 819–834.

Leijssen, M. (1998). Focusing microprocesses. In L. S. Greenberg, J. C. Watson, & G. Lietaer (Eds.), *Handbook of experiential psychotherapy* (pp. 121–154). New York: Guilford Press.

Lietaer, G. (1993). Authenticity, congruence and transparency. In D. Brazier (Ed.), *Beyond Carl Rogers: Towards a psychotherapy for the twenty-first century* (pp. 17–47). London: Constable.

Lietaer, G., Rombauts, J., & Van Balen, R. (Eds.). (1990). *Client-centered and experiential psychotherapy in the nineties*. Leuven, Belgium: Leuven University Press.

Lietaer, G., & Van Kalmthout, M. (Eds.). (1995). *Praktijkboek gesprekstherapie. Psychopathologie en experiëntiële procesbevordering*. Maarssen, the Netherlands: Elsevier/De Tijdstroom.

Lowenstein, J. (1985). *A test of a performance model of problematic reactions and an examination of differential client performances in therapy*. Unpublished masters thesis, Department of Psychology, York University.

Mahrer, A. R. (1978). *Experiencing: A humanistic theory of psychology and psychiatry*. New York: Brunner/Mazel.

Mahrer, A. R. (1989). *How to do experiential psychotherapy: A manual for practitioners*. Ottawa, Ontario, Canada: University of Ottawa Press.

Marcel, S. (1951). *Homo Viator: Introduction to a metaphysic of hope*. Chicago: Henry Regnery.

Maslow, A. H. (1961/1968). *Toward a psychology of being* (2nd ed.). New York: Van Nostrand Reinhold.

May, R. (1977). *The meaning of anxiety* (Rev. ed.) New York: W. W. Norton.

May, R., Angel, E., & Ellenberger, H. (Eds.). (1958). *Existence: A new dimension in psychiatry and psychology*. New York: Basic Books.

May, R., & Schneider, K. (1995). *Psychology of existence: An integrative, clinical perspective*. New York: McGraw-Hill.

May, R., & Yalom, J. (1989). Existential therapy. In R. J. Corsini & D. Wedding (Eds.), *Current psychotherapies* (4th ed., pp. 363–402). Itasca, IL: Peacock.

Mearns, D., & Thorne, B. (2000). *Person-centred therapy today: New frontiers in theory and practice*. London: Sage.

Merleau-Ponty, M. (1945/1962). *Phenomenology of perception*. London: Routledge and Kegan Paul.

*The Concise Oxford Dictionary*. (1990). Eighth edition. Oxford: Clarendan Press.

Paivio, S. C. (1997, December). *The outcome of emotionally-focused therapy with adult abuse survivors.* Paper presented at meeting of North American Society for Psychotherapy Research, Tucson, AZ.

Paivio, S. C., & Greenberg, L. S. (1995). Resolving "unfinished business:" Efficacy of experiential therapy using empty chair dialogue. *Journal of Consulting and Clinical Psychology, 63,* 419–425.

Paivio, S. C., & Nieuwenhuis, J. A. (2001). Efficacy of emotion focused therapy for adult survivors of child abuse: A preliminary study. *Journal of Traumatic Stress.*

Pascual-Leone, J. (1991). Emotions, development and psychotherapy: A dialectical constructivist perspective. In J. D. Safran & L. S. Greenberg (Eds.), *Emotion, psychotherapy, and change.* New York: Guilford Press.

Perls, F. S. (1947). *Ego, hunger, and aggression.* London: Allen and Unwin.

Perls, F. S., Hefferline, R. F., & Goodman, P. (1951). *Gestalt therapy.* New York: Julian Press.

Polster, E., & Polster, M. (1973). *Gestalt therapy integrated.* New York: Brunner/Mazel.

Prouty, G. (1994). *Theoretical evolutions in person-centered/experiential therapy. Applications to schizophrenic and retarded psychoses.* New York: Praeger.

Prouty, G., & Pietrzak, S. (1988). The pre-therapy method applied to persons experiencing hallucinatory images. *Person-Centered Review, 3,* 426–441.

Rennie, D. L. (1998). *Person-centred counselling: An experiential approach.* London: Sage.

Rice, L. N., & Greenberg, L. S. (Eds.). (1984). *Patterns of change: Intensive analysis of psychotherapy process.* New York: Guilford.

Rogers, C. (1951). *Client centered therapy.* Boston: Houghton Mifflin.

Rogers, C. R. (1957). The necessary and sufficient condition of therapeutic personality change. *Journal of Consulting Psychology, 21,* 95–103.

Rogers, C. R. (1958). A process conception of psychotherapy. *American Psychologist, 13,* 142–149.

Rogers, C. R. (1959). A theory of therapy, personality and interpersonal relationships, as developed in the client-centered framework. In S. Koch (Ed.), *Psychology: A study of a science* (Vol. 3, pp. 184–256). New York: McGraw Hill.

Rogers, C. (1961). *On becoming a person.* Boston: Houghton Mifflin.

Sachse, R. (1996). *Praxis der Zielorientierten Gesprächspsychotherapie.* Göttingen, Germany: Hogrefe.

Sachse, R. (1998). Goal-oriented client-centered therapy of psychosomatic disorders. In L. S. Greenberg, J. C. Watson, & G. Lietaer (Eds.), *Handbook of experiential psychotherapy* (pp. 295–327). New York: Guilford Press.

Safran, J. D., Crocker, P., McMain, S., & Murray, P. (1990). Therapeutic alliance rupture as a therapy event for empirical investigation. *Psychotherapy, 27,* 154–165.

Sartre, J. P. (1956). *Being and nothingness* (H. Barnes, Trans.). New York: Philosophical Library. (Original work published 1943)

Schmid, P. D. (1995). *Personale Begegnung. Der personzentrierte Ansatz in Psychotherapie, Beratung, Gruppenarbeit und Seelsorge* (2nd rev. ed.). Würzburg, Germany: Echter.

Swildens, J. (1997). *Procesgerichte gesprekstherapie* (Rev. ed.). Leusden: De Tijdstroom.

Teusch, L., & Bohme, H. (1999). Is the exposure principle really crucial in agoraphobia? The influence of client-centered "non-prescriptive" treatment on exposure. *Psychotherapy Research, 9*(1), 115–123.

Toukmanian, S. G., & Grech, T. (1991). *Changes in cognitive complexity in the context of perceptual-processing experiential therapy* [Department of Psychology Report No. 194]. York University, Toronto, Ontario, Canada.

van Deurzen-Smith, E. (1996). *Everyday mysteries: Existential dimensions of psychotherapy.* London: Routledge.

van Kessel, W., & Lietaer, G. (1998). Interpersonal processes. In L. S. Greenberg, J. C. Watson, & G. Lietaer (Eds.), *Handbook of experiential psychotherapy* (pp. 155–177). New York: Guilford Press.

Verhofstadt-Denève, L. (1999). *Theory and practice of action and drama techniques: Developmental psychotherapy from an existential-dialectical viewpoint.* London: Jessica Kingsley.

Warner, M. S. (1998). A client-centered approach to therapeutic work with dissociated and fragile process. In L. S. Greenberg, J. C. Watson, & G. Lietaer (Eds.), *Handbook of experiential psychotherapy* (pp. 368–387). New York: Guilford Press.

Watson, J. C., & Greenberg, L. S. (1997). Emotion and cognition in experiential therapy: A dialectical-constructivist position. In H. Rosen & K. Kuelwein (Eds.), *Construction realities: Meaning making perspectives for psychotherapists* (pp. 253–276). San Francisco: Jossey-Bass.

Wheeler, G. (1991). *Gestalt reconsidered.* New York: Gardner Press.

Whelton, W., & Greenberg, L. (2000). The self as a singular multiplicity: A process experiential perspective. In J. Muran (Ed.), *Self-relations in the psychotherapy process* (pp. 87–106). Washington, DC: APA Press.

Wilkins, P. (1999). *Psychodrama.* London: Sage.

Yalom, I. (1980). *Existential psychotherapy.* New York: Basic Books.

Yalom, I. (1995). *The theory and practice of group psychotherapy* (4th ed.). New York: Basic Books.

Yontef, G. M. (1993). *Awareness, dialogue and process: Essays on Gestalt therapy.* Highland, NY: Gestalt Journal Press.

Yontef, G. (1998). Dialogic gestalt therapy. In L. S. Greenberg, J. C. Watson, & G. Lietaer (Eds.), *Handbook of experiential psychotherapy* (pp. 82–102). New York: Guilford Press.

CHAPTER 13

# Psychotherapy Integration

LOUIS G. CASTONGUAY, JACK J. REID JR., GREGORY S. HALPERIN, AND MARVIN R. GOLDFRIED

*Alas, our theory is too poor for experience.*

ALBERT EINSTEIN

*No, no! Experience is too rich for our theory.*

NIELS BOHR

Things have changed in psychotherapy. Long past is the time when the majority of behavior therapists saw the psychodynamic tradition as an unworthy enterprise guided by unscientific minds and characterized by invalid theories and unsupported claims of therapeutic success (e.g., Eysenck, 1953). For their part, cognitive and behavior therapies have found ways to gain respectability and credibility in the eyes of many proponents of other orientations (Kendall, 1982). Indeed, over are the days when such therapies were viewed by many as effective treatments for meaningless problems or as dangerous interventions vandalizing human freedom and dignity (e.g., Koch, 1964; Winnicott, 1969). With a new generation of influential leaders and greater attention to research (see Greenberg, Watson, & Lieataer, 1998), the humanistic-existential orientation has—for the most part—left behind its reputation of an amalgam of eccentric practices that are based on superficial theories and that at best are only relevant to highly functioning individuals (see Landsman, 1974).

The old dismissive debates that characterized the field of psychotherapy for more than a half a century have given way to a new relationship among proponents of different

approaches—a relationship marked by mutual respect and serious efforts at conciliation (Gold, 1996; J. C. Norcross & Goldfried, 1992; Stricker, 1994; Stricker & Gold, 1993). The goal of this chapter is to present an overview of this movement of rapprochement and integration. First, we attempt to determine *why* the integration movement represents a significant force in the contemporary field of psychotherapy. We then describe *what* we perceive as the major trends within this movement. Finally, as a concluding note, we suggest *where* the integration movement should go in order to preserve its influence on the constantly evolving field of psychotherapy.

## INTEGRATION: WHY AND WHY NOW?

### Why?

In our view, the integration movement represents an attempt to deal with the complexity of the process of change and the factors that are involved in facilitating such change. Although this view will most certainly reflect an epistemologically naive perspective, we would like to suggest that there might be some parallel between the growth of a professional and scientific tradition (such as the specific schools of psychotherapy) and the development of individuals (therapists in this case) in their attempts to better understand and deal with complex phenomena (such as psychopathology and psychotherapy; see Goldfried, 2001). More specifically, we would like to suggest that the development of major orientations in

Preparation of this chapter was supported in part by National Institute of Mental Health Research Grant MH-58593.

psychotherapy has followed—more or less neatly—three phases that many clinicians will recognize as significant markers of their professional growth.

Beginning clinicians often experience an initial period of *excitement and discouragement*. The pride, relief, and joy of having developed a cohesive treatment plan, established a supportive relationship, implemented skillfully a difficult procedure, or simply conducted a good session often give way to feelings of confusion and self-doubt; this occurs when our first successful cases (or sessions) are followed by struggles to articulate an elegant case formulation, to use in a timely fashion a technique that is perfectly attuned to the client's need, to deal appropriately with a delicate problem in the therapeutic relationship, or simply to realize that session after session the client is not showing signs of improvement.

We would venture to guess that a similar process took place during the early days of the now well-established orientations and that the exhilaration of discovery experienced by pioneers of current forms of psychotherapy may have been quickly followed by frustrating discrepancies between their emergent theory and clinical observations. One can easily imagine how such a cyclical process of joys and tribulations might have prevailed in Freud's professional life during the 1890s, when his initial successes with the cathartic method were followed by unexpected difficulties—leading him to develop the psychoanalytic method for the cure for hysteria. It would not surprise us to learn that Carl Rogers and Joseph Wolpe went through similar experiences during the 1950s when they were discovering the power of empathy or the clinical relevance (and effectiveness) of laboratory procedures used with cats. As exciting as these times may have been, we would expect that both men experienced significant setbacks when trying to apply their brilliant ideas to complicated cases.

This first phase of excitement and discouragement is frequently followed, we believe, by a period of *confidence and rigidity*. After a lot of observations, thinking, and trial and error, theoreticians and clinicians adopt models that help them organize (cohesively and heuristically) their views on human suffering and the process of change. Systematic rules of practice are defined for the clinicians, and acceptable methods of knowledge acquisition are delineated for the theoreticians and researchers. This time is also when training programs are institutionalized and when clinicians who have mastered the model and its related techniques become not only healers but also supervisors.

At this point, a deep sense of conviction and high level of enthusiasm may well have taken place in the individual practitioner as well as in the professional field. With such elation,

however, then frequently comes the refusal to accept any dampening criticism that puts into question the brilliance of one's theory and the unmistakable effectiveness of one's interventions. Wariness of others' explanations and ways of intervening is also characteristic of clinicians and theoreticians who are deeply (and blindly) committed to a particular orientation. The hazards of this stage have been denounced by reputed members of cognitive-behavioral (e.g., Thoresen & Coates, 1978), psychodyanamic (e.g., Strupp, 1976), and humanistic traditions (Koch, 1969, as cited in Ricks, Wandersman, & Poppen, 1976). Donald Levis (1998) vividly illustrated some of the manifestations and costs of these hazards for the behavioral approach:

> Many behavioral therapists developed an extreme phobic reaction against anything that appeared to be Freudian in origin, to the point that even past history was considered unimportant, especially if it involved sexual or aggressive content. This phobic reaction soon developed in to an agoraphobic condition in which most, if not all, nonbehavioral contributions were avoided—even contributions that readily lend themselves to a learning interpretation. This myopic viewpoint created an anorexic condition for the field of behavior therapy which is leading to its ultimate starvation. It is ironic that the strengths of the behavior movement—its commitment to objective, scientific analysis, operational specificity, and principles of behaviorism—were overshadowed by the tendency to summarily dismiss without providing differential tests of a large body of existing literature, a literature which has evolved over the last 100 years as a result of extensive exposure to psychopathology and which, in most cases, is consistent with the tenets of behaviorism.

Although our theories and intervention methods allow us to assimilate clinical information and formulate various treatment plans, most of us (as therapists, theoreticians, or both) come to realize that there are some things we still cannot explain and some issues we cannot resolve successfully. Failures to understand and act effectively eventually lead most of us to adapt ourselves to a reality more complex than what we had originally recognized and adjust our theory and practice accordingly; this is when an individual clinician—or an orientation as a whole—emerges from the previous two stages with a sense of *humility and openness* for the potential contributions by those outside our domain. As described in the personal accounts of therapists who have gone through this developmental phase (Goldfried, 2001), the integration and eclectic movement in psychotherapy can be seen as a response (and by no means the only one) to the theoretical, clinical, and epistemological limitations of modern approaches to psychotherapy. It is a nondefeatist and noncomplacent response to the unsatisfactory status of our field—a response that is based on the assumption that the richness of plurality may be our best strategy to approach human complexity.

## Why Now?

Many factors have fueled the prevailing attitude of humility and openness in the field of psychotherapy (see Norcross & Newman, 1992). In our view, the main three interrelated sources of input for the integration are (a) the eye-opening quality of numerous research findings, (b) the shortcomings of the prevalent theoretical models, and (c) the deficiencies of our clinical methods. We first consider some of the outcome and process research that has facilitated the emergence and development of the integration movement. We then explore some of the conceptual and clinical limitations that have been identified by respected members of each major orientation and that have stimulated efforts of rapprochement and conciliation.

### Research

A cursory look to the psychotherapy outcome literature may lead one to feel quite positive about the field's ability to address human psychological suffering. After all, research spanning five decades definitively shows that psychotherapy works (Lambert & Bergin, 1994). In addition, a substantial number of specific treatments have met fairly stringent methodological and clinical criteria, allowing them to be defined as empirically supported (see Kendall, 1998).

A closer look at the same literature, however, clearly reveals that psychotherapy is far from being a panacea. Although it has been shown to be superior to the lack of treatment, placebo interventions, and pseudotherapy, there is also unmistakable evidence that some clients fail to achieve full improvement, that others terminate treatment prematurely, and that yet others deteriorate during therapy (Garfield, 1994; Lambert & Bergin, 1994). Furthermore, the list of empirically supported treatments has stirred considerable controversy, most notably in terms of their relevance to the day-to-day practice and actual efficacy. There are indeed substantial differences in the type of clients who are treated and the conditions under which therapy is conducted in the clinical trials (where empirically supported treatments are tested) compared to clients and conditions in the clinician's typical practice (see Jones in Castonguay, 1999).

Moreover, the success rate of many empirically supported treatments is not particularly impressive. For example, although cognitive-behavioral therapy (CBT) is the current gold-standard therapy for general anxiety disorder, only 50%

of the clients who complete treatment show full recovery. Even outcome studies on behavioral treatment for phobia—a therapeutic choice that is likely to meet unanimity among most contemporary practitioners—shows how far we as therapists still have to go with regard to our ability to reduce psychological difficulties. Although the success of this treatment is high for those who complete therapy (75%), it drops substantially when one also considers clients who refuse to participate in treatment or drop out (49%; Barlow & Wolfe, 1981).

Apart from failing to demonstrate extraordinary curative powers of psychotherapy, outcome research has also shattered the often-held assumption that a preferred approach by any therapist is superior to other approaches. With the exception of fairly specific clinical problems (e.g., panic disorder, obsessive-compulsive disorder), major forms of psychotherapy appear to have an equivalent impact. Although on the positive side, one can see in this empirical finding a dodo verdict (everyone has won and therefore deserves a prize; Luborsky, Singer, & Luborsky, 1975), many in the field have concluded from it that each form of therapy can be improved and that a consideration of the contributions of other orientations may be the most efficient avenue for improving our therapeutic impact as clinicians.

In addition to outcome research in psychotherapy, investigations into therapy processes similarly indicate the need for humility and openness with regard to this area. Although we know that psychotherapy works, many theoreticians and practitioners seem to have misattributed the reasons for its success. Although most classic books and training programs associated with each major orientation tend to emphasize the skillful implementation of particular technical interventions, research suggests that 45% of the variance in outcome can be explained by placebo effects and factors common to several approaches (Lambert, 1992). In fact, recent studies have suggested that the adherence to techniques specifically prescribed by particular approaches can—at least in certain contexts—interfere with the client's improvement (Castonguay, Goldfried, Wiser, Raue, & Hayes, 1996; Henry, Schacht, & Strupp, 1990; Henry, Strupp, Butler, Schacht, & Binder, 1993; Piper et al., 1999).

As described in the following discussion, a large number of therapeutic factors operating in several approaches (i.e., common factors) have been identified, and a number of them have been empirically investigated. Although the delineation of therapeutic commonalities represents an important contribution of the integration movement, it is also clear that variables that have been specifically associated with a particular orientation are related to treatment outcome. With recent scientific advances, however, it is becoming less certain that particular forms of therapy can actually claim sovereignty over some of these supposedly unique processes of change. For example, although emotional deepening has been highlighted as the fundamental route to therapeutic change in humanistic therapy, recent studies have demonstrated that such processes are also predictive of clients' improvement in CBT (Castonguay et al., 1996; Castonguay, Pincus, Agras, & Hines, 1998). The principles of operant conditioning, assumed to explain the therapeutic power of procedures unique to behavior therapy, have been found to operate in both humanistic and psychodynamic treatment (Murray & Jacobson, 1971). Furthermore, although the concept of alliance was developed within the psychodynamic tradition, numerous empirical studies have shown that this construct explains a significant part of outcome variance across a variety of theoretical orientations (Constantino, Castonguay, & Schut, 2001). As discussed by Schut and Castonguay (2001), other processes of change initially defined by Freud and his followers have not only been shown to explain the efficacy of CBT but have also served as the basis for recent efforts to improve the therapeutic benefit of this approach.

We find it interesting that although research has supported a number of seminal insights of Freud about the process of change in psychodynamic therapy (see Schut & Castonguy, 2001), it has also suggested that part of the success of this type of treatment may be due to interventions typically identified with CBT. In summarizing the findings of a 30-year study on the process and outcome of different forms of psychodynamic therapy (expressive, supportive, and a mixture of expressive and supportive treatment) conducted at the Menninger Clinic, Wallerstein and DeWitt (1997) arrived at the following conclusion:

1. The treatment results, with patients selected either as suitable for trials at psychoanalysis, or as appropriate for varying mixes of expressive-supportive psychotherapeutic approaches, tended—with this population sample—to converge rather than diverge in outcome.

2. Across the whole spectrum of treatment courses in the 42 patients, ranging from the most analytic-expressive, through the inextricably blended, on to the most single-mindedly supportive, in almost every instance—the psychoanalyses included—the treatment carried more supportive elements than originally intended, and these supportive elements accounted for substantially more of the change achieved than had been originally anticipated.

3. The nature of supportive therapy, or better the supportive aspects of all psychotherapy, as conceptualized within a psychoanalytic theoretical framework, and as deployed by psychoanalytic knowledgeable therapists, bears far more respectful specification in all its form variants than has usually been accorded it in the psychodynamic literature . . .

4. From the study of the kinds of changes reached by this cohort of patients, partly on an uncovering insight-aiming basis, and partly on the basis of the opposed covering-up varieties of supportive techniques, the changes themselves—divorced from how they were brought about—often seemed quite indistinguishable from each other, in terms of being so-called real or structural changes in personality functioning. (pp. 141–142)

Considering the importance revealed by these results of supportive interventions in different forms of psychodynamic therapy, it is particularly interesting to observe how similar these components are to CBT's technical repertoire. Included in Wallerstein and DeWitt's list of supportive components are "persuading the phobic patient to enter the phobic situation"; "intellectual guidance, advice, objective review of situation, assisting the patient's judgment"; "education in the form of advice, information, or suggestion in the direction of society's normative standards and expectations"; "reduction of environmental demands on the patient"; "prescription of daily activities"; "planned disengagement from unfavorable and noxious (specifically conflict triggering) life situation"; "maintained engagement in particular (necessary and challenging) life situations"; and "altered interactions with, or alteration of attitudes, of significant others" (see Wallerstein & Dewitt, 1997, pp. 147–148).

Although several studies suggest that the effectiveness of one approach is in part accountable by the active ingredients identified by other orientations, it would be wrong to infer that the theories of change underlying the major therapeutic orientations are completely divorced from reality—that there are no links between clinical textbooks and practice. In fact, a number of studies have shown that cognitive, interpersonal, and psychodynamic therapies can be distinguished and that therapists can and do behave in ways that are consistent with particular models of interventions (e.g., Hill, O'Grady, & Elkin, 1992). However, two recent studies appear to suggest that the correspondence between theory and practice may be stronger in research contexts than it is in day-to-day practice.

These two studies were based on the Coding System of Therapist's Focus (CSTF; Goldfried, Newman, & Hayes, 1989)—a process measure that allows for the identification of the therapist's focus (or target) of intervention, regardless of the specific technique or treatment approach used. In both studies, the same forms of treatments were investigated—that is, CBT and psychodynamic interpersonal (PI) therapy. Furthermore, in each study the focus of the therapist was assessed in therapy sessions (or segments of sessions) that were classified as *significant or helpful* and *less significant or less helpful.* The primary difference between the two studies is that the first was based on archived data taken from a controlled clinical trial (the Sheffield II Psychotherapy Project; Goldfried, Castonguay, Hayes, Drozd, & Shapiro, 1997), whereas the other was based on therapy conducted in naturalistic settings (Goldfried, Raue, & Castonguay, 1998). Put another way, whereas the first study involved experienced therapists implementing manualized protocols, the second included expert clinicians (chosen by leaders of the field) conducting therapy as part of their regular clinical practice.

In the Sheffield study, many significant differences were found with regard to the therapists' approaches. As would be predicted by the model of change of the investigated treatments, therapists in the PI (compared with therapists in CBT) focused more on emotion, discrepancies or incongruity between different aspects of client functioning, client avoidance, intrapersonal and interpersonal patterns in the client's life, client's expected reaction to others, impact of others on client's life, client's general interactions with others, parallels among people in client's life, therapists themselves, client's parents, client's past (childhood and adult past), events taking place during therapy, and trends that cut across different life stages of the client. CBT therapists, however, focused more on the external environment, choices and decisions, information, support, homework, and the future. As summarized by the authors, the results suggest that the PI therapists focused on *insight*—more specifically, what has not worked in the past—whereas CBT focused on *action*—or how to deal more effectively with external events, especially with stressful events in the future.

It is interesting to note that although several differences in therapists' focus were observed between the two therapies, only a small number of differences (slightly above chance level) were found between the types of session assessed—that is, therapists showed similar foci of interventions across helpful and less helpful sessions.

In the data set involving expert therapists, however, the opposite pattern of results was obtained. Specifically, although relatively few differences in therapists' focus emerged between therapeutic orientations, numerous significant differences were obtained between significant and less significant parts of treatment sessions. Among other things, therapists focused more frequently on themselves, parallels between time periods and people in the client's life, new information, and the future in significant segments as compared to less significant segments. As concluded by the authors, these targets of intervention reflect a blending of interventions strongly identified by each of the two approaches examined.

Taken together, the findings of these two studies appear to suggest that the day-to-day practices of expert therapists converge rather than diverge (regardless of their preferred

orientation) and that the intervention focus of such therapists in good therapy is different from that in therapy that is less good. The findings also suggest that when investigating the target of intervention in manualized treatments, it is easy to discriminate between different approaches, but it is hard to find differences between helpful and less helpful sessions. As argued by Goldfried et al. (1998), these findings raise some interesting but complicated questions: "How do we as psychologists define the 'state of the art': Is it by the treatment manuals included in clinical trials or is it by what master therapists, who have been nominated by those who wrote the manuals, actually do in clinical practice?" (p. 809).

This brief—and no doubt biased—survey of the process and outcome literature directly points to the *complexity* of the process of change. Although different approaches are assumed to rest on divergent models of human functioning and are supposed to capitalize on unique techniques, none has been able to rely on empirical findings to claim superiority over the others across a variety of clinical problems. Furthermore, although the procedures prescribed by different approaches are typically assumed to be responsible for the client's improvement, the percentage of outcome variance actually explained by these techniques is far from impressive. The success of one particular approach seems to be explained in part by variables that are common to all forms of psychotherapy and (ironically) by factors that have been closely associated with other orientations. To complicate things more, prescribed techniques have been shown to interfere with change, at least in certain contexts. Finally, despite the fact that the development of manualized treatments has been seen as indication of the field's progress (Agras, 1999, referred to manuals as "nothing less than a scientific revolution"), experts in the field seem not to adhere to theoretical protocol and may well behave more similarly than dissimilarly—a point that was made a long time ago by Fiedler (1950).

As a whole, these empirical results indeed suggest that our current theories may not be adequate to explain the process of change. These results also point to the merits of considering the models and interventions of other orientations.

### Theoretical and Clinical Disenchantments

Along with the research findings summarized previously, clinical and theoretical critiques voiced within each of the major orientations have also contributed to the current movement of reconciliation and integration in psychotherapy. In contrast to the enthusiasm (if not arrogance and complacence) for one's own approach that prevailed until the 1960s, the last three decades have seen many therapists pointing out inadequacies of their preferred models and intervention methods.

In a courageous and eloquent critique of the school of thought with which he has been identified, Strupp (1976) asserted that

> Once in the forefront of revolutionary change, psychoanalytic therapy is with increasing monotony described as antiquated, passé, and even defunct. Psychoanalytic theory is seen as based on formulations and working assumptions in dire need of massive overhaul . . . and psychoanalysis, as a branch of the behavioral sciences appears to be approaching its nadir. (p. 238)

Strupp further argued that instead of considering the writings of Freud and other analytic pioneers to be working hypotheses that can be improved, the closed-shop mentality that prevails in psychoanalytic training institutes has led psychoanalysts to treat them as gospel truth. He went on to say that the analytic establishment has discouraged collaboration between analytic therapists and researchers, and as a result the field of psychoanalysis has not benefited from advances in psychological and other behavioral sciences.

Like other influential psychoanalytic authors (e.g., Alexander, 1963; Grinker, 1976; Marmor, 1964), Strupp has convincingly argued that an adequate understanding of the process of change taking place within this orientation requires the consideration of many factors emphasized by learning theories. Marmor (1976, 1982), for instance, identified the following as key ingredients in psychoanalytic (or any other forms of) treatment: operant conditioning, suggestion and persuasion, cognitive learning, identification with the therapist, and explicit and implicit support from the therapist. Some psychodynamic authors have also emphasized the merit of considering the work of humanist-existential therapists in understanding the complexity of the process of change. For example, as part of an imaginary dialogue between a therapist of the traditional psychoanalytic approach and newer therapeutic approaches, Shectman (1977) has called attention to the existential therapy's emphasis on the therapeutic role of emotions.

Influential psychodynamic authors have also questioned the validity and efficacy of the clinical procedures deemed sacred in many psychoanalytic institutes. Appelbaum (1979), for example, wrote

> Some analytic thinkers believe, implicitly or explicitly, that overcoming repression will do it all, that once self-knowledge is achieved, nothing else needs to be done. This is, I assume, the way that most of those few but notorious ten to twenty years analyses come about, analyst and patient hooked on discovery, on the assumption that enough discovery will result in change, that around some corner is the 'crucial insight.' Such long-run analyses may make for good Woody Allen jokes, but to me they

are horror stories. Pursuing insight, making the unconscious conscious, bringing what is out of awareness into awareness, making overt what is covert is not an unalloyed good for everyone at all time. (p. 434)

Appelbaum's critical view of traditional psychoanalytic methods led him to explore many therapy centers closely identified with the humanistic movement. Although he relates having been shocked by some of the so-called interventions he witnessed, he also found practices that appeared complementary and therefore capable of improving psychodynamic technical repertoires. Similarly, Kahn (1991) also argued that a humanistic perspective has much to contribute to psychoanalytic practice, stating that "there is much to be learned by paying careful attention to Rogers' advice about the relationship between therapist and client" (pp. 35–36). In a similar way, Wachtel (1977) has argued that behavioral techniques can be help clients develop and implement solutions to the dilemma with which they been confronted (e.g., inhibitions, distortions). As he notes, behavioral techniques "seem particularly valuable for accomplishing what dynamic therapists have regarded as the 'working through' stage of therapy" (1977, p. 203).

Freud himself, it appears, failed to meet the standards of proper practice that have been ascribed to psychoanalysis. A number of authors have noted that he deviated considerably from a blank-screen attitude with some of his patients. As described by Gill (1982), for example, Freud gave a meal and sent a postcard to the Rat Man. According to Yalom (1980), he encouraged another patient (a young female named Elisabeth) to visit a young man whom she found attractive, interacted with members of her families on her behalf, begged her mother to communicate with the patient, and even helped untangle her family's financial problems. Moreover, at the end of this young woman's therapy, "Freud, hearing that Elisabeth was going to a private dance, procured an invitation to watch her 'whirl past in a lively dance' "(Yalom, 1980, p. 4).

Well-known cognitive-behavioral therapists have also offered specific criticisms of their approach—both at theoretical and clinical levels. Voicing concerns similar to those of Strupp (1976) about the complacency of psychoanalysts, Thorensen and Coates (1978) commented that

> The behavior therapies—born out of conflict with an authoritative and theoretically plump intrapsychic tradition, geared to survive in professionally tough clinical backgrounds, and recently afforded adult status as a legitimate professional approach—are showing signs of middle-aged bulge, theoretically, methodologically, and clinically. Success has bred a complacent orthodoxy which threatens to rob the behavior therapies of much of the scientific strength . . . For us an energy crisis clearly exists;

resources are being wasted in defending, confirming, and replicating without substantially advancing our understanding . . . Critically examining and revising our conceptual rationale offers the most useful allocation of professional energies. We need to hack at the conceptual roots of behavior therapies to cut away the dead material, plant new ones, and graft together others . . . Submerged in all this is the neglect, less tangible, and yet significant role of personal meanings, goals, and aspirations—the purpose of life. (pp. 15–16)

It is interesting to note that some of the originators of the cognitive-behavioral movement have avoided the trap of complacence denounced by Thorensen and Coates (1978), even though their obvious investment in their approach may have made them more vulnerable to intellectual and professional rigidity. Lazarus (1971), for example, has urged his colleagues to move beyond the narrow theoretical model and restrictive technical repertoires of behavior therapy, even though he was one of the leading figures who paved the way for the recognition of this approach. A few years after playing a predominant role in the birth and early development of the cognitive movement, Mahoney (1980) criticized this same approach by pointing out its narrow understanding and inadequate treatment of emotions, excessive emphasis on the role of rationality in adaptation, and neglect of unconscious processes. Echoing Thorensen and Coates's (1978) criticism of behavior therapy, Mahoney also condemned the attitude of orthodoxy and defensiveness that had begun to emerge in cognitive and cognitive-behavioral approaches.

Disenchantment within the cognitive-behavioral movement has not only been voiced by pioneer figures like Lazarus and Mahoney. A survey conducted in the mid-1970s showed that both behavioral and cognitive therapists considered their approach to poorly capture the complexity of the process of change (Mahoney, 1978). More recently, Goldfried and Castonguay (1993) have argued that CBT places excessive emphasis on situational determinants of specific cognitive and behavioral responses and have asserted that more attention needs to be paid to the role of complex intrapersonal and interpersonal patterns in clients' functioning.

As was the case with dynamic authors, some leading cognitive-behavioral therapists have recognized their own tendencies toward heresy in the practice of their art. In their classic *Clinical Behavior Therapy,* for example, Goldfried and Davison (1976, 1994) wrote

We found instances where 'insights' occur to us in the midst of clinical sessions, prompting us to react in specific ways that paid off handsomely in the therapeutic progress of our clients . . . In accordance with most common definitions of behavior therapy, this might be viewed as heresy. Perhaps in some way it is.

Nonetheless, our contact with reality is relatively veridical, and what we have observed under such instances is not terribly unique. If, in fact, some of these phenomena are reliable. . . . should we ignore them because we call ourselves behaviorists? (p. 16)

The importance of dealing with phenomena such as transference and resistance has been recognized by a number of cognitive-behavioral therapists (e.g., Beck et al., 1990; Goldfried, 1982; Rhoades & Feather, 1972). Authors such as Arnkoff (1981) and Goldfried (1985) have also demonstrated how the therapeutic relationship can be used to change cognitions and modify client's behaviors. Citing the work of humanistic therapists (Greenberg & Safran, 1987), Samilov and Goldfried (2000) have recently argued for the recognition, within CBT models, of two distinct types of cognitions: (a) hot cognitions that are inextricably linked to the client's immediate and prereflective sense of self-in-the-world and (b) cold cognitions that are governed by rules of logic and rationality and do not directly modify the client's immediate experience. Samilov and Goldfried (2000) also encouraged their cognitive-behavioral colleagues to use techniques developed by experiential therapists when addressing hot cognitions because traditional CBT is seen as ill-suited for targeting this realm of experience.

In their attempt to delineate the clinical strengths and weaknesses of behavior therapy, Goldfried and Castonguay (1993) have argued that cognitive-behavioral therapists have too often failed to appropriately consider some dimensions of psychotherapy process that have been the focus of other orientations. They have argued that successful therapy sometimes requires exploring the client's emotional experience and developmental history, recognizing and using the therapist's own reactions in therapy, and dealing appropriately with issues that interfere with the therapeutic relationship. They also have argued that cognitive-behavioral therapists could increase their intervention repertoires by paying more attention to general principles of change as opposed to specific techniques prescribed in typical treatment manuals. A focus on these principles of change would indeed allow them to recognize that numerous non-CBT techniques serve many of the therapeutic functions that CBT interventions were intended to perform and that the former may be more effective than the latter in some specific circumstances or with some particular clients (see Castonguay, 2000a).

The humanistic approach, like others, has not been shielded from conceptual and clinical disenchantment. Koch (as cited in Ricks et al., 1976), one of the most important figures of the humanism tradition of psychology, has denounced its theoretical stagnation, methodological anarchy, and dogmatism. Others, such as Landsman (1974), have decried the type of practice often encountered in growth centers:

> These, our finest jewels, offer a bewildering array of exotic mixtures, of sexuality unfettered, spirituality, meditation, and transcendence into infinity, solutions for the blahs, for Americans materialism, nude, erotic, and nonerotic massage, the most colorful exotic, light-headed excitements of all cultures and all times—and selling for about $75 to $150 per intimate, irresponsible weekend. (in Goldfried, 1982, p. 271)

Close examination of one of the most famous humanistic therapists, Carl Rogers, reveals that like preeminent psychodynamic and behavior therapists, he too employed methods other than those specified by his theory. Studies have indeed demonstrated that Rogers systematically and differentially applied reinforcements in reacting to client's utterances (Jacobson & Murray, 1971). Rogers himself eloquently and courageously recognized the potential importance of social influence. In a review of a book entitled *Models of Influence in Psychotherapy,* Rogers (1981) wrote that the author (P. Pentony)

> takes the multitude of present-day psychotherapies and, . . . with surgical objectivity, he analyzes each one—its premises, its strategies, its outcomes—and his knife often draws blood. I suspect most psychotherapists, as they see their work thus dissected, may react as I did—feeling first irritated, then disturbed, then challenged. The author's central theme is that all therapists accomplish their goals by exerting social influence, and he analyzes carefully the varying forms of that influence.

Rogers completed his review by describing Pentony's book as "a profound contribution." Consistent with such comments, Rogers also wrote that the inherent limitations of using a single theoretical orientation—even his client-centered therapy— were beginning to outweigh the benefits and that psychotherapy research should focus upon empirical descriptions of what happens in therapy (see Goldfried & Newman, 1992).

Some authors have attempted to bridge Rogerian client-centered therapy with psychodynamic self psychology (e.g., Tobin, 1990, 1991). These efforts at rapprochement are based on the premise that the developmental emphasis and interpersonal focus in self psychology can complement Rogerian therapy's exclusive attention to the therapist's relational skills (empathy, unconditional respect, authenticity). Others have encouraged humanistic therapists in general—not only those associated with a client-centered approach—to consider the merit of a rapprochement with other orientations (Greening, 1978; Landsman, 1974).

## CURRENT DEVELOPMENTS IN PSYCHOTHERAPY INTEGRATION

The complexity of human functioning and difficulty of facilitating change have thus forced greater humility and openness within each of the major orientations of psychotherapy; this in turn has laid the foundation for the current swell of efforts at rapprochement and integration. Such efforts may be categorized into five domains: eclecticism, theoretical integration, common factors, integrative approaches to specific clinical problems, and the improvement of major systems of psychotherapy.

### Eclecticism

Eclecticism is the application of diverse therapeutic techniques, without concern for whether the theoretical rationales behind the techniques are compatible (Lazarus, 1992). The greater emphasis on pragmatic utility over theoretical congruence has caused some to misattribute eclecticism as a hodgepodge of therapeutic techniques with no rhyme or reason (Eysenck, 1970). As cogently described by J. D. Norcross and Newman (1992), however, eclecticism needs to be differentiated from syncretism. Whereas eclecticism represents a systematic selection of "interventions based on patient need and comparative outcome research," syncretism reflects a combination of techniques that is both uncritical and unsystematic—a "muddle of idiosyncratic and ineffable clinical creation" (p. 20).

A large number of eclectic approaches have been developed over the last 30 years. One of the first and most influential among them is Arnold Lazarus's (1967, 1992) multimodal therapy. Based on an assessment of the client's strengths and weaknesses related to seven modalities of functioning (e.g., behavior, affect, sensation, cognition), multimodal therapists are trained to use techniques (derived from divergent orientations) that are most likely to be useful. As stated by Lazarus (1992), the practice of multimodal therapy is guided by

> (a) treatments of choice (i.e., knowing what the research literature has to say about specific remedies for particular problems); (b) tailored interventions (i.e., selecting psychotherapeutic strategies to fit patients' goals, coping behaviors, situational contexts, affective reactions, 'resistances,' and basic beliefs); and (c) therapists' styles (i.e., going beyond formal diagnoses to match treatment styles to specific client characteristics). (p. 237)

Developed by Larry Beutler, systematic eclectic therapy (Beutler, 1983; Beutler & Consoli, 1992) is aimed at matching the client with the most appropriate therapist and treatment. Considered in constructing the optimal therapeutic match are (a) therapist and client demographic and background variables (e.g., ethnic similarity, attitudes, values, beliefs); (b) client characteristics (i.e., degree to which the client can receive directives without feeling threatened or reactance, extent of impairment due to client's presenting problem or problem severity, whether the presenting problem is accompanied with an opaque or linear relation between symptoms and one's pattern of behaviors or problem complexity, and the typical method of coping with stressors—e.g., externalizing vs. internalizing—or coping style); (c) the functions of various intervention procedures in terms of "breadth of objectives, the level of experience addressed, the amount of therapist directiveness required, and preference for intratherapy vs. extratherapy material" (Beutler & Consoli, 1992, p. 276). With Beutler, like Lazarus's approach, priority is given to the individual client's needs over theoretical considerations when selecting treatments.

In an interesting extension of Beutler's client-treatment fit approach, Lampropoulos (2000a) has suggested a selective application of common factors depending on client and therapist styles and characteristics. For example, as the most robust common factor, the working alliance must still be tailored to each individual client's particular expectations for therapy and his or her level of openness to experience.

Interested readers can find in Norcross' (1986) *Handbook of Eclectic Psychotherapy* a description of other eclectic approaches, as well as a survey of eclectic efforts in Goldfried and Newman's (1992) historical account of the integration movement. Several examples of combinations of techniques from divergent theoretical models are also illustrated in a book by Marmor and Woods (1980) entitled *The Interface Between the Psychodynamic and Behavioral Therapies.*

**Theoretical Integration**

Whereas eclectic therapists are interested in finding out the best way to selectively prescribe or pragmatically blend different techniques, those involved in theoretical integration attempt to extract constructs and therapeutic principles across many orientations and shape them into a new, more comprehensive, and integrated theory of functioning and/or change. Implicit in this undertaking is the belief that such inclusive theories will hold greater explanatory power than do any of the single theories from which it draws (Norcross & Newman, 1992).

Under the rubric of theoretical integration falls Prochaska and DiClemente's (1992) transtheoretical model of therapeu-

tic change. This model encompasses a series of stages through which clients progress in trying to alter problematic states of being. A number of processes have been identified within each of these stages to help clients achieve different levels of change. For example, if a client is identified to be in a stage called *contemplation,* a therapist would be encouraged to apply interventions that raise the client's consciousness, engage the client's affect through role playing, reevaluate his or her environment, or any combination of these in order to achieve symptom relief (Prochaska & DiClemente, 1992).

Along the same lines as Prochaska and DiClemente's (1992) model of universal client change processes is William Stiles's assimilation model (1992). Stiles contends that therapy consists of the assimilation of an originally threatening-to-self experience into one's cognitive-affective schemas (Stiles et al., 1992). To accomplish this goal, the client must first allow a problematic experience into awareness and endure the resultant painful thoughts and feelings—that is, assimilation is preceded by accomodation. Stiles has described a series of continuous and predictable stages through which clients traverse while undergoing therapeutic change. These stages, or levels of engagement with a problematic experience, are described as follows (Stiles et al., 1992):

- *Stage 0:* Warded Off. The individual is successfully avoiding engagement with the problem. Very little of the individual's attentional resources are devoted to this issue (i.e., he or she is unaware of the problem).
- *Stage 1:* Unwanted Thoughts. The individual experiences unwanted thoughts about the problem. Strong negative affect occurs with the thoughts, and the individual still attempts to avoid the thoughts.
- *Stage 2:* Vague Awareness, Emergence. The problem is acknowledged as the ambiguous source of unwanted thoughts. Negative affect is very strong.
- *Stage 3:* Problem Statement, Clarification. Problem is clearly stated and acknowledged. Negative affect is present but less overwhelming.
- *Stage 4:* Understanding, Insight. The problematic experience is integrated into a schema with corresponding insight and understanding of the problem. Some affect may still be negative, but more positive emotions such as curiosity are also present.
- *Stage 5:* Application, Working Through. The individual uses newly gained understanding of the problem to devise problem-solving efforts (e.g., change in beliefs about the experience). Affect is primarily optimistic.

- *Stage 6:* Problem Solution. A solution is achieved for the problematic experience. Affect is positive with pride and satisfaction.
- *Stage 7:* Mastery. The individual successfully applies new solution automatically. Affect is neutral because the problem has lost its salience to the individual.

Although they focus on different dimensions of psychotherapy, both Prochaska and DiClemente and Stiles offer new insights into the nature of client change processes, above and beyond the models of change underlying particular brands of therapy.

Perhaps the author most strongly associated with the trend of theoretical integration is Paul Wachtel (1977). His classic *Psychoanalysis and Behavior Therapy: Toward an Integration* offers an elegant synthesis of psychodynamic, interpersonal, and behavioral principles and practices. At the heart of his integrative approach is the concept of the psychodynamic vicious cycle, which explains client maladaptive interpersonal patterns. True to his psychodynamic background, Wachtel employs insight to gain perspective on the origin and manifestations (including client's negative interpersonal expectations, the resulting problematic behaviors, and the expectation-confirming reactions of others) of such cycles. The major contribution of this approach, however, is Wachtel's contention that these self-fulfilling prophecies are currently reinforced through the client's distorted perception of his or her behavior toward others and their behavior towards him or her. Behavioral methods are thus used to modify client's ways of interacting with others (e.g., to bolster social skills), which helps break the current reinforcement of maladaptive interpersonal exchanges.

Several other integrative efforts have been described in collections edited by Goldfried (1982) and Marmor and Woods (1980). These efforts have also been reviewed in Arkowitz (1984) and Goldfried and Newman (1992). Integrative theories and practices have been described in an edited book by Stricker and Gold (1993), which in addition to including integrative approaches based on traditional forms of therapy (e.g., CBT and psychodynamic) also included examples of integration between traditional and nontraditional treatments (e.g., feminist therapy, Buddhism). Additionally, Arkowitz and Messer (1984) have edited a very interesting book on whether psychotherapy integration is possible or practical.

## Common Factors

A third strand of psychotherapy integration is the search for factors that cut across various therapeutic orientations. Common factors have triggered the interest of some authors several years ago (e.g., Rosenweig, 1936), but it is clearly the work of Jerome Frank (1961) that has paved the way for the current recognition of these variables. Frank identified several features (i.e., therapeutic environment, therapeutic relationship, therapeutic rationale, and therapeutic tasks prescribed by the rationale) and therapeutic functions (e.g., increase hope, achieve cognitive and emotional learning, increase sense of mastery) that are shared not only by many forms of psychotherapy but also by most forms of healing (such as nonmedical rites in non-Western cultures). A few authors (Garfield, 1957; Marmor, 1962) had also recognized the importance of common factors at the time of the publication of Frank's (1961) classic *Persuasion and Healing,* but no other work has had more influence on authors who later discussed common factors. These authors—just to name a few—represent a large group: Bandler and Grinder (1975), Ehrenwald (1967), Goldfried and Padawer (1982), Harper (1974), London (1964), Marks and Gelder (1966), Masserman (1980), Sloane (1969), Strupp (1973), Torrey (1972), and Tseng and McDermott (1975).

Over time, a bewildering number of common factors have been described—close to 90, according to Grencavage and Norcross (1990). In order to bring some cohesion to this field, Castonguay (1987; Castonguay & Borgeat, 2001; Castonguay & Lecomte, 1989) has developed a transtheoretical model that integrates similarities within major dimensions of psychotherapy: Therapeutic framework (e.g., setting, assessment, contract), basic processes (i.e, therapist influence, client and therapist engagement, therapeutic relationship) and therapeutic acts (i.e, processes of communication, techniques and strategies of interventions). With the same purpose in mind—or, as they elegantly put it, to delineate commonalities among common factors—Grencavage and Norcross (1990) have organized common factors within five superordinate categories: client characteristics, therapist qualities, change processes, treatment structure, and relationship elements. Based on extensive review of process and outcome research, Orlinsky and Howard (1987) have also offered a generic model of psychotherapy:

> to define the elements of the 'genus' psychotherapy—that is, the features that are common to the varied species of psychotherapy, however diverse the latter may be in the songs they sing and the colors they display to assure mutual recognition among colleagues.... [and] to formulate psychotherapy simply in terms of its 'active ingredients,' disregarding the appeals of familiar brand-name treatments whose patents on psychosocial therapies are expiring in this new age of eclecticism and integration. (pp. 6–7)

Despite the considerable attention they received, common factors were for a long time considered by many (especially behavior therapists) as secondary ingredients of change. Assumed to represent at best necessary but not sufficient conditions of change, common factors were frequently thought of as auxiliaries to the technique specifically prescribed by a particular approach (e.g., systematic desensitization). The accumulation of research findings, however, has forced most skeptics to reconsider the therapeutic role of these commonalities. Lambert (1992) argued that along with placebo effects, common factors explain about 45% of the outcome variance—compared to 15% of client improvement that appears to be due to specific techniques. Among these common factors, the working alliance now appears to be the most robust predictor of change across different forms and modalities of psychotherapy (Constantino et al., 2001).

In addition to being considered secondary variables in the process of change (or perhaps reflecting its second-class citizenship status), common factors have for a long time been equated to the so-called nonspecific variables. Inasmuch as nonspecific variables have been defined as interpersonal (or nontechnical) variables that have not yet been defined, equating the two types of variables has de facto imposed strict limitations on the types of variables that could be referred to as common factors. As pointed out by Castonguay (1993), this implies that no technical intervention has ever been used in more than one orientation. It also implies that none of the common factors so far have been clearly defined, operationalized, or both. It is clear, however, that a large number of techniques (e.g., reinforcement) and strategies of intervention (e.g., facilitating corrective experience) have been found to cut across different orientations. Moreover, a substantial number of them have been operationalized and measured reliably in many studies (e.g., working alliance, empathy). Fortunately, the field has become less inclined to use the term *nonspecific* (not only as a way to describe common factors, but in general) and has begun to refrain from relegating common factors to the status of nebulous (and inconsequential) processes of change. Lampropoulos (2000b) goes a step further in attempting to distinguish between the common factors that actually matter in a therapeutic sense and those common factors that either lack therapeutic potency or are too empirically vague to be studied. He suggests the following sequence of questions for determining whether a given variable is both common and therapeutically relevant: (a) Is the factor present in all or most therapies and (b) has the factor been empirically shown to relate to treatment outcome in most forms of therapy? An affirmative response to the aforementioned questions identifies a factor as both common and therapeutic.

## Integrative Approaches for Specific Clinical Problems

A number of integrative treatments have been developed for specific clinical problems. Perhaps the two best known among them are Linehan's dialectic-behavior therapy for borderline personality disorder and Wolfe's therapy for anxiety disorders.

Linehan's (1987) treatment rests on an eloquent etiological model, which posits that the combination of an early invalidating environment and a biological hypersensitivity to emotionality produces deficient emotional regulation processes that are central to the patient's intrapersonal and interpersonal difficulties. Embedded in a context of emotional validation (i.e., acceptance techniques), behavioral interventions (i.e. change techniques) are used to actively teach and apply coping strategies related to emotional dysregulation. The balance between the use of acceptance and change techniques represents one of the many dialectical principles intrinsic to this complex and innovative treatment. Also used in this integrative intervention are paradoxical techniques, process-experiential attempts to deepen and experience powerful emotions, and dynamic insights to relate current patterns to past distressful experiences (Koerner & Linehan, 1992; Linehan, 1993). At the core of dialectic-behavior therapy is also the implementation of Zen principles, which allow clients, for example, to own seemingly contradictory wishes (e.g. to be loved and to guard against vulnerability), such that the resultant behaviors are seen as understandable reactions to these wishes—yet another dialectical principle.

Central to Wolfe's approach is the premise that anxiety disorders are functionally related to many aspects of the client's life—environmental as well as intrapsychic. Wolfe draws attention to the phenomenological sense of dread and insecurity that many people with anxiety disorders constantly face. He advocates strategies for decreasing the resulting persistent experiential avoidance of painful emotions. Phobias, for example, are treated with the standard behavioral techniques but are also examined for what Wolfe says are possible symbolic reflections of vulnerabilities resulting from early traumatic abandonment experiences.

Other integrative approaches have also begun to emerge. McCullough (2000), for example, has designed an integrative treatment for chronic depression—a clinical problem that has been particularly resistant to previous treatment efforts. Reflecting the author's behavioral background, many components of this treatment involve the clinical implementation of conditioning principles, such as the identification of contingencies (especially negative reinforcements) and the modification of behaviors through techniques like assertion training. The treatment also includes interventions and intervention foci that have been associated with other theoretical traditions in psychology and psychotherapy. Among them are training in social problem solving reflective of Piaget's stage of formal operations, the use of therapist experience to provide feedback to clients on their impact on others, and identification and challenge of transference issues.

With the goal of improving the efficacy of CBT—the current gold-standard treatment—for generalized anxiety disorder, Newman, Castonguay, and Borkovec (1999; Newman, Castonguay, Borkovec, & Molnar, in press) have developed a treatment that combines CBT interventions with techniques used in humanistic, interpersonal, and psychodynamic therapies. The choice of the specific techniques added to CBT was based on both basic and applied research findings. For instance, procedures to deepen emotions (e.g., two-chair approach) have been added based on studies suggesting that worry, the central feature of generalized anxiety disorder, serves as a cognitive avoidance of painful emotion (Borkovec, Newman, & Castonguay, 1998). Also included are interventions designed to address interpersonal issues (in and outside the therapy) based on findings indicating that failure to solve interpersonal problems at the end of CBT predicts worse response at follow-up (Borkovec, Newman, Pincus, & Little, in press). Although process studies have demonstrated that emotional deepening and the exploration of specific interpersonal issues (e.g., relationship with parents or with therapist) are predictive of improvement in CBT (Castonguay et al., 1996; Castonguay et al., 1998; Hayes, Castonguay, & Goldfried, 1996; Jones & Pulos, 1993), research evidence has also shown that these issues are not typically emphasized in this approach, at least in comparison with psychodynamic therapy (Blagys & Hilsenroth, 2000). In contrast, this integrative treatment allows for a direct and systematic processing of these issues while continuing to emphasize the coping skills component that is part of CBT.

Other integrative approaches for specific problems (e.g., substance abuse, organic disorder, depression, chronic pain, severe mental disorders), populations (e.g., children, adolescents, older persons), and treatment modalities (e.g., couple, family, group, medication, and psychotherapy) have been described in Norcross and Goldfried (1992) and Stricker and Gold (1993).

## Improvement of Major Systems of Psychotherapy

The goal of the integration movement is not to create a new school of therapy, wherein all would define themselves as eclectic or integrative therapists. One can pursue the ultimate aims of integration (i.e., to deepen our understanding of change and increase the effectiveness of psychotherapy by considering the potential contributions of several orientations) while remaining primarily attached to one particular approach. Rapprochement with others, in other words, does not imply a rejection of one's own professional identity. As we have argued elsewhere (Goldfried & Castonguay, 1992),

the three major orientations (psychodynamic, humanistic, and CBT) are solidly entrenched in our professional landscape. On the other hand, respected members of each of these particular schools have attempted to improve their approach by integrating constructs and clinical venues developed in other traditions. This type of integration has been defined by Messer (1992, 2001) as *assimilative integration*. In Messer's (2001) words, this term refers to "the incorporation of attitudes, perspectives, or techniques from an auxiliary therapy into a therapist's primary, grounding approach" (p. 1).

Many of the contributions described in this chapter's section on theoretical and clinical disenchantment represent efforts of this sort. However, some authors have offered more extensive and elaborated assimilations of divergent concepts and methods, thereby offering new models within a particular tradition. For instance, arguing that humanistic-existential approaches have failed to provide an adequate understanding of character pathologies, Bouchard (1990) has demonstrated how such problems can be corrected by elegantly integrating psychoanalytic concepts (i.e., Fairbairn, 1954) within Gestalt theory. Gold and Stricker (2001) have argued that recent developments within the psychodynamic orientation have led to a cohesive framework (cogently described by Mitchell, 1988, as relational psychoanalysis) allowing psychodynamically oriented therapists to integrate within their clinical repertoire several strategies of interventions traditionally emphasized in nonpsychoanalytic orientations (e.g., interventions to change relationships outside therapy and to support clients' active efforts at change).

Perhaps the best-known attempt to improve one orientation by relying on the contributions of other tradition is the work of Jeremy Safran (Safran, 1990a, 1990b; Safran & Segal, 1990). As captured by the title of one of his books, a significant portion of his theoretical, clinical, and empirical contributions has been aimed at "widening the scope of cognitive therapy" (Safran, 1998). His consideration of humanistic, interpersonal, and psychodynamic traditions allows for a recognition of four dimensions of human functioning (i.e., emotional, developmental, interpersonal, and conflictual) that have been frequently disregarded in CBT models; it also allows for an integration of non-CBT methods to address the determinants of behaviors associated with these dimensions of functioning (see Castonguay, 2001, for a summary).

Expanding upon Messer's notion of assimilative integration, Lampropoulos (2000) offered concrete suggestions for how therapists can integrate other technical and theoretical components of other modalities in a cohesive and ultimately therapeutic manner. Specifically, he advocates that only empirically validated techniques be incorporated into one's main theoretical orientation, that to-be-integrated techniques fit the context already established by the main orientation, and that the final product of a theory with assimilated aspects of other theories remains internally consistent and the main theoretical and technical tenets stay intact.

## CONCLUDING NOTES: FUTURE DIRECTIONS

Despite being relatively young, the integration movement has served as the vehicle for several interesting developments in the field of psychotherapy. It seems clear, however, that more needs to be done for this movement to be able to fulfill its promise of significantly improving our understanding of the process of change and to substantially increase the efficacy of our interventions. It is clear to us that both theoretical and clinical advances can and should take place within each of the five domains of integration covered in the previous section. We also believe that to ensure its optimal development (if not survival), more attention should be given in the near future to two areas that are crucial to any school or trend in psychotherapy—training and research.

### Training

The quality of training can be seen as a barometer for the maturity of a professional domain. Reflecting their solid establishment in contemporary psychotherapy, humanistic, psychodynamic, and cognitive-behavioral approaches have generated systematic, rigorous, and cohesive training programs (both graduate and postgraduate). Until recently, however, training efforts in psychotherapy integration could be described for the most part as unsystematic and poorly articulated (Castonguay, 2000b). As Robertson (1986) cogently noted, one of the problems facing eclectic and integrative training is

> a scarcity of training faculty who are committed to and competent in the theory and practice of integrative-eclectic psychotherapy. Too often, therapy trainers (and I have to include myself) teach eclecticism in the form of value *statements* instead of value *actions*. It is hoped that we will not transmit this limitation to the generation of eclectic therapy trainers. (p. 432)

It would be inaccurate to say that training has not received attention in the integration movement. In fact, a training committee has for several years been an important part of the Society for the Exploration of Psychotherapy Integration (SEPI; for more information about the organization, please visit *http://www.cyberpsych.org/sepi/*). In addition, several important training issues have been debated for some time and continue to be the focus of current discussion within the integration movement (see Castonguay, in press; Consoli &

Jester, in press; Gold, in press; Lecomte, Castonguay, Cyr & Sabourin, 1993). Among these issues are the use of an integrative-eclectic model as a starting or ending point of one's training, the focus of supervision (exploring the supervisee-supervisor relationship or learning-specific techniques of interventions), characteristics required from students and trainers, the specific challenges and anxieties associated with integrative learning, and the place of formal training in research.

With a few exceptions (e.g., Lecomte et al., 1993), however, what has been missing is the articulation and implementation of structured and cohesive integrative training programs. In line with Robertson's (1986) hope that systematic training programs will be available to the next generation of eclectic-integrative trainers, a recent series of papers published in the *Journal of Psychotherapy Integration* has provided a description of current and future training efforts related to three major trends of psychotherapy integration: theoretical integration (Wolfe, 2000), pragmatic eclecticism (Norcross & Beutler, 2000), and common factors (Castonguay, 2000a). Each paper describes ways in which the authors are actually training students in their own preferred mode of integrative thinking and practice. Also presented are scaffolds of comprehensive training programs that the authors envisioned as ideal from their own perspective. Although such efforts and ideas represent good starting points, much more energy needs to be devoted in the future to articulate, build, and evaluate integrative training programs.

### Research

Research has clearly lagged behind the commitment shown toward theoretical and clinical development by individuals interested in psychotherapy integration. Nevertheless, empirical efforts have begun to provide support to this growing movement. In fact, a number of studies have been conducted within each of the trends described in the previous section.

A considerable number of studies have been conducted with respect to two of the approaches representing the theoretical integration perspective. As described by Prochaska and DiClemente (1992), the constructs of stages, processes, and levels of change (which are at the core of their transtheoretical approach) have been validated. In addition, the predictive validity of the stages and processes of change has been established with respect to premature termination, short-term outcome, and long-term outcome. Furthermore, stage-matching interventions for smoking cessation have shown promising results compared to those of the current gold-standard treatment. Both quantitative and qualitative research has also endorsed the construct and predictive validity of Stiles's assimilaton model (Field, Barkham, Shapiro, & Stiles, 1994; Stiles, Meshot, Anderson, & Sloan, 1992; Stiles, Shankland, Wright, & Field, 1997). For instance, clients who come to therapy with problems located at higher levels of assimilation achieved better outcomes in CBT compared to interpersonal therapy—a finding that is consistent with the assumption that well-assimilated problematic experiences require therapeutic techniques geared toward the client's activating new behaviors (Stiles et al., 1997). The findings of a qualitative study on the process of assimilation in process-experiential psychotherapy for depression suggest that progress in assimilation accounted for one client's superior outcome, whereas the lack of gains in assimilation across the course of treatment could plausibly explain another client's poor outcome (Honos-Webb et al., 1998).

With regard to eclecticism, the empirical work of Larry Beutler and his colleagues has provided helpful guidelines for prescribing the types of treatment that may be most indicated for particular clients (see Beutler & Consoli, 1992). For instance, their findings suggest that clients who tend to be highly reactive (i.e., reluctant to be controlled by others) should be prescribed interventions that are nondirective in nature (e.g., supportive therapy), whereas directive forms of interventions (e.g., CBT or focused-expressive therapy) appear to be indicated for individuals who are less reactive. In addition, insight-oriented therapies (e.g., supportive therapy or focused-expressive therapy) seem to be appropriate for individuals who cope with stress by internalizing their problems (e.g., self-blame), whereas symptom-focused treatment (e.g., CBT) may be a better fit for individuals who externalize (i.e., who blame others or external circumstances for their problems) when confronted with stress.

A number of common factors have been investigated. These factors include variables such as expectancies, working alliance, empathy, and corrective emotional experience (Arnkoff, Victor, & Glass, 1993; Castonguay & Borgeat, 2000; Lambert, 1992; Weinberger, 1993). As described earlier in this chapter, a variety of factors assumed to be unique to one orientation (e.g., emotional deepening, exploration of the past, behavioral activation techniques) also appear to cut across different approaches.

Several of the integrative treatments that have been developed to address particular forms of clinical problems have also been submitted to empirical investigations. Chief among them is Linehan's dialectic-behavior therapy for borderline personality disorder. A substantial number of efficacy studies have been conducted on this treatment and reviewed in several recent publications (e.g., Koerner & Dimeff, 2000; Koerner & Linehan, 2000; Linehan, Cochran, & Cochran,

2001). As summarized by Koerner and Linehan (2000),

> Research evidence to date indicates that, although DBT [dialectic-behavior therapy] was developed for the treatment of patients with suicidal behavior, it can be adapted to treat BPD [borderline personality disorder] patients with comorbid substance-abuse disorder and be extended to other patient populations and the treatment of other disorders. Across studies, DBT seems to reduce severe dysfunctional behaviors that are targeted for intervention (e.g., parasuicide, substance abuse, and binge eating), enhance treatment retention, and reduce psychiatric hospitalization. (p. 164)

Furthermore, process findings have provided support to one of the core aspects of Linehan's model of change by demonstrating that a balance of therapist acceptance and change was associated with clients' improvement (Shearin & Linehan, 1992).

Although its findings are preliminary, a recent study on the integrative therapy for generalized anxiety disorder described earlier indicates that a sequential combination of CBT and I/EP components is not only feasible (as suggested by numerous process measures, including the level of adherence and competence achieved by therapists), but it also appears to lead to higher pre-post treatment effect sizes than does traditional CBT for GAD (see Newman et al., in press). In addition, impressive findings for the efficacy of McCullough's cognitive behavioral-analysis system in combination with medication (Nefazodone) were recently published in the prestigious *New England Journal of Medicine* (Keller et al., 2000). A response rate of 85% (for completers) was obtained on a large sample of individuals suffering from chronic depression.

As an example of the fifth trend of the integration movement (i.e., efforts to improve effective forms of therapy), Castonguay (2000) provided a first efficacy test of an integrative-cognitive therapy (ICT) for depression. The study was based on earlier process findings, which suggested that therapists' adherence to the prescribed rationale and techniques in cognitive therapy may interfere with positive outcome when used to address alliance ruptures (Castonguay et al., 1996). Specifically, ICT requires therapists to follow the traditional cognitive therapy protocol (Beck, Rush, Shaw, & Emery, 1979), except when confronted with alliance ruptures. Following the guidelines described by Burns (1990), Safran and Segal (1990), and Linehan (1993), therapists are then instructed to use techniques derived from (or similar to interventions used in) humanistic and interpersonal therapies (e.g., empathy, exploration of therapist's contribution to ruptures) to resolve the relationship difficulties. Although findings are still preliminary, they suggest that ICT is not only superior to a waiting-list condition, but it also compares favorably to traditional cognitive therapy for depression.

Despite the promising nature of the aforementioned studies, it remains imperative for individuals invested in the integration movement to devote more energy into research. As Glass, Victor, and Arnkoff (1993) cogently argued, although current research represents a solid beginning, "it is clear that there are nearly unlimited avenues for future study" (p. 20). Considering the pressure for accountability that is imposed on mental health professionals, the onus is on integrative researchers to demonstrate that this movement can indeed lead to a better understanding of the complexity of the process of change and more effective ways of dealing with human suffering.

# REFERENCES

Alexander, F. (1963). The dynamics of psychotherapy in light of learning theory. *American Journal of Psychiatry, 120,* 440–448.

Appelbaum, S. A. (1979). *Out in inner space: A psychoanalyst explores the therapies.* Garden City, NY: Anchor.

Arkowitz, H. A. (1984). Historical perspective on the integration of psychoanalytic therapy and behavioral therapy. In H. Arkowitz & S. Messer (Eds.), *Psychoanalytic therapy and behavior therapy* (pp. 1–30). New York: Plenum Press.

Arkowitz, H., & Messer, S. B. (Eds.). (1984). *Psychoanalytic and behavior therapy: Is integration possible?* New York: Plenum Press.

Arnkoff, D. B. (1981). Flexibility in practicing cognitive therapy. In G. Emery, S. D. Hollon, & R. C. Bedrosian (Eds.), *New directions in cognitive therapy* (pp. 203–223). New York: Guilford Press.

Arnkoff, D. B., Victor, B. J., & Glass, C. R. (1993). Empirical research on integrative and eclectic psychotherapies. In G. Stricker & J. Gold (Eds.), *Comprehensive handbook of psychotherapy integration* (pp. 9–26). New York: Plenum Press.

Bandler, R., & Grinder, J. (1975). *The structure of magic.* United States: Science and Behavior Books.

Barlow, D. H., & Wolfe, B. E. (1981). Behavioral approaches to anxiety disorders: A report on the NIMH-SUNY, Albany, Research Conference. *Journal of Consulting and Clinical Psychology, 49,* 448–454.

Beck, A. T., Freeman, A., & Associates. (1990). *Cognitive therapy of personality disorders.* New York: Guilford Press.

Beck, A. T., Rush, J. J., Shaw, B. F., & Emery, G. (1979). *Cognitive therapy for depression.* New York: Guilford Press.

Beutler, L. E. (1983). *Eclectic psychotherapy: A systematic approach.* Elmsford, NY: Pergamon Press.

Beutler, L. E., & Consoli, A. J. (1992). Systematic eclectic psychotherapy. In J. C. Norcross & M. R. Goldfried (Eds.), *Handbook of psychotherapy integration* (pp. 264–299). New York: Basic Books.

Blagys, M. D., & Hilsenroth, M. J. (2000). Distinctive features of short-term psychodynamic-interpersonal psychotherapy: A review of the comparative psychotherapy process literature. *Clinical psychology: Science and practice, 7,* 167–188.

Borkovec, T. D., Newman, M. G., & Castonguay, L. G. (1998, November). *The potential role of interpersonal emotional processing in the treatment of Generalized Anxiety Disorder.* Paper presented at the Annual meeting of the Association for the Advancement of Behavior Therapy, Washington, DC.

Borkovec, T. D., Newman, M. G., Pincus, A., & Lytle, R. (in press). A component analysis of cognitive-behavioral therapy for generalized anxiety disorder and the role of interpersonal problems. *Journal of Consulting and Clinical Psychology.*

Bouchard, M. A. (1990). *De la phenomenologie a la psychanalyse.* Bruxelles: Pierre Mardaga.

Burns, D. D. (1990). *The feeling good handbook.* New York: Plume.

Castonguay, L. G. (1987). Rapprochement en psychotherapie: Perspectives theoriques, cliniques, et empiriques. In C. Lecomte & L. G. Castonguay (Eds.), *Rapprochement et integration en psychotherapie: Psychanalyse, behaviorisme et humanisme.* Chicoutimi: Gaetan Morin.

Castonguay, L. G. (1993). "Common factors" and "nonspecific variables": Clarification of the two concepts and recommendations for research. *Journal of Psychotherapy Integration, 3,* 267–286.

Castonguay, L. G. (2000a). A common factors approach to psychotherapy training. *Journal of Psychotherapy Integration, 10,* 263–282.

Castonguay, L. G. (2000b). Training in psychotherapy integration: Introduction to current efforts and future visions. *Journal of Psychotherapy Integration, 10,* 229–232.

Castonguay, L. G. (in press). Issues in psychotherapy training. *Journal of Psychotherapy Integration.*

Castonguay, L. G., & Borgeat, F. (2001). Les mécanismes de base en psychothérapie. In P. Lalonde, J. Aubut, & F. Grunberg (Eds.), *Psychiatrie clinique: Approche bio-psycho-sociale.* Chicoutimi: Gaetan Morin.

Castonguay, L. G., Goldfried, M. R., Wiser, S., Raue, P. J., & Hayes, A. H. (1996). Predicting outcome in cognitive therapy for depression: A comparison of unique and common factors. *Journal of Consulting and Clinical Psychology, 64,* 497–504.

Castonguay, L. G., & Lecomte, C. (1989, April). *The common factors in psychotherapy: What is known and what should be known.* Paper presented at the 5th Annual Meeting of the Society for the Exploration of Psychotherapy Integration, San Francisco.

Castonguay, L. G., Pincus, A. L., Agras, W. S., & Hines, C. E. (1998). The role of emotion in group cognitive-behavioral therapy for binge eating disorder: When things have to feel worst before they get better. *Psychotherapy Research, 8,* 225–238.

Consoli, A. J., & Jester, C. M. (in press). A model for teaching psychotherapy theory through integrative structure. *Journal of Psychotherapy Integration.*

Constantino, M. J., Castonguay, L. G., & Schut, A. J. (2001). The working alliance: A flagship for the scientific-practitioner model in psychotherapy. In G. Shick Tryon (Ed.), *Counseling based on process research* (pp. 81–131). New York: Allyn and Bacon.

Eysenck, H. J. (1953). *Uses and abuses of psychology.* Baltimore: Penguin Books.

Eysenck, H. J. (1970). A mish-mash of theories. *International Journal of Psychiatry, 9,* 140–146.

Fairbairn, W. R. D. (1954). *An object relations theory of the personality.* New York: Basic Books.

Field, S. D., Barkham, M., Shapiro, D. A., & Stiles, W. B. (1994). Assessment of assimilation in psychotherapy: A quantitative case study of problematic experiences with a significant other. *Journal of Counseling-Psychology, 41,* 397–406.

Fiedler, F. E. (1950). A comparison of therapeutic relationships in psychoanalytic, nondirective, and Adlerian therapy. *Journal of Consulting Psychology, 14,* 436–445.

Frank, J. D. (1961). *Persuasion and healing.* Baltimore: Johns Hopkins University Press.

Garfield, S. L. (1957). *Introductory clinical psychology.* New York: MacMillan.

Garfield, S. L. (1994). Research on client variables in psychotherapy. In A. E. Bergin & S. L. Garfield (Eds.), *Handbook of psychotherapy and behavior change* (4th ed., pp. 190–228). New York: Wiley.

Gill, M. M. (1982). *Analysis of transference, Vol. 1: Theory and technique.* New York: International Universities Press.

Gold, J. R. (in press). Anxiety, conflict and resistance in learning an integrative perspective on psychotherapy. *Journal of Psychotherapy Integration.*

Gold, J. R. (1996). *Key concepts in psychotherapy integration.* New York: Plenum Press.

Gold, J. R., & Stricker, G. (2001). A relational psychodynamic perspective on assimilative integration. *Journal of Psychotherapy Integration, 11,* 43–58.

Goldfried, M. R. (Ed.). (1982). *Converging themes in psychotherapy: Trends in psychodynamic, humanistic, and behavioral practice.* New York: Springer.

Goldfried, M. R. (1985). In vivo intervention or transference? In W. Dryden (Ed.), *Therapist's dilemmas.* London: Harper and Row.

Goldfried, M. R. (Ed.). (2001). *How therapists change: Personal and professional reflections.* Washington, DC: American Psychological Association.

Goldfried, M. R., & Castonguay, L. G. (1993). Behavior therapy: Redefining strengths and limitations. *Behavior Therapy, 24,* 505–526.

Goldfried, M. R., Castonguay, L. G., Hayes, A. H., Drozd, J. F., & Shapiro, D. A. (1997). A comparative analysis of the therapeutic focus in cognitive-behavioral and pychodynamic-interpersonal sessions. *Journal of Consulting and Clinical Psychology, 65,* 740–748.

Goldfried, M. R., & Davison, G. C. (1976). *Clinical behavior therapy.* New York: Holt, Rinehart, & Winston.

Goldfried, M. R., & Davison, G. C. (1994). *Clinical behavior therapy.* New York: Wiley.

Goldfried, M. R., & Newman, C. F. (1992). A history of psychotherapy integration. In J. C. Norcross & M. R. Goldfried (Eds.), *Handbook of psychotherapy integration* (pp. 46–93). New York: Basic Books.

Goldfried, M. R., Newman, C. F., & Hayes, A. M. (1989). *The coding system of therapeutic focus.* Unpublished manuscript, State University of New York, Stony Brook.

Goldfried, M. R., & Padawer, W. (1982). Current status and future directions in psychotherapy. In M. R. Goldfried (Ed.), *Converging themes in psychotherapy* (pp. 3–49). New York: Springer.

Goldfried, M. R., Raue, P. J., & Castonguay, L. G. (1998). The therapeutic focus in significant sessions of master therapists: A comparison of cognitive-behavioral and psychodynamic-interpersonal interventions. *Journal of Consulting and Clinical Psychology, 66,* 803–811.

Greenberg, L. S., & Safran, J. D. (1987). *Emotion in psychotherapy.* New York: Guilford Press.

Greenberg, L. S., Watson, J. C., & Lietaer, G. (1998). *Handbook of experiential psychotherapy.* New York: Guilford Press.

Greening, T. C. (1978). Commentary. *Journal of humanistic psychology, 18,* 1–4.

Grencavage, L. M., & Norcross, J. C. (1990). Where are the commonalties among the therapeutic common factors? *Professional Psychology: Research and Practice, 5,* 372–378.

Grinker, R. R. (1976). Discussion of Strupp's, "Some critical comments on the future of psychoanalytic therapy." *Bulletin of the Menninger Clinic, 40,* 247–254.

Harper, R. (1974). *Psychoanalysis and psychotherapy.* New York: Jason Aronson.

Hayes, A. H., Castonguay, L. G., & Goldfried, M. R. (1996). The effectiveness of targeting the vulnerability factors of depression in cognitive therapy. *Journal of Consulting and Clinical Psychology, 64,* 623–627.

Henry, W. P., Schacht, T. E., & Strupp, H. H. (1990). Patient and therapist introject, interpersonal process, and differential psychotherapy outcome. *Journal of Consulting and Clinical Psychology, 58,* 768–774.

Henry, W. P., Strupp, H. H., Butler, S. F., Schacht, T. E., & Binder, J. L. (1993). Effects of training in time-limited dynamic psychotherapy: Changes in therapist behavior. *Journal of Consulting and Clinical Psychology, 61,* 434–440.

Hill, C. E., O'Grady, K. E., & Elkin, I. (1992). Applying the collaborative study psychotherapy rating scale to rate therapist adherence in cognitive-behavior therapy, interpersonal therapy, and clinical management. *Journal of Consulting and Clinical Psychology, 60,* 73–79.

Jones, E. E., & Pulos, S. M. (1993). Comparing the process in psychodynamic and cognitive-behavioral therapies. *Journal of Consulting and Clinical Psychology, 61,* 306–316.

Kahn, M. (1991). *Between therapist and client: The new relationship.* New York: W. H. Freeman.

Keller, M. B., McCullough, J. P., Klein, D. N., Arnow, B., Dunner, D. L., Gelenberg, A. J., Markowitz, J. C., Nemeroff, C. B., Russell, J. M., Thase, M. E., Trivedi, M. H., & Zajecka, J. (2000). A comparison of nefazodone, the cognitive behavioral-analysis system of psychotherapy, and their combination for the treatment of chronic depression. *New England Journal of Medicine, 342,* 1462–1470.

Kendall, P. C. (1998). Empirically supported psychological therapies. *Journal of Consulting and Clinical Psychology, 66,* 3–6.

Koerner, K., & Dimeff, L. A. (2000). Further data on dialectical behavior therapy. *Clinical psychology: Science and Practice, 7,* 104–112.

Koerner, K., & Linehan, M. M. (1992). Integrative therapy for borderline personality disorder: Dialectical behavior therapy. In M. Goldfried & J. Norcross (Eds.), *Handbook of psychotherapy integration* (pp. 433–459). New York: Basic Books.

Lambert, M. J. (1992). Psychotherapy outcome research: Implications for integrative and eclectic therapists. In J. C. Norcross & M. R. Goldfried (Eds.), *Handbook of psychotherapy integration* (pp. 94–129). New York: Basic Books.

Lambert, M. J., & Bergin, A. E. (1994). The effectiveness of psychotherapy. In A. E. Bergin & S. L. Garfield (Eds.), *Handbook of psychotherapy and behavior change* (4th ed., pp. 143–189). New York: Wiley.

Lampropoulos, G. K. (2000a). Evolving psychotherapy integration: Eclectic selection and prescriptive applications of common factors in therapy. *Psychotherapy, 37,* 285–297.

Lampropoulos, G. K. (2000b). Definitional and research issues in the common factors approach to psychotherapy integration: Misconceptions, clarifications, and proposals. *Journal of Psychotherapy Integration, 10,* 415–438.

Lampropoulos, G. K. (2001). Bridging technical eclecticism and theoretical integration: Assimilative integration. *Journal of Psychotherapy Integration, 11,* 5–19.

Landsman, T. (1974, August). *Not an adversity but a welcome diversity.* Paper presented at the meeting of the American Psychological Association, New Orleans, LA.

Lazarus, A. A. (1967). In support of technical eclecticism. *Psychological Reports, 21,* 415–416.

Lazarus, A. A. (1971). *Behavior therapy and beyond.* New York: McGraw-Hill.

Lazarus, A. A. (1992). Multimodal therapy: Technical eclecticism with minimal integration. In J. C. Norcross & M. R. Goldfried (Eds.), *Handbook of psychotherapy integration* (pp. 231–265). New York: Basic Books.

Lecomte, C., Castonguay, L. G., Cyr, M., & Sabourin, S. (1993). Supervision and instruction in doctoral psychotherapy integration.

In G. Stricker & J. R. Gold (Eds.), *Comprehensive handbook of psychotherapy integration* (pp. 483–498). New York: Plenum Press.

Levis, D. J. (1988). Observations and experience from clinical practice: A critical ingredient for advancing behavior theory and practice. *The Behavior Therapist, 11,* 95–99.

Linehan, M. M. (1987). Dialectical behavior therapy for borderline personality disorder: Theory and method. *Bulletin of the Menninger Clinic, 51,* 261–276.

Linehan, M. M. (1993). *Cognitive-behavioral treatment of borderline personality disorder.* New York: Guilford Press.

Linehan, M. M., Cochran, B. N., & Cochran, C. A. (2001). Dialectical behavior therapy for borderline personality disorder. In D. Barlow (Ed.), *Clinical handbook of psychological disorders: A step-by-step treatment manual* (3rd ed., pp. 470–522). New York: Guilford Press.

London, P. (1964). *The modes and morals of psychotherapy.* New York: Holt, Rinehart, & Winston.

Luborsky, L., Singer, B., & Luborsky, L. (1975). Comparative studies of psychotherapies: Is it true that "Everyone has won and all must have prizes?" *Archives of General Psychiatry, 32,* 995–1008.

Mahoney, M. J. (1979). Cognitive and non-cognitive views in behavior modification. In P. O. Sjoden & S. Bates (Eds.), *Trends in behavior therapy* (pp. 39–54). New York: Plenum Press.

Marks, I. M., & Gelder, M. G. (1966). Common ground between behavior therapy and psychodynamic methods. *British Journal of Medical Psychology, 39,* 11–23.

Marmor, J. (1962). Psychoanalytic therapy as an educational process. *Science and Psychoanalysis, 7,* 286–299.

Marmor, J. (1964). Psychoanalytic therapy and theories of learning. *Science and Psychoanalysis, 7,* 265–279.

Marmor, J. (1976). Common operational factors in diverse approaches to behavior change. In A. Burton (Ed.), *What makes behavior change possible?* (pp. 3–12). New York: Brunner/Mazel.

Marmor, J. (1982). Change in psychoanalytic treatment. In S. Slipp (Ed.), *Curative factors in dynamic psychotherapy* (pp. 60–70). New York: McGraw-Hill.

Marmor, J., & Woods, S. M. (Eds.). (1980). *The interface between psychodynamic and behavioral therapies.* New York: Plenum Press.

Masserman, J. (1980). *Principles and practice of biodynamic psychiatry.* New York: Thieme-Stratton.

McCullough, J. P. (2000). *Treatment for chronic depression: Cognitive-behavioral analysis system of psychotherapy.* New York: Guilford Press.

Messer, S. B. (1992). A critical examination of belief structures in integrative and eclectic psychotherapy. In M. Goldfried & J. Norcross (Eds.), *Handbook of psychotherapy integration* (pp. 131–165). New York: Basic Books.

Messer, S. B. (2001). Introduction to the special issue on assimilative integration. *Journal of Psychotherapy Integration, 11,* 1–4.

Mitchell, S. (1988). *Relational concepts in psychoanalysis.* Cambridge, MA: Harvard University Press.

Murray, E. J., & Jacobson, L. I. (1971). Cognition and learning in traditional and behavioral psychotherapy. In M. Lambert & A. Bergin (Eds.), *Handbook of psychotherapy and behavior change* (pp. 661–688). New York: Wiley.

Newman, M. G., Castonguay, L. G., & Borkovec (1999, April). *New dimensions in the treatment of generalized anxiety disorder: Interpersonal focus and emotional deepening.* Paper presented at the 15th Annual Meeting of the Society for the Exploration of Psychotherapy Integration, Miami, FL.

Newman, M. G., Castonguay, L. G., Borkovec, T. D., & Molnar, C. (in press). Integrative therapy for generalized anxiety disorder. In R. G. Heimberg, C. L. Turk, & D. S. Mennin (Eds.), *Generalized anxiety disorder: Advances in research and practice.* New York: Guilford Press.

Norcross, J. C. (Ed.). (1986). *Handbook of eclectic psychotherapy.* New York: Brunner/Mazel.

Norcross, J. C., & Beutler, L. E. (2000). A prescriptive eclectic approach to psychotherapy training. *Journal of Psychotherapy Integration, 10,* 247–261.

Norcross, J. C., & Goldfried, M. R. (Eds.). (1992). *Handbook of psychotherapy integration.* New York: Basic Books.

Norcross, J. D., & Newman, C. F. (1992). Psychotherapy integration: Setting the context. In J. C. Norcross & M. R. Goldfried (Eds.), *Handbook of psychotherapy integration* (pp. 3–45). New York: Basic Books.

Orlinsky, D. E., & Howard, K. I. (1987). A generic model of psychotherapy. *Journal of Integrative and Eclectic Psychotherapy, 6,* 6–27.

Piper, W. E., Joyce, A. S., Rosie, J. S., Ogrodniczuk, J. S., McCallum, M., O'Kelly, J. G., & Steinberg, P. I. (1999). Prediction of dropping out in time-limited interpretive individual psychotherapy. *Psychotherapy, 36,* 114–122.

Prochaska, J. O., & DiClemente, C. C. (1992). The transtheoretical approach. In J. C. Norcross & M. R. Goldfried (Eds.), *Handbook of psychotherapy integration* (pp. 300–334). New York: Basic Books.

Rhoads, J. M., & Feather, B. W. (1972). Transference and resistance observed in behavior therapy. *British Journal of Medical Psychology, 45,* 99–103.

Ricks, D. F., Wandersman, A., & Poppen, P. J. (1976). Humanism and behaviorism: Toward new syntheses. In A. Wandersman, P. J. Poppen, & D. F. Ricks (Eds.), *Humanism and behaviorism: Dialogue and growth* (pp. 383–402). Elmsford, NY: Pergamon Press.

Robertson, M. H. (1986). Training eclectic psychotherapists. In J. Norcross (Ed.), *Handbook of eclectic psychotherapy* (pp. 416–435). New York: Brunner/Mazel.

Rogers, C. R. (1981). Book jacket comment. In P. Pentony (Ed.), *Models of influence in psychotherapy.* New York: Macmillan.

Rosenzweig, S. (1936). Some implicit common factors in diverse methods in psychotherapy. *American Journal of Orthopsychiatry, 6,* 412–415.

Safran, J. D. (1990a). Towards a refinement of cognitive therapy in light of interpersonal theory, I. Theory. *Clinical Psychology Review, 10,* 87–105.

Safran, J. D. (1990b). Towards a refinement of cognitive therapy in light of interpersonal theory, II. Practice. *Clinical Psychology Review, 10,* 107–121.

Safran, J. D. (1998). *Widening the scope of cognitive therapy.* Northvale, NJ: Aronson.

Safran, J. D., & Segal, Z. V. (1990). *Interpersonal process in cognitive therapy.* New York: Basic Books.

Samilov, A., & Goldfried, M. R. (2000). Role of emotion in cognitive-behavior therapy. *Clinical psychology: Science and Practice, 7,* 373–385.

Schut, A. J., & Castonguay, L. G. (2001). Reviving Freud's vision of a psychoanalytic science: Implications for clinical training and education. *Psychotherapy, 38,* 40–49.

Shearin, E. N., & Linehan, M. M. (1992). Dialectical behavior therapy for borderline personality disorder: Theoretical and empirical foundations. *Acta psychiatrica scandinavica, 92,* 155–160.

Shectman, F. (1977). Conventional and contemporary approaches to psychotherapy: Freud meets Skinner, Janov and others. *American Psychologist, 32,* 197–204.

Sloane, R. B. (1969). The converging paths of behavior therapy and psychotherapy. *American Journal of Psychiatry, 125,* 877–885.

Stiles, W. B., Meshot, C. M., Anderson, T. M., & Sloan, W. W. (1992). Assimilation of problematic experiences: The case of John Jones. *Psychotherapy-Research, 2,* 81–101.

Stiles, W. B., Shankland, M. C., Wright, J., & Field, S. D. (1997). Aptitude-treatment interactions based on clients' assimilation of their presenting problems. *Journal of Consulting and Clinical Psychology, 65,* 889–893.

Stricker, G. (1994). Reflections on psychotherapy integration. *Clinical Psychology: Science and Practice, 1,* 3–12.

Stricker, G., & Gold, J. R. (Eds.). (1993). *Comprehensive handbook of psychotherapy integration.* New York: Plenum Press.

Strupp, H. H. (1973). On the basic ingredients of psychotherapy. *Journal of Consulting and Clinical Psychology, 41,* 1–8.

Strupp, H. H. (1976). Some critical comments on the future of psychoanalytic therapy. *Bulletin of the Menninger Clinic, 40,* 238–254.

Thoresen, C. E., & Coates, T. J. (1978). What does it mean to be a behavior therapist? *Counseling Psychologist, 7,* 3–21.

Tobin, S. A. (1990). Self psychology as a bridge between existential-humanistic psychology and psychoanalysis. *Journal of Humanistic Psychology, 30,* 14–63.

Tobin, S. A. (1991). A comparison of psychoanalytic self psychology and Carl Rogers's person-centered therapy. *Journal of Humanistic Psychology, 31,* 9–33.

Torrey, E. F. (1972). What western psychotherapists can learn from witch-doctors? *American Journal of Orthopsychiatry, 42,* 69–76.

Tseng, W. S., & McDermott, J. F. (1979). Psychotherapy: Historical roots, universal elements, and cultural variations. *American Journal of Psychiatry, 132,* 378–384.

Wachtel, P. L. (1977). *Psychoanalysis and behavior therapy: Toward an integration.* New York: Basic Books.

Wallerstein, R. S., & DeWitt, K. N. (1997). Intervention modes in psychoanalysis and in psychoanalytic psychotherapies: A revised classification. *Journal of Psychotherapy Integration, 7,* 129–150.

Weinberger, J. (1993). Common factors in psychotherapy. In G. Stricker & J. Gold (Eds.), *Comprehensive handbook of psychotherapy integration* (pp. 9–26). New York: Plenum Press.

Winnicott, D. W. (1989). *Psychoanalytic explorations.* Cambridge, MA: Harvard University Press. (Original work published 1969)

Wolfe, B. E. (1992). Integrative psychotherapy of the anxiety disorders. In J. C. Norcross & M. R. Goldfried (Eds.), *Handbook of psychotherapy integration* (pp. 373–401). New York: Basic Books.

Wolfe, B. E. (2000). Toward an integrative theoretical basis for training psychotherapists. *Journal of Psychotherapy Integration, 10,* 223–246.

Yalom, I. D. (1980). *Existential psychotherapy.* New York: Basic Books.

CHAPTER 14

# Group Psychotherapy

ANNE ALONSO, SARAH ALONSO, AND WILLIAM PIPER

Human beings thrive in a community that values their participation and protects their dignity. We all need support, wisdom, and compassion throughout the life cycle, and we look to our natural groups for that kind of sustenance. When individual capacity fails and when suffering becomes too draining on one's resources, the therapy group can offer just such a community of peers to help heal human misery and to nurture continuing healthy development.

This chapter develops the concepts of group psychotherapy in the twenty-first century. For a host of reasons—the search for community because we have moved away from our natural villages, the added value that psychological theory places on the relational field, and the sheer economy of

the treatment model, given the financial constraints of the mental health field—group psychotherapy stands as a very viable and rich option for mental health care.

The initial section reviews some of the historical underpinnings and the basic concepts that hold across a range of theories. We summarize the main theories, paying attention to places where the theories inform the various goals and techniques. The larger part of this section is devoted to psychoanalytic group therapy and technique.

The second major section focuses on briefer group treatments and on inpatient and partial hospitalization groups. This section addresses aspects of symptom-specific and population-specific group therapy.

A third section reviews the current research about group psychotherapy.

## HISTORY AND EVOLUTION OF GROUP PSYCHOTHERAPY

### Early Beginnings

Group psychotherapy originated in America in 1905 and was first conducted at the Massachusetts General Hospital by an internist, Joseph H. Pratt (1922), who led groups composed of patients with tuberculosis. He referred to these groups as classes, and they bore remarkable similarity to those currently offered by cognitive-behavioral groups, psychoeducational groups, and self-help groups to alleviate the distress caused by commonly shared physical or psychological problems. A few years later, Trigant Burrow (1927) coined the term *group analysis* and conducted group therapy for noninstitutionalized patients. In the early 1930s Louis Wender (1940) introduced the notion of the group as a recreated family, applied psychoanalytic concepts to group therapy, and began the use of combined therapy.

Samuel Slavson (1951), an engineer by profession, founded the American Group Psychotherapy Association in 1948 and is regarded as having had the most influence on the development of American group psychotherapy. He referred to his method as analytic group psychotherapy and concentrated on the individual in the group rather than on the group itself. His greatest contribution is acknowledged to be the development of group psychotherapy with children. During the 1930s and 1940s Wolf and Schwartz (1962) actively applied the principles of psychoanalysis to groups of adults.

Group psychotherapy also created interest in Europe. A Romanian psychiatrist, Jacob L. Moreno (1898–1974), primarily identified with psychodrama, borrowed from his experience with the *Stegreiftheater* (Theater of Spontaneity in Vienna). Thus, his introduction of group psychotherapy in 1910 included role-playing and role-training methods (Moreno, 1947). Moreno may have coined the term *group therapy* in 1931. Although he never formally conducted group psychotherapy, Sigmund Freud called attention to group psychology in *Group Psychology and Analysis of the Ego* (1921/1962). Freud's insights into group formation and transference reactions form the underpinnings of modern psychoanalytically oriented group psychotherapy, from both the group to the individual and the individual to the group. Kurt Lewin (1947) introduced field theory concepts, emphasizing that the group is different from the simple sum of its parts. Lewin coined the term *group dynamics* in 1939 and is considered the pioneer of viewing the group as a whole.

In England, group therapy evolved largely as a result of the pressure to treat a large number of psychiatric casualties during World War II. Wilfred R. Bion (1959), an analysand of Melanie Klein's (1932), offered the hypothesis that the group has a separate mental life, with its own dynamics and complex emotional states, which he terms *basic assumption cultures*. His basic assumptions paralleled Klein's stages of infant development. Bion is best known for his work with the group as a whole, and his ideas have gained immense popularity in the United States. Henry Ezriel (1950) and John D. Sutherland (1952) were also active in group therapy, emphasizing the here-and-now and then-and-there perspectives. Ezriel is credited as the first person to describe the transferences between the members themselves and between the members and the group as a whole.

The distinction has been made between therapy *in* a group and therapy *through* a group. In the former case, the group leader administers the same therapy—either simultaneously or seriatim—to the entire group as that performed with individual patients. In therapy *through* the group, members play a critical role in the therapy—particularly through modeling and reinforcement procedures and other elements of group dynamics.

However, early in the study of groups, a fear of possible negative factors surfaced, voiced not only by Freud but also earlier by LeBon (1920) and others. When conditions are favorable, groups enjoy the power that comes from contagion. *Contagion* is a process by which members of a group are pulled into an activity in which they might not engage by themselves. At its most pernicious, it is the process that turns a group into a mob (LeBon, 1920). At its more benign, it is a centripetal force that entices a person—as a member of a cohesive group—to protect the cohesiveness by joining in the shared activity or pool of affects. When this activity takes the form of risking exposure to shame by disclosing and remembering hitherto-repressed material, the analytic process is moved along toward further resolution.

### History of Inpatient Groups

Since the time of Hippocrates (around 300 BC), mental illness has been viewed as a condition with similarities to medical illnesses, and hospitalization or institutionalization has been employed in an effort to heal the sick. The first psychiatric hospitals were established in Europe at the end of the eighteenth century and soon were followed by a handful of institutions in the United States that were devoted to the treatment and care of the mentally ill.

Inpatient group therapy in the United States can be traced to two roots: the therapeutic community or milieu therapy movement and the group therapy experiments of the early twentieth century. Among the first milieu therapies was that offered at the Menninger Foundation in Kansas in the 1930s. There, hospital treatment was based on the premise that different types of social interactions could be used to benefit individuals suffering from various mental disorders (Menninger, 1936). The earliest psychiatric groups offered in hospitals in this country were at Worcester State Hospital in Massachusetts (Sadock & Kaplan, 1983). There, a former minister-turned-physician named L. Cody Marsh began giving lectures about mental illness to patients over the loudspeaker and organizing discussion groups. Patients were required to pass an examination before they could be released. About the same time, Lazell (1921) was holding classes for patients with schizophrenia at St. Elizabeth's Hospital in Washington, DC, teaching them about the psychoanalytic roots of their problems. During World War II, groups were used in several military hospitals—in part as a way to treat many patients simultaneously with fewer demands on the staff. At the Northfield Military Hospital in England, Bion, Foulkes, Ezriel, and Main (1965) introduced the idea that the psychiatric unit in its entirety is a group, and as such, it had therapeutic benefit in all of its parts.

Foulkes' approach was to bring a psychoanalytic awareness to all types of group activities that occur in the hospital and to maintain sensitivity to the interaction between the group and the hospital unit (Rice & Rutan, 1987). He believed that the community in which the patient lived is a group with its own healing powers, thus emphasizing the importance of the milieu in the treatment of hospitalized patients. In particular, he was aware of how the hospital itself was a large group, of which the therapy group was a smaller part. Each part was affected by events in or around any other part. Theories of group therapy have evolved from these early experiments, and most hospitals have included group therapy since that time.

The concept of the milieu as therapeutic is generally attributed to the work of Maxwell Jones (1953) in England. Milieu therapy revolves around the belief that the social environment of the patient supports and enhances his or her recovery. All the relationships within the hospital unit are considered part of the milieu: patient to patient, patient to staff, staff to patient, and staff to staff. During the milieu therapy movement, patients and staff were jointly responsible for many decisions, such as medication changes, privileges on the unit, activities, and so on. Any interactions involving patients were seen as opportunities to learn about the patient's problems and make efforts toward change (Rice & Rutan, 1987). This concept—in one form or other—has been seen as a central organizing tenet in most inpatient settings since the middle of the twentieth century. It has suffered with the sweeping changes imposed on hospitals in the past decade or

so of managed care limitations, but it remains an essential tool in the treatment of psychiatrically hospitalized patients.

## MAINSTREAM GROUP THEORIES AND THERAPIES IN THE UNITED STATES

The field of group therapy has incorporated the historic influences into a solid clinical modality as articulated by the stellar work of a number of theorists in the United States and by their followers. Helen Durkin (1964) integrated principles of systems theory with group dynamics into the field of group therapy. Along with Durkin, Henrietta Glatzer (1962) became a prime force in the application of psychodynamic principles to group psychotherapy. She is known primarily for the concept of the *working alliance*. "She used the concept to emphasize the importance of the member-to-member interaction as a principal component of the working alliance in therapy groups" (MacKenzie, 1992, p. 305). Saul Scheidlinger's prolific output has set the stage for a broad-based view of group development; this view includes concepts such as the *mother-group* and the regressive pull in groups that activates early childhood patterns (1974).

## PRINCIPLES OF GROUP PSYCHOTHERAPY: BASIC THEORIES

Although group therapy was originally based on psychoanalytic principles, now a broad range of theories informs its practice.

### Psychodynamic Theorists

Most current analytic theorists define the psychodynamic umbrella as consisting of four major branches: classical theory, object relations theory, ego psychology, and self psychology. In addition, the scope of the analytic umbrella covers interpersonal theory, humanistic-existential theories, and feminist-analytic thought.

### Classical Analytic

The classical analytic emphasis on libido and aggression finds expression in the unconscious forces that propel the group as a whole along its epigenetic trajectory. In this model the group develops along the same epigenetic trajectory as the individual—namely, oral, anal, phallic, and genital imperatives dictating the movement from early to mature group stages.

## Object Relations

Object relations theory finds in groups a natural environment for the projections of internal part-objects onto the other people in the room (members and leader) and the gradual reintrojections of the split-off aspects of the self within the containment of the group envelope. This term defines a sense of impermeable cohesion among the group members. Internalized parts-object is a term to describe critical emotionally laden aspects of significant people, which the child incorporates into the self. These aspects then shape the person's views and expectations of important people in subsequent interpersonal contacts.

## Ego Psychology

Anna Freud's (1966) interest in ego defenses, by which an individual copes with potentially devastating anxiety, influences a host of group interventions having to do with recovery from physical or mental illness. Health psychology is a current branch of what the ego psychologists were addressing.

## Self Psychology

Self psychologists recognize the mirroring and empathic possibilities among committed members who can serve as self-object functions for one another. The term *selfobject* implies that other people are present only to gratify the needs of the nascent self and not as autonomous entities. As the members gratify this universal early need for one another, each can stabilize a sense of greater and more flexible self-esteem.

## Intersubjective Theorists and Relational Theorists

The obvious value of the group to people committed to the concept of a cocreated reality makes the group therapy a treatment of choice. There is no hidden place in the group transferences either among the members or with the leader. All are influenced and in turn influence one another in developing new sublimatory channels and emotional options. This synergy is consistent with the principles that undergird intersubjective theory.

## Related Analytic Theorists

Sullivanians and other interpersonalists such as Yalom and Lieberman (1971) stress the healing that comes from the real relationships among the members, and the feminists see in groups the opportunity to inspect the impact of gender on environment and vice versa. Existentialists depend on the group to explore, verify, and accept the individual's personal myth and intentionality in the world as they contribute to the individual's self-authenticity.

## Gestalt Theorists

Many of the theories that developed in the 1960s and 1970s utilized group models. The theory of Gestalt therapy is defined by two central ideas: First, the proper focus of psychology is the experiential present moment; second, it is only possible to know the self in relation to other things in the interactive field. Gestalt theory as developed by Perls, Goodman, and others from the Cleveland Gestalt Institute brought the field theory of Lewin and Goldstein (1947) to bear on patients' attempts to integrate action, affect, and cognition. While working with an individual protagonist within the group, these thinkers utilized the whole group as a supportive container and reactor to the protagonist's clinical development. In Gestalt theory, the focus is on organizing the accumulation of past experience into the present reality of the person. Thus, the balance between figure and ground (or content and process) is the direction toward health.

## Transactional Analysis

Transactional analysis divides personality into three phenomenological components or ego states, colloquially termed Parent, Adult, and Child. Berne (1959) developed a group therapy approach that understands social behavior in terms of strokes or transactions exchanged by people in maladaptive patterns called *games.*

The Redecision School of Transactional Analysis focuses on *ego state patterns,* which may be thought of as character patterns, as expressed in the individual's relationship with others; these clinicians seek to resolve maladaptive early life decisions through contracts for change (Kerfoot, G., & Gladfelter, J., personal communication).

## Nonanalytic Theorists

In addition to the psychodynamic theorists who have dominated the field of group therapy, a host of other theoreticians have contributed to the field of group psychotherapy. Some of them include the cognitive-behaviorists, the Gestalt theorists, transactional analysts, and the redecision therapists.

## Cognitive-Behavioral Theorists

Cognitive-behaviorists see in the group model the opportunity to rethink old cognitive schemas and to question some of the prior cognitive distortions. Behavioral clinicians address social and psychological problems within a testable conceptual framework; thus, the social influence that occurs in groups has a pivotal role in altering maladaptive responses by the use of modeling and reinforcement of new behaviors.

Group cognitive-behavioral therapy can be discussed in terms of skills that are taught, problems that are addressed, or specific behavioral techniques that are used. There are several critical skills that are taught to groups of people who may or may not have psychiatric-psychological dysfunction or impairment but who are suffering from the consequences of skills deficits and may experience an increase in well-being and gratification from the acquisition of such skills. Examples of skills that may be taught in a group therapy context are job-seeking skills, negotiating skills, parenting skills, and communication skills.

In behavioral group therapy, some structures exist that are similar to those in other orientations—the size of groups, matching with respect to the nature and severity of the problems (heterogeneous or homogeneous), age of the patients, open-ended or time-limited, single leader or coleaders, concurrent individual treatment for group members, agreements around confidentiality, and rules of conduct within the group and outside the group. Because of the short-term, problem-focused nature of behavior therapy, most groups are conducted at weekly intervals for 8–12 sessions of 1–2 hours duration. A greater number of fixed-session groups or open-ended groups are used for patients with multiple or complex problems requiring more time (Fay, cited in Alonso & Swiller, 1993).

## THERAPEUTIC FACTORS COMMON TO ALL GROUP PSYCHOTHERAPY

Whatever the model, group therapy rests on the assumptions that healing factors emerge and operate in all groups. Some of these factors can be brought into play to allow the individuals within the group to grow and develop beyond the constrictions in life that brought that person into treatment. Although some group theorists rely on a cluster of factors relevant to their models of the mind and of pathology, all utilize some of the whole group of therapeutic factors identified previously.

The analysts generally rely on the recapitulation of the family of origin and on the way the transferences develop relative to those early family experiences. The cognitive behaviorists exploit the factors that most rely on examining and clarifying schemas or thought patterns and cognitions.

## GROUP GOALS

It is obvious that to some extent, the theory used points toward the desired goals of the group, yet some goals are universal to all group therapy. These goals include offering a supportive community to the patient, relieving symptoms, increasing self-esteem, and freeing the patients to move toward their life goals. The particular directions that the work will take are more specific to the theoretical base of the leader and the treatment, as we discuss in the following sections.

### The Goals of the Open-Ended Psychodynamic Therapy Group

Character change is the main goal of the psychoanalytic group. The standard target for psychoanalytic groups in particular (as well as for many others) is the reawakening of early neurotic and characterological problems in the transference that emerges in the clinical hour. The emergence of repressed and avoided conflicts or of troubling internal part-object personification in the therapy group is facilitated by the multiplicity of transference targets and the powerful impact of the aforementioned curative factors. In this model it is assumed that people will have their problems in the context of relating to the other people in the room. As the transferences from member to member, from member to leader, and from member to the group as a whole develop, people reexperience some of their earliest conflicts. Resistance emerges and can be explored, thereby illuminating the underlying defensive structure of each individual. With increasing safety, members regress to earlier defensive modes and arrive at increasing insight into the underlying personality dilemmas. These dilemmas can then be experienced and analyzed in the group—both by the other members and by the leader. Initially this process can feel shaming and threatening in a number of dimensions. However, with each event all the members become more deeply aware of their own projections and displacements, and they can gradually reown those split-off parts of the self; when this happens, the splits, which had depleted the ego, are healed, and psychic energy is made available for the conscious goals of the ego. Transference distortions give way to clearer relatedness with others in the here and now. The individual is now available for true intimacy with a separate but related other.

Members in this kind of group are selected from along the whole spectrum of ego development. The main criterion is that individuals are able and willing to make a commitment to pursue in-depth exploration of their internal lives.

Some of the earlier literature on group treatment expressed doubts about the appropriateness of this uncovering kind of group for the sicker patients. Currently the tide has shifted; researchers (Kibel, 1991) argue that group therapy is the treatment of choice for the pre-Oedipal patient with early impairment that interferes with a mature and goal-directed life. These patients have been referred to as pre-Oedipal or characterologically impaired in either primary or secondary process organization (Axis I and Axis II). In fact, it seems that the distributed transferences in the group mitigate an overly threatening regression for such patients (Alonso & Rutan, 1983). Character difficulties are tenacious for all human beings—from the healthiest neurotic to the most regressed patient. For all people, character problems are

- Outside the patient's awareness.
- Syntonic—that is, perceived as *who I am* when brought into awareness.
- Resistant to change even when the patient wants to make such a change.
- Repeated compulsively until worked through—that is, they are robbed of some of their power with each experience of successful change to better alternatives.
- Difficult to change without strong motivation to overcome psychological inertia.

The tide of group belongingness provides the necessary motivation.

### The Goals of Cognitive-Behavioral Groups

The importance of practicing techniques and skills within the group cannot be overestimated. The group becomes a laboratory for trying out new behaviors in a supportive context. Reinforcement is provided by other members of the group to encourage practicing per se and also to support successive approximations to the desired level of proficiency. Finally, maladaptive schemas are adjusted so that a patient's thinking is more closely related to the reality principle. Thus, feelings about the self and others become less troublesome.

## SUPPORT GROUPS OF VARIOUS KINDS

### Symptom-Specific Groups

Since 1905 when Dr. Pratt offered his classes for patients with tuberculosis at the Massachusetts General Hospital, people have come together to commiserate with one another around the common symptom or set of symptoms, to share information, and to learn how to deal with that symptom's impact on their lives. Groups have been organized around medical illnesses such as cancer and diabetes; around psychological problems such as eating disorders, phobias, or bereavement; and around psychosocial sequelae of trauma such as war or natural disasters.

The goal of such groups is to provide support and information embedded in a socially accepting environment with people who are in a position to really understand what the

others are going through. The leader of such a group needs to be familiar with the symptoms, sophisticated in the treatment of these symptoms as well as the whole patient, and competent at providing and sustaining adjunctive care as needed. The treatment may emerge from cognitive-behavioral principles, psychodynamic principles, or psychoeducational ones. Frequently these groups tend to be time limited, and members often join at the same time and terminate together.

The emergent self-help movement has generated groups that differ from the previously mentioned ones in a number of ways. Self-help groups are egalitarian and leaderless, focused on the principles of universality and unconditional positive regard, and open-ended and variable in their membership. Their goal is not necessarily to promote interaction among members; indeed, most discourage the kind of interpersonal discourse that is commonly found in the group therapies described previously. The common enemy is the disease, and the common bond joins the members in a resistance to succumbing to the ravages of that disease.

### Self-Help Groups

Alongside group therapy offered by the professional community, a large array of self-help groups have emerged and flourished. The first of these was Alcoholics Anonymous, which became a model for many other problem-specific support groups led by their own members. These groups have become a major source of recovery and cure, and they illustrate the value of community and group cohesion for managing a range of human distresses. In particular, they focus on compulsive problems, such as substance addictions of all sorts, self-mutilation, and gambling.

All of the modalities listed previously have in common certain curative factors. Table 14.1 is a partial listing of the range of therapeutic factors in group therapy.

## THE DEVELOPMENTAL MAP OF A THERAPY GROUP

Since Bion's (1959) original work on group development, it has been customary to look at all therapy groups along a developmental trajectory. Although it is obvious that developmental theorists will emphasize a group development model consistent with their own branch of dynamic theory, there is nonetheless some agreement among all group therapists that any consistent group usually undergoes some initial stages of group formation and cohesion; it then moves to some level of differentiation among its members and then finally achieves a stage of integration of new learning and new maturity.

**TABLE 14.1    Therapeutic Factors in Group Psychotherapy**

| Factor | Definition |
| --- | --- |
| Acceptance | The feeling of being accepted by other members of the group; differences of opinion are tolerated, and there is an absence of censure. |
| Altruism | The act of one member's being of help to another; putting another person's need before one's own and learning that there is value in giving to others, and Freud believed it was a major factor in establishing group cohesion and community feeling. |
| Catharsis | The expression of ideas, thoughts, and suppressed material; it is accompanied by an emotional response that produces a state of relief in the patient. |
| Cohesion | The sense that the group is working together toward a common goal, also referred to as a sense of we-ness; it is believed to be the most important factor related to positive therapeutic effects. |
| Contagion | The process in which the expression of emotion by one member stimulates the awareness of a similar emotion in another member. |
| Family of origin | The group re-creates the family of origin for some members who can work through original conflicts psychologically through group interaction (e.g., sibling rivalry, anger toward parents). |
| Insight | Conscious awareness and understanding of one's own psychodynamics and symptoms of maladaptive behavior. Most therapists distinguish two types: (a) intellectual insight, or knowledge and awareness without any changes in maladaptive behavior; (b) emotional insight, or awareness and understanding leading to positive changes in personality and behavior. |
| Inspiration | The process of imparting a sense of optimism to group members; the ability to recognize that one has the capacity to overcome problems; it is also known as instillation of hope. |
| Interaction | The free and open exchange of ideas and feelings among group members; effective interaction is emotionally charged. |
| Interpretation | The process during which the group leader formulates the meaning or significance of a patient's resistance, defenses, and symbols; the result is that the patient develops a cognitive framework within which to understand his or her behavior. |
| Learning | Patients acquire knowledge about new areas, such as social skills and sexual behavior; they receive advice, obtain guidance, attempt to influence, and are influenced by other group members. |
| Reality testing | Ability of the person to evaluate objectively the world outside the self; includes the capacity to perceive oneself and other group members accurately. See also consensual validation. |
| Self-disclosure | The expression of suppressed feelings, ideas, or events to other group members; the sharing of personal secrets that ameliorate a sense of sin or guilt. |
| Universalization | The awareness of the patient that he or she is not alone in having problems, that others share similar complaints or difficulties in learning, and that the patient is not unique. |

## TECHNIQUES FOR CONDUCTING OPEN-ENDED PSYCHODYNAMIC GROUP THERAPY

This section focuses on open-ended psychoanalytic group psychotherapy as a basic model for treating patients with developmental conflicts and deficits. The first considerations for conducting a psychoanalytic group include

- Developing a contract that gives meaning and structure to the work in the group.
- Building the alliance both before and in the group. After the individual's personal dynamics are deemed as appropriate to group treatment, then the leader will want to explain the rationale by discussing the factors described previously, to help forge an alliance with the patient around the usefulness of such a focus, and to follow up with a careful description of how the group works, a preview of what the patient can expect to see unfold in the first meeting and in subsequent meetings, and a full discussion of the group agreements to which all the members of that group are agreed.
- Interviewing the patient to screen for the appropriateness of group treatment. The ideal composition of a psychoanalytic group is one in which the members share a fairly homogeneous level of ego development and are variable in character style and personality. This mix allows for a capacity of empathy among the members and at the same time avoids too common a set of defensive operations.
- Preparing the patient for working in the group. The value of preparing a patient for what to expect in a therapy group cannot be overemphasized. It is difficult to overcome the natural resistance to speaking with strangers about one's intimate life. Problems of early shame and exposure account for many early group dropouts and in either case are not conducive to trust building among the members. A frank discussion of the common fears, a clear description of how the group works, and some statement of the leader's role mitigates this resistance. It is also useful to explore the patient's wishes and fantasies about the group and to help detoxify the early intrusions of other members on the new members' privacy and equanimity.

### The Work of the Analytic Group

#### Sources of Conscious and Unconscious Data

The primary data in analytic treatment are basically what the patient *says,* what he or she *does,* and how he or she characteristically *is.* It is from these immediate behavioral data that we as therapists derive explanatory notions of unconscious material and defensive operations. Clearly, the more we have of such data, the better. The more we can see of our patient in action, the more the patient and we can understand about the patient and alter what is potentially alterable.

The group does allow for the direct observation of the patient's actual functioning, dysfunctioning, or both. The group allows for the patient's own reporting of internal and external experience and for his or her perceptions of and responses to the therapist. It also provides more people to whom he or she can respond and more people to react to those responses. The data are active, not passive. The arena for transference is extended from its traditional vertical axis to a horizontal one involving many different objects and—on occasion—transference is extended to the group as a whole.

Furthermore, because the stimulus conditions are not generally subject to the patient's control, his or her responses are likewise less controlled. Although we may not get as pure a picture of the transference, we do get a much more *complete* picture of the patient's character strength and pathology in action. Not only the therapist but also other patients and the patient him- or herself have the opportunity to observe these spontaneous, unedited responses and enduring behavior patterns reactive to both constant and occasional stimuli. This far more complex portrait of the patient with all his or her strengths and weaknesses—this kaleidoscopic view of the person—is a direct function of a multimodal treatment situation.

Group process is the closest analogue in the group setting to the free association process in the dyadic setting, and it is to facilitate this process that the leader is dedicated throughout group treatment. The unfolding of the group process resembles that of free association, but it exceeds intrapsychic boundaries and moves to both a horizontal plane (between members) and a vertical plane (member or members to therapist). It involves the whole array of transference and resistance, ego function and dysfunction, and symptoms and character defenses. The working assumption in this model of group therapy is that if the group process operates at full tilt (i.e., if the resistances—group or individual in origin—are consistently and successfully addressed) the many mutative forces of the group will also operate at maximum capacity to the benefit of each individual member. In this sense *the group process is both a product of and an agent of the analytic process as it is carried out in the group.* Thus, the group process has a curative force of its own while serving as a condition for individual growth (Kauff, cited in Alonso, 1993).

### Common Phenomena in Psychodynamic Group Therapy

Analytic groups rely on unconscious defenses to emerge in the interactions among the members. Groups have been described as a hall of mirrors, with each member seeing a disowned aspect of the self in the other faces in the mirror. Put another way, the members contain the projections of one another, and at times, they become the unconscious participants in each others' *projective identifications,* in which one person accepts the disowned parts of another in return for similar accommodations. It may well be that the exposure to and resolution of multiple oscillating projective identifications is the primary avenue for the healing and for allowing the patient to reintegrate the split-off pieces of the self and restore a previously compromised ego.

## ORGANIZING AND CONDUCTING AN OPEN-ENDED PSYCHODYNAMIC GROUP

The clinician needs to attend to a variety of factors in planning such a group. These factors include defining the meaning and goals of the work and describing them to potential group members. The composition in such a group ideally consists of people with fairly homogeneous levels of ego development, which maximizes the capacity of members to empathize with one another. The group members might be heterogeneous in most other respects. The leader should try to develop a clear set of shared group agreements relative to time, attendance, fees, and other external considerations, such as third-party payer intrusions into the work. As each individual is interviewed for the group, these goals and agreements should be fully discussed, including some awareness of how the group and the leader will in fact relate to one another in the room. Careful pregroup discussions can go a long way toward reducing early dropouts and the subsequent painful disorganization that can follow such disruptions.

After the group begins, the leader is in a position to observe member strengths and resistances, paving the way for healthy relatedness and analysis of neurotic patterns.

### Activity, Inactivity, and Neutrality

It is important to distinguish among inactivity, neutrality, and passivity. There is no room in any legitimate therapy for the clinician to remain intellectually and emotionally passive; he or she owes the patient full attention and deliberate concentration on all aspects of the treatment, in or outside the therapy hour—in this case, the group meeting. While remaining vitally ego-active, the psychodynamic clinician should avoid action that interferes with the flow of the patients' associations or that otherwise dictates the direction of the meeting. Similarly, the clinician in this model should strive to maintain a neutral stance toward the *material,* being careful to analyze and investigate all aspects of an event or a set of feelings; this does not mean that the clinician is neutral toward the *patients* in the sense of not caring about their well-being—or for that matter, avoiding feelings of concern, affection, irritation, or dismay about the patients in the course of a long-standing and emotionally involving treatment. Thus, what we are referring to in this paper is therapist inactivity and neutrality, which are expressed in a parsimony of words or action or direction on the part of the analytic clinician. We are therefore defining neutrality according to the terms of Anna Freud (1966)—that is, as a stance equidistant from id, ego, and superego positions, maintaining vigorous interest in all three. The involvement and participation of the members of a psychotherapy group facilitates the group leader's ability to maintain healthy neutrality and to contain the impulses to avoid neutrality in favor of judgment therapy, which may perhaps be open to him. The bulk of the literature on neutrality is confusing and contradictory. Neutrality tends to be defined by what it is not. Therapists are told that it is not indifference, coldness, remoteness, or blandness; it is not an armed truce or a lack of concern and devotion to the patient. It is further described as not taking action when abstaining is better; it is not making judgments or at least not imposing them on the patient. It is not giving advice.

Finally, the patient's problems emerge and are available for analysis in the interpersonal world of the group. When they do, the patient can make use of the interpersonal responses, which are not apt to be neutral at all; taken together, however, all the group's responses allow for a neutral interpretation on the part of the therapist.

Adopting this position informs the work of group clinicians and the control they exert on the treatment by virtue of how active or passive, how verbal or reticent, how interactive or reflective, how directive or nondirective to be—in the group or with any given patient.

In the early phase of the pregroup negotiation for treatment, the therapist must do quite a lot—actively and directly—in order to establish the *contract,* or the frame of the therapy. The clinician's tasks and responsibilities are numerous at this stage and form the indispensable basis for rapport and negotiation with the patient. These tasks range from the mundane—such as greeting the patient with respect—to setting the time and fee structure and arranging the details about third-party payment; they also include the task of providing more sophisticated explanations of the way this kind of treatment works, such as explaining the fundamental rule of free association and the importance of dreams.

Obviously, the role of the clinician here is more active and verbal. Lack of clarity or explicitness on the part of the clinician will interfere with the analytic work and confuse the

impact of the clinician's more neutral stance later. After the contractual parameters are well established, a phenomenon sometimes to referred to as the *therapeutic envelope* enfolds the members of the group in a sense of cohesion. Then the clinician's work is to stay out of the way, to sit still, and to allow the patient and the group to lead the way.

After the therapeutic envelope, or early cohesive stability, is intact, then the work of unfolding can begin. At this point, the patient and the group together are the composers of the aria, and the conductors of the orchestra. The clinician is more appropriately like the critic of the orchestra—listening with a hovering attention to the overall themes and caring less about the notes than about the music. As is the case with any critic, the analyst is quiet, but hardly passive. He or she is listening very intensely and is actively making links and associations that are personal and stimulated by the productions of the patient. Furthermore, the clinician is carefully monitoring the self, avoiding any acting out on his or her part that may compromise the best interest of the therapy group and any given patient.

### Contraindications for the Analytic Stance

Of course there are situations in which the inactive stance must be abandoned—for the safety of the patient or of others involved with the patient's life; when this occurs, psychodynamic treatment is in effect temporarily suspended, and safety considerations must take precedence. When the patient's ego is restored to a measure of intactness to tolerate the anxiety of an uncovering therapy, the analytic work can then resume.

### Working With Shame in Groups

Clinicians frequently worry about the shaming aspects of the disclosure that are part and parcel of the work in the group. It is true that going public with one's problems can be a daunting goal; after it has been done, however, shame is reduced, the patient begins to understand that he or she is part of the human condition and not subhuman or suprahuman, and development can resume. The group therapist sets the stage for the work of the group by developing a climate that is respectful, that avoids undue shaming of any one member by underscoring the universal quality of all human pain, and by encouraging frankness and empathic confrontation of the members by one another.

Because earliest shame is experienced in autistic isolation, the communication of it in an emotional field with another person occurs rarely and sometimes only serendipitously. Thus, the shame continues to flourish in an encapsulated, protected bubble. The bearer can neither expose it for fear of generating greater shame, nor can he or she work it through alone. As with other painful experiences, that which remains unspoken can more easily be repressed—or at least suppressed. Furthermore, should the individual have been exposed too early and too severely to repeated mortifications, then these experiences become a reservoir for humiliation. Because shame is related to the real or imagined loss of the object, the externally enforced constancy of the membership lends courage and the possibility of reestablishing empathic contact if that has been perceived as broken or withdrawn. This constancy provides the opportunity for a corrective emotional experience at its finest—not contrived, but negotiated and maintained by the goodwill of the group and the group ego as evidenced in the group contract. Thus, when empathic contact is broken—as it is repeatedly in a hard working group—there is an external, face-saving reason to come back and try again and again. The repetition compulsion is converted into working through with the continual analysis of the characterological dilemmas of each patient.

## COUNTERTRANSFERENCE PRESSURES IN THE ANALYTIC GROUP

Perhaps the more challenging tasks for the analytic group therapist have to do with maintaining a clinical equilibrium in the face of his or her own exposure to the contagious forces of the group. It is more difficult to hold to a quiet, nonactive therapeutic stance in a group, even for the analyst who is quite able to do so in dyadic treatment. The nongratifying, inactive clinician is subject to a variety of pressures that threaten to compromise even the most committed devotee to the theory of this technique. The pressures come from internal anxiety in the clinician, interpersonal pressure from colleagues, administrative pressures, and fashion.

If one avoids action and listens carefully to the pain of the patient in therapy, there will inevitably arise more areas of identification with the patient than the therapist might be comfortable to acknowledge and to bear. The wish then arises to heal the patient quickly and also to heal the self vicariously—a natural and healthy instinct in itself. However, if the combined pain is too great, the therapist will be tempted to take action to palliate the symptoms, if only to avoid even greater levels of regression and exposure to deeper levels of conflict for the whole group.

Even if a clinician is well established and working in a thriving private practice, the inevitable periodic discouragement that is part and parcel of the therapist's work can lead to a wish and a temptation to speed up the process, make the practice of psychotherapy more exciting, and generate more action in the hours. If, in addition, one is employed in a clinic or in a general hospital with colleagues from related fields who would like to see fast results, the difficulties with the less active stance multiply.

Furthermore, the fear of malpractice suits has added anxiety to already overburdened practitioners and has forced them to think more pragmatically. This situation makes it harder to have the courage for open-ended exploration, which is always accompanied by inevitable regressions.

## INPATIENT GROUP THERAPY

In many regards, groups in an inpatient hospital setting are like those outside the hospital. There are, however, important differences: Patients in the hospital are by definition disturbed enough to require confinement away from their homes and communities. With the increasing limitations of insurance coverage, patients may be in the hospital for only a few days and may not be there voluntarily. Group membership is likely to be much less controlled than it is in an outpatient setting because patients from different races, classes, cultures, ages, and diagnostic categories are apt to be on a unit at any given time.

In any given hospital, the groups are serving a patient population that includes chronic as well as acutely psychotic patients; decompensated, personality disordered patients; substance-abusing and dual-diagnosis patients; acutely depressed and suicidal patients; and patients from a forensic population. Lengths of stay are generally brief but may range anywhere from 24 hours to several months on the same hospital unit. Private and general hospitals with psychiatric units are usually quite short-term, and state psychiatric hospitals no longer routinely keep patients for lengthy periods of time; many stays are significantly less than a year. In general, most inpatient units are locked; very few maintain an open-door policy. Many of the patients in a typical hospital have been involuntarily hospitalized, a process that varies from state to state but in all cases allows hospitals to keep a patient against his or her will for a period of a few days, with the option for the hospital to apply to the local courts to legally commit the patient to the hospital for care. Other patients are receiving treatment voluntarily, and some may be in the hospital as an alternative to some other type of legal confinement—as in the case of some substance abusers. On some hospital units, patients are separated according to one criterion or other: diagnosis, severity of illness, and presence or absence of addiction, age, or gender. In other settings, patients from many or all of these categories coexist on the floor.

A psychiatric hospital unit is a great leveler of people. Patients come from all walks of life, have any sharp or potentially dangerous belongings removed from them, are checked every 15 min, may or may not be permitted to leave the unit, and in any event must ask permission to do so from someone with a key. Added to this humiliation is the stress of whatever life problems brought them to require such confinement in the first place. Whatever the modality or theory behind it, then, the goal of the hospitalization is to return people to whatever minimum level of functioning will permit them to live outside the locked doors. In some ways, this goal represents a change in thinking about the purpose of hospitalization that has occurred over the past couple of decades. It places more emphasis on outpatient treatments to provide for and accomplish significant, lasting change in a person's illness and life circumstances—a task that many hospitals sought to accomplish in years past. The question of whether this change is for better or for worse has been the source of much controversy, and in many hospitals the goals of the groups and other treatments provided are less than crystal clear. Differing opinions on this issue between and within members of various disciplines can make for a richly diverse or a fractious environment in which to help patients recover.

Partial hospitals are a natural outgrowth of inpatient hospitals—particularly in this age of decreasing lengths of inpatient stays. A partial hospital—like its sibling, the day treatment facility—is an intensive outpatient program that functions in a way similar to that of the daytime schedule of the inpatient unit (the term *day treatment* has come to imply a longer-term, more chronic program than does the *partial hospital,* which is generally 2–6 weeks in length). Typically, the patients in the partial hospital today were on the inpatient unit yesterday or are not quite acute enough for a locked setting, despite being in crisis. A patient in partial hospital attends community meetings and groups and then returns home in the evening and on weekends. There is limited medical and nursing attention, and the primary focus of the stay is that of ameliorating the patient's psychological distress. This arrangement differs from the hospital stay, which has as its focus (on an acute unit) the return of the patient to medical safety and stability; by and large, this translates to the resolution of acute psychoses and suicidal crises.

## TYPES OF INPATIENT GROUPS

Inpatient settings typically employ a variety of groups: educational, activity, behavioral, psychotherapy, and others, such as the community meeting. Each type of group serves both a specific and a more general purpose in the treatment of hospitalized patients.

### Educational Groups

These groups typically include information on medications, diagnoses, and conditions encountered by patients. They are generally led in a didactic fashion, sometimes with room left for members to ask questions or share some of their own experience. These groups are based on the premise that increasing the information available to a patient about an anxiety-laden topic helps to alleviate the anxiety he or she feels. Many hospitals use educational groups to help introduce patients to discussions of traumatic experiences in a structured manner. Because talking about traumas can be affectively flooding and retraumatizing to patients, educational groups are frequently used to help very disturbed patients safely begin work in these areas.

### Activity Groups

Activity groups usually involve some kind of physical action, such as craft projects, music, cooking, or calisthenics. They may also be organized around daily activities that are often abandoned in the hospital—for example, a beauty group in which patients are helped to attend to specifics of grooming, such as manicures, makeup, or hairstyling. For many hospitalized patients, daily activities have been anything but normal for some time, and many may have been unable to accomplish even simple tasks because of the interference of psychiatric symptoms (positive or negative). For the most regressed inpatients, an hour of having their hair brushed, putting on nail polish, drawing a picture in the company of others, or encountering and interacting with an animal (in the case of pet therapy) may be a highly significant event. In addition, activity groups allow the healthier patients to help the sicker ones, and they allow all the patients to access competencies that can otherwise be left behind the locked doors of the hospital.

### Behavioral Groups

Behavioral groups and cognitive-behavioral groups include skills training in areas such as communication, stress management, addictions, and management of self-injurious behaviors. These groups tend to be quite focused and may employ verbal or written exercises and homework outside the sessions. Such groups can be very helpful in allowing patients to gain greater control over their actions in an immediate way and can offer a language and framework in which to conceptualize the problems that may have led them to need hospitalization and therapy. Such groups are frequently used to introduce or reinforce cognitive-behavioral techniques for the management of anxiety and other overwhelming affective symptoms.

## Psychodrama

Psychodrama is another type of group used in inpatient settings. Introduced by Moreno in the 1920s, psychodrama involves the enactment of a patient's conflicted relationships on a stage, using other patients and staff to play the parts of the various members of that patient's social world. Patients are thus able to see their conflicts played out in front of them, given opportunities to rework and modify their interactions, and experience some of the emotions involved in a structured, contained setting.

## Psychotherapy Groups

Psychotherapy groups are most analogous to psychodynamic outpatient groups and may occur several times weekly. Opinions vary as to the appropriate goals and nature of such groups in this setting: Some theorists propose that it is the group itself that offers healing, and for others it is the individual interactions within the group. Kibel (1993) describes the overarching goal for an inpatient group as that of increasing the treatment alliance between staff and patients. He advocates for inclusive group membership (excepting only the most disruptive or cognitively impaired patients) and a focus on helping patients improve relatedness, reality testing, and management of affects by helping them understand their experience in the milieu. Yalom's (1983) nondynamic model is one of here-and-now, interpersonal learning that aims to help patients identify problem behavior and learn to manage it with their anxiety. Rice and Rutan (1987) defined a psychodynamic model predicated on the idea that even the most psychotic communications and behaviors have meaning in their context and that the task of the group is to help patients understand their fears and conflicts sufficiently to enable them to use defenses that are healthier than the ones that have currently broken down. They advocate dividing the population into higher- and lower-functioning groups in order to best address the needs of the members.

Brabender and Fallon (1993) describe several models of inpatient group psychotherapy and advocate for careful matching of the inpatient system to the group model chosen by the therapist. They include such factors as the clinical mission of the hospital setting, the theoretical orientation of the unit and its leaders, and the pace of turnover of patients and staff in

making their determinations as to choice of group model. Along with these factors, considering the patient population served and the value placed on groups by the institution helps group therapists to run successful groups on inpatient units. Each of the seven group models they describe (educative, interpersonal, object relations–systems, developmental, cognitive-behavioral, problem solving, and behavioral–social skills training) has its own theoretical underpinnings and technical aspects. Additionally, although each model can be placed within a framework of psychodynamic or psychoanalytic understanding, training in psychodynamics is not necessary to successfully lead groups in all of the models; this is especially helpful in institutions in which most group leaders are trainees who may have had little or no such theoretical instruction before coming to the hospital.

## The Change in the Model

The literature on inpatient group psychotherapy can be confusing to those entering the field in the new millennium. The vast majority of it was written more than a decade ago, and many readers conducting inpatient groups in today's hospitals express frustration at the difference between the hospital units described in the literature and their own. Most notably, the ascendance of the insurance review to a primary place in the treatment planning for hospitalized patients has resulted in a significant shift in clinical thinking. One of the most common questions asked in daily rounds is often *What will one more day benefit this patient that he could not get elsewhere?*

Such an approach can easily be seen as lending support, however irrationally, to the idea that medications are the only real benefit being offered a person who is hospitalized; yet as Kay Redfield Jamison, a psychologist with bipolar disorder, put it, "what good are medications when 40–50% of bipolar patients won't take them?" (personal communication, September 28, 2000). The change in insurance management has meant that often, doctors spend much of their time justifying treatments to reviewers in the form of lengthy paperwork and telephone calls. Group therapy in hospitals is more essential than ever if patients are to feel a sense of purpose in regaining control in their lives and to rise above the sea of hopelessness that threatens inpatient treaters and their patients alike. Stanton and Schwartz (1954) explained half a century ago that on an inpatient ward, confusion at the top of the administrative ranks is felt by everyone, including the most deluded and psychotic patient. The interpersonal, educative, and compassionate factors in group psychotherapy remain essential tools to help patients make use of the other treatments, including medications, that may help them live happier, less hospitalized lives.

## The Goal of Inpatient Psychiatric Groups

If the goal of a hospitalization is to achieve safety from harm, then the goal of the treatments within the hospital is to ameliorate unbearable pain. Medications provide some relief from the most acute symptoms, and their purpose is easy to understand. Individual meetings with a doctor help clarify the direction and nature of the hospital stay and offer some of the benefits of a short-term, individual therapy. The therapeutic action of inpatient groups occurs at many levels. Like other types of groups, they provide an enclosed arena for the reworking of recent and long-standing difficulties, and they offer an opportunity to help others on their journeys as well. Unlike many other treatments available in the hospital, the purpose of group therapy is sometimes harder to explain to acutely ill patients; this is especially true when people have been less exposed to psychological customs because of cultural, educational, or socioeconomic factors.

Patients in the hospital are often unable to articulate the nature of their difficulties and in many cases identify primarily external factors that cause them grief. More often than not, these groups are comprised of people with brittle, failing defenses—in an acute crisis. Inevitably, members are faced with a profound injury, humiliation, or loss that accompanied them to the hospital. It is unlikely that a psychotic patient who is experiencing command hallucinations and who believes he is being poisoned by the Nixon administration will enter a group for the stated purpose of reworking old psychic conflicts. Such a patient is far more likely to arrive in the group and explain to you his beliefs (or his confusion) about why he is here and what is wrong with the world outside. Attempts to direct him otherwise may be highly upsetting to him. Additionally, his neighbor in the group probably has her own ideas about what is dangerous in the world and about what is and is not true.

Accordingly, there are both explicit and implicit therapeutic agents in an inpatient group. After patients are safe and contained within the larger group setting of the hospital unit, the first task of the group is to allow members to tolerate being in the group. By and large, patients are in the hospital because they cannot tolerate being around others or because others cannot tolerate being around them. In the microcosm of the hospital ward, patients are continually attempting the impossible or the unlikely—coexisting relatively peacefully, with no one destroyed as a result. The manifest content of these groups is quite different from that of a high-functioning, outpatient group: Many members do not speak at all, some speak incomprehensibly, and others carry on seemingly intact conversations in their midst. There is often a focal subject to the group, such as a physical task

or a conversational topic. The stated goal may be psychoeducational or perhaps behavioral, but the implicit goal is to help patients tolerate their own and others' presence in the group. This goal is accomplished through shared learning of the rules of the unit, comparison of medications and symptoms, complaints about various hospital limitations, and so on. Through these learning experiences, patients begin to form a sense of themselves as a group with similar needs to be cared for.

In terms of group development, inpatient groups are generally preoccupied with the very earliest tasks because members are acutely ill and only stay a short time on the unit. These tasks are centered on dependency needs and conflicts as members come to terms with their presence in the hospital and grapple with whether the staff can save them. The development of these groups occasionally extends to include a reactive phase (Jones, 1953), in which members begin to emphasize their differences and dissatisfaction with the group leadership. Group action at this stage indicates the establishment of clearer boundaries between self and other, and it may be seen in partial or longer-term hospital groups more often than it is on the short-term inpatient ward.

Partial and longer-term hospital groups function in a way very similar to that of short-term inpatient groups, with some important exceptions. Depending on the length of stay and the severity of the population's pathology, partial hospital groups can expect to achieve greater cohesion and developmental progress than can groups in a very short-term hospital. Similarly, longer-term hospital settings such as state institutions, where patients may stay 3–6 months or more, offer opportunities for considerable stability in groups and the potential for long periods of productive group work.

## WHO LEADS INPATIENT GROUPS?

Anyone who works on the inpatient unit in a clinical capacity may run a group, and hospitals vary as to the structure and organization of these roles. Psychiatrists and psychologists, social workers, occupational therapists, nurses, counselors, and trainees all may lead groups, which provides an opportunity for members of the different disciplines to work together to help their patients. In many hospitals, groups are led by teams of one senior and one junior clinician, often a trainee. Coleadership offers therapists the support and camaraderie of another person in the trenches of the work, which can be difficult and stressful. It also adds complicating factors of its own: For instance, is one leader more in charge than the other? How will the roles be divided? What will patients be told about the coleadership arrangement?

Whatever the specifics of the coleadership arrangement, it is essential that the boundaries be explicit and that the leaders be prepared to discuss the process of their coleadership as an element of the group dynamic. Possible formats for group coleadership include having one leader's function as that of silent observer, one person as the leader and the other as the assistant, equal leadership, or alternating roles for leaders in the group. Coleadership introduces to the group elements of competition, dominance and submission, and negotiation (among others) that individual group leadership does not.

Whatever the theoretical model, group functioning depends on some sort of contract between patient, group leader, and hospital unit. Often, this contract is presented in the form of a brief, introductory statement at the beginning of each group session. Elements of the contract for an inpatient group by necessity differ some from those for an outpatient group; however, essential to any group is a contract that covers the boundaries of time, place, expectations of privacy, and attendance and participation. Whatever the theoretical model for inpatient group psychotherapy, attendance to the boundaries of the group is essential. Nevertheless, many inpatient group leaders find a lack of regard for these boundaries from busy medical and nursing staff, who may interrupt groups to handle other matters with patients during the group time. When there is limited institutional support for groups on a unit, group leaders find themselves called upon to provide the maximum possible degree of stability and safety within whatever frame actually exists in the setting. Although attendance at groups may be a requirement for privileges on some units, participation in psychotherapy groups should be fully voluntary, and in some cases, it may best be considered a privilege in itself. Unlike other groups, a psychotherapy group places demands on patients to speak in a relatively unstructured setting.

## Technical Considerations

Exactly how one leads groups on an inpatient unit depends on a number of factors. Length of stay, type of population, unit philosophy, and unit structure all contribute to the overall atmosphere of the hospital ward. Choosing the best group therapy model for a particular hospital unit depends on these elements as well as on the degree of progroup culture that exists in the ward at large (Brabender & Fallon, 1993). Some of the models Brabender and Fallon describe are best in a longer-term setting, in which groups can become more cohesive, whereas others can be used even in settings in which patients turn over very rapidly. The educative model, which has as its goal helping patients comprehend their problematic styles of coping so that they can modify them, is one model that is adaptable to the very short-term unit, as is the object relations–systems theory model. The techniques used in each model are different and based on varying theoretical underpinnings.

In the educative model, maladaptive behaviors are the target of the intervention; this is not a didactic model, but rather one in which the here-and-now behaviors of the group members are used as illustrations of members' interpersonal, behavioral style. In the educative group, members "learn to think clinically so that they can more effectively manage the sequelae of their mental illnesses" (Brabender & Fallon, 1993). Patients are directed to focus on those issues that brought them into the hospital and are encouraged to help each other understand where their coping skills and defenses break down. This is accomplished through a largely exclusive focus on events occurring within the group session. The group therapist has three tasks in this group: maintaining the boundaries of time, place, and so on; teaching patients to help one another identify and correct counterproductive behaviors; and facilitating the development of group norms such as the focus on the here and now, ensuring that group time is shared by members, and organizing discussions to be relevant to target behaviors.

In contrast, the object relations–systems group approach views the therapy group as a subset of the larger ward group (which is, in turn, a subset of the hospital as a whole). Group interventions are targeted at members' reactions to events on the unit or hospital overall. The theoretical assumption is a psychodynamic view: Inpatients, who are mostly psychotic or borderline patients, have regressed to the point at which they are no longer able to use splitting as an effective defense to keep good and bad representations separate. The defenses used by regressed patients are mostly projection and projective identification, and they have lost the ability to maintain separateness between good and bad, self and other. This problem is manifested as fears about aggression and negative affects, and patients tend to fear retaliation if they speak about their anger and frustration. This group model is predicated on the belief that helping patients articulate negative affect in a manageable way and demonstrating the absence of retaliation from such appropriate expression allows patients to regain the capacity for healthy splitting and thus to be more psychically intact.

The group leader in this model has the task of helping patients link their experiences to events that may have affected them on the unit. Here, it is essential that the leader be aware of what has been happening on the ward so that he or she can assist patients in seeing the ways in which their reactions—in context—are amplifications of ordinary responses to stressors that have a reasonable basis in normalcy. This group model allows even the most bizarre communications from patients to be used as valid information about tensions, frustrations, and fears of retaliation from authority within the system or its subset. The role of the group leader is to help patients speak what they fear is unspeakable, using the medium of the group as a whole (the ward) to help illustrate safe ways to articulate negative experiences. Interventions in this type of group may be directed to the individual or the group as a whole, and care is taken to support members' safe expression of difficult affect while avoiding interactions that might promote humiliation or greater vulnerability in the group. In contrast to the educative model, wherein members are asked to focus on behaviors that brought them into the hospital, the object relations–systems model avoids such direct focus as being too regressive. Instead, these interventions are directed toward reestablishing the successful defense of splitting through the tolerated expression of members' negative affects.

## CURRENT OUTPATIENT GROUP RESEARCH

### Focus on Efficacy, Applicability, and Efficiency

For much of the last quarter of the twentieth century, group therapy researchers have been preoccupied with demonstrating the efficacy of group therapy. They have used methodology and designs commonly used by individual therapy researchers to attempt to demonstrate that group therapy achieves clinical improvements that exceed control conditions (e.g., patients waiting for group therapy). In addition, group therapy researchers have been particularly interested in demonstrating that group therapy is as efficacious as individual therapy and is applicable to as many different types of patient problems. They have argued that if group therapy can be shown to be as efficacious and as applicable as individual therapy, it can also be shown to be more efficient (economical). In general, group therapy researchers have been successful in these pursuits.

### Evidence for Efficacy and Applicability

In 1980, Smith, Glass, and Miller published an extensive review of 475 controlled studies of psychotherapy outcome. They used the method known as meta-analysis. In meta-analysis, the outcome for each measure in a study is represented by a common unit known as an effect size. After they are calculated, effect sizes can be averaged across studies to arrive at general conclusions regarding the efficacy of different types of therapy. The two findings for which their review has become well known are (a) psychotherapy is clearly effective compared to control conditions, and (b) there are minimal

differences in the effectiveness of different types of psychotherapy. It is important to advocates of group therapy to know that almost half of the 475 studies involved group therapy and that the average effect size for group therapy was .83, which was almost identical to the average effect size for individual therapy, which was .87. Thus, on average, both were similarly effective. It should also be noted that most therapies were brief, which tends to characterize both the group and the individual outcome research literature. The average number of hours of therapy was 16 and the average duration of therapy was 11 weeks.

One limitation of their review was that each controlled study usually included group therapy or individual therapy but not both. Thus, differences between the studies could have influenced the comparisons that were made. In response to this problem, Tillitski (1990) conducted a meta-analysis based only on studies that included group therapy, individual therapy, and a control condition. He reported equivalent effect sizes for the two types of therapy. More recently, McRoberts, Burlingame, and Hoag (1998) published a similar review that used a larger number of studies and that used improved methodology. They also reported equivalent effect sizes for group and individual therapy.

A number of other reviews of group and individual therapies, some meta-analytic and some not, have been published during the past 20 years. In their book, *Handbook of Group Psychotherapy,* Fuhriman and Burlingame (1994) discussed 22 reviews. They reported that "the general conclusion to be drawn from some 700 studies that span the past two decades is that the group format consistently produced positive effects with diverse disorders and treatment models" (p. 15). From their perspective, there is considerable evidence for the efficacy of group therapy and its similarity to the efficacy of individual therapy. They also emphasized that most group therapies that have been studied are brief in duration.

In 1996, Piper and Joyce published a more recent review that examined the efficacy of time-limited, short-term group therapies and focused on 86 studies. In general, the methodology of the studies was strong. Most groups focused on a specific problem. They covered a wide range of problems, including lifestyle problems (e.g., smoking, drinking, social dysfunction); medical conditions (e.g., cancer); mood, anxiety, eating, and personality disorders; traumatic life experiences (e.g., abuse, loss); and anger control. There was also a diversity of theoretical and technical orientations, including behavioral, cognitive-behavioral, interpersonal, psychodynamic, psychoeducational, and others. The average length of the group therapies was 10 weeks. Each of the studies included multiple outcome variables. Thus, each study could provide more than one type of outcome evidence. Of the 50 studies that included a time-limited group therapy versus control condition comparison, almost all, 48 (96%), provided some evidence of significantly greater benefit for the therapy condition. Only one (2%) study provided evidence of greater benefit for the control condition. When this comparison was examined for each of the nine different categories of patient problems, the results were uniformly similar. For each category, nearly all of the studies provided evidence for the superiority of the therapy condition. Of the six studies that included a time-limited group therapy versus individual therapy comparison, only one provided evidence of superiority for the group therapy and only one provided evidence of superiority for the individual therapy. In contrast, all six provided evidence of no difference in benefit. Overall, the results of the review were consistent with those of previous reviews. There was clear evidence that short-term group therapies of different theoretical and technical orientations offered clinical benefits across a diverse range of patients, and approximately equivalent results were obtained for group and individual therapy. The authors concluded that the evidence for the efficacy and the applicability of time-limited group therapy was substantial.

### Evidence for Efficiency

In regard to the question of efficiency, Toseland and Siporin (1986) focused on studies that included both group therapy and individual therapy in the same study. Of 12 investigators who addressed the question of efficiency, 10 concluded that group therapy was more efficient. It seems clear that if one restricts the definition of efficiency to the average amount of time required to treat each patient, a clear figure can be calculated for each of the two therapies, and a straightforward comparison can be made. For example, in 1984, Piper, Debbane, Bienvenu, and Garant investigated four forms of psychotherapy: short-term individual, short-term group, long-term individual, and long-term group. Short-term was defined as 24 sessions over 6 months, and long-term was defined as 96 sessions over 2 years. Individual therapy was provided in sessions that lasted .9 hours, and group therapy was provided in sessions that lasted 1.5 hours. Groups consisted of eight patients. The time required per patient from the perspective of the therapist can be calculated for each therapy. For example, from the perspective of the therapist, short-term group therapy, which required 4.5 hours per patient, was more efficient than short-term individual therapy, which required 21.6 hours per patient, in a time ratio of approximately 1:5. Another example of the efficiency associated with short-term group therapy comes from a program that provides treatment for psychiatric outpatients who experience difficulty adapting to the loss of one or more persons

(Piper, McCallum, & Azim, 1992). A loss group meets once a week for 90 min for 12 weeks. It is possible to compare the average amount of therapist time allocated to each patient in a loss group with the average amount of therapist time allocated to a patient in short-term individual therapy. Based on an average of 7.5 patients in a group for twelve 90-min sessions, the average time per patient is 2.4 hours. For one patient in individual therapy for twelve 45-min sessions, the average time per patient is 9.0 hours. The ratio is approximately 1:4; this means that about four times as many patients can be treated in a group therapy program for loss. Of course, other factors such as compliance and outcome need to be taken into account in evaluating the overall success of the two types of therapy, but when therapist time is the criterion, the examples indicate that group therapy is more efficient.

### More Complex Questions

Overall, the findings concerning efficacy, applicability, and efficiency suggest that for a wide range of disorders, group therapy is as effective as individual therapy and that it is more efficient. In regard to practice, there is the clear implication that group therapy rather than individual therapy should be the treatment of choice for many disorders that have been studied. Although this conclusion is important, reviewers of group therapy research (e.g., Bednar & Kaul, 1994) have criticized researchers for being too preoccupied with issues of efficacy, applicability, and efficiency, to the exclusion of other important areas of research. These areas include efforts to answer the following questions:

- What types of patients benefit more from different types of group therapy? Patient types include personality, demographic, and diagnostic differences. Group therapy types include theoretical, technical, and duration differences.
- What types of patients benefit more from group therapy or individual therapy?
- What types of therapist characteristics and interventions lead to greater benefit?
- What underlying mechanisms are responsible for therapeutic change?
- What factors are responsible for maintenance of improvement?

These are indeed important questions whose answers would advance knowledge in the field. The question of why group therapy researchers have neglected such questions in favor of continuing to conduct studies that address efficacy, applicability, and efficiency is a legitimate one that requires an answer.

## Resistance to Group Therapy

Despite the evidence and the positive attributes associated with group therapy, it is not a readily embraced form of treatment; an indication of this was reported by Budman et al. (1988), who conducted a study that compared time-limited group therapy and time-limited individual therapy for psychiatric outpatients. These investigators found significant improvement for patients in both types of treatment. However, they also found that patients tended to prefer individual therapy. Other formal and informal reports in the literature suggest that if they are given the choice, many patients and many therapists would choose individual therapy.

A number of aspects of the group therapy situation can make it seem more intimidating and less appealing. Patients often experience a sense of less *control* in a group versus individual therapy; many people influence the flow of events. The sense of *individuality* may also diminish; the patient must accept that he or she is part of a group. There is also the potential for less complete *understanding* of the events that transpire in a session. Group discussions often jump from topic to topic and from person to person. In addition, the patient may experience feelings that initially are difficult to understand. Groups also offer less *privacy;* patients are continually exposed to others, and absolute confidentiality is impossible to guarantee. The sense of *safety* may diminish for many patients in a group; this is related to less control but more explicitly to the fact that criticism can come from many directions from a number of people. Thus, issues related to perceived or actual loss of control, individuality, understanding, privacy, and safety often lead to greater apprehension about participating in group therapy relative to individual therapy.

Resistance to participating in group therapy can also be experienced by therapists. They, too, are sensitive to the same features of groups that affect patients. In addition, groups are more complicated to organize. An entire set of patients must be assembled to begin at the same time. It may be difficult to obtain a sufficient number of referrals. If one or more patients back out, the onset of the whole group can be delayed, and if the group loses members after it has already started, the life of the group can be threatened. Also, therapists who feel that short-term group therapy is being forced upon them by managed care companies or other third-party payment sources with dubious financial motives resent and resist it.

Thus, a number of concerns and sources of resistance for both patients and therapists lead to apprehension about participating in group therapy; this may explain some of the motivation of group therapy researchers to provide even more data concerning the basic efficacy of group therapies in order to convince those who are ambivalent about participating. There are some additional reasons. With increasing pressure in the health care field to provide short-term group therapies, there is a genuine need to investigate the efficacy of new applications. Rather than abandon basic efficacy studies, researchers need to attain a balance between such studies and more complex studies; however, this brings us to a third reason. More complex studies (e.g., those that compare different types of patients and different types of group therapies) are considerably more difficult to conduct. These studies usually require multiple groups that run simultaneously. Researchers may face a lack of patient referrals to allow the simultaneous start of multiple groups, a lack of skilled group therapists to lead them, a lack of balance between groups due to differential dropouts, and a lack of patients who complete therapy. In order to have the statistical power to detect important effects, large samples are required. To accumulate sufficient numbers of patients and groups, even studies of short-term therapies inevitably become long-term research projects. Difficulties in organizing and maintaining a sufficient number of therapy groups for a complex research project can be quite formidable. The more groups that are involved, the more challenging is the task.

## Optimal Matching of Patients and Therapies

The optimal matching of patients and therapies appears to be one example of a complex research area that merits attempts to overcome the difficulties. Just because reviews of the literature indicate that two types of therapy have similar efficacy when averaged across patients does not prove that the choice between the two is not important for particular individuals. For example, in meta-analytic reviews, an average effect size usually represents the product of averaging across patients, therapists, and outcome variables across many studies. Patient characteristics such as personality variables tend to get lost in the mix and are thus ignored or discounted in importance. Because clinicians treat individuals, not averages, studies are needed that examine the interaction of patient characteristics and types of therapy. Those that have done so have provided promising findings.

A recent review of the predictive ability of patient characteristics in group therapy focused on interaction studies (Piper, 1994). The review covered a 40-year period (1952–1992). Twenty-three of the studies investigated the interaction between patient characteristics and other variables, usually different group therapies. Of the 23 studies, 19 or 83% reported significant interaction effects. This meant that the outcome of therapy depended on the combination of patient characteristics and type of therapy. Predictive patient characteristics included: internal locus of control, psychological mindedness, motivation, social competence, learned resourcefulness, ego strength, coping style, and defensive style. Forms of group therapy in the significant interaction effects differed on variables such as directiveness, insight orientation, structure, cognitive-behavioral orientation, and focus on group interaction. The implication of these findings for clinicians is that they should try to match patients and therapies when making treatment decisions. The evidence for the differential impact of patient characteristics on different forms of group therapy is fairly strong. Whether a similar situation exists for individual versus group forms of therapy is an empirical question that is worth examining.

### Pretherapy Preparation

As discussed in the preceding sections, a number of worthwhile group therapy research questions should be pursued beyond basic questions of efficacy. In order to carry out the appropriate studies, patient resistance to group therapy must be diminished. One means of accomplishing this objective is suggested by a previous line of group therapy research—that concerning pretherapy preparation or what alternatively is referred to as pretraining. Preparatory activities typically involve providing patients with information about what to expect, a model or example of how to conduct oneself, or a therapy-like experience. Therapeutic factors that are unique attributes of groups are often emphasized. These include opportunities for demonstrating one's interpersonal problems, opportunities for receiving feedback from peers, opportunities to be altruistic, and opportunities to share experiences and problems among similar people. The benefits attributed to preparation include improved attendance, retention, therapy process, and treatment outcome. A review of the literature (Piper & Perrault, 1989) indicated definite benefits to attendance, retention, and process, but it indicated rather minimal benefits to outcome. However, given the relatively small costs associated with preparatory activities, they appear to be well worth the effort.

### Therapeutic Factors

The unique therapeutic factors that tend to be emphasized in pretherapy training activities are among a set that is viewed as mediators of therapeutic change. Unfortunately the studies of therapeutic factors have remained at a rather primitive stage. Patients have usually been asked to rate the importance of each factor in bringing about useful change; although this is a useful way to begin, few studies have examined how strongly the ratings are associated with actual therapeutic change. Also, the patient's perception of what is useful is not synonymous with what was predominantly or actually useful in the group.

In addition, the therapeutic factors that have been described in the literature appear to overlap considerably. A more direct way of assessing and studying therapeutic factors is by the application of process analysis systems to the actual material of group therapy sessions. A number of promising systems are presented in the recent edited book by Beck and Lewis (2000). Of course, this approach requires considerably more time to implement.

### Inpatient Populations

Another important but problematic area of group research involves the investigation of efficacy in inpatient populations. A recent meta-analytic review (Mojtabai, Nicholson, & Carpenter, 1998) resulted in equivocal conclusions regarding the efficacy of group therapy. Given brief stays, rapid turnover of patients, and a host of confounding factors such as additional treatments, methodologically strong studies with this population are extremely difficult to conduct.

### Conclusion

In conclusion, considerable evidence supports the efficacy, applicability, and efficiency of many forms of group therapy. In comparisons with forms of individual therapy, they have performed very well. There will continue to be a need to evaluate new applications. However, an additional number of interesting and important research questions remain as a subsequent stage of research. In general, they involve more complex issues and require greater resources to investigate. We hope that group therapy researchers will continue to mobilize the resources and energy that are required to conduct the studies that will increase our understanding of how and why group therapies are effective; clearly this is what is needed to further advance knowledge in the field of group therapy.

## SUMMARY AND CONCLUSIONS

As in any maturing field of clinical endeavor, the general knowledge that sufficed at the beginning of the endeavor no longer suffice; the complexities increase and the subtleties matter, and the field of psychotherapy is left with an ever-greater mandate to train clinicians with greater rigor. Paradoxically, it is just at this moment in history that the support for training in clinical fields is threatened and attenuated. Cost containment for mental health care has delimited the learner-clinician's access to didactic and supervisory venues in which to begin to address the complexities addressed in this chapter. Some psychotherapy organizations, such as the American

Group Psychotherapy Association, are also feeling the squeeze, and local clinics have long since stopped encouraging their personnel to get training by paying for or releasing time for such intellectual endeavors. It becomes incumbent on the existing teachers to expand our own field of teaching and training to include a focus on group psychotherapy—one of the few affordable options left for extended treatment for the patients who struggle with lifelong problems that defy quick solutions. We hope this chapter will serve not only students but also our senior colleagues in deepening and fortifying the place of group theory, research, and treatment as we continue into the new century.

## REFERENCES

Alonso, A. (1993). Training for group psychotherapy. In A. Alonso & H. Swiller (Eds.), *Group therapy in clinical practice* (pp. 521–532). Washington, DC: American Psychiatric Press.

Alonso, A., & Rutan, J. S. (1983). Uses and abuses of transference interpretations in groups. In J. Aronson & L. R. Wolberg (Eds.), *Progress in group and family therapy* (pp. 23–30). New York: Brunner-Mazel.

Alonso, A., & Swiller, H. (1993). *Group therapy in clinical practice.* Washington, DC: American Psychiatric Press.

Beck, A. P., & Lewis, C. M. (Eds.). (2000). *The process of group psychotherapy.* Washington, DC: American Psychological Association.

Bednar, R. L., & Kaul, T. (1994). Experiential group research. In A. E. Bergin & S. L. Garfield (Eds.), *Handbook of psychotherapy and behavior change* (4th ed., pp. 631–663). New York: Wiley.

Berne, E. (1958). Transactional analysis: A new and effective method of group therapy. *American Journal of Psychotherapy, 12,* 735–743.

Bion, W. R. (1959). *Experiences in groups.* New York: Basic Books.

Brabender, V., & Fallon, A. (1993). *Models of inpatient group psychotherapy.* Washington, DC: American Psychological Association.

Budman, S. H., Demby, A., Redondo, J. P., Hannan, M., Feldstein, M., Ring, J., et al. (1988). Comparative outcome in time-limited individual and group psychotherapy. *International Journal of Group Psychotherapy, 38,* 63–86.

Burrow, T. B. (1927). The group method of analysis. *Psychoanalytic Review, 14,* 268–280.

Durkin, H. (1964). *The group in depth.* New York: International Universities Press.

Ezriel, H. (1950). A psychoanalytic approach to group treatment. *British Journal of Medical Psychology, 23,* 59–74.

Freud, A. (1966). *The writing of Anna Freud.* New York: International Universities Press.

Freud, S. (1962). Group psychology and analysis of the ego. In A. Strachey (Ed.), *The standard edition of the complete psychological works of Sigmund Freud* (Vol. 18, pp. 67–134). London: Hogarth Press. (Original work published 1921)

Fuhriman, A., & Burlingame, G. M. (1994). Group psychotherapy: Research and practice. In A. Fuhriman & G. M. Burlingame (Eds.), *Handbook of group psychotherapy: An empirical and clinical synthesis* (pp. 3–40). New York: Wiley.

Glatzer, H. (1962). Narcissistic problems in group psychotherapy. *International Journal of Group Psychotherapy, 12,* 448–455.

Jones, M. (1953). *The therapeutic community.* New York: Basic Books.

Kibel, H. (1991). The therapeutic use of splitting: The role of the mother-group in therapeutic differentiation. In S. Tuttman (Ed.), *Psychoanalytic group theory and therapy.* Madison, CT: International Universities Press.

Kibel, H. (1993). Inpatient group psychotherapy. In A. Alonso & H. Swiller (Eds.), *Group therapy in clinical practice* (pp. 93–111). Washington, DC: American Psychiatric Press.

Klein, M. (1932). *The psychoanalysis of children.* New York: Norton.

Lazell, E. W. (1921). The group treatment of dementia praecox. *Psychoanalytic Review, 8,* 168–179.

LeBon, G. (1920). *The crowd: A study of the popular mind.* New York: Fisher, Unwin.

Lewin, K. (1947). Frontiers in group dynamics: Concept, method, and reality in social science: Social equilibria and social change. *Human Relations, 1,* 5–41.

MacKenzie, K. R. (Ed.). (1992). *Classics in group psychotherapy.* New York: Guilford.

McRoberts, C., Burlingame, G. M., & Hoag, M. J. (1998). Comparative efficacy of individual and group psychotherapy: A meta-analytic perspective. *Group Dynamics: Theory, Research, and Practice, 2*(2), 101–117.

Menninger, W. C. (1936). Psychiatric hospital therapy designed to meet unconscious needs. *American Journal of Psychiatry, 93,* 347–360.

Mojtabai, R., Nicholson, R. A., & Carpenter, B. N. (1998). Role of psychosocial treatments in management of schizophrenia: A meta-analytic review of controlled outcome studies. *Schizophrenia Bulletin, 24,* 569–587.

Moreno, J. L. (1947). *Psychodrama.* New York: Beacon Press.

Piper, W. E. (1994). Client variables. In A. Fuhriman & G. M. Burlingame (Eds.), *Handbook of group psychotherapy* (pp. 83–113). New York: Wiley.

Piper, W. E., Debbane, E. G., Bienvenu, J. P., & Garant, J. (1984). A comparative outcome study of four forms of psychotherapy. *Journal of Consulting and Clinical Psychology, 52,* 268–279.

Piper, W. E., & Joyce, A. S. (1996). A consideration of factors influencing the utilization of time-limited, short-term group therapy. *International Journal of Group Psychotherapy, 46*(3), 211–328.

Piper, W. E., McCallum, M., & Azim, H. F. A. (1992). *Adaptation to loss through short-term group psychotherapy*. New York: Guilford.

Piper, W. E., & Perrault, E. L. (1989). Pretherapy preparation for group members. *International Journal of Group Psychotherapy, 39*, 17–34.

Pratt, J. H. (1922). The principles of class treatment and their application to various chronic diseases. *Hospital Social Services, 6*, 401–417.

Rice, C. A., & Rutan, J. S. (1987). *Inpatient group psychotherapy: A psychodynamic perspective*. New York: Macmillan.

Sadock, B. J., & Kaplan, H. I. (1983). History of group psychiatry. In B. J. Sadock & H. I. Kaplan (Eds.), *Comprehensive group psychotherapy* (2nd ed., pp. 2146–2157). Baltimore: Williams & Wilkins.

Scheidlinger, S. (1974). On the concept of "mother-group." *International Journal of Group Psychotherapy, 24*, 417.

Slavson, S. R. (1951). Current trends in group therapy. *International Journal of Group Psychotherapy, 8*, 36–43.

Smith, M., Glass, G., & Miller, T. (1980). *The benefits of psychotherapy*. Baltimore: Johns Hopkins University Press.

Stanton, A., & Schwartz, M. (1954). *The mental hospital: A study of institutional participation in psychiatric illness and treatment*. New York: Basic Books.

Sutherland, J. D. (1952). Notes on psychoanalytic group psychotherapy. *Psychiatry, 15*, 111–117.

Tillitski, L. (1990). A meta-analysis of estimated effect sizes for group versus individual versus control treatments. *International Journal of Group Psychotherapy, 40*, 215–224.

Toseland, R., & Siporin, M. (1986). When to recommend group treatment. *International Journal of Group Psychotherapy, 36*, 172–201.

Wender, L. (1940). Group psychotherapy: A study of its applications. *Psychiatric Quarterly, 14*, 708–719.

Wolf, A., & Schwartz, E. K. (1962). *Psychoanalysis in groups*. New York: Grune & Stratton.

Yalom, I. D. (1983). *Inpatient group psychotherapy*. New York: Basic Books.

Yalom, I. D., & Lieberman, M. A. (1971). A study of encounter group casualties. *Archives of General Psychiatry, 25*, 16–30.

# CHAPTER 15

# Family Psychotherapy

HAMID MIRSALIMI, STEPHANIE H. PERLEBERG, ERICA L. STOVALL, AND NADINE J. KASLOW

Since the emergence of civilization, scholars have recognized the central role that the family unit has played in human history. As long as families have been around, family problems have existed. Traditionally, families have turned to community members (e.g., extended family members, tribal elders, chiefs, clergy, health care providers) for help in resolving their difficulties. Only within the past century have we witnessed the emergence of the use of education, counseling, or therapy to assist families with their struggles.

The origins of family therapy can be traced to three roots. The first is the social work, marriage and family life education, and marriage counseling movements that began in the late 1800s and early 1900s (Broderick & Schrader, 1991; Kaslow & Celano, 1995; Kaslow, Kaslow, & Farber, 1999; Thomas, 1992). Toward the end of the nineteenth century, social workers began to provide classes to educate families (primarily women) to help prevent family problems. During such classes, participants often discussed their own problems; a family approach was adopted to view their problems in the context of the family. Many leaders of the marriage and family life education movement eventually became pioneers of the field of marital and family counseling.

The second root of the family therapy movement is clinical psychiatry. Several influential family therapy theoreticians were trained psychoanalytically, and their practices often began by treating individual patients. A common denominator among such psychiatrists was the recognition that certain problems of their individual patients were connected to current and family of origin dynamics. That recognition led the professionals to recognize that interventions at the family level constituted the treatment of choice even for their individual clients (e.g., Bateson, 1972; Bowen, 1988; Lidz, Cornelison, Fleck, & Terry, 1957a, 1957b; Minuchin, 1974). Ackerman, a child psychiatrist and psychoanalyst, arrived at similar conclusions in working with children and argued that the proper unit of diagnosis is the family rather than the child.

The third root of family therapy is that of general systems theory and communications theory and their application in understanding human interactions (e.g., Bateson, 1972). The application of the theory was influential in the famous double-bind explanation of the etiology of schizophrenia (Bateson, Jackson, Haley, & Weakland, 1956). Although double-bind messages are no longer considered the cause of schizophrenia, other constructs of general systems and communication theory continue to inform family therapy practice.

In addition to the aforementioned theoretical roots, the growth of a number of organizations was influential in advancing the family therapy movement (Kaslow et al., 1999). In the 1930s a number of marriage counseling centers were established, and the 1930s and 1940s witnessed the professional growth of the field of marital and family therapy. During that era two professional organizations were established. Family life educators established the National Council of Family Relations (NCFR), and marital counselors organized the American Association of Marriage Counselors (AAMC). During the 1970s the AAMC was renamed the American Association of Marriage and Family Therapy (AAMFT); both organizations remain active.

The field of family therapy has undergone a number of changes and expansions commensurate with cultural changes and technical and scientific advances. First, new theories of family therapy have emerged, and integrative models have expanded understanding of family functioning from multiple perspectives. Second, empirical analyses of family therapy tenets and the efficacy of the methods have advanced the field. Third, since the 1970s family therapy has enjoyed international recognition. In fact, the American family therapy movements both informed and were influenced by family therapy around the world. Fourth, ethical guidelines have been established for both research and practice of family therapy. Fifth, subspecialties of family therapy have emerged (e.g., sex therapy, divorce mediation). Sixth, the field has become more sensitive to diversity with regard to family structure, ethnicity and race, gender, social class, and sexual orientation.

In this chapter we provide a broad and comprehensive, albeit not complete, review of the theories and techniques of family therapy. After providing background information on family systems theory and characteristics of individual families, we turn to family intervention approaches. We discuss the major family intervention models and then examine culturally competent and gender-sensitive family therapies. This is followed by a look at specific applications of family therapy (e.g., medical family therapy, substance abuse, family violence). After reviewing the current state of the field of family therapy research, we offer directions for the future practice and research in family therapy.

## FAMILY SYSTEMS THEORY

Theories of family therapy are based on the assumption that an individual's behavior must be viewed and addressed within the context of the family. The family is seen as an evolving and developing living system whose members are interdependent. Each individual is influenced by the system as a whole and, at the same time, influences the functioning of the system. The family changes and develops over time, moving to different levels of organization and function during the course of the individual's and the family's life cycle. The family system struggles to maintain a balance between change and stability or homeostasis.

Systems theory assumes a hierarchical structure within the family based on the higher degree of responsibility and power of the executive subsystem (e.g., parents, mother, and grandmother) in comparison to the child subsystem. This structure is maintained by implicit rules, functional roles of individuals (e.g., primary breadwinner, primary caregiver, parentified child), and family routines. The components of the family structure are called subsystems and are delineated by boundaries. A subsystem may refer to an individual within the larger system or to a group of individuals connected by a common task or level of power within the family system. The boundary between the subsystems refers to the implied rules, activities, or behaviors that maintain some separation between the subsystems (e.g., parents sharing a bedroom, having routine periods of time away from the children). A variety of subsystems might be found in the family depending on the family's composition (e.g., sibships, same-sex family members, executive subsystem).

Most family systems theories acknowledge four aspects of functioning: cohesion, adaptability, communication, and organization. Cohesion refers to the level of interdependence between family members and is usually viewed on a continuum from overinvolvement (i.e., enmeshment) to complete detachment (i.e., disengagement). Healthy families maintain a balance between connectedness and respect for individuality; this balance changes over the life cycle of the family. Adaptability, ranging from chaotic to rigid, indicates the family's ability to make changes in certain circumstances while maintaining stability in values and rules for behavior. Communication processes in the family may involve verbal expression of content and emotions or nonverbal, less direct expression of feelings and relationships (e.g., silent treatment, physical signs of affection). Organization refers to the structure, rules, and roles of the family system. According to most theories of family therapy, the general goal of therapy is to create changes in family interaction patterns, which will in turn result in more adaptive family functioning and individual change.

Family systems theory also assumes that the family system as a whole interacts with other outside systems (e.g., educational system, community, government, work environment). The family as a whole is influenced by, and may have some influence on, the surrounding systems. A family therapist should always determine the extent to which a family is involved in outside systems and the degree to which family functioning is impacted by these interactions.

## CHARACTERISTICS OF INDIVIDUAL FAMILIES

### Family Development

Theories of family therapy assume that families change and develop, and much has been written about the changing family life cycle (e.g., Carter & McGoldrick, 1989). Family development most often is described in relation to the family's function of raising children. Stages of traditional family development include the commitment of two adults to a relationship, the decision to raise children and the increased responsibilities therein, boundary changes as children enter school and the outside world, increasing independence of family members as children enter adolescence, and the renegotiation of the parental relationship as the children leave home.

The family life cycle is influenced by family constellation (e.g., single-parent, remarried). For example, the divorce cycle varies depending on the state of the family's life cycle and includes the separation and divorce process, postdivorce, and the formation of a remarried family (Carter & McGoldrick, 1989). Other factors that impact the family life cycle include culture, ethnicity, immigrant status, chronic illness, death, substance abuse, and psychiatric disorders.

For some families migration is a significant life cycle transition that is often ignored. Immigrant families have myriad responses to this transition, based in part on their reasons for migration. Families who came to the United States for economic or educational reasons may adapt more easily than those seeking refuge or fleeing political persecution (McGoldrick, Giordano, & Pearce, 1996). Families who migrate within the United States for sociopolitical reasons (e.g., African Americans, Native Americans) also are faced with unique challenges. Families who effectively adapt to the migration experience are those with the capacity to alter family's structure and interactional processes to meet the demands of the new culture while keeping cultural patterns from their countries of origin (Bullrich, 1989).

The different stages of family life require adaptation to the developmental needs of the individuals within the family and to the demands of the outside world. The family system must change in order for individual members and the system as a whole to survive. Each stage of family development presents different tasks for the family and involves fluctuation in responsibilities and dependency needs of family members. Family development does not always follow a smooth path, but is often discontinuous. Periodically, the family must renegotiate implicit rules around behavior (e.g., how much time a child is allowed to spend away from the family with peers). As young family members mature, they are given new responsibilities and freedoms. Roles and relationships must be renegotiated. A child may take on more household responsibilities and in turn will earn age-appropriate freedoms. At this same time, the parent relinquishes some control over the child's choices and allows the child to differentiate from the family in order to develop as an individual. When the children leave their family of origin, the adults must renegotiate their relationship and develop new routines and goals. The process of development over the life span of a family calls for a certain degree of stability in order to provide for the health and safety of individual members. However, healthy family development requires flexibility within the family structure so that the changing needs of maturing members may be met.

### Family Structures and Types

Many theories of family therapy have been based on the model of a traditional nuclear family, consisting of two heterosexual parents and their biological children. Family therapists today, however, are faced with a wide variety of family configurations and living situations. Given the high divorce rate (40–50%; Bramlett & Mosher, 2001), over 20% of families in the United States are blended families including stepchildren or children who live with another parent outside of the home (Gorall & Olson, 1995). Single-parent families present different challenges because there is only one adult to assume parenting and financial responsibilities. Some families have multiple generations living in the home, or they have grandparents as the primary caretakers of children. Other nontraditional family constellations include adoptive and foster families, as well as gay and lesbian families (e.g., Dahlheimer & Feigal, 1994; Matthews & Lease, 2000; Scrivner & Eldridge, 1995; Settles, 1999). Still other families may have nonbiological relatives living in the home who are a very integral part of the family structure. Given the variability in family constellations, family therapists generally define "families" as natural social systems that function as a unit with common goals, rules, roles, power structure, routines, forms of communication, and strategies for negotiating and problem solving that allow for various tasks to be accomplished (Goldenberg & Goldenberg, 1999). Relationships among family members are significant and multifaceted and are impacted by a common history, shared perceptions and world beliefs, and a common purpose. Family members are connected by attachments and loyalties that persist over time even though the intensity and quality of these relationships may ebb and flow.

## Family Normalcy and Health Versus Dysfunction

The family therapy field increasingly has shifted from an emphasis on finding a singular, universal model for family normality and health to developing conceptualizations of normal family processes that take into account the diverse patterns of family functioning associated with differing family structures, sociocultural contexts, and developmental challenges (Walsh, 1993). Although there are varied viewpoints about what constitutes optimal family functioning, there is general agreement that normal family functioning implies cohesion among family members that helps to maintain a clear family structure while at the same time allowing for age-appropriate autonomy. The family is able to adapt to environmental and developmental demands by making shifts in power structure, role relationships, and rules. Communication is clear and effective, and family members are able to negotiate rule changes and solve problems together. Individual and subsystem boundaries are mutually understood and respected.

Family dysfunction occurs when the family is unable to adapt to the demands of normative development or of the environment. Systems theories assume that pathology lies within the system interactions, not within the individual. Family interaction patterns and structure become so rigid that the family system is unable to make the necessary changes to promote the health of the individual members or to allow expected changes in the family life cycle. According to systems theory, the psychological symptoms of any individual serve to maintain a certain balance, or equilibrium, within the family. If change threatens the family's established structure or pattern of interaction, an individual may develop psychological symptoms that perpetuate old patterns of family functioning. For example, if marital tension increases and the stability of the nuclear family is threatened, a child may begin to display behavioral symptoms that interrupt the marital conflict, focus parents on their roles as caregivers, and reduce the threat of destruction of the family unit.

When determining the relative health of a given family, a number of factors, in addition to the aforementioned constructs associated with theories of healthy family functioning, must be considered. Different phases of the family life cycle call for varying levels of cohesion and adaptability, and the current life cycle phase of a particular family must be taken into account. Patterns of family functioning that may be appropriate in one phase of a family's development (e.g.,

after the birth of a child) may impede development at another phase (e.g., adult children leaving home). Stressful life events (e.g., loss of a home, diagnosis of a chronic illness) may require different family interaction patterns, either on a temporary or on a long-term basis. When working with a family, the therapist must consider patterns of interaction in light of family stressors and recent events. In addition, family interaction patterns vary across cultures and ethnic groups. It is important for a family therapist to understand a particular family's sociocultural context before determining whether interactional patterns are maladaptive (Walsh, 1993).

Historically, definitions of family normalcy or health failed to acknowledge the influences of culture, social class, ethnicity, and race on family structure and process (Walsh, 1993). Family theorists and therapists have begun to understand the social construction of normal family functioning and have highlighted the fact that because definitions of normal behavior vary across cultures, therapists must not characterize certain family patterns as dysfunctional just because they deviate from the norms of the dominant culture or the norms that are held by the therapist or reflected in his or her theoretical view. They have also underscored the fact that culture contributes to how families define the nature, timing, tasks, and rituals related to life cycle phases and transitions (Carter & McGoldrick, 1989).

## Meaning, Beliefs, and Rituals

Family members share beliefs, values, and a worldview that are transmitted across generations. These beliefs provide connection with the nuclear family, as well as with the extended family in the past and future. Family beliefs provide a foundation and a lens through which each member filters life experiences and influence the meaning that family members attribute to certain situations, events, and life circumstances (e.g., death, prosperity, loss).

Family beliefs and values often are communicated and maintained through family rituals (Imber-Black, Roberts, & Whiting, 1988). For example, family celebrations highlight the value placed on certain life span events (e.g., birthdays, weddings, funerals). Rituals around holidays emphasize family values through inclusion of family members and repetition over time (e.g., Thanksgiving dinner, religious celebrations). Daily routines can also serve to communicate and perpetuate important values. For example, mealtime routines emphasize the importance of shared family time and nurturing. Family rituals and routines contribute to cohesion and stability within the nuclear family and across generations.

# FAMILY INTERVENTION APPROACHES

## Psychodynamically Oriented Family Therapy

Psychodynamically oriented family therapy, the nearest descendant of individual psychoanalytically oriented psychotherapy, is one of the few family models that acknowledges its ties to psychoanalytic thinking. Initially, psychodynamically oriented family therapists espoused a classical psychoanalytic or ego-psychological perspective. Ackerman, an early proponent of psychoanalytic family therapy, integrated psychoanalytic and systems theory (Ackerman, 1938). He viewed dysfunction as a failure in role complementarity between family members, as the product of persistent unresolved conflict within and between individuals in a family, and as a reflection of prejudicial scapegoating. His therapeutic interventions focused on disentangling interlocking pathologies. Framo (1981) postulated that unresolved intrapsychic conflicts, resulting from interactions with one's family of origin, are projected onto one's partner and children. Therefore, the goal of therapy is the working through of the negative introjects, which can be accomplished through a sequence of couples therapy, couples group therapy, and then family of origin meetings separately with each partner.

At the present time, the dominant form of psychoanalytic family therapy is object relations family therapy (Gerson, 1996; Leupnitz, 1988; Scharff, 1989; Scharff & Scharff, 1987, 1991; Slipp, 1988). Object relations family therapy, a long-term treatment approach, addresses unresolved intrapsychic conflicts that are reenacted in one's current life, causing interpersonal and intrapsychic difficulties. Therapy goals include delineating and redefining problems so that they are more accessible to resolution; clarifying boundary issues; explicating individual needs and desires and how these can be fulfilled within the partnership-family system; modifying narcissistic or inappropriate demands; increasing expressive and listening skills; diminishing coercive and blaming statements; facilitating problem solving and conflict resolution; modifying dysfunctional rules and communication patterns; helping family members achieve increased insight; strengthening ego functioning; acknowledging and reworking defensive projective identifications; attaining more mature internal self and object representations; developing more satisfying interpersonal relationships that support one's needs for attachment, individuation, and psychological growth; reducing interlocking pathologies among family members; and resolving partner and therapist-patient transferences. When these goals are achieved, they make possible the attainment of more ultimate goals including trust and closeness, role flexibility, appreciation of uniqueness, comfort with and enjoyment of one's sexuality, and an egalitarian power relationship between the couple as parents and partners, a balance between the cognitive and affective realms of living, positive self-image for each and family esteem for all, clear communication, and the resolution of neurotic conflicts.

To accomplish these goals, the therapist provides a holding environment (i.e., time, space, and a structure) that enables family members to feel secure enough to express their feelings and beliefs, feel intimate, and maintain a sense of self. The therapist reparents the family by providing consistent nurturance and a structure to enhance the development of individual members and the family unit. Once a therapeutic alliance is established and a thorough history is obtained, the therapist empathically interprets conflicts, resistances, negative transferences, defenses, and patterns of interaction indicative of unresolved intrapsychic and interpersonal conflicts. Effective interpretations link an individual's and a family's history with current feelings, thoughts, behaviors, and transactions, permitting more adaptive family interactional patterns and intrapsychic changes. Object relations family therapists address transference and countertransference dynamics to facilitate this endeavor. They use their own reactions to the family's interaction patterns (objective countertransference) to understand the shared yet unspoken experiences of each family member regarding family interactional patterns (unconscious family system of object relations). They use their objective countertransference reactions to interpret interpersonal patterns in which one family member is induced to behave in a circumscribed and maladaptive fashion (projective identification). Although there are specific techniques associated with object relations family therapy, techniques are considered secondary to the alliance between therapist and family.

## Experiential-Humanistic Family Therapy

Experiential-humanistic family therapy has its roots in individual schools of existential-humanistic therapy: Gestalt therapy, client-centered therapy, psychodrama, logotherapy, and the encounter group and sensitivity training movements (Wetchler & Piercy, 1996). Central tenets of family therapies based on the experiential-humanistic model include the belief in freedom of choice and the potentials for human (family) growth; the emphasis on the here and now (i.e., focus on the present as opposed to the past); the primacy of experience over rational thought (especially intellectualization); the importance of fostering open communication, genuineness, and authenticity in dyadic relationships in the family; and a positive and hopeful model of humanity. These therapies are unique in their emphases on the "person of the therapist" and on the belief that emotional interchanges between therapist and family members are key therapeutic elements.

According to existential-humanistic family therapy, family dysfunction arises from communication and interactional problems and their associated symbolic meaning. Goals of therapy include the development of awareness of experienced emotions; choosing to be honest in expressing genuine emotions with other family members; and the exploration of immediate inner experiences and relational interactions. The goals are achieved through the therapist's joining with the family; managing (not interpreting) resistance; pointing to and defining symptoms as efforts toward growth; explicating covert conflicts (e.g., battles for structure and initiative); and fostering open communication, genuineness, and authenticity in dyadic relationships in the family. The achievement of those goals is believed to manifest in the gaining of personal fulfillment and the growth of the family as a whole through increased self-awareness and self-esteem, clarity of communications, and the alteration of the meaning that family members attribute to family interactions.

Whitaker, a founder of experiential-humanistic family therapy, purported that his symbolic-experiential approach is atheoretical (e.g., Whitaker, 1976; Whitaker & Bumberry, 1988; Whitaker & Keith, 1981; Whitaker & Ryan, 1989). He believed that theories are hindrances to "being" and to genuine human experiences in therapy. However, a number of therapeutic emphases have been identified to represent his approach, including the importance of symbolic experience, spontaneity and creativity, growth, battles of structure and initiative, and issues related to psychotherapeutic impasse.

Other schools of experiential-humanistic family therapy include Gestalt (Kempler, 1974, 1981), human validation (e.g., Satir, Stachowiak, & Taschman, 1975), and emotion focused (Johnson & Greenberg, 1985, 1994; Johnson, Hunsley, Greenberg, & Schindler, 1999). Gestalt family therapists strive to help each person within the family attain maximum individuation combined with more vital relationships by facilitating self-exploration, risk taking, and spontaneity. In the human validation model, the therapist and family work together to stimulate an inherent health-promoting process within the family system that is characterized by open communication, emotional experience, and positive self-esteem in each member. This often is achieved through the use of such growth-enhancing techniques as family sculpting.

The most empirically supported form of experiential systems therapy is emotionally focused couple therapy. This approach helps couples identify repetitive negative interaction sequences that restrict accessibility to one another and redefine their problems as reflective of emotional blocks. As these rigid patterns are reprocessed and restructured, the partners are more capable of forming secure attachments and a better sense of connection with one another.

## Communication Model

The communication model, the dominant model in the 1960s, has contributed substantially to the field of family therapy. Indeed, one can recognize the far-reaching influences of this model in all schools of family therapy. Originally formulated at the Mental Research Institute (MRI) by Bateson, Jackson, Weakland, and Haley in Palo Alto, California, in the 1950s, the model gained prominence by providing a description of the etiology of schizophrenia based on family communication patterns. According to the double-bind formulation of schizophrenia, a form of paradoxical communication takes place in families with a member who has schizophrenia (Bateson et al., 1956). It was argued that in such families, contradictory messages are communicated along with a third message that the receiver of the message should not make the inconsistencies explicit. Such communication was theorized to cause confusion and pave the way for the emergence of symptoms characteristic of schizophrenia. Although double-bind communication is no longer believed to cause schizophrenia, the focus on maladaptive communication remains an influential aspect of the communication model. According to the model, all behavior is communication; the difference between various communications is whether they are at the surface or content level, or at the metacommunication or intent level.

Communications family therapy typically is time limited, with a maximum of 10 sessions. An individual clinician or cotherapy pair conducts the treatment, often with consultants behind a one-way mirror. The approach is problem focused and behaviorally oriented. It is believed that providing insight to the family is not a necessary agent of change. The goal of therapy is the reduction or elimination of suffering through problem resolution. Thus, therapy is focused on replacing repetitive, dysfunctional behaviors and communication patterns with healthier ways of behaving and communicating.

## Strategic Family Therapy

Strategic family therapy gained prominence in the 1970s and took center stage in the 1980s. The communication model and Erickson's strategic therapy heavily influenced this approach. Initially developed by Haley (1973, 1976, 1984) in Palo Alto, this approach was further developed by Haley at the Philadelphia Child Guidance Clinic and by Haley and Madanes at the Family Therapy Institute of Washington, DC

(Madanes, 1991). Central in the theoretical formulation of strategic family therapy is the notion that individual and family problems are maintained because of maladaptive family-interactional sequences that include inappropriate hierarchies within the family, as well as malfunctioning triangles. Failed attempts of family members to resolve problems are viewed as the very behaviors that perpetuate the problem (Haley, 1976). Hence, strategic interventions designed to alter the way family members interact and relate to one another are viewed as curative agents in strategic family therapy. Because family interactions are considered to be circular and nonlinear, it is theorized that fundamental changes in the way family members relate are necessary precursors to individual change.

Strategic family therapy is change rather than growth orientated, and little effort is made to provide the family with insight into their problems. The therapy tends to consist of brief interventions in which either the entire family or one or two family members are present. The therapist is active, authoritative, and directive. Goal setting is a major component of strategic family therapy, and two sets of goals are delineated. First, short-term goals are formulated based on the presenting problem; however, in an attempt to enhance motivation in the family, the goal is defined as an increase in positive behaviors rather than as a decrease in negative behaviors. Second, more long-term goals are set with a focus on altering the interactional sequences that have maintained the problem in the first place. In accordance with the above, Watzlawick has pointed out that successful family therapy would involve not only first-order changes (superficial changes that take place without meaningful alterations in the family structure) but also second-order changes, by which family structures are modified, resulting in long-lasting change (Watzlawick, Weakland, & Fisch, 1974).

Techniques of strategic family therapy include the initial interview, which is divided into five stages: social, problem, interaction, goal setting, and task setting. Once the therapist is able to derive an overall formulation, he or she develops a therapeutic approach involving a series of tactical interventions, called *directives*. Some such directives, categorized as straight directives, help maintain a cooperative stance between the therapist and the family. Other directives, labeled paradoxical directives, are utilized when the family is resisting change. Strategic family therapy also incorporates interventions designed to modify existing behavioral sequences. These include paradoxical interventions (e.g., therapeutic use of double-bind communication, positioning, restraining, symptom prescription), reframing, positive connotation, ordeals, pretending, and unbalancing. Because strategic family therapy is time limited and has a problem-solving focus, termination is often a natural process (Segal, 1991). When a family resists termination, termination is reframed as a break from therapy so that gains can be consolidated.

## Structural Family Therapy

The focus of structural family therapy, pioneered by Minuchin (e.g., Minuchin, 1974; Minuchin & Fishman, 1981; Minuchin, Lee, & Simon, 1996), is on family structure, which expresses itself through family interactions. The family experiences transitions to which the family structure must adapt in order to allow for individual growth and a stable environment. A well-functioning family has a well-defined, elaborated, flexible, and cohesive structure (Aponte & VanDeusen, 1981), allowing it to make the necessary adjustments. According to structural family therapy, dysfunctional families are marked by impairments in boundaries, inappropriate alignments (i.e., joining of one member with another), and power imbalances. These families become rigid in the face of stressors, unable to shift familiar patterns of interaction.

In structural family therapy, the course of treatment is typically brief, and the participants are usually those family members that interact on a daily basis. The therapist's role is that of a director who joins with the family and actively evaluates the family structure. This evaluation includes assessment of boundaries, flexibility, subsystems, the role of the symptomatic family member, the ecological context of the family, and the developmental stages of individuals and the family system. The primary goal of therapy is the resolution of the presenting problem. This goal is achieved through altering the family's conceptualization of the problem and restructuring the family to allow for more adaptive patterns of interaction.

## Behavioral and Cognitive-Behavioral Approaches

Approaches that fall within the rubric of behavioral and cognitive-behavioral family therapy include behavioral couple therapy (Gottman, 1999; Jacobson & Christiensen, 1996; Jacobson & Margolin, 1979), cognitive-behavioral family therapy (Dattilio, Epstein, & Baucom, 1998), behavioral parent training (Patterson, 1975), functional family therapy (Alexander & Parson, 1982; Morris, Alexander, & Waldron, 1988), and the conjoint treatment of sexual dysfunction (Heiman, Epps, & Ellis, 1995; Mason, 1991). Because couples therapy is covered in another chapter in this book (see chapter by Messer, Sanderson, & Gurman), we focus this section on cognitive-behavioral family therapy, behavioral parent training, functional family therapy, and sex therapy.

Cognitive-behavioral therapy emphasizes both the behaviors and the cognitive processes of family members. Cognitive-behavioral family therapy assumes that people's cognitive processes influence their behaviors, interactions with other family members, and emotional reactions. Cognitive-behavioral therapy involves the assessment of family members' beliefs, causal attributions, expectancies regarding the presenting problem, and logical analysis of distorted automatic thoughts. Techniques of therapy include cognitive restructuring aimed at changing dysfunctional interactive patterns and belief systems, communication skill building, problem-solving training, and homework.

Behavioral parent training aims to train parents in behavioral principles of child management. Strategies include teaching families to develop new reinforcement contingencies to increase the probability that new behaviors are learned. Commonly used techniques include skill acquisition, contingency contracting, and the imparting of behavioral principles.

Functional family therapy integrates systems theory, behaviorism, and cognitive therapy. The interactional sequences in which problems are embedded are addressed, and the function of these behaviors is ascertained. Family members' cognitions about one another and each other's problem behaviors are evaluated. Functional family therapy facilitates cognitive change and provides education in which specific strategies are provided to bring about behavior change. The goal is to provide new behavior patterns to meet individual functions of each family member.

## Transgenerational Family Therapy

Two major schools of transgenerational therapy are family-of-origin therapy and contextual therapy. Family-of-origin therapy is based on the work of Bowen (1988; Friedman, 1991; Kerr & Bowen, 1988), who views the family as an emotional relationship system. Dysfunction occurs when an individual is unable to differentiate from the family of origin and is thus unable to assert his or her feelings or thoughts, resulting in chronic anxiety. The interaction patterns within a family of creation (i.e., partners) are based on each individual's differentiation from his or her family of origin.

In family-of-origin therapy, the therapist works as a coach who develops a relationship with individual members but avoids becoming entangled in family relationships. The goal of therapy is for each individual to be differentiated within his or her family of origin. Typically, therapy involves the partners, but it can involve multigenerational sessions. One primary technique of therapy is the use of the genogram, a visual map of family history, structure, and relationships, to illustrate historical patterns of family interaction and behavior (Kaslow, 1995; McGoldrick & Gerson, 1985; McGoldrick, Gerson, & Shellenberger, 1999). From the genogram, hypotheses are formulated about the relationship between the presenting problem and family patterns. Key concepts of family-of-origin therapy include differentiation of self, triangulation, and the multigenerational process. Differentiation of self refers to an individual's ability to keep emotional and intellectual functioning distinct, being able to choose which system influences his or her activity at a given time. Triangulation occurs when two family members become aligned, or join together, in opposition to another family member. The concept of multigenerational process describes how the emotional process of a family can be transmitted across generations, with each successive generation being impacted by the levels of differentiation and relationship patterns of family members in previous generations.

Contextual family therapy is another form of transgenerational family therapy based on the writings of Boszormenyi-Nagy (e.g., Boszormenyi-Nagy & Krasner, 1986; Boszormenyi-Nagy & Spark, 1973). Whereas family-of-origin therapy focuses primarily on past relationships, contextual family therapy focuses more on current relationships with the family of origin. Goals of therapy are to reveal and address invisible loyalties, rebalance actual obligations to repair strained family relationships, and develop more trusting relationships with a balance of give and take among family members. The therapist works toward developing relational fairness in the family and attends to the sense of indebtedness between generations. Although the therapist serves as a catalyst for change, the family does much of the therapeutic work outside of the therapy sessions through homework assignments (e.g., writing letters, making phone calls, visiting the family of origin). Key concepts include relational ethics, family legacies, and family ledger. *Relational ethics* are concerned with fairness and equality among family members. *Family legacy* refers to the expectations passed from one generation to the next. The *family ledger* is the account of what family members have given to one another and what each family member owes.

## Psychoeducational Family Therapy

In psychoeducational family therapy, families are helped to remedy individual and family difficulties and to improve family functioning (McFarlane, 1991). The underlying principle of psychoeducational interventions is that family members can be educated to create an optimal environment for their disabled loved ones, an environment that minimizes stresses exacerbating the patient's illness and enhances the patient's capacity for adaptive functioning. In the past these approaches have been successfully used with families in which a member has severe psychopathology (e.g., schizophrenia or affective disorders; Anderson, Reiss, & Hogarty, 1986;

Falloon, Boyd, & McGill, 1984; Miklowitz & Goldstein, 1997). Other applications of this approach include sexual dysfunction, attention-deficit/hyperactivity disorder (ADHD), marriage enrichment, and family skills training. Generally speaking, psychoeducational interventions represent a variety of theoretical orientations, with no one orientation being predominant.

Psychoeducational approaches can be applied in an individual family format or with multiple families. There are four phases of treatment in the psychoeducational model as applied to work with families with a loved one who has been diagnosed with a schizophrenia spectrum disorder. The first phase coincides with relapse, followed by the education, reentry, and rehabilitation phases. Psychoeducational family therapy includes short-term, intermediate, and long-term goals. Short-term and intermediate goals include stabilizing symptoms, educating the family about the particular condition, educating the individual and family about pharmacology, establishing a treatment team, establishing the importance of continuity of care, identifying coping resources for the family, and developing and using social support. The long-term goals of this approach include relapse prevention and reintegration into the community.

## Systemic-Milan Family Therapy

The Milan group developed systemic family therapy in Italy (Boscolo, Cecchin, Hoffman, & Penn, 1987; Prata, 1990; Selvini-Palazzoli, 1974; Selvini-Palazzoli, Boscolo, Cecchin, & Prata, 1978; Selvini-Palazzoli, Cirillo, Selvini, & Sorrentino, 1989). The central theme of this approach is that dysfunctional families remain so because they follow belief systems that do not fit their realities. As such, family interactions often are destructive and perpetuate the negative symptoms that sustain the family's homeostasis. This treatment is process oriented and is viewed as an ecosystem in which each member can affect the psychological well-being of other members.

Family sessions range in number from 3 to 20 and are well spaced so that systemic change can occur. Sessions are led by an individual therapist or by cotherapists with interventions presented by a consulting team seated behind a one-way mirror. Systemic therapists often offer a directive for the family to complete between sessions. These directives include interventions such as circular questioning (one family member comments on the interactions of two other family members), rituals (prescribing an action that alters family roles by addressing spoken and unspoken family rules), counterparadoxical interventions (presenting a double bind that suggests the family not change), and second-order cybernetics (the cybernetics of cybernetics). These techniques highlight repetitive patterns of family behavior (games), introduce new conceptualizations of family problems, and encourage resolution of problems in new ways that result from systemic change. The specific goals of this treatment are determined by the family and are respected by the therapist (unless harm is being done to one of the family members). The general goals of systemic family therapy are to disrupt destructive patterns of family behavior and to enable the family to alter family belief patterns to fit their collective realities.

## Evolving Models

In addition to traditional approaches, a number of newer family therapy approaches have been proposed. Those evolving models can be classified under the general umbrella of postmodernist, second-order cybernetics, and social constructionist perspectives in family therapy. The postmodernist, social constructionist perspective differs from the modernist perspective in that the therapist is viewed as a participant observer and not as the agent of cure. Thus, the therapist collaborates with the client system (the partners or the family system) to create a new reality that is free of the presenting problem. Several such evolving models are reviewed below.

### Solution-Focused Family Therapy

Solution-focused family therapy, developed by O'Hanlon (O'Hanlon & Weiner-Davis, 1989), rests on the belief that meaning is a subjective experience. As such, the meaning a person, couple, or family attributes to a problem is also subjective, resulting in a problem formulation that is unique to them. At the heart of the solution-focused approach is the belief that reformulating the problem will result in new solutions that are likely to emerge and resolve the problem at hand. The transformation from a problem-focused to a solution-focused approach in therapy comes about through joining, describing the problem, finding exceptions to the problem, normalizing, and setting goals.

### Solution-Oriented Family Therapy

Although solution-oriented family therapy, developed by deShazer (deShazer, 1985, 1991), shares many similarities with O'Hanlon's solution-focused therapy, it differs from O'Hanlon's model in important ways. This model also espouses a solution approach to therapy, but it takes the position that one does not need to know the nature of the problem in order to work on resolving it, that the presenting problem is not necessarily related to the solution, and that the solution is not necessarily related to the problem. One of deShazer's more famous interventions, the *miracle question,* is descriptive of his approach: "Suppose that one night there is a miracle and while you were sleeping the problem that brought you to therapy is solved: How would you know? What would be different? What will you notice different the next morning that will tell you that there has been a miracle? What will your spouse [partner] notice?" (deShazer, 1991, p. 113). Such questions are useful in redefining the problem and its causes, as well as in moving toward solutions that would resemble ideal outcomes.

### The Reflecting Team Approach

The reflecting team approach, developed by Andersen (e.g., 1991, 1992), is similar to the Milan approach in many respects; however, it differs from the Milan approach in important ways. What is similar is the fact that the reflecting team approach also involves a group of consultants who view the family therapy session and make comments regarding both the therapeutic process and family interactions as they unfold. However, unlike the Milan approach, the reflecting team is not considered to be a panel of experts whose suggested interventions should be implemented by the therapist; instead, team members engage in the process as participant-observers. The reflections of the team are shared not only with the therapist but with the family as well. Then the family is free to examine the team's reflections, deciding whether team members are correct or incorrect in their comments. Reflecting team members engage in true reflections: they do not necessarily arrive at solutions or suggestions; instead, they reflect on the family process and the therapeutic process as it unfolds in front of them. The reflecting team approach is in line with the postmodernist, social constructionist approach in the way therapists try to understand interactions and engage the family in a therapeutic endeavor.

### Externalization and Reauthoring Lives and Relationships Approach

Central in the externalization and reauthorizing lives and relationships model, developed by White and Epston (White & Epston, 1990), is the notion of problem externalization, a method of redefining the problem as residing outside the individual or the family so that it can be viewed as an entity that can be looked at and worked on. White and Epston's approach involves helping the client develop an alternative story to the one that he or she believes to be the "true" story. Such true stories often involve normative societal beliefs that are devoid of the personal experiences of the individual or the

family. The individual or family often is troubled by such true stories; hence, developing alternative stories serves as the curative factor.

### Therapeutic Conversations Approach

According to the therapeutic conversations approach of Anderson and Goolishian, alternatively called *narrative therapy,* a collaborative conversation is not possible if the therapist takes the position of the expert (Anderson & Goolishian, 1988). Hence, the family therapist must approach the therapeutic situation from the position of not knowing, or "a kind of deliberate ignorance" (Hoffman, 1993, p. 127). Family members are encouraged to tell their story, and the expertise of both the therapist and the family members is utilized to resolve the family's problems. According to this model, the system does not create the problem; instead, the problem defines the system: "the system consists of a conversation or meaning system organized around the problem" (Becvar & Becvar, 1996, p. 287). For other second-order cybernetics models, such as Keeney's (1990) improvisational therapy and Flemons's (1991) relational orientation to therapy, see Becvar and Becvar (1996).

### Postmodern and Social Constructionist Approaches

Postmodern and social constructionist family therapies are relatively new approaches. These treatments move away from a systems view of the family, emphasizing individual experiences and viewpoints as well as the family's interactions with larger systems (Gergen, 1985). Language is used to construct subjectively a story that includes the family's view of reality. Problems are viewed as stories that families agree to tell about themselves.

A major concept underlying these therapies is that there are no fixed truths in the world, only multiple perspectives of reality. As such, the therapist encourages the family to define the goals of treatment. Postmodern therapists assume a collaborative role in the treatment and engage in therapeutic conversation with families to help them construct new meaning and understanding. The therapist helps the family reconstruct its story to include new interpretations of behavior that in turn encourage the development of new behaviors and solutions to problems.

## Integrative Models

The family therapy approaches covered so far can be viewed as being of relatively pure form, that is, one theoretical system per approach. More recently, however, integrative approaches have gained prominence (Carlson, Sperry, & Lewis, 1997). Even a cursory review of recent writing and clinical practice reveals how completely transformed the field of family therapy has become by the integrationist movement. This paradigm shift toward integration has evolved from many sources (Lebow, 1997). Integration occurs at the conceptual level, theoretical level, level of strategy or technique, and level of intervention.

Most of the efforts combine systems, psychodynamic, and behavioral conceptualizations (e.g., Feldman, 1992; Kirschner & Kirschner, 1986; Nichols, 1987, 1995; Pinsof, 1995; Wachtel & Wachtel, 1986). Other efforts mix here-and-now, transgenerational, and ecosystemic approaches (Seaburn, Landau-Stanton, & Horwitz, 1995). Narrative and strategic (Eron & Lund, 1993), strategic and behavioral (Duncan & Parks, 1988), experiential and systemic (Greenberg & Johnson, 1988), and structural and strategic (Liddle, 1984) are further examples of integrative models. Other leaders have focused on combination of treatment perspectives in the development of interventions for specific populations, such as intimate partner violence, substance abuse, sexual dysfunction, medical problems in a family member, and various forms of child and adolescent psychopathology (for a review, see Lebow, 1997). In addition, some authors have utilized an integrative approach for working with families from specific cultures (Boyd-Franklin, 1989; Boyd-Franklin & Bry, 2000; Falicov, 1998; Hardy, 1994).

Although the majority of integrative models involve the combination of two systems of marital and family therapy, most truly integrative approaches involve the combination of more than two systems. The following are a few examples of integrative, multisystemic family therapy models that include more than two models.

Feldman (1992) was one of the first to propose a multisystemic, integrative approach that combines psychodynamic, cognitive, behavioral, and family systems perspectives. He offered a model for determining how individual and family therapy can best be utilized in the treatment of a particular individual, couple, or family. Central in his approach is a detailed assessment of interpersonal and intrapsychic processes that involves individual, family, and family subgroup interviews. Based on those interviews, a formulation is derived and shared with the family. The ensuing treatment, which is determined collaboratively with the family, may involve all of psychodynamic, cognitive, behavioral, and family systems interventions.

Walsh's integrative family therapy approach is goal-directed and structured, typically lasts 10 sessions, and involves actively soliciting the family's involvement (Walsh, 1991). Central in Walsh's approach is an integrative evaluation of family structure, roles, communication patterns, perceptions, themes related to problems, and personality dynamics of key individuals. The integrative aspect of this model is readily recognizable because the family structure factors are based on Minuchin's work, the communication and perception factor is derived from Satir's work on communication and information processing, and the individual dynamics factor is influenced by Ackerman's work. Indeed, Walsh placed a great deal of emphasis on working with individual personality dynamics and recommended that the integrative family therapist espouse both an individual psychotherapeutic and an integrative family therapy model.

## CULTURALLY COMPETENT FAMILY THERAPY

As the demography of the United States has shifted, a growing body of literature addressing culturally competent family therapy has emerged (e.g., Ariel, 1999; McGoldrick et al., 1996; Piercy, Sprenkle, & Wetchler, 1996). As a result of the shifting demography, family therapists and theorists have directed their attentions to the diverse cultural contexts that their clients represent and have begun to focus on the impact of their own culture and their clients' culture on therapeutic process and outcome (Celano & Kaslow, 2000; Falicov, 1998; Kaslow, Celano, & Dreelin, 1995; Kaslow, Loundy, & Wood, 1998; McGoldrick, 1998; McGoldrick et al., 1996). Family therapists have come to understand that while family therapy theories reflect the culture in which they were developed, their clients do not always represent the same or even similar culture. As a result, therapists have come to appreciate that understanding the family's sociocultural and ecological context is essential for interpreting the meaning and function of family members' behavior and interactional patterns and for developing appropriate interventions (Tharp, 1991). The effectiveness of family therapy is increased when therapists recognize the dynamic interaction of cultural, individual, and family factors, including one's own ethnicity (actual and self-defined), the familial culture of origin, the culture in which the family is embedded, and the cultural groups with whom the family interacts (Szapocznik & Kurtines, 1993).

Ideally, the structure of family therapy is codetermined by cultural considerations combined with the therapist's theoretical orientation. Therapists treating families from culturally diverse backgrounds must incorporate flexibility into their work. Flexibility in therapy structure and format is warranted given the differential help-seeking patterns found among many families from ethnic minority groups (McGoldrick et al., 1996). Additional adaptations include varying the length and frequency of sessions, accepting the changing composition of family and nonfamilial participants in sessions, conducting family sessions in community settings or the family's home, and offering a gradual or delayed termination. Therapeutic goals are influenced by several cultural variables, including the role of authority (collaborative vs. hierarchical), decision-making processes (e.g., by whom and how implemented), perceptions of the cause of the problem (e.g., external, such as society, vs. intrafamilial, such as in-law difficulties, vs. internal, such as hormonal imbalances), meaning attributed to the problem, possible solutions for the problem (e.g., acceptable interventions), and therapist's and family's values (Celano & Kaslow, 2000; Kaslow et al., 1995, 1998).

Though there may be techniques and considerations unique to a particular cultural group, there are general guidelines and skills that are useful to incorporate into any culturally competent family therapy treatment. The therapist should endeavor to assess the importance of ethnicity and race to clients and families. This will allow the therapist to validate and empower clients within the appropriate cultural framework. In families where difficulties in cultural adaptation are associated with the presenting problem, the therapist should ensure that cultural concerns are made explicit rather than avoided. Placing a problem within the appropriate cultural context can enable a family to deconstruct problems as contextual rather than internal (Piercy et al., 1996). On the other hand, the therapist should also be aware of the attempts of some families to use culture as a defense against pain or a justification for resistance in the treatment.

Family therapists should work to create an atmosphere in which families feel that their culture is respected (Piercy et al., 1996). Sharing the same cultural background as the family in treatment does not ensure the creation of such an atmosphere, nor does coming from a different cultural background have to interfere with the creation of therapeutic comfort and safety. There are advantages and disadvantages in being in the same ethnic group as the client. Although there may be a natural rapport on which to build, there may also be overidentification with the family.

Another consideration in the conduct of culturally competent family therapy is the development of the therapeutic alliance. The family therapist is most effective in joining with the family if he or she exhibits an awareness of the family's culturally determined rules, roles, structure, communication, and problem-solving patterns (Sue & Zane, 1987). In addition, the family's structure and motivation for treatment, the family's and the therapist's own cultural contexts, and the cultural context that they cocreate influence the nature of the therapeutic alliance. Attention to joining is particularly important with families from ethnic minority groups given their increased risk for attrition from treatment (e.g., Kazdin, Stolar, & Marciano, 1995).

## GENDER-SENSITIVE APPROACHES TO FAMILY THERAPY

Gender-sensitive models are relative newcomers to the family therapy field. Although feminist critiques of other disciplines appeared in the 1960s, it was not until the late 1970s to early 1980s that they began to appear in the family therapy literature (e.g., Avis, 1985; Goldner, 1985; Hare-Mustin, 1978). Feminist models became more common in the late 1980s as theorists began developing new models of family therapy that considered gender as a major contextual factor (Ault-Riche, 1986; Avis, 1996; Bograd, 1991; Goodrich, Rampage, Ellman, & Halstead, 1988; Kaslow & Carter, 1991; Levant & Silverstein, 2001; McGoldrick, Anderson, & Walsh, 1988; Walters, Carter, Papp, & Silverstein, 1988). Literature addressing working with men in family therapy began to emerge in the 1990s (Bograd, 1991; Meth & Pasick, 1990).

In general, feminist approaches seek to underscore power imbalances; to highlight gender differences in relation to intimate relationships, parenting, and extended family relationships; and to discontinue social conditions that contribute to the maintenance of gender-prescribed behaviors (Avis, 1996). Such approaches also emphasize egalitarian relationships and the multiplicity of roles that men and women have in relationships. A major focus of male-oriented models of family therapy is the multiple images and roles of men (Bograd, 1990; Levant & Silverstein, 2001; Meth & Pasick, 1990; Philpot, Brooks, Lusterman, & Nutt, 1997). Such treatment seeks to support men as they value feelings related to their partners, children, and families of origin (Meth & Pasick, 1990). Male-oriented family therapy generally deemphasizes power, control, competition, and money in exchange for focus on the aforementioned topics. In general, interventions designed to acknowledge the importance of gender issues in family treatment should focus at least on the following steps: assessing the distribution of responsibility within the relationship, promoting shared responsibility between men and women, and addressing the balance of power within the relationship (Avis, 1996; Meth & Pasick, 1990).

## SPECIFIC APPLICATIONS

### Medical Family Therapy

Most families will face the challenge of chronic medical illness or disability at some point during the family life cycle. Illness and disability in elderly members may be anticipated but can be disruptive to family routines and relationships. Other families are confronted with illness or disability at unexpected times, such as when a family member is young or has a role of responsibility in the family. Given the demands of caring for an ill family member, a chronic illness can become a central organizing principle in the family. If the family becomes too rigidly organized around maintenance of the chronic illness, transitions in the family's development may be impeded (Reiss, Steinglass, & Howe, 1993). Nonillness family priorities may be suppressed, and normative family developmental issues can be ignored (Gonzalez, Steinglass, & Reiss, 1989).

Rolland (1994) discussed several aspects of chronic illness to be considered when examining the relation between family functioning and chronic illness: onset, course, outcome, type and degree of incapacitation, and degree of uncertainty. Illnesses with a gradual onset call for more measured alterations in family routines and structure than do those with a sudden onset. Families differ in their ability to mobilize rapidly when faced with sudden changes and to tolerate uncertainty over a prolonged period. The course of an illness can take one of three forms: progressive, constant, or relapsing or episodic. With a progressive illness, demands on the family continue to change over time. When the course is episodic, the demands of the illness require flexibility within the family. A constant course does not call for as many changes in demands on the family, but there is still the potential for exhaustion of resources and emotional strength. The outcome of chronic illnesses differentially affect family functioning due to varying degrees of anticipatory loss. Some illnesses have a more constant course with little chance of shortening an individual's life, whereas other illnesses follow a progressive course that almost certainly results in death. When faced with a fatal outcome, families experience grief and the expected loss of a family relationship, as they must adapt to the demands of the illness. The degree of incapacitation has a tremendous impact on families due to increased dependency of a family member, role changes within the family, and possibly social stigma. Rolland also emphasized the added difficulty of coping with illnesses that involve a high degree of uncertainty. The demands of constant adaptation and problem solving can exhaust the resources of even the most flexible families.

The family therapist's role with a family facing chronic medical illness may be to help the family find a place for the illness while working to maintain preillness family goals, routines, and rituals. The therapist must work to understand the demands of an illness and respect the family's need to be highly focused on illness tasks at certain times. At the same time, the therapist should help the family become aware of how illness demands can interfere with family and individual development. When working with families in which a member has a medical illness, it is recommended that a model of collaborative family health care be adopted in which family therapists collaborate with other professionals, the family, and the patient in order to coordinate care for the benefit of the patient and family (McDaniel, Hepworth, & Doherty, 1992).

## Substance Abuse

Given the tremendous negative impact of substance abuse and dependence on the lives of individuals, families, communities, and nations, prevention and intervention efforts have gained prominence on the national agenda. Substance abuse treatments have varied, extending from outpatient drug rehabilitation treatments to outpatient biological interventions (e.g., methadone treatment for heroin abusers) to inpatient therapies. For a number of reasons, delineated later, family therapy is an important and empirically supported therapeutic modality in the treatment of substance abuse (Edwards & Steinglass, 1995; Piercy et al., 1996).

Family therapy can be invaluable in substance abuse treatment because many substance abusers continue to desire a relationship with their families. However, due to behaviors related to substance abuse, family ties may be so strained that the abuser often is left without much remaining social support. In the life of a substance-dependent individual, the inability to go back home or to enjoy the support of family members is often synonymous with poor prognosis. Family therapy can be useful in helping to reconcile strained relationships and reestablishing family support for the patient. In addition to providing general support, the family can encourage the patient in the process of change and address other psychological difficulties such as depression (Piercy et al., 1996). Moreover, a family's active involvement in therapy is likely to motivate the individual with a substance abuse problem to engage in treatment, reducing the possibility of early termination or relapse.

Family therapy also can be very effective in addressing codependent behaviors that often are present in the families of substance abusers. The abuser uses substances, but his or her family members often engage in behaviors directly related to substance abuse. It is in this way that family members can fall into codependent patterns (Bernheim, 1997). Hence, substance abuse is a systemic mental health problem. Family therapy can help address such systemic issues, which go beyond the identified patient and may prolong or sustain the addictive behavior.

## Family Violence

Many family relationships are plagued by family violence, including child maltreatment (e.g., physical, sexual, and emotional abuse and neglect), intimate partner violence, and elder abuse. Given the severity, destructiveness, and pernicious nature of these problems, family therapists should be aware of key treatment issues: recognizing the need for safety within the family, focusing on individual responsibility, and acknowledging the role of culture in encouraging violent and abusive behavior (Carlson et al., 1997). Safety is the primary goal of any treatment where violence is present. When children or elderly family members are involved, mandatory reporting and involvement of the police or the appropriate government agency is the first step.

Although many people, including advocates, argue strongly against the use of couples therapy in cases of intimate partner violence, some therapists underscore the value of such an approach (e.g., Brooks, 1990; Geffner, Barrett, & Rossman, 1995; Hansen & Harway, 1993; Harway & Hansen, 1994; Mantooth, Geffner, Franks, & Patrick, 1987). The basic assumptions of this work are as follows: Each person is responsible for his or her behavior; batterers have the ability to stop the abusiveness; violence and intimidation are unacceptable; the clients have the resources to change their behaviors and the relationship; and the couples therapist can facilitate and motivate the couple in this process (Geffner et al., 1995). Treatment involves a thorough assessment of the relationship violence, relational dynamics, a determination of the appropriateness of couples therapy, a no-violence contract, and safety planning. The first stage of the therapy teaches the couple cognitive and behavioral skills to stop the violent behavior or defend against it and to address the emotions accompanying these changes. This includes anger management, behavioral controls, stress and anxiety management, addressing social roots of aggression, and developing plans for problematic substance use. The second stage emphasizes identifying intergenerational and social messages affecting the relationship and the working through of the emotional, cognitive, and behavioral consequences of these messages. Communication training, assertiveness and social skills training, conflict resolution and problem-solving training, skills in affect regulation, cognitive restructuring, and strategies to enhance self-esteem are also focal during this phase. The third stage includes an examination of the relationship and the decision whether to separate without violence or improve the relationship. In either case, couples therapy is used to help with the process. If the choice is to remain together, this work entails an in-depth analysis of power dynamics, expression of feelings with the goal of increased intimacy, and relapse prevention. In the final stage, the resolution stage, the treatment process comes to an end, and a long-term follow-up period begins.

Many therapists are also opposed to family treatment for childhood maltreatment. However, some family therapists have developed family-oriented treatment approaches for child abuse. For example, Barrett, Trepper, and Fish (1990) and Trepper and Barrett (1986) developed a comprehensive approach for the treatment of intrafamilial sexual abuse of children. In this model, the child's well-being is paramount, and the cessation of abuse is the primary treatment goal. Systemic approaches are used to equalize power in the family. The goal of the offender is to end his or her denial, engage in a nurturing role as a parent, and become actively involved in a sexual relationship with an age-appropriate partner. Their multiple systems model asserts that abuse results from a combination of external, family, and internal systems. They argue that attributing blame is insufficient and that other contributing factors must be examined for long-term change to occur. Although aware of the complexities of a family model for the treatment of intrafamilial sexual abuse, they advocate the use of conjoint treatment in conjunction with individual therapy for each family member, as well as addressing larger social systems. As another example of a family-oriented treatment for child maltreatment, Henggeler and colleagues have found that both multisystemic therapy and parent training are useful in the treatment of child abuse and neglect (Brunk, Henggeler, & Whelan, 1987).

Understanding the role of the cultural context in which families exist is of the utmost importance in cases of family violence (Brooks, 1990; Carlson et al., 1997). Feminist theorists suggest that acknowledging the effects of patriarchal culture on men and women can provide therapists with a more comprehensive understanding of the experiences of the family system (Walker, 1979). Theorists who work with men highlight the importance of understanding the ways that men have been socialized to use violence in their lives (Brooks, 1990). Therapists should pay attention to the myriad factors from the larger social system that contribute to and often exacerbate violence and abuse in couples and families. These factors often intensify and complicate the situations that present in treatment.

## FAMILY THERAPY RESEARCH

Similar to current trends in individual therapy research, advances in family therapy research have focused away from theoretical debates and toward empirical validations. The task of empirically validating family therapy has not been an easy one, and it continues to pose challenges. At the core of the difficulty lie some very basic questions: What constitutes a family? What is the domain of family therapy (Lebow & Gurman, 1995)? Should research focus primarily on traditional systems-focused family therapy, or is it acceptable to include family therapy approaches designed to help an individual client with his or her particular problems within a family therapy context (Baucom, Shohan, Mueser, Daiuto, & Stickle, 1998)? Should claims about the efficacy and effectiveness of family interventions be made when family therapy is the only therapeutic modality, or can such claims be made even in situations where family interventions are a part of a more comprehensive therapeutic approach (Pinsof, Wynne, & Hambright, 1996)? One can see that with such basic questions in setting the stage for research, methodological and statistical difficulties often pose a substantial, but only secondary, set of challenges.

To address some of these challenges, the trend in family therapy research has been to provide definitions up front as to how certain parameters are defined for the particular study. Likewise, review articles and meta-analyses typically explain how the investigators went about setting the stage for their analyses, describing their logic of why certain articles were included and others were excluded. There is often a definition of terms and a description of the criteria used to conduct the review or the meta-analyses (e.g., Pinsof, 1989; Pinsof et al., 1996). Recent methodologically well-designed reviews and meta-analyses of the family therapy research literature conclude that family therapy works (Dunn & Schwebel, 1995; Lebow & Gurman, 1995; Pinsof & Wynne, 1995; Pinsof et al., 1996; Shadish et al., 1993; Shadish, Ragsdale, Glaser, & Montgomery, 1995). The results also indicate that when comparing family therapy to no-treatment control groups, patients receiving family therapy do significantly better (statistically) at termination and follow-up. Pinsof et al. (1996) further delineated that when family therapy is used to treat a particular disorder, research results have revealed that the following disorders consistently responded well to family therapy treatment as compared to no-treatment controls: adult schizophrenia, adult alcoholism, dementia, cardiovascular risk factors in adults, adult and adolescent drug abuse, adolescent conduct disorders, adolescent anorexia of less than 3 years duration, adolescent and childhood obesity, childhood conduct disorders, childhood autism, chronic physical illness in children, and aggressive and noncompliance symptoms associated with ADHD (Pinsof et al., 1996). The investigators also pointed out the efficacy of couples therapy for the following disorders: marital distress and conflict, obesity, hypertension, and depressed women in distressed marriages.

Pinsof et al. (1996) focused next on comparing family therapy to alternative treatments. They concluded that when compared with medication treatment alone or with individual or group therapy, family therapy is a superior therapeutic modality for the following disorders and problems: adult schizophrenia, alcoholism, dementia, cardiovascular risk factors, adult and adolescent drug abuse, adolescent conduct disorder, childhood autism, and aggression and noncompliance

in ADHD. The authors also asserted that one of the strongest and most consistent findings about the superiority of any form of family therapy is in the application of psychoeducational family treatment of schizophrenia (Goldstein & Miklowitz, 1995; Pinsof et al., 1996). There is also growing evidence that in the treatment of childhood anxiety disorders, family therapy is superior to alternative treatments (Barrett, Dadds, & Rapee, 1996). Pinsof et al. (1996) also concluded that couples therapy is a superior therapeutic modality for depressed women in distressed relationships and for marital conflict and distress.

There is also a burgeoning and impressive body of research supporting the effectiveness of multisystemic family therapy for various family problems including juvenile offenders, adolescent sexual offenders, and substance abuse (e.g., Henggeler, Melton, Brondino, Scherer, & Hanley, 1997; Pickrel & Henggeler, 1996; Swenson, Henggeler, Schoenwald, Kaufman, & Randall, 1998). In addition, multisystemic family therapy is a more cost-effective treatment modality than individual therapy, hospitalization, incarceration, or standard treatments not involving the family (Hengeller, Melton, & Smith, 1992; Hengeller et al., 1999; Pinsof et al., 1996).

Pinsof et al. (1996) concluded that the available research does not support the notion than any particular family therapy is superior to any other form. Citing meta-analysis findings by Shadish et al. (1995), the authors stated that Shadish et al. "concluded that if all studies were comparably designed and implemented, orientation differences might disappear, suggesting that orientation outcome differences in meta-analyses may well be primarily a function of the quality of the research, as opposed to the quality of the therapies under investigation" (Pinsof et al., 1996, p. 325). Other investigators also point out that while research findings often support the efficacy of one treatment modality, the lack of outcome research or the scarcity of carefully designed studies makes it difficult to form conclusions about the superiority of one approach over another (Baucom et al., 1998; Dunn & Schwebel, 1995). Nonetheless, Pinsof et al. recognized that the failure of research findings to provide evidence in support of particular orientation differences is not proof that such differences do not exist.

## FUTURE DIRECTIONS

### Practice

Much of what has been discussed up to now has revolved around the development and evolution of the field of family therapy. However, at the beginning of the twenty-first century it seems important to ask the question, What is the future of family therapy? Goldenberg and Goldenberg (1999) delineated several topics in answering this question. The first involves a discussion of postmodern outlooks in family therapy. Postmodern philosophy challenges the modernist notion of the existence of an absolute reality that can be explained through cause-and-effect terms and measured by a detached observer. Instead, the postmodernist view postulates that truth is relative and that there are a variety of subjective beliefs in how the world really operates. Hence, truth and reality are relative and dynamic as opposed to absolute and static. The implication of the postmodernist approach to family therapy is that the previous beliefs about what constitutes family dysfunction and subsequent treatments are challenged. The role of the therapist is changed from one who has the knowledge to diagnose and treat to one whose job is to help the family recognize how its belief systems have created their own reality. The therapeutic impact of such an approach comes from the family's realization that the system of beliefs that has helped family members find meaning in their lives and construct their version of reality has also limited their options. The implication of the fact that there are multiple ways of viewing reality is that there are myriad ways of understanding assumptions, interactions, problems, and impasses. Such a realization has the potential of paving the way for adopting behavioral choices different from the ones that have led the family to the current state of problems. Therefore, the postmodernist, social constructionist approach has profound consequences for the practice of family therapy for several reasons: The therapist is permitted to be a nonexpert; there is a tremendous acceptance of eclecticism; there is an increased recognition of the need to recognize and address diversity issues; and family members and therapists are empowered by believing that the situation is changeable.

Future directions in the practice of family therapy will also be impacted by population diversity and multiculturalism. The fact that the population of North America is becoming increasingly diverse, both in terms of racial and ethnic makeup as well as socioeconomic and other cultural factors, is likely to force the field to adopt a more diverse and inclusive approach to the definition of family systems, the etiology of family dysfunction, beliefs about what constitutes dysfunction, and appropriate interventions given the diversity of belief systems. The multicultural view emphasizes the importance of the therapist's learning about the family's culture, the cultural background of family members, the culture of the agency where the therapist practices, and the dominant culture in which the therapist and the client family are working together. Once again, a multisystemic, integrative, and postmodernist approach is likely to be adopted in addressing those issues.

Gender-sensitive family therapy is another area that is likely to receive more prominence in the future of family therapy practice. Brooks (1996) noted that at the turn of the century, women and men are facing a period of profound gender role strain, putting into question traditional gender formulations. Hence, one challenge for family therapy is to address how client families could be helped to arrive at gender equity. To that end, Brooks encouraged family therapists to move beyond a stance of neutrality because to adopt such a stance is likely to perpetuate the society's traditional gender messages.

Goldenberg and Goldenberg (1999) also addressed the issue of same-sex coupling as a topic that needs to be addressed in the future of the field. As gay and lesbian partners have become more visible, family therapists, as well as many others, have become more aware of their own views and beliefs about the definition of what constitutes a family. Particular issues faced by same-sex couples and their families will need to be delineated, researched, and understood, and therapeutic approaches that are sensitive and effective in gay and lesbian families need to be recognized and adopted.

As the demographics and family constellations change in the United States, a number of family issues deserve greater attention in the next decade. These include the interface of family and work, family business consultation, the involvement of the family with the legal system, families with a member with a disability, families with adopted children (e.g., intercultural adoptions, same-sex adoptions), couples experiencing infertility, and elderly couples.

## Research

The past decade has seen an unprecedented flurry of activity on empirically supported family therapy outcome research, reviews of such research, and meta-analyses evaluating such research (e.g., Baucom et al., 1998; Diamond, Serrano, Dickey, & Sonis, 1996; Dunn & Schwebel, 1995; Estrada & Pinsof, 1995; Hampson & Beavers, 1996; Lebow & Gurman, 1995; Pinsof et al., 1996; Pinsof & Wynne, 1995; Shadish et al., 1993). While there is a tremendous need for further outcome research, there have been substantial advances to date as well. To go forward, it is important to recognize conclusions that can be drawn definitively about the efficacy and effectiveness of family therapy at this point in time; not doing so can amount to the proverbial reinventing of the wheel.

It has been argued that given the available outcome studies, we can conclude that further research comparing any form of family therapy with a no-treatment control condition, in order to show the efficacy of family therapy, is warranted only for disorders and problems that have not been studied so far. That is because we can conclude that for disorders and problems that have been studied up to now, the basic efficacy of family therapy has been proven (Lebow & Gurman, 1995; Pinsof & Wynne, 1995; Pinsof et al., 1996). So where do we go from here? It is time to determine what approaches are most effective in promoting specific types of changes, what approaches are useful to families from specific backgrounds, what processes unfold in each family therapy approach to sessions, and how the various approaches relate to particular outcomes from particular groups of clients who live in particular kinds of family units (Dunn & Schwebel, 1995). In addition, it is imperative that studies examine the efficacy of therapeutic approaches with individuals from other countries, ethnic-minority families within the United States, and sexually diverse families. Further, research must be conducted that focuses both on specific problems and comorbid conditions (e.g., families with a member with a comorbid schizophrenia spectrum disorder and substance abuse problem; Baucom et al., 1998; Pinsof et al., 1996). In addition, more research should be conducted with integrative models, as these are most commonly practiced within the community. Answers to the aforementioned questions and issues may be fruitfully found in effectiveness, efficacy, and dismantling and longitudinal research designs. Qualitative, as well as the traditional quantitative, research designs are important and will yield valuable insights (Lawson & Prevatt, 1999). These studies must better define, operationalize, and measure various forms of family therapy and address the cost effectiveness of family therapy (Pinsof et al., 1996). Further research addressing these recommendations will no doubt advance the field of family therapy in the current decade and beyond.

## REFERENCES

Ackerman, N. W. (1938). The unity of the family. *Archives of Pediatrics, 55,* 51–62.

Alexander, J. F., & Parsons, B. V. (1982). *Functional family therapy.* Pacific Grove, CA: Brooks/Cole.

Andersen, T. (Ed.). (1991). *The reflecting team: Dialogues and dialogues about the dialogues.* New York: W. W. Norton.

Andersen, T. (1992). Reflections on reflecting with families. In S. McNamee & K. J. Gergen (Eds.), *Therapy as social construction* (pp. 54–68). Newbury Park, CA: Sage.

Anderson, C. M., Reiss, D. J., & Hogarty, G. E. (1986). *Schizophrenia and the family.* New York: Guilford.

Anderson, H., & Goolishian, H. A. (1988). Human systems as linguistic systems: preliminary and evolving ideas about the implications for clinical theory. *Family Process, 27,* 371–393.

Aponte, H. J., & VanDeusen, J. M. (1981). Structural family therapy. In A. S. Gurman & D. P. Kniskern (Eds.), *Handbook of family therapy* (pp. 310–360). New York: Brunner/Mazel.

Ariel, S. (1999). *Culturally competent family therapy: A general model.* Westport, CT: Praeger.

Ault-Riche, M. (Ed.). (1986). *Women and family therapy.* Rockville, MD: Aspen Systems.

Avis, J. M. (1985). The politics of functional family therapy: A feminist critique. *Journal of Marital and Family Therapy. 11*(2). 127–138.

Avis, J. M. (1996). Deconstructing gender in family therapy. In F. P. Piercy, D. H. Sprenkle, & J. L. Wetchler (Eds.), *Family therapy sourcebook* (pp. 220–245). New York: Guilford Press.

Barrett, M. J., Trepper, T. S., & Fish, L. S. (1990). Feminist-informed family therapy for the treatment of intrafamilial child sexual abuse. *Journal of Family Psychology, 4,* 151–166.

Barrett, P. M., Dadds, M. R., & Rapee, R. M. (1996). Family treatment of childhood anxiety: A controlled trial. *Journal of Consulting and Clinical Psychology, 64,* 333–342.

Bateson, G. (1972). *Toward an ecology of mind.* New York: Ballantine Books.

Bateson, G., Jackson, D. D., Haley, J. E., & Weakland, J. (1956). Toward a theory of schizophrenia. *Behavioral Science, 1,* 251–264.

Baucom, D. H., Shohan, V., Mueser, K. T., Daiuto, A. D., & Stickle, T. R. (1998). Empirically supported couple and family interventions for marital distress and adult mental health problems. *Journal of Consulting and Clinical Psychology, 66,* 53–88.

Becvar, D. S., & Becvar, R. J. (1996). *Family therapy: A systemic integration* (3rd ed.). Boston: Allyn and Bacon.

Bernheim, K. F. (1997). *The Lanahan cases and readings in abnormal behavior.* Baltimore: Lanahan.

Bograd, M. (Ed.). (1991). *Feminist approaches for men in family therapy.* New York: Harrington Park Press.

Boscolo, L., Cecchin, G., Hoffman, L., & Penn, P. (1987). *Milan systemic family therapy: Conversations in theory and practice.* New York: Basic Books.

Boszormenyi-Nagy, I., & Krasner, B. R. (1986). *Between give and take: A critical guide to contextual therapy.* New York: Brunner/Mazel.

Boszormenyi-Nagy, I., & Spark, G. (1973). *Invisible loyalties: Reciprocity in intergenerational family therapy.* New York: Harper and Row.

Bowen, M. (1988). *Family therapy in clinical practice* (2nd ed.). Northvale, NJ: Jason Aronson.

Boyd-Franklin, N. (1989). *Black families in therapy: A multisystems approach.* New York: Guilford Press.

Boyd-Franklin, N., & Bry, B. H. (2000). *Reaching out in family therapy: Home-based, school, and community interventions.* New York: Guilford Press.

Bramlett, M. D., & Mosher, W. D. (2001). First marriage dissolution, divorce and remarriage: United States. *Advanced data from vital and health statistics: No. 323.* Hyattsville, MD: National Center for Health Statistics.

Broderick, C. B., & Schrader, S. S. (1991). The history of professional marriage and family therapy. In A. S. Gurman & D. P. Kniskern (Eds.), *Handbook of family therapy* (Vol. 2, pp. 3–40). New York: Brunner/Mazel.

Brooks, G. W. (1990). Traditional men in marital and family therapy. In M. Bograd (Ed.), *Feminist approaches for men in family therapy* (pp. 51–74). New York: Harrington Park Press.

Brooks, G. W. (1996). Gender equity in families: A promise worth keeping. *The Family Psychologist, 12,* 5–6.

Brunk, M., Henggeler, S. W., & Whelan, J. P. (1987). Comparison of multisystemic therapy and parent training in the brief treatment of child abuse and neglect. *Journal of Consulting and Clinical Psychology, 55,* 171–178.

Bullrich, S. (1989). The process of immigration. In L. Combrinck-Graham (Ed.), *Children in family contexts: Perspectives on treatment* (pp. 482–501). New York: Guilford Press.

Carlson, J., Sperry, L., & Lewis, J. A. (1997). *Family therapy: Ensuring treatment efficacy.* Pacific Grove, CA: Brooks/Cole.

Carter, E., & McGoldrick, M. (1989). *The changing family life cycle: A framework for family therapy* (2nd ed.). Boston: Allyn and Bacon.

Celano, M., & Kaslow, N. J. (2000). Culturally competent family interventions: Review and case illustrations. *American Journal of Family Therapy, 28,* 217–228.

Dattilio, F. N., Epstein, N. B., & Baucom, D. H. (1998). An introduction to cognitive behavioral therapy with couples and families. In F. M. Dattilio (Ed.), *Case studies in couple and family therapy: Systemic and cognitive perspectives* (pp. 1–36). New York: Guilford.

deShazer, S. (1985). *Keys to solution in brief therapy.* New York: W. W. Norton.

deShazer, S. (1991). *Putting difference to work.* New York: W. W. Norton.

Dahlheimer, D., & Feigal, J. (1994). Community as family: The multiple-family context of gay and lesbian clients. In C. H. Huber (Ed.), *Transitioning from individual to family counseling* (pp. 63–74). Alexandria, VA: American Counseling Association.

Diamond, G. S., Serrano, A. C., Dickey, M., & Sonis, W. A. (1996). Current status of family-based outcome and process research. *Journal of the American Academy of Child and Adolescent Psychiatry, 35,* 6–16.

Duncan, B. L., & Parks, M. B. (1988). Integrating individual and systems approaches: Strategic-behavioral therapy. *Journal of Marital and Family Therapy, 14,* 151–161.

Dunn, R. L., & Schwebel, A. I. (1995). Meta-analytic review of marital therapy outcome research. *Journal of Family Psychology, 9,* 58–68.

Edwards, M. E., & Steinglass, P. (1995). Family therapy treatment outcomes for alcoholism. *Journal of Marital and Family Therapy, 21,* 475–510.

Eron, J. B., & Lund, T. W. (1993). How problems evolve and dissolve: Integrating narrative and strategic concepts. *Family Process, 32,* 291–309.

Estrada, A. U., & Pinsof, W. M. (1995). The effectiveness of family therapies for selected behavioral disorders of childhood. *Journal of Marital and Family Therapy, 21,* 403–440.

Falicov, C. J. (1998). *Latino families in therapy: A guide to multicultural practice.* New York: Guilford.

Falloon, I. R. H., Boyd, J. L., & McGill, C. W. (1984). *Family care of schizophrenia.* New York: Guilford.

Feldman, L. B. (1992). *Integrating individual and family therapy.* New York: Brunner/Mazel.

Flemons, D. (1991). *Completing distinctions.* Boston: Shambala.

Framo, J. L. (1981). The integration of marital therapy with sessions with family of origin. In A. S. Gurman & D. P. Kniskern (Eds.), *Handbook of family therapy* (pp. 133–158). New York: Brunner/Mazel.

Friedman, E. H. (1991). Bowen theory and practice. In A. S. Gurman & D. P. Kniskern (Eds.), *Handbook of family therapy* (Vol. 2, pp. 134–170). New York: Brunner/Mazel.

Geffner, R., Barrett, M. J., & Rossman, B.-B.-R. (1995). Domestic violence and sexual abuse: Multiple systems perspectives. In R. H. Mikesell, D.-D. Lusterman, & S. H. McDaniel (Eds.), *Integrating family therapy: Handbook of family psychology and systems theory* (pp. 501–517). Washington DC: American Psychological Association.

Gergen, K. G. (1985). The social construction movement in modern psychology. *American Psychologist, 40,* 266–275.

Gerson, M. J. (1996). *The embedded self: A psychoanalytic guide to family therapy.* Hillsdale, NJ: Analytic Press.

Goldenberg, H., & Goldenberg, I. (1999). Current issues and trends in family therapy. In D. M. Lawson & F. F. Prevatt (Eds.), *Casebook in family therapy* (pp. 327–338). Belmont, CA: Wadsworth.

Goldner, V. (1985). Feminism and family therapy. *Family Process, 24,* 31–47.

Goldstein, M. J., & Miklowitz, D. J. (1995). The effectiveness of psychoeducational family therapy in the treatment of schizophrenic disorders. *Journal of Marital and Family Therapy, 21,* 361–376.

Gonzalez, S., Steinglass, P., & Reiss, D. (1989). Putting the illness in its place: Discussion groups for families with chronic medical illnesses. *Family Process, 28,* 69–87.

Goodrich, T. J., Rampage, C., Ellman, B., & Halstead, K. (1988). *Feminist family therapy: A casebook.* New York: W. W. Norton.

Gorall, D. M., & Olson, D. H. (1995). Circumplex model of family systems: Integrating ethnic diversity and other social systems. In R. H. Mikesell, D.-D. Lusterman, & S. H. McDaniel (Eds.), *Integrating family therapy: Handbook of family psychology and systems theory* (pp. 217–233). Washington, DC: American Psychological Association.

Gottman, J. M. (1999). *The marriage clinic: A scientifically based marital therapy.* New York: W. W. Norton.

Greenberg, L. S., & Johnson, S. M. (1988). *Emotionally focused therapy for couples.* New York: Guilford.

Haley, J. (1973). *Uncommon therapy: The psychiatric techniques of Milton H. Erickson, M. D.* New York: W. W. Norton.

Haley, J. (1976). *Problem-solving therapy.* San Francisco: Jossey-Bass.

Haley, J. (1984). *Ordeal therapy: Unusual ways to change behavior.* San Francisco: Jossey-Bass.

Hampson, R. B., & Beavers, W. R. (1996). Measuring family therapy outcome in a clinical setting: Families that do better or do worse in therapy. *Family Process, 35,* 347–361.

Hansen, M., & Harway, M. (Eds.). (1993). *Battering and family therapy: A feminist perspective.* Newbury Park, CA: Sage.

Hardy, K. (1994). Deconstructing race in family therapy. *Journal of Feminist Family Therapy, 5,* 5–33.

Hare-Mustin, R. (1978). A feminist approach to family therapy. *Family Process, 17,* 181–194.

Harway, M., & Hansen, M. (1994). *Spouse abuse: Assessing and treating battered women, batterers, and their children.* Sarasota, FL: Professional Resource Press.

Heiman, J. R., Epps, P. H., & Ellis, B. (1995). Treating sexual desire disorders in couples. In N. S. Jacobson & A. S. Gurman (Eds.), *Clinical handbook of couple therapy* (pp. 471–495). New York: Guilford Press.

Henggeler, S. W., Melton, G. B., Brondino, M. J., Scherer, D. G., & Hanley, J. H. (1997). Multisystemic therapy with violent and chronic juvenile offenders and their families: The role of treatment fidelity in successful dissemination. *Journal of Consulting and Clinical Psychology, 65,* 821–833.

Henggeler, S. W., Melton, G. B., & Smith, L. A. (1992). Family preservation using multisystemic therapy: An effective alternative to incarcerating serious juvenile offenders. *Journal of Consulting and Clinical Psychology, 60,* 953–961.

Henggeler, S. W., Rowland, M. D., Randall, J., Ward, D. M., Pickrel, S. G., Cunningham, P. B., Miller, S. L., Edwards, K., Zealberg, J. J., Hand, L. D., & Santos, A. B. (1999). Home-based multisystemic therapy as an alternative to the hospitalization of youths in psychiatric crisis: Clinical outcomes. *Journal of the American Academy of Child and Adolescent Psychiatry, 38,* 1331–1339.

Hoffman, L. (1993). *Exchanging voices: A collaborative approach to family therapy.* London: Karnac.

Imber-Black, E., Roberts, J., & Whiting, R. (Eds.). (1988). *Rituals in families and family therapy.* New York: W. W. Norton.

Jacobson, N. S., & Christiensen, A. (1996). *Integrative couple therapy: Promoting acceptance.* New York: W. W. Norton.

Jacobson, N. S., & Margolin, G. (1979). *Marital therapy: Strategies based on social learning and behavioral exchange principles.* New York: Brunner/Mazel.

Johnson, S. M., & Greenberg, L. S. (1985). Emotionally focused marital therapy: An outcome study. *Journal of Marital and Family Therapy, 11,* 313–317.

Johnson, S. M., & Greenberg, L. S. (Eds.). (1994). *The heart of the matter: Perspectives on emotion in marital therapy.* New York: Brunner/Mazel.

Johnson, S. M., Hunsley, J., Greenberg, L., & Schindler, D. (1999). Emotionally focused couples therapy: Status and challenges. *Clinical Psychology: Science and Practice, 6,* 67–79.

Kaslow, F. W. (1995). *Projective genogramming.* Sarasota, FL: Professional Resources Press.

Kaslow, N. J., & Carter, A. S. (1991). Gender-sensitive object-relational family therapy with depressed women. *Journal of Family Psychology, 5,* 116–135.

Kaslow, N. J., & Celano, M. P. (1995). The family therapies. In A. S. Gurman & S. B. Messer (Eds.), *Essential psychotherapies: Theories and practice* (pp. 343–402). New York: Guilford.

Kaslow, N. J., Celano, M., & Dreelin, E. D. (1995). A cultural perspective on family theory and therapy. *Psychiatric Clinics of North America, 18,* 621–633.

Kaslow, N. J., Kaslow, F. W., & Farber, E. W. (1999). Theories and techniques of marital and family therapy. In M. B. Sussman, S. K. Steinmetz, & G. W. Peterson (Eds.), *Handbook of marriage and the family* (2nd ed., pp. 767–792). New York: Plenum Press.

Kaslow, N. J., Loundy, M., & Wood, K. (1998). A cultural perspective on families across the life cycle: Patterns, assessment, and intervention outline. In C. D. Belar (Ed.), *Comprehensive Clinical Psychology: Vol. 10. Sociocultural and individual differences* (pp. 173–205). New York: Pergamon Press.

Kazdin, A. E., Stolar, M. J., & Marciano, P. L. (1995). Risk factors for dropping out of treatment among White and Black families. *Journal of Family Psychology, 9,* 402–417.

Keeney, B. (1990). *Improvisational therapy.* St. Paul, MN: Systemic Therapy Press.

Kempler, W. (1974). *Principles of gestalt family therapy.* Salt Lake City, UT: Desert Press.

Kempler, W. (1981). *Experiential psychotherapy within families.* New York: Brunner/Mazel.

Kerr, M., & Bowen, M. (1988). *Family evaluation: An approach based on Bowen theory.* New York: W. W. Norton.

Kirschner, D. A., & Kirschner, S. (1986). *Comprehensive family therapy: An integration of systemic and psychodynamic treatment models.* New York: Brunner/Mazel.

Lawson, D. M., & Prevatt, F. F. (1999). *Casebook in family therapy.* New York: Wadsworth.

Lebow, J. (1997). The integrative revolution in couple and family therapy. *Family Process, 36,* 1–17.

Lebow, J. L., & Gurman, A. S. (1995). Research assessing couple and family therapy. *Annual Review of Psychology, 46,* 27–57.

Leupnitz, D. A. (1988). *The family interpreted: Feminist theory in clinical practice.* New York: Basic Books.

Levant, R. F., & Silverstein, L. B. (2001). Integrating gender and family systems theories: The "both/and" approach to treating a postmodern couple. In S. H. McDaniel, D.-D. Lusterman, &

C. L. Philpot (Eds.), *Integrating family therapy: An ecosystemic approach* (pp. 245–252). Washington, DC: American Psychological Association.

Liddle, H. A. (1984). Toward a dialectical-contextual-coevolutionary translation of structural-strategic family therapy. *Journal of Strategic and Systemic Therapies, 3,* 66–79.

Lidz, T., Cornelison, A., Fleck, S., & Terry, D. (1957a). The intrafamilial environment of schizophrenic patients: I. The father. *Psychiatry, 20,* 329–342.

Lidz, T., Cornelison, A., Fleck, S., & Terry, D. (1957b). The intrafamilial environment of schizophrenic patients: II. Marital schism and marital skew. *American Journal of Psychiatry, 114,* 241–248.

Madanes, C. (1991). Strategic family therapy. In A. S. Gurman & D. P. Kniskern (Eds.), *Handbook of family therapy* (Vol. 2, pp. 396–416). New York: Brunner/Mazel.

Mantooth, C. M., Geffner, R., Franks, D., & Patrick, J. (1987). *Family preservation: A treatment manual for reducing couple violence.* Tyler: University of Texas at Tyler Press.

Mason, M. J. (1991). Family therapy as the emerging context for sex therapy. In A. S. Gurman & D. P. Kniskern (Eds.), *Handbook of family therapy* (Vol. 2, pp. 479–507). New York: Brunner/Mazel.

Matthews, C. R., & Lease, S. H. (2000). Focus on lesbian, gay, and bisexual families. In R. M. Perez, K. A. DeBord, & K. J. Bieschke (Eds.), *Handbook of counseling and psychotherapy with lesbian, gay, and bisexual clients* (pp. 249–273). Washington, DC: American Psychological Association.

McDaniel, S. H., Hepworth, J., & Doherty, W. J. (1992). *Medical family therapy: A biopsychosocial approach to families with health problems.* New York: Basic Books.

McFarlane, W. R. (1991). Family psychoeducational treatment. In A. S. Gurman & D. P. Kniskern (Eds.), *Handbook of family therapy* (Vol. 2, pp. 363–395). New York: Brunner/Mazel.

McGoldrick, M. (Ed.). (1998). *Re-visioning family therapy: Race, culture, and gender in clinical practice.* New York: Guilford.

McGoldrick, M., Anderson, C., & Walsh, F. (Eds.). (1988). *Women in families: A framework for family therapy.* New York: W. W. Norton.

McGoldrick, M., & Gerson, R. (1985). *Genograms in family assessment.* New York: W. W. Norton.

McGoldrick, M., Gerson, R., & Shellenberger, S. (1999). *Genograms: Assessment and intervention* (2nd ed.). New York: W. W. Norton.

McGoldrick, M., Giordano, J., & Pearce, J. K. (Eds.). (1996). *Ethnicity and family therapy* (2nd ed.). New York: Guilford Press.

Meth, R. L., & Pasick, R. S. (1990). *Men in therapy: The challenge of change.* New York: Guilford Press.

Miklowitz, D. J., & Goldstein, M. J. (1997). *Bipolar disorder: A family-focused treatment approach.* New York: Guilford.

Minuchin, S. (1974). *Families and family therapy.* Cambridge, MA: Harvard University Press.

Minuchin, S., & Fishman, H. C. (1981). *Family therapy techniques.* Cambridge, MA: Harvard University Press.

Minuchin, S., Lee, W.-Y., & Simon, G. M. (1996). *Mastering family therapy: Journeys of growth and transformation.* New York: Wiley.

Morris, S. B., Alexander, J. F., & Waldron, H. (1988). Functional family therapy. In I. R. H. Falloon (Ed.), *Handbook of behavioral family therapy* (pp. 107–127). New York: Guilford Press.

Nichols, M. P. (1987). *The self in the system: Expanding the limits of psychotherapy.* New York: Brunner/Mazel.

Nichols, W. C. (1995). *Treating people in families.* New York: Guilford.

O'Hanlon, W. H., & Weiner-Davis, M. (1989). *In search of solutions: A new direction in psychotherapy.* New York: W. W. Norton.

Patterson, G. (1975). *Families: Applications of social learning to family life.* Champaign, IL: Research Press.

Philpot, C. L., Brooks, G., Lusterman, D.-D., & Nutt, R. (1997). *Bridging separate gender worlds: How men and women clash and how therapists can bring them together.* Washington, DC: American Psychological Association.

Pickrel, S. G., & Henggeler, S. W. (1996). Multisystemic therapy for adolescent substance abuse and dependence. *Child and Adolescent Psychiatric Clinics of North American, 5,* 201–211.

Piercy, F. P., Sprenkle, D. H., & Wetchler, J. L. (Eds.). (1996). *Family therapy sourcebook* (2nd ed.). New York: Guilford Press.

Pinsof, W. M. (1989). A conceptual framework and methodological criteria for family therapy process research. *Journal of Consulting and Clinical Psychology, 57*(1), 53–59.

Pinsof, W. (1995). *Integrative problem centered therapy.* New York: Basic Books.

Pinsof, W. M., & Wynne, L. C. (1995). The efficacy of marital and family therapy: An empirical overview, conclusions and recommendations. *Journal of Marital and Family Therapy, 21,* 585–614.

Pinsof, W. M., Wynne, L. C., & Hambright, A. B. (1996). The outcomes of couple and family therapy: Findings, conclusions, and recommendations. *Psychotherapy, 33,* 321–331.

Prata, G. (1990). *A systemic harpoon into family games.* New York: Brunner/Mazel.

Reiss, D., Steinglass, P., & Howe, G. (1993). The family organization around the illness. In R. E. Cole & D. Reiss (Eds.), *How do families cope with chronic illness? Family research consortium: Advances in family research* (pp. 173–213). NJ: Erlbaum.

Rolland, J. S. (1994). *Families, illness, and disability: An integrative treatment model.* New York: Basic Books.

Satir, V., Stachowiak, J., & Taschman, H. (1975). *Helping families to change.* New York: Jason Aronson.

Scharff, D. E., & Scharff, J. S. (1987). *Object relations family therapy.* Northvale, NJ: Jason Aronson.

Scharff, D. E., & Scharff, J. S. (1991). *Object relations couple therapy.* Northvale, NJ: Jason Aronson.

Scharff, J. S. (Ed.). (1989). *Foundations of object relations family therapy.* Northvale, NJ: Aronson.

Scrivner, R., & Eldridge, N. S. (1995). Lesbian and gay family psychology. In R. H. Mikesell, D.-D. Lusterman, & S. H. McDaniel (Eds.), *Integrating family therapy: Handbook of family psychology and systems theory* (pp. 327–344). Washington, DC: American Psychological Association.

Seaburn, D. B., Landau-Stanton, J., & Horwitz, S. (1995). Core techniques in family therapy. In R. H. Mikesell, D.-D. Lusterman, & S. H. McDaniel (Eds.), *Integrating family therapy: Handbook of family psychology and systems therapy* (pp. 5–26). Washington, DC: American Psychological Association.

Segal, L. (1991). Brief therapy: The MRI approach. In A. S. Gurman & D. P. Kniskern (Eds.), *Handbook of family therapy* (Vol. 2, pp. 171–199). New York: Brunner/Mazel.

Selvini-Palazzoli, M. (1974). *Self-starvation.* London: Human Context Books.

Selvini-Palazzoli, M., Boscolo, L., Cecchin, G., & Prata, G. (1978). *Paradox and counterparadox.* Northvale, NJ: Jason Aronson.

Selvini-Palazzoli, M., Cirillo, S., Selvini, M., & Sorrentino, A. M. (1989). *Family games: General models of psychotic processes in the family.* New York: W. W. Norton.

Settles, B. (1999). The future of families. In M. B. Sussman, S. K. Steinmetz, & G. W. Peterson, *Handbook of marriage and the family* (2nd ed., pp. 143–175). New York: Plenum.

Shadish, W. R., Montgomery, L. M., Wilson, P., Wilson, M. R., Bright, I., & Okwumabua, T. (1993). Effects of family and marital psychotherapies: A meta-analysis. *Journal of Consulting and Clinical Psychology, 61*(6), 992–1002.

Shadish, W. R., Ragsdale, K., Glaser, R. R., & Montgomery, L. M. (1995). The efficacy and effectiveness of marital and family therapy: A perspective from meta-analysis. *Journal of Marital and Family Therapy, 21,* 345–360.

Slipp, S. (1988). *The technique and practice of object relations family therapy.* Northvale, NJ: Jason Aronson.

Sue, S., & Zane, N. (1987). The role of culture and cultural techniques in psychotherapy: A critiques and reformulation. *American Psychologist, 42,* 37–45.

Swenson, C. C., Henggeler, S. W., Schoenwald, S. K., Kaufman, K. L., & Randall, J. (1998). Changing the social ecologies of adolescent sexual offenders: Implications of the success of multisystemic therapy in treating serious antisocial behavior in adolescents. *Child Maltreatment, 3,* 330–338.

Szapocznik, J., & Kurtines, W. M. (1993). Family psychology and cultural diversity. *American Psychologist, 48,* 400–407.

Tharp, R. G. (1991). Cultural diversity and treatment of children. *Journal of Consulting and Clinical Psychology, 59,* 799–812.

Thomas, M. B. (1992). *An introduction to marital and family therapy: Counseling toward healthier family systems across the lifespan.* New York: Macmillan.

Trepper, T. S., & Barrett, M. J. (1986). *Treating incest: A multisystemic perspective.* New York: Haworth.

Wachtel, P. L., & Wachtel, E. F. (1986). *Family dynamics in individual psychotherapy: A guide to clinical strategies.* New York: Guilford.

Walker, L. E. (1979). *The battered woman.* Harper: New York.

Walsh, F. (1993). *Normal family processes* (2nd ed.). New York: Guilford.

Walsh, W. (1991). *Case studies in family therapy: An integrative approach.* Boston: Allyn and Bacon.

Walters, M., Carter, B., Papp, P., & Silverstein, O. (1988). *The invisible web: Gender patterns in family relationships.* New York: Guilford.

Watzlawick, P., Weakland, J., & Fisch, R. (1974). *Change: Principles of problem formation and problem resolution.* New York: W. W. Norton.

Wetchler, J. L., & Piercy, F. P. (1996). Experiential family therapies. In F. P. Piercy, D. H. Sprenkle, & J. L. Wetchler (Eds.), *Family therapy sourcebook* (2nd ed., pp. 79–105). New York: Guilford Press.

Whitaker, C. A. (1976). The hindrance of theory in clinical work. In P. J. Guerin, Jr. (Ed.), *Family therapy: Theory and practice* (pp. 154–164). New York: Gardner Press.

Whitaker, C. A., & Bumberry, W. M. (1988). *Dancing with the family: A symbolic-experiential approach.* New York: Brunner/Mazel.

Whitaker, C. A., & Keith, D. V. (1981). Symbolic-experiential family therapy. In A. S. Gurman & D. P. Kniskern (Eds.), *Handbook of family therapy* (pp. 187–225). New York: Brunner/Mazel.

Whitaker, C. A., & Ryan, M. O. (1989). *Midnight musings of a family therapist.* New York: W. W. Norton.

White, M., & Epston, D. (1990). *Narrative means to therapeutic ends.* New York: W. W. Norton.

# CHAPTER 16

# Child Psychotherapy

RICHARD J. MORRIS, HUIJUN LI, PATRICIA SÁNCHEZ LIZARDI, AND YVONNE P. MORRIS

Interest in the conduct and effectiveness of child and adolescent psychotherapy is a relatively recent event in the mental health treatment literature (e.g., Kazdin, Siegel & Bass, 1992; Kendall & Morris, 1991; Morris & Kratochwill, 1998c). Unlike the adult psychotherapy literature and related writings, which can be traced back to ancient times, the child and adolescent psychotherapy literature can be traced with any certainty only to the early twentieth century (e.g., Kanner, 1948; Kratochwill & Morris, 1993; Morris & Kratochwill, 1998b). The one notable exception involves research on those children who have been diagnosed as having a developmental disability such as mental retardation or autism. For these children, the child treatment literature can be traced to the work of Jean Itard in France and his attempts in the early 1790s to educate the "Wild Boy of Aveyron" (Itard, 1962; Morris, 1985).

The developments in the early twentieth century that contributed substantially to our present-day emphasis on child and adolescent psychotherapy were the following: (a) the *mental hygiene/mental health movement* in the early to mid-1900s, as well as the early-1900s advocacy work of Clifford Beers (1908), which focused on improving psychiatric services for people having emotional problems; (b) the introduction of *dynamic psychiatry* and Sigmund Freud's (1909)

detailed case of "Little Hans," as well as the psychoanalytic play therapy work in the 1920s and 1930s of Melanie Klein and Freud's daughter, Anna Freud, and Anna Freud's edited book series (with Heinz Hartmann & Ernst Kris) beginning in 1945, *The Psychoanalytic Study of the Child;* (c) the *intelligence testing movement* begun by Alfred Binet in France in the early 1900s; (d) the establishment of *child welfare professional associations* in the 1920s (e.g., the Council for Exceptional Children and the American Orthopsychiatry Association), as well as the formation at a much earlier time of the Association of Medical Officers of American Institutions for Idiots and Feebleminded (circa 1876; currently named the American Association on Mental Retardation); (e) *individualized instruction and special education classes* for mentally and emotionally disabled students, with the first teacher-training programs established for the latter students in the early 1910s in Michigan; and (f) the establishment of *child guidance clinics* throughout the United States in the early to mid-1900s (e.g., Kanner, 1948; Kauffman, 1981; Morris & Kratochwill, 1998b).

Other developments influencing our present day psychotherapy approaches with children and adolescents were quite different from the psychoanalytic emphases of Sigmund and Anna Freud and Melanie Klein. One development dates back almost as far as Freud's psychoanalysis but has its origins in the experimental psychology laboratory. This therapy approach became known as *behavior therapy* or *behavior modification* and was based on psychological theories of learning and conditioning (see, e.g., Bandura, 1969; Bandura & Waters, 1963; Hull, 1943; Mowrer, 1960; Pavlov, 1927; Skinner, 1938, 1953; Thorndike, 1913, 1931).

Preparation of this chapter was supported in part by the David and Minnie Meyerson Foundation's Project on Research, Advocacy, and Policy Studies on Disability at the University of Arizona. The authors wish to acknowledge the contribution of Mary Lucker to the word processing of this chapter. Portions of this chapter are based in part on R. J. Morris and Y. P. Morris (2000).

Two studies involving behavioral approaches gained early recognition for their attempts to understand and treat children's behavior disorders and each, like Freud's Little Hans case study, focused on children's fears. The first case study was by Watson and Raynor (1920), who investigated the development of fear in an 11-month-old boy named Little Albert; the second case study, by Jones (1924), involved the treatment of a fear in a 3-year-old boy named Peter.

A second nonpsychoanalytic development that impacted our present day approaches to child and adolescent therapy took place in the early 1940s. This new development was advocated by such writers as Frederick Allen (1942) and Virginia Axline (1947) and incorporated the psychoanalytic emphasis on the therapeutic relationship but deemphasized Freud's conceptualization of the unconscious and its role in explaining children's verbalizations and related play activities. In addition, unlike Freudian approaches, these writers emphasized the child's or adolescent's present life reality instead of his or her past experiences as the central focus of therapy. The emphasis, therefore, of these *relationship therapy* approaches was on providing the child with a warm, accepting, and permissive therapeutic environment in which few limitations were placed on him or her. By providing these "necessary" relationship and environmental conditions within the therapeutic setting, Allen, Axline, and others believed that the child or adolescent client would be provided with the opportunity to reach his or her highest level of psychological growth and mental health. Axline's writings followed the *client-centered approach* of Carl Rogers (1942), and Allen's therapeutic procedures were more consistent with an *ecological perspective* and the emerging area of social psychiatry.

In this chapter we present an overview of four major therapeutic approaches that are currently discussed in the child and adolescent psychotherapy literature (see, e.g., D'Amato & Rothlisberg, 1997; Kratochwill & Morris, 1993; Mash & Barkley, 1989; Morris & Kratochwill, 1998c). These therapies are behavior therapy and cognitive-behavioral therapy, child psychoanalysis, Adlerian therapy, and client-centered (humanistic) therapy. Before these therapies can be discussed in any detail, however, certain issues need to be discussed regarding the conduct of child and adolescent psychotherapy.

## ISSUES RELATED TO THE CONDUCT OF CHILD AND ADOLESCENT PSYCHOTHERAPY

Although early work by Levitt (1957, 1963) suggested that children and adolescents receiving "traditional" forms of psychotherapy did not improve appreciably more than those who did not receive treatment (i.e., approximately 66% of the treated children and 73% of the untreated children were rated as "improved"), a later meta-analysis by Casey and Berman (1985) indicated that there was a significant effect size for "treatment" (behavior therapy, psychodynamic therapy, or client-centered therapy) when compared to the control condition. Casey and Berman also reported that for certain types of outcome measures the behavior therapies were found to be better than the nonbehavioral therapies, but when the type of measure was controlled for, no differences were found in the effectiveness of the various psychotherapies. Weisz, Weiss, Alicke, and Klotz (1987), and Weisz, Weiss, Han, Granger, and Morton (1995), on the other hand, found in their respective meta-analyses that the average outcome for those children receiving a form of behavior therapy was appreciably better than was that for children receiving a nonbehavior therapy—with no particular behavior therapy procedure being better than any other behavioral procedure. Findings like these led Kazdin (1990) to conclude that "psychotherapy appears to be more effective than no treatment" and that "treatment differences, when evident, tend to favor behavioral rather than nonbehavioral techniques" (p. 28). Kazdin indicated that these meta-analytic studies highlighted the fact that the number of studies utilizing behavioral and cognitively based therapies outnumbered to a large extent those child and adolescent therapy studies, which incorporated such procedures as psychodynamic and client-centered approaches.

Research findings such as those from meta-analytic treatment outcome studies, as well as those involving the direct surveying of clinicians regarding treatment effectiveness (e.g., Kazdin, Siegel, & Bass, 1992), have led some writers to suggest—as has been discussed for more than 35 years in the adult psychotherapy literature (see, e.g., Beutler, 1997; Goldstein, Heller, & Sechrest, 1966; Huppert et al., 2001; Kazdin, 1997; Paul, 1967)—that we can no longer answer the question, "Is child or adolescent psychotherapy effective?" Instead, we need to answer the question, "Is this *particular type of child or adolescent therapy* effective for *this type of child or adolescent,* having *this presenting problem,* from *this family structure and background experiences,* with *this type of therapist,* from *this type of background,* with therapy being applied *under these environmental conditions or constraints?*" (see, e.g., Kazdin, 1990; Kendall & Morris, 1991; Morris & Morris, 2000). It is interesting to realize that a similar set of prescriptive questions in child psychotherapy was posed more than 40 years ago by Heinicke and Goldman (1960) but resulted in little or no subsequent therapy outcome research. Specifically, Heinicke and Goldman stated, "The question is no longer: Does therapy have an effect?—but rather: What changes can we observe in a certain kind of child or family which can be attributed to involvement in a certain kind of therapeutic interaction? Within this very broad question, we can vary the nature of the child's problem, the [therapeutic] orientation of the therapist, the frequency of the therapeutic contact, the length of the contact, the degree of involvement of parents, etc." (p. 492).

The success of child and adolescent therapies may also be influenced by comorbidity factors. For example, will children having attention-deficit/hyperactivity disorder (ADHD) improve equally using the same therapy procedure whether or not they have a comorbid diagnosis of conduct disorder? Or will adolescents having a diagnosis of agoraphobia with panic attacks improve as rapidly when receiving the same therapy method independent of the presence or absence of a comorbid diagnosis of dysthymia? Or will young adolescents who have obsessive-compulsive disorder (OCD) improve equally well with the same method of psychotherapy as will those young adolescents who have OCD and school refusal? Because few, if any, therapy outcome research studies exist that address these types of comorbidity questions (see, e.g., Kendall, Brady, & Verduin, 2001), no definitive answers can be given at this time. Although our current state of knowledge of child and adolescent psychotherapy procedures has not yet progressed to the point where specific prescriptive questions such as those listed can be answered at this time, there have nevertheless been some attempts in the literature to address more general prescriptive questions (see, e.g., Barkley, 1990; Bear, Minke, & Thomas, 1997; Kavale, Forness, & Walker, 1999; Morris & Kratochwill, 1998c).

The conduct of child or adolescent therapy is complicated also by the fact that it is not always clear who is the client (Kendall & Morris, 1991). Unlike psychotherapy with adults, the child or adolescent is not typically the person who initiates contact and an appointment with the clinician. Moreover, the child or adolescent may not be the only person who enters the therapist's office for the first visit, and it is rare that the child or adolescent pays for the therapy services. In most cases, the child's or adolescent's parent or guardian, teacher or other school personnel, or a representative of the juvenile justice system brings the "client" to the therapist's office, and it is one of these people (or, possible, an agency representative) who will probably pay for the therapist's services. In addition, unlike in adult psychotherapy, it is likely that one of these latter persons will have the legal right to review the therapist's session notes or request a report on the child's or adolescent's progress in therapy, therefore impacting the confidentiality between therapist and client (Arambulla, DeKraai, & Sales, 1993; DeKraai, Sales, & Hall, 1998). In addition, parents and teachers may believe

that the client is the child or adolescent and may thus become somewhat concerned later in the therapy process if they are asked to become integrally involved in the treatment plan that is developed. Therefore, defining "who is the client" early in the treatment program is important not only to reduce confusion on the part of the various participants but also to establish limits to confidentiality and establish who, other than the therapist, will be participating in the child's or adolescent's treatment plan. These types of decisions regarding who is the client and what the therapy process entails should only be made following a thorough intake assessment. Each person included in the therapy process should then give his or her consent to participate and specify the conditions (within the legal constraints imposed by state and federal laws) under which the therapist will be able to share each participating client's comments with the other participants and the therapist will be able to share his or her own perspective with the participating persons (Arambulla et al., 1993).

In terms of the therapeutic relationship, research in this area still lags far behind the adult literature even though several child therapy practices (e.g., child psychoanalytic therapy and client-centered therapy) indicate that the therapeutic relationship is at least a necessary condition for effecting positive behavior change. Kendall and Morris (1991) and Morris and Nicholson (1993) noted that although such "therapist variables" as therapist warmth, therapist empathy, model similarity, therapist ethnicity, and therapist verbal encouragement and physical contact have been discussed in the literature, as have such "client variables" as type of presenting problem, pretreatment level of prosocial functioning, and level of motivation, no firm conclusions can be made at this time regarding the contribution of these factors to therapy outcome. Moreover, a child's or adolescent's knowledge of the absence (or limited nature) of confidentiality in psychotherapy, although not yet studied, may influence therapy outcome as well as the individual's level of self-disclosure during therapy (Kendall & Morris, 1991).

The personal beliefs and related values of the therapist may also impact treatment outcome. The notion of therapist values is not only related, for example, to such areas as the cultural or ethnic values of the therapist vis-à-vis the client (and the client's family) or to the religious beliefs of the therapist versus those of the client (and his or her family), but also to situations in which the clinician sees the following individuals in psychotherapy: (a) gay or lesbian adolescents who do not construe their current psychological difficulties as related to their sexual preference, (b) a child or adolescent who has tested positive for the human immunodeficiency virus (HIV), (c) a child or adolescent who is living with drug-addicted parents, and (d) a physically or sexually abused child or adolescent who has been placed by the court back into the home where the perpetrator lives (Morris & Nicholson, 1993).

Little (or no) systematic research has been conducted on the contribution of these different factors on the outcome of child or adolescent psychotherapy or, for that matter, on the contribution of therapeutic relationship factors to therapy outcome. Instead, the literature has focused primarily on treatment effectiveness studies (i.e., empirically supported treatments) involving particular child or adolescent behavior disorders, school- or parent-based treatments, and community-based treatments (see, e.g., Morris & Kratochwill, 1998c; Morris & Morris, 2000). Within the structure of these studies, researchers have adopted the unspecified, undefined, and untested working assumption that therapy should be conducted within the framework of a sound therapeutic relationship between the therapist and adolescent client (e.g., Kendall & Morris, 1991; Morris & Morris, 2000). Consistent with this assumption, the therapies described next also presume the presence of a sound therapeutic relationship between the client and therapist.

## CHILD AND ADOLESCENT PSYCHOTHERAPY METHODS

### Behavior Therapy and Cognitive-Behavioral Therapy

Behavior therapy and cognitive-behavioral therapy approaches have their roots in the learning theory positions of Ivan Pavlov (1927), B. F. Skinner (1938, 1953), Clark Hull (1943), O. Hobart Mowrer (1960), and Albert Bandura (1969, 1977; Bandura & Walters, 1963). These researchers' respective theories of learning were tested and refined in experimental psychology laboratories during the previous century. The research findings from these theories demonstrated that people and animals behave in predictable ways and suggested that there are principles that can explain the manner in which people and animals behave. Researchers also found that intervention procedures based on these theories of learning could be developed to change people's behaviors (Morris, 1985). This largely laboratory-based research led, beginning in the 1960s, to the application of this knowledge to more practical or clinical areas such as behavior problems and behavior disorders in children and adolescents (see, e.g., Bandura, 1969; Gardner, 1971; Graziano, 1971; Lovass & Bucher, 1974; O'Leary & O'Leary, 1972). The findings from this more clinically oriented research were encouraging and led investigators and clinicians to expand their behaviorally

oriented treatment approaches to children and adolescents having a variety of behavioral difficulties.

Behaviorally oriented treatment approaches follow a general set of working assumptions (see, e.g., Kazdin, 1980; Morris, 1976; Morris & Kratochwill, 1983b; Rimm & Masters, 1979). First, it is assumed that children's and adolescents' behavior problems are learned unless there is genetic or biological evidence to the contrary. Second, behavior problems are learned separately from (and independently of) other behavior problems or related maladaptive behaviors that the child or adolescent may manifest, unless there is genetic or biological evidence or other objective data showing that a given set of behaviors are interconnected or occur together. Third, behavior problems are setting or situation specific. This suggests that unless there is contradictory evidence, it is assumed that a child's or adolescent's behavior problems that are observed in one setting will not generalize to other settings or situations. This is an important assumption within the behavioral view because it forces the clinician to look within the environmental setting where the behavior problem occurred for possible reasons that contributed to the performance of the behavior. It also encourages the clinician to look into those settings where the behavior problem has not occurred to determine what factors in these settings might be preventing the behavior problem from being performed.

The fourth assumption refers to the position that the emphasis of therapy is on the here and now. This assumption directs the clinician to focus on what is presently contributing to the child's behavior disorder or maladaptive behavior and to identify what in the child's present environment could be modified that might effect a positive behavior change in the child. The past history of the child, therefore, is important only to assist the clinician in determining (a) which intervention approaches have been effective or ineffective in the past (settings similar to the current setting) in changing the child's behavioral difficulties; (b) whether the frequency, severity, or duration of the behavior problem has gotten better or worse over time; and (c) whether a pattern has developed over time of the type of settings in which the behavior occurs on a regular basis (Morris & Morris, 1997). Behaviorally oriented therapists do not deny that historical events have, in some way, contributed to the development of the present behavior that the child is demonstrating; however, they maintain that because such events took place in the past, they cannot presently be manipulated unless the same causal (or maintaining) factors are still contributing to the child's behavioral difficulties. Historical causal events are therefore of low importance in the formulation of a treatment plan and in the conduct of behavior therapy and cognitive-behavioral therapy unless such events are presently contributing to the child's problem.

The fifth assumption indicates that the goals of behavior therapy and cognitive-behavioral therapy are specific. Because behaviorally oriented therapists maintain that children's and adolescents' behavior problems are learned in particular settings and are specific to those situations, it follows that the goals of therapy are specific—for example, the reduction of a targeted behavior within a particular setting. Sixth, consistent with the previous assumptions, unconscious factors play no essential role in the development, maintenance, or treatment of children's and adolescents behavior disorders. Moreover, insight is not necessary for changing a child's or adolescent's behavior problems. Because behaviorally oriented therapists do not accept the belief that there are underlying unconscious factors responsible for a child's or adolescent's behavior disorders, it follows that they do not maintain that insight is a necessary condition for effecting positive behavior change.

These latter assumptions represent a somewhat idealized position regarding the conduct of behavior therapy and cognitive-behavioral therapy. In actual practice, behaviorally oriented therapists may agree with all or only some of these assumptions.

The essential difference between behavior therapy and cognitive-behavioral therapy methods is the emphasis on the contribution of cognitive processes or private events as mediators in the child's or adolescent's behavior change. Specifically, in cognitive-behavioral therapy, the child's or adolescent's thoughts, feelings, attributions, self-statements, and other cognitive variables are viewed as important factors in effecting positive behavior change (e.g., Ellis & Wilde, 2002; McReynolds, Morris, & Kratochwill, 1988; Meichenbaum, 1977; Ramirez, Kratochwill, & Morris, 1987). In contrast, behavior therapy approaches typically focus on those directly observable variables within the child's or adolescent's immediate environmental setting that may be modified to effect positive behavior change. This behaviorally oriented approach is more consistent with the "applied behavior analysis" model of learning of B. F. Skinner (1938, 1953), whereas the cognitive-behavioral therapy approach is more consistent with Bandura's "social learning theory" (e.g., Bandura, 1969; Bandura & Walters, 1963), Ellis's "rational-emotive therapy" (e.g., Ellis, 1962; Ellis & Wilde, 2002), and Beck's "cognitive therapy" (e.g., Beck, 1976), as well as the writings of Meichenbaum (e.g., 1977), Karoly and Kanfer (1982), Mahoney (1974), and Kendall (1991, 1994). Each behavioral approach, however, shares the position that children's and adolescents' behavior problems are learned, are maintained by their consequences, and can be modified using procedures based on theories of learning.

The psychotherapy approaches most often used in behavior therapy and cognitive-behavioral therapy with children and adolescents involve the use of such *contingency management procedures* as reinforcement methods (including shaping, token economy program, schedules of reinforcement, self-reinforcement, contingency contracting, differential reinforcement of other behaviors, and differential reinforcement of incompatible behaviors), extinction, stimulus control, and time-out from reinforcement (see, e.g., Kazdin, 2000; Mash & Barkley, 1989; Mash & Terdall, 1997; Morris & Kratochwill, 1998c; Sulzer-Azaroff & Meyer, 1991). In addition, modeling methods are used (e.g., Bandura, 1969, 1977), as are relaxation training and systematic desensitization procedures (e.g., King, Hamilton, & Ollendick, 1988; Morris & Kratochwill, 1983b, 1998c; Wolpe & Lazarus, 1966), and *self-control and self-instructional training* (see, e.g., Bernard & Joyce, 1993; Hughes, 1988; Kendall, 1991, 1992; Kendall & Braswell, 1985; Meichenbaum & Goodman, 1971).

In terms of supportive research, a variety of behavior therapy and cognitive-behavioral therapy procedures have been used in the treatment of such child and adolescent behavior disorders as OCD, depression, fears and related anxieties, disruptive behavior disorders such as aggression and conduct disorder, ADHD, psychophysiological disorders including eating disorders, posttraumatic stress disorder, and autism (see, e.g., Mash & Terdall, 1997; Mash & Wolfe, 1999; Morris & Kratochwill, 1998c; Morris & Morris, 2000; Quay & Hogan, 1999). For example, regarding children's and adolescents' fears and phobias, four different types of behaviorally oriented methods have been used successfully to treat this disorder (see, e.g., Morris & Kratochwill, 1983a, 1998c). The first method, *systematic desensitization* and its variants, presumes that a child's fear or phobic response is learned and can, therefore, be counter conditioned by teaching the child to relax through the use of a relaxation protocol such as the one shown in Table 16.1. Calmness and trust in the therapeutic relationship has also been used in certain types of desensitization procedures such as in vivo and contact desensitization. The relaxed or calm state that the client experiences is then associated (either through imagination or in vivo) with a graduated hierarchy of fearful or anxiety-provoking situations that the client previously listed with the therapist's assistance. *Contingency management procedures* have also been used to treat these behavior difficulties. For example, positive reinforcement has been used to reduce the frequency and duration of social withdrawal and social isolation in young children, as well as to increase social interaction. When combined with shaping, positive reinforcement has also been used to treat school phobia.

Both live and symbolic *modeling* approaches have also been used to treat children's fears and phobias. Like

**TABLE 16.1   Relaxation Protocol**

| Steps in Relaxation |
|---|

1. Take a deep breath and hold it (for about 10 seconds). Hold it. Okay, let it out.
2. Raise both of your hands about halfway above the couch (or arms of the chair) and breathe normally. Now drop your hands to the couch (or arms).
3. Now hold your arms out and make a tight fist. Really tight. Feel the tension in your hands. I am going to count to three and when I say "three" I want you to drop your hands. One . . . two . . . three.
4. Raise your arms again and bend your fingers back the other way (toward your body). Now drop your hands and relax.
5. Raise your arms. Now drop them and relax.
6. Now raise your arms again, but this time "flap" your hands around. Okay, relax again.
7. Raise your arms again. Now relax.
8. Raise your arms above the couch (chair) again and tense your biceps. Breathe normally and keep your hands loose. Relax your hands. (Notice how you have a warm feeling of relaxation.)
9. Now hold your arms out to your side and tense your triceps. Make sure that you breathe normally. Relax your arms.
10. Now arch your shoulders back. Hold it. Make sure that your arms are relaxed. Now relax.
11. Hunch your shoulders forward. Hold it and make sure that you breathe normally and keep your arms relaxed. Okay, relax. (Notice the feeling of relief from tensing and relaxing your muscles.)
12. Now turn your head to the right and tense your neck. Relax and bring your head back into in its natural position. Turn your head to the left and tense your neck. Relax and bring your head back again to its normal position.
13. Turn your head to the left and tense your neck. Relax and bring your head back again to its natural position.
14. Now bend your head back slightly toward the chair. Hold it. Okay, now bring your head back slowly to its natural position.*
15. This time bring your head down almost to your chest. Hold it. Now relax and let your head come back to its natural resting position.
16. Now open your mouth as much as possible. A little wider, okay, relax (mouth should be partly open afterwards).
17. Now tense your lips by closing your mouth. Okay, relax.
18. Now put your tongue at the roof of your mouth. Press hard. (Pause.) Relax and allow your tongue to come to a comfortable position in your mouth.
19. Now put your tongue at the bottom of your mouth. Press down hard. Relax and let your tongue come to a comfortable position in your mouth.
20. Now just lie (sit) there and relax. Try not to think of anything.
21. To control self-verbalizations, I want you to go through the motions of singing a high note—not aloud. Okay, start singing to yourself. Hold that note. Okay, relax. (You are becoming more and more relaxed.)
22. Now sing a medium tone and make your vocal cords tense again. Relax.
23. Now sing a low note and make your vocal cords tense again. Relax. (Your vocal apparatus should be relaxed now. Relax your mouth.)
24. Now close your eyes. Squeeze them tight and breathe naturally. Notice the tension. Now relax. Notice how the pain goes away when you relax.
25. Now let your eyes relax and keep your mouth open slightly.
26. Open your eyes as much as possible. Hold it. Now relax your eyes.
27. Now wrinkle your forehead as much as possible. Hold it. Okay, relax.
28. Now take a deep breath and hold it. Relax.
29. Now exhale. Breathe all the air out . . . all of it out. Relax. (Notice the wondrous feeling of breathing again.)
30. Imagine that there are weights pulling on all your muscles making them flaccid and relaxed . . . putting your arms and body down into the couch.
31. Pull your stomach muscles together. Tighter. Okay, relax.
32. Now extend your muscles as if you were a prizefighter. Make your stomach hard. Relax. (You are becoming more and more relaxed.)
33. Now tense your buttocks. Tighter. Hold it. Now relax.
34. Now search the upper part of your body and relax any part that is tense. First the facial muscles. (Pause 3 to 5 seconds.) Then the vocal muscles. (Pause 3 to 5 seconds.) The neck region. (Pause 3 to 5 seconds.) Your shoulders . . . relax any part that is tense. (Pause.) Now the arms and fingers. Relax these. Becoming very relaxed.
35. Maintaining this relaxation, raise both your legs (about a 45-degree angle). Now relax. Notice how this further relaxes you.
36. Now bend your feet back so that your toes point toward your face. Relax your mouth. Bend them hard. Relax.
37. Bend your feet the other way . . . away from your body. Not far. Notice the tension. Okay, relax.
38. Relax. (Pause.) Now curl your toes together as hard as you can. Tighter. Okay, relax. (Quiet—silence for about 30 seconds.)
39. This completes the formal relaxation procedure. Now explore your body from your feet up. Make sure that every muscle is relaxed. Say slowly—first your toes, your feet, your legs, buttocks, stomach, shoulders, neck, eyes, and finally your forehead—you should be relaxed now. (Quiet—silence for about 10 seconds.) Just be there and feel very relaxed, noticing the warmness of the relaxation. (Pause.) I would like you to stay this way for about 1 minute, and then I am going to count to five. When I reach five, I want you to open your eyes feeling very calm and refreshed. (Quiet—silence for about 1 minute.) Okay, when I count to five I want you to open your eyes feeling very calm and relaxed. One . . . feeling very calm; two . . . very calm, very refreshed; three . . . very refreshed; four . . . and five.

*The child or adolescent should not be encouraged to bend his or her neck either all the way back or forward.

*Source:* Adapted in part from Jacobson (1938), Rimm (1967, personal communication), and Wolpe and Lazarus (1966). From *Treating children's fears and phobias: A behavioral approach* (p. 135) by R. J. Morris and T. R. Kratochwill, 1983, Elmsford, NY Pergamon Press. Copyright © 1983 by Pergamon Press. Reprinted by permission of Allyn & Bacon Inc.

contingency management methods, these procedures have been used more often to treat clearly identifiable fears and phobias such as phobias involving nondangerous animals, physical or dental examinations and receiving an injection, attending school, and darkness or sleep anxiety. *Cognitive-behavioral therapy* procedures that have been used have involved primarily self-instructional and self-control training where the therapist teaches the child how, when, and where to use various cognitions or self-statements to facilitate the learning of new and more adaptive nonfearful behaviors (Morris & Kratochwill, 1998a; Morris & Morris, 2000).

## Psychoanalytic Therapy

The origins of psychoanalysis as a psychotherapy method with children and adolescents can be traced back to Sigmund Freud's (1909) case of Little Hans. Hans was almost 5 years old and was very afraid of horses. His fear that a horse would bite him made him reluctant to leave the house. It was on the basis of these symptoms and other information conveyed to Freud by Hans's father that Freud formulated his theory of the development of phobias and his position on psychoanalytic therapy with children (Morris & Kratochwill, 1983b).

Freud never saw Hans in therapy. As Freud (1909) stated, "the treatment itself was carried out by the boy's father" (p. 149). Freud, however, did see Hans "on one single occasion," during which time he had a "conversation with the boy"; in that regard he stated that he "took a direct share" in the boy's treatment (p. 149). Freud did not participate directly in Hans's therapy because he felt that only a parent could adequately act as an analyst for a young child—he felt that a child could not form a trusting enough relationship with a stranger (e.g., analyst) to permit the normal therapeutic interchange that needs to take place in psychoanalysis (Kratochwill, Accardi, & Morris, 1988). Although he did not believe that an analyst could see children directly in therapy, he felt that the use of psychoanalysis with children had the purpose of "empirically" observing the origins of adult neuroses during childhood, and he wanted to confirm his own conceptualization of infantile sexuality, as he hypothesized in his (1905) article titled "Three Essays on the Theory of Sexuality."

In 1913, Hermine Hug-Hellmuth, the third woman to join Freud's Vienna Psychoanalytic Society, began conducting psychoanalytic work with children. She wrote about how she invited the children to speak to her using the metaphor of play rather than having them sit on the couch and use the psychoanalytic treatment tool of free association. Based on Hug-Hellmuth's initial work, Melanie Klein and Freud's daughter, Anna Freud, continued developing this area of play therapy, and during the 1920s to 1930s they established their respective schools of child analysis (Benveniste, 1998). Sigmund Freud's case of Little Hans therefore laid the groundwork for the formation of a new approach to the psychological treatment of children's and adolescents' behavioral and emotional disorders. As Anna Freud (1981) wrote,

> What the analysis of Little Hans opened up is a new branch of psychoanalysis, more than the extension of its therapy from adult to child—namely, the possibility of a new perspective on the development of the individual and on the successive conflicts and compromises between the demands of the drive, the ego, and the external world which accompany the child's laborious steps from immaturity to maturity (p. 278).

Both Klein and Anna Freud discovered that children using the medium of play will represent their inner conflicts, reflect on their views and perceptions of important relationships in their lives, and play out significant aspects of their unique pleasurable and traumatic experiences. The play medium, therefore, permits the child analyst to become attuned to the verbal and nonverbal communications of the child in order to further an understanding of the child's feelings, worries, wishes, motives, and conflicts (Warshaw, 1997).

Although Anna Freud and Melanie Klein were trained as psychoanalysts, their respective approaches to working with children were different. Anna Freud emphasized theory and pedagogy as part of her procedure, whereas Klein's approach focused on techniques (e.g., Donaldson, 1996; Viner, 1996). Specifically, Anna Freud believed that psychoanalysis should be a pedagogical tool used to educate children and strengthen their ego functioning. In her writings she emphasized the contribution of child development to the emergence of children's personality and general emotional functioning—maintaining that the interaction between mental functions and biology were very important in both the understanding of children's emotionality and the conduct of child psychoanalysis (e.g., Mayes & Cohen, 1996; Neubauer, 1996). She also believed that the transference relationship observed in adult psychoanalysis could not take place in child psychoanalysis, and that her father's notion of the Oedipus complex should not be an area of investigation with children because the revealing of Oedipal material was too traumatic for a child's immature ego (Donaldson, 1996; Viner, 1996). Moreover, consistent with Hug-Hellmuth's position, Anna Freud felt that children could not free associate during therapy because they were not capable of articulating their thoughts and that their play activity in therapy was not equivalent to (or a substitute for) free association (Solnit, 1998). As a result, insight from an analyst's interpretation of the patient's free association thinking was not possible with children. Interpretation of dream material was also to be limited to non-Oedipal content (Donaldson, 1996; Viner, 1996). Therapy therefore stressed the importance of the therapeutic relationship or therapeutic alliance, the emotional maturing of the child within the therapeutic alliance, and the use of interpretation of ego defenses versus interpretation of deeper unconscious material (O'Connor, Lee, & Schaefer, 1983).

Klein also recognized the language limitations of children. However, unlike Anna Freud, she viewed play activity as the equivalent to free association in adult psychoanalysis. This permitted her to interpret a child's play as being symbolic of various unconscious beliefs and motives and to introduce Sigmund Freud's notion of the transference relationship as a viable therapeutic tool in child psychoanalysis (e.g., Donaldson, 1996; Segal, 1990; Viner, 1996). Klein further maintained that although classical psychoanalytic theory does not consider as possible the development of superego functioning early in a child's life (i.e., prior to the internalization and resolution of the Oedipal conflict), she nevertheless believed that the child's first relationship with the mother in fact formed the basis of superego development in infancy. Specifically, she felt that the superego develops through the projection of aggressive feelings toward the mother and the introjection of these same feelings as hostile objects in the child's fantasy (Segal, 1990).

Other than these latter theoretical and treatment differences, Klein and Anna Freud agreed on many aspects of the conduct of child psychoanalysis. In this regard, Scharfman (as cited in O'Connor et al., 1983) pointed out the following similarities in the different forms of child psychoanalysis: (a) There should be few limitations on the direction of treatment, allowing for the analyst to follow the child's free expression of emotion; (b) interpretation is the basic technique used with defenses as they impede the flow of material that may need to be addressed in analysis; (c) the analyst restricts the use of educative materials or other means to change the child's environment, intervening only when it is necessary to maintain the continuity of analytic therapy; (d) the goal of therapy is to allow patients to fulfill their development as completely as possible by helping make conscious those unconscious elements that prevent movement toward effective functioning; and (e) the analyst does not place limitations on the various ways in which the patient perceives him or her—the analyst should be used by the patient as an object with whom he or she can interact and in whose presence he or she can feel comfortable with revealing thoughts and feelings about the past, present, and future.

To these latter similarities, we add the following general working assumptions of child and adolescent psychoanalysis:

(a) Behavioral problems are not construed as being situation or setting specific; (b) behavioral problems are a symptom of (and thereby caused by) an unconscious conflict—behaviors are viewed as serving a function for the person and represent his or her attempt to cope with inner needs and external realities, and one cannot assume that similar behaviors have the same or a similar cause; (c) the goal of psychoanalysis is specified in a general manner in order to provide the person with the opportunity to fulfill his or her psychological development as completely as possible and to clarify the person's basic motivations and ways of coping so that he or she can deal with them effectively and develop more adaptive capacities; (d) interpretation on the part of the analyst and insight by the patient are critical for the success of psychoanalysis; and (e) the therapeutic alliance is essential for providing the patient with the opportunity to make progress in fulfilling his or her psychological development.

Contemporary writers in child psychoanalysis have generally adopted Anna Freud's view that a child's or adolescent's developmental stage needs to be taken into consideration when conducting psychoanalysis (e.g., Kennedy & Moran, 1991; Yorke, 1996). For example, when treating children under 5 years of age, issues of cognitive capacity, reality testing, and the capacity for impulse control need to be taken into consideration (Kennedy & Moran, 1991). In the case of adolescents, because these individuals are typically verbal and can free associate, the analyst is more likely to follow a model that is consistent with adult psychoanalysis. The major exception, however, is the recognition by the analyst that the adolescent is still progressing through stages of development—each with its own tasks and conflicts that contribute to the adolescent's overall process of growth toward individuation and maturity. For example, this is a time when old patterns of relatedness to one's parents need to be resolved while beginning to establish new patterns based on various social, cognitive, and physiological competencies that take place (Blos, 1979). Moreover, when treating children or adolescents with developmental delays, psychoanalysis should address the developmental need in addition to the analysis of conflicts and defenses (Kennedy & Moran, 1991; Yorke, 1996).

In terms of supportive research, very few controlled outcome studies have documented the efficacy of child or adolescent psychoanalysis (Kazdin, 1990). Most of the literature in this area of psychotherapy is based on clinical case studies like those published in the multivolume compilation titled *Psychoanalytic Study of the Child*. Edelson (1993) suggested that the case study is especially appropriate for use to support claims concerning the scientific credibility of psychoanalytic explanations of behavior, and he felt that the empirical data derived from case studies further support treatment effectiveness. For example, by combining the results of several case studies regarding the psychoanalytic treatment of children's fears and anxiety disorders (e.g., A. Freud, 1977; Gavshon, 1990; Goldberg, 1993; Pappenheim & Sewwney, 1952; Sandler, 1989), the effectiveness of this approach can be demonstrated in successfully treating these anxiety disorders.

Although many proponents of child and adolescent psychoanalytic therapy would agree with Edelson regarding the value of case studies in supporting the treatment efficacy, at least one group of writers stated that the "research needs to catch up with the seasoned therapist" (Tuma & Russ, 1993, p. 155). They further suggested that psychoanalytic therapy (as well as psychodynamic therapy in general) "is still more of an art than a science and remains untested. This reality puts it at a disadvantage when compared with other treatment approaches such as behavioral therapy" (p. 155). Tuma and Russ also stated, however, that the "richness" of psychoanalytic and psychodynamic treatments, as well as their "wealth of knowledge" regarding child development, "make it imperative that we carry out sophisticated research studies that will answer specific questions about what interventions affect which specific processes" (p. 155). Moreover, Russ (as cited in Tuma & Russ, 1993) has indicated that if psychoanalytic therapy (and psychodynamic approaches in general) are to continue to be used with children and adolescents, clinical researchers will need to become as specific as behaviorally oriented researchers in analyzing the effectiveness of therapy outcome. Psychoanalytically oriented therapy researchers may also need to consider the findings of the Menninger Foundation's Psychotherapy Research Project (PRP; Wallerstein, 1994) when evaluating child and adolescent treatment efficacy. Specifically, the PRP reported that psychoanalysis and psychoanalytic therapies were found to be consistently modified in a supportive therapy direction and that more of the achieved changes were based on these supportive mechanisms rather than on interpretive resolution of intrapsychic conflict.

## Adlerian Approach

Alfred Adler was educated as a physician and was one of the charter members of Sigmund Freud's Vienna Psychoanalytic Society (which became known as the "Vienna Circle"), and later became one of its presidents. However, he resigned from the group in 1911 after becoming increasingly at variance with some of the basic tenets of psychoanalysis. Thereafter, he formed his own group, which was known as *individual psychology* (Kratochwill et al., 1988; Morris & Kratochwill, 1983b; Mosak & Maniacci, 1993). Although Adler's approach can be regarded in part as psychodynamic, it is distinguishable in a number of ways from Sigmund Freud's psychoanalysis. First, Adler's approach is "holistic" with the person being viewed as a "totality" that is

integrated into a social system. In this regard, the fundamental concepts in Adler's individual psychology are *holism, lifestyle, social interest,* and *directionality* or *goals* (Fadiman & Frager, 1976). Second, unlike Sigmund Freud, who assumed that human behavior is motivated by inborn instincts, Adler assumed that humans are motivated primarily by social factors (Kratochwill et al., 1988; Morris & Kratochwill, 1983b; Mosak & Maniacci, 1993).

Third, Adler introduced the concept of the *creative self,* which he conceptualized as a highly subjective individualized system that directs a person's experiences. Another difference between Adler and Sigmund Freud was Adler's view of the uniqueness of each individual personality. Thus, in contrast to Sigmund Freud's position, which indicated that sexual instincts were central in personality dynamics, Adler maintained that each individual was a unique configuration of social factors such as motives, interests, traits, and values. Adler's emphasis on conscious processes represented another major difference between his individual psychology and Sigmund Freud's psychoanalysis. For Adler, consciousness was the center of personality, whereas for both Sigmund and Anna Freud, as well as Melanie Klein, unconscious processes were the center of personality. Adler did not necessarily deny, however, personality dynamics where some unconscious processes directed the individual (Kratochwill et al., 1988; Morris & Kratochwill, 1983b; Mosak & Maniacci, 1993).

Adler did not view deviant behavior or behavior disorders as mental illness. Instead, individuals demonstrating these forms of behavior were said to be involved in mistaken ways of living or mistaken lifestyles. Consistent with his views regarding mistaken lifestyles, Adler believed that deviant behavior could occur in childhood because he felt that the first four or five years of life lay the foundation for the lifestyle. Thus, specific childhood behavior problems were not conceptualized any differently than was any other childhood behavior disorder. For Adler, mistaken lifestyles involve mistakes about oneself, the world, goals of success, and a low level of social interest and activity (Morris & Kratochwill, 1983b). As Mosak (1979) stated, "The neurotic, by virtue of his ability to choose, creates difficulty for himself by setting up a 'bad me' (symptoms, 'ego-alien' thoughts, 'bad behavior') that prevents him from implementing his good intentions" (p. 46).

The assumptions that therefore underlie Adler's individual psychology include the following: (a) The unconscious is deemphasized in the understanding and treatment of behavior disorders, and consciousness is the center of personality; (b) the theory and therapy are holistic in that the child or adolescent is seen as more than the sum of his or her parts without manifesting internal conflicts between underdeveloped forces such as from the id or ego; (c) the person is viewed as moving toward a goal with the purpose of behavior being goal attainment; (d) consistent with the creative self, an individual will find a way to achieve a goal; (e) behavioral problems are not construed as being situation or setting specific because they are directly related to goal attainment, which can take place in a variety of settings; and (f) behavior is understood within the individual's social context and social interest (i.e., sense of self-worth and feeling of belonging; Ansbacher, 1991; Dreikurs & Soltz, 1964; Edwards & Kern, 1995; Leak & Williams, 1991; Morris & Kratochwill, 1983b; Mosak & Maniacci, 1993).

Adler's notion of goal attainment is relevant to child and adolescent psychotherapy in that it implies that children's and adolescents' misbehaviors are best construed in terms of having a *purpose*. These purposes or goals are the following: (a) attention getting, (b) struggle for power or superiority, (c) desire to retaliate or get even, and (d) display of inadequacy or assumed disability (Dreikurs & Soltz, 1964). In this regard, Adlerian child and adolescent therapists believe that children who use attention-getting techniques desire attention so much that they will even seek attention by engaging in such negative behaviors as annoying others. Children whose goal is power or superiority will engage in behaviors or activities that show that they can do whatever they want and will not do what is asked of them by others. When the goal is retaliation or revenge, children or adolescents will engage in behaviors that will hurt others, embarrass others, or cause some sort of obvious discomfort in others—wanting, in essence, to create a mutual antagonism. When children or adolescents have a goal of displaying inadequacy, they will engage in behaviors that show that they are discouraged and cannot believe that they are important or significant. By engaging in these latter behaviors, the child or adolescent establishes a level of self-protection from failing at anything that is expected or asked of him or her and therefore decreases the chances that he or she will be required to do something. In other words, they are protected from trying and failing (Bitter, 1991; Dinkmeyer, Dinkmeyer, & Sperry, 1987; Kottman & Stiles, 1990; Mosak & Maniacci, 1993).

With respect to therapy outcome research, Mosak and Maniacci (1993) have indicated that research in this area is "generally geared to causalistic factors, and Adlerian psychology emphasizes purposes, not causes, making research appear somewhat too constraining" (p. 180). They concluded that "the literature on research in the area of [Adlerian] child psychotherapy research is severely lacking" (p. 180). Although therapy outcome research is sparse, there have been studies investigating the impact of various Adlerian constructs on children's behaviors (e.g., Appleton & Stanwyck, 1996; Clark, 1995; Edwards & Kern, 1995; Kern, Edwards, Flowers,

Lambert, & Belangee, 1999). For example, Edwards and Kern (1995) studied the impact of teachers' social interest on children's classroom behavior and found that teachers' social interest was negatively correlated with student disruptive behavior and scores on the Impatient-Aggression subtest of the Behavior Rating Checklist. A positive correlation was also found between teachers' social interest and children's cooperative attitudes. Edwards and Kern suggested that these results showed that teachers who have a positive sense of self, concern for others, and healthy psychological well-being may perceive their students as being less aggressive and impatient toward other students, themselves, and the teacher him- or herself. The researchers further suggested that these latter teachers may also be more likely to perceive students as not presenting typical classroom misbehaviors and may be more likely to attend to teacher instructions and work given by the teacher.

## Client-Centered (Humanistic) Therapy

The client-centered approach to child and adolescent psychotherapy is based on the personality theory and psychotherapy writings of Carl Rogers (1942, 1946, 1947, 1951, 1959). Although he is best known for his work with adults, Rogers's focus in graduate school was on children, as was his emphasis during his first 10 years of employment as a clinical psychologist at a child guidance clinic in Rochester, New York. In fact, his doctoral dissertation at the Teachers College of Columbia University was a study involving the clinical assessment of children. Moreover, his first book, *Clinical Treatment of the Problem Child* (Rogers, 1939), was in the area of child psychotherapy, and in the 1940s at Ohio State University Rogers taught a clinical practicum course involving the administration and interpretation of children's intelligence and personality tests (Ellinwood & Raskin, 1993).

It was not until Rogers went to the University of Chicago in 1945 that he focused his writings and practice entirely on counseling and psychotherapy with adults, refining his views and elaborating on them in later years at the University of Wisconsin (at Madison), Stanford University, Western Behavioral Sciences Institute, and the Center for Studies of the Person.

Although Rogers wrote about personality development and psychotherapy, he did not address in detail the development or etiology of specific types of behavior disorders or forms of psychopathology in either adults or children, preferring to focus on what he referred to as psychological maladjustment in the individual. For example, he listed the following conclusions regarding the characteristics of the individual:

1. The individual possesses the capacity *to experience in awareness* the factors in his *psychological maladjustment,* namely,

the incongruence between his *self-concept* and the totality of his *experience*.

2. The individual possesses the capacity and has the tendency to reorganize his *self-concept* in such a way as to make it more congruent with the totality of his *experience,* thus moving himself away from a state of *psychological maladjustment* and towards a state of *psychological adjustment.*

3. These capacities and this tendency, when latent rather than evident, will be released in any interpersonal *relationship* in which the other person is *congruent* in the *relationship,* experiences *unconditional positive regard* toward, and *empathic* understanding of, the individual, and achieves some communication of these attitudes to the individual. (Rogers, 1959, p. 221)

Certain assumptions regarding client-centered therapy are inherent in these statements. First, there is Rogers' central hypothesis, namely, that "the individual has the capacity to guide, regulate, and control himself, providing only that certain definable conditions exist" (Rogers, 1959, p. 221). Second, given the presence of the appropriate "definable conditions," the individual himself or herself is the only one capable of moving towards self-actualization. Third, the appropriate definable conditions for the individual to move away from "psychological maladjustment" are unconditional positive regard and empathic understanding provided within the context of a relationship with a therapist who is congruent with the individual. In this regard, the therapist does not act as an "advisor" to the individual or as an "expert analyst and interpreter, or galvanizer of emotional expression" (Ellinwood & Raskin, 1993, p. 259). Rogers also indicated that this latter assumption applies to children as well as adults. Thus, inherent in client-centered therapy is respect for the individual's self-directing capacities. Fourth, diagnostic or personality assessment of the individual is antithetical to the basic assumptions underlying client-centered therapy. From Rogers' point of view, diagnostic assessment is used in psychoanalysis to categorize the client within the context of the therapist's theory of psychopathology. Similarly, within a behavioral or Adlerian approach, the purpose of a diagnostic assessment is to focus on the specific problem or purpose that the therapist will select for intervention. Whereas each of these latter three approaches can be construed as problem-oriented therapies, client-centered therapy "does not have the goal of eliminating problems defined by the clinician, but rather the goal is to resolve conflicts that are meaningful [to the individual]" and in a manner consistent with the individual's movement toward self-actualization (Ellinwood & Raskin, 1993, pp. 262–263).

To these latter assumptions, we add the following general working assumptions of client-centered therapy:

(a) psychological maladjustment is not situation or setting specific; (b) instead of behavioral problems being the focus of therapy, resolving conflicts that are construed as meaningful to the individual is the focus of therapy; (c) therapy focuses not on the unconscious but on those issues and concerns that the individual experiences and is aware of in his or her movement toward psychological adjustment; and (d) the goal of client-centered therapy is specified in a general manner—to provide the individual with the opportunity to move himself or herself away from psychological maladjustment and toward a state of psychological adjustment and self-actualization (e.g., Ruthven, 1997).

The person who is most credited with advancing client-centered therapy with children and adolescents is Virginia Axline (1947), one of Rogers's former students who joined him at the University of Chicago's Counseling Center and later went to Columbia University's Teachers College (Ellinwood & Raskin, 1993). Axline was an outstanding writer who was able to capture in her writings the intricacies of conducting client-centered child therapy. Another early writer in client-centered child therapy was Elaine Dorfman (1951), who wrote a chapter on client-centered play therapy in Rogers's (1951) book *Client-Centered Therapy.*

In her book *Play Therapy,* Axline (1947) identified eight principles underlying a client-centered therapy approach to working with children:

1. The therapist must develop a warm, friendly relationship with the child, in which good rapport is established as soon as possible.
2. The therapist accepts the child exactly as he is.
3. The therapist establishes a feeling of permissiveness in the relationship so that the child feels free to express his feelings completely.
4. The therapist is alert to recognize the *feelings* the child is expressing and reflects those feelings back to him in such a manner that he gains insight into his behavior.
5. The therapist maintains a deep respect for the child's ability to solve his own problems if given the opportunity to do so. The responsibility to make choices and institute change is the child's.
6. The therapist does not attempt to direct the child's actions or conversation in any manner. The child leads the way; the therapist follows.
7. The therapist does not attempt to hurry the therapy along. It is a gradual process and is recognized as such by the therapist.
8. The therapist establishes only those limitations that are necessary to anchor the therapy to the world of reality and to make the child aware of his responsibility in the relationship. (Axline, 1947, pp. 73–74)

Consistent with Anna Freud and Melanie Klein, Axline believed that play formed an integral part of psychotherapy, permitting the child to express himself or herself through various verbal and nonverbal activities. However, unlike Freud and Klein, Axline believed that a child's activities in the play therapy room did not need to be directed or interpreted by the therapist. As Axline stated, "The child leads the way; the therapist follows" (p. 73). She also believed that some adolescents in client-centered therapy may choose to use the play therapy room whereas others may feel uncomfortable in this room. Similarly, she believed that some younger children may prefer the therapist's office over the play therapy room.

With respect to therapy outcome research, the amount of research supporting the efficacy of client-centered child therapy has lagged behind the quantity of similar research with adults (Ellinwood & Raskin, 1993). Dorfman (1951), for example, cited a number of process-oriented and therapy outcome studies with children, and other therapy process studies subsequent to Dorfman's review have been published (e.g., Lebo, 1955). She also pointed out the many difficulties in conducting this type of research with children in play therapy. Seeman (1983) also summarized some of the research findings in this area, as have Ellinwood and Raskin (1993). For example, using teacher and peer ratings, research has demonstrated that children undergoing client-centered therapy improve over those in a control group. In addition, client-centered therapy has contributed to improvement on personality and achievement scores of children.

## Comparison Outcome Studies

Research studies comparing the outcome of different types of child and adolescent psychotherapies is limited, although, as was mentioned earlier, several meta-analytic studies (e.g., Casey & Berman, 1985; Weisz, 1998; Weisz et al., 1987; Weisz et al., 1995) have suggested that the average outcome for children receiving child psychotherapy was appreciably better than those children not receiving therapy. The findings further suggested that the average positive outcome for the behavior therapies was appreciably higher than for the other types of child-oriented therapies, with no particular behavior therapy procedure found to be better than any other behavior therapy method. The results of two of these studies (i.e., Weisz et al., 1987; Weisz et al., 1995), however, were affected by whether the sample was limited to children versus adolescents, while the findings of another study (i.e., Casey & Berman, 1985) were influenced by certain child characteristics in that treatments involving children having aggression or social withdrawal were not as effective as treatments for hyperactivity, somatic difficulties, and phobias.

Consistent with the previous findings regarding behaviorally oriented therapies, Ellinwood and Raskin (1993) reported on a comparison outcome study conducted in Germany in 1981 by Dopfner, Schhluter, and Rey. Ellinwood and Raskin reported that these researchers compared client-centered play therapy with a behaviorally oriented social skills training (SST) program for nonassertive children. Dopfner et al. found that the SST approach was "effective in reducing social anxiety, low self-concept, low frequency of social interaction, low ability to behave normally in social interactions, and overall maladjustment. Play therapy appeared to reduce only social anxiety" (Ellinwood & Raskin, 1993, p. 273).

In one of the few data-based studies on the most frequently applied child and adolescent therapy procedures used by clinicians, Kazdin, Siegel and Bass (1990) found that behavioral, cognitive, eclectic, psychodynamic, and family therapies were rated as "most useful" by the psychologists and psychiatrists that were surveyed. The psychologists in the study rated behavior modification and cognitive therapy approaches as more useful than did the psychiatrists, whereas the psychiatrists rated psychoanalytic approaches as more useful than did the psychologists. In addition, Kazdin et al. stated, "The majority of either psychologists or psychiatrists, but not both, felt that psychodynamic therapy, play therapy, behavior modification, and cognitive therapy were very effective" (p. 196).

Comparison outcome studies are among the most difficult psychotherapy studies to conduct. The reasons for this are many (see, e.g., Kazdin, 1990, 1993, 1997; Kendall & Morris, 1991; Mash & Wolfe, 1999; Weisz, 1998). First, to be clinically meaningful, the studies should be conducted within clinic settings (vs. laboratory settings) by clinicians who are experienced (and competently trained) in the application of the particular method being used. Second, the child or adolescent clients should each be clinic-referred clients (vs. being recruited from advertisements), and the type, severity, and chronicity of each client's behavior disorder should be equated across treatment groups. Third, clients having comorbidity diagnoses should be equated across treatment groups, as should relevant demographic variables such as the gender, age, IQ, and socioeconomic status (SES) of clients. Fourth, treatment integrity across and within clinicians needs to be assessed for each type of therapy being administered to be assured that the treatments were carried out as intended. Fifth, follow-up assessment needs to take place to determine whether treatment outcome at posttest is maintained over time. Sixth, multimethod outcome assessments should be conducted in an objective manner, and where appropriate, interjudge reliability coefficients should be calculated to assure all involved that judges were in agreement regarding the observation of positive, negative, or no behavior change. Moreover, whenever possible, child or adolescent self-report, as well as behavior change data from parents, teachers, and peers should be obtained. Archived data, such as number of tardies at school, number of absences from school, number of trips to the principal's office, number of visits to the nurse's office, and so on, may also be useful in determining outcome in treatment comparison studies. Consistent with the more prescriptive questions posed earlier, it might be best initially to limit a comparison outcome study to the investigation of children or adolescents (not both) who have only one specific behavior disorder (e.g., ADHD, OCD, or separation anxiety). Additional limitations can be made regarding SES, duration of behavior disorder, no comorbidity diagnosis, and so on; however, it should be recognized that the generalizability of one's findings may appreciably decrease as the limitations imposed in the study increase.

In addition to the previous considerations, proponents of particular child and adolescent therapies have maintained that in order to make a fair comparison of their therapy approach with other approaches, certain assessment measures, which may be considered nontraditional dependent measures by proponents of other therapy approaches, need to be included in this type of outcome research. For example, Szapocznik et al. (1993) developed the Psychodynamic Child Ratings. They maintain that when child psychoanalysis is compared to other child therapies in terms of treatment outcome, an inaccurate assessment of its efficacy occurs because of the lack of "appropriate" measurement methods being utilized. Specifically, they believe that measures used in such outcome studies focus primarily on symptomatic and behavioral changes rather than on psychodynamic processes. As a result, they developed the Psychodynamic Child Ratings to evaluate the effect of child psychoanalysis. The scale produces a total score for psychodynamic functioning, as well as scores on two factorial derived scales: interpersonal and intrapersonal functioning. Little research, however, has been published using this scale.

Proponents of other child and adolescent therapies have made comments similar to those of Szapocznik et al. (1993). For example, Mosak and Maniacci (1993) indicated earlier that Adlerian psychology emphasizes purposes instead of causes and that this therefore makes outcome research "appear somewhat too constraining." Both positions seem to support the view that before any clinically meaningful comparison outcome research is conducted, not only do many of the aforementioned variables need to be taken into consideration, but also proponents of the child or adolescent therapies being

studied must agree to (and find acceptable) the dependent measures being utilized.

## CONCLUSIONS AND FUTURE DIRECTIONS FOR RESEARCH

There is little doubt from the child and adolescent psychotherapy literature that some form of treatment is better than no treatment and that for such behavioral problems as hyperactivity, somatic complaints, and phobias the behavior therapies are better than are other child psychotherapy approaches. We are also learning that the question, "Is child or adolescent psychotherapy effective?" is no longer a question that needs to be answered because any answer is not necessarily going to be clinically meaningful—that is, there is not a one-size-fits-all type of child or adolescent psychotherapy. The field needs to be oriented toward answering more prescriptive questions, such as "Which child therapy procedure is most effective for children having a primary diagnosis of ADHD and whose parents do not have sufficient time to be consultants to the clinician?" or "Which adolescent therapy method is most effective for inpatient female adolescents having a primary diagnosis of major depressive disorder and who are on a therapeutic dosage of antidepressant medication?" Answers to these types of questions will maximally advance the area of child and adolescent psychotherapy.

Other advances in research that need to take place involve making sure that psychotherapy outcome research focuses mainly on the treatment of children or adolescents who have a clinically derived (and independently verified) psychiatric diagnosis and are treated in mental health clinic or hospital settings versus university-based clinical laboratories or other institutional research settings. Moreover, the therapists providing the treatment should be experienced and competent in the application of the therapies being studied. Researchers also need to determine the contribution to treatment outcome of therapeutic relationship variables, as well as such variables as therapist and client ethnicity, cultural background, and values. In addition, as mentioned earlier, the relative contribution of a comorbid diagnosis needs to be assessed in relation to therapy outcome for both children and adolescents having the same primary diagnosis.

Child and adolescent psychotherapy has made many advances since the initial work of Anna Freud and Melanie Klein, and we fully expect great progress toward prescriptive treatments in this area and the development of empirically supported guidelines for treating children and adolescents with specific behavior disorders. At present, however, of the four forms of child and adolescent psychotherapy reviewed, no one can state with any certainty which types of treatment should be used with which types of children or adolescents under which types of conditions.

## REFERENCES

Allen, E. H. (1942). *Psychotherapy with children*. New York: Ronald Press.

Ansbacher, H. L. (1991). The concept of social interest. *Individual Psychology, 47,* 28–46.

Appleton, B. A., & Stanwyck, D. (1996). Teacher personality, pupil control, ideology, and leadership style. *Individual Psychology, 52,* 119–129.

Arambulla, D., DeKraai, M., & Sales, B. (1993). Law, children, and therapists. In T. R. Kratochwill & R. J. Morris (Eds.), *Handbook of psychotherapy with children and adolescents* (pp. 583–619). Boston: Allyn and Bacon.

Axline, V. (1947). *Play therapy: The inner dynamics of childhood.* Boston: Houghton Mifflin.

Bandura, A. (1969). *Principles of behavior modification.* New York: Holt, Rinehart, and Winston.

Bandura, A. (1977). *Social learning theory.* Englewood Cliffs, NJ: Prentice Hall.

Bandura, A., & Walters (1963). *Social learning and personality development.* New York: Holt, Rinehart, and Winston.

Barkley, R. A. (1990). *Attention deficit hyperactivity disorder: A handbook for diagnosis and treatment.* New York: Guilford Press.

Bear, G. C., Minke, K. M., & Thomas, A. (Eds.). (1997). *Children's needs: Vol. 2. Development, problems, and alternatives.* Bethesda, MD: National Association of School Psychologists.

Beck, A. T. (1976). *Cognitive therapy and emotional disorders.* New York: International Universities Press.

Benveniste, D. (1998). Play and the metaphors of the body. *The Psychoanalytic Study of the Child, 53,* 65–83.

Bernard, M. E., & Joyce, M. R. (1993). Rational-emotive therapy with children and adolescents. In T. R. Kratochwill & R. J. Morris (Eds.), *Handbook of psychotherapy with children and adolescents* (pp. 221–246). Boston: Allyn and Bacon.

Beutler, L. (1997). The psychotherapist as a neglected variable in psychotherapy: An illustration by reference to the role of therapist experience and training. *Clinical Psychology: Science and Practice, 4,* 44–52.

Bitter, J. R. (1991). Conscious motivations: An enhancement to Dreikurs' goals of children's misbehavior. *Individual Psychology, 47,* 210–221.

Blos, P. (1979). *The adolescent passage.* New York: International Universities Press.

Casey, R. J., & Berman, J. S. (1985). The outcome of psychotherapy with children. *Psychological Bulletin, 98,* 388–400.

Clark, A. J. (1995). The organization and implementation of a social interest program in the schools. *Individual Psychology, 51,* 317–331.

D'Amato, R. C., & Rothlisberg, B. A. (Eds.). (1997). *Psychological perspectives on intervention.* Prospect Heights, IL: Waveland Press.

DeKraai, M., Sales, B., & Hall, S. (1998). Informed consent, confidentiality, and duty to report laws in the conduct of child therapy. In R. J. Morris & T. R. Kratochwill (Eds.), *The practice of child therapy* (3rd ed., pp. 540–560). Needham Heights, MA: Allyn and Bacon.

Dinkmeyer, D. C., Dinkmeyer, D. C., Jr., & Sperry, L. (1987). *Adlerian counseling and psychotherapy* (2nd ed.). Columbus, OH: Merrill.

Donaldson, G. (1996). Between practice and theory: Melanie Klein, Anna Freud and the development of child analysis. *Journal of the History of the Behavioral Sciences, 32,* 160–176.

Dorfman, E. (1951). Play therapy. In C. R. Rogers (Ed.), *Client-centered therapy* (pp. 235–277). Boston: Houghton Mifflin.

Dreikurs, R., & Soltz, V. (1964). *Children: The challenge.* New York: Meredith Press.

Edelson, M. (1993). Telling and enacting stories in psychoanalysis and psychotherapy: Implications for teaching psychotherapy. *The Psychoanalytic Study of the Child, 48,* 293–325.

Edwards, D., & Kern, R. (1995). The implications of teachers' social interest on classroom behavior. *Individual Psychology, 51,* 67–73.

Ellinwood, C., & Raskin, N. J. (1993). Client-centered/humanistic psychotherapy. In T. R. Kratochwill & R. J. Morris (Eds.), *Handbook of psychotherapy with children and adolescents* (pp. 258–287). Boston: Allyn and Bacon.

Ellis, A. (1962). *Reason and emotion in psychotherapy.* New York: Stuart.

Ellis, A., & Wilde, J. (2002). *Case studies in rational emotive behavior therapy with children and adolescents.* Upper Saddle River, NJ: Merrill Prentice Hall.

Fadiman, J., & Frager, R. (1976). *Personality and personal growth.* New York: Harper and Row.

Freud, A. (1977). Fears, anxieties, and phobic phenomena. *The Psychoanalytic Study of the Child, 32,* 85–90.

Freud, A. (1981). Foreword to " 'Analysis of a phobia in a five-year-old boy'." In A. Freud (Ed.), *The writings of Anna Freud, 1970–1980* (Vol. 8, pp. 277–282). New York: International University Press.

Freud, A., Hartman, H., & Kris, E. (Eds.). (1945). *The psychoanalytic study of the child* (Vol. 1, pp. 1–423). New York: International Universities Press.

Freud, S. (1905). Three essays on sexuality. In J. Strachey (Ed.), *The Standard edition of the complete psychological works of Sigmund Freud* (Vol. 7, pp. 125–245). London: Hogarth.

Freud, S. (1909). The analysis of a phobia in a five-year-old boy. In J. Strachey (Ed.), *The Standard edition of the complete psychological works of Sigmund Freud* (Vol. 10, pp. 1–149). London: Hogarth.

Gardner, W. I. (1971). *Behavior modification: Applications in mental retardation*. Chicago: Aldine.

Gavshon, A. (1990). The analysis of a latency boy: The developmental impact of separation, divorce, and remarriage. *The Psychoanalytic Study of the Child, 45,* 217–233.

Goldberg, M. (1993). Enactment and play following medical trauma: An analytic case study. *The Psychoanalytic Study of the Child, 50,* 252–271.

Goldstein, A. P., Heller, K., & Sechrest, L. (1966). *Psychotherapy and the psychology of behavior change*. New York: Wiley.

Graziano, A. M. (Ed.). (1971). *Behavior therapy with children*. Chicago: Aline.

Heincke, C. M., & Goldman, A. (1960). Research on psychotherapy with children: A review and suggestions for further study. *American Journal of Orthopsychiatry, 30,* 483–494.

Hughes, J. (Ed.). (1988). *Cognitive behavior therapy with children in schools*. New York: Guilford.

Hull, C. (1943). *Principles of learning*. New York: Appleton-Century-Crofts.

Huppert, J. D., Bufka, L. F., Barlow, D. H., Gorman, J. M., Shear, M. K., & Woods, S. W. (2001). Therapists, therapist variables, and cognitive-behavior therapy outcome in a multicenter trial for panic disorder. *Journal of Consulting and Clinical Psychology, 69,* 747–755.

Itard, J. M. C. (1962). *L'enfant sauvage [The wild boy of Aveyron']* (G. Humphrey & M. Humphrey, Trans.). New York: Appleton-Century-Crofts.

Kanner, L. (1948). *Child psychiatry*. Springfield, IL: Charles C. Thomas.

Karoly, P., & Kanfer, F. H. (Eds.). (1982). *Self-management and behavior change: From theory to practice*. Elmsford, NY: Pergamon Press.

Kauffman, J. M. (1981). *Characteristics of children's behavior disorders*. Columbus, OH: Merrill.

Kavale, K. A., Forness, S. R., & Walker, H. M. (1999). Interventions for oppositional defiant disorder and conduct disorder. In H. C. Quay & A. E. Hogan (Eds.), *Handbook of disruptive behavior disorders* (pp. 441–454). New York: Kluwer Academic.

Kazdin, A. E. (1980). *Behavior modification in applied settings* (Rev. ed.). Homewood, IL: Dorsey Press.

Kazdin, A. E. (1990). Psychotherapy for children and adolescents. *Annual Reviews in Psychology, 41,* 21–54.

Kazdin, A. E. (1993). Research issues in child psychotherapy. In T. R. Kratochwill & R. J. Morris (Eds.), *Handbook of psychotherapy with children and adolescents* (pp. 541–565). Boston: Allyn and Bacon.

Kazdin, A. E. (1997). The therapist as a neglected variable in psychotherapy research [Special section]. *Clinical Psychology, Science and Practice, 4,* 40–89.

Kazdin, A. E. (2000). *Behavior modification in applied settings* (6th ed.). Belmont, CA: Wadsworth/Thomas Learning.

Kazdin, A. E., Siegel, T. C., & Bass, D. (1990). Drawing on clinical practice to inform research on child and adolescent psychotherapy: Survey of practitioners. *Journal of Consulting and Clinical Psychology, 21,* 189–198.

Kazdin, A. E., Siegel, T., & Bass, D. (1992). Cognitive problem-solving skills training and parent management training in the treatment of antisocial behavior in children. *Journal of Consulting and Clinical Psychology, 60,* 733–747.

Kendall, P. C. (Ed.). (1991). *Child and adolescent therapy: Cognitive-behavioral procedures*. New York: Guilford Press.

Kendall, P. C. (Ed.). (1992). *Child and adolescent therapy: Cognitive-behavioral procedures*. New York: Guilford Press.

Kendall, P. C. (1994). Treating anxiety disorders in children: Results of a randomized clinical trial. *Journal of Consulting and Clinical Psychology, 62,* 100–110.

Kendall, P. C., Brady, E. U., & Verduin, T. L. (2001). Comorbidity in childhood anxiety disorders: Effect on treatment outcome. *Journal of the American Academy of Child and Adolescent Psychiatry, 40,* 787–794.

Kendall, P. C., & Braswell, L. (1985). *Cognitive-behavioral therapy for impulsive children*. New York: Guilford Press.

Kendall, P. C., & Morris, R. J. (1991). Child therapy: Issues and recommendations. *Journal of Consulting and Clinical Psychology, 59,* 777–784.

Kennedy, H., & Moran, G. (1991). Reflections on the aim of child analysis. *The Psychoanalytic Study of the Child, 46,* 181–198.

Kern, R. M., Edwards, D., Flowers, C., Lambert, R., & Belangee, S. (1999). Teachers' lifestyles and their perceptions of students' behaviors. *Journal of Individual Psychology, 55,* 422–436.

King, N. J., Hamilton, D. I., & Ollendick, T. H. (1988). *Children's phobias: A behavioral perspective*. New York: Wiley.

Kottman, T., & Stiles, K. (1990). The mutual story-telling technique: An Adlerian application in child therapy. *Individual Psychology, 46,* 148–156.

Kratochwill, T. R., Accardi, A., & Morris, R. J. (1988). Anxiety and phobias: Psychological therapies. In J. Matson (Ed.), *Handbook of treatment approaches in child psychopathology* (pp. 249–276). New York: Plenum Press.

Kratochwill, T. R., & Morris, R. J. (Eds.). (1993). *Handbook of psychotherapy with children and adolescents*. Boston: Allyn and Bacon.

Leak, G., & Williams, D. (1991). Relationship between social interest and perceived family environment. *Individual Psychology, 47,* 159–165.

Lebo, D. (1955). Quantification of the nondirective play therapy process. *Journal of Genetic Psychology, 86,* 375–378.

Levitt, E. (1957). The results of psychotherapy with children: An evaluation. *Journal of Consulting Psychology, 21,* 189–196.

Levitt, E. (1963). Psychotherapy with children: A further evaluation. *Behaviour, Research, and Therapy, 6,* 326–329.

Lovass, I. O., & Bucher, B. D. (Eds.). (1974). *Perspectives in behavior modification with deviant children*. Englewood Cliffs, NJ: Prentice Hall.

Mahoney, M. J. (1974). *Cognition and behavior modification*. Cambridge, MA: Ballinger.

Mash, E. J., & Barkley, R. A. (Eds.). (1989). *Treatment of childhood disorders*. New York: Guilford Press.

Mash, E. J., & Terdall, L. G. (Eds.). (1997). *Assessment of childhood disorders* (2nd ed.). New York: Guilford Press.

Mash, E. J., & Wolfe, D. A. (1999). *Abnormal child psychology*. Belmont, CA: Brooks/Cole.

Mayes, L. C., & Cohen, D. J. (1996). Anna Freud and developmental psychoanalytic psychology. *The Psychoanalytic Study of the Child, 51,* 117–141.

Morris, R. J. (1976). *Behavior modification with children: A systematic guide*. Cambridge, MA: Winthrop Publishers.

Morris, R. J. (1985). *Behavior modification with exceptional children: Principles and practices*. Glenview, IL: Scott, Foresman.

Morris, R. J., & Kratochwill, T. R. (Eds.). (1983a). *The practice of child therapy*. New York: Pergamon Press.

Morris, R. J., & Kratochwill, T. R. (1983b). *Treating children's fears and phobias. A behavioral approach*. New York: Pergamon Press.

Morris, R. J., & Kratochwill, T. R. (1998a). Fears and phobias. In R. J. Morris & T. R. Kratochwill (Eds.), *The practice of child therapy* (3rd ed., pp. 91–131). Boston: Allyn and Bacon.

Morris, R. J., & Kratochwill, T. R. (Eds.). (1998b). Historical context of child therapy. In R. J. Morris & T. R. Kratochwill (Eds.), *The practice of child therapy* (3rd ed., pp. 1–4). Boston: Allyn and Bacon.

Morris, R. J., & Kratochwill, T. R. (Eds.). (1998c). *The practice of child therapy* (3rd ed.). Boston: Allyn and Bacon.

Morris, R. J., & Morris, Y. P. (1997). A behavioral approach to child and adolescent psychotherapy. In R. C. D'Amato & B. A. Rothlisberg (Eds.), *The quest for answers: A comparative study of intervention models through case study* (pp. 21–47). Prospect Heights, IL: Waveland Press.

Morris, R. J., & Morris, Y. P. (2000). Practice guidelines regarding the conduct of Psychotherapy with children and adolescents. In G. Stricker, W. Troy, & S. Shueman (Eds.), *Handbook of quality management in behavioral health* (pp. 237–264). New York: Plenum Press.

Morris, R. J., & Nicholson, J. (1993). The therapeutic relationship in child and adolescent psychotherapy: Research issues and trends. In T. R. Kratochwill & R. J. Morris (Eds.), *Handbook of psychotherapy with children and adolescents* (pp. 405–425). Boston: Allyn and Bacon.

Mosak, H. H. (1979). Adlerian psychotherapy. In R. J. Corsini (Ed.), *Current psychotherapies* (pp. 44–94). Itasca, IL: F. E. Peacock.

Mosak, H. H., & Maniacci, M. P. (1993). Adlerian child psychotherapy. In T. R. Kratochwill & R. J. Morris (Eds.), *Handbook of psychotherapy with children and adolescents* (pp. 162–184). Needham Heights, MA: Allyn and Bacon.

Mowrer, O. H. (1960). *Learning theory and behavior*. New York: Wiley.

Neubauer, P. B. (1996). Current issues in psychoanalytic child development. *The Psychoanalytic Study of the Child, 51,* 35–45.

O'Connor, K. O., Lee, A. C., & Schaefer, C. E. (1983). Psychoanalytic psychotherapy with children. In M. Hersen, A. E. Kazdin, & A. S. Bellack (Eds.), *The clinical psychology handbook* (pp. 543–564). New York: Pergamon Press.

O'Leary, K. D., & O'Leary, S. G. (1972). *Classroom management*. New York: Pergamon Press.

Pappenheim, E., & Sweeney, M. (1952). Separation anxiety in mother and child. *The Psychoanalytic Study of the Child, 2,* 95–114.

Paul, G. L. (1967). Outcome research in psychotherapy. *Journal of Consulting Psychology, 31,* 109–118.

Pavlov, I. P. (1927). *Conditioned reflexes* (G. V. Anrep, Trans.). London: Oxford University Press.

Quay, H. C., & Hogan, A. E. (Eds.). (1999). *Handbook of disruptive behavior disorders*. New York: Kluwer.

Ramirez, S. Z., Kratochwill, T. R., & Morris, R. J. (1987). Childhood anxiety disorders. In M. Ascher & L. Michelson (Eds.), *Cognitive behavior therapy* (pp. 149–175). New York: Guilford Press.

Rimm, D., & Masters, J. C. (1979). *Behavior therapy: Techniques and empirical findings* (2nd ed.). New York: Academic Press.

Rogers, C. R. (1939). *Clinical treatment of the problem child*. New York: Houghton Mifflin.

Rogers, C. R. (1942). *Counseling and psychotherapy*. New York: Houghton Mifflin.

Rogers, C. R. (1946). Significant aspects of client-centered therapy. *American Psychologist, 1,* 415–422.

Roger, C. R. (1947). Some observations on the organization of personality. *American Psychologist, 2,* 358–368.

Rogers, C. R. (1951). *Client-centered therapy: Its current practice, implications and theory*. Boston: Houghton Mifflin.

Rogers, C. R. (1959). A theory of therapy, personality, and interpersonal relationships as developed in client-centered framework. In S. Koch (Ed.), *Psychology: The study of a science* (Vol. 3). New York: McGraw Hill.

Ruthven, A. J. (1997). A person-centered/humanistic approach to intervention. In R. C. D'Amato & B. A. Rothlisberg (Eds.), *Psychological perspectives on intervention* (pp. 95–111). Prospect Heights, IL: Waveland Press.

Sandler, A. M. (1989). Comments on phobic mechanisms in childhood. *The Psychoanalytic Study of the Child, 44,* 101–113.

Segal, H. (1990). *Introducción a la obra de Melanie Klein* [Introduction to the work of Melanie Klein]. Mexico City: Paidós.

Seeman, J. (1983). *Personality integration: Studies and reflections*. New York: Human Sciences Press.

Skinner, B. F. (1938). *The behavior of organisms.* New York: Appleton-Century-Crofts.

Skinner, B. F. (1953). *Science and human behavior.* New York: Macmillan.

Solnit, A. J. (1998). Beyond play and playfulness. *The Psychoanalytic Study of the Child, 53,* 102–110.

Sulzer-Azaroff, B., & Mayer, G. R. (1991). *Behavior analysis and lasting changing.* Fort Worth, TX: Harcourt Brace Jovanovich.

Szapocznik, J., Rio, A. T., Murray, E., Richardson, R., Alonso, M., & Kurtines, W. (1993). Assessing change in child psychodynamic functioning in treatment outcome studies: The psychodynamic child ratings. *Revista Interamericana de Psicología/Interamerican Journal of Psychology, 27,* 147–162.

Thorndike, E. I. (1913). *Educational psychology: The psychology of learning* (Vol. 2). New York: Teachers College.

Thorndike, E. I. (1931). *Human learning.* New York: Century.

Tuma, J. M., & Russ, S. W. (1993). Psychoanalytic psychotherapy with children. In T. R. Kratochwill & R. J. Morris (Eds.), *Handbook of psychotherapy with children and adolescents* (pp. 131–161). Boston, MA: Allyn and Bacon.

Viner, R. (1996). Melanie Klein and Anna Freud: The discourse of the early dispute. *Journal of the History of the Behavioral Sciences, 32,* 4–15.

Wallerstein, R. S. (1994). Psychotherapy research and its implications for a theory of therapeutic change: A forty-year overview. *The Psychoanalytic Study of the Child, 49,* 120–141.

Warshaw, S. C. (1997). A psychoanalytic approach to intervention. In R. C. D'Amato & B. A. Rothlisberg (Eds.), *Psychological perspectives on intervention* (pp. 234–252). Prospect Heights, IL: Waveland Press.

Watson, J. B., & Raynor, R. (1920). Conditioned emotional reactions. *Journal of Experimental Psychology, 3,* 1–14.

Weisz, J. R. (1998). Empirically supported treatments for children and adolescents: Efficacy, problems, and prospects. In K. S. Dobson & K. D. Craig (Eds.), *Empirically supported therapies: Best practice in professional psychology* (pp. 66–92). Newbury Park, CA: Sage.

Weisz, J. R., Weiss, B., Alicke, M. D., & Klotz, M. L. (1987). Effectiveness of psychotherapy with children and adolescents: Meta-analytic findings for clinicians. *Journal of Consulting and Clinical Psychology, 55,* 542–549.

Weisz, J. R., Weiss, B., Han, S. S., Granger, D. A., & Morton, T. (1995). Effects of psychotherapy with children and adolescents revisited: A meta-analysis of treatment outcome studies. *Psychological Bulletin, 117,* 450–468.

Wolpe, J., & Lazarus, A. (1966). *Behavior therapy techniques.* New York: Pergamon Press.

Yorke, C. (1996). Anna Freud's contributions to our knowledge of child development: An overview. *The Psychoanalytic Study of the Child, 51,* 7–24.

CHAPTER 17

# Brief Psychotherapies

STANLEY B. MESSER, WILLIAM C. SANDERSON, AND ALAN S. GURMAN

Due to the rapid rise in both medical and mental health expenses, many cost-saving measures have been instituted in the health care arena that have included shorter stays in psychiatric hospitals and briefer outpatient therapies. The dramatic increase in dual-career families and the associated decrease in leisure time have made many people less available for longer term therapy. In addition, as the stigma attached to therapy has decreased, its popularity has increased, leading to greater demand for, and rationing of, therapeutic services. Scientific studies showing the value of brief therapy for a variety of problems have also helped to increase the use of this treatment modality.

Patients typically have opted for, or been offered, brief therapy but without the planfulness and focus of current models. Based on data from a large variety of settings where time-unlimited as well as time-limited therapy are practiced, Phillips

(1985) concluded that the modal number of therapy sessions is one, the median, three to five, and the mean, five to eight. More recently, the National Medical Expenditures Survey sampled 1,000 individuals about their use of psychotherapy (Olfson & Pincus, 1994). Thirty-four percent had 1–2 visits; 37% had 3–10; 13% had 11–20; and only 16% had over 20 visits. Stated differently, about 90% had fewer than 25 sessions, the usual cut-off point for labeling a therapy as brief. What distinguishes the current scene in terms of usage of brief therapy is that it is now more likely to be structured and planned. Factors such as formulating and working within a therapeutic focus, setting goals, having a known time limit, and increased therapist activity all have the potential to bring about change in a timely way. Before examining how the different brief therapies achieve that aim, we will present some of the main findings of research on the outcome of brief therapy.

## Empirical Studies of Brief Therapy

These studies include dose-effect relationships, a consumer survey, and meta-analyses comparing the relative value of different therapies. Process and outcome studies of each form of brief therapy can be found in the following sections.

### Dose-Effect Analysis

Howard, Kopta, Krause, and Orlinsky (1986) studied the relationship between dose (number of sessions) of therapy (largely open-ended) and the percentage of patients improved. They found that by 13 sessions 55–60% of patients had improved, as was true for 75% by 26 sessions. Figures differed according to diagnostic group, with borderline patients making gains more slowly. Their review of the literature yielded an even lower estimate of eight sessions for 50% improvement, but the same figure of 26 sessions for 75% improvement. Except for the 8-session finding, subsequent studies have tended to support these figures. For example, Kadera, Lambert, and Andrews (1996), employing the more stringent criterion of clinically significant change, found that 50% of patients had improved by 16 sessions, and 75% by 25 sessions. Similar to Howard et al.'s findings, Anderson and Lambert (2001) reported that 13 sessions were necessary before 50% of outpatients attained clinically significant change. Again, 25 sessions were required for 75% of patients to show such improvement.

In sum, it probably takes between 8 and 16 sessions for 50% of patients to improve and about 25 sessions for 75% of patients to show significant gains. It should be noted that change in these studies usually refers to symptom improvement or to feeling and functioning better, but does not include other kinds of outcomes measures valued in particular by experiential and psychodynamic therapists (e.g., Messer, 2001a).

### Survey of Consumer Satisfaction

An examination in a Consumer Reports survey of client-reported outcomes shows that the degree of felt improvement and satisfaction rises rapidly until 3–6 months of therapy have been experienced (Seligman, 1995). It then increases rather slowly until 2 years or more have passed, at which point it takes a further jump. The 3–6 month period would cover 12–25 sessions—the same as the figures for 50% to 75% improvement according to most of the dose-effect studies. It seems to be the case that a considerable amount of symptomatic and global change takes place within 12–25 sessions, with further improvement occurring slowly with more sessions.

### Meta-Analysis

In the meta-analysis carried out by Wampold et al. (1997), bona fide treatments—the great majority of them short-term—were compared. By *bona fide* the authors meant therapies that were delivered by trained therapists, about which there existed professional books or manuals, and that were tailored to the individual patient. They found that the therapies were not differentially effective. In general, this conclusion has been supported in meta-analyses but not necessarily in individual studies or meta-analyses employing specific diagnostic conditions (e.g., Dobson, 1989).

There seems to be a consensus that brief therapy is probably unsuitable for patients with more severe disturbances, including some of the personality disorders. In particular, borderline and avoidant personality disorders need more sessions to improve than the usual limits (25 sessions) of brief therapy (e. g., Barber, Morse, Krakauer, Chittams, & Crits-Christoph, 1997). On the other hand, obsessive-compulsive personality disorder (Barber et al.), and an undifferentiated group of the milder personality disorders, known as Cluster C (Winston et al., 1994), have been found to be responsive to brief-therapy approaches.

## Six Forms of Brief Therapy

This chapter describes six brief therapies, each stemming from a different theoretical tradition. Even if clinicians incorporate or assimilate techniques or perspectives from other models (Jensen, Bergin, & Greaves, 1990; Messer, 2001b), they continue to ground their therapeutic work in a particular theory. The six theories presented here include some of the most widely employed in the field of psychotherapy: psychodynamic, behavioral, couples and family systems, experiential, strategic, and integrative. All have well-worked-out brief forms of their traditional therapeutic outlooks, or are largely synonymous with brief therapy (e.g., strategic and family therapy).

In the case of three of these therapies—behavioral, systems, and strategic—the very way in which they were developed and are practiced predisposes them to be short term. That is, insofar as any therapy is symptom oriented or problem focused, it is more likely to be brief. On the other hand, therapies that developed as open-ended ventures, often emphasizing personality issues over symptoms per se, have made accommodations to a short-term format. These include the psychodynamic, experiential, and some varieties of integrative therapy.

The outline for the six sections typically included the following topics: (a) a brief historical introduction, (b) selection criteria, including diagnoses or problems treated, (c) techniques of the therapy, (d) the theory of change, (e) research supporting the approach, and (f) future directions. We start with the oldest of the therapeutic traditions—psychoanalytically based therapy.

## BRIEF PSYCHODYNAMIC THERAPY

### Introduction

*Brief psychodynamic therapy (BPT)* applies the principles of psychoanalytic theory and therapy to the treatment of selected disorders within a time frame of roughly 10 to 25 sessions. A time limit is usually determined at the outset of therapy, and sets in motion psychological expectancies regarding when change is likely to occur. In this way, BPT takes advantage of Parkinson's law that completion of a task is a function of the time allotted to it. BPT employs major concepts of psychoanalytic theory to understand clients, including the enduring importance and impact of psychosexual, psychosocial, and object relational stages of development; the existence of unconscious cognitive, emotional, and motivational processes; and the reenactment in the client's relationship to the therapist of emotion-laden issues from the past.

Principal techniques include reflection, clarification, interpretation, and in some models, confrontation of maladaptive interpersonal patterns, impulses, conflicts, and defenses along the axes of the *triangle of insight*. The latter refers to the threefold interpersonal context of (a) important current people in the client's life; (b) the transference, or perceived relationship to the therapist; and (c) childhood relationships, typically with parents and siblings. Links are made connecting various combinations of such past, present, and transferential relationships. In addition to its aim of enhancing insight, the therapy provides a corrective emotional experience in which old and current traumas, shameful secrets, and other warded-off feelings and memories are brought to light in the benign presence of the therapist. In the broadest sense it is the therapist's creation of a caring, empathically attuned relationship that allows therapy to bring about insight, healing, and growth in a suitably selected client.

BPT typically involves more active dialogue and challenge than long-term psychoanalytic therapy. There is an early formulation of a therapeutic focus that is expressed in psychodynamic terms such as core intrapsychic conflicts, maladaptive interpersonal patterns, or chronically endured psychic pain. Special attention is given to feelings that arise around termination, such as sadness, guilt, anxiety, and anger. Goals are set that are potentially achievable and might include conflict resolution, a changed interpersonal pattern, greater access to feelings, and more freedom of choice, as well as symptom

remission. For a historical overview of the roots of BPT, see Borden (1999) and Messer and Warren (1995).

### Selection Criteria

In general, brief dynamic therapists rule out those patients whose severity of disturbance precludes their ability to engage in an insight-oriented therapy, or who need more time to work through their problems. Although it is difficult to generalize because the different models set narrower or wider criteria, the following sections describe the general indicators in favor of and against recommending BPT.

#### Diagnostic Contraindications

These include serious suicide attempts or potential; current alcohol or other drug addiction; major depression; poor impulse control; incapacitating, chronic obsessional or phobic symptoms; some psychosomatic conditions, such as ulcerative colitis; and poor reality testing. With reference to the *Diagnostic and Statistical Manual of Mental Disorders (DSM)*, this would encompass major depressive disorder, schizophrenia, sociopathy, paranoia, and substance abuse, as well as the more severe personality disorders such as the borderline and narcissistic. Although the latter two syndromes can be treated with BPT, they require modifications in focus, technique, and goals that have been discussed at length elsewhere along with the treatment of other difficult patients (Messer & Warren, 1995). Examples of what such patients may require are a more adaptive, here-and-now focus; auxiliary modalities such as group therapy or family sessions; medication; and a more flexible approach to termination, such as the gradual tapering off of therapy.

#### Diagnostic Indications

In terms of *DSM*, these include the adjustment disorders; the milder personality disorders such as avoidant, dependent, and obsessive-compulsive; and the less severe anxiety and depressive disorders.

#### Psychotherapy Process Indications

Many of the diagnostic criteria stated previously are descriptive or static, based largely on the patient's history garnered from the initial interviews. Some BPT therapists such as Malan, Davanloo, and Sifneos (Davanloo, 1980), however, also stress a patient's response to the active, frequently confrontational techniques of their approach. Davanloo in particular refers to the importance of making trial interpretations in the initial interviews and noting whether the patient responds with deepened involvement versus some form of decompensation. If the latter occurred, he would consider the patient unsuitable for his form of brief therapy.

### Interpersonal or Motivational Indications

In a group of brief dynamic therapies referred to as *relational,* the criteria are expressed in interpersonal terms that are also best assessed from within the therapeutic situation. For example, Strupp and Binder (1984, pp. 57–58) list the characteristics they associate with a successful brief treatment as follows: The patient is sufficiently uncomfortable with his or her feelings or behavior to seek help via psychotherapy; has basic trust in the possibility of relief from distress through the therapist-patient relationship; is willing to consider conflicts in interpersonal terms and to examine feelings; can relate to others as separate individuals; allows his or her relationship predispositions to be played out in the therapy relationship and collaboratively examined; and is motivated, as determined by the extent of the previously listed characteristics.

For research findings on selection criteria for BPT, see Messer (2001c).

## Techniques of Therapy

All approaches to BPT rely on a number of common technical characteristics, including (a) an individualized central clinical focus, (b) a time limit, (c) a relative emphasis on the termination stage of treatment, (d) active techniques to accomplish therapeutic goals within the time limits, and (e) goals.

### Use of a Central Focus

This involves the formulation of a central clinical theme developed in the early sessions that serves to organize clinical observations and to guide therapist interventions. The central focus is a statement of the therapist's understanding of the patient's presenting problems as an expression of an underlying dynamic central issue or conflict. Such formulation seeks to incorporate as much of the current situation and relevant history as possible. This central focus may be verbalized directly to the patient as a form of a working contract or used to engage the patient in the therapy process. When this goes well one would expect the patient to feel understood and to become more motivated for further therapeutic exploration.

Although all forms of psychodynamic treatment rely on clinical formulations, in short-term therapy the central focus tends to be more circumscribed in scope, limiting the therapeutic inquiry so that clinical goals may be achieved within the time frame. In addition, the focus is generated more rapidly at the outset of treatment and is used more actively in brief therapy than in open-ended treatment.

### Use of a Time Limit

All brief psychodynamic treatments operate within implicit or explicit time limits. One brief therapist, James Mann (1973, 1991), makes the time limit a central theoretical and clinical construct, organizing his approach to brief therapy around the effects on the clinical process of a fixed number of sessions. He advocates the use of a 12-session time limit with a clear termination date that the therapist sets by the first or second session. Mann relies on the universality and poignancy of the experience of loss and on its impact at termination to make the time limit a central technical feature of his brief treatment. The patient's ambivalent responses to the issues of loss and separation are utilized therapeutically throughout the treatment, but especially at termination.

In models of BPT in which time limits are not made explicit, it is still utilized by the therapist to organize therapeutic activities and aims. In all psychodynamic approaches to brief treatment the time limit is understood to accelerate the process of psychotherapy by increasing the sense of urgency and immediacy and the emotional presence of the patient. Undoubtedly, the time limit influences the therapist as much as it does the patient, increasing, for example, therapist activity.

### Role of Termination

Termination is considered to be the phase of treatment in which the clinical gains of therapy thus far can be consolidated, and in which the issues of loss, separation, and individuation can be addressed directly within the here-and-now context of the ending of treatment. It is given a heightened importance in brief psychotherapy. Since the time limit is present from the beginning, the process of termination is activated at the start of the treatment. Resistances to termination can appear early in brief therapy, and are addressed throughout treatment. The brevity of treatment means that the pain of separating cannot be postponed to an indistinct and distant time and place, as is true of long-term therapy.

### Active Inquiry

The notion of *active technique* (Ferenczi, 1920/1950) can be contrasted to the traditionally lesser role of therapist activity in long-term psychoanalytic therapy. It refers to any of a variety of techniques aimed at accelerating the therapeutic process to make it possible to accomplish goals of psychodynamic importance in the more limited time frame of brief therapy. These have typically involved the use of time limits as already mentioned, direct suggestions (Ferenczi), the active confrontation and interpretation of defenses and resistances (Davanloo, 1980; Sifneos, 1972), and early and active interpretation of transference (Davanloo; Malan, 1976).

The use of confrontation and active interpretation of resistances and defenses is especially characteristic of the approaches of Malan, Davanloo, and Sifneos, and is intended to accelerate the emergence of unconscious conflicts, permitting their more rapid resolution. Advocates of such techniques tend to point out relentlessly to the patient where he or she is avoiding feelings, leaving out significant information, or being vague. Defenses may be interpreted in rapid-fire succession, with the therapist in persistent pursuit of the patient's authentic emotional experience. Such persistence is justified on the basis of the unconscious relief patients are said to feel when forced to recognize emotional truths—often unacceptable sexual or aggressive feelings—they have avoided and defended against. Breakthroughs are followed by the emergence of significant new clinical material, and the cycle of resistance, interpretation, and breakthrough is continuously repeated.

Other brief psychodynamic therapists in the more relational tradition (e.g., Book, 1998; Levenson, 1995; Luborsky, 1984) are less inclined to use confrontational techniques, but instead follow more in the tradition of conducting a *detailed inquiry*. This form of activity refers to a persistent curiosity on the part of the therapist that takes the form of ongoing clarification, questioning, seeking after more detail, and pointing out gaps or inconsistencies in the patient's narrative. These brief therapists also actively use their awareness of developing and ongoing interpersonal patterns in the patient-therapist relationship, and come to focus on these as a major source of clinical information. Such interpersonal transactions are thought to be indicative of enduring relationship patterns, and their active identification and clarification forms the basis of more relationally oriented brief-therapy technique.

The following clinical vignette illustrates the here-and-now focus on patient-therapist transactions. The therapist uses his own experience in the context of active transference interpretation linking past relationship patterns to the current therapeutic relationship.

> T: Each time I notice and comment that you are looking attractive or that you're doing well in your work you get tearful and cry.
> P: (crying) I feel I am not attractive. I feel I will be rejected. Father could never stand it. I won a ribbon in a race and he only could say the competition was not too great. Dad did

the same restricting with Mother. She even had to limit her vocabulary for him.

> T: I see, so you feel you have some well established old reasons for feeling that way with me. (Luborsky, 1984, p. 96)

## *Goal Setting*

Goal setting is linked to the use of a central focus, as well as to the time limit and the centrality of termination. It reflects the therapist's acceptance of limitations on what can be accomplished, and embodies an individualized approach to the aims of psychotherapy. It also requires assessing therapy outcome in an individualized and dynamically informed fashion. Although not necessarily a formal feature of all brief dynamic psychotherapies, the use of goal setting is at least implied. On the one hand, the concept reflects the greater degree of problem solving and symptom focus that is characteristic of time-limited treatments. On the other, it also includes psychoanalytically informed ideas about emotional health such as insight into personal conflicts, emotional maturity, and capacity for intimacy in relationships, as well as a lessening of anxiety and depression. Such goals are set with an individual patient in mind and directed at those problems that are of immediate concern.

## Theory of Change

For the more traditional models of BPT, it is patients' deep and emotionally meaningful realization of the impact of intrapsychic conflict on their lives that enables them to be freed from the emotional traps and pitfalls that have stymied them. In particular, these conflicts are interpreted in the context of the relationship with the therapist, which is understood in the light of the psychoanalytic concept of *transference*. Freud used this term originally to describe the repetition in the psychoanalytic situation of a relationship with a developmentally early, significant other, usually but not always a parent. The repetition for Freud represented the activation of early infantile sexual and aggressive impulses that had been frustrated. As the therapist articulates patterns in the current patient-therapist dyad, important clues are identified as to the patient's central emotional conflicts. When these come to light, they can be interpreted by the therapist and taken in by the patient, enabling significant modifications in the relationships among wishes, defenses, and anxieties, and thus in the symptoms that arise from them. There is very good evidence that outcome in BPT is related to the therapist's application of psychodynamic technique (Crits-Christoph & Connolly, 1999; Messer, 2001d).

From the viewpoint of relational theory, conflict is seen as arising in interpersonal relationships as the result of conflicting wishes in relation to others. Conflict need not be related to infantile sexual or aggressive drives as posited by Freud, but can instead include a wide range of affects, wishes, intentions, and subjectively experienced needs in relation to others (Sandler & Sandler, 1978). In addition, there tends to be more emphasis on the current maintaining factors in psychopathological transactions, with systemic notions such as cyclical and self-perpetuating dynamics, as opposed to strict causal linkages to the past (e.g., Wachtel, 1997). In this sense, psychopathology is understood to be a dynamic, self-fulfilling process in which feared and anticipated relational events tend to be enacted by individuals in their interactions with others, who will then tend to respond in complementary ways. The mechanism of change is not insight alone, but a corrective experience that takes place for the patient in the presence of a therapist who does not respond in the usual way to the patient's interpersonal expectations. This may be why measures of the therapeutic alliance between patient and therapist turn out to be such good predictors of therapy outcome (e.g., Barber, Connolly, Crits-Christoph, Gladis, & Siqueland, 2000; Martin, Garske, & Davis, 2000).

## Supporting Research

Brief psychodynamic therapy has been compared to wait-list controls and to alternative therapies; it has been studied via meta-analysis, which accumulates results from individual studies; it has been compared to long-term therapy; and it has been explored via dose-effect relationships in which number of therapy sessions is charted against the percentage of patients improved (Messer, 2001c; Messer & Warren, 1995).

As an example of a study comparing BPT to an alternative therapy, Piper, Joyce, McCallum, and Azim (1998) compared BPT to brief supportive therapy for patients with mixtures of depression, anxiety, low self-esteem, and interpersonal conflict. Both treatment groups showed significant improvement according to statistical and clinical criteria, but did not differ from each other. This finding, showing equivalence of different kinds of brief therapy, is typical when brief therapies (or longer ones) are compared via meta-analysis as well. For example, in their meta-analyses, both Crits-Christoph (1992) and Anderson and Lambert (1995) found, on average, no difference between BPT and other treatments across many studies. Both, however, found BPT to be superior to wait-list controls, which speaks to the benefits of brief dynamic therapy.

Piper, Debanne, Bienvenu, and Garant (1984) directly compared brief to longer term psychoanalytic therapy for patients suffering anxiety, depression, and mild to moderate characterological problems. BPT (about 22 sessions) was found to be as effective as and more cost-efficient than long-term therapy (about 76 sessions), and the findings held true at 6-month follow-up. To summarize, brief psychodynamic therapy is helpful to a substantial proportion of patients and its effects seem to continue beyond the termination of therapy.

## Future Directions

One of the prominent current trends is the application of BPT to the personality disorders where some degree of character change is called for. This means improvement not only in symptoms or target complaints but also in chronic maladaptive patterns or personality traits. Working with this population frequently brings another current trend to the fore, namely, the integration of techniques from outside the usual domain of psychodynamic therapy. For example, McCullough Vaillant (1997), in her book *Changing Character,* focuses on the elicitation of affect and the use of cognition to guide affect into more adaptive channels. The defenses are confronted, but in an empathic or supportive manner. She incorporates active interventions such as systematic desensitization (behavioral), dispute of logic (cognitive), guided imagery (experiential), or linking feelings to bodily experience (Gestalt; McCullough & Andrews, 2001). Similarly, Magnavita (1997), in his psychodynamically based volume on BPT entitled *Restructuring Personality Disorders,* describes anxiety-dampening techniques of a cognitive or behavioral origin. These might include teaching problem-solving skills, desensitizing patients through imagery work, or teaching more adaptive methods of dealing with defenses. Given the variable results of BPT with at least some personality disorders, the themes of integration, pragmatism, and flexibility are a welcome trend.

Other special populations to which BPT is being applied are children, adolescents, and the elderly (Messer & Warren, 1995, 2001). This brings in a developmental life-span approach to brief therapy, in which normative transitions, life stages, and developmental challenges are the focus of treatment. Within a developmental perspective, the patient's problem is defined in terms of an adaptive failure in light of situational factors and emotional crises. The goal of such an approach is to enable the patient to attain new and stable adaptive structures with a greater capacity to manage life stresses. There is less emphasis on conflict or personality structures and more on the interaction of patient and external events (Borden, 1999; Budman & Gurman, 1988; Warren & Messer, 1999). For example, the time-limited treatment setting recapitulates the central dilemmas of old age, namely, mortality and loss. This may permit a reworking of older patients' life stories to enable them to mourn, to accept what was, and to embrace their existence in a fresh way (Messer & Warren, 2001).

## COGNITIVE BEHAVIOR THERAPY

Cognitive behavior therapy (CBT) has been traditionally utilized as a short-term treatment for a wide range of emotional disorders and problems. Although CBT was not intentionally derived as a brief treatment, the nature of CBT lends itself to being relatively brief in comparison to more traditional psychotherapeutic modalities (cf. McGinn & Sanderson, 2001). Generally speaking, CBT maximizes its efficiency by utilizing manual-based empirically supported treatment strategies and defines specific, measurable, and achievable target goals. A focused assessment process and a relatively structured session format facilitate the implementation of treatment strategies and allow the therapist to make efficient use of session time. Once treatment is implemented, a periodic review of progress using objective criteria enables the therapist and client to make informed decisions about the direction of treatment. CBT utilizes strategies to enhance generalization and prevent relapse and empowers patients by providing them with skills they can use outside therapy sessions. Finally, the therapist's active, directive stance plays a critical role in making CBT time-efficient.

### Introduction

*Behavior therapy,* a term coined by Lazarus (1958), arose and gained prominence in the 1950s as an alternative to *psychodynamic psychotherapy.* In contrast to the practice of psychodynamic therapy, which relied on clinical judgment based on theory and experience, behavior therapy endeavored to apply principles of learning established in the laboratory toward the understanding and remediation of psychopathological behavior. The roots of behavior therapy may be traced as far back as the beginning of the twentieth century. Ivan Pavlov's seminal work on classical conditioning conducted in Russia (1927) may be credited with having the most influence on behavior therapy as we understand it today. Learning theory also played a significant role in the evolution of behavior therapy. *Behavior modification,* a term often used interchangeably with *behavior therapy,* has developed from the work of B. F. Skinner (1953), emphasizing operant or instrumental conditioning.

The cognitive influence on CBT was stimulated in the 1950s by the work of Aaron T. Beck, whose general theory of emotional disorders posited that emotions are mediated by ongoing cognitive appraisals and that biases in information processing are central to understanding psychopathology. Cognitive ther-

apy developed as a movement away from both the theoretical outlook and practical limitations of psychoanalysis and the restrictive nature of behaviorism (Dobson, 1988). In contrast to both the psychoanalytic model, which assumes that individuals are motivated by unconscious motives and impulses, and to the behavioral tradition, which assumes that individuals are controlled by external contingencies, Beck proposed that dysfunctional thoughts, which could readily be brought into conscious awareness, are responsible for emotional dysfunction.

Although a few cognitive and behavior therapists still conduct pure versions of these approaches, during the last quarter of the twentieth century, cognitive and behavioral traditions have been increasingly integrated in their treatment of emotional disorders. This marriage between cognitive and behavioral approaches has largely occurred due to their common emphasis on targeting symptoms and problems, and on their use of the experimental method to understand, remediate, and assess changes in psychopathology. Over the years, a variety of cognitive behavioral therapies have evolved and demonstrated efficacy in remediating a wide range of psychological problems.

### Selection Criteria

Cognitive behavioral therapies have been utilized and shown to be effective for a wide range of psychological problems experienced by children and adults (see the *Brief Overview of Research Supporting the Efficacy of CBT* later in this chapter). These include almost all of the *DSM* Axis I disorders (e.g., major depression, substance abuse, bulimia, enuresis, hypochondriasis) as well as a variety of other problems (e.g., headaches, stress, suicidal behavior, interpersonal communication, coping with chronic illness, procrastination). Essentially, CBT offers a range of strategies that can be tailored to address a number of psychological problems and disorders that individuals may experience.

However, the bulk of controlled evidence suggests that while brief CBT is effective in treating *DSM* Axis I disorders (cf. Nathan & Gorman, 1997), it may not be as effective in treating Axis II personality disorders. For example, although CBT appears to be an effective treatment for borderline personality disorder, the typical treatment is quite intensive (not limited to one session per week) and occurs over several years (Linehan, Armstrong, Suarez, Allmon, & Heard, 1991). Although treatment outcome data for other personality disorders are not available, innovative clinicians adapting CBT for these disorders suggest that the treatment is not brief (e.g., Young, 1999).

For the most part, the focus of treatment in CBT is the remediation or amelioration of symptoms (e.g., depression, panic attacks, negative self-image) or problems (e.g., social disconnection, lack of assertiveness, relationship distress), and on helping clients attain better functioning and quality of life. Treatment typically includes the use of strategies that focus on reducing symptoms directly (e.g., cognitive restructuring of depressive cognitions, exposure therapy for phobias) and strategies aimed at building skills (e.g., relaxation training, assertiveness training, problem solving) to increase the patient's ability to cope with situations that are problematic for the patient and that lead to negative emotional reactions. Specific and measurable outcomes are defined at the outset of treatment and success is defined by meeting these goals (e.g., reducing panic attacks to one per month, reducing the severity of depression to a score of 10 or below on the Beck Depression Inventory, etc.).

Once the stated goals are met, CBT aims to builds skills to maintain gains and prevent relapse and develops strategies that allow patients to alleviate symptoms or problems if they recur. The therapist and patient collaborate to decide on the intervention goals in CBT (i.e., which symptoms or problems will be targeted and which intervention techniques will be used). They also decide on what degree of improvement will be judged reasonable and what yardsticks they will use to decide whether set goals have been reached (e.g., an inventory, a behavioral measure such as no phobic avoidance of elevators). Reaching a consensus at this stage ensures that patient and therapist have similar expectations about how treatment will progress and when it will be terminated.

For the most part, treatment emphasis is on the present and future rather than on early childhood or historical antecedents (e.g., the parent-child relationship). The focus of treatment is to increase the patient's ability to function effectively within his or her current environment and on improving the client's sense of hope about the future. CBT theory posits that, ultimately, developing adaptive cognitions and behaviors will result in the modification of maladaptive core beliefs and schemas. To accomplish this, sessions focus on building the patient's available resources and developing new skills rather than solely providing insight into the patient's personality in an effort to transform it.

As outlined previously, the therapeutic relationship in CBT is quite different from the ones used in more traditional forms of therapy. The therapist and patient form a collaborative team and together identify maladaptive thoughts and behaviors and develop strategies to remediate them (Beck, 1995; Beck, Rush, Shaw, & Emery, 1979). Thus, the therapist is more active and directive in CBT than in BPT. Although the relationship between the patient and therapist is seen as playing an important role in CBT and a good therapeutic relationship is associated with better outcomes (e.g., Castonguay, Goldfried, Wiser,

Raue, & Hayes, 1996), it is not considered the primary vehicle of change. Instead, the specific cognitive and behavioral strategies employed within the treatment are believed to be responsible for change.

## Techniques of Therapy

CBT involves the application of specific, empirically supported strategies focused on maladaptive thinking (e.g., Beck et al., 1979) and behavior (e.g., Lewinsohn, Munoz, Youngren, & Zeiss, 1986). The techniques used for brief CBT are the same as those employed for more extensive therapy. Typically, treatment is directed at the following three domains that are present in most emotional disorders: cognition, behavior, and physiology. In the *cognitive* domain, patients learn to apply cognitive restructuring techniques so that negatively biased thoughts underlying negative emotional states can be modified to become more logical and adaptive, thereby leading to a less negative emotional response. Within the *behavioral* domain, techniques such as exposure to the feared stimulus, response prevention (e.g., stopping a maladaptive response that ultimately reinforces the problem, as when escaping from a feared stimulus), activity scheduling to increase reinforcement, skills training to remediate interpersonal deficits, contingency procedures (e.g., making reinforcement or punishment contingent on a particular response to increase or decrease its frequency), and problem solving are used to remediate behavioral deficits that contribute to and maintain negative emotional states (e.g., avoidance, escape, social withdrawal, loss of social reinforcement). Finally, within the *physiological* domain, patients experiencing negative affective states are taught to use imagery, meditation, and relaxation procedures to calm their bodies. It is important to note that the three domains are believed to influence each other in a reciprocal fashion. Hence, although interventions are directed at the individual domains, therapeutic effects are expected to occur in all three.

CBT attempts to empower patients and thus there is an emphasis on providing them with skills to offset their negative emotional states and dysfunctional behavior. The use of treatment strategies is not limited to the therapy session. A primary and perhaps unique goal of CBT is to facilitate the use of treatment techniques outside therapy sessions. Patients are strongly encouraged to implement specific strategies to deal with the problems experienced in their natural environments (e.g., cognitive restructuring is used to offset negative thought patterns elicited by an interpersonal conflict and thus to avoid the consequent depressive affect; breathing exercises are used at the first sign of anxiety to circumvent hyperventilation that may occur during a panic attack;

exposure therapy is used when someone encounters a phobic situation).

Although the specific details of treatment vary from disorder to disorder, in general each of these strategies is used to address the specific cognitive, behavioral, and emotional psychopathology for the respective disorder or problem (cf. Persons, 1989). Depending upon the presenting problem, some of these strategies may be more appropriate than others. Based on a case conceptualization and formulation of the nature of the problem, the clinician selects relevant strategies to address the patient's symptoms and problems. For example, the therapist may develop a case conceptualization that describes dysfunctional schemas (*I'm undesirable*), assumptions (*If people get to know me they won't like me*), automatic thoughts (*She would not go out with me if I asked her*), emotions (anxiety, depression), and maladaptive behaviors (social avoidance, not revealing information about oneself in social situations). The therapist then carries out interventions such as cognitive restructuring to produce changes in these areas, and thereby in the dysfunctional emotional states. (For a full description of CBT treatment strategies as applied to a wide variety of disorders, see Clark & Fairburn, 1997).

## Theory of Change

As mentioned previously, CBT utilizes strategies to change cognitions (e.g., to reduce harsh self-criticism that may lead to depression, and catastrophizing about events that may lead to anxiety) and behaviors (e.g., to decrease phobic avoidance; to increase assertiveness) related to the patient's psychopathology. Although cognitive and behavioral methods are aimed at different psychopathological processes, in fact, they have an overlapping effect (i.e., cognitive methods may produce a change in behavior, and behavioral methods may produce a change in cognition). For ease of discussion, the theory of change will be presented separately for cognitive and behavioral methods.

### Cognitive Model

Central to the cognitive model of emotional disorders (Beck, Emery, & Greenberg, 1985; Beck et al., 1979) is the notion that the thinking of emotionally disturbed individuals is characterized by faulty information-processing styles. In this model, affect and behavior are seen as being *mediated* by cognition. Thus, the focus is on understanding how patients interpret events in their lives. If maladaptive thoughts and images can be changed then the accompanying negative emotional states and behaviors will change as well. If the patient feels angry, then cognitions associated with threat should be identified and changed; if a patient feels anxious, then cognitions associated with danger should be modified; and so on. When these faulty appraisals are replaced with more adaptive perceptions, the negative emotional states decline without requiring the use of pathological coping methods such as avoidance, escape, distraction, and the like.

### Behavioral Model

*Learning theory* (e.g., Lewinsohn et al., 1986) posits that negative emotional states frequently are a result of changes in reinforcement from environmental interactions. For example, in depression there is a *loss of positive outcomes* (e.g., the loss of a relationship decreases satisfying interpersonal situations) and an *increase in negative outcomes* (e.g., being criticized by one's spouse). Changes in reinforcement may be a result of the unavailability of previous sources of positive outcomes (e.g., a relationship has ended, one retires from work) or the lack of skills to achieve positive outcomes (e.g., a lack of assertiveness results in continuous negative events at work, where the person is continually taken advantage of; a lack of social skills leads one to be alone frequently; one sets such high standards for performance at work that they are never met, leading to continuous dissatisfaction).

According to learning theory, the mechanism of action of cognitive behavioral treatment is a change in reinforcement, which is a result of instituting new sources of reinforcement (e.g., having an individual find a new relationship) or providing skills to allow patients to be more effective, thereby accessing positive reinforcement and feelings of mastery. At times, especially with anxiety disorders, directly altering the conditioning process is necessary. Patients suffering from anxiety typically engage in avoidance behavior of a feared stimulus. When the individual continues to avoid a phobic stimulus, this avoidance will lead to a decrease in anxiety and thereby negatively reinforce (strengthen) the avoidance behavior. In such cases, systematic exposure to feared situations is necessary to break the connection between avoidance and reduced anxiety (i.e., in *exposure therapy,* the anxiety is elicited but the avoidance behavior is blocked, leading to a disassociation between the two). Theories of the process of anxiety reduction from exposure emphasize both the cognitive aspects (e.g., one develops thoughts that the stimulus is no longer dangerous, and as a result, does not experience anxiety when confronted by the stimulus) and behavioral aspects (anxiety is a conditioned response that is reinforced by avoidance or escape; once the avoidance-escape is discontinued, the stimulus loses its ability to provoke anxiety).

## Supporting Research

Although space does not permit a thorough review of the research literature supporting the efficacy of CBT, one can say that short-term (12–15 sessions) cognitive behavioral treatment results in substantial improvement for patients with a wide range of disorders (Clark & Fairburn, 1997; Hollon & Beck, 1994; Nathan & Gorman, 1997). Perhaps the strongest support for the efficacy of CBT comes from the American Psychological Association Division of Clinical Psychology's Task Force on Psychological Interventions, a group whose mission has been to develop criteria to judge empirically supported psychological interventions (Chambless et al., 1998). The criteria are quite rigorous, requiring the inclusion of a comparison group such as an alternative treatment or placebo group. Cognitive behavioral treatments represent approximately 90% of empirically supported treatments identified by the task force.

Based upon the latest report, cognitive behavioral treatments have demonstrated efficacy in the treatment of panic disorder with and without agoraphobia, obsessive-compulsive disorder, social phobia, posttraumatic stress disorder, generalized anxiety disorder, specific phobia, stress and coping, depression, chronic headaches, bulimia, chronic pain, smoking cessation, enuresis, parent training for children with oppositional behavior, and marital discord. Cognitive behavior therapies have also demonstrated substantial efficacy in the treatment of substance abuse and dependence, obesity, binge eating, irritable bowel syndrome, encopresis, childhood anxiety, female hypoactive sexual desire, sex offenders, borderline personality disorder, family intervention and social adjustment in schizophrenia, and habit reversal and control. Typically, these treatments were implemented in protocols that were no longer than 15 sessions.

It is important to note that most of the efficacy studies used to determine empirically supported treatments examine outcome only at the end of treatment; thus whether these treatments have sustained effects is unclear. However, that being said, data that do exist on this topic (most extensively for treatment of depression and panic disorder) suggest that CBT has a lasting effect beyond the treatment period, and that it outperforms medication over the long run (cf. Sanderson & McGinn, 2000, on depression; Clark, 1999, on panic disorder).

## Future Directions

Although the scope and efficacy of brief CBT are impressive, much work remains to be done. In particular, future efforts of CBT clinical researchers must demonstrate the effectiveness of treatment outside research centers as well as turn more attention toward disorders overlooked by CBT (e.g., personality disorders).

Critics have pointed out that although brief CBT has been demonstrated to be an effective treatment in clinical research settings, few data are available on the effectiveness of CBT when delivered in settings to a diverse group of patients outside the research clinic. Clearly, the demonstration of treatment efficacy in controlled research environments is only the first step in treatment research. Once a positive therapeutic effect has been demonstrated under such conditions, generalizability becomes of paramount importance. This problem is not unique to CBT, but applies to other empirically supported treatments, such as pharmacological approaches, and is clearly an important area in need of further investigation. While caution may be warranted until data are generated, it is reassuring to note that data are beginning to appear that support the effectiveness of brief evidence-based treatments outside controlled research environments (e.g., Sanderson, Raue, & Wetzler, 1999; Wade, Treat, & Stuart, 1998; Wilson, 1998). In addition, a recent meta-analysis of psychotherapy studies found that the effect sizes of psychotherapy in clinically representative settings is only 10% lower than those obtained in clinical research settings (Shadish, Navarro, Crits-Cristoph, & Jorm, 1997). Thus, preliminary data are suggesting that in fact, the efficacy of CBT generalize beyond clinical research centers, even when administered during a brief course of treatment.

A second future direction of CBT is to focus on disorders that, to date, have been largely overlooked by CBT—most notably personality disorders. Critics of CBT have noted that the scope of CBT may be limited to straightforward Axis I disorders, such as anxiety and depressive disorders, for which specific symptoms are clearly the target of treatment. Patients experiencing personality disorders do not always have clear symptom patterns and may not fit into the standardized treatment protocols frequently utilized in CBT. In addition, patients with long-standing characterological problems may not be responsive to brief treatment. Fortunately, work has begun in this area and clinical theorists and researchers are beginning to turn their attention to the treatment of personality disorders (e.g., Linehan, 1993; Young, 1999). While preliminary data are promising (e.g., Linehan et al., 1991), it remains to be seen whether CBT is an effective treatment for personality disorders, especially in its traditional brief format.

## BRIEF FAMILY AND COUPLE THERAPY

### Introduction

Although the temporal standard for the length of a great many of the individual therapies discussed elsewhere in this volume historically has been quite long term, this has never been the case for family and couple therapy (Gurman, 2001). Family therapy emerged during midcentury as a challenge to dominant psychoanalytic ideas of the times, and most influential models of family therapy have strongly emphasized clinical efficiency, parsimony, and problem-centeredness, although family therapists rarely explicitly set time limits for treatment. Likewise, contemporary marital therapy methods, almost irrespective of their theoretical orientations, overwhelmingly tend to be short term (Gurman & Fraenkel, 2002). Indeed, there has never been an enduring, influential method of long-term marital or family therapy that has served as a standard for the ideal practice of systems-oriented treatment. Overall, then, Gurman (2001) has argued that the notion of *brief* family and couple therapy is largely redundant.

This is not to say that brief therapy and family and couple therapy are the same. They differ in terms of their dominant views of what maintains problems and what needs to be done to resolve them. Almost all influential theories of family and couple therapy tend to be brief by prevailing standards because they emphasize the central factors, discussed shortly, that characterize the conduct of all brief therapies. Unlike most discussions of family therapy, the present one will identify the conceptual commonalities between most family and couple therapy and most brief individual therapy (cf. Donovan, 1999; see also the chapter by Kaslow in this volume).

All of the controlled trials of the research that has been conducted on family and couple therapy (Pinsof & Wynne, 1995) have studied treatments that were time limited for research design purposes, so that the family and couple therapy research literature, in effect, is a literature of brief therapies. At the same time, all of these approaches and all of the family and couple therapy methods (Chambless et al., 1998) that have been empirically validated to date are decidedly brief even when practiced outside the research context. The irony in all this is that most family and couple therapy has been brief by default rather than by design. There is very clear evidence (Gurman, 2001) that most family and couple therapies inevitably tap into the major factors that tend to keep any treatment brief, although they do not necessarily do so for that explicit purpose.

## Selection Criteria

Although some family and couple interventions have been designed specifically for the treatment of patients with Axis I psychiatric disorders, such as schizophrenia and bipolar disorders, in general, family and couple therapists are not very interested in psychiatric diagnosis. Likewise, most family and couple therapists do not conduct broad-scale assessments at the outset of treatment, or do extensive history taking. Still, an active psychosis, a current episode of alcohol or other substance abuse, violence, and some personality disorders may preclude family and couple therapy.

At the same time, existing research (Lebow & Gurman, 1995) makes it clear that family and couple therapy, alone or in combination with other interventions, is indicated and is most likely the treatment of choice for the following common clinical problems: marital conflict and dissatisfaction, parent-child conflict, childhood conduct disorders, depression accompanying marital discord (especially in women), agoraphobia (especially in women), alcoholism (especially in men), adolescent drug abuse, and juvenile delinquency.

In terms of patient selection, what is generally more important than standard psychiatric diagnosis in the eyes of family and couple therapists is the problem-maintaining role of people involved in the lives of *index* (or so-called *identified*) *patients*. Family and couple therapists are primarily concerned with behavior that is functionally relevant to the symptoms or problems brought to their attention. That is, their primary assessment concern is to identify how problem behavior is currently reinforced. People who may be selected to be part of ongoing family therapy are those who appear to have leverage in everyday life to effect change for a given family or couple. Thus, it is not necessarily family members alone who comprise the treatment group in family therapy. Although others (e.g., treating physicians and school personnel) certainly may be appropriately included in treatment, most family and couple therapy occurs with members of the same household and extended family.

## Techniques of Therapy

With well over two dozen influential methods of family and couple therapy in existence (Gurman & Jacobson, 2002; Gurman & Kniskern, 1991; Nichols & Schwartz, 1998), the variety of frequently used therapeutic techniques available is enormous. Moreover, as family and couple therapy becomes more integrative (Gurman & Fraenkel, 2002; Gurman & Jacobson), techniques are commonly borrowed from alternative treatment approaches, sometimes systematically, sometimes not.

Although some family (and especially couple) therapies emphasize the development of insight, the majority of systems-oriented treatment methods emphasize behavior change, even those that are not rooted in behavior therapy per se. In-session techniques that are action focused may include, for example, a marital therapist's interdiction of a couple's persistent fighting and an urging of the couple to see aspects of one another's behavior that are (defensively) blocked from conscious awareness. A structural family therapist may challenge the overwhelmed parents of an acting-out child to find some new, more effective, and unified strategy to assert their executive power with the child in the session. Alternatively, a family and couple therapist may try to elicit previously unexpressed feelings among family members, not for cathartic reasons, but to change the way in which they communicate with one another.

Moreover, many family and couple therapists see real value in the use of out-of-session change-inducing experiences. The types of planned homework used in family and couple therapy vary considerably. Some, such as those used typically by behavior therapists and structural therapists, focus on very specific directives for behavior change, the results of which are explicitly followed up at subsequent sessions. Other family and couple therapists, such as those with psychodynamic or humanistic orientations, might be more inclined merely to suggest that their patients reflect on certain issues outside the sessions.

Family and couple therapists also commonly emphasize the use of techniques that are intended to change meaning and attribution in the present and in reference to the present (where the consequences of the past are to be found), although the techniques are not usually those rooted in cognitive therapy strategies per se. Such cognitively oriented techniques can take on many forms. For example, a therapist might attempt to externalize the behavior of a particular family member by examining how that person learned this typical behavior as a means of self-protection in the family of origin. This perspective would tend to lessen other family members' tendencies to see the undesired behavior as motivated by malevolence or a lack of caring. Alternatively, the therapist might attempt to shift the meaning attributed to a particular behavior pattern by positively reframing the behavior as having unacknowledged benefits for the family as a whole, and so forth. Interest among therapists in patients' internal experience, central to the work of more psychoanalytic practitioners in family therapy's early days, has been renewed in the last several years as family and marital therapy have become more integrated into the psychotherapy mainstream.

There are certain rather predictable attitudes of most family and couple therapists (cf. Budman & Gurman, 1988; Gurman, 2001) that enhance the likelihood that treatment will be relatively short term. Most family and couple therapists seek to define treatment goals relationally, as well as individually; to emphasize a developmental perspective on the family as well as on individual family members; to emphasize the strengths of family subsystems, as well as those of individuals; and to view the family or couple as the most powerful natural healing environment for change. A constellation of sociocultural factors involving race, ethnicity, and social class constitute significant elements in these natural healing environments, and family and couple therapists regularly consider such factors in planning and carrying our their work (e.g., Falicov, 1983; McGoldrick, Pearce, & Giordano, 1982).

In addition, most family and couple therapists seek relatively rapid change, value intermittent intervention, and prefer parsimonious interventions that may resolve presenting problems. These dominant values of most family and couple therapists, in combination with patient expectations that usually favor relatively briefer treatment experiences, may help to foster a collaborative set toward treatment. Such a *temporal alliance,* that is, a shared set of expectations about treatment length, may serve as an antidote to the affective intensity that occurs in most family and couple therapy, thereby facilitating the development of a relatively collaborative working relationship (Gurman, 2001).

### Establishing a Therapeutic Focus

Beyond these influential patient and therapist expectations, perhaps the most important factor in the conduct of brief marital and family therapy is the way in which most systems-oriented therapists highlight the nature of what is to be focused on in therapy sessions. In general, family and couple therapists focus on the relational patterns that center on the presenting problem or symptom; at the same time, they typically show relatively little interest in a family's or couple's general relationship style or patterns. As has often been said, "The system is its own best explanation." That is, no explanations of a system's ways of operating are needed beyond a careful observation of its dominant recurrent patterns. The best explanation of a particular family system, of course, necessarily includes a sensitive assessment of the role of sociocultural factors such as race, ethnicity, social class, religious affiliation, and sexual orientation. Note that in an eclectic or integrative style of family and couple therapy, which is probably the most common theoretical orientation among family therapists, problem-maintaining patterns need not be limited to observable behavior, but may include functionally relevant private experience as well (i.e., thoughts and feelings that precede or follow problematic interactions).

### The Meaning and Use of Time

In addition to the kinds of techniques used by family and couple therapists, and the ways in which they establish and maintain a treatment focus, there are certain recurring patterns of how systems-oriented therapists tend to view time in psychotherapy, and how they tend to use time. For example, in establishing a therapeutic focus and treatment goals family therapists emphasize the question, "Why *now*?" This question goes to the heart of the developmental or life-cycle view of problems that most family therapists adopt. That is, difficulties are almost always assessed in the context of the family's evolving life-transitions, both as a unit and as an interconnected collection of individuals. Moreover, recognizing that most families and couples do not expect protracted treatments, most family therapists attempt to initiate changes in families' functionally relevant transactional patterns quite early in treatment, often even as early as the first session.

Time is also used very flexibly by most family and couple therapists. The length of sessions is not the standard 50-min hour, and can change over time. In addition, family therapists often vary the interval between sessions to allow families and couples time to experiment with new interactional possibilities; to accommodate the family's sense of moving too fast therapeutically; or alternatively, to increase the pressure toward change. Indeed, an important aspect of the therapeutic focus in much family and couple therapy involves the many ways in which time is both respected and manipulated in order to achieve positive outcomes.

## Theory of Change

In addition to present-oriented techniques, and an emphasis on family behavior patterns centered on a problem or focus, the orientation of family and couple therapy toward the patient-therapist relationship has an enormous bearing on its brevity. In fact, the nature of this relationship captures the essence of the major mechanism of change in systems-oriented treatments. In contrast to psychoanalytic therapy, in which the transference relationship is often seen as the primary source of change, in family and couple therapy it is rather muted. Also in contrast to psychoanalytic therapy, the transferences and affective responses between and among family members are usually considered far more intense. The corrective emotional experience in systems-oriented therapy is seen as occurring within the family as patient, much more so than between therapist and patient.

## Supporting Research and Future Directions

Several types of family and marital therapy have been shown by empirical research to yield positive outcomes, with effect sizes comparable to those of individual psychotherapies (Gurman & Fraenkel, 2002; Lebow & Gurman, 1995). While such therapies are routinely given predetermined time limits in controlled clinical studies, these artificially applied limits closely approximate the usual duration of most family and couple therapy (Gurman, 2001). Thus, the most important questions calling for further empirical study in family therapy in general (e.g., Pinsof & Wynne, 1995) substantially overlap

the domain of brief family therapy. Certainly, among the most important directions for research in the study of therapeutic brevity is greater specification of the functional components of patients' and therapists' temporal expectations of therapy. It is when significant discrepancies between such expectations arise that the possibility of a strong early therapy alliance may be weakened or even precluded. Further study of the mechanisms of change in family therapy, and of how the formation of a patient-therapist temporal alliance (Gurman) may activate basic change mechanisms, is clearly called for.

## BRIEF EXPERIENTIAL THERAPY

### Introduction

Three distinct therapeutic traditions—client-centered, Gestalt, and existential—led to the development of *brief experiential therapy (BET)*. Appearing in the 1950s, they were referred to as the humanistic therapies or the so-called third force in psychology, alongside psychoanalysis and behaviorism. In Rogers's (1951) *client-centered therapy,* the therapeutic relationship was considered the primary vehicle of change insofar as the warmth, unconditional positive regard, and genuineness of the therapist (or parent) were considered the soil needed for the client (or child) to develop into a fully functioning person. In contrast to behavioral or psychoanalytic therapy, therapists are not seen as actively bringing about change through behavioral techniques or deep interpretations, respectively, but by giving clients their undivided attention and the psychological space in which to grow. Clients are viewed as the experts on their own experience. Rogers was prescient insofar as the therapeutic alliance, an important feature of the quality of the relationship between client and therapist, has been consistently found to be a good predictor of therapy outcome (Martin et al., 2000).

In *Gestalt therapy,* as in the client-centered model, it is the client who is viewed as discovering that which leads to change, but the role of the therapist is more active (Perls, Hefferline, & Goodman, 1951). To help clients resolve conflicts, the Gestalt therapist encourages expression of emotions and helps clients articulate what they are experiencing (Greenberg & Rice, 1997). They may use techniques such as the *empty chair,* in which clients are prompted to express their feelings aloud to a significant, albeit absent, party. It is not the therapist's interpretations that are said to bring about change, but the clients' enhanced awareness, especially of their own feelings.

In *existential therapy* (May, Angel, & Ellenberger, 1958) the concept of personal responsibility is paramount. Existential therapists strive to develop a climate of safety and security for clients before confronting them with their roles in, and responsibility for, creating their own life situations (Watson, Greenberg, & Lietaer, 1998). They attempt to direct clients' attention to fundamental and inescapable features of human existence such as loneliness, death, and existential anxiety. The last three are said to block a person's capacity for making authentic choices. Clients are helped to come to terms with these givens through the active support and even, at times, advice of the therapist.

*Process-experiential therapy,* whether in its brief or open-ended version, is an integration of client-centered, Gestalt, and existential therapies (especially the first two), with the addition of emotion theory, attachment theory, and constructivist, postmodern theories of knowledge and the self (Elliott, 2001). An authentic, *I-Thou* relationship between client and therapist is seen as central (Elliott & Greenberg, 1995). Process-experiential therapy focuses on the client's present experience and attention to bodily feelings. In addition, the person is regarded as being future oriented and goal directed rather than influenced primarily by the past, as claimed by psychoanalysis. Clients are also said to have a need for *agency.* Unlike in client-centered therapy, therapists may, at times, take the lead in guiding clients experiential processing while, at other times, clients' understanding of their own experience is paramount. The usual range of BET is 12–20 sessions.

### Selection Criteria

Elliott (2001), a prominent exponent of process-experiential therapy, considers BET to be suitable for clients with mild to moderate distress and symptoms. Potential clients should also be able and willing to focus on their inner experience and to express emotions. In diagnostic terms, included are the adjustment reactions and the depressive and anxiety disorders. Other suitable problems, expressed in nondiagnostic terms, are low self-esteem, internal conflicts, and interpersonal resentments and difficulties. For those clients who tend to focus on external factors as the cause of their problems, the therapist must try to create an internal focus by, at first, empathizing with the client's plight. More direct problem-solving tasks, which are a feature of BET, might be most appropriate for such clients. Because it would go against humanistic values to try to impose such a treatment (or any treatment) on clients, referral should be considered as well.

Watson and Greenberg (1998) point out that the quality of clients' introjects may affect their suitability for BET. That is, "Clients who are hostile and rejecting of themselves and who do not seem to have any complementary affirming, understanding, or nurturing attitudes towards themselves may not be good candidates for short-term therapy" (p. 140). In reviewing the research literature on brief dynamic

psychotherapy and in agreement with this viewpoint, Messer (2001d) found that such clients, often considered to have personality disorders, require a longer therapy to improve.

### Techniques of Therapy

In the space available, we can offer only an overview of the major techniques and methods of BET. Our discussion is based on several sources, to which the reader is referred for more in-depth consideration (Elliott, 2001; Elliott & Greenberg, 1995; Greenberg, Rice, & Elliott, 1993; Watson & Greenberg, 1998). To begin with, there is a distinction made between general treatment principles and therapeutic task facilitation. We will start with the *treatment principles* expressed in the form of guidelines to the BET therapist:

- *Enter and track the client's immediate and evolving experiencing.* The therapist enters the client's world, trying to grasp what is most central at any moment in time. There is an effort at empathic attunement that requires letting go of preformed ideas about the client.

- *Express empathy and genuine prizing.* Because the relationship is considered an important curative element in BET, the therapist conveys acceptance and prizing of the client.

- *Facilitate mutual involvement in goals and tasks of therapy.* The setting of goals should be a collaborative effort between client and therapist. The client should be helped to understand the specific therapeutic tasks that will be carried out in therapy, such as the empty chair or two-chair techniques described later.

- *Facilitate optimal client experiential processing.* The therapist should be flexible in recognizing that the client will be helped to work in different ways at different times. At one moment there may be the need for the client to tell his or her story and at another to work on emotional experiencing in connection with its more problematic aspects.

- *Foster client growth and self-determination.* Clients' agency is important in choosing their actions and constructing their experience. "The therapist also supports the client's potential for self-determination, empowerment, mature interdependence, mastery and self-development, by listening carefully for, and helping the client to explore 'growing edges' of, new experience" (Elliott, 2001, p. 41).

- *Facilitate client completion of key therapeutic tasks.* The therapist helps the client, especially in *brief* experiential therapy, to develop a clear therapeutic focus and keep that focus in mind in every session. The client is helped to resolve the issues encapsulated in that focus by a gentle guiding process.

One of the major ways in which process-experiential therapy differs from its client-centered progenitor is in its willingness to define specific *therapeutic tasks,* sometimes drawn from Gestalt therapy. The main elements of the tasks are (a) a *marker,* which indicates that the client is ready to work on a particular issue; (b) a *task intervention sequence* involving client and therapist task-relevant actions; and (c) a desired *resolution* of the task worked on. These tasks can be described as falling into one of the three following categories: basic exploratory, active expression, and interpersonal. In BET there is more use of the active expression tasks, whereas in the open-ended treatment of more chronic personality or interpersonal difficulties, the other two task modes predominate.

## Basic Exploratory Tasks

The therapist encourages clients to attend to and explore inner experience, and to verbalize it. That is, clients learn to symbolize their experience, constructing meaning out of it. This is probably the most frequent kind of activity engaged in by the experiential therapist. Examples of exploratory tasks are empathic exploration, experiential focusing (Gendlin, 1996)—used especially when clients feel overwhelmed or stuck—and facilitating retelling of traumatic or difficult experiences.

The therapist usually begins each session with *empathic exploration,* and the markers for other tasks eventually come into relief. Any experience that captures the client's attention can be explored and parsed, especially if it is unclear. With the help of the therapist, the client moves from a more intellectualized stance to one of personal evaluation and then to the generation and integration of new personal meanings about the self (Elliott & Greenberg, 1995). Other basic exploratory tasks are *systematic evocative unfolding* for unexplained client overreactions to specific situations (Watson & Rennie, 1994), and *meaning work* for life crises that challenge cherished beliefs.

## Active Expression Tasks

These stem from psychodrama and Gestalt therapy and are intended to bring hidden emotions to the fore. Best known among them are the *empty chair* (mentioned earlier) and *two-chair* techniques. The former is used for unfinished business, when there are lingering bad feelings toward a significant other. "In the presence of a strong therapeutic alliance, the therapist suggests that the client imagine the other in the empty chair and express any previously unexpressed feelings toward him or her. The therapist may also suggest that the client take the role of the other and speak to the self" (Elliott,

Davis, & Slatick, 1998, p. 265). Expression of strong feelings can lead to more positive views of self and other.

Whereas the empty chair technique is aimed at resolving conflicts between self and others, the two-chair technique is useful in resolving splits between two different aspects of the self, which are brought into dialogue with each other. It allows rapid contact with strong emotions and is particularly useful for uncovering clients' fears in anxiety disorders. Wolfe and Sigl (1998) give an example of how a person with panic disorder used it to reconcile one side of her self as "nice person" and another side as "angry bitch" (p. 287). The dialogue helped her to view her rage as based in legitimate grievances rather than as a totally unacceptable aspect of her self.

## Interpersonal Tasks

These include a therapeutic relationship characterized by empathic attunement, prizing, genuineness, and collaboration. When a client presents a vulnerability marker, indicating the emergence of strong emotional pain, the therapist offers *empathic affirmation.* Complaints about the therapist or treatment are dealt with through *alliance dialogue.*

Therapists practicing BET need to "establish a focus early in treatment and actively work toward an agreement with their clients on the goals of therapy in the first few sessions" (Watson & Greenberg, 1998, p. 132). In their research on depressed clients, these authors found that where therapists had not set a focus early on in either BET or person-centered therapy, clients had the poorest outcome.

## Theory of Change

The theory of experience-centered therapies is covered in detail in Greenberg and Van Balen (1998). Here we will highlight the most prominent current theoretical development in process-experiential therapy, which is *emotion theory* (Greenberg & Paivio, 1997; Greenberg & Rice, 1997). Emotions are seen as being important to peoples' well-being to the extent that they enhance orientation, adaptation, and problem solving. Within the safe environment of therapy, negative affects are evoked in the session in order to explore them and to access core maladaptive emotion schemes such as basic insecurity or worthlessness. *Emotion schemes* are structures that serve as the basis for human experience and as a way of organizing the self. They are made up of situational, bodily, affective, conceptual, and action elements. Different kinds of client *emotion reaction* require different therapist interventions and can serve different therapeutic purposes. For example, anger at being infringed upon can lead a client to set firmer personal boundaries; or an emotion reaction can lead to the incorporation of new experience, as when insecurity is restructured by accessing pride and mastery motivation.

Bohart (1993) has suggested that *experiencing* is a core change process in all therapeutic approaches. It is not only the symbolization of internal experience, it results from doing things in the world, that is, from behaving in new ways. *Empathy,* which has typically been defined as understanding the position of the other, is currently conceptualized as affective resonance with the other, which also contributes to change by its encouragement of unfolding and reflection.

## Supporting Research

Elliott (2001) conducted a meta-analysis of 28 studies (involving 20 treatment conditions) of BETs that consisted of individual, short-term (5–20 sessions), outpatient treatment of at least 10 clients. Seventeen of the studies were of client-centered, nondirective therapy, while 12 were of contemporary process-directive experiential therapy. Eight of the latter were of the process-experiential variety. The clients mostly suffered from anxiety or depression or, in some studies, personality disorders. The pre- to posttreatment changes were substantial (about 1.1 standard deviations), and were maintained at follow-up.

Analyses of the studies that had wait-list controls showed a similar advantage of treated over untreated clients. Comparing across different treatments, clients in the BETs changed as much as those in the other treatments. The finding of equivalence of BET and other therapies is in accord with recent meta-analyses that showed no differences among the therapies studied (Wampold et al., 1997). In a subanalysis, Elliott found that cognitive behavior therapy was superior to experiential therapy but that this difference disappeared when researcher allegiance to one or another of the therapies was controlled for.

## Future Directions

To attain research funding or insurance coverage, it has become increasingly important to gear treatment of any kind to the specific diagnostic categories encompassed by the *DSM.* Experiential treatment has been rising to the challenge by studying the kinds of therapist interventions that are necessary to treat a variety of disorders within this tradition. These include depression, posttraumatic stress disorder (PTSD), anxiety disorders, psychosomatic disorders, sexual abuse, and severe personality disorders such as borderline. Chapters on the treatment of each of these can be found in a volume edited by Greenberg, Watson, and Lietaer (1998). For example,

commonalities in emotion schemes appear to exist in the depressive disorders and certain types of in-session states emerge in their treatments. Greenberg, Watson, and Goldman (1998) present a model of the depressive process that requires evoking emotional memories and then helping the client reorganize them. The maladaptive depression-producing emotion schemes are challenged.

Likewise, Elliot et al. (1998) has found experiential states in clients suffering from PTSD differing from those arising in depression. This requires different techniques within the experiential tradition to treat PTSD. In dealing with flashbacks, for instance, renarrating traumatic episodes is helpful in order to symbolize traumatic affective experience in words. However, unless trauma was involved, this would not be especially helpful in depressives.

In addition to continuing studies of different diagnostic groups by means of randomized clinical trials, there has been a call for use of newer research methods to study BET. These include discovery-oriented, qualitative, and descriptive methods. One approach being adopted within the experiential tradition is intensive single-case research to track changes in key client issues across the course of therapy. Single case records that combine qualitative and quantitative data are particularly promising in providing explanations for within-session events. For example, Elliott (2000) has presented a hermeneutic single-case efficacy design that is systematic and self-reflective enough to provide an adequate basis for making inferences about what transpires in therapy. In his words, "The approach outlined here makes use of rich networks of information ("thick" description rather than elegant design) and interpretive (rather than experimental) procedures to develop probabilistic (rather than absolute) knowledge claims" (p. 3). For other emerging trends within the experiential therapy tradition, see Greenberg, Watson, and Lietaer (1998).

## STRATEGIC THERAPY

### Introduction

Strategic therapy is a brief, problem-focused psychotherapeutic approach developed by the Palo Alto Brief Therapy Group (Watzlawick, Weakland, & Fisch, 1974; Weakland, Fisch, Watzlawick, & Bodin, 1974). This mode of intervention is based upon the ironic notion that problems persist as a function of people's attempts to solve them. Thus, the focus of strategic therapy is on *ironic processes*. Since this treatment strategy is intended to break the vicious cycle that develops when the potential solution aggravates the problem, the goal of the therapist is to identify and develop a plan to interrupt the patient's well-intentioned solution efforts in order to re-solve the presenting problem (Fisch, Weakland, & Segal, 1982). This psychotherapeutic model is considered *strategic* in that the therapist develops interventions to deliberately interrupt ironic processes based upon a specific case conceptualization. Frequently, interventions include counterintuitive suggestions (e.g., to have the patient engage in the behavior he or she wants to eliminate, such as staying awake when having a problem with insomnia, or thinking an unwanted thought he or she is trying to suppress; Rohrbaugh & Shoham, 2001).

Regarding its historical origins, during the 1960s a group of psychotherapists associated with the Mental Research Institute (MRI) in Palo Alto were investigating therapeutic approaches to rapid problem resolution. The team became interested in the work of Milton Erickson, who was utilizing methods that were quite different than long-term psychodynamic psychotherapy—the dominant psychotherapeutic approach at the time (e.g., Haley, 1973). Rather than viewing problems as a function of underlying psychopathology, as did psychoanalysis, Erickson conceptualized them as stemming from the mishandling of common, everyday difficulties (Haley). Treatment was not focused on understanding psychopathology, but rather on solving problems as they cropped up. The Palo Alto group began testing a brief 10-session treatment based on the ironic process approach and Erickson's assumptions. From their clinical experience, a model of brief therapy emerged: focused problem resolution (Fisch et al., 1982; Weakland et al., 1974). This model was seen as strategic in that the clinician's interventions are deliberate and based upon a careful plan, and the clinician assumes responsibility for the outcome (Fisch et al.).

## Selection Criteria

Strategic therapy is considered appropriate for the entire range of problems for which people seek psychotherapeutic treatment. Thus, there are no specific selection criteria other than an individual presenting with at least one complaint (Rohrbaugh & Shoham, 2001). In fact, the clinical work that led to the development of this approach was based upon *unselected* cases seen at the Brief Therapy Center (BTC) and represented a wide range of problems. While almost half of the patients treated with strategic therapy at the BTC presented with an interpersonal problem such as marital discord or family conflict, many other individuals suffered from a range of problems, including anxiety, depression, procrastination, and eating disorders. Results from an archival study examining its effectiveness found that treatment outcome was not related to the presenting problem (Rohrbaugh, Shoham, & Schlanger, 1992). It is important to note, however, that given the limitations of the archival study (e.g., the lack of standardized diagnostic and assessment procedures and comparison group) one cannot be certain that strategic therapy is equally effective across all types and severities of presenting problems. Also worth noting, however, is that strategic interventions may be particularly useful for patients who are resistant to change, especially when compared to more straightforward skill-oriented approaches (cf. Rohrbaugh & Shoham).

## Techniques of Therapy

As succinctly summarized by Rohrbaugh and Shoham (2001, p. 71), the format for conducting brief strategic therapy is as follows:

> (a) define the complaint in specific behavioral terms; (b) set minimum goals for change; (c) investigate solutions to the complaint; (d) formulate ironic problem-solution loops (how "more of the same" solution leads to more of the complaint, and so on); (e) specify what "less of the same" will look like; (f) understand patients' preferred views of themselves, the problem, and each other; (g) use patient position to interdict problem-maintaining solutions; and (h) nurture and solidify incipient change.

Once the therapist has defined the problem or problems in specific, behavioral terms (e.g., taking 2 hr to fall asleep each evening) and set a minimum acceptable goal for change (e.g., taking 1 hr to fall asleep each evening), the intervention phase of therapy begins. The initial focus is to elucidate the solution patterns that maintain the complaint by assessing what the individual or others have been doing to solve the problem. Since the ironic process approach assumes that attempts to solve the problem are in fact maintaining it, illuminating cycles of problem-solving (i.e., problem-maintaining) strategies will highlight areas for intervention. Although the focus of problem-maintaining solutions is on the current period, previously attempted solutions can provide insight into what has and has not been effective.

Based upon the information obtained while evaluating current attempts to solve the problem, the therapist can conceptualize what "less of the same" will look like. Specifically, the goal is to reverse the problem-maintaining solution by identifying specific changes that need to be made. Ideally, this *strategic objective* constitutes a 180-degree reversal of what the patient has been doing (Rohrbaugh & Shoham, 2001). For example, if the problem-maintaining solution is the avoidance of social situations that cause anxiety, the objective of treatment might be for the patient to experience anxiety by entering a feared social situation, since the crucial element in planning an intervention is stopping the performance of the attempted solution (i.e., avoidance of social situations that cause anxiety). It is interesting to note that this strategy is similar to *systematic exposure,* a treatment strategy used within CBT. One of the marked differences however, is that in CBT the patient is typically given coping strategies to deal with the anxiety, whereas strategic therapy is not oriented toward providing such skills to patients.

To promote compliance, a hallmark of the Palo Alto strategic therapy model is framing therapeutic tasks and suggestions in terms compatible with the patients' own language, worldview, or position. To accomplish this, it is essential for the therapist to listen carefully to patients' comments in order to assess the way they see themselves and others and to determine what is important in their lives. In addition, the therapist attempts to determine patients' views of the problem, specifically, what they believe is causing it.

As part of setting the stage for effective problem resolution, the therapist not only elicits the patients' views, but also attempts to mold them to increase patients' receptivity to the intervention. For example, a therapist might accept a wife's position that her husband is demanding and controlling, and then extend this notion to suggest that the husband's behavior may indicate an underlying vulnerability. The therapist's extension creates a different way of looking at the problem, and thus a different solution to resolving it. The husband is now seen as vulnerable rather than controlling, and solving the problem requires dealing with his vulnerability, not his controlling nature. As the wife takes into account and responds to the husband's vulnerability, he becomes less controlling, and a positive feedback loop develops, leading to a resolution of the problem.

### Theory of Change

As noted before, the patient's presenting problem is believed to be maintained by his or her ongoing current attempt to control, prevent, or eliminate the problem. Thus, the focus of intervention and necessary condition for change is the interruption or elimination of the problem-maintaining behavior. From this viewpoint, resolving a problem does not require understanding or changing its antecedent cause, but simply the breaking of the ironic pattern of problem maintenance by promoting "less of the same" solutions (Rohrbaugh & Shoham, 2001). The theory of change is quite simple: If the problem-maintenance behavior can be reduced or eliminated, the problem will be resolved, regardless of its nature, origin, or duration. (Weakland et al., 1974).

### Supporting Research

There is a dearth of research on the Palo Alto strategic therapy model in its pure form. The only controlled study that exists was conducted by Goldman and Greenberg (1992), who compared a treatment based on the Palo Alto strategic therapy model to emotion-focused couples therapy and to a wait-list control condition. Whereas both treatments were superior to the control condition at posttreatment, couples who received strategic therapy reported better marital quality and more change in target complaints than the emotion-focused therapy group at the follow-up assessment (4 months after treatment).

The bulk of research support for this approach (for relationship distress as well as a variety of other problems) comes from the BTC's archives (Rohrbaugh et al., 1992; for a detailed description, see Rohrbaugh & Shoham, 2001). Since its inception, a standard procedure at the BTC has been for a team member to conduct a follow-up assessment with patients via telephone approximately 3 and 12 months following termination. The assessor (never the patient's primary therapist) evaluates changes in the presenting complaint, whether additional problems have developed, and whether additional treatment was sought elsewhere. On the basis of the patient's response to these questions, each case was classified into one of three categories: *success* (substantial or complete relief of the presenting complaint with no new problems), *significant improvement* (clear but incomplete relief of the complaint), or *failure* (little or no change, negative change, or further treatment for the presenting complaint).

In an initial report published by Weakland et al. (1974), the first 97 patients treated by the BTC group were categorized based upon their 1-year assessment. Forty percent achieved success status, 32% were rated as significantly improved, and 28% were considered treatment failures. Since this study neither included a comparison or control group nor used standardized assessment or diagnostic procedures, results must be interpreted with caution. However, as noted by Rohrbaugh and Shoham (2001), these data are comparable to success rates reported in the literature for other forms of psychotherapy (e.g., Smith, Glass, & Miller, 1980).

Rohrbaugh et al. (1992) updated the tabulation of outcome data for BTC cases seen through 1991 (a total of 285 patients). The results of this study essentially replicated the original findings. Furthermore, treatment outcome was unrelated to type of complaint, age, gender, educational level, and whether the patient had prior therapy, had been hospitalized, or carried a psychiatric diagnosis. (Since this archival data set is not published, the interested reader can see Rohrbaugh & Shoham, 2001, for a more detailed account.)

Finally, it is important to note that although they do not test the strategic therapy model per se, studies have supported the efficacy of a range of psychological treatments that include essential components of strategic therapy. Examples are the techniques based upon ironic-process principles, such as paradoxical interventions, that have been supported in a meta-analysis by Shoham-Salomon and Rosenthal (1987).

## Future Directions

Two areas stand out as requiring further attention. First, given the current emphasis on accountability in health care, if strategic therapy is to be a viable psychotherapeutic approach, treatment outcome data supporting its efficacy must be generated. As noted previously, to date only a handful of studies exist that support the effectiveness of strategic therapy. Collaborations between researchers and strategically oriented clinicians should be developed to generate research support for this approach (cf. Goldfried, Borkovec, Clarkin, Johnson, & Perry, 1999; Lambert, Okiishi, Finch, & Johnson, 1998). Second, research should be conducted to identify patients and problems particularly suited for this approach (e.g., Shoham, Bootzin, Rohrbaugh, & Urry, 1996). The existing research data suggest that strategic therapy is in fact quite effective for a reasonable proportion of patients. Thus, for some patients, interruption of the ironic process that is maintaining the problem behavior is effectively administered in a brief treatment. Identifying patients and problems most likely to benefit from strategic therapy would support its use in such cases in which a simple, parsimonious therapy may be the best first-line solution.

## BRIEF INTEGRATIVE-ECLECTIC THERAPY

## Introduction

Although most psychotherapists have been trained in one or more primary treatment approaches, the large majority of practitioners are eclectic or integrative in practice (Jensen et al., 1990). The terms *eclecticism* and *integration* have the common attribute of not using a pure approach to treatment, but have somewhat different meanings (Messer & Warren, 1995; Norcross, 1986). *Eclecticism* refers either to *technical eclecticism* (i.e., calling upon specific interventions from theoretically different methods) or to *prescriptive matching* (i.e., pairing the use of particular techniques with particular symptoms, syndromes, or patient personality types). *Theoretical integration* attempts to encompass different theories and the techniques deriving from them in one coherent theory. Finally, the *common-factors approach* to eclecticism emphasizes therapeutic variables and processes that are presumed to be common to all therapies and central to their efficacy.

Whereas most outpatient individual psychotherapy is eclectically brief, it is ironic that there are few explicit models of such therapy. Among the most influential are Bellak's (1992)

*brief and emergency psychotherapy,* Beutler's (1983) *systematic eclectic psychotherapy,* Budman and Gurman's (1988) *interpersonal-developmental-existential* approach, Garfield's (1989) *common-factors* approach, Klerman, Weissman, Rounsaville, and Chevron's (1984) *interpersonal psychotherapy,* Lazarus's (1981) *brief multimodal therapy,* and Wolberg's (1980) *flexible short-term psychotherapy.* A recent creative model is McCullough's *short-term anxiety-regulating therapy* (McCullough & Andrews, 2001).

## Selection Criteria

In the practice of some influential psychodynamic approaches to brief psychotherapy, discussed elsewhere in this chapter, the criteria for the selection of patients are quite exacting. In brief integrative-eclectic psychotherapy (BIEP), however, suitability criteria tend to be minimal and less stringent. Typically in BIEP, only the most severely disturbed candidates are excluded—for example, patients who are actively suicidal or dangerously impulsive, psychotic, drug abusing, or dealing with incapacitating chronic disorders such as schizophrenia. Even patients with personality disorders, especially those in the dramatic cluster and the anxious cluster, may be helped in brief treatment (Budman & Gurman, 1988). Generally, such diagnostic considerations aside, sufficient criteria for including a patient in BIEP are at least a moderate level of everyday psychosocial functioning, the capacity to form a working alliance with the therapist, and the ability either to identify a central focus (whether of the more symptomatic or thematic type, discussed later) or to agree upon such a focus with the therapist very early in treatment. Wolberg (1980, p. 140) captured the typical thinking of most BIEP-oriented clinicians about patient selection in urging that they "assume that every patient, irrespective of diagnosis, will respond to short-term psychotherapy unless he proves himself to be refractory to it."

## Techniques of Therapy

By its very nature, BIEP includes a very wide range of therapeutic techniques. Indeed, there are no techniques that are unique to BIEP. BIEP clinicians tend to be quite pragmatic in their choice and use of specific interventions, and regularly ignore the kinds of conceptual concerns expressed by clinical theorists about such indiscriminate borrowing. For example, Messer and Warren's (1995) concern that using a given technique out of the context of its originating theory may change its meaning does not usually deter workaday clinicians from incorporating varied techniques despite their possible incompatibility at a theoretical or even clinical level.

More than anything else, BIEP-oriented clinicians lean toward technical flexibility, often attempting to match particular interventions to particular problems. They usually do so somewhat intuitively rather than systematically, as is done in Beutler's (1983) and in Bellak's (1992) approaches. Thus, BIEP may include such interventions as interpretations to enhance insight, experiential exercises to enhance affective self-awareness, role playing to promote interpersonal effectiveness, and hypnosis or relaxation training to decrease anxiety. Essentially, in BIEP, the therapist's choice of techniques tends to be very patient-centered, in contrast to the more theory-centered choice of techniques usually found in pure approaches to therapy, including brief therapy. An increasingly important influence on the brief therapist's flexible selection of techniques involves an appreciation of potentially relevant patient sociocultural factors, such as race, ethnicity, and social class. As McGoldrick et al. (1982) have made clear, the fit between different styles and techniques of psychotherapy and patients of different cultural backgrounds varies significantly.

Still, most BIEP approaches are predominantly aligned with one conceptual orientation more than another. Thus, Bellak (1992) and Wolberg (1980) emphasize a psychodynamic foundation to their case conceptualization, Budman and Gurman (1988) and Klerman et al. (1984) have a strong interpersonal and adult-developmental slant, and Lazarus (1981) adopts a cognitive behavioral stance. In contrast, Beutler's (1983) approach is heavily influenced by social psychological theory, especially regarding interpersonal influence processes, and Garfield's (1989) common-factors approach deemphasizes techniques as major change-inducing elements of treatment, relying instead on such factors as empathic listening, reflection and reassurance, suggestion and explanation, and opportunities for catharsis.

In addition to selecting techniques that seem to fit the particular patient, BIEP therapists tend to choose interventions that have certain attributes that foster therapeutic brevity. These choices tend to be present-centered; to attend more to conscious and preconscious than to unconscious experience; to address interpersonal relationships more than inner fantasy life; to encourage, or at least suggest, taking action as much as engaging in reflection; and to acknowledge and build upon patient strengths and resources more than exposing deficits and limitations. A particular style of technical eclecticism in BIEP that is quite common involves the combination of different modalities of therapy, such as individual plus family/couple therapy, or individual plus drug therapy.

In general, the choice of therapeutic techniques, as in all brief therapy, should reinforce and be consistent with the maintenance of a clear, explicitly agreed upon *treatment focus*. The focus agreed upon can involve almost any life domain and problem description that allows the specification of achievable goals. A useful distinction in the setting of a focus is that between a *symptomatic focus* and *thematic focus*. The former refers to rather readily specified symptom complaints, usually of the sort associated with psychiatric diagnosis (e.g., depression, anxiety, or alcohol abuse). A thematic focus involves a broader pattern of behavioral or affective difficulty, or what behavior therapists call *response classes*—for example, interpersonal conflict, self-criticalness, or fear of commitment in relationships.

Budman and Gurman (1988) have offered a frame of reference to help therapists more rapidly assess a number of possible foci that are phenomenologically meaningful to patients. The five foci they described are losses, developmental dysynchronies, interpersonal conflicts, symptomatic presentations, and personality disorders. *Losses* can include any time frame (past, present, future), and may involve people (e.g., loved ones), position (e.g., job), or potential (e.g., permanent disability). *Developmental dysynchronies* refer to an individual's seeing him- or herself as being off track developmentally, and are often identified at nodal life-transition points (e.g., completion of formal education, marriage, etc.). *Interpersonal conflicts* commonly involve family and marital difficulties, although they may also center on friendships or workplace relationships. *Symptomatic presentations,* as noted, involve discrete symptoms such as anxiety or depression. *Personality disorders* may be gauged by chronic and constant loneliness, varied and repeated interpersonal conflicts, and anger and depression.

Budman and Gurman's (1988) five foci are not biased toward any particular theory of psychopathology or psychotherapy, and thus may serve as a template for the kind of rapid assessment and treatment planning that brief therapy requires. Moreover, the identification of a particular focus in their schema neither precludes nor preordains the use of any particular method of brief therapy or the selection of techniques within any given method.

Moreover, the use of such a template for focusing does not dictate how time is apportioned in BIEP. It is the manner of distributing time for treatment, not the setting of finite limits on the amount of available time (e.g., fixed termination date, fixed number of sessions), that typically distinguishes brief therapy from its longer term cousins (Budman & Gurman, 1988). Brief psychotherapy, and certainly BIEP, is very flexible in its distribution of treatment time. This temporal attitude has led some to assert that brief therapy could be more appropriately dubbed *time-sensitive* or *time-effective* therapy (Budman & Gurman). That is, BIEP is not necessarily continuous therapy, conducted weekly. Nor is BIEP necessarily provided as a course of treatment that comes to a final end. Rather, patients may be seen intermittently for successive periods of therapy, especially as changing life circumstances dictate a need to return for additional focused work. It is in this most concrete of ways that a life-cycle developmental perspective on clinical presentations (the all-important "Why *now?*" assessment question) has practical relevance.

## Supporting Research and Future Directions

BIEP, by its essential nature, lacks the panache to ever gain passionate adherents and become a therapeutic movement. Therefore, forces other than the conceptual and charismatic zealotry of BIEP's leaders will be called upon to maintain the widespread practice of these approaches. The first force that is likely to sustain and enhance BIEP's usage is the commonly encountered patient expectation that therapy should be brief and practical. Patients are generally not very interested in complex theories of treatment. They typically want to be offered what works, especially what is specifically likely to work for them. Likewise (although probably not with the same motivations), health care delivery systems and their administrators certainly favor whatever works, and whatever works the fastest.

The second major force that is likely to sustain the practice of BIEP is the corpus of existing research on psychotherapeutic outcomes. As noted earlier, the lion's share of outcome research on individual psychotherapy, which typically shows positive results, has involved brief treatment by any temporal standard (cf. Bergin & Garfield, 1994), and has tended not to favor one approach over the others. Many clinicians feel that if research has supported several different therapeutic approaches, combining them may enhance the overall effect. Process research has demonstrated that what appear to be pure approaches often are quite integrative (e.g., Jones & Pulos, 1993).

At the same time, there exists almost no research on what may be called *intentional integrative therapy,* in which intervention methods from disparate schools of thought are synergistically brought together in a coherent fashion, with adequate training and monitoring of therapists in the emerging integrative model. (See Glass, Arnkoff, & Rodriguez, 1998, for suggested directions for integrative psychotherapy research.) Likewise, the body of research on eclectic approaches is not large. It is best represented to date by Beutler's (1983) systematic approach, which attempts to match treatments to patients on the basis of potentially pertinent factors. A fundamental difficulty in studying eclectic treatments, of course, is that eclectic therapists typically use whatever techniques they think will benefit a given patient, rendering it difficult to standardize or manualize therapy for investigative purposes. Still, even in the face of these countervailing forces, brief integrative-eclectic styles of individual psychotherapy

are likely to continue to quietly dominate the landscape of contemporary practice.

## REFERENCES

Anderson, E. M., & Lambert, M. J. (1995). Short-term dynamically oriented psychotherapy: A review and meta-analysis. *Clinical Psychology Review, 15,* 503–514.

Anderson, E. M., & Lambert, M. J. (2001). A survival analysis of clinically significant change in outpatient psychotherapy. *Journal of Clinical Psychology, 57,* 875–888.

Barber, J. P., Connolly, M. B., Crits-Christoph, P., Gladis, P., & Siqueland, L. (2000). Alliance predicts patients' outcome beyond in-treatment change in symptoms. *Journal of Consulting and Clinical Psychology, 68,* 1027–1032.

Barber, J. P., Morse, J. Q., Krakauer, I. D., Chittams, J., & Crits-Christoph, K. (1997). Change in obsessive-compulsive and avoidant personality disorders following time-limited supportive-expressive therapy. *Psychotherapy, 34,* 133–143.

Beck, A. T., Emery, G., & Greenberg, R. L. (1985). *Anxiety disorders and phobias: A cognitive perspective.* New York: Basic Books.

Beck, A. T., Rush, A. J., Shaw, B., & Emery, G. (1979). *Cognitive therapy of depression.* New York: Guilford.

Beck, J. S. (1995). *Cognitive therapy: Basics and beyond.* New York: Guilford.

Bellak, L. (1992). *Handbook of intensive brief and emergency psychotherapy* (2nd ed.). Larchmont, NY: C.P.S. Inc.

Bergin, A. E., & Garfield, S. L. (Eds.). (1994). *Handbook of psychotherapy and behavior change* (4th ed.). New York: Wiley.

Beutler, L. E. (1983). *Eclectic psychotherapy: A systematic approach.* New York: Pergamon.

Bohart, A. (1993). Experiencing: The basis of psychotherapy. *Journal of Psychotherapy Integration, 3,* 51–67.

Book, H. E. (1998). *How to practice brief psychodynamic psychotherapy.* Washington, DC: American Psychological Association.

Borden, W. (1999). Pluralism, pragmatism and the therapeutic endeavor in brief dynamic treatment. In W. Borden (Ed.), *Comparative approaches in brief dynamic psychotherapy* (pp. 7–42). Binghamton, NY: Haworth Press.

Budman, S. H., & Gurman, A. S. (1988). *Theory and practice of brief therapy.* New York: Guilford.

Castonguay, L. G., Goldfried, M. R., Wiser, S., Raue, P. J., & Hayes, A. M. (1996). Predicting the effect of cognitive therapy for depression: A study of unique and common factors. *Journal of Consulting and Clinical Psychology, 66,* 7–18.

Chambless, D. L., Baker, M. J., Baucom, D. H., Beutler, L. E., Calhoun, K. S., Crits-Christoph, P., Daiuto, A., DeRubeis, R., Detweiler, J., Haaga, D. A. F., Johnson, S. B., McCurry, S., Mueser, T., Pope, K. S., Sanderson, W. C., Shoham, V., Stickle, T., Williams, D. A., & Woody, S. R. (1998). Update on empirically validated therapies: A project of the division of clinical psychology, American Psychological Association, Task Force on Psychological Interventions. *The Clinical Psychologist, 51*, 3–16.

Clark, D. M. (1999). Anxiety disorders: Why they persist and how to treat them. *Behavior Research and Therapy, 27*, 5–27.

Clark, D. M., & Fairburn, C. G. (1997). *Science and practice of cognitive behaviour therapy*. New York: Oxford University Press.

Crits-Christoph, P. (1992). The efficacy of brief dynamic psychotherapy: A meta-analysis. *American Journal of Psychiatry, 149*, 151–158.

Crits-Christoph, P., & Connolly, B. (1999). Alliance and technique in short-term dynamic therapy. *Clinical Psychology Review, 6*, 687–704.

Davanloo, H. (Ed.). (1980). *Short-term dynamic psychotherapy*. New York: Jason Aronson.

Dobson, K. S. (1988). *Handbook of cognitive-behavioral therapies*. New York: Guilford.

Dobson, K. S. (1989). A meta-analysis of the efficacy of cognitive therapy for depression. *Journal of Consulting and Clinical Psychology, 57*, 414–419.

Donovan, J. M. (Ed.) (1999). *Short-term couple therapy*. New York: Guilford.

Elliott, R. (2000, June). *Hermeneutic single case efficacy design (HSCED): An overview*. Paper presented at the meeting of the Society for Psychotherapy Research, Indian Lakes, IL.

Elliott, R. (2001). Contemporary brief experiential psychotherapy. *Clinical Psychology: Science and Practice, 8*, 38–50.

Elliott, R., Davis, K., & Slatick, E. (1998). Process-experiential therapy for posttraumatic stress difficulties. In L. Greenberg, J. C. Watson, & G. Lietaer (Eds.), *Handbook of experiential psychotherapy* (pp. 249–271). New York: Guilford.

Elliott, R., & Greenberg, L. S. (1995). Experiential therapy in practice: The process-experiential approach. In B. Bongar & L. E. Beutler (Eds.), *Comprehensive textbook of psychotherapy: Theory and practice* (pp. 123–139). New York: Oxford University Press.

Falicov, C. J. (1983). *Cultural perspectives in family therapy*. Rockville, ND: Aspen Systems.

Ferenczi, S. (1950). The further development of an active therapy in psychoanalysis. In J. Suttie (Ed.), *Further contributions to the theory and technique of psychoanalysis*. London: Hogarth. (Original work published 1920)

Fisch, R., Weakland, J. H., & Segal, L. (1982). *The tactics of change*. San Francisco: Jossey-Bass.

Garfield, S. L. (1989). *The practice of brief therapy*. New York: Pergamon.

Gendlin, G. T. (1996). *Focusing-oriented psychotherapy: A manual of the experiential method*. New York: Guilford.

Glass, C. R., Arnkoff, D. B., Rodriguez, B. F. (1998). An overview of directions in psychotherapy in integration research. *Journal of Psychotherapy Integration, 8*, 187–209.

Goldfried, M. R., Borkovec, T. D., Clarkin, J. F., Johnson, L. D., & Perry, G. (1999). Toward the development of a clinically useful approach to psychotherapy research. *Journal of Clinical Psychology, 55*, 1385–1406.

Goldman, A., & Greenberg, L. (1992). Comparison of integrated systemic and emotionally focused approaches to couples therapy. *Journal of Consulting and Clinical Psychology, 60*, 962–969.

Greenberg, L. S., & Paivio, S. (1997). *Working with emotions in psychotherapy*. New York: Guilford.

Greenberg, L. S., & Rice, L. N. (1997). Humanistic approaches to psychotherapy. In P. L. Wachtel & S. B. Messer (Eds.), *Theories of psychotherapy: Origins and evolution* (pp. 97–129). Washington, DC: American Psychological Association.

Greenberg, L. S., Rice, L. N., & Elliott, R. (1993). *Facilitating emotional change: The moment-by-moment process*. New York: Guilford.

Greenberg, L. S., & Van Balen, R. (1998). The theory of experience-centered therapies. In L. S. Greenberg, J. C. Watson, & G. Lietaer (Eds.), *Handbook of experiential psychotherapy* (pp. 28–57). New York: Guilford.

Greenberg, L. S., Watson, J. C., & Lietaer, G. (Eds.). (1998). *Handbook of experiential psychotherapy*. New York: Guilford.

Gurman, A. S. (2001). Brief therapy and family/couple therapy: An essential redundancy. *Clinical Psychology: Science and Practice, 8*, 51–65.

Gurman, A. S., & Fraenkel, P. (2002). The history of couple therapy: A millennial review. *Family Process, 41*, 199–260.

Gurman, A. S., & Jacobson, N. S. (Eds.). (2002). *Clinical handbook of couple therapy* (3rd ed.). New York: Guilford.

Gurman A. S., & Kniskern, D. P. (Eds.). (1991). *Handbook of family therapy* (Vol. 2). New York: Brunner/Mazel.

Haley, J. (1973). *Uncommon therapy: The psychiatric techniques of Milton H. Erickson, MD*. New York: Norton.

Hollon, S. D., & Beck, A. T. (1994). Cognitive and cognitive-behavioral therapies. In A. E. Bergin & S. L. Garfield (Eds.), *Handbook of psychotherapy and behavior change* (pp. 428–466). New York: Wiley.

Howard, K. I., Kopta, S. M., Krause, M. S., & Orlinsky, D. E. (1986). The dose-effect relationship in psychotherapy. *American Psychologist, 41*, 159–164.

Jensen, J. P., Bergin, A. E., & Greaves, D. W. (1990). The meaning of eclecticism: New survey and analysis of components. *Professional Psychology: Research and Practice, 21*, 124–130.

Jones, E. E., & Pulos, S. M. (1993). Comparing the process in psychodynamic and cognitive behavioral therapies. *Journal of Consulting and Clinical Psychology, 61*, 306–316.

Kadera, S. W., Lambert, M. J., & Andrews, A. A. (1996). How much therapy is really enough? *Journal of Psychotherapy Practice and Research, 5*, 132–151.

Klerman, G. L., Weissman, M. M., Rounsaville, B. J., & Chevron, E. S. (1984). *Interpersonal psychotherapy of depression*. New York: Basic Books.

Lambert, M. J., Okiishi, J., Finch, A. E., & Johnson, L. D. (1998). Outcome assessment: From conceptualization to implementation. *Professional Psychology, 29,* 63–70.

Lazarus, A. A. (1958). New methods in psychotherapy. *South African Medical Journal, 32,* 660–664.

Lazarus, A. A. (1981). *The practice of multimodal therapy.* New York: McGraw Hill.

Lebow, J., & Gurman, A. S. (1995). Research assessing couple and family therapy. *Annual Review of Psychology, 46,* 27–57.

Levenson, H. (1995). *Time-limited dynamic psychotherapy.* New York: Basic Books.

Lewinsohn, P. M., Munoz, R., Youngren, M., & Zeiss, A. M. (1986). *Control your depression.* New York: Fireside.

Linehan, M. M. (1993). *Cognitive-behavioral treatments of borderline personality disorder.* New York: Guilford.

Linehan, M. M., Armstrong, H. E., Suarez, A., Allmon, D., & Heard, H. L. (1991). Cognitive-behavioral treatment of chronically parasuicidal borderline patients. *Archives of General Psychiatry, 48,* 1060–1064.

Luborsky, L. (1984). *Principles of psychoanalytic psychotherapy: A manual for supportive-expressive treatment.* New York: Basic Books.

Magnavita, J. J. (1997). *Restructuring personality disorders: A short-term dynamic approach.* New York: Guilford.

Malan, D. (1976). *The frontier of brief psychotherapy.* New York: Plenum.

Mann, J. (1973). *Time-limited psychotherapy.* Cambridge: Harvard University Press.

Mann, J. (1991). Time limited psychotherapy. In P. Crits-Christoph & J. P. Barber (Eds.), *Handbook of short-term dynamic psychotherapy* (pp. 17–44). New York: Basic Books.

Martin, D. J., Garske, J. P., & Davis, M. K. (2000). Relation of the therapeutic alliance with outcome and other variables. *Journal of Consulting and Clinical Psychology, 68,* 438–450.

May, R., Angel, E., & Ellenberger, H. (Eds.). (1958). *Existence: A new dimension in psychiatry and psychology.* New York: Basic Books.

McCullough, L., & Andrews, S. (2001). Assimilative integration: Short-term dynamic psychotherapy for treating affect phobias. *Clinical Psychology: Science and Practice, 8,* 82–97.

McCullough Vaillant, L. (1997). *Changing character.* New York: Basic Books.

McGinn, L. K., & Sanderson, W. C. (2001). What allows cognitive behavioral therapy to be brief: Overview, efficacy, and crucial factors facilitating brief treatment. *Clinical Psychology: Science and Practice, 8,* 23–37.

McGoldrick, M., Pearce, J. K., & Giordano, J. (Eds.). (1982). *Ethnicity and family therapy.* New York: Guilford.

Messer, S. B. (2001a). Empirically supported treatments: What's a non-behaviorist to do? In B. D. Slife, R. N. Williams, & S. H. Barlow (Eds.), *Critical issues in psychotherapy: Translating new ideas into practice.* Thousand Oaks, CA: Sage.

Messer, S. B. (2000b). Introduction to the special issue on assimilative integration. *Journal of Psychotherapy Integration, 8,* 1–4.

Messer, S. B. (2001c). What allows therapy to be brief? Introduction to the series on brief therapy. *Clinical Psychology: Science and Practice, 8,* 1–4.

Messer, S. B. (2001d). What makes psychodynamic therapy time efficient. *Clinical Psychology: Science and Practice, 8,* 5–22.

Messer, S. B., & Warren, C. S. (1995). *Models of brief psychodynamic therapy: A comparative approach.* New York: Guilford.

Messer, S. B., & Warren, C. S. (2001). Brief psychodynamic therapy. In R. J. Corsini (Ed.), *Handbook of innovative psychotherapies* (2nd ed., pp. 67–85). New York: Wiley.

Nathan, P., & Gorman, J. (1997). *Treatments that work.* Oxford: Oxford University Press.

Nichols, M. P., & Schwartz, R. C. (1998). *Family therapy: Concepts and methods* (4th ed.). Boston: Allyn & Bacon.

Norcross, J. C. (1986). Eclectic psychotherapy: An introduction and overview. In J. C. Norcross (Ed.), *Handbook of eclectic psychotherapy* (pp. 3–24). New York: Guilford.

Olfson, M., & Pincus, H. A. (1994). Outpatient psychotherapy in the United States, II: Patterns of utilization. *American Journal of Psychiatry, 151,* 1289–1294.

Pavlov, I. P. (1927). *Conditioned reflexes* (G. V. Anrep, Trans.). London: Oxford University Press.

Perls, F. S., Hefferline, R. F., & Goodman, P. (1951). *Gestalt therapy.* New York: Julian.

Persons, J. B. (1989). *Cognitive therapy in practice: A case formulation approach.* New York: W. W. Norton.

Phillips, E. L. (1985). *Psychotherapy revised: New frontiers in research and practice.* Hillsdale, NJ: Erlbaum.

Pinsof, W. M., & Wynne, L. C. (Eds.). (1995). The effectiveness of marital and family therapy [Special issue]. *Journal of Marital and Family Therapy, 21,* 339–623.

Piper, W. E., Debbane, E. G., Bienvenu, J. P., & Garant, J. (1984). A comparative study of four forms of psychotherapy. *Journal of Consulting and Clinical Psychology, 52,* 268–279.

Piper, W. E., Joyce, A. S., McCallum, M., & Azim, H. F. A. (1998). Interpretive and supportive forms of psychotherapy and patient personality variables. *Journal of Consulting and Clinical Psychology, 66,* 558–567.

Rogers, C. R. (1951). *Client-centered therapy.* Boston: Houghton-Mifflin.

Rohrbaugh, M., & Shoham, V. (2001). Brief therapy based on interrupting ironic processes: The Palo Alto Model. *Clinical Psychology: Science and Practice, 8,* 66–81.

Rohrbaugh, M., Shoham, V., & Schlanger, K. (1992). *In the brief therapy archives: A progress report.* Unpublished manuscript, University of Arizona, Tucson.

Sanderson, W. C., & McGinn, L. K. (2000). Cognitive behavioral treatment of depression. In M. M. Weissman (Ed.), *Treatment of depression: Bridging the 21st century* (pp. 249–279). Washington, DC: American Psychiatric Association.

Sanderson, W. C., Raue, P. J., & Wetzler, S. (1999). The generalizability of cognitive behavior therapy for panic disorder. *Journal of Cognitive Psychotherapy, 12*, 323–331.

Sandler, J., & Sandler, A. M. (1978). On the development of object relationships and affects. *International Journal of Psychoanalysis, 59*, 285–296.

Seligman, M. E. P. (1995). The effectiveness of psychotherapy: The Consumer Reports study. *American Psychologist, 50*, 965–974.

Shadish, W. R., Navarro, A. M., Crits-Christoph, P., & Jorm, A. F. (1997). Evidence that therapy works in clinically representative conditions. *Journal of Consulting and Clinical Psychology, 65*, 355–365.

Shoham, V., Bootzin, R. R., Rohrbaugh, M. J., & Urry, H. (1996). Paradoxical versus relaxation treatment for insomnia: The moderating role of reactance. *Sleep Research, 24a*, 365.

Shoham-Salomon, V., & Rosenthal, R. (1987). Paradoxical interventions: A meta-analysis. *Journal of Consulting and Clinical Psychology, 55*, 22–28.

Sifneos, P. E. (1972). *Short-term psychotherapy and emotional crisis*. Cambridge: Harvard University Press.

Skinner, B. F. (1953). *Science and human behavior*. New York: Macmillan.

Smith, M. L., Glass, G. V., & Miller, T. I. (1980). *The benefits of psychotherapy*. Baltimore: Johns Hopkins University Press.

Strupp, H. H., & Binder, J. L. (1984). *Psychotherapy in a new key*. New York: Basic Books.

Wachtel, P. L. (1997). *Psychoanalysis, behavior therapy, and the relational world*. Washington, DC: American Psychological Association.

Wade, W. A., Treat, T. A., & Stuart, G. L. (1998). Transporting an empirically supported treatment for panic disorder to a service clinic setting: A benchmarking strategy. *Journal of Consulting and Clinical Psychology, 66*, 231–239.

Wampold, B. E., Mondin, G. W., Moody, M., Stich, F., Benson, K., & Ahn, H. (1997). A meta-analysis of outcome studies comparing bona fide psychotherapies: Empirically, "All must have prizes." *Psychological Bulletin, 122*, 203–215.

Warren, C. S., & Messer, S. B. (1999). Brief psychodynamic therapy with anxious children. In S. Russ & T. Ollendick (Eds.), *Handbook of psychotherapies with children and families* (pp. 219–237). New York: Kluwer Academic.

Watson, J. C., & Greenberg, L. S. (1998). The therapeutic alliance in short-term humanistic and experiential therapies. In J. D. Safran & J. C. Muran (Eds.), *The therapeutic alliance in brief psychotherapy* (pp. 123–145). Washington, DC: American Psychological Association.

Watson, J. C., Greenberg, L. S., & Lietaer, G. (1998). The experiential paradigm unfolding: Relationship and experiencing in therapy. In L. S. Greenberg, J. C. Watson, & G. Lietaer (Eds.), *Handbook of experiential psychotherapy* (pp. 3–27). New York: Guilford.

Watson, J. C., & Rennie, D. (1994). A qualitative analysis of clients' reports of their subjective experience while exploring problematic reactions in therapy. *Journal of Counseling Psychology, 41*, 500–509.

Watzlawick, P., Weakland, J. H., & Fisch, R. (1974). Change: Principles of problem formation and problem resolution. New York: Norton.

Weakland, J. H., Fisch, R., Watzlawick, P., & Bodin, A. (1974). Brief therapy: Focused problem resolution. *Family Process, 13*, 141–168.

Wilson, G. T. (1998). Manual-based treatment and clinical practice. *Clinical Psychology: Science and Practice, 5*, 363–375.

Winston, A., Laikin, M., Pollack, J., Samstag, L. W., McCullough, L., & Muran, J. C. (1994). Short-term psychotherapy of personality disorders. *American Journal of Psychiatry, 151*, 190–194.

Wolberg, L. R. (1980). *Handbook of short-term psychotherapy*. New York: Thieme-Stratton.

Wolfe, B. E., & Sigl, P. (1998). Experiential psychotherapy of the anxiety disorders. In L. Greenberg, J. C. Watson, & G. Lietaer (Eds.), *Handbook of experiential psychotherapy* (pp. 272–294). New York: Guilford.

Young, J. E. (1999). *Cognitive therapy for personality disorders: A schema-focused approach* (3rd ed.). Sarasota, FL: Professional Resource Press.

CHAPTER 18

# Crisis Intervention

LISA M. BROWN, JULIA SHIANG, AND BRUCE BONGAR

During the course of a lifetime all people experience a variety of personal traumas, such as divorce or illness, and many others will also live through cataclysmic events, such as natural disasters or acts of violence, that result in a state of crisis. An underlying assumption of crisis intervention theory is that crises are universal and can and do happen to everyone (James & Gilliland, 2001). International media coverage of earthquakes, floods, famine, war, and acts of terrorism provides poignant reminders of this fact.

The difference between a disaster and an accident is a matter of degree. In a disaster, the social structure is adversely affected, which in turn threatens the existence and functioning of an entire group, in contrast to the experience of individual trauma that results from an accident or act of crime (Eranen & Liebkind, 1993). The worldwide prevalence of people traumatized by disaster and war, terrorism, intrafamilial abuse, crime, and rape, as well as school and workplace violence, is significant. Indeed, some researchers found that approximately 40% of all children and teens will experience a traumatic stressor and that the lifetime prevalence for trauma exposure may be as high as 90% (Breslau et al., 1998; Ford, Ruzek, & Niles, 1996).

It is generally recognized that exposure to traumatic stressors without effective psychological intervention can trigger adverse, long-term effects that can become extremely difficult to resolve as an individual moves through subsequent developmental stages. The timely delivery of appropriate treatment is imperative during the acute crisis phase to mitigate the potential for psychopathological sequelae, such as posttraumatic stress disorder (PTSD).

However, it is important to note that not all individuals suffer physical and psychological deterioration in the aftermath of a crisis. Although exposure to traumatic stressors can be potentially hazardous to an individual's well-being, crisis states can also provide an avenue for personal growth (Tedeschi, Park, & Calhoun, 1998). In fact, Gerald Caplan, the founder of modern crisis intervention, argued that crisis is a necessary precursor to growth (1961, p. 19). The coping process, a time during which an individual strives for equilibrium or stability in response to a stressor, provides a venue for achieving either a higher or lower level of functioning than the precrisis state and creates a foundation for future development.

The idea that crisis can result in a positive or negative outcome is illustrated by two Chinese characters, one symbolizing "danger" and the other "opportunity." When combined to create the word "crisis," these symbols convey the potential as well as the dual meaning of the word. In the English language, the word "crisis" is derived from the Greek word "krinein," which translates as "to decide." As with the Chinese character for "crisis," derivatives of this term also capture the idea that the potential for either a detrimental or a beneficial outcome exists in the aftermath of a crisis.

Researchers and mental health clinicians have developed a number of definitions for the word "crisis" in the English language. In general, each of these definitions conveys a number of common concepts: Exposure to a traumatic or dangerous event leads to acute distress, which results in psychological disequilibrium, a state wherein the employment of familiar coping strategies has failed, creating the potential for cognitive, physical, emotional, and behavioral impairment.

Crisis intervention services are now widely recognized as an efficacious treatment modality for the provision of emergency mental health care to individuals and groups. In the past decade, there has been a proliferation of empirical outcome studies resulting in the development and refinement of a variety of effective assessment and intervention techniques. Psychologists need to be able to diagnose and treat disorders associated with trauma (e.g., PTSD, generalized anxiety disorder, and depression), provide consultation to medical personnel, educate the community and other crisis intervention service providers about normal responses to abnormal events, and assist in the implementation of emergency mental health care for communities, hospitals, and community agencies. It is critical for psychologists to be well trained in assessment, to have knowledge of useful crisis intervention techniques, and to be able to work effectively with other agencies in providing emergency mental health services.

### Chapter Overview

This chapter will present a summary of the historical highlights and the theoretical influences on the development of modern crisis intervention theory. As crisis intervention evolved into a recognized discipline, a number of models were developed that described, clarified, and formulated assessments and treatments used in providing emergency psychological care. These models provide the groundwork for our current understanding of crisis intervention and will be discussed along with newer models that have recently been advanced, such as Critical Incident Stress Management and Critical Incident Stress Debriefing.

Just as there are many different types of crises, health care professionals and agencies that provide crisis intervention services have developed a variety of effective assessments and treatments. An overview of solution-focused therapy, cognitive therapy, and other useful techniques will be presented, and the differences between brief psychotherapy and crisis inter-

vention will be delineated. The differences and similarities in the delivery of emergency mental health services to individuals and groups will be highlighted.

A conceptual overview will be described, along with a framework with which to identify, assess, and treat individuals or groups experiencing a crisis. We will specifically focus on three different events. Case examples will be used to illustrate the implementation of specific assessments and interventions in providing crisis intervention services to suicidal patients and victims of natural disaster and acts of terrorism, as well as patients and families struggling with debilitating illness.

A general framework for providing cross-cultural crisis intervention will also be presented. Sensitivity to and awareness of cultural differences, along with a basic knowledge of how different cultures respond to crisis and to therapeutic intervention, are necessary in providing an effective response. Crisis intervention terminology that is commonly used by health care providers, researchers, and social agencies will be noted and defined throughout this chapter. Additionally, current research and recent trends will be reviewed along with relevant legal issues.

Finally, most psychologists providing crisis mental health services will find themselves working in conjunction with other social agencies such as the police, hospital personnel, mobile crisis units, and the American Red Cross. Typically, a psychologist works as a member of a mental health team when providing crisis intervention services at the disaster site or in a variety of mental health care settings. A description of how such teams are formed and mobilized will be provided.

### HISTORY AND THEORY OF CRISIS INTERVENTION

During World War I, Salmon (1919) observed French and English medical teams treating soldiers suffering from war neuroses. He noted that timely interventions, conducted within close proximity to the battle zone, increased the number of soldiers who were able to return to combat and reduced the degree of adverse psychiatric consequences experienced by those traumatized by battle. World War I veterans who were psychologically disturbed by combat-related trauma, but were without physical wounds, were described as "shell-shocked" and were treated for combat neurosis. The long-endorsed idea that "time heals all wounds" was first challenged during World War I and would be further disputed during World War II.

During World War II, combat-related PTSD was referred to as "battle fatigue." The concepts of immediacy, proximity, and expectancy were acknowledged as critical elements in providing treatment to combat-fatigued soldiers during World War II. The goal was to treat distressed soldiers quickly and as close to the front line as possible in order to have them rapidly return to duty. However, recent research findings based on several decades of accumulated evidence indicate that many World War I and World War II veterans experienced the first onset of PTSD, or an exacerbation of symptoms, in late life (Ruskin & Talbott, 1996). Although it is unclear why the onset of combat-related PTSD was delayed for decades, some researchers hypothesized that many older adults were underdiagnosed because these veterans did not associate their postwar difficulties with their combat experiences. It also may be that health care clinicians attributed the symptoms experienced and reported by these veterans as solely related to alcoholism, depression, schizophrenia, or anxiety disorders. However, PTSD is often comorbid; in other words, a variety of mental illnesses can and do occur with PTSD (James & Gilliland, 2000; Zlotnick et al., 1999). Additionally, late-life stressors such as retirement, death, illness, economic hardship, and declining mental and physical well-being erode existing structure and social supports that earlier in life provided a modulating influence against the onset of PTSD symptoms (Hamilton & Workman, 1998).

Veterans suffering from combat neurosis, as well as bereaved family members, were treated with interventions that were adapted from those developed earlier by Erich Lindemann, a psychiatrist, to treat grieving family members who had lost a loved one in the 1942 Coconut Grove nightclub fire in Boston. Lindemann and his colleagues at Massachusetts General Hospital clinically observed the acute and delayed reactions of the relatives of the 492 victims who died in the fire. Although most individuals did not present psychopathological symptoms in response to the death of a loved one, some did develop acute grief reactions that appeared pathological. Lindemann (1944) found that these individuals exhibited temporary behavioral changes that were precipitated by the loss and were ameliorated by short-term interventions. He championed the idea that an individual's expression of grief after experiencing a significant loss should not be considered as abnormal or pathological but as a normal manifestation in reaction to a traumatic stressor. Historically, modern crisis intervention theory evolved from Lindemann's (1944) classic study of acute grief reaction.

Lindemann (1944) delineated five related normal grief reactions: (a) somatic distress; (b) preoccupation with the image of the deceased person; (c) guilt; (d) hostile reactions; and (e) the loss of patterns of conduct (Lindemann, 1944, p. 142). The extent of the individual's grief reaction was influenced by the degree of successful readjustment to the environment without the loved one, the ability to free himself or herself

from the deceased, and the facility to develop new relationships. Until this time, personality disorders or biochemical illnesses were thought to be the cause of grief-related depression or anxiety, and the provision of therapy to treat these symptoms was considered to be the exclusive domain of psychiatry. Notably, in the aftermath of this tragedy, Lindemann came to accept that community paraprofessionals and clergy could be just as effective in providing crisis intervention services as psychiatrists.

Lindemann and Gerald Caplan founded the Wellesley project, a community mental health program in Cambridge, Massachusetts, subsequent to the disastrous Coconut Grove nightclub fire, to provide crisis intervention and community outreach. An equilibrium/disequilibrium paradigm was developed that depicted the process of crisis intervention in treating an individual's reaction to a traumatic stressor. The paradigm included four stages: (a) The individual's equilibrium is disrupted, (b) the individual engages in grief work or brief therapy, (c) the individual experiences some resolution of the problem, and (d) the individual's equilibrium is restored.

The rationale for crisis intervention was that the provision of guidance and support to individuals in crisis would avert prolonged mental health problems. Lindemann and Caplan believed that when people are in a state of crisis they feel anxious, are more receptive to help and suggestion, and are motivated to change. Whereas Lindemann (1944) provided the foundation for understanding and treating acute grief reactions, Caplan (1964) used the concepts to expand the use of crisis intervention strategies in treating all developmental and situational traumatic events.

Crisis, as defined by Caplan (1961), is a state that results when an individual confronts obstacles to significant life goals that cannot be surmounted through the use of normal problem-solving efforts. Psychological homeostasis describes the balance or equilibrium between the affective and cognitive experience. When a disruption in psychological functioning occurs, an individual will engage in behaviors to restore balance or equilibrium. Traumatic events can create a state of disequilibrium.

Disequilibrium is defined as a time when an individual is unable to find a solution to a problem or when normal coping mechanisms fail, resulting in an inability to restore the state of equilibrium and disrupting homeostasis. The outcome, according to Caplan (1964), is acute distress accompanied by some level of functional impairment. Early intervention was the key to encouraging the potential for positive growth and, conversely, discouraging possible psychological impairment. Possible sequelae mentioned by Caplan (1969) included depression, panic, cognitive distortions, physical complaints, and maladaptive behavior.

Four stages of crisis reaction were described by Caplan (1964). The first stage involves an increase in tension that results from an emotionally threatening, crisis-precipitating event. The second stage is a period when daily functioning is disrupted because the individual experiences an increased level of tension and is unable to quickly resolve the crisis. The third stage may lead to depression when tension levels steadily increase to an intense level and the individual's coping mechanisms continue to fail. During the last stage, an individual may use different coping mechanisms to partly solve the crisis, or a mental breakdown may ensue.

In the late 1950s, several events accelerated the development of a diverse offering of crisis intervention services and fostered the growth of formalized crisis intervention programs. The advent of the Los Angeles Suicide Prevention Center, developed by suicidologists Norman Farberow and Edwin Shneidman, provided a successful template that would foster the growth of suicide prevention hot lines. In the 1960s, walk-in clinics and crisis hot lines, many of which were manned by nonprofessional volunteers, provided care for victims of rape and domestic violence and counseled those at risk for suicide.

The Short-Doyle Act, enacted by the California Legislature in 1957, laid the groundwork for the deinstitutionalization of many chronically mentally ill individuals who were placed indefinitely in locked wards of publicly funded mental hospitals. This act provided counties with funding to organize and operate mental health clinics for individuals with mental illness through locally controlled and administered health programs. The Community Mental Health Centers Act, passed by Congress six years later in 1963, was the outcome of President John Kennedy's vision for a new approach in the delivery of mental health services. The development of a national network of community-based mental health service centers was intended to provide services to chronically mentally ill patients. Crisis intervention services would be offered as a type of preventive outreach. Caplan (1961, 1964) defined the concepts of preventive psychiatry that would guide the delivery of these newly mandated services, the objective of which was to decrease "1) the incidence of mental disorders of all types in a community; 2) the duration of a significant number of those disorders which do occur; and 3) the impairment which may result from those disorders" (Caplan, 1964, pp. 16–17).

However, the goals established by the Community Mental Health Centers Act were not achieved, because the majority of mental health services provided by the clinics were not utilized by the seriously and chronically mentally ill but were being used by individuals with emotional and psychological problems that were previously treated by psychologists and psychiatrists in private practice. As a result, many individuals with chronic mental illness were not receiving adequate treatment.

In 1968 the Lanterman Petris Short Bill was passed by Congress to address this concern, and it placed new requirements on the type and delivery of mental health services made available through the clinics. Individuals without chronic mental illness were now offered short-term crisis intervention, whereas the seriously mentally ill were provided with long-term case management services.

Dramatic changes at the policy level have brought about (some might say forced) greater cooperation within the disciplines of mental health as well as across agencies. Since the passage of the Community Mental Health Centers Act, all community mental health centers receiving federal funding must provide 24-hour crisis and emergency services (Ligon, 2000). The focus at that time was to promote a transition from mental health services provided by institutions to services provided by the community. As deinstitutionalization continued over the years and the goal became focused on helping patients stabilize over a few days rather than providing long-term care, community programs have had to rapidly expand to accommodate the increased demand for emergency psychiatric services.

## Short-Term Crisis Intervention

The successful delivery of short-term crisis intervention services, coupled with the public's growing recognition that 24-hour psychiatric emergency treatment (PET) was effective and essential in responding to suicidal, homicidal, and psychotic crises, increased both the demand for and the development of community-based services. The theoretical basis for these programs is the principles of both public health and preventative mental health treatments and does not focus on identifying and treating psychopathology. Outreach programs were developed with the goals of identifying high-risk groups, promoting community recovery, and minimizing social disruption (Ursano, Fullerton, & Norwood, 1995). Emergency suicide hot lines, rape crisis centers, battered women's shelters, crisis intervention units, and community crisis centers flourished during the 1970s. In fact, the number of community mental health centers grew from 376 centers in 1969 to nearly 800 centers by the early 1980s (Foley & Sharfstein, 1983).

Three decades later, the short-term crisis intervention model continues to be used by community mental health centers and is also popular with health maintenance organizations (HMOs), preferred provider organizations (PPOs), and a number of insurance carriers. Managed care firms justify limiting their patients to four to six sessions with a trained mental health clinician based on their interpretation of community

**TABLE 18.1   Historical Milestones in Crisis Intervention**

- World War I: the first empirical evidence that early intervention reduces chronic psychiatry morbidity.
- World War II: the process of immediacy, proximity, and expectancy identified as important "active ingredients" in effective emergency psychological response.
- 1944: Lindemann's observations of grief reactions to the Coconut Grove fire begin "modern era" of crisis intervention.
- Late 1950s: community suicide prevention programs proliferate.
- 1963–64: Caplan's three tiers of preventive psychiatry delineated and implemented within the newly created community mental health system (primary, secondary, tertiary prevention).
- Late 1960s–early 1970s: crisis intervention principals applied to reduce the need for hospitalization of potentially "chronic" populations.
- 1980: formal nosological recognition of posttraumatic stress disorder in *DSM-III* "legitimizes" crisis and traumatic events as threats to long-term health.
- 1982: Air Florida 90 air disaster in Washington, D.C. prompts reexamination of psychological support for emergency response personnel; first mass disaster use of the group crisis intervention Critical Incident Stress Debriefing (CISD), which was originally formulated in 1974.
- 1986: "violence in the workplace" era begins with death of 13 postal workers on the job.
- 1989: International Critical Incident Stress Foundation (ICISF) formalizes an international network of over 350 crisis response teams trained in a standardized and comprehensive crisis intervention model (CISM); ICISF gains United Nations affiliation in 1997.
- 1992: American Red Cross initiates formal training for the establishment of a nationwide disaster mental capability; Hurricane Andrew tests new mental health function.
- 1993: Social Development Office (Amiri Diwam), ICISF, Kuwait University, et al. implement a nationwide crisis intervention system for postwar Kuwait.
- 1994: *DSM-IV* recognizes Acute Stress Disorder, emphasizes impairment in PTSD.
- 1995: bombing of the Federal Building in Oklahoma City underscores need for crisis services for rescue personnel, as well as civilians.
- 1996: TWA 800 mass air disaster emphasizes the need for emergency mental health services for families of the victims of trauma and disasters; OSHA 43148-1996 recommends comprehensive violence or crisis intervention in social service and health care setting.
- 1997: Gore Commission recommends crisis services for airline industry.
- 1998: OSHA 3153-1998 recommends crisis intervention programs for late-night retail stores.
- 1999: COMDTINST 1754.3 requires each U.S. Coast Guard region to develop an ICISF-model CISM team.
- 2001: terrorist attacks on the World Trade Towers and Pentagon Building result in the creation of the Office of Homeland Security to coordinate emergency services and efforts of federal, state, and local law enforcement agencies in responding to disasters.

Reprinted with permission from Everly and Mitchell, 1999.

center program evaluations that reported that short-term interventions were as beneficial as long-term psychotherapy (Kanel, 1999). In recent years, managed care has also had a significant effect on the delivery of services at the clinical level and in the administration of mental health services.

As part of a typical managed care treatment plan, patients are frequently referred to other community services, such as Alcoholics Anonymous and community-based support groups, to augment brief therapy. In general, managed care firms find short-term crisis interventions appealing because they are cost-effective therapeutic treatments.

More recently, Jeffrey Mitchell and George Everly developed a comprehensive, integrative, multicomponent program, Critical Incident Stress Management. A review of Critical Incident Stress Debriefing as a component of Critical Incident Stress Management is discussed later in this chapter (Everly & Mitchell, 1999). A summary of key historical events in crisis intervention theory and service development is presented in Table 18.1.

## STRESS AND COPING

Crisis intervention is now recognized as an effective component of a psychologist's therapeutic repertoire for helping individuals deal with the challenges and threats of overwhelming stress. As noted earlier, all individuals experience stress in the normal course of their lives. Although stress in and of itself is not harmful, it may precipitate a crisis if the anxiety accompanying it exceeds the individual's ability to cope.

### Stress

Stressful events may adversely impact everyday functioning and potentially lead to long-term impairment. A number of factors influence personal vulnerability. These include individual differences, such as age, personality type, health, worldview, life experiences, phase of development, support system, and cultural values. Also, the timing, intensity, and type of disturbance can be significant. Moreover, people possess different levels of stress tolerance, ways of coping with adversity, and access to social supports (Lazarus & Folkman, 1984; Myers, 1989). An individual's reaction to stress results from a complex interaction among these factors.

Some events that can potentially result in crisis are predictable, whereas others are not. Examples of unpredictable events include earthquakes or the sudden death of a loved one. In contrast, other situations are anticipated and gradually climax in a state of crisis. Examples include a long-distance move to another community, divorce, and death resulting from terminal illness.

Stressful events that evolve into an expected outcome offer the opportunity for gradual understanding and assimilation of the imminent loss or transition. The individual is not forced to abruptly absorb the distressing reality of an irrevocable event. A single stressful event may not be harmful, but the accumulative affects of such events over time can be intolerable. Therefore, the precipitating factor in a crisis may not be as significant as the series of events that precede it and create a vulnerable state for the person.

As noted earlier, people have different levels of stress tolerance, but cumulative crisis events exact demands for adaptation that ultimately exhaust emotional reserves, even in individuals possessing high tolerance levels. Although successful resolution of a crisis may result in personal growth and a higher level of functioning than in the precrisis state, psychic assaults from recurring, multiple crisis events would eventually lead to disorganization and disintegration of adequate coping abilities. If a person is able to cope with the stressful event without suffering subjective distress, then he or she will most likely experience stress and not a crisis.

## Coping

Coping and appraisal are closely related processes. The threat appraisal process involves three components: primary appraisal, secondary appraisal, and coping (Lazarus, 1966). Primary appraisal is the individual's perception of the event. It is important to note that the perception of an event, rather than the situation itself, is different for each individual. People experience the same event differently because of individual differences (as noted above) that influence their perception of the crisis. Hence, crisis is self-defined: It is the person's response to an internal or external event rather than the event itself. In other words, exposure to the same precipitating event may result in crisis for one person but not for another. A stressful event in and of itself does not constitute a crisis.

A crisis is determined by the individual's perception (primary appraisal) and his or her potential response to the event (secondary appraisal). The response that is executed in reaction to the stressful event is defined as coping. Coping can be either emotion focused or problem focused (Folkman & Lazarus, 1980; Lazarus, 1966). The goal of emotion-focused coping is to reduce emotional distress that is associated with the situation, whereas problem-focused coping strives to alter the relationship between the person and the source of the stress. Most stressors typically elicit both types of coping. Emotion-focused coping usually predominates when people feel that the stressor is something that must be endured, whereas problem-focused coping prevails when people feel that action can be taken to alter the source of the stress (Folkman & Lazarus, 1980).

If an event is perceived as threatening, and in response the individual's typical coping strategies fail and he or she is unable to pursue or is unaware of alternative coping strategies, then the precipitating event may result in a state of crisis, in which the person experiences feelings of helplessness, anger, anxiety, inadequacy, confusion, fear, disorganization, guilt, and agitation (Smead, 1988).

According to Roberts (2000), a crisis is "defined as a period of psychological disequilibrium, experienced as a result of a hazardous event or situation that constitutes a significant problem that cannot be remedied by using familiar coping strategies" (p. 7). James and Gilliland (2001) defined "crisis" as "a perception of an event or situation as an intolerable difficulty that exceeds the resources and coping mechanisms of the person. Unless the person obtains relief, the crisis has the potential to cause severe affective, cognitive, and behavioral malfunctioning" (p. 3).

Crises can be categorized as developmental, situational, existential, or environmental (James & Gilliland, 2001). Developmental crises arise from predictable, normal change and are internally caused situations that result from growth and role transitions, such as the onset of adolescence (Caplan, 1964; Erickson, 1950). Situational crises are externally caused situations that are unpredictable, such as the loss of a job, an accidental death, or natural disaster. The threat of loss (death, separation, illness) that occurs with a change in circumstances can precipitate a crisis reaction (Caplan, 1964). "The key to differentiating a situational crisis from other crises is that a situational crisis is random, sudden, shocking, intense, and often catastrophic" (James & Gilliland, 2001, p. 5).

Existential crisis acknowledges the turmoil of "inner conflicts and anxieties that accompany important issues of purpose, responsibility, independence, freedom and commitment" (James & Gilliland, 2001, p. 6). For example, the remorse that can accompany a person's knowledge that certain opportunities (career, marriage, children) are no longer available at age 60 that were once options at age 30 can result in feelings of emptiness for some individuals that can be difficult to remedy. Individuals or groups of people are at risk for exposure to environmental crises that are natural or human caused, biologically derived, politically based, or the result of severe economic depression (James & Gilliland, 2001).

To maintain equilibrium, people employ compensatory mechanisms when confronted with minor challenges and disturbances. "Commonly used compensatory mechanisms might include denial of the problem, rationalization, intellectualization, creation of a psychological carapace, and/or problem solving techniques" (Everly & Mitchell, 1999, p. 24). When coping and compensatory mechanisms fail and the threat of the situation cannot be adequately resolved, then most individuals are typically unable to reestablish psychological homeostasis, resulting in a state of crisis. It is at this point that symptoms of decompensation become evident: panic (psychological and physiological symptoms), depression, hypomania, somatoform conversion reactions (deficits in the motor or sensory systems), acute stress disorder (ASD), PTSD, grief or bereavement reactions, psychophysiological disorders (medical conditions that are exacerbated or caused by extreme stress; see Everly, 1989, for an in-depth discussion of the physiology of stress response mechanisms), brief reactive psychosis, obsessive-compulsive disorders, and other crisis-related symptoms (anger, violence, suicide; Everly & Mitchell, 1999, pp. 25–32).

Flight, fight, or freeze behaviors (survival-mode functioning) are specialized cognitive-affective mechanisms that are activated when individuals are confronted with life-threatening events (Chemtob, Roitblat, Hamada, & Carlson, 1988). These behaviors are adaptive in the context of a threatening incident but are deleterious to well-being if they persist after the event. Osterman and Chemtob (1999) posit that persistence of the survival-mode functioning accounts for the clinical presentation of traumatized patients. "High levels of anxiety and avoidance are associated with flight responses; increased anger and aggression represent the persistent mobilization of a fight response; and dissociative symptoms, emotional numbing, or depersonalization reflect freeze responses" (Osterman & Chemtob, 1999, p. 739). It is essential to start working with individuals as soon as possible after a crisis to prevent this chronic cycle of behaviors from developing.

### Acute Stress Disorder and Posttraumatic Stress Disorder

Posttraumatic stress disorder was first recognized as a diagnostic category, and was classified as a subcategory of anxiety disorders, in the 1980 *Diagnostic and Statistical Manual of Mental Disorders III* (American Psychiatric Association, 1980). The definition of ASD was included as an independent entity in the 1994 version of the *Diagnostic and Statistical Manual of Mental Disorders IV* (*DSM-IV;* American Psychiatric Association, 1994). The symptoms of ASD differ from those of PTSD in three ways. "The disturbance [for ASD] lasts for a minimum of 2 days and a maximum of 4 weeks and occurs within 4 weeks of the traumatic event" (APA, 1994, pp. 431–432), whereas the duration of the disturbance for PTSD is for at least 1 month (APA, 1994, pp. 427–429). Additionally, the person with PTSD experiences at least three symptoms signifying dissociation, and the dissociative symptoms may prevent the individual from effectively coping with the trauma.

The percentage of individuals exposed to severe trauma who eventually develop PTSD varies from 10% to 12%. The reader is encouraged to refer to the *DSM-IV* (APA, 1994) for a complete description of the criteria for ASD and PTDS. Clinicians providing crisis intervention to individuals and groups should be familiar with the diagnostic criteria for both these disorders.

## BRIEF AND LONG-TERM PSYCHOTHERAPY VERSUS CRISIS INTERVENTION

Crisis theory is comprised of an eclectic mix of theoretical modalities. It draws on cognitive-behavioral, psychoanalytic, existential, humanistic, and general systems theories (Callahan, 1998; Kanel, 1999). Although a number of models have been developed to describe the intervention process, they all share two characteristics. Crisis interventions are time limited and are designed to help individuals return to their precrisis level of functioning (Gilliland & James, 1993; Puryear, 1979; Roberts, 1991). The focus is on decreasing acute psychological disturbances rather than curing long-term personality or mental disorders. A principle of crisis intervention is that the person's symptoms are not viewed as indicative of personality deterioration or mental illness but, rather, are viewed as signs that the individual is experiencing a period of transition that is disruptive and distressing but relatively brief in duration. The goal is to help individuals and groups deal with the stressful transition period. Most people in crisis realize they need aid but do not perceive themselves as mentally ill.

As noted earlier, perception of, and the meaning ascribed to, an event is a critical factor in determining whether the individual can cope. The meaning a person gives to an event has been described as the "cognitive key" with which to unlock the door to understanding the patient's experience of the crisis (Slaikeu, 1990, p. 18). It affects what individuals do in response to the event and whom or what they blame for the incident. Meaning is dynamic, not static, and it changes over time as the context changes. By understanding the meaning of an event, clinicians can reframe their patients' cognitions to assist them in reducing their immediate suffering, increasing their coping capabilities, and preventing long-term adverse physical, affective, and behavioral consequences.

Crisis interventions differ from traditional psychotherapy in a number of significant ways. Crisis counseling typically takes place in community crisis clinics or at the site of the traumatic event, as in the case of natural disasters or violence at school or in the workplace. Crisis interventions are conducted immediately following a traumatic event, in contrast to an office-based therapy, in which patients usually schedule ongoing weekly appointments. Traditional therapy concentrates on diagnosis and treatment with collaborative goals of personal growth and improvement of functioning by encouraging insight (psychodynamic) or examination of thoughts, feelings, and behaviors (cognitive-behavioral therapy). An overview of how crisis intervention differs from psychotherapy is presented in Table 18.2.

In contrast, for individuals in crisis, the focus is on understanding the meaning of the crisis, assessing the idiosyncratic characteristics of the individual, learning about the strengths and weaknesses of the individual's support system, and adapting and developing the person's coping skills, all with the minimal goal of restoring precrisis levels of functioning. In general, crisis interventions are directive and supportive with the goal of lessening any adverse impact on future mental health.

Wainrib and Bloch (1998) noted that because a crisis can evoke either a positive or negative reaction, it creates an environment in which one "reassesses one's life" (p. 28). During this state people may be more receptive to new information and willing to try new coping strategies (Puryear, 1979). After a crisis, many individuals may strive to attain their precrisis level of functioning, whereas others may not be able to fully reconstruct their lives. However, some people may find that the successful resolution of a crisis serves as a catalyst that can bring about growth, positive change, and enhanced coping ability, as well as a decrease in negative behavior, resulting in a higher postcrisis level of functioning (Janosik, 1984, pp. 3–21). The acquisition of new skills and coping mechanisms to deal with the current crisis situation can foster psychological and emotional growth as well as benefiting the individual when he or she is confronted with new crisis or stressful situations in the future (Fraser, 1998).

TABLE 18.2   Crisis Intervention Versus Psychotherapy

|  | Crisis Intervention | Psychotherapy |
| --- | --- | --- |
| Context | Prevention, acute mitigation, restoration | Reparation, reconstruction, growth |
| Timing | Immediate, close temporal relationship to stressor or acute decompensation | Delayed, distant from stress or acute decompensation |
| Location | Close proximity to stressor or acute decompensation; anywhere needed | Safe, secure environment |
| Duration | One to three contacts, typically | As long as needed/desired |
| Therapist's role | Active, directive | Guiding, collaborative, consultative |
| Strategic foci | Conscious processes and environmental stressors or factors | Conscious and unconscious sources of pathogenesis |
| Temporal focus | Here and now | Past and present |
| Patient expectation | Directive, symptom reduction; reduction of impairment; directive support | Symptom reduction, reduction of impairment, personal growth; guidance and collaboration |
| Goals | Stabilize, reduce impairment, return to function, or move to next level of care | Symptom reduction, reduction of impairment, correction of pathogenesis, personal growth; personal reconstruction |

Reprinted with permission from Everly and Mitchell, 1999.

## Assessment and Intervention

Psychologists conducting standard diagnostic assessments in an office or hospital employ knowledge of life span development and psychopathology and utilize a diagnostic classification system such as the *DSM-IV* or ICD-10 to guide and organize their treatments.

A measurement of the severity of the psychosocial stressors experienced by the patient is noted on the *DSM-IV* Axis V (Generalized Assessment of Functioning). The patient's current level of functioning is determined by the clinician from a list of identified behaviors that are ranked from 0 to 100, with higher scores indicating greater overall functioning and coping (APA, 1994). Rating scores assigned at the beginning of treatment can be used to monitor the course of therapy. It is often helpful to compare the patient's current level of functioning to his or her highest level of functioning attained during the past year.

Crisis workers generally do not have the luxury of time to collect and analyze medical and mental health records that might be available under normal conditions. An abbreviated assessment process, whose objective is to quickly formulate an assessment and to understand the meaning the individual has ascribed to the crisis, should include an exploration of the precipitating event and past events that were similar, because memories of past losses and bereavement typically resurface in current loss situations.

An assessment of the individual must be made in conjunction with an appraisal of the nature and scope of the crisis in order to better delineate his or her experience. Was the individual a victim or a witness? The closer the proximity (temporal and physical) to the event and the greater the degree of perceived threat, the greater the potential for adverse physical and psychological sequelae.

Psychologists working with individuals in crisis must be able to quickly evaluate the degree of disequilibrium experienced by the individual and calmly convey support, acceptance, and confidence about the future. Assessments may have to be conducted at the site of the event and may be limited to less than 15 or 20 minutes. In instances in which a group has been exposed to a traumatic event, it is often beneficial to meet for a group assessment for a longer period of time. The "norm" of the group can be quickly determined, and individuals who deviate from the norm can be identified as being at high risk for adverse reactions (Wainrib & Bloch, 1998). Specific intervention plans can then be developed that address the needs of individuals, wherever they lie on the risk spectrum. Assessment is an overarching and ongoing process that takes place during each phase of crisis intervention.

Assessment should include asking about the individual's perception of the crisis, the sequence of events, current feelings, and a description of his or her attempts to deal with the problem. Is the individual safe? What is the individual's emotional affect, alcohol and drug usage, and current stress level? All individuals should be evaluated on an ongoing basis to determine if they pose a threat to themselves or others.

Although a number of protocols have been developed to guide clinicians in assessment and treatment, we present the steps for three that best represent key approaches to crisis intervention. An outline of the steps Puryear (1979) recommended includes the following: (a) immediate intervention, (b) action (actively assessing and formulating), (c) limited goal (averting catastrophe and restoring growth and hope), (d) hope and expectation, (e) support, (f) focused problem solving, (g) enhancement of self-image, and (h) encouragement of self-reliance.

A seven-stage approach to crisis intervention was developed by Roberts (1991, 2000): (a) Assess client lethality and safety needs, (b) establish rapport and communications, (c) identify the major problem, (d) deal with feelings and provide support, (e) explore possible alternatives, (f) assist in formulating an action plan, and (g) perform follow-up.

More recently, James and Gilliland (2001) created a six-step, "action-oriented situation-based method of crisis intervention," which includes the following steps: (a) Define the problem, (b) ensure client safety, (c) provide support, (d) examine alternatives, (e) make plans, and (f) obtain commitment to positive actions (p. 33). Within this framework, the clinician should assess (a) the severity of the crisis; (b) the client's current emotional status; (c) the alternatives, coping mechanisms, support systems, and other available resources; and (d) the client's level of lethality (danger to self and others). Although experts in this area may differ on the terms and number of steps required, they do agree that specific elements are essential and fundamental to intervention.

### Planning and Implementing the Intervention

Planning and implementing the intervention occur after one has completed an assessment of the individual and the crisis. Basic concepts from each of these models include the following:

1. Establishing therapeutic rapport with the person. With open-ended questions, support, and empathy, encourage expression of feelings and thoughts without lecturing or using clichés such as "I understand" or "Be strong." Helpful remarks should be clear and straightforward, with the intent of assuring, normalizing, validating, and empowering the individual. Overwhelming emotions can block an individual's ability to think and cope.

2. Assisting the person with describing the problem to help find his or her own solution. When people develop their own solutions, they are more likely to follow through with them and are more willing to learn and use new coping skills.

3. Helping the person identify available resources, coping strategies, and sources of support. An examination of coping strategies helps the individual determine what worked and what did not in the past when dealing with stressors. With this knowledge the individual can develop new coping strategies to deal with the current and future difficulties. Providing advice or giving answers to people in crisis lowers self-esteem and fosters feelings of dependency on others to provide solutions.

4. Selecting one or more specific, time-limited goals that take into consideration the person's significant others, social network, culture, and lifestyle. Collaboratively develop a plan of action for recovery to help the person restabilize and begin moving toward the future. Assist the individual as he or she explores advantages and disadvantages of possible options. Summarize, focus, and clarify.

5. Implementing the plan and evaluating its effectiveness. Adjust the plan as necessary, and if ongoing care is needed, refer the individual to appropriate community resources that can provide it.

### CASE EXAMPLES

#### Suicide

Whether a psychologist works in a college counseling center, community mental health agency, inpatient setting, or outpatient private practice or with individuals in the aftermath of a disaster, he or she is likely to see people who present with an elevated risk for suicide. The psychologist must have readily at hand the crisis intervention and emergency management tools necessary to deal with the problem of patient suicidality as well as a familiarity with state laws. Psychologists should have a clear idea of what steps they can and should take once they believe that "an attempted suicide is likely: use of crisis intervention techniques, referral to an emergency service, referral to a psychiatrist for medication, and/or civil commitment" (Stromberg et al., 1988, p. 469). It is critical for the psychologist who assesses or treats suicidal patients to know the resources that are available for emergencies and outpatient crises. Specifically, the psychologist must know community crisis intervention resources and which hospital he or she might use for voluntary or involuntary hospitalization of suicidal patients, as well as having a thorough understanding of the procedures for each setting (Pope, 1986).

Suicide can result from any development or situational crisis. Individuals who feel overwhelmed and confused, along with experiencing intense loss, anger, and grief, can view suicide as a viable alternative. There is a consensus that crisis management principally entails therapeutic activism, the delaying of the patient's suicidal impulses, the restoring of hope, environmental intervention, and consideration of hospitalization (Fremouw, de Perczel, & Ellis, 1990).

### Case Vignette

Sonya recently moved from the Midwest to a large city to start a new job. Shortly after she arrived she lost her job when her company downsized her division. A week later her apartment was burglarized. A strained relationship with her parents prevented Sonya from asking them for financial help, and returning home was not an option. As the days passed, Sonya found it increasingly difficult to concentrate, eat, get out of bed, and look for employment. She was running short of funds and realized that she would not be able to pay her rent and was facing eviction. A counselor at her church met with her and learned that Sonya viewed suicide as a way to escape an intolerable situation and that she felt hopeless about the future.

### Assessment and Risk Factors

Because the suicidology literature is voluminous, diverse, and sometimes contradictory, psychologists may have difficulty determining the relative importance of various factors when assessing individuals for suicide risk. Simon (1987) stated, "there are no pathognomic predictors of suicide" (p. 259). Because each individual is unique, the nature of assessment and measurement is difficult. Motto (1991) noted that a measure or observation that may determine suicide risk in one person might have different significance or no relevance at all for another. Clinicians need an opportunity to establish a level of trust that assures candor and openness in order to be in an optimal position to assess risk (Motto, 1991). Sonya's counselor was able to establish a relationship with her and indeed found, upon direct query, that she had experienced a series of acute stressors and in response, as she felt increasingly depressed and hopeless, developed a specific plan for committing suicide.

A complete evaluation of risk factors, including Sonya's psychiatric diagnosis, substance abuse, previous suicide attempts, a family history of suicide, and current level of functioning, should be considered in conjunction with psychological assessment results (Bongar, 1992; Maris, Berman, Maltsberger, & Yufit, 1992). An integrated perspective on assessment and treatment of Sonya's suicidality must be maintained (Simon, 1992). However, it should be emphasized that the assessment of Sonya's risk for suicide should never be based on a single score, measure, or scale (Bongar, 2002).

Any suicidal crisis (ideation, threat, gesture, or actual attempt) is a true emergency situation: It must be dealt with as a life-threatening issue in clinical practice and should prompt an examination of the lethality potential of present or previous suicidal situations. Factors that substantially increase Sonya's imminent risk include the presence of a specific plan by the patient, accessibility of lethal means, the presence of syntonic or dystonic suicidal impulses, behavior suggestive of a decision to die, and admission of wanting to die (Bongar, 2002).

Among the most serious risk factors are those of various psychiatric disorders, such as schizophrenia, major depression, bipolar disorder, borderline personality disorder, and alcoholism or drug abuse (Asnis et al., 1993; Linehan, 1997, 1999; Stoelb & Chiriboga, 1998). In a comprehensive review of the literature, Tanney (1992) found that more than 90% of adults who have committed suicide were suffering from a diagnosable psychiatric disorder at the time of their death. It is clear that proper diagnosis and treatment of acute psychiatric illness can lower the risk for suicide, and it is necessary to recognize that "the most basic management principle is to understand that most suicide victims kill themselves in the midst of a psychiatric episode" (Brent, Kupfer, Bromet, & Dew, 1988, p. 365). Brent and his colleagues (Brent, Bridge, Johnson, & Connolly, 1996) noted the need to involve the family for support and improved treatment compliance.

There are a number of social clues, including Sonya's putting her affairs in order, giving away her prized possessions, behaving in any way that is markedly different from her usual pattern of living, saying good-bye to her friends or psychotherapist, and settling her estate (Beck, 1967; Shneidman, 1985). The presence of one or more of the following psychological variables represents increased risk for completed suicide (Shneidman, 1986).

- Acute perturbation (the person is very upset or agitated).
- The availability of lethal means (e.g., purchasing or having available a gun, rope, poison, etc.).
- An increase in self-hatred or self-loathing.
- A constriction in the person's ability to see alternatives to his or her present situation.
- The idea that death may be a way out of terrible psychological pain.

- Intense feelings of depression, helplessness, and hopelessness.
- Fantasies of death as an escape, including retrospectives, on patient's own funeral (imagined scenes of life after death increase the risk).
- A loss of pleasure or interest in life.
- The feeling that he or she is a source of shame to his or her family or significant others, or evidence that the patient has suffered a recent humiliation.

Five specific components in the general formulation of suicide risk were identified by Maltsberger (1988):

1. Assessing the patient's past responses to stress, especially losses.
2. Assessing the patient's vulnerability to three life-threatening affects: aloneness, self-contempt, and murderous rage.
3. Determining the nature and availability of exterior sustaining resources.
4. Assessing the emergence and emotional importance of death fantasies.
5. Assessing the patient's capacity for reality testing (p. 48).

The following brief inquiry developed by Motto (1989) is appropriate in settings where rapid decisions must be made (e.g., the emergency room, or consult service of a general hospital) or when a brief screening device is needed. This approach rests on the premise that "going directly to the heart of the issue is a practical and effective clinical tool, and patients and collaterals will usually provide valid information if an attitude of caring concern is communicated to them" (p. 247).

1. Do you have periods of feeling low or despondent about how your life is going?
2. How long do such periods last? How frequent are they? How bad do they get? Does the despondency produce crying or interfere with daily activities, sleep, concentration, or appetite?
3. Do you have feelings of hopelessness, discouragement, or self-criticism? Are these feelings so intense that life doesn't seem worthwhile?
4. Do thoughts of suicide come to mind? How persistent are such thoughts? How strong have they been? Did it require much effort to resist them? Have you had any impulses to carry them out? Have you made any plans? How detailed are such plans? Have you taken any initial action (such as hoarding medications, buying a gun or rope)? Do you have lethal means in your home (e.g., firearms, pills, etc.)?

5. Can you manage these feelings if they recur? If you cannot, is there a support system for you to turn to in helping to manage these feelings?

### Intervention and Patient Management

It is crucial that psychologists are well trained and knowledgeable about assessing for and managing potential suicidality. When is the right time to hospitalize a patient who professes suicidal ideation? How can psychologists best manage and provide treatment to patients? An important issue is the patient's competency and willingness to participate in management and treatment decisions (Gutheil, 1984, 1999).

The first management decision in treating a suicidal patient is to determine treatment setting, which includes consideration of characteristics of both the patient and therapist, and a careful evaluation (including a clear definition of the risks and the rationale for the decisions that one is making; Motto, 1979). For acute crisis cases of suicidality, provide a relatively short-term course of psychotherapy that is directive and crisis focused, emphasizing problem solving and skill building as core interventions.

Slaby (1998) described 13 elements in managing the outpatient care of suicidal patients.

1. Conduct initial and concurrent evaluations for suicidal ideation and plans.
2. Eliminate risk, by enhancing or diminishing factors that influence self-destructive behaviors.
3. Determine the patient's need for hospitalization.
4. Evaluate and instigate psychopharmacotherapy to treat the underlying disorder (i.e., depression).
5. Encourage increasing social support with the patient's friends and family.
6. Provide individual and family therapy.
7. Address concurrent substance use.
8. Refer for medical consultation, if needed.
9. Refer for electroconvulsive therapy (ECT), if appropriate.
10. Use psychoeducation with patient and significant others to manage and treat suicidality.
11. Arrange for emergency coverage for evenings and weekends.
12. Help patient and significant others set realistic goals for management and treatment of suicidal behaviors.
13. Keep current, accurate records.

It is important to note that although these treatment guidelines will enhance patient care, implementation of some or all of these elements does not insure that a patient will not commit suicide.

Some people will kill themselves because of abrupt changes in clinical status. Others may lie to their therapist to avoid interference with their plan. Most who die, however, will show signs of a deteriorating condition and will confirm in words that they require more intensive treatment (Slaby, 1998, pp. 37–38).

The psychologist must not hesitate to contact others in the life of the patient and enlist their support in the treatment plan (Slaby, Lieb, & Trancredi, 1986). Litman (1982) recommended that if a therapist treats a high-risk outpatient who thinks he or she can function as an outpatient, it is the therapist's responsibility to ensure that the risk is made known to all concerned parties (i.e., the family and significant others).

Seek professional consultation, supervision, and support for difficult cases. Consultation may be either formal (involving written documentation and possibly payment) or informal and may take place with a senior colleague, an expert in the area of concern, a peer, or a group of peers. Additionally, one may wish to consult with an individual outside of one's own professional domain, such as an attorney or physician; this is referred to as interprofessional consultation (Appelbaum & Gutheil, 1991; Bongar, 2002).

## Natural Disasters and Acts of Terrorism

Disasters often occur with unexpected swiftness and overwhelming force, adversely affecting ordinary people who were in "the wrong place at the wrong time" (Charney & Pearlman, 1998). Natural disasters, man-made disasters, and acts of terrorism shatter the assumptions of control, personal safety, and the predictability of life. When a cataclysmic event occurs, the function of the community is disrupted, causing a breach in the individual's emotional and physical support system. Worksites and homes may have been destroyed, people may be injured or dead, and lives are irrevocably altered. The impact of the trauma coupled with the fear that the event could recur fuels our deepest fears and impacts the lives of all within the community.

### Case Vignette

In late August, the community of St. Petersburg was hit by a devastating hurricane that destroyed homes and property. Flooding damaged John's home, and he moved to temporary housing provided by the American Red Cross. When offered crisis intervention services John declined, stating that others were in greater need. Upon further discussion, the therapist learned that John felt he should be able to provide for himself and viewed outside assistance as a sign of weakness and failure on his part.

### Assessment and Intervention

In the aftermath of this disaster, John may be experiencing a sense of unreality and dissociation, although the hurricane is over and the disaster site is calm. Basic needs, such as water, food, and a safe place, are the initial focus following a disaster because "physical care is psychological care, and this is the prime and essential function of relief organizations" (Kinston & Rosser, 1974). It is frustrating when victims of disaster refuse services. Psychologists faced with this dilemma should be empathetic and strive to normalize the person's reaction to the disaster during the initial interview. John's cultural norms should be considered when one assesses for acute and long-term problems, and at the same time one should promote positive coping strategies.

It should be determined if John would be amenable to receiving support and treatment from another local community, cultural, or religious organization engaged in providing relief care. Disaster victims rarely present to traditional mental health services (Lindy, Grace, & Green, 1981). However, most individuals who experience a disaster will do well and will not develop PTSD. The development of psychological sequelae depends on the nature of the disaster, the type of injuries sustained, the level of life threat, and the period of community disruption.

### The Four Phases of Disaster Response

Four phases have been identified that describe how people response to disaster (Cohen, Culp, & Genser, 1987). When natural disasters or acts of terrorism result in death, and the news media besieges the community, the people affected may feel overwhelmed and experience a range of reactions including shame, hatred, and guilt (Shneidman, 1981). It is normal during the first phase for people to experience feelings of disbelief, numbness, intense emotions, fear, dissociation, and confusion in immediate reaction to a disaster. People may appear apathetic and dazed, unable to grasp the reality and impact of the event.

It is during the second phase, in the days and months following a disaster, that aid from organizations and agencies outside the area assist the community with cleanup and rebuilding. At this time many individuals may experience denial and intrusive symptoms that are accompanied by autonomic arousal (e.g., a heightened startle response, insomnia, hypervigilance, and nightmares). As people start to realize the reality of the loss, common affects that may be evident include apathy, withdrawal, guilt, anger, anxiety, and irritability.

The third phase may last up to a year and marks a time when individuals typically shift their focus from the survival of the group or community back to the fulfillment of their individual needs. Individuals may feel disappointment and resentment when hopes of restoration and expectations of aid are not realized. Reconstruction, the final phase, can last for years as survivors gradually rebuild their lives and establish new goals and life patterns. Recovery from disaster involves the resolution of psychological and physiological symptoms through reappraising the incident, ascribing meaning, and integrating new self-concept (Cohen et al., 1987).

Green (1990) explicated the mediating characteristics of disasters. He noted that the greater the person's perceived threat of death or injury, the more likely the potential for adverse psychological functioning. Injury and physical harm, exposure to dead and mutilated bodies, and the violent, sudden death of a friend, co-worker, or loved one can cause traumatic stress. It is not necessary to witness such an event to experience intrusive thoughts and stress. For example, news broadcasts that replayed the horrific events of the terrorist attack on September 11, 2001, that killed thousands of people when a highjacked jet airliner crashed in Pennsylvania and the World Trade Towers and when a portion of the Pentagon Building burned and collapsed after being attacked by terrorists manning hijacked commercial airplanes created considerable distress for most viewers. Research needs to be conducted to elucidate the impact the news media has in creating collective traumatic stress many miles away from the catastrophic event. Intentional death and harm, resulting from man-made disasters and terrorist attacks, is viewed as particularly heinous and incites strong emotions.

Following a disaster, rapid response teams must mobilize rapidly, often with little warning. A multidisciplinary team that includes psychologists, physicians, social workers, nurses, and other mental health paraprofessionals is an ideal way to quickly identify high-risk groups and behaviors, to promote recovery from acute stress, and to decrease the likelihood of long-term adverse effects. Teams that arrive from outside the geographic area often benefit from working collaboratively with local community members who can assist them with integrating into the disaster environment. Psychologists should possess basic knowledge of the culture and norms of the group they are trying to assist. School systems, workplaces, communities, and foreign nations all have their unique customs and culture.

### Debriefing the Members of the Crisis Response Team

Members of rapid response teams providing crisis intervention are not immune to the stressors of the disaster and of caring for the victims. Rescue workers, heroes, people who are injured in the event, and children are at increased risk for stress-related sequelae. Crisis workers often experience the symptoms of PTSD, ASD, depression, and anxiety (Durham, McCammon, & Allison, 1985; Fullerton, McCarroll, Ursano, & Wright, 1992). Vicarious traumatization results when the crisis worker is adversely affected by the trauma that is manifested by the individuals in crisis.

Although debriefing is valuable in helping crisis workers "regain a state of emotional, cognitive, and behavioral equilibrium" (James & Gilliland, 2001), it is not recommended that debriefing be employed as an intervention for distressed crisis workers during or at an early stage of disaster response, because it is intended to "facilitate psychological closure to a traumatic event" (Everly & Mitchell, 1999; Shalev, 1994). Debriefing is a group intervention in which team members are guided through a chronological reconstruction of the disaster. The objective is to gain an understanding of the events related to and surrounding the disaster before the trauma becomes concretized, but it can only be effective if individuals are able to listen, express feelings, and cognitively restructure the experience.

James and Gilliland (2001) compiled a list of six precautions from a review of the literature that should be considered when providing crisis intervention and during the debriefing process:

1. Crisis work should be done in teams.
2. Time for sleep and to decompress is critical.
3. Crisis team members should not debrief each other.
4. Debriefing should take place away from the site of the disaster.
5. The structure of the organization and the way in which it provides disaster relief services affect how the team copes at the disaster site.
6. Excellent physical and mental health is required to conduct crisis work.

### Critical Incident Stress Debriefing and Critical Incident Stress Management

Critical Incident Stress Debriefing (CISD) was developed by Jeffery Mitchell in response to his reactions to traumatic incidents he witnessed as a firefighter and paramedic. It was originally formalized to be used with emergency workers but is now used with a wide range of individuals who have experienced trauma, including crisis workers, primary victims, and secondary observers (Everly & Mitchell, 1999). Critical Incident Stress Debriefing is used to mitigate acute stress that results from traumatization, to help crisis workers attain precrisis equilibrium and homeostasis, and to identify individuals who require additional mental health care (Everly & Mitchell, 1999).

Formal CISD is conducted approximately 24 hours after the event by a trained and certified CISD mental health professional. It was not designed as a substitute for psychotherapy or individual debriefing or as a stand-alone intervention (Everly & Mitchell, 2000). The "seven-phase group crisis intervention process" lasts approximately two to three hours and follows a prescribed format that consists of seven segments: (a) introduction, (b) fact finding, (c) thoughts, (d) reaction, (e) symptoms, (f) teaching, and (g) reentry (Everly & Mitchell, 1999).

Critical Incident Stress Debriefing is a component of Critical Incident Stress Management (CISM). Critical Incident Stress Management is a term that describes an integrated and comprehensive collection of "crisis response technologies for both individuals and groups" (Everly & Mitchell, 1999).

The purpose of CISM interventions is to reduce the impairment from traumatic stress and to facilitate needed assessment and treatment. The core eight CISM components are summarized in Table 18.3.

### Illness

Although illness is a common occurrence for many older adults, the advent of a chronic or terminal illness is life altering and places permanent restrictions on the individual's life. For example, adjustment to bodily changes resulting from surgery or illness, altered expectations of the future, environmental restrictions such as a lack of physical mobility or confinement to a wheelchair, and changed relationships with significant others are typically experienced as losses. One or any combination of these illness-related losses constitutes a serious threat to an individual's sense of body integrity, which in turn compounds the stresses related to treatment and invasive medical procedures.

**TABLE 18.3   Core Critical Incident Stress Management**

| Intervention | Timing | Activation | Goal | Format |
|---|---|---|---|---|
| Precrisis preparation | Precrisis phase | Crisis anticipation | Set expectations, improve coping, stress management | Groups/organizations |
| Demobilization and staff consultation (rescuers) | Shift disengagement | Event driven | To inform and consult, allow psychological decompression; stress management | Large groups/ organizations |
| Crisis Management Briefing (CMB) (civilians, schools, business) | Any time postcrisis | | | |
| Defusing | Postcrisis (within 12 hours) | Usually symptom drive | Symptom mitigation; possible closure; triage | Small groups |
| Critical Incident Stress Debriefing (CISD) | Postcrisis (1 to 10 days; 3–4 weeks for mass disasters) | Usually symptom driven; can be event driven | Facilitate psychological closure; symptom mitigation; triage | Small groups |
| Individual crisis intervention (1:1) | Any time, anywhere | Symptom driven | Symptom mitigation; return to function, if possible; referral, if needed | Individuals |
| Pastoral crisis intervention | Any time, anywhere | Whenever needed | Provide spiritual, faith-based support | Individuals/groups |
| Family CISM | Any time | Either symptom driven or event driven | Foster support and communications; symptom mitigation; closure, if possible; referral, if needed | Families/ organizations |
| Organizational consultation | | | | |
| Follow-up/referral | Any time | Usually symptom driven | Assess mental status; access higher level of care, if needed | Individual/family |

Reprinted with permission from Everly and Mitchell, 2000.

## Case Vignette

Mary was a 78-year-old retired teacher who lived alone in her home in a suburb of Chicago. Her daughter noticed that she was forgetting to bring in the newspaper and that she was no longer tending her garden, a long-standing source of enjoyment and pride. She was having problems finding her keys and remembering to turn the stove off when she was done cooking. Mary's daughter had her evaluated by a neuropsychologist and it was determined that she was experiencing the early stages of Alzheimer's dementia.

## Assessment and Intervention

The news that a loved one has a progressive, terminal illness like Alzheimer's disease is frightening and difficult to accept. Although new medications, such as Aricept, and some herbal supplements like vitamin E and ginkgo may slow the dementing process, at this time there is no cure. It is important for psychologists to have an understanding of not only the short- and long-term cognitive, emotional, and eventual physical changes, but also an appreciation of the ramifications of the disease process on the caregiving spouse and family members.

## Alzheimer's Disease

Approximately 4 million Americans are afflicted with Alzheimer's disease and this number is expected to grow to 14 million by the year 2050. Notably, an estimated 2.7 million spouses and family members provide care for a family member with the disease. On average, most individuals survive for 8 to 10 years after being diagnosed with Alzheimer's disease and will spend five of those years closely supervised by family or living in a skilled nursing home facility (Hendrie, 1998). The chronic, debilitating aspects of the disease are stressful for caregivers.

As the years pass and the disease progresses, the coping mechanisms of the caregiver may breakdown. The symptoms during the early stages of the disease, typically lasting 2 to 4 years, are progressive confusion and forgetfulness. The symptoms occurring during the middle stage, lasting approximately 2 to 10 years, include increased confusion and memory loss, decreased attention span, and difficulty recognizing family and close friends. The symptoms during the final stage, roughly 1 to 3 years, include diminished ability to communicate, impaired swallowing, weight loss, and inability to recognize self or family members. Mary and her daughter need empathy, support, and education regarding the disease process and community resources. Many caregivers will seek out or be referred to crisis intervention services.

## Five Stages of Death and Dying

The initial reactions of Mary and her mother may be similar to those described as the five stages of death and dying (Kübler-Ross, 1969). The five stages consist of (a) denial and isolation, (b) anger, (c) bargaining, (d) depression, and (e) acceptance. Individuals do not necessarily progress through each stage, nor do they experience the stages in a linear, sequential order. Some people may experience a stage more than once, whereas others may be unable to progress beyond a given stage. Awareness of these stages may be of value to the clinician working with a patient or a caregiver in crisis. Both Mary and her daughter will grieve and mourn in response to the losses that result from Alzheimer's disease. As with any crisis situation, psychologists need to provide treatment or make referrals to appropriate health care clinicians, if normal grieving evolves into major depression.

## Elder Abuse

A review of the literature shows that Alzheimer's caregivers are at increased risk for depression, elder abuse, illness, burnout, and social isolation (Dippel, 1996). All caregivers have normal life stressors to deal with, but if the stress of caring for a cognitively impaired loved one becomes intolerable, it can sometimes result in abuse. Psychologists should be aware of local laws regarding elder abuse. A multidisciplinary approach that includes psychologists, physicians, and social workers can be useful when treating the abused victim. In many instances, both the victim and the caregiver should receive social services. The attainment of new, adaptive coping skills and, in some instances, breaking the cycle of abuse is the focus of the intervention for the caregiver. It is important to remember that in cases of physical abuse, some suggest that the cycle of violence theory holds, in that the abusive children of the elderly parents were abused by them when they were children. They then act out their anger on the dependent elder parent because the use of violence has become a normal way to resolve conflict in their family. The crisis worker must help the adult child caregiver address his or her own past history of child abuse to stop the cycle (Kanel, 1999, p. 204).

## Caring for the Caregiver

It is beneficial for the caregiver, as well as the patient, to have regularly scheduled respite care. This may entail the use of a community day care program, a volunteer respite companion, or home health service. Frustration, burnout, and social isolation can adversely affect the functioning of the caregiver.

Although Mary's daughter may feel guilty about leaving her mother, regular breaks will help her maintain her well-being.

A caregiver's psychoeducation and support group not only provides support but is also an invaluable source of information regarding community resources. It can be overwhelming for a caregiver to deal with numerous medical specialists, community agencies, insurance forms, and more. Caregivers may benefit from working with a caseworker or healthcare specialists who can provide training to manage cognitive changes (e.g., use of a memory book) and ensure safety (e.g., with alarms or locks on doors).

Psychologists who work with caregivers can encourage them to utilize the ten steps to enhance caregivers' coping that were compiled from national experts by Castleman, Gallagher-Thompson, and Naythons (1999). These are the recommendations for caregivers:

1. Be confident of the diagnosis (seek a second opinion).
2. Be realistic (become educated about the disease process and know your options).
3. Enjoy any pleasant surprises (some personality changes resulting from Alzheimer's disease may be positive).
4. Treat everything (other medical and psychiatric conditions should be appropriately treated).
5. Combine medication with psychological and complementary therapies (consider attending a support group, exercising, or engaging in therapy).
6. Assemble an extensive support network (ask other family members, friends, and neighbors for help when needed).
7. Take good care of yourself (physically, emotionally, and socially).
8. Take good care of the person with Alzheimer's.
9. Plan for the future early (make legal, financial, and medical decisions during the early stages of the disease).
10. Stay informed (keep updated about new medications and treatments).

## CULTURAL CONSIDERATIONS

An additional pressure in providing effective services has been the diversification of our society, especially in urban settings. The projection for the year 2050 is that many urban settings will be predominately populated by people whose heritages are from Latin and Central America, Asia, and Africa (U.S. Bureau of the Census, 1996). The person taking the initial crisis call must be able to correctly evaluate the emergent nature of the problem; this is particularly difficult when he or she is not familiar with the background (not to mention the language) of the caller. Familiarity with diverse cultural norms is relevant here: What is considered a crisis in one cultural group might not be a crisis in another group. Responses that will be considered helpful may also vary according to cultural or ethnic group practices.

In cultural groups whose orientation is more toward an interdependent focus (the needs of the group are more important than the individual), family members tend to delay seeking help until the family can no longer cope with the problem (Tracey, Leong, & Glidden 1986; Triandis, Kashima, Shimada, & Villereal, 1986). Cultural considerations at the individual level can be determined by using a modification of the Systematic Treatment Selection approach to consider patient characteristics, relationship variables, treatment selection, and the cultural variable that affect decision making (Shiang, Kjellander, Huang, & Bogumill, 1998).

Some general guidelines can be suggested for crisis situations:

1. Become familiar with case studies of representative local cultural groups.
2. Seek consultation with people who have detailed knowledge of the cultural norms and their psychiatric manifestations.
3. Ask the person or other people in the person's environment about the level of abnormality or normality of this behavior.
4. Ask about consequences for endorsing abnormal behaviors.
5. Apply Western-based categories of illness only after the culture-specific categories have been reviewed and considered nonapplicable.
6. At all stages of a crisis, consider the cultural meanings of the psychosocial impact, the type of plan developed to resolve the immediate crisis, the ways of implementing the plan, and the types of follow-up to the implementation.

In the section related to mobile crisis units we present a brief case study to highlight the cultural considerations in the context of a crisis with an elderly client.

## COLLABORATIONS WITHIN THE MENTAL HEALTH FIELD

Hospital settings have traditionally provided services using a multidisciplinary team approach. In a crisis situation it has been found that this type of teamwork is critical; not all the needs of a person in crisis can be effectively handled by a person trained in one approach. Further, once the team operates in the environment of the person in crisis, general rules of hierarchy and authority necessarily become of secondary importance to the need to help the person resolve the "problem." Thus, distinctions between the disciplines are less clearly drawn. For example, consult-liaison teams that link to crisis teams and primary care facilities can provide assessment, diagnosis, and knowledge about where the client can best be treated in their particular system. Once the crisis has been resolved, follow-up with the multidisciplinary team can cast a wider net to provide services that help prevent relapse (Shiang & Bongar, 1995).

## Collaborations Across Agencies: Mobile Crisis Intervention Teams

One program that exemplifies the collaboration between multiple agencies is the use of mobile crisis units, which are community-based entities that dispatch professionals to a scene in the field to provide outreach and treatment (Ligon, 2000). The intent of these units is to address the "problem" using both law enforcement capabilities and mental health services to assess and "talk down" a crisis, to evaluate for restraint (via hospitalization or jail), and to ensure the safety of the community. An additional objective was to reduce the amount of resources and funding needed by using the most effective and efficient means of intervention possible (i.e., save money by allowing first-response police officers to return to duty more quickly, reduce admissions to hospitals, and provide repeat visits for volatile ongoing situations).

As of 1995, at least 39 states had some mobile capacity, and almost all of these states were sending teams to sites such as homes, hospital emergency rooms, residential programs, and shelters (Geller, Fisher, & McDermeit, 1995). In comparison to use of the emergency room, these mobile crisis units generally provided (a) greater accessibility of services to an indigent population, (b) more accurate assessments by observing more of the patient's environment and functioning in the real world, (c) earlier interventions in the phase of decompensation to help prevent hospitalization, and (d) superior liaisons with other agencies to facilitate referrals for the patient. In addition, the mobile crisis intervention teams identified strengths and weaknesses in past training and were able to offer intensive further training and public education (Zealberg, Santos, & Fisher, 1993).

A national survey found that most states believed mobile crisis units had helped to reduce hospital admissions. However, there has been little formal evaluation of their effectiveness. Geller et al. (1995) cautioned that the beliefs about the benefits of mobile crisis units tend to outnumber the facts. The authors suggest that, in the past, the use of descriptive reports

to encourage further funding was misleading; few states regularly evaluated the effectiveness of their programs.

Only recently have some of these benefits been examined through research. Deane, Steadman, Borum, Veysey, and Morissey (1999) surveyed police departments nationwide and found that of those police departments with mobile crisis teams (52 programs), 82% (43 programs) reported that they were moderately to very effective in their ability to respond to mental health crises. Guo, Biegel, Johnsen, and Dyches (2001) conducted a study using two samples that were matched on variables (e.g., demographics, diagnosis, substance use, and psychiatric history). It was found that there was a significant difference in the rate of hospitalization between the two groups. Patients presenting at the psychiatric emergency room for crisis services using a traditional model of care were 51% more likely to be hospitalized than were similar patients who had been serviced by the mobile crisis unit.

This study's finding supported the belief that mobile crisis units do in fact prevent hospital admissions by stabilizing the client, recommending services, and providing follow-up. The use of these more comprehensive research methodologies to formally evaluate and gain a more accurate understanding of the proposed effectiveness of community-based mobile crisis units is critical to addressing effectiveness and allocating resources.

## Collaboration With Law Enforcement Agencies

Although individual mobile crisis teams may see different populations depending upon the communities they service, they all have found it necessary to collaborate with the police and other law enforcement agencies. The collaboration of mobile crisis units and police is a unique and innovative one and requires mutual communication and trust. It has been conceptualized as two roles: The role of the mental health professional is to work with the person in crisis to establish rapport and problem solve in the moment, whereas the role of the police is to provide "the level of security necessary to do [the] work" (Zealberg, Christie, Puckett, McAlhany, & Durban, 1992, p. 613). Each discipline brings its respective training strengths: The police provide security, law enforcement resources, and the knowledge of how to deal with dangerous individuals, and mental health professionals provide knowledge of crisis evaluation, diagnosis, mental health resources, and the ability to relate with difficult patients. This collaborative, reciprocal interaction allows the team to respond to potentially violent situations and intervene. The benefit for society is that both hospital and jail space are used only for those patients that need this type of restriction (Lamb, Shaner, Elliot, DeCuir, & Foltz, 1995).

To achieve this collaboration, groups must communicate reliably at many levels. Successful programs indicate that the following are minimal requirements: a direct phone line or police radio to handle crises in the moment; ongoing meetings with police to jointly plan expectations and responsibilities; and regular meetings to provide feedback, share training efforts and observation shifts, and debrief the officers who experience critical stress incidents (Zealberg et al., 1992). Mutual respect in both directions is key: Mental health professionals must learn to respect the police's expertise in regard to safety and be able to be flexible in their actions.

At times the mental health person is acting as the primary communicator with the person in trouble, and at other times the police may want the professional to be there just to advise (Zealberg et al., 1992). Lamb and colleagues (1995) found that when there was an effective and close collaboration between mental health workers and the police, there was a substantial decrease in the criminalization of the chronically and severely mentally ill population, many of whom are at high risk for being placed in the criminal justice system.

The Berkeley Mobile Crisis Team (MCT) has been in operation since 1979. The program began after it became evident that police spent a large amount time providing crisis intervention and mental health services, and the city felt that a specialized mental health team would be able to more appropriately handle these services. The MCT is available every day of the year from 10:30 a.m. to 11:00 p.m. to citizens of Berkeley and Albany. There is a daytime shift from 10:30 a.m. to 4:00 p.m. and an evening shift from 4:00 p.m. to 11:00 p.m. The day shifts are usually covered by one paid professional staff member who is either a psychologist, social worker, or marriage and family counselor. The evening shift consists of a staff member joined by a graduate student volunteer intern.

Mobile Crisis Team service providers are contacted through police radio via the police dispatcher or via telephone and cell phone. During 1996–1997, police made 60% of the referrals to the team. Typical calls request assessment for involuntary psychiatric evaluation, support to families and individuals following a critical incident such as an unexpected death or traumatic incident, mitigation of domestic disputes, and outreach to the homeless. Occasionally, the MCT will provide training and debriefing to the police and outreach and debriefing to large groups in the community. In the 1996–1997 fiscal year, the MCT served 7,582 people, which was 6.2% of Berkeley and Albany's combined population of 122,000 (Vogel-Stone, 1999).

## Case Vignette

One September evening, the police summoned the Berkeley MCT to the home of a landlady who owned and managed a multi-unit apartment complex. She was a frail, elderly, monolingual Chinese woman who was reported to have had an altercation with a tenant and, as a result, was feeling threatened. The tenant complained about living in a water-damaged area of the building. Additionally, he admitted that he had not been paying rent for many months.

## Assessment and Intervention

When the call came in to the team, it was determined that, because the woman was monolingual Chinese, speaking Toisan, it was absolutely necessary to (a) provide a Toisan speaker who knew the cultural customs, (b) assess the dangerousness of the tenant, (c) make contact with her family as potential support, and (d) determine what other services might be needed.

Berkeley was fortunate to have the resources to provide four Chinese-speaking responders as the team, one of whom spoke Toisan. The two police officers and two mental health worker were all of Chinese ethnicity and familiar with traditional customs. When the landlady invited them into her home and brought out food to greet her visitors, they understood that she was not trying to "bribe" or coerce them into her way of thinking but attempting to establish a relationship with them through the exchange of normal social behaviors. The police officer who was fluent in the Toisan dialect helped to translate the interaction.

After interviewing the landlady and acknowledging her concerns, the professionals set out a plan of action. The mental health workers contacted the adult children to see if they would be able to provide additional help to the mother. The elderly woman had been reluctant to get her family involved, but by having "outside" agencies make the request (appeal to support network), she felt justified that she was not overreacting to the tenant. In addition, MCT convinced the landlady that an inspection of the water damage to the building needed to be scheduled, and they then provided the landlady with a referral to a Chinese-speaking property manager who could assist the landlady in her functions. She was fearful because she did not want to sell the building; she was afraid that, after many years of saving money with her husband, she would lose her place to live and become a "burden to her children."

The police interviewed the difficult tenant, who admitted that, due to his frustration, he had been hostile and had threatened violence. They encouraged him to pay rent or face the possibility of being evicted. He was relieved to hear that there would be an inspection of the water damage by the housing authority (appeal to the law). The MCT and the police planned a periodic following up of the situation. In this circumstance, the situation might have easily degenerated into a hostile and violent incident, because neither side of the conflict could communicate with the other and intermediaries had not been called. The consideration of cultural norms helped facilitate greater understanding and brought about specific interventions that were culturally acceptable to the parties (Chiu, 1994).

## SUMMARY

This chapter was written to provide the reader with an overview of the history and theory of crisis assessment and intervention and some of the challenges and opportunities for psychologists providing this care. The terrorist attacks that took place in the United States on September 11, 2001 will undoubtedly heighten the public's awareness of, and increase the demand for, crisis intervention services. It seems safe to predict that researchers and practioners will continue to hone assessments and treatments, using findings from outcome studies to guide the clinician's response to a range of events. Crisis intervention services will continue to provide a venue for change to individuals who are feeling overwhelmed, experiencing psychological disequilibrium, struggling to cope, and suffering personal distress.

## REFERENCES

American Psychiatric Association. (1980). *Diagnostic and Statistical Manual of Mental Disorders* (3rd ed.). Washington, DC: American Psychiatric Press.

American Psychiatric Association. (1994). *Diagnostic and Statistical Manual of Mental Disorders* (4th ed.). Washington, DC: American Psychiatric Press.

Appelbaum, P. S., & Gutheil, T. G. (1991). *Clinical handbook of psychiatry and the law* (2nd ed.). Baltimore: Williams and Wilkins.

Asnis, G. M., Friedman, T. A., Sanderson, W. C., Kaplan, M. L., van Praag, H. M., & Harkavy-Friedman, J. M. (1993). Suicidal behaviors in adult psychiatric outpatients, I: Description and prevalence. *American Journal of Psychiatry, 150,* 108–112.

Beck, A. T. (1967). *Depression: Clinical, experimental, and theoretical aspects.* New York: Harper and Row.

Bongar, B. (1992). The ethical issue of competence in working with the suicidal patient. *Ethics and Behavior, 2,* 75–89.

Bongar, B. (2002). *The suicidal patient: Clinical and legal standards of care* (2nd ed.). Washington, DC: American Psychological Association.

Brent, D. A., Bridge, J., Johnson, B. A., & Connolly, J. (1996). Suicidal behavior runs in families: A controlled family study of adolescent suicide victims. *Archives of General Psychiatry, 53,* 1145–1152.

Brent, D. A., Kupfer, D. J., Bromet, E. J., & Dew, M. A. (1988). The assessment and treatment of patients at risk for suicide. In A. J. Frances & R. E. Hales (Eds.), *American Psychiatric Press review of psychiatry* (Vol. 7, pp. 353–385). Washington, DC: American Psychiatric Press.

Breslau, N., Kessler, R., Chilcoat, H., Schultz, L., Davis, G., & Andreski, P. (1998). Trauma and posttraumatic stress disorder in the community. *Archives of General Psychiatry, 55,* 626–633.

Callahan, J. (1998). Crisis theory and crisis intervention in emergencies. In P. M. Kleespies (Ed.), *Emergencies in mental health practice* (pp. 22–40). New York: Guilford.

Caplan, G. (1961). *An approach to community mental health.* New York: Grune and Stratton.

Caplan, G. (1964). *Principles of preventive psychiatry.* New York: Basic Books.

Caplan, G. (1969). Opportunities for school psychologists in the primary prevention of mental health disorders in children. In A. Bindman & A. Spiegel (Eds.), *Perspectives in community mental health* (pp. 420–436). Chicago: Aldine.

Castleman, M., Gallagher-Thompson, D., & Naythons, M. (1999). *There's still a person in there: The complete guide to treating and coping with Alzheimer's.* New York: Putnam.

Charney, A. E., & Pearlman, L. A. (1998). The ecstasy and the agony: The impact of disaster and trauma work on the self of the clinician. In P. M. Kleespies (Ed.), *Emergencies in mental health practice* (pp. 418–435). New York: Guilford.

Chemtob, C. M., Roitblat, H. L., Hamada, R. S., & Carlson, J. G. (1988). A cognitive action theory of Post-Traumatic Stress Disorder. *Journal of Anxiety Disorders, 2,* 253–275.

Chiu, T. L. (1994). The unique challenges faced by psychiatrists and other mental health professionals working in a multicultural setting. *International Journal of Social Psychiatry, 40,* 61–74.

Cohen, R., Culp, C., & Genser, S. (1987). *Human problems in major disasters: A training curriculum for emergency medical personnel* [DHHS Pub. No. (ADM) 88-1505]. Washington, DC: U.S. Government Printing Office.

Deane, M., Steadman, H., Borum, R., Veysey, B., & Morrissey, J. (1999). Emerging partnerships between mental health and law enforcement. *Psychiatric Services, 50,* 99–101.

Dippel, R. L. (1996). The caregivers. In R. L. Dippel & J. T. Hutton (Eds.), *Caring for the Alzheimer patient.* Amherst, NY: Prometheus Books.

Durham, T. W., McCammon, S. L., & Allison, E. J. (1985). The psychological impact of disaster on rescue personnel. *Annals of Emergency Medicine, 14,* 664–668.

Eranen, L., & Liebkind, K. (1993). Coping with disaster: The helping behavior of communities and individuals. In J. P. Wilson & B. Raphael (Eds.), *International handbook of traumatic stress syndromes* (pp. 957–964). New York: Plenum Press.

Erickson, E. (1950). *Childhood and society.* New York: W. W. Norton.

Everly, G. S., Jr. (1989). *A clinical guide to the treatment of the human stress response.* New York: Plenum Press.

Everly, G. S., & Mitchell, J. T. (1999). *Critical Incident Stress Management (CISM): A new era and standard of care in crisis intervention* (2nd ed.). Ellicott City, MD: Chevron.

Everly, G. S., & Mitchell, J. T. (2000). The debriefing "controversy" and crisis intervention: A review of lexical and substantive issues. *International Journal of Emergency Mental Health, 2,* 211–225.

Foley, H. A., & Sharfstein, S. S. (1983). *Madness and government: Who cares for the mentally ill?* Washington, DC: American Psychiatric Press.

Folkman, S., & Lazarus, R. S. (1980). An analysis of coping in a middle-aged community sample. *Journal of Health and Social Behavior, 21,* 219–239.

Ford, J. D., Ruzek, J., & Niles, B. (1996). Identifying and treating VA medical care patients with undetected sequelae of psychological trauma and posttraumatic stress disorder. *NCP Clinical Quarterly, 6,* 77–82.

Fraser, J. S. (1998). A catalyst model: Guidelines for doing crisis intervention and brief therapy from a process view. *Crisis Intervention and Time-Limited Treatment, 4,* 159–177.

Fremouw, W. J., de Perczel, M., & Ellis, T. E. (1990). *Suicide risk: Assessment and response guidelines.* New York: Pergamon Press.

Fullerton, C. S., McCarroll, J. E., Ursano, R. J., & Wright, K. M. (1992). Psychological responses of rescue workers: Fire fighters and trauma. *American Journal of Orthopsychiatry, 62,* 371–378.

Geller, J., Fisher, W., & McDermeit, M. (1995). A national survey of mobile crisis services and their evaluation. *Psychiatric Services, 46,* 893–897.

Gilliland, B. E., & James, R. K. (1993). *Crisis intervention strategies* (2nd ed.). Belmont, CA: Brooks/Cole.

Green, B. L. (1990). Defining trauma: Terminology and generic dimension. *Journal of Applied Social Psychology, 20,* 1632–1642.

Guo, S., Biegel, D., Johnsen, J., & Dyches, H. (2001). Assessing the impact of community-based mobile crisis services on preventing hospitalization. *Psychiatric Services, 52,* 223–228.

Gutheil, T. G. (1984). Malpractice liability in suicide. *Legal aspects of psychiatric practice, 1,* 1–4.

Gutheil, T. G. (1999). Liability issues and liability prevention in suicide. In D. G. Jacobs (Ed.), *The Harvard Medical School guide to suicide assessment and intervention* (pp. 561–578). San Francisco: Jossey-Bass.

Hamilton, J., & Workman, R. (1998). Persistence of combat-related posttraumatic stress symptoms for 75 years. *Journal of Traumatic Stress, 11,* 763–768.

Hendrie, H. C. (1998). Epidemiology of Alzheimer's disease. *American Journal of Geriatric Psychiatry, 6,* S3–S18.

James, R. K., & Gilliland, B. E. (2001). *Crisis intervention strategies* (4th ed.). Belmont, CA: Brooks/Cole.

Janosik, E. H. (1984). *Crisis counseling: A contemporary approach.* Monterey, CA: Wadsworth Health Sciences Division.

Kanel, K. (1999). *A guide to crisis intervention.* Pacific Grove, CA: Brooks/Cole.

Kinston, W., & Rosser, R. (1974). Disaster: Effects on mental and physical state. *Journal of Psychosomatic Research, 18,* 437–456.

Kübler-Ross, E. (1969). *On death and dying.* New York: Macmillan.

Lamb, H., Shaner, R., Elliot, D., DeCuir, W., & Foltz, J. (1995). Outcome for psychiatric emergency patients seen by an outreach police-mental health team. *Psychiatric Services, 46,* 1267–1271.

Lazarus, R. S. (1966). *Psychological stress and the coping process.* New York: McGraw-Hill.

Lazarus, R. S., & Folkman, S. (1984). *Stress, appraisal, and coping.* New York: Springer.

Ligon, J. (2000). Mobile Crisis Units: Frontline community mental health services. In R. R. Albert (Ed.), *Crisis intervention handbook: Assessment, treatment, and research* (2nd ed., pp. 357–372). New York: Oxford University Press.

Lindemann, E. (1944). Symptomatology and management of acute grief. *American Journal of Psychiatry, 101,* 141–148.

Lindy, J. D., Grace, M. C., & Green, B. L. (1981). Survivors: Outreach to a reluctant population. *American Journal of Orthopsychiatry, 51,* 468–478.

Linehan, M. M. (1997). Behavioral treatments of suicidal behaviors. In D. M. Soff & J. J. Mann (Eds.), *Annals of the New York Academy of Sciences: The neurobiology of suicidal behavior* (pp. 302–328). New York: New York Academy of Sciences.

Linehan, M. M. (1999). Standard protocol for assessing and treating suicidal behaviors for patients in treatment. In D. G. Jacobs et al. (Ed.), *The Harvard Medical School guide to suicide assessment and intervention* (pp. 146–187). San Francisco: Jossey-Bass.

Litman, R. E. (1982). Hospital suicides: Lawsuits and standards. *Suicide and Life-Threatening Behavior, 12,* 212–220.

Maltsberger, J. T. (1988). Suicide danger: Clinical estimation and decision. *Suicide and Life Threatening Behavior, 18,* 47–54.

Maris, R. W., Berman, A. L., Maltsberger, J. T., & Yufit, R. (Eds.). (1992). *Assessment and prediction of suicide.* New York: Guilford.

Motto, J. A. (1979). Guidelines for the management of the suicidal patient. *Weekly Psychiatry Update Series Lesson, 20*(3), 3–7. (Available from Biomedia, Inc., 20 Nassau Street, Princeton, NJ 08540)

Motto, J. A. (1989). Problems in suicide risk assessment. In D. G. Jacobs & H. N. Brown (Eds.), *Suicide: Understanding and responding. Harvard Medical School perspectives on suicide* (pp. 129–142). Madison, CT: International Universities Press.

Motto, J. A. (1991). An integrated approach to estimating suicide risk. *Suicide and Life-Threatening Behavior, 21,* 74–89.

Myers, D. G. (1989). Mental health and disaster: Preventative approaches to intervention. In R. Gist & B. Lubin (Eds.), *Psychosocial aspects of disaster* (pp. 190–228). New York: Wiley.

Osterman, J. E., & Chemtob, C. M. (1999). Emergency intervention for acute traumatic stress. *Psychiatric Services, 6,* 739–740.

Pope, K. (1986, January). Assessment and management of suicidal risks: Clinical and legal standards of care. *Independent Practitioner,* 17–23.

Puryear, D. A. (1979). *Helping people in crisis.* San Francisco: Jossey-Bass.

Roberts, A. R. (1991). Conceptualizing crises theory and the crisis intervention model. In A. R. Roberts (Ed.), *Contemporary perspectives on crisis intervention and prevention* (pp. 3–17). Englewood Cliffs, NJ: Prentice Hall.

Roberts, A. R. (2000). An overview of crisis theory and crisis intervention. In A. R. Roberts (Ed.), *Crisis intervention handbook* (2nd ed., pp. 3–30). New York: Oxford University Press.

Shalev, A. Y. (1994). Debriefing following traumatic exposure. In R. J. Ursano, B. G. McCaughey, & C. S. Fullerton (Eds.), *Individual and community responses to trauma and disaster* (pp. 201–219). London: Cambridge University Press.

Shiang, J., & Bongar, B. (1995). Brief and crisis psychotherapy in theory and practice. In B. Bongar & L. Beutler (Eds.), *Comprehensive textbook of psychotherapy* (pp. 380–401). New York: Oxford University Press.

Shiang, J., Kjellander, C., Huang, K., & Bogumill, S. (1998). Developing cultural competency in clinical practice: Treatment considerations for Chinese cultural groups in the U.S. *Clinical Psychology: Science and Practice, 5,* 182–209.

Shneidman, E. S. (1981). Postvention: The care of the bereaved. *Suicide and Life-Threatening Behavior, 11,* 349–359.

Shneidman, E. S. (1985). *Definition of suicide.* New York: Wiley.

Shneidman, E. S. (1986). Some essentials of suicide and some implications for response. In A. Roy (Ed.), *Suicide* (pp. 1–16). Baltimore: Williams and Wilkins.

Simon, R. I. (1987). *Clinical psychiatry and the law.* Washington, DC: American Psychiatric Press.

Simon, R. I. (1992). *Concise guide to psychiatry and the law for clinicians.* Washington, DC: American Psychiatric Press.

Slaby, A. E. (1998). Outpatient management of suicidal patients. In B. Bongar, A. L. Berman, R. W. Maris, M. M. Silverman, E. A. Harris, & W. L. Packman (Eds.), *Risk management with suicidal patients* (pp. 34–64). New York: Guilford.

Slaby, A. E., Lieb, J., & Tancredi, L. R. (1986). *Handbook of psychiatric emergencies* (3rd ed.). New York: Medical Examination Publishing.

Slaikeu, K. A. (1990). *Crisis intervention: A handbook for practice and research* (2nd ed.). Boston: Allyn & Bacon.

Smead, V. S. (1988). Best practices in crisis intervention. In A. Thomas & J. Grimes (Eds.), *Best practices in school psychology* (pp. 401–414). Washington, DC: National Association of School Psychologists.

Stoelb, M., & Chiriboga, J. (1998). A process model for assessing adolescent risk for suicide. *Journal of Adolescence, 21,* 359–370.

Stromberg, C. D., Haggarty, D. J., Leibenluft, R. F., McMillian, M. H., Mishkin, B., Rubin, B. L., & Trilling, H. R. (1988). *The psychologist's legal handbook.* Washington, DC: Council for the National Register of Health Service Providers in Psychology.

Tanney, B. (1992). Mental disorders, psychiatric patients, and suicide. In R. Maris, A. Berman, J. Maltsberger, & R. Yufit (Eds.), *Assessment and prediction of suicide* (pp. 277–320). New York: Guilford.

Tedeschi, R. G., Park, C. L., & Calhoun, L. G. (1998). Posttraumatic growth: Conceptual issues. In R. G. Tedeschi, C. L. Park, & L. G. Calhoun (Eds.), *Posttraumatic growth: Positive changes in the aftermath of crisis* (p. 2). Mahwah, NJ: Erlbaum.

Tracey, T. J., Leong, F. T., & Glidden, C. (1986). Help seeking and problem perception among Asian Americans. *Journal of Counseling Psychology, 33,* 331–336.

Triandis, H., Kashima, Y., Shimada, E., & Villareal, M. (1986). Acculturation indices as a means of confirming cultural differences. *International Journal of Psychology, 21,* 43–70.

U.S. States Bureau of the Census. (1996). Population projections of the U.S. by age, sex, race, and Hispanic origin: 1995–2050. Washington, DC: U.S. Government Printing Office.

Ursano, R. J., Fullerton, C. S., & Norwood, A. E. (1995). Psychiatric dimensions of disaster: Patient care, community consultation, and preventive medicine. *Harvard Review of Psychiatry, 3,* 196–209.

Vogel-Stone, C. (1999). Outcomes of mobile crisis intervention services: Impressions from service recipients and service providers. Unpublished doctoral dissertation, California School of Professional Psychology, Alameda.

Wainrib, B. R., & Bloch, E. L. (1998). *Crisis intervention and trauma response: Theory and practice.* New York: Springer.

Zealberg, J., Christie, S., Puckett, J., McAlhany, D., & Durban, M. (1992). A mobile crisis program: Collaboration between emergency psychiatric services and police. *Hospital and Community Psychiatry, 43,* 612–615.

Zealberg, J., Santos, A., & Fisher, R. (1993). Benefits of mobile crisis programs. *Hospital and Community Psychiatry, 44,* 16–17.

CHAPTER 19

# Psychotherapy With Older Adults

BOB G. KNIGHT, INGER HILDE NORDHUS, AND DEREK D. SATRE

In the final 30 years of the twentieth century, there was an increasing focus within psychotherapy on older adult clients (Knight, Kelly, & Gatz, 1992). In the United States, the expansion of Medicare coverage for outpatient psychotherapy services led to a dramatic increase in the delivery of psychotherapy to older adults in the closing decade of the century (Knight & Kaskie, 1995). On a largely parallel track, there has been increasing focus on psychotherapy integration (e.g., Stricker & Gold, 1993). These two trends will likely continue in the future, with important implications both for theorists and for practicing clinicians. In this chapter, we discuss psychotherapy with older adults in an integrative framework. In the first section, we review briefly the evidence for the effectiveness of various psychological interventions with a range of problems faced by older clients. In the next three sections, we discuss integrative trends in psychotherapy with older adults using the common-factors theme, the metatheoretical framework, and the prescriptive eclecticism integrative approach. In the final section, we begin to explore the potential for theoretical integration in psychotherapy with older adults, using the integrative model developed at the older adult clinical program associated with the University of Bergen (Norway). Our intertwined themes in the chapter are that the integrative approaches are useful in thinking about psychotherapy with older adults, and that working with older clients may provide particular impetus to thinking in integrative terms.

It is hoped that these discussions will contribute to improved treatment access for older adults. Facilitating patients' access to therapy and establishing an effective therapeutic relationship are crucial to all forms of psychotherapy and to all groups of patients. Several factors may combine to undermine the utilization of mental health services by older adults (Gallo, Marino, Ford, & Anthony, 1995; Zivian, Larsen, Gekoski, Hatchette, & Knox, 1994). These include inadequate detection of mental health illness among elderly patients (e.g., due to insufficient geriatric assessment), reluctance on the part of elders to seek mental health care (e.g., because of fear of stigma), and failures to recognize an older adult's need for psychotherapy by referral sources and mental health professionals (e.g., due to ageism or to poor training).

A recent investigation of attitudes toward mental health services held by older adults is of special relevance in this respect. In this study, Currin, Hayslip, Schneider, and Kooken (1998) found that younger cohorts of older adults held more positive attitudes toward mental health services than did older age cohorts. These data suggest that deficits about knowledge regarding aging and mental health, impediments to financial support of the cost of therapy, barriers to the availability of services, and negative expectations about effectiveness of treatment all decrease among the later born cohorts of older adults. The authors also suggested that younger cohorts expect mental health professionals to be of help and in turn may be more likely to actively seek therapeutic help. Epidemiological trends may mirror this cohort-linked shift in attitudes toward mental health treatment. Koenig, George, and Schneider (1994) argued that the increasing prevalence of mental disorders in successively later born cohorts implies a greater need for mental health services among the older adults of coming decades than in those generations who have been elderly in the past. These shifts clearly have implications for clinical management and implementation of psychological treatment, such as an increased need for mental health professionals skilled in providing mental health services to older adults.

## EMPIRICAL SUPPORT FOR THE EFFECTIVENESS OF PSYCHOTHERAPY

The following section reviews the empirical evidence for the effectiveness of psychotherapy with older adults. Standards for evaluation of therapy effectiveness are found in the work of task forces on empirically supported psychological treatments within the American Psychological Association's (APA's) Division 12. The task forces have concentrated on treatments for specific psychological problems (Chambless et al., 1998; Task Force on Promotion and Dissemination of Psychological Procedures, 1995). These guidelines have been applied to the literature on psychological interventions with older adults by Gatz and associates (1998). They report that behavioral and environmental interventions for older adults with dementia meet the standards for "well-established, empirically supported" therapy. "Probably efficacious" therapies for the older adult include cognitive behavioral treatment of sleep disorders and psychodynamic, cognitive, and behavioral treatments for clinical depression. For anxiety disorders, the authors conclude that the few treatment studies of psychological interventions conducted to date do not meet these standards, due to lack of a control group and concomitant treatment with anxiolytic drugs. Life review and reminiscence, techniques discussed later in this chapter, are probably efficacious in improvement of depressive symptoms or in producing higher life satisfaction. In the following summary we examine the application of psychological interventions to specific problems faced by older adults, with attention to available empirical literature.

### Chronic Illness and Disability

Conducting psychotherapy with emotionally distressed older adults very often means working with older adults who are chronically ill or physically disabled, and who are struggling to adjust to these problems while suffering concurrent depression (Zeiss, Lewinsohn, Rohde, & Seeley, 1996). Estimates of the prevalence of adults over the age of 56 with at least one chronic illness range from 50% to 86% (Boczkowski & Zeichner, 1985; Ham, 1983; National Center for Health Statistics, 1987). Important components of working with this population include learning about chronic illnesses and their psychological impact, control of chronic pain, adherence to medical treatment, rehabilitation strategies, and assessment of behavioral signs of medication reactions.

There has been little study of the effectiveness of psychotherapy with medically ill older adults. However, the few studies completed to date have been encouraging. Arean and Miranda (1996) found cognitive and behavioral approaches effective in relieving symptoms of depression in medically ill outpatients. In another study, Lopez and Mermelstein (1995) found cognitive and behavioral interventions successful in treating depression with inpatients in a hospital geriatric unit. The authors of this study described a treatment program in which patients received 30-min therapy sessions three to four times per week, with an emphasis on increasing pleasant events and cognitive restructuring. Psychological treatment was coordinated with physicians and nurses involved in patient care.

In addition to treating depression in medically ill or disabled elders, psychotherapy can also be used to help manage pain. It has been estimated that 25% to 50% of community-dwelling elderly suffer from chronic pain (Crook, Ridout, & Browne, 1984), with rates of 45% to 80% for elderly who live in nursing homes (Roy & Michael, 1986). Chronic pain is associated with rheumatoid arthritis and delayed healing from injuries. Pain management methods that may be incorporated into psychotherapy sessions include distracting oneself from the pain, reinterpreting pain sensations, using pleasant imagery, using calming self-statements, and increasing daily pleasurable activities (Widner & Zeichner, 1993). Employment of these cognitive and behavioral techniques in therapy may help clients reduce dependence on medication to manage pain. Because chronic pain is associated with depression in older adults (Ferrell, Ferrell, & Osterweil, 1990; Parmalee, Katz, & Lawton, 1991), effective pain management has the potential to reduce risk of depression.

Although medication is frequently indicated to help relieve pain in older adults, outcome studies have shown that cognitive and behavioral techniques are also effective in helping clients manage pain (Cook, 1998). In this study, which included a treatment group of 22 nursing home residents, participants who received cognitive behavioral pain management training reported less pain and less pain-related disability than those in an attention/supportive-control group. Participants were randomized in this study, and were screened to eliminate subjects with serious cognitive impairment. Treatment gains in the cognitive behavioral group were maintained at a 4-month follow-up.

## Depression

Depression is prevalent in older adults who are chronically ill (if disability is present) or grieving. However, research findings contradict the stereotype of the older person as frequently depressed, since depression is actually less prevalent in older adults than it is in younger ones: 1% of older adults have a lifetime prevalence of major depression, whereas 6% of younger adults have been diagnosed with a major depressive episode (Robins et al., 1984).

Fortunately, depression in older people appears to respond well to psychological interventions. Gallagher and Thompson (1983) compared cognitive, behavioral, and brief insight-oriented therapy with a total of 38 adults over the age of 55. All three groups showed reduction in symptoms of depression, but the cognitive and behavioral groups maintained gains better at follow-up. A similar study with 115 subjects over the age of 60, with the same three treatment conditions and a waiting-list control, found all three treatment approaches superior to the control group, with each mode of psychotherapy equally effective. At follow-up, all three treatment groups maintained gains equally (Thompson, Gallagher, & Breckenridge, 1987; see also Teri, Curtis, Gallagher-Thompson, & Thompson, 1994). Arean et al. (1993) compared group reminiscence therapy, problem-solving therapy, and a waiting-list control. Both groups showed reduction in depressive symptoms in comparison to the control, although the problem-solving group showed greater improvement, a difference that was maintained at a 3-month follow-up. In a recent study that examined the effectiveness of interpersonal psychotherapy for maintenance following treatment of recurrent major depression with antidepressants, Reynolds et al. (1999) found that both interpersonal therapy and nortriptyline were superior to a placebo in preventing relapse, and that combining both treatment methods was superior to either one in isolation.

## Anxiety

Although prevalence rates have varied among studies, results from epidemiological investigations indicate that symptoms of anxiety, as well as recognized anxiety disorders, constitute a significant problem among older adults (Blazer, George, & Hughes, 1991; Robins & Regier, 1991). As with depression, anxiety frequently occurs in association with physical illness and disability in late life (Fisher & Noll, 1996).

The few intervention studies conducted to date suggest that behavioral interventions for anxiety symptoms are promising. Progressive muscle-relaxation training appears to be effective in reducing levels of anxiety as well as self-reported psychiatric symptoms among community-dwelling samples of older adults. Rankin, Gilner, Gfeller, and Katz (1993) found that one session of relaxation training significantly reduced trait anxiety according to a modified version of the Spielberger State-Trait Anxiety Inventory. Yesavage (1984) found that older adults were less anxious than a control group after 3 weeks of progressive muscle-relaxation training. Scogin, Rickard, Keith, Wilson, and McElreath (1992) investigated the effects of relaxation on a group of older adults with high self-reported anxiety. They found that progressive muscle-relaxation and imaginal relaxation techniques were equally effective in increasing relaxation level and in reducing anxiety and psychiatric symptoms. In this study, imaginal relaxation entailed participants' visualizing the tensing and releasing of each muscle group, rather than actually doing so. These gains were maintained at follow-up 1 month after training. A follow-up study conducted on the participants 1 year later found that both treatment groups showed continued improvement in relaxation levels, with gains maintained on measures of anxiety and psychiatric symptoms (Rickard, Scogin, & Keith, 1994). This report did not indicate how often participants continued to use relaxation techniques in the intervening year. However, other studies have suggested that continued practice of relaxation techniques is necessary to maintain anxiety symptom reduction (De Berry, 1982; De Berry, Davis, & Reinhard, 1988).

The positive effects of relaxation training appear to be quite broad. De Berry (1981–82) found that a group of anxious widows reported less anxiety, less muscle tension, better sleep, and fewer headaches following 10 weeks of combined progressive muscle relaxation and guided visual imagery. Reduction in anxiety was maintained at follow-up 10 weeks later, although the study did not make clear whether the other improvements were maintained. Relaxation has also been useful in reducing anxiety and breathing problems in older medical patients (Gift, Moore, & Soeken, 1992). In the context of group psychotherapy, relaxation training may also reduce symptoms of generalized anxiety disorder (Wetherell, personal communication, June 19, 2000).

## Alcohol Problems

Although rates of alcohol abuse and dependence are lower for older adults than for younger ones, drinking remains a serious problem among the elderly. Aside from the psychological and social problems accompanying addiction, alcohol-related health risks to older adults include adverse interactions with medications, liver damage, increased risk of falling, and negative effects on cognitive functioning (see Bucholz, Sheline, & Helzer, 1995, for review). Bienenfeld (1987) found that elderly alcoholics were at 5 times greater risk for suicide than non-alcoholic elderly.

Empirical studies suggest that psychotherapy can be useful in treating older alcoholics. In a review of published outcome studies of psychological interventions, Schonfeld and Dupree (1995) found the empirical evidence for the effectiveness of cognitive and behavioral interventions superior to that of 12-step and social support treatment models. However, not all of the studies they review that support cognitive and behavioral treatment were controlled (e.g., Dupree, Broskowski, & Schonfeld, 1984). In one study that did include a control group, Kashner, Rodell, Ogden, Guggenheim, and Karson (1992) compared subjects randomly assigned to a mixed-age confrontational treatment group to those in an age-specific group treatment for older adults, called Older Adult Rehabilitation (OAR). Therapy for this group included a reminiscence component. Seventy-two male participants completed OAR treatment. Participants in OAR were more than twice as likely to maintain abstinence at a 1-year follow-up. In another study that also addressed the long-term impact of intervention, Carstensen, Rychtarik, and Prue (1985) found that a behavioral treatment program for older males was successful in maintaining treatment gains at a 2-year follow-up. In conjunction with a cognitive behavioral treatment approach, these studies suggest that older adults benefit both from being in a group setting with other older alcoholics and from a less confrontational style on the part of group leaders.

Recent studies of intervention for alcohol problems have focused on brief interventions. These interventions include psychoeducational sessions for at-risk drinkers, in which information regarding the risk of excessive alcohol use is offered. Blow and Berry (2000) found that a single-session intervention was useful in decreasing the amount of alcohol consumed by older adults. It seems likely that this strategy may be usefully incorporated into more formal therapy, when the therapist has recognized a possible alcohol problem.

## Sleep Disorders

Insomnia is a frequent problem for older adults, and may interfere significantly with day-to-day functioning. Between 12% and 25% of adults over the age of 65 complain of chronic sleep difficulties (Ford & Kamerow, 1989). In *sleep-maintenance insomnia,* the individual may awaken in the middle of the night and be unable to get back to sleep. He or she may then take naps during the day in order to make up the sleep time lost, resulting in greater and greater time spent in bed in order to receive a normal amount of sleep.

Although insomnia is sometimes thought of as a medical problem or an inevitable result of aging, studies have found that psychological interventions can be very effective in treating this disorder. Zeiss and Steffen (1996) have recommended a combination of education, sleep restrictions, and stimulus-control interventions in treating sleep-maintenance insomnia in older adults. In *sleep education,* the client is taught about the effects of alcohol, caffeine, nicotine, exercise, sleeping aids, and nutrition on sleep, as well as about age-related changes in sleep. The latter information can help reduce unrealistic expectations regarding sleep time because the client may be relieved to know that older people generally sleep less than younger ones.

This approach has been found effective in controlled-outcome studies, with gains maintained up to 1 year following treatment (Morin, Kowatch, Barry, & Walton, 1993). The outcome study conducted by Morin and his colleagues found that treatment was effective in reducing *sleep latency* (difficulty falling asleep), waking after sleep onset, and early morning waking; for each of these problems, sleep efficiency was increased. In another outcome study, Morin, Colecchi, Stone, Sood, and Brink (1999) found that combined pharmacotherapy and cognitive behavioral therapy was most effective in treating insomnia in a sample of older adults. However, cognitive behavioral treatment was more effective in treating insomnia than pharmacotherapy alone. Treatment gains were better maintained at follow-up by those study participants who had received cognitive behavioral therapy.

The effectiveness of treating insomnia with cognitive and behavioral methods represents an important advance, given the high prevalence of insomnia and the negative side effects of sedative-hypnotic medications in older adults. These include cognitive impairment, increased risk of falls, and the fact that most medications lose their effectiveness over time (Morin & Kwentus, 1988).

Given the growing empirical evidence for the efficacy of a number of psychological interventions with a wide variety of problems faced by older adults, as described in the previous section, and positive clinical experiences reported over a period of 80 years or more (Knight et al., 1992), the stage is set for an exploration of integration issues in psychotherapy with older adults. Four strands of psychotherapy integration will be pursued in the following sections: common factors in psychotherapy; Knight's contextual, cohort-based, maturity, specific-challenge (CCMSC) model as a transtheoretical framework for therapy with older adults; the CCMSC model as a guideline for prescriptive eclecticism; and theoretical integration as exemplified by the Bergen model.

## COMMON FACTORS IN PSYCHOTHERAPY WITH THE OLDER ADULT

Probably most closely identified with the work of Jerome Frank, especially his classic book *Persuasion and Healing* (1961), an early and consistent theme of psychotherapy integration has been the concept that there are common factors in change processes that are effective ingredients in psychotherapy and that likely cut across theoretical systems. Frank (1982) has described potential common factors as including an intense and confiding relationship with the therapist that inspires hope, a healing setting, a rationale that explains the person's difficulties and provides methods for change or relief, and a set of prescribed treatments.

Knight (1996a) noted that older adults seem especially responsive to simply being listened to, and speculated that this may be a somewhat unusual experience for many older adults experiencing psychological problems. To the extent that societal attitudes about aging and about older adults tend to be negative in tone and pessimistic in expectations (e.g., Butler, 1975), a relationship that provides support and hope is likely to have a powerful impact on older adults. Although the psychotherapeutic relationship is more explicitly discussed in psychodynamic and humanistic approaches to therapy, Castonguay (1997) cites evidence for its salience and importance in behavioral approaches as well. In fact, Bruninck and Schroeder (as cited in Castonguay, 1997) found evidence that behavioral therapists can be more supportive than psychodynamic and Gestalt therapists.

In one of the few empirical studies of the effects of the therapeutic relationship in therapy with older adults, Marmar, Gaston, Gallagher, and Thompson (1989) found independence of therapist and client ratings of the alliance, and a stronger association of alliance with outcome in cognitive therapy. In a different article, the same group reported a stronger correlation of patient defensiveness with patient commitment to treatment in cognitive therapy than in psychodynamic therapy (Gaston, Marmar, Thompson, & Gallagher, 1988). The researchers speculated that cognitive therapy requires a stronger commitment from the patient and that cognitive therapists may not handle defensiveness well. These findings are reminiscent of work by Beutler and colleagues (e.g., 1991) finding that cognitive therapy works better with younger adults who have externalizing coping styles and are low on reactance. Further research is needed on the importance of the therapeutic relationship in therapy with older adults, and on the need to match therapy to the characteristics of older adults that may influence therapy effectiveness.

In a somewhat similar manner, the provision of a rationale for the problem and a potential way to achieve relief may have a great effect on older adults. Older adults seem less likely than younger ones (at least in current and recent cohorts) to identify problems as psychological in nature (Lasoki & Thelen, 1987). The identification of a set of symptoms, perceived as unrelated and possibly physical in origin, as due to depression may in itself be a relief for an older client. The rationale for the problem and the description of a potential treatment also serve to correct the likely attribution of the problem to aging processes, which are assumed to be irreversible (Knight & Satre, 1999). These common aspects of therapy are likely to be even more effective with older clients than with younger ones, given their presumed lack of experience in conceptualizing problems in psychological terms and the pessimism likely to be associated with aging-based attributions.

This brief exploration of common factors in psychotherapy points to the importance of further exploration of this area of potential commonalities across therapy systems used with older adults, so far generally neglected in research and scholarship on therapy with the elderly. The salience of the therapeutic relationship and of the provision of a rationale for the psychological problem and its treatment may be of particular benefit to older clients. Other potential common factors with some empirical support in research with younger adults include self-efficacy and corrective emotional experience (Weinberger, 1993) and should be further explored with older persons as well. As with younger adults, it appears that there are powerful basic elements to psychotherapy with older adults that may play a central role in treatment. In the next section, we turn to the CCMSC model and its potential role as a transtheoretical framework and as a guide for prescriptive therapy with older adults.

## THE CCMSC MODEL AS A TYPE OF TRANSTHEORETICAL FRAMEWORK

Another type of approach to psychotherapy integration is to construct an overarching framework that can organize differing theoretical approaches and inform their application to different types of clients, to different types of problems, or to different ways of approaching problems. Rather than reducing apparently different therapies to a set of common factors (as discussed previously) or trying to achieve a theoretical integration (as will be discussed later), the *transtheoretical approach* organizes the differing theories within an overarching framework. In discussing integration with younger adult clients, Prochaska (1984) is a major proponent of this effort. For older adults, the proposed framework of therapy is based on key research findings from life span developmental psychology and social gerontology. Knight (1996a) proposed a *contextual, cohort-based, maturity, specific-challenge (CCMSC) model* as a way of addressing the questions of whether and how psychotherapy needs to be adapted for work with older adults. Briefly, the model proposes that differences could be due to the following factors:

1. *Social contextual factors,* or the ways in which older adults are segregated within social contexts such as nursing homes, medical settings, and age-segregated living environments and are treated differently by both formal laws and regulations (e.g., Medicare, the Older Americans Act) and by informal social norms and attitudes (ageism, age stereotypes of all kinds).

2. *Cohort effects,* or differences that arise from being born into a specific set of social historical circumstances that influence the length and nature of educational experience, social values, normative life experiences, and so forth (focusing, e.g., on differences among generations of the Jazz Age, the Depression era, World War II, and the baby boom as older adult cohorts).

3. *Maturational effects,* or the changes that occur during adult development and aging (life span psychology would suggest that these can involve improvement and stability as well as decline).

4. *Specific challenges* of later life, chronic illness, disability, grief, and caregiving. Not unique to later life but stochastically more common, these issues require specific knowledge and skills that therapists who primarily work with older populations may need to acquire.

In general, Knight (1996a) argued that differences in therapy with older adults, when they occur, are more often due to contextual influences, cohort differences, or the nature of the specific challenges than to maturational changes.

Over the past several years, Knight and his colleagues have applied the CCMSC model to a variety of specific therapy systems to explore issues related to therapy with older adults. In a discussion of CCMSC and psychodynamic therapy, Knight (1996b) argued that the CCMSC model can assist developmental views of adulthood and aging within the psychodynamic model by extending them into later life in a way that draws upon research in gerontology and life span developmental psychology and the writings of those with specific clinical expertise in work with older adults. He argued that this knowledge base provides a more optimistic view than is found in much psychodynamic writing about later life. Grief work, psychodynamic work on illness-related issues, and the importance of transference and countertransference issues were all seen as strengths of the psychodynamic approach.

On the other hand, the CCMSC model calls attention to social-context effects and cohort effects in ways that are often neglected in noncontextual intrapsychic theorizing. Knight argued, for example, that retirement is better conceptualized as a social role than as a developmental stage. As a social role, the psychological effects of retirement are expected to vary by occupation, social class, and gender and can be expected to change over time. The individual's task is changed from adjusting to a developmental stage of loss of work to creating a meaningful, optimal role as a retired person. Therapy within residential care is unlinked from the developmental-stage framework and is seen as specific to the setting and to the illnesses that cause people to live there. Different cohorts (e.g., Depression-era vs. baby boom cohorts) differ in diagnostic profiles, common character disorders, and typical childhood experiences.

Knight and Fox (1999) discussed the relationship of the CCMSC model to behavior therapy approaches. Behavior therapists have argued that their approaches may be more acceptable to older clients who have grown up in less psychologically minded eras and want relatively quick, practical solutions to problems. The CCMSC model would see this as a cohort effect, and one that would be expected to change as the baby boomers become older adults. Knight and Fox reviewed evidence that learning may take longer with older adults and that classical conditioning may reach a lower asymptote than in younger adults. Operant conditioning appears to be relatively well preserved in older adults, including those with psychosis and with dementia. The behavioral approach has been used a great deal with older adults in nursing homes and in other institutional settings and is well suited to analyzing and changing the contextual settings in which older adults are sometimes located as a way of resolving their problems.

Knight and Satre (1999) discussed cognitive behavioral approaches as related to the CCMSC model. Maturation was argued to affect cognitive behavioral therapy (CBT) by suggesting a slower pace and possibly simpler presentation of some concepts, and by providing a push toward higher levels of abstraction (i.e., working on schemas more frequently than on automatic thoughts). Cohort effects were seen as influencing many proposed changes in assessment and in therapy with older adults, in that changes in the presentation of questions or of therapy materials may be due to lower educational levels in earlier born cohorts and to their differing life experiences, rather than to effects of aging as a developmental process. The importance of understanding older adults' social context as they perceive it and changing these perceptions was seen as critical in CBT work with older clients. Finally, the literature on psychological interventions with older adults was reviewed as organized around the treatment of specific challenges in later life (e.g., coping with disability, pain management, sleeping disorders, caregiving issues).

Knight and McCallum (1998) applied the CCMSC model to family systems approaches to therapy. The maturity component of the model called attention to the question of what defines a family as an *aged family*. That is, virtually all families contain aged members; so how is it that some families define themselves or come to be seen by the therapist as having specific aging issues? The cohort effects part of the model calls attention to the misunderstandings and values conflicts that arise within families in part because families are composed of persons from a variety of cohorts with differing social-historical contexts for their own maturation. The special contexts in which older family members may be living can be difficult for younger family members to comprehend and negotiate, precisely because they are different from the contexts with which younger family members are familiar. As in other models, much of what makes family therapy with "older families" different (and likely often answers the question of why we think of them as older families) has to do with the specific challenges faced in later life by some older family members.

This overview of the CCMSC's application to four types of psychotherapy systems illustrates several points about this framework for thinking about psychotherapy with older adults. The framework is transtheoretical in the sense that it can be applied to all of these theoretical approaches to inform their use with older adults. In doing so, it often raises questions and issues not typically addressed by the individual systems. In part, this comes from the nature and history of the CCMSC, which is rooted in life span developmental psychology and social gerontology. Each of these is, in turn, influenced in varying degrees by the need to integrate physiology of aging, psychology of aging, sociology of aging, and social policy about the aged when addressing older adults and the problems they face. Older adults often have multiple problems from more than one of the domains of medicine, psychology, and social issues, domains that have typically been kept separate when addressing the problems of younger adults. This separation, quite possibly not a great idea for younger adults but workable to the extent that younger adults often have a principal problem falling in only one of these domains, is neither defensible nor practicable with older adults who commonly have multiple problems in multiple domains.

As seen in this section, the CCMSC model can guide the discussion of whether various theories of psychotherapy need modification when used with older adults. In the next section, we turn to the question of whether specific problems frequently faced by older adults call for the use of different therapy theories and techniques. In integrative therapy, matching therapies to problems is called *prescriptive eclecticism*.

## THE CCMSC MODEL AS A FRAMEWORK FOR PRESCRIPTIVE ECLECTICISM

The proponents of prescriptive psychotherapy, primarily Beutler and his colleagues (e.g., Beutler & Hodgson, 1993) have positioned themselves within the *technical eclecticism* approach to psychotherapy integration. This approach focuses on techniques rather than theoretical systems and advocates that selection be based on what is empirically known to work with specific problems, specific types of clients, and so forth. As Gold (1996) noted, the methods and the recommendations stemming from this approach can be quite similar to those of the transtheoretical approach. The principal difference would be that the selection of techniques would be guided by empirical findings, rather than by conceptual guidelines. Technical eclecticism can also be viewed as a consequence of therapeutic experience, to the extent that therapist behavior is shaped by the reinforcement of seeing clients improve; observers have often noted that the techniques of experienced therapists from different schools of thought are more similar than different (e.g., Jacobson, 1999; note that Jacobson was not an integrationist, however).

Some reflection on the history of psychotherapy with older adults reveals an apparent tendency for experience with older clients to pull the therapist somewhat out of model. From at least the middle of the twentieth century, psychodynamically oriented therapists have written about needing to be more active, more goal-directed, and more practical with older clients (see Rechtschaffen, 1959, for an early review). More recently, Nordhus, Nielsen, and Kvale (1998) wrote about the use of a *psychodynamic theory* with older adults, while drawing extensively upon the writing of CBT therapists who work with the elderly. In the other direction, *life review* is at times included or incorporated into discussions of CBT (e.g., Gallagher-Thompson & Thompson, 1996), even though its conceptual roots and the nature of its practice are much more similar to psychodynamic therapy. Knight and Satre (1999) noted that the natural tendency of older adults to reminisce, noted by Butler (1963) in a classic article, may pull CBT practitioners toward this more abstract and life-historical level of analysis. The problems of later life, and possibly the nature of older clients themselves, would appear to exert a certain pull toward eclectic use of techniques.

The CCMSC framework suggests that there may be a degree of pragmatic prescriptive psychotherapy being practiced with older adults. As with other applications of this framework, the prescription is not based so much on maturation as on other domains included in the framework. For example, consideration of context effects can call attention to the extensive use of behavioral techniques within medical and nursing home settings. This focus on behavioral technology is no doubt determined in part by the nature of the residents' problems, and so could be placed under specific challenges as well. The great majority of nursing home residents have dementia or chronic medical disorders, or both. These disorders seem especially amenable to behavioral intervention (Fisher & Carstensen, 1990; Gatz et al., 1998). In addition, however, the nursing home environment itself often needs behavioral analysis and intervention (Spayd & Smyer, 1996), and evidence suggests that behavioral interventions are needed to set up contingency systems that reward staff for using behavioral interventions with the residents (Stevens et al., 1998). Older adults are often heavily involved in medical contexts and tend to bring psychological problems to medical offices. Adaptations for behaviorally oriented consultations in doctors' offices, clinics, and hospitals are also likely to be needed (Haley, 1996).

Cohort effects are most likely to affect the selection of psychological interventions by their effect on the prevalence of psychological disorders, the educational levels of clients, and the typical psychological-mindedness of clients. Depression seems to vary by cohort, and it can be predicted that the prevalence of depression among older adults in later born cohorts (e.g., the baby boomers, now poised on the brink of older-adult status) will be higher than in the past (Koenig et al., 1994). Suicide rates are also higher in later born cohorts (McIntosh, Santos, Hubbard, & Overholser, 1994). Knight (1996b) speculated that some apparent age differences in character disorders may be cohort based rather than the results of maturation. Educational levels have increased in consecutive cohorts through the twentieth century. Changes in psychotherapy approaches that have been responsive to lower educational levels and lower prior exposure to psychological thinking should become unnecessary in the next decade or so.

Maturational changes as we age are thought to have relatively little effect on determining the type of technique that can be used with older adults (Knight, 1996a). However, therapists from a number of systems have recognized a need to talk more slowly, to present ideas one at a time, and to be prepared to accommodate changes in sight, hearing, and mobility that are common with aging.

The specific challenges of late life may themselves pull for certain prescriptive practices when one is selecting techniques for use with older clients. Much work with chronic illness and disability with any age of client draws heavily upon CBT techniques (Knight & Satre, 1999). Griefwork, in contrast, seems to pull for a more life-review or psychodynamic focus on emotions and on the meaning of life with and without the deceased. It must be noted, however, that there is scant evidence on the effectiveness of grief work. Knight and McCallum (1998) noted that family caregiving issues would

seem to call for the use of family systems approaches; however, most of what has been done with caregivers uses CBT techniques with the individual caregiver, with rather modest results (Gatz et al., 1998; Knight, Lutzky, & Macofsky-Urban, 1993).

Life review and reminiscence in therapy with older adults may take a variety of forms. As noted previously, older patients often tend to reminisce in therapy, particularly when dealing with grief. In this way, life review helps to integrate the patient's current distress into the context of his or her entire life, which may serve as a useful tool in coping with present suffering. Life review has also been advocated as a more formalized tool in both individual and group psychotherapy for older adults. In guided life review, the patient explores his or her experiences and values in key areas, such as relationships, work, and spirituality, as a way of understanding these experiences and identifying goals for personal growth (Birren & Deutchman, 1991).

Although prescriptive eclecticism suggests a pragmatic use of techniques developed in different theoretical contexts, theoretical integration would provide a conceptual basis for drawing upon differing theoretical systems when working with older adults. To date, there has been little work on psychotherapy with older adults that crosses traditional theoretical boundaries. In the next section, the Bergen model is presented as an example of this type of integration.

## THE BERGEN INTEGRATIVE PSYCHODYNAMIC MODEL

The Bergen integrative psychodynamic model has its roots in life span developmental psychology. Within the framework of psychotherapy following psychodynamic principles, Erikson's (1959, 1982) psychosocial developmental theory is the only one containing a specific focus on aging, and thus, a theoretical basis for an age-specific therapeutic approach. He was the first to describe the developmental tasks of later life and relate them to the psychotherapy endeavor, and based on this perspective, the life-review intervention strategy was described (Butler, 1963). From the early formulations by Butler (1963), several modifications of the basic life-review format have been elaborated; central among these more recent approaches is the development of *autobiography* (Birren & Deutchman, 1991). The common principle in all these approaches, and basic in classical psychoanalytic approaches, is to prompt early recollections, and thus facilitate the process of gaining an integrated perspective on one's life. Different authors may vary in their emphasis on the universality of the life-review process, but the process is more often than not described in normative terms—that is, as a process that is normal and particularly beneficial for older adults (see Nordhus & Nielsen, 1999).

More recently, therapists adhering to basic psychodynamic principles have changed from the traditional normative stance as we know it from classical ego psychology formulations (e.g., Silberschatz & Curtis, 1991). A more time-limited treatment course is increasingly being used, with goals formulated in terms of the presence of pathogenic beliefs (e.g., Curtis & Silberschatz, 1997) or of maladaptive interpersonal patterns (e.g., Levenson & Strupp, 1997). A basic observation that engendered concepts such as transference and resistance to change is that people tend to repeat their typical relationship patterns—even when such patterns are associated with distress. Thus, the repetition of early relationship patterns was traditionally conceived of as a means of meeting one's infantile security and attachment needs.

A contemporary life span–psychodynamic understanding would maintain that security and attachment are lifelong needs that continue to exert their influence throughout adulthood and into later life, rather than aims that ought to be relinquished in adulthood. *Attachment theory* introduces a general motivational factor for the repetition of interactional patterns as a way of rendering the world predictable and manageable (Bretherton, 1987). What needs to be modified in therapy is the maladaptive way in which one goes about meeting these needs in order to stop repeating early dysfunctional relationship patterns. Essentially, this is a learning perspective, in which the individual learns mental representations that are generally resistant to change and that have a strong effect on later relationship patterns. Generally, this perspective allows for a greater flexibility in therapy, in that it allows a focus either on the past or on the here and now. Also, it provides the possibility of using behavioral and cognitive techniques to optimize the therapeutic process (Nordhus et al., 1998). The clinical focus on problems that originate with beliefs, relationship behaviors, and the perception of relationships invites the use of cognitive behavioral and interpersonal intervention strategies.

Modifications suggested when working with older patients focus primarily on the relationship between the therapist and the patient. The therapist may often be encouraged to take a more active stance than typically seen with younger individuals and may need to educate the client about the nature of the psychotherapy endeavor. With regard to the process of therapy, the therapist may need to be more flexible in setting the duration and frequency of sessions, as well as in the interactions with family or other professionals being involved with the patient (Knight, 1996a). This flexibility primarily relates to the specific challenges that the patient faces

(e.g., recently bereaved), and not to the therapeutic potential of older patients.

## The Value of Case Formulation

Psychotherapy literature on aging generally tends to be well described clinically but not necessarily supported by extensive empirical research findings (Gallagher-Thompson & Thompson, 1995). The need to further develop empirically validated therapeutic approaches toward older adults is indisputable. For one thing, evaluation of the individual case in clinical descriptions of older patients has to a large extent relied on anecdotal methods in the absence of more informative and specific coding procedures. Although the study of individual cases has been a fundamental source of data in the clinical literature in general, there are long-recognized difficulties in using data so derived for hypothesis testing or for verification of clinical constructs. The critical task is to identify and operationalize clinical constructs in a way that permits continuous assessment and evaluation. One way to do this is to formalize the case study method by focusing on specific therapist-patient interactions and demonstrate how they develop through the course of therapy.

A case formulation is tailored to the specific individual's life circumstances, needs, thought patterns, and so on. The therapist must, nevertheless, rely upon general clinical knowledge, including knowledge about older adults, as well as experiences from working with other individuals, including supervised experience working with older adults. The repetitive, dysfunctional interaction construct is rooted in general and familiar theoretical language (e.g., attachment theory and transference). Staying close to the descriptive data, however, provides us with an empirical underpinning for aspects of these concepts as these unfold in each individual case. This may in turn counteract a tendency to overgeneralize about persons with whom we have little knowledge or experience. For example, therapists without appropriate knowledge and experience may stereotype clients' psychological needs in terms of age.

## The Cyclical Maladaptive Pattern

The Bergen model was developed in the context of a clinical training program conducting individual psychotherapy with older adults in the outpatient clinic in the Department of Clinical Psychology at the University of Bergen in Norway, and is described in detail elsewhere (e.g., Nordhus & Nielsen, 1999; Nordhus et al., 1998). At a general level, the Bergen approach can be classified as integrative psychodynamic (Wachtel, 1993, 1997), and utilizes a specific format of case formulation:

the *cyclical maladaptive pattern* (*CMP*; Levenson & Strupp, 1997; Strupp & Binder, 1984). The *integrative psychodynamic* label implies that various therapeutic techniques and interventions may be productively combined within the same, psychodynamically informed, course of treatment. This type of theoretical integration may also be described as *assimilative integration* of psychotherapeutic theory and technique (e.g., Messer, 2001).

A basic assumption of the Bergen model is that psychopathology can be described in terms of vicious cycles or maladaptive interpersonal functioning in the patient's interaction with others. In the patient's attempt to satisfy basic needs or to establish and maintain satisfying relationships, he or she typically acts in ways that unintentionally elicit repetitions of negative experiences or traumas. Erikson's shift to a life span developmental model argued that these negative experiences could have occurred in adulthood and are not limited to childhood events. In older clients, it is as likely that presenting problems will have had their origin in adulthood.

The persistence of these vicious interpersonal cycles results from an interplay among the patient's characteristic coping styles, inaccurate and maladaptive beliefs about herself or himself and others (Weiss & Sampson, 1986), and the inadvertent reinforcement provided by the responses of others. These maladaptive circles involve inflexible and self-perpetuating behaviors, and in turn negative self-appraisals by the patients leave them vulnerable to various feelings of psychological distress and observable symptoms. In different words, much of this description would be consistent with cognitive behavioral or interpersonal theories of therapy

Adhering to basic psychodynamic concepts such as unconscious motivation, conflict, defense, and so forth, the integrative model implies cyclical processes by which internal states and external events each continually recreate the conditions for the recurrence of the other (Wachtel, 1994). Internal processes such as wishes, fantasies, and motives are as likely to result from as to cause a patient's behavior. A central element in the model, therefore, is that causality is circular rather than linear. This implies that the traditional question of *What comes first, insight or behavioral change?* no longer is meaningful. Nor is insight conceived of as the final result, or an end product. Most insights are *partial insights,* and positive change typically develops gradually and may imply recurrent or intermittent brief therapy encounters (Cummings, 1986; Levenson & Strupp, 1997). In this way, while the theory of problem etiology is psychodynamic, the change processes might be seen as cognitive behavioral or interpersonal as well as psychodynamic.

A typical therapeutic challenge ensuing from this way of reasoning is to help the patient interrupt cyclical maladaptive patterns by learning new ways of integrating interpersonal experience, and to adopt more flexible and adaptive ways of relating. This new learning might most profitably start within the relatively safe and confiding climate of the consulting room. The psychotherapeutic process, therefore, is viewed as a set of collaborative interpersonal transactions, and the relationship between patient and therapist is used as a vehicle for bringing about change (Binder & Strupp, 1991). Because of the patient's unwitting tendency to cast the therapist into the roles of significant others and to enact with the therapist maladaptive behavior rooted in earlier conflicts, this process holds a fundamental therapeutic potential for new and experientially based learning. Evoking therapeutic change, however, requires that the therapist *actively* identify and attend to the repetitive, cyclical maladaptive patterns that unfold within the therapeutic encounter (the transference). The patient's past may be helpful to understanding the origin and development of a particular maladaptive pattern, and to help place a particular transference enactment between the therapist and patient into a broader perspective. However, focusing on the self-perpetuating behaviors in the patient's present life may be more strategically useful than focusing on the original or initiating causes (Nordhus et al., 1998). Thus, this perspective does not rule out a life span developmental framework, but it is a question of therapeutic choice whether the unique developmental story should be the focus. Therefore, the therapeutic focus may vary, balancing past history and present needs.

The pursuit of insight into the distant past as a critical agent of change may be overvalued, often at the neglect of focusing on interpersonal exchange that takes place in the therapeutic transaction. The classical ideas of Alexander and French (1946) served as an impetus for the development of contemporary short-term psychodynamic psychotherapies by questioning the traditional analytic assumption that depth and enduring change were proportionate to the prolonged reconstruction of childhood conflictual experiences. Erikson's (1982) life span approach moved theoretical attention away from the exclusive focus on childhood conflict to include those arising during adult developmental stages. Alexander and French (1946) asserted that substantial change may result from new corrective emotional experiences provided by the very interaction between patient and therapist in the here and now of the transference. In our own model, we have found the corrective emotional experience to be a very useful clinical concept also in terms of keeping the therapist on target and close to clinical phenomena as opposed to getting caught up in defeatist ageist stereotypes. The CMP is a way of organizing interpersonal information as it unfolds in the therapeutic encounter and is briefly illustrated in the following vignette.

## Case Illustration

Mr. A., a 76-year-old retired businessman, presented his problems as lack of confidence and strong feelings of worthlessness. He described himself as one who tended to feel uncomfortable when expressing irritation and anger, which were often followed by negative feelings and depression. In his retirement years he had more or less withdrawn from social life except for relatively frequent contact with his two grown children and their families. He lived with his 74-year-old wife, whom he described as a considerate woman, but he communicated openly that he wanted to be more cared for by his wife and sometimes felt rejected by her. Mr. A. was a kind, introspective, sensitive man who nevertheless had difficulty interacting comfortably with people. His father died when Mr. A. was 17 years old, and it appeared that his mother had a history of recurrent periods of depression during his adolescent years. At intake, the patient met the criteria for major depressive disorder.

In terms of a developmental diagnosis, it seemed reasonable to focus on how the patient's past behavior persisted in his current relationships, and how it colored the therapeutic connection. The historical information provided a context for understanding the vulnerability of the patient that was unfolding in the therapeutic setting. It seemed likely that his mother's depression and the early loss of his father, at the time when he was entering manhood, helped to form relationship patterns that were still causing problems in late life. He developed negative expectancies and a conditioned depressive response to situations that required assertiveness and an explicit voicing of his needs. In terms of a CMP, however, it is what goes on in the therapeutic interaction in the here and now that serves as central descriptive clinical data (Strupp & Binder, 1984). That is, rather than focusing on reviewing the history of relationships with mother and father, the therapeutic focus was the relationship with the therapist and with the wife.

In the following excerpt, the therapist's initial formulation of a CMP is presented. The CMP is composed of four categories that were used to organize the interpersonal information about the client. It was formulated by the end of the third session, including the reenactment experienced in the therapeutic setting by the therapist.

### Acts of the Self

Mr. A. presented as a person who was conflicted about his relational wishes. On the one hand, he wanted to be closer to people, especially to his wife, but he was frightened that he would be rejected. He wished to express his irritation and anger when feeling rejected, but would frequently be passive or self-punitive rather than appropriately assertive. ("I observe that my wife is helping others rather than me. If I say something about it, we always end up quarreling. The best thing to do is to say nothing at all.")

### Expectations of Others' Reactions

Mr. A.'s experiences with others left him with somewhat negative views of what he could expect to happen in relationships (which was not altogether unrealistic, given his experiences). He validated his general expression of being ignored by saying that "If I tell my family, and especially my wife, that I am depressed, the risk of being asked to count my blessings and pull myself together is too high."

### Acts of Others Toward the Self

Mr. A.'s feelings of being left outside his family were explicitly communicated. He expected that others perceived him as too weak to be heard in things that mattered ("I have always tried to solve conflicts by being diplomatic, something that is not considered to be a positive characteristic").

### Acts of the Self Toward the Self

By withdrawing and by refraining from voicing his problems and complaints, Mr. A. thought that he would appear less troublesome and more acceptable to his family. He acknowledged his own vulnerability and was constantly blaming himself for not being able to interact in a more assertive way. After the first session, he was blaming himself for not showing any progress in therapy, and "for not bringing good news to the therapist."

### Therapist's Reaction to Client

Based on the previous formulation, the therapist prepared herself for identifying recurrent themes that in one way or another were related to Mr. A.'s cyclical maladaptive patterns. Central to this approach was the therapist's own experience of frustration resulting in a feeling of not knowing how to help the patient. By communicating his needs for help in a self-blaming manner, the patient contributed to the therapist's growing feeling of not being able to help the patient. In this way, Mr. A. verified his own assumption of being weak and a hopeless case. An important element of this approach is that the therapist's sense of impotence was analyzed in a client-specific manner rather than being accepted as being due to the client's age and limited potential for change due to being old.

The central question for planning intervention was to focus on what kinds of new experiences and understanding (or *corrective emotional experience*) will support Mr. A. in identifying and communicating his own need in a more direct way. This would imply encouraging behaviors that signify a new manner of acting toward the therapist.

The therapist assumed that the type of new experience that might facilitate change in Mr. A.'s maladaptive interpersonal style would be the following:

1. Mr. A.'s experience of the therapist as one who accepted him as a person with a legitimate need for help (communicated by the therapist in a safe and supportive climate), and

2. Mr. A.'s experience of himself as a person who asks for help in an explicit and nondefensive way (e.g., using assertiveness training or role play).

In subsequent sessions, the therapist maintained a persistent focus on the interactive style of the patient. Whenever the patient demonstrated self-reproach and mistrustful expectations toward others' ability to help him, the therapist confronted him with direct questions such as "How can I know how to help you, when you keep telling me that you do not expect anyone to be able to help you?" Questions like these were followed by the therapist's confirming that she observed his pain and discomfort and by encouraging him to verbalize what he ideally would expect from therapy.

By confronting the patient with the vague and passive way he presented his needs, the therapist was able to have Mr. A. experience the confusion that his communicative style created. By taking part in the patient's mode of relatedness instead of focusing primarily on symptoms or past developmental history, the therapist was working at the core of the therapeutic process, in the here-and-now transaction (Levenson, 1995). In order to stay in that transaction, the therapist utilized assertiveness training and role playing, and eventually a joint focus on parallel interaction problems outside of therapy was established. These interventions, while chosen within a psychodynamic framework, are fairly commonly used cognitive behavioral techniques. In the following videotaped sessions, Mr. A. appeared to be more engaged and spontaneous in the therapeutic exchange. He gradually realized (somewhat reluctantly) his own responsibility in producing positive change in his relation with his wife.

## Summary of the Bergen Model

According to the Bergen model, the cyclical and integrative psychodynamic perspective is a sound foundation for developing competencies in clinical practice with older adults (Nordhus & Nielsen, 1999). Within the framework of brief psychodynamic therapy, it incorporates current developments in interpersonal, object relations as well as cognitive behavioral approaches. Yet to what extent is chronological age an informative variable for therapeutic work, let alone a matter of therapeutic adaptation? Generally, the therapist is challenged to understand how much emphasis to place on the individual's being old, and how much to place on his or her being a patient. Therapeutic work with older adults requires an understanding of both psychotherapy and aging, as well as how to use each understanding in the service of the other (Kivnick & Kavka, 1999).

First, working within an outpatient clinic like the one in Bergen necessitates that we do not offer psychotherapeutic services to patients with severe cognitive and psychotic symptoms. On the other hand, the majority of our patients aged 60 years and older report moderate to severe medical problems. This means that we typically have a community-dwelling older patient with medical problems, who is either self-referred or referred by a family physician, other medical units, or a family member. He or she may enter therapy with various forms of depression, anxiety, somatoform disorders, or minor to moderate adjustment disorders. Medical problems and medication use often imply that we coordinate our strategies with medical care, but these seldom negatively interfere with the therapeutic course.

Second, patients often seek therapeutic help in the clinic, because they are enmeshed in an unsatisfying relationship or are suffering from symptoms and dysphoric feelings that appear to be linked to troubled relationships. Recent empirical findings indicate that conflicts in current, close relationships are commonly presented complaints of older patients (e.g., Miller & Silberman, 1996). Such facts serve as important corrections to the traditional one-sided perception of the normative needs of the older patient, which would have the therapist focus on reconciling the patient to the life that has already passed. In the Bergen model, with an interactional and mastery-oriented approach to therapy, we emphasize the cooperative working relationship between therapist and patient. By focusing on the patient's present reality, current life situation, and interpersonal relationships, the therapist becomes an active participant in the therapeutic exchange.

Third, with regard to the process of therapy, our experience is that the therapist may need to be more flexible in setting the duration and the frequency of sessions, compared to therapeutic work with younger adults. Under certain circumstances, for instance with a patient under great stress, the therapist might find it appropriate to offer direct advice. Generally, we adhere to setting a time limit, also aiming at reinforcing the patient's confidence in his or her ability to resolve the current complaint. Nearly two thirds of the therapies last fewer than

20 sessions, but the older patients tend to have their sessions given at a more flexible schedule with more sparsely distributed sessions (e.g., every 2nd week). The most common reason for this is that concomitant physical decline and illness is making them less mobile, although it is also true that our patients (especially those aged 80 years and older) may expect that psychologists are like their primary physicians, implying fewer scheduled sessions. In conclusion, then, it seems that reasons for adaptations in therapy with older adults are primarily due to medical and contextual factors rather than limitations in the psychological potential for change. The cyclical maladaptive patterns format seems valuable for the therapeutic endeavor itself as well as for supervising psychotherapy training. In terms of contributing to the geropsychology field, specific case formulations, like the CMP, keep the therapist focused on a remediable problem rather than forming abstract and vague formulations, including age stereotypes. In addition, these formulations keep the therapist close to ongoing observable clinical data and encourage the use of active, present-oriented intervention techniques.

## SUMMARY AND CONCLUSIONS

In this review of psychotherapy with older adults, we have examined the literature within a framework of integrative approaches to psychotherapy. As with younger adults, outcome studies with an older adult population have largely been done within a cognitive behavioral theoretical framework, but there is evidence for the effectiveness of other therapies as well. First considering a common factors approach to integrative psychotherapy, there is some reason to believe that older adults may be especially responsive to the common relational elements of psychotherapy and to the hope imparted by the identification of a problem as a psychological disorder that can be treated. In a second type of integrative model, Knight's CCMSC model can be seen as a type of transtheoretical framework for thinking about the need to adapt therapy for working with older clients. Psychotherapy with older adults, driven by the interdisciplinary nature of gerontology and by the fact that older clients typically have problems from multiple domains, has always been integrative in the sense of crossing disciplinary lines to create a knowledge base for understanding aging and older clients, but has not been integrative in drawing on differing therapy theories. Third, the CCMSC model can also be seen as guiding a kind of prescriptive eclecticism with regard to the specific challenges of later life: CBTs for coping with the effects of functional disability and chronic illness, active listening and life review with grief, and family-oriented interventions with caregiving. Finally, the Bergen model is offered as a first example of

theoretical integration or assimilative integration in work with older clients: a model that is rooted in psychodynamic theory and uses many concepts and techniques from cognitive behavioral work with older adults.

Clearly there is much more work to be done to develop a truly integrative psychotherapy with older adults. Research in clinical geropsychology could be planned to investigate the role of common factors in therapy with older adults and could explore prescriptive approaches to matching therapies to presenting problems. Theoretical integration or assimilative integration could be used to reconcile the use of techniques by therapists whose theories do not easily support them: the commonly cited idea that psychodynamic therapists have to be more active and problem focused with older clients or that cognitive behavioral therapists engage in some degree of reminiscence or life review with older clients. Within integrative therapy, a focus on older clients and on life span developmental ideas could expand the integrative discussion into the consideration of lifelong development, the role of societal context, and the constantly shifting historical context in which psychological development unfolds. At present, integrative therapy, like much of psychology, risks being a de facto specialty concerning young adults (and sometimes including children and adolescents).

The ideas covered in this chapter can be seen as pioneering steps toward this goal. Bringing clinical geropsychology into the dialogue about integrative psychotherapy could advance theory and research about the nature of psychotherapy with older adults and also enrich thinking about therapy with adults by introducing a life span perspective into the ongoing debate about integrative psychotherapy.

## REFERENCES

Alexander, F., & French, T. M. (1946). *Psychoanalytic psychotherapy*. New York: Ronald Press.

Arean, P. A., & Miranda, J. (1996). The treatment of depression in elderly primary care patients: A naturalistic study. *Journal of Clinical Geropsychology, 2,* 153–160.

Arean, P. A., Perri, M. G., Nezu, A. M., Schein, R. L., Christopher, F., & Joseph, T. X. (1993). Comparative effectiveness of social problem-solving therapy and reminiscence therapy as treatments for depression in older adults. *Journal of Consulting and Clinical Psychology, 61,* 1003–1010.

Beutler, L. E., Engle, D., Mohr, D., Daldrup, R., Bergan, J., Meredith, K., & Merry, W. (1991). Predictors of differential response to cognitive, experiential, and self-directed psychotherapeutic procedures. *Journal of Consulting and Clinical Psychology, 59,* 333–340.

Beutler, L. E., & Hodgson, A. B. (1993). Prescriptive psychotherapy. In G. Stricker & J. R. Gold (Eds.), *Comprehensive handbook of psychotherapy integration* (pp. 151–163). New York: Plenum Press.

Bienenfeld, D. (1987). Alcoholism in the elderly. *American Family Physician, 36,* 163–169.

Binder, J. L., & Strupp, H. H. (1991). The Vanderbilt approach to time-limited psychotherapy. In P. Crits-Christoph & J. Barber (Eds.), *Handbook of short-term dynamic therapy* (pp. 137–165). New York: Basic Books.

Birren, J. E., & Deutchman, D. E. (1991). *Guiding autobiography groups for older adults: Exploring the fabric of life.* Baltimore: Johns Hopkins University Press.

Blazer, D., George, L., & Hughes, D. (1991). The epidemiology of anxiety: An age comparison. In C. Salzman & B. D. Liebowitz (Eds.), *Anxiety in the elderly* (pp. 17–30). New York: Springer.

Blow, F., & Berry, K. L. (2000). Older patients with at-risk and problem drinking patterns: New developments in brief interventions. *Journal of Geriatric Psychiatry and Neurology, 13,* 115–123.

Boczkowski, J., & Zeichner, A. (1985). Medication compliance and the elderly. *Clinical Gerontologist, 4,* 3–15.

Bretherton, I. (1987). New perspective on attachment relations: Security, communication, and internal working models. In J. D. Osofsky (Ed.), *Handbook of infant development* (2nd ed., pp. 1061–1100). New York: Wiley.

Bucholz, K. K., Sheline, Y. I., & Helzer, J. E. (1995). The epidemiology of alcohol use, problems and dependence in elders. In T. Beresford & E. Gomberg (Eds.), *Alcohol and aging* (pp. 19–41). New York: Oxford University Press.

Butler, R. N. (1963). The life-review: An interpretation of reminiscence in the aged. *Psychiatry, 26,* 65–75.

Butler, R. N. (1975). *Why survive? Growing old in America.* New York: Harper and Row.

Carstensen, L. L., Rychtarik, R. G., & Prue, D. M. (1985). Behavioral treatment of the geriatric alcohol abuser: A long-term follow-up study. *Addictive Behavior, 10,* 307–311.

Castonguay, L. G. (1997). Support in psychotherapy: A common factor in need of empirical data, conceptual clarification, and clinical input. *Journal of Psychotherapy Integration, 7,* 99–103.

Chambless, D. L., Baker, M. J., Baucom, D. H., Beutler, L. E., Calhoun, K. S., Crits-Christoph, P., Daiuto, A., DeRubeis, R., Detweiler, J., Haaga, D. A. F., Bennett Johnson, S., McCurry, S., Mueser, K. T., Pope, K. S., Sanderson, W. C., Shoham, V., Stickle, T., Williams, D. A., & Woody, S. R. (1998). Update on empirically validated therapies, II. *The Clinical Psychologist, 51,* 3–16.

Cook, A. J. (1998). Cognitive-behavioral pain management for elderly nursing home residents. *Journal of Gerontology: Psychological Sciences, 53B,* P51–P59.

Crook, H., Ridout, E., & Browne, G. (1984). The prevalence of pain complaints among a general population. *Pain, 18,* 299–314.

Cummings, N. A. (1986). The dismantling of our health system. *American Psychologist, 41,* 426–421.

Currin, J. B., Hayslip, B., Schneider, L. J., & Kooken, R. A. (1998). Cohort differences in attitudes toward mental health among older persons. *Psychotherapy, 35,* 506–518.

Curtis, J. T., & Silberschatz, G. (1997). The plan formulation method. In T. D. Eells (Ed.), *Handbook of psychotherapy case formulation* (pp. 116–136). New York: Guilford.

De Berry, S. (1981–82). An evaluation of progressive muscle relaxation on stress related symptoms in a geriatric population. *International Journal of Aging and Human Development, 14,* 255–269.

De Berry, S. (1982). The effects of meditation-relaxation on anxiety and depression in a geriatric population. *Psychotherapy: Theory, Research and Practice, 19,* 512–521.

De Berry, S., Davis, S., & Reinhard, K. E. (1988). A comparison of meditation-relaxation and cognitive/behavioral techniques for reducing anxiety and depression in a geriatric population. *Journal of Geriatric Psychiatry, 22,* 231–247.

Dupree, L. W., Broskowski, H., & Schonfeld, L. (1984). The Gerontology Alcohol Project: A behavioral treatment program for elderly alcohol abusers. *Gerontologist, 24,* 510–516.

Erikson, E. H. (1959). *Identity and the life cycle.* New York: W. W. Norton.

Erikson, E. H. (1982). *The life cycle completed.* New York: W. W. Norton.

Ferrell, B. A., Ferrell, R. R., & Osterweil, D. (1990). Pain in the nursing home. *Journal of the American Geriatrics Society, 38,* 409–414.

Fisher, J. E., & Carstensen, L. L. (1990). Behavioral management of the dementias. *Clinical Psychology Review, 10,* 611–629.

Fisher, J. E., & Noll, J. P. (1996). Anxiety disorders. In L. L. Carstensen, B. A. Edelstein, & L. Dornbrand (Eds.), *The practical handbook of clinical gerontology* (pp. 304–323). Thousand Oaks, CA: Sage.

Ford, D. E., & Kamerow, D. B. (1989). Epidemiologic study of sleep disturbances and psychiatric disorders: An opportunity for prevention? *Journal of the American Medical Association, 262,* 1479–1484.

Frank, J. D. (1961). *Persuasion and healing.* Baltimore: Johns Hopkins University Press.

Frank, J. D. (1982). Therapeutic components shared by all psychotherapies. In J. H. Harvey & M. M. Parks (Eds.), *The master lecture series: Vol. 1. Psychotherapy research and behavior change* (pp. 9–37). Washington, DC: American Psychological Association.

Gallagher, D. E., & Thompson, L. W. (1983). Treatment of major depressive disorder in older adult outpatients with brief psychotherapies. *Psychotherapy: Theory, Research, and Practice, 19,* 482–490.

Gallagher-Thompson, D. E., & Thompson, L. W. (1995). Psychotherapy with older adults in theory and practice. In B. Bongar & L. E. Beutler (Eds.), *Comprehensive textbook of psychotherapy: Theory and practice* (pp. 359–401). New York: Oxford University Press.

Gallagher-Thompson, D. E., & Thompson, L. W. (1996). Applying cognitive-behavioral therapy to the psychological problems of late life. In S. Zarit & B. G. Knight (Eds.), *A guide to psychotherapy and aging* (pp. 61–82). Washington, DC: American Psychological Association.

Gallo, J. J., Marino, S., Ford, D., & Anthony, J. C. (1995). Filters on the pathway to mental health care, II. Sociodemographic factors. *Psychological Medicine, 25,* 1149–1160.

Gaston, L., Marmar, C. R., Thompson, L. W., & Gallagher, D. (1988). Relation of patient pretreatment characteristics to the therapeutic alliance in diverse psychotherapies. *Journal of Consulting and Clinical Psychology, 56,* 483–489.

Gatz, M., Fiske, A., Fox, L. S., Kaskie, B., Kasl-Godley, J., McCallum, T., & Wetherell, J. (1998). Empirically-validated psychological treatments for older adults. *Journal of Mental Health and Aging, 4,* 9–46.

Gift, A. G., Moore, T., & Soeken, K. (1992). Relaxation to reduce dyspnea and anxiety in COPD patients. *Nursing Research, 41,* 242–246.

Gold, J. R. (1996). *Key concepts in psychotherapy integration.* New York: Plenum Press.

Haley, W. E. (1996). The medical context of psychotherapy with the elderly. In S. H. Zarit & B. G. Knight (Eds.), *A guide to psychotherapy and aging: Effective interventions in a life stage context* (pp. 221–240). Washington, DC: American Psychological Association.

Ham, R. J. (1983). *Primary care geriatrics.* Boston: Jon Wright.

Jacobson, N. S. (1999). An outsider's perspective on psychotherapy integration. *Journal of Psychotherapy Integration, 9,* 219–234.

Kashner, T. M., Rodell, D. E, Ogden, S. R., Guggenheim, F. G., & Karson, C. N. (1992). Outcomes and costs of two VA inpatient treatment programs for older alcoholic patients. *Hospital and Community Psychiatry, 43,* 985–989.

Kivnick, H. Q., & Kavka, A. (1999). It takes two: Therapeutic alliance with older adults. In M. Duffy (Ed.), *Handbook of counseling and psychotherapy with older adults* (pp. 107–132). New York: Wiley.

Knight, B. G. (1996a). *Psychotherapy with older adults* (2nd ed.). Thousand Oaks, CA: Sage.

Knight, B. G. (1996b). Psychodynamic therapy with older adults: Lessons from scientific gerontology. In R. Woods (Ed.), *Handbook of clinical psychology and ageing.* London: Wiley.

Knight, B. G., & Fox, L. S. (1999). La practica de la terapia conductual [The practice of behavior therapy]. In I. Montorio & M. Ezal (Trans. & Eds.), *Intervencion psicologica in la vejez [Psychological interventions in late life]* (pp. 101–110). Madrid: Sintesis.

Knight, B. G., & Kaskie, B. (1995). Models for mental health service delivery to older adults: Models for reform. In M. Gatz (Ed.), *Emerging issues in mental health and aging* (pp. 231–255). Washington, DC: American Psychological Association.

Knight, B. G., Kelly, M., & Gatz, M. (1992). Psychotherapy with the elderly. In D. K. Freedheim (Ed.), *The history of psychotherapy* (pp. 528–551). Washington, DC: American Psychological Association.

Knight, B. G., Lutzky, S. M., & Macofsky-Urban, F. (1993). A meta-analytic review of interventions for caregiver distress: Recommendations for future research. *Gerontologist, 33,* 240–249.

Knight, B. G., & McCallum, T. J. (1998). Family therapy with older clients: The contextual, cohort-based, maturity/specific challenge model. In I. H. Nordhus, G. VandenBos, S. Berg, & P. Fromholt (Eds.), *Clinical geropsychology* (pp. 313–328). Washington, DC: American Psychological Association.

Knight, B. G., & Satre, D. D. (1999). Cognitive behavioral psychotherapy with older adults. *Clinical Psychology: Science and Practice, 6,* 188–203.

Koenig, H. G., George, L. K., & Schneider, R. (1994). Mental health care for older adults in the year 2020: A dangerous and avoided topic. *Gerontologist, 34,* 674–679.

Lasoki, M. C., & Thelen, M. H. (1987). Attitudes of older and middle-aged persons toward mental health intervention. *Gerontologist, 27,* 288–292.

Levenson, H. (1995). *Time-limited psychodynamic psychotherapy: A guide to clinical practice.* New York: Basic Books.

Levenson, H., & Strupp, H. E. (1997). Cyclical maladaptive patterns: Case formulation in time-limited dynamic psychotherapy. In T. D. Eells (Ed.), *Handbook of psychotherapy formulation* (pp. 84–115). New York: Guilford.

Lopez, M. A., & Mermelstein, R. J. (1995). A cognitive-behavioral program to improve geriatric rehabilitation outcome. *The Gerontologist, 35,* 696–700.

Marmar, C. R., Gaston, L., Gallagher, D., & Thompson, L. W. (1989). Alliance and outcome in late life depression. *Journal of Nervous and Mental Disease, 177,* 464–472.

McIntosh, J. L., Santos, J. F., Hubbard, R. W., & Overholser, J. C. (1994). *Elder suicide: Research, theory, and treatment.* Washington, DC: American Psychological Association.

Messer, S. B. (Ed.). (2001). Assimilative integration [Special issue]. *Journal of Psychotherapy Integration, 11.*

Miller, M. D., & Silberman, R. L. (1996). Using interpersonal psychotherapy with depressed elders. In S. H. Zarit & B. G. Knight (Eds.), *A guide to psychotherapy and aging: Effective clinical interventions in a life-stage context* (pp. 83–100). Washington, DC: American Psychological Association.

Morin, C. M., Colecchi, C., Stone, J., Sood, R., & Brink, D. (1999). Behavioral and pharmacological therapies for late-life insomnia: A randomized controlled trial. *JAMA, 281,* 991–999.

Morin, C. M., Kowatch, R. A., Barry, T., & Walton, E. (1993). Cognitive-behavior therapy for late-life insomnia. *Journal of Consulting and Clinical Psychology, 6,* 137–146.

Morin, C. M., & Kwentus, J. A. (1988). Behavioral and pharmacological treatments for insomnia. *Annals of Behavioral Medicine, 10,* 91–100.

National Center for Health Statistics. (1987). *Statistical abstract of the United States* (108th ed.). Washington, DC: U.S. Government Printing Office.

Nordhus, I. H., & Nielsen, G. H. (1999). *Brief dynamic psychotherapy with older adults. In Session: Psychotherapy in Practice, 55,* 935–947.

Nordhus, I. H., Nielsen, G. H., & Kvale, G. (1998). Psychotherapy with older adults. In I. H. Nordhus, G. R. Vandenbos, S. Berg, & P. Fromholt (Eds.), *Clinical geropsychology* (pp. 289–313). Washington, DC: American Psychological Association.

Parmalee, P. A., Katz, I. R., & Lawton, M. P. (1991). The relation of pain to depression among institutionalized aged. *Journals of Gerontology, 46,* P15–P21.

Prochaska, J. O. (1984). *Systems of psychotherapy: A transtheoretical analysis* (2nd ed.). Homewood, IL: Dorsey.

Rankin, E. J., Gilner, F. H., Gfeller, J. D., & Katz (1993). Efficacy of progressive muscle relaxation for reducing state anxiety among elderly adults on memory tasks. *Perceptual and Motor Skills, 77,* 1395–1402.

Rechtschaffen, A. (1959). Psychotherapy with geriatric patients: A review of the literature. *Journal of Gerontology, 14,* 73–84.

Reynolds, C. F., Frank, E., Perel, J., Imber, S., Cornes, C., Miller, M. D., Mazumdar, S., Houck, P. R., Dew, M. A., Stack, J. A., Pollock, B. G., Kupfer, D. J. (1999). Nortriptyline and interpersonal psychotherapy as maintenance therapies for recurrent major depression: A randomized controlled trial in patients older than 59 years. *Journal of the American Medical Association, 281,* 39–45.

Rickard, H. C., Scogin, F., & Keith, S. (1994). A one-year follow-up of relaxation training for elders with subjective anxiety. *The Gerontologist, 34,* 121–122.

Robins, L. N., Helzer, J. E., Weissman, M. M., Orvaschel, H., Gruenberg, E., Burke, J. D., & Regier, D. A. (1984). Lifetime prevalence of specific psychiatric disorders in three sites. *Archives of General Psychiatry, 41,* 949–958.

Robins, L. N., & Regier, D. A. (Eds.). (1991). Psychiatric disorders in America: The epidemiological catchment area study. New York: Free Press.

Roy, R., & Michael, T. (1986). A survey of chronic pain in an elderly population. *Canadian Family Physician, 32,* 513–516.

Schonfeld, L., & Dupree, L. W. (1995). Treatment approaches for older problem drinkers. *International Journal of the Addictions, 30,* 1819–1842.

Scogin, F., Rickard, H. C., Keith, S., Wilson, J., & McElreath, L. (1992). Progressive and imaginial relaxation training for elderly persons with subjective anxiety. *Psychology and Aging, 7,* 419–424.

Silberschatz, G., & Curtis, J. T. (1991). Time-limited psychodynamic therapy with older adults. In W. Myers (Ed.), *New techniques in the psychotherapy of older patients* (pp. 95–108). Washington, DC: American Psychiatric Press.

Spayd, C. S., & Smyer, M. A. (1996). Psychological interventions in nursing homes. In S. H. Zarit & B. G. Knight (Eds.), *A guide to psychotherapy and aging: Effective interventions in a life stage*

*context* (pp. 241–268). Washington, DC: American Psychological Association.

Stevens, A. B., Burgio, L. D., Bailey, E., Burgio, K. L., Paul, P., Capilouto, E., et al. (1998). Teaching and maintaining behavior management skills with nursing assistants in a nursing home. *Gerontologist, 38,* 379–384.

Stricker, G., & Gold, J. R. (Eds.). (1993). *Comprehensive handbook of psychotherapy integration.* New York: Plenum Press.

Strupp, H. H., & Binder, J. L. (1984). *Psychotherapy in a new key: A guide to time-limited dynamic psychotherapy.* New York: Basic Books.

Task Force on Promotion and Dissemination of Psychological Procedures. (1995). Training in and dissemination of empirically validated psychological treatments: Report and recommendations. *The Clinical Psychologist, 48,* 3–23.

Teri, L., Curtis, J., Gallagher-Thompson, D., & Thompson, L. W. (1994). Cognitive-behavior therapy with depressed older adults. In L. S. Schneider, C. F. Reynolds, B. Liebowitz, & A. J. Friedhoff (Eds.), *Diagnosis and treatment of depression in late life* (pp. 279–292). Washington, DC: American Psychiatric Press.

Thompson, L. W., Gallagher, D., & Breckenridge, J. S. (1987). Comparative effectiveness of psychotherapies for depressed elders. *Journal of Consulting and Clinical Psychology, 55,* 385–390.

Wachtel, P. L. (1993). *Therapeutic communication: Principles and effective practice.* New York: Guilford.

Wachtel, P. L. (1994). Cyclical processes in personality and psychopathology. *Journal of Abnormal Psychology, 103,* 51–54.

Wachtel, P. L. (1997). *Psychoanalysis, behavior therapy, and the relational world.* Washington, DC: American Psychological Association.

Weiss, J., & Sampson, H. (1986). Testing alternative psychoanalytic explanations of the therapeutic process. In J. M. Masling (Ed.), *Empirical studies of psychoanalytic theories* (Vol. 2, pp. 1–26). Hillsdale, NJ: Analytic Press.

Weinberger, J. (1993). Common factors in psychotherapy. In G. Stricker & J. R. Gold (Eds.), *Comprehensive handbook of psychotherapy integration* (pp. 43–56). New York: Plenum Press.

Widner, S., & Zeichner, A. (1993). Psychologic interventions for the elderly chronic pain patient. *Clinical Gerontologist, 13,* 3–18.

Yesavage, J. (1984). Relaxation and memory training in 39 elderly patients. *American Journal of Psychiatry, 141,* 778–781.

Zeiss, A. M., Lewinsohn, P. M., Rohde, P., & Seeley, J. R. (1996). Relationship of physical disease and functional impairment to depression in older people. *Psychology and Aging, 11,* 572–581.

Zeiss, A. M., & Steffen, A. (1996). Behavioral and cognitive-behavioral treatments: An overview of social learning. In S. Zarit & B. G. Knight (Eds.), *A guide to psychotherapy and aging* (pp. 35–60). Washington, DC: American Psychological Association.

Zivian, M. T., Larsen, W., Gekoski, W., Hatchette, V., & Knox, V. J. (1994). Psychotherapy for the elderly: Public opinion. *Psychotherapy, 31,* 492–502.

# PART THREE

# PROFESSIONAL ISSUES

CHAPTER 20

# North American Perspectives on Education, Training, Licensing, and Credentialing

JUDY E. HALL AND GEORGE HURLEY

This chapter is designed to familiarize readers with the broad realm of education, training, licensing, and credentialing in professional psychology across the North American continent. Particular attention is paid to the development and implementation of these components in both the United States and Canada because of their similar developmental histories and strong cross-border interchanges and influences.

Clearly, the description of education, training, and credentialing of clinical psychology is not brief. We describe each component from the perspective of the major organizations in the United States and Canada, and to some degree in Mexico, that participate in the structures established to educate, train, accredit, identify, and certify programs and individuals. We

examine some influences from external forces that have shaped these developments. We cover what would be important from the perspective of an individual student or professional looking for a single source.

## Clinical Versus Clinical Psychology: The Evolution of Definitions in the United States and Canada

### The U.S. Experience

Psychology's history of attempts to differentiate types of psychologists have been either resisted or encouraged, often depending on what organization or constituent group was likely to benefit. Defining the profession broadly in state licensing laws and regulations made sense in terms of enhancing the overall political and professional power of psychology. The scope of practice and the group of psychologists licensed influenced decisions about diagnosis, assessment, and reimbursement and also provided the profession with prestige needed to compete with more senior professions. The American Psychological Association (APA) acted quickly 45 years ago to define entry to the profession as a person with a doctoral degree (APA Committee on Legislation, 1955). Then, for a licensed psychologist to be seen as distinctive, a specialty label was chosen, typically based on the name of the program completed. Today, debating the differences between clinical psychology and counseling psychology, as only one example, divides the profession at times and occupies incredible energy that might be better spent elsewhere.

After many battles and no winners, the fervor that once attached itself to being a clinical psychologist has moved to a different position that appears somewhat accepted, namely that professional psychology is made up of many types of psychologists, typically identified initially by the title of the doctoral program (and thus affected by the training philosophy in that area), but all being trained at ameliorating some type of dysfunction or discomfort in humans or organizations. As a result, the word *clinical* embraces a wider array of psychologists, helps focus on their commonalities, and positions psychology to speak with something closer to one voice (Belar & Perry, 1992).

It has taken us 55 years to reach some degree of comfort with that perspective, and although it is not universal, it is the approach that we bring to this review of education, training, licensing, and credentialing in North America. Although we later introduce some history of the development of professional psychology and attendant national conferences for perspective, we do not limit ourselves to describing the developmental status and future of clinical psychology only. Instead, we include "clinical psychology" or "professional psychology" as identifiers of the broad set of applied psychologists who carry on a vast array of professional activities. (The histories of several branches of applied psychology are elaborated in vol. 1 of this Handbook.)

Recently, APA has acted on petitions from different areas of psychology practice to determine whether (a) the area should be approved officially as a "specialty" in professional psychology (e.g., clinical neuropsychology), (b) the area should be clearly labeled with "clinical" as a prefix (e.g., clinical health), (c) the area should be officially approved as a specialty based on a de jure review instead of the de facto

approval that occurred at various stages throughout the development of the profession (e.g., clinical, counseling, and school psychology), or (d) the area qualifies for a proficiency but not a specialty (e.g., clinical child).

What are the current and official U.S. definitions? Following we excerpt part of the definitions approved by APA at the time that these three de facto specialties were officially continued as specialties:

> Clinical psychologists assess, diagnose, predict, prevent, and treat psychopathology, mental disorders and other individual or group problems to improve behavior adjustment, adaptation, personal effectiveness and satisfaction.
>
> Counseling psychologists help people with physical, emotional, and mental disorders improve well-being, alleviate distress and maladjustment, and resolve crises.
>
> School psychologists . . . provide a range of psychological diagnosis, assessment, intervention, prevention, health promotion, and program development and evaluation services.

These definitions can be accessed in full from the following websites: www.apa.org/crsppp/clinpsych.html, www.apa.org/crsppp/counseling.html and www.apa.org/crsppp/schpsych.html.

A more inclusive definition of practice was provided by the National Register of Health Service Providers in Psychology (hereafter National Register) when it defined without reference to specialty title the health service provider in psychology. This 1974 definition has been incorporated into the statute or regulations by nine state licensing boards to identify the health service providers among all those licensed and approved by APA (APA Council of Representatives, 1996) and the Association of State and Provincial Psychology Boards (ASPPB, 1998):

> A "Health Service Provider in Psychology" is "a psychologist currently and actively licensed/certified/registered at the independent practice level in a jurisdiction, who is trained and experienced in the delivery of direct, preventive, assessment and therapeutic intervention services to individuals whose growth, adjustment, or functioning is impaired or to individuals who otherwise seek services." (Council for the National Register of Health Service Providers in Psychology, 2000, p. 11)

The necessity to be as inclusive as possible is highlighted by U.S. federal legislation for purposes of Medicare reimbursement. A clinical psychologist was originally defined as someone who graduated from a clinical psychology program. Although this narrower legal definition would have applied to the majority of graduates of professional psychology programs, it would have eliminated many qualified health service psychologists from providing needed services to Medicare patients. Responding to public comments, the Center for Medicare and Medicaid Services (CMS) now defines clinical psychologists as persons who hold doctoral degrees in psychology and are state licensed at the independent practice level of psychology to furnish diagnostic, assessment, preventive, and therapeutic services. Those psychologists who do not meet those requirements are limited to providing diagnostic testing services for Medicare reimbursement (Federal Register, 1998).

### The Canadian Experience

Much as in the United States, the term *clinical* has created taxonomic confusions in Canadian psychology that had to be addressed. The collective remedy to date in Canada is to endorse the term *professional psychology* to denote the larger set of more direct service and applied branches of psychology. As an example of this issue, Dobson and Dobson (1993) noted that "there remains a tendency to equate professional psychology with clinical psychology. However, the following (chapters) amply demonstrate the falsity underlying this statement—professional psychology in Canada exists in a diverse range of work settings, practice areas and work activities" (p. 5). Likewise, Goodman (2000) stated that "clinical psychology is not synonymous with professional psychology. It is a subset along with school psychology, counseling psychology, forensic-correctional psychology, neuropsychology, rehabilitation psychology, and industrial organizational psychology. While there is overlap among the subsets, each has its own unique features" (p. 25).

Canadian clinical psychology (historically read "applied psychology," now "professional psychology")—much like U.S. clinical psychology—represents a story of ongoing broad-based development rooted in historic circumstances, emerging societal and professional needs, and somewhat unique Canadian academic and practice traditions. Likewise, clinical psychology as a formalized branch or subset of the larger Canadian professional psychology arena also draws its own identity in Canada from many of the larger formative forces impacting Canadian professional psychology.

Given the somewhat parallel problems in both the United States and Canada with the term *clinical,* we propose to use the term *professional psychologist* for those psychologists in both countries who provide health and other similar services aimed at ameliorating and addressing problems presented by individuals or organizations.

## ASSESSING PROFESSIONAL COMPETENCE: THE ROLE OF CERTIFICATION MECHANISMS IN PROFESSIONAL PSYCHOLOGY

The terms *credentialing* and *certification* are often used interchangeably. Credentialing typically refers to individuals who have been certified as having met some standard. For instance, the university or professional school certifies to the public that the graduate has met the requirements of the degree by awarding the diploma. Credentialing and certification thus usually refer to an individual achievement. Certification indicates quality, "especially in the absence of knowledge to the contrary" (Drum & Hall, 1993, p. 151). According to Stromberg (1990), "certification is a process by which government or a private association assesses a person, facility, or program and states publicly that it meets specific standards"—these standards are considered to be significant measures. Thus, we will see the term *certification* again when we discuss licensing of individual psychologists. Accreditation and designation refer to the certification of programs, as opposed to individuals. These three terms, *credentialing, accreditation,* and *designation,* are certification mechanisms.

### Self-Regulation and Government Regulation of Education and Training Programs

Part of the responsibility of belonging to a profession includes the responsibility to regulate that profession. Regulating a profession includes many activities, one of which is the establishment of education and training standards, followed by the application of those standards to education and training programs. Psychology has at least three major players in its self-regulation of education and training: (a) the professional associations (APA and Canadian Psychological Association, or CPA, Committees on Accreditation), (b) the licensing and credentialing bodies (ASPPB's National Register Designation Project), and (c) statewide or provincial review or approval of programs, such as in Ontario or New York State (New York State Doctoral Evaluation Project, 1990). Accreditation and designation of training programs, such as internships and postdoctoral residencies, involve the accrediting bodies as well as the Association of Psychology Postdoctoral and Internship Centers (APPIC) programs. Future psychologists are affected by these organizations and the standards they employ as illustrated by the person moving through the education, training, licensing, credentialing, and certification process as illustrated in Figure 20.1. The organizations identified are described by function in Table 20.1.

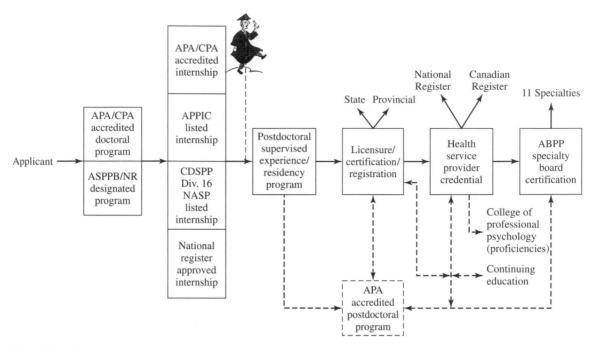

**Figure 20.1**    Typical doctoral sequence in the United States and Canada from entry into graduate school to Health Service Provider in Psychology (HSPP) and specialty board certification.

**TABLE 20.1    Designation, Accreditation, and Credentialing: Three Modes of Assessment of Competence**

| Competence Level and Scope | Program | Example | Individual | Example |
|---|---|---|---|---|
| Basic and minimal | Criteria-based designation of doctoral programs that produce professional psychologists | Association of State and Provincial Psychology Boards (ASPPB)–National Register of Health Service Providers in Psychology Designation Project | Certification of individual's degree and training in professional psychology | Universities and professional schools |
| Basic and extensive | Criteria-based accreditation of doctoral programs and internships that produce professional psychologists | American and Canadian Psychological Associations Committees on Accreditation | License to practice as a professional psychologist | State, provincial, and territorial licensure bodies in United States and Canada |
| | Criteria-based listing and review of internship sites and internship completed | Association of Psychology Postdoctoral and Internship Centers (APPIC) | Credentialing of licensed psychologists as health service providers in psychology | National and Canadian Register of Health Service Providers in Psychology |
| Advanced and specialized or generic | Criteria-based accreditation of postdoctoral programs in professional psychology in specialized and generic areas | American Psychological Association Committee on Accreditation (COA) | Board certification through examination of advanced skills in 11 specialty areas | American Board of Professional Psychology (ABPP) |
| | Criteria-based listing of postdoctoral training programs | APPIC | | |

Armed with an overview of these private and public influences that constitute part of organized psychology, we now consider the various educational levels and models for training of professional psychologists, especially as relating to the competencies expected of psychologists in North America.

## PROFESSIONAL EDUCATION

### Doctoral-Level Education Versus Subdoctoral-Level Education

In both the United States and Canada, doctoral-level education has been seen as the long-desired entry practice level for clinical psychologists. In the United States there has been a general consensus about this educational requirement for the autonomous professional practice of psychology, whereas in Canada there is widespread autonomous practice at both the master's and the doctoral level of education. Autonomous practice for master's level psychologists exists only in Vermont, West Virginia, and Kentucky (except for the case of school psychologists practicing in educational settings). Other states do have master's-level practitioners, but such individuals are typically supervised or restricted in their practice roles (ASPPB, 2001).

These differential degree requirements for autonomous practice in Canada and the United States reflect a number of different national factors. In Canada such entry-level educational criteria reflect a somewhat different level of general availability of doctoral-level training programs in relation to applicant pool combined with a far more restrictive view on private graduate education programs. In Canada there are currently 17 doctoral clinical programs that accommodate approximately 10% of clinical applications (Robinson et al., 1998), whereas there is a much wider availability of both university-based and freestanding doctoral-level clinical training programs and available training slots in the United States. Unlike in the United States, the almost complete absence of freestanding, for-profit, doctoral-level professional psychology training institutions in Canada (i.e., entities outside the publicly funded Canadian university system) has also meant that doctoral-level clinical psychology has been much slower to develop. Finally, unlike in the United States, where there has been rapid development of doctoral-level clinical training and commensurate doctoral-level state licensing requirements, the far slower growth of Canadian clinical training has meant that Canadian jurisdictions and licensing boards have necessarily made far greater use of master's degree programs as sources for generating autonomous psy-

chologist practitioners—especially in the Atlantic provinces of Newfoundland, Prince Edward Island, Nova Scotia, and New Brunswick. In addition, Quebec has had a longstanding tradition of master's-level practitioner programs. In effect, about two thirds of the 12,000 practicing Canadian psychologists are trained at the master's level (Gauthier, 1997; Robinson et al., 1998). Canada is still grappling with how to provide increased numbers of doctoral-level professional psychology training programs.

In Mexico (and for most of Europe and Latin America), the typical psychologist—whether licensed or not—is trained at the subdoctoral level following an introduction to professional training that begins after two years of high school (*bachillerato*). The U.S. and Canadian pattern of obtaining a bachelor's degree prior to entry to graduate training is not typical in many of these countries. In most, obtaining a master's degree and a doctoral degree is a route chosen only for those intending to teach and do research in a university setting. A comparison of the education, training, and licensure of psychologists in North American is illustrated in Table 20.2.

### Sequence and Models of Education

#### The Scientist-Practitioner Model

In both the United States and Canada the sequence of doctoral-level training for students following the scientist-practitioner model (the *Boulder-model PhD*) is largely similar, although there are a few notable differences. In the United States students normally begin graduate education with a set of basic core courses prescribed for their first year. In Canada students are normally only admitted to clinical psychology graduate programs based on an undergraduate bachelor of science honors degree in psychology, which affords much of the preparation normally provided in the first year of psychology graduate training in the United States.

Overall, content of training for Canada and the United States is quite similar. Each country requires that doctoral-level clinical training be conducted in the four primary areas of (a) biological bases of behavior, (b) cognitive and affective bases of behavior, (c) social bases of behavior, and (d) individual differences in behavior, as well as statistics, research design, psychological measurement, ethics and standards, and history and systems of psychology. Training in specific skills such as psychodiagnosis, assessment, individual and group intervention, consultation, and program evaluation also constitute part of formal training (APA, 2000; CPA, 1991).

TABLE 20.2   Education and Training for a License in Psychology in the United States, English Canada, Quebec, and Mexico

| | Licensed Psychologists Requirements by Country | | | |
| --- | --- | --- | --- | --- |
| | United States | English Canada | Quebec | Mexico |
| Regulated by | State or territory | Province or territory | Province | Federal government |
| Degree required | Doctoral | Doctoral or master's degree | Master's degree in a professional area | *Licenciado* (professional masters degree) |
| Degrees granted | PhD, PsyD, and EdD | PhD, EdD, and master's | MPs, PhD, and DPs | Licentiate diploma |
| Total years of education and training for licensure | 23 years | Doctorate = 23 years, master's = 17–20 years | Doctorate = 23 years, master's = 19 years | 16.8 years |
| Location of educational offerings | University or private, freestanding institution | University | University | Autonomous university or private, freestanding institution |
| Responsible for quality of education | State, national | Provincial, national | Provincial, national | Federal |
| Extent of undergraduate studies | 4-year bachelor's degree program following 12 years of elementary and secondary school | Honors program = 4 years, general program = 3 years | Because of 2- or 3-year CGEP, honors program is 3 years | *Bachillerato* = 3 years following 9 years of elementary and secondary school |
| Major in psychology required for admission | No, special courses may be required | Yes, or equivalent | Yes, or equivalent | General education and introduction to psychology in *bachillerato* |
| Internship required for graduation | Yes, 1 year | For doctoral degree, 1 year | For doctoral degree, 1 year | No, social service is required |
| Post degree year of supervised experience required | In 49 out of 50 states | Yes, for those provinces with doctoral registration | Entry is master's level, currently no internship or post degree experience required | Not for *licenciado* |

After 3 years of full-time study, including various practicums, graduate students typically undertake a comprehensive examination of their knowledge in the required areas of study. Afterward, work begins on the doctoral thesis. Usually after approval of the dissertation topic (and data collection), students embark on a full-time year of internship training designed to anchor their knowledge, values, and skills in a practice setting relevant to their career goals. The end result of the scientist-practitioner model of training is intended to be a doctoral-level clinical psychologist who is both a producer of research and a high-quality, competent practitioner. The Boulder model of training has been reaffirmed in the United States and Canada on a number of occasions and continues as an important framework for psychologists pursuing more academically oriented careers as well as for psychologist practitioners. The scientist-practitioner PhD is the only model endorsed by *Counseling Psychology* (Gelso & Fretz, 2001). O'Sullivan and Quevillon (1992) surveyed APA-accredited programs, and with 90 of the programs responding, there was a 98% conformance to the Boulder model.

Maher (1999) recently compared research-oriented to professional-applied PhD programs using National Research Council (NRC) data published in 1995. The professional applied programs (a) were rated lower in quality of faculty, who in turn had a lower average publication record; (b) depended more on a part-time faculty and on assigning more students to each faculty member; (c) admitted students with lower GRE scores; and (d) awarded more PhDs since the 1982 NRC data. Maher concluded that a PhD means something very different when awarded by a professional school that is not seated within a research-oriented institution.

### The Practitioner Model

The first practice-oriented doctorate of psychology (PsyD) programs in the late 1950s and 1960s soon led to a rapid growth of PsyD programs by the 1980s (D. R. Peterson, Eaton, Levine, & Snepp, 1982). Based on information collected and compiled by APA Research Office in 2000 on 1998 graduates, about 41% of all clinical graduates in the United States (2,302) were granted PsyD degrees (952), with approximately 58% of PsyDs and PhDs in clinical psychology (1333) awarded by professional schools. The existence of large class size in both university-based and freestanding schools of professional psychology in the United States means that a majority of clinical students are now coming from professional school backgrounds. Therefore, in the United States the practitioner model (PsyD) is a well-developed and now quite well-accepted doctoral degree for clinical psychology. Here the emphasis is on developing a strong and knowledgeable practitioner who understands and is a knowledgeable consumer of research but who may not necessarily produce research as part of his or her career path.

Notwithstanding the notable strengths of the scientist-practitioner model of training, the history of the PsyD model in the United States stems from a number of disparities in objectives and dissatisfactions with the first model of training for clinical psychologists. Perhaps the most notable disparity in the Boulder model of training has been the fact that few U.S. PhD clinicians outside of academic settings have devoted time to research and that most have published virtually nothing after having received their PhDs. In general, the PhD model takes an excessive amount of time (6.8 years) to complete relative to the 5.1-year completion time for the PsyD (Gaddy, Charlot-Swilley, Nelson, & Reich, 1995). See Table 20.3 for the components that make up doctoral training in the United States.

In Canada the PsyD is only beginning to come to gestation. The relatively recent and slower evolution of doctoral-level clinical training from a predominantly research-oriented to a more balanced scientist-practitioner orientation is a function both of the exclusively university-based departmental training approach and of the historic desire to embed clinical training in a predominantly research-oriented framework. Nonetheless, similar criticisms about the scientist-practitioner have emerged in Canada. Hunsley and Lefebvre (1990) found that most PhD-trained Canadian professional psychologists neither are significant producers of research nor wish to pursue research as part of their careers. Moreover, much like the

United States, most students in Canadian doctoral programs take about seven years to complete their PhDs—in large part because of the growing dual curricula demands to cover both strong research components and an ever expanding professional component (Robinson et al., 1998). Finally, there is very little opportunity in the Canadian scientist-practitioner model to accommodate the estimated 40% of those master's-level psychologists who might wish to upgrade their training to a doctoral-level standard (Handy & Whitsett, 1993).

Notwithstanding that most of the clinical training programs for master's degrees in Canada have been quite rigorous precisely because they have often led to autonomous practice, the resultant professional practice mosaic across Canada is now a major focus of concern for Canadian professional psychology. Serious national efforts to arrive at some kind of national mobility mechanism for Canadian professional psychologists are now being driven by Canada's Agreement on Internal Trade, which aims, among other things, to foster the mobility of professional services across Canada. Among options being considered—beside grandparented mutual recognition agreements for currently practicing psychologists—is a more flexible doctoral training model, that is, a PsyD that might help bridge the training gap across provinces with differential autonomous practice requirements (Hurley, 1998; Robinson et al., 1998).

What will a made-in-Canada scholar-practitioner program look like? Serious work has already begun in Quebec to offer a university-based competency-driven PsyD based on eight core domains of training (Poirier et al., 1999). Drawing on the recommendations of the CPA PsyD Task Force (Robinson et al., 1998) and the work of Poirier et al. (1999) in Quebec, and with Quebec governmental approval, several Quebec universities have now developed PsyD program tracks and curricula that will soon admit students. Offered as a complementary model to the scientist-practitioner PhD, the Quebec PsyD will seek to highlight core practice-oriented competencies that are based in a grounding of scientific knowledge and critical thinking and will be of shorter duration than the typical PhD. Such programs should help students attain the necessary training skills at a doctoral level, which otherwise would have required extended master's training and supervision.

Other provinces are also either considering or developing PsyD-model training plans. However, noting U.S. outcome research (Yu et al., 1977) on attributes of quality PsyD training programs (e.g., smaller student bodies, low faculty-student ratios, and being university-based rather than freestanding), the CPA PsyD task force's final report recommendation for similar attributes for Canadian PsyD programs will most likely serve as a defining template across the country. Finally, given the very large financial burden for students

**TABLE 20.3   Education and Training Sequence for a License in Psychology in the United States**

| Licensed or Certified Psychologist = 23 years | | |
|---|---|---|
| Academic Level | Years | Education Received |
| Postdoctoral supervised experience-residency program | 1 year | Doctoral training |
| Internship | 1 year | Doctoral training |
| PhD, PsyD, or EdD | 4–5 years | Graduate education and practicum training |
| Master's degree | 2–3 years | Graduate education and practicum training |
| Bachelor's degree | 4 years | Postsecondary education |
| High school | 4 years | Secondary education |
| Junior high school | 2 years | Basic education |
| Elementary school | 6 years | Basic education |

often accompanying more profit-driven PsyD programs in some areas of the United States and given the strong Canadian tradition endorsing lower cost publicly funded Canadian universities, the made-in-Canada PsyD programs may well look for a variety of cost-offset mechanisms for moderating the impact of such student debt on early career development.

In Table 20.4 the similarities between the English Canada sequence of training and that in Quebec are presented side by side. With the exception of the doctorate in psychological services (DPs) in Quebec, there is little difference in the doctoral degree offered. The main difference exists in the two foundations for graduate education and any requirement for admission to graduate study. In English Canada, an honors

**TABLE 20.4    Education and Training Sequence for a License in English Canada and Quebec**

| Licensed or Registered Psychologist in English Canada = 23 Years (Doctorate), 17–20 Years (Master's) | | |
|---|---|---|
| Academic Level | Years | Education Received |
| Postdoctoral | 1 year | Doctoral training |
| Internship | 1 year | Doctoral training |
| PhD/EdD | 4–5 years | Graduate education and practicum training |
| Master's degree | 2 years | Graduate education and practicum training |
| Honors BA or BSc | 4 years | Postsecondary education/ undergraduate education |
| General BA or BSc | 3 years | Postsecondary education/ undergraduate education |
| High school | 6 years | Secondary education |
| Elementary school | 6 years | Basic education |

| Licensed or Registered Psychologist in Quebec = 23 years (Doctorate), 19 years (Master's) | | |
|---|---|---|
| Academic Level | Years | Education Received |
| Postdoctoral | 1 year | Doctoral training |
| Internship | 1 year | Doctoral training |
| PhD/DPs | 4 years | Graduate education and practicum training |
| MPs | 2 years | Graduate education and practicum training |
| BA or BSc major | 3 years | Postsecondary education/ undergraduate education |
| BA or BSc honors | 3 years | Postsecondary education/ undergraduate education |
| CEGEP professional or technical | 3 years | Postsecondary education/ undergraduate education |
| CEGEP General | 2 years | Postsecondary education/ undergraduate education |
| Postdoctoral | 1 year | Doctoral training |
| High school | 5 years | Secondary education |
| Elementary school | 6 years | Basic education |

**TABLE 20.5    Education and Training Sequence for a *Cédula* in Mexico**

| *Cédula* (Ministry-Awarded National Practitioner License) = 17.3 Years, Specialist = 19.3 Years | | |
|---|---|---|
| Academic Level | Years | Education/Experience |
| Specialist | 2 years | Additional experience and training |
| Social service | 480-hr minimum | Experience |
| *Licenciado* in psychology | 4.5 years | University or college education |
| Bachelor's (*bachillerato*) | 3 years | Postsecondary education |
| Secondary school | 3 years | Secondary education |
| Elementary school | 6 years | Basic education |

degree in psychology is typically required; in Quebec, students go to the Collèges d'Enseignement Général et Professionnel (CEGEP) immediately after high school and take either a 2-year general program that corresponds to the last year of high school and first year in a university in English Canada or a 3-year terminal program for technical or professional studies that do not require a university education.

The training of professional psychologists in Mexico (as well as in Europe and Latin America) is closest to an almost exclusively professional training program. In fact, the practitioner's degree (licentiate) often comes first and leads immediately to a permanent license (*cédula*), with a small portion of individuals then deciding to get the necessary research degree or other training needed for employment in an academic setting. This is almost the opposite of what occurs in the United States and Canada, where academic-scientific foundational work precedes professional training. As illustrated in Table 20.5, the time to independent practice is considerably shorter than for the United States or Canada.

## PROFESSIONAL TRAINING: PRACTICUMS, INTERNSHIP, AND POSTDOCTORAL COMPONENTS

One of the distinguishing features of any profession is hands-on training. Professionals are expected to be not only knowledgeable about their subject area but also able to perform competently. Professional psychology is no different in this regard from other professions, and the field has spent much collective time and resources in developing coherent, sequential training experiences to integrate the knowledge, skills, and attitudes necessary to become a competent professional. We now examine each of the typical training experiences that psychologists undertake as part of their formal professionalization.

## Practicums

### Developing Basic Practice Competence

Practicum experience is often the first professional training encounter for professional psychology students. Here, the Oxford American Dictionary's various definitions of *practice* all weigh heavily in the equation of practicum training, that is, (a) "action as opposed to theory," (b) "a habitual action," (c) "repeated exercise to improve one's skill," and (d) "professional work" (Ehrlich, Flexner, Carruth, & Hawkins, 1980, p. 700). Having acquired the fundamental knowledge and basic skills required for beginning the practice of clinical work through various courses, students are now expected to begin putting such knowledge, skills, and ethical values to use in real-life encounters with clients and patients.

As the first formalized training component, the practicum is often both quite challenging and exciting for students. Practicum goals usually include the strengthening of interviewing skills, the basics of translating theory into practice through direct clinical encounters (and through supervision), and the development and refinement of basic assessment, report writing, and consultation skills. Such exercises are normally part of a course requirement and are usually conducted in training clinics, university counseling centers, or in school settings, which often translates into direct involvement with a wide variety of clients and presenting problems.

Although cases are usually selected and assigned to students based on their incoming skill levels, many challenges and surprises often await as clinical work progresses. Here, the clinical student begins to encounter and cultivate "an important characteristic of the clinician—*the capacity to tolerate ambiguity*" (Phares, 1988, p. 33). Such personal characteristics as interpersonal awareness and sensitivity, basic respect for diversity in human living, and—perhaps most importantly—respect for the dignity of persons —all relate not only to the capacity to tolerate ambiguity but also to the capacity to appreciate a broad range of human behaviors and customs with their attendant avenues of adaptation and growth as well as dysfunction and potential pathology. These characteristics also set the stage for appreciation of the broad range of other strengths as students later advance through their own career steps in the profession.

In summary, practicums are generally sequenced in difficulty and variety in order for students to develop systematically their clinical skills and intervention techniques. Although students in both Canada and the United States are expected to complete at least 600 to 1,000 hours of practicum training prior to admission to the internship, the actual figures reported as part of the application for the internship are much higher than that, as students increasingly feel that they are more marketable for an internship with more and diverse hours. Depending on the internship setting (community mental health centers, medical centers, hospitals, or university counseling centers) and the information on which it is based (an internship application or independent survey) and realizing that beyond direct client contact and supervision there is disagreement on which activities should count (scoring psychological tests, report writing, attending staff meetings, peer supervision, etc.), the average total number of practicum hours now reaches around 1,800 hours, the equivalent of 1 full year of supervised experience.

### The Role of Supervision in Training

One of the hallmarks of professional psychology training is the introduction of the direct supervision of students' clinical skills, typically on a one-to-one basis with a clinical supervisor. The supervisory relationship has been a rich source of study in professional psychology, and numerous models abound regarding stages and styles of supervision that foster skills and the development of professionalism. Most important, however, is the potential to work directly with a mentor and begin more self-directed learning as a budding psychologist. Supervision as a direct form of training will continue throughout internship and the postdoctoral supervision sequence and will serve as one of the major avenues for fine-tuning a variety of clinical skills before launching as a licensed professional psychologist.

Typically, supervision takes the form of case review by direct observation or video or audiotape of sessions with one's supervisor, and students can expect to meet in direct supervision at least once a week. Other supervision may take the form of case review involving either the practicum group or agency staff. In all, students can expect that their early clinical work will be closely scrutinized and that they will have the opportunity to consult regularly with their supervisors as required. Finally, a practicum journal is often a part of course requirements and, among other training goals, helps students begin to track direct service hours with clients and patients as well as the numbers of hours of supervision received—an exercise that will lay the groundwork for tracking later internship and postdoctoral direct service and supervision hours for licensure and credentialing purposes.

## Internship

One of the major defining components in professional psychology training is the internship requirement for doctoral programs in professional psychology. Typically, the internship occurs after completion of course work and required practicums and precedes granting of the doctoral degree. The internship year is designed to strengthen and refine existing basic competencies as well as introduce new or more advanced competencies that are expected of a newly licensed professional psychologist.

### Certification Mechanisms for Assessing Programmatic Competence of Internship Training Programs

As mentioned earlier, assessing professional competence through certification mechanisms is an important part of both self-regulatory and external regulatory components of professional psychology education and training. In the case of internship training programs, four major professional psychology mechanisms are involved in the United States and Canada in providing basic and extensive reviews of programmatic competence level and scope. Referring to the typical doctoral education and training sequence again, these components are the APA-CPA-accredited internship, the APPIC-listed internship, the Joint Committee on Internships of the Council of Directors of School Psychology Programs (CDSPP), APA's Division of School Psychology, and National Association of School Psychologists–listed internship, and the individual approval of the internship submitted by an applicant for credentialing by the National Register.

### APA-CPA Accreditation of Doctoral Internships

Both APA and CPA consider doctoral internship training to be a capstone experience in the formalized doctoral training component prior to awarding of the doctoral degree. Testifying to its central importance, the CPA accreditation manual (1991) notes the following:

> The internship is an essential component in the preparation of the doctoral level, professional psychologist. . . . It presents the opportunity for a more sophisticated integration of graduate education, psychological theory and professional skills. The internship serves as an important step in the socialization process of the professional psychologist. . . . The preparation of a doctoral level professional psychologist is facilitated by exposure to experiences in the evolution of personal growth and in the evolution of dysfunctional clinical or adjustment entities over time. The internship contributes to this experience by requiring a full time experience for one calendar year or a half time experience over two years, comprising in either case a minimum of 1600 hours. (p. 17)

Similar descriptors exist for the APA with regard to internship training and reflect the intent that program accreditation of internship training is an important indicator of a quality programmatic training environment.

With regard to actual accreditation procedures, CPA and APA differ somewhat in their respective approaches. CPA accreditation of doctoral internships is based on a criterion-based certification of program quality and addresses a series of five major criteria and 33 subcriteria that the internship setting must or ideally should possess in order to be accredited (CPA, 1991). APA, on the other hand, has moved to an outcome-based model and congruence philosophy of accreditation for training programs (APA Council of Representatives, 1996). As an example of this (eight-) domain approach for professional psychology internship accreditation, Domain B (Program Philosophy, Objectives and Training Plan) of the APA 1996 Guidelines and Principles for Accreditation of Programs in Professional Psychology states the following:

> The program has a clearly specified philosophy of training, compatible with the mission of its sponsor institution and appropriate to the practice of professional psychology. The internship is an organized professional training program with the goal of providing high quality training in professional psychology. The training model and goals are consistent with its philosophy and objectives. (p. 12)

In the end, however, both approaches seem to offer very similar outcomes—at least in terms of accreditation status. Where Canadian doctoral programs and internships have applied for concurrent accreditation by both CPA and APA, independent decisions reached by both accrediting bodies have virtually a 100% overlap (J. Gauthier, personal communication, August 1998).

### APPIC-Listed Internships

The APPIC was formed in the mid-1960s in the United States originally to address only internship training, and although not a formal accrediting agency, it does offer U.S. and Canadian professional psychology internship programs a paper review process that allows programs that meet all criteria and that conform to APPIC policies to be listed as an APPIC member. To quote from APPIC's 2000–2001 Directory,

> The Association has been organized to facilitate the achievement and maintenance of high quality training in professional psychology; to facilitate exchange of information between institutions and agencies offering doctoral internship and/or postdoctoral training in professional psychology; to develop standards for such training programs; to provide a forum for exchanging views, establishing policies, procedures and contingencies on training matters and selection of interns, and resolving other problems and issues for which common agreement is either

essential or desirable; to provide assistance in matching students with training programs; and to represent the views of training agencies to groups and organizations whose functions and objectives relate to those of APPIC. (R. G. Hall & Hsu, 2000, p. 1)

For APPIC listing, internships that either are accredited by APA or CPA or otherwise meet the current 14 APPIC criteria may be listed. This process of approval could also be considered a designation process because it is parallel to that performed with doctoral educational programs by the ASPPB's National Register Designation Project.

Perhaps the most important APPIC function is the matching of students with training programs through its uniform application procedure and computerized matching service. This newly instituted service follows the matching programs already in existence for a number of other health care disciplines and now allows both professional psychology students and internship training programs a more streamlined and orderly matching process. In terms of match results, APPIC match statistics suggest that about half of all matched applicants received their top-ranked choice of sites and that about 80% of students match with one of their top three sites.

In all, more than 80% of the 3,000-plus U.S. and Canadian match applicants in 2001 ended up matching with an internship program (APPIC, 2001), and in terms of supply and demand, it appears that there has been somewhat less disparity over the last few years between excess supply of applicants and available internship sites in the United States. (Canada generally remains balanced with regard to available applicants and internship sites.)

A corollary of APPIC is the Canadian Council of Professional Psychology Programs (CCPPP), but the latter represents both internships and doctoral programs. CCPPP sends a representative to the APPIC Board of Directors meetings and to the Council of Chairs of Training Councils to facilitate solution of problems as they arise for Canadian students and to find ways to harmonize the Canadian standards and procedures with those in the United States. There are 40 internships listed on CCPPP's Web site at www.usask.ca/psychology/ccppp.

### Directory of Internships for Doctoral Students in School Psychology

In order to promote awareness of training sites for doctoral-level school psychologists, the CDSPP approved in 1983 and revised in 1998 the Guidelines for Meeting Internship Criteria in School Psychology. Individual sites submit an entry for the yearly directory and attest to the fact that their site meets the CDSPP guidelines. Then the CDSPP, School Psychology Division 16 of APA, and the National Association of School Psychologists, through a jointly supported committee, publish a list of internship sites that provide training appropriate for school psychologists. The impetus for this initiative was the small number of sites available generally, with no APA-accredited internships in school districts at the time that this effort began.

The CDSPP guidelines are based on the National Register criteria modified slightly to meet school psychology needs, based on consultation and assistance provided by the National Register. Over the past 18 years, the National Register worked with the CDSPP to articulate how students completing such sites can be credentialed by the National Register. The main differences between the CDSPP and the National Register guidelines are the accommodation of the possibility of only one intern at a site and the cosigning of intern reports by the supervisor, as well as the requirement that the internship occur prior to the granting of the degree.

Based on the 2000 edition of this directory, 36 school sites report being APA accredited, and an additional 69 are listed, representing a total of 376 full-time and 49 half-time positions available. Updates are conducted yearly, and as of this writing the list of internships is not available online.

### National Register Approved Internships

The National Register created the first criterion-based model for evaluating internship training. The history of the National Register's involvement was prompted by the need to approve internships submitted by applicants for credentialing as a health service provider in psychology. As a result of the large number of quite varied training experiences submitted to meet the internship criterion, in 1980 the Appeal Board of the National Register developed the Guidelines for Defining an Internship or Organized Health Service Training Program in Psychology (National Register, 2000, pp. 13–14). APPIC then adopted these criteria for use in their review of internship programs; APA incorporated these criteria in their internship accreditation standards; and, more recently, CDSPP modified these criteria to meet their special needs. However, the APPIC, APA, and CDSPP require the internship to occur prior to the granting of the degree.

In 1990 the National Register reviewed every file of its 16,000 psychologists and developed a comprehensive list and classification of all the internship training programs completed by those psychologists. This is a unique database that provides a snapshot of internships over a 50-year time period, most of which were not accredited.

## Postdoctoral Training and Accreditation

After successful completion of internship training and the completion of all other doctoral requirements, the student is awarded the doctoral degree in professional psychology. At this juncture most new doctorates seek postdoctoral supervised experience, whereas others may pursue a formalized postdoctoral training experience, all for the purpose of meeting the state license requirement of a year of postdoctoral experience. The history of formalized postdoctoral training is relatively recent in the United States, and APA has essentially just begun the accreditation of postdoctoral residencies (or fellowships). For example, whereas there are approximately 570 internship programs participating in APPIC, only 66 agencies offer postdoctoral fellowship training (R. G. Hall & Hsu, 2000). Canada also offers the rare formalized postdoctoral training opportunity in some settings, but there is as yet no concomitant accreditation mechanism through CPA, and no Canadian postdoctoral training programs have yet listed with APPIC.

Much like the earlier history of internship training, formalized postdoctoral training is just beginning to come into the mainstream of professional psychology. In the case of postdoctoral training, however, the needed groundwork development for generic advanced and specialty training came via proactive involvement from a number of national professional psychology organizations in both the United States and Canada. Following on the draft standards created at the Ann Arbor Conference on Postdoctoral Residencies in Professional Psychology, the Interorganizational Council (IOC) formed by seven North American psychology bodies met for five years and produced standards and procedures that later led to the 1996 APA adoption of the eight domains and numerous standards now required for the APA accreditation of postdoctoral training programs for professional psychologists. Room exists within these structures to accommodate both generic advanced training and specialty training, depending on the postdoctoral program's requirements and content. APA has now approved six residencies in the advanced general area. Specialty residencies have yet to be accredited by APA, although clinical neuropsychology has adopted and tested its own standards. Again, accreditation is voluntary for postdoctoral training programs.

Based on the success of the IOC, another U.S./Canadian interorganizational professional psychology group known as the Council of Credentialing Organizations in Professional Psychology (CCOPP) began work on developing a conceptual model and taxonomy of specialization for the area of health service psychology (Drum, 2001). In general, work by such groups as IOC and CCOPP represent a shift toward a more North American–integrated formulation and enactment of professional psychology training designed to lend greater coherence to competency-based outcomes for general practice and other specialization routes for professional psychologists.

## APA Commission on Education and Training Leading to Licensure in Psychology Versus Current APA Policy

Since 1955 APA has promulgated two additional models for what should be required education and training for professional psychologists. The latest (APA, 1987) specified that by 1995 an applicant for licensure must have been graduated from an APA accredited program or from a program that met the standards of the board (in most instances this would be an ASPPB- or National Register–designated doctoral program in psychology). In addition, the applicant was to complete 2 years of supervised professional experience, one of which was postdoctoral. Note that the emphasis was on the timing of the experience, with no reference to completion of an internship. The internship was left to the doctoral programs to regulate. In addition, these standards were written broadly so that all specialties could be eligible for licensing.

Over a dozen years later, the landscape has changed. Students are completing a year of practicum experience prior to internship so that they are more competitive in the internship match. Increased numbers of health care practitioners are competing for the same health care dollar and providing what they consider to be the equivalent service provided by psychologists. A significant portion of the clinical, counseling, and school psychology programs is now accredited. Internship programs are increasingly seeking APA accreditation. The training requirement is due for reexamination from a competency perspective. The question really is, At what point is basic readiness for independent practice achieved?

To begin addressing that question, a presidentially appointed commission of 30 individuals met twice in 2000, chaired by the president elect of APA, Norine Johnson, and staffed jointly by the practice and the education directorates of APA. The draft statements of the commission and the strategies for implementation have been circulated for comment by internal and external bodies affected by the potential policy. The major suggested modifications to APA policy include setting the standard of an APA-CPA-accredited internship or one that meets APPIC or CDSPP guidelines being required for a license, and by 2010 requiring all internships to be accredited. The second major suggestion relates to the 2 years of experience required for the license. One of the 2 years of experience could be completed prior to the degree, as long as the internship is completed prior to the granting of the degree. The commissioners were not suggesting the elimination of the year of postdoctoral training. In fact, post-doctoral education and training are emphasized as an important part of the continuing professional development and credentialing process for professional psychologists (APA Commission on Education and Training Leading to Licensure in Psychology, 2001).

This proposed policy threatens established structures and thus has met with resistance from some organizations committed to the requirement of the postdoctoral year of experience for licensure. One of the arguments is that it took 20 years to get that standard enacted in most states; to change it now might have a costly impact on the standing of the profession of psychology and destabilize the consensus around having a national standard for some time to come.

No matter what the outcome is of the deliberations and debates around this issue, it promises to have a major impact on APA's position on the standards for education and training leading to licensing and perhaps even the standards legislated by states for entry to the profession.

## DEVELOPING STANDARDS FOR THE REGULATION OF PROFESSIONAL PSYCHOLOGY

Essential to defining, evaluating, and promoting the education, training, and credentialing of psychologists is incorporation of the opinions of those affected by the services or training provided—the faculty, the institution, the students, the graduates, the users, and consumers. Following consensus about educational standards, self study, on-site peer review, and a review of internal and external assessments by those affected, a decision is made regarding adherence to those standards as part of the process of accreditation, which is defined as a "nongovernmental process of quality assessment and assurance applied to general, technical, and professional programs and institutions of higher education" (Nelson & Messenger, 1998, p. 4).

Accreditation is only one example of self-regulation (Drum & Hall, 1993). Consensual agreement among the various constituencies is difficult, time-consuming, and expensive. It may be easy to identify difficulties with particular approaches and recommend changes. It is another thing to accomplish those changes. Then, once standards are established, a subsequent modification threatens established structures. Examples of continuing debate topics are the doctoral-level standard for entry to the profession versus the master's level and, more recently, the requirement of a postdoctoral year of experience for admission to licensure (APA Commission, 2000).

## APA Accreditation: Public Accountability Leading to Outcomes Assessment

A major change in the APA accreditation process has taken place in the past dozen years, stimulated by a national meeting in 1990 of relevant constituencies to suggest changes to the accreditation process, including the broadening of input to the Committee on Accreditation (COA; Sheridan, Matarazzo, & Nelson, 1995). There were many changes made, including the decisions to render the COA—to the greatest extent possible—independent of forces external to its own operating policies and procedures in the accreditation review and recognition of individual programs and to increase the COA's responsibility in the formulation of accreditation policies and procedures based on good practices of accreditation nationally (P. Nelson, personal communication, May 2001). In addition, the COA was to be expanded from 10 to 21 members representing various domains. The APA guidelines and procedures for accreditation were revised and approved in 1996, and they are still being amended. Although public accountability was hardly a new concept, these guidelines and procedures emphasize quality by measuring program goals and outcomes, focusing on competencies rather than curriculum, and stressing self-study rather than external reviews. The influences that brought all those changes were many. The COA outcomes model was a compromise among converging and diverging forces operative within the professional practice and credentialing community, professional educators and trainers, and the educational institutions in which accredited programs are hosted (P. Nelson, personal communication, May 2001). The U.S. Department of Education, which recognizes accrediting bodies such as the APA COA for purposes of student financial aid under Title IV of the Higher Education Act, played a role in this process by including in their 1994 regulations a requirement that student achievement be measured in terms of course completion, state licensing examination, and job placement rates (U.S. Department of Education, 1994). However, the major influence occurred earlier in 1991 by APA's participation in the Council on Postsecondary Accreditation (COPA), a private, voluntary accreditor of the accreditors that no longer exists. (The function previously served by COPA had been partially replaced by the Council on Higher Education Accreditation, or CHEA.) In 1999 "targeted changes were made . . . to enable the COA to come into full compliance with the [U.S. Department of Education] regulations for recognition of accrediting agencies." (APA, 2000, foreword)

Although this topic is too complex for complete exposition here, the reader can get a flavor of the energy placed on defining the proper education and training by examining some of the attempts to bring organized psychology together. Often, the term *organized psychology* is used to describe the coming together of different constituencies for the collective good. To define these issues, organized psychology typically appoints task forces, holds conferences, and invites representatives to address definitional issues and set standards. In order to understand the development of professional psychology, it is helpful to revisit briefly its early history.

## The Historic Road to Modern-Day Licensing and Credentialing of Professional Psychologists

U.S. psychology emerged as a profession following World War II. The Veterans Administration (VA) and the Public Health Service (PHS) needed a way to identify acceptable education and training programs in clinical and counseling psychology, whose graduates were needed to serve veterans returning from the war. The choice for conducting a system of quality control was between a federal government agency or the APA. APA answered by accrediting the first set of programs in 1948 (Sheridan et al., 1995). At the same time, graduatess of programs sought recognition as psychologists. There were two mechanisms available: a short-lived state association certification process in a few states and specialty certification by the American Board of Professional Psychology (ABPP). The first state licensure law was passed in 1945 and was followed soon by several others. Thus, within a short time in the United States, accreditation of doctoral programs in psychology and the concomitant licensing and credentialing of psychologists began.

However, unlike the medical profession, these laws did not require the completion of an accredited psychology program. Partly because psychology is an academic discipline and a profession, the requirement of graduating from an accredited program has been more of an aspirational standard that is restricted to programs in professional psychology, defined eventually as clinical, counseling, and school psychology. Credentialing of psychologists also began as a voluntary activity but increasingly became required for certain roles as each state passed a licensing law. As a result, exceptions in the law often allow persons with doctoral degrees in psychology to refer to themselves as psychologists and their work as psychological (e.g., those in state, academic, or industrial settings). Organized psychology was unwilling to make the commitment that other health care professions made, which required graduates to complete an approved program and become licensed. Many exemptions remain even today, more than 56 years after the passage of the first licensing law.

The small number of U.S. programs initially applying for accreditation underscored the fact that accreditation was voluntary. Psychology licensing laws, in turn, allowed

individuals to be licensed as psychologists on the basis of a wide range of credentials and degrees. Recognizing that psychology was behind other professions in regulating the education and training sequence required for entry to practice, in 1976–1977 two U.S. national conferences on education and training in psychology convened by APA and the National Register brought together organized psychology to establish guidelines for the identification of doctoral programs in psychology for credentialing purposes (Wellner, 1978). This effort intended to present a unified front to state legislatures as to who was a "psychologist" by defining the required educational curriculum. The Guidelines for Defining a Doctoral Program in Psychology were adopted as the standard for evaluating programs by the National Register and ASPPB and, as a result, had a major impact on licensing and credentialing standards. The foundation knowledge areas for practice were also incorporated formally into the 1979 APA accreditation criteria.

In 1980 the National Register used the designation criteria (as they became known) to review all doctoral training programs purporting to train psychologists and published the first list of designated doctoral programs in psychology. This occurred for two main reasons: One was the absence of agreement on the admission criteria for licensing of psychologists, and the other related to the dissatisfaction in using a more qualitative review process (accreditation) for licensing purposes. The latter dissatisfaction emanated primarily from variability in the curriculum content of graduates from APA accredited programs.

With the federal and private health care systems seeking qualified providers, with variable criteria for definition of an acceptable program, and with more practitioners outside and inside psychology competing for the health dollar, the standard of completing an accredited or designated program in professional psychology was increasingly being included in state legislation. The "other" or "equivalent" category, which had been described as a euphemism for "not psychology," began to disappear from state laws. Because the designation criteria are applicable to any area of professional psychology, designation gave licensing bodies a mechanism for evaluating programs that APA accreditation did not. A current list of programs meeting the designation criteria is available at www.nationalregister.org.

Parallel development of internship criteria occurred when internship training was defined as a component essential to the Boulder model. Accredited internship programs in professional psychology appeared in 1956. As a result of the variability in training experiences submitted by licensed psychologists to meet the internship criterion for credentialing by the National Register, in 1980 the Appeal Board of the National Register developed internship criteria, and these were adapted by APPIC, APA (1979), and CDSPP to meet their own needs.

Today, most graduates of professional psychology programs become licensed as psychologists. Licensing criteria are set by each jurisdiction but are greatly influenced by guidelines for state legislation of the APA in 1955, 1967, and 1987 (APA, 1987; APA Committee on Legislation, 1955, 1967). In 1992 the ASPPB adopted its own model of state legislation. As a result, completion of an APA-accredited or ASPPB-National Register-designated program now meets the educational requirements of most state licensing statutes and regulations. Many states require an internship, but all states except one require a year of postdoctoral experience for a license.

Canada has not adopted these criteria as universally as has the United States and does not have its own model legislation guidelines. The CPA accreditation program, begun in 1984, reviews both Canadian programs and internships and now encourages Canadian programs to apply for CPA accreditation first with the understanding that APA may recognize CPA.

## THE LICENSING PROCESS

Licensing laws were established to define the practice of the profession; to set educational, training, and examination standards for the profession; and, most of all, to assist the public in identifying who is qualified to practice the profession. This is different from saying that the license assesses quality. Being licensed provides the potential consumer with the reassurance that the state, province, or territory has determined that the individual has met minimal standards.

There are now 62 jurisdictions in the United States and Canada that regulate the practice of psychology or the title of psychologist. Both types of laws attempt to protect the public by clearly identifying who is qualified to practice as a psychologist (practice act) or present as a psychologist (certification of title act). Stromberg et al. (1988) explained the difference best in the following:

> *Licensure* is a process by which individuals are granted permission to perform a defined set of *functions*. If a professional performs those functions (such as diagnosing or treating behavioral, emotional or mental disorders) regardless under what name (such as therapist, psychologist or counselor), he is required to be licensed. In contrast, *certification* focuses not on the function performed but on the use of a particular *professional title* (such as "psychologist"), and it limits its use to individuals who have met specified standards for education, experience and examination performance. (pp. 1–2)

Only a small number of jurisdictions have true licensure laws. The majority have certification laws, including those called permissive acts, requiring the person to be licensed if he or she practices psychology and uses the title. We use the term *license* to refer to either type of regulation.

Legislation also differs with regard to which psychologists are covered. Generic laws, such as in New York, require persons presenting themselves as psychologists, regardless of specialty area, to be licensed unless otherwise exempted. However, in a jurisdiction with a "health service provider" or "clinical" type definition of practice, only psychologists with that education and training sequence would even qualify for a license. Thus, industrial and organizational psychologists would not be eligible. However, exemptions to the statute may allow other psychologists to practice. Some states have a two-tier process by which the individual is first licensed as a psychologist and then may be certified as a health service provider. Specialty licensing, though attempted in certain jurisdictions, is rare, with the exception of the title of school psychologist, but entry is typically at the master's level (exceptions are Texas and Virginia).

In Canada the regulatory laws are generic, requiring any practicing psychologist to be "registered," "chartered," or "certified" (the terms often seen in Canada). "Health service provider in psychology" is restricted to the voluntary listing of registered psychologists who meet the application criteria for the Canadian Register of Health Service Providers in Psychology. No specialty licensing exists in Canada.

### Education and Training Requirements

#### Degree

The degree required for independent practice in the United States is the doctorate, with the exception of Vermont, West Virginia, and now Kentucky, where entry is available with a master's degree. A significant number of states (approximately 40) also have provisions for recognition of the master's-level trained person, although not for independent practice.

In Canada approximately two thirds of the 12,000 registered psychologists have entered practice at the master's level. In addition, approximately 40% of the psychologists in Canada reside in Quebec, where the minimum educational requirement for a license includes completion of a Master of Professional Studies degree (MPs). Several of the Canadian provinces were originally doctoral entry only. With the exception of British Columbia, all provinces either admit to independent practice at the master's level or allow practice at that level with some restrictions and a different title (Ontario). When one considers professional practice in North America, only the United States adheres to a doctoral degree entry standard as policy.

## *Curriculum*

Psychology also varies from other professions in that the curriculum requirements are not as consistent as found in medicine, social work, nursing, and other health care professionals graduating from professional schools. When U.S. licensing began, the degree completed was a Ph.D., typically from a department of psychology in the college of arts and sciences in a major university. The curriculum was designed to train a researcher, even though many of the students were asking for training for practice. This need eventually led to the creation of U.S. practitioner degree programs. This PsyD offered students an option similar to the medical degree (MD). However, some of the larger professional schools granted a PhD, which led to confusion about the meaning of the PhD. As the PsyD became more accepted, those same professional schools added a PsyD track to parallel the PhD track in the same specialty area. Today, the largest number of graduates in psychology comes from professional schools, and soon the number of PsyDs granted will equal the number of PhDs awarded (Belar, 1998). The other degree in psychology, the doctorate of education (EdD), is now becoming increasingly rare. As a result of these three degrees, most licensing statutes say a "doctoral degree in psychology" rather than name a specific degree.

## *Experience*

The 2 years of experience required for licensure, which is the norm today, typically specifies that one of those years include a year of postdoctoral experience. At that point any similarity among the 62 standards for the 2 years evaporates. There are standards for internships that are fairly universal; however, there is no consistent standard for the year of postdoctoral experience (ASPPB, 2001).

As noted earlier, whether those standards should remain the same is under debate. Not being able to practice independently on receipt of the doctoral degree puts psychology graduates at a disadvantage in the marketplace in competing not only against doctoral-level providers such as physicians but also against master's-level providers such as social workers and counselors.

## Examination Components: Exam for Professional Practice in Psychology and Oral-Jurisprudence Exams

After meeting the education and training requirements, the license applicant takes the Exam for Professional Practice in Psychology (EPPP). The exam is available throughout the year in a computer-generated version, with four forms available at any one time. This examination is properly validated through multiple studies on psychologists in the United States and Canada, including the original job analysis by Rosenfeld, Shimberg, and Thornton (1983) and the recent practice analysis conducted in 1995. For more detailed information, visit www.asppb.org.

Of the 15,095 exams administered in 1997–1999, 81% of the candidates reported that they had a doctoral degree (data are available from ASPPB Web site). In a separate analysis approximately 89% of the doctoral psychologists taking the examination reported that they completed an APA-accredited program (ASPPB, 2000). The national pass point is 70% of the items correct, typically only for the doctoral-level candidate, and this has been adopted by the majority of members of the ASPPB, the association that develops and sells the exam to the member jurisdictions. Not all jurisdictions require the exam (Quebec, Prince Edward Island, Northwest Territories); not all have adopted the recommended pass point (Washington, DC, Maryland, North Dakota, and South Dakota in the United States, and New Brunswick in Canada); and most use a lower pass point for the master's-level candidate.

Following a successful performance on the EPPP, there may be an oral or a jurisprudence exam, or both. In general, these exams are developed and administered by the licensing body and have not been subjected to psychometric validation. The oral exams also differ greatly in the degree of structure and the approach, in many instances involving only an interview. These complementary exams give the board the opportunity to assess what they believe is lacking in a multiple choice exam; offer the opportunity to meet each potential licensee, depending upon the size of the jurisdictions; and, because few fail, are rarely challenged.

## License Maintenance Requirements

### *Adherence to Ethical Standards and Jurisdictional Regulations*

The licensed psychologist is required to adhere to ethical and professional standards, with the former referring to the APA or CPA codes of ethics and the latter to any regulations developed by the jurisdiction. Failure to adhere to these standards if followed by a complaint to the licensing body may bring about an investigation and prosecution. If found guilty, the license may be restricted in some material way. If the psychologist is disciplined, there may be ramifications in terms of provider status (e.g., potential removal from the HMO-PPO provider panel of a health care organization or from Medicare provider status), professional and credentialing status (e.g., sanctioned by APA, National Register, or ABPP), or malpractice coverage.

## Continuing Education

Another component in maintaining a license to practice is the requirement for continuing professional education. In the United States and Canada 44 of the 62 jurisdictions require the licensee to complete a certain number of hours in continuing education (CE) for renewal of the license. This requirement makes sense in theory, given that professionals may practice for 40 years after receiving their degrees. However, the course quality and level of sophistication vary, and actual learning achievement is typically not measured. Credits are awarded if the participants complete the course evaluation form, regardless of whether they learned anything that was useful to their practice.

The only formal study of the effectiveness of CE for a professional took place in New York by the state board for the certified public accountants profession. The New York State Board of Regents took the position that if a profession wanted to require CE for renewal of a license, the profession needed to undertake a study of the CE requirement and fund it out of licensing fees, as the members of the CPA profession were required to do. However, this study did not examine whether what was studied improved practice; it examined the impact on knowledge (J. E. Hall, 1993). To date, the New York State Board of Regents has not approved a CE requirement for psychology.

## Mobility of the Psychologist's License to Practice

Once an individual is licensed to practice, it would seem logical that any subsequent license would be relatively easy to get, should the individual move or need to be licensed in another jurisdiction (assuming that there is no history of discipline). Clearly the licensed psychologist has to complete an application and pay the fee. However, the jurisdiction may also require primary source verification of credentials and submission of the applicant's EPPP score. While the state or province to which the psychologist is applying has the responsibility to protect the public, the verification process may place incredible barriers or lengthy delays on people who have been licensed, often for years, without any incident.

### Reciprocity Agreements

Several professions, not just psychology, have recently attempted to facilitate mobility of licensed practitioners by two basic methods: multijurisdictional agreements or individual endorsement of credentials. Reciprocity agreements involve the acceptance of licensees without question. For instance, Texas currently has a reciprocity agreement with Louisiana. That means that anyone licensed in Louisiana could be licensed automatically in Texas and vice versa. These agreements are legally binding until rescinded. Although this may be acceptable from the psychologist perspective, the idea that a licensing body has no control over each person who would be licensed in that jurisdiction causes boards to avoid such agreements. Even after ASPPB put enormous resources into encouraging jurisdictions to sign on to its reciprocity agreement, only 10 have done so. A few that signed it later withdrew. One difficulty is that the agreement often necessitated the jurisdiction's changing its law to meet the contractual specifications, including conducting an oral examination. California has eliminated its oral examination as of January 2002, even though it has had a long history of oral examinations.

### Credentials Endorsement Agreements

Another form of mobility is offered through use of individual credentialing mechanisms that employ recognized national standards and reflect primary source verification procedures. Expediting the granting of a license to a person because he or she possesses a credential involves endorsement of that credential. One of the earliest examples is ABPP and the diploma privilege. If a state accepts ABPP for endorsement purposes, it usually involves waiver of the license examination, either the oral or the EPPP, on the basis of the applicant's having previously taken the ABPP exam. Although 34 states have this provision, ABPP has 3,200 active diplomates, so endorsement affects a small portion of psychologists.

In the late 1990s an individual mobility certificate was created by ASPPB, the Certificate of Professional Qualification (CPQ). Although it is new, few people have applied for the CPQ, even though it recently completed its 2-year grandparent period, which allowed licensees without doctoral degrees in psychology to qualify. By the conclusion of the grandparent period on December 31, 2001, approximately 4,000 applications were received. The requirements of the CPQ involve the jurisdiction's accepting these certificate holders without implementing any additional barriers other than a jurisprudence examination, although Ohio requires that the transcript still be submitted. For more information, visit www.asppb.org.

Another approach to facilitating mobility is to use an established credential such as the National Register, which applies to 14,000 psychologists, for endorsement. As primary source documentation of education, training, licensing, board certification, and proficiency certification are on file, a growing number of jurisdictions have agreed. These psychologists have taken the licensing examinations required by at least one jurisdiction and have been monitored for disciplinary activity while credentialed by the National Register. For more information, visit www.nationalregister.org.

### Government-Initiated Agreements

In Canada, because of the Agreement on Internal Trade, movement of professionals across Canada will be based on demonstrating the requisite competencies. In order to develop an agreement that met with acceptance by professionals and the government, psychology established a working group. After several years of work and a lot of negotiation, the Mutual Recognition Agreement (MRA) became effective June 24, 2001, and includes several fast-track mechanisms for granting a license to psychologists: (a) holding the Canadian or National Register Health Service Provider in Psychology credential, (b) having graduated from a CPA- or APA-accredited doctoral program, or (c) holding the CPQ. Any psychologist licensed for 5 years in 1 of the 11 signatory jurisdictions prior to July 1, 2003, may also be licensed. In addition, psychology regulatory bodies agree to perform a competency assessment of applicants for a license beginning July 1, 2003. Although consonant with the intent of the provisions of the North American Free Trade Agreement (NAFTA), this agreement goes beyond harmonization of education and training that Canada, the United States, and Mexico may negotiate under NAFTA. Visit www.cpa.ca for a copy of the MRA.

Another example of facilitating mobility exists in Europe. As a consequence of a country's membership in the European Union (EU), regulated professionals are free to move and practice in another country participating in the EU. The main barrier to practicing in another country is language. However, if language is not an issue and the practitioner has met standards in one country, he or she can practice in another country for a year without any restrictions and regardless of the disparity in the two sets of standards. However, after that time period, the individual may be required to make up certain deficiencies for the right to continue practicing in the second jurisdiction.

## CERTIFICATION BY PRIVATE CREDENTIALING ORGANIZATIONS

Once licensed, psychologists have the opportunity to be credentialed for specific purposes. These voluntary credentials are chosen by a portion of those who are potentially qualified, and not to the degree as they are in medicine, where 80% of physicians are board certified (J. E. Hall, 2000). These

voluntary credentials may have standards that are higher than is required for a license.

> Therefore, the goal of licensing—to serve the public need—is furthered by credentialing organizations' assessment of specialized education and training and specialty competence. At the same time, these voluntary certification bodies are dependent upon licensing for certain protections, such as the investigation of complaints of professional misconduct. . . . Neither licensing nor certification alone is sufficient as a mechanism to protect the public and ensure minimum competence; both are needed. (J. E. Hall, 2000, pp. 317–318)

The typical doctoral sequence (as noted in Figure 20.1) reflects the credentialing organizations that are members of the CCOPP. There are also many other credentialing organizations that exist for psychologists, although many are small, have no central office or full-time staff, may credential multiple disciplines, have no publicly available list of credentialed practitioners, and fail to meet the standards met by the credentialing organizational members of CCOPP. Because of the existence of "unrecognized" or "undesignated" credentialing organizations, the public, including psychologists, needs to be wary of relying on such credentials and seek out those that are generally accepted in professional psychology. With those concerns in mind, we chose to focus on the National and Canadian Register, ABPP, and the College of Professional Psychology.

### National and Canadian Registers of Health Service Providers in Psychology

The concept of health service or health care provider is present throughout health care and is not specific to psychology. However, when the National Register was established in 1973, it was a new concept for psychology partly because the focus had been previously on mental health. The broad concept of a health service provider in psychology was developed especially to address psychology's uniqueness as both a profession and an academic discipline, as it didn't prescribe a specialty area but offered a definition of services delivered tied to education, training, and licensing credentials.

> A "Health Service Provider in Psychology" is a psychologist currently and actively licensed/certified/registered at the independent level in a jurisdiction, who is trained and experienced in the delivery of direct, preventive, assessment, and therapeutic intervention services to individuals whose growth, adjustment, or functioning is impaired or to individuals who otherwise seek services. (Council for the National Register, 2000, p. 11)

Although licensed, not all psychologists are qualified to provide direct health services to the public. Because many laws are generic, any person with a degree in psychology may apply for a license. In order to address this, the National Register was established so that qualified psychologists could be identified by insurers, governmental agencies, and health care organizations as well as by the individual consumers. This organization was established first in the United States in 1973 and later in Canada in 1985. There are approximately 14,000 registrants (National Register) and 3,000 Listees (Canadian Register). Access to the list of qualified psychologists is available online at www.nationalregister.org and www.crhspp.ca.

Credentialing by the National Register is offered to licensed practitioners. However, now there is a special stepwise credentialing procedure for students in training. At the completion of the internship, psychology graduate students can plan ahead and have their credentials placed in a "savings bank" for access later. As students submit primary source documentation of the internship, the doctoral degree, and the postdoctoral year of experience as each is completed, each credential is evaluated. Approval leads to the placement of the doctoral student's name on the National Psychologist Trainee Register (NPTR). With the addition of a credential, the information on the Web site is updated. Upon licensure, the graduate is automatically credentialed by the National Register. Visit www.nationalregister.org for the frequently updated NPTR list. Similarly, for the Canadian Register there is a temporary register for those licensed in a jurisdiction but still engaged in meeting the remaining supervised experience requirements for listing.

### American Board of Professional Psychology

Although the National Register is the largest and most successful credentialing organization in terms of numbers credentialed, it is not the oldest. The ABPP was created in 1947 (under a different name) to identify specialists in professional psychology using training and experience criteria and a specialty examination process, initially in clinical, counseling, and industrial and organizational psychology and, later in 1967, school psychology. (See Bent, Packard, & Goldberg, 1999, for a comprehensive history of the ABPP.) Today, approximately 3,200 active board-certified specialists exist, with much of the recent growth due to the emergence of new specialties in professional psychology, such as clinical neuropsychology, forensic, family, rehabilitation, psychoanalytic, behavioral, clinical health, and group psychology. After adopting the ASPPB–National Register Designation Criteria and the National Register internship criteria, ABPP decided

that psychologists credentialed by the National Register automatically meet the fundamental requirements for being evaluated as a specialist in professional psychology. Thus, the ABPP has endorsed the National Register credential. For access to their Web page, visit www.abpp.org.

### College of Professional Psychology

The College of Professional Psychology was established by APA in the 1990s to evaluate members of APA, either at the master's or doctoral level, who are health service providers and have experience specific to the treatment of alcohol and other psychoactive substance abuse disorders. There are 1,000 individuals who have met the criteria and passed the multiple-choice examination developed and administered by the College (Jan Ciuccio, personal communication, May 2001). In addition, the College developed an examination in psychopharmacology that is available to state licensing bodies or to individuals as evidence of competency in the psychopharmacology knowledge base. For current information go to www.apa.org/college/homepage.html.

### Credentialing and Credentials Verification

Health care delivery systems also seek to be accredited, much as occurs for education and training programs. This quality assurance mechanism supports the licensing and credentialing of psychologists. The Joint Commission on Accreditation of Healthcare Organizations (JCAHO) and the National Committee on Quality Assurance (NCQA), as well as others, evaluate delivery systems using a set of criteria addressing quality improvement, customer satisfaction, and credentialing of practitioners. Accrediting bodies such as these require primary source verification of credentials.

The Health Care Quality Improvement Act of 1986 mandated the federal government's establishment of a National Practitioner Data Bank (NPDB) where licensing sanctions on physicians and dentists are housed, as well as malpractice actions and hospital sanctions on all practitioners. The Health Insurance Portability and Accountability Act of 1996 requires the reporting of licensing sanctions on all practitioners to the Health Integrity and Protection Data Bank (HIPDB). State psychology licensing boards are now mandated to report disciplinary sanctions to the HIPDB. Visit www.npdb-hipdb.com for more information.

Today, health care companies verify the credentials of practitioners and query the federal and state data banks for sanctions. Credentialing organizations that use primary source verification methods and monitor practitioner discipline are seen as more credible than organizations that appear to grant a credential on the basis of minimal information that may not be verified. NCQA recently recognized organizations that meet acceptable standards by including in their 2001 accreditation standards (Standards 3.3 and 3.4) criteria for an organization having "deemed status." The National Register is the organization that has deemed status for psychology.

In an attempt to eliminate duplicate applications by practitioners and create a repository of credentials that will need only periodic updating, the Federal Credentialing Program (FCP) was established to assist federal agencies that also need to credential practitioners. The FCP is also developing criteria for determining which credentialing organizations and other similar bodies are eligible for deemed status, partly derived from the model that NCQA uses. For more information on the FCP, visit http://bhpr.hrsa.gov/dqa/fcppg.htm.

### Challenges to Expanding Practice

The culmination of the proper education, training, and experience for a psychologist is a license followed by credentialing as a health service provider, as a specialist or a proficiency. Whereas the credentialing organizations are national and not subject to borders, a license is for a specific jurisdiction. Because of telephone, video and audio conferencing, and online access to the service delivery to individuals, the concept of borderless practice threatens the right of a jurisdiction to regulate practice. Psychologists are faced with the dilemma of where and when to be licensed and which licenses to maintain. For example, approximately 25% of psychologists credentialed by the National Register maintain more than one license. Now that standards are more consistent from one state to another, psychologists have the potential to be more mobile. Should they have to acquire additional licenses, or is there a more parsimonious way of handling the global health care delivery system?

The real interest in borderless practice occurs when telehealth service delivery occurs. Both the U.S. and Canadian federal governments view this issue differently from licensing bodies, so it is too soon to predict how and when it will be resolved. From an education and training perspective, however, meeting national standards and qualifying for national credentials, such as the National Register–Canadian Register Health Service Provider in Psychology, may well offer the greatest protection to psychologists and the clients they serve. If a national license is not acceptable to state licensing boards, being licensed in one jurisdiction, which maintains disciplinary authority, and holding a national credential in health service delivery, such as from the National or Canadian Register, would seem an ideal foundation on which to allow psychologists to offer telehealth services.

## A HISTORICAL ADDENDUM ON CLINICAL PSYCHOLOGY: A CHRONOLOGY OF NATIONAL CONFERENCES IN THE UNITED STATES AND CANADA

Problem solving by organized psychology in the United States and Canada often occurs in conferences to which diverse representatives are invited. These meetings may lead to structures, agreements, or consolidation of opinions that change the direction in which the profession is moving. It would be almost impossible to articulate the real outcomes of all the numerous conferences in the United States and Canada. The proximal point is clearly the proceedings; the distal point is the structures or the standards that are created. Often, those structures take years to be created, refined, and approved, and by then the tie to the originating conference may have been forgotten. The expenses in mounting conferences are great, in terms of both financial resources and professional time. However, those who attend each take away their own personal reaction to the success of the conference. For all these reasons conferences are difficult to success, so in the following we simply list the names, dates, and reference for many of the conferences that have shaped U.S. and Canadian professional psychology. All have endorsed the scientist-practitioner Boulder model of training even though some have addressed other models.

### U.S. Conferences

**1949 Boulder Conference on Training in Clinical Psychology.** Creation of the Boulder model (scientist-practitioner) involving the integration of academic and applied training, followed by a 1-year internship culminating in a PhD degree in clinical psychology (Raimy, 1950). The only topical appendix contains David Shakow's 1947 report on clinical training.

**1951 Northwestern Conference.** Description of the roles and functions of counseling psychologists stimulated by a request to create standards of training and practice for these psychologists employed by the U.S. Veterans Administration (APA, 1952).

**1955 Thayer Conference.** Sought accreditation for school psychology training centers before doctoral school psychology programs were eligible for accreditation by APA and before school psychology was a specialty recognized by ABPP (Cutts, 1955).

**1956 Stanford Conference.** Reviewed and reaffirmed the Boulder training model and unsuccessfully promoted a 2-year postdoctoral internship (Belar, 1992).

**1958 Miami Beach Conference on Graduate Education in Psychology.**    Addressed all of psychology but affirmed the scientist-practitioner model (Roe, Gustad, Moore, Ross, & Skodak, 1959).

**1964 Greyston Conference.**    Recognized counseling psychology's overlap with other specialties in professional psychology—an issue that permeates counseling and school psychology's conferences and position papers. APA addressed this issue by accrediting programs in professional psychology and defining "professional" as including clinical, counseling and school psychology (Thompson & Super, 1964).

**1965 Chicago Conference on the Professional Preparation of Clinical Psychologists.**    Stressed diversity in the training and the preparation of psychologists for meeting wide societal needs. Endorsed psychological service settings tied to university departments (Hoch, Ross, & Winder, 1966).

**1974 Vail Conference.**    Addressed society's concerns in education, encouraged master's-level training programs, and endorsed the PsyD program model in settings other than a traditional psychology department in a large university. Originally titled the "National Conference on Levels and Patterns of Professional Training in Psychology," the conference stressed cultural diversity and social responsibility in graduate education (Korman, 1974).

**1976–1977 Conferences on Education and Credentialing of Psychologists.**    Sponsored by APA and the National Register, these two conferences led to the Guidelines for Defining a Doctoral Degree in Psychology. These criteria were adopted by licensing bodies and credentialing organizations and were used to evaluate doctoral programs beginning in 1980 (National Register, 2000; Wellner, 1978).

**1981, 1986, and 1987 National Council of Schools of Professional Psychology Conferences.**    Focused on issues of education and training in professional schools by faculty and administrators in professional schools that are members of National Council of Schools of Professional Psychology (NCSPP). The first of these was titled the "La Jolla Conference on Quality Control" and was followed in 1986 by the "Mission Bay Conference" (Bourg, Bent, McHolland, & Stricker, 1989) and the "San Antonio Core Curriculum in Professional Psychology" in 1987 (R. L. Peterson et al., 1991). The latter "continued the work of articulating professional psychology models of education and training begun at the Mission Bay

conference . . . and led to the fourth book in the NCSPP series" (p. 375).

**1982 Spring Hill Symposium on the Future of Psychology in the Schools.**    First major meeting of school psychologists about school psychology since the Thayer Conference. Reexamined the provision of school psychology services given the social and economic considerations at that time (Ysseldyke, 1982).

**1983 National Working Conference on Education and Training in Health Psychology.**    Formalized education and training sequence and the definition of one of the most popular areas found in clinical psychology training programs, which at that time represented 42 programs. This conference is referred to as the Arden House Conference, which is the location in New York where the meeting was held (Stone, 1983).

**1985 Conference on Training Clinical Child Psychologists.**    Held at Hilton Head Island, South Carolina, this conference focused on training of clinical child psychologists (Tuma, 1985), an area of practice that recently was approved as a specialty by APA.

**1987 National Conference on Internship Training in Psychology.**    Focused on the role of internship training in the preparation of professional psychologists and recommended a 2-year internship, 1 year pre- and the other postdoctoral. Held in Gainesville, Florida (Belar et al., 1987).

**1987 National Conference on Counseling Psychology.**    Held in Atlanta, Georgia, this third national conference confirmed the scientist-practitioner (or scientist-professional) model for counseling psychology (Resolutions Approved by the National Conference, 1987).

**1987 National Conference on Graduate Education in Psychology.**    Known as the Utah conference, these conferees attempted to address the full scope of graduate education in psychology. The conference emphasized research and having diversity in settings and in the way individuals are trained and recommended that professional schools affiliate with universities (Bickman & Ellis, 1990).

**1990 National Conference on the Education and Training of Scientist Practitioners for Professional Practice.**    Held in Gainesville, Florida, and cosponsored by 20 organizations, this conference reframed the necessity for science to inform practice and practice to inform science by emphasizing the integration of the scientific method with professional practice (Belar & Perry, 1992).

**1992 National Conference on Postdoctoral Fellowship Training in Professional Practice.** Known as the Ann Arbor Conference, the distal outcome was the implementation of postdoctoral accreditation conceptualized and tested by the IOC and implemented by APA (Belar et al., 1993).

**1997 National Working Conference on Supply and Demand.** Attempted to focus on supply and demand issues regarding internship and employment. However, the conference largely initiated a dialogue over a wide range of issues in professional psychology—including whether licensure could occur prior to completion of the postdoctoral year of experience. Sponsored by the APA and the APPIC, the proceedings are available on the APA web site (http://www.apa.org).

### Canadian Conferences

As John Conway (1984) wryly noted in his history of the development of clinical training in Canada, "The history of clinical psychology in Canada is a short one; and its past, though hardly as ancient as that of psychology, is longer than its history" (p. 177). Canada has also had fewer conferences, and they are somewhat unknown in the United States. Hence, we provide more detail here.

Much as in the United States, World War II served to accelerate the development of applied psychology in Canada. The founding of the first national psychology organization in Canada in 1938—the Canadian Psychological Association— reflected both an increased interest in psychology's contribution to Canada's war effort and a desire by Canadian psychologists to better organize, share, and disseminate their collective work. Applied psychologists were finding their skills in demand in peacetime Canada, and initial federal funding began to flow for graduate students and for faculty positions in clinical psychology (Conway, 1984, p. 178). Unlike in the United States, where postwar clinical psychology began to specialize rapidly due to the VA, Canadian university-based training programs in the late 1940s and early 1950s were mostly organized and oriented toward broad-based applied psychology perspectives with little interest in specialization (Conway, 1984).

**1960 Opinicon, Ontario.** The first national conference on the state of psychology in Canada was sponsored by CPA. Although intended to address professional training and research training issues, the actual conference was directed largely to the concerns of academic research psychologists.

After proclaiming that a clinical PhD should follow a scientist-professional model, the conference delegates reframed clinical psychology as a PhD research degree to the exclusion of any real concept of a profession (Conway, 1984).

**1965 Couchiching, Ontario.** CPA's next national training conference was designed to address some of the neglected issues of professional psychology and the training of professional psychologists. At this conference, a university-based, psychology department–driven, scientist-professional model leading to the PhD was again endorsed by most attendees. The conference also requested that CPA establish accreditation procedures for applied programs. Although arguments continued about the merits of various types of professional training models (as well as whether importing a U.S.-style Boulder model was truly the best model for training Canadian clinicians), younger Canadian universities with newer psychology departments began to design more clinical training programs and began hiring more clinical faculty members (Conway, 1984).

**1997 Vancouver, British Columbia, Conference.** Professional issues in Canadian psychology began to assert themselves loudly in the late 1960s and early 1970s through a variety of venues. Chief among these were the licensing of psychologists by various provinces and the formation of the Advisory Council of Provincial Associations of Psychologists (ACPAP)—the forerunner of the Council of Provincial Associations of Psychology (CPAP)—a national council of fraternal and regulatory bodies organized to increase national communication and advocacy with regard to professional issues. The Vancouver Conference recommended not only increased voice in CPA for professional issues but also the development of a Canadian Code of Ethics for psychologists as well the development of accreditation criteria for clinical psychology (Dobson & Dobson, 1993).

**1984 Opinicon II.** Opinicon II again reaffirmed the scientist-professional model for graduate training of Canadian professional psychologists (Ritchie, Hogan, & Hogan, 1988). This same year, CPA formally adopted accreditation criteria for clinical psychology following a scientist-practitioner template, thus institutionalizing the scientist-practitioner model for at least the next two decades. Clinical psychology training programs were gradually becoming more balanced with regard to research and practice by the mid-1980s. In addition, Opinicon II recommended the use of a Canadian-oriented designation system much like the United States' ASPPB– National Register designation system for U.S. psychology graduate programs (Dobson & Dobson, 1993). However, the exclusively university-based nature of clinical training programs as endorsed in CPA accreditation criteria meant that little or no attention continued to be given to other possible training models such as the U.S.-developed PsyD with its attendant increased professional focus.

**1994 Mississauga, Ontario, Conference on Professional Psychology.** The Mississauga Conference in many ways represented a radical departure from earlier conferences. Ironically, while professional psychology was developing new practice areas and new marketplaces for services, more traditional training and practice areas (e.g., hospital psychology departments) were being cut back or reorganized toward program management models. National federal cuts to health care funding not only led to decreased federal and provincial health funding to psychology, but also reflected a growing skepticism regarding the cost-effective role that psychologists traditionally played in the health care system. In response to this rapidly shifting landscape, CPA, together with the Canadian Register and provincial partners, funded and convened the Mississauga Conference.

The theme of Mississauga could perhaps best be summarized as "moving the markers" (and fast!) for professional psychology. Rather than focus on the whole discipline, this conference was carefully designed to "develop guiding principles and specific action plans for professional psychology for implementation immediately upon completion of the conference" (Dobson & King, 1994, p. 3). As relayed by Dobson and King, who were coeditors of the final report on Mississauga, earlier Delphi polls of leading professional psychologists taken just prior to the conference showed that funding of psychological services, advocacy for professional psychology, and training emerged as the three most pressing challenges the conference should address. Based on the same spirit of action-based principles and concepts as the APPIC-sponsored Ann Arbor Conference held a year earlier in the United States, the Mississauga Conference set to work to address these three major challenges in Canada.

The Mississauga delegates came forward with a number of bold and forward-thinking recommendations. Among the most striking recommendations for professional psychology education, training, and practice was the explicit endorsement of the need for and development of psychologist entrepreneurs with business knowledge embedded in core training and practice skills originating in graduate and internship training. Among other important recommendations were the reaffirmation of the doctoral standard (flexibly defined as the national entry standard for professional psychology practice in Canada), the endorsement of professional mobility across Canadian jurisdictions through such mechanisms as mutual recognition of

practice credentials, and the development of enhanced advocacy capacity for professional psychology. Delegates also called for strategic alliances and more continued coordinated initiatives as had been previously designed by such entities as the National Professional Psychology Consortium. Blessed by the three major national psychology organizations involved with professional psychology practice (i.e., the Canadian Register, CPA, and CPAP), the Mississauga Conference set the stage for the endorsement of clinical psychology—among other branches of professional psychology—as both an advocacy-oriented and a business-oriented professional practice branch for psychological health services in Canada.

**2001 Winnipeg, Manitoba, Conference.** The Winnipeg conference addressed whether psychology should restructure itself in response to the multiple collective challenges that face Canadian psychology today. Besides the perennial issue of limited resources for near-unlimited challenges, other 21st-century issues such as globalization of the profession, issues of professional mobility (both inside Canada and across nations) and the rapid evolution of professional psychologists from mental health providers to primary care providers (i.e., "health service providers in psychology") make for a heady mix of challenges and opportunities for the profession over the next 10 years. In the history of Canadian psychology, perhaps the only certain outcome will be that clinical psychology, as well as other branches of professional psychology, will continue to respond to the pressing internal and external needs of the day with careful consideration and a variety of actions whose outcomes are often truly measured only in the historical mirror of retrospect.

Canadian clinical psychology—as a major subset of professional psychology—has, in many ways, come full circle from its earliest beginnings during World War II. Beginning as a broad-based and socially relevant area of psychology in the 1940s and moving to a near–second class existence as a practice area in the 1950s, to a cautiously reaffirmed area in the 1960s, to a CPA-accredited specialty in the 1980s, and to a major professional psychology constituent group at beginning of the 21st century, Canadian clinical psychology does indeed have a longer past—and probable future—than its formal existence implies.

## CONCLUSION

The education, training, licensing, and credentialing of clinical psychologists represent a product of longstanding quality assurance goals inside and outside the profession as well as the process of professional development of the discipline within the context of the countries of the United States, Canada, and Mexico. None of these pieces can be separated from the other as they represent the historic and contemporary collective impact of the internal and external influences on professional psychology in North America.

As is evident from this overview, there remains a diversity of views regarding the best ways to educate, train, and sustain highly competent professional psychologists that represent the best interests of clients/patients, the profession, and the public, despite the truly impressive, broad-based, and substantive progress made to date by professional psychology. In general, where agreement has been reached, professional psychology has moved forward and prospered. Where international dialogue has occurred, such as at the seven yearly meetings of the Trilateral Forum on Professional Psychology, representatives of the three North American countries have reached a better understanding of each other's methods of training. Perhaps as a consequence of that dialogue, changes have occurred at the same time, many of which are summarized in these pages and are reflected in the tables. However, the basic foundations of the discipline and profession essentially require that the road to progress entails many possible pathways and vigorous debate regarding best roads to travel at any given time. Probably the only certainty is that this debate and dialogue will continue to be *the process* that propels professional psychology into this yet very new millennium.

As professional psychology continues to develop in the countries of North America and beyond, it may be wise to recollect the spirit of progress envisioned by Stricker and Trierweiler (1995) when they spoke of the local clinical scientist as a bridge between the science and practice of professional psychology. They noted, "If science and practice are regarded as activities—research and praxis—then there may be fundamental incompatibilities between the two. . . . However, if science and practice are regarded as attitudes or identities, the incompatibility may be resolved to the benefit of each, despite the general obstacles that exist" (p. 996). With this view, the portrait of the local clinical psychologist becomes "a vibrant scientist-professional, a local clinical scientist who enters the world of the profession, providing assistance to patients but never forgetting his or her roots in the discipline of psychology, both as a science and as a practice" (p. 999).

Although clinical psychology has come a very long way in a relatively brief period of time, many challenges—current and future—remain. The frontiers of psychological knowledge are expanding at ever-increasing velocity as the planet simultaneously shrinks in the face of new information and communication technologies. North American professional psychology, professional psychologists, and the now near-global public are all a part of these trends as ideas, structures, and methods are compared and tested against a backdrop of developing, evaluating, and monitoring competency-based professionals. Increasing numbers of countries worldwide are now addressing how best to produce and sustain highly competent, ethical, and wise professional psychologists who embrace the best that the discipline and profession has to offer and who will practice in the emerging global community. Despite the challenges, it is an exciting and heady time for professional psychology, and—most important of all—the journey continues.

## REFERENCES

American Psychological Association. (1979). *Criteria for accreditation of doctoral training programs and internships in professional psychology.* Washington, DC: Author.

American Psychological Association. (1987). Model act for state licensure of psychologists. *American Psychologist, 42,* 696–703.

American Psychological Association. (2000, January 1). *Book 1: Guidelines and principles for accreditation of programs in professional psychology.* Washington, DC: Author.

American Psychological Association. (2001, February). *Report by the commission on education and training leading to licensure in psychology.* Washington, DC: Author.

APA Committee on Legislation. (1955). Joint report of the APA and CSPA (Conference of State Psychological Associations). *American Psychologist, 10,* 727–756.

APA Committee on Legislation. (1967). A model for state legislation affecting the practice of psychology 1967: Report of the APA Committee on Legislation. *American Psychologist, 22,* 1095–1103.

American Psychological Association Council of Representatives. (1996, February). *Minutes.* Washington, DC: Author.

Association of Psychology Postdoctoral and Internship Centers. (2001). *APPIC Match Statistics.* Washington, DC: Author.

Association of State and Provincial Psychology Boards. (1992). *Model act for licensure of psychologists.* Montgomery, AL: Author.

Association of State and Provincial Psychology Boards. (1998). *Model act for licensure of psychologists.* Montgomery, AL: Author.

Association of State and Provincial Psychology Boards. (2000). *ASPPB educational reporting service: EPPP performance by designated doctoral program in psychology.* (Available from the ASPPB, PO Box 241245, Montgomery, AL 36124-1245)

Association of State and Provincial Psychology Boards. (2001). *Handbook of licensing and certification requirements for psychologists in the US and Canada.* Montgomery, AL: Author.

Belar, C. (1992). Conference on internship and postdoctoral training. In A. E. Puente, J. R. Matthews, & C. L. Brewer (Eds.),

*Teaching psychology in America: A history* (pp. 301–310). Washington, DC: American Psychological Association.

Belar, C. D. (1998). Graduate education in clinical psychology: "We're not in Kansas anymore." *American Psychologist, 53,* 456–464.

Belar, C. D., & Perry, N. W. (1992). National conference on scientist-practitioner education and training for the professional practice of psychology. *American Psychologist, 47,* 71–75.

Belar, C. D., Bieliauskas, L. A., Larsen, K. G., Mensh, I. N., Poey, K., & Roehlke, H. J. (Eds.). (1987). *Proceedings: National Conference on Internship Training in Psychology.* Baton Rouge, LA: Land and Land.

Belar, C. D., Zimet, C. N., Bieliauskas, L., Klepac, R. K., Larsen, K. G., & Stigall, T. T. (Eds.). (1993). *Proceedings: National Conference on Postdoctoral Fellowship Training in Professional Psychology.* Baton Rouge, LA: Land and Land.

Bent, R. J., Packard, R. E., & Goldberg, R. W. (1999). The American Board of Professional Psychology, 1947 to 1997: A historical perspective. *Professional Psychology: Research and Practice, 29,* 65–73.

Bickman, L., & Ellis, H. (Eds.). (1990). *Preparing psychologists for the 21st century.* Hillsdale, NJ: Erlbaum.

Bourg, E. F., Bent, R. J., McHolland, J., & Stricker, G. (1989). Standards and evaluation in the education and training of professional psychologists. *American Psychologist, 44,* 66–72.

Canadian Psychological Association. (1991). *Accreditation manual.* Ottawa, ON: Author.

Conway, J. B. (1984). Clinical psychology training in Canada: Its development current status, and the prospects for accreditation. *Canadian Psychology, 25,* 177–191.

Council for the National Register of Health Service Providers in Psychology. (2000). *National Register of Health Service Providers in Psychology* (18th ed.). Washington, DC: Author.

Cutts, N. E. (Ed.). (1955). *School psychologists at mid-century: A report of the Thayer Conference on the functions, qualifications, and training of school psychologists.* Washington, DC: American Psychological Association.

Dobson, K. S., & Dobson, D. J. G. (Eds.). (1993). *Professional psychology in Canada.* Seattle: Hogrefe and Huber.

Dobson, K. S., & King, M. C. (1994). *The Mississauga Conference on professional psychology.* Ottawa, ON: Canadian Psychological Association.

Drum, D. J. (2001). *A conceptual model of health service providers in psychology.* (Available from author at 100 A West 26th St., Counseling and Mental Health Center, University of Texas, Austin, TX 78712-1001)

Drum, D. J., & Hall, J. E. (1993). Psychology's self-regulation and the setting of professional standards. *Applied and Preventive Psychology, 2,* 151–161.

Ehrlich, E., Flexner, S. B., Carruth, G., & Hawkins, J. M. (1980). *Oxford American dictionary.* New York: Avon Books.

*Federal Register.* (1998, April 23). Vol. 63, No. 78.

Gaddy, C. D., Charlot-Swilley, D., Nelson, P. D., & Reich, J. N. (1995). Selected outcomes of accredited programs. *Professional Psychology: Research and Practice, 26,* 507–513.

Gauthier, J. (1997, Winter). President's column. *Psynopsis,* p. 2.

Gelso, C., & Fretz, B. (2001). *Counseling psychology.* Orlando, FL: Harcourt Brace.

Goodman, J. T. (2000). Three decades of professional psychology: Reflections and future challenges. *Canadian Psychology, 41,* 25–33.

Hall, J. E. (1993). The role of the state. In P. Wohlford, H. F. Myers, & J. E. Callan (Eds.), *Serving the seriously mentally ill: Public-academic linkages for improving psychological services, research and training* (pp. 195–205). Washington, DC: American Psychological Association.

Hall, J. E. (2000). Licensing and credentialing as quality management tools in behavioral health care. In G. Stricker, W. G. Troy, & S. A. Shueman (Eds.), *Handbook of quality management in behavioral health* (pp. 317–332). New York: Kluwer Academic/Plenum.

Hall, R. G., & Hsu, J. (Eds.). (2000). *Internship and postdoctoral programs in professional psychology: 2000–2001* (29th ed.). Washington, DC: Author.

Handy, L., & Whitsett, S. (1993). Continuing education in professional psychology. In K. S. Dobson & D. J. G. Dobson (Eds.), *Professional psychology in Canada* (pp. 107–121). Toronto: Hogrefe and Huber.

Health Care Quality Improvement Act of 1986, Title IV of P.L. 99-660. (42 U.S.C. 11101 et. seq.).

Health Insurance Portability and Accountability Act of 1996, § 221, Title XI of P.L. 104-191 (41 U.S.C. 1301 et seq.).

Hoch, E. L., Ross, A. O., & Winder, C. L. (1966). Conference on the professional preparation of clinical psychologists: A summary. *American Psychologist, 21,* 42–51.

Hunsley, J., & Lefebvre, M. (1990). A survey of the practices and activities of Canadian clinical psychologists. *Canadian Psychology, 31,* 350–358.

Hurley, G. (1998, August). Mobility for Canadian health service psychologists? The Canadian conundrum and possible compromise. In P. Nelson (Moderator), *Education, training and credentialing standards for health service providers in psychology: Consensus and controversy within and between national communities.* Panel discussion conducted at the 24th International Congress of Applied Psychology, San Francisco, CA.

Korman, M. (1974). National Conference on Levels and Patterns of Professional Training in Psychology: The major themes. *American Psychologist, 29,* 441–449.

Maher, B. (1999). Changing trends in doctoral training programs in psychology: A comparative analysis of research-oriented versus professional-applied programs. *Psychological Science, 10,* 475–481.

*Mutual Recognition Agreement of the Regulatory Bodies for Professional Psychologists in Canada.* (2001). (Available from Joseph S. Rallo, Chair, Council of Provincial Associations of Psychologists, 825 Sherbrook Street, Winnipeg, MB R3A 1M5, Canada)

Nelson, P. D., & Messenger, L. C. (1998, Winter). APA encourages multi-cultural dialogue on accreditation. *Psychology International, 9*(1), 1, 4–5.

New York State Doctoral Evaluation Project. (1990). *Doctoral education in psychology.* (Available from Doctoral Evaluation Project, New York State Education Department, Cultural Education Center, Room 5a43, Albany, NY 12230)

O'Sullivan, J. J., & Quevillon, R. P. (1992). 40 years later: Is the Boulder model still alive? *American Psychologist, 47,* 67–70.

Peterson, D. R., Eaton, M. M., Levine, A. R., & Snepp, F. P. (1982). Career experiences of doctors of psychology. *Professional Psychology, 13,* 268–277.

Peterson, R. L., McHolland, J. D., Bent, R. J., Davis-Russell, E., Edwall, G. E., Polite, K., Singer, D. L., & Stricker, G. (Eds.). (1991). *The core curriculum in professional psychology.* Washington, DC: American Psychological Association.

Phares, E. J. (1988). *Clinical psychology: Concepts, methods and profession* (3rd ed.). Chicago: Dorsey Press.

Poirier, M., Lafond, G., Ritchie, R., Cyr, M., Forget, J., & Desgagnes, M. (1999, November). *La Formation du Psychologies: Le Doctoral en Psychologie axe sur les competences professionnelles* [Training of psychologists: A PsyD based on professional competencies] (H. P. Edwards, Trans.). (Available from Ordre des psychologues du Quebec, 1100, avenue Beaumont, bureau 510, Ville Mont Royal, Montreal, Quebec H3P 3H5, Canada)

Raimy, V. C. (Ed.). (1950). *Training in clinical psychology.* New York: Prentice Hall.

Resolutions Approved by the National Conference. (1987). *American Psychologist, 42,* 1070–1084.

Ritchie, P. L.-J., Hogan, T. P., & Hogan, T. V. (Eds.). (1988). *Psychology in Canada: The state of the discipline: 1984.* Old Chelsea, ON: Canadian Psychological Association.

Robinson, B., Brooker, H., Carpenter, P., DeKoninck, J., Dobson, K., Doyle, A. B., Dozois, D., Granger, L., McIvor, J., & Mureika, J. (1998, November). *Psy.D. task force: Final report to the Canadian Psychological Association Board of Directors.* Ottawa, ON: Canadian Psychological Association.

Roe, A., Gustad, J. W., Moore, B. V., Ross, S., & Skodak, M. (Eds.). (1959). *Graduate education in psychology.* Washington, DC: American Psychological Association.

Rosenfeld, M., Shimberg, B., & Thornton, R. F. (1983). *Job analysis of licensed psychologists in the United States and Canada: A study of responsibilities and requirements.* Princeton, NJ: Educational Testing Service.

Sheridan, E. P., Matarazzo, J. D., & Nelson, P. D. (1995). Accreditation of psychology's graduate professional education and training programs: An historical perspective. *Professional Psychology: Research and Practice, 26,* 386–392.

Stone, G. C. (Ed.). (1983). National working conference on education and training in health psychology. *Health Psychology, 2*(Suppl.).

Stricker, G., & Trierweiler, S. J. (1995). The local clinical scientist: A bridge between science and practice. *American Psychologist, 50,* 995–1002.

Stromberg, C. D. (1990, May). *Associations' certification programs: Legal and operational issues.* Paper presented at a meeting of the American Speech and Hearing Association, Rockville, MD. (Available from the author at Hogan & Hartson, 555 13th Street, NW, Washington, DC 20005)

Stromberg, C. D., Haggarty, D. J., Leibenluft, R. F., McMillian, M. H., Mishkin, B., Rubin, B. L., & Trilling, H. R. (1988). *The psychologist's legal handbook.* Washington, DC: Council for the National Register of Health Service Providers in Psychology.

Thompson, A. S., & Super, D. E. (Eds.). (1964). *The professional preparation of counseling psychologists: Report of the 1964 Greyston Conference.* New York: Bureau of Publications, Teacher's College, Columbia University.

Tuma, J. M. (Ed.). (1985). *Proceedings: Conference on training clinical child psychologists.* Washington, DC: American Psychological Association.

U.S. Department of Education. 34 C. F.R. § 602 (1994). Secretary's procedures and criteria for recognition of accrediting agencies; final rule.

Ysseldyke, J. E. (1982). The Spring Hill Symposium on the future of psychology in the schools. *American Psychologist, 37,* 547–552.

Yu, L. M., Rinaldi, S. A., Templer, D. I., Colbert, L., Siscoe, K., & Van Patten, K. (1997). Score on the examination for professional practice in psychology as a function of attributes of clinical psychology graduate programs. *Psychological Science, 8,* 347–350.

Wellner, A. M. (Ed.). (1978). *Education and credentialing in psychology.* Washington, DC: Steering Committee of APA, ASPPB, and National Register.

CHAPTER 21

# Ethical Issues in Clinical Psychology

STANLEY E. JONES

Good ethical practice includes striving to the highest aspirations of the profession as well as adhering to the minimal standards that are enforced as part of ethics codes. It necessarily involves not only knowledge about and compliance with ethical standards, but competence in and adherence to clinical and legal standards as well. The duty to abide by standards is one of the elements that make professions distinctive. Aspirational ethics is closest to the traditional definition of "ethics," synonymous with "moral philosophy." Application of moral reasoning weighs a variety of ethical principles to a situation and considers the best options. Minimal standards are part of what is more properly labeled a code of conduct. Application of such codes is more likely to consider the rules that may be applicable and to ensure that behavior does not violate one or more rules. A psychologist who does not behave according to the minimal standards is subject to being investigated and being found to have behaved unethically. A psychologist can deserve sanction for committing a forbidden act, as well as for failing to engage in a required behavior. A focus on measuring up to minimal standards overlooks the practical value of aiming for the aspirational standards and thereby being very likely to also meet the enforceable rules.

The focus of this chapter includes the sources of ethical principles and standards, the major ethical issues in clinical practice, and methods of regulation.

## ETHICS CODES AND REGULATIONS

The American Psychological Association's (APA) ethics code has been the primary ethics document in psychology since the first APA ethics code, then called the Ethical Standards of Psychologists, was adopted (APA, 1953). The APA ethics code was commonly adopted as the disciplinary standards for states' psychology licensure boards. However, this adoption has varied over the years. Some licensure laws write the content of a particular version of the APA ethics code into law, and others simply refer to the APA ethics code generally or to a particular version. When the content of a code has been written into law, changes may also be made so that individual standards may vary from the code used as the pattern. In addition, the same range of methods may be used in adopting disciplinary standards into licensure board regulations, rather than into the licensure law itself. Some states have adopted a model code of conduct recommended by the Association of State and Provincial Psychology Boards (ASPPB; 1991).

### The American Psychological Association's Ethics Code

#### Current Ethics Code and Revisions

APA adopted its first ethics code in 1951, and there have been several revisions since then. The version current as of this writing is the Ethical Principles of Psychologists and Code of

Conduct (APA, 1992), and a revision of this code was nearing completion. A new code was projected for adoption in August 2002.

This makes writing about specific provisions in the ethics code difficult, but it also highlights a continuing problem for practicing psychologists. It is not enough for a psychologist to learn the version of the ethics code that was current when he or she was in training or sat for the licensure exam. As stated in the Preamble to the 1992 APA ethics code, "The development of a dynamic set of ethical standards for a psychologist's work-related conduct requires a personal commitment to a lifelong effort" (p. 1599). The last two ethics codes, the versions adopted in 1981 and 1992, have been in effect for about 10 years each. The practicing psychologist must be prepared to learn each new code as it is implemented. Of course, when considering the real life changes that occur in licensure and other laws, court decisions, practice standards, new treatment methods, and other practice conditions, this requires an ongoing effort of continuing education. New ethics codes are simply one of the changes.

Current information on the ethics code is available on the APA Web site at http://www.apa.org/ethics or through APA.

### Aspirational and Enforceable

The first APA ethics code was distinctive in APA's use of the critical incident method for its development. Although the form of the original code and the critical incident method were not continued, it was considered important to maintain some kind of tie to behavioral examples. The casebooks were the primary method for this, but this has proven increasingly difficult, as improved legal defensibility of the code for enforcement has made this a lower priority.

The 1992 Ethical Principles of Psychologists and Code of Conduct (APA, 1992), was the first APA code to differentiate explicitly between statements intended to be "aspirational" and those to be enforced. A casebook did not follow it, but an unofficial commentary was published by APA (Canter, Bennet, Jones, & Nagy, 1994).

Many psychologists argue for inclusion of more specific guidance in the ethics code. Others argue against including anything in an enforceable code that might add unreasonable or unnecessary standards. A reality is that the separation of aspirational from enforceable elements in the code does present some limits to the content of ethical standards. The ethics code cannot provide a full statement of how to behave ethically, and the "Ethical Standards" section in the 1992 ethics code is a statement of a minimum standard or code of conduct. Guidance for practice is more likely to be found in documents that focus on a limited content area and provide guidelines or

principles that are not intended to be binding. APA has adopted the strategy of providing such information in guidelines such as the General Guidelines for Providers of Psychological Services (APA, 1987), the *Standards for Educational and Psychological Testing* (American Educational Research Association, APA, and National Council on Measurement in Education, 1999), and *Publication Manual of the American Psychological Association–Fifth Edition* (APA, 2001). Materials adopted by groups other than APA as a whole may also provide helpful information, including the APA Division 41 (Forensic Psychology)/American Psychology-Law Society's Specialty Guidelines for Forensic Psychologists (Committee on Ethical Guidelines for Forensic Psychologists, 1991). In addition, groups may facilitate projects published as individuals that apply the ethics code to particular content areas, such as a book of cases related to industrial and organizational psychology (Lowman, 1998).

### Revisions

Two changes to the APA ethics code in the 1980s and 1990s are of special importance to understanding the nature of the ethics code and its implied limitations. The first is related to the emergency revision of the code made by APA to produce the "Ethical Principles of Psychologists (Amended June 2, 1989)" (APA, 1990). The Bureau of Competition of the Federal Trade Commission (FTC) investigated APA regarding the code's content related primarily to advertising and referral fees. The emergency revision was part of a negotiation to end the investigation (FTC, 1993). For example, the previous referral fee provision was being interpreted in such a way as to prohibit preferred provider organizations and the like.

Another change of special importance was the clearer conceptualization of aspirational as opposed to enforceable ethics provisions just discussed and first implemented in the 1992 APA ethics code (APA, 1992). Part of the legal impetus for this change was found in a court decision (*White v. the North Carolina State Board,* 1990) that found some provisions in the 1981 ethics code to be unconstitutionally vague in one state. A fundamental legal principle in enforcing ethics codes is that the rules must provide fair notice to the professional as to what behavior will lead to a sanction.

More complete descriptions of the history of the APA ethics code may be found in Canter et al. (1994) and Koocher and Keith-Spiegel (1998).

### Content of the 1992 Ethics Code

The 1992 ethics code (APA, 1992) contains an introduction, the aspirational Preamble and General Principles, and the enforceable Ethical Standards. The introduction provides an overview and information regarding enforcement of the code and application of the code to other professional standards and to the law. It notes that the code may be adopted by licensure boards and may otherwise be applied to psychologists who are not members of APA. The Preamble and General Principles sections state aspirational goals that apply broadly.

The Ethical Standards section provides enforceable rules. The standards are divided into seven sections. Three sections are intended to apply more generally to all psychologists: groups 1 ("General Standards"), 3 ("Advertising and Other Public Statements"), and 5 ("Confidentiality"). The other groups are "Evaluation, Assessment, or Intervention"; "Therapy"; "Teaching, Training Supervision, Research, and Publishing"; and "Forensic Activities." Even though some sections may apply more consistently to some groups of psychologists than to others, it is important for all psychologists to consider the entire code when making ethical decisions. A psychologist in practice may rarely need to consider the section on research but must do so if doing research or engaging in other activities covered by that section. If the psychologist engages in research, it is not a defense to argue that the psychologist did not think he or she was engaging in research or did not know the relevant provisions of the ethics code.

The 1992 ethics code included a number of changes from previous codes. For the first time in an APA code, rules to be enforced were differentiated from aspirational statements, and the enforceable standards were more specific. Standards were also organized differently and limited as much as possible to single-behavior "unitary" concepts in individual standards. New provisions provided explicit guidance regarding sexual involvement with former clients (Standard 4.07) and with certain students (Standard 1.19), barter (Standard 1.18), informed consent to therapy (Standard 4.02), withholding records for nonpayment (Standard 5.11), and forensic services (Standards 7.01–7.06). There were also modified provisions regarding advertising (Standards 3.01–3.03) as well as referrals and fees (Standard 1.27), testimonials (Standard 3.05), and in-person solicitation (Standard 3.06). The advertising standards included provisions believed to be acceptable to the FTC as replacements for some standards rescinded in the 1989 revision.

### Pending Revision

Most revisions have made only modest changes to content, and only the 1959 (APA, 1959) and 1992 revisions altered the format substantially. The pending revision, however, is the first since the major change in 1992, so it is more likely to involve changes in structure and content. Drafts of the pending

revision suggest that there will be substantial changes to the General Principles and to the order and organization of the ethical standards. There are likely to be new standards and substantial changes to some ethical standards. However, many standards will remain unchanged or with modest changes. There is, of course, no way to predict the final decisions, which are made by the APA Council of Representatives.

Comment on revision drafts by practicing psychologists is very important and potentially influential on the groups drafting revision language. The pending revision is the first to post drafts on the APA Web site and to provide for making comments online. However, comments are most effective when the commenter understands points such as those just made about guidelines and enforceable standards. For example, some psychologists might suggest that the enforceable standards explicitly list all the elements required to be in psychological treatment records. While a benefit might be that the psychologist would know precisely the minimum required, it would also mean that any less in a record would subject the psychologist to a potential ethics violation. As noted, APA has taken the approach of providing such detail in guidelines, here in the form of the APA Record Keeping Guidelines (APA, 1993).

Arguments that a particular provision is undesirable because it may result in psychologists' being sued is not likely to persuade drafters because a purpose of the enforceable provisions in ethics codes is, in fact, to set standards. The important issue is to set the correct standards.

### Other Codes and Standards

In addition to the APA ethics code, a variety of other ethics codes may be relevant to individual psychologists. For example, the Canadian Psychological Association (CPA, 2000) has adopted its own code. The CPA code incorporates a decision-making process into the code itself and structures the code by relating each general principle to the more specific provisions. A psychologist who belongs to a variety of mental health professional organizations may be subject to multiple ethics codes.

As noted earlier, ASPPB adopted a model code of conduct in 1990. This was a recommendation to state boards, and it is effective only if adopted in a state. Some state licensure boards adopted this code. The scope of this code is different from APA's because it substantially addresses only those areas needed in regulating licensed psychologists. Psychologists do not need to know this code independently; if it has been used in the psychologist's state, the psychologist simply needs to know his or her own state's laws and regulations.

Ethics codes do not provide all the information needed for psychologists to do good work. The 1992 APA ethics code says that psychologists should "consider other professional materials" (p. 1598) when the Code alone is not sufficient. As "most helpful in this regard" are the many "guidelines and standards that have been adopted or endorsed by professional psychological organizations" (p. 1598). A footnote lists guidelines, such as APA's (1987) General Guidelines for Providers of Psychological Services. Guidelines are, of course, constantly being revised, adopted, and, occasionally, rescinded or otherwise determined to be out of date. The code clarifies that "such guidelines . . . , whether adopted by the American Psychological Association (APA) or its Divisions, are not enforceable as such by this Ethics Code, but are of educative value to psychologists, courts, and professional bodies" (p. 1598). Psychologists may be concerned that courts or others may use guidelines as if they were standards. This does in fact happen, as at least one state licensure board has used the APA's (1994) Guidelines for Child Custody Evaluations in Divorce Proceedings in reviewing complaints about such practice. The point is not that this is either good or bad but that psychologists need to know what standards are being applied to them, to learn the standards, and to follow them.

In addition to ethics codes and practice guidelines and standards, there will be other standards that psychologists must know and follow. For example, psychologists need to know laws related to child abuse reporting and, if practicing in a particular hospital, professional staff regulations.

### Licensure Board Regulations

As suggested earlier, the actual disciplinary standards written into psychology licensure laws and established by licensure boards through regulations vary from state to state and may or may not be based on a version of the APA ethics code. The actual contents of the major provisions, however, are very similar. For example, all such standards address a prohibition against sexual misconduct and improper multiple relationships, requirement to keep confidentiality, and so on. Such regulations also, however, address the mechanics of licensure, requiring such things as specific requirements for renewal of licensure, display of license, and payment of fees.

### MAJOR ETHICAL PRACTICE ISSUES

A review of the content of the APA ethics code makes it apparent that clinical practice is constantly involved with ethics. Many other chapters in these volumes will address content that is at the heart of many ethical issues. For example, Standard 2.02 in the 1992 ethics code, "Competence and Appropriate Use of Assessments and Interventions," states in part (a) that

"Psychologists who develop, administer, score, interpret, or use psychological assessment techniques, interviews, tests, or instruments do so in a manner and for purposes that are appropriate in light of the research on or evidence of the usefulness and proper application of the techniques" (p. 1603). Obviously, there is a great deal of information related to the research and evidence related to assessment. In providing information on these topics, authors are also providing information that is useful to interpreting the ethics code.

However, there are several major practice issues with special ethical relevance, and some key considerations are reviewed next.

### Competence

Psychologists have an ethical responsibility to know their competencies and to practice only within those competencies. Professions are licensed based on a determination that the public lacks sufficient understanding to know who is qualified to provide the relevant professional services. But it is not possible for a licensure entity to determine the specific competencies possessed by each licensed professional. Accordingly, it is a primary requirement, ethically and in licensure laws and regulations, for each professional to practice within the limits of his or her competence.

Standards related to competence (e.g., 1992 ethics code Standard 1.04, "Boundaries of Competence") may leave questions as to how one can establish competence in a specific, limited area. Competence in the major areas, however, is easy to consider. For example, a psychologist who had no academic coursework and no supervised experience in working with children has not established competence in working with children. A psychologist who had some coursework in developmental issues and completed some supervised experience in working with children might have his or her competence in working with children challenged but would have some basis for arguing that he or she was competent. It would be important for the psychologist to show evidence of training in the actual services that he or she was providing.

Using the Standard 1.04 as an example, competence can be established in a variety of ways. As Standard 1.04 states in part (a), "Psychologists provide services, teach, and conduct research only within the boundaries of their competence, based on their education, training, supervised experience, or appropriate professional experience" (p. 1600). This indicates that any of the four listed activities may be considered as a basis for competence. Continuing education is generally included in the methods by which a psychologist may develop competence.

The ethical principles of beneficence and nonmaleficence provide an important ethical basis for the emphasis on practicing within one's competence. Maximizing benefit is achieved by ensuring that the psychologist knows what he or she is doing. Minimizing harm is achieved by not practicing in an area in which the psychologist is not trained.

In actual ethics cases, competence becomes an issue most frequently by an instance of practice that is clearly in error, not by a debate over precisely how many courses or supervised assessments are required for competence. In that context, demonstrating some basis for competence in training or other preparation might be a defense for not being competent by training. However, being unable to show clearly adequate preparation in the face of poor practice makes an easy case of unethical behavior. When a person is well trained and nonetheless makes an error in performance, this raises a question of malpractice more than one of ethics. Depending on the circumstances, of course, poor performance may also raise ethics concerns.

A credential such as a license may be required to practice legally but is not, in itself, required to practice ethically. (However, see the later discussion regarding public representations.) A credential that includes review of education and training and that assesses performance may itself establish that a psychologist is competent. Some credentials (e.g., vanity boards or most grandfathered credentials) do not establish competency, even if they otherwise give credibility to the psychologist's services.

Graduate training in clinical psychology is the primary way to establish a credential in clinical psychology. But this relates more to the comments about a credential and not to competence, which relates more to actual practice activities such as techniques and populations. In other words, a psychologist may be competent as a clinical psychologist yet not be competent in working with children or doing a particular form of therapy.

The most common way in which a psychologist practices outside his or her competence is when beginning to work in a new area of practice. For example, this frequently happens when a psychologist without training in child custody evaluations accepts work in this area.

There are, of course, situations in which psychologists begin work in an area that is new to the field. Generally, this involves experimental work, whether those engaging in such work acknowledge this or not. The psychologist can still ensure that the work is grounded in methods for which he or she is competent and that all parties are informed of the nature of the work. (See the later discussion of informed consent.)

## Confidentiality

Confidentiality is of special importance in clinical psychology because almost all clinical material carries with it the potential for harm if improperly revealed. Without confidence that their privacy will be respected, clients will be unable to provide information that is of critical importance to the success of interventions. Psychology has long recognized the importance of confidentiality and has always placed a high ethical value on maintaining confidentiality.

However, there are increasing compromises in this principle, and psychology's ethics codes have recognized these limits. While psychologists have complained that such compromises are a problem, there appears to be little choice based on the types of situations that prompt compromises.

When a client is suicidal and unwilling to make an agreement to protect him- or herself, the psychologist may need to reveal confidential information (such as the client's threat) in order to take appropriate protective action. Clinical psychology tends, of course, to focus on the welfare of the individual client, but society's interests are served at times by compromise of the individual's rights. Such analyses led to the Tarasoff ruling and are credited with stimulating a variety of laws and rulings that defined the circumstances in which psychologists have a duty to warn others about harm threatened by a client. Despite the extensive treatment of this topic in terms of the ethical issues, this is often a legal issue rather than a fundamentally ethical one. Where a duty to warn is required (e.g., in a jurisdiction in which case law applies or by state statute), the law, in essence, requires an action by the psychologist. No ethical rule or analysis is required to determine this. The psychologist's most critical review is largely one of the clinical facts. Has this client threatened another person? Does the psychologist's assessment of the client's mental status meet a duty-to-warn test in the relevant jurisdiction? If the tests are met, the action is required. The primary ethical issue is whether confidential information may be provided, and the ethics code allows such reporting (e.g., in the 1992 APA ethics code, divulging confidential information without release in such a circumstance would be allowed because it is mandated by law).

There may be a variety of other situations in which providing confidential information is required, based on the welfare of someone other than the client, such as child abuse reporting when someone other than the child is the client. Some of the compromises in confidentiality, however, are the consequence of psychology's success in offering useful information in situations such as malpractice litigation and family courts. The client may sign a release and in any event is told up front that the information that he or she will be providing is not going to remain confidential. The psychological relationship operates without the benefit of confidentiality from the other parties in the proceeding at least. If psychology insists on confidentiality, psychologists would simply not be used in such matters.

## Autonomy and Informed Consent

Informed consent is based in part on a belief in individuals' rights to autonomous choice and self-determination. Informed consent is addressed from the perspective of a person who has the capacity (legal and mental) to consent. In order for a person to give consent, it must be given without coercion and with sufficient information for the consent to be meaningful.

In the realities of modern practice, there are many situations in which treatment conditions are less than optimal. For example, the client's ability to pay, whether due to personal financial limitations or the nature of the client's insurance, may have an impact on the treatment itself or on adjunctive methods (e.g., in-patient treatment). One of the ways to address this is through informed consent. Even if conditions are not optimal, the client can participate in the decisions to maximize appropriate care.

Although informed consent is a primary issue in ethics, informed consent procedures and forms may also have clinical and risk management functions.

## Multiple Relationships

The prohibition against certain dual or multiple relationships has been an important feature of ethics codes for psychologists. The problems for clients at issue include harm, exploitation, loss of the psychologist's objectivity or other factors that would limit the psychologist's effectiveness, and conflicts of interest for the psychologist. The multiple relationship prohibition is in addition to rules that prohibit actual exploitation of a client. Psychological treatment relationships involve a variety of emotional and cognitive reactions by both the client and the psychologist. Addition of roles other than the treatment relationship, such as friend or business associate, are likely to create problems. Accordingly, the multiple relationship rule prohibits addition of relationships that would be likely to create problems.

The rule, since the 1992 APA ethics code's Standard 1.17, makes it clearer that such multiple relationships cannot always be avoided and provides more guidance for determining when to avoid becoming involved and also how to deal with relationships that result in problems despite the psychologist's attempts to avoid them. The rule also makes it clearer that not all multiple relationships must be avoided, but only those that are likely to create problems. Some concern about the appearance of prohibiting all multiple relationships has been present among rural psychologists who may be involved with clients in a variety of situations that are unavoidable. This may also be true when dealing with small ethnic or other cultures within metropolitan areas.

It is important that those psychologists who have such concerns recognize that the real problem is not the ethics code, but the real dangers of multiple relationships. In most circumstances, it is prudent to use a more practical rule than the ethics code: When in doubt, avoid any multiple relationship that has any likelihood of creating even the most minor problem.

## Sexual Misconduct

Some combined relationships have been considered to be so likely to be harmful that they are prohibited always; sexual relationships with clients are a primary example. Over several revisions, the APA ethics codes made rules more explicit, so that in addition to prohibiting sexual involvement with current clients, explicit prohibitions were added regarding therapy with former sexual partners and sexual involvement with former clients.

The 1992 rule regarding sexual involvement with former clients is best understood as an "almost never" rule stated in two parts. It first provides that it is always wrong to become sexually involved with a former client "for at least two years after cessation or termination of professional services" (p. 1605). Second, it provides that "psychologists do not engage in sexual intimacies with former therapy . . . clients even after a two-year interval except in the most unusual circumstances" (p. 1605) and provides a list of variables that the psychologist would have to address in order to demonstrate that no harm to the former client occurred. Both the use of the phrase "most unusual circumstances" and the extensive list of factors to consider signal that it would be very rare to find a circumstance in which such involvement would be ethical.

## Advertising and Public Statements

The ethical principle of integrity requires that public statements, such as advertising, be truthful and not misleading. Blatant violations of standards in this area are claiming a degree that the psychologist has not been awarded and claiming publications that were not published. Claims of particular results (e.g., "95% of our patients achieve treatment goals") must be supported with reasonable data. Most of these standards related to accurate representations are in section 3 of the 1992 ethics code, "Advertising and Other Public Statements." As stated in Standard 3.01, "Public statements include but are not limited to paid or unpaid advertising, brochures, printed matter, directory listings, personal resumes or curriculum vitae, interviews or comments for use in media, statements in legal proceedings, lectures and public oral presentations, and published materials" (p. 1604).

Psychologists should also make sure that others issuing statements on their behalf (e.g., a company hired to produce a brochure for the psychologist's practice) are accurate, and the psychologist should review materials at various points. Although an error in the final version may not be preventable, the psychologist can prevent fraudulent or misleading statements that were present in earlier drafts. The psychologist can do so by providing good information in the beginning and reviewing later drafts and proofs. Such oversight may be less certain in large organizations such as hospitals and universities, but psychologists can still do much to keep such materials accurate.

In clinical practice one of the most contentious issues has been who has the right to claim the title "clinical psychologist." Psychologists are typically licensed with a generic title ("licensed psychologist"), so this rarely resolves the issue. Although some psychologists would like to argue that only a graduate of an accredited clinical psychology program can claim the title, there are in fact a number of legitimate ways to argue that one is making an accurate statement in claiming the title "clinical psychologist." The obvious, and not disputed, methods include receipt of a doctoral degree in clinical psychology from an APA-accredited institution, completion of a formal retraining program, receipt of an ABPP in clinical psychology, and receipt of licensure with a designation of "clinical psychologist." Other methods that may be appropriate would take into account FTC guidelines for statements that are accurate and the APA's (1987) General Guidelines for Providers of Psychological Services, which states in footnote 7 that "APA defines the term *clinical psychologist* in health service delivery legislation in a generic sense to include all qualified professional psychologists who provide relevant services" (p. 721). The fact that this statement occurs in an APA guideline does not mean that a particular psychologist's use of the title is appropriate. An ultimate test is whether a particular title is "false or deceptive" in the context in which it is used and as defined in whatever ethics code or regulation is at issue. Some of these points were covered in a 1995 letter to the Division of Clinical Psychology expressing the position of the APA Ethics Committee.

One of the most serious problems involving misrepresentation is fraud in knowingly submitting false claims to payers, such as insurance companies. Psychologists may also be held accountable for the actions of office staff members who may file fraudulent claims in a manner that indicates that the psychologist did not exercise appropriate oversight. To avoid any argument that such claims were made privately and not in a public statement, the 1992 ethics code covers this in Standard 1.26, "Accuracy in Reports to Payors and Funding Sources."

As noted earlier, an important change in APA's ethics code in 1989 came about in part by an investigation by the FTC. This resulted in a consent order that restricted enforcement actions by APA but also explicitly allowed restrictions against almost all the types of advertising that APA would want to limit. Although the completion date of the cease and desist portion of the order is December 2002, the order uses concepts that are useful in understanding this area of ethics. These concepts are that psychologists should not use false or deceptive information in advertising, that individuals who are vulnerable should not be directly solicited for business or asked for testimonials, and that referral fees should be subject to disclosure.

## Supervision

Both ethics codes and licensure regulations require that psychologists delegate to supervisees only clinical services for which the supervisees are competent and for which they will actually be supervised. In addition, psychologists must in fact provide as much supervision as is required by the services and level of preparation of the supervisee. Psychologists' services frequently deal with very sensitive aspects of clients' lives and have the potential for serious harm. Accordingly, services provided by supervisees must be considered and overseen carefully.

This level of risk is one reason why psychologists found guilty of ethics violations for improper supervision may be severely sanctioned. For example, consider a psychologist who is supervising an unlicensed therapist who is accused of sexual misconduct with a client. The psychologist's defense is that he did not engage in the misconduct and believed that the therapist knew the behavior was wrong and had not revealed signs of the misconduct in the office. But the psychologist was not conducting regular supervision meetings with the therapist and was not actually reviewing other indications of the handling of the case, such as the case record or the office staff's reports about appointments and billing. If the therapist who engaged in the misconduct had, over several months, failed to follow office policies on reporting nonpayment to the office manager and had exceptions to office policy by scheduling appointments after regular hours when there were no other staff members present, the psychologist's failure to supervise is likely to be seen as a substantial factor in the occurrence of the misconduct.

It should also be noted that requirements to keep records to ensure accountability suggest that records should be kept of supervision. (See, e.g., the 1992 ethics code's Standard 1.23, "Documentation of Professional and Scientific Work.")

## FREQUENT PROBLEMS

Several subjects are among the more frequent areas of complaints or deserve special comment. These include sexual misconduct, forensic and child custody evaluations, managed care and insurance complaints, and raw data release.

### Sexual Misconduct

Despite clear ethics prohibitions for many years and psychologists' recognition that sexual involvement with current clients is harmful, such misconduct continues to be one of the most frequent major violations. A full consideration of this topic is beyond the scope of this chapter, and the reader is referred to other sources for more information. (See, e.g., Pope, 1994; Pope, Sonne, & Holroyd, 1993; Schoener, Milgrom, Gonsiorek, Luepker, & Conroe, 1990; as well as sections on sexual misconduct in ethics texts such as Koocher & Keith-Spiegel, 1998.)

However, three elements to this situation will be discussed briefly. Sexual attraction to clients is relatively common, and psychologists generally handle such attraction in ways that are therapeutic or at least that avoid involvement or harm. However, therapeutic relationships can be intense, and psychologists who are in isolated practice situations may be more vulnerable to establishing an inappropriate relationship that can be the beginning of an even more dysfunctional relationship. Psychologists should stay involved with colleagues, especially if in a solo practice, and seek consultation about any cases that involve personal, emotional reactions.

An extension of such emotional reactions, which can occur at any time in a psychologist's life, are the special vulnerabilities that occur when psychologists are experiencing problems. Such problems can include marital difficulties, depression, or the classic midlife crisis. Colleagues become especially important in attempting to intervene with a psychologist who has fallen in love with a client and who no longer cares about professional reputation or future. Earlier intervention is obviously easier, but it may still be difficult. The 1992 ethics code (Standard 1.13, "Personal Problems and Conflicts") attempted to focus responsibility on dealing with problems such as depression at a point where a psychologist should know there is a problem but before the psychologist is actually impaired.

Many psychologists see clients who have been involved sexually with a prior therapist, and it is important to seek continuing education for addressing such issues if it was not covered in graduate training (see Pope, 1994).

### Forensic and Child Custody Evaluations

Psychologists play increasingly important roles in a variety of court and legal activities. This is true for psychologists who have prepared for such roles, as well as for psychologists who are subpoenaed or otherwise asked to become involved in particular cases. In these activities psychologists have an important impact on the rights of individuals, families, and society. As such, practicing within the limits of the psychologist's competence is very important, as is doing good and careful work.

There are more guidelines available now than in the past, but the guidelines are written in such a way that the psychologist still must exercise judgment in applying the guidelines to each case. Staying current on prevailing practices both locally and nationally is important. Any psychologist doing court work must be prepared to document the basis for his or her competence in terms of coursework, continuing education, and supervised experience. Also, doing any less than what would be considered excellent work risks criticism later. This is an area in which one should be very careful to avoid cutting corners, whether requested by the attorneys or the judge.

An example of what was once an evolving issue is the importance of including both parents in an assessment in issues in a child custody or visitation matter. Psychologists have been criticized when doing less, even when the fact that only one parent was involved in the assessment was understood and agreed to by all parties and the court. This is now treated as an established practice.

An example of a still evolving area is the importance of collateral information. Even though the psychologist has collected information from both parents and has assessed them and the children individually and jointly, the psychologist risks sanction if he or she has not obtained collateral support for important information that is in dispute. Also, expert forensic reviewers may expect to see reports that provide detailed information about the assessment. A reviewer may consider a report with less information to be inadequate, even if the psychologist provided detailed information later in the process, for example, in court testimony.

Since the mid-1980s, child custody–related complaints have been a significant proportion of the complaints filed with the APA Ethics Committee. In the article reporting on activity for 2000, 18 cases were opened that were not brought to the committee's attention by other reviewing bodies (e.g., licensure boards). Of those 18, 5 were child custody matters.

The fact that there are a significant number of child custody complaints does not necessarily mean that there are more problems in this area than in other areas of practice. In part, the level of complaints is a measure of the contentiousness of the area. Once a child custody or visitation matter has gone to the level of court involvement, there is going to be a winner and loser. And the extreme emotions that result may be targeted at a psychologist who testified adversely.

## Managed Care

If the ethics code discusses "managed care" explicitly, it will only be with a code subsequent to the 1992 APA ethics code. Even without explicit discussion, however, many sections of the ethics codes have direct applicability.

It should be noted that since managed care is not a single behavioral situation, no single ethical analysis will apply to it. In addition, the APA ethics code is applied to individual psychologists, and many of the basic concerns raised about managed care plans are not with regard to the behavior of the psychologist, but of the managed care review. Whether more explicit guidance regarding managed care is included in the ethics code, such provisions will be limited by the multifaceted nature of managed care and limitations to the length of the code.

Important elements in existing codes include provisions for informed consent, with an emphasis on describing relevant aspects of the nature of services and limits to confidentiality. Psychologists need to consider that clients may not understand provisions of their mental health coverage for a variety of reasons, including misrepresentation by managed care company, complicated materials, and failure of the client to read materials. Some managed-care review processes involve more extensive intrusion into records than do others, so there are limits to what the psychologist can anticipate.

Competence bears special importance to any managed care situations that involve direct or indirect pressure to provide services without referring. Psychologists must be very careful not to provide services (or to supervise services) for which they do not have competence. In addition, pressure to deliver high levels of services may interfere with quality of care. One of the most often raised problems is concern about professional reviewers disapproving continuing treatment based on contract limitations rather than treatment needs.

An ethical dilemma presented in some managed care cases occurs when the psychologist provider, who remains responsible for the actual treatment plan delivered, is unable to get approval for appropriate treatment. The provider may be charged with providing inadequate care if inappropriate treatment is provided. A legal case led to recommendations that providers always appeal denial of care when the psychologist believes that continued care was needed.

Several specific sections of the 1992 ethics code have direct relevance to managed care circumstances and dilemmas.

Important provisions are any regarding contracts, for example, Standard 4.08, "Interruption of Services." Part (a) includes the requirement that "Psychologists make reasonable efforts to plan for facilitating care in the event that psychological services are interrupted" (p. 1606) by several factors. Included in a nonexhaustive list are "the client's . . . financial limitations" (p. 1606). Managed care plans often involve explicit limitations in the financing of individual clients' care, which are known ahead of time. Accordingly, the psychologist is in a position to "make reasonable efforts" to plan for facilitating care in the event of interruption due to the limitations. The psychologist who makes no effort may be in violation of the code. Part (b) is an explicit requirement to take action at the point of entering into contractual relationships:

> When entering into employment or contractual relationships, psychologists provide for orderly and appropriate resolution of responsibility for patient or client care in the event that the employment or contractual relationship ends, with paramount consideration given to the welfare of the patient or client. (p. 1606)

Note that the criterion to be used is "paramount consideration given to the welfare of the client." This suggests that the psychologist must avoid a contract that does not allow consideration of client welfare in determining client treatment issues in the event that the contract ends.

Other important provisions relate to financial limitations. For example, requirements to discuss financing limitations are addressed by Standard 1.25. Part (e) of Standard 1.25, "Fees and Financial Arrangements," is relevant when "limitations to services can be anticipated because of limitations in financing" (p. 1602). It requires that under those circumstances, the limitations must be discussed with the client as early as is feasible. Of particular concern here are managed care provisions that seek to prevent the psychologist from having such discussions.

Another provision deals with conflicts between provisions of the ethics code and organizational rules or agreements. Standard 8.03 is titled "Conflicts Between Ethics and Organizational Demands" and states that

> If the demands of an organization with which psychologists are affiliated conflict with this Ethics Code, psychologists clarify the nature of the conflict, make known their commitment to the Ethics Code, and to the extent feasible, seek to resolve the conflict in a way that permits the fullest adherence to the Ethics Code. (p. 1611)

Unethical behavior is doing nothing when faced with such a conflict.

Psychologists who work as reviewers for managed care companies and who are APA members are subject to the ethics code, but only in their discretionary actions as individuals. To the extent that they are implementing provisions in a plan, their accountability to an otherwise unethical provision may be limited.

**Raw Data Release**

One of the most frequent ethics questions regards requests for raw data or other testing records to be released to attorneys, courts, and others. Concerns relate both to test security and to harm that may result to clients if test data are misinterpreted. While confidentiality is an obvious issue, it can be addressed by a client release. Ethics codes have discouraged release if it would constitute misuse of the tests by releasing raw materials especially to those who are not qualified to interpret the data. The dilemma for psychologists is that there has been relatively little guidance as to how far a psychologist must go before releasing data in response to a legal demand and as to who is qualified to receive test data. This provision was receiving substantial attention in the pending revision.

Because the most substantial question is the legal strategies available for responding to requests, the best guidance available has been a document by the APA Committee on Legal Issues (COLI) titled "Strategies for Private Practitioners Coping With Subpoenas or Compelled Testimony for Client Records or Test Data" (APA COLI, 1996). In addition, the APA Committee on Psychological Tests and Assessment (CPTA) issued a "Statement on the Disclosure of Test Data" in 1996 (APA CPTA, 1996). This article includes a discussion of what constitutes raw data as opposed to other information such as normalized scores.

The language in Standard 2.02b from the 1992 ethics code regarding release to clients was confusing to some psychologists, who wondered if it meant that clients had a special right to receive test data even if they were not qualified to use them. An alternative interpretation was that in some states clients have a right to review their files, and "as appropriate" in the phrase "to patients or clients as appropriate" (p. 1603) refers to such a situation. Generally, clients should be provided information so that it is clearly understood, and release of raw data from records is not likely to be understood without other explanation.

**ETHICAL DECISION-MAKING MODELS**

A single ethics code rule or legal statute rarely provides a full answer to a real-life situation. Psychologists regularly encounter situations that require a consideration of the proper

ethical decision, and a number of decision-making models are available. (See, e.g., Canter et al., 1994; Haas & Malouf, 1989; Kitchener, 1984; Koocher & Keith-Spiegel, 1998.)

Most models include identifying the ethical aspects of the problem, identifying relevant ethical and other standards, determining relevant facts and collecting additional information as needed, identifying options and selecting an action plan, taking the action, and evaluating the results. Models also emphasize consultation with experts. It is generally recommended that psychologists document the process used, factors considered, action taken, and outcome observed.

Canter et al. (1994) emphasized actions taken prior to a point in time when an actual dilemma is encountered. This includes knowing the ethics code and applicable laws and legal and institutional regulations, taking continuing education workshops in ethics, and learning a formal method for analyzing ethical dilemmas. Obviously, having good ethics education during graduate training is critical. Identifying ethical challenges before they become problems is a key goal. The emphasis on preparation is especially important because many ethical problems require immediate action and a formal system for considering ethical options is not practical.

A simple method is helpful for situations in which action must occur quickly. For example, a psychologist may ask, "Is my action ethical, practical, and reasonable?" or "Am I acting in a responsible and accountable manner?" A method by Callahan, cited by Haas and Malouf (1989), is for the psychologist to imagine him- or herself in a "clean, well-lit room" in order to gauge the acceptability of a planned action taken with the full understanding of colleagues. Psychologists should also attend carefully to cautions from others, whether colleagues, students, clients, or others. Psychologists should resist the temptation to dismiss such cautions as unwarranted and instead to see them as invitations to review the situation in depth through an ethical analysis and consultation.

The following steps are one decision-making system.

- *Identify the ethical aspects.* Sometimes these are apparent at the beginning of the analysis but may become clearer later in the process. It can be instructive to ask the following: What ethical issues are involved? Are the ethical issues ones of aspirational ethics or enforceable ethics rules? What legal (statutory, case law, licensure board regulations) are involved, if any? What clinical, scientific, or technical issues are involved? (Clinical opinions and strategies are often important in issues of "fact," as mentioned later.)

- *Identify the ethical problems.* This is a tentative identification. Be general and specific. Consider whether there is a single problem or multiple dilemmas. What priority do the various problems have?

- *Identify relevant ethical and other standards.* Are there specific rules that will address all or part of the problem? Consider ethics codes, licensure laws and regulations, other laws, institutional rules, and professional guidelines.

  *Consider whether there is an uncomplicated resolution or whether this is an ethical dilemma in which there are specific conflicting duties or rights.*

- *Determine the facts.* What do you actually know? What additional information is needed to clarify the situation? Consider clinical opinions that, for the purpose of the ethical analysis, are facts. For example, if you are considering the ethics of violating confidentiality to protect a suicidal client, your clinical opinion that he or she is at imminent risk to make a suicide attempt is a "fact" in your ethical analysis. How you formed the opinion is a clinical issue.

- *List options for resolving the problem.* If the situation is complex, write down the options. For each option, ask whether the option is ethical, practical, and reasonable. Consider consultation to review the options.

- *Decide on and evaluate an action plan.* Ask whether the means and ends are morally acceptable. Use the "clean, well-lit room" exercise to consider the plan's acceptability. Consider consultation if it is not already part of the plan.

- *Take action.* Document the decision process, action, and outcome.

- *Evaluate the action.* Is the outcome as expected? Were there negative consequences that need to be addressed?

## ENFORCEMENT OF CODES

The APA ethics code is used in various types of disciplinary and corrective actions against psychologists. The APA ethics code is directly enforced by APA and by state or other psychological associations that adopt it and apply it to their members. Such enforcement is limited to members of such groups. The APA ethics code is also enforced by states that incorporate the code into licensure legislation or licensure board regulations as the profession's code of conduct. In such cases, the ethics code has the force of law and is enforced by the licensure board, or more commonly now, by a professional discipline agency of the state. If the code is used as a standard for psychologists working in settings such as a hospitals or universities, action might be taken against a psychologist on the staff or faculty if the professional is alleged to have violated the code.

In addition to such direct application of a code in reviewing for an ethics or licensure violation, the ethics code is also used as a set of standards of practice in malpractice or other civil litigation. The plaintiff uses the code to show what the standards were that the psychologist did not uphold, just as the defendant psychologist would use it to demonstrate that appropriate procedures were used. An important difference is that an ethics complaint review looks at whether the psychologist complied with the ethics code as such. It need not be shown that the client was necessarily harmed. The profession has an interest in enforcing the ethics code even if no harm was shown because the content of the code is determined based on a belief that not complying with the code is likely to be harmful to the profession and clients. In a malpractice review the plaintiff must show harm by a psychologist who owed him or her a professional duty. Only after that is established is the psychologist's compliance with the ethics code relevant.

Of course, ethics codes and licensure regulations are not the only bases for review of psychologists' behavior. A psychologist may be found guilty of having broken an independent (even if related) law. Psychologists may have such action taken against them without having been found to have violated the ethics code or even if it has been shown that they have not violated the code. For example, a psychologist might be charged with insurance fraud based on laws independent of ethics or licensure rules. In such situations, laws may be more stringent than a particular ethics code or licensure provision. For example, there may be situations in which laws against fee splitting may be violated without violating the 1992 APA ethics code provision.

For APA members and others who file complaints against APA members, it is important to understand the APA Ethics Committee's (1996) Rules and Procedures that govern the process for conducting ethics investigations of members. The current version is typically posted on the APA's Web site at www.apa.org/ethics, and amendments were adopted in 2001 that were planned for publication in 2002. Changes that may be made to the rules can have a substantial effect on investigations. For example, the 1996 rules revision resulted in new APA student affiliates being subject to jurisdiction of the Ethics Committee. (This jurisdiction is limited to review of activities not under the scrutiny of the student's graduate program and of affiliates who join after the provision was put in place.) Also, that revision changed the time limit for a member filing a complaint against another member from 1 to 3 years. Beginning with the 1992 revision (APA Ethics Committee, 1992b), the rules include a brief overview that is likely to be included in the future and to be helpful when reviewing future revisions.

The APA procedures provide two types of investigations. One is called a *show cause proceeding* and provides for review of an APA member if the member has lost his or her professional license, been convicted of a felony, or lost membership in a state psychological association due to unethical conduct. Because another authoritative body has sanctioned the member, the burden is on the member to convince APA that he or she should not be expelled. (The name comes from the member's being given an opportunity to "show cause" why the member should not be expelled.) In 2001 changes were adopted to provide that such matters would result in an automatic expulsion from APA unless the member appealed the expulsion.

The other type of investigation is based on a complainant's alleging that the psychologist violated the ethics code. The complaint is usually filed by an individual but may also be filed by the Ethics Committee acting on its own, called a *sua sponte review*. These complaint investigations allege a violation of the ethics code, and the burden is on the Committee to prove the charges. The complaint is judged by the version of the ethics code in effect at the time the behavior occurred.

In both types of APA investigations, members are not allowed to resign membership in APA (directly or by nonpayment of dues) while under scrutiny of the Ethics Committee. However, changes adopted in 2001 included an option for resignation under investigation.

The Rules and Procedures provide a great deal of detail. For example, there are time limits for filing complaints; nonmembers have 5 years in which to file a complaint, and APA members have 3 years. There are limited provisions for waiving the time limit.

## STAYING UP TO DATE

Information about the APA ethics program can be found in the Ethics Committee's annual article in *American Psychologist*. This includes information about ethics code and rules and procedures revisions, the Committee's investigation activities, and educational activities. In recent years the article has carried a table identifying published statements of the Committee. These can be important to interpreting provisions in the ethics code. As noted earlier, the APA Web site is a source of current information.

For example, the Committee issued a statement in 1995 regarding services by telephone or Internet and issued a revised statement in 1997 (APA Ethics Committee, 1998). A primary point of both statements was that even though the Ethics code did not include explicit mention of such services, provisions such as informed consent and confidentiality apply.

## REFERENCES

American Educational Research Association, American Psychological Association, and National Council on Measurement in Education. (1999). *Standards for educational and psychological testing.* Washington, DC: American Educational Research Association.

American Psychological Association. (1953). *Ethical standards of psychologists.* Washington, DC: Author.

American Psychological Association. (1959). Ethical standards of psychologists. *American Psychologist, 14*(6), 279–282.

American Psychological Association. (1987). General guidelines for providers of psychological services. *American Psychologist, 42,* 712–723.

American Psychological Association. (1990). Ethical principles of psychologists (amended June 2, 1989). *American Psychologist, 45,* 390–395.

American Psychological Association. (1992). Ethical principles of psychologists and code of conduct. *American Psychologist, 47,* 1597–1611.

American Psychological Association. (1994). Guidelines for child custody evaluations in divorce proceedings. *American Psychologist, 49,* 677–680.

American Psychological Association. (2001). *Publication manual of the American Psychological Association* (5th ed.). Washington, DC: Author.

American Psychological Association Committee on Legal Issues. (1996). Strategies for private practitioners coping with subpoenas or compelled testimony for client records or test data. *Professional Psychology: Research and Practice, 27*(3), 245–251.

American Psychological Association Committee on Psychological Tests and Assessments. (1996). Statement on the disclosure of test data, 1996. *American Psychologist, 51,* 644–648.

American Psychological Association Ethics Committee. (1992). Rules and procedures. *American Psychologist, 47,* 1612–1628.

American Psychological Association Ethics Committee. (1996). Rules and procedures. *American Psychologist, 51,* 529–548.

American Psychological Association Ethics Committee. (1998). Report of the Ethics Committee, 1997. *American Psychologist, 53,* 969–980.

Association of State and Provincial Psychology Boards. (1991). *Code of conduct.* Montgomery, AL: Author.

Canadian Psychological Association. (2000). *Canadian code of ethics for psychologists* (3rd ed.). Ottawa, Ontario, Canada: Author.

Canter, M. B., Bennet, B. E., Jones, S. E., & Nagy, T. F. (1994). *Ethics for psychologists: A commentary on the APA Ethics Code.* Washington, DC: American Psychological Association.

Federal Trade Commission. Consent order. (1993, January 6). *Federal Register, 58*(3), 557.

Haas, L., & Malouf, J. (1989). *Keeping up the good work: A practitioner's guide to mental health ethics.* Sarasota, FL: Professional Resource Exchange.

Kitchener, K. (1984). Intuition, critical evaluation, and ethical principles: The foundation for ethical decisions in counseling psychology. *Counseling Psychologist, 12*(3), 43–55.

Koocher, G., & Keith-Spiegel, P. (1998). *Ethics in psychology: Professional standards and cases* (2nd ed.). New York: Oxford University Press.

Lowman, R. L. (1998). *The ethical practice of psychology in organizations.* Washington, DC: American Psychological Association.

Pope, K. S. (1994). *Sexual involvement with therapists: Patient assessment, subsequent therapy, forensics.* Washington, DC: American Psychological Association.

Pope, K. S., Sonne, J. L., & Holroyd, J. (1993). *Sexual feelings in psychotherapy: Explorations for therapists and therapists-in-training.* Washington, DC: American Psychological Association.

Schoener, G. R., Milgrom, J. H., Gonsiorek, J. C., Luepker, E. T., & Conroe, R. M. (Eds.). (1990). *Psychotherapists' sexual involvement with clients: Intervention and prevention.* Minneapolis, MN: Walk-In Counseling Center.

*White v. the North Carolina State Board of Examiners of Practicing Psychologists.* 8810SC1137 North Carolina Court of Appeals, Wake County No. 86-CVS-8131 (February 6, 1990).

# CHAPTER 22

# Health Care Marketplace in the United States

DAVID J. DRUM AND ANDREW SEKEL

As the twenty-first century begins, the U.S. health care system has endured a turbulent, unremitting change cycle for over two decades. It is truly a system in motion, configuring and reconfiguring itself on a regular basis in response to the forces fueling change. The genesis of this turmoil has been the efforts for economic reform on the part of both business and government, motivated by the desire to reduce health care costs. The health care system has been restructured around free-market principles, and there has been a dramatic shift in the way health care services are organized, delivered, and financed. In the past, health care was seen as a profession in which professional authority held sway. Today it has been transformed into a marketplace, where it is being treated like other commodities. Behavioral health care, as part of the larger system, has also experienced change, notably in the way it is financed and in its unfortunate segmentation from medical and surgical care. Practicing psychologists are in a very different health care world than existed through the mid-1980s.

In many other countries in the world, health care is centralized, with the government both financing and paying for the care. This is not the case in the United States, which has not adopted such a single-payer system. The way health care is financed in this country lies at the heart of the problems that the system faces today. The consumer (the patient) does not pay for most of the expenses associated with an episode of care. Rather, either the patient's employer or a govern-

mental agency bears the costs. The arrangement is called a third-party payer system, and health care in the United States is completely dependent on it. Almost four out of every five dollars flowing into and supporting the health care enterprise come not from the consumer, but from either the government or employers. Medicare, Medicaid, and other local- and state-government-sponsored programs pay 47% of the nation's health care bills. Group health plans funded by employers as part of benefit packages pay 32% of the total cost (VHA Inc., Deloitte, & Touche, 2000).

Beginning in the 1970s, health care costs began to increase dramatically, a trend that would continue into the mid-1980s. At that time, businesses started to feel the strain on their profits and began to exert pressure on health plan administrators to contain costs. They were joined in this effort by State and Federal governments eager to avoid tax increases. The concerted efforts of government and industry to contain costs through various mechanisms have provided the impetus for economic reform in health care. Cost containment has not proven an easy goal to achieve, however, because of a number of factors. First of all, medical practitioners have been reluctant to change from a system of finance in which they dominated. From the late 1930s to the 1980s, the standard method of reimbursing providers and service facilities was the fee-for-service/third-party Payer system (FFS/TPP). This system was built on provider-oriented principles that considered medical practitioners to be members of a protected guild, similar to medieval guilds. It virtually eliminated price competition as a cost-containment mechanism and prevented free enterprise marketplace forces from operating naturally in the health care system. A further impediment to cost containment is the fact that the primary purchaser (employer or government) is not the recipient of the care. In the FFS era, not only did patients not pay for care directly, but also they were largely unaware of the true costs of the care received. Physicians themselves often remained uninformed about costs. Finally, it must be observed that change does not come easy in any enterprise grounded on the ethical principle that both life and quality of life are precious. Legitimate concerns that efforts to contain costs will lead to deterioration in quality of care abound in the health care marketplace today.

However difficult it has proven to contain costs, the efforts to do so by purchasers have led to dramatic changes. An entirely new health care environment has been created, one with serious implications for all health care stakeholders. Purchasers ceased accepting the cost increases of the FFS system and became active promoters of price competition via a competitive bidding process. They no longer favor purchasing traditional indemnity or service insurance coverage; where permissible, they self-insure, either passing on financial risk or engaging in shared financial risk arrangements with health plans. Health plans now find themselves in a difficult situation. They promised purchasers that they could reduce expenditures while retaining and even improving quality of care. This has proved daunting, to say the least, because purchasers have continued to cut funding—although expecting health plans to deliver the same level of quality. Purchasers are asking their employees to participate in the cost-containment effort. Employers no longer advocate for employees. They now support efforts by health plans to reduce expenditures. They attempt to increase employee cost sensitivity by forcing higher contributions to premium charges and supporting higher copay, coinsurance, and deductibles.

Because the hallmark of the health care environment today is rapid change and because stakeholder roles and relationships are not in stable alignment, a purely descriptive approach to the health care marketplace would have a short shelf life. In this chapter, therefore, the focus is on understanding the forces driving change, including marketplace dynamics. To build a foundation, the chapter begins with a discussion of the primary stakeholders in health care, followed by a brief explanation of how two categories of forces, sustaining and disruptive, are able to shape a marketplace. Next are described the three distinct eras in health care from the late 1880s to the present: (a) the self-regulatory era, (b) the FFS/TPP era, and (c) the present-day cost containment era. During the first and second periods, stakeholder revolts against the prevailing system ultimately ushered in the next era, establishing the principles by which it would function. The market and service delivery features of the FFS/TPP era are described in detail because they became the health care standard against which the stakeholders of the current cost-containment era are now in revolt. The current revolt seeks to replace the cost-increasing, noncompetitive features of the FFS/TPP system with market-based, price-competition approaches. During the current era, a number of disruptive innovations altered important features of the FFS/TPP system, and these are discussed. Next, the impact of the cost-containment era on health care stakeholders is analyzed, with an emphasis on how health care is financed and delivered, in particular behavioral health care. The dynamics of health care that continue to create a changing environment are explained, and the chapter examines some future trends.

## STAKEHOLDERS AND THEIR STRATEGIES

Marketplace dynamics operate continuously in the health care arena. All free markets have stakeholder groups, which are either part of the supply or part of the demand side of the market. The various stakeholders vie for supremacy, attempting to promote their own interests by modifying the market to achieve their particular economic goals. The stakeholders are often the instigators of two categories of change forces: sustaining forces and disruptive forces. Both types of change forces are capable of altering the marketplace dynamics, and the various stakeholders can and do employ them to further their own goals. The interplay and competition among stakeholders in the health care marketplace has driven change for over a century.

### The Four Stakeholders

The four key health care stakeholder constituencies in the United States are (a) purchasers, (b) health plans, (c) providers, and (d) consumers. The *purchasers* are largely the employers who pay health plan premiums for employees; alternatively, they represent governmental agencies that pay for health care costs for enrollees in their programs. The various state and federal governmental entities also serve as the regulators of health care. Through antitrust enforcement, national and state rule-making authority, and legislative actions, governmental power takes a large role in shaping and defining the health care system in the United States. *Health plans* typically define and administer the benefit system used by the consumer and contract with providers and their service facilities (particularly hospitals) to provide health care services for enrollees. Using a variety of insurance or financial arrangements, health plans contract with purchasers who pay premiums on behalf of employees or, in the case of governmental entities, on behalf of beneficiaries. The *provider* stakeholder constituency consists of the clinicians who provide care (physicians, psychologists, physical therapists, nurses, etc.) and the service facilities in which care is provided. *Consumers,* the largest stakeholder constituency, include the patients who receive care and the families affected by the nature and quality of the care provided.

## Forces for Change: Sustaining and Disruptive Innovations

Even given the imperative for reduced health benefit expenditures stimulated by health care purchasers, change of the magnitude being experienced in the health care marketplace could not occur without additional powerful forces disrupting the status quo. Christensen, Bohmer, and Kenagy (2000) described two categories of change forces that have altered the way free markets operate and evolve. *Sustaining innovations* represent advancements that move technology forward, extend or expand capability, or improve precision. Health care examples include discovering the importance of antiseptics in preventing infection during treatment, developing antibacterial agents, improving imaging of internal body systems, and finding treatments for previously untreatable conditions. Sustaining innovations typically extend or enhance the prevailing technological or business paradigm and thus expand the market. The second category of change forces is *disruptive innovations*. Because they significantly transform the prevailing business or technical paradigm, disruptive innovations create more turbulence than do sustaining innovations and therefore are more difficult for stakeholders in the marketplace to incorporate to their advantage. Disruptive innovations are usually adopted when they decrease the cost of a product or service for the majority of the market by introducing new, more effective technology or business models. Disruptive innovations make it possible for services to be provided with equal effectiveness for less cost.

About 25 years ago the health care system began to be bombarded by disruptive innovations aimed at changing the prevailing paradigms for finance and service delivery. These innovations are linked to a specific category of stakeholders: the purchasers. Normally, disruptive innovations in free markets have direct, apparent benefits or appeal to the true consumer of the product or service. The benefits resulting from these recent disruptive innovations in health care have accrued more to the purchaser, however. Change is not being driven directly by consumer needs, and it has complicated the

change process. The actual consumer of health care has had to adjust to alterations that in many cases have led to increased out-of-pocket expenses, have disrupted relationships with providers, or have created more complicated rules regarding access to care. With the stakeholders in mind and an understanding of the change forces operating in the marketplace, it is time to examine the evolution of health care from the late nineteenth century through the current period.

## EVOLUTION OF HEALTH CARE IN THE UNITED STATES

Current health care in the United States, including its service delivery and finance systems, stems from an evolutionary process that began in the late nineteenth century. Over the last 120 years, certain key historical actions have defined how health care coverage is obtained, how services are financed, and how competition and choice operate in the health care marketplace. It is possible to divide health care in the United States into three eras, employing a framework similar to Weller (1984; for a more detailed description of the social, political, and economic factors at work in transforming the health care system up through approximately 1980, see Starr, 1982, and Weller, 1984). In the self-regulatory era of the late nineteenth century, a free-market environment for health care was operating and evolving in response to the economic and social conditions of the time. This era ended as a result of actions taken by a particular stakeholder constituency: the provider, representing the interests of physicians and hospitals. In the 1930s a new era was launched, guided by provider-based principles and interests. It is known as the FFS/TPP era, and it would be the dominant health care model until the mid-1980s. At that time another stakeholder group, the purchaser, initiated changes that resulted in the currently unfolding cost-containment era.

### The Self-Regulatory Era

The self-regulatory era in health care began in the late 1800s and lasted until the late 1930s. During this early period health care in the marketplace evolved naturally in response to existing conditions and without much governmental involvement or interference from professional associations of providers. In the beginning health care stakeholders consisted primarily of consumers and providers (physicians and hospitals). Consumers were the *purchasers* of health care services. They paid for care directly, usually by a per-visit charge. The physicians and hospitals were the *sellers* of health care. In addition to the predominant self-pay system, however, a new form of arranging and paying for health care services emerged during this period.

By the late 1800s the leading manufacturing, mining, and transportation industries in the United States began to arrange and subsidize health care services for their employees' job-related illnesses and injuries, particularly in rural areas where health care was virtually nonexistent. The industries found that they required a mechanism to ensure that care would be available when needed and that there would be a way to compensate the provider. They began to hire physicians as employees or, as became more common, went directly to health care entities, usually hospitals, to develop contractual arrangements for the care of workers. These industries became a third stakeholder: the purchaser. The typical service delivery arrangement was a contract for care with a specific hospital and its associated physicians. The mechanism created to pay for that care was a *prepayment system* in which the employer agreed to pay a fixed amount to cover the anticipated health care needs of its employees. Health care costs would be covered by the contractual arrangement only if the employee received care from the contracted hospital or physician. Because these prepayment plans typically were linked to a single hospital and its core of affiliated physicians in a community, not all physicians or hospitals in a given community participated.

Over time, and with the increasing economic uncertainty of the 1920s and 1930s, prepayment health plans proliferated. They diversified their plan structures; expanded benefits to include general medical care; and included arrangements with trade unions, fraternal organizations, employee associations, and other entities. As the Great Depression approached, consumers became anxious about access to health care. Hospitals began searching for financial vehicles to ensure a steady income stream. A robust market for prepaid health plans emerged, creating a price competitive, self-regulatory market environment. Physicians and hospitals, however, began to resist this free-market system on the grounds that it divided physicians into economic entities competing for business on the basis of price. It also limited the ability of consumers to choose freely among all legally qualified physicians and did not include all hospitals and physicians in a given community. Physicians, through county and state medical societies and the American Medical Association (AMA), began to oppose the prepayment health plan arrangements and the resulting selective contracting and price competition. Their efforts were successful. The provider stakeholder community would eventually dismantle the self-regulatory era of health care.

During this first era, however, several key elements of the nation's health care finance and delivery system emerged. First, *employer participation* in the payment of employee health care was initiated. Although the actual percentage of people receiving employer-financed health care remained small, the precedent of employer involvement would prove to be increasingly important throughout all three eras of health care. Second, group health plans were financed on a *preservice payment system*. This innovation introduced financial risk to the hospital-physician provider system. If the prepaid premium negotiated was insufficient to cover costs of care, the provider system still was obligated to provide the care. Third, the notion of *selective contracting* with hospitals and physicians was introduced. Without selective contracting it would not be possible for hospital-physician systems to divide into competing economic units vying for enrollees. Of course, without competing health care systems, *price competition,* the fourth key element from this period, would have been severely curtailed. In short, a classic free-enterprise marketplace was unfolding in health care. It is significant that no stakeholder constituency was in a dominant market position relative to the other stakeholders. Providers, consumers, purchasers, and the health plans that increasingly emerged toward the end of the self-regulatory era, were aligning and realigning themselves as marketplace conditions changed.

This period was notable for other reasons. Notably, it would demonstrate that a stakeholder constituency could, through concerted effort and under favorable conditions, dismantle a particular market system. This fact would not be lost on those promoting price competition and cost-containment in the current period. It also established a precedent for today's price competition. And it established that provider organizations and hospitals were capable of contracting directly with employers and other organizations without using a third-party, managed-care organization or an insurance intermediary. However, a crucial concept was lost when the free-market system was destroyed: the ability to understand the relationship between price competition and quality of care. For all practical purposes, price competition was eliminated before its full and true effects could be discerned.

The success of the provider community of physicians and hospitals working through their professional associations to defeat and eventually eliminate the self-regulatory era of price competition would be the first of two stakeholder revolts against a prevailing health care finance and delivery system. Each revolt would lead to fundamental changes in health care finance, delivery, and management, and would decidedly slant the marketplace in favor of the desires of the dominant stakeholders.

**Fee-for-Service/Third-Party Payer Era**

The beginning of the FFS/TPP era of health care in the United States can be traced to the mid-1930s. At that point in time, provider advocacy organizations representing physicians and hospitals began to alter the existing free-market economic system for health care in a way that would be favorable to their membership. Weller (1984) described this as the *guild free choice era* because the provider organizations operated in a manner similar to guilds. At heart, the economic environment that was to be created would be anticompetitive: Each physician and each hospital would become a self-contained market free of competitive pressures.

The manner in which the physicians and hospitals set about defeating the popular free-market health care system of the 1930s would determine to a great degree the elements of the second era. They successfully shifted the health care focus from the goal of the purchaser for a low-cost system to the needs of providers and facility operators. Because this provider revolt took place during the Great Depression, the advocacy organizations were able to operate without serious concerns about antitrust actions. Led primarily by the AMA, these organizations employed a three-part approach to assure that the interests of the medical community were met. First, they began a campaign to discredit prepayment plans. They drew the attention of both the consumer and the physician to the drawbacks of these plans: namely, restrictions on free choice of physicians, intimating that prepayment plans might fail financially and that "contract medicine" diminishes quality of care.

In the second and most effective part of the strategy, the AMA and the American Hospital Association (AHA) established policy positions that enumerated the principles and standards of their respective associations and were incorporated into the related medical ethics codes that practitioners were expected to follow. Through these actions the AMA and AHA were able to blunt and almost eliminate hospital and physician participation in prepayment plans. Two key policy statements set the rules. In 1933 the AHA issued its policy on hospital participation in *The Periodic Payment Plan for the Purchase of Hospital Care* (Weller, 1984). Basically, this policy stipulated that group hospitalization plans should include all hospitals in each community in which a plan operates, that subscriber benefits should apply at any hospital in which the person's physician practices, and that all plans must be controlled and administered by nonprofit organizations largely composed of representatives of hospitals in good standing in the community. Application of these principles in the marketplace would severely curtail price competition in the hospital sector.

In 1934 the AMA House of Delegates adopted a policy stipulating 10 principles it required private health insurance plans to meet if they were to avoid resistance from the provider community (Starr, 1982). This policy in effect stated that all aspects of medical care should be controlled by the medical profession; that there should be no third-party intermediary in the medical care process; that there should be

participation by any willing, legally qualified physician; that there should be no restrictions on patients' choice of physicians; and, finally, that all aspects of medical care, regardless of setting, should remain under the control of a medical professional. Through application of these principles, "the AMA insisted that all health insurance plans accept the private physicians' monopoly control of the medical market and complete authority over all aspects of medical institutions" (Starr, 1982, p. 300). These principles for private health plans were enforced through accreditation standards, and some were incorporated into state insurance codes and related association ethics codes. Physicians and hospitals faced severe consequences if they did not comply.

In the third prong of the approach to changing the health care system, the AMA did not oppose the development of health plans that were in keeping with its principles. Indeed, in the mid- to late-1930s, hospital systems and medical societies participated in establishing medical insurance plans that adhered to the policies and standards set forth by the AMA and AHA. Designed to compete against the existing commercial forms of health coverage, the first Blue Cross plans for hospital care reimbursement and Blue Shield health plans for physician services were established. They rapidly became the dominant forms of health insurance coverage. Fundamental to these plans was the elimination of price competition by including all hospitals of standing in a community in Blue Cross and community-wide eligibility for physician participation in Blue Shield. By achieving community-wide participation, the division of hospitals and physicians into competing economic units, in which closed panels of providers aligned with a specific hospital and competed for business with other similar systems, was effectively curtailed. Acceptance and enforcement of these principles in the marketplace and, in particular, in how health insurance was structured, brought to a close the self-regulatory era of health care. The variety of prepayment health plans and various health insurance arrangements of the self-regulatory era were replaced by two types of health insurance arrangements: indemnity and service plans. Indemnity plans reimbursed patients directly for most of the costs associated with health care. Except for those too poor to pay at the time of service, patients paid the physicians directly. Service plans, usually developed and managed under the watchful eyes of medical personnel, paid providers directly and usually for the full cost of care. Both types of plans were deemed acceptable because they respected physician sovereignty, kept intermediaries out of the care process, and minimized price competition. Having achieved a favorable structure for health insurance, professional associations more consistently embraced it as a financing mechanism for health care.

Over time, the professionally derived and promulgated principles served as a blueprint for the structure of a new health care market in which the finance and service delivery systems conformed to these principles. The emergence and refinement of this new marketplace structure coincided also with a several-decade upsurge in employer and government financing of health care. Sustaining innovations within the field of medicine during this same time were extending the range and effectiveness of medical care. Because in the new system physicians were paid a defined amount for each specific service provided and hospitals were reimbursed for their costs in providing care, it became known as the fee-for-service (FFS) system. The indemnity and service insurance entities created to pay providers and hospitals for services became known as third-party payers (TPPs), further highlighting the restriction of their role to that of financial intermediaries. The new system eventually became known as the FFS/TPP system. This system would increasingly dominate health care finance and service delivery systems in the United States, fueling a 50-year period of prosperity for providers and service facilities.

As the FFS/TPP system developed, certain of its marketplace and service delivery features became integral parts of almost every aspect of health care, from state insurance regulations to Medicare and Medicaid rules. In addition, the system set the guidelines for competition among providers and for relationships among health insurance intermediaries and physicians and patients. A close look at the system's structure reveals that by nullifying price competition, it encouraged inflation of prices. This eventually would cause the FFS/TPP system to become the target of a number of disruptive innovations aimed at containing health care costs by modifying or eliminating its key principles. The FFS/TPP system also had a lasting effect on psychology. During this era psychology matured as a health service profession and entered the marketplace as a provider group eligible for third-party reimbursement. As such, it had to abide by the principles of the marketplace. Being part of the health service provider profession, psychology structured its educational and training programs as well as its service delivery system to fit harmoniously within features of the system.

As the FFS/TPP system evolved and the principles on which it was based became entrenched in the marketplace, the following key features emerged:

1. The person who receives health care typically is not the true purchaser of that care. Rather, that person's employer or a governmental body more typically purchases the care. This is the central dynamism of the FFS/TPP system. A fundamental disconnect exists between the patient and the true cost and payment for medical care. The patient is virtually cost unconscious.

2. Care may be accessed without preauthorization. In the FFS/TPP indemnity insurance system, consumers have the right to access primary, specialty, and emergency care without obtaining preauthorization from health plan personnel. Medical necessity was determined largely by the provider, not by the insurer or the health plan.

3. The care reimbursement system must be open to all legally qualified providers. A central tenet of the FFS/TPP system is known as community-wide eligibility of providers for reimbursement by third-party payers. FFS/TPP principles stipulate that health insurance plans operating in a given community should allow all legally qualified providers to participate. Health plans operated by insurers are not to contract selectively with providers by creating closed or limited panels of providers. This prohibition against horizontal market division ensures that each provider is a separate economic entity in the marketplace and significantly reduces price competition among providers.

4. Care management is the exclusive right of the provider. Fundamental to the FFS/TPP system is the principle that third parties, such as health plan personnel, should not be allowed to participate in utilization management of patients. Such decisions are to be made within the context of the provider-patient relationship without the involvement of an intermediary.

5. The FFS/TPP system is cost generating because of its capability to stimulate price-inelastic demand. The FFS/TPP system promotes price-inelastic as opposed to price-elastic demand. In a typical economic market the price of a product or service is considered to be elastic if it is lowered to increase revenue. If a provider can raise revenue by increasing fees or by increasing utilization rates at the same or higher fees, demand is considered to be price inelastic (Enthoven, 1993). The FFS/TPP era created a price-inelastic health care system. Providers are reimbursed for each procedure performed and at a rate that equals the usual, customary, and reasonable (UCR) rate for that procedure in that provider community. Hospitals are reimbursed for the costs associated with providing care in their settings. Rather than having to reduce fees to increase revenue, as is typical in a competitive free market, providers and hospitals are able to stimulate demand for more procedures and then also raise revenue by increasing fees or charges. By engaging in a form of shadow pricing (i.e., raising charges for procedures, which then become reflected over time by increases in the UCR and cost of care reimbursement rates), providers and hospitals are able to increase the amount of revenue received from third-party payers.

6. Financial risk for health care is borne by purchasers and their contracted insurance carriers. The FFS/TPP system discourages providers and the facilities with which they are associated from joining forces to create a prepayment health plan and then marketing that plan directly to purchasers. In this way the system minimizes the amount of financial risk that providers and service facilities might incur in open market arrangements. In the FFS/TPP indemnity insurance and service models, health insurers are largely financial intermediaries who pay providers and facility operators for the procedures and services provided to patients.

7. The FFS/TPP system delimits stakeholder roles in the marketplace. The principles on which the FFS/TPP system is constructed discourage cross-market competition. There is rigid segmentation or partitioning of the finance, service delivery, and management of health care according to stakeholder function. The system is designed to dissuade one type of stakeholder from taking on another's role or function: for example, health plans combining an insurance function with a service delivery function or a purchaser contracting directly with a hospital and its medical staff. Keeping the health care market segmented into distinct stakeholder roles prevents the division of providers and treatment facilities into economic units that compete with each other on price.

The FFS/TPP era is historically important not only because of the key features just described but also because it demonstrated that a stakeholder constituency—the provider—could dramatically change the dynamics of the marketplace. And it could do so in a way that was favorable to its interests. During the self-regulatory era, no single stakeholder held a dominant position relative to the others. However, in the FFS/TPP era, the provider clearly dominated. All other stakeholders are confined to a specific function in the marketplace. In addition, during this period the health care system in the United States became dependent on the third-party purchaser to provide the financial resources to fund health care. The elimination of price competition, the fact that consumers were increasingly cost unconscious, and the dramatic rise during the period in medicine's capacity to intervene effectively in illnesses combined to create an expensive, heavily utilized health care system with an enormous appetite for more funding. The stage was now set for a second revolution.

## Cost-Containment Era

The third and current period of health care in the United States began in earnest in the early 1980s when the purchasers, increasingly and with steadfastness, began to resist paying more for health coverage. Purchasers forced health plans and eventually providers and facility operators to reduce costs. Much like the previous stakeholder revolt led by providers, this one was aimed at eliminating those features of the prevailing health care system that the stakeholder in revolt deemed objectionable. This time the focus was on eliminating the cost-increasing incentives of the FFS/TPP system. In some interesting respects the period represents a return to the early 1930s, when marketplace forces were shaping health care.

Whereas the change effort of the previous rebellion was guided from the start by principles articulated by professional associations and enforced through their codes of ethics, the cost-containment era began without a guiding blueprint or mechanism for enforcement of changes in the health care marketplace. Purchasers had a common goal of reducing the financial burden on employers and the government, but they lacked a unified and clear strategy for reducing health care expenditures. For this reason, the cost-containment era unfolded not as a concerted, well-orchestrated effort, but rather in reaction to a string of discrete disruptive innovations. These innovations have had the cumulative effect of changing the health care finance and service delivery systems in profound ways, moving health care in the United States toward a price-competitive, market-based enterprise.

Five key disruptive innovations were either introduced into the health care marketplace by government, employers, or insurance intermediaries or embraced by them as effective cost-saving measures. The first two innovations, the Employee Retirement Income Security Act (ERISA) and the Federal Tax Equity and Fiscal Responsibility Act (TEFRA), in effect paved the way for the emergence of the next two: managed competition and managed care. Managed competition would eventually provide a market-based framework for containing health care costs; managed care would provide procedures for managing providers and consumers. Simultaneously introduced into the marketplace would be carve-outs and the resultant carving out of behavioral health care from the rest of the health care system. The importance of these disruptive innovations cannot be underestimated, for they will continue to have a profound influence on the health care marketplace. The following describes these innovations, demonstrating how each changed an important feature of the finance or service delivery system of the previous FFS/TPP era or affected behavioral health care.

### Employee Retirement Income Security Act

In 1974 ERISA became law. Prior to its passage employers had to purchase health care coverage through a state-regulated insurance carrier. After ERISA, businesses with 50 or more employees could self-insure their health benefits programs. ERISA would prove to be a vitally important disruptive innovation for several reasons. First, if employers chose to self-insure, they would not have to comply with state insurance regulations, including requirements to pay health insurance premium taxes and to provide state-mandated health benefits. This preemption from state regulation has meant considerable savings for employers. Second, because ERISA preempts employer-based self-insurance plans from state regulation, providers desiring to blunt or counter the effect of managed care on their practice would find the state legislative pathway to be of only marginal benefit. For example, after the introduction of managed care, providers wishing to eliminate the managed care strategy of using limited provider panels by working toward the passage of "any willing provider" statutes would discover that self-insurance plans are exempt from compliance with such laws. Thus, ERISA makes it more difficult for the provider stakeholders to counter managed care arrangements, something they were able to do successfully in the 1930s to bring a close to the self-regulatory era. Third, ERISA gave purchasers financial incentive to control costs because any reduction in expenditures was retained by employers rather than becoming profit for an insurance carrier.

The ability to retain savings from cost-containment activities provided ERISA's greatest impact: changing the flow of the revenue stream in health care and providing a fertile environment for the growth of managed care, itself a disruptive innovation. Under the FFS/TPP system, the original revenue flow progressed from the purchaser to the indemnity insurance carrier. Revenue then passed through the carrier to the patient, who had already paid the provider directly. Over time, the insurance industry would develop service plans that would allow for direct reimbursement of the provider. Regardless of which way the provider was reimbursed, the insurance carrier in the FFS/TPP model was essentially a financial intermediary who did not engage in cost-containment activities. Rather, the carrier simply provided reimbursement on a FFS basis, based on UCR rates.

As employers availed themselves of the option to self-insure, they became ever more sophisticated health care purchasers, able to intensify price competition in the marketplace. As a result, two new patterns of revenue flow emerged. In the first, revenue progressed from the purchaser to a cost-containment entity, usually a managed care organization (MCO), before reaching the provider. The MCO became an intermediary working on behalf of the purchaser to contain costs by actively managing both providers and patients. MCOs limited access to the new revenue flow to those providers who accepted participation in cost-containment activities. MCOs

thus became agents of change for the provider reimbursement and service delivery systems.

As MCOs evolved, they used more aggressive mechanisms to manage costs. They encouraged the formation of multispecialty provider organizations, channeling patients to those organizations via contracts. This accelerated the development of what became known as organized delivery systems (ODSs; Zelman, 1996). ODSs are groups of providers linked through various administrative and contractual arrangements to each other and to service facilities for the purpose of providing health care. As a result of their work with MCOs in cost containment activities, ODSs have the capability of managing utilization, conducting quality improvement procedures, and even accepting financial risk for providing health care.

With the maturation of the ODSs, a second new pattern of revenue flow emerged, one which eliminated the MCO intermediary altogether. The success of managed care in getting these ODSs to assume financial risk via capitated or prepayment systems provided incentives for ODSs to improve their ability to reduce unnecessary utilization, manage quality of care, and carry out other care management functions. Many ODSs in essence were becoming provider-initiated and administered care management systems capable of controlling costs. Hence, a new, viable health care avenue was available to purchasers. It created a fresh revenue stream that began with the purchasers who directly contracted with an ODS, eliminating both traditional insurance carriers and MCOs from the revenue stream. It was not long before sophisticated ODSs were competing with MCOs for health care contracts with purchasers. The increased viability of ODSs to engage in direct contracting with purchasers—combined with greater purchaser knowledge and competence in self-insuring health care benefits—added a new dimension to price competition. The resulting tension created further instability in an already unstable marketplace as MCOs sought to limit the potential threat represented by ODSs.

ERISA has proven to be a particularly powerful disruptive innovation. By giving employers the right to self-insure, it enabled them to have more options in contracting with health plans, including bypassing the health plans and contracting directly with provider organizations. In essence, it simultaneously undermined another principle of the FFS system and elevated the purchaser to a position of greater authority over health plans in the marketplace. ERISA also gave rise to an intermediary in the care-giving process, one which identified with the needs of health plans and purchasers to contain costs. This had the effect of defeating another FFS principle: the prohibition of an intermediary from involvement in the physician-patient relationship. It also elevated health plan authority above the providers in a newly emerging stake-holder hierarchy.

## Tax Equity and Fiscal Responsibility Act and the Prospective Payment System

The 1982 Federal Tax Equity and Fiscal Responsibility Act (TEFRA) was targeted at controlling Medicare costs, but it had an unexpected effect on all health care costs and on behavioral health in particular. The most salient and well-known cost-containment mechanism proposed by TEFRA was diagnostic related groups (DRGs). DRGs contain costs by establishing the reimbursement rate that providers will receive for treatment of a specific condition in advance. By setting fixed payment rates for inpatient treatment of medical conditions, DRGs create what has become known as the prospective payment system (PPS), yet another important modification of the existing FFS system. TEFRA moved reimbursement for inpatient hospital services from a fee per unit of service to a fee per episode of treatment. This was a radical change. Before DRGs, hospitals were reimbursed for all charges related to inpatient treatment. Through the use of DRGs, TEFRA set the number of allowable days for a hospital stay for a specific illness or procedure. Whether a patient stayed more or fewer days than the prescribed number, hospitals received the same reimbursement rate. Strong incentives were thus created for hospitals to control utilization as a way to maximize profits, versus increasing utilization to maximize profits, as had been the case in the FFS/TPP era.

The DRGs established because of TEFRA did not apply to behavioral health conditions, however. TEFRA codified what many health care payers already knew: In behavioral health care, diagnosis of conditions did not lead to predictable treatment courses or reliable estimates for the time of treatment. Most providers of behavioral health care greeted the passage of TEFRA with great relief, not realizing that it would eventually lead to a separation of behavioral health care from the rest of medicine and cause it to be viewed as the chief spur to high inflation in health care costs. In the absence of any other cost-containment mechanisms for behavioral health, mental health care emerged as the only sector of the inpatient market still operating under the unmodified FFS reimbursement method.

The health care marketplace proved quick to adjust to regulatory changes. Many of the large hospital corporations, which saw their revenues drop as a result of TEFRA, found relief by shifting their focus onto psychiatric inpatient care. Venture capitalists and entrepreneurs rushed in to take advantage of the last unregulated part of the FFS system. Psychiatric inpatient facilities grew at a prolific rate, outstripping any

reasonable projection for the need for inpatient care. Four large hospital corporations (Charter Hospitals, Community Psychiatric Center [CPC] Hospitals, Psychiatric Institutes of America, and the psychiatric division of HCA, Inc. [formerly Hospital Corporation of America]) saw double- and triple-digit growth in their facilities between 1980 and 1990 (Bassuk & Holland, 1987). A significant cause of the rapid rise in all health care costs during that decade was the exploitation by hospitals and providers of the rich benefits for psychiatric inpatient care unregulated by DRG prospective payment methods. The standard of care for chemical dependency rapidly became 28 days, regardless of the severity or duration of the problem. Hospital stays became lengthy for behavioral health disorders. By 2000 these same disorders would most commonly be treated on an outpatient basis. The excesses of the psychiatric hospitals came to a halt in the early 1990s due to high profile investigations of their operations and subsequent significant fines (Lodge, 1994). For purchasers, there was perhaps no better marketing campaign for the emergence of managed behavioral health care organizations (MBHOs).

As a disruptive innovation, TEFRA made two important contributions to restructuring the health care marketplace along cost-containment lines. First, by reintroducing a PPS, it overrode one of the basic principles of the FFS system. Second, it eventually resulted in a separate method for managing rising behavioral health care costs. Although no DRGs applicable to behavioral health inpatient care developed as a result of TEFRA, purchasers began seriously to seek other solutions to contain the steadily rising costs of behavioral health care. Eventually they would embrace carve-out MBHOs, the final disruptive innovation of the cost-containment era.

## Managed Competition

In the early 1980s another disruptive innovation appeared. Enthoven and others began to propose ways to reintroduce price competition into the health care marketplace (e.g., Ellwood & Enthoven, 1995; Enthoven, 1993; Enthoven & Kronick, 1989a, 1989b; Enthoven & Singer, 1997, 1998). The price competition movement that these authors stimulated eventually would become known as managed competition. Managed competition proposes to change the nature of the health care marketplace in fundamental ways by introducing competitive pressures for cost containment and then managing how the marketplace responds to those pressures in order to prevent market failure. It intends to create conditions and forces that will compel health plans and their associated providers to manage carefully the care provided. The theory and strategies of managed competition guided the development of President Bill Clinton's Health Security Act (1993).

Although Clinton's efforts failed to result in legislation, managed competition principles were increasingly adopted by business and government.

Managed competition can be defined as the process of structuring the health care marketplace so that rational microeconomic market forces produce a more cost-conscious, publicly accountable, quality-focused health care system. In essence, managed competition is a blueprint for increasing competition in health care by structuring and managing a fluid market environment in such a way so as to contain costs while at the same time attempting to maintain quality of care and preventing market failure. Its fundamental goal is to change the health care paradigm from the traditional FFS model to a managed competition model that is capable of containing costs.

An idea of the magnitude of the change contemplated by managed competition can be gleaned from Table 22.1, which compares specific elements of the FFS health care system with the managed competition alternatives. An entire chain of change—a linked series of events among stakeholders—results from this alteration of the health care paradigm. First, managed competition advocates the need to convert purchasers into sponsors of the change process. Then they must provide those sponsors with strategies designed to change the structure of the marketplace so that health plans operate equitably and so that the more generally accepted microeconomic forces (e.g., supply and demand, price elasticity, etc.) operate to contain costs without sacrificing quality. If microeconomic forces fail to produce the desired competitive

market, sponsors must adjust the strategies used to protect against market failure. Because the sponsors are really purchasers implementing managed competition strategies, they will most likely try to prevent market failure by having an effect on the stakeholders they influence the most: the health plans. In turn, health plans, in order to survive and gain market share, will need to influence the behavior of providers, service facilities, consumers, and the pharmaceutical industry through various managed care arrangements. Managed competition, should its full implementation be achieved, has the potential for the greatest impact of all the disruptive innovations to date. Even though its goals and strategies have been only partially realized up to this point, it still has had a profound effect.

Managed competition employs numerous strategies to accomplish its various goals. It aims to make the consumer more cost conscious and thus to change consumer behavior; it seeks to stimulate competition among health plans and to eliminate the noncompetitive features in the health care system; and it has attempted to develop a sponsor system capable of implementing key managed competition strategies. Making health plans compete for the business of purchasers on the basis of cost and quality through a competitive bidding process is a key strategy. By standardizing plan benefits and requiring the plans to provide performance data, the bidding process enables purchasers to compare price and quality. Managed competition also seeks to make the consumer more cost conscious by changing the degree to which and the manner in which premiums charged by health plans are subsidized by employers and the federal government. Managed competition would index an employer's contributions to health plan premiums to the lowest cost plan available to the employees. Those employees opting to enroll in a higher cost health plan would have to pay the difference in premium charges between the lowest cost plan and the plan chosen. The goal, of course, is to encourage consumers to be sensitive to cost when selecting among health plans offered during enrollment, thereby forcing health plans to contain costs in order to be attractive to potential enrollees. Managed competition proponents also call for changing government-based tax subsidies to ensure that competition is supported and promoted, as well as to encourage businesses to continue to provide health care for their employees. Managed competition has also set into motion certain initiatives focused on changing consumer behavior. It applies financial incentives to persuade consumers to accept reduced autonomy to initiate care and to accept a limited choice of provider. It attempts to intensify cost consciousness when the consumer contemplates use of benefits by imposing higher copayments and coinsurance and by establishing financial penalties for not using the authorized provider system.

**TABLE 22.1  Comparison of Fee-for-Service and Managed Competition Paradigms**

| Traditional Fee for Service | Managed Competition |
| --- | --- |
| Separate finance and delivery of health care. | Integrated finance, delivery, and management of health care. |
| Competition for patients at individual provider level. | Competition for patients at health plan level. |
| All licensed providers eligible to participate. | Selective and exclusive contracting with providers. |
| Unfettered choice of provider by consumer. | Restricted choice of provider. |
| Solo practice or single-specialty practice groups. | Integrated multispecialty practice associations. |
| Inelastic price demand. | Elastic price demand. |
| Medical necessity determined by provider and consumer. | Medical necessity determined by health plan. |
| Nonstandardized insurance benefit packages with risk-based selection of enrollees. | Standardized benefits and no risk selection. |
| No financial risk for provider and facility operators. | Financial risk to health plans and provider care organizations. |
| Level of care continuum not managed. | Level of care managed across entire continuum. |
| Low cost attunement of consumer. | Cost-sensitive consumer. |

To stimulate competition among health plans, managed competition encourages the establishment of certain rules of equity. These are designed to structure the business environment in which health plans operate for the purpose of eliminating the noncompetitive features of the traditional FFS health insurance system. To accomplish this goal, health plans are required to bid on standardized benefit packages so that purchasers can more easily compare premium rates. When benefits are standardized, it is more difficult for health plans to avoid enrolling potential high-cost subscribers by not offering benefits that would adequately cover their care. Under managed competition rules, payments to health plans would be risk adjusted to ensure that the plans are adequately compensated for costs associated with treatment of high-need patients. Further, health plans are prevented from denying enrollment or limiting coverage for preexisting medical conditions. Once a person is enrolled, the health plan is guaranteed to be renewable, regardless of medical conditions, thus making coverage continuous. Health plans must accept all eligible participants who choose them. Finally, the premium level is set on a community-rating basis; that is, the premium charge is the same regardless of the health status of people eligible to enroll. Managed competition also seeks to promote direct competition among health plans in order to control costs without adversely affecting quality. To do so, it encourages the division of providers into competing economic units at the health plan level. It then encourages health plans to contract with distinct panels of providers in order to reduce the anticompetitive effects of competing health care systems that have virtually identical or highly overlapping providers. An additional approach to deepening competition at the health plan and multispecialty level is to require these entities to provide performance data on patient satisfaction, access, and quality of care. By implementing these strategies, managed competition advocates hope to make the provision of health care more price elastic, as compared with the inelastic price of the FFS system.

A final key strategy is to transform purchasers into sponsors of managed competition and then to develop a sponsor system. Sponsors contract with health plans for large groups of beneficiaries and manage the health care market environment in a way that maintains price competition. A well-orchestrated, viable system of sponsors is central to the success of managed competition. Sponsors have several important roles. They must contain cost and maintain quality; take corrective action to protect against tendencies toward market failure in a fluid, evolving market; and guide the system in the direction of greater efficiency. In order for sponsors to gain the leverage necessary to structure and adjust the market, they must represent and purchase care for a substantial portion of the market. Three types of sponsors, all major purchasers of health plans

on behalf of employees or beneficiaries, are envisioned in a managed competition market: (a) large employers like IBM or the California Public Employees Retirement System (CALPERS), which purchase health care services on behalf of hundreds of thousands of beneficiaries; (b) purchasing cooperatives composed of a coalition of employers and self-employed individuals; and (c) government-based sponsors that purchase care on behalf of millions of Medicare- and Medicaid-eligible beneficiaries.

The various strategies collectively known as managed competition are meant to be implemented as an interlocking package in an integrated and balanced way. If this does not occur, it is unlikely that the twin goals of producing a cost-conscious, price-competitive health care environment and maintaining or improving the quality of care from that offered under the traditional FFS system could be achieved. There are obvious critical challenges to the full implementation of the managed competition model. First, it must have the ability to decrease the fragmentation present in the purchaser segment of the marketplace and to create a sponsor system capable of managing change of the magnitude demanded. Second, health plans in managed care systems must have the ability to develop sustainable partnerships with provider organizations. These provider organizations must be able to engender loyalty and develop allegiance among consumers while simultaneously managing the care that they provide.

Managed competition strategies and challenges apply equally to the medical, surgical, and behavioral health components of the health care system. Their state of implementation and impact to date are described later. Managed competition is the third purchaser-linked disruptive innovation. Much like ERISA, it strengthened the authority of purchasers relative to the health plans with which they contract. It increased the number and effectiveness of strategies that purchasers had at their disposal to pressure health plans to contain costs, and it shifted a greater burden of the cost-containment mission to health plans. The stage is now set for health plans to introduce two disruptive innovations of their own: managed care and carve-outs.

### Managed Care

Unlike managed competition, which is aimed at restructuring the economic principles of health care, managed care attempts to influence the health care behavior of providers and consumers. In the world of health care finance, health plans and purchasers view providers and consumers as cost centers. MCOs were formed to enable health plans to satisfy the demands from purchasers that they contain or reduce expenditures. Following passage of ERISA, purchasers understood that if they self-insured their company's health benefits and contracted with a health plan to manage costs, they could reduce premium increases for employees' health care benefits. Managed care consists of an evolving set of interventions focused on containing or reducing health care expenditures while attempting to maintain or enhance the quality of care provided. Although the cost reduction benefits accrue to the health care purchaser, it falls to the health plans to implement managed care strategies. In fact, as the health plan market has consolidated, the term *managed* has become virtually synonymous with health plans. Only a small and decreasing fraction of health plans do not manage the care that patients receive.

The beginning of attempts by purchasers to contain health care costs can be traced back to passage of the 1973 Health Maintenance Organization (HMO) act. That act provided startup grants and loans for HMOs and required employers to offer an HMO as an option when a qualified one became available. Until recently, the standard HMO service delivery system was a multidisciplinary staff model clinic that integrated finance, management, and service delivery systems. The proponents of HMOs hoped that these new ODSs would stimulate price competition in the marketplace and eventually replace FFS systems or at least force them to be more cost conscious. The competitive advantage that HMOs were supposed to have was based on their incentives to contain costs. Despite financial support for their development, HMOs emerged much more slowly than anticipated. They also engaged in shadow pricing, setting their premium rates just below that of traditional FFS plans. The anticipated competition and reduction in costs never materialized, despite the fact that HMOs managed utilization more carefully than did the FFS systems.

Within the managed care movement, preferred provider organizations (PPOs) appeared as the next cost-containment approach. PPOs divide providers into two groups: those in their network who are eligible for higher levels of reimbursement and those out of network who are reimbursed at lower rates. The patient is responsible for paying the difference between the reimbursement levels provided by the health plan and the fee charged by the provider. PPOs developed networks of providers who were willing to accept discounted FFS rates and abide by the PPOs' utilization review guidelines in return for preferred access to their enrollees. This form of managed care immediately began to express its disruptive effects on the prevailing health care system. Reluctant as it was, provider acceptance for participating in PPOs resulted in further erosion of the FFS principles as a bedrock structure for health care. PPOs began to use selective contracting with providers, dealing a serious blow to the community-wide provider concept of the FFS system. PPOs had a second major impact: The right to

set prices no longer rested with the provider. Now it was the PPO that set a reimbursement rate for services. However, PPOs did continue to use the concept of reimbursing providers on an FFS basis.

As networks became more sophisticated in terms of utilization management, the next generation of managed care systems would attack another key element of the FFS system. These newer forms of managed care would begin to erode provider authority by becoming involved in more aggressive utilization management. Case managers would become active in helping to determine level, duration, and intensity of care that providers offered. The rise of an intermediary's involvement in the care process would become one of the most problematic aspects of managed care for providers. Along with the rise of case managers came a new method of payment that directly attacked the heart of the FFS system. Managed care began to operate under a prepayment arrangement. This form of health care finance became known as *capitation*, and it greatly increased pressure on provider systems and health plans to contain costs. Capitation created incentives for both health plans and provider organizations to reduce expenditures in order to increase profitability. Capitation arrangements led to yet more aggressive utilization management, fears about denial of care, and concerns that quality of care would be sacrificed to maximize profits.

As MCOs gained experience in controlling health care expenditures, purchasers increasingly sought to contract with health plans that had strong managed care systems. Despite the switch from unmanaged indemnity plans to managed care plans, above-average inflation returned to health care by 1999 and 2000. This fact calls into question the actual effectiveness of the current managed care strategies in containing health care expenditures. Perhaps the enduring contribution of this phase of the managed care movement will be its disruption and nullification of key FFS principles in the marketplace. Specifically, it reintroduced the concept of financial risk to provider organizations, brought an intermediary deeper into the caregiving process, intensified selective contracting with providers and their facilities, and divided providers into competing economic entities.

### Carve-Outs and Behavioral Health Care

Carve-outs represent the most important disruptive innovation developed to contain costs. They were introduced into the marketplace almost simultaneously with the larger managed care movement. Carve-outs segment one health care benefit from the rest, providing specialized administration and cost-containment controls to that segment. Pharmaceutical benefits, laboratory services, occupational medicine, and others were subject to carve-outs. But behavioral health care would experience the greatest disruption from this innovation.

Carve-outs were increasingly applied when costs rose significantly in a segment of the market, when it was hard to determine medical necessity because of the level of provider discretion in determining the amounts or types of care given, or when the dynamics in that segment of the market were different from those that mainstream MCOs could handle effectively. Health plans and the purchasers with which they interacted came to view behavioral health care as meeting all three of these criteria. There is an inherent problem with carve-outs, however: They create an artificial division in the health care continuum, in effect separating a part from the main body. Carve-out companies emerged that were separately financed, and they developed independent service delivery systems. These service delivery systems were often inconvenient. For example, when laboratory services are carved out, there can be a lack of integration of that function within the medical practitioner's office. The patient must go to a separate facility for laboratory work, frequently having to fill out additional paper work and then wait for service. There sometimes can be difficulty in reintegrating the information into the physician's setting in a timely fashion.

Behavioral health care carve-outs posed a more serious problem. Because functions overlap between primary care and behavioral health care, consumers may not know where to access care for behavioral health concerns. In fact, a significant portion of the care is still provided by primary care physicians. Even more serious, behavioral health carve-outs make it more difficult to coordinate care for a broad range of medical conditions that have high comorbidity rates for behavioral health problems. In addition, they impede the ability of the rest of the health care system to utilize fully the skills of the behavioral health specialist. Such specialists have the capability to help patients change health practices or make lifestyle adjustments that would prevent chronic health conditions from developing or prevent exacerbating already existing conditions. Behavioral health carve-outs have come to have broader implications than being simply a different company managing mental health benefits; they have also come to represent a separation of the skills of the behavioral health specialist from the broader needs of medical and surgical care patients.

Behavioral health care was among the first areas singled out by health plans for management via carve-outs. The use of carve-outs as cost-containment strategies in behavioral health care gave rise to a new form of MCO, the MBHO. Two distinct types of MBHOs quickly emerged: the multidisciplinary staff model clinic (the *clinic model*) and the external intermediary utilization review organization (the *network model*). The clinic-model MBHOs were staffed by salaried providers and

were often funded by capitation, a new form of financial risk taking that was similar to the older prepayment system of the self-regulatory era. Capitation funding arrangements pay a fixed dollar amount per enrollee per month to a clinic; the clinic in turn is expected to provide all medically necessary behavioral health care. Capitation funding is viewed by purchasers as a method to predetermine their costs for behavioral health care and as a way to create incentives for providers and their clinics to contain costs.

The early clinic-model carve-out MBHOs frequently had contracts with one or more local employers to provide behavioral health care services. Direct contracting with purchasers gave these companies a connection to employers similar to the ones that had developed during the self-regulatory era. Seeing a business opportunity, entrepreneurs quickly began to develop clinic-model carve-out companies in behavioral health care. Soon a variety of clinic-model MHBOs became active in the marketplace. Despite their variety, they continued to manage utilization and coordinate care internally. No external intermediary was involved in utilization management.

The network model represents the second type of MBHO to develop. It grew out of utilization review organizations that had been active for several years in general medical and rehabilitation care sectors of the health care market. These organizations saw the opportunity to expand into behavioral health care. They extended and modified their care management and utilization control procedures and then began marketing themselves to purchasers as MBHOs. Early on the utilization review organizations did not have contractual relationships with providers; their only contact was with purchasers to contain costs. However, they quickly realized that it was difficult to manage providers with whom they did not have a contractual arrangement. This gave rise to the network model of behavioral health care, which enabled utilization review organizations to develop contractual relationships with providers. Unlike in the clinic model, these companies did not directly employ behavioral health care providers. They contracted with providers on a discounted, FFS basis. One key element of the contract was the provider's agreement to abide by the company's utilization management standards. Utilization review organizations thus were transformed from those that could only attempt to influence providers to curtail services to ones with power to dismiss from the networks those providers who did not abide by their utilization management principles.

The network-model MBHOs developed a number of utilization management strategies to contain costs. First, they began requiring precertification for inpatient facility treatment. Next, they developed guidelines that specified intensity and duration of treatment for major disorders. At the same time, they began contracting with psychiatric inpatient facilities to align their own financial incentives more closely with those of the hospital. They also promoted development of a broader continuum of care, encouraging partial hospitalization programs, intensive outpatient care systems, and other forms of care that could contribute to cost containment. This necessitated coordination of care across the range of interventions and accelerated the rise of the case manager who is external to the provider-patient relationship.

The network utilization management model established several key precedents in behavioral health care. First, it initiated selective contracting with behavioral health care providers. Second, it introduced discounted FFS rates and prevented the practice of billing patients for the difference between the full fee of the provider and discounted rates. Third, it reduced provider authority by imposing an intermediary in the provider-patient relationship. Eventually, these intermediaries began to rely on treatment protocols to manage utilization; many of these protocols were not based on empirically validated principles. Fourth, they contributed to the migration of the psychotherapy function from a primarily doctoral-based activity to the subdoctoral level. The network model, along with the clinic model, also set important precedents by taking on financial risk through capitation and other funding methods. The use of risk-based funding mechanisms led to concerns among providers and patients about denial of care and quality issues. In response, MCOs established quality improvement programs and participated in health care accreditation processes.

Each of the two MBHO models would in turn develop a variety of service delivery and finance systems, which actively competed among themselves for marketplace dominance. In the 1990s eight network, clinic, or combination care management models were in use in the marketplace (Drum, 1995). By the turn of the century, the network model dominated. The clinic model proved to be expensive and complicated to create. To enable a group of providers to work together required setting up facilities, administrative support structures, and quality and utilization management systems. In addition, the clinic model proved difficult to expand beyond local markets and could not compete for contracts with large purchasers who needed regional and national provider systems. Network models, on the other hand, could quickly establish networks in virtually all areas of the country. In a classic market oversupply situation, network-style MBHOs were able to find an ample supply of providers willing to contract with them at steeply discounted rates. MBHOs could expand and contract networks as market forces required, and they could do so inexpensively. They could reconfigure their products according to the needs of purchasers. In a given region where multiple MBHOs operate, provider networks often use the same providers. Consequently, differences in quality are not significant among the

various MBHO networks. Price reduction thus becomes the only competitive advantage that MBHOs have as they seek contracts from purchasers.

The inability to apply DRGs to behavioral health care, the receptivity of self-insured purchasers to contract with MBHOs on a carve-out basis, and the use of managed competition principles to promote competition among providers and stimulate cost consciousness of consumers all provided a robust environment for MBHOs. Their success in containing and reducing costs for self-insured health plans stimulated insurance companies to begin using their services. The growing market for MBHOs attracted venture capitalists and entrepreneurs, signaling that the race for market share was underway. Competition for market share played into the hands of purchasers who continue to seek price reductions.

Most insurance companies did not have the expertise to construct an MBHO internally. They either contracted with carve-out MBHOs or purchased them. MBHOs that contracted with or were acquired by insurance companies gained immediate access to a large number of insured lives, expanded their national presence, and, of course, gained market share. The MBHOs that did not develop contractual relationships with insurance companies often merged and consolidated with other smaller MBHOs and employee assistance program (EAP) companies. This consolidation began in the late 1980s and occurred throughout the 1990s. The drive for growth frequently overlooked the differences in culture and style between many of these companies, as well as the unique and often-incompatible information and technology systems they had developed. By early 2001, the largest MBHOs reported covering over 100 million lives (according to the following behavioral health care company Web sites consulted on May 29, 2001: United Behavioral Health at http://www.unitedbehavioralhealth.com/ ubh/ubhmain/aboutus.html, Magellan Behavioral Health at http://www.magellanhealth.com/mbh/about_us/fast_facts.html, ValueOptions at http://www.valueoptions.com/news.htm, and CIGNA Behavioral Health at http://www.cignabehavioral.com/ about_corp.htm). Clinic-model MBHOs in the year 2000 did not fare as well as did network models. Of the small percentage of clinic models that managed to make the transition from local to regional clinic systems, few of those survived the shift from contracting on a regional basis to a national level in this highly fluid environment.

By the beginning of 2001, the consolidation of MBHOs had resulted in two types of network-based MBHOs: independents and affiliated or owned. Each has fundamental weaknesses as well as strengths. The independent model enjoys tremendous flexibility in selling its products to any health care organization in the marketplace. But it lacks a stable base of contracts from which to build its operations, and it may not have access to the type of technology required to execute core functions—a technology that large insurance companies have in ample supply. Managing a large number of contracts with various requirements across different information systems in use as a result of mergers is difficult and expensive. Owned-affiliated MBHO companies, on the other hand, do not have the same difficulties. They often have access to systems and technology that otherwise would not be affordable for an independent model. They also may have exclusive contracts to manage the behavioral health care benefits on a national basis for their owners or affiliates, thus attaining a stable source of revenue.

The managed behavioral health care industry has seen rapid development and change in the last 18 years. An industry that started as a collection of small entrepreneurial companies has grown into a highly consolidated one. The diversity of models that were implemented when the industry began has evolved into a network model dominated by large MBHOs that manage millions of lives. Large MBHOs are plagued, however, by the same problems that derailed large national health care organizations: the lack of adequate technology and systems to manage rapid growth. The competition for market share has driven prices so low that companies are now struggling to make sufficient profits to invest adequately in their infrastructures.

MBHOs had a substantial impact on providers, in particular the psychiatric hospitals. By the end of 2000 all the major psychiatric hospital chains were out of business, either sold or bankrupt, leaving many parts of the country without a psychiatric hospital. Individual practitioners have lost some autonomy. They are often asked to follow treatment guidelines that are not empirically validated. Also during this period there has been a dramatic increase in the number of behavioral health professionals eligible to be licensed to provide care. States passed legislation allowing professional counselors to practice independently at the master's-degree level. The result has been a downward migration of the psychotherapy function. Once practiced primarily by psychiatrists and doctoral-level psychologists, psychotherapy is now increasingly practiced by providers with 1 to 2 years of graduate education.

The behavioral health care carve-out has proved to be a vitally important disruptive innovation for several reasons. First, it contributed to a mind-body split in health care that reduced reliance on the use of more biopsychosocial approaches to the treatment of health conditions. Second, it brought a unique form of managed care to behavioral health care—one with its own industry dynamics and cost-containment procedures. Last, carve-outs further emphasized that psychotherapy was not a physician activity. As a result, the scope-of-practice laws, which constrain medical functions from migrating to other types of providers, do not apply to psychotherapy.

## The Impact of the Cost-Containment Era of Health Care: An Analysis

The disruptive innovations described in this chapter have had a profound effect on reshaping the structure and dynamics of health care in the United States. In the absence of an entity empowered by all stakeholders to organize and lead the transformation of the health care system, change will doubtless continue to occur in response to existing disruptive innovations or ones that are yet to be introduced. A good example of the former is the PPS, introduced as a result of TEFRA. It originally focused on containing inpatient hospital costs but is now slated to be extended by Medicare to treatment of patients in rehabilitation facilities. If health plans are successful in developing and enforcing provider compliance with clinical pathways, they could extend the PPS as a method of payment for a broad range of outpatient services. (During the 1980s the search for clinical pathways—i.e., the most effective and efficient treatment pathway for a given disorder—began as a way to ensure high quality of care. Clinical pathways define expected patient outcomes, associated care provider interventions, and expected treatment time for specific diagnoses or surgical procedures.) Now that the cost-containment era has been underway for over two decades, it is possible to discuss its impact on key stakeholder constituencies and to demonstrate how it has changed the dynamics operating in the health care system.

### Effect on Health Care Stakeholders

**Purchaser Stakeholders.** Since the mid-1980s health care purchasers have begun to resist paying higher premiums and have clamored for cost containment to reduce the growth in expenditures. In contrast to their predecessors who made the shift from the self-regulatory era to the FFS era, 1980s purchasers were neither organized nor particularly inclined to orchestrate or manage the change process once it was underway. They began the change effort without a guiding blueprint, relying instead on disruptive innovations to accomplish their goals. Nonetheless, the health care environment has been transformed in fundamental ways.

During the cost-containment era, a clearly defined stakeholder hierarchy unfolded that was quite different from the FFS era, when providers occupied the top of the stakeholder food chain. The purchasers now have the power. They guide and influence the behavior of the two stakeholder constituencies with which they have direct contact: health plans and employees. Even though the entire array of managed competition strategies has not been implemented, those strategies that were successfully put into place by purchasers have had a formidable impact. Purchasers have been able to restructure the marketplace and change the business model in which health care operates. As change agents, they have taken on the implementation of some of the roles assigned by managed competition to sponsors. They have promoted greater equity on the part of health plans, increased cost-consciousness among consumers through cost shifting, standardized health benefits packages in order to make it easier to compare health plans bids on the basis of price, and implemented competitive bidding among health plans to encourage price competition. The issue of quality is another matter. These same purchaser-sponsors have been less successful in risk-adjusting payments to health plans in order to compensate them adequately for providing care for the chronically ill. They have also been unsuccessful in providing information about access, quality, and satisfaction data on plan performance to enrollees and in getting health plans to create distinct versus highly overlapping provider networks. It could be said that the purchaser-sponsors more successfully implemented the managed competition strategies for cost containment than they did those for ensuring quality.

Advocates of managed competition now face a crucial issue. Is it possible for purchasers, who are also major stakeholders in the health care enterprise, to serve as the sponsor of change and achieve a system as equally attentive to cost containment as it is to quality of care? Or will this dual role fuel, as some fear, a race to the bottom, where cost issues dominate over quality? Attentiveness to quality of care unfortunately has been compromised by the degree of fragmentation within the purchaser stakeholder community; the incomplete transformation of purchasers into true, effective, unbiased sponsors of change; and the incomplete development of the crucial sponsor system.

As initiators of the cost-containment era, purchasers have been its main beneficiaries. It is unlikely that they will return to the passive role they played in the FFS era. Rather, they are likely to continue to apply managed competition strategies in order to increase their leverage with health plans and to find ways to block initiatives by other stakeholders in order to counteract their growing influence. As will be made evident in the section titled "Dynamics of Health Care," because of fragmentation within the stakeholder community, purchasers have been a major source of instability in the marketplace and an unreliable change agent.

What will be the future for purchaser stakeholders? They are likely to continue to influence the health care marketplace through two avenues: (a) applying pressure on health plans to contain costs and (b) shifting the costs of health care to employees. If these two strategies prove effective in containing costs, marketplace change should unfold incrementally. However, if they prove ineffective and coincide with a period of economic stagnation or recession, employers are likely to move aggressively to limit the impact of health care costs on their competitive position in a global economy. If this scenario occurs, the purchaser will likely seriously consider moving to a system in which a fixed contribution is offered to employees for their health care. With a fixed contribution system, the employer gives each employee a specific amount for health care coverage; it becomes the employee's responsibility to use that contribution to purchase health care on the open market from health plans operating in the community. A change of this magnitude would qualify as a new disruptive innovation that would ripple throughout the entire stakeholder system. If such a cost-containment mechanism becomes prevalent, it would alter the relationships and dynamics among the key stakeholders. Clearly, as health care costs escalate and the fixed contribution of employers remains the same or lags behind inflation, the employee's stake in controlling health care costs will change.

**Health Plan Stakeholders.** Health plan stakeholders find themselves pressured from all sides. This stakeholder constituency has not been doing well financially. Market consolidation and the resulting increased market share have not given birth to the expected financial benefits. Price competition stimulated by the purchaser has required health plans to take increasingly aggressive action with both providers and consumers. To persuade purchasers to support the bitter fruit of cost-containment procedures, health plans have promised that they could contain costs and maintain quality through a variety of managed care arrangements. Fearing that the purchaser might engage in direct contracting with organized health care delivery systems and also worrying about loss of market share, health plans have been unable to counteract the power of the purchaser. Increasing consolidation in the marketplace among health plans should eventually give them more leverage in markets in which they have a dominant share. For the foreseeable future, however, health plans will focus increasingly and with greater intensity on managing the behavior of providers and consumers. Advances in information technology, along with the shift away from establishing clinical pathways to monitoring their enforcement, will take health plans deeper into actual medical management of a patient's care. The focus will move from proxies of quality (credentialing, accreditation, and quality improvement programs) to the application of clinical pathways and assessment of outcomes. Health plans will also learn to risk-adjust payments to providers because of advancements in information technology and will attempt to extend the PPS to outpatient care by reimbursing providers on a fee-per-episode instead of a FFS basis. Behavioral health care will once again feel pressure as health plans face daunting challenges in extending the fee-per-episode payment system to this segment of health care.

Ever since purchasers gained the right to self-insure their health care programs as a result of ERISA, their power relative to health plans has increased. Therefore, health plans and their care management systems are likely to continue to occupy the pressure-filled environment where the demands of the purchaser and consumer must be balanced with the dissatisfaction and demands of the provider community.

**Provider Stakeholders.**  The provider stakeholder community has experienced the brunt of the cost-containment changes. No longer dominant in the stakeholder hierarchy, providers are now situated below both purchasers and health plans. The hardest blow has been the defeat of the protections offered by the FFS principles. Providers have had to cope with an intermediary becoming involved in the provider-patient relationship, selective contracting by MCOs, increased administrative costs, decreased rates of reimbursement, and, in some cases, assumption of financial risk. The provider protections that were built into the FFS-era market structure have been largely nullified, and to date, providers have been ineffective in establishing a new path to marketplace supremacy. Although they are advocating for quality of care for consumers, promoting direct contracting with purchasers, and organizing and possibly unionizing for greater leverage with health plans, providers will have to struggle in the future to prevent further erosion of their authority.

The behavioral health care component of the provider community will face the greatest challenge in retaining authority. The difficulty will arise from the supply-demand imbalances (an oversupply of psychiatrists, psychologists, social workers, licensed professional counselors, etc.), problems agreeing on clinical pathways because of the multiple disciplines and their different perspectives, and a marginalized place in the health care environment due to being carved out from medical and surgical care.

**Consumer Stakeholders.**  The consumer stakeholder community has experienced much of the discomfort resident in the cost-containment era. The consumers' right to unfettered choice of providers has been narrowed. The competitive bidding process that employers use in selecting a health plan has meant that many patients have had to switch providers because employers switch health plans more frequently. The right to access care that is unimpeded by precertification procedures has been severely diminished. Purchasers have required employees or beneficiaries to pay a larger share of their health care premiums and bills. Added to these changes is the fact that funding sources for the safety-net provider system for the poor and uninsured consumer have decreased, reducing the safety net's ability to supply needed services.

In response to their losses, consumers have complained to employers about restrictions in choice of provider and sought protection via legislative channels. Although consumers have relinquished a great many of their rights, in the future they will increasingly demand that health plans allow reimbursed access to state-of-the-art medical care. They will also become more informed about best practices as a result of medical information available on the Internet and the interactions that the Internet makes possible with other consumers.

### Dynamics of Health Care

To gain a broader perspective on the state of the health care marketplace, it is important to understand the dynamics in place today among the various stakeholders as they struggle for position. These new dynamics emphasize how changeable an environment is the cost-containment era.

**Interstakeholder Boundaries and Functions Are Fluid.** Unlike the FFS era, where stakeholder functions were carefully defined and stakeholders were confined to their assigned role in the health care system, the cost-containment era allows stakeholders to perform multiple functions, including those of other stakeholders. Purchasers can directly contract with provider health care organizations; health plans can form their own provider organizations and be involved in service delivery; and purchasers can assume insurance functions through self-insurance arrangements. The marketplace has not fully adjusted to these shifting stakeholder roles. Until predictable patterns emerge, all stakeholders will be caught in a cycle of perpetual change and adjustment. Stakeholders will continue to vie for position in the health care marketplace by attempting to reduce intrastakeholder fragmentation, thereby increasing their leverage.

**Provider Functions Are Capable of Migrating Among Levels and Types of Providers, if Unimpeded by Artificial Marketplace Barriers.**  The cost-containment movement stands to benefit considerably from the natural migration of functions that occurs in self-regulatory free markets. However, powerful restrictions exist in the health care marketplace that prevent or severely limit migration of function among health care providers. The FFS era, with its guild-like protection of physician prerogatives, resulted in a health care system built on elevated physician authority and backed up by scope-of-practice laws resistant to function migration. Migration of function in this instance means that the function shifts primarily to another level of provider or expands to include a broader community of providers. Battles will necessarily occur as other types of providers seek to remove barriers to assuming some of the functions of physicians.

Nowhere will there be greater conflict than in the behavioral health care arena, as psychologists press for prescription drug privileges and access to a broader range of Current Procedural Terminology (CPT) codes.

**Treatment Authority Fluctuates Among Providers, Consumers, and Health Plans.** If, as a hypothetical example, there were only 100 units of authority to divide among purchasers, consumers, and health plans, the way the units are shared will change as the health care system changes. In the FFS era the vast majority of those units of authority rested with the providers. In the cost-containment era some of the providers' authority for treatment decisions has been shifting to health plans. As health plans focus on enforcement of the use of clinical pathways and become involved in medical management of patients in other ways, provider authority will shift even further.

In the future the amount of authority that the provider holds will continue to erode as consumers take advantage of health information and the personal exchanges that the Internet makes possible. Consumers will also seek a share of the growing authority of health plans as they press for access to state-of-the-art treatments and push for inclusion of specific medications in health plan formularies.

**Cost-Containment Strategies Change in Response to Stakeholder Actions.** During the first 20 years of the cost-containment era, strategies employed by health plans to reduce expenditures underwent changes in response to feedback from consumers and providers. For example, after consumers clamored for more choice, health plans eventually accommodated by broadening their health plan options and networks. When providers and consumers alike complained forcefully about overly restrictive and cumbersome utilization management mechanisms, these were modified. It can be anticipated that cost-containment strategies in use today will be replaced as various stakeholders find ways to neutralize their impact. Given that cost-containment mechanisms will be continuously evolving, it will be important for providers in particular to be able to anticipate the direction of change because change differentially affects the viability of the various service delivery systems active in the marketplace.

**Fragmentation of the Purchaser Stakeholder Community Creates Instability Among All Stakeholders.** Managed competition theorists recognize that unless purchasers reduce fragmentation within their ranks, they will be poorly positioned to lead the change effort and will lack sufficient leverage to stimulate reliable change. From a market perspective, the purchaser stakeholder community, like the provider community, is fragmented. It consists of thousands of employers of varying size. They differ in the amount of leverage that they can exert in the marketplace, how sophisticated they are in applying managed competition strategies, the economic condition of their segment of the market, and other factors that they must consider in deciding how aggressively to push for cost containment. Purchaser diversity results in conflicting signals to health plans regarding cost-containment initiatives. For example, some purchasers staunchly support the aggressive cost-reduction mechanisms that health plans use, regardless of employee reaction. Others seek relaxation of those same mechanisms in response to employee dissatisfaction. When this happens, health plans of course adjust their cost-containment strategies; in turn, consumers and providers must likewise adjust. Governmental entities further complicate the situation. They are not only the largest purchasers, but they also act as regulators who must be responsive to concerns of consumers, insurers, providers, and employers. As regulators, governmental entities take certain actions that at some points in time block the use of specific cost-containment mechanisms and at others support them. A good example of the latter would be enforcement of antitrust regulations with respect to providers.

## FUTURE TRENDS

It is difficult to forecast the future when the health care marketplace is evolving without a clear managing entity to direct the change process and when new dynamics are emerging among stakeholders. Nonetheless, five possible changes are explored: the rise of disease management programs, the delivery of medical information over the Internet (or telemedicine), the possibility of a single-payer system, the potential demise of the independent MBHOs, and a movement toward a carved-in health care system.

### Disease Management

Disease management programs are comprehensive strategies that connect a set of interventions to a larger change model designed to treat and improve the health status of people with a specific chronic health condition. Typically, these programs contain elements that help reduce or eliminate barriers to coordination of care across settings, employ evidence-based clinical pathways, stay involved with participants throughout the life of the illness (not just when flareups occur), and represent collaborative efforts requiring active and willing participants.

There are several reasons why disease management programs will become increasingly important. In the years to come, the aging population of baby boomers means that there will be more people with chronic health conditions. Because the cost of care for this group will be substantially higher than for other health plan enrollees, disease management programs will be explored as a way of reducing expenditures. Because a few large MCOs now enroll a substantial share of the market (and in many communities a single MCO dominates), MCOs will not be able to avoid enrolling people with chronic conditions through risk avoidance, benefit design, or network gap strategies. They thus will have a greater incentive to learn how to care effectively for people with chronic health conditions. Decreased effectiveness of current cost-containment strategies will lead MCOs into more active involvement in medical care processes. Within a decade progress is expected to be made in establishing widely agreed-upon clinical pathways for specific diseases and their symptoms, leading to more effective disease management change models. Similarly, information systems essential to gathering data about participants, effectively communicating with them, and evaluating outcomes will improve and become more widespread among health care and their provider systems.

Regardless of the pace of adoption of disease management programs, psychologists should be well positioned to develop, administer, and provide disease management services—and not only in the behavioral health care sector. The skills of the psychologist in program design and evaluation are essential elements of all disease management programs. Sophisticated change models, which will be at the heart of each program, require knowledge about how to match the program design to people's readiness to change, motivate people to participate, change their relationship with their disease, sequence and pace the elements of a change process, and use peer and group reinforcement for change. Also, because disease management programs are broad in scale, involving multiple providers in multiple settings, it is necessary to develop the proper organizational climate for their implementation. The skills that psychologists have in organizational intervention and executive coaching will be invaluable for successful implementation of disease management programs.

## Tele-Medicine

The Internet has the possibility of revolutionizing various parts of the health care marketplace. There is already a vast amount of information available to consumers about medical issues and the treatment of illness. The Internet allows consumer stakeholders to become better informed. It gives them easy access to a much broader range of information, including clinical pathways or treatment protocols, which allows them to measure their treatment against established benchmarks. As interactive video improves and becomes increasingly available on the Internet, it will have the greatest impact on behavioral medicine. Because most of the functions that are needed to conduct an assessment and treatment of a behavioral health patient are available through the use of interactive video, access to treatment will change significantly.

The location of the provider and the patient will no longer be a critical factor. The definition of seeing someone for treatment in a community will change to include anyone who is in the network anywhere in the world. Networks will cross community and state boundaries. Providers who are viewed as experts in the treatment of a specific condition will now have a national audience. This phenomenon will greatly enhance consumer choice and will provide potential access to previously unavailable specialists in a specific disorder. Video conferencing will allow care to be delivered directly to the patient. Tele-medicine has the potential to put further pressure on providers. Membership in a network will no longer be determined by community reputation or location. MBHOs will have access to providers on a national basis and potentially will have a greater ability to direct referrals and negotiate fees. Because most national networks are not dependent on location, MBHOs will be able to develop much smaller national networks that still give consumers a wide range of choices.

## Single-Payer System

A single-payer system has been adopted throughout much of Europe; however, it is unlikely that the health care marketplace in the United States will move to such a system unless the current cost-containment strategies fail. For a single-payer system to contain costs effectively, it must be accompanied by a budget that puts a national limit on health care spending. The level of resistance by all stakeholders to a single-payer system appears to be high. As purchasers, employers would probably be taxed as a form of contribution to a single-payer system. Health plans as they are structured today would be out of business. Consumers would have to tolerate rationing of care in a model that would probably be experienced as even more adverse than current cost-containment strategies. Providers would have their fees set at a national level and would not have the option to treat patients outside the regulated system. Given the amount of resistance by all stakeholders, it is unlikely that there will be an emergence of a single-payer system as a viable model for cost containment.

## Further Consolidation of MBHOs

Many MBHOs are experiencing significant financial problems as the twenty-first century begins. There likely will be
further consolidation and the potential breakup of some of
these as a result. Most vulnerable will be those that are independent of large insurance companies. The instability that
these independent MBHOs experience in contracts and the increased demands that various health plans make on MHBOs
will continue to raise costs. The continued pressure to build
out an expensive infrastructure at a time of continued price decline will cause more company failures. Further consolidation
will reduce competition and slow the trend to lower prices.

## Carve-Ins

Although for almost a decade more voices have been raised in
favor of carving in, or including, behavioral health care within
the medical and surgical care system, little actual movement
in that direction has occurred. Because carve-out companies
currently hold the vast majority of MBHO contracts, there
would have to be a significant shift in the marketplace in order
to initiate and sustain a movement toward behavioral health
care carve-ins. A carve-in model offers many potential benefits to patients and could also create savings in medical costs.
The most appropriate placement for mental health practice
in a care delivery system is with primary care. Medical patients often are influenced by psychological problems. The
comorbidity of medical and psychiatric disorders is well documented. There is significant scientific support for the usefulness of behavioral medicine practices in medical clinics and
hospitals (Chiles, Lambert, & Hatch, 1999). The placement of
behavioral health care within medical clinics has the potential
to increase quality and contain costs.

## CONCLUSION

The cost-containment era is in its early phases. The turbulence it has caused in the health care environment is likely to
continue into the future. The dominant stakeholder, the purchaser, will likely continue to apply and possibly even intensify pressure on health plans to reduce expenditures. Health
plans in turn will cascade that pressure downward in the system to providers and consumers. The disruptive innovations
already active in the marketplace will continue to spawn incremental changes in the managed care systems of health
plans and modify the provider payment and service delivery
systems. The ascendancy of the network-managed care
model as the dominant service delivery system over the clinic
model ensures that providers and patients alike will have to

cope with the presence of an external intermediary in the
treatment process. In fact, the role of the external intermediary is expected to move deeper into the medical management
of patient care. The tools that managed care systems use will
continue to evolve and become more sophisticated.

The stakeholders will continue re-sorting their roles and relationships, but the stakeholder hierarchy that exists now will
not change substantially. Purchasers have been the primary
beneficiaries of the cost-containment era. They have achieved
significant cost reductions and have replaced providers in the
dominant position. Purchasers and health plans are likely to
occupy the top range of the hierarchy well into the future, although providers and consumers will search for ways to improve their standing. It is highly improbable that providers
will reoccupy the top range of the stakeholder hierarchy now
that the cost-containment era has undone all the key provider
protections that were at the heart of the FFS/TPP system. The
FFS principles that effectively prohibited selective contracting with providers, the involvement of intermediaries in the
provider-patient relationship, and the shifting of financial risk
to purchasers have been removed. Also, the marketplace principles of the FFS system that limited stakeholders to specific
functions and blocked cross functioning are no longer in operation. Ironically, although the principles that structured the
health care marketplace during the FFS era essentially have
been undone, FFS as a payment method (albeit with reduced
fees for services) remains active in the marketplace.

Whereas the changes stimulated by disruptive innovations
have effectively nullified the principles undergirding the FFS-
era system, they have not been as effective in providing a new,
stable marketplace structure. The absence of such a structure
will ineluctably lead the federal government to use its regulatory authority to address difficult-to-resolve issues. As both a
purchaser and regulator of health care, the federal government seems to be the only entity in a position to address such
key issues as the growing legion of people without health insurance and the challenge to maintain quality of care in a
high-priced, competitive environment. It probably will require both federal and state governmental entities to address
the anticompetitive features of medical scope of practice
laws. These laws undermine the potential cost savings that accrue when functions legitimately migrate from more expensive to less expensive providers.

The behavioral health care sector of the marketplace will
likely remain carved from general health care. There will be
increased battles over migration of functions within behavioral health care. Because psychotherapy essentially has
become a nonphysician activity, it has been unimpeded by
medical barriers to migration of function. Health plans,
through their managed care contracting systems, have caused

psychotherapy to move to a shared doctoral and subdoctoral activity. Medical associations will oppose extending prescription privileges to psychologists, and medical scope-of-practice laws will further impede this migration in function. Similar migration-of-function battles will become more frequent and intense within the behavioral segment of the health care continuum. This will make it hard for behavioral health care practitioners to organize along multidisciplinary lines in order to engage in direct contracting with purchasers and to resist reimbursement compression. Significant disciplinary differences and conflicts will have to be overcome, or MHBOs will continue to be the integrators of the different disciplines in behavioral health care.

# REFERENCES

Bassuk, E. L., & Holland, S. K. (1987). Accounting for high cost psychiatric care. *Business and Health, 4*(9), 38–41.

Chiles, J., Lambert, M. J., & Hatch, A. (1999). The impact of psychological interventions on medical cost offset: A meta-analytic review. *Clinical Psychology: Science and Practice, 6*(2), 204– 220.

Christensen, C. M., Bohmer, R., & Kenagy, J. (2000). Will disruptive innovations cure health care? *Harvard Business Review, 78*(5), 102–112.

Clinton, W. J. (1993). Health security: The president's report to the American people (U.S. DOCS. No. PREX 1.2:H 34/4). Washington, DC: U.S. Government Printing Office.

Drum, D. J. (1995). Changes in the mental health service delivery and finance systems and resulting implications for the national register. I. *Register Report, 21*(1), 4–10.

Ellwood, P. M., & Enthoven, A. C. (1995). Responsible choices: The Jackson Hole Group for Health Reform. *Health Affairs, 14*(2), 24–39.

Enthoven, A. C. (1993). The history and principles of managed competition. *Health Affairs, 12*(Suppl.), 24–48.

Enthoven, A. C., & Kronick, R. (1989a). A consumer-choice health plan for the 1990s, universal health insurance in a system designed to promote quality and economy. I. *The New England Journal Of Medicine, 320*(1), 29–37.

Enthoven, A. C., & Kronick, R. (1989b). A consumer-choice health plan for the 1990s, universal health insurance in a system designed to promote quality and economy. II. *The New England Journal Of Medicine, 320*(2), 94–101.

Enthoven, A. C., & Singer, S. J. (1997). Market and collective action in regulating managed care. *Health Affairs, 16*(6), 26–32.

Enthoven, A. C., & Singer, S. J. (1998). The managed care backlash and the task force in California. *Health Affairs, 17*(4), 95–110.

Lodge, B. (1994, June 29). Medical firm to plead guilty in fraud probe $362.7 million fine would set record. *Dallas Morning News.* Retrieved June 26, 2002, from http://www.ect.org/nme2 .html

Starr, P. (1982). *The social transformation of American medicine.* New York: Basic Books.

VHA Inc., Deloitte, & Touche. (2000). *Health care 2000: A strategic assessment of the health care environment in the United States.* Irving, TX: Author.

Weller, C. D. (1984). "Free choice" as a restraint of trade in American health care delivery and insurance. *Iowa Law Review, 69,* 1351–1392.

Zelman, W. A. (1996). The changing health care marketplace: Private ventures, public interests. San Francisco: Jossey-Bass.

CHAPTER 23

# Role of Technology in Clinical Psychology

KJELL ERIK RUDESTAM, RONALD A. GIANNETTI, AND B. HUDNALL STAMM

Clinical psychology has always maintained a fascination with technology. Unlike many other health professions, clinical psychology emerged from a discipline that was deeply rooted in the scientific laboratory, and early twentieth-century behaviorists such as J. B. Watson and B. F. Skinner relied upon laboratory instrumentation and measurement technology both to stimulate their ideas and to enrich and support their contributions to the field. Meanwhile, it is easy to overlook the fact that consumers of applied psychology have always been intrigued by the trappings of technology in the guise of promoting mental health. Witness the popularity, both in Europe and in the United States, of Anton Mesmer, the charismatic Austrian physician, and his pseudoscientific approach to curing a wide range of psychological and physical complaints using a mythical spiritual fluid called "animal magnetism." Blending hypnotism and medicine, Mesmer asked patients to hold onto electric wires that had been inserted, together with magnets, in a large tub of water, while, dressed flamboyantly in flowing purple robes, he moved around the tub, dancing, chanting, and putting the patients into deep curative trances (Cushman, 1995).

At a more mundane level, no doctoral student or clinical psychologist working in an academic institution in the 1960s and 1970s can forget using typewriters to write multiple drafts of dissertations, professional papers, and research articles, relying on hand calculators to compute most statisti-

cal analyses, or, eventually, lugging IBM cards to mainframe computers for more prodigious analyses. What has changed, of course, is the sophistication of the available technology and its widespread availability to working psychologists, as well as to the public.

The advent of the widespread adoption of technology by clinical psychology came with the personal computer in the 1980s and proliferated with universal access to the Internet in the following decade. There were, of course, a few clinicians who made noteworthy use of mainframe computers in clinical practice long before this time. The earliest software program that could be used for a computer and a person to engage in a therapeutic discussion using ordinary language was created by Joseph Weizenbaum at MIT in 1966 and dubbed ELIZA. Intended more as an experiment in artificial intelligence than as an attempt to devise a talking therapist, ELIZA could answer questions. The first part of Weizenbaum's program extracted information from material typed into it by the patient; the second part used a script that formulated an appropriate reply. The computer program might be viewed as a primitive Rogerian therapist, kind, nonjudgmental, and simplistic, but realistic enough that people would "forget" that they were interacting with a machine. Another experiment in creating a software program that could conduct psychotherapy was initiated by William Colby at about the same time (Colby, Watt, & Gilbert, 1966). Although Colby and his colleagues hoped that their program might eventually serve as a low-cost provider of psychotherapy in hospitals and mental health centers but expressed reservations about its efficacy, Weizenbaum retained considerable misgivings about the ethics of using a computer to substitute for a respectful, caring human being as a psychotherapist (Bloom, 1992).

## Technology Usage by Clinical Psychologists

In many ways it is a shame that the computer entered the psychology field as a psychotherapist, since that is among the most difficult and controversial activities that it might perform (Bloom, 1992). With the exception of a few adventurous psychologists, there appears to be a significant lag between the advent of technology in everyday life and the use of technology by the practicing clinical psychologist. According to Kemenoff (1999), the primary use of computers in clinical practice appears to be for administrative and clerical purposes. McMinn, Buchanan, Ellens, and Ryan (1999) recently conducted a survey of 420 American Psychological Association (APA) members in clinical practice (out of 1,000 possible respondents) regarding their use of and attitudes toward the implementation of technology to assist their office practices. McMinn et al. divided technological advances into three tiers based on level of advancement. The first wave consists of tools for keeping records and maintaining an office more efficiently and includes devices such as fax machines, photocopiers, and computerized software for billing purposes. The second wave refers to current tools that directly affect patient care, such as computer applications of test administration and interpretation, and adjunctive computerized educational programs to increase self-esteem or reduce drug and alcohol use. The third wave represents more emerging technologies, such as videoconferencing and using virtual reality programs for overcoming phobias. The authors were surprised to find that computer usage in office practice had not increased appreciably since a comparable survey by Farrell (1989) a decade earlier. A majority of respondents employed computers to assist in patient billing, but only a minority used computers fairly or very often for test scoring (26%), test interpretation (20%), maintaining patient records (22%), and more esoteric applications such as teleconferencing for psychotherapy (.2%) or virtual reality for treating anxiety disorders (.2%). By far the most common "technological" practices were consulting with colleagues on the telephone (95%) and providing crisis intervention on the telephone (96%).

The lag in adopting available technological tools to assist in clinical practice is accompanied by—or perhaps affected by—the respondents' concerns about the ethics of such behavior. Significant numbers of psychologists were concerned about the confidentiality implications of, for instance, using the computer to store patient records or a fax machine to forward confidential records. Providing direct clinical services on the Internet seemed fraught with ethical concerns, as did providing regular psychotherapy on the telephone (although adjunctive telephone therapy, as in crisis intervention or screening, seemed to be acceptable). A majority of psychologists (60%) thought that the adoption of therapy via computer was probably unethical, an opinion seemingly based not only on confidentiality considerations but also on "reticence to embrace technologies that usurp or supplant the therapeutic relationship" (p. 169). In short, third-wave technologies raised the most concerns, and second-wave technologies raised more concerns than first-wave technologies. The unfamiliar is suspect.

One might argue that change in the field of psychology proceeds at a glacial pace, but one cannot apply that argument to the availability of technology that promises (or threatens) to impact current practice in the field. The real hazard in writing this chapter is that the content will become obsolete upon the date of publication. Thus, we are more interested in exploring the issues than in reviewing available software and hardware. The fact is that all sorts of technological gadgets and programs are becoming available for streamlining the office practice of clinical psychology, ranging from computerized billing programs to automated test scoring systems to hi-tech relaxation chairs. Rather than describing the kinds of products that can currently be found in a good mail-order catalog from a respectable mental health vendor, we will focus on what seems to be most germane to the practice of clinical psychology and divide the chapter into three broad areas: (a) technology in the education and training of clinical psychologists, (b) technology in supervision and consultation, and (c) technology in psychological assessment and treatment.

## TECHNOLOGY IN EDUCATION AND TRAINING

In a recent invited address to the APA, Diane Halpern, winner of an Award for Distinguished Career Contributions to Education and Training in Psychology, noted that changing the university is like changing a cemetery: You don't get help from the inhabitants (Halpern, 1998). Nonetheless, with or without the sanction and blessing of faculty and students, technology-mediated instruction has taken the university by storm.

The history of computer-assisted instruction, first attempted using time-sharing computers in the 1960s, has been clearly described by Linda Harisim and her colleagues (Harasim, Hiltz, Teles, & Turoff, 1995). Communication took place over dumb terminals connected to mainframe computers or dial-up telephone lines. In 1969, the U.S. government experimented with dedicated telephone lines for data exchange by constructing the Advanced Research Projects Agency Network (ARPANET) to connect researchers with remote computer centers to share resources. It was not long before these researchers wanted to exchange messages with one another about their projects. The electronic mail (e-mail) function was born and became immensely popular. Other communication networks (e.g., USENET, BITNET, CSNET) followed, still predominantly connecting researchers and scientists. Eventually, the Internet, a global network of networks, supplanted these individual efforts.

Murray Turoff is given credit for designing the first computer conferencing system in 1970 (Hiltz & Turoff, 1978). Today there are many conferencing systems available that support not only the discussion feature but other, more sophisticated features as well, including personal messaging and audio and video capability. Bulletin boards, common spaces for posting messages over the computer, were developed in the late 1970s (Sterling, 1992) but did not proliferate until a decade later. Both of these functions are at the heart of the implementation of computer networks for training and education.

Computer conferencing systems were applied to course activity in higher education in the 1980s and remain a prominent feature of online education today. According to Harasim (1998), there are three major applications of computer conferencing technology in education: (a) as the primary teaching mechanism for one or more courses, (b) as an enhancement to traditional face-to-face courses, and (c) as a forum for discussions and information exchange with peers and experts and a means of accessing online resources. All of these variants have found their way into the training of clinical psychologists.

The use of the Internet has been well integrated into higher education at the present time and augurs to increase. Almost every institution of higher learning has incorporated some aspects of the new technology into its curriculum delivery system. Most universities and training institutions of clinical psychologists still rely on traditional methods of face-to-face education, and there is doubt among many that computer networks can replace the personal touch in training students in the more interpersonal skills of the psychologist. Most institutions use computer networks as an adjunct to more traditional classroom experiences. Some assignments or the occasional course might be offered online, where discussion can run more freely and library resources are more available. In other schools the online environment is fully integrated into the curriculum and plays a major role in the delivery of education.

The Fielding Institute, Union Institute, Walden University, and Saybrook Institute are among the few major graduate institutions that have, for several decades, been training students who are dispersed from one another and from the institution itself to become clinical psychologists. They represent what has historically been known as "distance education." According to the U.S. Congress for Technology Assessment, distance education refers to "linking of a teacher and students in several geographic locations via technology that allows for interaction" (Daniel & Stevens, 1998, p. 162). However, many distance learning institutions that have come to adopt a strong online presence were functioning prior to the Internet by relying upon individually directed study, mail, the telephone, and/or infrequent residential sessions for contact between students and instructors. They usually established a distance education model in order to provide an educational opportunity for a group of geographically dispersed students, such as midlife, midcareer professionals who could not easily give up their family and work responsibilities in order to move to a campus-based institution for a lengthy period of time.

It is important to clarify that there is a difference between distance education and computer-networked education. Adherence to a distributed model of training does not necessarily imply the adoption of an online teaching environment. Distance education flourished long before the advent of the personal computer (Maehl, 2000). Distance education institutions have not necessarily embraced online learning, but when they have done so, the transition to a communication-based technology has often gone more smoothly because of the overlap of values and skills required to succeed in the setting.

More recent entrants into the online education field include Capella University, which offers a totally online degree program in clinical psychology; the American Schools of Professional Psychology, which is developing an online presence through Argosy Online, started in 1999; and the University of Phoenix, which offers a host of academic programs and continuing education courses online. The Fielding Institute, which has the only distributed APA-accredited PhD program in clinical psychology, uses a blended model, which relies on a combination of distance activities and residential activities. Students come together for national and regional sessions with faculty and one another and participate in face-to-face seminars, colloquia, and other learning activities at those times. They also participate in monthly residential "cluster groups" led by core faculty who are distributed throughout the United States. The computer augments the educational experience rather than defining it. Students and faculty communicate regularly via e-mail (an increasingly common practice in more traditional schools as well), access bulletin boards for course and institutional information, deliberate online in faculty and committee meetings, and have the option of taking or offering several of their courses online.

Fielding's approach to incorporating online coursework into the clinical psychology curriculum is illustrative of creative efforts currently being conducted by many other academic institutions. By and large, courses are offered as asynchronous online seminars, although students have the opportunity to select face-to-face seminars and tutorial options to taking courses online. The asynchronous format has the advantage of allowing students to participate in a class whenever and wherever they wish, within the time constraints and requirements of a particular course. It is also true that various faculty are experimenting with real-time teaching aids, including chat rooms and audio and visual displays. Each "class" is limited to about eight students, so there is ample opportunity for online discussion. Students post assignments and papers on an electronic forum and respond to one another's work with both critical feedback and motivational support. Over time a clear set of norms has developed in order to maximize the use of the electronic medium for academic coursework. The norms include clear deadlines for work, the types of messages that are appropriate and inappropriate, the number of log-ons required per week, and the role of the instructor in terms of facilitation, modeling, and structuring boundaries (Stevens-Long & Crowell, 2002).

## Learning Outcomes of Online Education

At this point in time, there are no definitive outcome data that allow us to argue for the superiority of online learning to classroom learning. There are some studies accumulating that find online classes, that is, courses that use computer networking as the university classroom, to be at least as effective in producing learning outcomes, as measured by exam scores and student feedback, as the traditional classroom. One recent study reported better examination performance from students taking a web-based introductory psychology course than those taking a traditional lecture course and attributed the findings to the fact that online sections force students to interact with the course material (Maki, Maki, Patterson, & Whittaker, 2000).

There is also an emerging literature on the dynamics of online groups and how they are similar to and different from face-to-face work groups or therapy groups (see, for example, Sproul & Kiesler, 1991). One consistent advantage of online groups is that the lack of social and visual cues that characterize the asynchronous learning environment helps to level the playing field for students: quiet and reserved students in traditional classes are often equal participants in online classes; gender and ethnicity diminish as concerns of engagement. Moreover, evidence suggests not only that students learn the course content as well as they do in traditional

classrooms, but that a significant amount of metalearning takes place. Students learn how to communicate in writing, how to give and receive feedback sensitively and effectively, how to manage time and collaborate, and how group dynamics evolve over the course of time.

As universities and training institutions scramble to keep up with the onslaught of Internet-based distance education, there are scant data available to offer guidance to what works and what does not work. A recent report produced by The Institute for Higher Education Policy, funded by the National Education Association (2000), offers benchmarks for success. The following ingredients are distilled from those that were determined to be essential for quality education over the Internet:

- A reliable, optimally fail-safe technology delivery system with a well-supported and maintained centralized infrastructure.

- Clear guidelines and faculty-student agreement regarding times for completion of assignments and faculty response, including timely, constructive feedback to students.

- The development, design, and delivery of courses based on clear guidelines regarding minimal standards, with the selection of technology used to deliver the course content determined by desired learning outcomes.

- Courses designed to require students to demonstrate the skills of analysis, synthesis, and evaluation and the methods of effective research.

- Facilitated interaction among students and between students and faculty.

- Students prepared to participate on the basis of self-motivation, commitment, and access to the technology requirements.

- Student access to electronic libraries on the Internet and training to obtain the necessary information.

- Student and faculty access to adequate technical assistance and training prior to and during the courses.

## Pedagogy

Electronic teaching developed from advances in communication technology, not from innovative changes in pedagogy (Stevens-Long & Crowell, 2002). This fact has profound implications for identifying a suitable place for technology in the training and education of clinical psychologists. Generally speaking, educational institutions that experiment with the incorporation of sophisticated technology into their training programs do so within the context of their dominant pedagogical principles and historical attitudes toward education.

When that pedagogy relies upon the authoritative expertise of the instructor, who disseminates knowledge and information to relatively passive students using lectures supported by audiovisual aids, that same pedagogy is transposed to the electronic environment. In that context, instructional materials would be presented to the student online in the form of lecturettes (either in real time or in archived video form), which the student downloads and provides evidence of absorbing through the completion of exams or papers. These measures of competence might take the form of responding to a set of exam questions on a website or writing a term paper and submitting it to the professor by e-mail. The professor evaluates the material, perhaps provides some feedback, and the student receives a grade in the course. Thus, reliance on a prevailing educational paradigm in the guise of computer-mediated coursework means that face-to-face instructional practices (and distance learning by correspondence) are now being replicated in a new medium. However, this may not be the best and most effective use of the online environment.

In one study, 176 teachers were surveyed regarding differences and similarities between teaching online using computer networks and teaching in the traditional classroom (Harasim & Yung, 1993). Ninety percent of the respondents articulated the following kinds of differences characteristic of the online experience:

- The teacher becomes a facilitator and mentor.
- Students become active participants in discussion.
- Students and faculty have more access to resources.
- Students become increasingly independent.
- Students develop more equal learning opportunities with significantly more group interactions.
- Learning and teaching become more collaborative.
- Teachers and students operate more as equals with less hierarchy.
- Students have more time to reflect on ideas and exchange ideas.

Such statements suggest that computer-mediated communication technology has the potential to radically alter the graduate training experience. We would argue that to take full advantage of the opportunities of communication technology for training purposes implies significant shifts in thinking about educational pedagogy. Michael Schrage (1990) suggests that we need to shift our thinking from viewing technology as a means of managing information to regarding technology as a medium of relationships. As Schrage puts it, "Technology is really a medium for creating productive environments" (p. 67). Technologies can be effective if they are designed to empower students' engagement with the learning process and collaboration. Computer networks lend themselves well to the training of clinical psychologists, moving students beyond simply assimilating information to engaging in a "community of practice" (Brown & Duguid, 2000). This is what accreditation agencies refer to as "professional socialization," an enculturation process that extends beyond the warranting or credentialing function of psychology training programs.

## Implications for the Future

It appears that networked learning needs to be part of a larger strategy to reconceptualize education and build learning organizations and a knowledge society (Senge, 2000). The status of the university as the core training site for clinical psychologists is threatened by the possibility of creating an international university without walls enabled by communication-mediated technology. The debate about the future form and function of the university promises to be ferocious (Noam, 1995; Tehranian, 1996). Building training programs to grow tomorrow's psychologists and meet the continuing education needs of today's psychologists will require principled design that focuses on collaboration rather than competition; reflective thinking (Schon, 1987); and active self-directed learning that includes creative, real-world problem-solving.

Cynthia Belar, chief of APA's Education Directorate (1998), has recently noted that psychology seems to be slipping behind other disciplines in the adoption of telecommunication and computer-based learning programs. The trick is to determine what aspects of clinical training can be automated and which require extensive faculty time and attention. For instance, there is no reason why certain core courses, those that stipulate a standard curriculum, cannot be offered on CD-ROM and other self-paced learning programs that students can master individually (or in groups). This could extend to the core clinical service curriculum as well, perhaps including interviewing skills, mental status exams, test administration, and some intervention principles. Belar suggests adding a virtual reality component to training graduate students in skill development in assessment and intervention. In this way, the public is protected from inexperienced therapists and assessors who are low on the learning curve. It may also mean that there will be greater cooperation among institutions and training programs, which might share programs easily, because space and time would cease to be mitigating factors.

In sum, we agree with Dede's (2000) futuristic vision of a gradual erosion of the distinction between distance education and classroom-based education to a model that negotiates a balance between the two approaches based on the particular subject matter, group of students, and learning objectives. It will be an ongoing challenge to design effective learning environments that are responsive to the changing face of educational institutions, as training programs seek to respond appropriately to a clientele that is demanding increasing flexibility due to issues of work, age, geography, and experience. Thus, we will need to know how each interactive medium shapes the cognitive, affective, and social interactions of participants.

## TECHNOLOGY IN SUPERVISION AND CONSULTATION

A number of individuals and institutions have explored the application of computer technology to supervising or training clinical psychology students or mental health practitioners in clinical skill acquisition. One is a software tutoring system for helping develop entry-level family therapy skills called The Therapist Education and Supervision System (TESS; R. C. Smith, 1996). Another is a self-instructional, video-based package that has been successfully used to teach basic clinical interviewing skills, including the ability to ask open-ended questions, paraphrase content, reflect feelings, and engage in confrontation (Carter, 1997).

A time-honored supervision and training method, the group case presentation, has been modified using computer software (Homrich, 1997). Group Support Systems (GSS), a computerized method of facilitating work-group tasks, was used to structure the psychotherapy case presentations and was compared with a more traditional format. The discussions using GSS yielded higher levels of participation, greater trainee satisfaction, a higher level of perceived quality of interaction, and superior learning.

Janoff and Schoenholtz-Read (1999) have introduced web-based collaboration into the clinical training and supervision of clinical psychology students. The core components of their group psychotherapy training model include theory presentations, experiential work on group leadership facilitation, and clinical case consultations. They blend face-to-face meetings between students and faculty supervisors with online posting of documents and threaded conversations on a discussion forum.

### Telehealth

The introduction of online supervision of graduate students within a psychology training program is but part of a larger domain, called telehealth, which supports a variety of health-related activities, including providing psychological and medical supervision and consultation at a distance. One recent source defines telehealth as "the use of telecommunications and information technology to provide access to health assessment, diagnosis, intervention, consultation, supervision, education and information across distance" (Nickelson, 1998, p. 527).

The number of papers associated with telehealth has grown rapidly over the last decade, as has the number of telehealth programs. The first telehealth program opened at the University of Nebraska in 1959. In 1994, there were 17 telehealth programs; by 1995, there were 50 (Telemedicine Information Exchange, 2000). Since 1995, mental health has become one of the most important telehealth applications, with a variety of activities, including use of websites, telephones, e-mail, online videoconferencing, store and forward applications, virtual reality, and information transmission from peripherals and tests (Jerome et al., 2000; Rothchild, 1999; Stamm, 1998, 2000). The role of psychologists in this emerging and varied market has yet to be determined (Jerome et al., 2000; Stamm, 1998).

Supervision and consultation are common and can include activities such as specialists supervising generalists, doctoral-level psychologists supervising midlevel or paraprofessional caregivers, supervision for licensure, and peer-to-peer supervision to prevent burnout and vicarious or secondary trauma (Stamm, 1999). An extension of supervision and consultation is professional-to-professional consultation, in which the primary care provider introduces the patient to an expert at a distant location. As patients become more comfortable with the technology and, particularly, with the provider at the remote location, there is a decreasing need for two professionals. For example, a teacher or principal in a rural school might initiate the relationship between his or her student and a distant school psychologist. As the student gains confidence in the relationship, he or she may meet directly with the remote professional with only modest technical assistance to begin and end the session.

Telehealth is increasingly common in correctional settings, linking inmates with their families to improve family function and to speed reintegration into the community (Magaletta, Fagan, & Ax, 1998). Similarly, telehealth is used with families who are separated by institutionalization for serious mental illnesses (Stamm, 1998). Telehealth also supports the mental health of caregivers, by reducing the effects of isolation, such as burnout and compassion fatigue, and restoring competency and positive control (Stamm, 1999; Terry, 1999).

Because of reductions in cost and technological difficulty, the choice to participate in a telehealth system can be made by small organizations, by individual providers, and even by consumers. This allows patients to play an ever-expanding role in selecting their own health care.

Telehealth distributes control for care to a larger circle of people than has heretofore been common. At the same time, there is a digital divide that augments health disparities. Income is a major predictor of accessing the Internet (National Telecommunications and Information Administration, 1999), and the divide between rich and poor is increasing in severity: the gap between the highest and lowest income widened 29% between 1997 and 1999. Whites are more likely to have Internet access than any other racial group, and urban areas are more likely to have access than rural areas (National Telecommunications and Information Administration, 1999).

## Models of Training and Supervision

Binder (1999) has argued persuasively that interactive computer technology can significantly alter and improve training and supervision in therapy technique. He distinguishes between "declarative knowledge" and "procedural knowledge." Declarative knowledge relates to how therapists employ "working models" to organize clinical information and ascribe meaning to it, draw on clinical data from previous and current experiences, and use theoretical concepts to organize the data. Beginning therapists have relatively unformed, primitive working models; over time, new information and conceptual knowledge become integrated with previous experiences. Declarative knowledge becomes transformed as the novice eventually becomes an expert. Historically, according to Binder, students obtain declarative therapeutic knowledge through course work and direct supervision, in which the supervisor offers suggestions and points out missed opportunities and poor decision-making from clinical sessions that have already taken place. Increasingly, therapy treatment manuals are available to help students acquire declarative knowledge in more precise ways.

However, how does an inexperienced clinical psychologist learn when and how to implement theories and concepts of practice? One does not learn to ride a bicycle by reading and talking about it! This is where procedural knowledge comes in, the application of declarative knowledge to real-work situations, what Donald Schon (1987) described as "knowing-in-action." As Binder (1999) puts it, "The competent practitioner is capable of constructing a working model of a problem situation that effectively guides problem-solving behavior" (p. 711). Whereas declarative knowledge may be learned from didactic experiences, including progressively sophisticated treatment manuals, procedural knowledge requires the active involvement of the learner, who is exposed to a "prearranged

sequence of progressively more complex clinical problems, knowledge and methods" (p. 715). Supervision based on therapy audiotapes or videotapes does not afford this level of controlled learning. However, the simulation of real clinical experiences, based on structured sequences of events, can now be captured using interactive, multimedia computer technology, providing the student with guided interactive practice with immediate feedback.

At this point in time, developments are under way to improve this technology. Engen, Finken, Luschei, and Kenney (1994) and Maple (as cited in McMinn, 1998) have designed interactive videodisks that offer psychology students choice points during simulated psychotherapy sessions. Each choice point invites an action and an outcome, which can be used for learning purposes. So-called expert system-based, computer-assisted training programs (ESCATs) are also proliferating. They draw on artificial intelligence technology to model the decision-making processes of experts within specialty fields. Thus, the Rorschach Trainer (McMinn & Scanish, 1996) helps students learn Exner's Comprehensive System for scoring the Rorschach on their own, and an ESCAT designed by Todd (1996) helps students learn how to diagnose eating disorders.

## Technology and Research Training

We would be remiss not to include some commentary regarding technological developments in research training and application as pertaining to the practice of clinical psychology. In this context we will briefly describe four general applications of computer-enhanced communication to research activities, as opposed to more technical advancements in measurement technology and data analysis. First, research training, as part of the curriculum, can also take place over the Internet. One pertinent example is the online teaching of statistics, a content area that requires a great deal of individual tutoring and practice. Many statistics texts now come with software for acquiring mastery of data analysis concepts and applications, and there are sophisticated training programs available through vendors such as SPSS and SYSTAT. These programs typically take a modular approach and include exposure to concepts and provide problem-solving experience with detailed feedback until the student meets the criteria for competence. Saba and Hodges (2002) regularly teach a popular graduate-level course in statistics to clinical psychology students online. It is a multimodal approach that includes group discussion, individualized exercises, and a chat room in which students can see, work on, and confer about statistical problems while receiving real-time consultation and feedback from the instructor. Other examples of teaching statistics online can be found in Harasim et al. (1995).

Second, psychologists are now engaged in trying to understand the impact of technology on human behavior and attitudes. Consequently, there is a growing literature on the influence of cyberspace on personality (Pratt, 1995). Moreover, the Internet is quickly becoming a viable new laboratory for experimentation and a wonderful environment for studying psychological concepts such as collaboration, aggression, leadership, friendship, romance, and group behavior (Wallace, 1999).

Third, we are all aware that the research dissertation (and, for that matter, much of university-based research) has historically been oriented around obtaining data from undergraduate psychology students at the university that the student researcher is attending. Research in clinical psychology cries out for real-world application, and the opportunity to capitalize on computer-based communication methods is notable. It now becomes much easier for psychologists in different parts of the world to collaborate on research projects not only by communicating via e-mail but also by instantaneously sharing data and research records with one another. Multisite research becomes convenient and economical, a particular benefit for researchers without access to major funding or alternative resources. Faculty and students in different areas can each collect data on the same phenomenon and readily share their findings, thus claiming a truly representative and heterogeneous sample. The Internet also becomes a viable means of data collection. Participants who share a particular characteristic or interest can be sought and accessed through listservs, news groups, chat rooms, or search engines. The same scales or surveys can be distributed readily to many more people than can practically be reached face-to-face, and responses can be simply—and anonymously—returned and data downloaded and analyzed automatically by the researcher. In effect, the Internet becomes an entry point for global access to a mother lode of rich and diverse real-world research data. This fact has not been lost on the American Psychological Society, which maintains a listing of Web-based studies on its home page (Jerome et al., 2000).

Finally, the world of electronic publishing is exploding. Within the profession of clinical psychology, it becomes increasingly possible to disseminate papers and articles to peers and students using the Internet. Jerome et al. (2000) have recently discussed how technological changes are affecting the editorial review process of psychology journals. Electronic journals are still in their infancy but are certain to multiply in the near future. Martin Seligman, former APA president and highly regarded spokesperson for clinical

psychology, led the way in 1998 by inaugurating the publication of the electronic journal *Prevention and Treatment* under his editorship.

## TECHNOLOGY IN PSYCHOLOGICAL ASSESSMENT AND TREATMENT

### Public Use of the Internet for Education and Psychotherapy

The Internet is currently being used by the public to obtain counseling and psychotherapy both in self-help form and from licensed professionals. As of 1999 there were over 28,000 newsgroups on the Internet (Fink, 1999), and many of these have a focus of sharing and responding to specific types of psychological problems. There are online groups for every conceivable type of shared interest or problem, ranging from infertility to financial setbacks.

Virtual support groups have multiplied by the ease at which they can be created using listservs. The popularity of many of these online support groups is astounding. This should come as no surprise because the market for self-help books and videotapes has been huge for many years and online groups can be viewed as a more technological iteration of the same need. As might be anticipated from self-help groups, responses are uneven in quality, often validating, but not necessarily wise or insightful.

People who might not otherwise seek treatment or possess accurate knowledge regarding mental health issues now have a wealth of information and access to resources readily available. Search engines are a rapid vehicle for locating useful information and dialogue on health promotion and health maintenance. Widespread access to information, which is what the Internet offers, can help demystify psychology, which for many remains an esoteric discipline. For others the possibility of revealing deep secrets online seems safe, since the home computer coupled to the Internet allows the opportunity to hide in anonymity. In this regard, there is empirical evidence available to suggest that there is therapeutic value in personal, diarylike writing about traumatic events and personal frustrations (Pennebaker & Beall, 1986; Pennebaker, Colder, & Sharp, 1990).

One can also be concerned about the limitations of nonprofessional help for serious mental disorders. There is reason to believe that vulnerable people do express suicidality in cyberspace (Baume, Rolfe, & Clinton, 1998) and suicidologists are concerned about the so-called Werther effect, which refers to the potential for distressed individuals to become suicidal through social learning, contagion, imitation, or suggestion, processes that can easily be facilitated by electronic newsgroups.

Some professionals have noted that many consumers are using contacts with anonymous others on the Web as surrogates for significant others in daily life. It is quite easy to construct a "virtual community" in cyberspace. How do these communities function like psychotherapy, and, more importantly, are they a threat to the professional practice of psychotherapy? Moreover, if they are, what negatives arise from the threat, and what might that threat produce that is positive?

It could be said that we have been here before. The advent of the telephone certainly made it possible to be connected to others at great distance. However, there are differences. Miller and Gergen (1998) have noted eight of them:

1. The Internet allows for immediate contact with large numbers of individuals who share a specific problem.

2. Numbers of contacts and geographical distance do not influence the cost, which is low.

3. Bulletin boards and e-mail provide the option of asynchronous communication, allowing ample time for reflection and reply. Telephones do not.

4. It is elementary to maintain a written record of online communications.

5. The lack of social markers, such as age, gender, ethnicity, and physical appearance, reduces the risk of prejudice in communications.

6. The sheer scope of the Internet allows for a wide array of opinions from individuals from very different walks in life.

7. The medium offers anonymity.

8. Communications tend to be two-way, and recipients of help can easily shift into the role of helpers.

Miller and Gergen (1998) conceived an elegant study of tracking conversations across one Internet discussion group (chat room) for a period of 11 months to explore the similarity between the conversations that take place online with those more characteristic of traditional psychotherapy. As an exemplar they chose a discussion group on suicide from an Issues in Mental Health forum. They divided the discourse among participants into five domains: (a) help-seeking interchanges, (b) informative interchanges, (c) supportive interchanges, (d) growth-promoting interchanges, and (e) punitive interchanges. They discovered that punitive interchanges were rare, informative interchanges were moderately available, and supportive interchanges were very common. Participants provided sympathy and encouragement, validated one another's experiences, offered helpful (and nonhelpful) advice,

and even asked provocative questions. However, they rarely provided the interpretations, reflections, reframing, and metacommentary that we associate with experienced psychotherapists. Thus, the authors concluded that Internet discussion groups are useful for helping others help themselves and have therapeutic potential, but that the field of professional psychotherapy is probably safe from this competition because it promises to offer a level of reflective understanding rarely seen in cyberspace self-help groups. They suggest that the real challenge ahead for clinical psychology is how to effectively combine the power of the Internet with what we have traditionally been trained to do face-to-face.

## Professional Use of the Internet

Russ Newman (2000), executive director of the APA, recently declared in the *Monitor on Psychology* that

> We have an opportunity to be a preeminent profession within the Internet culture . . . the question is not simply whether health services should be delivered via the Internet, but rather what services under *what conditions* can be effectively delivered through the Internet or other telecommunications technologies. (p. 24)

Professional mental health workers, including psychologists, have discovered the Internet as a business opportunity. The first for-profit psychological practice that is administered by professionals on the Internet goes by the name Shrink-Link (Binik, Cantor, Ochs, & Meana, 1997). A standard procedure is for clients to post questions online to an expert panel and receive an e-mail response within 24–72 hours, together with a bill for services. There is even a Directory of Internet Psychotherapists (Ainsworth, 1997) who practice what is commonly called "cybertherapy." Fee setting is innovative because session time takes on a whole new meaning in cyberspace. Thus, charges either accrue per minute of response time ($1.50–$2.00 a minute is typical) or per e-mail ($20.00–$25.00; Fink, 1999). Patients approach therapists online for either single interactions, in the same way that they might write Dear Abby, or multiple contact. Is this psychotherapy? Probably not in terms of how most psychologists define the term, but reports suggest that customer satisfaction is high (Fink, 1999), and it is accessible to individuals who have physical disabilities or who live in remote areas.

It seems evident that there will be an increasingly creative use of the Internet to provide psychological services in the near future. Online group psychotherapy (Colon, 1999) and crisis intervention (Wilson & Lester, 1998) are just two recent innovations. This growth will be accompanied by the need to resolve concerns raised by the professional community, such as concerns about confidentiality (Pope & Vetter, 1992) and cross-jurisdictional licensing and accountability. Fundamentally, should the provider of care be licensed in the state where the care originates or the state to which the care goes? (Nickelson, 1998)

Koocher and Morray (2000) surveyed state attorney generals regarding the delivery of mental health services via telemetry and discovered no established standards across the states. Rural states are more advanced than their urban counterparts. Koocher and Morray predict increasing regulatory and legal precedent and recommend that psychologists (a) assess their competency in providing care through the medium, (b) consult with their professional liability insurance carrier, (c) seek consultation from their colleagues, (d) provide patients written emergency procedure information, (e) inform clients of the standard limitations and cautions regarding mental health care as well as potential risks to privacy due to the technology used, and (f) clearly inform patients what types of services can be offered.

### Computer-Assisted Assessment

Most applications of computers in clinical assessment are in the areas of computerized assisted interviewing or in psychological test administration, scoring, and interpretation. This discussion is limited to initial assessment in general practice. The interested reader can find excellent and relatively recent revues of computer applications in neuropsychological assessment (Kane & Kay, 1997) and behavioral medicine (Werner, 1995). In addition, edited volumes are available on adaptive testing (Drasgow & Oslo-Buchanan, 1999) and behavioral health care management (Trabin, 1996).

Computerized interviewing began at the University of Wisconsin. A group of researchers experimented with using computers to collect medical history information directly from patients (Slack, Hicks, Reed, & Van Cura, 1966). Although this was labeled "interviewing," it amounted to programming a computer to administer a questionnaire. The branching logic capabilities of the computer permitted questions to be presented contingent upon the responses to previous questions. This was possible only to a very limited degree with pencil and paper. The enthusiasm for this research found its way into taking psychiatric histories (Greist, Klein, & Van Cura, 1973; Maultsby & Slack, 1971). Others attempted to collect and report more comprehensive descriptive data such as patient problem lists (D. R. Fowler, Finkelstein, Penk, Bell, & Itzig, 1987) and psychosocial histories (Giannetti, 1987).

In the early 1970s most clinicians had little or no knowledge of computers. Many resisted the very idea that computers might be used to collect data directly from patients. They viewed computers as a dehumanizing hazard when applied to any aspect of patient care. The early studies on computer-administered interviews served to establish their credibility. The majority of patients enjoyed responding to computer-administered questionnaires and frequently preferred them to clinician interviews (e.g., Angle, Ellinwood, Hay, Johnsen, & Hay, 1977; Card et al., 1974; Lucas, 1977; Lucas, Mullin, Luna, & McInroy, 1977), and the agreement between information collected by computer and clinical interview was very high (Carr, Ghosh, & Ancill, 1983; Grady & Ephross, 1977).

Other computer applications were based upon a formalization of the clinical diagnostic interview. Clinicians would conduct an interview by following a structured interview schedule and record their observations on rating scales and checklists. Presumably, a structured interview process could yield more complete and reliable data than an informal interview. The data were then input into a computerized decision-tree program that would make DSM-II diagnostic classifications. An early example was the Current and Past Psychopathology Scales (CAPPS; Endicott & Spitzer, 1972). The CAPPS data were processed by a computer algorithm (DIAGNO-II; Spitzer & Endicott, 1969) to yield one or more DSM-II diagnoses. The authors found that computer diagnoses agreed with clinicians' diagnoses as well as clinicians agreed with each (Fleiss, Spitzer, Cohen, & Endicott, 1972).

A number of other computerized structured diagnostic interviews have been developed. These include the Diagnostic Interview Schedule (DIS; Robins, Helzer, Croughan, & Ratcliff, 1981), DTREE (First, Williams, & Spitzer, 1989), Structured Clinical Interview for DSM-IIIR (SCID; Spitzer, Williams, Gibbon, & First, 1990) and its successor versions, and the Composite International Diagnostic Interview (CIDI; World Health Organization, 1993). The DIS, CIDI, and SCID have both clinician-administered and patient self-administered capabilities.

Parallel with these developments, the computer was being applied to the administration, scoring, and interpretation of psychological tests. The first interpretive program was the Mayo Clinic MMPI (Rome et al., 1962). This application, intended for psychological screening of medical patients, produced a brief list of likely symptoms or characteristics. A number of other researchers were working on more comprehensive interpretive systems at that time (e.g., R. D. Fowler, 1980). Commercial services for MMPI mail-in scoring and interpretation emerged in the late 1960s and early 1970s. The introduction of the microcomputer permitted practitioners to have office-based testing systems (Johnson, Giannetti, & Williams, 1978). These computers were still very expensive, and the available software was limited.

The introduction of the desktop personal computer changed everything. Computer-assisted testing became industrialized rather rapidly as new and existing assessment companies entered the field. The number of available computerized self-report tests increased geometrically. Scoring and interpretive aids for clinician-administered intellectual and projective tests soon followed. Today, the clinician can select from a wide array of products.

Computer-based diagnostic interview programs vary in their coverage of diagnostic classifications, and none of them cover all possible diagnoses. The reliability and validity of these interviews have been evaluated in several studies (e.g., Dreesen & Arntz, 1998; Peters & Andrews, 1995; Rosenman, Korter, & Levings, 1997). Diagnostic agreement varies substantially by diagnostic category. If there is an advantage to this approach in clinical practice, it would be in the structured and reliable collection of data. The advantage does not lie in diagnostic accuracy.

There is little doubt that computerized administration and scoring of psychological tests is more convenient, faster, less expensive, and less error prone than conventional administration and hand scoring. It is also advantageous to have data electronically stored for other analyses. Studies mentioned earlier established that most patients do not object to interacting with a computer and many enjoy the process. Once we get beyond these basic findings, however, matters become decidedly more ambiguous.

Moreland (1987) observed that most assessment tools available for computer administration were developed for conventional administration: "Therefore, as a practical matter, one must be concerned that factors indigenous to computerized administration, but irrelevant to the purposes of the test, may alter test performance" (p. 32). He also noted that that there had been little research on this matter. Fifteen years later, Butcher, Perry, and Atlis (2000) reviewed available studies on the equivalence of booklet and computer administered tests. They found a substantial number of studies on the MMPI/MMPI-2, including one meta-analysis of 14 studies (Finger & Ones, 1999). They concluded that the two methods of administration are psychometrically equivalent. However, they found very few studies on tests other than the MMPI, and some of those did show differences between administration methods. Another review (Schulenberg & Yutrzenka, 1999) presents good evidence for the equivalence of conventional and computerized versions of the Beck Depression Inventory. For any other tests that were developed and normed based upon conventional administration, one cannot assume that scores obtained from a computer-administered version are equivalent to the original version.

Even with the MMPI and the BDI, for which group statistics on equivalency are good, the practitioner should be aware that other factors could conceivably affect the results for individuals. Schulenberg and Yutrzenka (1999) have argued that recent studies indicate computer aversion can have an effect on scores on measures of negative affect. Spinhoven, Labbe, and Rombouts (1993) asked 343 patients admitted to an outpatient clinic to volunteer for computerized assessment, and 186 refused. Those who refused tended to be older, female, less educated, and less experienced with computers than those who volunteered. Those who completed the computerized assessment tended to rate the experience positively. Even within this group, sex, age, education level, and computer experience correlated with attitudes toward the use of computers.

Beyond administration and scoring, many programs are on the market that provide computer-based test interpretations (CBTI) for, primarily, tests of personality. Evaluating the validity of CBTIs is a very complex matter. Snyder (2000) summarized many of the issues. The validity of the instrument itself and the availability and quality of clinical correlate information limit the validity of any interpretation, whether it is generated by a computer or an individual clinician. The decision rules used to generate narrative statements are almost always proprietary and, hence, cannot be examined as part of any study. The sample in any given study is likely to trigger only a subset of the available narrative statements in the CBTI pool. Evaluation of the statements can vary from global judgments about the entire report, to comments on subsections of the report or individual statements.

Moreland's (1987) review concluded that CBTI research had produced mixed but generally positive results and was well worth pursuing further. A more recent review of CBTI research (Butcher et al., 2000) presents a grand total of four additional CBTI studies in the 13 years since Moreland's review. Our search discovered one additional study on the Millon Adolescent Personality Inventory (Rubenzer, 1992) and one on the WISC-R (Tsemberis, Miller, & Gartner, 1996). Taken together, these newer studies would not alter Moreland's original conclusions. Despite their popularity, there are no adequately validated CBTIs. The validities of CBTIs are essentially unknown, and apparently there has been very little interest in conducting validation studies.

A recent departure from the traditional CBTI approach attempts to tie assessment more closely to treatment planning. It is a computer program designed to implement Beutler and Clarkin's (1990) Systematic Treatment Selection (STS) model. The software has a variety of features, including projection of treatment course based on similar patients in its database, graphs of the patient's relative standing on assessed variables, assessment of probable risk, and a list of the most pressing problems. The distinguishing feature is the assessment of patient characteristics that have been empirically shown to predict differential responses to different interventions (Beutler & Harwood, 2000), permitting the clinician to select treatment strategies tailored to the individual patient.

The four patient characteristics currently assessed using the STS Clinician Rating Form (Fisher, Beutler, & Williams, 1999) are level of functional impairment; characteristic ways of coping with stress, particularly externalization and impulsivity; traitlike levels of interpersonal resistance to external influence; and current level of distress. As an example of the implications for treatment selection, patients who cope with stress by internalizing responsibility and blaming themselves respond better to insight-oriented treatments. Patients who cope by externalizing blame, by acting out, or by avoidance respond better to behaviorally oriented treatments (Fisher et al., 1999). The output identifies the patient's likely coping style and lists suggestions for interventions suitable to that style.

## Computer-Assisted Psychotherapy

DeWeaver (1983) described the microcomputers available in the early 1980s and the ways they might contribute to an independent psychotherapy practice. Today many computer-assisted educational programs exist to prevent alcohol and drug abuse, increase responsible sexual behavior, prevent delinquent behavior, enhance self-esteem, modify self-destructive lifestyles, and reduce disruptive classroom behavior (Bloom, 1992). Professional software programs are increasingly available to address specific psychopathologies. An example is Student Bodies, a self-help eating disorder prevention treatment that includes a multimedia program and a computer-mediated discussion group (Winzelberg, 1998). Another program is designed for treating posttraumatic stress and pathological grief through the Internet (Lange et al., 2000).

Most computer-assisted therapy applications are automated versions of traditional cognitive behavioral therapy techniques used to address specific problems of anxiety, affective disorders, sexual dysfunction, and habit control. They range from those intended for use by clinicians as adjuncts to treatment to applications that are more self-help-based and intended to extend services to primary care settings or to persons who are reluctant or unable to seek professional assistance. Examples are a self-directed graduated exposure treatment program for phobics (Ghosh, Marks, & Carr, 1988); a computer-assisted vicarious exposure treatment program (K. L. Smith, Kirkby, Montgomery, & Daniels, 1997); an individualized program for dysfunctional beliefs and automatic thoughts in mild to moderate depression (Selmi, Klein, Greist, Sorrell, & Erdman, 1990); a weight loss program using behavior therapy with a palmtop computer offering treatment regimes, feedback, and reinforcement (Burnett, Tayloy, & Agras, 1985); a behavioral self-control program for problem drinkers (Hester & Delaney, 1997); use of a palmtop computer

for self-monitoring and reinforcement in the treatment of panic disorder (M. G. Newman, Kenardy, Herman, & Taylor, 1997); and a couples therapy program for sexual dysfunctions called Sexpert that simulates therapeutic dialogue and responds differentially to a client's input (Binik et al., 1997). All of these programs have provided some evidence to suggest that they can be effective with regard to clinical outcomes and useful at least as adjuncts to traditional interventions. They have the further virtue of saving valuable therapist time.

One of the limitations of the older generation of computer-assisted treatment programs is their "one form fits all" approach. Recent programs offer individualized treatment and are more sensitive to specific client goals and circumstances. Although the examples above are automated techniques applied to specific problems, the Therapeutic Learning Program (TLP; Gould, 1990) is intended to help patients identify and solve their own problems. The application is grounded in Gould's theory of adult development. It is a short-term, goal-oriented approach in which the computer program assists the patient in defining problems, identifying actions that will address the problems, and dealing with conflicts and irrational thoughts about engaging in those actions. After a session with the computer, the patient receives a printout and interacts with the therapist in an individual or group session (Gould, 1996). A randomized controlled study comparing TLP-assisted therapy groups to traditional cognitive-behavioral stress reduction groups found them equally effective in reducing depression and anxiety, but the TLP groups used one-third to one-half less of the therapist's time (Dolezal-Wood, Belar, & Snibbe, 1998).

The most cutting-edge software treatment programs make use of virtual reality technology to produce a perceptual world that captures the patient's experiences and responds to the patient's actions. Virtual reality (VR) therapy operates under the principle of providing the patient with the illusion that an experience that is computer-mediated is not mediated but direct (Fink, 1999). Where control is an important therapeutic issue, such as in phobias, VR software typically enables the user to exercise control in terms of the rate and extent of exposure to feared objects and situations. Virtual reality equipment usually consists of a head-mounted visual display with earphones that is connected to a computer. The computer generates the audio and visual stimuli to produce simulations of feared or unknown situations. The therapist can experience what the patient is experiencing and can speak with the patient through a microphone. The patient "moves" through the environment by a sensor that tracks head position and orientation. The position of other parts of the body can be tracked as well so that, for example, the patient's hand movements interact with objects in the simulation.

An early desensitization of phobias program using VR was instituted at Clark University in 1992 to study the fear of flying (Williford, Hodges, North, & North, 1993). The most commonly simulated environments are still associated with phobias, and the treatments employ some form of graduated exposure therapy. For a statement of the theoretical rationale for its use and examples of applications, see Rothbaum and Hodges (1999). The two available controlled studies of VR are both for agoraphobia and used wait list controls (North, North, & Coble, 1998; Rothbaum, Hodges, & Kooper, 1997). Although the findings are quite positive, there have been no studies to date directly comparing the effectiveness of VR exposure to imaginal or in vivo exposure.

Virtual reality therapy offers numerous advantages for the practice of psychotherapy. Exposure therapy can be conducted without the time involved in leaving the therapist's office, and it reduces the risk of harm or public embarrassment to the patient. The therapist has more precise control of exposure stimuli. It is more convenient than in vivo exposure and more realistic than imaginal exposure. It can be used in situations in which in vivo exposure is quite expensive (fear of flying) or impossible (combat-related posttraumatic stress disorder).

There are a couple of disadvantages to the use of virtual reality therapy. One is the financial cost involved, since computer programs and head-mounted displays can cost several thousand dollars. However, as with most of the new technology, these costs will surely come down in the near future. Second, some individuals complain of dizziness and nausea when they participate in VR (Regan & Price, 1994).

Although the initial VR work was on anxiety disorders, there have been attempts to apply VR technology to the treatment of eating disorders (Riva, Bacchetta, Baruffi, Rinaldi, & Molinari, 1998) and impotence (Optale et al., 1998). Virtual reality has the potential to simulate the social, as well as the physical, environment (Glance, Durlach, Barnett, & Aviles, 1996). Social simulations would permit the therapist to accompany the patient into current and past situations, interacting with simulated people significant in the patient's life to assist the patient in solving problems or mastering skills. The technology necessary for such applications is still in its infancy.

A more sophisticated form of VR, called augmented reality, refers to the manipulation of environments to enhance rather than replace the physical world (Fink, 1999). The patient, for instance, might project his or her image into a crowded football stadium or experience dental treatment minus the pain of the actual scene. An extension of this technology is the creation of virtual reality communities on the Internet. These are called Multi-User Dimensions (MUDs), and although they could theoretically be used for therapy purposes they typically have no such explicit purpose. There is no reason, for instance, that a therapist could not "accompany" a patient into a MUD and encourage the patient to experiment with new behaviors in the virtual environment.

## Summary and Future Directions

There is reason to believe that the resistance to computers may come more from therapists than patients (Ben-Porath & Butcher, 1986). After all, although computer-programmed clinicians may lack nonverbal skills, they are apt to remain polite and friendly; never become angry, bored, or fatigued; and tend to be relatively inexpensive in comparison to their human counterparts (Bloom, 1992). Clinical psychologists, on the other hand, often have an aversion to computer technology because they fear its dehumanizing implications. Moreover, clinicians express deep reservations about adopting computer-assisted interventions with patients. Not surprisingly, these reservations are more common among psychodynamically oriented psychologists than among cognitive-behavioral psychologists or family systems–oriented psychologists. This is probably because the latter models place less emphasis on therapist-patient relationship issues within the therapy session and anticipate new behaviors to occur primarily outside of the session (Bloom, 1992). It is also timely to note that the brief, focused therapy models of a cognitive-behavioral persuasion that so far lend themselves more to computerized applications are precisely the types of therapy that managed care providers tend to appreciate. One might predict the development and adoption of computer-assisted interventions to find a receptive home in this environment.

Dobson and Khatri (2000) exemplify both the enthusiasm and the apprehension of psychologists regarding the proliferation of computerized approaches to psychotherapy. On the one hand, they note, manualized therapies are probably the most easily modified for computer delivery, and that will most certainly take place very soon. On the other hand, we need to remind ourselves that acquiring information is not the same as gaining knowledge, and gaining knowledge is not the same as having wisdom. Cognitive therapists are already vulnerable to criticism of being overly mechanical and minimizing the human relationship factor in psychotherapy. The acquisition of greater competence via the electronic medium always runs the risk of further de-emphasizing skill training in human interactions. The risk is that, with the widespread implementation of computerized treatment, time and money will be targeted to the training of students in computer skills rather than in the ability to construct effective personal interactions.

Technological advancements in the field of clinical psychology are now sufficiently developed to make them practical for use by most educators, researchers, and practitioners. The pressing issues today are less related to the development of technology per se than they are to the fit between the technology and the human aspects of service delivery. It is critical to remember that, as clinical mental health professionals, our value as academicians and caregivers rests on our commitment to psychological knowledge and human service, not on our skills as technologists. Technology is a far-sighted tool, but a near-sighted master.

## REFERENCES

Ainsworth, W. (1997). Directory of internet psychotherapists. *Metanoia and Mental Health Net*. Retrieved February 3, 2001, from http://www.metanoia.org/imhs/directry.htm.

Angle, H. V., Ellinwood, E. H., Hay, W. M., Johnsen, T., & Hay, L. R. (1977). Computer-aided interviewing in comprehensive behavioral assessment. *Behavior Therapy, 8,* 747–754.

Baume, P., Rolfe, A., & Clinton, M. (1998). Suicide on the Internet: A focus for nursing intervention? *Australian and New Zealand Journal of Mental Health Nursing, 7*(4), 134–141.

Belar, C. D. (1998). Graduate education in clinical psychology: "We're not in Kansas anymore." *American Psychologist, 53*(4), 456–464.

Ben-Porath, Y. S., & Butcher, J. N. (1986). Computers in personality assessment: A brief past, an ebullient present, and an expanding future. *Computers in Human Behavior, 2,* 167–182.

Beutler, L. E., & Clarkin, J. F. (1990). *Systematic treatment selection: Toward targeted therapeutic interventions.* New York: Bruner/Mazel.

Beutler, L. E., & Harwood, T. M. (2000). *Prescriptive psychotherapy: A practical guide to systematic treatment selection.* New York: Oxford University Press.

Binder, J. L. (1999). Issues in teaching and learning time-limited psychodynamic psychotherapy. *Clinical Psychology Review, 19*(6), 705–719.

Binik, Y. M., Cantor, J., Ochs, E., & Meana, M. (1997). From the couch to the keyboard: Psychotherapy in cyberspace. In S. Kiesler (Ed.), *Culture of the Internet* (pp. 71–102). Mahwah, NJ: Erlbaum.

Bloom, B. L. (1992). Computer-assisted psychological intervention: A review and commentary. *Clinical Psychology Review, 12*(2), 169–197.

Brown, J. S., & Duguid, P. (2000). *The social life of information.* Cambridge, MA: Harvard Business School Press.

Burnett, K. F., Taylor, C. B., & Agras, W. S. (1985). Ambulatory computer-assisted therapy for obesity: A new frontier for behavior therapy. *Journal of Consulting and Clinical Psychology, 53,* 698–703.

Butcher, J. N., Perry, J. N., & Atlis, M. M. (2000). Validity and utility of computer-based test interpretations. *Psychological Assessment, 12,* 6–18.

Card, W. I., Nicholson, M., Crean, G. P., Watkinson, G. E., Evans, C. R., & Russell, D. (1974). A comparison of doctors and computer interrogation of patients. *International Journal of Biomedical Computing, 5,* 175–181.

Carr, A. C., Ghosh, A., & Ancill, R. J. (1983). Can a computer take a psychiatric history? *Psychological Medicine, 13,* 151–158.

Carter, J. A. (1997). The systematic development of a video-based self-instructional interview training package (Doctoral dissertation, University of Mississippi, 1997). *Dissertation Abstracts International, 58*(11B), 6229.

Colby, K. M., Watt, J. B., & Gilbert, J. P. (1966). A computer method of psychotherapy: Preliminary communication. *Journal of Nervous and Mental Disease, 142*(2), 148–152.

Colon, Y. (1999). Digital digging: Group therapy online. In J. Fink (Ed.), *How to use computers and cyberspace in the clinical practice of psychotherapy* (pp. 65–82). New York: Jason Aronson.

Cushman, P. (1995). *Constructing the self, constructing America: A cultural history of psychotherapy.* Reading, MA: Addison-Wesley.

Daniel, J., & Stevens, A. (1998). The success stories: The use of technology in "out-of-school education." In C. de M. Moura Castro (Ed.), *Education in the information age* (pp. 156–167). New York: Inter-American Development Bank.

Dede, C. (2000, September). Comments. *APS Observer, 13*(7), 3, 7–8.

DeWeaver, K. L. (1983). Evolution of the microcomputer: Technological implications for the private practitioner. *Psychotherapy in Private Practice, 1*(3), 59–69.

Dobson, K. S., & Khatri, N. (2000). Cognitive therapy: Looking backward, looking forward. *Journal of Clinical Psychology, 56*(7), 907–923.

Dolezal-Wood, S., Belar, C. D., & Snibbe, J. (1998). A comparison of computer-assisted psychotherapy and cognitive-behavioral therapy in groups. *Journal of Clinical Psychology in Medical Settings, 5,* 103–115.

Drasgow, F., & Olson-Buchanan, J. B. (Eds.). (1999). *Innovations in computerized assessment.* Mahwah, NJ: Erlbaum.

Dreesen, L., & Arntz, A. (1998). Short-interval test-retest interrater reliability of the structured clinical interview for DSM-III-R personality disorders (SCDI-II) in outpatients. *Journal of Personality Disorders, 12,* 138–148.

Endicott, J., & Spitzer, R. L. (1972). Current and past psychopathology scales (CAPPS): Rationale, reliability, and validity. *Archives of General Psychiatry, 27,* 678–687.

Engen, H. B., Finken, L. J., Luschei, N. S., & Kenney, D. (1994). Counseling simulations: An interactive videodisc approach. *Computers in Human Services Special Topic: Electronic Tools for Social Work Practice and Education, 11*(3–4), 283–298.

Farrell, A. D. (1989). Impact of computers on professional practice: A survey of current practices and attitudes. *Professional Psychology: Research and Practice, 20,* 172–178.

Finger, M. S., & Ones, D. S. (1999). Psychometric equivalence of the computer and booklet forms of the MMPI: A meta-analysis. *Psychological Assessment, 11,* 58–66.

Fink, J. (1999). *How to use computers and cyberspace in the clinical practice of psychotherapy.* New York: Jason Aronson.

First, M. B., Williams, J. B. W., & Spitzer, R. L. (1989). *DTREE: The electronic DSM-III-R.* Washington, DC: American Psychiatric Press.

Fisher, D., Beutler, L. E., & Williams, O. B. (1999). Making assessment relevant to treatment planning. *Journal of Clinical Psychology, 55,* 825–842.

Fleiss, J. L., Spitzer, R. L., Cohen, J., & Endicott, J. (1972). Three computer diagnosis methods compared. *Archives of General Psychiatry, 27,* 643–649.

Fowler, R. D. (1980). The automated MMPI. In J. B. Sidowski, J. H. Johnson, & T. A. Williams (Eds.), *Technology in mental health care delivery systems* (pp. 69–84). Norwood, NJ: Ablex.

Fowler, D. R., Finkelstein, A., Penk, W., Bell, W., & Itzig, B. (1987). An automated problem-rating interview: The DPRI. In J. N. Butcher (Ed.), *Computerized psychological assessment: A practitioner's guide* (pp. 87–107). New York: Basic Books.

Ghosh, A., Marks, I. M., & Carr, A. C. (1988). Therapist contact and outcome of self-exposure treatment for phobias: A controlled study. *British Journal of Psychiatry, 152,* 234–238.

Giannetti, R. A. (1987). The GOLPH psychosocial history: Response-contingent data acquisition and recording. In J. N. Butcher (Ed.), *Computerized psychological assessment: A practitioner's guide* (pp. 124–144). New York: Basic Books.

Glance, K., Durlach, N. I., Barnett, R. C., & Aviles, W. A. (1996). Virtual reality (VR) for psychotherapy: From the physical to the social environment. *Psychotherapy, 33,* 464–473.

Gould, R. L. (1990). *Therapeutic learning program: Therapist's manual.* Santa Monica, CA: Interactive Health Systems.

Gould, R. L. (1996). The use of computers in therapy. In T. Trabin (Ed.), *The computerization of behavioral healthcare* (pp. 39–62). San Francisco: Jossey-Bass.

Grady, M., & Ephross, P. H. (1977). A comparison of two methods for collecting social histories of psychiatric hospital patients. *Military Medicine, 142,* 524–526.

Greist, J. H., Klein, M. H., & Van Cura, L. J. (1973). A computer interview for psychiatric patient target symptoms. *Archives of General Psychiatry, 29,* 247–253.

Halpern, D. (1998, August 16). *Designing the 21st-century university: Pedagogy, technology, and lifelong learning.* Presidential address, Division 2, Society for the Teaching of Psychology, San Francisco.

Harasim, L. M. (1998). The internet and intranets for education and training: A framework for action. In C. de Moura Castro (Ed.), *Education in the information age* (pp. 181–201). New York: Inter-American Development Bank.

Harasim, L. M., Hiltz, S. R., Teles, L., & Turoff, M. (1995). *Learning networks.* Cambridge, MA: MIT Press.

Harasim, L. M., & Yung, B. (1993). *Teaching and learning on the Internet.* Burnaby, British Columbia, Canada: Simon Fraser University, Department of Communication.

Hester, R. K., & Delaney, H. D. (1997). Behavioral self-control program for Windows: Results of a controlled clinical trial. *Journal of Consulting and Clinical Psychology, 65,* 686–693.

Hiltz, S. R., & Turoff, M. (1978). *The network nation: Human communication via computer.* Reading, MA: Addison-Wesley.

Homrich, A. M. (1997). *Effects of group support system interactive computer technology on task-group processes of psychology case presentations* (Doctoral dissertation, University of Georgia, 1997). *Dissertation Abstracts International, 58*(06B), 3316.

Janoff, D. S., & Schoenholtz-Read, J. (1999). Group supervision meets technology: A model of computer-mediated group training at a distance. *International Journal of Group Psychotherapy, 49*(2), 255–272.

Jerome, L. W., DeLeon, P. H., James, L. C., Folen, R., Earles, J., & Gedney, J. J. (2000). The coming of age of telecommunication in psychological research and practice. *American Psychologist, 55*(4), 407–421.

Johnson, J. H., Giannetti, R. A., & Williams, T. A. (1978). A self-contained microcomputer system for psychological testing. *Behavior Research Methods and Instrumentation, 10,* 579–581.

Kane, R. L., & Kay, G. G. (1997). Computer applications in neuropsychological assessment. In G. Goldstein & T. M. Incagnoli (Eds.), *Contemporary approaches to neuropsychological assessment* (pp. 359–392). New York: Plenum Press.

Kemenoff, L. A. (1999). *Clinician acceptance of computer-assisted psychotherapy* (Doctoral dissertation, California School of Professional Psychology, 1999). *Dissertation Abstracts International, 60*(05B), 2346.

Koocher, G. P., & Morray, E. (2000, October). Regulation of telepsychology: A survey of state attorneys general. *Professional Psychology: Research and Practice, 31*(5), 503–508.

Lange, A., Schrieken, B., van de Ven, J.-P., Bredeweg, B., Emmel Kamp, P. M. G., van der Kolk, J., Lydsdottir, L., Massaro, M., & Reuvers, A. (2000). "Interapy": The effects of a short protocol led treatment of posttraumatic stress and pathological grief through the Internet. *Behavioural and Cognitive Psychotherapy, 28*(2), 175–192.

Lucas, R. W. (1977). A study of patients' attitudes to computer interrogation. *International Journal of Man-Machine Studies, 9,* 69–86.

Lucas, R. W., Mullin, P. J., Luna, C. B. X., & McInroy, D. C. (1977). Psychiatrists and a computer as interrogators of patients with alcohol-related illnesses: A comparison. *British Journal of Psychiatry, 131,* 160–167.

Maehl, W. H. (2000). *Lifelong learning at its best.* San Francisco: Jossey-Bass.

Magaletta, P. R., Fagan, T. J., & Ax, R. K. (1998). Advancing psychology services through telehealth in the Federal Bureau of Prisons. *Professional Psychology: Research and Practice, 29*(6), 543–548.

Maki, R. H., Maki, W. S., Patterson, M., & Whittaker, P. D. (2000). Evaluation of a web-based introductory psychology course: Learning and satisfaction in online versus lecture courses.

*Behavior Research Methods, Instruments and Computers, 32,* 230–239.

Maultsby, M. C., & Slack, W. V. (1971). A computer based psychiatry history system. *Archives of General Psychiatry, 25,* 570–572.

McMinn, M. R. (1998). Technology in practice. In A. S. Bellack & M. Hersen (Eds.), *Comprehensive clinical psychology: Vol 2. Professional issues* (pp. 363–375). New York: Pergamon Press.

McMinn, M. R., Buchanan, T., Ellens, B. M., & Ryan, M. K. (1999). Technology, professional practice, and ethics: Survey findings and implications. *Professional Psychology: Research and Practice, 30*(2), 165–172.

McMinn, M. R., & Scanish, J. D. (1996). *The Rorschach trainer.* Lutz, FL: Psychological Assessment Resources.

Miller, J. K., & Gergen, K. J. (1998). Life on the line: The therapeutic potentials of computer-mediated conversation. *Journal of Marital and Family Therapy, 24*(2), 189–202.

Moreland, K. L. (1987). Computerized psychological assessment: What's available. In J. N. Butcher (Ed.), *Computerized psychological assessment: A practitioner's guide* (pp. 26–49). New York: Basic Books.

National Education Association. (2000). *Benchmarks for success in Internet-based distance education.* The Institute for Higher Education Policy. Retrieved December 21, 2000, from http://www.ccsf.cc.ca.us/Pub/Mj/TLTR.

National Telecommunications and Information Administration. (1999). *Falling through the 'Net:' Defining the digital divide.* Retrieved December 21, 2000, from http://www.ntia.doc.gov/ntiahome/fttn99/contents.html.

Newman, M. G., Kenardy, J., Herman, S., & Taylor, C. B. (1997). Comparison of palmtop-computer-assisted brief cognitive-behavioral treatment to cognitive-behavioral treatment for panic disorder. *Journal of Consulting and Clinical Psychology, 65,* 178–183.

Newman, R. (2000). Comments. *Monitor on Psychology, 31*(9), 24.

Nickelson, D. W. (1998). Telehealth and the evolving health care system: Strategic opportunities for professional psychology. *Professional Psychology: Research and Practice, 29,* 527–535.

Noam, E. M. (1995, October 13). Electronics and the dim future of the university. *Science, 270,* 247–249.

North, M., North, S. M., & Coble, J. R. (1998). Virtual reality therapy: An effective treatment for phobias. In G. Riva, B. K. Widerhold, & E. Molinari (Eds.), *Virtual environments in clinical psychology and neuroscience* (pp. 112–119). Amsterdam: IOS Press.

Optale, G., Munari, A., Nasta, A., Pianon, C., Verde, J. B., & Viggiano, G. (1998). A VR based therapy for the treatment of impotence and premature ejaculation. In G. Riva, B. K. Widerhold, & E. Molinari (Eds.), *Virtual environments in clinical psychology and neuroscience* (pp. 136–139). Amsterdam: IOS Press.

Pennebaker, J. W., & Beall, S. K. (1986). Confronting a traumatic event: Toward an understanding of inhibition and disease. *Journal of Abnormal Psychology, 95*(3), 274–281.

Pennebaker, J. W., Colder, M., & Sharp, L. K. (1990). Accelerating the coping process. *Journal of Personality and Social Psychology, 58*(3), 528–537.

Peters, L., & Andrews, G. (1995). Procedural validity of the computerized version of the Composite International Diagnostic Interview (CIDI-Auto) in the anxiety disorders. *Psychological Medicine, 25,* 1269–1280.

Pope, K. S., & Vetter, V. A. (1992). Ethical dilemmas encountered by members of the American Psychological Association: A national survey. *American Psychologist, 47*(3), 397–411.

Regan, E. C., & Price, K. R. (1994). The frequency of occurrence and severity of side-effects of immersion virtual reality. *Aviation Space and Environmental Medicine, 65*(6), 527–530.

Riva, G., Bacchetta, M., Baruffi, M., Rinaldi, S., & Molinari, E. (1998). Experiential cognitive therapy: A VR based approach for the assessment and treatment of eating disorders. In G. Riva, B. K. Widerhold, & E. Molinari (Eds.), *Virtual environments in clinical psychology and neuroscience* (pp. 120–135). Amsterdam: IOS Press.

Robins, L. N., Helzer, J. E., Croughan, J., & Ratcliff, K. (1981). National Institute of Mental Health Diagnostic Interview Schedule. *Archives of General Psychiatry, 38,* 381–389.

Rome, H. P., Swenson, W. M., Mataya, P., McCarthy, C. E., Pearson, J. S., Keating, F. R., & Hathaway, S. R. (1962). Symposium on automation techniques in personality assessment. *Proceedings of the Staff Meetings of the Mayo Clinic, 37,* 61–82.

Rosenman, S. J., Korter, A. E., & Levings, C. T. (1997). Computerized diagnosis in acute psychiatry: Validity of the CIDI-Auto against routing clinical diagnosis. *Journal of Psychiatric Research, 31,* 581–592.

Rothbaum, B. O., & Hodges, L. F. (1999). The use of virtual reality exposure in the treatment of anxiety disorders. *Behavior Modification, 23,* 507–525.

Rothbaum, B. O., Hodges, L., & Kooper, R. (1997). Virtual reality exposure therapy. *Journal of Psychotherapy Practice and Research, 6,* 219–226.

Rothchild, E. (1999). Telepsychiatry: Why do it? *Psychiatric Annals, 29,* 394–401.

Rubenzer, S. (1992). A comparison of traditional and computer-generated reports in an adolescent inpatient setting. *Journal of Clinical Psychology, 48,* 817–827.

Saba, L., & Hodges, P. (2002). Teaching statistics online. In K. E. Rudestam & J. Schoenholtz-Read (Eds.), *Handbook of online learning: Innovations in higher education and corporate training.* Newbury Park, CA: Sage.

Schon, D. (1987). *Educating the reflexive practitioner.* San Francisco: Jossey-Bass.

Schrage, M. (1990). *Shared minds: The new technologies of collaboration.* New York: Random House.

Schulenberg, S. E., & Yutrzenka, B. A. (1999). The equivalence of computerized and paper-and-pencil psychological instruments:

Implications for measures of negative affect. *Behavior, Research Methods, Instruments, and Computers, 31,* 315–321.

Selmi, P. M., Klein, M. H., Greist, J. H., Sorrell, S. P., & Erdman, H. P. (1990). Computer-administered cognitive-behavioral therapy for depression. *American Journal of Psychiatry, 147,* 51–56.

Senge, P. (2000). *Schools that learn: A fifth discipline fieldbook for educators, parents, and everyone who cares about education.* New York: Doubleday.

Slack, W.V., Hicks, G. P., Reed, C. Z., & Van Cura, L. J. (1966). A computer based medical history system. *New England Journal of Medicine, 274,* 194–198.

Smith, K. L., Kirkby, K. C., Montgomery, I. M., & Daniels, B. A. (1997). Computer-delivered modeling of exposure for spider phobias: Relevant versus irrelevant exposure. *Journal of Anxiety Disorders, 11*(5), 485–495.

Smith, R. C. (1996). *The introduction of preference and choice in the computer-assisted supervision of marriage and family therapists during pre-practicum* (Doctoral dissertation, Brigham Young University, 1996). *Dissertation Abstracts International, 57*(12A), 5080.

Snyder, D. K. (2000). Computer-assisted judgment: Defining strengths and liabilities. *Psychological Assessment, 12,* 52–60.

Spinhoven, P., Labbe, M. R., & Rombouts, R. (1993). Feasibility of computerized psychological testing with psychiatric outpatients. *Journal of Clinical Psychology, 49,* 440–447.

Spitzer, R. L., & Endicott, J. (1969). DIAGNO II: Further developments in a computer program for psychiatric diagnosis. *American Journal of Psychiatry, 125*(Suppl.), 12–21.

Spitzer, R. L., Williams, J. B. W., Gibbon M., & First, M. B. (1990). *Structured Clinical Interview for DSM-III-R, Patient Edition (SCID-P)/Non-patient Edition (SCID-NP).* Washington, DC: American Psychiatric Press.

Sproul, L. S., & Kiesler, S. (1991). *Connections: New ways of working in the networked organization.* Cambridge, MA: MIT Press.

Stamm, B. H. (1998). Clinical applications of telehealth in mental health. *Professional Psychology Research and Practice, 29*(6), 536–542. Retrieved December 21, 2000, from http://www.apa.org/journals/pro/pro296536.html.

Stamm, B. H. (1999). Creating virtual community: Telehealth and self care updated. In B. H. Stamm (Ed.), *Secondary traumatic stress: Self-care issues for clinicians, researchers and educators* (2nd ed., pp. 179–208). Lutherville, MD: Sidran Press.

Stamm, B. H. (2000), Shifting gears: Integrating models of telehealth and telemedicine into current models of mental health care. In L. G. Lawrence (Ed.), *Innovations in clinical practice* (Vol. 18, pp. 385–400). Sarasota, FL: Professional Resource Press.

Sterling, B. (1992). *The hacker crackdown: Law and disorder on the electronic frontier.* New York: Bantam Books.

Stevens-Long, J., & Crowell, C. (2002). The design and delivery of online graduate education. In K. E. Rudestam & J. Schoenholtz-Read (Eds.), *Handbook of online learning: Innovations in higher education and corporate training.* Newbury Park, CA: Sage.

Tehranian, M. (1996). The end of the university? *Information Society, 12,* 442.

Telemedicine Information Exchange. (2000, November). *Program Database.* Portland, OR. Retrieved November 5, 2000, from http://tie.telemed.org/.

Terry, M. J. (1999). Kelengakutelleghpat: An Arctic community-based approach to trauma. In B. H. Stamm (Ed.), *Secondary traumatic stress: Self-care issues for clinicians, researchers and educators* (2nd ed., pp. 149–178). Lutherville, MD: Sidran Press.

Todd, L. K. (1996). A computer-assisted expert system for clinical diagnosis of eating disorders: A potential learning tool for practitioners. *Professional Psychology: Research and Practice, 27,* 184–187.

Trabin, T. (Ed.). (1996). *The computerization of behavioral healthcare.* San Francisco: Jossey-Bass.

Tsemberis, S., Miller, A. C., & Gartner, D. (1996). Expert judgments of computer-based and clinician-written reports. *Computers in Human Behavior, 12,* 167–175.

Weizenbaum, J. (1966). ELIZA: A computer program for the study of natural language communication between man and machine. *Communications for the Association for Computer Machinery, 9,* 36–45.

Werner, G. (1995). Computer applications in behavioral medicine. In A. J. Goreczny (Ed.), *Handbook of health and rehabilitation psychology* (pp. 605–635). New York: Plenum Press.

Williford, J. S., Hodges, L. F., North, M. M., & North, S. M. (1993). Relative effectiveness of virtual environment desensitization and imaginal desensitization in the treatment of acrophobia. *Proceedings Graphics Interface, 162.* Toronto, Ontario.

Wilson, G., & Lester, D. (1998). Suicide prevention by e-mail. *Crisis Intervention and Time-Limited Treatment, 4*(1), 81–87.

Winzelberg, A. J. (1998). *Evaluation of a computer-mediated eating disorder prevention program* (Doctoral dissertation, Stanford University, 1998). *Dissertation Abstracts International, 59*(10B), 5590.

World Health Organization. (1993). *Composite International Diagnostic Interview—Version 1.1.* Geneva, Switzerland: Author.

CHAPTER 24

# Expanding Roles for Psychologists in the Twenty-First Century

PATRICK H. DeLEON, KRISTOFER J. HAGGLUND, STEPHEN A. RAGUSEA, AND MORGAN T. SAMMONS

The science of psychology is merely a century old—and clinical psychology has existed for only half that time—yet the scope of psychology's impact on the culture has already expanded beyond the dreams of its founders. As we enter the twenty-first century, it is more than prudent that we peer into the near and distant future of human psychology. However, as is often observed, predicting the future is always difficult, particularly predicting it correctly. Therefore, what the authors of this chapter offer is not a prediction of psychology's future. Rather, it is a look at the horizon, as seen by four leaders in the field. As the authors see it, psychology has just begun to actualize its potential, and the roles psychologists fill will grow in number and form as far into the future as can be seen. Expanding roles in health care, the formulation of public policy, business, social planning, and leadership are all part of a bright future for the next generation of young psychologists and the society they serve.

---

The opinions expressed by Morgan T. Sammons are his personal views and do not reflect the official policies or positions of the U.S. Navy or Department of Defense.

## PSYCHOLOGY'S VISION

As one of the learned professions, psychology possesses very few external constraints upon its ability to effectively expand its scope of influence. Within the health care arena, for example, professional psychology has been extraordinarily successful over the past several decades in incorporating into its domain any clinical functions that it has pursued, notwithstanding the concerted opposition of organized psychiatry (e.g., the authority to independently diagnose and treat, regardless of the locus of service; DeLeon, Rossomando, & Smedley, in press). Within the educational arena, the essence of the national dialogues championed by the Reagan, Bush, Clinton, and most recently the G. W. Bush administrations has been psychological issues (e.g., lifelong learning and the appropriate role of standardized testing). The authors have been personally involved in the public policy arena for a considerable period of time, and from our collective perspective, we are confident that as our nation enters into the twenty-first century we shall see a continued expansion of psychology's influence into a wide range of public policy areas. In fact, we fully expect that psychology's vision will ultimately become the defining factor in shaping a number of future national debates (DeLeon,

VandenBos, Sammons, & Frank, 1998). However, we are also all too aware that it is impossible to predict with any sense of certainty the specifics of what will come to pass.

## Blueprint for Change

Whenever professional psychology (or any other discipline, for that matter) has evolved from the status quo, it has been our observation that there have been several underlying systemic principles involved. Perhaps the most important has been that the profession's leaders have possessed a clear vision of where they wanted to evolve, including a substantively solid rationale. Unanimity of opinion among the general membership has never been required; nor, in all candor, should it even be expected. Change is always unsettling, and one soon finds that there are highly vocal individuals who remain personally vested in maintaining the status quo. Second, timing is extraordinarily important, both within the profession and external to it. To succeed, there must be a critical mass of dedicated colleagues who share the vision of the leadership. However, it is equally important that the proposed changes ultimately fit into a broader societal perspective. To be meaningful and to flourish, the way an individual profession seeks to evolve must be fundamentally consistent with related developments external to it. For psychology, the past decade has seen a virtual explosion of scientific knowledge within the mental health and broader behavioral health arenas. Even more recently, there have been unprecedented advances within the computer and technological arenas (including a growing appreciation for the applicability of telehealth). Third, it is impossible to overemphasize the extent to which those within a profession desiring change must be willing to be patient and persistent. Rarely do substantive modifications in laws, administrative regulations, or educational priorities occur the first time proposed. A clear and understandable rationale for the proposed change, including a distinct public policy foundation, must often be first articulated. It is especially important that this proposed change make conceptual (e.g., intuitive) sense to those who are not personally aware of the nuances of psychology's expertise. It is as if one must first create a visual image of why the change *will* naturally occur. Fourth, within both the legislative and administrative arenas, those who are ultimately in a position to prioritize proposed modifications more often than not have a fundamental budgetary (rather than programmatic) background and orientation. Finally, those seeking change must become attuned to, and proactively address, the perceptions of other organizations (e.g., interest groups) that eventually will be affected by the envisioned modifications—particularly those groups that at first

consideration might seem to be only tangentially relevant to the immediate policy discussions.

## The Maturation of the Profession of Psychology

When President Carter signed Executive Order no. 11973 on February 19, 1977, thereby establishing his landmark President's Commission on Mental Health (1978), there were approximately 59,900 members and affiliates of the American Psychological Association (APA). That same year, the state of Missouri became the last state in the nation to license or certify practicing psychologists. A decade later (1988), the Committee for the American Psychological Association of Graduate Students (APAGS) was established by the APA Council of Representatives. Over the years, psychology continued to be one of the most popular undergraduate majors. As we enter the twenty-first century, the comparable APA membership numbers have grown to 155,000, with APAGS possessing 59,700 members. These are very impressive numbers, and they speak well for the future of the profession. Stated slightly differently, within the public policy arena, psychology's collective voice *will* be heard.

At the same time, however, we feel that it is important to emphasize that psychology is a relatively young profession and that, in particular, its members are only in the beginning stages of appreciating the importance of their personal involvement in the public policy (e.g., political) process. Although the discipline of psychology dates back to the founding of Wundt's laboratory in 1879, it was on September 21, 1970 that classes began at the first independent professional school of psychology—the California School of Professional Psychological (CSPP; Street, 1994). This was to be the era of the Doctor of Psychology degree (PsyD), the first program being launched in the Department of Psychology at the University of Illinois at Champaign-Urbana in 1968. There can be little disagreement that the paradigm shift to the professional-oriented PsyD degree represented a fundamental change in psychology's self-image and underlying mission. Today there are 48 accredited PsyD programs, most of which are within professional schools that graduate 58% of all clinical students (P. Nelson, personal communication, September 5, 2001).

Along with the increasing emphasis on professional psychology (e.g., clinical rather than experimental), the field has also seen the gradual development of "hands-on" public policy training initiatives. In 1974, Pam Flattau served as the first APA Congressional Science Fellow, under a program established in conjunction with the American Association for the Advancement of Science (AAAS). Today, over a quarter of a century later, approximately 125 colleagues have had the opportunity of serving on Capitol Hill (or in the administration) as APA or Robert Wood Johnson Health Policy Fellows or in other similar national programs. These farsighted and dedicated individuals have experienced first hand the excitement of personal involvement in the public policy process, with many subsequently returning to academia or public service dedicated to encouraging the profession's increased public policy involvement. During their service to Congress or the executive branch, fellows learn about public policy development by participating in its formation. Fellows typically serve as legislative assistants (LAs), with all of the duties thereof, including meeting constituents, "staffing" senators or representatives in committee meetings and hearings, drafting legislation, writing speeches, and attending debates and votes on the floor of the House and Senate. Recent fellows have worked on the development of such legislation as mental health parity, the National Health Service Corps, patients' bill of rights, rural mental health, and psychology's participation in graduate medical education funding (to name a few).

Initially, APA focused only on providing this experience for recent doctoral graduates; as the program matured, however, a concerted effort was made to attract more senior fellows as well. The APA fellows have included individuals from almost every psychological specialty area, including several who also possessed degrees in law (Fowler, 1996). The Robert Wood Johnson Foundation fellowship and several of the other congressional fellowship programs select mid-career professionals who show promise to be leaders in their respective fields. Additionally, more senior fellows are better able to use their fellowships to learn about and to influence policy. Congressional offices typically feel fortunate to recruit an accomplished professional and appreciate the experience that more senior fellows bring to policy debates. Senior fellows are usually given responsibility for developing or augmenting their senator's or representative's policy in the fellows' general area of expertise (e.g., mental health, health care, education).

Over the years, we have been very impressed by the increasing numbers of individual psychologists who have gravitated to positions of high-level public policy responsibility. During the era of the Great Society, John Gardner served as secretary of the Department of Health, Education, and Welfare. Psychologists have served as departmental assistant secretaries, subject to U.S. Senate confirmation; director of a National Institute of Health (NIH), as well as of other federal research institutes; head of the federal Bureau of Prisons; commanders of federal health care facilities; and chief state mental health officials. Former APA President Dick Suinn served as mayor of Ft. Collins, Colorado.

In the 107th Congress (2001–2002) three psychologists were elected to the U.S. House of Representatives, and 12 psychologists served in the various state legislatures. Within university administrations, our colleagues have served at all levels of responsibility. In the private sector, psychologists have been owners and administrators of the entire range of health care facilities. Psychologists' expertise as clinicians is independently recognized throughout the judicial system and under all federal and private reimbursement systems. Moreover, psychology's graduate students are supported under almost every federal training and service delivery initiative. One could suggest that collectively, psychology has done very well in insuring that the profession can fully participate in initiatives that have been conceptualized, and ultimately crafted, by other professional disciplines. The underlying unanswered question is whether professional psychology has matured sufficiently to establish its own programmatic agenda via the public policy process.

## SYSTEMIC CHANGES WITHIN THE HEALTH CARE ARENA

As we have indicated, over the past several decades there has been a gradually increasing awareness of the importance of the psychosocial, environmental, and behavioral aspects of health care for both individual clinical concerns (e.g., the impact of stress upon heart disease) and for more generic population-based concerns (e.g., adverse ethnic health disparities or the incidence of family violence). From a psychological perspective, this concerted focus on behavioral (e.g., nonbiological) events represents an extraordinarily fertile ground for proactive interventions. The relevant scientific knowledge base is rapidly increasing. However, we would rhetorically ask: What is the availability of psychological interventions? To what extent have our nation's health delivery systems, the all-important reimbursement mechanisms, and society's fundamental definition of "quality of care" actually incorporated psychological (e.g., behavioral science) expertise? In our collective judgment, this will be one of the profession's major challenges for the twenty-first century.

### Historical Perspective

In a historical context, the Lalonde report of 1974 effectively laid out the broad parameters for the health policy discussions of the 1990s and the twenty-first century. The Canadian minister of national health and welfare intuitively recognized the extraordinary impact educated consumers would ultimately have, as well as the critical importance of systematically seeking objective (e.g., data-based) programmatic goals. Interestingly, throughout his report and the subsequent policy documents that we will reference, mental health care per se was specifically noted by the highest level of health policy experts. Minister Lalonde prophetically noted that

> Good health is the bedrock on which social progress is built. A nation of healthy people can do those things that make life worthwhile, and as the level of health increases so does the potential for happiness. The Governments of the Provinces and of Canada have long recognized that good physical and mental health are necessary for the quality of life to which everyone aspires. Accordingly, they have developed a health care system which, though short of perfection, is the equal of any in the world. . . . For the[se] environmental and behavioral threats to health, the organized health care system can do little more than serve as a catchment net for the victims. Physicians, surgeons, nurses and hospitals together spend much of their time in treating ills caused by adverse environmental factors and behavioural risks. . . . It is therefore necessary for Canadians themselves to be concerned with the gravity of environmental and behavioural risks before any real progress can be made. There are encouraging signs that this concern is growing; public interest in preserving a healthy environment, in better nutrition and in increasing physical recreation has never been higher. (Lalonde, 1974, pp. 5–6)

> In most minds the health field and the personal medical care system are synonymous. This has been due in large part to the powerful image projected by medicine of its role in the control of infective and parasitic diseases, the advances in surgery, the lowered infant mortality rate and the development of new drugs. This image is reinforced by drug advertising, by television series with the physician as hero, and by the faith bordering on awe by which many Canadians relate to their physicians. The consequence of the traditional view is that most direct expenditures on health are physician-centered, including medical care, hospital care, laboratory tests and prescription drugs. . . . (O)ne finds that close to seven billion dollars a year are spent on a personal health care system which is mainly oriented to treating existing illness. (Lalonde, 1974, pp. 11–12)

The Minister went on to state that "When the full impact of environment and lifestyle has been assessed . . . there is little doubt that future improvements in the level of health of Canadians lie mainly in improving the environment, moderating self-imposed risks and adding to our knowledge of human biology" (Lalonde, 1974, p. 18).

Five global strategies were proposed:

1. A *Health Promotion Strategy* aimed at informing, influencing, and assisting both individuals and organizations so that they would accept more responsibility and be more active in matters affecting mental and physical health.
2. A *Regulatory Strategy* aimed at using federal regulatory powers to reduce hazards to mental and physical health

and at encouraging and assisting provinces to use their regulatory powers to the same end.
3. A *Research Strategy* designed to help discover and apply knowledge needed to solve mental and physical health problems.
4. A *Health Care Efficiency Strategy,* the objective of which would be to help the provinces reorganize the system for delivering mental and physical health care so that the three elements of cost, accessibility, and effectiveness are balanced in the interests of Canadians.
5. A *Goal-Setting Strategy,* the purpose of which would be to set, in cooperation with others, goals for raising the level of the mental and physical health of Canadians and improving the efficiency of the health care system.

From a slightly different perspective, APA Past President George Albee has been heralding the critical importance of prevention and of educated consumers for nearly a half century, while steadfastly further urging his colleagues to also systematically address the economic and broadly defined environmental aspects of mental health care (Albee, 1986).

**Healthy People**

Approximately half a decade later, during President Carter's administration, the surgeon general of the United States issued *Healthy People: The Surgeon General's Report on Health Promotion and Disease Prevention* (U.S. Department of Health, Education, and Welfare [HEW], 1979). To our knowledge, this was the first time within the American health policy debates that the importance of behavioral health had been raised to the level of presidential consideration. In his receiving statement, the president stated, "I have long advocated a greater emphasis on preventing illness and injury by reducing environmental and occupational hazards and by urging people to choose to lead healthier lives. So I welcome this Surgeon General's Report on Health Promotion and Disease Prevention. It sets out a national program for improving the health of our people—a program that relies on prevention along with cure. This program is ambitious but achievable. It can substantially reduce both the suffering of our people and the burden on our expensive system of medical care" (HEW, 1979, p. v).

Secretary Califano said,

> It gives me great pride that virtually my final official act as Secretary of Health, Education, and Welfare is to release this report. . . . Its purpose is to encourage a second public health revolution in the history of the United States. And let us make no mistake about the significance of this document. It represents an

emerging consensus among scientists and the health community that the Nation's health strategy must be dramatically recast to emphasize the prevention of disease. That consensus is as important as the consensus announced in 1964 by the first Surgeon General's Report on Smoking and Health—a document now remembered as a watershed. This nation's first public health revolution, of course, was the struggle against infectious diseases which spanned the late nineteenth century and the first half of the twentieth century. (HEW, 1979, p. vii)

*Healthy People* proclaimed the following:

- Prevention is an idea whose time has come. We have the scientific knowledge to begin to formulate recommendations for improved health.

- Of the 10 leading causes of death in the United States, at least seven could be substantially reduced if persons at risk improved just five habits.

- Because there are limits to what medical care can do for those already sick or injured, people clearly need to make a greater effort to reduce their risk of incurring avoidable diseases and injuries. People must make personal lifestyle choices, too, in the context of a society that glamorizes many hazardous behaviors through advertising and the mass media.

Five data-oriented national goals were proposed, focusing upon the various age groups constituting our nation's population. Addressing the unique health care needs of healthy adolescents and young adults, the publication expressly discussed mental health, including the impact of sociocultural factors and society's expectations. It noted that reaching these goals will require a national effort and the commitment of people extending far beyond what is traditionally considered the health sector.

In addressing healthy adults, the report noted that mental health is a substantial contributor to disability and suffering for American adults. The report's perspective was that "Beginning in early childhood and throughout life, each of us makes decisions affecting our health. They are made, for the most part, without regard to, or contact with, the health care system. Yet their cumulative impact has a greater effect on the length and quality of life than all the efforts of medical care combined" (HEW, 1979, p. 119). Again, the fundamental policy question for professional psychology is whether the nation's health care system has yet incorporated psychological and behavioral science expertise within its priorities. Also, will professional psychology accept the challenge of ensuring that this occurs in a timely fashion?

## The Institute of Medicine

Over the years the Institute of Medicine (IOM) has served as a health policy think tank for various administrations and Congress. The IOM was chartered in 1970 by the National Academy of Sciences, acting under the academy's 1863 congressional charter responsibility to be an advisor to the federal government. In 1982, the IOM released its report: *Health and Behavior: Frontiers of Research in the Biobehavioral Sciences* (Hamburg, Elliott, & Parron, 1982). Once again, the underlying policy theme stressed the importance of integrating the behavioral sciences throughout the nation's health delivery system both clinically and—in our judgment, equally importantly—when designing research protocols and programmatic strategies. The report noted that

The heaviest burdens of illness in the United States today are related to aspects of individual behavior, especially long-term patterns of behavior often referred to as "lifestyle." As much as 50 percent of mortality from the 10 leading causes of death in the United States can be traced to lifestyle. . . . One important advance of the twentieth century is recognition that it is possible to employ scientific methods to gain a better understanding of human behavior. The task is difficult and complex, but human behavior can be observed systematically, reliably, and reproducibly. As knowledge progresses, observations can become increasingly quantitative and have considerable predictive power. (Hamburg et al., 1982, pp. 3–4)

The report went on to note that "Diseases for which lifestyle factors are especially significant have a dominant position in causes of mortality and morbidity. . . . The chronic nature of many mental disorders leads to a relatively large demand on the health care system; for instance, patients with schizophrenia occupy about 25 percent of *all* hospital beds in the United States" (Hamburg et al., 1982, p. 7). It continued, "Much remains to be learned, but the existing research base provides strong evidence that the biobehavioral sciences can make substantial and unique contributions to dealing with much of the disease that now constitutes the main burdens of illness in this country" (Hamburg et al., 1982, p. 16).

The IOM noted the following points:

- The primary care sector has a major role in caring for 60% of the adults and a large proportion of the children who have a discernible mental disorder. Thus, there is a clear need for a concerted effort to overcome the serious deficiencies in communications between mental health and general health services.

- Interdisciplinary collaboration is not an end in itself but rather a means to a higher goal—solving a problem.

- Essential to the success of the mission of the report is the attraction of talented and dedicated young people to health and behavior research The first step is wider recognition of the importance of these problems, the burden of illness they impose, their human impact, and the urgency of progress. The second is awareness that scientific opportunities exist for grappling with the problems.
- One of the significant changes of the twentieth century is the growing recognition that the methods of science can be employed in understanding human behavior, even though the task is difficult and complex.

The IOM was careful to provide concrete examples of the very dramatic impact of behavioral interventions on both specific disease entities (e.g., cessation of smoking on blood pressure and on cancer) and also more generic descriptions of systematic implications (e.g., weight reduction on a wide range of clinical complications). It was noted that physical disorders in which stressors have been implicated as risk factors include bronchial asthma, influenza, peptic ulcers, hypertension, hyperthyroidism, and sudden cardiac death. Stressors also seem to be risk factors in the precipitation of such mental disorders as depression, schizophrenia, alcoholism, and drug abuse.

From our public policy perspective, what seems notably absent from the IOM discussion was an appreciation for how difficult it would be over the next two decades for our nation's health professions' training programs to be responsive to their vision. Further, the discussion overlooked how slow those who are essentially responsible for paying for our nation's health services would be in appreciating the long-term cost-effectiveness of the IOM's underlying message. In our judgment, as one of the learned professions, psychology has a special societal responsibility to address this nexus and to clearly demonstrate to the nation that the ongoing advances in the behavioral sciences can be effectively integrated into the health care delivery in a highly cost-effective manner.

Demonstration of behavioral intervention effectiveness will require both high-quality science and continued education and training in health-related areas, as well as persistent advocacy and lobbying at state and federal levels. Over the twentieth century, the U.S. health care system evolved to treat acute illnesses, and it continues to treat all illnesses from that perspective. The acute illness approach to care is subtly affirmed by the messages in pharmaceuticals advertising, the persistence of outdated educational training, the predomination of federal research funding for basic sciences, and the public's passion about "finding cures." New models of care, such as the Cardinal Symptoms Management, have been proposed for the ever-growing segment of the population with chronic illness or disabilities, but few of these models have been tested on a large scale or over a number of years (Frank, Hagglund, & Farmer, in press). Trials of prevention interventions have been more common but remain outside mainstream health care. Large-scale evaluations of care models that integrate psychological, behavioral, and social interventions are rarely designed or implemented without support from major corporate sponsors or the federal government. Gaining support for large-scale demonstrations involving behavioral interventions, let alone payment for behavioral interventions from the public and private sectors, will require persistent, skilled advocacy to counteract the presumption of the need for acute care and cure-oriented science. Similarly, training programs often remain entrenched in traditional values and approaches. Reformations in health care training are occurring (e.g., expansion of problem-based learning), but there is virtually no effort to develop interdisciplinary health training programs or to overlap "medical" and "behavioral" sciences training. Without question, these will be among the most critical challenges facing the profession, and health care, in the twenty-first century.

## Healthy People 2010

In many ways, perhaps the most significant change that has evolved within our nation's health policy leadership since the release of *Healthy People* has been the growing high-level institutional appreciation for the importance (and "achievability") of long-range strategic planning, based upon objective goals and standards. In 2000, the surgeon general issued an impressive follow-up policy document: *Healthy People 2010: Understanding and Improving Health* (U.S. Department of Health and Human Services [HHS], 2000), which was committed to the single, overarching purpose of promoting health and preventing illness, disability, and premature death. Not surprisingly, the underlying policy themes remained highly consistent:

> Over the years, it has become clear that individual health is closely linked to community health—the health of the community and environment in which individuals live, work, and play. Likewise, community health is profoundly affected by the collective behaviors, attitudes, and beliefs of everyone who lives in the community. Indeed, the underlying premise of *Healthy People 2010* is that the health of the individual is almost inseparable from the health of the larger community and that the health of every community in every State and territory determines the overall health status of the Nation. That is why the vision for *Healthy People 2010* is "Healthy People in Healthy Communities." (HHS, 2000, p. 3)

It is important to appreciate the significance of the fact that although we are specifically addressing "health care" and reflecting upon the policy thinking occurring at the highest levels of the U.S. government, much of the terminology being utilized is essentially that of social and community psychology (or public health nursing), and not the traditional reductionism to biomedical concepts. For example, community partnerships, particularly when they reach out to nontraditional partners, can be among the most effective tools for improving health in communities. Moreover, life expectancy and quality of life can be increased over the next 10 years by helping individuals gain the knowledge, motivation, and opportunities they need to make informed decisions about their health. Also, the leading causes of death in the United States generally result from a mix of behaviors; injury, violence, and other factors in the environment; and the unavailability or inaccessibility of quality health services. Furthermore, mental health is sometimes thought of as simply the absence of a mental illness but is actually much broader. Mental health is a state of successful mental functioning, resulting in productive activities, fulfilling relationships, and the ability to adapt to change and cope with adversity. Mental health is indispensable to personal well-being, family and interpersonal relationships, and one's contribution to society. Additionally, although the diversity of the American population may be one of our nation's greatest assets, diversity also presents a range of health improvement challenges—challenges that must be addressed by individuals, the community and state in which they live, and the nation as a whole. It would be a significant understatement to suggest that what is being discussed today has not been our nation's traditional concept of health care.

## Additional Institute of Medicine Reports

Since the beginning of the twenty-first century, the IOM has released several additional policy documents that continue to emphasize the trends just described in several dimensions. In *Promoting Health: Intervention Strategies from Social and Behavioral Research* (Smedley & Syme, 2000), the IOM focused in depth upon promising areas of social science and behavioral research that would improve the public's health:

- The vast majority of the nation's health research resources have traditionally been directed toward biomedical research endeavors with less than 5% of the approximately $1 trillion spent annually on health care in the nation being devoted to reducing risks posed by preventable conditions. By itself, however, biomedical research cannot address the most significant challenges to improving the public's health in the new century. Behavioral and social interventions offer great promise to reduce disease morbidity and mortality, but as yet their potential has been relatively poorly tapped.

- Behavior change is a difficult and complex challenge. It is unreasonable to expect that people will change their behavior easily when so many forces in the social, cultural, and physical environment conspire against such change. If successful programs are to be developed to prevent disease and improve health, attention must be given not only to the behavior of individuals but to the environmental context within which people live.

- Children should be a major focus of intervention efforts. Risk factors observed in adults can be detected in childhood. Interventions in early life can change the trajectory of these risk factors.

- Differences across socioeconomic and racial or ethnic groups, or combinations thereof, range up to 10 or more years in life expectancy and 20 or more years in the age at which significant limitations in functional health are first experienced.

- Socioeconomic policy and practice and racial or ethnic policy and practice are the most significant levers for reducing socioeconomic and racial or ethnic disparities and hence improving overall population health in our society, more important even than health policy.

The juxtaposition of the continued prosperity of America and the lack of high-quality health care for a substantial number of Americans also gives us pause. What is the role of psychology in advocacy for those who lack health insurance or are underserved by the health care delivery system? The populations who do not have access to quality health care are vastly overrepresented by people with low incomes, people with disabilities and/or chronic illnesses (including mental illnesses), immigrants, racial and ethnic minorities, those who live in rural areas, and those who are homeless. Obviously, these are diverse groups, but they share two commonalities: They have much poorer access to health care, education, and other resources to maintain health, and they frequently have little voice in public policy. In 2000, approximately 43 million Americans lacked health insurance. It is striking that 69% of these Americans have at least one family member who is working full time (Kaiser Commission on Medicaid and the Uninsured, 2001).

## Crossing the Quality Chasm

*A New Health System for the 21st Century* (IOM, 2001) addresses the extent to which the current American health care system is significantly behind other segments of the economy in utilizing advances in relevant technology and in ensuring that scientific advances are employed in a timely fashion. The American health care delivery system is in need of fundamental change. Americans should be able to count on receiving care that meets their needs and is based on the best scientific knowledge. Yet there is strong evidence that this frequently is not the case. The lag between the discovery of more efficacious forms of treatment and their incorporation into routine patient care is unnecessarily long, in the range of about 15 to 20 years. Even then, adherence of clinical practice to the evidence is highly uneven.

## TECHNOLOGICAL ADVANCES

Perhaps the single most significant societal change affecting professional psychology is the extraordinary advances that are occurring almost daily within the technology and communications fields, and their direct applicability to health care. The Robert Wood Johnson Foundation (Institute, 2000) recently noted, "The health industry has lagged behind other industries in implementing information technologies that streamline business and clinical processes. We forecast that changes in information technology as applied to health care will be a prime catalyst of change in the future" (p. xviii). Technological change is accelerating in two areas that will affect health care dramatically: medical and information technologies. Medical technology has been one of the major drivers of the health care system since the introduction of effective pharmacological agents in the early part of this century. Its impact will continue in the next decade. However, health care has not made significant use of the advances in information technology that have transformed most other industries. That situation will not continue for much longer as the boundaries between information and medical technologies begin to blur. Telehealth, a combination of computer-supported case management, remote telemetry via sensors, and better-informed consumers, will create new ways of delivering care. Chronically ill patients will be monitored remotely through the use of a variety of sensor devices, such as video cameras, blood pressure monitors, and smart pill boxes. These will be linked to computer systems that will allow the provider to catch potential adverse events before they happen.

The IOM proclaimed that "Health care delivery has been relatively untouched by the revolution in information technology that has been transforming nearly every other aspect of society. The majority of patient and clinician encounters take place for purposes of exchanging clinical information. . . . Yet it is estimated that only a small fraction of physicians offer

e-mail interaction, a simple and convenient tool for efficient communication, to their patients" (IOM, 2001, p. 15). The number of Americans who use the Internet to retrieve health-related information is estimated to be about 70–100 million. Currently over half of American homes possess computers, and although information presently doubles every 5 years, it will soon double every 17 days, with traffic on the Web already doubling every 100 days (Jerome et al., 2000).

Within organized psychology, we are very pleased to see that there has been a growing awareness of the potential impact of technological advances upon the entire profession, not to mention considerable membership interest. The APA Board of Professional Affairs (BPA) established a special task force on telehealth issues, which has been working collaboratively with a similar task force created by the board of directors. The APA journal *Professional Psychology: Research and Practice* has featured three special sections composed of articles focusing upon telepsychology initiatives (i.e., October 2000, April 2000, and December 1998), and the *APA Monitor,* as well as various divisional newsletters, now regularly publishes articles on membership activities in this arena. Public service psychologists, in particular, have been on the cutting edge of demonstrating telepsychology's clinical applicability. It is expected that the newest revision of the APA ethical standards will specifically address telepsychology concerns. Nevertheless, in many ways, one might also suggest that professional psychology has just begun to explore the extent to which technological advances will radically alter the manner in which psychological services will be offered in the twenty-first century, including making psychological diagnostic interviews and testing readily available to more Americans and in locations (e.g., nursing homes and prisons) where psychologists are virtually absent today.

## PUBLIC POLICY REFLECTIONS

As we have suggested, it is our collective judgment that psychology possesses the clinical and scientific expertise necessary, and the societal recognition (e.g., status) and membership numbers, to become a *major* player in our nation's public policy arena. What the profession must do first, however, is begin shaping psychology's *own* legislative agenda and, in so doing, directly respond to society's perceived needs. As but one example, professional psychology must take a proactive stance in ensuring that psychological expertise will be reimbursed when its practitioners engage in providing the psychosocial and preventive care that for decades progressive health policy experts have agreed is absolutely critical (Conrad, 1998; VandenBos, DeLeon, & Belar, 1991). To accomplish this objective, psychology's training programs may well have to emulate the successful efforts of our colleagues in medicine and professional nursing in order to establish treatment "homes of our own" (Rodgers, 1980). During the coming decade we should expect to see behavioral science–based teaching in nursing homes and adolescent runaway shelters, administered by professional psychology training programs. State and federal authorities should be provided with targeted financial resources to support psychology's graduate students who are actively participating in these programs (e.g., pre- and post-doctoral fellowships).

Professional psychology's educational institutions should take the lead in establishing collaborative interdisciplinary training programs, for example, with colleagues in business, law, nursing, pharmacy, and public health. Similarly, it should be psychology's educators, clinicians, and scientists who are on the cutting edge of determining how the ever-escalating advances occurring in information technologies can be effectively utilized to provide enhanced access to quality health care. Reflecting upon medicine's and nursing's historical successes, we would predict that it will become psychology's professional schools that ultimately subsume this charge within their fundamental educational mission. Nonetheless, to date, this element of the profession has been relatively absent from the public policy (and political) process. The time has come for psychology's educational leaders to be considerably more proactive, rather than reactive. Professional psychology must develop the policy vision required for professional psychology to continue its impressive maturation as we enter the twenty-first century. We would strongly urge that, as psychology moves forward, we never forget that our underlying policy vision must always focus on how society's interests can best be served.

## THE RELEVANCE OF CLINICAL PSYCHOLOGY: THE NEED TO CONVERSE WITH OUR COLLEAGUES AND OUR CULTURE

How can psychology best serve society's interests? That single question may best reflect the necessary, evolving, paradigmatic shift in psychology's perceived mission. The ancient professions of architecture, law, nursing, medicine, and, for that matter, tax accounting all had their historical foundations in the needs established by their social environment. The foundations of the young science of psychology, however, were in the respected but impractical academic realm of philosophy. Indeed, it was not until the early twentieth century that academic courses such as "mental philosophy" began to evolve into what we would now recognize as the first examples of Psychology

101 (C. E. Rice, 2000). Because of these foundations, philosophical considerations in psychology were viewed as vastly more important than the solution of real-world problems. To this day, many research psychologists in academia remain primarily focused on the philosophical underpinnings of therapeutic interventions, whereas most practicing psychologists are posing the more pragmatic question, "What works?"

Moreover, although we now know a good deal about which interventions work (Chambless et al., 1996), we remain poorly equipped to address many of the common clinical problems presented daily in a typical psychology practice. The etiology of this professional weakness is partially attributable to the disconnect that unfortunately developed between psychology's academic and practice communities. In order for psychology to mature and expand, researchers must conduct *relevant* as well as scientifically rigorous research, and practitioners must be involved in the critical process of advancing the profession's knowledge base. One approach to this challenge is exemplified by the concept of the Practice Research Network as organized by the Pennsylvania Psychological Association (Borkovec, Echmendia, Ragusea, & Ruiz, 2001). Such research would serve to unite the elements of the profession while increasing the likelihood of scientific and professional activities that are more likely to directly and immediately serve society.

Psychology's scores of journals are burgeoning with solid empirical research that has, in only a century, established psychology as the preeminent mental health profession. However, much of this research meets academic, not clinical, needs, and the profession of psychology will surely be replaced by others to the degree that psychology's research and practice are irrelevant to society's needs. Toward this end, in addition to basing clinical work more on relevant research, practitioners must move their interventions out of comfortable consultation rooms, into the rapidly changing, technological world of the modern family. Very briefly, here are four examples of social trends that the profession of psychology should be addressing with much greater vigor.

First of all, in a very real way, the American family is in crisis. The divorce rate, which now stands at approximately 50%, has a profound impact on human life. Factors such as personal happiness, vocational stability, income, suicide rates, and longevity have been found to be seriously and negatively affected by divorce (Tucker et al., 1997). What can psychologists do to predict successful marriages through the premarital screening of potential newlyweds? What can psychologists do to improve the success rate of existing marriages? Where is the clarifying body of research to guide family psychologists in their efforts to positively impact the lives of married couples? Given the importance of this social problem, psychology's response is woefully inadequate.

Second, too few clinical psychologists are preparing for the technological revolution afforded by the internet in general and telehealth in particular, although these technologies dominate our lives more with each passing day. The truth clearly remains that psychologists are ill prepared to defend either diagnosis or treatment of psychopathology facilitated by television or computer. According to an acknowledged leader in this field, Leigh Jerome, as quoted in APA's *Monitor on Psychology,* "Unfortunately, there remains a paucity of empirical data that assesses the efficacy and feasibility of telehealth capabilities for clinical applications," Indeed, most investigators find that there remains a lack of fundamental research in all major areas related to online therapy, including the questions of which technologies are best for delivering which type of services and under what conditions telehealth services lead to improved outcomes (Rabasca, 2000). Unfortunately, recent literature searches have demonstrated that psychology is still well behind the curve in terms of adjusting and incorporating this world-changing technology into psychology's vast existing base of knowledge (Ragusea, personal communication, 2001).

Third, the Human Genome Project is unlocking the human genetic code. If it is not already in progress, we will certainly soon commence human cloning. As important as that statement is, it addresses a matter that is minor when compared to the greater importance of a change in our genetic reality. We must all fully understand that people will soon be making conscious decisions about how to *adjust the human chromosome.* As we complete the genetic map and learn how to change design elements, we will begin changing the genes that influence height, weight, intelligence, assertiveness, creativity, memory, athletic skill, and so on. Is there anyone on the planet who seriously thinks that the human race is currently prepared to face the challenges inherent in making these decisions? Psychology has much to contribute in this realm, but, as Shiloh notes,

> Despite general agreement about the importance of psychological issues in genetic counseling, the entry of psychologists into this highly professional, competitive, and rapidly developing field will not be easy. The pace will depend in part on their efforts to adapt psychological knowledge to the highly complex subject matter of medical genetics. Nevertheless, considering the rising needs, it is reasonable to assume that more and more psychologists will be engaged in the future in genetic centers and will have to address the implications of genetic counseling in their general practice. (1996)

It can be argued that psychology should be leading the culture's advances into genetic manipulation by investigating (a) the psychological factors that contribute to the making of such decisions, (b) the impact of such decisions on individuals and families, and (c) how psychologists can best work with physicians, ethicists, and social planners to enhance the likelihood that this genetically enhanced chapter of humanity's book of life will be a rich and joyous tale, not a horror story. However, there is virtually no psychological research published in this critically important, rapidly emerging realm, and therefore psychologists remain ill prepared for challenges of this nature and magnitude.

Fourth, the problem of America's response to the twin issues of crime and punishment remains. Make no mistake about it: America has won the Worldwide Incarceration Invitational. We in the United States have demonstrated that we have the will and financial resources to put more of our citizens behind bars than any other nation. Indeed, throughout most of the the past decade, America has incarcerated a higher percentage of its population *than any other country on Earth* (U.S. Department of Justice, 1998). According to a 2001 report by ABC News, 25% of the entire world's prison population is in U.S. prisons.

Most people tend to forget that prisons, as we know them, are really a very modern invention. For most of human history, with few exceptions, jails were a place to keep prisoners for a short time—until they were punished using techniques such as public humiliation in the stocks, whipping, or hanging. Over the last hundred years, America has embraced a model that involves incarcerating people in prison for very long periods of time. Commonly, people are sentenced to jail terms of 18 months or 5 years or 25 years. Time in prison has itself become the punishment. There are lots of problems with this technique. First, it is expensive. It currently costs approximately $25,000 to keep one prisoner in jail for one year, and that does not include the cost of building the prison itself! Even worse, all that money does not buy much of a solution, given that the recidivism rates for prisoners commonly approach 40–50%.

Most people can agree that some people need to be behind bars. The truth is that there are some people who are so psychosocially disturbed or dangerous that they must to be kept where they cannot hurt other people. That precise number, while unknown, is likely to be relatively small. However, the number of individual human beings we choose to imprison is *not* small; it is huge.

As of February 2001, the United States of America had more than 2 million of its citizens behind bars. That equals the entire population—every man, woman, and child—in the three states of North Dakota, South Dakota, and Delaware, at an annual cost of approximately $50 billion. Who are those people behind bars? Some of them are violent, dangerous people. Approximately half are in jail for drug- and/or alcohol-related offenses. Additionally, according to a 1998 survey done by the U.S. Department of Justice, 238,000 prisoners are known to be mentally ill, a population approximately equal to that of the city of St. Petersburg, Florida or Akron, Ohio.

How did this happen to our mentally ill? We all know the history of deinstitutionalization. Nationally, state mental hospital populations peaked in 1955 at 559,000 people. By contrast, today's public mental hospital population is approximately 70,000, and *25,000 of these cases are for forensic evaluation!* Thus, although the specific numbers are not available, what we have experienced is nothing short of a mass migration from mental hospitals to prisons (M. E. Rice & Harris, 1997).

Let us not be mistaken for Pollyannas: Some people *should* be behind bars. A small percentage of prisoners will need to be incarcerated for extended periods, and for some that means a lifetime. None of us wants somebody like John Wayne Gacy living next door to our children or grandchildren. However, not every criminal is a monster, and we do not have enough money to put every lawbreaker in jail. We need to start trying a different approach to crime and punishment.

A new movement called Restorative Justice is gathering strength. It is an approach that combines justice with mercy and common sense. Restorative Justice is based upon a redefinition of crime as injury to the victim and the community rather than a challenge to the power of the government. Victims help define the harm of the crime and identify how the harm might be repaired. The essence of the punishment is to fix that which has been damaged. This model of crime resolution has proven very successful and costs much less money as well. What better techniques might be considered? There are, undoubtedly, many alternatives.

It is psychology that should lead the way in prison reform. What other profession has our expertise in human behavior? Using our research methodologies, psychologists could explore a range of new alternatives to our existing criminal justice system. All we lack is the will. The APA's Task Force on Envisioning, Identifying, and Accessing New Professional Roles (Levant et al., 2001) recently reflected that "Approximately 1% of the population is currently in prison, on probation, or on parole. Many billions of dollars are spent annually to support this massive incarceration effort. Psychologists have not effectively contributed to the resolution of this massive societal problem. Psychologists must become involved at the center of what is fundamentally a psychological problem of learning and behavior."

Unfortunately, psychologists, like most people, would rather not think of their failures. Prisoners are society's failures, and many prisoners are psychotherapy failures. We all want to forget about the people who live inside that gray, cold cement-and-steel world of American's prisons. We are willing to think about the issue of crime and punishment only when it invades *our* world, *our* neighborhood, *our* family. We must do better. Moreover, although prison reform is one of our particular interests, there many cultural challenges for psychologists to tackle.

Psychology must become more actively involved with humanity's social reality. If psychologists take care of society, society will take care of psychology. If psychology ignores the culture's needs, however, psychology risks being discarded into the dustbin of history.

## CAMOUFLAGED PSYCHOLOGISTS: THE STEALTH LEADERSHIP INSTITUTE OF PSYCHOLOGY

Our discussion of the mysterious Stealth Leadership Institute of Psychology (SLIP) will be brief. As business consultants, growing numbers of "professional psychologists by training" are advocating change in public and corporate policy *implementation.* Often, they do so without much mention of their background in professional psychology or a license to *do* anything as a scientist or health professional. They are hired as business consultants with contracts for services and the delivery of results, usually with the intent of mutual profit. Many of these "psychologists by training" hire on as apprentice business consultants in lieu of calculating but inexperienced and sometimes interpersonally inadequate MBA graduates. According to Interaction Associates Senior Associate Daniel J. Anderson, "My experience is that business can genuinely appreciate smart, honest, interpersonally facile professionals. Thus, the creation of the Stealth Leadership Institute of Psychology, the extent of [whose] informal membership is, unfortunately, unknown" (personal communication, 2001).

Psychologists are not the only professionals engaged in such activities. In early 2001, McKinsey & Co., Bain, and Deloitte Consulting, to name a few among many multibillion-dollar business consulting firms, recruited new PhDs and postdocs in the "hard" sciences (e.g., neurology, economics, physics) from MIT and Harvard for positions starting in the middle six figures with a 30% bonus. These scientists are being hired not to function as professionals in their fields but, rather, as agents of change with or without professional titles or licenses.

In psychology, George Albee has long argued that psychologists would be better off as educators and consultants, not reimbursable health care providers. Even in these capacities, however, they remain psychologists in mind, heart, and soul; no one becomes a licensed psychologist by accident. These stealth psychologists are now business consultants, and most don't include their professional psychology degrees on their business cards. Advertising one's profession—even psychology—may actually *limit* the perceived value of the services in the business reality of an increasingly global capitalist economy. Most often we hear our stealth colleagues dropping phrases such as "I was trained as a psychologist" as a validation for their scientific rigor and discipline. However, their statement is immediately followed by a sharp focus on the particular organization, profession, agency, legislature, and business in need of their specific consulting services.

How much influence for socially responsible consulting—for productive change in policy, corporate or public—do these stealth psychologists have? This is difficult to measure. It is our understanding that one SLIP PhD colleague is responsible for the collaborative design to execute a peace strategy in Belfast.

Some of these psychologists have become scoundrels-for-hire, and some are great psychologists practicing for the common good—public and private—in all but name. According to Daniel J. Anderson, "There are early indicators that the informal membership in SLIP is growing daily as psychologists seek greater growth opportunities beyond the traditional boundaries of professional identity."

## POLICY OPPORTUNITIES BY "WORKING FROM THE INSIDE"

State and federal governments are open opportunities for the growth of psychology because of the nature of the health, social, and environmental challenges facing our public leaders. Many psychologists are already in policy positions, some identifying themselves clearly as psychologists and others working in a stealth role. The growing acceptance of psychology as a learned profession and valued contributor to public policy, however, presents an opportunity for expanded policy making by *psychologists,* rather than those "trained as psychologists." The APA has a large and well-coordinated government liaison office that is well respected on Capitol Hill. Moreover, most, if not all, states and territories have hired lobbyists to work for their interests at the state level. Psychology interests are sometimes also represented by lobbyists from universities or nonprofit organizations. These groups will occasionally form coalitions, such as those recently formed to

support the Mental Health Equitable Treatment Act (S. 543, 107th Congress), which mandates that insurers provide equal coverage of mental health benefits to those of medical and surgical benefits, if mental health benefits are offered. These types of coalitions are found on most major issues and can be highly effective. Advocacy and lobbying are clearly an area in which psychology can benefit from increased participation. During a recent "11th-hour" amendment-drafting session of a major health care bill, a representative of the American Medical Association (AMA) was in one of the democratic "warm rooms" in the Capitol. The bill was already being debated on the Senate floor, but the "manager's" amendment contained several important changes to the bill, changes that were to be incorporated into the House version (which was debated at a later date). The manager's amendment was accepted by a voice vote in the final moments of the debate. The final version of the bill that passed the Senate was acceptable to the AMA. Psychology is working toward that level of participation in policy formation.

In addition to the "outside looking in" approach of lobbying and advocacy, psychology has potential to grow within federal and state governments. Inside the halls of Congress, psychology's legislative initiatives do not often face hostile objection (with some exceptions, such as that regarding prescription privileges), but psychology often suffers from benign neglect. Few federal or state leaders or their staff have a good understanding of the potential contributions of psychologists to health care, criminal justice, education, industry, social system development, and community building. Few federal or state legislators *fail* to understand or consider the potential contributions of medicine. For example, the initial language for a recent bill to reauthorize large federal programs that provide health care to the underserved diminished the emphasis on mental and behavioral health despite the recent reports by the surgeon general and the IOM. However, in concert with other staff members and with strong, persistent advocacy support by the Education Directorate of the APA, a psychologist congressional fellow was able to expand the role of mental and behavioral health in these high-profile programs. However, this relatively small success came only through several staff-to-staff meetings, phone calls to advocates encouraging them to contact their legislators, and participation in the final drafting of the bill at 10:00 p.m. the night before the committee markup in which the bill was "voted out" and sent to the floor for full debate. Late in that evening drafting session, it was suggested for one particular section of the bill that "we just go back to the old language" in order to reach a compromise on an issue that did not pertain to mental health. The staff member making this suggestion had forgotten, however, that the "old language" of this section did not include mental and behavioral health specialists. It was the psychologist fellow who reminded the staffer that the old language failed to include mental and behavioral health specialists. Psychologists would have been cut out of a major component of the federal program had the old language been used. Working from the inside is an effective method to reduce the benign neglect of psychology on Capitol Hill and in state legislative chambers, and it is best accomplished with psychologists' serving as staff or fellows. Psychologists' (who identify themselves as psychologists) working "on the inside" would go a long way toward increasing inclusion in policy. It would also go a long way toward improving society.

The view from the "inside" is unique, highly energizing, and informative. The two most common ways to become involved are to become a congressional fellow and to be employed as a staffer. Staff members often start as interns or volunteers from campaigns or through personal contacts. Some congressional fellows accept positions on staff after their fellowship year(s). There are many misperceptions about congressional staff, but the truth is that they are bright, articulate, energetic, and hardworking individuals who care about policy as much as or more than they care about politics. A substantial portion of their activity involves reliance on personal relationships, because so much of their job performance relies on negotiation skills. Negotiations occur with staff from the other party, with the administration, and with constituents regarding their desires and needs. Staff members are also ravenous consumers of information, although not typically scientific journal articles. Psychologists have proven to be effective staff members, and some have proven to be effective legislators because of the overlap in skills necessary to succeed in both professions. However, there are too few psychologist congressional or state staff members or legislators. Psychologists have an opportunity to increase their "stock" in the legislative hallways by participating in policy as paid staff or through fellowships. Only four psychologists have been Robert Wood Johnson Fellows health policy fellows, and not many more have applied but not been selected. Increasing the numbers of psychologists who are Robert Wood Johnson Fellows is largely a function of having more psychologists apply to the program.

## PRESCRIPTIVE AUTHORITY: PSYCHOLOGY'S RESPONSIBILITY TO IMPROVE PSYCHOPHARMACOLOGICAL SERVICE PROVISION

A central paradox in the provision of modern psychopharmacological agents is that, in spite of their known efficacy, and in spite of tremendous increases in their use over the past

decade, they have done little to reduce the societal burden of mental disease—that is, their effectiveness is open to question. This phenomenon has been directly studied in depression (Moncrieff, 2001), but evidence also exists for schizophrenia (Harding, Brooks, Ashikaga, Strauss, & Breir, 1987a, 1987b; Harrison et al., 2001; Hegarty, Baldessarini, Tohen, Waternaux, & Oepen, 1994) and undoubtedly for other mental conditions as well. Numerous explanations for this phenomenon are possible, among the most plausible being (a) that psychotropics are not appreciably more efficacious than placebo; (b) that the effects of psychotropics are insufficiently specific to provide significant amelioration for any one particular disorder; (c) that psychotropics are incorrectly employed—chronically overdosed or, more likely, underdosed—in everyday clinical practice, and (d) that psychotropic medications are, when used as single modalities, insufficient to bring about lasting improvement.

All of these speculations have varying degrees of merit, and all have been the subject of investigation. The placebo issue has come under increasing scrutiny in the past decade (Greenberg & Fisher, 1989; Kirsch, 1997; Kirsch & Sapirstein, 1998; Shapiro & Shapiro, 1998), and it is likely that the placebo response rate to antidepressants approaches 40% (Khan, Warner, & Brown, 2000). Placebo responding is less studied in other conditions, but it is reasonable to assume that a fairly robust placebo response exists even in psychotic conditions and mania. As many as 30% of patients (Emsley, 1999) treated with antipsychotics show essentially no improvement, and the placebo response to antipsychotics, even during an acute psychotic episode, can be relatively robust (Marder & Meibach, 1994). Although antipsychotics are of demonstrable efficacy in controlling, but not ablating, the acute symptoms of psychosis and may be of material assistance in preventing relapse, a "substantial minority" of patients derive little benefit from drug treatment (Wirshing, Marder, van Putten, & Ames, 1995).

On the other hand, it is equally true that most studies of antidepressants and other psychotropics find that active agents not only are more efficacious than placebo in ameliorating acute symptoms but are also effective in preventing relapse to a more significant degree than placebo. Antipsychotics are clearly effective in preventing relapse, but, again, they should not be considered a panacea. Approximately 50% of patients treated with placebo relapse within 4–6 months, as compared with 20% on antipsychotics (Csernansky & Newcomer, 1995).

The placebo response is a function of not only medication but also diagnosis, patient, and even phase of treatment. It is endemic in psychopharmacology, just as it is in all types of allopathic treatment. Discussion of the role of placebo in treatment of mental distress is essential to good clinical use of psychopharmacological agents, because of the repeatedly demonstrated, often substantial, placebo effect associated with them. To acknowledge this response is not to deny the utility of these agents: A substantial number of patients show a robust placebo response to narcotic analgesic, yet we do not question the value of those agents. Nonetheless, this response must be clearly understood by clinicians in order to allow optimum use of antidepressants and other psychotropics.

Also related to the issue of placebo responding is the question of the degree of specificity of response to antidepressants. Kirsch and Sapirstein (1998) argued that much of the response to antidepressants cannot be ascribed to a specific effect on neurotransmitter function or other cause, and that up to 75% of response to an antidepressant is either a placebo or a nonspecific response. This speculation has merit, and is an issue in clear need of further study, but it should not be interpreted to mean that there is not a substantial population that does respond specifically to antidepressants, and that their use has not enhanced both short- and long-term outcome of depression and other mental disorders. Like the placebo response, the degree of nonspecificity of response will vary across patient, diagnosis, and phase of treatment dimensions. A clearer definition of the nonspecific response to psychotropics will aid both researchers who strive to identify biological substrates to mental distress and clinicians who seek guidance as to how to use these agents most effectively. Again, however, we must take great care to avoid the politics surrounding allopathic versus nonallopathic treatments. Hollon (1996) observed that "if psychotherapy works (that is, if it has causal agency), then it really does not matter if it works for specific or nonspecific reasons" (p. 1028)—an observation that remains as trenchant when applied to pharmacotherapy as when applied to psychotherapy.

Of the five points outlined above, we believe the last two—the misuse of psychotropics and the overreliance on psychotropics as a single modality—provide the most compelling explanation as to why psychotropics have not reduced the burden of mental disorders, in spite of their greatly increased use. An understanding of these issues is important in demonstrating how psychologists, using psychotropics in an adjunctive manner and in combination with psychosocial and behavioral treatments of demonstrated effectiveness, can improve the provision of psychotropics and make substantial contributions to the public weal.

Antidepressant medications were the highest-selling category of prescription drugs in 2000 (Pear, 2001), and over $6 billion was spent on antidepressants alone in the 1990s (Croghan, 2001). Surveys of practice patterns in primary care and psychiatry reveal that a significant majority of patients

(Pincus et al., 1998)—indeed, as many as 97% (National Depressive and Manic Depressive Association, 2000) of patients—are treated with medication, a trend that has been particularly noticeable in the past decade (Olfson et al., 1998). In psychiatry, the likelihood of a patient's receiving medication for depression has increased significantly over the past 15 years, to the point that currently approximately 90% of all patients receive medication, most commonly for depression (Pincus et al., 1998). At the same time, other data suggest that many patients in primary care prefer counseling to medication to treat mental distress and that counseling is as effective as medication in managing mild to moderate depression (Chilvers et al., 2001).

Depression is by all standards undertreated using routine primary care (Lin et al., 1998; Nierenberg & Alpert, 2000). The recent large-scale survey of over 1,000 patients and 800 non–psychiatrically trained primary care physicians (National Depressive and Manic Depressive Association, 2000) underscore this point. Although an extraordinary number of people were treated with medication, most patients were not compliant with a treatment regimen, and over one half experienced side effects that were significant enough to cause them to discontinue or switch antidepressants. Even after taking medication for 3–5 years, most patients had significant residual symptoms of depression. Another finding of importance from this survey was that, although the majority of primary care physicians felt they had adequately informed patients about side effects of medication, only a small number of patients believed they had received sufficient information.

However, poor adherence to drug regimens is only one variable in an equation resulting in suboptimal outcomes. Simon, von Korff, Rutter, and Peterson (2001) compared outcomes for treatment of depression in primary care and psychiatry and concluded that outcomes were poor in either setting. Their data revealed that, regardless of setting, patient visits were few (even among patients of psychiatrists, only 57% made more than three visits in 90 days). These authors commented that systematic issues, such as the fact that Health Plan Employer Data and Information Set (HEDIS) criteria suggest only three visits in 3 months, rather than the care itself, might be responsible for the poor record of treatment of depression. Another large-scale survey of depressed patients revealed that only half of all patients had continuous treatment for more than 6 months (Tierney, Melfi, Signa, & Croghan, 2000). These data indicate that depression, by definition a chronic, relapsing condition, is not only being undertreated in primary and specialty care but, perhaps more importantly, is being treated in a fashion that essentially guarantees that medication will be the most likely treatment—at the expense of either psychotherapy alone, or combinations of medication and psychotherapy, both of which are of apparently greater value in treating depression and other mental conditions.

This situation persists despite data indicating that collaborative (psychologist-physician) care leads to better outcome (Katon et al., 1996). It also appears that minimum improvements in routine care, particularly via the addition of psychotherapy or closer medication management, can improve outcome for depression treated in primary care. Schoenbaum et al. (2001) prospectively studied depressed patients assigned to routine primary care, augmented medication management (monthly contact with nurse specialists to determine medication adherence), and a cognitive behavioral therapy arm. Addition of medication or psychotherapy (sometimes in combination) led to substantially greater improvements in quality of life and productivity. The benefits of added psychotherapy were substantially greater than those of the addition of medication only. The added cost of providing these services was well in keeping with benefits derived.

In summary, all available data suggest that psychotropics, particularly antidepressants, are misused and generally overused. Further, in the vast majority of cases they are used as single therapeutic modalities, and most patients do not receive psychological treatments, either singly or in combination, for mental distress. This had led to a situation wherein the costs of mental health treatment have escalated, but the societal burden of mental distress has not been ameliorated and the vast majority of patients with mental distress do not experience substantive relief. The training of psychologists makes them the most appropriate profession to provide a full spectrum of interventions for mental distress, from appropriate assessment and diagnosis, to empirically validated psychotherapeutic and behavioral intervention, to accurate monitoring of the process of change. Until the recent past, psychologists have not sought to expand their scope of practice to include prescriptive authority. Within the past decade, this has emerged as a priority for the profession, but in the face of considerable opposition. The medical profession views this as a major infringement on their professional territory. In spite of the fact that most psychologists endorse prescriptive authority (Sammons, Gorny, Zinner, & Allen, 2000), some psychologists remain opposed, fearing that the ability to prescribe will be a de facto endorsement of the medical model of treatment for mental disorders (Adams & Bieliauskas, 1994).

## Will Prescribing "Medicalize" Psychology?

Some opponents of prescriptive authority for psychologists, both within and outside the profession, believe that those who choose to prescribe will succumb to the medical model

of treatment of mental disorders. As cited above, current standards under the medical or psychiatric model for treatment of depression require no more than three visits in 3 months, of which one is recommended to be to a prescriber—a situation essentially guaranteed to produce overreliance on pharmacological interventions.

Medical managed care treatment standards such as HEDIS criteria attract considerable and justifiable criticism from psychologists, few of whom believe that an episode of depression can be appropriately managed in three visits over a 3-month span. It is the fear of these psychologists that much of our practice will be reduced to medication checks and perfunctory management of the symptoms of depression, as is often the case in modern psychiatric treatment of the disorder. On the other hand, psychiatrists and other physicians who oppose psychologists' prescribing do not do so on the basis of such standards but, rather, argue that psychiatrists are physicians and that a comprehensive medical evaluation is requisite in order for psychologists to learn to prescribe safely and effectively.

Numerous data exist to contradict this. First, we know that psychiatrists rarely practice medicine after completing their residency training. Only about 5% of outpatient psychiatrists ever perform a physical examination on their patients (Kick, Morrison, & Kathol, 1997; Krummel & Kathol, 1987): Physical exams have become so uncommon by psychiatrists that they essentially do not exist. Additionally, most psychiatrists do not take a comprehensive medical history but leave this to other medical professionals to perform. Thus, in terms of performance of one of the basic components of "medical" treatment, the history and physical, psychiatry does not conform to the standards that apply to the rest of the profession. Some attempt has been made to alter this situation in recent years, with the development of residency programs designed to train physicians in primary care or internal medicine and psychiatry. However, these programs are in short supply and typically attract few applicants. In any event, the result is the same. What is produced is a generalist or an internist specializing in psychiatry, not a psychiatrist specializing in internal medicine or primary care.

Many have argued that prescribing psychologists will not become "junior psychiatrists"—that their practice will be fundamentally different from their medical colleagues and will represent a truly psychological model of pharmacologic service provision (Cullen & Newman, 1997). All data accrued to date support this perspective. Prescribing psychologists, just as do their psychiatric counterparts, will probably rely in a collegial manner on the medical skills of colleagues, who are internists, pediatricians, neurologists, other physicians, and midlevel practitioners (e.g., advanced practice nurses and physician's assistants). The practice of psychiatry is not the practice of medicine; nor will be the practice of psychologists who prescribe.

Nevertheless, the profession must be sensitive not only to our own definition of various forms of mental distress and our notions of the most appropriate treatment but also to changing societal expectations and definitions of mental disorders and their treatment. Depression as currently conceptualized (the "common cold" of mental distress) is far different from the definitions that existed prior to the advent of drugs that could effectively treat the condition in outpatient settings. Indeed, as Healy (1997) commented, prior to the psychopharmacological era, depression was considered to be of sufficient rarity that the existence of an economically viable market for antidepressants was questioned. In other words, depression was defined in the severest terms—as an incapacitating illness with profound effects on every aspect of daily living, most likely requiring long-term institutionalization to manage.

Definitions have changed, and obviously for the better. We now acknowledge less severe forms of depression as true manifestations of mental distress that, while not incapacitating, result in suffering and prevent optimum functioning. However, we must be sensitive to the fact that this redefinition, coupled with the successful marketing of allopathic treatments for depression, has led to significant misperceptions of effective treatment by both the public and the medical profession. The response of many psychologists to this situation has not been adaptive: We characterize the debate in moral terms and argue that nonallopathic treatments represent a morally superior alternative to drugs. Not only is this incorrect, but it also further widens the perceptual divide between allopathic and nonallopathic treatments and perpetuates a situation in which patients and providers are forced to make false choices between drug and nondrug treatments. Evidence suggests that for many forms of mental distress, nonpharmacological treatments are appropriate, but for significant numbers of patients, combined pharmacological and psychological treatments are superior (Sammons & Schmidt, 2001). Psychopharmacological agents can be added to the armamentarium of psychologists without the need to embrace the medical model of mental health service provision. In order to offer the most effective form of treatment to the greatest number of patients, it is incumbent on the profession that we do so (DeLeon, 2001).

## REFERENCES

Adams, K. M., & Bieliauskas, L. A. (1994). On perhaps becoming what you had previously despised: Psychologists as prescribers of medication. *Journal of Clinical Psychology in Medical Settings, 1,* 189–197.

Albee, G. W. (1986). Toward a just society: Lessons from observations on the primary prevention of psychopathology. *American Psychologist, 41,* 891–898.

Borkovec, T. D., Echemendia, R. J., Ragusea, S. A., & Ruiz, M. (2001). The Pennsylvania practice research network and future possibilities for clinically meaningful and scientifically rigorous psychotherapy effectiveness research. *Clinical Psychology: Science and Practice, 8,* 155–167.

Chambless, D. L., Sanderson, W. C., Shoham, V., Johnson, S. B., Pope, K. S., Crits-Christoph, P., Baker, M., Johnson, B., Woody, S. R., Sue, S., Beutler, L., Williams, D. A., & McCurry, S. (1996). An update on empirically validated therapies. *The Clinical Psychologist, 49,* 5–18.

Chilvers, C., Dewey, M., Fielding, K., Gretton, V., Miller, P., Palmer, B., Weller, D., Churchill, R., Williams, I., Bedi, N., Duggan, C., Lee, A., & Harrison, G. (2001). Antidepressant drugs and generic counseling for treatment of major depression in primary care: Randomised trial with patient preference arms. *British Medical Journal, 322,* 1–5.

Conrad, K. (1998). Making telehealth a viable component of our national health care system. *Professional Psychology: Research and Practice, 29,* 525–526.

Croghan, T. W. (2001). Increased spending for antidepressants. *Health Affairs, 20,* 129–135.

Csernansky, J. G., & Newcomer, J. G. (1995). Maintenance drug treatment for schizophrenia. In F. E. Bloom & D. J. Kupfer (Eds.), *Psychopharmacology: The fourth generation of progress* (pp. 1267–1275). New York: Raven Press.

Cullen, E. A., & Newman, R. (1997). In pursuit of prescription privileges. *Professional Psychology: Research and Practice, 28,* 101–106.

DeLeon, P. H. (2001). 2000 APA annual President's report. *American Psychologist, 56,* 556–558.

DeLeon, P. H., Rossomando, N. P., & Smedley, B. D. (in press). Foreword: The future is primary care. In R. Frank, S. McDaniel, J. Bray, & M. Heldring (Eds.), *Psychology in primary care.* Washington, DC: American Psychological Association.

DeLeon, P. H., VandenBos, G. R., Sammons, M. T., & Frank, R. G. (1998). Changing health care environment in the United States: Steadily evolving into the 21st century. In A. S. Bellack & M. Hersen (Series Eds.) & A. N. Wiens (Vol. Ed.), *Comprehensive clinical psychology: Vol. 2. Professional issues* (pp. 393–401). UK: Elsevier Science.

Emsley, R. A. (1999). Partial response to antipsychotic treatment: The patient with enduring symptoms. *Journal of Clinical Psychiatry, 60*(Suppl. 23), 10–13.

Fowler, R. D. (1996). Foreword: Psychology, public policy, and the congressional fellowship program. In R. P. Lorion, I. Iscoe, P. H. DeLeon, & G. R. VandenBos (Eds.), *Psychology and public policy: Balancing public service and professional need* (pp. ix–xiv). Washington, DC: American Psychological Association.

Frank, R. G., Hagglund, K. J., & Farmer, J. E. (in press). Cardinal symptoms management: An alternative to traditional primary care? In R. G. Frank, S. McDaniel, J. Bray, & M. Heldring (Eds.), *Primary care psychology*. Washington, DC: American Psychological Association.

Greenberg, R. P., & Fisher, S. (1989). Examining antidepressant effectiveness: Findings, ambiguities, and some vexing puzzles. In S. Fisher & R. P. Greenberg (Eds.), *The limits of biological treatment for mental distress: Comparisons with psychotherapy and placebo* (pp. 1–37). Hillsdale, NJ: Erlbaum.

Hamburg, D. A., Elliott, G. R., & Parron, D. L. (1982). *Health and behavior: Frontiers of research in the biobehavioral sciences*. Washington, DC: National Academy Press.

Harding, C. M., Brooks, G. W., Ashikaga, T., Strauss, J. S., & Breier, A. (1987a). The Vermont longitudinal study of persons with severe mental illness, I: Methodology, study sample, and overall status 32 years later. *American Journal of Psychiatry, 133*, 718–726.

Harding, C. M., Brooks, G. W., Ashikaga, T., Strauss, J. S., & Breier, A. (1987b). The Vermont longitudinal study of persons with severe mental illness, II: Long-term outcome of subjects who retrospectively met DSM-III criteria for schizophrenia. *American Journal of Psychiatry, 144*, 727–735.

Harrison, G., Hooper, K., Craig, T., Laska, E., Siegel, C., Wanderling, J., Dube, K. C., et al. (2001). Recovery from psychotic illness: A 15 and 25 year international follow up study. *British Journal of Psychiatry, 178*, 506–517.

Healy, D. (1997). *The antidepressant era*. Cambridge, MA: Harvard University Press.

Hegarty, J. D., Baldessarini, R. J., Tohen, M., Waternaux, C., & Oepen, G. (1994). One hundred years of schizophrenia: A meta-analysis of the outcome literature. *American Journal of Psychiatry, 151*, 1409–1415.

Hollon, S. M. (1996). The efficacy and effectiveness of psychotherapy relative to medications. *American Psychologist, 51*, 1025–1030.

Institute for the Future. (2000). *Health and health care 2010: The forecast, the challenge*. San Francisco: Jossey-Bass.

Institute of Medicine (IOM). (2001). *Crossing the quality chasm: A new health system for the 21st century*. Washington, DC: National Academy Press.

Jerome, L. W., DeLeon, P. H., James, L. C., Folen, R., Earles, J., & Gedney, J. J. (2000). The coming of age of telecommunications in psychological research and practice. *American Psychologist, 55*, 407–421.

Kaiser Commission on Medicaid and the Uninsured. (2001). *The uninsured: A primer*. Washington, DC: The Henry J. Kaiser Family Foundation.

Katon, W., Robinson, P., von Korff, M., Lin, E., Bush, T., Ludman, E., Simon, G., & Walker, E. (1996). A multifaceted intervention to improve treatment of depression in primary care. *Archives of General Psychiatry, 53*, 924–932.

Khan, A., Warner, H. A., & Brown, W. A. (2000). Symptom reduction and suicide risk in patients treated with placebo in antidepressant clinical trials: An analysis of the Food and Drug Administration database. *Archives of General Psychiatry, 57*, 311–317.

Kick, S. D., Morrison, M., & Kathol, R. G. (1997). Medical training in psychiatry residency: A proposed curriculum. *General Hospital Psychiatry, 19*, 259–266.

Kirsch, I. (1997). Specifying nonspecifics: Psychological mechanisms of placebo effects. In A. Harrington (Ed.), *The placebo effect: An interdisciplinary exploration* (pp. 166–186). Cambridge, MA: Harvard University Press.

Kirsch, I., & Sapirstein, G. (1998, June 26). Listening to Prozac but hearing placebo: A meta-analysis of antidepressant medication. *Prevention and Treatment, 1*, Article 0002a. Retrieved from http://www.apa.org.

Krummel, S., & Kathol, R. G. (1987). What you should know about physical evaluations in psychiatric patients. *General Hospital Psychiatry, 9*, 275–279.

Lalonde, M. (1974). *A new perspective on the health care of Canadians: A working document*. Ottawa: Government of Canada.

Levant, R., Reed, G., Ragusea, S., Stout, C., DiCowden, M., Murphy, M., Sullivan, F., & Craig, P. (2001). Envisioning and accessing new professional roles. *Professional Psychology: Research and Practice, 32*, 79–87.

Lin, E. H. B., Katon, W. J., von Korff, M., Russo, J. E., Simon, G. E., Bush, T. M., Rutter, C. M., Walker, E. A., & Ludman, E. (1998). Relapse of depression in primary care: Rate and clinical predictors. *Archives of Family Medicine, 7*, 443–449.

Marder, S. R., & Meibach, R. C. (1994). Risperidone in the treatment of schizophrenia. *American Journal of Psychiatry, 151*, 825–835.

Moncrieff, J. (2001). Are antidepressants overrated? A review of methodological problems in antidepressant trials. *Journal of Nervous and Mental Disease, 189*, 285–295.

National Depressive and Manic Depressive Association. (2000). *Beyond diagnosis: Depression and treatment: A call to action to the primary care community and people with depression*. Retrieved from http://www.ndmda.org.

Nierenberg, A. A., & Alpert, J. E. (2000). Depressive breakthrough. *Psychiatric Clinics of North America, 23*(4).

Olfson, M., Marcus, St. C., Pincus, H. A., Zito, J. M., Thompson, J. W., & Zarin, D. A. (1998). Antidepressant prescribing practices of outpatient psychiatrists. *Archives of General Psychiatry, 55*, 310–316.

Pear, R. (2001, May 8). Spending on prescription drugs increases by almost 19 percent. *New York Times*. Retrieved from http://www.nytimes.com.

Pincus, H. A., Tanielian, T. L., Marcus, S. C., Olfson, M., Zarin, D. A., Thompson, J., & Zito, J. M. (1998). Prescribing trends in psychotropic medications: Primary care, psychiatry, and other medical specialties. *Journal of the American Medical Association, 279*, 526–531.

President's Commission on Mental Health. (1978). *Report to the President from The President's Commission on Mental*

*Health* (Vol. 1). Washington, DC: U.S. Government Printing Office.

Rabasca, L. (2000). Taking telehealth to the next step. *The Monitor on Psychology, 31*(4). Retrieved September 8, 2001, from http://www.apa.org/monitor/apr00/telehealth.html.

Rice, C. E. (2000). Uncertain genesis: The academic institution of American psychology in 1900. *American Psychologist, 55,* 488–491.

Rice, M. E., & Harris, G. T. (1997). The treatment of mentally disordered offenders. *Psychology, Public Policy, and the Law, 3,* 126–183.

Rodgers, D. A. (1980). The status of psychologists in hospitals: Technicians or professionals. *The Clinical Psychologist, 33*(4), 5–7.

Sammons, M. T., Gorny, S. W., Zinner, E. S., & Allen, R. P. (2000). Prescriptive authority for psychologists: A consensus of support. *Professional Psychology: Research and Practice, 31,* 604–609.

Sammons, M. T., & Schmidt, N. B. (2001). *Combined treatments for mental disorders: A guide to psychological and pharmacological interventions.* Washington, DC: American Psychological Association.

Schoenbaum, M., Unutzer, J., Sherbourne, C., Duan, H., Rubenstein, L. V., Miranda, J., Meredith, L. S., Carney, M. F., & Wells, K. (2001). Cost-effectiveness of practice initiated quality improvement for depression: Results of a randomized controlled trial. *Journal of the American Medical Association, 288,* 1325–1330.

Shapiro, A. K., & Shapiro, E. (1997). The placebo: Is it much ado about nothing? In A. Harrington (Ed.), *The placebo effect: An interdisciplinary exploration* (pp. 12–36). Cambridge, MA: Harvard University Press.

Shiloh, S. (1996). Genetic counseling: A developing area of interest for psychologists. *Professional Psychology: Research and Practice, 27,* 475–486.

Simon, G. E., von Korff, M., Rutter, C. M., & Peterson, D. A. (2001). Treatment process and outcomes for managed care patients receiving new antidepressant prescriptions from psychiatrists and primary care physicians. *Archives of General Psychiatry, 58,* 393–401.

Smedley, B. D., & Syme, S. L. (Eds.). (2000). *Promoting health: Intervention strategies from social and behavioral research.* Washington, DC: National Academy Press.

Street, W. R. (1994). *A chronology of noteworthy events in American psychology.* Washington, DC: American Psychological Association.

Tierney, R., Melfi, C. A., Wigna, W., & Croghan, T. W. (2000). Antidepressant use and use patterns in naturalistic settings. *Drug Benefit Trends, 12*(6), 7–12.

Tucker, J. S., Friedman, H. S., Schwartz, J. E., Criqui, M. H., Tomlinson-Keasey, C., Wingard, D. L., & Martin, L. R. (1997). Parental divorce: Effects on individual behavior and longevity. *Journal of Personality and Social Psychology, 73,* 381–391.

U.S. Department of Health, Education, and Welfare (HEW). (1979). *Healthy people: The surgeon general's report on health promotion and disease prevention* [DHEW Pub. No (PHS) 79-55071]. Washington, DC: U.S. Government Printing Office.

U.S. Department of Health and Human Services (HHS). (2000). *Healthy people 2010: Understanding and improving health.* Washington, DC: U.S. Government Printing Office.

U.S. Department of Justice. (1998). *Sourcebook of criminal justice statistics, 1997* (K. Maguire & A. Pastore, Eds.). Washington, DC: U.S. Government Printing Office.

VandenBos, G. R., DeLeon, P. H., & Belar, C. D. (1991). How many psychologists are needed? It's too early to know! *Professional Psychology: Research and Practice, 22,* 441–448.

Wirshing, W. C., Marder, S. R., van Putten, T., & Ames, D. (1995). Acute treatment of schizophrenia. In F. E. Bloom & D. J. Kupfer (Eds.), *Psychopharmacology: The fourth generation of progress* (pp. 1259–1266). New York: Raven Press.

# Author Index

Appelbaum, S. A., 268, 332
Apple, R. F., 284
Applegate, B., 12, 33, 48
Appleton, B. A., 398
Appleyard, G., 291
Apter, A., 186
Arambulla, D., 391
Arbisi, P., 105
Archer, R., 154
Arcus, D. M., 42, 130
Arean, P. A., 454, 455
Argyropoulos, S., 130
Ariel, S., 377
Arkowitz, H., 29, 264, 336
Arkowitz, H. A., 336
Arlow, J. A., 257
Armentano, C., 213
Armstrong, H. E., 292, 413, 416
Armstrong, J., 183
Arndt, S., 79, 80
Arnesen, H., 133
Arnkoff, D. B., 333, 340, 427
Arnold, L. E., 33, 46
Arnow, B., 285, 286, 340
Arntz, A., 543
Aron, L., 259, 262–263
Arons, B. S., 288
Arrindell, W. A., 104
Arroyo, W., 39
Arsenault, L., 198
Asamen, J., 77
Asarnow, R. F., 77
Ashikaga, T., 563
Ashman, S. B., 29
Ashmore, R. D., 48
Askari, H., 187
Asnis, G. M., 440
Asnis, J., 132
Assenheimer, J. S., 10, 11, 16
Association of Psychology Postdoctoral and
    Internship Centers, 480, 481
Association of State and Provincial Psychology
    Boards, 472, 475, 486, 497
Astatham, D. J., 237
Astrachan, B. M., 67
Atchison, M., 232
Atlis, M. M., 543
Attkisson, C. C., 28
Atwood, G. E., 263
Augustyn, M., 39
Ault-Riche, M., 378
Aurbach, M., 132
Autry, J. H., 286–287
Aviles, W. A., 545
Avshalom, C., 196
Ax, R. K., 538
Axelrod, S. R., 156, 160, 161, 163, 164
Axline, V., 390, 399
Azim, H. F. A., 362, 412

Ba, P., 134
Babor, T. F., 203
Bacchetta, M., 545
Bachman, J. G., 204
Bachrach, H., 267, 269

Backmund, H., 181
Bagby, R. M., 129
Baider, L., 233
Bailey, E., 460
Bak, R. M., 127
Baker, A., 291
Baker, L., 34
Baker, M., 559
Baker, M. J., 416, 454
Baker, S. L., 132
Baldessarini, R., 106, 107
Baldessarini, R. J., 288, 563
Baldwin, D. S., 129
Balint, M., 259, 261, 263
Ball, S. A., 13, 167
Ballenger, J. C., 109, 175
Baltazar, P. L., 133
Bandler, R., 336
Bandura, A., 127, 281, 389, 392, 393
Banks, S. M., 214
Banon, E., 152
Baptista, M. A., 202
Barbaccia, M., 215, 216
Barban, L., 240
Barbar, J. P., 408, 412
Barbato, N., 106
Barberesi, W. J., 28
Bardone, A., 97
Barkeley, R. A., 33
Barkham, M., 340
Barkley, R. A., 12, 27, 32, 33, 34, 35, 36, 47, 51,
    390, 391, 393
Barlow, D. A., 40
Barlow, D. H., 11, 12, 37, 39, 42, 43, 46, 82,
    120, 122, 128, 131, 132, 133, 134, 135,
    136, 137, 138, 281, 282, 283, 288, 292,
    329, 390
Barnardeschi, L., 133
Barnes, G., 214
Barnes, G. E., 199
Barnes, T. R. E., 291
Barnett, P. A., 99, 104
Barnett, R. C., 545
Baron, E., 197
Baron, M., 81, 108
Baron-Cohen, S., 45
Barr, H. M., 35
Barra, M., 268
Barrett, M. J., 380
Barrett, P. M., 43, 381
Barrett-Lennard, G. T., 301
Barrowclough, C., 284
Barry, T., 456
Barsky, A. J., 132
Barth, N., 186, 187
Bartholomew, K., 159, 164
Bartholow, B., 197, 205, 209
Bartholow, B. D., 198
Bartko, J. J., 20, 67
Bartolozzi, D., 129
Barton, K. A., 232
Bartush, D. J., 196
Baruffi, M., 545
Barwick, M., 34
Basch, M., 262

Basco, M. R., 97
Basile, V., 186
Basoglu, M., 124
Bass, D., 389, 390, 400
Bass, E., 103
Bassett, A. S., 68, 69, 70, 74
Bassuk, E. L., 519
Bates, M. E., 198
Bates, W., 198
Bates, W. M., 203
Bateson, G., 367, 372
Battaglia, M., 77, 133
Battaglia, M. M., 15
Batten, N., 128
Baucom, D. H., 373, 381, 382, 383, 416, 454
Bauer, D. H., 127
Bauer, M., 110
Bauermeister, J. J., 33
Baugher, M., 104
Baum, A., 266, 267
Baum, A. W., 292
Baume, P., 540
Baumeister, R. F., 161, 163
Bavly, L., 13, 19, 201, 202
Baxter, L. R., 293
Beach, S. R. H., 287
Beahr, D., 231, 241
Beall, S. K., 540
Bean, J. A., 185
Bear, G. C., 391
Beardslee, W., 37, 39
Beardslee, W. R., 99, 100
Beaufils, B., 108
Beaumont, P. J. V., 284
Beauvais, F., 209
Beavers, W. R., 382
Bebbington, P., 291
Beck, A. T., 6, 10, 11, 20, 96, 102, 152, 155, 162,
    280, 287, 291, 292, 333, 340, 393, 414,
    415, 416, 440
Beck, A. T., Freeman, A., & Associates, 152, 155,
    162, 333
Beck, G. J., 134
Beck, J. G., 137
Beck, J. S., 11, 280, 414
Becker, B., 50
Becker, D., 15
Becker, D. F., 8, 9
Becker, I., 106, 107
Becker, J., 104
Becker, R. E., 283
Beckett, R., 291
Becvar, D. S., 376
Becvar, R. J., 376
Bedi, G., 32
Bedi, N., 564
Bednar, R. L., 362
Bedrick, J., 198
Beebe, B., 263
Begg, D., 198
Begg, D. J., 34
Begin, A., 235
Begleiter, H., 206
Behan, P. O., 6
Beidel, D. C., 39, 42, 43, 122, 129, 130, 233

Friedman, M. C., 34
Friedman, R. M., 29
Friedman, S., 40, 133, 134
Friedman, T. A., 440
Friis, S., 133
Frijda, N. H., 305, 308
Frischholz, E. J., 240
Fromm, E., 259
Fromme, K., 206, 216
Fromm-Reichmann, F., 258, 259
Frone, M. R., 207, 208
Froom, J., 288
Frosch, A., 270
Frosch, W. A., 163
Frueh, B. C., 233
Fruzetti, A. E., 287
Fuchs, M., 152, 160
Fudge, H., 97
Fuentes, J., 12
Fuetsch, M., 129
Fugere, C., 43
Fuhriman, A., 361
Fulimtot, K., 184
Fulker, D. W., 134
Fulkerson, J., 218
Fulkerson, J. A., 48
Fullerton, C. S., 230, 231, 434, 443
Fulton, M., 156
Furer, P., 130
Furmark, T., 281
Furnham, A., 184
Fux, M., 135
Fyer, A. J., 126, 128, 130, 133

Gabbard, G. O., 241
Gaboury, A., 218
Gaddy, C. D., 477
Gade, R., 215
Gaffney, F. A., 135
Galatzer-Levy, R., 269
Galatzer-Levy, R. M., 267, 269
Gales, M., 262
Gallacher, F., 9
Gallagher, D., 266, 455, 457
Gallagher, D. E., 455
Gallagher-Thompson, D., 446, 455
Gallagher-Thompson, D. E., 461
Gallo, J., 13
Gallo, J. J., 453
Gallow, J. J., 19
Gallups, M. S., 128
Gambino, B., 215
Gamble, W., 104
Garant, J., 362, 412
Garb, H. N., 153, 154
Garber, J., 29, 95, 96, 102
Garbin, M. G., 96
García Coll, C., 29, 48
Garcia, L., 133
Gard, M. C. E., 175
Gardner, C. O., 101, 104
Gardner, W. I., 392
Garety, P., 291
Garfield, S. L., 329, 336, 425, 426, 427
Garfinkel, B., 12, 33

Garfinkel, P., 178, 184, 188
Garfinkel, P. E., 174, 175, 176, 181, 186
Garmezy, N., 11
Garner, D., 178, 184, 188
Garner, D. M., 181, 184, 284
Garrido, M., 48
Garske, J. P., 412, 419
Gartner, D., 543
Garvey, M. J., 287, 288
Gary, M. L., 48
Gaston, L., 266, 457
Gatz, M., 453, 454, 456, 460
Gaub, M., 32, 33
Gauthier, J., 475
Gauvin, L., 177, 181, 183
Gavshon, A., 397
Gay, P., 263
Ge, X., 29
Gebhart, J., 72
Gedney, J. J., 538, 540, 558
Geffken, G. R., 123
Geffner, R., 380
Gekoski, W., 453
Gelder, M., 282
Gelder, M. G., 128, 129, 130, 336
Gelenberg, A. J., 286, 340
Geller, B., 37, 106, 121
Geller, J., 214, 217, 218, 447
Gelso, C., 476
Gemar, M., 103
Gendall, K. A., 187
Gendlin, E. T., 301, 302, 303, 305, 306, 308, 312, 314, 317, 322
Gendlin, G. T., 421
Genser, S., 442, 443
George, C. F., 132
George, D. T., 187
George, E. A., 289
George, E. L., 289
George, L., 455
George, L. K., 126, 233, 454, 460
George, T., 200
Gergen, K. G., 376
Gergen, K. J., 541
Gerhard, D. S., 108
Gerlinghoff, M., 181
Gerlsma, C., 104
Gershon, E. S., 100
Gershuny, B. S., 156, 160, 161, 163, 164
Gerson, J., 264
Gerson, M. J., 371
Gerson, R., 374
Gerstein, D., 213, 214
Gersten, M., 128, 130
Geyer, B., 121
Gfeller, J. D., 455
Ghadirian, A. M., 175
Ghaemi, S. N., 105, 106, 108, 109, 110
Ghosh, A., 542, 544
Giacopassi, D., 216
Giannetti, R. A., 542
Gianoulakis, C., 207
Giardinelli, L., 136
Giardino, N. D., 133
Gibbon, M., 96, 542

Giedd, J. N., 36
Gift, A. G., 455
Gift, T. E., 68
Gilbert, J. P., 533
Gilbert, P., 131
Gilboa-Schechtman, E., 131
Gilger, J. W., 35
Gill, M., 35
Gill, M. M., 263, 332
Gillberg, C., 46, 178
Gillberg, I. C., 178
Giller, E., Jr., 233
Giller, E. L., Jr., 233
Gilligan, C., 263
Gilliland, B. E., 431, 433, 436, 437, 439, 443
Gillin, C., 109
Gillin, M. D., 15
Gilliom, M., 32
Gilmore, M., 48
Gilmore, M. M., 151
Gilner, F. H., 455
Ginsburg, G., 40
Giordano, J., 369, 377, 418, 426
Giorgino, D., 291
Girgus, J. S., 100
Gitlin, M., 108
Gitlin, M. J., 104
Gitow, A., 129
Gladis, P., 412
Gladsjo, J. K., 132
Gladstone, T. R., 99, 100
Glance, K., 545
Glaser, R. R., 381
Glass, C. R., 340, 427
Glass, D. R., 287, 288
Glass, G., 361
Glass, G. V., 424
Glassgold, J. M., 270
Glassman, N. S., 266, 267
Gleaves, D. H., 174, 177, 237, 240
Glidden, C., 446
Glowinski, A., 237
Glowinski, H., 184
Gniwesch, L., 98
Goate, A., 206
Godart, N. T., 176
Goedde, H. W., 206
Goering, P., 174, 175, 176
Goetz, D., 283
Goetz, R. R., 235
Gold, J. R., 327, 336, 338, 339, 453, 459
Gold, P. W., 101, 177
Goldberg, A., 262
Goldberg, D., 258, 269
Goldberg, J., 101, 134, 206, 211, 212, 215, 216, 217, 218
Goldberg, J. F., 81, 108
Goldberg, M., 397
Goldberg, R. W., 489
Goldberg, S., 43
Goldbloom, D. S., 174, 175, 176
Goldenberg, H., 369, 382
Goldenberg, I., 369, 382
Goldfried, M. R., 327, 328, 329, 330, 331, 333, 334, 335, 336, 338, 340, 414, 425

# Subject Index